Canada
2000-2001

3rd Edition

Travel better, enjoy more
ULYSSES
Travel Guides

Publisher
Pascale Couture

Copy Editing
Jacqueline Grekin
Anne Joyce
Wayne Hiltz

Editing Assistance
Cindy Garayt
Natalie Philpot

Computer Graphics
Stéphanie Routhier

Artistic Director
Patrick Farei (Atoll)

Page Layout
Typesetting
Elyse Leconte
Julie Brodeur
Alexandra Gilbert
Visuals
Anne Joyce
Caroline Béliveau

Cartographers
André Duchesne
Patrick Thivierge
Yanik Landreville

Illustrations
Lorette Pierson
Myriam Gagné
Marie-Annik Viatour
Jenny Jasper

Photography
Cover Page
Tibor Bognár
Inside Pages
Guy Dagenais
Jacqueline Grekin
Megapress Images:
K. Cooke, E. Dugas,
J. Pharand, P. Quittemelle
Roger Michel
Reflexion: Walter Bibikow,
Tibor Bognár,
Anne Gardon, Paul Jensen,
Jerg Kroener, Mauritius-
Rosing, Sean O'Neill,
Troy & Mary Parlee, B.
Terry, Y. Tessier,
P. Renaud

Research and Writing : Atlantic Provinces (Benoit Prieur), Québec (François Rémillard, Gabriel Audet, Caroline Béliveau, Daniel Desjardins, Stéphane G. Marceau, Judith Lefebvre, Claude Morneau, Yves Ouellet, Joël Pomerleau, Yves Séguin), Ontario (Pascale Couture), Toronto (Jennifer McMorran, Alain Rondeau and Jill Borra), Manitoba (Paul Karr and Stephanie Heidenreich), Saskatchewan (Paul Karr and Stephanie Heidenreich), Alberta (Jennifer McMorran and Alexis De Gheldere), Rockies (Lorette Pierson and Alexis De Gheldere), British Colombia (Pierre Longnus, P.-É. Dumontier, François Rémillard and Alexis De Gheldere), Yukon (François Brodeur and Pierre Longnus), Northwest Territories (Lorette Pierson), Nunavut (Jacqueline Grekin), Portrait (François Brodeur and Benoit Prieur; *collaboration* Nathalie Garneau).

Distributors

AUSTRALIA: Little Hills Press, 11/37-43 Alexander St., Crows Nest NSW 2065, ☎ (612) 437-6995, Fax: (612) 438-5762

CANADA: Ulysses Books & Maps, 4176 Saint-Denis, Montréal, Québec, H2W 2M5, ☎ (514) 843-9882, ext.2232, 800-748-9171, Fax: 514-843-9448, info@ulysses.ca, www.ulyssesguides.com

GERMANY and **AUSTRIA**: Brettschneider, Fernreisebedarf, Feldfirchner Strasse 2, D-85551 Heimstetten, München, ☎ 89-99 02 03 30, Fax: 89-99 02 03 31, cf@brettschneider.de

GREAT BRITAIN and **IRELAND**: World Leisure Marketing, Unit 11, Newmarket Court, Newmartket Drive, Derby DE24 8NW, ☎ 1 332 57 37 37, Fax: 1 332 57 33 99, office@wlmsales.co.uk

ITALY: Centro Cartografico del Riccio, Via di Soffiano 164/A, 50143 Firenze, ☎ (055) 71 33 33, Fax: (055) 71 63 50

PORTUGAL: Dinapress, Lg. Dr. Antonio de Sousa de Macedo, 2, Lisboa 1200, ☎ (1) 395 52 70, Fax: (1) 395 03 90

SCANDINAVIA: Scanvik, Esplanaden 8B, 1263 Copenhagen K, DK, ☎ (45) 33.12.77.66, Fax: (45) 33.91.28.82

SPAIN: Altaïr, Balmes 69, E-08007 Barcelona, ☎ 454 29 66, Fax: 451 25 59, altair@globalcom.es

SWITZERLAND: OLF, P.O. Box 1061, CH-1701 Fribourg, ☎ (026) 467.51.11, Fax: (026) 467.54.66, Fax: 800-820-2329, sales@globe-pequot.com

OTHER COUNTRIES: Ulysses Books & Maps, 4176 Saint-Denis, Montréal, Québec, H2W 2M5, ☎ (514) 843-9882, ext.2232, 800-748-9171, Fax: 514-843-9448, info@ulysses.ca, www.ulyssesguides.com

Canadian Cataloguing in Publication Data (see page 6)
© May 2000, Ulysses Travel Guides.
All rights reserved
Printed in Canada
ISBN 2-89464-299-7

"The world is all of space and all of time. We can choose to return home through the garden or by the street; but we can also come back from the summer or another season. To travel the world is to reinvent history."

"Le monde, c'est tout l'espace et tous le temps. On peut rentrer chez soi par le jardin ou par la rue; mais on peut aussi venir de l'été et des autres saisons. Parcourir le monde, c'est réinventer l'histoire."

Antonine Maillet
Par derrière chez mon père

Table of Contents

Cataloguing

Canadian Cataloguing in Publication Data

Main entry under title :

    Canada

    (Ulysses travel guide)
    ISSN 1486-1933

    ISBN 2-89464-299-7

    1. Canada - Guidebooks. I. Series.

FC38.C23   917.104'648   C98-301057-9   F1009.C23

Map List

Map Symbols

?	Tourist Information (permanent)	▲	Mountain
?	Tourist Information (seasonal)	△	Glacier
?	Tourist Information	◯	Beach
	Car Ferry	⚡	Downhill Ski Centre
	Ferry	†	Church
	Bus Station	⊠	Border Crossing
	Train Station		Funicular
✈	Airport	Ⓗ	Hospital
Ⓜ	Métro Station (Montréal)	Ⓟ	Parking Lot
⌇	Golf Course		

Write to Us

The information contained in this guide was correct at press time. However, mistakes can slip in, omissions are always possible, places can disappear, etc. The authors and publisher hereby disclaim any liability for loss or damage resulting from omissions or errors.

We value your comments, corrections and suggestions, as they allow us to keep each guide up to date. The best contributions will be rewarded with a free book from Ulysses Travel Guides. All you have to do is write us at the following address and indicate which title you would be interested in receiving (see the list at the end of the guide).

Ulysses Travel Guides
4176 Rue Saint-Denis
Montréal, Québec
Canada H2W 2M5
www.ulyssesguides.com
E-mail: text@ulysses.ca

Symbols

🛶	Ulysses's Favourite
☎	Telephone Number
⇄	Fax Number
≡	Air Conditioning
⊗	Fan
≈	Pool
ℜ	Restaurant
ℑ	Fireplace
⊕	Whirlpool
ℝ	Refrigerator
K	Kitchenette
△	Sauna
☉	Exercise Room
tv	Colour Television
pb	Private Bathroom
sb	Shared Bathroom
fb	Full Board (Lodging + 3 Meals)
bkfst incl.	Breakfast Included
🐾	Pets allowed
♿	Wheelchair Access
✿	Health Centre

ATTRACTION CLASSIFICATION

★	Interesting
★★	Worth a visit
★★★	Not to be missed

The prices listed in this guide are for the admission of one adult.

HOTEL CLASSIFICATION

The prices in this guide are for one room, double occupancy
in high season.

RESTAURANT CLASSIFICATION

$	$10 or less
$$	$10 to $20
$$$	$20 to $30
$$$$	$30 and more

The prices in the guide are for a meal for one
person, not including drinks and tip.

All prices in this guide are in Canadian dollars.

We acknowledge the financial support of the Government of Canada through the Book Publishing Industry Development Program (BPIDP) for our publishing activities.

We would also like to thank SODEC (Québec) for its financial support.

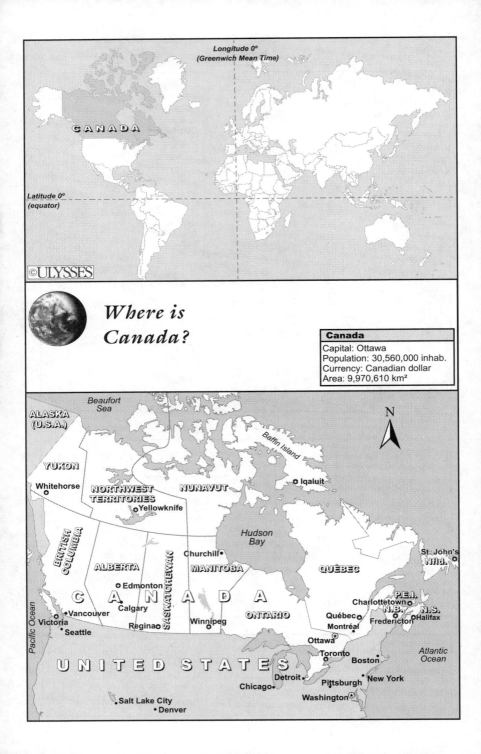

Longitude 0°
(Greenwich Mean Time)

Latitude 0°
(equator)

CANADA

©ULYSSES

*Where is
Canada?*

Canada
Capital: Ottawa
Population: 30,560,000 inhab.
Currency: Canadian dollar
Area: 9,970,610 km²

N

Beaufort
Sea

ALASKA
(U.S.A.)

Baffin Island

YUKON

Whitehorse

NORTHWEST
TERRITORIES

NUNAVUT

Iqaluit

Yellowknife

Hudson
Bay

BRITISH
COLUMBIA

ALBERTA

SASKATCHEWAN

MANITOBA

QUÉBEC

St. John's
Nfld.

Churchill

C A N A D A

Edmonton

P.E.I.

Pacific Ocean

Vancouver

Calgary

ONTARIO

Charlottetown

N.B.

N.S.

Victoria

Regina

Winnipeg

Québec

Fredericton

Halifax

Seattle

Montréal

Ottawa

Atlantic
Ocean

Toronto

U N I T E D   S T A T E S

Boston

Detroit

Pittsburgh

New York

Chicago

Salt Lake City

Washington

Denver

Portrait

How to describe Canada?

It's simply too vast to be characterized by any one cliché, except maybe the one regarding winter.

Canadians themselves subdivide their country in different ways. For some there are simply two large regions: Eastern Canada and Western Canada, or even French and English, while for others the question is much more complicated. There is Atlantic Canada, which includes the three maritime provinces (Nova Scotia, New Brunswick and Prince Edward Island) and the province of Newfoundland and Labrador; then Québec and Ontario, which stand alone, the latter occasionally being referred to (perhaps tongue-in-cheek) as the centre of Canada; next, Manitoba and Saskatchewan are called prairie provinces, despite the fact

that 50% of both provinces is forested; Alberta is also considered a prairie province, though from a touristic point of view, its mighty Rocky Mountains imply a stronger connection to its neighbour to the west, British Columbia, and these two provinces are often grouped together as Western Canada; finally, there is the Yukon, the Northwest Territories and Nunavut, which occupy a vast northern region extending from east to west above the 60th parallel.

To say simply there is an East and a West is to deny that each of these areas has its own history, economy and demographic composition. As for a common identity, some will argue there is no such thing, that Canada hasn't had time to develop one. The framework for the first Canadian constitution was only laid out in 1867 and the country's current borders have existed as such for less than 50 years ago. Perhaps this multiplicity is what defines and strengthens Canada.

It is not surprising that Canadians have difficulty defining themselves collectively. Most of the time they do it by differentiation. They'll tell you that they're not Americans, pointing out that they live in a society where the State plays an important social role, priding themselves for being nicer, more polite and more considerate and that their country is safer. Also, the 'melting pot' concept promoted in the United States isn't used as a model here; multiculturalism has become one of the ideologies on which Canadian society is being built. But whether English-speaking or French-Speaking, Canadians work, construct and consume in much the same way as in the rest of North America.

Regardless of how Canadians respond to the questions of their existence, it's almost certain that they will continue to live in a free and peaceful democracy. And how could it be otherwise? The Canadian substratum is rich, the earth is fertile and the climate is just harsh enough to remind people that it is a waste of energy not to live in peace. On top of that, Canada has something precious that is missing elsewhere and that can give life to an idea, build a different future or simply be admired: space.

Geography

A bit bigger than the United States, Canada is 13 times the size of France and the United Kingdom. It occupies the whole northern part of North America, with the exception of Alaska, and spans five and a half time zones. To the north, the Arctic Ocean is the only boundary. Greenland lies to the northeast. To the east and west, the Atlantic Ocean and Pacific Ocean, respectively, put several thousand kilometres between Canada and its neighbours, except for the tiny French islands of St-Pierre and Miquelon located between Nova Scotia and Newfoundland. Finally the United States lies across all of Canada's land-based borders. This is actually the world's longest undefended border.

The most striking thing about Canada when looking at a map is that there's water everywhere. A large part of the world's fresh water supply flows across this land or is stored in the form of ice. Some huge bodies of water stand out, such as Great Slave Lake, Bear Lake, Lakes Superior, Erie, Huron and Ontario, and the reservoirs in the Québec mid-north. Rivers are also abundant.

The country is much hillier in the western region, where three mountain chains running north-south succeed each other. The highest peak in Canada, Mount Logan, whose summit reaches an altitude of 6,054m, is here. East of these mountains, great plains stretch across Alberta, Saskatchewan and Manitoba, as well as in the continental part of the Northwest Territories and

Nunavut to the Canadian Shield. From north to south, these flatlands go from tundra to boreal forest to the prairies which are mainly consecrated to grain farming. The prairies are known as Canada's bread basket.

Northern Ontario and Québec are part of the same geological formation, the Canadian Shield. This undulating terrain is the last vestige of what was, during the Precambrian period, an imposing mountain massif. There are major metal deposits here. This area is also dominated by tundra and boreal forest. The Québec peninsula becomes more hilly toward the Atlantic Ocean and the Gulf of St. Lawrence. The coast is a succession of sometimes very impressive fjords and cliffs. Southern Ontario borders the Great Lakes. This is the most populated region of Canada; it includes Toronto, the largest city in Canada and the fourth largest in North America by population.

The St. Lawrence River originates from the Great Lakes, quickly enters Québec territory, surrounds the island of Montréal, and flows below the walls of Québec City before widening into the gulf. The St. Lawrence is one of the continent's main points of entry and remains the main focus of Québec's history, population and economy. In the late 1950s, channels and locks opened up the Great Lakes to ocean traffic thousands of kilometres from the coast. Southern Ontario and the St. Lawrence Valley offer rich soil and a slightly milder climate favouring agriculture. Along the Atlantic coast, originating in the southern U.S., the Appalachians shape the landscape of southern Québec. These mountains aren't very high, especially in western Québec.

To the east, beyond the Appalachians, New Brunswick, Prince Edward Island and Nova Scotia along with Newfoundland and Labrador make up the Atlantic provinces. Fishing, sea traffic, farming and forestry have characterized their economies for a long time. For centuries, the shallow waters of the Grand Banks have been an ideal habitat for bottom feeders, at least until overfishing decimated cod stocks and led to the collapse of the fishery in the early 1990. This is possibly the worst ecological disaster to have occurred in Canada and the country is still lost in conjectures about what became of the Grand Banks.

Finally, way in the north, large islands form a triangle-shaped archipelago, a paradise for arctic explorers in search of a challenge. The magnetic North Pole is found here and, by logical conclusion so is Santa Claus. This distinguished guest has no neighbours except for the odd military base "occupying" the territory.

The Canadian climate gets more and more harsh the farther you are from the temperate south. With respect to climate, the eastern part of the country is quite similar to Scandinavia except for the southernmost regions, where the climate resembles that of Poland or Slovakia. The Pacific coast enjoys the warmest temperatures, comparable to the weather in England, with just as much rain...

Climate is the primary factor in agriculture, which in turn affects how Canada is populated. So it's not surprising that the vast majority of Canada's 30,560,000 inhabitants live less than 300 km from the country's southern border. Microclimates, Aboriginal settlement, the exploitation of natural resources and concerted efforts to colonize regions have nonetheless led to the creation of pockets of populated areas in the north.

The Provinces and Territories

Canada is a federation divided into 10 provinces not including the vast northern regions above the 60th parallel. The great Canadian North is divided into three territories, Yukon, the Northwest Territories and Nunavut, which are under the tutelage of the federal government. There is no international airport in the territories, which makes access more difficult.

The last province to enter Canadian confederation was **Newfoundland and Labrador.** The majority of its 552,000 inhabitants live around the perimeter of a large island, called Newfoundland or "The Rock" in the Gulf of St. Lawrence. The capital, St. John's, overlooks the Atlantic. **Labrador**, the provincial territory extending from the Québec peninsula, including the whole eastern border, was granted to Newfoundland after lengthy proceedings pitting the two British colonies against each other.

Newfoundland has for a long time been the poorest of Canada's provinces, its main resources coming from the sea. Significant petroleum discoveries off its coast bring hopes of better days to come. In order to exploit these resources, a consortium has just started operating the biggest petroleum platform in the world, Hibernia.

The smallest Canadian province is an island in the Gulf of St. Lawrence, between Québec, New Brunswick and Nova Scotia. **Prince Edward Island** has only 137,000 residents. Charlottetown is its capital. The island has always relied on fishing, agriculture (primarily potatoes) and tourism; its beaches are among the most beautiful in Canada. Nineteen-ninety-seven was a memorable year for islanders: it is the year the Confederation Bridge, linking the island to the mainland, was opened.

Nova Scotia is linked to the continent by a narrow strip of land, the Chignecto Isthmus. Its shores are washed by waters from the Gulf of St. Lawrence, the Atlantic and the Bay of Fundy. North of the peninsula, Cape Breton Island completes the province's territory. This was the first place in North America settled by Europeans, namely the French, who baptised it Acadia. Acadians were later deported by the English who then settled the area and built Halifax, the provincial capital and one of Canada's busiest ports. Some Acadians stayed in Nova Scotia or returned; they remain a small minority in the overall population of 941,000. The sea is omnipresent in Nova Scotia. Other resources are agriculture, forestry and coal mining.

Over 761,000 people live in **New Brunswick**, Canada's only officially bilingual province. One third of the population is French-speaking; they are Acadians with their unique accent, their own flag and a history that is distinct from that of the French population in the rest of Canada. Fishing, farming and forestry have for a long time fed, however meagrely, the New Brunswick economy. It was one of the main beneficiaries, along with Newfoundland, of wealth redistribution programs instituted by the federal government. The situation is changing, however. New Brunswick's government resolved to improve public finances here long before this became common practice in the rest of Canada. The provincial government also conducted an aggressive campaign to attract leading businesses, especially in the telecommunications sector.

Québec is unique in Canada. It's vast territory is three times the size of France and yet it has a population of only 7,420,000. Its French-speaking majority distinguishes it not only from the rest of Canada but all of North America as well. The use of French has been legislated in order to counteract the assimilation that has led to the near extinction of Francophone communities elsewhere in Canada. This protection of the French language also directs immigrants toward inclusion into the Francophone majority. Anglophones, however, have been established here for a long time, particularly in southwestern Québec and on the West Island of Montréal and obviously don't favour local language laws. Since Québec started seriously questioning its place in Canada, many Anglophones have

left the province. Almost half of Québec's population and almost all new immigrants live in the Montréal area, the focus of the province's industrial and service sectors. Québec City is the capital.

As in Ontario, the substratum is rich in minerals. The St. Lawrence Valley is very well suited to agricultural activities, and forestry in the north has already made Québec the world's primary paper producer. The eastern part of the province, which is more reliant on natural resources, doesn't enjoy the same economic prosperity as the more industrialized regions. Sparsely populated northern Québec has seen a boom since the decision to exploit the hydro-electric potential of the many rivers leading to either James Bay or the Gulf of St. Lawrence estuary.

Ontario is geographically the second largest province in Canada but the most highly populated with 11,407,000 inhabitants. It's also the most prosperous province, as it is responsible for 40% of Canada's gross national product. Ontario is rich in natural resources with mineral deposits and vast forests. Heavy industry, notably the automobile manufacturing industry has chosen this province over others. Finally, Toronto, the capital of Ontario and Canada's biggest city, is home to most of Canada's major businesses. This huge cosmopolitan city rivals those in the United States. The proximity of U.S. markets contributes to the province's wealth: the Canadian city of Windsor, for example, is just north of Detroit. The warm climate in this southern region permits fruit growing

on the same scale as in southern British Columbia. Southern Ontario's white wines, particularly the ice wines, have acquired an international reputation.

Much of the Québec-Ontario border follows the Ottawa River. The National Capital Region includes **Ottawa**, the capital, located on the Ontario side of the river, the city of Hull, on the Québec side, and the surrounding area. The wealth of museums, public buildings and other attractions has made the region a showcase for Canadian culture, politics and tourism. Civil service and high-technology industry are predominant here.

In **Manitoba**, you have to cover hundreds of kilometres before the landscape starts getting a bit hilly. The major city and capital of this province, Winnipeg, was built south of the lake of the same name, on the shores of the Red River. The local economy had for a long time been dominated by wheat farming, until progress in agricultural techniques made it possible to diversify. Nickel mining was one notable new activity. The whole northeastern part of the province opens onto Hudson Bay, and from there, onto the Atlantic. Having to transport grain to the east necessitated the construction of the major sea port of Churchill. For many years, the province had a Francophone majority, until the arrival of new Anglophones and the banning of the official use of French. It would take a court decision a few decades later to recognize the rights of what, in the meantime, had become a persistent yet very small community in the midst of a total population of 1,139,000.

The straight borders of **Saskatchewan** say a lot about its geography. It is a vast, flat terrain where grain farming has been favoured since its colonization, notably by a wave of Ukrainian immigrants. Farming is closely supervised by the federal government as is the sale and transport of the wheat harvest. Saskatchewan has a population of 1,023,000. The two main cities are Saskatoon, world potash capital, and Regina, the provincial capital. Saskatchewan was the first region to implement aspects of the social safety net, in particular, health insurance. In fact, the political landscape would very likely not be as it is today were it not for the spirit of initiative and co-operation that developed on the plains of Manitoba, Saskatchewan and Alberta. It was in Saskatchewan that the first ever North American socialist government was elected. This success was not repeated on the federal level but the political shock was enough to force other political parties to reconsider some of the ideas put forth by the socialists.

Saskatchewan's neighbour to the west is **Alberta**. Incidently, these are the only two provinces that are completely landlocked. Alberta's territory is divided into various zones: mountains (the Rockies offer breathtaking views), boreal forests, wheat fields, pastures and even deserts. Edmonton is the provincial capital. Alberta is the domain of cowboys: pointy boots and cowboy hats are still a common sight in downtown Calgary, and the annual Calgary Stampede is indeed

the greatest outdoor show on Earth. But the best thing in Alberta, economically speaking, is the oil that's pumped out of it. The prosperity brought by this black gold has caused the population to climb to 2,847,000, has brought about the re-stabilization of government finances and has made Calgary one of the country's most important business centres. In terms of politics, Alberta is also the most established seat of the Canadian right. In the last few years, it has led to some administrative reforms that would be considered unthinkable elsewhere in Canada.

British Columbia covers some 950,000km². Its Pacific coastline stretches from Alaska to Washington State. The most striking thing about this province is its geography. Three quarters of the territory lies above 930m and a mountain chain reaching 3,000m stands between the coast and the horizon. The choppy coastline is dotted with hundreds of islands. The biggest one, Vancouver Island, which is the size of the Netherlands, is home to Victoria, the province's capital. Vancouver is also the name of the province's major city; it is situated on the coast of the mainland. The climate is much milder here in winter than in the rest of Canada. Nature is equally generous in providing fruit, fish and timber. Over 3,933,000 people live in British Columbia, including a very vibrant Asian community.

The **Yukon** is located in the mountainous region between Alaska, Mount Mackenzie to the east and British Columbia to the south. Whitehorse is the administrative capital for the 31,500 inhabitants of

the territory, but the most famous spot in the Yukon remains Dawson. Not far from this small town, a little river called the Klondike is associated with the most famous goldrush in the west.

The land east of the Yukon forms the **Northwest Territories**. There are 41,000 people living here, about half of whom are Aboriginal. Yellowknife is the capital and largest city. On April 1, 1999, this territory was divided in two. The northeastern section, including most of the Arctic islands, became **Nunavut**, a territory whose population of 25,000 people is 85% Inuit.

Flora

Considering the climatic differences, the flora varies markedly from one region to another; in the north, it is either scraggly or non-existent and in the south it may be lush. Generally the vegetation is divided according to the four strata, from north to south: tundra, subarctic forest, boreal forest and mixed forest. The distinct climates in British Columbia and the Rocky Mountains have given these areas unique vegetation.

Maple Leaf

Tundra is the northernmost type of vegetation. It exists where ice limits the growing season to a few weeks per year. Only the top layer of the ground is free of permafrost and the only things that grow are miniature trees, moss and lichen.

The subarctic forest, or transition forest, comes after the tundra. It has sparse vegetation; trees are small and grow extremely slowly. Spruce and larch in particular are present here.

The boreal forest is next. It's a very homogeneous forest region consisting of coniferous trees, mainly white spruce, black spruce, balsam, jackpine and larch. This area is exploited for paper pulp and timber.

The mixed forest is the southernmost forest in Canada. In particular, it is found in the St. Lawrence Valley and consists of both coniferous and deciduous trees. There are many species of trees including eastern white pine, red pine, hemlock spruce, spruce, wild cherry, maple, birch and aspen. Every year, the landscape is ablaze with colour as maple trees turn from green to yellow to bright red.

Along the British Columbia coastline and on the neighbouring islands, 60% of the land is covered with such a forest so lush that it is known as a temperate rain forest, the northern counterpart to the tropical rain forest. Douglas firs, red cedars and giant sitka spruces reach impressive proportions. For example, a Douglas fir lucky enough to survive the local lumber industry can reach 90m in height with a trunk 4.5m in diameter at its base.

There are also several unique ecosystems. This is the case from Alberta to Manitoba where the prairies regain the soil, confined in the north by bordering aspens. In the boreal forest, parasitic invasions, forest fires and large-scale cutting often lead to the planting of a provisional forest that encourages regeneration of the original forest. And, of course, a country with as many lakes and rivers as Canada also has many wetlands and bogs that are among the richest and most interesting environments to observe.

Fauna

With all this land, diverse geography and varied climates, it is no wonder that Canada's wildlife is one of its riches. A multitude of animals populates the vast forests, plains and northern regions, and the oceans, lake and rivers are teeming with fish and aquatic animals. Here are a few of the main mammals found in Canada.

Beaver

The **Beaver**, a tireless worker, is a Canadian icon. The beaver-pelt trade was at the origin of the European colonization of the country. It can be recognized by its heavy body, its short, webbed hind feet, and its wide, flat, scaly tail that serves as a rudder when swimming. Its incisors are constantly growing and allow it to cut down the trees required to built its shelter on the water. It then builds a dam to create a pond that will submerge the entrance to its home. Finally, the beaver lays down small trees in this pond. In winter, the hut will be safe from predators and open to an underwater food-storage space that is protected by a layer of ice.

The **white-tailed deer** is the smallest species of deer in eastern North America, attaining a maximum weight of about 150kg. This graceful creature lives at the forest's edge and is one of the most commonly hunted animals in Québec. The male's antlers fall off each winter and grow back in the spring.

The **wolf** is a predator that lives in packs. It measures between 67 and 95cm, and weighs no more than 50kg. Wolves attack their prey (often deer) in packs, and their viciousness makes them rather unsympathetic creatures. Wolves keep their distance from humans.

The **skunk** is known mostly for its defence mechanism: it sprays its attackers with a foul-smelling liquid. The first European settlers called this mammal *bête puante* or "stinking beast". The animal is common to eastern North America, even to some cities and, while it is attractive, it is a good idea to keep your distance.

The **moose** is the largest member of the deer family in the world; it can measure more than 2m in height and weigh up to 600kg. The male is distinguished by its broad, flattened antlers, large head, rounded nose and by the hump on its back.

Most often found in forests, the **black bear** is the most common species of bear in eastern Canada, it is also found in the West. It can weigh up to 150kg when fully grown, yet is the smallest type of bear in Canada. Be careful – the black bear is unpredictable and dangerous.

The **grizzly bear** is not only the biggest bear, but also the biggest land predator. Grizzlies are found mostly in the mountains and on the coast in northwestern Canada. They are extremely dangerous.

Polar bears are very large bears that live in the Far North. They are powerful swimmers and great seal hunters. This bear is just as deadly as the grizzly, perhaps because there's hardly ever a place to hide on the ice field.

Polar Bear

Found in significant numbers in both deciduous and coniferous forests, the **porcupine** is famous for the way it defends itself. When threatened, the quills covering its body stand on end, turning the porcupine into a kind of unassailable pin cushion. Some Aboriginals used it as an emergency food source, as the meat can be eaten raw.

Lynxes are members of the cat family, weighing about 11kg. Their bob tails and pointed ears topped with little tufts of longer fur make them easy to identify. They are nocturnal and hard to spot.

The **raccoon** is a nocturnal and particularly crafty animal found in southeastern Canada. It has a reputation for cleanliness because of its habit of plunging its food underwater before eating it.

The **red fox** has striking auburn fur and is found throughout the forests of eastern Canada. A cunning creature, it keeps its distance from humans and is rarely seen. It hunts small animals and also feeds on nuts and berries.

Beluga whales are white and measure about 5m in length. These marine mammals live mainly in polar waters, but can be found in the estuary of the St. Lawrence at the mouth of the Saguenay. This is the smallest species of whale in the St. Lawrence.

Countless **orcas** inhabit the waters around Vancouver Island and are commonly spotted from the ferries that link this island with the mainland. They are the only marine mammals that eat warm-blooded animals like seals, belugas and other smaller whales, which probably explains their more common appellation, killer whales.

Bigger than its European relative, the **bison** (American buffalo) was the high lord of the American plains for many years. Millions of them lived here and migrated over long distances. Their meat, leather and tendons fulfilled the essential needs of nomadic Aboriginal people. Over-hunted, it has come very close to extinction. It is now found on breeding farms and in national parks.

Bison

A bit smaller than an ox, the **musk ox** lives on the tundra and travels in herds. It's easy to recognize by its long, woolly fleece, and big stumpy horns. When under attack, musk oxen will form a circle to collectively protect themselves.

History

This vast continent had already been home to a medley of Aboriginal peoples for several thousands of years when the Europeans discovered the New World. These populations' ancestors, nomads originating from northern Asia, had crossed the Bering Strait toward the end of the Ice Age, over 12,000 years ago, slowly appropriating the entire continent. It was in the course of the following thousands of years, as the glaciers receded, that some of them began emigrating to more northern lands, notably those of Canada.

There is some doubt, however, as to whether the Aboriginal presence on the West Coast originated with these same vast waves of immigration. According to one theory, the ancestors of the West Coast peoples came here more recently (around 3000 BC) from islands in the Pacific. Proponents of this hypothesis base their argument on the natives' art, traditions and spoken languages, which are not unlike those of the Aboriginal peoples of the Pacific islands.

Nevertheless, Aboriginals were still moving about when the Europeans established themselves here. The bands of the Iroquois confederacy, for instance, were then on the run from powerful rivals who were constantly pushing them farther north, all the way to the St. Lawrence River. Farther west, the populating of the Prairies by the Cree, the Assiniboines and the Blackfoot would occur mainly in the mid-18th century. They came, for the most part, in pursuit of wild horses and buffaloes. In fact, only the Inuit, formerly referred to as Eskimos, were able to enjoy their hunting grounds in peace – but only just.

When the Europeans launched their first intensive explorations of North America, several Aboriginal peoples, often united in the bosom of linguistic families, shared or vied for a place in Canada. The Far North belonged to the Inuit, who speak Inuktitut. The island of Newfoundland was home to the Beothuk nation. The St. Lawrence Valley was occupied by the Iroquois, Huron-Wendat, Pétun and Neutral nations.

Almost the entire Canadian Shield as well as the north and west of the Prairies accommodated the Algonquin nation. From east to west lived the Welustuk (Malecites), Mi'gmaq (Micmacs), Innu (Montagnais), Ottawa, Ojibwa, Noooheenoos (Cree), Blackfoot, Blood, Peigans and Gros Ventres. In Manitoba lived the Sioux communities. The Yukon and the southern part of the Northwest Territories were inhabited by communities belonging to the Athabaskan linguistic family. In the Rockies, to the south, were the Kootenay and the Salish.

Finally, from north to south on the west coast, what was to become British Columbia was occupied by Nootka, Coast Salish, Kwakiutl, Bella Coola, Tsimshian, Haida and Tlinkit. Tagish, Tahltan, Testsaut, Carrier, Chilcotin, Interior Salish, Nicola and Kootenays occupied the interior.

Some of these nations would be exterminated or repelled by neighbouring communities before the continent was even explored by the Europeans. Moreover, the wars between European colonies would lead to more shifts in Aboriginal populations.

Living in groups, Aboriginal peoples in this vast country developed societies whose customs were distinct from one another. Nations in the St. Lawrence Valley, for example, lived mainly on produce from their vegetable gardens, supplementing this with fish and game, while the more northern and nomadic communities in the western plains essentially depended on hunting to survive.

With the passing centuries, a communication network was woven over the entire continent. Many Aboriginal peoples made ample use of the canoe and maintained very close commercial ties with neighbouring nations. From the 16th century on, these First Nations peoples, who were well adapted to the rigours and particularities of the land, were marginalized by the coming of the Europeans.

First Contacts

The first Europeans came to Canada via the Atlantic Ocean, reaching the shores of what we now refer to as the Atlantic provinces. The first to undertake this venture were the Vikings, circa AD 1000. They took advantage of a temporary warm spell to fish and attempt to settle on the island of Newfoundland, which they named Vinland. In 1497, Giovanni Caboto, rechristened John Cabot in English, left

Bristol for Newfoundland. The navigator was seeking a direct route to China. Though he failed to find it, he did report back to England the existence of inestimable amounts of cod in the gulf and on the open sea. From that moment on, British, French, Spanish and Basque fishers flocked to the Grand Banks and put into port on a regular basis to smoke or salt their catch.

In 1534, Francis I, who was also keen on finding gold and the mythical route that would put the riches of the Orient within the grasp of French vessels, commissioned navigator Jacques Cartier, who made three voyages to the New World. These voyages marked an important stage as they constituted France's first official contacts with the peoples and land in this part of North America.

During these expeditions, the Breton navigator travelled far up the St. Lawrence River, to the Aboriginal villages of Stadacona (Québec City) and Hochelaga (the island of Montréal). Cartier's discoveries, however, received little consideration from the French authorities, who were solely interesting in Asia. Following this failure, the French Crown ignored this inhospitable land for several decades.

Acadia

It was the growing fashion for fur hats and coats in Europe as well as the benefits this trade promised that later rekindled France's interest in North America. Because the fur trade required close and constant ties to local suppliers, a permanent presence soon became essen-

tial. Up to the end of the 16th century, several attempts were made to set up trading posts on the Atlantic coast or inland.

Finally, in 1604, in the reign of King Henry IV, the Frenchman Pierre du Gua, sieur de Monts, established the first colony. He did so with 80 men, on a small island in the Bay of Fundy, naming it "Acadie" (Acadia). It was an unfortunate choice, for winter completely cut the island off from the mainland, which provided them with wood, game and drinking water. Close to half of the new colonists would not survive the winter. In the spring, those that did moved to the other side of the bay and founded the Port Royal colony. The Micmac, who looked favourably on trade with the Europeans, welcomed them and came to the new colony's assistance. They would have cause to regret it, for the Europeans passed on diseases their immune systems were unable to fight. Nine-tenths of the Micmac population would perish as a result.

The Port Royal colony was later abandoned as Henry IV proved rather unimpressed by the trade results of the venture. It was nevertheless reopened in 1610 by a companion of de Monts's, who pointed out to wealthy French Catholics the possibility of converting Aboriginals to their faith. The Micmac actually acquiesced in good faith, without ever really renouncing their own beliefs.

Port Royal was not destined to know peace, however. Between 1613 and 1690, the British seized the colony on three occasions, occupying it for varying

periods of time. The resolution of conflicts in Europe and the Saint-Germain-en-Laye, Breda and Ryswick treaties returned it to the French every time. Finally, in 1710, the British seized Acadia once more and did not surrender it again. They renamed it "Nova Scotia."

The seizure was hardly symbolic, though, as the French colonists, mainly Poitevins, succeeded in founding several other colonies and becoming self-sufficient, practising farming, fishing, hunting and trade.

The French

Populating efforts by the French were not confined to Acadia. From 1608, Samuel de Champlain undertook the adventure, which he shared with the Sieur de Monts. He ventured up the St. Lawrence River and settled at the foot of a cliff facing a narrowing of the river, where he built a few fortified buildings. This was the "Abitation de Québec" (in Algonquin, "Québec" means "where the river narrows"). For the merchants financing the operation, the Québec settlement was meant to secure and facilitate fur trade on the St. Lawrence. Their suppliers, the Innu (Montagnais), were in fact at war with the Iroquois, who fully intended monopolizing the sale of furs to the French. Champlain, for his part, wished to found a genuine populated colony.

Their first winter in Québec was an extremely hard one. Indeed, 20 of the 28 men died of scurvy and malnourishment before the supply ships arrived in the spring of 1609. Be that as it may, this date marks the beginning of a permanent French presence in North America. When Samuel de Champlain died on Christmas day of 1635, New France already boasted about 300 pioneers, and the French had explored the entire St. Lawrence River and the Great Lakes region.

Between 1627 and 1663, the Compagnie des Cents Associés had the purchasing monopoly of furs and was slowly populating New France. Moreover, French religious circles began taking a growing interest in the colony. The Recollet priests were the first to arrive, in 1615. They would be replaced by the Jesuits in 1632. In 1642, it was first the will for evangelization that justified the creation of a small village, Ville-Marie, which would later become Montréal. The missionaries settled in Huronnie, where they were very likely tolerated because of trade agreements.

Five Jesuits perished in1648-49 during the defeat of the Huron-Wendat at the hands of the Iroquois. This war was, in fact, part of a huge military campaign waged by the mighty Five Nations Iroquois confederacy, which annihilated all rival nations between 1645 and 1655. The Huron-Wendat, Pétun, Neutral and Erie nations, each numbering at least 10,000, were almost entirely decimated in the space of a decade. The offensive even threatened the existence of the French colony. In 1660-61, Iroquois warriors struck throughout New France, bringing about the ruin of crops and the decline of the fur trade.

Louis XIV, king of France, thus decided to govern the colony himself. New France, comprising approximately 3,000 inhabitants, consequently became a French province. The royal government recruited farm workers and even sent a full regiment to put down the Iroquois. This proved effective, and the soldiers were encouraged to stay on as colonists. To make up for an insufficient female population, the king dowered close to 800 volunteers, who came here to enter into marriage. These women became known as *les filles du roi* (the king's daughters). This period of New France's history is also that of the famed *coureurs des bois* (trappers) era. Forsaking their lands for the fur trade, these young intrepid men went far into the interior in order to trade directly with Aboriginal trappers. Nevertheless, most of the colonists' main occupation remained the cultivation of the soil.

Society revolved around the seigneurial system; land in New France was divided into seigneuries, which were further subdivided into lands held by commoners. The land was partitioned into deep and narrow strips to allow everyone access to waterways. This system obliged eligible voters to pay an annual allowance and fulfill a series of duties for their seigneur. As there were few eligible voters and a certain rivalry between seigneurs, these voters benefited from living conditions far superior to those of French peasants.

French territorial claims in North America grew rapidly at this time due to expeditions undertaken by trappers, the clergy and

explorers, who were to discover virtually the entire North American continent. New France reached its peak at the dawn of the 18th century, when it monopolized the fur trade in North America, controlled the St. Lawrence River and undertook the development of Louisiana. These positions enabled it to keep the expansion of British colonies in check, despite the fact that these were far more populous between the Atlantic Ocean and the Appalachian Mountains. A new word referring to French colonists who had opted for New France rather than their mother country thus emerged: these were Canadians. This designation would take on its current meaning considerably later, much like the word "Canada" would come to refer to a much larger territory than it had originally.

The West: A Source of Fur

In 1670, the territory now known as the prairies, made up of the provinces of Manitoba, Saskatchewan and Alberta, was ceded by the British Crown to the Hudson's Bay Company (HBC), which took over the economic and political administration of the region, called Rupert's Land.

The HBC controlled trade in Rupert's Land, which encompassed all land that drained into Hudson Bay, therefore covering much of present-day Canada. In 1691, Henry Kelsey, an employee of the company, was the first to set sight on the eastern boundary of Alberta. HBC traders, however, had competition from French fur trappers, who headed inland to the source of the fur instead of waiting for the natives to bring the pelts to the trading posts. Ultimately, it was Anthony Henday, an independent trader, who became the first white man to trade in Alberta in 1754-55. Encouraged by favourable reports, independent fur traders in Montréal formed the North West Company in 1787, and then founded the first trading post in Alberta, Fort Chipewyan, on Lake Athabasca.

The 18th century saw an increase in exploration and colonization all over the world by European sea powers, but there was an immense area that still seemed inaccessible: the far-off and mysterious Pacific Ocean. Some of the many peoples inhabiting its shores were completely unknown to French, Spanish and English navigators. The Panama Canal had not yet been dug, and sailing ships had to cover incredible distances, their crews braving starvation, just to reach the largest of the Earth's oceans.

In 1792, English explorer James Cook's compatriot George Vancouver (1757-1798) took possession of the territory surrounding the city that now bears his name for the King of England, and by so doing put an end to any plans the Russians and Spaniards had of laying claim to the region. The former would have liked to extend their empire southward from Alaska, while the latter, firmly entrenched in California, were looking northward. Spanish explorers had even made a brief trip into Burrard Inlet in the 16th century. This far-flung region was not coveted enough to cause any bloody wars, however,

and was left undeveloped for years to come.

The Vancouver region was hard to reach not only by sea, but also by land, with the virtually insurmountable obstacle of the Rocky Mountains blocking the way. Imagine setting out across the immense North American continent from Montréal, following the lakes and rivers of the Canadian Shield, and exhausting yourself crossing the endless Prairies, only to end up barred from the Pacific by a wall of rock several thousand metres high. In 1808, the fabulously wealthy fur merchant and adventurer Simon Fraser became the first person to reach the site of Vancouver from inland. This belated breakthrough had little impact on the region, though, since Fraser was unable to reach any trade agreements with the coastal nations and quickly withdrew to his trading posts in the Rockies.

In 1818, Great Britain and the United States created the condominium of Oregon, a vast fur-trading zone along the Pacific bounded by California to the south and Alaska to the north. In so doing, these two countries excluded the Russians and the Spanish from this region once and for all. The employees of the North West Company combed the valley of the Fraser River in search of furs.

The Decline of New France

Conquered in Europe, France agreed to hand control of Hudson Bay, Newfoundland and French Acadia over to England in accordance with the 1713

Treaty of Utrecht. With this treaty, New France lost much of its stake in the fur trade as well as its strategic military positions. Severely weakened, it was unable to resist for very long. Even the construction of an impressive fortress, Louisbourg, on the island of Cape Breton, would prove futile.

In 1749, 2,500 British colonists and two regiments founded Halifax, in proximity of the Acadian communities already in place. From 1755, the British colonel, Charles Lawrence, ordered what he believed to be a preventive measure: the deportation of Acadians he suspected had remained faithful to France. This great upheaval led to the exodus of at least 7,000 Acadians. Some would take years to come home, ultimately to find British colonists on their lands, which they had been clearing and farming for over a century. The Acadians therefore settled in New Brunswick, on the northwest coast of Nova Scotia, in Québec and even in Newfoundland, taking the memory of Acadia with them. Other Acadians reached the French colony of Louisiana and became "Cadiens," or "Cajuns."

The showdown for the control of North America concluded a few years later with the final victory of British troops over the French. Montréal was the last to fall, in 1760, though the outcome had ultimately been settled since the capture of Québec City the previous year. General Wolfe's British troops, who arrived aboard a 200-ship fleet, conquered those of General Montcalm after a summer of siege. At the time of the British conquest, New France boasted approximately 60,000 inhabitants, 8,967 of whom lived in Québec City and 5,733 in Montréal.

The British Regime and Loyalist Settlement

In accordance with the 1763 Treaty of Paris, France officially ceded Canada, its possessions east of the Mississippi and what it had left of Acadia to England. The first years of British government were very trying for the former subjects of the French Crown. First, the provisions of the Royal Proclamation of 1763 instituted territorial divisions that deprived the colony of its most lucrative sector, the fur trade. Moreover, the setting up of British civil laws and the refusal to recognize papal authority meant the destruction of the two pillars on which colonial society had rested up to then: the seigneurial system and religious hierarchy. Finally, Catholics were excluded from administrative duties. A good many of the elite left the country for France, while British merchants gradually took control of trade.

England later agreed to rescind the Royal Proclamation, for it had to increase its hold over Canada and win over its population in order to better resist the upsurge of independence movements in its 13 Southern Colonies. As such, from 1774, the Québec Act replaced the Royal Proclamation and inaugurated a more realistic policy toward this British colony, whose population was predominantly Catholic and French-speaking.

The Canadian population remained almost essentially of French stock until the end of the War of American Independence, which brought about a first wave of Anglo-Saxon colonists. U.S citizens wishing to remain faithful to the British Crown, the Loyalists migrated to Nova Scotia as well as other maritime territories in the region. Their arrival spawned the first real colonies in New Brunswick, Prince Edward Island and Cape Breton Island. Between 5,000 and 6,000 Loyalists also settled upriver from Canadians, mainly on the shores of Lake Ontario and, though more seldomly, in the regions populated by the French. Aboriginal peoples who had supported the cause of the British against the American revolutionaries would also obtain territories in the region. In what would later become Upper Canada and finally Ontario, the Loyalists settled en masse in the open spaces. Though the French had recognized and explored the Great Lakes well before, their only settlements there were trading posts and forts, which controlled the roads, including the Fort Rouillé, later to become Toronto.

Wherever colonists chose to settle and whatever their ethnic group, their lives were very difficult, often amounting to a race against winter. Indeed, they had to be sufficiently set up to withstand the cold season. This compelled them to build rudimentary and uncomfortable shelters and clear the land, which they could then sow as quickly as possible. And there was no plough that could lift soil in which stumps and stones remained.

It goes without saying that for Loyalists and British colonists who would later join their ranks, being part of the Empire was a major advantage. They looked upon French-speaking Canadians, who considered the pope to have higher authority than that of the king, with suspicion. The British authorities wanted the Loyalists to keep their customs, and in 1791, divided Canada into two provinces: Upper and Lower Canada. The former was situated west of the Ottawa River and mainly inhabited by Anglo-Saxons, with British civil laws henceforth in current use. The latter, which consisted mainly of French Canadians, remained governed according to the French tradition of common law. Moreover, the Constitution Act of 1791 introduced an initial parliamentary government in Canada by creating a House of Assembly in each of the two provinces. At the time, the term "Canada" did not yet encompass the British Atlantic colonies, which led a completely separate existence. The Act aimed to restrict the powers of the legislative assemblies elected by the people.

Under the terms of the act, the executive functions of government were carried out by a governor appointed by the British government, who in turn would name the members of the executive council who were to assist him. The legislature took the form of an elected legislative assembly holding very little real power and subject to vetos by the governor and the executive council. Loyalists in Upper Canada first chose Newark (now Niagara-on-the-Lake) for a capital, but soon moved it to York (which would later become Toronto) in fear of an American invasion.

They had reason to be wary of their southern neighbours, for in 1812 the United States took advantage of the Napoleonic wars to attempt an invasion of both Canadas, and in so doing set York ablaze. The U.S. military was remarkably ineffective, however, and none of the British colonies fell completely into their hands. The Americans even suffered stinging defeats, the British having managed to seize a part of Maine, set fire to the White House and burn Buffalo. At the end of the war, both sides assumed their former positions.

The British government came to the conclusion that the loss of 13 of its colonies (creating the United States) had been caused by the excessive freedom they had enjoyed. The governors surrounded themselves with some of the colony's most powerful and influential men. Together they ruled, taking little account of the wishes of the people's elected representatives. This oligarchy became known in Upper Canada as the Family Compact and in Lower Canada as the *Clique du Château*.

Meanwhile, Napoleon's Continental System forced Britain to get its lumber from Canada. From an economic standpoint, this was good for the colony. The development of a new industry was especially timely, as the fur trade, the original reason for the existence of the colony, was in steady decline. In 1821, the takeover of the Montréal-based North West Company by the Hudson's Bay Company

marked the end of Montréal as the centre of the North American fur trade. Meanwhile, rural Québec suffered through an agricultural crisis caused by the exhaustion of farmlands and rapid population growth resulting from high birth rates among French-Canadian families.

These economic difficulties and the struggle for power between Francophones and Anglophones in largely French-speaking Lower Canada kindled the Patriotes Rebellions of 1837-38. French-Canadians chose Louis-Joseph Papineau as spokesman. The period of political conflict that fuelled the rebellion was initiated by the 1834 publication of the *92 Résolutions*, a scathing indictment of British colonial policy. The authors of the resolutions, a group of parliamentarians led by Papineau, decided to hold back from voting on the budget until Britain addressed their demands. Britain's response came in 1837 in the form of the *10 Resolutions*, written by Lord Russell, which categorically refused any compromise with their opponents in Lower Canada.

In the fall of 1837, Montréal was the scene of violent clashes between the Fils de la Liberté (Sons of Liberty), made up of young French Canadians, and the Doric Club, composed of Loyalists. Further confrontations occurred in the Richelieu valley region and in the county of Deux-Montagnes, where small insurgent groups stood up to the British army before being crushed. The following year, a group of Patriotes met with the same fate in Napierville where they confronted 7,000 British troops. This time, how-

ever, colonial authorities sent a strong message to prospective rebels. In 1839, they hanged 12 Patriotes and deported many others.

Meanwhile, the farming and working classes of Upper Canada became convinced that the Family Compact was using its political monopoly to assure its economic one. Two political parties emerged, the Conservatives, also known as Tories, who wanted to maintain the status quo, and the Reformists, whose aim was to make the government more democratic. Despite the absence of intense cultural conflicts, there was a call for reform in Upper Canada. The reformist leader was William Lyon Mackenzie, a Torontonian of Scottish descent who launched his first attacks against the government and the Family Compact in his newspaper, *The Colonial Advocate*. He was later elected to the Legislative Assembly, where he immediately attacked government finances. As time went on, Mackenzie's remarks became ever harsher regarding the protectionism and abusive powers of the Family Compact, which expelled him from the Assembly for defamation. In 1835, he was elected the first mayor of Toronto, but his increasingly extreme views worried some of his more moderate supporters, who ended up rejecting his program completely. The ideas put forth by Mackenzie were shared by a great number of those who expressed their discontent with the Family Compact, but many were unwilling to break ties with Britain.

A powerful new governor quashed hopes for change

through constitutional means with Mackenzie's more radical supporters. When Mackenzie learned of this, he decided to launch his revolutionary forces. Unfortunately, despite its leader's enthusiasm, this movement of workers and small farmers was very poorly organized, and its attempt to capture Toronto was put down quickly, with little violence. A vanquished Mackenzie would follow Papineau into exile in the United States, where they would try in vain to reassemble their troops and to win U.S. support.

When hostilities first broke out, London had sent an emissary, Lord Durham, to study the colony's problems. Expecting to find a population in revolt against colonial authority, Durham found instead two peoples, one French and one British at odds. The solution he later proposed in his report, known as the *Durham Report*, was radical. He suggested to authorities in Britain that gradual efforts should be made to assimilate French Canadians.

The Union Act, laid down by the British government in 1840, was largely based on the conclusions of the *Durham Report*. A new parliamentary system was introduced giving the two former colonies the same number of delegates, despite the fact that Lower Canada had a much larger population than Upper Canada. Public finances were also consolidated and finally, English was made the sole official language. As armed insurrection had proven futile in the past, French Canada's political class sought to align itself with progressive Anglophones in an attempt to resist these

changes. Later, the struggle for responsible government became the central goal of this coalition.

The agricultural crisis, intensified by the arrival of immigrants and the high birth rate, resulted in a massive emigration of French Canadians to the United States. Between 1840 and 1850, 40,000 French Canadians left the country to seek employment in the factories of New England. To counteract this exodus, the Catholic Church and the government launched an extensive campaign to colonize outlying regions, such as Lac Saint-Jean. Nevertheless, the mass exodus from Québec did not stop until the beginning of the next century. It is estimated that about 750,000 French Canadians left the province between 1840 and 1930.

From this point of view, the colonization campaign, which doubled the amount of farmland in Lower Canada, ended in failure. The swelling population of rural Québec was not effectively absorbed until several decades later with the start of industrialization.

The Canadian economy received a serious blow during this era when Britain abandoned its policy of mercantilism and preferential tariffs for its colonies. To counter the effects of this change in British policy, United Canada signed a treaty in 1854, making it possible for certain goods to enter the United States without import duties. The Canadian economy recovered, albeit slowly, until U.S. industrialists lobbied to have the treaty revoked in 1866. Resolving these economic difficulties was the impetus

behind Canadian confederation in 1867.

The Confederation and Expansion of Canada

In 1867, confederation reshaped the entities formerly known as Upper and Lower Canada into the provinces of Ontario and Québec, respectively. Two other provinces – Nova Scotia and New Brunswick – adhered to this pact, which would later unite a vast territory stretching from the Atlantic to the Pacific. For Francophone Canadians, this new political system confirmed their minority status set up by the Union Act of 1840. A bilingual central government and provincial legislatures (bilingual in Québec only) shared the various legislative powers. It was not until the latter half of the following century that New Brunswick became officially bilingual, thus recognizing the role of its significant Acadian minority. The province obtained jurisdiction in the sensitive areas of education, culture and civil laws, while the central government was entrusted with wide powers of taxation and economic regulation. The pact that created modern-day Canada was markedly favourable to Ontario. This province's population did in fact top that of Québec's, with the result that the former's proportional representation gave it an advantage over the latter.

Though, in 1867, Canada did not extend beyond Ontario to the west, the British Empire did, including Canadian territory all the way to the Rockies in the west and to the north pole. The fur trade being the principle activity of the HBC, the Company had done all it could to discourage colonization in the region, which explains why the population had only reached 12,000 by 1871.

The fur-trading companies offered nothing in the way of law enforcement. American whisky traders were thus drawn north to this lawless land. With dwindling buffalo herds, Aboriginal were exploited and generally taken advantage of by the Americans; the whisky trade also has deleterious effects on them on them. Uprisings, including the Cypress Hills Massacre, prompted the formation of the North West Mounted Police and the March West began. Starting from Fort Garry in Winnipeg, the police crossed the plains lead by James Macleod. They got rid of the whisky traders at Fort Whoop-Up in 1874, and they then set about establishing four forts in southern Alberta including Fort Macleod and Fort Calgary.

This police corps, which would become the Royal Canadian Mounted Police (RCMP), had much more in common with the French police force than with the British. Offenders were arrested by privates and judged by their officers, which was altogether exceptional in British judicial tradition. The opening of Western territories to colonization was also preceded by treaties with First Nations peoples and by land surveying. This is probably what spared Canada from the serious wars between European and Native American communities the United States had experienced.

Following the United States' purchase of Alaska from Russia in 1867, and the 1868 resolution by Minnesota favouring the annexation of the Canadian prairies, leaders of the fledgling Canadian Confederation (1867) were forced into action. They negotiated with Great Britain and the Hudson's Bay Company to acquire the Northwest Territories (which at the time included present-day Alberta, Saskatchewan, Manitoba and the Northwest Territories) in 1868 without so much as consulting the people who had settled there, for the most part French-speaking Metis.

Land in Manitoba began to be surveyed, but the Metis had no intention of letting themselves be dispossessed. They resisted and prevented the governor appointed by Canada from taking power. Their leader, Louis Riel, attempted to obtain recognition of his people's rights. The Canadian government turned a deaf ear. Pressure from the Americans, who were just waiting for a reason to intervene, the difficulty of taking military action against the well-organized Metis in a region so far from the central government, fear the First Nations would back the Metis and finally Québec support for the Metis forced the federal government to negotiate. Finally, the bilingual province of Manitoba was created in 1870 on a minuscule territory, smaller than Belgium, granted most of the powers that the other provinces enjoyed, except those related to natural resources and the development of the land.

Some 15 years later, the Metis would recall their leader from exile to face a

similar situation, in Saskatchewan at this time. However, Ottawa was in a better position and had troops at its disposal that quashed the rebellion. Riel was accused of treason under an antiquated British law, then hung. His prosecution and execution deeply divided public opinion in Ontario and Québec, where he was considered a compatriot fallen victim to Ottawa's colonial policies.

By 1871, only the British possessions of Newfoundland, Prince Edward Island (which joined the country in 1873), the Far North and British Columbia, had yet to join Confederation. Unlike the prairies, which were simply annexed to the Canadian Confederation in 1868, British Columbia was already a British colony and was thus able to negotiate its entrance into confederation. Isolated on the Pacific coast, British Columbia's principal trading partner was California. As its population grew with the gold rush of the 1850s, certain residents even dreamed of creating an independent country. But these hopes were dashed at the end of this prosperous period, when in 1871, British Columbia's population was only 36,000. Great Britain had already joined its colony on Vancouver Island with British Columbia in anticipation of their eventual integration into the new Canadian Confederation.

But Canada remained far away. With a promise from Canada that a pan-Canadian railway would reach the coast by 1881, British Columbia agreed to join confederation in 1871. However, all sorts of problems delayed the construction of the railroad, and in

1873, as a severe recession gripped Canada, causing major delays in the railway, British Columbia threatened to separate. It wasn't until November 7, 1885 that the railway from Montréal to Vancouver was finally completed, four years late.

As the railway expanded, more and more farmers settled in the region known as the Northwest Territories, which had no responsible government on the provincial level. You will recall that Canada had annexed the territories (prairies) without giving them provincial status, except for a small parcel of land, which became the province of Manitoba. Inevitably, the federal government was compelled to expand Manitoba and create the provinces of Saskatchewan and Alberta in 1905.

Most settlers arrived in Alberta when the Canadian Pacific Railway reached Fort Calgary in 1883 and eight years later in 1891 when the Grand Trunk Railway's northern route reached Edmonton. Ranchers from the United States and Canada initially grabbed up huge tracts of land with grazing leases. Much of this open range land was eventually granted to homesteaders. To Easterners, the West was ranches, rodeos and cheap land, but the reality was more often a sod hut and loneliness. Though a homestead could be registered for $10, a homesteader first had to cultivate the land and own so many head of cattle. But the endless hope for a better future kept people coming from far and wide.

In 1895, London officially granted Canada the Far North; the Yukon territory

was officially ceded in 1898 to ensure Canadian jurisdiction over that area during the Klondike gold rush. Contacts between the Inuit and Europeans here had been constant since the 16th century, when the Nordic waters first attracted whalers.

From an economic standpoint, Confederation failed initially to provide the expected results. It was not until three decades had passed, characterized by sharp fluctuations, that Canada really experienced its first great period of rapid economic growth. The foundations for this growth were laid several years after Confederation by Sir John A. Macdonald, the federal Conservative Prime Minister re-elected in 1878 after five years out of office. His electoral campaign had centred around his National Policy, a series of measures aimed at protecting and promoting Canada's nascent industries by means of protective tariffs, the creation of a big internal market unified by a transcontinental railway, and the growth of this internal market by a policy of populating the Prairies through massive immigration. At the same time, the arrival in Canada of the industrial revolution and the use of steam as a power source brought about enormous changes. Though Montréal and Toronto remained the undisputed hubs of this movement, numerous other smaller cities were also affected. The lumber industry, which had been one of the mainsprings of the economy during the 19th century, began exporting more cut wood than raw lumber, giving rise to a processing industry. The expansion of the railway, the hub of which was Montréal, led to spe-

cialization in the production of rolling stock. The leather goods, clothing and food industries also enjoyed significant growth.

This wave of industrialization accelerated the pace of urbanization and created a large, poor working class. Factory neighbourhoods were terribly unhealthy – coal mines in Alberta and British Columbia were the most dangerous in the world. Strikes broke out, but were soon suppressed by the public authorities.

The Golden Age of Economic Liberalism

With the beginning of the 20th century, a period of prodigious economic growth in Canada started and lasted until the Great Depression of the 1930s. Sharing the optimism and euphoria of Canadians, Prime Minister Wilfrid Laurier predicted that the 20th century would be Canada's.

Manufacturers profited during this period of growth. Thanks to new technology and new markets, the abundance of natural resources was the principal catalyst of this second wave of industrialization. Central to the new era was the production of electrical power. With its numerous powerful rivers, Québec became a major producer of hydroelectric power in a matter of years. The pulp and paper industry found huge markets in the United States, due to the depletion of forests in the United States and the rise of the popular press.

This new period of industrialization differed from the first one in several ways. Taking place largely outside the major cities, it led to an increase in urban growth in outlying regions. In some cases, cities sprang up in a matter of a few years. Unlike the manufacturing industries, the exploitation of natural resources required more qualified workers and a level of financing far beyond local means. Britain's stake in the economy, which up until now had been the largest, gave way to the triumphant rise of American capitalism. The Canadian population was then in full transformation. Half the population became urban as of 1921.

When the First World War broke out in Europe in 1914, the Canadian government gave its full support to Britain without hesitation. A significant number of French Canadians voluntarily enrolled in the army, although the percentage of volunteers per capita was far lower than that in other provinces. This lack of enthusiasm can doubtless be attributed both to Québec's long severed ties with France and, what is more important, to Francophones' somewhat ambivalent feelings toward Britain. Canada soon set a goal of inducting 500,000 men. Since there were not enough volunteers, the government voted, in 1917, to introduce conscription. Reaction to this in Québec was violent and marked by fights, bombings and riots. In the end, conscription failed to increase appreciably the number of French-Canadian recruits. Instead, it simply underlined once again the ongoing friction between English and French Canada.

The two wars would at least have one positive result in Canada in that the

departure of such a great number of able-bodied men was to oblige companies to replace them with women. These women were never to forget that they were entirely qualified to fulfill the same duties as their "menfolk." They would later demand and, after a concerted and lengthy struggle, obtain the right to vote.

Life in Western Canada was difficult around the turn of the century. In British Columbia, a strike by 7,000 miners looking to improve their working conditions lasted two years, from 1912 to 1914, and finally had to be broken by the Canadian army. For the farmers who came here to grow wheat, the high cost of rail transport, lack of rail service, low wheat prices and bad harvests, along with duties too high to protect the fledgling industry in central Canada, all came together to make for miserable and desperate times. The First World War created a temporary boom, which lasted until 1920, causing a rise in the price of raw materials and wheat. The workers remained dissatisfied, though, and in 1919, the workers' unions of the West created their own central union, the One Big Union. As supporters of Russian Bolsheviks, the union's goal was to abolish capitalism. However, a general strike in Winnipeg, Manitoba quickly created a rift between the workers with respect to their objectives, and demonstrated Canada's determination not to let the country fall into the Marxist ideology. The 1920s again proved prosperous for the West, and Alberta, at the time an essentially agricultural province, was able finish clearing its territory.

The Great Depression

Between 1929 and 1945, two international-scale events, the Depression and Second World War, greatly disrupted the country's political, economic and social progress. The Great Depression of the 1930s, originally viewed as a cyclical, temporary crisis, lengthened into a decade-long nightmare and put an end to the country's rapid economic expansion. With Canada strongly dependent on foreign markets, the country as a whole was hard hit by the international stock market crash. Exporting industries were the hardest hit. The textile and food industries, which sold to the Canadian market, held up better during the first years of the Depression, before foundering as well. The trend towards urbanization slowed as people began to view the countryside as a refuge where they could grow their own food. Poverty became more and more widespread, and unemployment levels reached 27% in 1933. Governments were at a loss in the face of this crisis, which they had expected to be short-lived. Massive public works projects were introduced to provide jobs for the unemployed.

Western Canada was devastated, in particular the Prairie provinces, which saw their agricultural revenues drop by 94% between 1929 and 1931! And the fact that their farms specialized almost exclusively in wheat made the situation even worse. This period was marked by the evolution of two Western Canadian political movements, both of which remained almost exclusively local, the Social Credit and the

Co-operative Commonwealth Federation (CCF). The doctrine of the Social Credit, which supported the small farmers' and workers' stand against the capitalist ascendancy by providing interest-free credit, reached its height under William Aberhart, who was elected premier of Alberta in 1935. His government dared to defy the capitalist system like no Canadian government ever had before (or has since).

The federal government was also compelled to question the merits of economic liberalism and to redefine the role of the state. Part of this trend included establishing the Bank of Canada in 1935, which permitted greater control over the monetary and financial system. However, it was not until the ensuing war years that a full-scale welfare state was created. In the meantime, the crisis that shook liberalism continued to engender ideologies. In Québec, for example, traditional nationalism secured a place of choice, lauding traditional values typified by the rural world, the family, religion and language.

The Second World War

The Second World War began in 1939, and Canada became officially involved on September 10 of that year. The Canadian economy received a much-needed boost as industry set out to modernize the country's military equipment and to meet the requirements of the Allies. Canada's close ties to Great Britain and the United States gave it an important diplomatic role,

as indicated by the Québec conferences of 1943 and 1944. Early in the war, however, the problem of conscription surfaced again. While the federal government wanted to avoid the issue, mounting pressure from the country's Anglophones forced a plebiscite on the issue. The results once again showed the division between Francophones and Anglophones: 80% of English Canadians voted in favour of conscription, while the same percentage of French Canadians was opposed to the idea. Mixed feelings toward Britain and France left French Canadians very reluctant to become involved in the fighting. However, they were forced to follow the will of the majority. In the end, 600,000 Canadians were recruited, 42,000 of whom died in action.

Canada was profoundly changed by the war. Its economy became much stronger and more diversified than before. The federal government's massive intervention during the war marked the beginning of its increased role in the economy and of the relative marginalization of provincial governments. In addition, the contact thousands of Canadians had with European life and the jobs women held in the factories modified people's expectations. The winds of change were blowing.

The Post-War Period

Canada's current borders have only existed as such since 1949, when Newfoundland chose to join confederation. A dire economic situation was the deciding factor in its becoming the 10th Canadian province.

The end of the Second World War signalled a period of considerable economic growth, during which consumer demands repressed by the economic crisis and wartime rationing could finally be satisfied. Despite a few fluctuations, the economy performed spectacularly until 1957.

It became increasingly evident that the real Canadian market was located south of the border. Trade proliferated to the point that Canada and the United States became the two most active mutual economic trading partners. Moreover, Canada was in need of capital to ensure its development and could no longer count on the support of British money-lenders. The Americans would take over, more often than not as majority shareholders in the growing heavy-industry sector.

The St. Lawrence Seaway was dug, opening the Great Lakes to Atlantic navigation. Montréal lost its place as the main trans-shipment port and maritime traffic in its port fell significantly. The city, which had been *the* Canadian metropolis since the British conquest, consequently yielded its place to Toronto.

This prosperity was not equally felt by the various social and ethnic groups. Francophone communities were increasingly lagging behind the Anglophone majority. Economic development in Québec allowed Maurice Duplessis – a premier at once conservative, capitalist and nationalist – to maintain control and prevent the emergence of modern and secular institutions. The Duplessis era can only be explained by the tacit co-operation of much of the traditional and business elite, both Francophone and Anglophone. Though seemingly in its finest hour, the church felt its authority weakening, which prompted it to support, and to encourage its followers to support, the Duplessis government in full measure.

Despite Duplessis's iron hand, opposing voices nonetheless emerged. The most organized opposition came from union leaders, journalists and the intellectual community. All these groups wanted modernization for Québec and endorsed the same neoliberalist economic credo favouring a strong welfare system.

In 1960, the Québec Liberal Party under Jean Lesage was elected on a platform of change and stayed in power until 1966. This period, referred to as the Révolution Tranquille, or Quiet Revolution, was indeed marked by a veritable race for modernism that put Québec "in line with the rest of the world." Religion lost its place at the centre of French-Canadian culture. Language would henceforth define the identity of francophones. The steps taken by the Québec State would repeatedly gain widespread acceptance elsewhere in Canada, notably with regard to the powerful economic levers put into place.

Politics and the Constitutional Crisis

The lively nature of Québec society in the 1960s engendered a number of new ideological movements there, particularly on the left. The extreme

was the Front de Libération du Québec (FLQ), a small group of radicals who launched a series of terrorist strikes in Montréal. In October 1970, the FLQ abducted James Cross, a British diplomat, and Jean Laporte, a Québec cabinet minister. The Canadian Prime Minister at the time, Pierre Elliot Trudeau, fearing a political uprising, called for the War Measures Act to be enforced. The Canadian army took to the streets of Montréal and Québec City. Shortly afterward, Pierre Laporte was found dead. The crisis finally ended when James Cross's kidnappers agreed to let him go in exchange for their safe conduct to Cuba.

The most significant political event in Canada between 1960 and 1980 was the rapid rise of moderate nationalism in Québec. Since the Quiet Revolution, successive Québec governments have all considered themselves the spokespeople of a distinct nation, demanding special status and increased powers for Québec to the detriment of the Canadian government. For nationalist Québecers, Canada is the work of two founding peoples, one of which, Francophones, resides mainly in Québec. They are therefore opposed to the present situation in which this population is simply a minority in an increasingly integrated Canadian whole.

Pierre Trudeau's federal government put up staunch resistance. At once Anglophone and Francophone, Trudeau was also an ardent nationalist. His allegiance was nonetheless to a strong and united Canadian state where there would be but one people. His vision of a

multicultural Canada denied Québec nationalists their place as one of the two founding peoples. Trudeau's idealized policy of bilingualism was seen to deny Québec's desire to become the champion of the official linguistic minority. Trudeau's nationalism led him to cut certain symbolic ties uniting Canada to London. The goal was to repatriate the constitution and, with it, the power to amend the Canadian constitution. London proved willing, but the provinces' consent was required. Fearing an even more centralized Canada where it would not obtain desired recognition, Québec opposed all attempts to repatriate the constitution. It was not the only province to be concerned about Ottawa's plans.

Breaking with the traditionalism of the past, Québec nationalism championed a strong, open and modern Québec with increased powers for the provincial government and, ultimately, political independence for the province. The nationalist forces rallied around René Lévesque, who eight years after founding the Parti Québécois, surprised everyone with a stunning victory in the 1976 provincial election. With a mandate to negotiate sovereignty for Québec, the party called a referendum in 1980. From the beginning, the referendum campaign revived the division between Québec sovereignists and federalists. The struggle was intense and mobilized the entire population right up until the vote. Finally, after a campaign based on promises of a new style of federalism, the "No" (No to Sovereignty Association) side won with 60% of the vote. Despite this loss, sovereigntists were consoled by how far their cause had come in only a few years. From a fringe movement in the 1960s, nationalism quickly proved itself to be a major political phenomenon.

The federal government finally unveiled its reworked constitutional plan. This consisted of repatriating the constitution by including the Canadian Charter of Rights and Freedoms and an amending formula that would allow a change in the balance of powers without the consent of all provinces. Ottawa followed up on its plan with the consent of nine provinces, despite the unanimous opposition of Québec's National Assembly, sovereigntists and federalists alike. By doing so, the federal government itself plunged Canada into a constitutional crisis, one which has been monopolizing Canadian politics ever since.

The 1980s and 1990s

For many, the 1980s began with a post-referendum depression, accentuated by a period of economic crisis in Canada unmatched since the 1930s. Though the economy improved slightly over time, the unemployment rate remained very high and government spending resulted in a massive deficit. Like many other western governments, the provincial and federal governments had to reassess the policies of the past.

The 1980s and early 1990s were a time of streamlining and one that saw the creation of global markets and the consolidation of

large economic blocks. Canada and the United States signed the Free-Trade Agreement in 1989. The 1994 North American Free Trade Agreement (NAFTA) brought Mexico into this market, creating the largest tariff-free market in the world.

In 1984, a new federal government was ushered in, that of Conservative Brian Mulroney. As regards the constitution, he would take it upon himself, in 1982, to repair the damage done by his predecessor. The context was also right, particularly since Québec's separatist government itself had been replaced. All 10 premiers got together at Meech Lake in 1987 and came to an agreement. Robert Bourassa, the premier of Québec at the time, was willing to let bygones be bygones if five conditions were met, including the recognition of Québec as a distinct society.

To become official, the Accord had to be ratified by the legislative assemblies of the 10 provinces before June 24, 1990. This seemed simple enough. However, the situation turned into a monumental fiasco when certain provincial premiers were elected out of office and replaced by opponents of the deal, when the Premier of Newfoundland changed his mind on the matter, and when public opinion in English Canada turned against the agreement.

In an attempt to avert a major swing towards sovereignty, Premier Bourassa resolved to present the federal government with an ultimatum. He announced that a referendum would be held before October 26, 1992, either on an acceptable federalist

offer or on the proposition of sovereignty for Québec. Until the last moment, Robert Bourassa truly believed the other provinces and the federal government would produce, for the first time in the recent history of the country, an agreement responding to the demands of a majority of Québecers. The governments did consent to return to the negotiation table shortly before the deadline. A general agreement, the Charlottetown Accord, was put together in a few days. This was presented not only as a response to Québec's aspirations but also to those of the other Canadian provinces and Canada's Aboriginal peoples. October 26, 1992, the date originally planned for a provincial referendum on Québec's future, was kept as the date for this Canada-wide referendum. For Québecers, the Accord was deemed an unacceptable setback with regard to the prior agreement. They therefore refused to endorse it. The rest of Canada also refused, considering the offer still too generous to Québec.

Worn out by the fruitless discourse around their place within Canada, many Québecers, since the failure of the "Meech Lake Accord," were impatiently awaiting the opportunity to express their desire for change. This opportunity would first present itself during the 1993 federal elections. For the first time, Québecers had the option of voting for a well-structured sovereignist party, the Bloc Québécois, which would represent them within Canadian Parliament. The Bloc Québécois would ultimately walk off with more than two-thirds of the ridings at stake in Québec and form the official opposition in Ottawa. The following year, the people of Québec were destined to elect a new government to manage the province, the Parti Québécois, the main standard bearer of the Québec separatist cause in the course of the last quarter century.

Fifteen years after the 1980 referendum, federalist and sovereignist forces embarked on a new referendum campaign. No one could then have predicted such a close final result. On the night of the referendum, the counting of the very last vote had to be made before the verdict could finally be determined. Québecers voted 49.4% in favour ("Yes") of the sovereignist plan, while 50.6% voted against it ("No"). Only one percentage point divided the two options; Québec was literally split in two. The day after the referendum, Jacques Parizeau tendered his resignation as leader of the Parti Québécois and premier of Québec. He would be replaced by Lucien Bouchard, at that time leader of the Bloc Québécois in Ottawa; he remains premier of Québec.

Toward the 21st Century

Federalists, who had always believed themselves immune to a potential majority vote of Québecers in favour of sovereignty, were badly shaken up by the close results of the 1995 referendum. It was a brutal wake-up call. The federal government was fully resolved to prevent Québec separatists from following up on their plan. The strategies put forth aimed to dissuade Québec

nationalists by threatening them with a potential division of their territory, by praising the merits of Canada and discussing the legality of potential secession. The Supreme Court of Canada delivered its verdict on this issue in 1999.

In 1997, federal Prime Minister Jean Chrétien wished to take advantage of the favourable economic situation and launched early elections. The Liberal Party was re-elected, though with a smaller majority despite massive support from Ontario, the most populous Canadian province. The Reform Party was once again the big winner in the West, claiming even more seats than in the previous election. The Bloc Québécois's performance was not as strong as in 1993. They nevertheless won 45 of the 75 seats in Québec. As for the Progressive Conservatives and the New Democrats, they regained some of their former strengths thanks to voters in Atlantic Canada. The Canadian political map has never been so complex. The Liberal Party's inability to gain much support outside of Ontario, Reform's performance in the West and the large contingent of Bloc Québécois members of parliament certainly puts in question the idea of a Canadian consensus.

Québec, in fact, has not been the only region to question its place within Canada. The 20th century has made governments into much more active participants than the fathers of Canadian confederation had anticipated. Ottawa has increasingly expanded its role, often by curtailing the legislative powers of the provinces.

From a confederation, Canada has thus slowly become a much more centralized federation. This centralization is generally to the advantage of poorer or weaker provinces, which former get part of a redistribution of the national wealth. Moreover, they need not assume all the obligations of a modern government. The system also favours Ontario, which takes advantage of its demographic strength to guide national policies.

A certain dissatisfaction arose elsewhere, too. The Albertan example is revealing. At the end of the 1970s, the oil boom, combined with an economic slowdown in Ontario and Québec, gave Alberta almost total employment and made it the province with the highest revenue per capita. Though growth was phenomenal, it was not as marked as anticipated. Alberta's demands for larger control of its oil and gas widened the split between the province and the federal government, and in the 1980 federal elections, the Liberal Party, the party ultimately brought to power, failed to elect any members of parliament from British Columbia or Alberta. The Liberals thus led the country until 1984 without any representation from these two provinces.

The National Energy Program tabled by the Trudeau government was the straw that broke the camel's back as far as Albertans were concerned. Under this program, the federal government was to claim a greater and greater share of the price of Canadian oil and natural gas, leaving only a very marginal amount of the profits generated by the explosion of the world markets for the provinces and producers.

This appropriation by the federal government of natural resources, which had been regulated and private since Confederation, was strongly repudiated by Alberta and was one of the reasons for the federal Liberals' defeat in the 1984 election. The Conservative government's attempts to make amends to Québec further alienated Albertans, who finally turned to the Reform Party. In fact, in the early 1980s, separatist movements in Alberta even succeeded in gaining the support of 20% of the population and in electing a member to the Alberta legislature in 1981.

Another bone of contention between the provinces and Ottawa stemmed from the fact that the federal government had unlimited powers of taxation at it's disposal (which was not the case with the provinces) and the right to spend this money in whatever sphere it chose. The federal government used these powers to impose national standards in sectors clearly outside provincial jurisdiction. These standards had no legal merit, but any province neglecting to respect them could see itself deprived of major funding. The yoke was that much heavier for the provinces as the economic situation led the federal government to reduce the extent of what it paid out.

Are all these tensions cause for concern? Probably not. The political conflicts that have occupied Canada over the last 25 years are simply signs of the current restoration of balance. The issues at the heart of the dispute often date back to the British conquest. It is therefore virtually certain that they are not about to find a definitive answer. One of Canadian democracy's greatest strengths is nevertheless to tackle these issues peacefully, respecting democratic rules. And there is nothing to indicate that this is about to change.

Demography

The population of Canada, much like that of the rest of the Americas for that matter, springs from very diverse origins. In the land that would become Canada, Aboriginal people were joined by French colonists, whose descendants now make up the most significant national minority, as early as the 16th century. And, in the course of the last two centuries, Canada has, by turns, grown richer with immigrants from the British Isles and the United States, then Europe and eventually from all over the world. This infusion of new blood will only inten-

Inuit Woman

sify, given that the Canadian population is aging.

Aboriginal Peoples

The first nations to people what is now known as Canadian territory, the Inuit and First Nations peoples, now represent, numerically speaking, a small fraction of the total population. First Nations peoples are scattered throughout Canada and remain under the injudicious and scurrilous aegis of the federal government. Though some still have the use of hunting and fishing territories, their traditional way of life has, to a large extent, been annihilated.

Aboriginals are currently facing major social problems as a result of such factors as loss of traditional lands and attempts to assimilate them. For the last few decades, however, they have become more vocal and adopted more effective political structures to put forward their claims. Today, it is no longer possible to disregard Aboriginal dynamics when it comes to planning regional development or exploiting natural resources in Canada.

The Aboriginal lobby remains a powerful moral lever on the Canadian government. These last few years, Aboriginal people have also succeeded in attracting the attention of both the media and the general population. Interest has primarily focussed on their political and territorial claims. Armed standoffs over land claims have made the news across the country. Most land claims, which result from hundred-year-old treaties, are far from being resolved. Nevertheless, important steps have been taken, most notably when the principle of autonomy for aboriginal governments was tackled during the 1992 constitutional talks. Aboriginal claims now find very solid support throughout most of Canada.

Francophones

The Francophone population forms the majority in Québec and a significant minority in New Brunswick. Its endurance throughout the rest of Canada, however, can hardly be considered a success, despite its own efforts and the support of the federal government.

A large percentage of Québec's Francophones are descendants of the original French colonists who arrived in the country between 1608 and 1759. These immigrants arrived gradually. By 1663, there were only 3,000 settlers in New France. With an increased number of immigrants starting to arrive and with settlers starting families, the population of Québec stood at about 60,000 at the time of the British conquest of 1759. The settlers were mostly farmers from western France.

Today, after just over two centuries, the descendants of these 60,000 French-Canadians number in the millions, seven million of whom still live in Canada. Some interesting comparisons have been made between Québec's sharp rate of population growth and the growth rates seen elsewhere between 1760 and 1960. For example, while the population of the world during this same 200 year period grew three times, and the population of Europe grew five times,

the population of Francophone Canada grew 24 times. This statistic is particularly surprising given that immigration from France had dwindled to almost nothing and that there were very few marriages between British and French families (with the exception of a number of Irish-French unions). In addition, between 1840 and 1930, about 900,000 Québecers, most of them Francophone, left Canada for the United States.

The phenomenal growth of Canada's French population resulted largely from a remarkably high birth rate. Indeed, for a long time, French-Canadian women had an average of eight children. Families of 15 or 20 children were not unusual. This trend can be attributed to the influence of the Catholic church which sought to counterbalance the growth of the Protestant church in Canada. Interestingly, Francophone Québecers now have one of the lowest birth rates in the world, similar to that found in Germany and other western European countries.

The French majority in Québec had long been deprived of control over the economy of the province. In 1960, Francophones earned on average 66% of what Anglophones did. With the Quiet Revolution, Francophones began to take control of their economy. At the same time, they stopped thinking of themselves as French-Canadians and began to define themselves as Québecers. Québec's total population, 82% of which is Francophone, is characterized by an increasing number of immigrants. Unfortunately, French communities outside Québec, particularly

in the west, are steadily declining.

Anglophones

The first Anglophones, most of whom were merchants, when they began to arrive in Canada, only represented a minute portion of the population, even more than 20 years after the conquest of 1759. The British established various trading posts, notably in the west and on Hudson Bay. At the time, populated colonies were already prospering in the Maritime provinces.

The American Revolution would provoke a veritable influx of British immigrants, who would populate the territories now grouped within Canada. Whether because they wished to seek new lands or to remain faithful to England, Loyalists left the United States for Canada between 1783 and the beginning of the 19th century. No matter where they settled, these Loyalists were anxious to show their attachment to the laws, customs and religions their ancestors had brought over from Great Britain. Generally farmers rather than merchants, they did not mix much with the established English communities that controlled business in Québec City and Montréal.

These colonists settled in the Anglophone colonies of Nova Scotia, Prince Edward Island and New Brunswick. They soon became the majority in the latter colony. Farther west, in what constituted Canada at the time, they settled in the southwest of what is now Québec territory and, most particularly, to the north of the Great Lakes, in what would become

Ontario. They prospered and populated the plains stretching from Ontario to the Rockies, as the railway progressed and opened these territories up to colonization. Finally, on the other side of the mountains, two more British colonies established themselves, one on Vancouver Island, the other on the coast. They would later unite to create the province of British Columbia.

Later, others from the United Kingdom joined the Loyalists, often through necessity rather than choice. Thus arrived the Scottish and Irish, many of latter were driven from their homelands by the potato famine. The decline of British immigration from the end of the 19th century was offset by the integration of newcomers of other nationalities.

Other Cultural Communities

Immigration from countries other than France, the United States or England only really began in the late 19th century. In the first part of the century, before the economic crisis of the 1930s and Second World War put a stop to immigration to Canada, most new arrivals were mainly of Central European origin: Jews, Ukrainians and Italians. Postwar prosperity brought immigrants in even greater numbers than before. Most were from Southern and Eastern Europe. Starting in the 1960s, Canada began to see the arrival of immigrants from every continent including many from Indochina and the West Indies, and more recently, Chinese nationals fleeing Hong Kong before its return to Beijing China.

Even though these new arrivals tended to preserve their own culture as much as possible, they eventually adopted either the English or the French language, and were then integrated into that particular community. For the most part, English was the chosen language as it is often one of the languages spoken in their native countries and perceived as the language of North America, indeed, as that which ensures greater success. This caused problems in Québec, where the use of French was quickly being supplanted by English. Strict language laws now oblige new immigrants to send their children to French schools.

Economy

Canada emerged from the 1980s with a colossal national debt, incurred by all its governments in order to sustain and generate economic activity. Only Alberta and New Brunswick managed to come out of it relatively unscathed. The former owes this to the wealth generated by its oil industry, the latter to clear-sightedness and heavy sacrifices. By 1990, a quarter or more of the State's tax revenues were used neither to finance its activities nor to reimburse the accumulated debt.

This money only paid the interest due and payable on the accumulated debt. The governments were thus left with very little room for manoeuvre, obliging politicians to make battling the deficit a priority. Federal government spending cuts have since allowed the State to envisage budget surpluses.

Provincial deficits, however, were harder to fight because federal transfers melted away and every cutback directly affected voters. Certain more right-wing governments, notably those of Ontario and Alberta, made drastic cuts, notably in social programs, to get rid of their deficits. Other governments set cutback targets and gave themselves leeway to meet them despite financial restraints. The whole country was nevertheless well on its way to getting out of the downward spiral begun in the 1970s. Today, most provincial governments have balanced budgets.

The globalization of markets and free trade with the United States and Mexico seemed to have benefitted Canada, which was thus able to increase the volume of its exports. On the other hand, unemployment rates hovered steadily around 10% (8.3% in 1998). The fact that employment has proved less and less directly linked to the volume of investments during the last few years is a disturbing phenomenon.

All this has resulted in a widening gap between the rich and poor in Canada, with the middle-class quality of life diminishing because they are more taxed and less well served. That said, the situation in Canada is hardly desperate. It remains a country in which citizens enjoy a very high standard of living. The United Nations named Canada as the country with the highest standard of living. State-of-the-art Canadian industries, notably as regards transport, media, electronics, engineering, services and biotechnology, are the largest in their sector on the world market. New models have emerged to sustain entrepreneurship. Tax reliefs have even been obtained by unions to set up investment funds meant to support private enterprise.

Politics

The British North America Act of 1867 is the constitutional document on which Canadian Confederation is based. It creates a division of powers between the levels of government. In addition to a central government based in Ottawa, therefore, the ten Canadian provinces each have a government with the power to legislate in certain domains. The constitutional conflict between Québec and the Canadian government is largely a product of disagreements over precisely how these powers should be divided.

Canada is a constitutional monarchy. The Head of State is the Queen, Elizabeth II of England. Royal prerogatives are generally delegated to the Governor General, appointed for five years by the Queen upon the Prime Minister's recommendation. If the powers assigned to the Governor are in theory unlimited, it is because these are not exercised, British parliamentary tradition requiring the strictest reserve and co-operation with the people's elected representatives. In every province, a Lieutenant Governor fulfills duties analogous to those of the Governor General.

In Canada, as in all Western democracies, legislative, executive and judicial powers do not all rest in the same hands. Technically speaking, the most

important of these is legislative power, which, in Ottawa, is exercised by Parliament, independent of the Government. This Parliament is divided into two Houses, according to the English model of Lower and Upper Chambers. The Senate is the Upper Chamber. Senators are appointed by the Governor General on the Prime Minister's recommendation, and their task is to examine and amend bills, which are ultimately passed by the House of Commons. Because they are not elected representatives, senators are not empowered to obstruct the wishes expressed by the votes of Members of Parliament. Elected Members of Parliament (MPs), who each represent a riding for a four to five year mandate, sit in the House of Commons, or Lower Chamber. Elections function according to the single ballot majority system. This kind of system generally leaves room for only two major political parties. It also, however, has the advantage of ensuring greater stability between each election, while making it possible to identify each MP with a particular riding.

Members of the same party generally all vote the same way after having adopted their position in caucus. The House of Commons passes laws, but also oversees the actions of the Government, which the Members can question on any matter. Moreover, the Auditor General, the Chief Electoral Officer and, in certain legislatures, the Public Protector are directly responsible to Parliament. In every province, a Legislative Assembly operates according to the same rules, with the exception

that almost all have abolished their Senate.

The party leader who wins the largest number of seats is invited by the Governor General to become Prime Minister and select the Ministers who will form the Cabinet with him or her. By custom, almost all Cabinet Ministers must already be Members of the House of Commons, as they are responsible to Parliament for their official actions and those of their departments. Tradition dictates that the Cabinet resign if defeated by a majority in the House of Commons. This is very rare since the Prime Minister usually has a majority of Members of the Commons at his or her service. The Cabinet is responsible for most legislation, the administration of the Government and the establishment of its policy, as well as the Treasury Department. It is the real seat of power in Canada.

Finally, judicial power is exercised by judges. These are appointed by the federal Minister of Justice and Attorney General if pertaining to courts of law, and by provincial counterparts in other cases. Judges' independence and impartiality are guaranteed by the permanence of their appointment and by the fact that they are very generously remunerated for their services.

At the federal level, two parties, the Liberal Party and the Conservative Party, have each governed the country at various times since Confederation in 1867. The more left-wing New Democratic Party (NDP) was long the only third party worthy of the name in the Commons. In the last two general elections, however, two new regional parties have emerged, the Reform Party which recently became the Canadian Conservative Reform Alliance, and the Bloc Québécois. The Liberal Party, headed by Prime Minister Jean Chrétien, is currently in its second term as government.

Diplomacy

Canada occupies an enviable place on the international scene. It sits at the table of the seven most industrialized countries (known as the G7) as well as on the Organization for Economic Cooperation and Development (OECD). It is a member of the United Nations Organization (UNO) and one of its staunchest supporters. It is, for that matter, a Canadian Prime Minister, Lester B. Pearson, who created the United Nations peacekeeping force. Moreover, the Canadian armed forces have served as peacekeepers on numerous occasions. Because of Canada's position as a former colony and a current industrial power, it often finds itself in a diplomatic position. Canada has held a seat in the United Nations Security Council since October 1998.

Canada is both a member of the Commonwealth and the French-speaking world. On the trade level, it is a member of the World Trade Organization (WTO). What is more, its North American trade is governed by the North American Free Trade Agreement (NAFTA). Militarily, Canada is a member of the North Atlantic Treaty Organization (NATO). More-

over, Canada has forged a particular alliance with the United States to ensure continental defence. This alliance, the North American Aerospace Defence Command, is better known by the acronym NORAD.

Arts

When it comes to the arts, it is impossible to avoid the influence of the United States. Many Canadians, particularly English-Canadians, have ambiguous feelings towards their U.S. neighbours. American popular culture is omnipresent in their everyday lives. It is fascinating, but also troubling, and much time and energy are invested in defining just what distinguishes Canadian culture from that found south of the border. Nevertheless, countless extremely talented artists of all kinds have gained international renown and have established cultural trends that are uniquely Canadian.

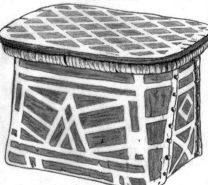

Aboriginal Craft

The aspirations and the concerns of a society are reflected in the work of its artists. For a long time, artistic expression in French Canada presented

an image of a people constantly on the defensive, tormented by an unsatisfactory present situation and filled with doubt over the future. However, after World War II, and particularly after the Quiet Revolution, Québec culture evolved and became more affirming. Open to outside influences, and often very innovative, Québec culture is now remarkably vital.

Aboriginal Art

Aboriginal art has long been considered anthropological specimens and collected almost exclusively by ethnography museums. It is only in the 20th century that it has gradually obtained the status of "works of art." Since First Nations did not traditionally disassociate art from everyday objects, their work did not measure up to the canons of conventional European art. It is only after many struggles, some of which have yet to be won, that Aboriginal works were introduced into art museums. Canadians have showed an increased interest in Aboriginal art since the 1960s and 1970s, with over 100 Canadian museums today carrying collections of Aboriginal art. While artistic practices vary greatly from region to region, the differences between First Nations and Inuit art are the most marked.

Inuit art is very popular in Canada; it is regularly exhibited in museums and

Portrait

appreciated by numerous collectors. Cooperatives were formed in the 1950s to promote and disseminate the arts of the Far North, which marked a major turning point in the history of Inuit art. Before this time, the objects created were small: toys, tools and sacred amulets. Near the end of the 1940s, however, sculptures began to appear as they do today, sometimes reaching 1m in height and assuming a variety of shapes and colours. These sculptures were made of bone, ivory, caribou tines and, occasionally, antler or wood. The most popular material, however, remains stone, sculpted by the Inuit for millennia. Also known as «soapstone», this rock comes from the steatite family and its colour varies between grey, green and black; the darker it is, the denser it is. Stonecut printing is a recent practice that has become popular due to the simplicity of the lines and the quality of the product. Some Inuit art forms are exclusively feminine: basketry, dollmaking, sewing, embroidery, beadwork as well as hide and leather work.

The Inuit call their art *sananquaq*, which means "small portrayal of reality." For the artists, who are often hunters and fishers, the best works are those that faithfully capture human or animal movement. Sculptures, like carvings, told the stories that made up a heritage passed down through the oral tradition: myths and legends, dreams, the forces of nature, relationships between people and animals and the work of daily life. Themes and styles varied from one region to another.

First Nations people practice sculpture less than their northern neighbours, except for those on the West Coast, a region renowned for its totemic art. While those in eastern and northern Canada preferred creating in the realm of the infinitely small, perhaps because most First Nations' peoples were nomadic, it was quite the opposite for those on the Pacific coast. Their totems, which represented the lineage of different tribes, could reach heights of 20 to 25m. The motifs were inspired by the spirit world, the animal world, as well as from mythology. Totemic culture has existed for thousands of years, but the only totems we see are preserved in museums or in parks. The oldest of them is about 300 years old. Generally speaking, the works of First Nations artists were made with materials such as wood, leather or cloth. They also created many three-dimensional works (masks, dream catchers, decorated objects), silk-screen prints and works on paper.

Many First Nations and Inuit artists have adopted contemporary materials and practices such as video, installation work, performance or new technologies. Contemporary Aboriginal art, present throughout Canada, is laden with political innuendo.

Painting

Québec

Through most of the 19th century, visual art in Québec displayed a rather antiquated aesthetic. With the support of major art collectors in Montréal, Québec artists began to

experiment somewhat towards the end of the 19th and the beginning of the 20th century. Landscape artists, including Lucius R. O'Brien, achieved a certain success during this period. The Barbizon school, characterized by representations of rural life, was also influential. Inspired by the La Haye school, painters like Edmund Morris began to introduce a hints of subjectivism into their work.

The works of Ozias Leduc, which are attributed to the Symbolism trend, began to show a tendency towards the subjective interpretation of reality, as did the sculptures of Alfred Laliberté at the beginning of the 20th century. Some works completed around this time exhibit a certain receptiveness of European styles, among them the paintings of Suzor-Côté. It is however, in the work of James Wilson Morrice, who was inspired by Matisse, that the influence of the European School is most explicitly detectable. Morrice, who died in 1924, is considered by most as the forerunner of modern art in Québec. It would, however, take several years, marked notably by the work of landscape and urban artist, Marc-Aurèle Fortin before visual arts in Québec were in line with contemporary trends.

Québec modern art began to affirm itself during World War II thanks to the leaders of the group, Alfred Pellan and Paul-Émile Borduas. In the 1950s, two major trends developed in Québec's art community. The most significant of these involved non-figurative works, of which there were two general categories: abstract expressionism, as seen in the works of Marcelle Ferron, Marcel

Barbeau, Pierre Gauvreau and Jean-Paul Riopelle, and geometric abstraction, represented by artists such as Jean-Paul Jérôme, Fernand Toupin, Louis Belzile and Redolphe de Repentigny. The other major trend in art was a new wave of figurative painting by artists including Jean Dallaire and Jean-Paul Lemieux.

Post-war trends continued into the 1960s. The emergence of new painters, such as Guido Molinari, Claude Tousignant and Yves Gaucher brought increased attention to the geometric abstraction style. Engraving and print-making became more common mediums of expression, art "happenings" were frequent and artists began to be asked to provide work for public places. Styles and influences diversified greatly in the early 1970s, resulting in the eclectic art scene found in Québec today.

English Canada

It was not until the 19th century that it became possible to speak of Ontario art movements. At the turn of the 1840s, a few artists began to stand out, producing paintings that extolled the land, portraying the immensity of a scarcely inhabited territory, with pastoral scenes and typical landscapes. Encouraged by local collectors, a few artists gradually began to develop personal styles. This was true, for instance, of Cornelius Krieghoff, a painter of Dutch descent whose canvases evoke the rustic lives of the new settlers, and of Robert R. Whale, a landscape painter.

At the beginning of the 20th century, the creation of the Canadian Art Club set out to promote painting in Canada and to raise the profile of Canadian artists, some of whom had emigrated to Europe, through a series of exhibitions held between 1907 and 1915. Among Ontario-born painters who spent much of their lives in Europe, James Wilson Morrice is no doubt the most famous, creating works that show the mark of European masters, especially of the impressionists and of Matisse.

In the early years of the 20th century, some of the great Ontario landscape painters achieved renown for creating genuinely Canadian art. Tom Thomson, whose paintings provide a distinctive portrayal of landscapes unique to the Canadian Shield, was an originator of this movement. He died prematurely in 1917 at the age of 40, though his work had an indisputable effect over one of the most notable groups of painters in Ontario, the Group of Seven, whose first exhibition was held in Toronto in 1920. These artists, Franklin Carmichael, Lawren S. Harris, Frank H. Johnson, Arthur Lismer, J.E.H. Mac-Donald, Alexander Young Jackson and Frederick Varley, were all landscape painters. Although they worked closely together, each developed his own pictorial language. They were distinguished by their use of bright colours in their portrayal of typical Canadian landscapes. Their influence over Canadian painting is substantial, and only a handful of contemporary artists distinguished themselves from the movement, among them David Milne Brown, developed a technique inspired by Fauvism and impressionism.

Painters gradually began to put landscapes aside and exploit social themes instead. This was true of Peraskeva Clark, whose canvasses evoke the difficult years of the Great Depression, and of Carl Schaefer, who chose to reproduce rural scenes from his home region of Hanover, Ontario, using them to portray the Depression's harsh consequences.

Abstract art, which flourished in Québec around the 1940s, also had its disciples in Ontario, among them Lawren Harris, a former member of the Group of Seven, and also the Painters Eleven, Ontario's second great pictorial movement, created in 1954.

The stark landscape of the Canadian prairie with its cold winters and fields are typical of artist William Kurelek. Of Ukrainian descent, Kurelek has recreated scenes from across Canada.

It is impossible to cast a cursory glance at Canadian painting without treating the work of Emily Carr, who rendered all the splendour of British-Columbian landscapes in shades of green and blue and conveyed something of the First Nations spirit. Jack Shadbolt and Gordon Smith would also convey the particular vision of the surrounding landscapes shared by those living on the West Coast.

At the other end of the country, in the white light of the Atlantic, Alex Coleville paints. His hyperrealist style, great technical mastery and the gaze of his characters are spellbinding.

Literature

English Literature

Over the years, Canadian literature has sought to create its own space among English-language literatures. Although Britain and the United States have had a commanding influence in defining this identity, English-speaking Canadian authors have gradually given shape to a literary thinking they can call their own.

Although trading posts were set up at points across Ontario and there was a small population of settlers in the 17th century, it was not until the end of the 18th century that colonization began in earnest, with towns and villages developing along the St. Lawrence and the Great Lakes. One cannot really speak of Canadian literature in English until the 1820s.

The first writers, mostly poets, set out to describe the geographic reality that surrounded them, with its wild, untamed nature. This movement can well be described as realist literature and is representative of the concerns of Canadian society of that era, with a vast space to occupy. Several works mark these early moments in English-Canadian literature, such as those of William Kirby and Alexander McLachlan. There gradually developed a desire to create a romantic literature with Canadian accents. In Eastern Canada, Lucy Maud Montgomery wrote her most famous work *Anne of Green Gables*. She is doubtless the most widely renowned of local writers and her book, perhaps the most famous Canadian novel. Literary works reflecting urban realities and their harmonization with nature also began to evolve, giving a foretaste of important urban developments in the 20th century and issuing warnings of their dangers. These themes are brought out in the works of Archibald Lampman, Duncan Campbell Scott and Isabella Valancy Crawford.

The beginning of the 20th century was marked by a tragic world event, the outbreak of the First World War which had a profound influence on English-Canadian thinking. Some people began to feel a need to face up to the British Empire and seek a more equal position for Canada. Writers were hardly exempt from this movement, and the first demands for the development of Canadian culture began to be heard. Writers felt a need to break away from the omnipresent British cultural domination. In the United States, many authors had established themselves not merely as writers of English but as American writers. This emancipation drew envy from several English-speaking Canadian authors and spurred them to create a style of their own. But this movement did not enjoy unanimous support, and some authors, such as Mazo de la Roche in her chronicles, still called for solid links with the British Empire.

This movement would grow all the same, allowing modern Canadian literature in English to define itself more clearly. Hugh McLennan, in his novel *Two Solitudes*, speaks of relations between English- and French-speakers, creating a work with distinctly Canadian themes. The 20th century was also the era of industrialization and of the deep social upheavals that came in its wake, bringing on a more active social engagement and the denunciation of injustice and social evils. This led to a protest movement reflecting the need to build a more just Canadian society. Many voices were heard, including those of authors such as Morley Callaghan, who depicted the hard life of city-dwellers and promoted a stronger social engagement; Stephen Leacock, whose works offer humorous criticisms of Canadian society, and Raymond Souster, a Toronto writer known for his political engagement.

The theatre world has also blossomed thanks, among others, to the works of playwright and novelist Robertson Davies. His *Deptford Trilogy* and *Cornish Trilogy*, both set in Toronto, are analytical and thoughtful looks at the growth of the city from provincialism to sophistication. *The Cunning Man*, the last novel in the latter trilogy, is particularly noteworthy. Summer theatre festivals have become an important element in Ontario cultural life, in particular the Shakespeare festival held every year in Stratford since 1953, and the Shaw festival in Niagara-on-the-Lake.

Margaret Atwood, a feminist, satirist, nationalist, poet and novelist carried modernism into the 1970s. Her literary and critical writings have contributed much to the attempt to define Canadian culture and literature. The 1970s saw the appearance of modern movements such as Open Letter in Toronto, seeking to bring new contributions to old ideas. Several authors have also distinguished themselves, notably John Ralston Saul for his essay *Voltaire's Bastards*; Michael Ondaatje, the Sri Lankan-born Toronto author who won Britain's prestigious Booker Prize in 1993 for his novel *The English Patient* (which became an Academy-Award winning film in 1997), and, more recently, Toronto writer Timothy Findley, upon whom the French government conferred the title of *chevalier des arts et lettres* for his body of work.

One of the earliest pieces of Western Canadian literature is *David Thompson's Narrative of his Explorations in Western North American 1784-1812*. Earle Birney was born in Alberta, and was brought up there and in British Columbia. His belief that geography links human beings to their history is evident in his poetry and its attempts to define the significance of place and time.

Born in 1920 in the Yukon, which was overrun by gold-diggers in the 19th century, to a father who participated in the Klondike gold rush, Pierre Berton lived in Vancouver for many years. He has written many accounts of the high points of Canadian history including *The Last Spike* which recounts the construction of the later Canadian railway across the Rockies all the way to Vancouver.

Renowned for her powerful paintings of Canada's Pacific coast, Emily Carr wrote her first book at the age of 70, just a few years before her death. The few books she wrote are autobiographical works, which vividly portray the atmo-

sphere of British Columbia and exhibit her extensive knowledge of the customs and beliefs of the First Nations.

Robert Kroetch and Rudy Wiebe are two of Alberta's most well-respected writers. Kroetch is a storyteller above all, and his *Out West* trilogy offers an in-depth look at Alberta over four decades. *Alberta* is part travel guide, part wonderful collection of stories and essays, and captures the essence of the land and people of Alberta. *Seed Catalogue* is another of his excellent works. Rudy Wiebe is not a native Albertan but spent most of his life there. He was raised as a Mennonite, and the moral vision instilled in him by his religious background is the most important feature of his writing. *The Temptations of Big Bear*, for which he won the Governor General's Award, describes the disintegration of First Nations culture caused by the growth of the Canadian nation.

The writings of Jane Rule, an American who has lived in British Columbia since 1956, reflect a mentality that is typical of both the American and Canadian west. However, she is better known for her efforts to bridge the gap between the homosexual and heterosexual communities. Other notable western writers include poets Patrick Lane from British Columbia and Sid Marty from Alberta. More recently, however, Vancouver can be proud of its native son Douglas Coupland, who in 1991 at the age of 30, published his first novel, *Generation X*. His work coined a new catch-phrase that is now used by everyone from

sociologists to ad agencies to describe this young, educated and underemployed generation. Coupland's novel *Microserfs*, is just associally relevant, as he describes the world of young computer whizzes, making sweeping generalizations about American popular culture that are both ironic and admiring. *Life After God* explores spirituality in a modern world and the impact of a generation raised without religion. *Girlfriend in a Coma* (1997) criticizes society's progress through a woman who wakes up from an 18-year coma to find out nothing has changed for the better. Coupland's other works include *Polaroids From the Dead* (1996) and *Shampoo Planet* (1993). His most recent novel is *Miss Wyoming* (2000).

Vancouver playwrite George Ryga's play *Ecstasy of Rita Joe* marked a renewal for Canadian theatre in 1967. This work deals with the culture shock experienced by Aboriginal communities, inherently turned towards nature yet existing in a dehumanized western society. Albertan Brad Fraser's powerful play *Unidentified Human Remains or the True Nature of Love* analyzes contemporary love in an urban setting. The play was adapted for the cinema by Denys Arcand under the title *Love and Human Remains*.

French Literature

Literary output in Québec began with the writings of early explorers, like Jacques Cartier, and members of religious communities. These manuscripts were usually intended to describe the New World to authorities back in France.

The lifestyles of the Aboriginals, the geography of the region and the beginnings of colonization were the topics most often covered by authors of the period, such as Père Sagard (*Le Grand Voyage au Pays Hurons*, 1632) and Baron de La Hontan (*Nouveaux Voyages en Amérique Septentrionale*, 1703).

Oral tradition dominated literature during the 18th and early 19th centuries. Most of the literary output of this period dealt with the theme of survival and reflected nationalist, religious and conservative values. The romanticization of life in the country, far from the temptations of the city, was a common element. Glorifying the past, particularly the period of French rule, was another common theme in the literature of the time. With the exception of certain works, most of the novels from this period are only of socio-historic interest.

Traditionalism continued to influence literary creation profoundly until 1930, when certain new literary movements began to emerge. The École Littéraire de Montréal (Montréal Literary School), and particularly the works of the poet Émile Nelligan, who was inspired by Baudelaire, Rimbaud, Verlaine and Rodenbach, stood in contrast to the prevailing style of the time. Nelligan, who remains a mythical figure, wrote poetry at a very young age, before lapsing into mental illness. Rural life remained an important ingredient of Québec fiction during this period, though certain authors began to put country life in a different light. Louis Hémon, in *Maria*

Chapdelaine (1916), presented rural life more realistically, while Albert Laberge (*La Scouine*, 1918) presented the mediocrity of a country existence.

During the Great Depression and Second World War, Québec literature began to reflect modernism. Literature with a rural setting, which continued to dominate, gradually began to incorporate themes of alienation. Another major step was taken when cities, where most of Québec's population actually lived, began to be used as settings in Francophone fiction, in books such as *Bonheur d'Occasion* (*The Tin Flute*, 1945), by Franco-Manitoban Gabrielle Roy.

Modernism became a particularly strong literary force with the end of the war, despite Maurice Duplessis's repressive administration. Two genres of fiction dominated this period: the urban novel, and the psychological novel. Québec poetry entered a golden era distinguished by the work of a multitude of writers such as Gaston Miron, Alain Grandbois, Anne Hébert, Rina Lasnier and Claude Gauvreau. This era essentially saw the birth of Québec theatre as well. With regard to essay writing, the *Refus Global* (1948), signed by a group of painters, was the most incisive of many diatribes critical of the Duplessis administration.

Québec writers gained greater prominence with the political and social vitality brought about by the Quiet Revolution in the 1960s. A great number of political essays, such as *Nègre Blanc d'Amérique* (1968), by Pierre Vallière, reflected an era of reap-

praisal, conflict and cultural upheaval. Through the plays of Marcel Dubé and those of rising talents such as Michel Tremblay, Québec theatre truly came into its own during this period. The use by novelists, poets and dramatists of idiomatic French-Canadian speech, called *joual*, was an important literary breakthrough of the time.

Nancy Huston was born in Calgary and lived there for 15 years. More than 20 years ago, after a five-year stay in New York City, she decided to relocate to Paris, where she finished her doctoral studies in semiology under the tutelage of Roland Barthes. After winning the Governor General's Award in 1993 for her novel *Cantique des Plaines* (*Plainsong*), she became a major contributor to French-language literature. Since then she has published, among other things, *Tombeau de Romain Gary*, another brilliant work.

Contemporary literature is rich and diversified. New writers, such as Victor-Levy Beaulieu, Alice Parizeau, Roch Carrier, Jacques Poulin, Louis Caron, Yves Beauchemin and Christian Mistral, have joined the ranks of previously established authors.

Music

Music entered a modern era in Canada after The Second World War. World renowned symphony orchestras and operas make their homes in Canadian cities from east to west. Major music festivals including the Scotia Music Festival in Halifax, International Baroque Music Festival on Lameque Island in New Brunswick, the

Portrait

International Music Festival in the Québec's Lanaudière region, Montréal, Toronto and Vancouver's famous jazz festivals, Edmonton's Folk Music Festival, the list goes on and on.

The Canadian Radio-television and Telecommunications Commission (CRTC) supervises all types of broadcasting in Canada, ensuring, among other things, Canadian content. For example, any non-Canadian songs are limited to 18 airplays per week. Though this may seem restrictive, it has gone a long way to promoting Canadian music and television in all its forms and languages, and to ensuring that Canadian artists get a fair chance in an area that is all too often dominated by the sleeping giant to the south.

With the Quiet Revolution, song writing in Québec entered a new and vital era. Singers like Claude Leveille, Jean-Pierre Ferland, Gilles Vigneault and Claude Gauthier won over crowds with nationalist and culturally significant lyrics. In 1968, Robert Charlebois made an important contribution to the Québec music scene by producing the first French-language rock album.

Currently, established performers like Plume Latraverse, Michel Rivard, Diane Dufresne, Pauline Julien (who died in 1998), Claude Dubois, Richard Seguin, Paul Piché are being joined by newcomers like Jean Leloup, Joe Bocan, Sylvie Bernard, Vilains Pingouins and Richard Desjardins. The best known name these days is Céline Dion, who sings in both French and English. Her amazing voice has made her *the* pop diva

around the world. There is also the particular achievement of songwriter Luc Plamondon and his participation in the production of *Starmania*. Québec also has its share of non-Francophone artists, like singer and poet Leonard Cohen, 1980s pop star Corey Hart and the Innu musical group Kashtin. The year 1998 brought local Québec artists Bran Van 3000 and Lhasa international acclaim.

English-Canadian artists working in the greatest variety of genres have made their mark on the world music scene. In classical music, Toronto's Glen Gould stood out very quickly as an exceptionally gifted pupil who learned musical composition starting at age 5. His virtuosity was recognized unanimously and he is remembered on the world scene as one of the most talented musicians of his period.

Neil Young was born in Toronto but only spent part of his youth there before moving with his mother to Winnipeg, Manitoba. At first he was a member of various groups, including The Squires, Buffalo Springfield and, most notably, Crosby, Stills, Nash and Young. He began his solo career in 1969, and in 1972 he recorded *Harvest*, his most popular and best known album. Today, he lives in the United States.

Bruce Cockburn was born in Ottawa. Widely recognized in the United States and Europe, especially in Britain, as well as in Canada, Cockburn sits atop many lists of pop music writers, composers and singers. His words, often poetic, offer thoughts on rural life, as in his early albums, mystical connota-

tions, or political and environmental commitment, as in his album *Humans*. Among his recordings, some that stand out are *High Winds, White Sky* (his second album), *Dancing in the Dragon's Jaws* (nominated for various awards), *Stealing Fire*, *Humans* and *Big Circumstance*. He also wrote musical scores for famous films such as *Goin' Down the Road*, which won him a BMI Award as well as a Juno Award for Canadian popular singer of the year.

Among other musicians who have become noted on the international scene are the hard-rock group Rush, the crooner Paul Anka and, a few years back, Barenaked Ladies, whose music moves between rock, jazz and folk. But Canada's number one band is probably the Tragically Hip. Alanis Morissette exploded onto the scene in 1996, and, more recently Shania Twain contributed has to country's move into the mainstream. Country music is most representative of Alberta music. Wilf Carter, from Calgary, became famous in the United States as a yodelling cowboy. More recently, k.d. lang, of Consort, Alberta, became a Grammy-winning superstar. In her early days with the Reclines, she was known for her outrageous outfits and honky-tonk style, but of late, her exceptional voice and blend of country and pop are her trademarks. A rarity in show business, she has always had the courage to be open about her homosexuality. Alberta also has its share of more mainstream stars, among them Jann Arden.

British Columbia, and more particularly cosmopolitan Vancouver, prefer a little more variety and have produced some significant mainstream stars. Bryan Adams was actually born in Kingston, Ontario, but eventually settled in Vancouver. This grammy-nominated rock and roll performer is known the world over. Grammy-winner Sarah McLachlan, herself born in Halifax, Nova Scotia, now calls Vancouver home and has set up her own record label, Nettwerk, in the city.

In Atlantic Canada, the Celtic and Irish influences make for wonderfully melodious music that is very much a part of everyday life. The growing mainstream popularity of this kind of music is thanks in part to artists like the famous rock-fiddler Ashley McIsaac, the Rankin Family, songstress Rita McNeil and Newfoundland group Great Big Sea.

Film

The weak sister of the arts scene, the Canadian film industry has developed only slowly, financially unable to match the big-budget films produced by the major U.S. studios. As a result, it has not achieved much recognition among the Canadian public. During the 1950s, the creation of the National Film Board paved the way for the emergence of many documentaries and other quality films, as well as bringing fame to Canadian film-makers.

In French Canada, however, the film industry has been free to flourish. With documentaries and realistic films, directors focussed primarily on a critique of Québec society. Later, the full-length feature film dominated with the suc-cess of certain directors like Claude Jutras (*Mon Oncle Antoine*), Jean-Claude Lord (*Les Colombes*), Gilles Carle (*La Vraie Nature de Bernadette*), Michel Brault (*Les Ordres*), Jean Beaudin (*J.A. Martin Photographe*) and Frank Mankiewicz (*Les Bons Débarras*). The NFB-ONF and other government agencies provided most of the funding for these largely uncommercial works.

Import feature films of recent years include those of Denys Arcand (*Le Déclin de l'Empire Américain*, and *Jésus de Montréal*, 1989, both available in English), Jean-Claude Lauzon (*Un Zoo la Nuit*, and *Léolo*) Léa Pool (*À Corps Perdu*) and Jean Beaudin (*Being at Home With Claude*).

The 1970s were important for the English-Canadian film industry, with the production of certain films that finally found favour with the public. Some producers, such as Don Shebib with his film *Goin' Down the Road*, even achieved commercial success.

Despite difficult beginnings, Canadian cinema has recently achieved greater recognition thanks to talented producers such as David Cronenberg, with his films *Rabid*, *The Fly*, *Naked Lunch*, *M. Butterfly*, and *Crash*, which won the jury prize at Cannes in 1996. His most recent film is *Existenz*. Others include Robin Spry, with *Flowers on a One-Way Street* and *Obsessed*, and Atom Egoyan, with *The Adjuster, Family Viewing, Exotica* and *The Sweet Hereafter*. Several avant-garde film-makers have also stood out, notably Bruce MacDonald, with *Road Kill* and *Highway 61*. Sticking more to the mainstream, director James Cameron spent a lot of Hollywood dollars on blockbusters like *Terminator* and *Titanic*.

Animated films from the early days of the National Film Board achieved great success on the international scene. Norman McLaren, who developed various techniques that revolutionized this art such as painting directly onto the film, won an Oscar for his 1952 film *Neighbours*. Other contributions to this field include J. Hoedman with *Sand Castle* and John Weldon and Eunice Macaumay with *Special Delivery*. Director Frédérick Back won an Academy Award in 1988 for his superbly animated film, *The Man who Planted Trees*.

Table of distances (km)
Via the shortest route

	Calgary (AB)	Charlottetown (PE)	Edmonton (AB)	Fredericton (NB)	Halifax (NS)	Montréal (QC)	Ottawa (ON)	Québec (QC)	Regina (SK)	Saskatoon (SK)	St. John's (NF)	Toronto (ON)	Vancouver (BC)	Whitehorse (YT)	Winnipeg (MB)
Charlottetown (PE)	4847														
Edmonton (AB)	278	5125													
Fredericton (NB)	4461	386	4739												
Halifax (NS)	4931	265	5209	469											
Montréal (QC)	3643	1207	3921	820	1290										
Ottawa (ON)	3508	1403	3786	1017	1487	197									
Québec (QC)	3894	984	4173	598	1068	254	449								
Regina (SK)	758	4092	1036	3706	4176	2888	2753	3139							
Saskatoon (SK)	825	4380	523	3994	4464	3176	3041	3427	257						
St. John's (NF)	5742	957	6020	1281	1020	2101	2296	1879	4987	5275					
Toronto (ON)	3427	1747	3706	1361	1831	542	402	795	2673	2961	2642				
Vancouver (BC)	967	5814	1245	5428	5898	4610	4475	4861	1725	1792	6709	4387			
Whitehorse (YT)	2330	7177	2051	6791	7261	5973	5838	6224	3088	2579	8072	5758	1919		
Winnipeg (MB)	1329	3518	1607	3131	3601	2314	2179	2565	574	862	4412	2098	2296	3659	
Yellowknife (NT)	1733	6580	1454	6194	6664	5376	5241	5627	2491	1979	7475	5161	2700	2685	3062

Example: The distance between Montréal and Toronto is 542 km.

Practical Information

I nformation in this chapter will help you better plan your trip, not only well in advance, but once you've arrived in Canada.

I mportant details on entrance formalities and other procedures, as well as general information, have been compiled for visitors from other countries. Finally, we explain how this guide works, which will benefit both tourists from other countries and Canadians. Bon voyage in Canada!

Entrance Formalities

Passport

A valid passport is usually sufficient for most visitors planning to stay less than three months in Canada; visas are not required. U.S. citizens do not need a passport, but it is, however, a good form of identification. A three-month extension is possible, but a return ticket and proof of sufficient funds to cover this extension may be required.

Caution: some countries do not have an agreement with Canada concerning health and accident insurance, so it is advisable to have the appropriate coverage. For more information, see the section entitled "Health" on page 54.

Canadian citizens who wish to enter the United States, to visit Alaska or Washington State for example, do not need visas, nor do citizens of the majority of Western European countries. A valid passport is sufficient for a stay of less than three months. A return ticket and proof of sufficient funds to cover your stay may be required.

Extended Visits

Visitors must submit a request to extend their visit **in writing** and **before** the expiration of the first three months of their visit or of their visa (the date is usually written in your passport) to an Immigration Canada office. To make a request you must have a valid passport, a return ticket, proof of

sufficient funds to cover the stay, as well as the $65 non-refundable filing fee. In some cases (work, study), however, the request must be made **before** arriving in Canada.

Customs

If you are bringing gifts into Canada, remember that certain restrictions apply:

Smokers (minimum age is 16) can bring in a maximum of 200 cigarettes, 50 cigars, 400g of tobacco, and 400 tobacco sticks.

For **Wine and alcohol,** the limit is 1.1 litres; in practice, however, two bottles per person are usually allowed. The limit for beer is 24 cans or bottles, the 355 ml size.

There are very strict rules regarding the importation of **plants**, **flowers**, and other **vegetation**; it is therefore not advisable to bring any of these types of products into the country. If it is absolutely necessary, contact the Customs-Agriculture service of the Canadian embassy **before** leaving.

If you are travelling with your **pet**, you will need a health certificate (available from your veterinarian) as well as a rabies vaccination certificate. It is important to remember that the vaccination must be carried out **at least** 30 days **before** your departure and should not have been administered more than one year ago.

Finally, visitors from out of the country may be reimbursed for certain taxes paid on purchases in Canada. (see p 35).

Embassies and Consulates

Canadian Embassies and Consulates Abroad

AUSTRALIA
Canadian Consulate General
Level 5, Quay West
111 Harrington Road, Sydney
N.S.W., 2000
☎ *(61) 2364-3000*
⇒ *(61) 2364-3098*

BELGIUM
Canadian Embassy
2 Avenue de Tervueren
1040 Brussels
Métro Mérode
☎ *(2) 741.06.11*
⇒ *(2) 741.06.19*

DENMARK
Canadian Embassy
Kr. Bernikowsgade 1, DK=
1105 Copenhagen K
☎ *(45) 12.22.99*
⇒ *(45) 14.05.85*

FINLAND
Canadian Embassy
Pohjos Esplanadi 25 B
00100 Helsinki
☎ *(9) 171-141*
⇒ *(9) 601-060*

GERMANY
Canadian Consulate General
Internationales Handelszentrum
Friedrichstrasse 95, 23rd Floor
10117 Berlin
☎ *(30) 261.11.61*
⇒ *(30) 262.92.06*

GREAT BRITAIN
Canada High Commission
Macdonald House
One Grosvenor Square
London, W1X 0AB
☎ *(171) 258-6600*
⇒ *(171) 258-6384*

ITALY
Canadian Embassy
Via Zara 30, 00198 Rome
☎ *(6) 44.59.81*
⇒ *(6) 44.59.87*

NETHERLANDS
Canadian Embassy
Parkstraat 25, 2514JD
The Hague
☎ *(70) 361-4111*
⇒ *(70) 365-6283*

NORWAY
Canadian Embassy
Oscars Gate 20, Oslo 3
☎ *(47) 46.69.55*
⇒ *(47) 69.34.67*

PORTUGAL
Canadian Embassy
MCB Buildin
Avenida Liberdade no. 144
2nd and 3rd floors
1200 Lisboa
☎ *213 47 48 92*
⇒ *213 47 64 66*

SPAIN
Canadian Embassy
Edificio Goya, Calle Nunez de Balboa 35
28001 Madrid
☎ *(1) 423.32.50*
⇒ *(1) 423.32.51*

SWEDEN
Canadian Embassy
Tegelbacken 4, 7th floor
Stockholm
☎ *(8) 613-9900*
⇒ *(8) 24.24.91*

SWITZERLAND
Canadian Embassy
Kirchenfeldstrasse 88
3000 Berne 6
☎ *(31) 357.32.00*
⇒ *(31) 357.32.10*

UNITED STATES
Canadian Embassy
501 Pennsylvania Ave. NW
Washington, DC, 20001
☎ *(202) 682-1740*
⇒ *(202) 682-7726*

Canadian Consulate General
Suite 400 South Tower
One CNN Center
Atlanta, Georgia, 30303-2705
☎ *(404) 577-6810 or 577-1512*
⇒ *(404) 524-5046*

Canadian Consulate General
Three Copley Place
Suite 400
Boston, Massachusetts, 02116
☎ *(617) 262-3760*
⇒ *(617) 262-3415*

Canadian Consulate General
Two Prudential Plaza
180 N. Stetson Ave.
Suite 2400
Chicago, Illinois, 60601
☎ *(312) 616-1860*
⇒ *(312) 616-1877*

Canadian Consulate General
St. Paul Place, Suite 1700
750 N. St. Paul St.
Dallas, Texas, 75201
☎ *(214) 922-9806*
⇒ *(214) 922-9815*

Canadian Consulate General
600 Renaissance Center
Suite 1100
Detroit, Michigan, 48234-1798
☎*(313) 567-2085*
⇥*(313) 567-2164*

Canadian Consulate General
300 South Grande Ave.
10th Floor, California Plaza
Los Angeles, California, 90071
☎*(213) 687-7432*
⇥*(213) 620-8827*

Canadian Consulate General
Suite 900, 701 Fourth Ave. S.
Minneapolis, Minnesota, 55415-1899
☎*(612) 333-4641*
⇥*(612) 332-4061*

Canadian Consulate General
1251 Ave. of the Americas
New York, New York
10020-1175
☎*(212) 596-1600*
⇥*(212) 596-1793*

Canadian Consulate General
One Marine Midland Center
Suite 3000
Buffalo, New York, 14203-2884
☎*(716) 852-1247*
⇥*(716) 852-4340*

Canadian Consulate General
412 Plaza 600
Sixth and Stewart Streets
Seattle, Washington 98101-1286
☎*(206) 442-1777*
⇥*(206) 443-1782*

Foreign Consulates in Ottawa, Ontario

AUSTRALIA
Australian High Commission
50 O'Connor St.,
K1N 5R2
☎*(613) 236-0841*
⇥*(613) 236-4376*

BELGIUM
80 Elgin St.
4th Floor
K1P 1B7
☎*(613) 236-7267*
⇥*(613) 236-7882*

DENMARK
47 Clarence
K1N 9K1
☎*(613)236-2389*
⇥*(613) 562-1812*

FINLAND
55 Metcalfe, Suite 850
K1P 6L5
☎*(613) 236-2389*
⇥*(613) 238-1474*

GERMANY
1 Waverly St.
K2P 0T8
☎*(613) 232-1101*
⇥*(613) 233-1484*

GREAT BRITAIN
80 Elgin
K1P 5K7
☎*(613) 237-1303*
⇥*(613) 237-6537*

ITALY
275 Slater St.
21st Floor
K1P 5H9
☎*(613) 232-2401*
⇥*(613) 232-1484*

NETHERLANDS
350 Albert, Suite 2020
K1R 1A4
☎*(613) 237-5030*
⇥*(613) 237-6471*

NORWAY
90 Sparks St.
K1P 5B4
☎*(613) 238-6571*
⇥*(613) 238-2765*

SPAIN
74 Stanley Ave.
K1M 1P4
☎*(613) 747-2252*
☎*(613) 747-7293*
⇥*(613) 744-1224*

SWEDEN
377 Dalhousie
K1N 9N8
☎*(613) 241-8553*
⇥*(613) 241-2277*

SWITZERLAND
5 Malborough Ave.
K1N 8E6
☎*(613) 235-1837*
⇥*(613) 563-1394*

UNITED STATES
2 Wellington
K1P 5T1
☎*(613) 238-5335*
⇥*(613) 238-5720*

Foreign Consulates in Toronto, Ontario

AUSTRALIA
175 Bloor St. E.
Suite 316,
M4W 3R8
☎*(416) 323-1155*
⇥*(416) 323-3910*

BELGIUM
2 Bloor St. W.
Suite 2006, Box 88
N4W 3E2
☎*(416) 944-1422*
⇥*(416) 944-1421*

DENMARK
151 Bloor St. W.
Suite 310,
M5S 1S4
☎*(416) 962-5661*
⇥*(416) 962-3668*

FINLAND
1200 Bay St.
M5R 2A5
☎*(416) 964-7400*
⇥*(416) 921-0318*

GERMANY
77 Admiral Rd.
M5R 2L4
☎*(416) 925-2813*
⇥*(416) 925-2818*

GREAT BRITAIN
777 Bay St., suite 2800
M5G 2G2
☎*(416) 593-1290*
⇥*(416) 593-1229*

ITALY
136 Beverly St.
M5T 1Y5
☎*(416) 977-1566*
⇥*(416) 977-1119*

NETHERLANDS
1 Dundas St. W., Suite 2106
M5G 1Z3
☎*(416) 598-2520*
⇥*(416) 598-8064*

Practical Information

NORWAY
2 Bloor St. W. Suite 504
☎*(416) 920-5229*
≈*(416) 920-5982*

SPAIN
55 Bloor St. W.
Suite 1204
M5R 2A5
☎*(416) 967-0488*
≈*(416) 968-9547*

SWEDEN
2 Bloor St. W. Suite 1504
M4W 3E2
☎*(416) 963-8768*

SWITZERLAND
154 University Ave.
Suite 601
M5H 3Y9
☎*(416) 593-5371*
≈*(416) 593-5083*

Foreign Consulates in Montréal, Québec

AUSTRALIA
Australian High Commission
(*no office in Montréal*)
See listing under Ottawa.

BELGIUM
Belgium Consulate General
999 Boulevard De Maisonneuve W.
Suite 1250
H3A 3C8
☎*(514) 849-7394*
≈*(514) 844-3170*

DENMARK
Consulate General of Denmark
1 Place-Ville-Marie, 35th Floor
H3B 4M4
☎*(514) 871-8977*

FINLAND
Consulate General of Finland
800 Square Victoria, Suite 3400
H4Z 1E9
☎*(514) 397-7600*

GERMANY
Consulate General of Germany
1250 Boulevard René-Lévesque
Ouest, Suite 4315, H3B 4X1
☎*(514) 931-2277*

GREAT BRITAIN
British Consulate General
1000 de la Gauchetière Ouest
Suite 901, H3B 3A7
☎*(514) 866-5863*

ITALY
Consulate General of Italy
3489 Rue Drummond, H3G 1Z6
☎*(514) 849-8351*
≈*(514) 499-9471*

NETHERLANDS
Consulate General of the Netherlands
1002 Rue Sherbrooke Ouest
Suite 2201, H3A 3L6
☎*(514) 849-4247*
≈*(514) 849-8260*

NORWAY
Consulate General of Norway
1155 Boulevard René-Lévesque W.
Suite 3900, H3B 3V2
☎*(514) 874-9087*

SPAIN
Consulate General of Spain
1 Westmount Sq., H3Z 2P9
☎*(514) 935-5235*
≈*(514) 935-4655*

SWEDEN
Consulate General of Sweden
8400 Boulevard Décarie, H4P 2N2
☎*(514) 345-2727*

SWITZERLAND
Consulate General of Switzerland
1572 Avenue Dr. Penfield, H3G 1C4
☎*(514) 932-7181*
≈*(514) 932-9028*

UNITED STATES
American Consulate General
Place Félix-Martin
1155 Rue Saint-Alexandre
☎*(514) 398-9695*
≈*(514) 398-9748*
Mailing address:
C.P. 65 Stations Desjardins
Montréal, H5B 1G1

Foreign Consulates in Vancouver, B.C.

AUSTRALIA
Australian Consulate
888 Dunsmuir St.
V6C 3K4
☎*(604) 684-1177*

BELGIUM
Honourary Consulate of Belgium:
Birks Place, Suite 570
688 West Hastings
V6B 1P4
☎*(604) 684-6838*

FINLAND
Consulate of Finland
1188 Georgia St. West
Apt. 1100
V6E 4A2
☎*(604) 688-4483*

GERMANY
Consulate General of Germany
World Trade Centre,
999 Canada Place, Suite 704
V6C 3E1
☎*(604) 684-8377*

GREAT BRITAIN
British Consulate General
111 Melvílle St., Suite 800
V6E 3V6
☎*(604) 683-4421*

ITALY
Consulate General of Italy
1200BurrardSt., Suite 705
V6Z 2C7
☎*(604) 684-7288*
≈*(604) 685-4263*

NETHERLANDS
Consulate General of the Netherlands
475 Howe St., Suite 821
V6C 2B3
☎*(604) 684-6448*

NORWAY
Royal Norwegian Consulate General
1200 Waterfront Centre
200 Burrard St.
V6C 3L6
☎*(604) 682-7977*
≈*(604) 682-8376*

SPAIN
Consulate General of Spain:
See listing under Toronto.

SWEDEN
Consulate of Sweden:
1188 Georgia St. W.
Apt. 1100
V6E4A2
☎*(604)683-5838*

SWITZERLAND
Consulate General of Switzerland:
999 Canada Place
V6C 3E1
☎*(604)684-2231*

UNITED STATES
U.S. Consulate General
1095 West Pender
V6E 2M6
☎*(604)685-4311*

Tourist Information

Each province has its own ministry of tourism in charge of promoting tourism development in its respective province. Tourist information is distributed to the public by regional offices. You can get details on the sights, restaurants and hotels in the region. Besides these numerous information centres, most large cities also have their own tourism associations. These offices are open year-round whereas the regional offices are generally only open in the high season. The addresses of the various regional tourist information offices are located in the "Practical Information" section of each chapter.

For Canada-wide information, contact the Canadian Tourism Comission, public/private sector organization devoted to marketing Canada.

Canadian Tourism Commission
8th Floor West
235 Queen St.
Ottawa, ON
K1A 0H6
☎*(613) 946-1000*
www.travelcanada.ca

Tourist Information Offices Abroad

BELGIUM
Comission Canadienne du Tourisme
Rue Américaine, 27
1060 Bruxelles
☎*(02) 538-5792*
≈*(02) 539-2433*

SWITZERLAND
Welcome to Canada!
22, Freihofstrasse, 8700 Küsnacht
☎*(1) 910 90 01*
≈*(1) 910 38 24*

UNITED STATES
Tour & Travel
140W, 69th St., New York
NY 10023-5107
☎*(718) 579-8401*

Getting to Canada

By Plane

Canada has several international airports. For information on each, see the "Practical Information" section at the beginning of each chapter.

From Europe

There are two possibilities: direct flights or flights with a stopover in Montréal, Toronto or Calgary. Direct flights are of course much more attractive since they are considerably faster than flights with a stopover (for example expect about nine hours from Amsterdam for a direct flight compared to 13 hours).

In some cases, however, particularly if you have a lot of time, it can be advantageous to combine a charter flight from Europe with one of the many charter flights within Canada from either Montréal or Toronto. Prices for this option can vary considerably depending on whether you are travelling during high or low season.

The major airlines flying to Canada are **Air Canada, KLM, Air France** and **British Airways**.

Air Canada Offices

BELGIUM
Lufthansa
Rue de Trone 130
B-1050 Brussels
☎*(02) 627 4088*
≈*(02) 627 4012*

DENMARK
Suite 2356
Vester Farimagsgade 1
2 DK-1606
Copenhagen
☎*(33) 11 45 55*
≈*(33) 11 80 55*

GERMANY
Kurfurstendamm 209
10719
☎*(30) 882 5879*
≈*(30) 882 3679*

Marienstraße 32
40210 Dusseldorf
☎*(211) 16 25 85*
≈*(211) 16 25 29*

Lyoner Stern
Hahnstrasse 70
60528 Frankfurt
☎*(069) 27 11 51 11*
≈*(069) 27 11 51 12*

GREAT BRITAIN
Conduit St.
London W1R 9TG
☎*(208) 08705 247226*
≈*(208) 750 8495*

Practical Information

ITALY
Viale Regina
Giovanna N8
Milan
☎*2940 9189*
⇆*201810*

NETHERLANDS
☎*020 346 9539*
⇆*00 44 181 750 8495*

SPAIN
Paseo de Garcia 69
Planta 6 - Offficina 31
Barcelona 08008
☎*(93) 215 0089*
⇆*(93) 215 6497*

Gran Via 86, Edificio España
Madrid 28013
☎*(91) 547 9304 / 547 6136*
⇆*(91) 542 7331*

SWITZERLAND
1-3, rue Chantepoulet
Geneva
☎*(22) 731 4980*
⇆*(22) 732 1554*

Lowenstraße 56
Zurich 8001
☎*(1) 224-4545*
⇆*(1) 211 0793*

From the United States

American Airlines, Delta Airlines, Northwest Airlines, United Airlines, Air Canada and their affiliates offer daily direct or connecting flights between major U.S. and Canadian cities.

From Oceania

Air Canada, in cooperation with United Airlines, offers three daily flights from Sydney to Vancouver via Los Angeles or San Francisco; one continues on to Calgary.

Quantus flies twice daily between Sydney and Los Angeles, where there are connecting flights to Vancouver and other Canadian cities.

Air Canada Offices

AUSTRALIA
Level 12 - 92 Pitt St., Sydney
☎*(61-2) 9232 5222*
Inuvats: 1-300 656 232
⇆*(61-2) 9223 7606*

NEW ZEALAND
Dingwall Building 3/F
87 Queen Street, Auckland
☎*(64-9) 379 3371*
⇆*(64-9) 302 2912*

From Asia

Both Air Canada and Canadian Airlines offer direct flights between Vancouver and Hong Kong.

Air Canada Offices

HONG KONG
Room 1601-4 Wheelock House
20 Pedder Street Central
☎*(852) 2522 1001*
⇆*(852) 2810 1117*

Within Canada

Air Canada has just bought Canadian Airlines, but both are being administered as separate entities until spring 2000. With their respective local partners (**Air BC** offers flights within Alberta and British Columbia, as does Canadian Airlines' regional partner, **Canadian Regional**), these companies offer regular and connecting flights to Western Canada. Daily flights to the cities of Vancouver, Victoria, Edmonton and Calgary as well as many other cities are offered from all the major cities in the country. Flights from eastern Canada often have stopovers in Montréal or Toronto. For example Air Canada flies to Vancouver, Calgary, Edmonton and Victoria 14 times a week. During the high season, the charter companies such as **Air Transat, Royal** and **Canada 3000** offer flights to Vancouver and

Calgary. These flights are subject to change regarding availability and fares.

Air Canada

Calgary
☎*(403) 265-9555*

Edmonton
☎*(780) 423-1222*

Montréal
☎*(514) 393-3333*

Regina
☎*(306) 525-4711*

Saskatoon
☎*(306) 652-4181*

Toronto
☎*(416) 925-2311*

Vancouver
☎*(604) 688-5515*

Victoria
☎*(250) 360-9074*

Winnipeg
☎*(204) 943-9361*

Canadian Airlines

All Provinces and Territories
☎*800-665-1177*

Hearing Impaired (TTY)
☎*800-465-3611*
(Continental US/Canada)

U.S.A
(Including Hawaii)
☎*800-426-7000*

Montréal
☎*(514)845-PLUS (7587)*

Toronto
☎*(416) 675-PLUS*

Calgary
☎*(403) 236-PLUS*

Vancouver
☎*(604) 270-PLUS*

Anywhere else in Canada
☎*800-663-0290*

Continental USA and Hawaii
☎*800-426-7007*

Getting Around

By Car

Good road conditions and cheaper oil prices than in Europe make driving an ideal way to travel all over Canada. Excellent road maps published in Canada and regional maps can be found in bookstores and in tourist information centres

Things to Consider

Driver's License: As a general rule, foreign driver's licenses are valid for six months from the arrival date in Canada.

Highway Code: turning right on a red light when the way is clear is permitted everywhere in Canada except in Québec.

When a school bus (usually yellow in colour) has stopped and has its signals flashing, you must come to a complete stop, no matter what direction you are travelling in. Failing to stop at the flashing signals is considered a serious offense and carries a heavy penalty.

Wearing of seatbelts in the front and back seats is mandatory at all times.

On highways, the speed limit on secondary highways is 90km/h, and 50km/h in urban areas.

Gas Stations: Because Canada produces its own crude oil, gasoline prices are much less expensive than in Europe, and only slightly more than in the United States. Some gas stations (especially in the downtown areas) might ask for payment in advance as a security measure, especially after 11pm.

Winter driving: Though roads are generally well plowed, particular caution is recommended. Watch for violent winds and snow drifts and banks. In some regions gravel is used to increase traction, so drive carefully.

Car Rentals

The best way to get a good price for car rental is to reserve well in advance. Many travel agencies have agreements with the major car-rental companies (Avis, Budget, Hertz, etc.) and offer good values; contracts often include added bonuses.

When renting a car, find out if the contract includes unlimited kilometres,and check that the insurance provides full coverage (accident, property damage, hospital costs for you and passengers, theft).

Caution:
To rent a car you must be at least 21 years of age and have had a driver's license for **at least** one year. If you are between 21 and 25, certain companies (for example Avis, Thrifty, Budget) will ask for a $500 deposit, and in some cases they will also charge an extra sum for each day you rent the car. These conditions do not apply for those over 25 years of age.

A credit card is extremely useful for the deposit to avoid tying up large sums of money, and can in some cases (gold cards) cover the collision and theft insurance.

Most rental cars come with an automatic transmission, however you can request a car with a manual shift.

Child-safety seats cost extra.

Accidents and Emergencies

If you run into trouble on the highway, pull onto the shoulder of the road and turn the hazard lights on. If it is a rental car, contact the rental company as soon as possible. Always file an accident report. If a disagreement arises over who was at fault in an accident, ask for police help.

If you are a member of an automobile association (Canada: Canadian Automobile Association; U.S.A.: American Automobile Association; Switzerland: Automobile Club de Suisse; Belgium: Royal Automobile Touring Club de Belgique; Great-Britain: Automobile Association; Australia: Royal Australian Automobile Association), you have access to some free services provided in Canada by the CAA.

By Bus

Besides cars, buses are the easiest way to get around, are relatively cheap and provide access to most of Canada. It takes only three and a half days to cross the country. Except for public transportation in cities, which is government-run, there is no national transportation company; many private coach lines share the road.

Greyhound
☎*800-661-8747*
Covers all of Western Canada to Ottawa.

Practical Information

Orléans
☎(514) 842-2281
The main company in
Québec.

Smoking is prohibited on
most bus lines and pets
are not allowed. In general, children under five
travel free of charge and
people aged 60 and over
are granted significant
discounts.

Sample Travel Times

Montréal - Ottawa
2hrs 10 min

Montréal - Québec City
2hrs 45 min

Montréal - Toronto
6hrs 10 min

Calgary - Vancouver
14 hrs

Toronto - Vancouver
3 days

Bus Tours

Some companies also offer
package deals on excursions of a day or more,
which (depending on the
length of the tour) include
accommodation and
guided tours. There is
quite a variety of tours
available – too many to list
here. For further information on these tours, contact
the tourist information
centres.

By Train

Travellers who are not
pressed for time may want
to consider the train, one
of the most pleasant and
impressive ways to discover Canada. Via Rail
Canada is the only company that offers train travel
between the Canadian
provinces. This mode of
transportation can be
combined with air travel
(various packages are

offered by Air Canada and
Canadian Airlines) or on
its own from big cities in
Eastern Canada like Toronto or Montréal. This last
option does require a lot
of time however. It takes a
minimum of five days to
get from Montréal to Vancouver.

The CANRAILPASS
☎888-842-7245
www.viarail.ca
This pass offers unlimited
travel in economy class for
a period 12 days in one
month. This package is an
economical way of seeing
the country.

By Bicycle

Bicycling is very popular
in Canada, especially in
big cities like Montréal,
Vancouver and Ottawa.
Bicycle paths have been
set up so that cyclists can
get around easily and safely, but caution is always
recommended, even on
these paths. Bicycle touring is possible throughout
Canada.

Hitchhiking

There are two types: "free"
hitchhiking, which is
prohibited on highways,
and "organized" hitchhiking with a group called
Allo-Stop. "Free" hitchhiking is more common,
especially during the
summer, and easier to do
outside the large city
centres, but is not
particularily safe.

Money and Banking

Most banks readily exchange U.S. and European
currency but almost all will
charge **commission**. There
are exchange offices that

have longer hours, and
some don't take commission. Just remember to **ask
about fees** and **to compare
rates**.

Currency

The monetary unit is the
dollar ($), which is divided
into cents (¢). One dollar=100 cents.

Bills come in 5-, 10-, 20-,
50-, 100-, 500- and
1000-dollar denominations,
and coins come in 1-
(pennies), 5- (nickels), 10-
(dimes), 25-cent pieces
(quarters), and in 1-dollar
(loonies) and 2-dollar
coins.

In Québec, Francophones
sometimes speak of
"piastres" and *"sous"* which
are dollars and cents
respectively.

Traveller's Cheques

Remember that Canadian
dollars are different from
U.S. dollars. If you do not
plan on travelling to the
United States on the same
trip, it is best to get your
traveller's cheques in
Canadian dollars. Traveller's cheques are accepted
in most large stores and
hotels, however it is easier
and to your advantage to
change your cheques at an
exchange office.

Credit Cards

Most major credit cards are
accepted at stores, restaurants and hotels. While the
main advantage of credit
cards is that they allow
visitors to avoid carrying
large sums of money,
using a credit card makes
leaving a deposit for car
rental much easier. Also
some cards, gold cards for
example, automatically

insure you when you rent a car. In addition, the exchange rate with a credit card is generally better. The most commonly accepted credit cards are Visa, Master-Card, and American Express.

Credit cards offer a chance to avoid service charges when exchanging money. By overpaying your credit card (to avoid interest charges), you can then withdraw against it. You can thus avoid carrying large amounts of money or traveller's cheques. Withdrawals can be made directly from an automatic teller if you have a personal identification number for your card.

Banks

Banks can be found almost everywhere and most offer the standard services to tourists. Visitors who choose to stay for a long period of time should note that **non-residents** cannot open bank accounts. If this is the case, the best way to have ready money is to use traveller's cheques. Withdrawing money from foreign accounts is expensive. However, several automatic teller machines accept foreign bank cards, so that you can withdraw directly from your account. Money orders are another means of having money sent from abroad. No commission is charged, but it takes time. People who have residence status, permanent or not (such as landed-immigrants or students), can open a bank account. A passport and proof of residence status are required.

Taxes and Tipping

Taxes

The ticket price on items usually **does not include tax**. In most provinces there are two taxes, the GST (federal Goods and Services Tax, TPS in French) of 7% which is payable throughout Canada, and a provincial tax, which varies from province to province. The provincial and federal sales taxes are cumulative in Newfoundland and Labrador, Prince Edward Island, New Brunswick, Nova Scotia and Québec.

Tax Refunds for Non-Residents

Non-residents can be refunded for taxes paid on their purchases made while in Canada. To obtain a refund, it is important to keep your receipts. A separate form for each tax (federal and provincial) must be filled out to obtain a refund. Conditions for refunds are different for the GST and the PST. For further information, call ☎ *800-668-4748*.

Tipping

Tipping applies to all table services, that is in restaurants or other places where customers are served at their tables (fast-food service is therefore not included in this category). Tipping is also compulsory in bars, nightclubs and taxis.

Depending on the quality of the service, patrons must leave approximately 15% of the bill before tax. Unlike in Europe, the tip is not included in the bill,

and clients must calculate the amount themselves and give it to the server.

Business Hours and Holidays

Business Hours

Stores

Stores are generally opened the following hours:

- Monday to Wednesday 10am to 6pm

- Thursday and Friday 10am to 9pm

- Saturday from 9am or 10am to 5pm

- Sunday noon to 5pm Not all stores open on Sundays.

Convenience stores, called *dépanneurs* or "deps" in Québec, are found throughout Canada and are open later, sometimes 24hrs a day.

Banks

Banks are open Monday to Friday from 10am to 3pm. Most are open on Thursdays and Fridays, until 6pm or even 8pm. Bank machines operate 24hrs a day.

Post Offices

Large post offices are open from 9am to 5pm. There are several smaller post offices located in shopping malls, convenience stores and even pharmacies; they are open much later than the larger ones.

Practical Information

Holidays

The following is a list of public holidays. Administrative offices and banks are closed on these days and some stores may also be closed.

January 1 and 2
New Year's Day

Easter Monday

3rd Monday in May
Fête de Dollard and Victoria Day

June 24
Saint-Jean Baptiste Day (Québec)

July 1
Canada Day

1st Monday in Aug
Civic Holiday (except in Québec)

1st Monday in Sep
Labour Day

2nd Monday in Oct
Thanksgiving

November 11
Remembrance Day

December 25 and 26
Christmas & Boxing Days

Time Difference

Canada has six time zones: from Halifax to Vancouver there are five (Pacific, Mountain, Central, Eastern and Atlantic), and then Newfoundland, which is a half-hour ahead of Atlantic Standard Time. Eastern Standard Time is five hours behind Greenwich Mean Time and six hours behind continental Europe.

Climate

The climate of Canada varies widely both by region and season. Winters are generally very cold with temperatures reaching as low as -20°C throughout most of the country. British Columbia (temperatures range between 0°C and 15°C in Vancouver) is the biggest exception and receives rain instead of snow. The Northwest Territories, Nunavut , the Yukon and other northern regions endure extremely cold temperatures in winter – it is not unusual to see the thermometer drop to -30°C. Throughout the country, summer is a beautiful season, and temperatures can reach above 30°C. In certain coastal areas, particularly in Newfoundland and Nova Scotia, it is often rainy and foggy.

Health

Vaccinations are not necessary for people coming from Europe, the United States, Australia and New Zealand. On the other hand, it is strongly suggested, particularly for medium or long-term stays, that visitors take out health and accident insurance. There are different types so it is best to shop around. Bring along all medication, especially prescription medicine. Unless otherwise stated, the water is drinkable throughout Canada.

During winter, lip balm and moisturizers are often used by people with sensitive skin, since the air inside buildings is often very dry.

Emergencies

Many municipalities in Canada have the **911** service, allowing you to dial only three digits to reach the police, firefighters or ambulance service, in case of emergency. You can also dial **0** to contact an operator who will supply you with the appropriate numbers.

Security

There is far less violence in Canada than in the United States. A genuine non-violence policy is advocated throughout the country. If you run into problems, **911** is the emergency number in most places, otherwise dial **0** to reach an operator.

Insurance

Cancellation

Your travel agent will usually offer you cancellation insurance when you buy your airline ticket or vacation package. This insurance allows you to be reimbursed for the ticket or package deal if your trip must be cancelled due to serious illness or death. Healthy people are unlikely to need this protection, which is therefore only of relative use.

Theft

Most residential insurance policies protect some of your goods from theft, even if the theft occurs in a foreign country. To make a claim, you must fill out a police report. It may not be necessary to take out further insurance, depending on the amount covered by your current home policy. As policies vary considerably, you are advised to check with your insurance company. European visitors should take out baggage insurance.

Life

Several airline companies offer a life insurance plan included in the price of the airplane ticket. However, many travellers already have this type of insurance and do not require additional coverage.

Health

This is the most useful kind of insurance for travellers and should be purchased before your departure. Your insurance plan should be as complete as possible because health care costs add up quickly. When buying insurance, make sure it covers all types of medical costs, such as hospitalization, nursing services and doctor's fees. Make sure your limit is high enough, as these expenses can be costly. A repatriation clause is also vital in case the required care is not available on site. Furthermore, since you may have to pay immediately, check your policy to see what provisions it includes for such situations. To avoid any problems during your vacation, always keep proof of your insurance policy with you.

Senior Citizens

Reduced transportation fares and entertainment tickets are often made available to seniors. Do not hesitate to ask.

Children

Facilities for children are available almost everywhere you go, whether it be transportation or leisure activities. Generally, children under five travel for free, and those under 12 are eligible for fare reductions. The same rules apply for various leisure activities and shows. Find out before you purchase tickets. High chairs and children's menus are available in most restaurants, while some larger stores and malls provide a babysitting service while parents shop.

Telecommunications

Local area codes are clearly indicated in the "Practical Information" section of each chapter. Dialling these codes is unnecessary if the call is local. For long-distance calls, dial 1 for the United States and Canada, followed by the appropriate area code and the subscriber's number. Phone numbers preceded by 800 or 888 allow you to reach the subscriber without charge if calling from Canada, and often from the U.S. as well. If you wish to contact an operator, dial 0.

When calling abroad you can use a local operator and pay local phone rates. First dial 011 then the international country code and then the phone number.

For example, to call Belgium, dial 011-32, followed by the area code (Antwerp 3, Brussels 2, Ghent 9, Liège 41) and the subscriber's number. To call

Switzerland, dial 01-41, followed by the area code (Bern 31, Geneva 22, Lausanne 21, Zurich 1) and the subscriber's phone number.

Another way to call abroad is by using the direct access numbers below to contact an operator in your home country.

United States
AT&T
☎*800-CALL ATT*
MCI
☎*800-888-8000*

British Telecom Direct
☎*800-408-6420*
☎*800-363-4144*

Australia Telstra Direct
☎*800-663-0683*

New Zealand Telecom Direct
☎*800-663-0684*

Considerably less expensive to use than in Europe, public phones are scattered throughout the city, easy to use and some even accept credit cards. Local calls cost 25¢ for unlimited time. For long distance calls, equip yourselves with quarters (25¢), or purchase a $10, $15 or $20 card, on sale at newsstands and most convenience stores. For example, a call from Montréal to Toronto will cost $2.50 for the first three minutes and 38¢ for every additional minute. Calling a private residence will cost even less. Paying by credit card or with the prepaid "HELLO!" card is also possible, but be advised that calling by such means is considerably more expensive.

Exploring

Every chapter in this guide leads you through a Canadian region, territory or province, including major tourist attractions, followed by a historical and cultural description. Attractions are classified according to a star rating system, so you don't miss the must-sees if time is lacking.

★   Interesting
★★   Worth a visit
★★★   Not to be missed

The name of each attraction is followed by its address and phone number. The price of admission for one adult is included in brackets. It is best to make inquiries, for several places offer discounts for children, students, senior citizens and families. Several are only open during tourist season, as indicated within these same brackets. Even in the off-season, however, some of these places welcome visitors, particularly groups, upon request.

Accommodations

A wide choice of accommodations to fit every budget is available in most regions of Canada. Most places are very comfortable and offer a number of extra services. Prices vary according to the type of accommodation and the quality/price ratio is generally good, but remember to add the 7% G.S.T (federal Goods and Services Tax) and the provincial sales tax, which varies from province to province. The Goods and Services Tax is refundable for non-residents in certain cases (see p 56).

A credit card will make reserving a room much easier (strongly recommended in summer!), since in many cases payment for the first night is required.

Most tourist information centres provide a free hotel-room reservation service.

Hotels

There are countless hotels across Canada, and they range from modest to luxurious. Most hotel rooms come equipped with a private bathroom. The prices we have listed are rack rates in the high season. In the majority of establishments, however, a whole slew of discounts, up to 50% in some cases, is possible. Weekend rates are often lower when a hotel's clientele is mostly business people. There are also corporate rates, rates for auto-club members, and seniors discounts to take advantage of. Be sure to ask about package deals, promotions and discounts when reserving.

Bed and Breakfasts

Unlike hotels or inns, rooms in private homes do not always have a private bathroom. Bed and breakfasts are well distributed throughout Canada, in the country as well as the city. Besides the obvious price advantage, is the unique family atmosphere. Credit cards are not always accepted in bed and breakfasts.

Youth Hostels

Youth hostel addresses are listed in the "Accommodations" section for the cities in which they are located.

Motels

There are many motels throughout the country, and though they tend to be cheaper, they often lack atmosphere. These are particularly useful when pressed for time.

University Residences

Due to certain restrictions, this can be a complicated alternative. Residences are only available during the summer (mid-May to mid-August); reservations must be made several months in advance, usually by paying the first night with a credit card.

This type of accommodation, however, is less costly than the "traditional" alternatives, and making the effort to reserve early can be worthwhile. Visitors with valid student cards can expect to pay approximately $20 plus tax, while non students can expect to pay around $30. Bedding is included in the price, and there is usually a cafeteria in the building (meals are not included in the price).

Staying in Aboriginal Communities

The opportunities for staying in Aboriginal communities are limited but are becoming more popular. As reserves are managed by band councils, in some cases it is necessary to obtain authorization from the prior to your visit.

Camping

Next to being put up by friends, camping is the most inexpensive form of accommodation. Unfortunately, unless you have winter-camping gear, camping is limited to a short period of the year, from June to August. Services provided by campgrounds can vary considerably. Campsites can be either privately or publicly owned. The prices listed in this guide apply to campsites without connections for tents, and vary depending on additional services.

Restaurants

Many restaurants offer set menus, complete meals for one price, which is usually less expensive than ordering individual items from the menu. The price usually includes a choice of appetizers and main dishes, plus coffee and sometimes dessert.

Prices in this guide are for a meal for one person, before taxes and tip (see p 53).

$	$10 or less
$$	$10 to $20
$$$	$20 to $30
$$$$	$30 or more

These prices are generally based on the cost of evening set menus, but remember that lunchtime meals are often considerably less expensive.

Bars and Danceclubs

Most pub-style bars do not have a cover charge (although in winter there is usually a mandatory coat-check). Expect to pay a few dollars to get into discos on weekends. Most provinces stop the sale of alcohol at 2am, except for Québec where it ends at 3am. Some bars remain open past these hours but serve only soft drinks. Drinking establishments that only have a liquor license must close at midnight. In small towns, restaurants also frequently serve as bars. For entertainment come nightfall consult the "Restaurant" and "Entertainment" sections in every chapter.

Wine, Beer and Alcohol

In Canada, provincial governments are responsible for regulating alcohol, sold in special liquor stores throughout the country. For example, Québec has the *Société des Alcools du Québec* (SAQ.) with many branches all over the province. Also in Québec, convenience and grocery stores are authorized to sell beer and a few wines, but the choice is slim and the quality of wines mediocre. Other provinces have State-run beer and wine stores, the only places where alcohol can be purchased.

The legal drinking age in Canada is 19, except in Québec, Manitoba and Alberta where it is 18. Note that certain northern communities are dry towns, where the sale of alcohol is strictly forbidden.

Gay and Lesbian Life

In 1977, Québec became the second place in the world, after Holland, to include in its charter the principle of not discriminating on the basis of sexual orientation. Other Canadian provinces later followed suit (most recently Alberta).

Canadians are generally open and tolerant towards homosexuality. Over the years, legislation, particularly at the federal level, has been reformed, to an extent, in favour of gays and lesbians, thus reflecting changing attitudes in society, especially in Québec, Ontario and British Columbia. However, the government sometimes seems to be living in the dark ages when Canada Customs does everything in its power to ban the importation of Marcel Proust's novels in English Canada! Little Sisters bookstore in Vancouver has been putting up a brave legal battle against these inspectors who believe they are *the* authority on censorship.

Generally speaking, rural areas tend to be more homophobic and Western Canada is not as tolerant of gays and lesbians. Yet, the Prairies have their share of queer celebrities, including country-singer, k.d. lang. Atlantic Canada seems to display a similar attitude to the west, however, Nova Scotia has attracted some attention to this issue with the film *The Hanging Garden*, by Halifax playwright Thom Fitzgerald. Famous gay rocker Ashley MacIsaac is also from Cape Breton Island, Nova Scotia. In Québec, society on the whole is

Practical Information

very tolerant; famous artists an politicians have
come out about them-
selves at an early age, as
did the renowned play-
wright, Michel Tremblay.
Ontario's gay community
tends to stand out in the
news the most, since To-
ronto is the most popu-
lated city in Canada and
probably because the city
has a more politically active nature.

Montréal constitutes one of
the most important gay
communities in the world
along with San Francisco,
New York and Amsterdam.
The **Village**, regrouping
most of the services and
businesses catering to gays
and lesbians, has become
a tourist attraction. Québec
City also has a gay quarter
on Rue Saint-Jean, outside
the walls.

In English Canada, To-
ronto, Ottawa and Van-
couver have the largest
established gay communi-
ties. In Toronto, it is found
around Church and
Wellesley Streets, in Vancouver it is mainly in the
West End.

Important celebrations
mark gay pride each year
in Toronto towards the
end of June and in
Montréal the first weekend
of August (Divers Cité).

For more information on
gay and lesbian life:

In Montréal
L'Androgyne Bookstore
3636 Boulevard Saint-Laurent

In Toronto
Glad Day Bookshop
598a Yonge Street

In Vancouver
Little Sister Book and
Art Emporium
1221 Thurlow Street

Advice For Smokers

Smoking is prohibited in
most shopping centres, on
buses and on subways,
and in government offices.

Most public places (restaurants, cafés) have smoking
and non-smoking sections.
Cigarettes are sold in bars,
grocery stores, newspaper
and magazine shops. The
legal age for smoking is 16
years old.

Shopping

In most retail stores, prices
are fixed and as indicated.
However, some bargaining
is expected, at flea mar-
kets, for example.

What to Buy

Alcohol
A number of alcoholic
beverages are produced in
Canada, such as wine in
Ontario and ciders in
British Columbia.

Electronics
Canada is one of the
biggest manufacturers of
telecommunications prod-
ucts. The industry is centred in Montréal. It therefore might be a good idea
to buy some gadgets such
as answering machines,
fax machines or cordless
telephones and cellular
phones. However, be
aware that these devices
may require a special
adaptor for use in your
home country. Importing
these items may be illegal
in certain European coun-
tries.

Compact Discs
Compact discs are much
less expensive than in
Europe, however, they

may be more expensive
than in the United States.

Furs and Leather
Clothes made from animal
skins are of very good
quality and their prices are
relatively low. Approxi-
mately 80% of fur items in
Canada are made in the
"fur area" of Montréal.

Local Arts & Crafts
These consist of items
such as paintings, sculp-
tures, woodwork, ceram-
ics, coppered enamel and
weaving.

Aboriginal Arts & Crafts
There are beautiful sculptures made by Inuit and
First Nations artists from
different types of stone,
wood and even animal
bone that are generally
quite expensive. Make
sure the sculpture is au-
thentic by asking for a
certificate of authenticity
issued by the Canadian
government. Good quality
imitations are widely available and are much less
expensive.

Festivals and Cultural Events

Canada is rich in cultural
activities. Given the
impressive number of festivals, annual expositions,
exhibitions, fairs, gatherings and otherwise, it is
impossible to list them all.
We have, however, se-
lected a few of the high-
lights, which are described
in the "Entertainment"
sections of each chapter.

Pets

The restrictions on animal
companions vary from one
province to another. Pro-
vincial and national parks
in Québec do not accept
dogs, even on leashes,

whereas the opposite is true of Ontario. Pets are not allowed in restaurants. Some hotel chains in Canada allow domestic animals.

Miscellaneous

Drugs

Recreational Drugs are against the law and not tolerated (even "soft" drugs).

Electricity

Voltage is 110 volts throughout Canada, the same as in the United States. Electricity plugs have two parallel, flat pins, and adaptors are available here.

Laundromats

Laundromats are found almost everywhere in urban areas. Bring your own detergent. Although change machines are sometimes provided, it is best to bring plenty of coins with you.

Pharmacies

In addition to the smaller drug stores, there are large pharmacy chains that sell everything from chocolate to laundry detergent, as well as the more traditional items such as cough drops and headache medications.

Restrooms

Public washrooms can be found in most shopping centres. If you cannot find one, it usually is not a problem to use one in a bar or restaurant.

Markets

There are many outdoor and indoor markets. Besides good bargains and fresh produce and goods, they can give you a feel for a place.

Weight and Measures

Although the metric system has been in use in Canada for several years, many people continue to use the Imperial system in casual conversation. Here are some equivalents:

Weights

1 pound (lb) =
454 grams (g)

1 kilogram (kg) =
2.2 pounds (lbs)

Linear Measure

1 inch =
2.54 centimetres (cm)

1 foot (ft) =
30 centimetres (cm)

1 mile =
1.6 kilometres (km)

1 kilometre (km) =
0.63 miles

1 metre (m) =
39.37 inches

Land Measure

1 acre =
0.4 hectare (ha)

1 hectare (ha) =
2.471 acres

Volume Measure

1 U.S. gallon (gal) =
3.79 litres

1 U.S. gallon (gal) =
0.83 imperial gallon

Temperature

To convert °F into °C:
subtract 32, divide by 9, multiply by 5

To convert °C into °F:
multiply by 9, divide by 5, add 32.

Canada boasts vast,
untouched stretches of wilderness, some of which is protected by national and provincial parks that visitors can explore on foot, by bicycle, by car, on horseback, on skis or by snow-mobile.

There are coasts washed by the waters of the Pacific and Atlantic oceans, vast rain forest harbouring centuries-old trees, majestic mountains that form the spine of the American continent, as well as prairies, coniferous forests, lakes and more. The following pages contain a description of the most popular outdoor activities that can be enjoyed in these unspoiled areas.

Parks

Throughout Canada there are national parks administered by the federal government and provincial parks administered by the provincial governments. Most of the parks offer a variety of services and facilities: information centres, maps, nature interpretation programs, guides, lodging informa-tion (B&B, inns, camping) and restaurant information. Since these services often depend on the season and are not available in all parks, it is best to check with the park offices ahead of time. Provincial parks are generally smaller and offer less services.

A number of parks are crisscrossed by marked trails stretching several kilometres that are perfect for hiking, cycling, cross-country skiing and snow-mobiling.

Primitive campsites or shelters can be found along some of these paths. Some of the camp sites are very rudimentary, and a few don't even have water; it is therefore essential to be well equipped. Take note, however, that in the national parks in the Rocky Mountains, wilder-ness camping is strictly forbidden due to the pres-ence of bears and other large animals.

Since some of the trails lead deep into the forest far from all human habita-tion, visitors are strongly advised to heed all signs. This will also help protect the fragile plant-life. Useful maps showing trails, camp sites and shelters are available for most parks.

It is important to be well aware of the potential dangers before heading off into the wild of the provincial and national parks. Do not forget that each individual is ultimately responsible for his or her own safety. Dangers to watch out for include avalanches and rock slides, risks of hypothermia or sunstroke,

rapid changes in temperature (especially in mountainous regions), non-potable water, glacier crevasses concealed by a thin layer of snow, strong waves or tides on the coasts and wild animals like bears and rattlesnakes.

Never stop in an avalanche or rock-slide area. Cross-country skiers and hikers must take particular care when passing through these areas. It is always best to check with park staff about the stability of the snow before heading out.

Hypothermia begins when the internal body temperature falls below 36°C, at which point the body loses heat faster than it can produce it. Shivering is the first sign that your body is not able to warm itself. It is easy to disregard the cold when hiking in the summer. However, in the mountains, rain and wind can lower the temperature considerably.

Imagine sitting above the tree line in a downpour,

with the wind blowing at 50 km/h. Then imagine that you are tired and have no raincoat. In such conditions, your body temperature drops rapidly and you run the risk of hypothermia. It is therefore important to carry a change of warm clothes and a good wind-breaker with you at all times.

When hiking, it is preferable to wear several layers instead of a big jacket that will prove too warm once you start exercising intensely, but too light when you stop to rest. Avoid wet clothes at all costs.

Water can be found in most Canadian parks, but it is not always clean enough to drink. For this reason, be sure to bring along enough water for the duration of your hike, or boil any water you find for about 10 minutes.

Visitors who enter the national and provincial parks run the risk of encountering wild, unpredictable and dangerous animals. It is irresponsible and illegal to feed, trap or bother wild animals in a national park. Large mammals like bears, elk, moose, deer and buffalo may feel threatened and become dangerous if you try to approach them. It is even dangerous to approach animals in towns where wild animals roam about in an urban setting. Stay at least 30m from

large mammals and at least 50m from bears and buffalo.

Summer Activities

As soon as the temperature inches above 0°C and the ice starts to melt, Canadians and visitors alike start to look forward to days in the country. Below we mention some of the most popular activities to enjoy in the great Canadian outdoors.

While your choice of clothing will vary with the season, do not forget that evenings and nights are often quite chilly throughout the year depending on the latitude. In certain regions, regardless of the temperature, a long-sleeved shirt is indispensable unless you want to serve yourself as dinner to the mosquitoes and black flies. If you plan on venturing into the woods in the month of June, bring insect repellent and use it!

Hiking

Hiking is widely accessible and practised all over the country. Many parks have hiking trails of varying length and difficulty. A few have longer trails that head deep into the wilderness for 20 to 40km. Respect the trail markings and always leave well prepared when you follow these trails. Maps that show the trails, campsites and shelters are available.

You will find suggested hikes in the "Outdoor Activities" section of many of the chapters in this guide. Suggested parks are described in the "Exploring" sections.

The Trans Canada Trail, an exciting new multipurpose trail, will be inaugurated on September 9, 2000. The longest such trail in the world, it will span a stunning 16,000km that will cross Canada from St. John's, Newfoundland, to Victoria, British Columbia, and head northward from Calgary, Alberta to Tuktoyaktuk, Northwest Territories and Chesterfield Inlet, Nunavut. The trail will be used for hiking as well as cross-country skiing, snowshoeing, cycling, horseback riding and snowmobiling, drawing on both existing and newly converted trails.

Cycling

Visitors can go cycling all over Canada, along the usually quiet secondary roads or the trails crisscrossing the parks. The roads offer prudent cyclists one of the most enjoyable means possible of touring these picturesque regions. Keep in mind, however, that distances can be very long.

If you are travelling with your own bicycle, you can bring it on any bus; just be sure it is properly protected in an appropriate box. Another option is to rent one on site. For bike rental locations, check under the "Bicycles-Rentals" heading in the *Yellow Pages*. Many bike shops also offer rentals and can direct you to tourist information offices. Adequate insurance is a good idea when renting a bicycle. Some places include insurance against theft in the cost of the rental. Inquire before renting.

Canoeing

Canada's vast territory is spotted with a multitude of lakes and rivers, making it a canoe-enthusiast's dream. Many of the parks and reserves are departure points for canoe trips of one or more days. On longer trips backwoods campsites are available for canoeists. Maps of the canoe trips and trails, as well as canoe-rental services are available at the information centre of all parks.

Kayaking

Kayaking isn't a new sport but its popularity is on the rise. More and more people are discovering this wonderful way to travel on water in a safe and comfortable vessel at a pace well suited to appreciating the surrounding nature. In fact, being in a kayak gives you the impression of sitting right on the water and being a part of nature: an experience that is both disorienting and fascinating! There are three types of kayaks with varying curvatures: lake kayaks, river kayaks and sea kayaks. The latter kind can hold one or two people depending on the model, and is the most popular because it is the easiest to manoeuvre. Many companies offer kayak rental and organize guided expeditions on Canada's waterways.

Rafting

Rafting, which involves tackling rapids in an inflatable dingy, is perfect for thrill seekers. These rafts hold around 10 people and offer the strength and flexibility required to take on the rapids. People particularly relish the sport in the spring when river waters are high and the current is faster. It goes without saying that you should be in good physical condition to take part in this type of excursion, all the more so because between rapids, the boat is manoeuvred by the strength of the rowers. A well-organized trip, with an experienced guide is much safer. Generally, companies that offer rafting provide all the equip-

Outdoors

ment necessary to ensure the comfort and safety of the participants. So, hop in and let the freshly thawed rivers make you jump and twirl among huge splashes!

Beaches and Swimming

Whether on the Atlantic or Pacific shores, or on a lake or tumultuous river in the forest, Canada's waterways await you. Soft white sand, and pebble and rocky beaches are numerous. But don't expect warm waters everywhere; the farther north, the colder the water, especially in rivers. Canadians and visitors alike can soak up the sun on the coasts, lakes and rivers of the country.

Hunting and Fishing

Hunting and fishing are both strictly regulated. Given the complexity of the regulations, it is a good idea to check with Natural Resources Canada or with Environment Canada.

Free brochures containing the essentials regarding hunting and fishing regulations and restrictions are available.

As a general rule, the following applies:

A permit is required to hunt or fish. Hunting of migratory birds is only allowed with a federal permit which can be purchased in any post office. A certificate to bear firearms or a permit by the province or country of origin is required when requesting this type of permit.

At press time, a fishing permit cost around $20 (up to $50 for non-residents). The price of a hunting permit depends on the type of game hunted and can cost up to $300 for non-residents. Permits are issued depending on the hunting zone, time of year, the species and the existing quotas. It is a good idea to obtain your permit well in advance since there are numerous restrictions.

Fishing and hunting seasons are established by the government and must be respected at all times. While hunting, always wear an orange fluorescent singlet. Hunting at night is not permitted.

In the interests of conservation, the number of game is limited, and protected species cannot be hunted. All hunters must declare their kill at one of the registration centres (most of which are located on access roads to the hunting zones) within 48 hours of leaving the zone.

Hunting and fishing are permitted in wildlife reserves and parks according to certain rules. Reservations are required for access to waterways. For more information, check directly with the park or reserve office where you plan to hunt or fish.

Winter Activities

In winter, most of Canada is covered with a blanket of snow, creating ideal conditions for a slew of outdoor activities. Most parks with summer hiking trails are converted into cross-country skiing trails in winter. Dress warmly or the cold will bite you. Despite the low temperature, winter offers many outdoor activity possibilities for your enjoyment.

Downhill Skiing and Snowboarding

There are many downhill skiing and snowboarding centres in the country. Known the world over for its downhill skiing, the Rocky Mountains attract millions of powder hounds, who are whisked to the highest summits by helicopter and dropped off to enjoy the ski of their lives.

Some hills have lighting systems and offer night skiing. The hotels located near the ski hills often offer package-deals including accommodation, meals and lift tickets. Check when reserving your room.

Lift tickets are very expensive; in an effort to accommodate all types of skiers and snowboarders most centres offer half-day passes, whole-day and night passes. Some centres have even started offering skiing by the hour.

Skating

Most municipalities have public skating rinks set up in parks, on rivers or lakes. Some places have rental services, and even a little hut where you and your skates can warm up.

Cross-country Skiing

There are many parks and ski centres with well kept cross-country trails. In most ski centres you can rent equipment by the day.

Many places offer longer trails, with shelters alongside them offering accommodation and even food delivered by snowmobile.

Snowmobiling

Now this is a popular Canadian sport! Quebecer Joseph-Armand Bombardier, better know for his company that builds aircraft and railway material, invented the snowmobile.

Trails cross diverse regions and lead adventurers into the heart of the wilderness. Along the trails are all the necessities for snowmobiling: repair services, heated sheds, fuel, and food services. It is possible to rent a snowmobile and the necessary equipment in certain snowmobiling centres. Don't forget that a permit is required. It is also advisable to take out liability insurance.

Certain safety rules apply. A helmet is mandatory and driving on public roads is forbidden unless the trail follows it. Headlights and brake lights must be lit at all times. The speed-limit is 70 km/h. It is preferable to ride in groups. Finally, always stick to cleared trails.

Dogsledding

Used by the Inuit for transportation in the old days, today dogsledding has become a respected sporting activity. Competitive events abound in northern countries all over the world. In recent years, tourist centres have started offering dogsled trips running anywhere from a few hours to a few days in length. In the latter case, the tour organizer provides the necessary equipment and shelter. In general, you can cover 30km to 60km per day, and this sport is more demanding than it looks, so good physical fitness is essential for long trips.

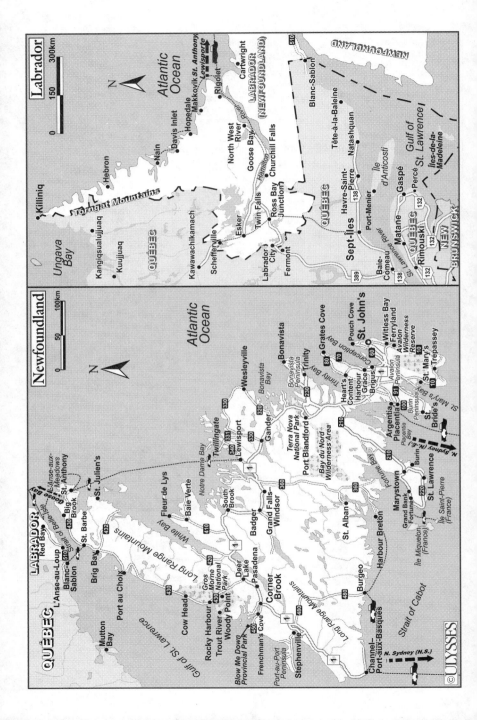

Newfoundland and Labrador

S till a little known corner of the world, Newfoundland is very different from Canada's other Atlantic provinces – not just geographically but historically and culturally as well.

T he province's geo-graphical isolation, at the northeasternmost edge of North America, has helped forge its unique character. "The Rock," as it is aptly nicknamed, is a rocky island ill-suited to agriculture, a hostile re-gion whose landscape, often very rugged, is so splendid that you can't help but stand back and marvel.

T he west part of the island is shaped by the ancient Long Range Moun-tains, the tail end of the Appalachians. Gros Morne National Park, a UNESCO World Heritage Site, offers visitors a remarkable chance to explore these mountains, which in many places plunge straight into the limpid waters of deep fiords. Farther north, to-ward L'Anse aux Mead-ows, the former site of a Viking camp, the road runs along flat and strik-ingly desolate coastal land-scapes. Elsewhere, lofty cliffs, pebble beaches and tiny fishing villages punc-tuate the shore, providing scenes of picturesque en-chantment.

T he capital of the prov-ince, St. John's, lies in a magnificent natural setting on the shores of a long harbour rimmed with high, rocky hills. In addition to the island of Newfound-land, the province also includes Labrador covered with subarctic forests and tundra. Labrador, sparsely populated with just a few thousand inhabitants, cov-ers nearly 300,000km². Both the island of New-foundland and Labrador, far off the beaten tourist track, offer outdoor enthu-siasts countless opportuni-ties to explore a rich wil-derness. Without much difficulty, visitors can ob-serve caribou and moose, colonies of puffins and gannets, and, from the coast, whales swimming about and icebergs slowly drifting by.

T he numerous traces of Aboriginal communities that have been discovered along its shores indicate that this province has been inhabited almost continuously for over 8,000 years. The first people to settle here were Aboriginals belonging to the Maritime Archaic nation and Dorset culture, predecessors to today's Inuit. The Aboriginals encountered by European explorers, however, were Beothuk, who came to Newfoundland around the year 200. Due to its relative proximity to the European continent, the island of Newfoundland was one of the very first places in the New World to be known to Europe. Legend has it that at the end of the fifth century, St. Brendan, an Irish abbot, crossed the Atlantic in his search for new peoples to convert to Christianity and landed on this island.

The first Europeans whose presence here can actually be proved, however, were the Vikings, who, toward the year 1000, apparently used the island as a base for exploring the continent. Leif's camp, in L'Anse-aux-Meadows, is the oldest European site in North America. It wasn't until several centuries later that Europeans rediscovered Newfoundland.

In the 15th century, Europeans learned of the teeming waters around the island through Basque fishers. Each summer, the Basques would come to this region to fish cod in the Grand Banks and hunt whales in the Strait of Belle Isle. Officially, however, the credit for discovering Newfoundland goes to Giovanni Caboto (John Cabot), who came here in the service of England in 1497.

Over the following centuries, the French and the English competed for control of Newfoundland and the rest of North America. In 1558, the English founded their first permanent settlement in Trinity, on the Bonavista Peninsula. Then, in 1583, Sir Humphrey Gilbert officially claimed St. John's harbour and the rest of the island of Newfoundland for Queen Elizabeth I of England. This did not, however, prevent the French from establishing their own permanent settlement, known as Plaisance (now Placentia), on the coast of the Avalon Peninsula in 1662.

Plaisance remained the capital of the French colony of Terre-Neuve (Newfoundland) until the signing of the Treaty of Utrecht in 1713. Though the island was ceded to England under this treaty, the French continued to take an interest in it; in fact, the last battle of the Seven Years' War (or French and Indian War) took place in St. John's. The war ended with the signing of the Treaty of Paris in 1673, under which

France lost its North American empire. Over the following centuries, more people, many from Ireland, settled along the coast of Newfoundland. In 1867, the year the Canadian Confederation was created, the islanders decided that Newfoundland should remain a British colony. It wasn't until 1949 that Newfoundland became the tenth and final province to join Canada.

This chapter is divided into six tours: five for Newfoundland and one for Labrador :

Tour A : St. John's ★★
Tour B : The Avalon Peninsula ★★
Tour C : Eastern and Central Newfoundland ★
Tour D : Western Newfoundland ★
Tour E : The Viking Route ★★★
Tour F : Labrador ★

Finding Your Way Around

By Ferry

The island of Newfoundland is accessible by ferry from North Sydney, on Cape Breton Island, Nova Scotia. These ferries, operated by the Marine Atlantic company, offer service to Port aux Basques (in southwestern Newfoundland) and Argentia (on the Avalon Peninsula, in southeastern Newfoundland). The crossing between North Sydney and Port aux Basques usually takes about 5hrs. With a few exceptions, there is at least one crossing per day, each way, between North Sydney and Port aux Basques. The one-way fare is $60 per car and $19 per adult. It takes about 14hrs to travel between North Sydney and Argentia. There is at least one crossing, each way, every Monday, Wednesday and Friday. The one-way fare is $124 per car and $55 per adult. Reservations: ☎800-341-7981.

It is also possible to take the ferry from Goose Bay, Labrador to the island of Newfoundland. This ferry, which travels to Lewisporte, in north-central Newfoundland, runs several times a week from the beginning of June to the beginning of September *(Reservations: ☎1-800-341-7981)*. There is a good road from Goose Bay to Churchill Falls and Labrador City, then on to Baie Comeau (Québec). Reservations: ☎800-563-6353.

By Plane

The province's major civilian airport is located in St. John's. There are direct flights between St. John's and a number of large Canadian cities, including Halifax, Montréal and Toronto. Air Canada also offers direct service to St. John's from London, England, while Royal Airlines offers a direct flight from Dublin, Ireland. The two main airlines that serve the island of Newfoundland are Air Canada, with its subsidiary **Air Nova** *(☎800-463-8620)* and Canadian International *(☎800-426-7000)*. The airport is only 6km from downtown St. John's.

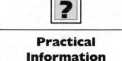

Practical Information

Area code: **709**

Tourist Information

Destination Newfoundland and Labrador
P.O. Box 8730
St. John's, Newfoundland
A1B 4K2
☎**729-2830**
or 800-563-6353
⇒**729-1965**

There are about 30 tourist information centres scattered across the province, notably in St. John's and in the major ports of entry.

Exploring

★★

Tour A: St. John's

St. John's, the provincial capital, occupies a spectacular site on the Avalon Peninsula, at the eastern tip of the island, and of Canada. The city is built like an amphitheatre around a well-protected harbour that opens onto the Atlantic Ocean by way of a narrow channel aptly known as the Narrows and is flanked on either side by tall, rocky peaks. About 1.6km long and 800m wide, St. John's harbour is an excellent inland port that is frequented by ships of all sizes and flying the flags of various countries. Hidden behind the port installations lies a charming city whose winding

streets are lined with pretty, brightly coloured wooden houses. European fishers of various nationalities were already coming regularly to the site of modern-day St. John's as early as the 15th century. In 1583, Sir Humphrey Gilbert officially claimed the harbour and the rest of the island of Newfoundland for the Queen of England. Later, St. John's was often at the centre of rivalries between the French and the English and fell into the hands of the French on three different occasions. Signal Hill was subsequently fortified to protect the city.

Commissariat House *(free admission; Jun to Sep; King's Bridge Rd., ☎729-2460)*. This Georgian-style wooden building, completed in 1821, was first used as the residence of the commissariat of the local military base and then served as the vicarage of **St. Thomas Anglican Church** *(Military Rd.)*. This church, also known as the Old Garrison Church (1836), was the chapel of the British garrison of Fort William. Commissariat House and St. Thomas Church are among the few buildings in downtown St. John's to have survived the great fires of 1846 and 1892. Now a provincial historic site, Commissariat House was restored some time ago and furnished in the style of the 1830s.

Government House *(Military Rd., ☎729-4494)*, another building that escaped the flames, was erected in 1831 as the official residence of the governor of Newfoundland. It has served as the Lieutenant Governor's house since the province joined the Canadian Confederation. The beautifully landscaped

Newfoundland
and Labrador

grounds are open to the public every day, but the house itself may only be visited by appointment. The frescoes adorning the ceiling were executed by Polish painter Alexander Pindikowski in 1880 and 1881. He would paint during the day then return for the night to the local prison, where he was serving a sentence for counterfeiting.

Built on a promontory overlooking the city, the **Roman Catholic Basilica of St. John the Baptist** *(Military Rd.)* was designed by Irish architect John Jones in 1855. Originally a cathedral, it was converted into a basilica in 1955. Its facade is graced with two 43m high towers. The interior is richly decorated; the left transept contains a statue of Our Lady of Fatima, a gift from some Portuguese sailors who survived a shipwreck on the Grand Banks. The front of the basilica is a splendid vantage point from which to view the city.

The elegant **Anglican Cathedral of St. John the Baptist** *(at the corner of Church Hill and Gower St.)*, with its pure Gothic lines, was designed by English architect Sir George Gilbert Scott in 1847. It was completed in 1885 but was totally destroyed by a fire in 1892. The cathedral was rebuilt a few years later under the supervision of Sir George's son. Its magnificent stained-glass windows are particularly noteworthy. Established in 1699, the parish of St. John the Baptist is the oldest Anglican parish in Canada.

The **Newfoundland Museum** *(Tue, Wed, Fri 9am to 5pm, Thu 9am to 9pm, Sat and Sun 10am to 6am; 285 Duckworth St., ☎ 729-0916)* houses permanent exhibitions that offer an excellent overview of the human history of Newfoundland and Labrador.

Signal Hill

The collections also examine the way of life of the six First Nations that live or once lived in these regions: the Maritime Archaic who left traces of their existence in Port au Choix, among other places; the Dorset, who lived on the shores of the island until beginning of the first century AD; the Beothuk, the predominant First Nation in Newfoundland when the Europeans arrived, which has since been completely wiped out; the Micmac, the largest nation in Atlantic Canada; the Inuit, once called Eskimos, who still inhabit the northernmost shores of Labrador; and the Montagnais, who live in Labrador, along the shores of the Gulf of St. Lawrence. The exhibitions also explore the lives of 19th-century settlers and fishers.

Signal Hill National Historic Site, visible from all over St. John's, is a rocky hill topped by a tower that looks out over the mouth of the harbour. The hilltop commands magnificent **views** of the Atlantic, the harbour and the city both day and night. Because of its strategic location, Signal Hill was long used as an observation and communications post. As early as 1704, flags were flown here to inform the military authorities and merchants of St. John's when ships were arriving. It was also on Signal Hill that the city's defences were erected from the 18th century to the Second World War. Vestiges of 19th-century military installations can still be found here. In 1762, Signal Hill was the scene of the final North American battle of the Seven Years' War (also known as the French and Indian War).

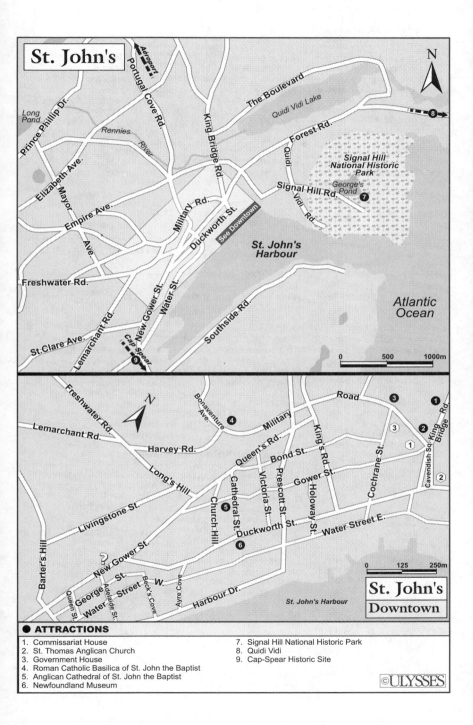

St. John's

N

Aéroport

Portugal Cove Rd.

The Boulevard

Quidi Vidi Lake

8

Long Pond

Prince Phillip Dr.

Rennies

River

King Bridge Rd.

Forest Rd.

Quidi

Signal Hill National Historic Park

George's Pond

7

Elizabeth Ave.

Mayor Ave.

Empire Ave.

Military Rd.

Duckworth St.

See Downtown

Signal Hill Rd.

Vidi Rd.

St. John's Harbour

Atlantic Ocean

Freshwater Rd.

St.Clare Ave.

Lemarchant Rd.

New Gower St.

Water St.

Cap. Spear

9

Southside Rd.

0   500   1000m

Freshwater Rd.

N

Bonaventure Ave.

Road

3

1

Military

4

Lemarchant Rd.

Harvey Rd.

Queen's Rd.

Bond St.

King's Rd.

3

2

1

Long's Hill

Prescott St.

Gower St.

Cochrane St.

1

Livingstone St.

Cathedral St.

Victoria St.

Holoway St.

Cavendish Sq.

King Bridge Rd.

2

Barter's Hill

Church Hill

5

Duckworth St.

Water Street E.

0   125   250m

New Gower St.

6

George St.

Adelaide St.

Street W.

Beck's Cove

Ayre Cove

Harbour Dr.

St. John's Harbour

St. John's
Downtown

Queen St.

Water St.

● **ATTRACTIONS**

1. Commissariat House
2. St. Thomas Anglican Church
3. Government House
4. Roman Catholic Basilica of St. John the Baptist
5. Anglican Cathedral of St. John the Baptist
6. Newfoundland Museum

7. Signal Hill National Historic Park
8. Quidi Vidi
9. Cap-Spear Historic Site

©ULYSSES

The French, who had been defeated in Québec City and Louisbourg several years earlier, managed to seize St. John's for a few months, after which they were ousted by English troops led by Lieutenant Colonel William Amherst. During summer, visitors can see the **Signal Hill Tattoo**, a re-enactment of 19th-century military exercises complete with period costumes and gun and cannon salvos.

At the Signal Hill welcome centre, there is a small **museum** *($2.50; mid-Jun to beginning of Sep, every day 8:30am to 8pm, rest of the year 8:30am to 4:30pm* ☎772-5567) with an exhibition on fishing and the history of St. John's and Newfoundland. **Cabot Tower**, the main building on Signal Hill, was erected in 1897 in honour of the 400th anniversary of John Cabot's arrival in North America and Queen Victoria's diamond jubilee. The tower was a maritime signal station until 1960 and now houses an exhibition on the history of maritime signalling on this hill.

The exhibition also takes a close look at the life of Guglielmo Marconi, who, on December 12, 1901, received the first transatlantic wireless message at Signal Hill. This message, an "S" in Morse code, was sent from Cornwall, England. From the top floor of Cabot Tower, visitors can enjoy a splendid view of the ocean. For a view of the harbour, head to the ruins of the **Queen's Battery**. From the foot of the cliff, you can see the rock to which the chain used to seal off the harbour in the 18th century was fastened.

On the other side, you'll see the ruins of Fort Amherst, now topped by a lighthouse. Signal Hill's well laid out paths make it a pleasant place for a walk. Another trail runs along the harbour from Signal Hill to St. John's.

Quidi Vidi, one of the most picturesque villages in the province, stands proudly at the foot of Signal Hill, flanked by rock walls. It is made up of a few dozen brightly coloured houses, a small chapel and, of course, a fishing port, which has been in use since the 17th century. Nearby **Quidi Vidi Lake** is the scene of the annual **St. John's Regatta**, held on the first Wednesday in August. On a nearby promontory, visitors will find the remains of the **Quidi Vidi Battery** *(free admission; mid-Jun to early Sep, every day 9am to 5pm)*. Built in 1762 by the French, who occupied St. John's and its surrounding area for several months, this battery was later used by the British and was abandoned in 1870.

The **Cape Spear National Historic Site** *(11km south of St. John's, on Hwy. 11 mid-May to mid-Oct, 10am to 6pm,* ☎772-5367*)*. Cape Spear is the easternmost point on the North American continent. In 1863, it was thus graced with a lighthouse, which became the most important one in the province after the lighthouse in St. John's harbour. Originally, the lighthouse was a square structure built around a tower, at the top of which were seven parabolic reflectors that reflected the light from seven lamps. The lighthouse was modernized over the years, and a new one was erected right nearby in 1955.

The **old lighthouse** *($2.50; all year, every day 9am to 5pm),* furnished the way its keeper's house was in 1939, is open to the public. Close by, visitors can see the remnants of the extensive military installations built here during the Second World War. Cape Spear is also a pleasant place to stroll along the shore. In fine weather, the view of the ocean and the coast is spectacular.

Tour B: The Avalon Peninsula

Highway 10 leads south from St. John's to Witless Bay.

Witless Bay

The **Witless Bay Ecological Reserve** (see p 77) comprises three islands offshore from the villages of Witless Bay and Bauline. Each summer, these islands serve as a refuge for hundreds of thousands of seabirds, who come here to lay their eggs and raise their nestlings.

From Witless Bay, Highway 10 leads south to Ferryland.

Ferryland

A pretty fishing village that feels as if it has been left behind by time, Ferryland was the site of one of the first English colonies in North America (1621). The settlers were sent here by George Calvert who only stayed here for a few years before moving to present-day Maryland, thus becoming the first Lord Baltimore. Calvert's departure did not mean the end of the colony of Ferryland, however, which was taken in hand by English navigator David Kirke.

At the **Colony of Avalon Archaeology Site** *($3; mid-May to mid-Oct, every day 9am to 7pm; Hwy. 10; ☎432-3200)*, where excavations have been carried out over the past few years, visitors can see the foundations of the colony and tour the research and analysis facilities. To learn more about the history of Ferryland and its surrounding area, head to the **Historic Ferryland Museum** *(free admission; mid-Jun to mid-Sep, every day 9am to 5pm; Hwy. 10, ☎432-2711)*, whose exhibitions deal, most notably, with the colony's earliest days.

The 1,070km² **Avalon Wilderness Reserve** ★, located in the southeastern part of the Avalon Peninsula, attracts fishing buffs and hikers. To visit the reserve, you must obtain a permit at La Manche Provincial Park (Hwy. 10, 11km from Cape Broyle). The Avalon Wilderness Reserve is the natural habitat of tens of thousands of caribou. In the southernmost part of it, families of **caribou** can frequently be seen crossing Highway 10.

Cape St. Mary's is located at the southwesternmost tip of the Avalon Peninsula.

Cape St. Mary's

The **Cape St. Mary's Ecological Reserve** ★★ *(May to Oct, every day 9am to 7pm; along Hwy. 100, ☎729-2424)* (see p 77) protects the most spectacular and most easily accessible colony of seabirds in North America.

From Cape St. Mary's, Highway 100 leads to Placentia, on the west coast of the Avalon Peninsula.

★
Placentia

This picturesque village on the shores of Placentia Bay became closely associated with the European presence on the island at a very early date. Basque fishers were already stopping here by the early 16th century, as the pebble beach proved a particularly suitable spot for drying cod.

Caribou

Later, in 1662, the French established the first permanent settlement here. Known as Plaisance, it was the capital of the French colony of Terre-Neuve until the signing of the Treaty of Utrecht in 1713.

Under the French Regime, Plaisance's role was to contain English expansion in Newfoundland, defend the French fleet based in Newfoundland, and protect Canada from invasion in times of war. France kept only limited military forces in Plaisance, which didn't stop the little garrison from attacking St. John's, the English capital of Newfoundland, in 1696, 1705 and 1709. The 1705 expedition was the only

one in which the French failed to seize Fort William, which overlooked St. John's, though they did burn the city. **Castle Hill National Historic Park** ★ *(free admission; mid-Jun to beginning of Sep, every day 8:30am to 8pm; beginning of Sep to mid-Jun, every day 8:30am to 4:30pm; on Hwy 100, ☎227-2401)* protects the ruins of various 17th- and 18th-century French and English fortifications. To defend Plaisance, the French built the Vieux Fort in 1662, Fort Louis in 1691 and Fort Royal in 1693. After seizing control of the region, the English erected little Fort Frederick in 1721, then, during the War of the Austrian Succession (1740-1748), the New Fort. Castle Hill commands an outstanding view of Placentia and its bay.

From the Trans-Canada Highway, Highway 80 leads north to Heart's Content.

The Bonavista Peninsula

★
Trinity

A village with particularly well-preserved 19th-century architecture, Trinity sits on a promontory alongside an excellent natural harbour on the **Bonavista Peninsula** ★★. The site was named by explorer Gaspar Corte Real, who explored its bay on Trinity Sunday in the year 1501. In 1558, the English made Trinity their first permanent settlement in Newfoundland. Thanks to its fisheries and its commercial ties with London, Trinity managed to attain a certain level of prosperity.

Newfoundland and Labrador

In 1615, it became the seat of the first maritime court in the history of Canada, for a case involving a conflict between local and seasonal fishers.

Trinity offers visitors all sorts of opportunities to step back into the past: the **Trinity Interpretation Centre** *($2.50; mid-Jun to early Sep, every day 10am to 17pm; Hwy. 239, ☎464-2042)* boasts an excellent collection of maps, illustrations and period photographs; the **Green Family Forge** *($2; mid-Jun to early Sep, every day 10am to 18pm; Church Rd., ☎464-2244)* presents an exhibition on the history of a forge dating back to the 1750s and **Hiscock House** *($2.50; mid-Jun to early Sep, every day 10am to 5h30pm, Hwy. 239, ☎464-2042)*, open to the public, is a typical turn-of-the-century merchant's house. The most novel way to learn about Trinity's history, however, is the **Trinity Pageant** ★, a series of plays about local history, presented in different places around town. The shows are held daily during summer, starting at 2pm.

From May to August, several kinds of whales come to the waters off Newfoundland. They can often be spotted from the shore. For a closer look, we recommend going on a whale-watching excursion. Trinity is a good point of departure, and a number of tour agencies organize outings.

★
Cape Bonavista

Did John Cabot really open the way to the exploration of Canada? Newfoundlanders swear that he did and maintain that it was at Cape Bonavista that Cabot and his crew stopped for the first time in the summer of 1497, after sailing across the Atlantic from Bristol, England. In reality, no one really knows where Cabot arrived in the New World. Cape Bonavista is fighting over the honour with several other sites along the Canadian coast. In any case, it was in Cape Bonavista that Newfoundlanders celebrated, with great pomp, the 500th anniversary of Cabot's landing in 1997.

The village of Bonavista is the largest community on the peninsula. Its pretty, brightly coloured houses are surrounded by a rolling landscape that opens onto a bustling port. Bonavista was frequented by fishers of all different nationalities throughout the 16th century, before the English settled here around 1600.

At the beginning of the 19th century, the government of Newfoundland started building lighthouses along the shores of the island to make the waters safer for ships. In 1843, the first lighthouse on the north shore of the island was erected on Cape Bonavista. Today, you can visit the **old lighthouse** *($2.50 mid-Jun to early Oct, every day 10am to 5h30pm; Hwy. 230; ☎468-7444)*, which has been restored and furnished the way it was in the 1870s. It houses an exhibition on the history of lighthouses and the daily life of their keepers. The point offers a magnificent **view** ★ of the sea and the rocky shoreline. Whales can often be spotted offshore in summer. If you keep your eyes peeled, you can see these giant mammals from many spots along Bonavista Bay.

Tour E: The Viking Highway

There is an excellent road from Deer Lake to **Gros Morne National Park** ★★★ (see p 76), one of the jewels of the Atlantic provinces and a UNESCO World Heritage Site. The Viking Highway runs along the Strait of Belle Isle from the park, through strikingly desolate, rocky landscapes.

Port au Choix

Port au Choix, where fishing is still the major activity, was an important port for Basque fishers for many years. Its name comes from "Portuchoa," which means "little port" in Basque. The Basques were not the first people to take advantage of Port au Choix's excellent location, however. The **Port au Choix National Historic Site** ★ *($2.75; mid-Jun to mid-Sep, every day 9am to 5pm; ☎861-3522)* displays archeoligical evidence of peoples who inhabited this region long before any Europeans arrived. In the 1950s, archaeologists uncovered traces of a Dorset Eskimo community that occupied the site of nearby Phillip's Gardens, between the years 200 and 600. Dorset culture was sophisticated, as evidenced by the finely worked bone and stone carvings discovered here.

In 1967, other major digs in the region led to the uncovering of a Maritime Archaic burial ground containing human bones, tools and weapons that date back 3,200 to 4,300 years. The Maritime Archaic survived essentially on fishing and hunting. They developed an artistic tradition and decorated their clothing with shells, seal's claws and pendants made of bone. The tools, weapons and ornaments found in the tombs indicate that these people would prepare for a life after death not unlike their life on earth.

At the Port au Choix National Historic Site, visitors can see some of the artifacts found in this area and watch a documentary on the lifestyle of these Aboriginal peoples. The short walk to the Phillip's Garden's archaeological site offers a chance to contemplate the region's rugged landscape.

★
L'Anse aux Meadows

The **L'Anse aux Meadows National Historic Site** ★★ *($5; mid-Jun to early Sep, every day 9am to 8pm; Hwy. 436, ☎623-2608)* is the only place where traces of the presence of Norwegian sailors – or Vikings, as they are sometimes called in North America – have been discovered. L'Anse-aux-Meadows has been designated a World Heritage Site by UNESCO. A group of Norwegian sailors, led by Leif Eriksson, came here from Greenland and set up a camp around the year 1000. This camp consisted of eight buildings and was home to an estimated 80 to 100 people. The Norwegians used it as a base for their expeditions along the Atlantic coast. According to the sagas, on their expeditions from Leif's camp, Leif Eriksson and his family discovered the shores of Labrador, Newfoundland and regions farther south on the Gulf of St. Lawrence. Eriksson named the southernmost lands "Vinland," after the wild vines that grew there.

The L'Anse-aux-Meadows site was discovered by Helge Ingstad and Anne Stisne Ingstad in 1960. Visitors can see the foundations of the eight buildings uncovered by the Ingstads, and later by Parks Canada. Three buildings from Eriksson's era have been reconstructed right nearby.

Excellent guided tours are available. The welcome centre presents an interesting exhibition on the vestiges found on the site and also shows a film on the captivating story of the excavations conducted by Helge Ingstad and Anne Stisne Ingstad, and later by Parks Canada.

★
St. Anthony

Located on the shores of an excellent inland harbour, St. Anthony is the largest community in the northern part of the peninsula. Since 1922, it has been the headquarters of the **Grenfell Mission**, which provides medical care for the isolated communities of northern Newfoundland and Labrador. The mission was founded by Dr. Wilfred Grenfell (1865-1940), who started developing the region's first real network of hospitals, infirmaries and orphanages in 1894. To finance his projects, Grenfell created a company called Grenfell Crafts, which sold winter clothing made by local craftspeople; the profits would go to the mission.

Cape Bonavista

Newfoundland and Labrador

Today, you can visit the **Grenfell House Museum** *($5; 9am to 8pm; Hwy. 430, 454-2281)*, the Grenfell family's former home, which houses a collection of objects used by fishers at the turn of the century. The museum's shop sells pretty winter clothing made on the premises, as well as local crafts. From the centre of St. Anthony, visitors can go to nearby **Fishing Point**, which offers a splendid **view ★** of the ocean. Whales and icebergs can often be spotted from here during the summer. There is also a good restaurant at Fishing Point.

Parks

Tour C:
Eastern and Central
Newfoundland

Terra Nova National Park ★ *(☎533-2801)* covers just over 400km² of wooded, gently rolling terrain. It is bounded by Newman Sound and Clode Sound, inlets of Bonavista Bay. The park is home to numerous animal species, including moose, black bears, martens, beavers and lynxes. The waters of the sounds, particularly during May and August, attract various species of whales, including humpbacks. **Ocean Watch Tours** *(☎533-6024)* hosts cruises in the sounds for people interested in observing whales and other aquatic species.

The main activities to be enjoyed in the park are camping, hiking, fishing, canoeing and, in winter, cross-country skiing; most

organized outings start at Newman Sound. The Twin Rivers Golf Course is located at the park's south entrance. Two lookouts, both accessible by car, offer **panoramic views ★** of the park: the **Blue Hill Exhibit** *(drive 7km from the north entrance, then take a side road for 1.5km)* and the **Ochre Hill Exhibit** *(drive 23km from the north entrance, then take a side road for 3km)*.

The internationally renowned **Gros Morne National Park ★★★** *(☎458-2417)* boasts 1,805km² of spectacular scenery: fiords, lakes, high plateaus, coastal dunes and boreal forests. The Long Range Mountains run the entire length of the park; Gros Morne is the highest, at 850m. In 1987, UNESCO designated Gros Morne National Park a World Heritage Site, primarily because of its geological make-up: in the southern part of the park **Tablelands** formed by the shifting of two tectonic plates, serve as an eloquent testimony to continental drift. The park's landscape was also shaped by the retreat of the glaciers at the end of the Glacial Epoch.

Gros Morne National Park protects numerous wild mammals, including bears, moose and caribou. It is not uncommon to see moose along the park's main roads, and various species of whales can be spotted from the shore during summer. In addition to wildlife observation, other activities to be enjoyed here include camping, hiking (over 100km of trails), swimming, boat rides, fishing and, in winter, cross-country skiing. Lodgings are available at Trout River,

Woody Point, Rocky Harbour and Cow Head.

Its splendid scenery and distinctive geological characteristics make the park's **south sector** well worth exploring. From the south entrance, Highway 431 runs through a rolling landscape, then along one of the arms of **Bonne Bay ★**, a deep fiord surrounded by the Long Range Mountains. The road leads to **Woody Point**, a pretty fishing village, then on to **Trout River Pond ★★**. This 15km-long freshwater fiord lies in a glacial valley at the edge of the **Gregory Plateau** and **Tablelands ★★**, created by the shifting of the tectonic plates about 500 million years ago. Visitors can explore this part of the park by taking a **boat ride** *(mid-Jun to mid-Sep; three departures per day from Trout River; ☎951-2101)* on Trout River.

The landscape of the **north sector** is dominated by the Long Range Mountains. The park's welcome centre, on Highway 430, a few kilometres from **Rocky Harbour**, shows an excellent documentary on the flora, fauna and geological features of Gros Morne National Park. It also provides information on the various activities to be enjoyed in the park and hosts a number of nature talks. From Rocky Harbour, the road leads to the **Lobster Cove Head lighthouse**. The old lighthouse keeper's house now contains an exhibition on the history of the settlement of the coastline in this area. There is a trail leading from the lighthouse to a rocky beach.

Much farther north in the park, a 3km trail offers access to **Western Brook**

Pond ★★, a 16km-long, 165m-deep inland fiord created during the Glacial Epoch. The rock walls that plunge into its crystalline waters reach as high as 650m in places. A **cruise** is the most pleasant way to take in the fiord's spectacular beauty. The outing lasts about 2.5hrs; for reservations, inquire at the Ocean View Motel (☎458-2730) in Rocky Harbour. Trimmed with beaches and sand dunes, **Shallow Bay**, at the north end of the park, is a good place to go swimming.

Outdoor Activities

Bird-watching

Tour B: The Avalon Peninsula

At the **Witless Bay Ecological Reserve** ★, the main avian attraction is the Atlantic puffin, the provincial bird. Though bird colonies can be seen from the shore, you can get a much closer look by taking a cruise. A number of tour agencies, including **Bird Island Charters** (*$25 per person;* ☎753-4850) offer excursions from the villages along the coast.

The **Cape St. Mary's Ecological Reserve** ★★ (*9am to 5pm; on Hwy. 100,* ☎729-2424), on the southwest tip of the Avalon Peninsula and washed by the Atlantic Ocean is home to some 60,000 seabirds. The most interesting place to observe them is along Bird Rock, a tall rock a few

metres from the shore, where a number of species nest. Visitors will also find the largest gannet colony in Newfoundland, the southernmost colony of thick-billed murres in the world, and many other species of birds, including eagles. Furthermore, humpback whales can be spotted offshore in July. The welcome centre provides fascinating information on the behaviour of seabirds.

Accommodations

Tour A: St. John's

The Roses B & B
$60 bkfst incl.
K, tv
4 rooms
9 Military Rd.
☎726-3336
⇝726-3483
Laid out in a Victorian house that is typical of downtown St. John's, this bed and breakfast is a friendly and very charming spot. Its high ceilings, rich mouldings, and wood floors give it a warm atmosphere. Its always inviting rooms are decorated with a heterogenous mix of antiques of greater or lesser value and modern furniture. Some of the rooms are equipped with fireplaces. Days at this welcoming inn always begin on the right foot with a copious breakfast served on the top floor of the house, from which there is a panoramic view of the port.

Compton House
$69 bkfst incl.
ℜ, ⊛, pb
10 rooms
26 Waterford Bridge Rd., A1E 1C6
☎739-5789
⇝739-1770
This majestic Victorian residence, converted into an inn, occupies a vast, prettily landscaped property near the Waterford River valley, about 15min by foot from the centre of the city. Guests quickly feel right at home in this lovely, elegant and inviting house brimming with period charm. The front living room is particularly pleasant and has a fireplace as do the little library and the dining room. Guest rooms are well furnished, very comfortable and all equipped with private bathrooms. If a little extra luxury is in order, visitors can stay in suites, each of which is equipped with a balcony or a patio, a whirlpool and a fireplace.

Waterford Manor
$85 bkfst incl.
⊛, ℜ, tv
7 rooms
185 Waterford Bridge Rd., A1E 1C7
☎754-4139
⇝754-4155
Built at the end of the last century for the family of a local merchant, this sumptuous Queen Anne house is now a beautiful inn. Recent renovation work has restored its former grandeur and adapted it to meet modern expectations of comfort. Guest rooms, each of which has its own special character, are furnished with antiques and decorated with meticulous attention to detail. They are all very pleasant, but the most beautiful one, on the top floor, offers a fireplace and a whirlpool. Breakfast may be served in guests' rooms or in the

Newfoundland and Labrador

dining room on the ground floor. The Waterford Manor, tucked away in a pretty residential neighbourhood on the outskirts of the Waterford River valley, is about a 15min walk from downtown St. John's.

Quality Hotel by Journey's end
$90
ℜ, *tv*
162 rooms
2 Hill O'Chips, A1C 6B1
☎ *754-7788 or 800-228-5151*
≈ *754-5209*
Quality Hotel by Journey's end is always a sure bet. It is a welcoming, well-situated establishment near downtown that offers good value for your money. Although the rooms are comfortable, well kept and functional, there is nothing especially original about them. Since it sits on a rise near the port, the Quality Hotel offers a lovely view of the bay.

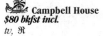 **Hotel Newfoundland**
$129
ℜ, ≈, ☺
Cavendish Square, P.O. Box 5637
A1C 5W8
☎ *800-441-1414 or 726-4980*
≈ *726-2025*
The most prestigious establishment in St. John's, a member of the Canadian Pacific hotel chain, is a modern, 301-room hotel in the heart of the city. Its interior decor is a brilliant success: it is both original and inviting. From the lobby visitors can go into the Court Garden, where terraced plant beds are interspersed with waterfalls. The warmth and brightness of this spot are in singular contrast to the cool, rainy climate that so often shrouds the city. Guest rooms are spacious, charming and comfortable – they have been designed as much to please vacationers as to meet the

needs of business travellers – and most of them offer breathtaking views of the port, the city and the bay.

Tour B: The Avalon Peninsula

Ferryland

Downs Inn
$55 bkfst incl.
sb, tv
4 rooms
Rte. 10, AOA 2H0
☎ *(877) 432-2808*
≈ *432-2659*
Lodging is available about an hour from St. John's at Downs Inn, a pleasant bed and breakfast laid out in an old Presbyterian convent. Erected in 1914, this building was home to about 15 nuns until the 1980s; renovation work has managed to preserve the spirit of the house. Each of the spacious, clean, comfortable rooms is equipped with a fireplace, but none of them have private washrooms.

Placentia

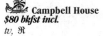 **Rosedale Manor**
$50 bkfst incl.
4 rooms
Riverside Dr., AOB 2Y0
☎ *227-3613*
Guests of the Rosedale Manor, one of the lovely inns on this part of the peninsula, feel right at home. Located in the heart of the village, just across from the bay, this pretty, historic house offers carefully decorated rooms embellished with antique furniture and equipped with private bathrooms. The owner is both attentive and discreet. If you have an interest, she will be happy to fill you in on the local history.

The Bonavista Peninsula

Trinity

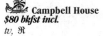 **Campbell House**
$80 bkfst incl.
tv, ℜ
5 rooms
High St.
☎ *464-3377 ou 877-464-7700*
≈ *464-3377*
Campbell House is a bed and breakfast set up in a lovely house that dates from the 1840s. The old-fashioned appeal of this stately residence, which stands in the middle of the town's historic area, has been well preserved thanks to meticulous renovation work. The rooms are charming and prettily decorated. From Campbell House there is a beautiful view of the town and the ocean.

The Village Inn
$52
ℜ, *tv*
7 rooms
Taverner's Path
☎ *464-3700*
Despite its relatively modest size, the Village Inn is the largest hotel establishment in Trinity. It has occupied this building in the heart of the village since the beginning of the 20th century. Its rooms vary greatly in comfort and quality. There is a good family restaurant on the premises and whale-watching trips are organized here.

Terra Nova National Park

Terra Nova Park Lodge
$90
79 rooms
ℜ, ≈, ≡, *tv*
AOC 2G0
☎ *543-2525*
⇆ *543-2201*

Terra Nova Park Lodge stands on a large lot near the national park and close to an excellent 18-hole golf course. Naturally, it attracts a clientele of golfers, but it also appeals to travellers who simply want to enjoy its peaceful setting. This luxurious establishment offers all of the comforts and the excellent cuisine served in its restaurant adds to the pleasure of a stay here.

Tour E: The Viking Route

Norris Point

 Sugar Hill Inn
$156
pb, △, ℜ, tv
7 rooms
Rte. 431, P.O. Box 100, A0K 3V0
☎ *458-2147 ou 888-299-2147*
⇆ *458-2166*

The Sugar Hill, one of the best places to stay on the western half of the island, comes into view on a beautifully landscaped hillside as you enter Norris Point in the southern part of Gros Morne National Park. All of its rooms are charming and equipped with private bathrooms. A sauna and a whirlpool are at guests' disposal and excellent fare is served in the inn's dining room.

Ocean View Motel
$65
ℜ, tv
44 rooms
Main St.
☎ *458-2730 ou 800-563-9887*
⇆ *458-2256*

The Ocean View Motel offers rooms that are spacious, comfortable and clean, but of no particular charm. This establishment is well kept and houses a good family restaurant.

Cape Onion

Tickle Inn
$60 bkfst incl.
ℜ
4 rooms
R.R. 1, A0K 4J0
☎ / ⇆ *452-4321*

A little over half an hour from L'Anse-aux-Meadows road and from St. Anthony is the Tickle Inn, an appealing little inn in an enchanting setting facing the ocean and surrounded by valley landscapes. This spot is perfect for long walks and for spotting whales and icebergs on the open sea. The rooms are well kept and inviting. The Tickle Inn's dining room serves some of the best cuisine in the area.

Restaurants

Tour A: St. John's

 Stella's
$
106 Water St.
☎ *753-9625*

Stella's is absolutely perfect for a quick bite or for a tea break. This warm, welcoming spot offers a menu made up of fish and chicken dishes, vegetarian dishes, sandwiches, salads and soups. The seafood chowder is especially comforting on a rainy day.

Taj Mahal
$$
203 Water St.
☎ *576-5500*

Taj Mahal, lavishly decorated in Victorian style, prepares authentic Indian cuisine. Its elaborate menu highlights various tandoori specialties. The chicken *tikka*, the *tandoori* shrimp and the *malai tikka* fish are especially delicious. The *nan* bread is succulent, as is the steamed rice. Most of the main dishes cost about $10. A complete dinner for two can be enjoyed here for under $40.

 Cellar
$$-$$$
Bird's Cove, Water St.
☎ *579-8900*

One of the best restaurants in the province, the Cellar earns its reputation with an innovative menu that seduces the senses. Whether in a pasta, seafood or meat dish, the originality of the flavours and the freshness of the produce are as impressive as the beautiful presentation. The pleasant atmosphere of the dining room and its low-key lighting are perfect for intimate evenings.

 Stone House
$$$
8 Kenoa's Hill
☎ *753-2380*

The magnificent Stone House, built in the 1830s, is comprised of four dining rooms and offers an interesting menu that mingles nouvelle cuisine with the culinary traditions of Newfoundland. It lists an appetizer of cod tongue, of course, as well as a wide selection of seafood- and fish-based main courses. In addition there is an excellent choice of game, such

Newfoundland and Labrador

as caribou, moose, wild goose and pheasant. The wine cellar is well stocked and may be visited upon request.

Tour B: The Avalon Peninsula

Trepassey

Trepassey Restaurant
$-$$
Rte. 10
☎438-2934
The magnificent Trepassey Restaurant, in the Trepassey Motel, is the perfect spot for lunch. The dishes on offer, mainly seafood and fish, are simple but well prepared and inexpensive. The layout of the restaurant is inviting and offers a pretty view of the bay.

The Bonavista Peninsula

Trinity

Eriksson
$$
☎464-3698
Eriksson simmers up simple dishes composed mainly of seafood and fish in the warm atmosphere of a stately old home.

Tour E: The Viking Route

Trout River

Seaside Restaurant
$$-$$$
☎451-3461
Seaside Restaurant owes its renown to the freshness and quality of its fish and seafood, which make up the greater part of its menu. The cuisine is delicate and well-prepared, while the service allows for plenty of time (sometimes a bit too much) to contemplate the fascinating motion of the ocean through the dining room's large picture window.

Rocky Harbour

Fisherman's Landing
$$
☎458-2060
An unpretentious family restaurant, Fisherman's Landing proposes a menu of fish and seafood, with some meat and poultry items for good measure. The service is courteous, although somewhat businesslike, and the prices are reasonable. Copious breakfasts are served.

St. Anthony

Lightkeepers' Café
$$-$$$
Fishing Point
☎454-4900
There could be no better location for a restaurant than that of the Lightkeepers' Café at the very tip of Fishing Point. It offers a remarkable view of the ocean, an entrancing tableau occasionally enhanced by the slow drift of an iceberg or the to and fro of a whale. This beautiful panorama is happily complemented by excellent fare. The menu lists mainly fish and seafood dishes, including succulent snow crab, and the wine list is quite varied. Sunrise over the sea is a sight that can be enjoyed here starting at 7am.

Atlantic Puffin

Nova Scotia

The magnificent province

of Nova Scotia looks like a long peninsula; it is connected to the continent by nothing more than a narrow strip of land known as the Isthmus of Chignecto.

In "Canada's Ocean Playground," the sea is never far away. In fact, no part of the territory of Nova Scotia is more than 49km from the water, be it the Atlantic Ocean, the Northumberland Strait or the Bay of Fundy. The proximity of the coast has shaped the character and lives of Nova Scotians as much as it has the splendid maritime landscape.

The coastline, stretching hundreds of kilometres, is punctuated with harbours and bays, their shores dotted with fishing villages and towns. What is most striking about Nova Scotia is the way its architectural heritage blends so harmoniously with the natural setting.

From the tiniest fishing village to Halifax, the capital, there are few places where the architecture of the houses and buildings, often dating back to the 19th century, does not fit in beautifully with the surrounding landscape.

At one time, the magnificent land of Nova Scotia was the focus of the rivalry between the French and British empires. Originally inhabited by the Micmac (Mi'qmaq) First Nation, it was the site of the first European colony in America north of Florida.

Visitors will discover many fascinating sites bearing witness to Nova Scotia's turbulent history, such as the Fortress of Louisbourg on Cape Breton Island, Citadel Hill in Halifax, the Grand-Pré National Historic Site, commemorating the deportation of the Acadians, and the Abitation de Port-Royal, a replica of the first permanent French settlement in North America (1605).

Finding Your Way Around

By Car

Halifax

Entering Halifax and reaching the downtown area is generally very easy by car; many road signs clearly indicate the way. If in doubt, remember that Halifax lies on the southwest side of the harbour (Dartmouth is on the other side), and the downtown area faces right onto the port. Visitors will have little trouble finding their bearings downtown, since Citadel Hill and the port serve as landmarks. The most important downtown artery is Barrington Street.

Cape Breton Island

The quickest way to get to Cape Breton Island from Halifax is via Highway 102, and then the TransCanada to Port Hastings. The island is also accessible by taking Highway 7 which follows the Atlantic Ocean.

The route passes through peaceful rural communities and a few fishing ports, among them Musquodoboit Harbour with its superb stretches of sand at **Martinique Beach**.

Either of these routes will take you to Cape Breton Island. Once there, you

can go either to Sydney, Louisbourg or near Baddeck, which marks the beginning of the Cabot Trail.

By Plane

Halifax International Airport is served by planes from Europe and the United States. Air Canada and Canadian Airlines offer flights from major Canadian cities. For more information, please refer to the "Practical Information" chapter. There is shuttle service from the airport to the big hotels downtown.

By Bus

Visitors can reach a variety of destinations within Nova Scotia, as there are buses running from Halifax to Yarmouth, Amherst and Sydney (*Acadian Lines,* ☎454-9321) and along the southern coast of the province.

Cape Breton Island

From Halifax, visitors can take the bus as far as Sydney. It is worth noting, however, that no bus goes all the way around the island (aside from private tour buses). There is no way to get around easily, except in Sydney, so it is best either to rent a car or rely on your own resources (hitchhiking, cycling).

Acadian Lines
Halifax to Sydney
☎(902) 454-9321

Transit Cap Breton *around Sydney*
☎(902) 539-8124

By Train

VIA, the Canadian railway, ends at Halifax. The station is near downtown. To find out the passenger train schedule :
☎800-561-3952

By Ferry

From Saint John (New Brunswick) to Digby (Nova Scotia):
MV Princess of Acadia
☎888-249-7245
☎(902) 566-3838
Departure: three times daily during summer.

From Portland (Maine) to Yarmouth (Nova Scotia):
Prince of Fundy Cruise
Box 4216, Station A, Portland Maine, 04101
☎800-341-7540 *from Canada and the U.S.*
www.princeoffundy.com
Departure: daily from May to Oct.

From Bar Harbor (Maine) to Yarmouth (Nova Scotia):
Marine Atlantic
☎888-249-7245
Departure: once daily, mid-May to mid-Sep.

The ferry linking Caribou (Nova Scotia) to Wood Islands (Prince Edward Island) provides daily service from May to Dec :

Northumberland Ferry
Box 634, Charlottetown, P.E.I. C1A 7L3
☎888-249-7245

A ferry links North Sydney with Argentia, Newfoundland three times a week in summer.

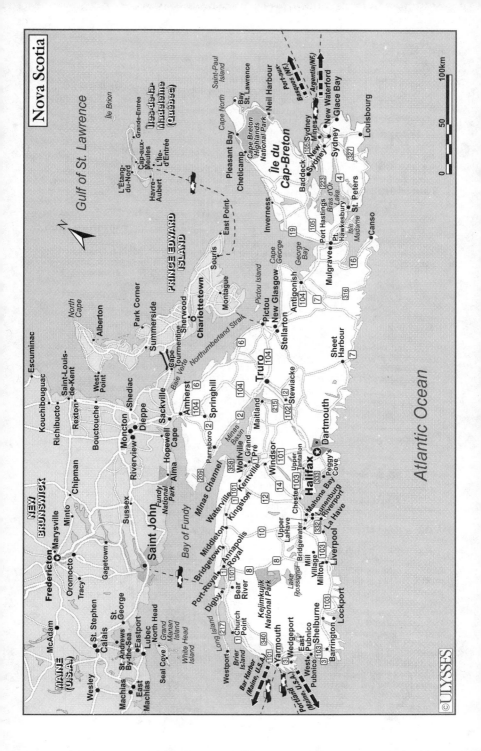

Nova Scotia

Gulf of St. Lawrence

Atlantic Ocean

© ULYSSES

Practical Information

Area code: **902**

Tourist Information Office

Visitor Centre
1595 Barrington St.
☎ **490-5946**
⌐ **490-5973**

The provincial government operates a reservation service for hotels, bed & breakfasts, campgrounds and car rentals. Information on festivals, ferry service and weather forecasts is also available. Dial ☎ **800-565-0000** in North America or ☎ **(902) 425-5781**.

Exploring

Halifax

A city with a rich architectural heritage built at the foot of a fortified hill overlooking one of the longest natural harbours in the world, Halifax is a delightful place to visit. The city's location, which is outstanding from both a navigational and a strategic point of view, has been the deciding factor in its growth. In 1749, the British began developing the site, which had long been frequented by the Micmac First Nation. That year, 2,500 British soldiers and colonists led by Governor Edward Cornwallis settled

here with the aim of securing Britain's claim to the territory of Nova Scotia. At the time, France and its North American colonies were the enemy. Over the following decades, Halifax served as a stronghold for British troops during the American Revolution and the War of 1812. A military past is evident in the city's present-day urban landscape, its most striking legacy being, of course, the Citadel, whose silhouette looms over the downtown area. Not only a military city, Halifax has always been a commercial centre as well. Its access to the Atlantic, its excellent port and, starting in the late 19th century, its connection to the Canadian rail network have all favoured trade. Historic Properties, made up of warehouses built on the pier, is the oldest architectural grouping of its kind in the country, bearing witness to the city's long-established commercial tradition.

Halifax is now the largest urban centre in the Atlantic provinces, with a population of over 330,000 (including the inhabitants of Dartmouth, its twin city).

It has a more varied, even cosmopolitan appearance than the rest of Atlantic Canada, and #boasts several superb museums and a whole slew of other attractions. Visitors are sure to enjoy strolling around Halifax and scouting out its restaurants, bustling streets and wide assortment of shops.

The Citadel and its Surrounding Area

The **Halifax Citadel National Historic Site ★ ★ ★** *($6; early May to late Oct, 9am to 5pm; Jul and Aug until 6pm; Citadel Hill;* ☎ *426-5080)* is the most striking legacy of the military history of Halifax, a city that has played an important strategic role in the defence of the East Coast ever since it was founded in 1749. The fourth British fort to occupy this site, this imposing star-shaped structure overlooking the city was built between 1828 and 1856. It was the heart of an impressive network of defences intended to protect the port in the event of an attack.

Visitors can explore the Citadel alone or take part in an interesting guided tour, that traces the history of the various fortifications that have marked the city's landscape since 1749 and explains their strategic value.

Old Town Clock

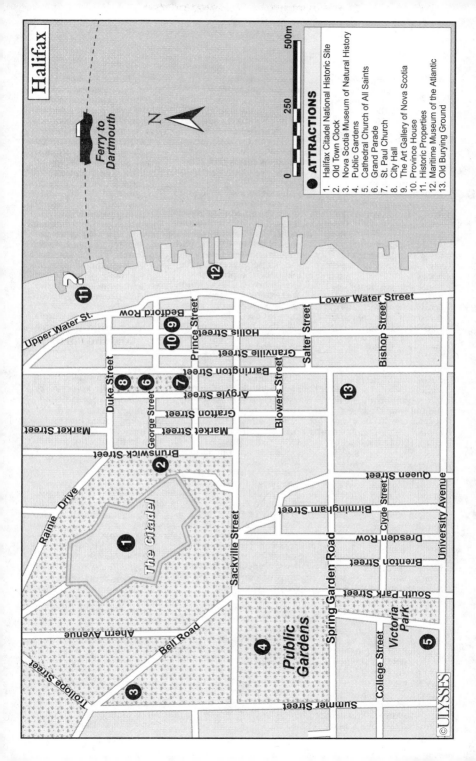

Halifax

Ferry to Dartmouth

N

0   250   500m

● ATTRACTIONS

1. Halifax Citadel National Historic Site
2. Old Town Clock
3. Nova Scotia Museum of Natural History
4. Public Gardens
5. Cathedral Church of All Saints
6. Grand Parade
7. St. Paul Church
8. City Hall
9. The Art Gallery of Nova Scotia
10. Province House
11. Historic Properties
12. Maritime Museum of the Atlantic
13. Old Burying Ground

Upper Water St.
Bedford Row
Lower Water Street
Prince Street
Hollis Street
Granville Street
Barrington Street
Salter Street
Argyle Street
Grafton Street
Market Street
Blowers Street
Bishop Street
Duke Street
George Street
Market Street
Brunswick Street
Rainie Drive
The Citadel
Sackville Street
Ahern Avenue
Bell Road
Trollope Street
Queen Street
Birmingham Street
Clyde Street
Dresden Row
Brenton Street
South Park Street
Spring Garden Road
University Avenue
College Street
Summer Street
Public Gardens
Victoria Park

© ULYSSES

All of the rooms used to accommodate soldiers and store arms and munitions are open to the public, and visitors can move about through the corridors leading from one room or level to another. It is also possible to walk along the ramparts, which offer an incomparable view of the city and its port. In summer, students dressed and armed like soldiers of the 78th Highlanders and the Royal Artillery perform manoeuvres within these walls. The site also includes a **military museum** (☎427-5979) that houses an extensive collection of British and Nova Scotian arms and uniforms. A fascinating 15min audiovisual presentation on the history of Halifax may be viewed as well.

Right in front of the Citadel, towards the port, stands one of the most famous symbols of Halifax, the **Old Town Clock** ★ (*Citadel Hill, opposite the main entrance of the Citadel*), with its four dials. The clock was presented to the city in 1803 by Prince Edward, son of George III of Britain, who served as commander in chief of the Halifax garrison from 1794 to 1800. It serves as a reminder that the prince was a great believer in punctuality.

Northwest of the Citadel, visitors will find the **Nova Scotia Museum of Natural History** ★ (*$3.50; Jun to mid-Oct, Mon, Tue, Thu and Fri 9:30am to 5:30pm, Wed 9:30am to 8pm, Sun 1pm to 5:30pm; mid-Oct to late May, Tue, Thu, Fri and Sat 9:30am to 5pm, Wed 9:30am to 8pm, Sun 1pm to 5pm; 1747 Summer St.; ☎424-6099*), whose mission is to collect, preserve and study the objects and specimens most representative of Nova Scotia's geology, plant and animal life and archaeology.

The museum features exhibits on subjects such as botany, fossils, insects, reptiles and marine life. One of the most noteworthy items on display is a whale skeleton.

Visitors can also view a film on the birds living along the province's coast. The archaeology exhibit is particularly interesting, presenting the lifestyle and material possessions of the various peoples who have inhabited the province's territory over the centuries. The exhibit is organized in chronological order, starting with the Palaeolithic age, then moving on to the Micmacs, the Acadians and finally the British.

Stretching southwest of the Citadel are the lovely, verdant **Public Gardens** ★★ (*main entrance on South Park St.*), a Victorian garden covering an area of 7m, that dates back to 1753. Originally a private garden, it was purchased by the Nova Scotia Horticultural Society in 1836. The present layout, completed in 1875, is the work of Richard Power. A fine example of British know-how, the Public Gardens are adorned with stately trees concealing fountains, statues, charming flowerbeds, a pavilion and little lakes where ducks and swans swim about.

This is an absolutely perfect place to take a stroll, far from the occasionally turbulent atmosphere of downtown Halifax. During summer, concerts are held here on Sunday afternoons, and the Friends of Public Gardens organization offers guided tours of the garden (☎422-9407).

South of the Public Gardens, near Victoria Park, stands the **Cathedral Church of All Saints** ★ (*free admission; mid-Jun to mid-Sep, 1:30pm to 4:30pm; 1320 Tower Rd.; ☎424-6002*), whose remarkable stained-glass windows and exquisite woodwork will take your breath away.

The structure was completed in 1910, two centuries after the first Anglican service was held in Canada. It is located in a pretty part of the city, where the streets are flanked by stately trees. Some of Halifax's most prominent educational establishments can be found nearby.

Downtown Halifax and the Port

As early as a decade after Halifax was founded, **Grand Parade** (*between Harrington and Argyle Sts.*) had become a trading and gathering place for city residents. It is now a garden in the heart of the downtown area, flanked by tall buildings on all sides.

At the south end of Grand Parade, visitors will find **St. Paul Anglican Church** ★ (*free admission; Jun to Sep, Mon to Sat 9:30am to 5pm; Oct to May, Mon to Fri 9am to 4:30pm; 1749 Argyle St., Grand Parade*), the oldest Protestant church in Canada, built in 1750 after the model of St. Peter's Church in London, England. Despite the wearing effects of time and the addition of several extensions, the original structure has been preserved.

Inside, visitors can examine a piece of metal from the *Mont Blanc*, one of the ships that caused a terrible explosion in Halifax in

1917. On the north side of Grand Parade stands **City Hall** *(free admission)*, an elegant Victorian-style building dating back more than a century.

In the Dominion Building, a fine example of the city's rich architectural heritage erected at the end of the last century, is the **Art Gallery of Nova Scotia** ★★★ *($5; Tue to Fri 10am to 6pm, Sat and Sun noon to 5pm; 1741 Hollis St., opposite Province House; ☎424-7542)*, four flours of modern exhibition space containing the most remarkable art collection in Nova Scotia.

The permanent collection, consisting of nearly 3,000 pieces, is devoted to both popular and contemporary art. Although many works are by painters and sculptors from Nova Scotia and the Atlantic provinces in general, artists from other Canadian provinces, the United States and Europe are also represented. The Art Gallery presents the occasional touring exhibition as well. Finally, there is a wonderful boutique selling local crafts.

Seat of the government of Nova Scotia, **Province House** ★ *(free admission; Jul and Aug, Mon to Fri 9am to 5pm, Sat and Sun 10am to 4pm; Sep to Jun, Mon to Fri 9am to 4pm; Hollis St.; ☎424-4661)*, an elegant Georgian style edifice dating from 1819, is the oldest provincial legislature building in Canada. Visitors can take a guided tour through the Red Chamber, the library and the legislative assembly chamber.

The buildings and old warehouses along the Halifax pier, the oldest of their kind in Canada, have been renovated and now form an attractive and harmonious architectural grouping known as **Historic Properties** ★★★ *(bordered by Duke and Lower Water Sts., ☎429-0530)*. Numerous shops, restaurants and cafés have set up business here, along with an excellent provincial tourist information office.

This is a very popular, pleasant place, whose narrow streets lead to a promenade along the pier. The *Bluenose II* is often moored here during the summer. Built in Lunenberg in 1963, the *Bluenose II* is a replica of the most beloved ship in Canadian history, the *Bluenose*, which sailed the seas from 1921 to 1946 and is depicted on the Canadian ten-cent piece. When it is moored here, the *Bluenose II* offers 2hr cruises around the Halifax harbour.

A tour of Halifax's impressive port aboard this or any other ship offering similar excursions is a marvellous way to get to know the city *(for more information, contact the tourist information office,* Historic Properties; ☎424-4247).

Looking right out onto the harbour, the **Maritime Museum of the Atlantic** ★★ *($6; Jun to mid-Oct, Mon to Sat 9:30am to 5:30pm, Tue until 8pm; mid-Oct to May, Wed to Sat 9:30am to 5pm, Tue until 8pm, Sun 1pm to 5pm; 1675 Lower Water St., near the port; ☎424-7490)* presents a wonderful exhibition that offers a comprehensive overview of the city's naval history.

On the ground floor, there is a reconstruction of William Robertson and Son, a store that supplied shipowners, shipbuilders and captains for a century. On the same floor, visitors will find an assortment of historical artifacts related to Halifax's military arsenal and a varied collection of small craft, particularly lifeboats. The second floor features an absolutely extraordinary assortment of model boats, from sailboats to steamships.

Visitors can also tour the *Acadia*, which is moored at the pier behind the museum. This ship first sailed out of Newcastle-on-Tyne, England back in 1913 and spent most of the following 57 years gathering information for charts of the Atlantic coast and the shores of Hudson Bay. Close to the museum is the *HMCS Sackville*, a convoy ship that was used in World War II and has now been converted into a museum dedicated to the sailors who served in that war. At the **interpretive centre**, located in an adjacent building, visitors can view a 15min film on the Battle of the Atlantic.

Canada has given refuge to thousands of people. For more than 40 years, from 1928 to 1971, many of the men and women who came to the country stopped in Halifax at **Pier 21** (*$6; 9am to 8pm; 1055 Marginal Rd., ☎425-7770*). The pier also welcomed thousands of refugees during the Second World War and was the departure point for Canadian soldiers heading off to battle in foreign lands.

A former transit point, this pier has since been transformed into a museum in memory of these people. Interactive exhibits attempt to bring these memorable moments back to life, and a slide show tells about the lives of the people in transit. There's also a café, a tourist information centre and a store.

Farther south, on Barrington Street, at the corner of Spring Garden Road, lies the **Old Burying Ground** ★ (*free admission; Jun to Sep, 9am to 5pm; Barrington St. and Spring Garden Rd.*), Halifax's first cemetery, which is now considered a national historic site. Some of the old tombstones are veritable works of art. The oldest, marking the grave of John Connor, was erected in 1754. A map containing information on the cemetery is available at St. Paul Church (*Grand Parade*).

While visiting Halifax, make sure to stroll along **Spring Garden Road** ★, the busiest and most pleasant commercial street in Atlantic Canada. Lined with all sorts of interesting shops, restaurants and cafés, it looks like the local Latin

Quarter. Parallel to Spring Garden Road, but farther north, **Blowers Street** is another attractive artery, flanked by somewhat less conventional shops and businesses.

On the Outskirts of Halifax

Point Pleasant Park ★ (*at the end of Young Ave.*) covers an area of 75ha on Halifax's south point. Here, visitors will find kilometres of hiking trails along the coast, offering lovely views through the forest. Due to its location at the entrance of the harbour, Point Pleasant was of great strategic importance to the city for many years.

The first Martello tower in North America, now the **Prince of Wales Tower National Historic Site** ★ (*free admission; Jul to Sep, 10am to 6pm; Point Pleasant Park; ☎426-5080*), was erected here in 1796-97. Drawing inspiration from a supposedly impregnable tower on Corsica's Martello Point, the British erected this type of structure in many places along the shores of their Empire. The Prince of Wales Tower was part of Halifax's extensive network of defences. It now houses a museum on its history.

McNabs Island, measuring 4.8km by 1.2km and located right at the entrance to the harbour, was also part of the city's defenses. The British erected Fort McNab here between 1888 and 1892, equipping it with what were then the most powerful batteries in all of the city's fortifications.

Visitors can examine the vestiges of the structure at the **Fort McNab Historic**

Site ★ (*☎426-5080*), while enjoying a stroll around this peaceful, pretty island, which features a number of hiking trails. The ferry to McNabs Island leaves from Cable Wharf. For the schedule, contact the tourist information office (*Historic Properties, ☎424-4247*).

Dartmouth

From the pier in front of Historic Properties in Halifax, visitors can take a **ferry** (*about $1*) to Dartmouth, on the opposite shore, which offers a splendid view of both the port and McNabs Island. The town of Dartmouth boasts an attractive waterfront, beautiful residences, a variety of shops and restaurants and several tourist attractions, including the **Historic Quaker House** ★ (*free admission; early Jun to early Sep; 57-59 Ochterlaney St., ☎464-2300*). This is the only remaining example among some 22 similar houses built around 1785 by Quakers who came to Dartmouth from New England. Guides in period dress tell visitors about the Quaker lifestyle.

Springhill

Springhill was founded in 1790 by Loyalist colonists who intended to support themselves by farming. The area did not actually develop, however, until 1871, when the Springhill Mining Company coal mine opened. For nearly a century after, Springhill was one of the largest coal producers in Nova Scotia. The difficulties and dangers of coal mining were not without consequence. In 1891, 125 men and boys lost their lives in an accident in one of the galleries. Two more catastrophes, in 1956 and 1958, claimed the lives of 39 and 75 men respectively. After that, several mines remained in operation, but large-scale coal mining came to an end in Springhill. To add to this string of bad luck, the city was also the victim of two devastating fires (1957 and 1975).

To find out everything there is to know about popular singer Anne Murray, a Springhill native, head to the **Anne Murray Centre** (*$5.50; mid-May to early Oct, 9am to 5pm; Main St.; ☎597-8614*). Her fans will be delighted by the exhaustive collection of objects that either belonged to Murray at one time or summon up key moments in her life and career. Audiovisual aids frequently complement the presentation. Few details have been neglected; the exhibit starts off with a family tree tracing Murray's family origins back two centuries.

The **Springhill Miners' Museum ★★** (*$4.50; mid-May to early Oct, 9am to 5pm; on Rte. 2, take Black River Rd.; ☎597-3449*) offers an excellent opportunity to discover what life was like for Springhill's miners. A visit here starts out with a stop at the museum, which explains the evolution of coal mining and tells the often dramatic history of Springhill's mining industry. Visitors are then invited to tour an old gallery.

Parrsboro

At the edge of the Minas Basin, marking the farthest end of the Bay of Fundy, Parrsboro is a small community graced with several pretty buildings dating back to the 19th century.

The region's tide-sculpted shoreline is a treasure-trove for geologists. It is therefore no surprise that Parrsboro was chosen as the location for the **Fundy Geological Museum ★** (*$3; early Jun to mid-Oct, every day 9:30am to 5:30pm; Two Island Rd., near the centre of Parrsboro; ☎254-3814*), a provincial museum devoted to the geological history of Nova Scotia and other regions. Various types of fossils, rocks and stones are on display. The exhibit is lively and interesting, created with the lay person in mind. There is also a fun video, designed to teach children about geography.

Windsor

The site now occupied by Windsor, at the confluence of the Avon and Sainte-Croix Rivers, was frequented by Micmacs for many years before being colonized. They referred to it as Pisiquid, meaning "meeting place." Acadians began settling here in 1685 and succeeded in cultivating the land by creating a network of dykes. Although this part of Acadia was ceded to Great Britain under the terms of the Treaty of Utrecht in 1713, the British presence was not felt in the area until Charles Lawrence erected Fort Edward here in 1750. By building the fort, Lawrence was attempting to strengthen Britain's authority over the territory and protect the British from the Acadians. In 1755, about 1,000 of the region's Acadians were rounded up here before being deported. During the 19th century, Windsor was an important centre for shipbuilding and the exporta-

tion of wood and gypsum. Despite major fires in 1897 and 1924, the town has managed to preserve some lovely residences. It is the starting point of the Evangeline Route.

The **Fort Edward National Historic Site ★** (*free admission; early Jun to early Sep, 10am to 6pm; in the centre of Windsor; ☎542-3631*) consists only of a blockhouse, the oldest fortification of its kind in Canada. This structure is all that remains of Fort Edward, erected in 1750. An interpretive centre provides information on the history of the fort. The site also offers a gorgeous view of the Avon River.

Erected in 1835, **Haliburton House ★** (*free admission; early Jun to mid-Oct, Mon to Sat 9:30am to 5:30pm; Sun 1pm to 5:30pm; 414 Clifton Ave.; ☎798-2915*), also known as **Clifton House**, was the residence of Thomas Chandler Haliburton (1796-1865), judge, politician, businessman, humorist and successful author. This plain-looking wooden house is adorned with magnificent Victorian furniture. It stands on a large, attractively landscaped 10ha property. Haliburton made a name for himself in Canada and elsewhere by writing novels featuring the character Sam Slick, an American merchant who comes to Nova Scotia to sell clocks. Through this colourful character, Haliburton offered a harsh but humorous critique of his fellow Nova Scotians' lack of enterprise. A number of the expressions Haliburton created for his character, such as "Truth is stranger than fiction," are commonly used today in both French and English.

Shand House *(free admission; early Jun to mid-Oct, Mon to Sat 9:30am to 5:30pm, Sun 1pm to 5:30pm; 389 Avon St.; ☎798-8213)*, a fine example of Victorian architecture, was built between 1890 and 1891. The furniture inside belonged to the family of Clifford Shand, the house's original owner.

Grand-Pré

The **Grand-Pré National Historic Site** ★ ★ *($2.50; site year-round, church mid-May to mid-Oct, 9am to 6pm; Rte. 1 or Rte. 101, Exit 10; ☎542-3631)* commemorates the tragic deportation of the Acadians. Here, visitors will find Église Saint-Charles, a replica of the Acadian church that occupied this site before the Deportation, which houses a museum. The walls are hung with six large, extremely moving paintings by Robert Picard, depicting life in colonial Acadia and the Deportation. The stained-glass windows, designed by Halifax artist T.E. Smith-Lamothe, show the Acadians being deported at Grand-Pré. Visitors will also find a bust of American author Henry Wadsworth Longfellow and a statue of Evangeline. In 1847, Longfellow wrote a long poem entitled *Evangeline: A Tale of Acadie*, which told the story of two lovers separated by the Deportation.

The site also includes a smithy and a placard explaining the principal behind the dykes and aboiteaux (sluice gates) developed by the Acadians before they were expelled from the region.

Wolfville

Wolfville is a charming little university town. Its lovely streets are lined with stately elms concealing sumptuous Victorian residences. The city has about 3,500 permanent residents, while the university, **Acadia University**, founded in 1838, welcomes about 4,000 students a year. With its Victorian atmosphere, excellent cafés and restaurants and magnificent inns, this beautiful town is a perfect place to stay during a tour of the region. Wolfville was founded in 1760, several years after the deportation of the Acadians, by Planters from New England who were attracted by the excellent farmland available here. The community was known as Upper Horton and then Mud Creek before being christened Wolfville in honour of local judge Eilsha DeWolf in 1830.

Grand Pré

Twice a day, from the shores of the small, natural harbour, visitors can observe the effects of the high tides in the Bay of Fundy. Aboiteaux constructed by the Acadians in the 17th century can be seen nearby.

While touring the pretty university campus, take the time to stop in at the **Acadia University Art Gallery** *(free admission; early Jun to Aug, every day noon to 5pm; Sep to May, Mon to Fri 11am to 5pm, Sat and Sun 1pm to 4pm; Beveridge Art Centre, at the corner of Main St. and Highland Ave.; ☎585-1373)*, which often presents interesting exhibitions of contemporary art, as well as works from other periods.

The **Randall House Historical Museum** *(free admission; mid-Jun to mid-Sep, 10am to 5pm, Sun 2pm to 5pm; 171 Main St.; ☎542-9775)* displays objects, furniture, paintings and photographs from the region dating from 1760 to the present day.

The Route to Cape Split

After passing through some of the region's magnificent rolling landscape and picturesque little villages, take a few moments to stop at the **Lookoff** ★ *(Rte. 358)*, which offers an extraordinary view of Minas Basin and the Annapolis valley. Then go to the end of Route 358, where a trail (13km return) leads to the rocky points of **Cape Split** ★ ★.

Port-Royal

In 1604, one year after the king of France granted him a monopoly on the fur trade in Acadia, Pierre du Gua, Sieur de Monts, accompanied by Samuel de Champlain and 80 men, launched the first European attempt to colonize North America north of Florida. In the spring of 1605, after a difficult winter on Île Sainte-Croix, De Monts and his men settled at the mouth of the waterway known today as the Annapolis River, where they founded Port-Royal. From 1605 to 1613, the settlement of Port-Royal occupied the area now known as the Port-Royal National Historic Site. After efforts to colonize this region were abandoned, the capital of Acadia was moved first to La Have (on the Atlantic coast) for several years, and then to the present site of Annapolis Royal.

The **Port-Royal National Historic Site ★★** *($2; mid-May to mid-Oct, 9am to 6pm; from Rte. 1, take the road leading to Granville Ferry;* ☎*532-2898)* is an excellent reconstruction of the small wooden fortification known as "Abitation" as it appeared in 1605. It was here that fruitful, cordial relations were established between the French and the Micmacs. This site also witnessed the first performance of the Neptune Theatre and the founding of the first social club in North America, known as "L'Ordre du Bon Temps." Today, visitors can see the various facilities that enabled the French to survive in North America. Staff in period costume take visitors back to those long-lost days. One of the guides is of Micmac origin

and can explain the relationship between the French and the Micmacs, who were always allies.

Fort Anne

Acadian visitors can ask to see a map of the region, which shows where each Acadian family resided in the mid-17th century.

The **Annapolis Tidal Project** *(Upper St. George St.; Rte. 1,* ☎*532-7018)* is an experimental project where visitors can discover how the powerful tides in the Bay of Fundy can be used to produce electricity. There is a tourist information office here as well.

Annapolis Royal

It was here that Port-Royal, the capital of Acadia, was established in 1635. Because of its advantageous location, the settlement was able to control maritime traffic. In 1710, the British took over the site and renamed the town Annapolis Royal in honour of Queen Anne. Until Halifax was founded in 1749, Annapolis Royal was the capital of the British colony of Nova Scotia. Today, Annapolis Royal is a peaceful village with a rich architectural heritage, graced with residences dating back to the early

18th century. Wandering along its streets is a real pleasure. It is also possible to stay in some of the lovely houses here.

At the **Fort Anne National Historic Site ★★** *($2.75; mid-May to mid-Oct, 9am to 6pm, until 5pm the rest of the year; St.George St.;* ☎*532-2397)*, visitors will find an old fort, in the heart of which lie the former officers' quarters, now converted into a historical museum. The exhibition provides a detailed description of all the different stages in the history of the fort, which was French before being taken over by the British. Visitors can enjoy a pleasant stroll around the verdant grounds, which offer lovely views of the surrounding area.

While in the area, make sure to take a walk in the **Annapolis Royal Historic Gardens ★★** *($5; late May to mid-Oct, 8am until dark;* ☎*532-7018)*, which have been carefully laid out according to British and Acadian horticultural traditions.

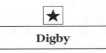

Digby

A charming town with a picturesque fishing port, Digby lies alongside Annapolis Basin and the Digby Strait, which opens onto the Bay of Fundy. It is known for its scallop-fishing fleet, the world's largest. Its port is therefore a very lively place, where visitors will be tempted to linger, fascinated by the comings and goings of the boats. From Digby, visitors can also head over to Saint John, New Brunswick aboard the ferryboat *MV Princess of Acadia*, which sets out from the port.

Long Island and Brier Island

Veritable havens of peace, Long Island and Brier Island attract thousands of visitors each year because the waters off their shores are frequented by sea mammals, especially whales who come to the Bay of Fundy to feed during summertime. Whale-watching cruises set out from Westport (Brier Island) and Tiverton (Long Island) every day during summer. Many walking trails on Brier Island allow for pleasant strolls along the island's rocky shore and offer very lovely views of the bay.

Pointe-de-l'Église (Church Point)

Farther along the coast, the road passes through another little Acadian village, Pointe-de-l'Église (Church Point), which is home to the splendid **Église Sainte-Marie** ★. Built between 1903 and 1905, it is the largest and tallest wooden church in North America. The interior has a very harmonious appea-

rance. Right next door stands **Université Sainte-Anne**, Nova Scotia's only French-language university, which plays an important cultural role in the province's Acadian community. The university houses a museum containing objects related to the history of the local Acadians. A visit to Pointe-de-l'Église and its surroundings would not be complete without taking the time to eat a *pâté de râpure*, a local dish available at the university snack-bar, among other places. The Acadian flag is flown in front of many residences along the road to Yarmouth. In Meteghan, travellers can stop a spell at **La Vieille Maison** *(free; mid-Jun to early Sep, every day 9am to 7pm; Meteghan, ☎645-2389)*, a 19th-century house in which the lifestyle of Acadians of the period is exhibited.

Yarmouth

Yarmouth was founded in 1761 by colonists from Massachusetts. Life here has always revolved around the town's bustling seaport, which is the largest in western Nova Scotia. Now a major port of entry for visitors from the United States, Yarmouth has a large selection of hotels and restaurants, as well as an excellent **tourist information office** *(288 Main St.)*.

Two ferries link Yarmouth to the state of Maine: the *Bluenose* *(☎800-341-7981)*, which shuttles between Yarmouth and Bar Harbor all year round, and the *MS Scotia Prince* *(☎800-341-7540)*, which offers service between Yarmouth and Portland from the beginning of May to the end of October.

A good way to learn about Maritime history and the town's heritage is to view the extraordinarily rich collection on display at the **Yarmouth Country Museum** ★ *($2.50, 22 Collins St., ☎742-5539)*, a small regional museum set up inside a former Presbyterian church. This vast jumble of objects includes miniature replicas of ships, furniture, old paintings and dishes. The museum's most important piece, however, is an octagonal lamp formerly used in the Cape Fourchu lighthouse.

Equally remarkable is the **Firefighters Museum** ★ *($2; Jun, Sep and mid-Oct, Mon to Sat 9am to 5pm; Jul and Aug, Mon to Sat 9am to 9pm, Sun 10am to 5pm; mid-Oct to Jun, Mon to Fri 9am to 4pm, Sat 1pm to 4pm; 451 Main St.; ☎742-5525)*, which displays two full floors of fire engines. The oldest vehicle, which the firefighters had to pull, dates back to the early 19th century.

Ross Thompson House

Cape Fourchu ★ *(turn left after the hospital and continue for 15km)* is undeniably less spectacular than Peggy's Cove, but much more peaceful. Its lighthouse, erected in 1839, stands on a rocky promontory. Visitors who arrive at the right time will be able to see Yarmouth's impressive fishing fleet pass by just off shore.

Shelburne

Shelburne was founded in 1783, the final year of the American Revolution, when about 30 ships carrying thousands of Loyalists arrived in Nova Scotia. By the following year, the town already had over 10,000 inhabitants, making it one of the most densely populated communities in North America. Today, Shelburne is a peaceful village. **Dock Street ★**, which runs alongside the natural harbour, is flanked by lovely old buildings that form a harmonious architectural ensemble.

This historic section features several points of interest, including the **Ross Thomson House ★** *($2; early Jun to mid-Oct, every day 9:30am to 5:30pm; 9 Charlotte Lane; ☎875-3141)*, whose general store dates back to the late 19th century. It is furnished in a manner typical of that type of business at the time.

In the same neighbourhood, visitors can stop in at the **Dory Shop ★** *($2; mid-Jun to Sep, every day 9:30am to 5:30pm; Dock St.; ☎875-3219)*, a workshop where fishing vessels were built in the last century.

Also noteworthy is the **Shelburne County Museum** *($2; mid-May to mid-Oct, every day 9:30am to 5:30pm; Dock St.; ☎875-3219)*, whose collection deals with the arrival of the Loyalists and the history of shipbuilding in this area, among other subjects.

Lunenburg

Lunenburg is definitely one of the most picturesque fishing ports in the Maritimes. Founded in 1753, it was the second British settlement in Nova Scotia, Halifax being the first. Its original population consisted mainly of "foreign Protestants" from Germany, Montbelliard and Switzerland. German was commonly spoken in Lunenburg up until the end of the 19th century, and various culinary traditions have survived to the present day. The village occupies a magnificent site on the steep shores of a peninsula with a natural harbour. A number of the colourful houses and buildings here date back to the late 18th and early 19th centuries. In fact, because of the architecture, parts of Lunenburg are somewhat reminiscent of the Old World. Lunenburg was recently named a Unesco World Heritage Site, because of its architecture. A very busy fishing port, Lunenburg also has a long tradition of shipbuilding. The celebrated *Bluenose*, a remarkable schooner never defeated in 18 years of racing, was built here in 1921. Lunenburg is an extremely pleasant place to visit in the summertime. Its streets are lined with shops selling quality products. The art galleries are

particularly interesting. The atmosphere here is also animated by all sorts of activities, including the **Nova Scotia Fisheries Exhibition and Fisherman Reunion**, a celebration of the world of fishing, which has been held each year at the end of August since 1916.

The **Fisheries Museum of the Atlantic ★★** *($7; mid-May to mid-Oct, every day 9:30am to 5:30pm, mid-Oct to mid-May, Mon to Fri 8:30am to 4:30pm; on the waterfront; ☎634-4794)*, set up inside an old fish-processing plant, commemorates the heritage of the fishers of the Atlantic provinces. Visitors will find an exhaustive, three-floor introduction to the world of fishing, including an aquarium, an exhibit on the 400-year history of fishing in the Grand Banks of Newfoundland, a workshop where an artisan can be observed building a small fishing boat, an exhibit on whaling and another on the history of the *Bluenose*, and more. Three ships are tied to the pier behind the building, including the *Theresa E. Connor*, a schooner built in Lunenburg in 1938 and used for fishing on the Banks for a quarter of a century. Expect to spend at least 3hrs for a full tour of the museum.

Make sure to take the opportunity to visit the little fishing hamlet of **Blue Rock ★**, located a short distance from Lunenburg. Peaceful and picturesque, this handful of houses lies on a rocky cape overlooking the ocean.

Mahone Bay

Mahone Bay

Mahone Bay is easily recognizable by its three churches, each more than a century old, built side by side facing the bay. Like Lunenburg, it was first settled by "Protestant foreigners" in 1754, and like a number of other communities on the Atlantic coast, its port served as a refuge for privateers. Until 1812, these individuals pillaged enemy ships and village, while paying British authorities to protect them. Later, until the end of the 19th century, Mahone Bay enjoyed a period of great prosperity due to fishing and shipbuilding. The lovely old houses lining the streets of the village bear witness to this golden era. Mahone Bay has a pretty sailing harbour and several good inns and bed & breakfasts. Visitors can also go to the **Settlers Museum** *(free admission; mid-May to early Sep, Tue to Sat 10am to 5pm, Sun 1pm to 5pm; 578 Main St.; ☎624-6263)*, which features a collection of antique furniture, dishes and other old objects from the area. The house itself dates back to 1850.

★
Chester

Chester was founded in the 1760s by New England families. It has been a popular vacation spot since the beginning of the 19th century. Many well-heeled residents of Halifax have second homes here, and visitors will find a number of quality hotels and restaurants, an 18-hole golf course, three sailing harbours, several craft shops and a theatre, the **Chester Playhouse** *(22 Pleasant St.)*. Perched atop a promontory overlooking Monroe Bay, Chester cuts a fine figure with its lovely residences and magnificent trees.

From Chester, Route 12 leads to the **Ross Farm Living Museum of Agriculture** ★ *($5; early Jun to mid-Oct, every day 9:30am to 5:30pm; New Ross; ☎689-2210)*, a 23ha farm inhabited by five successive generations of the Ross family from 1916 onwards. Guides in period dress liven up the museum, which has about 10 buildings typical of those found on large farms in the 19th century.

★★
Peggy's Cove

The picturesque appearance of the tiny coastal village of Peggy's Cove has charmed many a painter and photographer. The little port, protected from turbulent waters, is lined with warehouses standing on piles. Farther along, visitors can stroll across the blocks of granite that serve as a base for the famous lighthouse of Peggy's Cove, which houses a post office during summertime. It is best to be careful when walking here, especially when the water is rough. On the way out of Peggy's Cove, visitors can stop at the **William F. de Garthe Memorial Provincial Park** ★ to see a sculpture of 32 fishers, along with their wives and children, carved into a rock face 30m-long. William de Garthe, who spent five years creating this sculpture, was fascinated by the beauty of Peggy's Cove, where he lived from 1955 until his death in 1983, and by the lifestyle and courage of the local fishers.

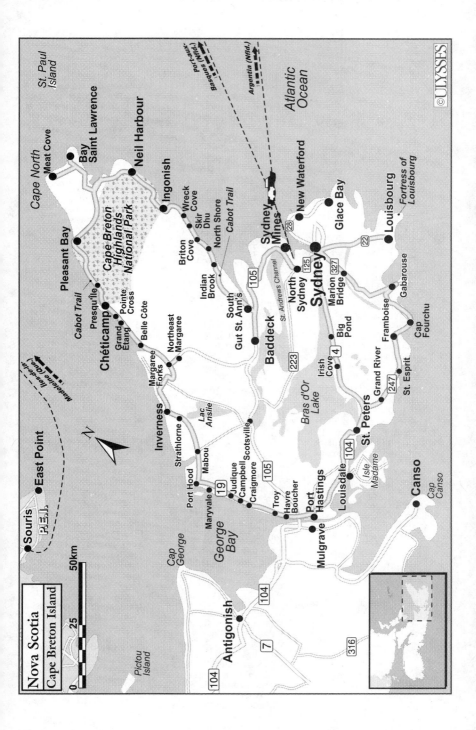

Cape Breton Island

In addition to its historic sites, Cape Breton boasts marvellous stretches of wilderness, to the delight of the countless nature lovers who visit each year. One of these is Cape Breton Highlands National Park, with its hiking trails and spectacular vantage points.

The Cabot Trail is the best way to enjoy and appreciate the beauty of Cape Breton Island. This steep winding road makes a complete circle around the island, passing through dense forests and charming villages along the way. No visit to Nova Scotia would be complete without seeing Cape Breton Island.

Port Hastings

The small town of Port Hastings is the gateway to Cape Breton Island. Although not a particularly pretty town, it is a major crossroads for travellers, with highways leading to both Baddeck and Sydney. Port Hastings does offer many practical facilities, including restaurants, service stations and most important, a tourist information office.

Isle Madame

This tranquil peninsula covers an area of 42.5km² and has some nice picnic areas. Isle Madame was settled by the Acadians and a francophone presence remains.

St. Peters

St. Peters is situated on the narrow strip of land that separates the Atlantic Ocean from Bras d'Or Lake. Colonists settled here in 1630 and built Fort Saint-Pierre. About 20 years later, Nicolas Denys took over the fort and turned it into a trading and fishing post. To learn more about this French pioneer, visit the **Nicolas Denys Museum** *($0.50; Jun to Sep, open everyday 9am to 5pm; 46 Denys St.)*.

The trading post developed gradually, but business really took off 140 years ago, when a canal was dug between Bras d'Or Lake and the ocean to provide a passage for boats. Each year, many ships (maximum 4.88 tons) can be seen passing through the canal from the park on either side. An outdoor display shows how the locks work.

★
Bras d'Or Lake

Bras d'Or Lake is an inland sea with 960km of shoreline. It thus occupies a good part of the island, dividing it into two areas, the Cape Breton Lowlands and Highlands. This vast expanse of water attracts many animal species, including the magnificent bald eagle that can be seen on occasion. For those who like to fish, trout and salmon abound in the lake and its many channels (St. Andrews Channel, St. Patrick Channel).

Aboriginal peoples have long been attracted to the shores of this lake with its abundance of fish. The Micmacs established themselves permanently here. Their presence remains constant to this day on four reserves – the Whycocomagh, Eskasoni, Wagmatcook and Chapel Island. Besides the reserves, there are several villages around the lake. The **Bras d'Or Scenic Drive** ★ *(follow the signs marked with a bald eagle)* goes all the way around the lake.

From St. Peters to Sydney

The road to Sydney passes through small towns along the shores of Bras d'Or Lake. It also goes through some Aboriginal reserves.

Another option: from St. Peters, take Rte. 247 along the ocean. At Marion Bridge take Rte. 327 to Sydney.

This road winds along the coast and passes through several charming fishing villages, including l'Archevêque. Unfortunately, the road is in poor condition.

Sydney

With a population of 25,000, Sydney is the largest town in the area. J.F.W. DesBarres, a Loyalist from the United States, founded the town in 1785. A few years later, Scottish immigrants settled here. Sydney grew quickly at the beginning of the 20th century, when coal-mining industries were established here. Coal-mining is still Sydney's primary industry. The town has all the services necessary to accommodate visitors and is a good place to stop for a rest before going on to Louisbourg. Otherwise, Sydney offers few attractions.

Cossit House *(free admission; Jun to mid-Oct, 9:30am to 5:30pm; 75 Charlotte St., ☎539-7973)* is the oldest house in town. Restored and decorated with period furniture, it looks just as it did long ago. Guides dressed in period costume lead tours through the house and are available to answer any questions.

Nearby, also on Charlotte Street, is the **Jost House** *(free admission; Jul and Aug, Mon to Sat 9:30am to 5:30pm; Sep and Oct, Mon to Sat 10am to 4pm ; 54 Charlotte St., ☎539-0366)*, which was the home of a rich merchant.

To find out more about Sydney's history, visit **St. Patrick's Church Museum** *(87 Esplanade)*. Built in 1828, this Catholic church is the oldest in Cape Breton. It features an exhibit on the town's past.

Louisbourg

Visitors are drawn to Louisbourg because of the nearby Fortress of Louisbourg, the area's main attraction. Many of the local businesses, including hotels, motels and restaurants, are geared towards tourists. It takes a full day to see the fortress, while the town itself offers few attractions.

The **Fortress of Louisbourg** ★ ★ ★ *($11, children $5.50; Jun and Sep 9:30am to 5pm, Jul and Aug 9am to 7pm; ☎733-2280)* was strategically built at the water's edge, where enemy ships could be seen and attacks could be countered. The fortress is ideally located since it was built outside of the town itself and is removed from all the modern development. It has therefore been easier to recreate the atmosphere of the fledgling French colony back in 1744. Cars are not permitted close to the fortress, and a bus provides transportation to the site.

Louisbourg

During the 18th century, France and England fought over territory in America. The French lost Acadia, which then became Nova Scotia. It was during this turbulent period in 1719, that French authorities decided to build a fortified city on Île Royale and began construction of the Fortress of Louisbourg. As the most complex system of fortifications in New France, this undertaking presented some major challenges.

Besides being a military stronghold, Louisbourg was also a fishing port and a commercial centre. Within a short time, its population had grown to 2,000 inhabitants. Everything was designed to enable colonists and soldiers to adjust to their new environment and barracks; houses and garrisons were all erected.

Nevertheless conditions were rough, and colonists sometimes had difficulty adapting. Despite the hardships, the colony grew and local business flourished.

The French presence on Île Royale was a thorn in the side of the English colonies stationed further south. In 1744, when war was declared in Europe between France and England, the Louisbourg garrison took advantage of its position to attack the English villages in the area and thus take over an English outpost. The situation incensed the English in New England, and provoked William Shirley, governor of Massachusetts, to send his troops to attack the offending French bastion in 1745. Four thousand New England soldiers ventured an attack on the supposedly impenetrable Fortress of Louisbourg. Despite this reputation, the

French troops were underequipped and poorly organized. They had never even imagined such an attack possible, and could not defend themselves. After a six-week-long siege, the Louisbourg authorities surrendered to the British troops.

A few years later, in 1748, Louisbourg was returned to France when the two nations signed a peace treaty. Life carried on in the fortress, and within a year Louisbourg was as active as ever before. This renewed prosperity was short-lived, however, since in 1758 the fortress was conquered once and for all by British troops, thus ending the French presence in the area.

Hardly 10 years after this conquest, the fortress was left to ruin, and only much later was it rebuilt. Today, almost one quarter of the fortress has been restored and, during the summer, people dressed in period costume bring it to life again, recreating the Louisbourg of long ago. There are soldiers, a baker and a fisher with his family. The scene is most convincing, and a stroll down the streets of this old French fortress is a fascinating experience.

Glace Bay

Glace Bay lies on the Atlantic coast. The area is rich in coal which forms the base of Glace Bay's industry. The name of this town is of French origin and refers to the pieces of ice *(glace)* that can be seen drifting along the coast. This small town, which has a population of about 20,000, features two interesting attractions.

Guglielmo Marconi (1874-1937) became famous for proving that it was possible to send messages using a wireless telegraph. At the age of 22, Marconi had already developed a wireless station from which messages could be sent over a short distance. In 1902, he sent the first trans-Atlantic message from his transmitting station at Table Head. At the **Marconi National Historic Site ★** *(free admission; Jun to mid-Sep, every day 10am to 6pm; Timmerman St., ☎295-2069)* visitors can learn about Marconi's discoveries and see his work table, as well as the radio station from which the first message was sent. The Glace Bay area's mining industry dates back many years. As long ago as 1790, French soldiers from Louisbourg were already coming to Port Morien for coal. The industry really took off at the beginning of the 20th century, when mines were dug here, most importantly at New Waterford. Today, Glace Bay produces more coal than any other town in Eastern Canada.

To learn more about this industry, visit the **Miner's Museum ★★** *($3.50; Jun to early Sep, 10am to 6pm, Tue until 7pm; rest of the year, every day Mon to Fri 9am to 4pm; 42 Birkley St., ☎849-4522)*, which has exhibits showing the various tools and techniques used in coal mining. There is also a recreation of a typical mining town from the beginning of the century. Finally, the most fascinating part of the museum is a guided tour of a coal mine.

★★
Baddeck

Baddeck is a charming village, perfect for taking a stroll or enjoying a bite to eat on a terrace. Whether you decide to stay for a few days to enjoy the comfortable hotels and calm atmosphere, or simply stop for a few hours before heading off on the Cabot Trail, Baddeck offers many attractions that make it worth the detour. One fascinating sight is the summer home of the inventor Alexander Graham Bell.

The **Alexander Graham Bell National Historic Site ★★** *($4.25; every day, Jun 9am to 6pm, Jul and Aug 8:30am to 7:30pm, Sep to mid-Oct 8:30am to 6pm; town's east exit, Chebucto St., ☎295-2069)* displays many of Bell's inventions and the instruments he used in his research. Bell's life story is also told. Visitors will learn, for example that after teaching sign language for many years, he created an artificial ear that recorded sounds. This experiment led to his invention of the telephone.

★★★
The Cabot Trail

The Cabot Trail follows steep, precipitous cliffs that plunge out over the Atlantic Ocean, and passes through some picturesque little villages. Leaving Baddeck, the road follows the shore before climbing up to the plateau on the north end of the island. The many lookouts along this road offer magnificent panoramic views. It's worth taking the time to stop and appreciate the wild beauty of the landscape, where a restless sea with steep hills and a dense forest are home to a variety of animal species.

The first village after Baddeck is tiny **South Gut St. Ann's**, home to the **Gaelic College**, an institution devoted to the survival of Gaelic culture in North America. Courses are offered in Gaelic language, singing and bagpipe playing.

The road continues along the coast to **Ingonish Ferry**, where it begins to mount the vast plateau occupying the north end of the island at an elevation of 366m. The scenery grows increasingly spectacular.

Cape Breton Highlands National Park ★ ★ ★ (see p 100).

This road leads first to the charming fishing village of **Bay St. Lawrence ★**. Built at the water's edge, the village has little wooden houses and a picturesque port, where cormorants can be seen gliding above the waves. The road climbs along the **cliffs ★ ★** and winds its way to **Meat Cove**, a perfect place to stop for a picnic and enjoy the **superb view ★** over the ocean waves.

The road continues west. From Cape North to **Pleasant Bay**, visitors can gaze at the canyon formed by the sides of the hills. The **view ★ ★** is stunning. After being on the move for a while, Peasant Bay truly is a welcome and *pleasant* spot to rest.

The plateau ends near **Petit Étang**. The road heads back down and follows the Gulf of St. Lawrence to the Acadian region of Cape Breton. The landscape is surprising, as forests and steep cliffs give way to a barren plateau

studded with Acadian villages. Among these is **Chéticamp**, a quiet village with simple little houses and a fishing port. It is a departure point for seal and whale-watching excursions. More villages with French names follow, including **Grand Étang**, **Saint-Joseph du Moine**, **Cap-Lemoine** and **Belle Côte**.

The west part of the Cabot Trail ends at Margaree Harbour. You can continue your journey by cutting across the plateau back to Baddeck. The highlight along this route is the **Margaree Salmon Museum** *($0.50, mid-Jun to mid-Aug, 9am to 5pm;* ☎248-2848) in **Northeast Margaree**. The museum displays the various implements used for salmon fishing.

Ceilidh Trail

The road along the west coast of the island leads to the Ceilidh Trail. This region was settled by Scots, and vestiges of Gaelic culture still remain. More than anywhere else on Cape Breton Island, the villages along the Ceilidh Trail offer an excellent opportunity to discover Scottish heritage. Gaelic music is heard throughout this region, and a few musicians here are now famous on the national and international music scenes. Furthermore, the warm waters here wash up against a few of the island's beautiful beaches, especially near **Mabou ★**. There are a number of modest little villages along the Gulf of St. Lawrence. In this region, Mabou is definitely the nicest place to stay. A few kilometres past Mabou is the **Glenora Distillery**, which produces a single malt whisky. There is also an inn and a pub here.

Pictou

Pictou holds symbolic importance in Nova Scotia's history. This is where the *Hector*, a ship carrying the first Scottish settlers to Nova Scotia, dropped anchor. Many Scots later followed, seduced by a climate and geography reminiscent of home. They colonized other parts of the coast and Cape Breton Island. Pictou's lively downtown streets are lined with handsome buildings dating back to those early years of settlement.

A ferry service runs between Caribou, just beside Pictou, to Wood Islands, on Prince Edward Island. Close by, **Caribou Provincial Park** has a beautiful beach that is perfect for swimming.

Hector Heritage Quay ★ ★ *($3.50; mid-May to mid-Oct, every day 10am to 8pm; downtown, at the port,* ☎485-6057) is an interpretive centre devoted to the history of the *Hector*, the schooner that carried the first Scottish settlers to Pictou in 1773. The exhibition is very thorough. Behind the building, visitors can watch artisans build an exact replica of the *Hector*.

The **McCulloch House ★** *($1; early Jun to mid-Oct, Mon to Sat 9:30am to 5:30pm, Sun 1pm to 5:30pm; Old Haliburton Rd.,* ☎485-4563) is a modest house built in 1806 for Reverend Thomas McCulloch, one of the most influential people in the Pictou area at the time. The house is furnished with original pieces.

Housed in the old railway station, the **Northumberland**

Fisheries Museum ★ *($3; late Jun to early Sep, every day 9:30am to 5:30pm; Front St.)* contains a collection of items related to the history of fishing in this region, and features an authentic fishing hut.

Parks

Cape Breton Highlands National Park ★★★ begins here. The park, created in 1936, protects 950km² of wilderness inhabited by moose and bald eagles. A wide range of activities is offered throughout the oldest park in Eastern Canada, with just about everything an outdoor-enthusiast could desire: magnificent views, a forest inhabited by fascinating animal life, beaches, camp-sites, 27 hiking trails and even a golf course.

Beaches

Sandy beaches that are ideal for swimming can be found in various parts of Nova Scotia. Two regions have pleasant beaches: the north coast of the province along the Northumberland Strait, where the shore is washed by delightfully warm waters; and the Atlantic coastline. A number of provincial parks have been established in order to protect these areas, and we have selected some of those with the loveliest beaches.

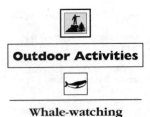

Outdoor Activities

Whale-watching

Every year, whales come to the Gulf of St. Lawrence and the waters south of the island, in the Atlantic Ocean. During this period, visitors can take part in one of the 3hr whale-watching expeditions organized by various local companies.

Brier Island Whale & Seabird Cruises
$37
Westport
☎*839-2995*
two to five departures daily, May to mid-Oct

Pirate's Cove
$35
Tiverton
☎*839-2242*
three departures per day, Jun to Oct

The southwest coast has a variety of marine animal life. Seals, humpback whales and Atlantic puffins are just a few of the numerous species that you can see by taking one of the boat trips departing from different towns in the region.

Lunenburg Whale Watching Tour
P.O. Box 475
Lunenburg, B0J 2C0
☎*527-7175*
Jun to Oct

Peggy's Cove Water Tours

Peggy's Cove, B0J 2N0
☎823-1060
Jun to mid-Oct

Cape Breton

Atlantic Whale Watch
Ingonish Beach
☎285-2320
departures at 10am, 1:30pm and 4:30pm

Island Whale Watch and Nature Tours
Bay St. Lawrence
☎*383-2379*
departures at 10:15am, 1:30pm and 4:30pm

Whale and Seal Cruise
Pleasant Bay
☎*224-1316*
departures at 9am, 1pm and 6pm

Seaside Whale & Nature Cruises
Laurie's Motor Inn, Chéticamp
☎*224-3376 or 800-95-WHALE*
three departures daily

Whale Cruisers
$25
Cheticamp
☎*224-3376*
Jul and Aug
departures at 9am, 1pm and 6pm

Deep-sea Fishing

Various outfits organize deep-sea fishing expeditions. Participants are provided with all necessary equipment and instruction.

Whale Island
$25
Ingonish
☎*285-2338 or 800-565-3808*
≈*285-2338*

Deep-Sea Fishing Chéticamp
$25
P.O. Box 221, Chéticamp, B0E 1H0
☎*224-3606*

Accommodations

Halifax

Halifax Heritage House Hostel
$18 for members
$22 for non-members
1253 Barrington St., B3J 1Y3
☎422-3863
A few hundred metres from the train station and about 15min by foot from the city's main attractions, the Halifax Heritage House Hostel is part of the International Youth Hostel Federation. A pretty, historic building, it can accommodate about 50 people and is equipped with a kitchenette.

Waverley Inn
$79 bkfst incl.
tv, ℜ
1266 Barrington St., B3J 1Y5
☎423-9346
≈425-0167
The Waverley Inn boasts a rich tradition of hospitality dating back more than a century. This sumptuous house, built in 1865-66, was the personal residence of wealthy Halifax merchant Edward W. Chipman until 1870, when a reversal of fortune plunged him into bankruptcy.

A few years later, sisters Sarah and Jane Romans purchased the house for $14,200. In October 1876, the Waverley Inn threw open its doors and was considered the most prestigious hotel in the city for several decades to follow. It has welcomed many famous individuals, including English author Oscar Wilde, who stayed here in 1882.

Despite the passing of time, the Waverley Inn has managed to preserve most of its original grandeur. Nevertheless, its rooms, decorated in a rather heavy style, do not conform to modern standards of luxury amd comfort. However, this inn is sure to interest visitors seeking a truly authentic Victorian atmosphere. The Waverley Inn is located near the train station, about a 15min walk from the city's major attractions.

Halliburton House Inn
$120 bkfst incl.
tv, ℜ
5184 Morris St., B3J 1B3
☎420-0658
≈423-2324
The Halliburton House Inn lies tucked away on a quiet residential street near the train station, just a short distance from Halifax's main attractions. A pleasant, elegant place, it offers an interesting alternative to the large downtown hotels. In terms of comfort, Halliburton House Inn has all the angles covered.

The pleasant rooms are well-decorated and adorned with period furniture, giving them a lot of character. There are also several lovely common rooms, including a small living room to the left of the entrance, a library and an elegant dining room where guests can enjoy excellent cuisine.

The inn's three buildings look out on a peaceful, pretty garden full of flowers, where guests can sit at a table beneath a parasol. Halliburton House Inn, erected in 1809, was originally the home of Sir Brenton Halliburton, chief justice of the Supreme Court of Nova Scotia.

Citadel Inn Halifax
$125
tv, ℜ, ≈, ⊘
1960 Brunswick St., B3J 2G7
☎422-1391 or 800-565-7162
≈429-6672
Comfortable but somewhat lacking in charm, the Citadel Inn Halifax is attractively located just a stone's throw away from the Citadel. Guests have access to an indoor pool and a gym, as well as to a dining room and a bar. Furthermore, parking is free, which is a real bonus in Halifax.

Chateau Halifax
$135
tv, ℜ, ⌂, ⊛, ≈
1990 Barrington St., B3J 1P2
☎425-6700 or 800-268-1133
≈425-6214
The Chateau Halifax offers superior accommodation in spacious, sober and very comfortably furnished rooms. The friendly, pleasant hotel bar, Sam Slick's Lounge, is a perfect spot to enjoy a drink with friends or hold an informal meeting.

The Chateau features an indoor pool and numerous sports facilities. It provides access to a shopping centre with stores and restaurants, and is just minutes away from the city's main sights and the World Trade and Convention Centre.

Sheraton Halifax
$139
tv, ℜ, ⌂, ≈
1919 Upper Water St., B3J 3J5
☎421-1700 or 800-325-3535
≈422-5805
Halifax is home to a good number of luxury hotels. None of these, however, boasts a more spectacular or enchanting site than the Sheraton Halifax, located right on the pier, next to Historic Properties. Furthermore, particular care was taken to ensure that

the building would blend harmoniously with its surroundings, which make up the oldest part of the city.

The rooms are spacious, well-decorated and inviting. The hotel has two restaurants as well as conference rooms, an indoor pool and several other athletic facilities. In addition to all this, the Sheraton houses the only casino in Halifax, which is very busy evenings and weekends.

Wolfville

Blomidon Inn
$89
℞, tv
127 Main St., B0P 1X0
☎*542-2291 or 800-565-2291*
⇌*542-7461*
At the elegant Blomidon Inn, visitors can stay in a sumptuous manor built in 1877. At the time, costly materials were used to embellish the residence, which still features marble fireplaces and a superb, carved wooden staircase. This place has all the ingredients of a top-notch establishment: a splendid dining room where guests can enjoy refined cuisine, impeccable, friendly service and richly decorated sitting rooms. This majestic building stands in the centre of a large property bordered by stately elms. The Blomindon Inn is a veritable symbol of Nova Scotian hospitality. All of the rooms are adorned with antique furniture and include private baths.

Tattingstone Inn
$89
tv, ≈, △, ℞, pb
10 rooms
434 Main St., B0P 1X0
☎*542-7696 or 800-565-7696*
⇌*542-4427*
The superb Tatting-stone Inn offers tastefully deco-

rated rooms, some containing 18th-century furniture. The accent here is on comfort and elegance. Guests can stay in one of two buildings; the main residence has the most luxurious rooms.

Annapolis Royal

Garrison House Inn
$90
℞, pb/sb
open Apr to Dec
350 George St., B0S 1A0
☎*532-5730*
⇌*532-5501*
Several bed & breakfasts and excellent inns offer visitors the pleasure of staying in the heart of Annapolis Royal, one of the oldest towns in North America. One of these is the Garrison House Inn, a magnificent hotel located in the heart of Annapolis Royal, facing Fort Anne. Its antique-filled rooms are simply gorgeous. The top-floor room, with bay window and many skylights and a real view is defenetely the most stunning ; reservations are a good idea, for this room in particular. Very inviting common areas, including a delightful library and a restaurant on the ground floor, contribute to the pleasure of a stay here.

Digby

Pines Resort Hotel
$140
≈, ☺, ℞, K, tv
Shore Rd., B0V 1A0
☎*245-2511 or 800-667-4637*
⇌*245-6133*
The impressive Pines Resort Hotel stands on a hill overlooking the bay in a lovely natural setting. Every part of this hotel was conceived to ensure an excellent stay, from the superb interior design and

pretty, comfortable rooms to the excellent restaurant and inviting bar. Guests also have access to a wide range of athletic facilities, including tennis courts, a swimming pool and a gym; there is also a golf course nearby.

Yarmouth

Rodd Colony Harbour Inn
$100
tv, ℞
6 Forest St., B5A 3K7
☎*742-9194 or 800-565-7633*
⇌*742-6291*
The Rodd Colony Harbour Inn lies directly opposite the boarding point for the ferry to Maine. Since it is located on a hillside, there is a lovely view from the back. The rooms are spacious and well designed. The bar is a pleasant place for a drink.

Shelburne

Cooper's Inn
$75
℞
875 Dock St., B0T 1W0
☎/⇌*875-4656*
☎*800-688-2011*
Located in the very heart of Shelburne's historic section looking out on the harbour, lovely Cooper's Inn is one of the best hotels in the province. It occupies a magnificently renovated old house that was built for a wealthy Loyalist merchant in 1785. The decor of each room and the choice of furniture for the house were carried out with such minute attention to detail that a simple visit to Cooper's Inn is a pleasure in itself. All of the rooms are comfortable and equipped with private bathrooms. A splendid, very bright suite has been laid out on the top floor; it is well worth

the $135 rate. In addition, one of the rooms is easily accessible to travellers with disabilities. Each room is named for one of the house's former owners. To top it all off, the inn's dining room serves up cuisine that pleases the most distinguishing palates.

White Point

White Point Beach Resort
$110
tv, ℜ, ≈
Rte. 3, Exit 20A or 21 off of Hwy. 103, B0T 1G0
☎354-2711 or 800-565-5068
↝354-7278
The White Point Beach Resort offers luxurious, modern accommodation in small cottages or in a large building facing directly onto a beach that stretches 1.5km. The complex is attractive and has been carefully and tastefully laid out in order to make the most of its beautiful surroundings. In addition to swimming at the beach or in the pool, visitors can play golf or tennis or go fishing. The pleasant bar offers a magnificent view of the ocean.

Lunenburg

Bluenose Lodge
$60 bkfst incl.
ℜ, tv
corner Falkland Ave. and Dufferin St., B0J 2C0
☎/↝634-8851 ☎800-565-8851
The Bluenose Lodge is a splendid Victorian house located a few minutes' walk from the centre of Lunenburg. Furnished with antiques, the rooms are full of character, and all include a private shower.

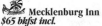 ### Marinee King Inn
$60 bkfst incl.
open mid-Feb to Dec
15 King St., B0J 2C0
☎800-565-8509
A visit to Lunenburg offers an opportunity to discover the old fashioned charm of the town's numerous 19th-century residences, many of which have been converted into pleasant inns. One good, relatively inexpensive option is the Marinee King Inn, a lovely Victorian house built around 1825. The decor remains quite typical of that era, when tastes leaned towards heavily furnished rooms. In the evening, guests can enjoy a delicious meal in the dining room.

Brigantine Inn
$65 bkfst incl.
ℜ, tv
82 Montague St., B0J 2C0
☎634-3300 or 800-360-1181
The Brigantine Inn is extremely well located facing the port. Most of the spotless, attractively decorated rooms feature large windows and balconies with splendid views.

Boscawen Inn
$90 bkfst incl.
ℜ
open mid-Apr to Dec
150 Cumberland, B0J 2C0
☎634-3325 or 800-354-5009
A superb Victorian house dating from 1888, Boscawen Inn lies in the heart of Lunenburg, on a hillside overlooking the port. The location is spectacular, and the pleasant terrace offers an unimpeded view of the town's historic section. Guests can also relax in one of three sitting rooms, which, like all the other rooms in the house, are adorned with period furniture.

Mahone Bay

Sou'Wester Inn
$75
788 Main St., B0J 2E0
☎624-9296
The village of Mahone Bay is sure to please visitors with a taste for large 19th-century houses. Some of these residences are now high-quality B&Bs. One of the best is the Sou'Wester Inn, a magnificent Victorian residence originally owned by a shipbuilder. The entire house is furnished in the style of the period. Guests are invited to relax on the terrace overlooking the bay.

Chester

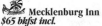 ### Mecklenburg Inn
$65 bkfst incl.
open late May to late Oct
78 Queen St., B0J 1J0
☎275-4638
A charming residence built at the end of the 19th century, the Mecklenburg Inn has adorable rooms, a terrace and a charming, relaxing sitting room. The dining room is open in the evening.

Cape Breton Island

Sydney

 ### Rockinghorse Inn
$70
tv
259 Kings Rd., B1S 1A7
☎539-2696 or 800-664-1010
↝539-2696
For charming accommodation in a peaceful environment that is also close to the downtown area, head to the Rockinghorse Inn. This renovated Victorian residence has eight charming rooms, each with its own private bath. Staying here makes it easy to for-

get that Sydney is an industrial town.

Delta Sydney
$109
≈, ℜ, tv, ○, ⊘, ⊛
300 Esplanade, B1P 1A7
☎562-7500
☎800-268-1133 from Canada
☎800-887-1133 from the U.S.
⇌562-3023
Downtown Sydney consists mainly of a few streets alongside the river, and it is here that most of the town's hotels are located. One of these is the Delta Sydney, whose facade looks out on the Sydney River. The rooms are a bit lacking in charm, but thoroughly functional. As a bonus, the hotel features a lovely swimming pool with a slide, a sure hit with the children.

Cambridge Suites Hotel
$109 bkfst incl.
tv, ≈, K, ℜ, ○, ⊘
380 Esplanade, B1P 1B1
☎562-6500 or 800-565-9466
⇌564-6011
Right next-door stands the Cambridge Suites Hotel, which is about as comfortable as the Delta, although more care has been taken with the decor. The rooms are actually small apartments equipped with kitchenettes. The hotel is also home to an excellent restaurant called Goodies.

Louisbourg

Point of View Suites
$115
ℜ, K, tv
5 Lower Commercial St., B0A 1M0
☎733-2080 or 888-374-8439
A lovely new establishment was recently built near the Louisbourg Fortress.. It has attractively designed, modern rooms and a warm ambience. Each room has a kitchenette and a balcony. There is also a restaurant that offers excellent dishes, such as snow crab (in

season). As its name suggests, this facility offers a magnificent view of the sea.

Baddeck

Auberge Gisèle
$85
ℜ, ⊛, ≈, ○
open early May to late Oct
Rte. 205 exit 8, 387 shore Rd.,
B0E 1B0
☎295-2849 or 800-304-0466
⇌295-2033
Auberge Gisèle is a good place to keep in mind. Located on the shore of Bras d'Or Lake, its rooms offer lovely views. Upon arriving, visitors will be enchanted by the pine-bordered lane leading up to this lovely residence, whose rooms are all attractively decorated. There are a few more rooms in a nearby annex.

Inverary Inn
$95
tv, ℜ
Hwy. 105 exit 8, B0E 1B0
☎295-3500 or 800-565-5660
⇌295-3527
At the cozy Inverary Inn, guests can either stay in the main building or in charming little wooden cottages. The decor and the vast grounds give this place a rustic feel well-suited to the Nova Scotian countryside.

Ingonish Beach

 **Keltic Lodge**
$298
≈, K, ℜ, tv
open Jun to Oct and Jan to Mar
Middle Head Peninsula, B0C 1L0
☎285-2880 or 800-565-0444
⇌285-2859
The Keltic Lodge boasts a spectacular location alongside a cliff overlooking the sea. Slightly removed from the access roads, in the heart of a veritable oasis of peace, the Keltic Lodge

offers top-notch accommodation just a short distance from the Cabot Trail. The buildings are handsome and the rooms, some of which are in cottages, are both charming and comfortable. The dining room features a gourmet menu.

Dingwall

Markland Coastal Resort
$90
K, ℜ, tv
3km from Dingwall, B0C 1G0
☎383-2246 or 800-872-6084
⇌383-2092
An excellent place to relax, admire the sea, walk along the beach or depart from to explore the Cabot Trail, the Markland Coastal Resort offers comfortable accommodation in wooden cottages with a cozy, rustic-looking interior. Each cottage has several rooms equipped with a terrace. The large, grassy piece of land opposite the cottages leads to an untouched beach. The Markland is an ideal spot for couples or families who enjoy a peaceful, secluded setting and wide open spaces. The fine food served in the dining room hits the spot after a long day in the fresh air.

Chéticamp

Laurie's Motor Inn
$85
K, ℜ, tv
Main St., B0E 1H0
☎224-2400
⇌224-2069
There are several places to stay in the centre of the Acadian community of Chéticamp. One of these is Laurie's Motor Inn, a motel stretching alongside the Gulf of St. Lawrence. Although the decor is not very original, the rooms are clean and comfortable. If you're famished or just

want to enjoy a satisfying meal, don't hesitate to stop in at the motel's dining room, which has a very decent menu. The seafood is especially good.

Pictou

Walker Inn
$75 bkfst incl.
ℜ, *tv*
34 Coleraine St., B0K 1H0
☎ 485-1433 or 800-370-5553 for reservations

Located in the heart of Pictou, the Walker Inn is a pretty brick building dating back to 1865. This place is charming, each of its renovated rooms has a private bath. The Walker Inn is kept by a friendly French Canadian couple. Evening meals may be enjoyed in the inn's beautiful dining room, by reservation only.

Restaurants

Halifax

Trident Booksellers & Café
$
1570 Argyle St.
☎ 423-7100

What a pleasure it is to enjoy an excellent cup of coffee while poring over a book! That's the concept behind the Trident Booksellers & Café, an extremely friendly, airy place located a few steps away from Blowers Street. The menu includes a good choice of coffees, hot chocolates, teas and summer refreshments. There is also a choice of pastries. Newspapers are always available for customers, and books (often secondhand), are sold at modest prices.

La Maison
$$-$$$
1541 Birmingham St.
☎ 492-4339

Much more than a simple French restaurant, La Maison offers a whirlwind tour of the flavours of French-speaking America and Europe. There are many appetizers to choose from, including steak tartar, warm goat-cheese salad, and an excellent bouillabaisse of mussels, scallops and shrimp. Mouth-watering lamb chops, seafood papillote, duck in Grand Marnier sauce and a variety of steaks are some of the main dishes prepared at La Maison. The food is served either in the relaxing atmosphere of the dining room, which has a classic decor, or, when the weather is fair, on the peaceful terrace.

Halliburton House Inn
$$$
5184 Morris St.
☎ 420-0658

The dining room at the elegant Halliburton House Inn is a perfect place to enjoy a long, intimate dinner for two or linger over a meal among friends. Furnished in a tasteful, elegant manner, the place has a lot of style and emanates opulence. Aside from a few exceptions, like the alligator appetizer, the menu is made up of classics, including an excellent *steak au poivre* flambéd with brandy, lamb *à la Provençale*, Atlantic salmon and *coquilles Saint-Jacques*.

Five Fishermen
$$$
1740 Argyle St.
☎ 422-4421

Set up inside one of the oldest buildings in town, an old renovated school, the Five Fishermen is a great favourite with fish and seafood lovers. Lob-

ster obviously gets top billing on the menu. Other dishes include Atlantic salmon and trout, as well as a variety of steaks. It is worth noting that the kitchen closes later than most others in town, around 11pm on Sundays and at midnight during the rest of the week. The wine list, furthermore, is very extensive.

Wolfville

Coffee Merchant
$
at the corner of Main and Elm Sts.
☎ 542-4315

If you're craving a good cup of coffee, head over to the Coffee Merchant, which serves good cappuccino and espresso. This is a pleasant place, where it is tempting to linger, read a newspaper or gaze out the window at the comings and goings of the people on the street. The menu is limited to a few sandwiches and muffins.

Blomidon Inn
$$-$$$
127 Main St.
☎ 542-229

The Blomidon Inn has two dining rooms – a small, very cozy one in the library and a larger one richly decorated with mahogany chairs. The latter is embellished by a picture window that looks out onto a beautiful landscape. The menu is equally exceptional, featuring such delicious dishes as poached salmon and scallops and salmon Florentine.

Chez La Vigne
$$-$$$
117 Front St.
☎ 542-5077

Chez La Vigne, renowned for excellence for many years now, offers fine

Nova Scotia

regional cuisine made with fresh products from the valley. Every evening, an interesting and reasonably priced, table d'hôte menu is set; the wine and beer selection is also impressive. Weather permitting, it is possible to dine al fresco on an attractively landscaped back terrace.

Digby

Digby's famous scallops are of course *the* local specialty, and most of the town's restaurants are in proximity to the port. **The Red Raven Pub** (*$-$$; Water St.,* ☎245-5533), a family restaurant, dishes up simple, inexpensive fare. Just nearby, the **Fundy Restaurant** (*$-$$; Water St.,* ☎245-4950), just a shade more elegant than the Rod Raven, presents a slightly more varied menu. Scallops are the stars on both menus.

Shelburne

Cooper's Restaurant
$$$
Cooper's Inn
36 Dock St.
☎875-4656
Cooper's Restaurant offers the elegance and ambiance of a historic house built in 1785 and the flavours of refined regional cuisine. For starters there is a choice of dishes such as smoked salmon wrapped in a spinach crepe. About 10 main dishes are offered, including succulent sautéed scallops and excellent pasta topped with lobster. A selection of some 20 wines, including some excellent vintages, as well as a great variety of aperitifs and digestifs, rounds out the menu.

Lunenburg

Boscawen Inn
$$
150 Cumberland St.
☎634-3325
Lunenburg boasts a magnificent location overlooking a natural harbour. The Boscawen Inn, a Victorian house standing on a hillside, is a good place to appreciate the natural beauty of the surroundings and the harmony of the local architecture. The dining-room menu consists mainly of excellent fish and seafood dishes.

Cape Breton Island

Sydney

On Charlotte Street, there are a number of little snack bars serving hamburgers and fries.

Restaurant at the Delta Hotel
$$
300 Esplanade
☎562-7500
The Restaurant at the Delta Hotel has a very decent menu featuring a fair number of fish dishes. With its large picture windows looking out onto the water, the place also offers a lovely view. Breakfast served.

Joe's Warehouse
$$
424 Charlotte St.
☎539-6686
Don't be scared off by the Western look of Joe's Warehouse, which happens to be a local institution. Although the decor is not exactly sophisticated and the music sounds like what you'd hear in a shopping mall, the atmosphere is still very inviting. In any case, people come to Joe's for the generous portions of delicious prime rib.

Seafood is also on the menu.

Louisbourg

At the fortress, a restaurant has been set up in one of the buildings facing the water. The food is no more than decent, but at least visitors can eat lunch without leaving the site.

Baddeck

Baddeck Lobster Suppers
$$
Ross St.
☎295-3307
If you are hungry for lobster, head over to Baddeck Lobster Suppers. The main dish includes lobster and unlimited seafood chowder, mussels, salad and dessert.

McCurdy's
$$
Silver Dart Lodge, Shore Rd.
☎295-2340
The Silver Dart Lodge is pleasantly located on the shores of Bras d'Or Lake. Its restaurant, McCurdy's, which looks out onto this magnificent body of water, offers its guests an unbeatable atmosphere. In addition to the view, people come here to sample the tasty seafood dishes and savour the Scottish cuisine.

Dingwall

Markland Hotel
$$
☎383-2246
The restaurant at the Markland Hotel has a pine-panelled dining room with a decor that is stylish without being extravagant. The menu is extremely interesting, however; simply reading it over will whet your appetite. The offerings include grilled salmon with Mousseline sauce and grilled filet of pork with plums in a red-wine and onion sauce.

Chéticamp

Laurie's
$-$$
☎*224-2400*
At Laurie's, visitors might be surprised to discover that the menu lists both lobster and hamburgers. In fact, this restaurant has something for every taste and budget. Guests are offered such succulent dishes as the fisherman's platter, which includes lobster, crab and shrimp. The Acadian staff is as friendly as can be, amiably telling their guests to "enjoy *le repas.*"

Pictou

Stone House Café and Pizzeria
$-$$
11 Water St.
☎*485-6885*
Established in a lovely house in Pictou's historic district, the Stone House Café and Pizzeria is a very appealing family restaurant that serves simple, well-prepared food that will please fans of American-style pizza. In nice weather it is possible to sit on the restaurant's terrace facing the port.

Entertainment

Halifax

Bars and Danceclubs

Lower Deck Pub
Privateer's Warehouse
In the historic district, there is the Lower Deck Pub, which presents performances of traditional music from Atlantic Canada some evenings.

Theatres

Halifax's most renowned theatre company, the **Neptune Theatre** *(5216 Sackville St.,* ☎*429-7070)* is devoted to presenting classic plays.

Large-scale rock concerts are held at the **Halifax Metro Centre** *(1284 Duke St.,* ☎*451-1221).* For that matter, when artists of international renown come to the Maritimes, they usually choose to play in Halifax.

Fans of classical music can attend concerts given by the **Symphony Nova Scotia** *(1646 Barrington St.,* ☎*421-7311).*

Wolfville

Atlantic Theatre Festival 356 Main St.
☎*542-4242 or 800-337-6661*
Excellent classic plays are presented from mid-June to early September in the city's 500-seat amphitheatre. Ticket prices vary between $22 and $34 per person.

Annapolis Royal

The Fat Pheasant
200 St. George St.
☎*526-0042*
The main floor of the Fat Pheasant is delightful. This cozy room has a bookcase and beautiful woodwork – the perfect place to sip a drink. There's a friendly Irish pub in the basement, where you can have a beer and light snack (typical pub fare). The place gets hopping on weekends with a variety of live entertainment.

Chester

During July and August, the **Chester Playhouse** *(about $18; 22 Pleasant St.,* ☎*275-3933)* presents plays and concerts in the evening.

Shopping

Halifax

Without a doubt, the most pleasant place to shop is **Historic Properties** *(bordered by Duke and Lower Water Sts.),* the historic neighbourhood alongside the Halifax wharves. Shops selling crafts and clothing take up a large portion of the space in this harmonious 19th-century architectural grouping.

The **Gallery Shop** *(Art Gallery of Nova Scotia, 1741 Hollis,* ☎*424-2836)* offers an excellent selection of local crafts as well as works by painters, sculptors and other artists from Nova Scotia. Pieces by Micmac artists are also available.

The **Micmac Heritage Gallery** *(Barrington Place Shops, Granville Level,* ☎*422-9509)* is the most impressive gallery dedicated to Micmac arts and crafts in the Atlantic provinces. Articles on display include leather mittens and moccasins, woven baskets, jewelry and paintings.

The **Houston North Gallery** *(Sheraton Hotel, 1919 Upper Water St.)* presents a remarkable collection of First Nations and Inuit sculptures and paintings.

Nova Scotia

Shelburne

Charlotte Lane Café & Craft
13 Charlotte Lane
☎*875-3314*
Not only is it one of the best places to eat in town, Charlotte Lane Café also sells a variety of beautiful crafts created by Nova Scotian artists.

Lunenburg

Houston North Gallery
110 Montague St.
☎*634-8869*
Visitors interested in First Nations and Inuit art should make sure to stop in at the Houston North Gallery, which displays a remarkable assortment of sculptures and paintings.

Bluenose II Company Store
121 Bluenose Dr.
☎*634-1963*
The famous *Bluenose* is honoured at the Bluenose II Company Store. Those looking for a memento of this schooner will have an endless selection to choose from. The profits go to a good cause: keeping the *Bluenose II* in operation.

Carriage House Gallery
290 Lincoln St.
☎*634-4010*
The Carriage House Gallery exhibits and sells works by a variety of Scottish artists.

Chester

The Warp & Woof Gifts & Gallery
81 Walter St.
☎*275-4795*
The Warp & Woof Gifts & Gallery sells carvings, pottery, woolen sweaters and other beautiful crafts made by Maritime artists.

Pictou

Grohmann Knives
1168 Water St.
☎*485-4224*
Grohmann Knives is a family business founded in the 1950s. Their high-quality knives are now sold in many countries around the world.

Green Thumb Farmer's Market
exit 20
The Green Thumb Farmer's Market is a great place to buy fresh fruits and vegetables as well as numerous local products.

Prince Edward Island

Prince Edward Island
is a rare harmony of rural and maritime landscapes, the epitome of a simple, serene way of life.

Set back from the peaceful roads and tucked away behind rolling valleys of farmland lie picturesque little fishing villages, adorable white clapboard churches, and the pulsing glow of a lighthouse towering over the sea from isolated rocky outcrops. Most striking in these charming scenes is the brilliant palette of colours: the vibrant yellow and green of the fields falling over the cliffs of deep rust red into the lapis blue of the sea.

Bathed to the north by the Gulf of St. Lawrence and to the south by the Strait of Northumberland, this island is above all known for its magnificent white sand dunes and beaches, often deserted and extending between sea and land as far as the eye can see. It goes without saying that these ribbons of sand are among the most beautiful on the east coast of the continent. They offer great spots for swimming, long walks and discoveries. The beaches may be what initially attract most visitors, but they quickly discover the many

other treasures Prince Edward Island (P.E.I.) has to offer. For starters, the small capital city of Charlottetown, whose architecture and unique atmosphere give it an antique charm; from there the possibilities are virtually endless, the friendliest fresh lobster feasts you can imagine, the storybook world *Anne of Green Gables*, the kindness of the inhabitants, and the richness of the magnificent plants and wildlife of Prince Edward Island National Park.

Finding Your Way Around

By Car

Prince Edward Island has a good road network. Due to the lack of adequate public transit, the best way to tour the island is either by bike or by car.

The island is accessible from Cape Tormentine, New Brunswick, via the 13km-long **Confederation Bridge** *($35.50/ car, round-trip;* ☎*437-7033 or 888-437-6565, www.confederationbridge. com)*, which spans Northumberland Strait. For islanders, the bridge's inauguration in 1997 marked a veritable revolution: crossing the strait now takes 10min by car compared to a half hour by ferry. You can pay the toll with cash, credit card or debit card.

By Plane

Visitors flying to the island arrive at **Sherwood** airport, about 4km north of downtown Charlottetown (☎566-7992). **Air Canada** (☎894-8825 or 892-1007), and its partner **Air Nova**, as well as **Canadian Airlines** (☎892-5358) and its partner Air Atlantic, are the major airline companies serving this airport. Four car-rental agencies have offices in the airport such as **Budget** (☎566-5525).

By Ferry

From May to December, you can reach P.E.I. by taking the **Northumberland Ferries**, which link Caribou (Nova Scotia) to the Wood Islands (May to Nov, no reservation; car $47, passenger $10.75; ☎888-249-7245). The trip takes 75min.

P.E.I. is also accessible by ferry from the Îles-de-la-Madeleine (Québec) aboard the **Lucy Maud Montgomery** (car $64.25, adults $33.75; one ferry/day, reserve if possible; ☎418-986-3278), which arrives in Souris, near the northeastern point of the island.

By Bus

Prince Edward Island has limited bus service. However, there is a bus to Cavendish from the big hotel chains in downtown

Charlottetown (departure 9am, return 6pm).

Practical Information

Area Code: **902**

Tourist Information

Provincial Tourist Information Office
The island's main provincial tourist information office is in Borden-Carleton, right at the foot of the Confederation Bridge, ☎800-463-4734 or 629-2428, ⇌629-2428, www.peiplay.com

Charlottetown
at the corner of Water and Prince Sts.

Borden-Carleton
at the foot of Confederation Bridge

Cavendish
on Rte. 6

Brackley Beach
on Rte. 15

Poole's Corner
at the intersection of Rtes. 3 and 4

Wood Islands
on the road that leads to the ferry

Souris
on Rte. 2

Summerside
on Rte. 1A

Portage
on Rte. 2

Exploring

Charlottetown

Charming and quaint, Charlottetown has a unique atmosphere. Despite its size, it is more than just a small, typical Maritime town; it is a provincial capital with all the prestige, elegance and institutions one would expect for its status. Though everything here seems decidedly scaled down, the capital of Prince Edward Island has its parliament buildings and sumptuous lieutenant-governor's residence, a large performance and visual-arts complex, pretty parks and rows of trees concealing beautiful Victorian residences, a prestigious hotel and several fine restaurants. Adding to its charm is its picturesque location on the shores of a bay at the confluence of the Hillsborough, North and West Rivers. A meeting place for the Micmac, the site was known to explorers and French colonists in the 18th century. It was not until 1768, however, that British settlers actually founded the city, naming Charlottetown in honour of the wife of King George III of Great Britain. Less than a century later, Charlottetown made its way into history books as the cradle of Canadian Confederation. It was in this little town, in 1864, that the delegates of the North American British colonies met to discuss the creation of the Dominion of Canada.

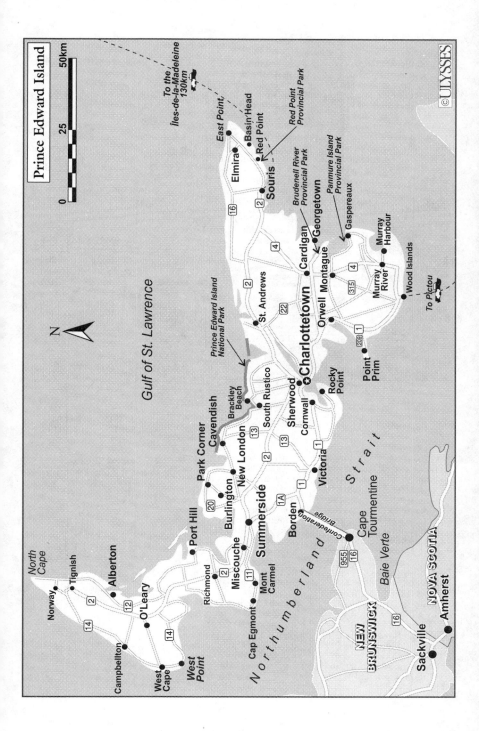

Prince Edward Island

Gulf of St. Lawrence

North Cape
Norway
Tignish
Alberton
O'Leary
Campbellton
West Cape
West Point
Cap Egmont
Mont Carmel
Richmond
Miscouche
Summerside
Borden
Confederation Bridge
Port Hill
Burlington
New London
Park Corner
Cavendish
Brackley Beach
South Rustico
Prince Edward Island National Park
St. Andrews
Sherwood
Cornwall
Victoria
Rocky Point
Point Prim
Charlottetown
Orwell
Montague
Cardigan
Georgetown
Gaspereaux
Brudenell River Provincial Park
Panmure Island Provincial Park
Souris
Elmira
East Point
Basin Head
Red Point
Red Point Provincial Park
Murray Harbour
Murray River
Wood Islands
To Pictou

To the Îles-de-la-Madeleine 130km

Northumberland Strait

NEW BRUNSWICK
Cape Tourmentine
Baie Verte
NOVA SCOTIA
Sackville
Amherst

0   25   50km

© ULYSSES

The **Confederation Arts Centre** ★★ *(free admission; Jul to Aug, 9am to 9pm; Sep to Jun, Mon to Sat 9am to 5pm, Sun 2pm to 5pm; 145 Richmond St., ☎628-1864 or 800-565-0278, ≈566-4648, www.confederationcentre.com)* was constructed in 1964, one century after the decisive meeting of the Fathers of Confederation in Charlottetown.

Confederation Arts Centre

The complex was designed to increase public knowledge of current Canadian culture and its evolution. The Arts Centre has many facets, including a museum with several impressive exhibits, an art gallery and a public library. There are also several beautiful auditoriums where visitors can take in a performance of *Anne of Green Gables*. Presented every summer for more than three decades now, this musical is a fun way to spend an evening in Charlottetown and become immersed in the world of Prince Edward Island's most famous author, Lucy Maud Montgomery.

The **Province House National Historic Site** ★★ *(free admission; Jul and Aug, 9am to 6pm; Sep to Jun, Mon to Fri 9am to 5pm; corner of University Ave. and Grafton St., beside the Confederation Art Centre, ☎566-7626)* can honestly be considered the cradle of Canadian Confederation. It was here that the 23 delegates from United Canada (present-day Ontario and Québec), Nova Scotia, New Brunswick and Prince Edward Island assembled in 1864 to prepare the Confederation of 1867.

Ironically, the host of this decisive conference, Prince Edward Island, did not join the Dominion of Canada until a few years later, in 1873. Visitors can see the rooms where the Canadian Confederation was worked out and watch a short film explaining the significance of the event. Province House is now the seat of the Legislative Assembly of Prince Edward Island.

St. Paul's Anglican Church ★ *(free admission; corner of Grafton and Prince Sts.)* was erected in 1896 to replace several Anglican churches built in the previous century. Its interior is splendid, especially the wooden vault and stained-glass windows.

St. Dunstan's Basilica ★ *(free admission, donations accepted; corner of Great George and Sydney Sts.)*, a beautiful example of the Gothic style, is the most impressive religious building on Prince Edward Island. Its construction began in 1914, on the same site occupied successively by three Catholic churches during the previous century.

Pretty Great George Street, where you can browse through many shops and second-hand stores, ends up at the small **port of Charlottetown**, a pleasant area where visitors will not only find a park and marina but also **Peake's Wharf** ★ *(at the end of Great George St.)*, a collection of shops in charming renovated old buildings. Close by stands the classy **Prince Edward Hotel** (see p 120), as well as a few restaurants.

Beaconsfield Historic House ★ *($2.50; Jul to early Sep, every day 10am to 5pm; Sep to Jun, Tue to Fri and Sun 1pm to 5pm; early Nov to mid-Jun, Tue to Fri and Sun 1pm to 5pm; 2 Kent St., ☎368-6603)* was built in 1877 for wealthy shipbuilder James Peake and his wife Edith Haviland Beaconsfield. It is one of the most luxurious residences in the province,

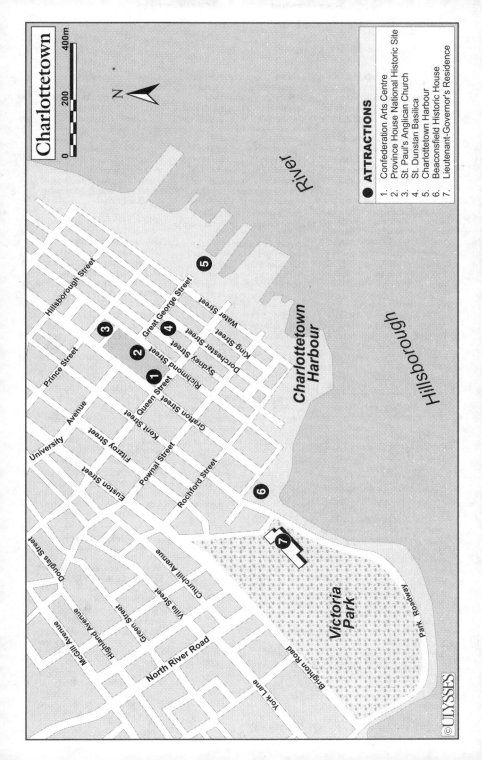

Charlottetown

ATTRACTIONS

1. Confederation Arts Centre
2. Province House National Historic Site
3. St. Paul's Anglican Church
4. St. Dunstan Basilica
5. Charlottetown Harbour
6. Beaconsfield Historic House
7. Lieutenant-Governor's Residence

River

Hillsborough Street

Prince Street

Great George Street

Sydney Street

Richmond Street

Dorchester Street

King Street

Water Street

Charlottetown Harbour

Hillsborough

University Avenue

Kent Street

Queen Street

Grafton Street

Fitzroy Street

Pownal Street

Euston Street

Rochford Street

Douglas Street

Churchill Avenue

Villa Street

Green Street

Highland Avenue

McGill Avenue

North River Road

York Lane

Brighton Road

Park Roadway

Victoria Park

© ULYSSES

N

0   200   400m

with 25 rooms and nine fireplaces. After James Peake declared personal bankruptcy in 1882, his creditors, the Cunall family, moved in. The family had no descendants, so Beaconsfield House served as a training school from 1916 on, and was converted into a museum in 1973.

On the other side of Kent Street, shielded behind a stately row of trees, stands the splendid **Lieutenant-Governor's residence** *(corner of Kent St. and Pond Rd.).* It has been the official residence of the British crown's representative on Prince Edward Island since 1835. Magnificent, beautifully designed **Victoria Park ★**, which spreads out before the residence, is a lovely place for a stroll.

Rocky Point

Rocky Point is located at the end of a point of land at the mouth of the West River, facing the Hillsborough River, historically a strategic point in the defense of Charlottetown and the back-country against a possible attack from the sea. Early on, this site was of particular interest to the colonial empires that would battle for control of the island. The French were the first to establish themselves here in the 1720s, when they founded Port la Joye, captured in 1758 by the British who then founded Fort Amherst. The fine-tuning of the fort came that same year when the war between France and England began in earnest. The British garrison had the important role of protecting the island from French invasion and

controlling maritime traffic in the Northumberland Strait throughout the whole war. However, with the end of the war in 1763, the fort's importance decreased significantly and was abandoned by the British in 1768. The **Port La Joye - Fort Amherst National Historic Site ★** *($2.25; mid-Jun to early Sep, every day 9am to 5pm; Rte. 19;* ☎*566-7626)* houses a small interpretive centre presenting an exhibit on the various documents related to the French colony (Port La Joye) and the British presence at the site (Fort Amherst). There is also a short documentary film on the history of the Acadians of Prince Edward Island. Very little remains today of Fort Amherst. There is, however, a lovely view of the surrounding fields and of the city of Charlottetown from the site.

The **Micmac Village** *($3.25; mid-Jun to early Sep, every day 9am to 5pm; Rte. 19,* ☎*566-7626)* is also worth a stop when visiting Rocky Point. There is a small museum, a gift shop and a reconstruction of a Micmac village, the Aboriginal people that inhabited the island before the arrival of European colonists.

Victoria

The beautiful residences lining the streets of this charming and peaceful coastal town attest to the opulence of another era. Founded in 1767, this seaport played a significant role in the local economy up until the end of the 19th century, when bit by bit the development of the railway on Prince Edward Island outmoded

it. Fishing trawlers can still be seen, however, bobbing about just beyond the once busy harbour. Today the interest in Victoria lies mostly in its old-fashioned character and in the friendliness of its residents. Country life on the island is best represented here. There are two inns, a few restaurants, and a famous chocolatier...

When arriving from the east you'll first come to **Victoria Provincial Park**, which extends to the water and includes a small beach and a picnic area. The **Victoria Seaport Museum** *(free admission; Jul to early Sep, Tue to Sun 10am to 5pm; Rte. 116;* ☎*658-2602)* is located close by in a lighthouse. Besides the several photographs of Victoria on display, you can also climb to the top of the lighthouse for a view of the village, the coast and the surroundings.

The centre of Victoria is made up of just a few streets. There are several shops, restaurants, as well as **The Victorian Playhouse** *(*☎*658-2025),* which presents, topnotch concerts and theatre all summer long, adding to the charm of the town.

Park Corner

Anne of Green Gables Museum at Silver Bush ★ *($2.50; Jun and Sep to Oct, every day 9am to 6pm; Jul and Aug, 9am to 7pm;* ☎*886-2807)* was actually a favourite house of Lucy Maud Montgomery. It belonged to her aunt and uncle, Annie and John Campbell. She adored it and was married here in July 1911. Today it is a historic house, decorated with period furniture and many of the author's and her family's personal effects.

New London

The small community of New London has the distinguished honour of being the birthplace of the writer who has made Prince Edward Island famous internationally. The main attraction is the house where she was born, the **Lucy Maud Montgomery Birthplace** *($2; late May and Jun, Sep to mid-Oct, every day 9am to 5pm; Jul and Aug, 9am to 7pm; intersection of Rtes. 6 and 8, ☎886-2099 or 436-7329)*. Personal objects, including Montgomery's wedding dress, can be viewed in this simple house.

Cavendish

The Cavendish area is a sacred spot for tourists to P.E.I. Located next to some of the most beautiful beaches on the island and several big tourist attractions, Cavendish has many lodging possibilities, restaurants and shops. It is a gateway to the national park and therefore has an excellent tourist information centre.

Green Gables House ★ *($2.50; mid-May to late Jun, 9am to 5pm; late Jun to late Aug, 9am to 8pm; late Aug to late Oct, 9am to 5pm; Rte. 6, west of Cavendish, ☎672-6350, ≈672-6370)* is the house that Lucy Maud Montgomery used as the main setting for her famous novel *Anne of Green Gables*. Built towards the middle of the 19th century, the house belonged to David

and Margaret MacNeil, older cousins of the author's. Montgomery used to love strolling down "lover's lane," located in the woods on her cousins' property. She was so inspired by the surroundings that it became the backdrop for her novel. By 1936, the novel was so popular that the federal government made a classified the house as an historic site/national site, and thus today it can be visited.

A visit to the island would not be complete without at least a one- day trip to **Prince Edward Island National Park** ★★★ *(three welcome centres: in Cavendish, near the intersection of Rtes. 6 and 13, ☎963-2391; opposite the Dalvay-by-the-Sea Hotel, ☎672-6350; Brackley, at the intersection of Rtes. 6 and 15, ☎672-2259)*, which stretches for kilometres along the northern coast of the island, from Blooming Point to New London Bay. The park was created in 1937 with the goal of preserving a unique natural environment, including sand dunes (with their fragile ecosystem), red sandstone cliffs, magnificent beaches and saltwater marshes. While exploring the park, visitors will be constantly delighted by stunning views of the sheer coastline, the sudden appearance of a red fox or one of the many activities that may be enjoyed here.

The park was expanded in February 1998 and now includes the Greenwich Peninsula, which extends to the east of St. Peters Bay.

South Rustico

South Rustico itself is actually a crossroads in the middle of the countryside around which stand the main institutions of the Acadian community: the church, the presbytery, the cemetery, the school and the **Farmer's Bank of Rustico** ★ *($1; Jul to Aug, Tue to Sun 10am to 4pm; Rte. 243, ☎963-2304)*. This farmer's bank was founded in 1864 by Father George-Antoine Belcourt, to give Acadians the opportunity to participate in the economy. It was the first people's bank in the country, and for a certain time, the smallest chartered bank in Canada. It is now a museum and the exhibit tells of Father Belcourt's work and the historic location. Right next door, the modest **Saint Augustine Church** *(Church St.)* is the oldest Acadian church on the island.

Green Gables

Brackley Beach

This small hamlet on the shores of Rustico Bay is worth a visit to see the

Baywatch Lighthouse *($1.50. early Jun to mid-Sep, 10am to 10pm; at the intersection of Rtes. 15 and 16,* ☎*672-3478)* and its exhibit of photographs of island lighthouses. Another recommended stop close by is **The Dunes Art Gallery** *(free admission; May, 10am to 6pm; Jun to Sep, 9am to 10pm; Oct, 10am to 6pm; Rte. 15,* ☎*672-2586)* where the works of the biggest artists of the island are on display. There is also a charming little restaurant. With Prince Edward Island National Park right nearby, Brackley Beach provides plenty of accommodations.

Orwell Corner

A visit to the **Orwell Corner Historic Village** ★ *($3; late Jun to early Sep, every day 9am to 5pm; Trans-Canada Hwy. 30km east of Charlottetown;* ☎*651-8510)* is a must for anyone interested in discovering what life was like in rural Prince Edward Island back in the 19th century. This delightful village is made up of restored buildings, including a pretty little school that looks as if it came straight out of a Lucy Maud Montgomery novel, a church, a shingle factory, several barns, a forge and a farmhouse that doubles as a general store and a post office. The atmosphere is animated by characters in period dress, who are available to answer visitors' questions. Orwell Corner may be smaller than other similar historic villages, such as Kings Landing in New Brunswick, but its size

gives it a charming authenticity.

A few hundred metres from Orwell Corner, tucked away in an enchanting setting, lies the **Sir Andrew Macphail Homestead** *(free admission, suggested donation; late Jun to early Sep, every day, 10am to 5pm; Jul and Aug, every day, 10am to 9pm; 30km east of Charlottetown, Rte.1,* ☎*651-2789)*. A native of Prince Edward Island, Andrew Macphail (1864-1938) had an extraordinary career in the fields of research and medicine, as well as in writing and journalism His house, furnished as it was at the beginning of the 20th century, is a lovely part of the local heritage. There is a small dining room where light meals are served. Visitors can also explore the vast grounds by taking a pleasant walk along a 2km trail.

Point Prim

Not far from the village of Eldon, Route 1 intersects with Route 209, a small road leading to the **Point Prim Lighthouse** *(free admission; Jul and Aug, 9am to 7pm; Rte. 209,* ☎*659-2412)*, designed and built in 1845 by Isaac Smith, architect of Charlottetown's Province House. The lighthouse is open to the public, and the surrounding area is perfect for a picnic. The **view** ★ of the sea is worth the short detour.

Montague

Montague might not be very big, but it is nevertheless one of the largest communities in the eastern part of the province. It is home to several busi-

nesses, shops and restaurants, as well as the interesting **Garden of the Gulf Museum** ★ *($3; Jun to late Sep, Mon to Sat 9am to 5pm; 2 Main St. S.,* ☎*838-2467)*, set up inside the former post office. The exhibit deals with both local and military history. Montague is also the point of departure for excursions organized by **Cruise Manada Seal Watching Boat Tours** (see p 119). Other excursions start at the Brudenell Marina.

Souris

The little town of Souris, with its 1,600 or so inhabitants, is the largest community on the eastern part of Prince Edward Island. Accordingly, it offers a wide range of services, including several restaurants and hotels and a tourist information centre. Not far away lies **Souris Beach Provincial Park**, with a picnic area and an unsupervised beach. Main Street is graced with several pretty buildings that bear witness to Souris's prominent role in this region. The most striking of these are the **Town Hall** and **St. Mary's Church**. The town port is the boarding point for the ferry (see p 110) to Québec's Îles-de-la-Madeleine, situated in the heart of the Gulf of St. Lawrence.

Basin Head

Ideally located on one of the island's loveliest **sandy beaches** ★★, not far from some magnificent dunes, the **Basin Head Fisheries Museum** ★★ *($3; mid-Jun and late Sep, Mon to Fri, 10am to 5pm; Jul and Aug.*

10am to 7pm; Rte.16. ☎*357-7233)* offers visitors an opportunity to learn about all different facets of the wonderful world of fishing around Prince Edward Island. The museum exhibits an interesting collection of artifacts related to the lives and occupation of the fishers of old. The building itself is flanked by sheds in which vessels of various sizes and periods are displayed, as well as a workshop where local artisans make wooden boxes like those used in the past for packing salted fish. An old canning factory stands a little farther off. In all respects, this is one of the most interesting museums in the province. To make the most of your visit, take a stroll along the neighbouring beaches and dunes, as well.

East Point

For a magnificent view of the ocean and the area's coastal landscape, head to the **East Point Lighthouse ★** *(free admission, guided tours $2.50; Jul to mid-Aug; Rte. 16;* ☎*357-2106),* which stands on the easternmost tip of the island. During summer, visitors can climb to the top of this old lighthouse, which dates back to 1867.

Elmira

A tiny rural village near the easternmost tip of the island, Elmira is home to the **Elmira Railway Museum ★** *($1.50; mid-Jun to early Sep, every day 10am to 6pm; Rte.16A;* ☎*357-7234),* one of the six museums of the Prince Edward Island Museum and Heritage Foundation. Located in a bucolic setting, it occupies the town's former train station, which

has been closed since 1982. In addition to the main building, there is a warehouse and a railway car stationed on one of the tracks. This museum's excellent exhibit is a reminder of the glorious sense of adventure that accompanied the construction of Prince Edward Island's railway.

Summerside

With a population of around 10,000 people, Summerside is Prince Edward Island's second-largest town. It is presently experiencing an economic boom, due to the nearby Confederation Bridge to New Brunswick, completed in 1997. It is a pleasant town, graced with lovely Victorian residences and a pretty waterfront. As the chief urban centre on the western part of the island, Summerside also has a number of shops, restaurants and places to stay.

Eptek *($2; Jul to early Sep, every day 9:30am to 6:30pm; Sep to Jun, Tue-Fri 10am to 4pm; on the waterfront, Water St.,* ☎*888-8373)* is a national exhibition centre that presents travelling exhibits of Canadian art. The same building also houses Prince Edward Island's Sports Hall of Fame.

West Point

Through a collection of photographs and other articles, the **International Fox Museum ★** *(free admission, donations accepted; May to Oct, 10am to 6pm; 286 Fitzroy St.,* ☎*436-2400)* traces the history of fox-breeding on Prince Edward Island. After a timid start at the end of the 19th century, this activity represented 17% of the province's economy by the 1920s. In those years, a pair of silver foxes could fetch as much as $35,000. Efforts are now being made to revive this once prosperous industry.

Mont-Carmel

Mont-Carmel, known for many years as Grand-Ruisseau, was founded in 1812 by the Arseneault and Gallant families. The splendour of the **Église Notre-Dame-du-Mont-Carmel ★** *(Rte. 11),* which lies in the heart of the parish, bears eloquent witness to the prominent role played by Catholicism in Acadian culture.

Located on the site of the very first settlement, Grand-Ruisseau (now known as Mont-Carmel), the **Acadian Pioneer Village ★** *($3.50; Jun to mid-Sep, 9am to 7pm; Rte. 11; 1.5km west of the church,* ☎*800-567-3228)* recreates the rustic lifestyle of early 19th-century Acadians. The village includes a church and presbytery, two family homes, a smithy, a school and a barn.

Most of the furniture in the buildings was donated by citizens of neighbouring villages. There is a comfortable hotel at the entrance of the pioneer village, as well as the restaurant Étoile de Mer, which offers visitors a unique opportunity to enjoy Acadian cuisine.

West Point

A stop at West Point offers an opportunity to explore one of the most peaceful, picturesque spots on the island, **Cedar Dunes Provincial Park ★** *(Rte. 14)*, which features endless deserted beaches and dunes and is an excellent spot for observing wildlife and vegetation. Another interesting nearby spot is the **West Point Lighthouse** *($2.50; late Jun to late Aug, 8am to 9:30pm; May to mid-Jun and Sep, 8am to 8pm; Rte. 14;* ☎*859-3606)*, which dates back to 1875 and is one of the largest in the province. In addition to housing a museum and a restaurant, it is the only lighthouse in Canada that is used as an inn.

North Cape

The scenery around North Cape, the northernmost tip of the island, is not only pretty, but often spectacular, with red sandstone cliffs plunging into the blue waters of the Gulf of St. Lawrence. North Cape itself occupies a lovely site along the coast. Here, visitors will find the **Atlantic Wind Test Site** *($2; Jul and Aug, 10am to 8pm; at the end of Rte. 12;* ☎*882-2746)*, where wind technology is

tested and evaluated. A small exhibit explains the advantages of using this type of energy.

Parks and Beaches

The craggy, breathtakingly beautiful landscapes, endless beaches and unique plant and animal life are among the most spectacular attractions of this red crescent-shaped island, which lies 40km east of continental Canada. A number of parks have been created to highlight the natural beauty of parts of the island. The most renowned is Prince Edward Island National Park, but there are also 29 provincial parks. More than 40 lovely beaches with sands in countless shades of pink also help make this island a veritable paradise for vacationers.

Parks

The province's parks provide all sorts of services for vacationers (campsites, picnic areas, supervised beaches) and feature a variety of activities intended to familiarize visitors with various natural settings; nature trails and welcome centres offer information on the local plant and animal life. These parks are an inexhaustible source of discovery for the entire family.

About 15 of the provincial parks have **camping** facilities *(☎652-2356 for reservations in the eastern part of the island, and* ☎*859-8790 for the western part)*. Visitors can also camp in the national park, but the conditions vary (see p 61).

Beaches

The island is fringed with a series of exquisite white- and red-sand beaches, especially along the north coast. Magnificent sandy **beaches ★** which are ideal for swimming and undoubtedly among the most beautiful on the Eastern Seaboard, run along the entire shoreline of **Prince Edward Island National Park**. Some have been landscaped and are supervised; they usually have showers, changing rooms and often small restaurants. Other beaches, just as beautiful but unsupervised, stretch as far as the eye can see. The eastern part of Prince Edward Island boasts equally beautiful sandy beaches. The splendid **beach ★** at **Basin Head**, also accessible from **Red Point Provincial Park**, is kilometres long. Another exceptional **beach ★** is located at **Panmure Island Provincial Park**, in the eastern section of the island. Along Northumberland Strait, where the water is considerably warmer than it is in the Gulf of St. Lawrence, there are also a few lovely beaches: **Wood Islands Provincial Park**, in the southeast, is a very pleasant place to swim.

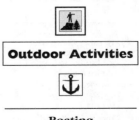

Outdoor Activities

Boating

Visitors wishing to head out to sea can take part in one of a variety of short cruises offered by these local companies.

Mill River Boat Tour
$15
☎*856-3820*

Cardigan Sailing Tours
$50
☎*583-2020*

Charlottetown Peake's Warf boat cruises
various tours/ 70min $14
☎*566-4458*

Seal-watching

Groups of seals regularly swim near the shores of the island. Visitors interested in observing these large sea mammals can take part in an excursion organized for that purpose.

Cruise Manada
$17, children under 12 $8.50
☎*838-3444 or 800-986-3444*
Departure: from the Montague Marina, mid-May to late Jun and early Sep to early Oct every day 10am and 2pm, early Jul to late Aug every day 10am, 1pm, 3:30pm and 18:30pm, Jul and Aug every day 2:30pm.

Garry's Seal Cruises
$15.50, children $7.50
☎*962-2494 or 800-561-2494*
Departure: Murray River pier, May to mid-Jun every day 1pm, 3:30pm and 6:30pm, mid-Jun to mid-Sep every day 8:30am, 10:30am, 1pm, 3:30pm and 6:30pm, mid-Sep to late Oct 10:30am, 1pm, 6:30pm.

Fishing

Several companies offer deep-sea fishing excursions, giving visitors a chance to test their fishing skills while enjoying an exciting outing on the water.

Excursions of this type set out from **Covehead Harbour**:

Richard's Deep-Sea Fishing
$15
☎*672-2376*

Salty Seas Deep-Sea Fishing
$15
☎*672-3246*

A company in **Alberton** arranges similar outings:
Andrew's Mist
$25
☎*853-2307*

North Rustico:

Aiden Poiron's
☎*963-2442*
Also offers deep-sea excursions

Accommodations

Charlottetown

Youth Hostel
$12.50 members
$15 non-members
153 Mount Edward Rd.
☎*894-9696*
The Youth Hostel provides the least expensive lodging in the provincial capital region. It's a friendly spot set up in a barn-like building about 3km west of downtown, near the university. During summer, rooms are also available at the **University of Prince**

Edward Island *($26 single, 32 double;* ☎*566-0442)*.

Heritage Harbour House Inn
$70 bkfst incl.
early Jun to late Sep
4 rooms
9 Grafton St., C1A 1K3
☎*892-6633*
☎*800-405-0066*
The Heritage Harbour House Inn is an excellent bed and breakfast located on a residential street just a stone's throw from the Arts Centre. The rooms are impeccably clean, as are the shared bathrooms. The house itself is warm and inviting, and guests have use of a day room where they can relax, read or watch television. Bonnie, the owner and a charming hostess, serves a continental breakfast each morning.

The Charlottetown Rodd Classic
$85-$135
tv, ℜ, ≈
109 rooms
corner of Kent and Pownal Sts.
C1A 1L5
☎*894-7371*
☎*800-565-7633*
The Charlottetown Rodd Classic is an excellent downtown hotel with a rather stately appearance, built to meet the needs of both business people and vacationers. Renovated in 1998, the inviting rooms are modern and tastefully furnished. The hotel also houses a good restaurant.

Charlotte's Rose Inn
$115
tv
4 rooms
11 Grafton St., C1A 1K3
☎*892-3699 or 894-3699*
Charlotte's Rose Inn is also an elegant, 19th-century Victorian home. Originally built in 1884, it has since been meticulously renovated. In addition to its old-world charm, its rooms are furnished with antiques and private bath-

rooms. Great location on a peaceful street in the old part of town.

Dundee Arms
$120
tv, ℜ
18 rooms
200 Pownal St., C1A 8C2
☎ *892-2496*
⇄ *368-8532*
The Dundee Arms, built in 1903, is an elegant inn set up inside a large Queen Anne style residence built at the beginning of the century. The beautifully decorated bedrooms and common rooms will take you back in time. The inn also features a highly-reputed dining room. Finally, there are comfortable, slightly less expensive motel rooms available in an adjoining building.

🌴 Prince Edward Hotel
$159
tv, ℜ, ≈
211 rooms
18 Queen St., C1A 8B9
☎ *566-2222 or 800-441-1414*
⇄ *566-2282*
Part of the Canadian Pacific hotel chain, The Prince Edward Hotel is without a doubt the ritziest and most comfortable hotel on the island. It is also perfectly situated, looking out over the port of Charlottetown. The interior is modern and well designed, with four restaurants and all the facilities one would expect to find in a hotel of this calibre. Business meetings and conferences are often held at the Prince Edward. Its conference rooms can accommodate up to 650 people.

Cavendish

Kindred Spirits Country Inn
$65 bkfst incl.
135 bkfst incl. suite or cottage
pb, ≡, tv
mid-May to mid-Oct
14 rooms
Rte. 6, C0A 1N0
☎ / ⇄ *963-2434*
Furnished with antiques and exquisitely decorated, the Kindred Spirits Country Inn offers quality accommodation less than 1km from the Cavendish beach. Guests can relax in one of several common rooms, including a superb living room. Kindred Spirits has 25 rooms, 14 of which have whirlpools. The establishment also offers suites with more luxurious accommodation, as well as 12 fully equipped, charming cottages, more suitable for families.

🌴 Shining Water Country Inn and Cottages
$75-$130
ℜ, pb, tv
May to mid-Oct
10 rooms
Rte. 13, C0A 1N0
☎ *963-2251*
In the heart of Cavendish, the Shining Water Country Inn and Cottages is a - lovely old house with spacious porches all around. This inn features comfortable rooms and friendly service. Guests can relax in a pleasant, airy living room. There are cottages behind the house that are available for about $15 extra.

Cavendish Motel
$78
tv, ℜ
early Jun to mid-Sep
35 rooms
intersection of Rtes. 6 and 13
C0A 1M0
☎ *963-2244 or 800-565-2243*
In the centre of what could be considered the village of Cavendish, the

Cavendish Motel offers clean, pleasant, modern rooms.

South Rustico

Barachois Inn
$125
ℜ
May to late Oct
7 rooms
Church Rd., C1A 7M4
☎ *963-2194*
The heart of South Rustico is in fact a crossroads where all of the main francophone institutions from this part of the island are located. The Barachois Inn, located nearby, is an additional to this pretty architectural grouping. Built in the 1870s, this lovely patrician house was renovated just a few years ago and includes two rooms and two suites, all furnished in period style and each equipped with a private washroom. With its large porches and beautiful gardens, the Barachois is very appealing. It is especially suited to those who enjoy the charms of its quiet, country setting.

Little Rock

🌴 Dalvay-by-the-Sea
$190 bkfst incl.
ℜ, ≈, pb
P.O. Box 8, C0A 1P0
☎ *672-2048*
⇄ *672-2741 www.aco.ca/dalvay*
Dalvay-by-the-Sea is an impressive Victorian house located at the eastern tip of the park, a few hundred metres from magnificent white-sand beaches. It is also the only hotel establishment within the perimeter of the national park. Built in 1896, the Dalvay was once the summer residence of Alexander Macdonald, one of the most powerful American industrialists of his era and

a business partner of John D. Rockefeller. Nowadays, the house has about 20 very elegantly decorated rooms and cottages, all of them with private bathrooms. As much because of its unique location as for its splendid design, Dalvay-by-the-Sea is one of the best hotels on the island; advance reservations for summertime stays are strongly recommended. Visitors who lodge elsewhere should stop by for a peek at the building's splendid dining and living rooms. Tennis court.

Little Pond

 Ark Inn
$85
ℜ, tv
mid-Jun to Sep
8 rooms
R.R.4, C0A 2B0
☎*583-2400 or 800-665-2400*
⇌*583-2176*
A haven of peace, the Ark Inn stands on a large property with access to a private beach. The comfortable rooms feature futons, modern furniture and large windows. One thing that sets the Ark Inn apart is that most of its rooms are split-level, with the upper portion affording a lovely view. Some rooms are also equipped with a whirlpool. There is a pleasant restaurant on the ground floor.

Bay Fortune

 Inn at Bay Fortune
$125 bkfst incl.
ℜ, tv, 11 rooms
late May to mid-Oct
Rte. 310, C0A 2B0
☎*687-3745*
⇌*687-3540*
www.innatbayfortune.com
One of the most sumptuous and charming inns on

the island, the Inn at Bay Fortune offers high-quality food and accommodation. The building has a unique architectural design; it stands on a lovely, verdant site, offering a superb view of the bay after which it is named. The rooms are furnished in an elegant and original, fashion, each one different from the last. Some even have a fireplace. An excellent choice!

Summerside

 Silver Fox Inn
$75
ℜ
6 rooms
61 Granville St., C1N 2Z3
☎*436-4033 or 800-565-4033*
The beautiful Silver Fox Inn lies a short distance from the port in an old residential neighbourhood and is surrounded by a pretty little garden. All of the rooms are well furnished, inviting and equipped with a private bathroom. Overall, the inn is elegantly decorated and has an atmosphere reminiscent of turn-of-the-century high-society.

Loyalist Country Inn
$99
tv, ℜ
50 rooms
195 Harbour Dr., C1N 5R2
☎*436-3333*
⇌*436-4304*
The most comfortable hotel in Summerside, the Loyalist Country Inn boasts an excellent location in the heart of town, with a view of the nearby port. Although they are modern, the rooms still have character, and are tastefully furnished. This hotel is a real favourite with business people. Its restaurant, the Prince William Dining Room, is highly recommended (see p 123).

West Point

 West Point Lighthouse
$75
tv, ℜ
late may to late Sep
10 rooms
O'Leary, R.R.2, C0B 1V0
☎*859-3605 or 800-764-6854*
⇌*859-1510*
The only inn in Canada set up inside a lighthouse (only one room is actually inside the lighthouse; the others are in the adjoining building), the West Point Lighthouse is a good spot to stop for a day or two, long enough to explore the magnificent dunes and beaches along the nearby shore. This is a friendly place, and the rooms are decent.

Woodstock

Rodd Mill River Resort
$67
tv, ℜ
May to Oct
90 rooms
O'Leary, R.R.2, C0B 1V0
☎*859-3555 or 800-565-7633*
⇌*859-2486*
The Rodd Mill River Resort is ideal for sports buffs. Not only is there an excellent golf-course nearby, but the resort itself has an indoor pool, tennis courts, a gym and squash courts. The rooms, furthermore, are very comfortable.

Tyne Valley

Doctor's Inn Bed & Breakfast
$55
ℜ
2 rooms
Rte. 167, C0B 2C0
☎*831-3057*
The Doctor's Inn Bed & Breakfast is a country home typical of the 1860s with a pleasant garden. Its two decent, but not very luxurious rooms are avail-

able year-round. The place is very quiet, and excellent evening meals are available.

Restaurants

Charlottetown

Anchor and Oar House Grub & Grog
$
mid-May to mid-Oct
behind the Prince Edward Hotel
Water St.
☎*894-1260*
Just outside the Prince Edward Hotel, on the same side as Peake's Wharf, the Anchor and Oar House Grub & Grog has a simple menu idea for lunch. Most dishes are less than $6. There is a selection of salads and sandwiches, and several fish and seafood dishes round out the offerings.

Cedar's Eatery
$
81 University St.
☎*892-7377*
Centrally located, Cedar's Eatery offers an inexpensive, change of pace. *Kebab, falafel, shawarma* and *shish taouk*, Lebanese cuisine's most famous exports, are the headliners. The atmosphere is young, friendly and unpretentious, and the portions are generous.

Peake's Quay
$-$$
May to Sep
36 Water St.
☎*368-1330*
Peake's Quay should win the trophy for the best-situated restaurant in Charlottetown. The pleasant terrace looks directly out over the city's marina. An economical menu of

simple dishes, including excellent seafood crepes, is offered at breakfast time. In the evening, the menu is more elaborate but still affordable. For less than $20, you can have a delicious plate of lobster, among other things. Peake's Quay is also a pub where people linger over a drink or two.

 **Off Broadway Café**
$$
125 Sydney St.
☎*566-4620*
Perhaps surprisingly for a city of this size, Charlottetown's collection of restaurants includes a few gems, namely the Off Broadway Café. Its relaxing, romantic and tasteful atmosphere and its excellent menu make it the hottest restaurant in town. A variety of dishes, many with a French touch, are served. And seafood connoisseurs will not be disappointed by the main dishes and appetizers featured. Rounding up the menu is a choice selection of desserts, including many crepes.

Victoria

 **Landmark Café & Craft**
$
Jul to Sep
Main St.
☎*658-2286*
In the centre of the charming little village of Victoria, near the two inns and almost directly opposite the chocolate shop, visitors will find the Landmark Café & Craft an extremely friendly, warm and simple place whose walls are adorned with pretty handicrafts. The menu consists of light home-made dishes – quiche, *tourtière* (meat pie), pasta, salads and desserts.

St. Ann

 **St. Ann's Church Lobster Supper**
$$
Jun to Oct
Rte. 224
☎*621-0635*
For more than 30 years now, St. Ann's Church Lobster Supper, a non-profit organization, has been serving lobster everyday from 4pm to 9pm. The menu, like those of other similar local restaurants, consists of a salad, fish soup, mussels, lobster and dessert – all for about $20. This is the type of tradition that visitors to Prince Edward Island should definitely not miss out on.

New Glasgow

Prince Edward Island Preserve Co.
$
Rte. 13, intersection of Rtes. 234 and 258
☎*964-2524*
The Prince Edward Island Preserve Co. is actually a shop selling delicious natural products. It also has a café that serves good sandwiches and salads, as well as other dishes, including lobster quiche, a smoked fish platter and mussels *à la provençale*.

New Glasgow Lobster Suppers
$$
Jun to mid-Oct
Rte. 258
☎*964-2870*
Looking out on the Clyde River, the New Glasgow Lobster Suppers is one of the island's classic eateries. Since opening, it has served over a million customers! During summer, hundreds of people pass through its two dining rooms every evening between 4pm and 8:30pm.

The charm of this place lies in its simplicity; in the dining rooms, there are rows of plain tables covered with red-and-white-checkered tablecloths. Obviously, the menu revolves around lobster. Each meal includes an all-you-can-eat appetizer, one lobster and a home-made dessert. Prices vary depending on the size of the lobster you choose, but $20 per person is about average.

North Rustico

Fisherman Wharf Lobster Suppers
$$
mid-May to mid-Oct
Rte. 6
☎963-2669
A well-known local institution, Fisherman Wharf Lobster Suppers also serves traditional lobster meals, with unlimited fish and seafood soup, a vast choice of salads, bread, a lobster and a dessert for about $20. The place can seat approximately 500 people, which doesn't exactly make it intimate, but that's part of its charm.

Oyster Bed Bridge

Café St-Jean
$$
early Jun to late Sep
Rte. 6
☎963-3133
Both elegant and inviting, the Café St-Jean is a small restaurant set up inside a rustic-looking house with a view of the Wheatley River. In the evening, the food is fairly elaborate, with not only seafood on the menu, but also a fair number of other well-prepared, original dishes and cajun specialities. The less expensive lunch menu consists of light dishes.

The name of the café refers to the time before the British conquest, when the island was known as Île-St-Jean and the Acadian presence was very strong in this region.

Brackley Beach

Dunes Café
$$
Jun to Sep
10am to 10pm
Rte. 15
☎672-2586
The Dunes Café is the only place of its kind on the island. Set up in a complex with original modern architecture that also houses a remarkable art gallery, it serves local and international cuisine in an airy decor. The lunch menu is less elaborate and easier on the pocketbook. Live music is often featured in the evening

Orwell Corner

Sir Andrew McPhail Restaurant
$
late Jun to early Sep
Rte. 1
☎651-2789
Located on the historic site of the Sir Andrew Macphail Homestead, the Sir Andrew McPhail Restaurant is a pleasant place to enjoy a good, light meal at lunchtime or take a break in the afternoon. Though the menu is simple, the food is tasty. Reservations are required for dinner ($$). The elegance and atmosphere of the Macphail Homestead make this a very appealing little restaurant.

Summerside

Prince William Dining Room
$$
195 Harbour Dr. in the Loyalist Country Inn
☎436-3333
The Prince William Dining Room offers well-prepared food and a fairly elaborate menu, including a wide choice of appetizers and main dishes. Seafood and fish make up a good part of the offerings, but various steak and chicken dishes are also available. On some evenings, a specific dish is featured, such as the excellent surf and turf, consisting of a small steak and a lobster tail. The service is courteous, and the atmosphere elegant but relaxed.

West Point

West Point Lighthouse
$-$$
late May to late Sep
Rte. 14
☎859-3605
A good place to stop for a break during a tour of western Prince Edward Island, the West Point Lighthouse is an inn whose restaurant is open from daybreak to 9:30pm. The lunch menu consists of a variety of light dishes, including the usual lobster rolls, chowders and other seafood. In the evening, the cuisine is a bit more sophisticated, with more elaborate appetizers and main courses, such as a fisherman's platter, made up of five different kinds of seafood or fish for less than $20. The menu also lists steak, chicken Kiev and pasta. The restaurant is laid out in a simple fashion in the building adjoining the lighthouse. Guests can also eat on the outside terrace.

Prince Edward Island

Entertainment

Charlottetown

Each summer for more than three decades now, the Confederation Arts Centre has presented the musical **Anne of Green Gables** *(Confederation Arts Centre,* ☎*566-1267 or 800-566-1207)*, inspired by the work of Prince Edward Island's favourite daughter, Lucy Maud Montgomery. Both funny and touching, the story of little "Anne with an e" is now a classic of children's literature all over the world. It is amazing to see to what point Anne has affected young Japanese, who now make up a significant percentage of tourists to the island. The musical is enjoyable and makes for a fun night out.

Victoria

Almost every night in July and August, the **Victoria Playhouse** *(about $12;* ☎*658-2025 or 800-925-2025)* presents entertaining plays and concerts in its little theatre. With its quality performances, the Victoria Playhouse is as charming as the city itself.

Shopping

Charlottetown

In Charlottetown, visitors can go to **Peake's Wharf** to stroll along the pier and enjoy the seashore while doing some shopping in the pretty boutiques. There is something for everyone here – crafts, souvenirs, T-shirts, etc.

Clothing

Both children and their parents will enjoy picking out one of the funny T-shirts and sweatshirts available at **Cow's** *(opposite the Confederation Arts Centre).* Make sure to sample the store's excellent ice cream at the same time.

La Cache *(119 Kent St.,* ☎*368-3072)* sells comfortable clothing as well as kitchen goods and tablecloths.

Visitors looking for warm woolens should head over to the **Wool Sweater Factory Outlet** *(Prince Edward Hotel,* ☎*566-5850),* which offers a lovely selection of high-quality, casual sweaters.

Crafts and souvenirs

All sorts of beautiful crafts, books and souvenirs are available at **The Two Sisters** *(150 Richmond St.,* ☎*894-3407).*

Anne of Green Gables fans can poke around in the **Anne of Green Gables Souvenirs shop** *(110 Queen St.;* ☎*368-2663).*

Victoria

The melt-in-your-mouth home-made chocolates at **Island Chocolate** *(Main St.,* ☎*658-2320)* are an absolute delight.

Cavendish

The **Cavendish Boardwalk** *(Rte. 6)* has all kinds of adorable little shops, some, like **Two Sisters**, specializing in T-shirts and souvenirs. Visitors will also find a branch of **Roots** (sportswear) and **Cow's**, with its cute clothing and terrific ice cream. At the front of the store, there is a selection of slightly defective Cow's clothing at reduced prices.

The **Island Treasures** *(at the intersection of Rtes. 6 and 13;* ☎*963-2350)* shop is another good place to purchase local crafts and many other articles for the home.

New Brunswick

New Brunswick, gateway to Atlantic Canada, is enchanting in its diversity.

Geographically, it is remarkably varied, combining more than a 1,000km of shoreline and seascapes with picturesque farmlands and endless stretches of often mountainous wilderness. Forests cover a full 85% of the territory. It is traversed from north to south by the majestic St. John River, whose source lies in the Appalachian foothills. This river has always been essential to the province's development, and charming towns and villages have sprung up along its richly fertile banks.

Among these are Fredericton, New Brunswick's pretty capital with its old-fashioned feel, and Saint John, the province's chief port city and industrial centre.

After winding its way through a pastoral landscape, the St. John River empties into the Bay of Fundy, whose often spectacularly steep shores mark the southern border of New Brunswick. An amazing natural phenomenon occurs in this bay twice a day when the highest, most powerful tides in the world surge up onto the shores. They reshape the landscape in sometimes unusual ways, and actually reverse the current of the rivers! Without question, the Bay of Fundy's giant tides constitute one of the greatest natural attractions in the eastern part of the continent.

The bay's shoreline, furthermore, is of incomparable beauty. Be that as it may, New Brunswick's other coast, on the Atlantic Ocean, has charms of its own. It is here, from the border of Nova Scotia to that of Québec, that visitors will find the province's most beautiful sandy beaches, washed by uncommonly warm waters that are perfect for swimming. Most importantly, however, this is the Acadian coast. In towns and villages like Caraquet, Shippagan and Shediac, visitors can learn about Acadia and its warm, hospitable inhabitants.

Finding Your Way Around

By Car

The city of Fredericton grew up on either side of the St. John River, but the downtown area and most tourist attractions lie on the west bank. Visitors will have no difficulty finding their way around the small city centre, which may be explored on foot. The two main downtown arteries are Queen and King Streets – both of which run parallel to the river. Most attractions, as well as many restaurants and businesses, lie on one or the other of these streets.

From St. Stephen to Saint John, and then on to Sussex, the major road is Highway 1. In Sussex, that route connects with Highway 2 which leads to Moncton and Aulac at the border of Nova Scotia where the tour ends. To reach Deer Island, take the exit for St. George from Highway 2, and then follow the signs to the tiny village of Letete. A ferry crosses from there to Deer Island. It is possible to reach Campobello Island from the state of Maine by taking the road from Calais to Lubec. To reach Grand Manan Island, visitors must take the ferry from Blacks Harbour.

Except for a small section between Cape Tourmentine and Shediac, Highway 11 is the main road used on this tour. The highway passes through most of the towns and villages on the coast, skirts around the peninsula, and then runs alongside Baie des Chaleurs to the Québec border. From Newcastle, visitors can cross New Brunswick from east to west on Highway 8 that runs through the Miramichi River valley.

Highway 180 also leads from Bathurst to Saint-Quentin, passing near Mont Carleton, while Highway 17 heads from Campbellton to Saint-Leon-ard (on the St. John River). These two highways also cross the mountainous Appalachian countryside.

By Plane

Fredericton's Airport is located about 16km southeast of the city, on Lincoln Road (☎451-8011). It is served mainly by Air Canada (☎458-8561) and its partner, Air Nova, and Canadian Airlines (☎446-6034 or 800-665-1177) and its partner, Air Atlantic. Visitors can take a taxi to the downtown area.

St. John Airport: About 10km east of the city. A shuttle carries passengers from the large downtown hotels to the airport several times a day. The airport is served mainly by Air Canada (☎632-1517) and its partner, Air Nova, and Canadian Airlines (☎698-2630) and its partner, Air Atlantic.

Moncton Airport: Located on Champlain Street, in Dieppe. The downtown area may be reached by taxi. The airport is served mainly by Air Canada (☎857-1044) and its partner Air Nova, and Canadian Airlines (☎857-0620) and its partner, Air Atlantic.

Bus Station

Fredericton
at the corner of Brunswick and Regent Streets
☎458-6000

Saint John
300 Union St., at the corner of Carmarthen St.
☎658-4700

Moncton
downtown, at 961 Main St.
☎859-5060

Train Stations

Saint John
Station St.
☎800-561-3952

Moncton
Downtown, on the west side, near Main St.
☎859-3917

By Ferry

St. John: A ferry makes the crossing from Saint John to Digby, Nova Scotia three times a day except for Sunday, setting out from a dock on the west bank of the St. John River.
☎636-4048

Grand Manan Island: A ferry makes its way five or six times a day from Blacks Harbour.
☎662-3724

Practical Information

Area Code: **506**

Tourist Information Offices

New Brunswick Tourist Information Centre
☎800-561-0123

Fredericton Tourism
CB 130 Fredericton, N.B.
E3B 4Y7
☎(506) 460-2129
☎888-4768
≈(506) 460-2474
www.city.fredericton.nb.ca

Saint-Jacques
Trans-Canada Highway
☎735-2747

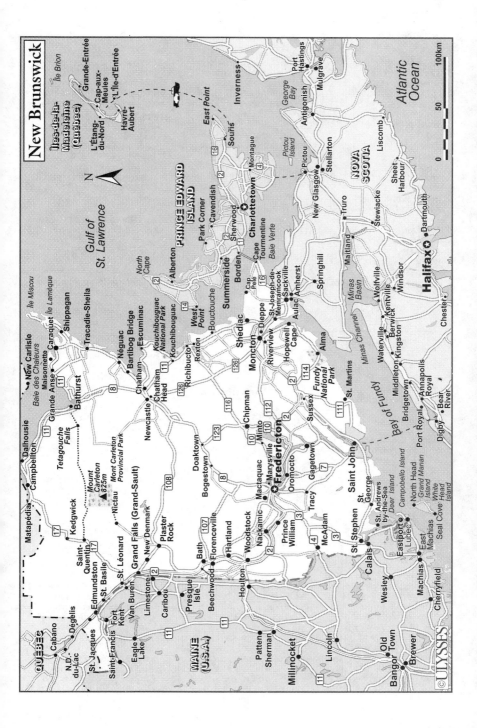

New Brunswick

St. Stephen
King St.
☎466-7390

St. Andrew
Hwy. 1
☎466-4858

Saint John
Hwy. 1
☎658-2940
near the Reversing Falls
☎658-2937
downtown, in the market
☎658-2855

Moncton
Main St., close to Boreview Park
☎856-4399
City Hall, 665 Main St.
☎853-3590
www.greater.moncton.nb.ca

Exploring

★ ★

Fredericton

Fredericton is definitely one of the most precious jewels in the province's crown. As capital of New Brunswick, it has managed to preserve the remarkable historical legacy and architectural harmony handed down to it from the previous century, giving it a subtle elegance and old-fashioned character.

Adorned with magnificent churches and government buildings, as well as large green spaces, some of which lie alongside the St. John River, Fredericton is one of those cities that charms visitors at first sight. Its quiet streets, lined with stately elms, are graced with vast, magnificent Victorian residences.

With their invariably well-tended front gardens, these pretty houses abound in Fredericton and contribute greatly to the city's charm.

The site now occupied by the city was originally an Acadian trading post named Sainte-Anne that was founded in the late 17th century. Acadians lived here until 1783, when they were driven away by arriving Loyalists. The city of Fredericton was founded the following year. It became the provincial capital and was named Fredericton in honour of the second son of George III, Great Britain's king at the time. Over the years, very few industries have set up shop here, opting instead for Saint John. Today, Fredericton's chief employers are the provincial government and the universities.

Downtown

The best place to start off a tour of downtown Fredericton is at the excellent tourist office located inside City Hall *(at the corner of Queen and York Sts., ☎452-9616)*. It also offers very good guided bus tours of the city. The oldest part of the **City hall** ★ *(free admission; mid-May to early Sep, every day 8am to 7:30pm; early Sep to mid-May, by appointment)* was built in 1876 when it included not only the municipal offices and council rooms but also an opera house, a farmer's market and a number of prison cells. The fountain in front of City Hall dates from 1885 while the building's second wing was erected between 1975 and 1977. The Council Chamber, open to the public during summer, makes for an interesting visit.

On the other side of York Street, visitors will see the **courthouse** *(no tours; at the corner of Queen and York Sts.)*, a large stone building erected in the late 1930s. The edifice was used as a high school before being adopted for its present purpose in 1970. Right next to the courthouse stands the **New Brunswick College of Craft and Design** *(no tours)*, the only post-secondary school in Canada to offer a program devoted entirely to training artisans.

A little further, visitors will see the **Military Compound and Guard House** ★ ★ *(free admission; Jun to early Sep, every day 10am to 6pm; at the corner of Queen and Carleton Sts., ☎453-3747)*. Erected in 1827 as replacements for the city's original wooden military buildings, these stone buildings served as barracks for British troops until 1869. One room has been restored to illustrate the building's initial use, and a soldier in period dress serves as a guide. A sundial was reconstructed on the barracks wall. Up until the beginning of this century, residents of Fredericton could check the time by referring to devices such as this one.

Head up Carleton Street to the corner of King Street where **Wilnot United Church** ★ ★ *(at the corner of Carleton and King Sts.)* is located. Its rather austere facade conceals a superb, exceptionally colourful interior abounding in hand-carved woodwork. This church was built in 1852, although the Fredericton Methodist Society, which joined the United Church of Canada in 1925, was founded back in 1791.

The morning fog rising gently on Bonne Bay and the small village of Rocky Harbour, Newfoundland, at the eastern limits of Canada.
- *B. Terry*

The moose is an impressive animal that lives in Canada's forests, especially in marshy areas.
- *Jerg Kroener*

The Atlantic puffin can be found in many different places on Canada's east coast and has a distinctive beak that earned it the nickname "parakeet of the sea."
- *P. Quittemelle*

There are plenty of small, friendly fishing ports in the Maritimes, such as this one in Little River, Nova Scotia. Of course, the forest is never too far away.
- *K. Cooke*

Despite its small size, Prince Edward Island is covered from coast to coast by imposing fields that tickle the eye with their striking colours.
- *P. Quittemelle*

The Acadian coast is well known for its small, charming villages scattered about along the coast. Located on the shores of the Northumberland strait, Cap-Lumière is certainly no exception to this rule.
- *Roger Michel*

Confederation Bridge measures 13km and connects Canada's smallest province, Prince Edward Island, to New Brunswick, on the continent. - *P. Quittemelle*

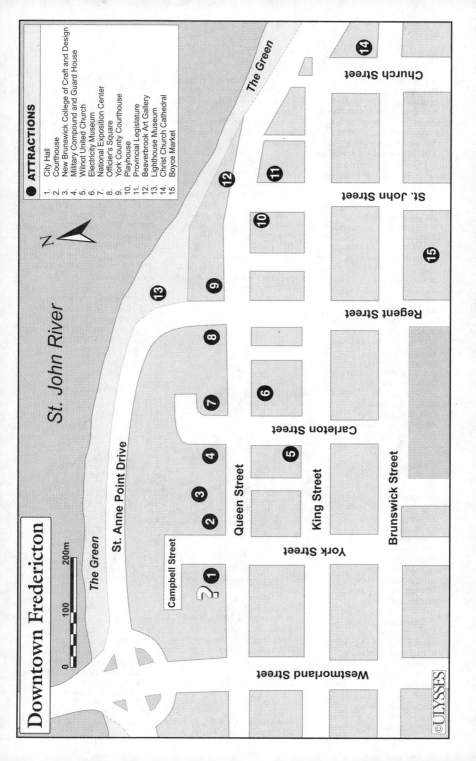

Downtown Fredericton

St. John River

ATTRACTIONS

1. City Hall
2. Courthouse
3. New Brunswick College of Craft and Design
4. Military Compound and Guard House
5. Wilmot United Church
6. Electricity Museum
7. National Exposition Center
8. Officer's Square
9. York County Courthouse
10. Playhouse
11. Provincial Legislature
12. Beaverbrook Art Gallery
13. Lighthouse Museum
14. Christ Church Cathedral
15. Boyce Market

N

The Green

St. Anne Point Drive

Campbell Street

Queen Street

York Street

King Street

Carleton Street

Regent Street

Church Street

St. John Street

Brunswick Street

Westmorland Street

The Green

0   100   200m

© ULYSSES

A beautiful Second-Empire-style building erected in 1881 houses the **New Brunswick Sports Hall of Fame** *(free admission, early Jun to early Sep, every day 10am to 6pm; early Sep to Jun, Mon to Fri noon to 4pm; ☎453-3747)*, dedicated to New Brunswick's finest athletes.

Also on Queen Street, **Officer's Square ★★** *($2; Jun 1 to Sep 30, Tues to Sat 10am to 5pm, Sun noon to 5pm; rest of the year, Tue to Sat 10am to 5pm; 571 Queen St., near Regent St., ☎455-6041)* is an attractive park. Facing it is the building once used as officers' quarters, erected in two stages : from 1839 to 1840 and in 1851. Its bow-shaped stone columns, railings and iron stairs are typical of architecture designed by royal engineers during the colonial era. The former quarters now house the **York-Sunbury Museum**, devoted to the province's military and domestic history.

Continue along Queen Street to the pretty **York County Courthouse ★** *(no tours; Queen St., after Regent St.)*, erected in 1855. In those years, there was a market on the ground floor. Today, the building houses the services of the Ministry of Justice as well as a courtroom.

A little further along Queen Street, on the opposite side of the street, stands the **Playhouse** *(Queen St., at the corner of St. John St., ticket sales: ☎506-458-8344)*, built in 1964. Since 1969, it has served as home base for the only English-speaking theatre company in the province,

The New Brunswick Theatre. Construction of the Playhouse was financed by Lord Beaverbrook, a British newspaper tycoon who lived in New Brunswick as a child.

Not far from the Playhouse, visitors will see the **Provincial Legislature ★★** *(free admission; Jun to Aug, every day 9am to 7pm; late Aug to early Jun, Mon to Fri 9am to 4pm; Queen St., at the corner of St. John St., ☎453-2527)*, seat of the provincial government since 1882. Inside, an impressive spiral wooden staircase leads to the library that contains over 35,000 volumes, some of which are very rare.

Legislature

Of particular interest are the Assembly Chamber, where the members of Parliament gather, and the portraits hang of King George III and Queen Charlotte, by British painter Joshua Reynolds.

Across from the Legislative Building stands the **Beaverbrook Art Gallery ★★★** *($3; Jun and*

Sep, Mon to Fri 9am to 6pm, Sat and Sun 10am to 5pm, guided tours at 11am; Queen St., ☎458-8545), another of Lord Beaverbrook's gifts to the city of Fredericton. The gallery houses, among other things, a superb collection of works by highly renowned British painters as well as a number of other lovely canvases by Canadian artists such as Cornelius Krieghoff and James Wilson Morrice. Without question, however, the most impressive piece on display is Catalan artist Salvador Dali's *Santiago el Grande*.

After touring the fascinating Beaverbrook Art Gallery, summer visitors can enjoy a delightful stroll on Fredericton's splendid **Green**.

Stretching 4km alongside the St. John River, it enables both walkers and cyclists to explore the banks of the river. The Green contributes greatly to the quality of life in the city. Visitors can stop at the **Lighthouse Museum** *($2; May to Jun, Mon to Fri 10am to 4pm, Sat and Sun 10am to 9pm, Jul to*

Aug every day 10am to 9pm; ☎459-2515) which presents a historical exhibit.

Take Queen Street to Church Street in order to visit the Gothic style **Christ Church Cathedral ★★** *(at the corner of Queen St. and Church St., ☎506-450-8500)* whose construction, completed in 1853, was largely due to the efforts of Fredericton's first Anglican bishop, John Medley.

University, a Catholic institution originally located in Chatham, on the Miramichi River. Together, the two universities have 8,000 students. This is a wonderful spot from which to view the city below.

Christ Church Cathedral

From the cathedral, take Brunswick Street to Regent Street. On the left-hand side stands **Boyce Market** *(Sat 6am to 1pm; 665 George St., at the corner of Brunswick and Regent Sts., ☎506-451-1815)*, a public market where farmers, artisans and artists sell their products every Saturday morning. Right next door, on the left side of Brunswick Street, lies Fredericton's **Old Loyalist Cemetery**. It was here that the most notable figures in Fredericton's early history were buried from 1787 to 1878.

Outside Downtown

The **University of New Brunswick** *(at the end of University St.)*, founded in 1785 by newly arrived Loyalists, is made up of several different edifices. Its arts building is the oldest university building still in use in Canada.

On the same site, visitors will also find **St. Thomas**

Odell Park ★ *(Rockwood Ave., northwest of the city)* covers over 175ha and includes 16km of trails. This beautifully preserved, peaceful natural area has been enhanced by the addition of an enclosure for deer, duck ponds, picnic tables and a play area for children.

Saint-Jacques

This is the first village that many travellers (or at least those arriving from Québec) will encounter on their tour of New Brunswick. There's no coincidence that Saint-Jacques is home to one of the province's largest tourist-information centres as well as a provincial park, **Les Jardins de la République**. It has campsites, a pool and play area for children as well as hiking and cycling trails. There are also two major attractions nearby.

The **New Brunswick Botanical Garden ★★** *($3; Jun to Sep; Hwy. 2, Exit 8, ☎735-2699 or 735-2525)*, destined to become one of the region's greatest draws, is worth visiting for a number of reasons. Some 75,000 plants have been distributed over a well laid-out area of 7ha that offers a lovely panoramic view of the region's gentle, wooded valleys. The garden's designers had the clever idea of installing an unobtrusive sound system, enabling visitors to explore the garden with the music of Bach, Chopin or Mozart in the background.

The **Antique Automobile Museum ★** *($2.50; late May to mid-Sep; right beside the Garden, ☎735-2525)* grew up around the private collection of Edmundston resident Melvin Louden. It displays a lovely selection of antique cars, some of which are very rare nowadays, including the Bricklin – the only automobile made in New Brunswick – and the 1933 Rolls Royce Phantom.

Grand Falls (Grand-Sault)

A charming little town on the banks of the St. John, at the point where the river plunges 23m, Grand Falls is a dynamic, engaging community whose mostly French-speaking population has Québécois and Acadian roots. This pretty spot was frequented by the Malecite First Nations for many years before becoming a British military post in 1791. The city was finally established in 1896. In addition to its attractive location, Grand Falls has a charming town centre. Its wide boulevard, flanked by low houses facing right onto the street, gives it a slightly midwestern character. It is worth noting that Grand Falls is the only town in Canada with an officially bilingual name–Grand Falls-Grand Sault. With its green valleys, the surrounding region, known for its potatoes, makes for a lovely outing.

The magnificent **waterfall** ★★ that inspired the town's name is the largest and most impressive in Atlantic Canada. The waters of the St. John plunge 23m, then rush for about 2km through a gorge whose sides reach as high as 70m. At the far end of the gorge, the turbulent water has eroded the rock, creating cavities known here as "wells," since water stays in them after the river rises. Visitors can start off their tour by dropping by the **Malobiannah Centre** *(on Chemin Madawaska, alongside the falls)*, that is both an interpretive centre and a regional tourist-information centre. From here, there is a splendid view of the falls and the hydroelectric dam. A footpath heading out from the centre makes it possible to observe the falls and the gorge from all different angles. At the **Centre La Rochelle** *($1; Centennial Park)*, on the opposite bank right in the centre of town, there is a staircase that leads down to the river bed, offering a better view of the gorge, the wells and the waterfall.

Hartland

Home town of Richard Hatfield, the province's eccentric former prime minister, Hartland is an adorable village typical of the St. John River Valley. It is known for its remarkable **covered bridge** ★★, the world's longest. Stretching 390m across the river, the structure was built in 1899 at a time when simply covering a bridge made its skeleton last up to seven times longer. Today there are more covered bridges in New Brunswick than anywhere else on Earth. Visitors who would like to stop for a picnic and admire the local scenery will find an attractive park on the west bank of the river.

Prince William

A wonderful open-air museum covering 120ha on the banks of the St. John, **Kings Landing** ★★★ *($10; Jun to mid-Oct, every day 10am to 5pm; along the Trans-Canada Highway in Prince-William, ☎363-4999, ₌363-4989)* is a reproduction of an early 19th-century Loyalist village. It includes more than 20 historic buildings and about 30,000 objects that help illuminate the area's past, including furniture, clothing and tools.

To enliven the atmosphere, there are people dressed in period clothing, who perform the daily tasks of 19th-century villagers, as well as answering visitors' questions. There is no more pleasant and effective means of learning about Loyalist history than a visit to Kings Landing, the best museum on the subject.

Gagetown

After winding its way through the fields of a prosperous farming region, the little road heading out of Oromocto leads to Gagetown, a tiny village on the banks of the majestic St. John. Everything here —the church, the general store, the handful of houses, the very location – is so pretty that you'd think it is straight out of a fairy tale. This peaceful spot has retained the old-fashioned character of a Loyalist village as well as an atmosphere that couldn't possibly be more Anglo-Saxon. With all that charm, it is hardly surprising that each year Gagetown attracts artists seeking inspiration, as well as vacationers looking for a place to relax. Sailors stop here, too, tying their yachts or sailboats to the village wharf.

Covered Bridge

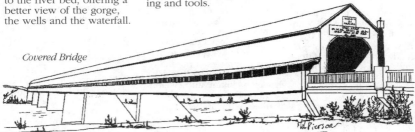

Algonquin

Although Gagetown is small, it nevertheless boasts several bed and breakfasts, a very good inn, an art gallery and several craft shops. There is also a free ferry service to the other side of the river.

The **Tilley House** ★ *($2; mid-Jun to mid-Sep, every day 10am to 5pm; Front St., ☎488-2966)* was built in 1786, making it one of the oldest residences in New Brunswick. It now houses the Queens County Museum, which displays all sorts of objects relating to local history and the life of the house's most illustrious owner, Samuel Leonard Tilley, one of the Fathers of Canadian Confederation (1867).

At the **Loomcrofter Studio** ★ *(south of the village, near the school, ☎488-2400)*, visitors will find the studios of various designers and weavers of tartan cloth. The building itself is one of the oldest in the St. John River Valley.

St. Stephen

The most important border town in Atlantic Canada, St. Stephen is a small, lively community that was founded in 1784 by American colonists wishing to remain loyal to the British crown after the Revolutionary War. Today, ironically, St. Stephen and

Calais, its twin town in the state of Maine, could easily be mistaken for a single town if it weren't for the St. Croix River which forms a natural border. This lively community is celebrated on both sides of the border each year during the **International Festival**, which takes place at the end of August. In early August, another festival, this time dedicated to **chocolate**, is held only in St. Stephen, which has the distinction of being the birthplace of the chocolate bar, invented here in 1910 by the Ganong company. The ever successful **Ganong Chocolatier** *(73 Milltown Blvd., ☎465-5611)* shop is a must for anyone with a sweet tooth.

The **Charlotte County Museum** *(free admission; Jun to Aug, Mon to Sat 9:30am to 4:30pm; 443 Milltown Blvd., ☎466-3295)* is set up inside a Second Empire style residence built in 1864 by a prosperous local businessman. It now houses a collection of objects related to local history, especially the period when St. Stephen and the small neighbouring villages were known for shipbuilding.

The **Crocker Hill Garden & Studio** *(by reservation only; 2.4km east of St. Stephen, on Ledge Rd., ☎466-4251)* is a magnificent garden looking out on the St. Croix River.

★★

St. Andrews by-the-Sea

The most famous vacation spot in Southern New Brunswick, St. Andrews is a lovely village facing the bay. It has managed to benefit from its popularity by highlighting its astonishingly rich architectural heritage. Like many other communities in the area, St. Andrews was founded by Loyalists in 1783. Then in enjoyed a period of great prosperity during the 19th century as a centre for shipbuilding and the exportation of billets. A number of the opulent houses flanking its streets, particularly **Water Street** ★, date back to that golden era. At the end of the century, St. Andrews's began welcoming affluent visitors who came here to drink in the invigorating sea air. St. Andrews' new vocation was clearly established in 1889 with the construction of the magnificent **Algonquin** ★★ hotel on a hill overlooking the village. In addition to the picturesque charm of its many historic buildings and its location alongside the bay, with its giant tides, St. Andrews now boasts a wide selection of accommodations and fine restaurants, numerous shops and a famous golfcourse. All of this makes

St. Andrews by-the-Sea a perfect place to stay during a tour of the region and its islands.

Erected in 1820, **Sheriff Andrews's House** ★ *(free admission; late Jun to early Sep 9:30am to 4:30pm; 63 King St.,* ☎*453-2324)* is one of the town's best-preserved homes from that era. It was built by Elusha Shelton Andrews, sheriff of Charlotte County and son of distinguished Loyalist Reverend Samuel Andrews. Since 1986, it has belonged to the provincial government, which has turned it into a museum. Guides in period costume explain the sheriff's life and times.

A sumptuous 19th century neoclassical residence, the **Ross Memorial Museum** ★ *(free admission, late May to early Oct, Tue to Sat 10am to 4:30pm, Sun 1:30pm to 4:30pm; 188 Montague St.,* ☎*529-1824)* contains an antique collection, that Henry Phipps Ross and Sarah Juliette Ross, assembled over their lifetime. Living in St-andrews from 1902 until they dies, they had a passion for travelling and antiques. They acquired some magnificent pieces of Chinese porcelain and other now priceless imported objects as well as some lovely furniture made in New Brunswick.

There are several remarkable churches in St. Andrews. The most flamboyant is **Greenock Church** ★★ *(at the corner of Montague and Edward Sts.)*, a Presbyterian church completed in 1824. Its most interesting feature is its pulpit, which a good part is made of Honduran mahogany.

Until very recently, the **St. Andrews Blockhouse** *(on the west end of Water St.)*, a national historic site, was the last surviving blockhouse from the War of 1812. Unfortunately, it was damaged by fire, but necessary repairs are being made. Pretty **Centennial Park** lies opposite.

The **Sunbury Shores Arts & Nature Centre** *(139 Water St.,* ☎*529-3386)* houses a small art gallery where visitors can admire the work of New Brunswick artists. The centre is better known, however, for its summer courses on art, crafts and nature, for groups of children and adults.

At the **Huntsman Marine Science Centre and Aquarium** ★★ *($4.50; Jul to Oct, 10am to 4pm; Brandy Cove Rd.;* ☎*529-1202)*, visitors can learn about the bay's natural treasures. Several animal species may be observed here, including seals who are fed every day at 11am and 4pm. There is also a touch-tank where visitors can touch various live species of shellfish. This is an important research centre.

At the beginning of the 19th century, the **Ministers Island Historic Site** ★ *($5 per car includes tour of house; Jun to mid-Oct; Mowat Drive Rd., take Bar Rd. only at low tide until the end)* was the property of Reverend Samuel. It was purchased in 1890 by Sir William Van Horne, a Montréal resident famous for building the Canadian Pacific Railway – the first railroad linking Montréal to Vancouver. On this large estate, Van Horne erected an immense 50-room summer home. Minister's Island is only accessible at low tide. To arrange a visit, contact the tourist information office *(*☎*529-3000 or 529-5081)*.

At the **Atlantic Salmon Centre** *($4; Apr to Oct 9am to 5pm; Chamcook, 8km from St. Andrews on Rte. 127,* ☎*529-4581)*, visitors can learn about the life cycle of Atlantic salmon, most importantly by viewing the fish in its natural environment through a window.

Deer Island

After cruising through a scattering of little islands covered with birds, the free ferry from Letete lands at Deer Island, which features wooded landscape, untouched beaches and tiny fishing villages. Three hours before high tide each day, visitors can view an interesting natural phenomenon from the southern point of the island – one of the largest whirlpools in the world, known locally as the **Old Sow** ★. In summertime, a private ferry makes the crossing between Deer Island and Campobello Island about every hour.

Campobello Island

Campobello, the beloved island of former U.S. president Franklin D. Roosevelt (1882-1945), is a good place for fans of history and the great outdoors to unwind. People come here to enjoy the lovely untouched beaches, go cycling on the quiet roads or walk along the well-maintained trails that follow the shoreline. On the eastern tip, the picturesque lighthouse at **East Quoddy Head** ★ occupies a magnificent site on the bay from which it is sometimes possible to spot whales and other sea mammals. In the early 19th century, Campobello's beauty

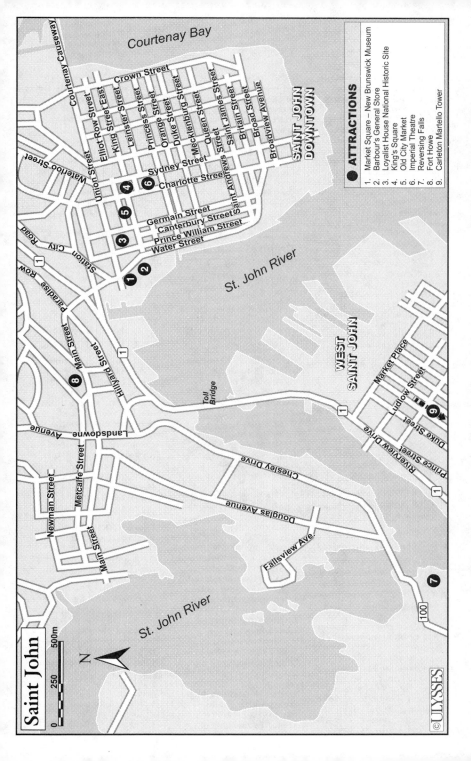

Saint John

ATTRACTIONS

1. Market Square – New Brunswick Museum
2. Barbour's General Store
3. Loyalist House National Historic Site
4. King's Square
5. Old City Market
6. Imperial Theatre
7. Reversing Falls
8. Fort Howe
9. Carleton Martello Tower

Courtenay Bay

Crown Street
Union Street
Elliot Row Street
King Street
Leinster Street
Princess Street
Orange Street
Duke Street
Mecklenburg Street
Queen Street
Saint James Street
Britain Street
Broad Street
Broadview Avenue

SAINT JOHN DOWNTOWN

Waterloo Street
Sydney Street
Charlotte Street
Germain Street
Canterbury Street
Prince William Street
Water Street
Saint Andrews Street
Station
City Road

St. John River

WEST SAINT JOHN

Market Place
Ludlow Street
Duke Street
Riverview Drive
Prince Street

Paradise Row
Main Street
Hillyard Street
Landsdowne Avenue
Metcalfe Street
Newman Street
Main Street

Toll Bridge

Chesley Drive
Douglas Avenue
Fallsview Ave.

St. John River

N

0   250   500m

© ULYSSES

began to attract the attention of wealthy families living in the northeastern cities of the United States who built lovely summer homes here. The most famous of these families was that of Franklin D. Roosevelt, whose father, James, purchased 1.6ha on the island in 1883. Franklin himself, and then his own family, spent most of his summers here from 1883 to 1921, the year he contracted polio. He returned on several later occasions to visit his friends on the island while serving as President of the United States. Although Campobello lies within Canada, it is most easily accessible from the border town of Lubec, Maine. During the summer months, a private ferry also shuttles hourly between Deer Island and Campobello.

Roosevelt House

Roosevelt-Campobello International Park ★★ *(free admission; late May to early Oct, 10am to 6pm; Rte. 774,* ☎ *752-2922)* is a joint project of the Canadian and U.S. governments. It was launched in 1964 with the aim of increasing public awareness of Roosevelt's special attachment to Campobello Island and his magnificent property there. The visitor's centre shows a short film on Roosevelt's sojourns on the island. Afterward, visitors can tour the extraordinary **Roosevelt**

House, most of whose furnishings belonged to the former U.S. president. Then you can stop at the **Prince House**, the site of the **James Roosevelt House** and the **Hubbard House**. The park also includes a beautiful natural area, south of the visitor's centre, where lovely hiking trails have been cleared along the shore.

Grand Manan Island

For many years, Grand Manan's 275-odd bird species and unique rock formations mainly attracted scientists, including the famous James Audubon in the early 19th century. More recently, however, Grand Manan has begun to benefit from the current ecotourism craze since the island obviously has a lot to offer nature lovers.

It is a pleasant place to explore by bicycle and even better on foot, thanks to the excellent network of trails running alongside the jagged shoreline with its often spectacular scenery. Without question, one of the most picturesque places on the island is the lighthouse known as **Swallowtail Light ★**, which stands at the tip of a peninsula at North Head. From here, whales can regularly be seen swimming off the shores of the island. Grand Manan also features a **museum** *(Grand Harbour,*

☎ *662-3524)* and serves as the point of departure for numerous whale-watching excursions and expeditions to **Machias Seal Island ★**, a remarkable bird sanctuary.

The island has several lighthouses, beaches and great bird-watching spots. Travellers have a choice of several B&Bs as well as an excellent **campground** *(The Anchorage,* ☎ *662-7022).*

To reach Grand Manan Island, visitors must take the ferry from Blacks Harbour *(☎662-3724),* which makes five or six trips a day.

Saint John

Saint John, New Brunswick's largest city, occupies a hilly area on either side of the St. John River, at the point where it flows into the Bay of Fundy. A perfect example of the old, industrial port cities in the eastern part of North America, it has a unique, slightly mysterious charm. Lofty cranes and warehouses line the docks, that look strangely like wooden fences rising high out of the river at low tide. To add to its mysterious character, Saint John is often blanketed with a thick fog that can envelop the city at any moment, and then disappear just as quickly. The growth of the city's industries is due largely to its port which is ice-free all year long.

The site itself was scouted out for the first time on June 24, 1604 by explorer Samuel de Champlain, who christened the river St. John (Saint-Jean) in honour of the patron saint of that day. Later, in 1631, Charles de La Tour established a trading post here. The city's history didn't really start, however, until 1783 under the English regime. From May 10 to May 18 of that year, about 2,000 Loyalists landed in Saint John, seeking a fresh start in life after the defeat of British forces by American revolutionaries. More arrived before winter, doubling the population of Saint John.

The city then absorbed a large number of immigrants, most from the British Isles. In those years, Partridge Island, in the port, was Canada's chief point of entry and quarantine station for immigrants. Today, Saint John has a higher concentration of Irish-Canadians than any other city in the country. It is a pleasant place to visit, particularly in mid-July during **Loyalist Days** which commemorate the arrival of the Loyalists in 1783. In August, the excellent **By-the-Sea Festival** celebrates the performing arts while the **Franco-Frolic**, held in June, honours Acadian culture and traditions.

Downtown

Downtown Saint John ★★, with its narrow streets lined with historic buildings and houses, lies on a hill on the east side of the river. A tour of the area usually starts at **Market Square**, laid out a little more than a decade ago as part of an effort to revitalize the city centre. The square includes a shopping mall, a convention centre, several restaurants and a hotel that combines modern construction with 19th century buildings. An excellent **tourist information office** is located at the entrance to Market Square. The **New Brunswick Museum** ★ *($6; year-round,*

Mon to Fri 9am to 9pm, Sat 10am to 6pm, Sun noon to 5pm; Market Sq., ☎643-2300, ⇒643-6081) was recently moved and is now also located in Market Square. As the oldest museum in Canada, it is devoted not only to the work of New Brunswick artists, but also to the history of the province's inhabitants – Aboriginals, Acadians, Loyalists, and others. The permanent collection features also certain imported objects, including pieces of Chinese porcelain.

On the south side of Market Square stands **Barbour's General Store** *($2; mid May to mid Oct; ☎658-2939)*, a small brick building displaying consumer goods typically available in this type of shop during the 19th century. Guided tours of the city are offered from here. Visitors can head up Union Street to the **Loyalist House National Historic Site** ★ *($3; mid-May to mid-Sep; 120 Union St., ☎652-3590)*. Built in the first decade of the 19th century, this is a very simple house decorated with elegant period furniture. Union Street later intersects with Charlotte Street where visitors can turn right to reach **King's Square** ★ a pretty urban park marking the centre of Saint John. The paths in the park are laid out in the pattern of the Union Jack what better way for the inhabitants of Saint John to express their attachment to their mother country? Standing opposite the park on Charlotte Street is the **Old City Market** ★ *(free admission; year-round, Mon to Thu 7:30am to 6pm, Fri 7:30am to 7pm, Sat 7:30am to 5pm; 47 Charlotte St., ☎658-2820)*, dating back to 1876, where shoppers can still purchase fresh produce from local

fai
du
tha
use
cor
disl
the
the .... **imperial Theatre** ★ *(24 King Sq. South, ☎634-8355 or 674-4111)*. Built in 1913 and restored in 1994, it is dedicated to the performing arts.

The **Aitken Bicentennial Exhibition Centre** *(free admission; Jun to Sep, every day 10am to 5pm; Sep to Jun, Tue to Sun 11:30am to 4:30pm; 20 Hazen Ave., ☎633-4870)* presents exhibits specifically designed to teach children about various facets of science in an exciting way.

Outside Downtown

The **Reversing Falls** ★★ *(on Rte. 100, at the river)* is a unique natural phenomenon that occurs twice a day at high tide. The current of the river at this point drops 4m at low tide, reversing at high tide when the water level of the bay is several metres higher than that of the river. This countercurrent is felt as far upriver as Fredericton.

For an excellent **view** ★ of the city, head to the site of **Fort Howe** *(Main St., ☎658-2090)*. At the same location, there is a wooden blockhouse that was built in Halifax and moved here in 1777 to protect the port of Saint John in the event of a U.S. attack.

The **Carleton Martello Tower** ★★ *($2.50; Jun to Oct 9am to 5pm; on the west bank, Whipple St., ☎636-4011)* is a circular tower built during the War of 1812 to protect the port

.s. attacks. It was used as a command ost for the Canadian army during the Second World War. Guides in 19th-century dress explain the history of both the tower and the city of Saint John. From the top, visitors can enjoy a magnificent panoramic view of the city, the port and the bay.

If Saint John were a person, **Rockwood Park** *(main entry on Mt. Pleasant Ave.)* would be its lungs. Covering 890ha, it is Canada's largest city park. All sorts of outdoor activities may be enjoyed here, including hiking, swimming, fishing, canoeing and pedal-boating. A number of other activities are organized just for children. In the park's northern section, is the **Cherry Brook Zoo** *($3.25; open all year 10am to nightfall; Sandy Point Rd., in the north part of Rockwood Park, ☎634-1440)*, the only zoo in the Maritimes featuring exotic animals. About 100 or so different species may be found here.

For many years, **Partridge Island** ★ *($10; May to Nov; from the port of St. John, for information ☎693-2598)* was the main point of entry for immigrants coming to Canada from the British Isles and the European continent. Between 1785 and 1942, it was the transition point and quarantine station for some three million immigrants who then either settled in Saint John or, more commonly, elsewhere in Canada or the United States. About 2,000 of these individuals died here. Having survived the often difficult journey across the Atlantic, they never had the chance to see anything beyond Partridge Island. They were buried in one of the six cemeteries located here. The island is also the site of New Brunswick's oldest lighthouse as well as a historical museum.

St. Martins

St. Martins is one of New Brunswick's best-kept treasures. An idyllic fishing village looking out on the Bay of Fundy, St. Martins is adorned with numerous houses built in the 19th century when it was known as a major producer of large wooden ships.

Today, the village is very picturesque with local fishing boats moored in its little port.

It also has two covered bridges, one of which leads to the famous **echo caves** ★ – cavities created in local cliffs by the action of the tides in the Bay of Fundy. Nature lovers will find long, untouched beaches in St. Martins, as well as attractive **Lions Park** which is a good place to take a walk or go swimming. As home to two of the province's best inns, the village also has something to offer connoisseurs of fine cuisine. Finally, to enjoy a **spectacular view** ★ of the local red cliffs, head to the **Quaco Head light-**

house, located several kilometres west of St. Martins.

Hopewell Cape

Hopewell Cape's rock formations, nicknamed the **flower pots** ★★, are one of the province's most famous attractions. All by themselves, they symbolize the massive force of the tides in the bay. At high tide, they look like small wooded islands right off the coast. As the waters recede at low tide, they expose lofty rock formations sculpted by the endless coming and going of the tides. When the tide is at its lowest, visitors can explore the sea bed. Numerous water sports are organized from Hopewell Rock.

Moncton

Due to its location in the heart of Atlantic Canada, as well as its qualified, bilingual workforce, Moncton is now New Brunswick's rising star. Up until the Acadians were expelled from the region, this site on the banks of the Petitcodiac River was a small Acadian trading post. Colonists from the United States then settled here and founded the city which thrived in the mid-19th century as a ship

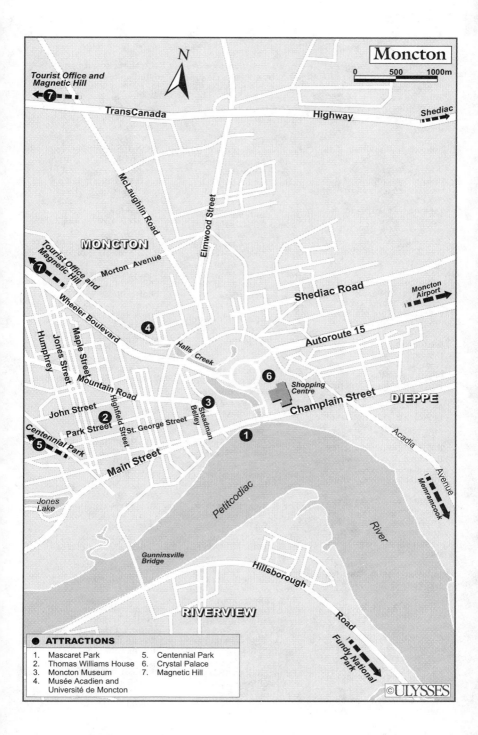

Moncton

0   500   1000m

N

Tourist Office and
Magnetic Hill
7

TransCanada   Highway   Shediac

McLaughlin Road

Elmwood Street

MONCTON

Morton Avenue

Shediac Road

Moncton
Airport

Tourist Office and
Magnetic Hill
7

Wheeler Boulevard

4

Autoroute 15

Halls Creek

Humphrey

Jones Street

Maple Street

Mountain Road

6

Shopping
Centre

Champlain Street

DIEPPE

John Street

Highfield Street

3

Steadman

Belley

Acadia

2

Park Street

St. George Street

Centennial Park

5

1

Main Street

Jones
Lake

Petitcodiac

River

Avenue
Memramcook

Gunninsville
Bridge

Hillsborough

RIVERVIEW

Road

Fundy National
Park

● ATTRACTIONS

1. Mascaret Park
2. Thomas Williams House
3. Moncton Museum
4. Musée Acadien and
    Université de Moncton

5. Centennial Park
6. Crystal Palace
7. Magnetic Hill

©ULYSSES

building centre and later as a transportation hub for the Intercolonial Railway. The economy is now based chiefly on commerce and the service sector.

For Acadians, who constitute 35% of the population, Moncton offers a unique opportunity to face the challenges and savour the pleasures of city living. Despite their minority status, they have made Moncton a base for their most important economic and social institutions and the home of the province's only French-speaking university, the Université de Moncton. Ironically, the city and by extension the university were named after officer Robert Monkton, commander of the British forces during the capture of Fort Beauséjour in 1755, that heralded the fall of the French Empire in North America.

Moncton is now the centre of Acadian rebirth and the vibrant energy in the air here is due in good part to the entrepreneurial spirit that characterizes today's Acadians. Moncton's immediate surroundings include such varied communities as **Dieppe**, most of whose inhabitants are Acadian, and the very English-speaking **Riverview**. An excellent time to visit the city is in early July when the atmosphere is enlivened by the **Moncton Jazz Festival**.

The Petitcodiac River, known locally as the Chocolate River because of the colour of its waters, empties and then fills back up again twice a day in accordance with the tides in the Bay of Fundy. The rise in the river's water level is always preceded by an interesting phenomenon

known as a **tidal bore ★**, a wave up to several dozen centimetres high that flows upriver. The best spot to watch this wave is at **Bore Park** (downtown on Main St.). To know what time of the day the tidal bore will occur during your stay, contact Moncton's tourist information office (at the corner of Main St., facing Bore Park, ☎856-4399).

The Second Empire style **Thomas Williams House ★** (free admission; May, Mon, Wed and Fri 10am to 3pm; Jun, Tue to Sat 9am to 5pm, Sun 1pm to 5pm; Jul and Aug, Mon to Sat 9am to 5pm, Sun 1pm to 5pm; Sep, Mon, Wed and Fri 10am to 5pm; 103 Park St., ☎857-0590) is a 12-room residence built in 1883 for the family of Thomas Williams who then an accountant for the Intercolonial Railway. His heirs then lived here for nearly a century. Today, the house is a museum where visitors can learn about the lifestyle of the Moncton bourgeoisie during the Victorian era. Back in 1883, Moncton was no more than a tiny village, and the house lay outside its boundaries in the middle of the countryside.

The **Moncton Museum ★** (free admission; Jul and Aug, Mon to Sat 9am to 4:30pm, Sun 1pm to 5pm; 20 Mountain Rd., ☎856-4383, ≈856-4355) houses a lovely collection of objects linked to the history of the city and its surrounding area. During summertime, the museum often presents large-scale temporary exhibits. The sumptuous facade was salvaged from the city's former city hall. Moncton's oldest building, dating back to 1821 and very well preserved, stands right next door.

The **Musée Acadien ★** (free admission; Jun to Sep, Mon to Fri 10am to 5pm, Sat and Sun 1pm to 5pm; Oct to May, Tue to Fri 1pm to 4:30pm, Sat and Sun 1pm to 4pm; Université de Moncton, Clément Cormier Bldg., ☎858-4088) displays over 30,000 objects, including a permanent collection of Acadian artifacts dating from 1604 up to the last century. The museum was founded in Memramcook in 1886 by Père Camille Lefebvre of the Collège Saint-Joseph. It was moved to its present location in 1965. In the same building as the museum, visitors will find the **Centre d'Art de l'Université de Moncton ★★** where works by Acadian artists are exhibited. On the west side of the city, **Centennial Park** (St. George Blvd.) is a place where the whole family can come to relax any time of the year. The area includes hiking trails, a small beach, tennis courts and a playground. Canoe and pedal-boat rentals are also available.

The **Magnetic Hill ★** ($2 per car; west of Moncton, Exit 88 from the Trans-Canada Hwy.) is an intriguing optical illusion that gives people the impression that their car is climbing a slope. The staff ask drivers to stop their engines at what seems to be the bottom of a very steep hill. Then, as if by miracle, the car seems to climb the slope. This remarkable illusion is a must for families. Other family attractions have sprung up around Magnetic Hill, including a park, a zoo, a mini-train, a go-kart track, a miniature golf course, and most of all, the superb **Magic Mountain ★** water park. Here you will also find shops, restaurants and a hotel.

Saint-Joseph-de-Memramcook

A rural town in the pretty Memramcook valley, Saint-Joseph is of great symbolic importance to the Acadian people. This is the only region on the Bay of Fundy where Acadians still live on the farmlands they occupied before the Deportation. It thus serves as a bridge between pre- and post-Deportation Acadia. Collège Saint-Joseph, where the Acadian elite was educated for many years, was founded here in 1864. The college hosted the first Acadian national convention in 1881. At the **Historic Site of the Lefebvre Monument** ★ *($2; Jun to early Sep, everyday 9am to 5pm; Monument Lefebvre,* ☎758-9783), visitors can learn about Acadian history by viewing an exhibition on the key factors and pivotal moments leading to the survival of the Acadian people.

Sackville

A subtle aura of affluence and a unique awareness of the past emanate from Sackville whose beautiful residences lie hidden behind the stately trees that flank its streets. The city is home to **Mount Allison University**, a small, highly reputable institution whose lovely buildings stand on beautiful, verdant plots of land in the centre of town. On campus, visitors will find the **Owens Art Gallery** ★ *(on campus,* ☎364-2574) which displays a large collection of paintings by New Brunswick artists, including several works by master Alex Colville.

Waterfowl Park ★★ *(free admission; every day until nightfall; entrance on East Main St.)* is an interpretive centre focussing on the plant and animal life in salt-water marshes. Thanks to 2km of trails and wooden footbridges, visitors can enter a world of unexpected richness and diversity. In addition to being exceptionally informative, this park is a wonderful place to relax.

Aulac

After British forces captured Fort Beauséjour in 1755, the Deportation, a tragic event in Acadian history, was initiated in Aulac. Built in 1751, Fort Beauséjour occupied a strategic location on Chignecto Bay, on the border of the French and British colonial empires. The **Fort Beauséjour National Historic Site** ★ *(free admission; mid-May to mid-Oct; Hwy. 2, Exit 550A,* ☎876-2443) includes an interpretive centre that deals with Acadian history and the Deportation. Visitors can also stroll around several of the remaining fortifications of the star-shaped structure. The view of the bay and of New Brunswick and Nova Scotia is excellent from here.

★
Cap-Pelé

Cap-Pelé offers visitors a wonderful opportunity to discover the fascinating world of fishing. Founded at the end of the 18th century, this Acadian community still depends on the riches of the sea for its survival. The village is also home to *boucanières* (smokehouses), barn-like buildings where fish is

smoked before being exported. The 30-odd *boucanières* in the Cap-Pelé region provide 95% of the world's smoked herring.

Beautiful **Plage de l'Aboiteau** ★★ is not far from Cap-Pelé. This splendid beach, located near a fishing port, is ideal for swimming and much less crowded than Parlee Beach Provincial Park. It is hidden from the road by an embankment of boulder and rock for which the beach was named. An «aboiteau" is a type of seawall that protects coastal farmland; it is a word primarily used in Acadia). There are also two other beautiful beaches in the Cap-Pelé area: Gagnon Beach and Sandy Beach.

The region occupies a little plateau that is almost completely denuded of vegetation and offers lovely views of the ocean. Further along the same road, visitors will reach **Barachois**. In the centre of the village stands the oldest wooden Acadian church in the Maritimes, the **historic church of Saint-Henri-de-Barachois** ★ *(free admission; Jul and Aug, 11am to 5pm; Rte. 133,* ☎532-2976), built in 1824.

★
Shediac

The town of Shediac is the best-known vacation spot on the east coast of New Brunswick. Its popularity is due largely to the magnificent beach in **Parlee Beach Provincial Park** ★★ *(Rte. 15)* whose surprisingly warm waters are perfect for swimming.

Shediac

Because of this popularity, a number of recreational facilities have sprung up in and around Shediac, including a lovely golf course and some amusement parks. The town's reputation, however, is also due in good measure to the abundance of lobster found off its shores which can be savoured fresh any time. The town has even proclaimed itself the lobster capital of the world and holds an annual **lobster festival** in mid-July. Right next to the tourist information centre, there's a gigantic lobster that is 11m long and 5m wide and weighs 90 tonnes. It's meant to remind visitors of the regional importance of this crustacean. Shediac was founded as a fishing port in the 19th century. A handful of lovely buildings have endured from that era and contrast sharply with the chaotic atmosphere that characterizes the town during the busy summer season. Heading northward along the coast, visitors will pass through several tiny Acadian communities that survive mainly on fishing.

Bouctouche

A pleasant little town looking out on a large, calm bay, Bouctouche was founded at the end of the 18th century by Acadians driven from the Memramcook valley. It has the distinction of being the birthplace of two celebrated New Brunswickers, Antonine Maillet and K.C. Irving. Winner of the 1979 Prix Goncourt for her novel *Pélagie-la-Charrette*, Antonine Maillet has gained more international recognition than any other Acadian author. She first came into the public eye in the 1960s with *La Sagouine*, a remarkable play that evokes the lives and spirit of Acadians at the turn of the 20th century. K.C. Irving, who died recently, built a colossal financial empire involved in widely diversified operations, most importantly in the oil industry. He started out with nothing and died one of the wealthiest individuals in the world.

The relatively new **Pays de la Sagouine** ★★ *($10; mid-Jun to early Sep, everyday*

10am to 6pm; at the southern entrance of the village on Rte. 134; ☎743-1400, ≈743-1414) a re-creation of early 20th-century Acadia, draws inspiration from Antonine Maillet's highly successful play, *La Sagouine*. Its creators cleverly decided to enliven the atmosphere with characters from the famous play who perform theatrical and musical pieces. The highlight is Île-aux-Puces in the centre of the bay. It is here that the Pays de la Sagouine is the liveliest, and visitors can learn about the lifestyle of early-20th-century Acadians by talking with the characters on site. The restaurant l'Ordre du Bon Temps, located at the entrance, serves tasty, traditional Acadian cuisine. In the evenings, guests can enjoy theatre productions and musical performances.

The **Kent County Museum** ★ *($3; late Jun to early Sep, Mon to Sat 9am to 5:30pm, Sun noon to 6pm; on the east side of the village, 150 Convent St., ☎743-5005)* is one of the most interesting regional museums in the province. The building itself was used as a convent until 1969. Its various rooms contain period furniture and pieces of sacred art that evoke the history of the convent and the daily life of the nuns and their students. The museum's friendly guides give interesting tours.

Irving Eco-Centre La Dune de Bouctouche ★★ *(Rte. 475, about 5km north of Bouctouche).* The Bouctouche dune extends over 12km into Bouctouche Harbour. It is the habitat of a great variety of aquatic plants and animals as well as of migratory birds and waterfowl including great blue herons, piping plovers and long-winged terns. The dune protects the calm waters and salt marshes of the bay, was formed over the course of centuries by the ceaseless action of winds, tides and ocean currents.

The twofold goal of the Irving Eco-Centre is to preserve this fragile ecozystem and to educate the public about it. A 2km-long boardwalk has been built to facilitate wildlife viewing, and guides give interpretive tours of the dune.

For many years now, the spectacular fine-sand beach that borders the entire perimeter of the dune has been a very popular destination for summer outings. Surrounded by particularly warm waters, this is one of the best spots for swimming on the coast. The dune is located a few kilometres north of Bouctouche and can be reached by bicycle or on foot by trail through the forest.

Tracadie-Sheila

After passing through the villages of **Néguac** and **Val-Comeau**, each of which has beaches and a provincial park, Route 11 leads to Tracadie-Sheila, a little town with numerous restaurants and hotels as well as an attractive wharf. As the institutional buildings attest, the town's history was marked for

many years by the presence of the Religieuses Hospitalières de Saint-Joseph (Sisters of Mercy). They nursed the sick – especially lepers – here from 1868 to 1965. Every year in late June and early July, Tracadie-Sheila hosts the **Festival International de la Francophonie**, that highlights French-language music and arts.

The **Tracadie Historical Museum ★** *(free admission; Jun to mid-Aug; on the 3rd floor of the Académie Sainte-Famille, Rue du Couvent, ☎395-6366)* houses an exhibit on the various stages in the history of Tracadie and its surroundings.

Visitors will find a selection of Micmac artifacts, religious objects and 19th-century tools. Not far from the museum lies the **leper cemetery** where about 60 identical crosses stand in rows.

★
Shippagan

Protected by the strait that separates it from Île Lamèque, the site now occupied by Shippagan was originally a trading post that gave way to a sea port at the end of the 18th century. Now a bustling little community, Shippagan hosts several industries and, more importantly, a port that accommodates one of the largest fishing fleets on the Acadian peninsula. Fishing has been the mainspring of the Acadian economy for

over 200 years now. Its charm lies not only in its seaside location, but also in the unique atmosphere created by its port. Anyone interested in learning more about the fishing industry should stop in Shippagan, explore the town, stroll along the wharf and visit the marine centre. In addition, each year around the third week of July, the town holds a **Fishing and Aquatic Culture Festival** *(☎336-8726)*, made up of a number of fishing related activities, including the blessing of the boats.

Most Acadians who succeeded in avoiding deportation fled from the fertile shores of the Bay of Fundy through the woods to the province's east coast. Since the soil there was much poorer, they turned to the sea for survival, taking up fishing that has long been an integral part of Acadian culture. To discover the fascinating world of modern fishing in Acadia and the Gulf of St. Lawrence, especially the rich animal life inhabiting the seabed in this region, visitors can head to the **Marine Centre and Aquarium ★★** *($5; mid-May to Sep, every day 10am to 6pm; near the Shippagan wharf, ☎336-3013)*. A visit to the Aquarium offers a chance to view tanks with a variety of fish species from the Gulf of St. Lawrence and from the lakes and rivers of the province as well as lobster and, notably, blue lobster. The fish and crustaceans swim about the viewing tanks which recreate their natural environment. This makes the visit particularly interesting. But the most fascinating exhibit has to be the seal tank, especially during feeding time (11am to 4pm). There's also a video for those who would like to learn more about the history of fishing in the region. The complex also is a scientific research centre.

Île Lamèque

A ramp connects Shippagan to Île Lamèque. With its flat landscape and handful of tiny hamlets made up of pretty white or coloured houses, this island is a haven of peace where time seems to stand still. A visit to the **Église Sainte-Cécile** ★ in Petite-Rivière-de-l'île is a must. This charming, colourful wooden church provides an enchanting setting for the **International Baroque Music Festival**, a wonderful event held each year during the last week of July.

Île Miscou

Just a short ferry ride from Île Lamèque lies Île Miscou, another sparsely populated peaceful place renowned for its lovely, often deserted beaches. At the far end of the island stands the **Île Miscou Lighthouse** ★ *(at the end of Rte. 133)*, one of the oldest in New Brunswick and a marvellous spot from which to view the ocean. A few kilometres before the lighthouse, on the same road, visitors will find an **interpretive site** ★ *(Rte. 133)* with a path and footbridges leading through a peat bog.

★★

Caraquet

Caraquet's charm lies mainly in the warmth and vitality of its inhabitants. The largest town on the peninsula, it is equipped with a number of hotels and restaurants. Caraquet is also considered the cultural hub of Acadia and with good reason. It is probably this town and its residents' lifestyle that best illustrate modern Acadian culture that draws on a variety of influences without renouncing its rich past. August is by far the best time to visit Caraquet, since August 15 is the Acadian national holiday. The Tintamarre and Frolic (August 15) alone make for a memorable experience. The **Acadian Festival** *(☎727-6515 or 727-6540)* also takes place in August. At other times, visitors can attend performances by the excellent theatre company of the **Théâtre Populaire d'Acadie** *(276 Blvd. Saint-Pierre O., ☎727-0920)*, relax on one of the town's little beaches or set off on a cruise from the **Carrefour de la Mer** *(51 Blvd. Saint-Pierre Est)*.

The **Acadian Museum** ★ *($3; mid Jun to mid Sep; 15 Blvd. Saint-Pierre Est, ☎727-1713)* houses a small collection of everyday objects from the past two centuries.

An important place of pilgrimage in a lovely natural setting, the **Sanctuaire Sainte-Anne-du-Bocage** ★ *(free admission; everyday, all year round; Blvd. Saint-Pierre O.)* includes a small wooden chapel, the Stations of the Cross and a monument to Alexis Landry, the ancestor of most of the Landry families in Acadia.

No history book on Acadia could ever be as an effective an educational tool as the **Village Historique Acadien** ★★★ *($10; mid-Jun to early Sep; on Rte. 11, about 10km west of Caraquet, ☎726-2600)*. Here, on a vast piece of land, visitors will find a reconstructed village. It includes about 40 houses and other buildings, most of which are authentic, dating from 1770 to the beginning of the 20th century. The atmosphere is enlivened by performers in period costume who carry out everyday tasks using traditional methods and gladly inform visitors about customs of the past. A film at the interpretive centre presents a brief history of the Acadian people. You can now stay in town at the Hôtel Château Albert, a replica of an establishment from the early 1900s.

The **Musée de Cire d'Acadie** ★ *($6; Jun to Sep, 9am to 6pm; Jul and Aug, every day 9am to 7pm; Rte. 11, near the Village Historique Acadien, ☎727-6424)* is a wax museum that re-creates the main historical events that marked Acadia from its foundation to the Deportation and illustrates the daily life activities of Acadians of that era. In all, 23 scenes, eight of which are animated, present 86 figures. The reconstructions are skilfully accomplished and the tour is instructive. Each visitor is allotted a cassette guide.

Caraquet has been the oyster capital for ages. As far back as 1758, the first Acadians fished for oysters which grow in the Bay of Caraquet. Oyster harvesting eventually became oyster farming, thanks to the creation of ostreicultural farms. You can now find out more about oyster production by going to the **Ferme Ostréicole Dugas** *(free admission; beginning of May to mid-Nov, Mon to Sat, 9:30am to 5:30pm; 675 Blvd. Saint-Pierre O., ☎727-3226)*, that has been converted into an ecomuseum. The Dugas family presents traditional know-how which they have developed over many years. Visitors can look at a variety of exhibits, such as the oysters and old oyster-farming implements. Workshops on oyster-box making are also offered. The visit ends with an oyster-tasting session.

Grande-Anse

At Grande-Anse, another tiny coastal village, visitors will find pretty **Ferguson Beach** that lies at the foot of a cliff, and the unique **Pope Museum** ★ *($5; mid-Jun to early Sep; 184 Rue Acadie, ☎732-3003)*. The museum's exhibit includes a model of Saint Peter's in Rome, clothing and pieces of sacred art as well as a collection of papal iconography. A number of these objects are both rare and interesting. The museum serves as a reminder of the important role that religion has played in Acadian history.

Parks

The perfectly marvellous **Irving Nature Park** ★★ *(free admission; at the end of Sand Cove Rd., ☎632-7777)* has a great deal to offer nature lovers. Located just a few kilometres west of the industrial city of Saint John, this magnificent park

covers a 225ha peninsula trimmed with untouched beaches. The city seems a million miles away from here. Visitors can also enjoy a pleasant stroll along one of the park's trails, communing with nature and observing the plant and animal life in southern New Brunswick.

Fundy National Park ★★★ *(Rte. 114, near Alma, ☎887-6000 or 887-2005)* is the best place to explore the shores of the bay, observe its plant and animal life and grasp the power of its tides. It covers a densely wooded, mountainous territory of 206km², abounding in spectacular scenery, lakes and rivers and nearly 20km of shoreline. All sorts of athletic activities can be enjoyed here. With its 120km of trails running through the forest, near lakes and alongside the magnificent bay, the park is a hiker's paradise. Visitors can also enjoy fishing, camping on one of the many equipped or natural sites, playing a game on the excellent golf course or swimming in the heated pool. Travellers pressed for time should make sure at the very least to visit **Pointe Wolfe** ★★ where nearby trails offer spectacular views of cliffs plunging straight into the waters of the bay. At each entrance to the park, employees offer information on the various activities available.

Outdoor Activities

Whale-watching

Because of its rich feeding grounds, the **Bay of Fundy** is one of the best places in the world to observe certain species of whales. Whale-watching excursions are organized throughout the summer in the following places: **St. Andrews by-the-Sea**, **Deer Island**, **Campobello Island** and **Grand Manan Island**, in the southwestern part of the province. Count on around $45 per 3hr excursion. Contact:

Cline Marine
☎529-4188 or 747-2287
Departures from St. Andrews: Deer Island and Campobello Island

Atlantic Marine Wildlife Tours
☎459-7325
Departures from St. Andrews

St. Andrews by-the-Sea

Outdoor Adventure
☎755-6415

Tide Runner
16 King
☎529-4481

S/V Cory
St. Andrews Wharf
☎529-8116
Excursions on yachts that can carry up to 40 passengers

St. George

Adventure Destination Centre
15 Adventure Lane
☎755-2699

Island Coast Boat Tours
☎662-8181
Departures from Grand Manan Island

Ocean Search
☎662-8488
Departures from Grand Manan Island

Seawatch
☎662-8552
Departures from Grand Manan Island

Starboard Tours
☎662-8545 or 663-7525
Departures from Grand Manan Island

Accommodations

Fredericton

University of New Brunswick
20 Bailey Dr., end of University Ave.
May to mid-Aug
200 beds
☎453-4891
≈453-3585
During the summer, rooms in the student residence can be rented at the University of New Brunswick. Expect to pay around $41.50 for a double-occupancy room, or $28.40 for a single room.

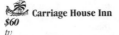 **Carriage House Inn**
$60
tv
230 University Ave., E3C 4H7
☎452-9924 or 800-267-6068
≈458-0799
The many opulent Victorian residences lining the streets of Fredericton provide much of its charm. The Carriage House Inn is one of these magnificent houses, built in 1875 and transformed into an inn with a unique atmosphere that transports guests to another era. There are several large rooms including a ballroom, a library and a solarium as well as 10 guest rooms furnished with antiques. The inn looks out onto a quiet, well-to-do street shaded by large elm trees and lies just a few minutes' walk from downtown. It is best to reserve in advance, regardless of the season. Breakfast is served in a cheerful solarium frequented by businesspeople.

Fredericton Country Inn & Suites
$94 bkfst incl
tv, ℂ
445 Prospect St. W., E3B 6B8
☎459-0035
≈458-1011
Located outside of town, this hotel offers decent rooms. Guests enjoy many little extras, such as free newspapers and all-day coffee long, which make the stay quite enjoyable. For longer stays in Fredericton, travellers can rent a room with a kitchenette and living room.

Lord Beaverbrook Hotel
$108
tv, ℜ, ℜ, ≡, △, ✿, ⊙, P, ≈
659 Queen St., E3B 5A6
☎455-3371 or 800-561-7666
≈455-1441
You won't find a hotel more centrally located than the Lord Beaverbrook Hotel – that has been a

landmark in downtown Fredericton for half a century. With its back to the St. John River, it faces the Legislative Assembly of New Brunswick. The hotel's prestigious history is evident in the richly decorated entrance hall and the aristocratic air about the Governor's Room, a small dining room tucked away. Despite renovations, the rooms are not as luxurious as you might expect.

Sheraton Inn
$109
tv, K, △, ⊙, ℜ, ≈
225 Woodstock Road, E3B 2H8
☎457-7000 or 800-325-3535
≈457-4000
The elegant Sheraton Inn is beautifully located on the shore of the St. John River, just outside of downtown Fredericton. It is by far the most luxurious hotel in the capital and one of the nicest in the province. The architects made the most of the location including a superb terrace looking out over the river, the ideal spot for cocktails, a dip in the pool or a relaxed meal while taking in the scenery. The rooms are very comfortable, pretty and functional, and several offer great views. As you might expect, the recently built Sheraton is equipped with an indoor pool and exercise facilities, a very good restaurant, a bar and conference rooms. It has clearly been designed to please both business people and travellers.

Grand Falls

Maple Tourist Home
$55
tv
142 Main St., E3Z 2V9 ☎473-1763
An excellent bed and breakfast located in downtown Grand Falls, the Maple Tourist Home has

three spotless rooms.
Guests can also relax in a
comfortable common
room.

Hill Top Motel
$63
tv, ℜ
131 Madawaska Rd., E3Y 1A7
☎*473-2684 or 800-496-1244*
⇌*473-4567*
The Hill Top Motel is the
only motel located in the
heart of Grand Falls, just a
few hundred metres from
the Interpretive Centre. As
its name implies, the Hill
Top is located atop a
promontory offering a
view of the city's hydro-
electric dam. The rooms
are clean but decorated
with little imagination.

Motel Léo
$66
tv, ℜ
2.5km north of Grand Falls,
E0J 1M0
☎*473-2090 or 800-661-0077*
Along the Trans-Canada
Highway, 2.5km north of
Grand Falls, the Motel Léo
rents inexpensive, well-
appointed rooms. This is a
fairly typical motel, where
most guests only stop for
one night to take a break
on a long trip. The staff is
very friendly.

Lakeside Lodge & Resort
$69
ℂ, *tv*, ⌂, ℨ, ⊛, ℜ, ≡
590 Gillespie Rd., Lake Pirie
E0J 1M0
☎*473-6252*
Not far from Lake Pirie,
about 5km south of Grand
Falls, the Lakeside Lodge
& Resort offers nature-lovers an excellent alternative
to the local motels. Seven
cottages with fireplaces
and kitchenettes are available, as well as eight
rooms, two of which have
a fireplace and a sauna.

Auberge Près du Lac
$81
tv, ℜ, ≈
2.5km north of Grand Falls E0J 1M0
☎*471-1300*
for reservations:
☎*888-473-1300*
⇌*473-5501*
Right next door to the
Motel Léo is the Auberge
Près du Lac. Offering quality lodging, the complex
includes motel rooms as
well as cottages on the
shores of an artificial lake.
Guests can choose a stan-
dard room or a wedding
suite. Activities, ranging
from pedal-boating on the
lake, to mini-golf, basketball, working out and
swimming in the indoor
pool, make this a popular
spot for families.

Hartland

Campbell's Bed & Breakfast
$35
tv, K
1km north of Hartland, E0J 1N0
☎*375-4775*
⇌*375-4014*
It is hard to imagine a
more peaceful spot than
Campbell's Bed & Break-
fast, a farmhouse built
along the St. John River
near the town of Hartland.
Sitting on the large porch,
it is easy to appreciate the
tranquillity of Richard
Hatfield country. Although
a bit over-decorated, the
rooms are comfortabl and
guests have use of a fully-
equipped kitchen at all
times. Mrs. Campbell
doesn't actually live in the
B&B, but rather in a little
house about 200m away
on the same property.

Gagetown

🏖 **Steamers Stop Inn**
$75
tv, ℜ
74 Front St., E0G 1V0 ☎*488-2903*
⇌*488-1116*
A rather austere-looking
house in the heart of town
along the shore of the St.
John River, the Steamers
Stop Inn fits right in with
the pastoral charm that
characterizes Gagetown.
There is definitely no
better place to get a real
feel for this little vacation
spot since everything is
close by. Rooms are well
appointed, and five of
them provide a view of the
river. The inn also has a
decent restaurant.

St. Andrews
by-the-Sea

🏖 **Rossmount Inn**
$95
tv, ≈, *ℜ*, ⊗, ⊛
a few km from St. Andrews on Hwy.
127 heading east, E0G 2X0
☎*529-3351*
⇌*529-1920*
Set in the middle of a large
property overlooking the
surrounding countryside,
the Rossmount Inn is a
magnificent inn with an-
tique furniture in each
room. The Rossmount Inn
also offers an excellent
dining room.

St. Andrews Motor Inn
$125
tv, ℜ
111 Water St., E0G 2X0
☎*529-4571*
St. Andrews Motor Inn,
right on the bay, offers
comfortable, modern
rooms with balconies or
terraces. Some rooms even
have a kitchenette. The
outdoor pool behind the
building looks out over the
bay.

New Brunswick

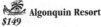 **Algonquin Resort**
$149
tv, ℜ, K, ≈, =, ◔, △
May to Oct
Hwy. 127, 184 Adolphus St. E0G 2X0
☎ *529-8823 or 800-441-1414*
≈ *529-7162*
Dominating the quaint setting of St. Andrews by-the-Sea is the best and most reputed hotel in the Maritimes, the Algonquin Resort. A majestic neo-Tudor grouping in the centre of a large property, this dream hotel has withstood the test of time by carefully preserving the aristocratic refinement and Anglo-Saxon character of an elite resort of the late 1800s. Built in 1889, the Algonquin was completely devastated by fire in 1914. Most of it was rebuilt the next year. Then, in 1991, a new convention centre was added, followed by a new wing with 54 rooms and suites in 1993. The Algonquin offers superb, modern and very comfortable rooms and suites, excellent food at the Passamaquoddy Veranda dining room, flawless service and a whole slew of activities. If the nightly rate is beyond your budget, do at least visit the hotel and treat yourself to Sunday brunch, lunch or supper, a drink in the Library Bar or stop at the gift shop.

Campobello Island

Lupin Lodge
$50
tv, ℜ
Jun to Oct
E0G 3H0
☎ *752-2555*
Well situated near the park, the Lupin Lodge offers relatively comfortable accommodation. During the summer season, the neighbouring restaurant is busy, all day long until evening falls.

Grand Manan Island

Fisherman's Haven Cottages
$80
Grand Harbour, E0G 1X0
☎ *662-8919 or 662-3389*
≈ *662-6246*
Lots of families spend at least a few days of their vacation on Grand Manan Island. A popular option for such vacationers is to rent a cottage like the ones offered at Fisherman's Haven Cottages, which have two or three bedrooms. Weekly rates are available.

Saint John

 Parkerhouse Inn
$89 bkfst incl.
ℜ, pb, tv
71 Sydney St., E2L 1L5 ☎ *652-5054 or 888-457-2520* ≈ *636-8076*
The Parkerhouse Inn occupies a pretty, turn-of-the-century house that has preserved all of its original splendour. A magnificent dining room, richly ornamented with woodwork, occupies almost the entire ground floor. A beautiful staircase leads to the upper floors, where the antique-furnished guestrooms are located. Each room has its own special charm and all have private washrooms. The Parkerhouse Inn is set right in the heart of Saint John, just behind the Imperial Theatre. The inn's restaurant has an outstanding reputation.

Inn on the Cove
$95 bkfst incl.
tv, ⊛, ⟋
1371 Sand Cove Rd., E2M 4X7
☎ *672-7799*
≈ *635-5455*
If you don't see Saint John as an idyllic spot to take a relaxing and revitalizing vacation, it must be because you've never come

across the Inn on the Cove, probably one of the best inns in the province. Located in a quiet setting with a spectacular view of the Bay of Fundy, the inn is actually only 5min by car from downtown. Nature-lovers will find beautiful, wild beaches to explore close by and trails leading to Irving Nature Park. The house is furnished with taste and a particular attention to detail while the comfortable rooms are decorated with antiques. All of the rooms are lovely, but the two located on the second floor and facing the back of the house are even better. They are larger, have their own bathrooms and offer a stunning view of the bay. The owners are friendly but discreet, and prepare excellent breakfasts.

Delta Brunswick Hotel
$95
tv, ℜ, ≈
39 King St., E2L 4W3
☎ *648-1981 or 800-268-1133*
≈ *658-0914*
In the heart of downtown on the busiest street, the Delta Brunswick Hotel is the largest hotel in Saint John with 255 deluxe rooms and suites. Attached to a shopping mall, the building itself lacks a bit of charm. The hotel is best known for the gamut of services for vacationers and businesspeople.

Hilton
$154
tv, ℜ, ≈, ◔, ⊛
1 Market Sq., E2L 4Z6
☎ *693-8484 or 800-561-8282*
≈ *657-6610*
The Saint John Hilton, offering high quality accommodation, lies in a beautiful setting at the end of the pier close to the market. It is a great spot to enjoy the singular beauty of this sea port whose

activity is dictated by the continuous ebb and flow of the tides. Its rooms are spacious and decorated with furniture that is both modern and inviting. Obviously, the rooms at the back of the building, overlooking the port of Saint John, are most desirable. The Hilton also has a good restaurant, Turn of the Tide (see p 152) with a view of the piers.

St. Martins

St. Martins Country Inn
$95
tv
Hwy. 111, E0G 2Z0
☎833-4534 or 800-565-5257
⇄833-4725
The divine St. Martins Country Inn is situated in the enchanting setting of a large property overlooking the town. Built in 1857 for the most important shipbuilder in St. Martins, it has maintained the serene and perhaps slightly snobby atmosphere befitting the residence of a highly- visible member of the Anglo-Saxon upper class of that era. Everything to satisfy the discerning tastes of the epicurean traveller is in place: beautifully decorated rooms filled with period furniture; a highly reputed kitchen; three splendid dining rooms; and impeccable service. Reserve in advance.

Fundy National Park

Fundy Park Chalets
$73
tv, K, ℜ, ≈
E0A 1B0
☎887-2808
Visitors to Fundy National Park can choose between campsites and Fundy Park Chalets. These rather rustic-looking cottages are

located near the park administration office and the golf course, not far from the coast. Each one is equipped with a room with two beds, a bathroom and a kitchenette. Provisions are available just a few kilometres away in Alma.

Moncton

Canadiana Inn
$90
open Mar to Nov
tv
46 Archibald St., E1C 5H9
☎382-1054
Set in a quiet neighbourhood not far from the city's liveliest streets, the Canadiana Inn occupies a large, lovely Victorian house built at the end of the 19th century. Its rooms, equipped with comfortable furnishings, are handsomely decorated and inviting. The establishment has a pleasant upstairs terrace as well as two dining rooms where generous breakfasts are served. The service here is very congenial.

Hotel Beauséjour
$109
tv, ℜ, ≈, △, ◔, ≡
750 Main St., E1C 1E6
☎854-4344 or 800-441-1414
⇄858-0957
For those travellers in search of some pampering, elegance and comfort, there is Hotel Beauséjour, Moncton's finest establishment and a member of the Canadian Pacific hotel chain. The quality of service that has made the reputation of this chain is here as well as beautifully-decorated and spacious rooms, an excellent restaurant and piano bar. Along with a lovely indoor swimming pool, it is easy to put the bustle of urban life behind you, or perhaps below you. Right in the

heart of Moncton, the hotel could not be more suitably located for business people and travellers hoping to take advantage of the nearby restaurants and bars.

Sackville

Marshlands Inn
$89
tv, ℜ
55 Bridge St., E4L 3N8
☎536-0170 or 800-561-1266
⇄536-0721
The charm of Sackville is due in good part to the multitude of large, beautiful houses from the 1800s. One of these has been converted into the outstanding Marshlands Inn, once a sumptuous residence offered as a wedding gift by William Crane, an important man of that era, to his daughter. The inn has more than 20 rooms, each one impeccably furnished. Several have private bathrooms.

Shediac

Chez Françoise
$60
open Apr to Dec
tv
293 Main St., E0A 3G0
☎532-4233
⇄532-8423
Located on a beautifully-maintained piece of property in the heart of Shediac, Chez Françoise is a wonderful inn. Built at the turn of the century, it was originally the residence of a wealthy family. With its wood trim, sumptuous staircase and large front porch ideal for coffee or an apéritif, the elegant interior make for a charming little spot.

New Brunswick

Four Seas Motel
$60
tv, ℜ, K
762 Main St., E0A 3G0
☎*532-2585*
≈*855-0809*
Near the entrance to the
provincial park, the Four
Seas Motel is a good
choice for families. The
service is efficient and
friendly, the restaurant is
very good and the rooms
are clean and well fur-
nished, mostly with mod-
ern pieces. During the
summer season, it is best
to reserve early in the
morning if you want one
of the less expensive
rooms since they go fast.

Belcourt Inn
$109
tv
112 Main St., E0A 3G0 ☎*532-6098*
A member of the Associa-
tion des Auberges du
Patrimoine du Nouveau-
Brunswick, Belcourt Inn
occupies a sumptuous
patrician house that has
belonged to such notables
as former premier of New
Brunswick Judge Allison
Dysart. Erected in 1912,
this three-storey Victorian
building has preserved all
of its olden-day splendour
and charm, both inside
and out. The common
rooms are spacious and
furnished with antiques
and richly ornamented
with woodwork. The inn's
seven individually deco-
rated guestrooms are also
decked out in period furniture. A very inviting porch
provides an ideal setting
for reading and relaxing.
Belcourt Inn is situated in
the heart of Shediac, just
across from Chez
Françoise.

Bouctouche

 **Old Presbytery of
Bouctouche**
$75
ℜ
157 Chemin du Couvent, E0A 1G0
☎*743-5568*
≈*743-5566*
The Old Presbytery of
Bouctouche actually occu-
pies a presbytery con-
structed at the end of the
19th century. Today it is a
superb family inn just
outside the centre of
Bouctouche with beautiful
views of the bay. It has a
first-rate atmosphere that is
ideal for relaxation while
the renovated building is
full of charm. An old
chapel has been converted
into a reception hall. Its
restaurant has an excellent
reputation.

Caraquet

Hôtel Paulin
$45-$80
tv, ℜ
open May to Oct
143 Blvd. St-Pierre O., E1W 1B6
☎*727-9981*
≈*727-3165*
Also part of the Caraquet
skyline for many years, the
Hôtel Paulin is actually a
pleasant inn that has been
run by the Paulin family
for the last three generations. The rooms vary in
quality. Some have re-
cently been nicely reno-
vated while others are
quite out of date but are
still very clean. In all cases,
however, the rooms are of
good value. There is a
very pretty suite at the
back of the building with a
view of the ocean. Guests
can relax in the sitting
room and enjoy the restaurant's excellent food.

Le Poirier
$45
98 Blvd. St-Pierre Ouest., E1W 1B6
Caraquet also has a pleasant inn, Le Poirier, which
was originally built in 1928
and has managed to keep
its old-world charm. Its
four simply decorated
rooms are all cozy.

Maison Touristique Dugas
$55
tv
683 Blvd. St-Pierre Ouest., E1W 1A1
☎*727-3195*
≈*722-3193*
There is truly something
for all tastes and all budgets at the Maison
Touristique Dugas. The
main building, a beautiful,
massive house built in
1926, numbers over
10 impeccable, pretty
rooms of varying sizes. In
addition to these rooms,
campsites and fully
equipped rental cottages
are available on the
grounds. Located a little bit
west of Caraquet, the Maison Touristique Dugas
offers a very friendly welcome and excellent break-
fasts in the morning. From
the house, a trail winds
through the woods to the
Dugas's private beach, just
a 10min walk away.

Auberge de la Baie
$59
tv, ℜ
139 Blvd. St-Pierre Ouest., E1W 1B7
☎*727-3485*
≈*727-3634*
The Auberge de la Baie
provides comfortable,
modern motel-style accom-
modation. It has, however,
an unusual principal ar-
rangement with most of
the rooms opening onto
an interior hallway instead
of outdoors. There is a
good restaurant with po-
lite, friendly and attentive
service. Finally the ample
grounds offer access to a
small deserted beach lo-
cated behind the inn.

Restaurants

Fredericton

 The Lobster Hut
$$
1216 Regent St., City Motel
☎*455-4413*
The Lobster Hut could almost be listed as a Fredericton attraction. Its bizarre, almost psychedelic decor is made up of an eclectic collection of photos, posters and gadgets that all have to do with maritime life. The restaurant is as friendly as can be and, as you may have guessed, specializes in fish and seafood. The food is good and relatively inexpensive.

The Dip
$$-$$$
Sheraton Inn
During mild, summertime weather, it would be hard to imagine a better spot for a drink, light snack or meal than The Dip, a terrace restaurant with a bistro menu. Besides the attentive and courteous service, it offers an absolutely unbeatable view of the St. John River.

Bruno's Seafood Café
$$$
Sheraton Inn
If the weather proves prohibitive, you can always take shelter at Bruno's Seafood Café, the indoor restaurant at the Sheraton Inn (see p 146). The cuisine is just as good along with an impeccable service and a cozy ambiance. The highlights of the menu are excellent scallops Florentine and pepper shrimp. There is also a children's menu. In addi-

tion, Bruno's usually offers a seafood buffet on Friday evenings for about $20 per person.

St. Andrews by-the-Sea

Chef Café
$
180 Water St.
☎*529-8888*
Imagine America in the '50s and you've got the decor of the Chef Café, a popular but rinky-dink restaurant that clashes with the inherent chic that is St. Andrews. The menu includes simple dishes like fish and chips and lobster rolls as well as several inexpensive breakfasts. For a more sophisticated menu, pick a spot at the back of the restaurant in the cozier dining room known as the Captain's Table.

The Lighthouse Restaurant
$$-$$$
Patrick St.
☎*529-3082*
For many visitors, fresh lobster at a reasonable price is in itself enough of a reason to visit Atlantic Canada. When passing through St. Andrews, these seafood fanatics converge on The Lighthouse Restaurant. This pretty spot looking out over Passamaquoddy Bay is on the last street at the eastern edge of St. Andrews.

Passamaquoddy Veranda
$$$
Algonquin Hotel
☎*529-8823*
The Passamaquoddy Veranda offers an outstanding dining experience as much for the elegance of its decor as for the exceptional quality of its international and regional cuisine. A meal at the

Veranda is not within everyone's budget. Fortunately, there is a much less expensive lunch menu and a Sunday brunch that starts at $18.50.

Saint John

Grannan's Seafood Restaurant and Oyster Bar
$$
Market Sq.
☎*634-1555*
Grannan's Seafood Restaurant and Oyster Bar has become an institution in Saint John. The restaurant's decor is a hodgepodge of eccentric maritime-related relics and photos, a real fishmonger's paradise. It opens onto an outdoor terrace that's perfect for those warm summer evenings. Often quite crowded in the evening, this restaurant's menu is predictably composed mainly of fish and seafood dishes.

Incredible Edibles Café
$$
42 Princess St.
Without question one of the trendiest spots in Saint John, the Incredible Edibles Café serves excellent continental cuisine and superb desserts. Feasters can sit out in the garden or in the delightful interior dining room. Among other dishes, the menu includes excellent pasta with mussels as well as a succulent filet of salmon. To top off a delectable meal, or simply to satisfy a mid-afternoon craving, the raspberry cheesecake hits the spot. This café also has a reasonably priced lunch menu.

New Brunswick

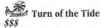 **Turn of the Tide**
$$$
Hilton Hotel
☎**632-8564**
The Turn of the Tide (see p 148) offers a varied menu, typical of a hotel of this calibre, with a vast choice of meat, game, and of course the requisite fresh seafood and fish. The menu is a bit pricey, but the food is sure to please, and the view of the port makes it all the more worthwhile. The decor is classic, airy and tasteful.

Moncton

Café Joe Moka
$
corner Robinson and Main Sts.
Practically facing the Café Robinson, the Café Joe Moka offers a similar menu and an equally pleasant patio.

Shediac

Paturel
$$-$$$
Cape Bimet Rd.
☎**532-4774**
About 5 km outside of Shediac towards Cap-Pelé, a small road leads to the famous Paturel. It's a simple restaurant with an ocean view that   serves fresh seafood at prices that are reasonable, all things considered. Portions, especially the Seafood Platter, which includes a variety of seafood from the region. To add to the maritime atmosphere, the restaurant lies right next to Paturel Seafood Ltd., a seafood-processing plant.

Chez Françoise
$$$
93 Main St.
☎**532-4233**
Undeniably one of the best restaurants in the region, Chez Françoise offers refined French cuisine and an excellent wine list. And to add to your dining pleasure, the dining room is decorated with elegance and style. On lazy summer afternoons, the establishment's front porch is the perfect place for sipping a cool drink.

Bouctouche

L'Ordre du Bon Temps
$-$$
entrance to Pays de la Sagouine
☎**743-1400**
L'Ordre du Bon Temps is the restaurant at the Pays de la Sagouine. It offers visitors the chance to sample traditional Acadian specialties like *fricot de poulet*, *poutine râpée*, *poutine à trou*, *pâté à la râpure* or *pâté aux palourdes*. The menu probably has the most extensive selection of Acadian dishes in all of Acadia, so take advantage of it.

 Tire-Bouchon
$$-$$$
Old Presbytery
☎**743-5568**
Acadian hospitality is at its best at Tire-Bouchon the excellent dining room in the Old Presbytery where chef Marcelle Albert introduces diners to the most refined regional specialties. The name, which means "corkscrew," is quite fitting considering the fine bottles stocked in the wine cellar.

Shippagan

 Abri des Flots
$$-$$$
next to the Aquarium
☎**336-8454**
Very elegant and endowed with a splendid view of the port, the Abri des Flots is, as one might expect, an excellent fish and seafood restaurant. When the lobster rolls and other small meals are available at relatively reasonable prices, lunchtime is a good time to stop in for a bite. During the evening, gourmets benefit from a wide choice. Those with a big appetite can attempt to discover all the wonders of the sea in one meal with the "Sea in Your Plate."

Caraquet

Auberge de la Baie dining room
$$
139 Blvd. St-Pierre Ouest.
☎**727-3485**
Airy and modern, yet still friendly and inviting, the Auberge de la Baie dining room offers a good variety of dishes, including seafood and steaks. The service is very attentive. Some of this restaurant's specialties are baked scallops, *Coquilles St. Jacques au gratin* and Provençal frogs' legs.

Paquetville

La Crêpe Bretonne
$-$$
1085 Rue Du Parc
☎*764-5344*
If your tummy starts to grumble as you pass through the little town of Paquetville, silence it with a stop at La Crêpe Bretonne, a small restaurant whose specialties are crepes and seafood. These two are sometimes combined in scallops and béchamel crepes, lobster and béchamel crepes or crab and béchamel crepes. A good place for an inexpensive lunch or a good evening meal.

Entertainment

Fredericton

The Upper Deck Sports Bar
2nd floor, Queen St.
Always hopping, even on a Sunday night, The Upper Deck Sports Bar is one of the most popular spots with young Frederictonians. The place features pool tables and regular live music. This bar has a large back patio where people can eat and sip drinks in a relaxing atmosphere.

Saint John

O'Leary's
46 Princess St.
The Irish influence is known to be very strong in Saint John. It is therefore no surprise to find O'Leary's, an excellent Irish pub. The clientele is generally young, and musicians are often presented.

Moncton

Capitol Theatre
811 Main St.
☎*856-4377*
The sumptuous Capitol Theatre is the main performing arts centre in Moncton. After renovations restored the panache of days gone by, the theatre re-opened in 1993 presenting a variety of quality productions.

Shopping

Fredericton

No visit to Fredericton would be complete without a stop at **Gallery 78** *(796 Queen St.)*, which exhibits and sells works by some of the best-known New Brunswick artists. It is also a wonderful way to visit a sumptuous Victorian house overlooking the St. John River. With its high ceilings, large rooms, hardwood floors and stately staircase, you'll be wishing it was for sale too!

The **Arts Council of New Brunswick Gallery** *(103 Church St.,* ☎*450-8989)* exhibits and sells a superb collection of high quality products created by the province's artists and crafts-people. It is one of the best craft boutiques in New Brunswick.

Gagetown

Acadia Gallery of Canadian Art
late Jun to late Sep, everyday 11am to 4pm
1948 Lakeview Rd.
☎*488-1119*
The charming contemporary Acadia Gallery of Canadian Art, located in the centre of Gagetown, exhibits a particularly interesting selection of works by artists using a variety of media. Since the gallery also serves as a workshop, it is often possible to meet some of the artists inspired by this enchanting site along the St. John River.

St. Stephen

Ganong Chocolatier
73 Milltown Blvd.
☎*465-5611*
The oldest candy maker in Canada (1873), Ganong Chocolatier was also the first to produce the chocolate bar. Today, the shop sells about 75 different varieties of chocolate. Just try to choose...

St. Andrews by-the-Sea

North of Sixty Art
238 Water St.
☎*529-4148*
North of Sixty Art is an Inuit art gallery that can be visited like a museum. Works exhibited include uniquely diverse and beautiful sculptures. Among the dozens of boutiques along Water Street, this one is probably the most interesting.

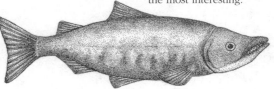

Québec

Situated in the northeast of the American continent, Québec is Canada's largest province. It covers a surface area of 1,550,000km², roughly equivalent to the size of France, Germany and the Iberian peninsula put together, or slightly larger than the state of Alaska.

With the exception of certain southern regions, Québec is sparsely populated and is characterized by an expansive wilderness of lakes, rivers and forests.

The province forms a huge northern peninsula, with James Bay and Hudson Bay to the west, Hudson Strait and Ungava Bay to the north, and the Gulf of St. Lawrence to the south. Québec also shares very long land borders with Ontario to the west and southwest, with New Brunswick and the state of Maine to the southeast, with the states of New York, Vermont and New Hampshire to the south and with Labrador, part of the province of Newfoundland, to the northeast.

Québec's geography is dominated by the St. Lawrence River, the Appalachian Mountain range and the Canadian Shield, three of the most distinct geographical formations in North America. More than a 1000km long, the St. Lawrence is the largest river leading to the Atlantic Ocean on the continent. Traditionally the primary route into the continent, the St. Lawrence played a central part in Québec's development. Even today, most of the province's population lives along the river, particularly in the Montréal region where nearly half of Québec's population resides.

To the south, near the U.S. border, the Appalachian mountains cross the St. Lawrence lowlands from southwestern Québec to the Gaspé peninsula. The remaining 80% of Québec's land mass is part of the Canadian Shield, a very old, heavily eroded mountain range extending over all of northern Québec. This region of the province has a tiny population and abundant natural resources, including vast forests and mighty rivers, some of which are used in the production of hydroelectric power.

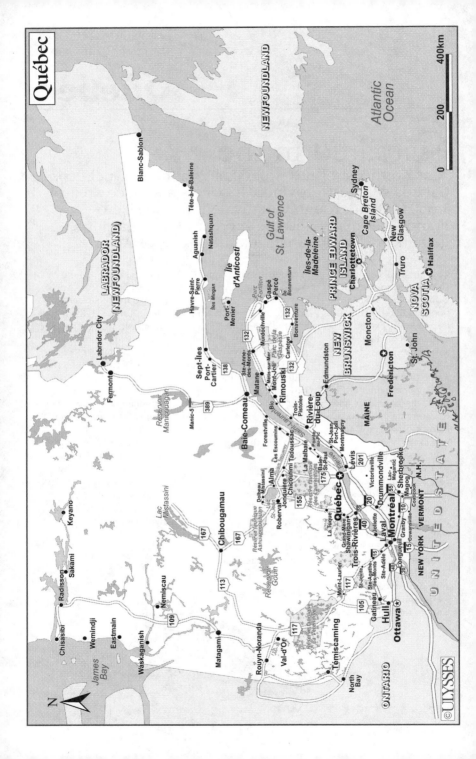

Montréal

A city of paradoxes at the crossroads of America and Europe, seen as both Latin and northern, cosmopolitan and unmistakably the metropolis of Québec, Montréal holds nothing back.

It succeeds in delighting American tourists with its so-called European charm, but also manages to surprise overseas travellers with its haphazard character and nonchalance. Montréal is an enchanting city to visit, an exhilarating place to discover; it is generous, friendly and not at all mundane. And, when it comes time to celebrate jazz, film, humour, singing or Saint-Jean-Baptiste Day, hundreds of thousands of people flood into the streets, turning events into festive public gatherings.

This festive spirit lasts all year in the city's countless cafés, nightclubs and bars of all different kinds, which are constantly packed by a joyful, urban crowd. While Montrealers know how to party, they also enjoy celebrating the arts. With French and North American influences, as well as the vitality of new arrivals, Montréal is an international city and the primary centre of culture in Québec. The abundance of high quality work produced here, most notably in the fields of theatre, fashion, literature and music, attests to the dynamism and creativity of the local population. The city has also earned an enviable reputation among food-lovers; many believe that one can eat better in Montréal than anywhere else in North America.

Finding Your Way Around

There are 28 municipalities on the island of Montréal, which measures 32km by 16km at its widest. Montréal proper, with a population of over one million, is the main urban area in the Communauté Urbaine de Montréal (Montréal Urban Community), which encompasses all of the boroughs on the island. Greater Montréal also includes the Rive-Sud (South Shore), Laval and the Rive-Nord (North Shore), totalling 3,326,510 inhabitants (1996).

Downtown runs along the St. Lawrence, south of Mont Royal (234m), which is one of the 10 hills of the Montérégie region.

By Car

There are two possible routes from Québec City. The first is via Highway 20 West to the Pont Champlain, then follow Autoroute Bonaventure (10) straight into the centre of town. The other route is via Highway 40 West to Autoroute Décarie (15), and follow the signs for downtown, *centre-ville*.

Visitors arriving from Ottawa should take Highway 40 East to Autoroute Décarie (15), then follow the signs for downtown, while those arriving from Toronto should take Highway 20 East onto the island, then follow the signs for downtown via Autoroute Ville-Marie (720).

Visitors arriving from the United States on Highway 10 (Autoroute des Cantons de l'Est) or Highway 15 will enter Montréal via the Pont Champlain and Autoroute Bonaventure (10).

Car Rentals

Avis
1225 Rue Metcalfe
☎*866-7906*

Budget
1240 Rue Guy
☎*937-9121*
Complexe Desjardins
☎*842-9931*

Hertz
1475 Rue Aylmer
☎*842-8537*

National
1200 Rue Stanley
☎*878-2771*

Via Route
1255 Rue Mackay
☎*871-1166*

Airports

Dorval International Airport

Dorval airport is located approximately 20km from downtown Montréal, and is 20min by car. To get downtown from here, take Highway 20 East to the junction of Highway 720 (the Ville-Marie) and follow signs for "Centre-ville, Vieux-Montréal."

For information regarding airport services (arrivals, departures, other information), an information counter is open from 6am to 10pm seven days a week: ☎*394-7377*.

Dorval to downtown

La Québécoise
☎*931-9002*
Departure: Mon to Fri every 20min from 7am to 11pm, every 30min from 11pm to 1am; Sat and Sun every 30min from 7am to 1pm
Cost: $11 one way and $19.75 return; free for children under five.
The bus stops at the train station (*777 De La Gauchetière*), and the bus terminal (*505 Boulevard de Maisonneuve Est, métro station Berri-UQAM*).

The major car rental companies have offices at the airport.

A Thomas Cook counter is open from 6am to 11pm, but a commission is charged. Better exchange rates are available in downtown Montréal.

Mirabel Airport

This airport is located approximately 50km north of Montréal, in Mirabel. To reach downtown Montréal from Mirabel, follow the Autoroute des Laurentides (Hwy. 15) S. until it intersects with Autoroute Métropolitaine (Hwy. 40) E., which you follow for a few kilometres, then continue once again on the 15 S. (which is now called Autoroute Décarie) until Autoroute Ville-Marie (Hwy. 720). Follow the signs for "Centre-ville, Vieux-Montréal." The trip takes 40 to 60min.

For information concerning airport services (arrivals and departures), an information counter is set up for visitors (*Mon, Wed, and Fri 3:35pm to 11:45pm, Tue 7:45am to 3:45, Fri to Sun 24hrs; ☎394-7377*).

Mirabel to downtown Montréal

La Québécoise Bus Company
☎*931-9002*
Departure: schedule varies according to flight arrivals and departures
Cost: $18 one-way, $25 return
The bus stops at the train station (*777 De La Gauchetière, corner University*), and the bus terminal (*505 Boul. de Maisonneuve Est, Métro Berri-UQAM*).

Mirabel to Dorval

La Québecoise
☎*931-9002*
Departure: schedule varies according to arrivals and departures
Cost: $15 one-way, $19.75 return, free for passengers with transfers in under 15hrs.

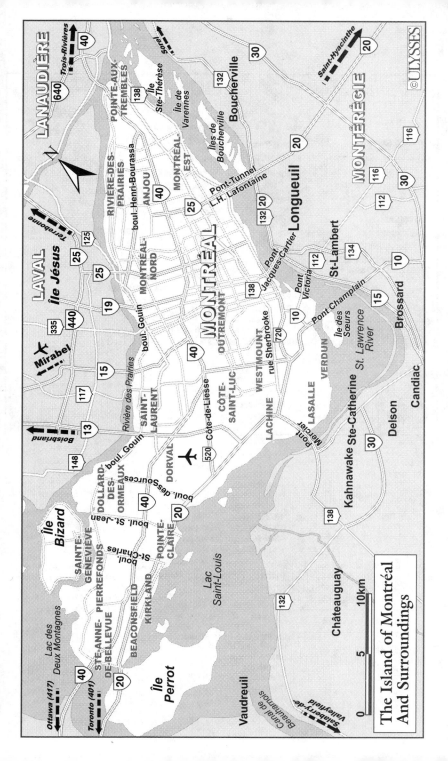

The Island of Montréal
And Surroundings

©ULYSSES

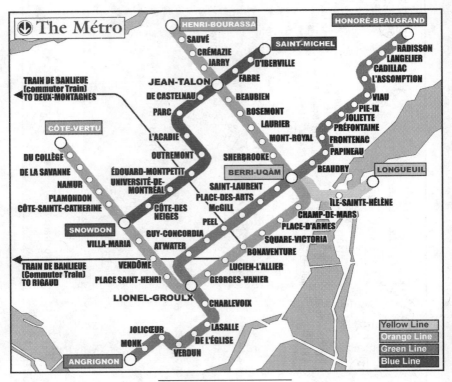

The Metro

TRAIN DE BANLIEUE
(commuter Train)
TO DEUX-MONTAGNES

HENRI-BOURASSA
SAUVÉ
CRÉMAZIE
JARRY
D'IBERVILLE
SAINT-MICHEL
HONORÉ-BEAUGRAND
RADISSON
LANGELIER
CADILLAC
L'ASSOMPTION
JEAN-TALON
FABRE
DE CASTELNAU
BEAUBIEN
VIAU
PARC
ROSEMONT
PIE-IX
JOLIETTE
LAURIER
PRÉFONTAINE
CÔTE-VERTU
L'ACADIE
MONT-ROYAL
FRONTENAC
DU COLLÈGE
OUTREMONT
SHERBROOKE
PAPINEAU
DE LA SAVANNE
ÉDOUARD-MONTPETIT
BERRI-UQÀM
BEAUDRY
LONGUEUIL
NAMUR
UNIVERSITÉ-DE-MONTRÉAL
SAINT-LAURENT
PLAMONDON
PLACE-DES-ARTS
ÎLE-SAINTE-HÉLÈNE
CÔTE-SAINTE-CATHERINE
CÔTE-DES-NEIGES
McGILL
CHAMP-DE-MARS
SNOWDON
PEEL
PLACE-D'ARMES
GUY-CONCORDIA
VILLA-MARIA
ATWATER
SQUARE-VICTORIA
BONAVENTURE
TRAIN DE BANLIEUE
(Commuter Train)
TO RIGAUD
VENDÔME
LUCIEN-L'ALLIER
PLACE SAINT-HENRI
GEORGES-VANIER
LIONEL-GROULX
CHARLEVOIX
JOLICŒUR
LASALLE
MONK
DE L'ÉGLISE
VERDUN
ANGRIGNON

Yellow Line
Orange Line
Green Line
Blue Line

All the large car-rental companies have offices at the airport (see p 158).

Devises Internationales is open during flight arrivals and departures, but they charge a commission. Better exchange rates are available in downtown Montréal. This bank, however, has various automatic teller machines to exchange more common currencies.

Bus Terminals

505 Boulevard de Maisonneuve Est
(Métro Berri-UQAM)
☎ *842-2281*

Train Station

Gare Centrale
895 Rue de la Gauchetière Ouest
(Métro Bonaventure)
☎ *871-7765*
☎ *800-361-5390 (from Québec)*
☎ *800-561-8630 (from Canada)*
⇒ *(514) 871-7766*

Public Transportation

Montréal's métro (subway) and bus network covers the entire metropolitan region. A $47 pass entitles the holder to unlimited use of these services on the island for one month. To use it for a week only, purchase the Cam-Hebdo for 12.50$.

You can also purchase the Tourist Pass, that allows unlimited usage for one day (*$7*) or three days (*$14*) at a time. Alternatively, visitors can purchase six tickets for the price of $8.25, or single tickets at $2 a piece. If a trip involves a transfer (from the bus to the métro or vice versa), passengers must ask the bus driver for a transfer ticket when boarding, or take one from a transfer machine in the Métro station. Free subway maps and timetables for each line are available inside all stations.

For more information on the public transportation system, call:
STCUM
☎ *288-6287*
(A-U-T-O-B-U-S)

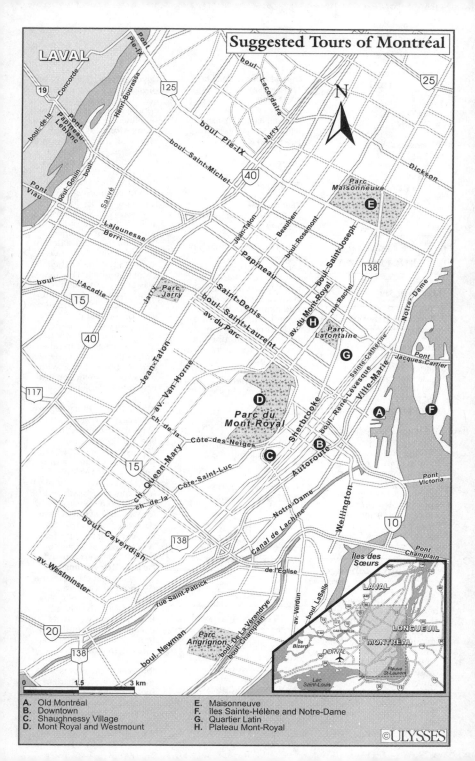

Suggested Tours of Montréal

LAVAL

N

A. Old Montréal
B. Downtown
C. Shaughnessy Village
D. Mont Royal and Westmount

E. Maisonneuve
F. Îles Sainte-Hélène and Notre-Dame
G. Quartier Latin
H. Plateau Mont-Royal

©ULYSSES

Taxis

Co-op Taxi
☎725-9885

Diamond
☎273-6331

Taxi LaSalle
☎277-2552

Practical Information

Area code: *514*

Tourist Information

Centre Infotouriste
1001 Rue du Square-Dorchester
at the corner of Metcalfe and
Square-Dorchester
(Peel Métro station)
☎873-2015
www.tourisme-montreal.org

The centre is open from
8am to 7pm, every day
during summer, and from
9am to 6pm every day
from November to April.

There is a small tourist
booth, which provides
information only on
Montréal, at 174 Rue
Notre-Dame Est (Champ-
de-Mars Métro station)

Foreign Exchange

A number of downtown
banks offer currency ex-
change services. In most
cases, there is a service
charge. Foreign exchange
offices don't always charge
a fee, so it is best to inquire beforehand. Most
banks are able to ex-
change U.S. currency.

Bank of America Canada
1230 Rue Peel
☎392-9100

National Bank of Canada
1001 Rue Sainte-Catherine Ouest
☎281-9640

Forexco
1250 Rue Peel
☎879-1300

Thomas Cook
625 Boulevard René-Lévesque Ouest
☎397-4029

Automatic teller machines
that exchange foreign currency have been installed
in Complexe Desjardins
(on Sainte-Catherine Ouest,
between Jeanne-Mance
and Saint-Urbain). They are
open from 6am to 2am.
These machines can pro-
vide Canadian funds in
exchange for various for-
eign currencies, or U.S. or
French funds for Canadian
currency. There are similar
machines at Mirabel Air-
port.

Post Offices

1250 Rue University
☎283-4506

1695 Rue Sainte-Catherine Est
☎522-5191

Exploring

★★★

Vieux-Montréal

In the 18th century,
Montréal, like Québec City,
was surrounded by stone
fortifications. Between
1801 and 1817, these ram-
parts were demolished due
to the efforts of local merchants, who saw them as
an obstacle to the city's

development. The network
of old streets, compressed
after nearly a century of
confinement, nevertheless
remained in place. Today's
Vieux-Montréal, or Old
Montréal, thus corresponds
quite closely to the area
covered by the fortified
city. During the 19th century, this area became the
hub of commercial and
financial activity in
Canada. Banks and insur-
ance companies built
sumptuous head offices
here, leading to the demolition of almost all buildings erected under the
French Regime. The area
was later abandoned for
nearly 40 years in favour
of the modern downtown
area of today. Finally, the
long process of putting
new life into Old Montréal
got underway during the
preparations for Expo '67
and continues today with
numerous conversion and
restoration projects.

In the 19th century, **Square
Victoria** was a Victorian
garden surrounded by
Second-Empire and
Renaissance-Revival-style
stores and office buildings.
Only the narrow building
at 751 Rue McGill survives
from that era. North of Rue
Saint-Antoine, visitors will
find a **statue of Queen Victoria**, executed in 1872 by
English sculptor Marshall
Wood, as well as an au-
thentic Art-Nouveau-style
Parisian Métro railing. The
latter, designed by Hector
Guimard in 1900 and
given to the city of
Montréal by the city of
Paris for Expo '67, was
installed at one of the entrances to the Square-Victoria métro station.

Rue Saint-Jacques was the
main artery of Canadian
high finance for over a
century. This role is re-
flected in its rich and varied architecture, which

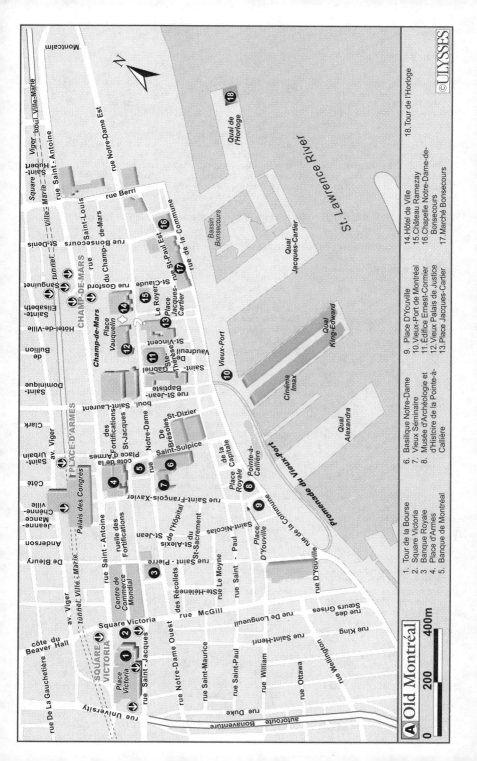

A Old Montréal

0   200   400m

1. Tour de la Bourse
2. Square Victoria
3. Banque Royale
4. Place d'Armes
5. Banque de Montréal
6. Basilique Notre-Dame
7. Vieux Séminaire
8. Musée d'Archéologie et d'Histoire de la Pointe-à-Callière
9. Place D'Youville
10. Vieux-Port de Montréal
11. Édifice Ernest-Cormier
12. Vieux Palais de Justice
13. Place Jacques-Cartier
14. Hôtel de Ville
15. Château Ramezay
16. Chapelle Notre-Dame-de-Bonsecours
17. Marché Bonsecours
18. Tour de l'Horloge

© ULYSSES

St. Lawrence River

Bassin Bonsecours

Quai Jacques-Cartier

Quai King-Edward

Quai Alexandra

Cinéma Imax

Vieux-Port

Promenade du Vieux-Port

Place Royale

Place D'Youville

Place de la Capitale

Pointe-à-Callière

rue de la Commune

rue St-Paul Est

Place Jacques-Cartier

rue Le Royer

rue Gosford

rue St-Claude

rue St-Vincent

Place Vauquelin

Saint-Gabriel

Sainte-Thérèse

Vaudreuil

rue St-Jean-Baptiste

St-Dizier

De Brésoles

Saint-Sulpice

rue Notre-Dame

côte de la Place d'Armes

PLACE D'ARMES

des Fortifications

St-Jacques

boul. Saint-Laurent

rue Saint-François-Xavier

rue de l'Hôpital

St-Sacrement

St-Alexis

Saint-Jean

Saint-Pierre

Saint-Nicolas

Place D'Youville

rue de la Commune

rue Saint-Paul

Saint-Henri

rue De Longueuil

rue Saint-Maurice

rue McGill

Ste-Hélène

des Récollets

rue Le Moyne

rue Saint - Paul

rue des Sœurs Grises

rue King

rue William

rue Wellington

rue Ottawa

rue Duke

autoroute Bonaventure

côte du Beaver Hall

rue De La Gauchetière

rue University

Place Victoria

SQUARE VICTORIA

Square Victoria

av. Viger

tunnel Ville-Marie

De Bleury

Anderson

Jeanne-Mance

Chenneville

Côté

Saint-Urbain

av. Viger

Clark

Saint-Dominique

de Bullion

Hôtel-de-Ville

Sainte-Élisabeth

Sanguinet

Saint-Denis

Saint-Louis

rue Berri

Saint-Hubert

Square Saint-Hubert

boul. Ville-Marie

Viger

rue Saint-Antoine

rue Notre-Dame Est

CHAMP-DE-MARS

Champ-de-Mars

du Champ-de-Mars

rue Bonsecours

rue Saint-Jacques

rue Saint - Antoine

Palais des Congrès

Centre de Commerce Mondial

ruelle des Fortifications

rue Notre-Dame Ouest

N

Montcalm

Montcalm

Vieux-Port

serves as a veritable encyclopedia of styles from 1830 to 1930. In those years, the banks, insurance companies and department stores, as well as the nation's railway and shipping companies, were largely controlled by Montrealers of Scottish extraction, who had come to the colonies to make their fortune.

Begun in 1928 according to plans by New York skyscraper specialists York and Sawyer, the former head office of the **Banque Royale ★ ★** (*360 Rue Saint-Jacques, Square Victoria métro station*), or Royal Bank, was one of the last buildings erected during this era of prosperity. The 22-floor tower has a base inspired by Florentine palazzos, which corresponds to the scale of the neighbouring buildings. Inside the edifice, visitors can admire the high ceilings of this "temple of finance," built at a time when banks needed impressive buildings to win customers' confidence. The walls of the great hall are emblazoned with the heraldic insignia of eight of the 10 Canadian provinces, as well as those of Montréal (St. George's cross) and Halifax (a yellow bird), where the bank was founded in 1861.

The square, which is in fact shaped more like a trapezoid, is surrounded by several noteworthy buildings. The **Banque de Montréal ★ ★** (*119 Rue Saint-Jacques, métro station Place-d'Armes*), or Bank of Montreal, founded in 1817 by a group of merchants, is the country's oldest banking institution. Its present head office takes up an entire block on the north side of Place d'Armes. A magnificent building by John Wells,

built in 1847 and modelled after the Roman Pantheon, it occupies the place of honour in the centre of the block, and offers customer banking. Its Corinthian portico is a monument to the commercial power of the Scottish merchants who founded the institution. The capitals of the columns, severely damaged by pollution, were replaced in 1970 with aluminum replicas. The pediment includes a bas-relief depicting the bank's coat of arms carved out of Binney stone in Scotland by Her Majesty's sculptor, Sir John Steele.

Under the French Regime, **Place d'Armes ★ ★** (*Place-d'Armes métro station*) was the heart of the city. Used for military manoeuvres and religious processions, the square was also the location of the Gadoys well, the city's main source of potable water. In 1847, the square was transformed into a lovely, fenced-in Victorian garden, which was destroyed at the beginning of the 20th century in order to make room for a tramway terminal. In the meantime, a **monument to Maisonneuve** was erected in 1895. Executed by sculptor Philippe Hébert, it shows the founder of Montréal, Paul de Chomedey, Sieur de Maisonneuve, surrounded by prominent figures from the city's early history, namely Jeanne Mance, founder of the Hôtel-Dieu (hospital), Lambert Closse, along with his dog Pilote, and Charles Lemoyne, head of a family of famous explorers. An Iroquois warrior completes the tableau.

In 1663, the seigneury of the island of Montréal was acquired by the Sulpicians from Paris, who remained

its undisputed masters up until the British conquest of 1760. In addition to distributing land to colonists and laying out the city's first streets, the Sulpicians were responsible for the construction of a large number of buildings, including Montréal's first parish church (1673). Dedicated to *Notre Dame* (Our Lady), this church had a beautiful Baroque facade that faced straight down the centre of the street of the same name, creating a pleasant perspective characteristic of classical French town-planning. At the beginning of the 19th century, however, this rustic little church cut a sorry figure when compared to the Anglican cathedral on Rue Notre-Dame and the new Catholic cathedral on Rue Saint-Denis, neither of which remains today. The Sulpicians therefore decided to make a decisive move to surpass their rivals once and for all. In 1823, to the great displeasure of local architects, they commissioned New York architect James O'Donnell, who had an Irish Protestant background, to design the largest and most original church north of Mexico.

Basilique Notre-Dame ★ ★ ★ (*$2; 110 Rue Notre-Dame Ouest, Place d'Armes métro station, ☎842-2925*), built between 1824 and 1829, is a true North American masterpiece of Gothic-Revival architecture. It should be seen not as a replica of a European cathedral, but rather as a fundamentally neoclassical structure characteristic of the Industrial Revolution, complemented by a medieval-style decor that foreshadowed the historicism of the Victorian era. These elements make the building remarkable.

Basilique Notre-Dame

all that remain of the exuberant, Spanish-style Gothic-Revival decor of the original.

The **Vieux Séminaire** ★ (*116 Rue Notre-Dame Ouest, métro Place-d'Armes*), or old seminary, was built in 1683 in the style of a Parisian *hôtel particulier*, with a front courtyard and a rear garden. It is the oldest building in the city. For more than three centuries, it has been occupied by Sulpician priests, who, under the French Regime, used it as a manor from which they managed their vast seigneury. At the time of the building's construction, Montréal had barely 500 inhabitants, and was constantly being terrorized by Iroquois attacks. Under those circumstances, the seminary, albeit modest in appearance, represented a precious haven of European civilization in the middle of a wild, isolated land. The public clock at the top of the facade was installed in 1701, and may be the oldest one of its kind in the Americas.

The **Musée d'Archéologie et d'Histoire de la Pointe-à-Callière** ★★ (*$8.50; Sep to Jun, Tue to Fri 10am to 5pm, Sat and Sun 11am to 5pm; Jul to Sep, Tue to Fri 10am to 6pm, Sat and Sun 11am to 6pm; 350 Place Royale, Pointe-à-Callière, Place-d'Armes métro station, ☎872-9150*). This archaeology and history museum lies on the exact site where Montréal was founded on May 18, 1642. The Rivière Saint-Pierre used to flow alongside the area now occupied by Place d'Youville, while the muddy banks of the St. Lawrence reached almost as far as present-day Rue de la Commune. The first colonists built Fort Ville-Marie out of earth and

O'Donnell was so pleased with his work that he converted to Catholicism before dying, so that he could be buried under the church. Between 1874 and 1880, the original interior, considered too austere, was replaced by the fabulous polychromatic decor found today. Executed by Victor Bourgeau, then the leading architect of religious buildings in the Montréal region, along with about 50 artists, it is made entirely of wood, painted and gilded with gold leaf. Particularly noteworthy features include the baptistery, decorated with frescoes by Ozias Leduc, and the powerful electro-pneumatic Casavant organ with its 5,772 pipes, often used

during the numerous concerts given at the basilica. Lastly, there are the stained-glass windows by Francis Chigot, a master glass artist from France, which depict various episodes in the history of Montréal. They were installed in honour of the church's 100th anniversary.

To the right of the chancel, a passage leads to the Chapelle du Sacré-Cœur (Sacred Heart Chapel), added to the back of the church in 1888. Nicknamed the Chapelle des Mariages (Wedding Chapel) because of the countless nuptials held there every year, including singer Celine Dion's in 1994, it was seriously damaged by fire in 1978. The spiral staircases and the side galleries are

wooden posts on the isolated point of land created by these two bodies of water. Threatened by Iroquois flotillas and flooding, the leaders of the colony soon decided to establish the town on Coteau Saint-Louis, the hill now bisected by Rue Notre-Dame. The site of the fort was then occupied by a cemetery and the château of Governor de Callière, hence the name.

The museum uses the most advanced techniques available to provide visitors with a survey of the city's history. Attractions include a multimedia presentation, a visit to the vestiges discovered on the site, excellent models showing the different stages of Place Royale's development, holographic conversations and thematic exhibitions. Designed by architect Dan Hanganu, the museum was erected for the celebrations of the city's 350th anniversary in 1992.

Stretching from Place Royale to Rue McGill, **Place d'Youville** owes its elongated shape to its location on top of the bed of the Rivière Saint-Pierre, which was canalized in 1832.

Musée d'Archéologie de la Pointe-à-Callière

In the middle of the square stands the **Centre d'Histoire de Montréal** (*$4.50; May to Sep, every day 9am to 5pm; Sep to May, closed Mon 10am to 5pm, closed Dec 8 to Jan 25; 335 Place d'Youville, Square-Victoria métro station, ☎872-3207*), a small, historical museum presenting temporary exhibitions on various themes related to life in Montréal. The building itself is the former fire station number 3, one of only a few examples of Flemish-style architecture in Québec. The Marché Sainte-Anne once lay to the west of Rue Saint-Pierre and was, from 1840 to 1849, the seat of the Parliament of United Canada. In 1849, the Orangemen burned the building after a law intended to compensate both French and English victims of the rebellion of 1837-38 was adopted. The event marked the end of Montréal's political vocation.

The Port of Montréal is the largest inland port on the continent. It stretches 25km along the St. Lawrence, from Cité du Havre to the refineries in the east end. The **Vieux-Port de Montréal ★★**, (*Place-d'Armes or Champs-de-Mars métro stations*) or old port, corresponds to the historic part of the port, located in front of the old city. Abandoned because of its obsolescence, it was revamped between 1983 and 1992, following the example of various other centrally located North American ports. The old port encompasses a pleasant park, laid out on the embankments and coupled with a promenade, which runs alongside the piers or *quai*, offering a "window" on the river and the few shipping activities that have fortunately been maintained. The layout accents the view of the water, the downtown area and Rue de la Commune, whose wall of neoclassical, greystone warehouses stands before the city, one of the only examples of so-called "waterfront planning" in North America.

From the port, visitors can set off on an excursion on the river and the Lachine canal aboard **Le Bateau Mouche** (*$21.50 taxes included; mid-May to mid-Oct, departures every day at 10am, noon, 2pm, 4pm, 7pm; Quai Jacques-Cartier; ☎849-9952*), whose glass roof enables passengers to fully appreciate the beauty of the surroundings. The *navettes fluviales* or river shuttles (*late May to mid-Oct, weekends 11am to 7pm, mid-summer every day 11am to 7pm; Quai Jacques-Cartier, ☎281-8000*) ferry passengers to Île Sainte-Hélène (*$2.75*) and Longueuil (*$3.25*), offering a spectacular view of the old port and Old Montréal along the way.

From the time it was inaugurated in 1926 until it closed in 1970, the **Édifice Ernest-Cormier** ★ (*100 Rue Notre-Dame Est, Champ-de-Mars métro station*) was used for criminal proceedings. The former courthouse was converted into a conservatory and was named after its architect, the illustrious Ernest Cormier, who also designed the main pavilion of the Université de Montréal and the doors of the United Nations Headquarters in New York City. The Courthouse is graced with outstanding bronze sconces, cast in Paris at the workshops of Edgar Brandt. Their importation in 1925 ushered in the Art Deco style in Canada. The main hall, faced with travertine and topped by three dome-shaped skylights, is worth a quick visit.

The **Vieux Palais de Justice** ★ (*155 Rue Notre-Dame Est, Champ-de-Mars métro station*), the oldest courthouse in Montréal, was built between 1849 and 1856, according to a design by John Ostell and Henri-Maurice Perrault, on the site of the first courthouse, which was erected in 1800. It is another fine example of Canadian neoclassical architecture. After the courts were divided in 1926, the old Palais was used for civil cases, judged according to the Napoleonic Code. Since the opening of the new Palais to its left, the old Palais has been converted into an annex of City Hall, located to the right.

Place Jacques-Cartier ★ (*Champ-de-Mars métro station*) was laid out on the site once occupied by the

Château de Vaudreuil, which burned down in 1803. The former Montréal residence of the governor of New France was without question the most elegant private home in the city. Designed by engineer Gaspard Chaussegros de Léry in 1723, it had a horseshoe-shaped staircase leading up to a handsome cut-stone portal, two projecting pavilions (one on each side of the main part of the building) and a formal garden that extended as far as Rue Notre-Dame. After the fire, the property was purchased by local merchants, who decided to give the government a small strip of land on the condition that a public market be established there, thereby increasing the value of the adjacent property, which remained in private hands. This explains Place Jacques-Cartier's oblong shape.

The **Hôtel de Ville** ★ (*275 Rue Notre-Dame Est, Champ-de-Mars métro station*), or City Hall, a fine example of the Second-Empire, or Napoleon III, style, is the work of Henri-Maurice Perrault, who also designed the neighbouring courthouse.

In 1922, a fire (yet another!) destroyed the interior and roof of the building, later restored in 1926, modeled after the city hall in Tours, France. Exhibitions are occasionally presented in the main hall, which is accessible via the main entrance. Visitors may also be interested to know that it was from the balcony of City Hall that France's General de Gaulle cried out his famous "*Vive le Québec libre!*" ("Freedom for Québec!") in 1967, to the great delight of the crowd gathered in front of the building.

The humblest of all the "châteaux" built in Montréal, the **Château Ramezay** ★★ (*$5; summer, every day 10am to 6pm; rest of the year, Tue to Sun 10am to 4:30pm; schedule subject to change; 280 Rue Notre-Dame Est, Champ-de-Mars métro station, ☎861-3708*), is the only one still standing. It was built in 1705 for the governor of Montréal, Claude de Ramezay, and his family. In 1745, it fell into the hands of the Compagnie des Indes Occidentales (The French West India Company), which made it its North American headquarters.

Québec

Hôtel de Ville

Precious Canadian furs were stored in its vaults awaiting shipment to France. After the conquest (1760), the British occupied the house, before being temporarily removed by American insurgents, who wanted Québec to join the nascent United States. Benjamin Franklin even came to stay at the château for a few months in 1775, in an attempt to convince Montrealers to become U.S. citizens.

In 1896, after serving as the first building of the Montréal branch of the Université Laval in Québec City, the château was converted into a museum, under the patronage of the Société d'Histoire et de Numismatique de Montréal (Montréal Numismatic and Antiquarian Society), founded by Jacques Viger. Visitors will still find a rich collection of furniture, clothing and everyday objects from the 18th and 19th centuries here, as well as a large number of native artifacts. The Salle de Nantes is decorated with beautiful Louis XV-style mahogany panelling, designed by Germain Boffrand and imported from the Nantes office of the Compagnie des Indes (circa 1750).

This site was originally occupied by another chapel, built in 1657 upon the recommendation of Saint Marguerite Bourgeoys, founder of the Congregation de Notre-Dame. The present **Chapelle Notre-Dame-de-Bonsecours** ★ (*400 Rue Saint-Paul Est, Champ-de-Mars métro station,* ☎*845-9991*) dates back to 1771, when the Sulpicians wanted to establish a branch of the main parish in the eastern part of the fortified city.

In 1890, the chapel was modified to suit contemporary tastes, and the present stone facade was added, along with the "aerial" chapel looking out on the port. Parishioners asked God's blessing on ships and their crews bound for Europe from this chapel. The interior, redone at the same time, contains a large number of votive offerings from sailors saved from shipwrecks. Some are model ships, hung from the ceiling of the nave. At the back of the chapel, the little **Musée Marguerite-Bourgeoys** (*$2; May to Oct, Wed to Sun 9am to 4:30pm; Nov to Apr 10:30am to 4:30pm*) displays mementos of the saint. From there, visitors can reach a platform adjoining the "aerial" chapel, which offers an interesting view of the old port.

The **Marché Bonsecours** ★★ (*350 Rue Saint-Paul Est*) was erected between 1845 and 1850. The lovely grey stone neoclassical edifice with sash windows was erected on **Rue Saint-Paul**, for many years Montréal's main commercial artery. The building is adorned with a portico supported by cast-iron columns moulded in England, and topped by a silvery dome, which for many years served as the symbol of the city at the entrance to the port. The public market, closed since the early 1960s following the advent of the supermarket, was transformed into municipal offices then an exhibition hall before finally reopening partially in 1996. The building originally housed both the city hall and a concert hall upstairs. The market's old storehouses, recently renovated, can be seen on Rue Saint-Paul, while from the large balcony on Rue de la Commune you can see the partially reconstructed **Bonsecours dock**, where paddle-wheelers full of farmers came to the city to sell their wares.

The **Tour de l'Horloge** ★ (*at the end of the Quai de l'Horloge; May to Oct*) is visible to the east from the end of Quai Jacques-Cartier. Painted a pale yellow, the structure is actually a monument erected in 1922 in memory of merchant marine sailors who died during WWI. It was inaugurated by the Prince of Wales (the future Edward VIII) during one of his many visits to Montréal. An observatory at the top of the tower provides a clear view of Île Sainte-Hélène, the Jacques-Cartier bridge and the eastern part of Old Montréal. Standing on Place Belvédère at the base of the tower, one has the impression of standing on the deck of a ship as it glides slowly down the St. Lawrence and out to the Atlantic Ocean.

Downtown

The downtown skyscrapers give Montréal a typically North American look. Nevertheless, unlike most other cities on the continent, there is a certain Latin spirit here, which seeps in between the towering buildings, livening up this part of Montréal both day and night. Bars, cafés, department stores, shops and head offices, along with two universities and numerous colleges, all lie clustered within a limited area at the foot of Mont-Royal.

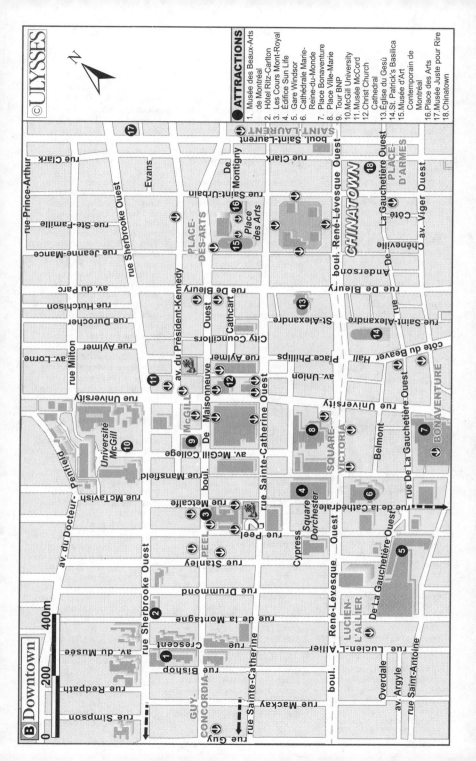

B Downtown

© ULYSSES

N

0 200 400m

● ATTRACTIONS

1. Musée des Beaux-Arts de Montréal
2. Hôtel Ritz-Carlton
3. Les Cours Mont-Royal
4. Édifice Sun Life
5. Gare Windsor
6. Cathédrale Marie-Reine-du-Monde
7. Place Bonaventure
8. Place Ville-Marie
9. Tour BNP
10. McGill University
11. Musée McCord
12. Christ Church Cathedral
13. Église du Gesù
14. St. Patrick's Basilica
15. Musée d'Art Contemporain de Montréal
16. Place des Arts
17. Musée Juste pour Rire
18. Chinatown

At the beginning of the 20th century, Montréal's central business district gradually shifted from the old city to what was up until then a posh residential neighbourhood known as the "Golden Square Mile," inhabited by upper-class Canadians. Wide arterial streets such as Boulevard René-Lévesque were then lined with palatial residences surrounded by shady gardens. The city centre underwent a radical transformation in a very short time (1960-1967), marked by the construction of Place Ville-Marie, the métro, the underground city, Place des Arts, and various other infrastructures which still exert an influence on the area's development.

Sherbrooke (*1379 Rue Sherbrooke Ouest*), opened its doors in 1912. Its facade, made of white Vermont marble, is the work of the Scottish merchants' favourite architects, the prolific Edward and William Sutherland Maxwell. The building became too small for the museum's collection and was enlarged towards the back on three different occasions. Finally, in 1991, architect Moshe Safdie designed the Pavillon Jean-Noël-Desmarais, just opposite on the south side of Rue Sherbrooke. This new wing includes the red brick facade of a former apartment building and is linked to the original building by tunnels under Rue Sherbrooke.

The last of Montréal's old hotels, the **Ritz-Carlton Kempinski ★** (*1228 Rue Sherbrooke Ouest*) was inaugurated in 1911 by César Ritz himself. For many years, it was the favourite gathering place of the Montréal bourgeoisie. Some people even stayed here year-round, living a life of luxury among the drawing rooms, garden and ballroom. The building was designed by Warren and Wetmore of New York City, the well-known architects of Grand Central Station on New York's Park Avenue. Many celebrities have stayed at this sophisticated luxury hotel over the years, including Richard Burton and Elizabeth Taylor, who were married here in 1964.

Montréal has the most extensive **underground city** in the world (see p 194). Greatly appreciated in bad weather, it provides access to over 2,000 shops and restaurants, as well as movie theatres, apartment and office buildings, hotels, parking lots, the train station, the bus station, Place des Arts and even the Université du Québec à Montréal (UQAM) via tunnels, atriums and indoor plazas. The **Cours Mont-Royal ★★** (*1455 Rue Peel*) are duly linked to this sprawling network, which centres around the various métro stations. A multipurpose complex, the Cours consist of four levels of stores, offices and apartments laid out inside the former Mount Royal Hotel.

Musée des Beaux-Arts

The **Musée des Beaux-Arts de Montréal ★★★** (*free admission; $1 for temporary exhibits, half-price Wed 5:30pm to 9pm; Tue to Sun 11am to 6pm; 1380 Rue Sherbrooke Ouest, ☎285-2000*). Montréal's Museum of Fine Arts is the oldest and largest museum in Québec.

It was founded in 1860 by the Art Association of Montréal, a group of Anglo-Saxon art lovers.

The Pavillon Beniah-Gibb, on the north side of Rue

The museum's main entrance is now in the new wing, at the corner of Rue Crescent.

At Montréal's **Musée des Arts Décoratifs** (*free admission; Tue to Sun 11am to 6pm, Wed 11am to 9pm; 2200 Rue Crescent, ☎284-1252*), visitors can see International-style (1935 to the present day) furniture and decorative objects from the Liliane and David Stewart collection, as well as travelling exhibitions on glass, textiles and other materials.

The **Édifice Sun Life ★★** (*1155 Rue Metcalfe*), erected between 1913 and 1933 for the powerful Sun Life insurance company, was for many years the largest building in the British Empire. It was in this "fortress" of the Anglo-Saxon establishment, with its colonnades reminiscent of ancient mythology, that the British Crown Jewels were hidden during World War II. In 1977, the company's head office was moved to Toronto, in protest against provincial language laws excluding English. Fortunately, the chimes that ring at 5pm every day are still in place and remain an integral part of the neighbourhood's spirit.

A number of churches clustered around Square Dorchester before it was even laid out in 1872. Unfortunately, only two of the eight churches built in the area between 1865 and 1875 have survived. One of these is the beautiful Gothic-Revival-style **St. George's Anglican Church ★★** *(at the corner of Rue de la Gauchetière and Rue Peel)*. Its delicately sculpted sandstone exterior conceals an interior covered with lovely, dark woodwork. Particularly noteworthy are the remarkable ceiling, with its exposed framework, the woodwork in the chancel, and the tapestry from Westminster Abbey, used during the coronation of Elizabeth II.

In 1887, the head of Canadian Pacific, William Cornelius Van Horne, asked his New York friend Bruce Price (1845-1903) to draw up the plans for **Gare Windsor ★** *(corner of Rue de la Gauchetière and Rue Peel)*, a modern train station that would serve as the terminus of the transcontinental railroad, completed the previous year. At the time, Price was one of the most prominent architects in the eastern United States, where he worked on residential projects for high-society clients, as well as

skyscrapers like the American Surety Building in Manhattan. Later, he was put in charge of building the Château Frontenac in Québec City, thus establishing the Château style in Canada.

*Cathédrale
Marie-Reine-du-Monde*

Cathédrale Marie-Reine-du-Monde ★★ *(Boulevard René-Lévesque Ouest corner of Mansfield)* is the seat of the archdiocese of Montréal and a reminder of the tremendous power wielded by the clergy up until the Quiet Revolution. It is exactly one third the size of St. Peter's in Rome. In 1852, a terrible fire destroyed the Catholic cathedral on Rue Saint-Denis. The ambitious Monseigneur Ignace Bourget (1799-1885), who was bishop of Montréal at the time, seized the opportunity to work out a grandiose scheme to outshine the Sulpicians' Basilique Notre-Dame and ensure the supremacy of the Catholic Church in Montréal. What could accomplish these goals better than a replica of Rome's St. Peter's, right in the middle of a Protestant neighbourhood? Despite reservations on the part of architect Victor Bourgeau, the plan was carried out. The bishop even made Bourgeau go to

Rome to measure the venerable building. Construction began in 1870 and was finally completed in 1894. Copper statues of the 13 patron saints of Montréal's parishes were installed in 1900.

An immense, grooved concrete block with no facade, **Place Bonaventure ★** *(1 Place Bonaventure)*, completed in 1966, is one of the most revolutionary works of modern architecture of its time. Designed by Montrealer Raymond Affleck, it is a multi-purpose complex built on top of the railway lines leading into the Gare Centrale. It contains a parking area, a two-level shopping centre linked to the métro and the underground city, two large exhibition halls, wholesalers, offices, and an intimate 400-room hotel laid out around a charming hanging garden, worth a short visit.

A railway tunnel leading under Mont Royal to the downtown area was built in 1913. The tracks ran under Avenue McGill College, then multiplied at the bottom of a deep trench that stretched between Rue Mansfield and Rue University. In 1938, the subterran-

Québec

ean **Gare Centrale** was built, marking the true starting point of the underground city. Camouflaged since 1957 by the **Hôtel Reine-Elizabeth**, the Queen Elizabeth Hotel, it has an interesting, streamline-Deco waiting hall. **Place Ville-Marie** ★★★ (*1 Place Ville-Marie, Bonaventure* métro station), was erected above the northern part of the formerly open-air trench in 1959. The famous Chinese-American architect Leoh Ming Pei (Louvre Pyramid, Paris; East Building of the National Gallery, Washington, D.C.) designed the multipurpose complex, which is built over the railway tracks and contains vast shopping arcades now linked to most of the surrounding edifices. It also encompasses a number of office buildings, including the famous cruciform aluminum tower, whose unusual shape enables natural light to penetrate all the way into the centre of the structure, while at the same time symbolizing Montréal, a Catholic city dedicated to the Virgin Mary.

In the middle of the public area, a granite compass card indicates true north, while **Avenue McGill College**, which leads straight toward the mountain, indicates "north" as perceived by Montrealers in their everyday life. This artery, lined with multicoloured skyscrapers, was still a narrow residential street in 1950. It now offers a wide view of Mont Royal, crowned by a metallic cross erected in 1927 to commemorate the gesture of Paul Chomedey de Maisonneuve, founder of Montréal, who climbed the mountain in January 1643 and placed a wooden cross at its summit to

thank the Virgin Mary for having spared Fort Ville-Marie from a devastating flood.

The **Tour BNP** ★ (*1981 Avenue McGill College*), certainly the best designed building on Avenue McGill College, was built for the Banque Nationale de Paris in 1981 by the architectural firm Webb, Zerafa, Menkès, Housden Partnership (Tour Elf-Aquitaine, Paris; Royal Bank, Toronto). Its bluish glass walls tower over a sculpture entitled *La Foule Il-luminée* (The Illuminated Crowd), by the Franco-British artist Raymond Mason.

McGill University ★★

(*805 Rue Sherbrooke Ouest, McGill métro station*) was founded in 1821, thanks to a donation by fur-trader James McGill. It is the oldest of Montréal's four universities. Throughout the 19th century, the institution was one of the finest jewels of the Golden Square Mile's Scottish bourgeoisie. The university's main campus lies nestled in greenery at the foot of Mont Royal. The entrance is located at the northernmost end of Avenue McGill College, at the Roddick Gates, which contain the university's clock and chimes. On the right are two Romanesque-Revival-style buildings, designed by Sir Andrew Taylor to house the physics (1893) and chemistry (1896) departments. The Faculty of Architecture now occupies the second building. A little farther along, visitors will see the Macdonald Engineering Building, a fine example of the English baroque-Revival style, with a broken pediment adorning its rusticated portal (Percy Nobbs, 1908). At the end of the drive stands the

oldest building on campus, the Arts Building (1839). For three decades, this austere neoclassical structure by architect John Ostell was McGill University's only building. It houses Moyse Hall, a lovely theatre dating back to 1926, with a design inspired by antiquity (Harold Lea Fetherstonaugh, architect).

The **Musée McCord d'Histoire Canadienne** ★★ (*$8.50 taxes included, free on Sat 10am to noon; late Jun to mid-Oct, every day 10am to 6pm; mid-Oct to May, Tue to Fri 10am to 6pm, Sat and Sun 10am to 5pm; 690 Rue Sherbrooke Ouest, McGill Métro, ☎398-7100*), the McCord Museum of Canadian History, occupies a building formerly used by the McGill University Students' Association. Designed by architect Percy Nobbs (1906), this handsome building of English baroque inspiration was enlarged toward the back in 1991. Along Rue Victoria, visitors can see an interesting sculpture by Pierre Granche entitled *Totem Urbain/Histoire en Dentelle* (Urban totem/History in lace). For anyone interested in First Nations people and daily life in Canada in the 18th and 19th centuries, this is *the* museum to see in Montréal. It houses a large ethnographic collection, as well as collections of costumes, decorative arts, paintings, prints and photographs, including the famous Notman collection, composed of 700,000 negatives on glass plates. This last collection constitutes a veritable portrait of Canada at the end of the 19th century.

The first Anglican cathedral in Montréal stood on Rue Notre-Dame, not far from Place d'Armes. After a fire in 1856, **Christ Church Cathedral** ★★ (*at the corner of Rue University*) was relocated closer to the community it served, in the heart of the nascent Golden Square Mile. Using the cathedral of his hometown, Salisbury, as his model, architect Frank Wills designed a flamboyant structure, with a single steeple rising above the transepts. The soberness of the interior contrasts with the rich ornamentation of the Catholic churches included in this walking tour. A few beautiful stained-glass windows from the workshops of William Morris provide the only bit of colour.

After a 40-year absence, the Jesuits returned to Montréal in 1842 at Monseigneur Ignace Bourget's invitation. Six years later, they founded Collège Sainte-Marie, where several generations of boys would receive an outstanding education. **Église du Gesù** ★★ (*1202 Rue de Bleury*) was originally designed as the college chapel. The grandiose project begun in 1864 by architect Patrick C. Keely, of Brooklyn, New York, was never completed, due to lack of funds. Consequently, the church's Renaissance-Revival-style towers remain unfinished. The *trompe-l'œil* decor inside was executed by artist Damien Müller. Of particular interest are the seven main altars and surrounding parquetry, all fine examples of cabinet work. The large paintings hanging from the walls were commissioned by the Gagliardi brothers of Rome. The Jesuit college, erected to the south of the church, was demolished in 1975, but the church was

fortunately saved, and then restored in 1983.

Fleeing misery and potato blight, a large number of Irish immigrants came to Montréal between 1820 and 1860, and helped construct the Lachine Canal and the Victoria Bridge. **St. Patrick's Basilica** ★★ (*Rue Saint-Alexandre*) was thus built to meet a pressing new demand for a church to serve the Irish Catholic community. When it was inaugurated in 1847, St. Patrick's dominated the city below. Today, it is well hidden by the skyscrapers of the business centre. Architect Pierre-Louis Morin and Père Félix Martin, the Jesuit superior, designed the plans for the edifice, built in the Gothic Revival style favoured by the Sulpicians, who financed the project. One of the many paradoxes surrounding St. Patrick's is that it is more representative of French than Anglo-Saxon Gothic architecture. The spectacular interior encourages prayer. Each of the pine columns that divide the nave into three sections is a whole tree trunk carved in one piece.

Formerly located at Cité du Havre, the **Musée d'Art Contemporain** ★★ (*$6; Tue to Sun 11am to 6pm, free on Wed 6pm to 9pm; 185 Rue Sainte-Catherine Ouest, at the corner of Rue Jeanne-Mance, ☎847-6212*), Montréal's modern art museum, was moved to this site in 1992. The long, low building, erected on top of the Place des Arts parking lot, contains eight rooms, where post-1940 works of art from both Québec and abroad are exhibited. The interior, which has a decidedly better design than the exterior, is laid out around a circular hall. On the lower level, an amusing

metal sculpture by Pierre Granche entitled *Comme si le temps... de la rue* (As if time... from the street), shows Montréal's network of streets crowded with helmeted birds, in a sort of semicircular theatre.

During the rush of the Quiet Revolution, the government of Québec, inspired by cultural complexes like New York's Lincoln Center, built **Place des Arts** ★ (*260 Boulevard de Maisonneuve Ouest, through to Rue Sainte-Catherine Ouest, Place-des-Arts métro station*), a collection of five halls for the performing arts. Salle Wilfrid Pelletier, in the centre, was inaugurated in 1963 (2,982 seats). It accommodates both the Montreal Symphony Orchestra and the Opéra de Montréal. The cube-shaped Théâtre Maisonneuve, on the right, contains three theatres: Théâtre Maisonneuve (1,460 seats), Théâtre Jean-Duceppe (755 seats) and the intimate little Café de la Place (138 seats). The Cinquième Salle (350 seats) was built in 1992 during the construction of the Musée d'Art Contemporain. Place des Arts is linked to the governmental section of the underground city, which stretches from the Palais des Congrès convention centre to Avenue du Président-Kennedy. Developed by the various levels of government, this portion of the underground network distinguishes itself from the private section, centred around Place Ville-Marie, farther west.

Set up inside the former buildings of the Ekers brewery, the **Musée Juste Pour Rire** ★★ (*$5; Mon to Fri 9:30am to 3:30pm, Sat and Sun 10am to 5pm;*

Québec

2111 Boulevard Saint-Laurent, Saint-Laurent métro station, ☎845-4000), or Just for Laughs Museum, opened in 1993. This museum, the only one of its kind in the world, explores the different facets of humour, using a variety of film clips and sets. Visitors are equipped with infrared headphones that enable them to follow the presentation. The building itself was renovated and redesigned by architect Luc Laporte, and has some 3,000m² of exhibition space.

Montréal's **Chinatown** ★ may be rather small, but it is nonetheless a pleasant place to walk around. A large number of the Chinese immigrants who came to Canada to help build the transcontinental railroad, completed in 1886, settled here at the end of the 19th century.

Though they no longer live in the neighbourhood, they still come here on weekends to stroll about and stock up on traditional products. Rue de la Gauchetière has been converted into a pedestrian street lined with restaurants and framed by lovely Chinese-style gates.

Village Shaughnessy

When the Sulpicians took possession of the island of Montréal in 1663, they kept a portion of the best land for a farm and an Iroquois village there in 1676. Following a fire, the village was relocated several times before being permanently established in Oka. Part of the farm, corresponding to the area now known as Westmount, was then granted to French settlers.

The Sulpicians planted an orchard and a vineyard on the remaining portion. Starting around 1870, the land was separated into lots. Part of it was used for the construction of mansions, while large plots were awarded to Catholic communities allied with the Sulpicians. It was at this time that Shaughnessy House was built – hence the name of the neighbourhood. During the 1970s, the number of local inhabitants increased considerably, making Shaughnessy Village the most densely populated area in Québec.

The Sulpicians' farmhouse was surrounded by a wall linked to four stone corner towers, earning it the name Fort des Messieurs. The house was destroyed when the **Grand Séminaire** ★★ (1854-1860) (*2065 Rue Sherbrooke Ouest*) was built, but two towers, erected in the 17th century by François Vachon de Belmont, superior of the Montréal Sulpicians, can still be found in the institution's shady gardens. It was in one of these that Saint Marguerite Bourgeoys taught young Aboriginal girls. Around 1880, the long neoclassical buildings of the Grand Séminaire, designed by architect John Ostell, were topped by a mansard roof by Henri-Maurice Perrault. Information panels, set up on Rue Sherbrooke directly in line with Rue du Fort, provide precise details about the farm buildings.

Founded in 1979 by Phyllis Lambert, the **Centre Canadien d'Architecture** ★★★ (*$6; free admission Thu 6pm to 8pm; Jun to Sep, Tue to Sun 11am to 6pm, Thu to 8pm; Oct to May, Wed to Fri 11am to 6pm, Thu to 8pm; Sat and*

Chinatown

*Sun 11am to 5pm; 1920 Rue
Baile,* ☎939-7026), or Canadian Centre for Architec-
ture, is both a museum
and a centre for the study
of world architecture. Its
collections of plans, drawings, models, books and
photographs are the most
important of their kind in
the entire world. The Centre, built in 1989, has six
exhibition rooms, a book-
store, a library, a 217-seat
auditorium and a wing
specially designed for researchers, as well as vaults
and restoration laborato-
ries. The main building,
shaped like a "U," was
designed by Peter Rose,
with the help of Phyllis
Lambert. It is covered with
grey limestone from the
Saint-Marc quarries near
Québec City. This material,
which used to be extracted
from the Plateau Mont-
Royal and Rosemont quar-
ries in Montréal, adorns
the facades of many of the
city's houses.

The centre surrounds the
Maison Shaughnessy ★,
whose facade looks out on
Boulevard René-Lévesque
Ouest. This house is in fact
a pair of residences, built
in 1874 by architect Wil-
liam Tutin Thomas. It is
representative of the mansions that once lined Boulevard René-Lévesque (formerly Boulevard
Dorchester). In 1974, it
was at the centre of an
effort to salvage the neighbourhood, which had
been torn down in a num-
ber of places. The house,
itself threatened with demolition, was purchased at
the last moment by Phyllis
Lambert. She set up the
offices and reception
rooms of the Canadian
Centre for Architecture
inside. The building was
named after Sir Thomas
Shaughnessy, a former
president of Canadian Pa-
cific, who lived in the
house for several decades.

The inhabitants of the
neighbourhood, grouped
together in an association,
subsequently chose to
name the entire area after
him.

The amusing **architecture
garden**, by artist Melvin
Charney, lies across from
Shaughnessy House, be-
tween two highway on-
ramps. It illustrates the
different stages of the
neighbourhood's develop-
ment, using a portion of
the Sulpicians' orchard on
the left, stone lines to indicate borders of 19th-cen-
tury properties and rose
bushes reminiscent of the
gardens of those houses. A
promenade along the cliff
that once separated the
wealthy neighbourhood
from the working-class
sector below offers a view
of the lower part of the city
(Little Burgundy,
Saint-Henri, Verdun) and
the St. Lawrence River.
Some of the highlights of
this panorama are repre-
sented in a stylized manner
atop concrete posts.

Like the Congrégation de
Notre-Dame, the Sœurs
Grises had to relocate their
convent and hospital,
which used to be situated
on Rue Saint-Pierre in Old
Montréal. They obtained
part of the Sulpicians' farm,
where a vast convent, de-
signed by Victor Bourgeau,
was erected between 1869
and 1874. The **Couvent des
Sœurs Grises** ★★ (*1185 Rue
Saint-Mathieu*) is the product of an architectural
tradition developed over
the centuries in Québec.
The chapel alone reveals a
foreign influence, namely
the Romanesque Revival
style favoured by the
Sulpicians, as opposed to
the Renaissance and Ba-
roque Revival styles pre-
ferred by the church.

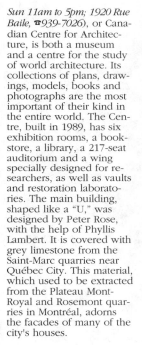

Mont Royal and Westmount

Montréal's central neigh-
bourhoods are distributed
around Mont Royal, an
important landmark in the
cityscape. Known simply
as "the mountain" by
Montrealers, this squat
mass, measuring 234m at
its highest point, is composed of intrusive rock. It
is in fact one of the seven
hills studding the St. Lawrence plain in the
Montérégie region. A
"green lung" rising up at
the far end of downtown
streets, it provides
Montrealers with a healthy
dose of nature. The moun-
tain actually has three
summits; the first is occupied by Parc du Mont-
Royal, the second by the
Université de Montréal,
and the third by
Westmount, an independ-
ent city with lovely
English-style homes. In
addition to these areas,
there are the Catholic,
Protestant and Jewish
cemeteries, which, considered as a whole, form the
largest necropolis in North
America.

From the **Belvédère
Camilien-Houde** ★★ (*Voie
Camilien-Houde*), a lovely
scenic viewpoint, visitors
can look out over the
entire eastern portion of
Montréal. The Plateau
Mont-Royal lies in the
foreground, a uniform
mass of duplexes and
triplexes pierced in a few
places by the oxidized-
copper bell towers of
parish churches, while the
Rosemont and
Maisonneuve quarters lie
in the background, with
the Olympic Stadium
towering over them. In
clear weather, the oil
refineries in the east end

Québec

can be seen in the distance. The St. Lawrence River, visible on the right, is actually 1.5km wide at its narrowest point. The Belvédère Camilien-Houde is Montréal's version of Inspiration Point and a favourite gathering place of sweethearts with cars.

Pressured by the residents of the Golden Square Mile, who saw their favourite playground being deforested by various firewood companies, the City of Montréal created **Parc du Mont-Royal** ★★★ in 1870. Frederick Law Olmsted (1822-1903), the celebrated designer of New York's Central Park, was commissioned to design the park. He decided to preserve the site's natural character, limiting himself to a few lookout points linked by winding paths. Inaugurated in 1876, the park, which covers 101ha on the southern part of the mountain, is cherished by Montrealers as a place to enjoy the fresh air (see also p 182).

The **Chalet du Mont Royal** ★★★ (*Mon to Fri 9:30am to 8pm; Parc du Mont-Royal, ☎844-4928*), located in the centre of the park, was designed by Aristide Beaugrand-Champagne in 1932 as a replacement for the original structure, which was threatening to collapse. During the 1930s and 1940s, big bands gave moonlit concerts on the steps of the building. The interior is decorated with remounted paintings depicting scenes from Canadian history. These were commissioned from some of Québec's great painters, such as Marc-Aurèle Fortin and Paul-Émile Borduas. Nevertheless, people go to the chalet mainly to stroll along the lookout and take

in the exceptional view of downtown, best in the late afternoon and in the evening, when the skyscrapers light up the darkening sky.

Both the cemetery and the roads leading to it offer a number of views of the **Oratoire Saint-Joseph** ★★ (*free admission; every day 9am to 5pm, mass between 6:30am and 9:30pm, nativity scene Nov 15 to Feb 15; 3800 Chemin Queen Mary, ☎733-8211 for information*). The enormous building topped by a copper dome, the second-largest dome in the world after that of St. Peter's in Rome, stands on a hillside, which accentuates its mystical aura. From the gate at the entrance, there are over 300 steps to climb to reach the oratory. Small buses are also available for worshippers who do not want to climb the steps. It was built between 1924 and 1956, thanks to the efforts of the blessed Frère André, porter of Collège Notre-Dame (across the street), to whom many miracles are attributed. A veritable religious complex, the oratory is dedicated to both Saint Joseph and its humble creator. It includes the lower and upper basilicas, the crypt of Frère André and two museums, one dedicated to Frère André's life, the other to sacred art. Visitors will also find the porter's first chapel, built in 1910, a cafeteria, a hostelry and a store selling devotional articles.

Aiming to preserve its monopoly on French-language university education in Québec, Québec City's Université Laval, after

Oratoire Saint-Joseph

many attempts, finally opened a branch of its institution in the Château Ramezay. A few years later, it moved to Rue Saint-Denis, giving birth to the Quartier Latin (see p 181). The **Université de Montréal** ★ (*2900 Boulevard Édouard-Montpetit*) finally became autonomous in 1920, enabling its directors to develop grandiose plans. Ernest Cormier (1885-1980) was approached about designing a campus on the north side of Mont Royal. The architect, a graduate of the École des Beaux-Arts in Paris, was one of the first to acquaint North Americans with the Art Deco style.

Westmount is like a piece of Great Britain in North America. Its **City Hall** ★ (*4333 Rue Sherbrooke Ouest*) was built in the Neo-Tudor style, inspired by the architecture of the age of Henry VIII and Elizabeth I. During the 1920s this style was regarded as the national style of England because it issued exclusively from the British Isles. It is characterized, in part, by horizontal openings with multiple stone transoms, bay windows and flattened arches. The impeccable green of a lawn-bowling club lies at the back, frequented by members wearing their regulation whites.

Take Chemin de la Côte-Saint-Antoine to Parc Murray. In Québec, the term *côte*, which translates literally as "hill," usually has nothing to do with the slope of the land, but is a leftover of the seigneurial system of New France. The roads linking one farm to the next ran along the tops of the long rectangles of land distributed to colonists. As a result, these plots of land gradually became known as *côtes*, the French word for "side." Côte Saint-Antoine is one of the oldest roads on the island of Montréal. Laid out in 1684 by the Sulpicians on a former trail used by Aboriginals, it is lined with some of Westmount's oldest houses. At the corner of Avenue Forden is a **milestone** dating back to the 17th century, discreetly identified by the pattern of the sidewalk, which radiates out from it. This is all that remains of the system of road signs developed by the Sulpicians for their seigneury on the island of Montréal.

Parc Westmount ★ and the **Westmount Library** ★ (*4575 Rue Sherbrooke Ouest*). The park was laid out on swampy land in 1895. Four years later, Québec's first public library was erected on the same site. Up until then, religious communities had been the only ones to develop this type of cultural facility – the province was somewhat

behind in this area. The recently restored red-brick building is the product of the trends toward eclecticism, picturesqueness and polychromy that characterized the last two decades of the 19th century.

Maisonneuve

In 1883, the city of Maisonneuve was founded in eastern Montréal, thanks to the initiative of farmers and French-Canadian merchants; port facilities expanded into the area and the city's development picked up. Then, in 1918, the formerly autonomous city was annexed to Montréal, becoming one of its major working-class neighbourhoods, with a 90% francophone population. In the course of its history, Maisonneuve has been profoundly influenced by men with grand ideas, who wanted to make this part of the country a place where people could thrive together. Upon taking office at the Maisonneuve town hall in 1910, brothers Marius and Oscar Dufresne instituted a rather ambitious policy of building prestigious Beaux-Arts-style public buildings intended to make "their" city a model of development for French Québec. Later, in 1931, Frère Marie-Victorin founded Montréal's Jardin Botanique in Maisonneuve; today, it is the second largest botanical garden in the world. The last major episode in the area's history was in 1971, when Mayor Jean Drapeau initiated the construction of the immense sports complex used for the 1976 Olympic Games.

The **Jardin Botanique, Maison de l'Arbre** and **Insectarium** ★ ★ ★ (*$9.50 high season, 7$ low season for the greenhouses and Insectarium; 2-day ticket with the Biodôme and the Tour Olympique $22.50; Sep to May, every day 9am to 5pm, May to Sep, every day 9am to 7pm; 4101 Rue Sherbrooke Est, ☎872-1400*). The 73ha Jardin Botanique was begun during the economic crisis of the 1930s on the site of Mont-de-La-Salle, home base of the brothers of the Écoles Chrétiennes. Behind the Art Deco building occupied by the Université de Montréal's institute of biology, visitors will find a stretch of 10 connected greenhouses, which shelter, notably, a precious collection of orchids and the largest grouping of bonsais and *penjings* outside of Asia. The latter includes the famous Wu collection, given to the garden by master Wu Yee-Sun of Hong Kong in 1984.

Thirty outdoor gardens, open from spring through autumn, and designed to inform and amaze visitors, stretch to the north and west of the greenhouses. Particularly noteworthy are the symmetrical display gardens around the restaurant, the Japanese garden and its *sukiya*-style tea pavilion, as well as the very beautiful Chinese Lac de Rêve, or Dream Lake garden, whose pavilions were designed by artisans who came here from China specifically for the task. Since Montréal is twinned with Shanghai, it was deemed appropriate that it should have the largest such garden outside of Asia.

The northern part of the botanical garden is occupied by an arboretum. The

Québec

Maison de l'Arbre, literally the "tree house" was established in this area to familiarize people with the life of a tree. The interactive, permanent exhibit is actually set up in an old tree trunk. There are displays on the yellow birch, Québec's emblematic tree since 1993. The building's structure, consisting of beams of different types of wood, reminds us how leafy forests really are. Note the play of light and shade from the frame onto the large white wall, meant to resemble trunks and branches. A terrace in the back is an ideal spot to contemplate the arboretum's pond; it also leads to a charming little bonsai garden. To reach the Maison de l'Arbre, climb on board the *Balade*, the shuttle that regularly tours the garden, or use the garden's northern entrance located on Boulevard Rosemont.

The complementary **Insectarium** (☎872-8753) is located to the east of the greenhouses. This innovative living museum invites visitors to discover the fascinating world of insects.

The **Château Dufresne ★★** (*2929 Rue Jeanne-d'Arc, métro Pie-IX*) is, in fact, two 22-room private mansions behind the same facade, built in 1916 for brothers Marius and Oscar Dufresne, shoe-manufacturers and authors of a grandiose plan to develop Maisonneuve. The plan was abandoned after the onset of World War I, causing the municipality to go bankrupt. Their home, designed by Marius Dufresne and Parisian architect Jules Renard, was supposed to be the nucleus of a residential upper-class neighbour-

hood, which never materialized. It is one of the best examples of Beaux-Arts architecture in Montréal. From 1979 to March of 1997, the château was home to the Musée des Arts Décoratifs de Montréal (☎259-2575) now located downtown (see p 170).

Stade Olympique

The **Stade Olympique ★★★** (*guided tour $5.25, package with tour and funicular $10.25; guided tours in English at 12:40pm and 3:40pm; closed mid-Jan to mid-Feb; 4141 Avenue Pierre-de-Coubertin*, ☎252-8687) is also known as the Olympic Stadium and the "Big O." Jean Drapeau was mayor of Montréal from 1954 to 1957, and from 1960 to 1986. He dreamed of great things for "his" city. Endowed with exceptional powers of persuasion and unfailing determination, he saw a number of important projects through to a successful conclusion, including the construction of Place des Arts and the métro, Montréal's hosting of the World's Fair in 1967 and, of course, the 1976 Summer Olympics.

The latter event required the construction of appropriate facilitiès. In spite of the controversy this caused, the city sought out a Parisian visionary to de-

sign something completely original. A billion dollars later, the major work of architect Roger Taillibert, who also designed the stadium of the Parc des Princes in Paris, stunned everyone with its curving, organic concrete shapes. The 56,000-seat oval stadium is covered with a kevlar roof supported by cables stretching from the 190m leaning tower. In the distance, visitors will see the two pyramid-shaped towers of the **Olympic Village**, where the athletes were housed in 1976.

The stadium hosts a variety of annual events, such as the Salon de l'Auto (Car Show) and the Salon National de l'Habitation (National Home Show). From April to September, Montréal's National League baseball team, the Expos, plays its home games here.

The stadium's tower, which is the tallest leaning tower in the world, was rebaptised the **Tour de Montréal**. A funicular (*$9; Mon noon to 9pm, Tue to Thu 10am to 9pm, Fri to Sun 10am to 11pm;* ☎252-8687) climbs the structure to an interior observation deck which commands a view of the eastern part of Montréal. Exhibits are presented on the upper levels. There is also a rest area with a bar.

The foot of the tower houses the swimming pools of the Olympic Complex, while the former cycling track, known as the Vélodrome, located nearby, has been converted into an artificial habitat for plants and animals called the **Biodôme** ★★★ (*$9.50; every day 9am to 5pm; mid-Jun to early Sep, to 7pm; 4777 Avenue Pierre de Coubertin;* ☎868-3000). This new type of museum, associated with the Jardin Botanique, contains four very different ecosystems – the Tropical Rainforest, the Laurentian Forest, the St. Lawrence Marine Ecosystem and the Polar World – within a space of 10,000m².

Penguins

These are complete microcosms, including vegetation, mammals and free-flying birds, and close to real climatic conditions.

★★

Île Sainte-Hélène and Île Notre-Dame

When Samuel de Champlain reached the island of Montréal in 1611, he found a small rocky archipelago located in front of it. He named the largest of these islands in the channel after his wife, Hélène Boulé. Île Sainte-Hélène later became part of the seigneury of Longueuil. Around 1720,

the Baroness of Longueuil chose the island as the site for a country house surrounded by a garden. It is also worth noting that in 1760, the island was the last foothold of French troops in New France, commanded by Chevalier François de Lévis. Recognizing Île Saint-Hélène's strategic importance, the British army built a fort on the eastern part of the island at the beginning of the 19th century. The threat of armed conflict with the United States having diminished, the Canadian government rented Île Sainte-Hélène to the City of Montréal in 1874, at which time the island was turned into a park and linked to Old Montréal by ferry, and, from 1930 on, by the Jacques-Cartier bridge.

In the early 1960s, Montréal was chosen as the location of the 1967 World's Fair (Expo '67). The city wanted to set up the event on a large, attractive site near the downtown area; such a site such, however, did not exist – it had to be built. Using earth excavated during the construction of the métro tunnel, Île Notre-Dame was created, doubling the area of Île Sainte-Hélène. From April to November 1967, 45 million visitors passed through Cité du Havre, the gateway to the fairground, and crisscrossed both islands. Expo '67, as Montrealers still refer to it, was more than a jumble of

pavillions; it was Montréal's awakening. The city opened itself to the world that year, and visitors from all over discovered a new art of living, including mini-skirts, colour television, hippies, flower power and protest rock.

Parc Hélène-de-Champlain ★★ lies on Île Sainte-Hélène, which originally covered an area of 50ha, but was enlarged to over 120ha for Expo '67. The original portion corresponds to the raised area studded with boulders made of breccia. Peculiar to the island, breccia is a very hard, ferrous stone that takes on an orange colour when exposed to air for a long time. In 1992, the western part of the island was transformed into a vast open-air amphitheatre, where large-scale shows are presented. On a lovely park bordering the river, across from Montréal, visitors will find *L'Homme* ("Humankind"), a large metal sculpture by Alexandre Calder, created for Expo '67.

After the War of 1812 between the United States and Great Britain, the **Fort de l'Île Sainte-Hélène** ★★ was built so that Montréal could be properly defended if ever a new conflict were to erupt. Supervised by military engineer Elias Walker Durnford, it was completed in 1825. Built of breccia stone, the fort is in the shape of a jagged "U," surrounding a drill ground, used today as a parade ground by the Compagnie Franche de la Marine and the 78th Regiment of the Fraser Highlanders as a parade ground. These two costumed mock regiments delight visitors by reviving Canada's French and Scot-

Québec

tish military traditions. The drill ground also offers a lovely view of both the port and **Pont Jacques-Cartier**, inaugurated in 1930, which straddles the island, separating the park from La Ronde.

The arsenal is now occupied by the **Musée David-M.-Stewart** ★★ (*$6; Sep to May, Wed to Mon 10am to 5pm; Jun to Aug, every day 10am to 6pm;* ☎*861-6701*), which exhibits a collection of objects from the 17th and 18th centuries, including interesting collections of maps, firearms, and scientific and navigational instruments put together by Montréal industrialist David Stewart and his wife Liliane. The latter heads both the museum and the Macdonald-Stewart Foundation, which also manages the Château Ramezay and the Château Dufresne (the former Musée des Arts Décoratifs).

La Ronde ★ (*$27.50; Jun to Sep, every day 11am to 11pm, Fri and Sat to midnight.;* ☎*872-6222*), an amusement park set up for Expo '67 on the former Île Ronde, opens its doors to both the young and the not so young every summer. For Montrealers, an annual trip to La Ronde has almost become a pilgrimage. An international fireworks competition is held here on Saturdays or Sundays during the months of June and July.

Very few of the pavilions built for Expo '67 have survived the destructive effects of the weather and the changes in the islands' roles. One that has is the former U.S. pavilion, a veritable monument to modern architecture. The first complete geodesic dome to be taken beyond the stage of a model, it

was created by the celebrated engineer Richard Buckminster Fuller (1895-1983). The **Biosphere** ★★ (*$6.50; Jun. 24 to Sep. 1, every day 10am to 6pm; off-season, Tue to Sun, 10am to 5pm;* ☎*283-5000, Île-Sainte-Hélène* métro station), built of tubular aluminum and measuring 80m in diameter, unfortunately lost its translucent acrylic skin in a fire back in 1978. An environmental interpretive centre on the St. Lawrence River, the Great Lakes and the different Canadian ecosystems, is now located in the dome. The permanent exhibit aims to sensitize the public to issues of sustainable development and the conservation of water as a precious resource. There are four interactive galleries with giant screens and hands-on displays to explore and delight in. A terrace restaurant with a panoramic view of the islands completes the museum.

Île Notre-Dame emerged from the waters of the St. Lawrence in no less than 10 months, with the help of 15 million tonnes of rock and soil transported here from the métro construction site. Because it is an artificial island, its creators were able to give it a fanciful shape by playing with both soil and water.

The island, therefore, is traversed by pleasant **canals and gardens** ★★, laid out for the 1980 Floralies Internationales, an international flower show. Boats are available for rent, enabling visitors to ply the canals and admire the flowers mirrored in their waters.

Montréal's **Casino** ★ (*free admission, parking and coat check; every day 24hrs; Île-Sainte-Hélène métro station, bus #167;* ☎*392-2746*) occupies the former French and Québec pavilions of Expo '67. The main building corresponds to the old **French Pavilion** ★, an aluminum structure designed by architect Jean Faugeron. It was renovated in 1993 at a cost of $92.4 million in order to accommodate the Casino.

The upper galleries offer some lovely views of downtown Montréal and the St. Lawrence Seaway.

Immediately to the west of the former French pavilion, the building shaped like a truncated pyramid is the **former Québec pavilion** ★ (*every day 9am to 3am*). It was incorporated into the Casino after being raised and recovered with gold-tinted glass in 1996.

Casino

Nearby, visitors will find the entrance to the **Plage de l'Île Notre-Dame**, a beach enabling Montrealers to lounge on real sand right in the middle of the St. Lawrence. A natural filtering system keeps the water in the small lake clean without chemical additives. The number of swimmers allowed on the beach is strictly regulated, however, in order to maintain the balance of the system.

There are other recreational facilities here as well, namely the Olympic Basin created for the rowing competitions of the 1976 Olympics and the **Circuit Gilles-Villeneuve**, where Formula One drivers compete every year in the Grand Prix Player's du Canada, part of the international racing circuit.

Quartier Latin

People come to this university neighbourhood, centred around Rue Saint-Denis, for its theatres, cinemas and countless outdoor cafés, which offer a glimpse of the heterogeneous crowd of students and revellers. The area's origins date back to 1823, when Montréal's first Catholic cathedral, Église Saint-Jacques, was inaugurated on Rue Saint-Denis. This prestigious edifice quickly attracted the cream of French-Canadian society, mainly old noble families who had remained in Canada after the conquest. In 1852, a fire ravaged the neighbourhood, destroying the cathedral and Monseigneur Bourget's bishop's palace in the process. Painfully reconstructed in the second half of the 19th century, the area remained residential

until the Université de Montréal was established here in 1893, marking the beginning of a period of cultural turmoil that would eventually lead to the Quiet Revolution of the 1960s. The Université du Québec, founded in 1974, has since taken over from the Université de Montréal, now located on the north side of Mont Royal. The prosperity of the quarter has thus been ensured.

After the great fire of 1852, a reservoir was built at the top of the hill known as Côte-à-Barron. In 1879, it was dismantled and the site was converted into a park by the name of **Square Saint-Louis ★★**. Developers built beautiful Second-Empire-style residences around the square, making it the nucleus of the French-Canadian bourgeois neighbourhood. These groups of houses give the area a certain harmonious quality rarely found in Montréal's urban landscape. To the west, **Rue Prince-Arthur** extends west from the square. In the 1960s, this pedestrian mall (between Boulevard Saint-Laurent and Avenue Laval) was the centre of the counterculture and the hippie movement in Montréal. Today, it is lined with numerous restaurants and terraces. On summer evenings, street performers liven up the atmosphere.

The **Bibliothèque Nationale ★** (*1700 Rue Saint-Denis*), the national library, was originally built for the Sulpicians, who looked unfavourably on the construction of a public library on Rue Sherbrooke. Even though many works were still on the *Index*, and thus forbidden reading for the clergy, the new library was seen as unfair competition. Known in the past as

Bibliothèque Saint-Sulpice, this branch of the Bibliothèque Nationale du Québec was designed in the Beaux-Arts style by architect Eugène Payette in 1914. This style, a synthesis of classicism and French Renaissance architecture, was taught at the Paris École des Beaux-Arts, hence its name in North America. The interior is graced with lovely stained-glass windows created by Henri Perdriau in 1915.

The screening room and rental service of the **Office National du Film du Canada (ONF) (National Film Board of Canada)** are located at the corner of Boulevard de Maisonneuve. The ONF-NFB has the world's only *cinérobothèque* (*$5 for 2hrs, 3$ for 1hr; Tue to Sun noon to 9pm; 1564 Rue St-Denis, ☎496-6887*), enabling about 100 people to watch different films at once. The complex also has a movie theatre (*$5; every day, monthly schedule*) where various documentaries and NFB films are screened. Movie lovers can also visit the **Cinémathèque Québécoise** (*335 Boulevard de Maisonneuve Est, ☎842-9763*), a little farther west, which has a collection of 25,000 Canadian, Québec and foreign films, as well as hundreds of pieces of equipment dating back to the early history of film (see also p 193). The Cinémathèque recently reopened after extensive renovations. UQAM's new concert hall, **Salle Pierre-Mercure**, is across the street.

Unlike most North American universities, with buildings contained within a specific campus, the campus of the **Université du Québec à Montréal (UQAM) ★** (*405 Rue Sainte-*

Québec

Catherine Est, at the corner of Rue Saint-Denis) is integrated into the city fabric like French and German universities built during the Renaissance. It is also linked to the underground city and the métro. The university is located on the site once occupied by the buildings of the Université de Montréal and the Église Saint-Jacques, which was reconstructed after the fire of 1852. Only the wall of the right transept and the Gothic-Revival steeple were integrated into Pavillon Judith-Jasmin (1979), and have since become the symbol of the university. UQAM is part of the Université du Québec, founded in 1969 and established in different cities across the province. Every year, over 40,000 students attend this flourishing institution of higher learning.

Plateau Mont-Royal

If there is one neighbourhood typical of Montréal, it is definitely this one. Thrown into the spotlight by writer Michel Tremblay, one of its illustrious sons, the "Plateau," as its inhabitants refer to it, is a neighbourhood of penniless intellectuals, young professionals and old francophone working-class families. Its long streets are lined with duplexes and triplexes adorned with amusingly contorted exterior staircases leading up to the long, narrow apartments that are so typical of Montréal. Flower-decked balconies made of wood or wrought iron provide box-seats for the spectacle on the street below. The Plateau is bounded by the mountain to the west, the

Canadian Pacific railway tracks to the north and east, and Rue Sherbrooke to the south. It is traversed by a few major streets lined with cafés and theatres, such as Rue Saint-Denis and Avenue Papineau, but it is essentially a tranquil area. A visit to Montréal would not be complete without a stroll through this area to truly grasp the spirit of Montréal. This tour starts at the exit of the Mont-Royal métro station. Turn right on Avenue du Mont-Royal, the neighbourhood's main commercial artery.

At the end of Rue Fabre, visitors will find **Parc Lafontaine**, the Plateau's main green space, laid out in 1908 on the site of an old military shooting range. Monuments to Sir Louis-Hippolyte Lafontaine, Félix Leclerc and Dollard des Ormeaux have been erected here. The park covers an area of 40ha, and is embellished with two artificial lakes and shady paths for pedestrians and bicyclists. There are tennis courts and bowling greens for summer-sports enthusiasts, and in the winter, the frozen lakes form a large rink, which is illuminated at night. The

Théâtre de Verdure (outdoor theatre) is also located here. Every weekend, the park is crowded with people from the neighbourhood, who come here to make the most of beautiful sunny or snowy days.

Église Saint-Jean-Baptiste ★★ (*309 Rue Rachel Est*), dedicated to the patron saint of French Canadians, is a gigantic symbol of the solid faith of Catholic working-class inhabitants of the Plateau Mont-Royal at the turn of the 20th century, who, despite their poverty and large families, managed to amass considerable amounts of money for the construction of sumptuous churches. The exterior was built in 1901 by architect Émile Vanier. The interior was redone after a fire, and is now a veritable Baroque Revival masterpiece designed by Casimir Saint-Jean that is not to be missed. The pink-marble and gilded wood baldaquin in the chancel (1915) shelters the altar, made of white Italian marble, which faces the large Casavant organs – among the most powerful in the city – in the jube. Concerts are frequently given at this church. It can seat up to 3,000 people.

Parks

Mount-Royal

All year round, Montrealers flock to **Parc du Mont-Royal**, a huge green expanse in the middle of the city, to enjoy a wide range of athletic activities. During summer, footpaths and mountain-bike trails are maintained. Bird feeders have been set up along one trail for bird-watchers. During winter, the paths serve as cross-country ski trails, leading across the snowy slopes of the mountain, and Lac aux Castors becomes a big, beautiful skating rink, where people of all ages come to enjoy themselves.

Île Sainte-Hélène and Île Notre-Dame

Parc des Îles (☎*872-4537*) encompasses both Île Sainte-Hélène and Île Notre-Dame. In summer, Montrealers flock here on sunny days to enjoy the beach and the swimming pools. Footpaths and bicycle trails crisscross the park. In wintertime, a whole host of activities is organized here, including cross-country skiing (14km), tobogganing, ice fishing and skating on the 2km-long Olympic rowing basin.

The island of Montréal is strewn with parks where visitors can enjoy all sorts of activities. **Parc Angrignon** (*3400 Boulevard des Trinitaires*), **Parc Lafontaine** (see p 182), **Parc du Mont-Royal** (see p 182), **Parc Jeanne-Mance** (*Avenue de l'Esplanade, between Avenue du Mont-Royal and rue Duluth*) and **Parc René-Lévesque** (*at the west end of the Canal de Lachine*) are all very pleasant places to relax in a peaceful atmosphere. Year-round, Montrealers take advantage of these small islands of greenery to unwind far from the urban tumult, while remaining right in the heart of the city.

Outdoor Activities

Cycling

The area around the **Canal de Lachine** has been redesigned in an effort to highlight this communication route, so important during the 19th and early 20th centuries. A pleasant bike path was laid out alongside the canal. Very popular with Montrealers, especially on Sundays, the path leads out to **Parc René-Lévesque**, a narrow strip of land jutting out into Lac Saint-Louis, which offers splendid views of the lake and its surroundings. There are benches and picnic tables in the park and plenty of seagulls to keep you company. The path leads around the park, returning beside the river and the Lachine rapids. Many birds frequent this side of the park, and if you are lucky you might see some great herons.

Île Notre-Dame and **Île Sainte-Hélène** are accessible from Old Montréal. The path runs through an industrial area, then through the Cité du Havre before reaching the islands (cyclists cross the river on the Pont de la Concorde). It is easy to ride from one island to the other. The islands are well maintained and are a great place to relax, stroll and admire Montréal's skyline.

Accommodations

Gîte Montréal
3458 Avenue Laval, H2X 3C8
☎*289-9749*
☎*800-267-5180*
≠*287-7386*
Gîte Montréal is an association of nearly 100 bed & breakfasts (*gîtes*), mostly Victorian houses in the Latin Quarter. In order to make sure that all rooms offered are comfortable, the organization visits each one. Reservations required.

Relais Montréal Hospitalité
3977 Avenue Laval, H2W 2H9
☎*287-9635*
☎*800-363-9635*
≠*287-1007*
About 30 bed & breakfasts are also registered with the Relais Montréal Hospitalité. All have been carefully inspected, and the rooms are clean and comfortable. The establishments are located throughout Montreal, though many are on on Rue Laval.

Québec

Vieux-Montréal

Auberge Alternative
$17 dormitory
$50 double room
K
358 Rue Saint-Pierre, H2Y 2M1
☎282-8069
www.odyssee.net/eber/intro.html
The Auberge Alternative, located in Old Montréal, opened in April 1996. Run by a young couple, it is a renovated building dating from 1875. The 34 beds in the rooms and dormitories are rudimentary but comfortable, and the bathrooms are very clean. Brightly coloured walls, lots of space and a large common room and kitchenette with stone walls and old wooden floors complete the facilities. A blanket costs $2 per night, and guests have laundry machines at their disposal. Twenty-four hour access.

Passants du Sans-Soucy
$125 bkfst incl.
9 rooms
171 Rue Saint-Paul Ouest
Place d'Armes métro station
☎842-2634
≈842-2912
Even though Old Montréal is visited by thousands of tourists, it has little to offer in the way of accommodations. There is, however, the Passants du Sans-Soucy, an extremely pleasant inn set in the heart of the old city whose charming rooms are furnished with antiques. Built in 1723, the building was renovated eight years ago. Reservations required.

Hôtel Inter-Continental
$199 bkfst incl.
357 rooms
≈, ⊖, △, ℜ
360 Rue Saint-Antoine Ouest
H2Y 3X4
☎987-9900
☎800-327-0200
≈847-8550
www.interconti.com
Except for one of its wings, the Hôtel Inter-Continental, located on the edge of Old Montréal, is a fairly new building (1991) that is linked to the Centre de Commerce Mondial (World Trade Centre) and several shops. The Palais des Congrès (convention centre) is right nearby. It has an original appearance, due to its turret with multiple windows, where the living rooms of the suites are located. The rooms are tastefully decorated with simple furniture. Each one is equipped with a spacious bathroom, among other nice touches. Guests are courteously and attentively welcomed. Business people will enjoy all the necessary services, such as computer hook-ups, fax machines and photocopiers. Parking $12 per day.

Maison Pierre-du-Calvet
$195 bkfst incl.
6 rooms
pb, ℜ
405 Rue Bonsecours
Champ-de-Mars métro station
☎282-1725
≈282-0456
Built in 1725, the Maison Pierre-du-Calvet is one of Montréal's oldest homes, discretely tucked away at the intersection of Bonsecours and Saint-Paul streets. It has recently been entirely renovated, as have many other older houses in the neighbourhood. The rooms and suites, each different from the next and each with its own fireplace, exude an irresistible charm, with lovely antique wood panelling accentuated by oriental rugs, stained glass and beautiful antiques; the ancestral yet refined setting gives visitors the illusion of travelling back in time. Moreover, the bathrooms are immaculately clean and tiled in Italian marble. A pretty indoor courtyard and day room allow guests to escape from the swarming crowds. Breakfast is served in a lovely Victorian dining room. The service is attentive and meticulous. In short, this inn, located in the heart of the city's historic district is a real gem, and will make your stay absolutely unforgettable.

Downtown

Auberge de Jeunesse
$18-$26/pers. for members
$22-$30/pers. for non-members
1030 Rue Mackay, H3G 2H1
☎843-3317
☎800-663-3317
≈934-3251
The Auberge de Jeunesse (youth hostel), located a stone's throw from the downtown area, is one of the least expensive places to sleep in Montréal. Two-hundred and fifty beds occupy rooms that can accommodate from four to 10 people, as well as 15 private rooms. Breakfast is served in the café, which opened in 1996. Guests have access to a laundry room, a TV room, a pool table and a kitchen. Finally, a variety of reasonably priced activities and excursions are organized by the hostel; these can include anything from trips to a sugar-shack or guided tours of the city. This is a non-smoking hostel.

YMCA
$40

tv, ≈, ⊙, ◠

1450 Rue Stanley, H3A 2W6
Peel métro station

☎ *849-8393*
⇻ *849-8017*

The downtown YMCA, the oldest YMCA in North America, was built in 1851 and has 331 basic but comfortable rooms with one or two beds each. Men, women and children are welcome. Most of the rooms are equipped with a telephone and a television; some have a sink or a bathroom. The cafeteria on the ground floor serves morning and evening meals (*$3-$6*). Guests enjoy free access to the YMCA's swimming pool, fully equipped gym and locker room. The Young Men's Christian Association (YMCA) was founded in London in 1844 to help young English workers.

Manoir Ambrose
$50 bkfst incl.

22 rooms
sb/pb, tv
3422 Rue Stanley, H3A 1R8

☎ *288-6922*
⇻ *288-5757*
http://interresa.ca/hotel/mambr
ose.htm

Manoir Ambrose is set in two big, beautiful Victorian houses made of hewn stone, which are located side by side on a peaceful street. It has several little rooms scattered all over the house. The outdated decor will amuse some guests, but the rooms are well-kept and the service is friendly. Laundry service for a fee (*$5*).

Hôtel de la Montagne
$144

ℜ, ⊛, ≈, ≡

1430 Rue de la Montagne
H3G 1Z5

☎ *288-5656*
☎ *800-361-6262*
⇻ *288-9658*

Besides its 134 rooms on 19 floors, the Hôtel de la Montagne also offers a pool, an excellent restaurant and a bar, as well as friendly and courteous staff. The pool (which it is known for) is found outside, on the roof, and is only open in the summer.

Marriott Château-Champlain
$165

611 rooms

≈, ☀, ⊙, ◠, ℜ, ♿

1 Place du Canada, H3B 4C9

☎ *878-9000*
☎ *800-228-9290*
⇻ *878-6761*
www.marriott.com/
marriott/cana-321.htm

The Marriott Château-Champlain is a very original-looking white building with semicircular windows, much resembling a cheese-grater. Unfortunately, this renowned hotel has small but elegant rooms. Direct access to the underground city (see p 194).

Queen Elizabeth
$195

1,022 rooms

⊙, ♿, ≈, ℜ, ◠, ≈, ☀

900 Boulevard René-Lévesque Ouest
H3B 4A5

☎ *861-3511*
☎ *800-441-1414*
⇻ *954-2256*
www.cphotels.ca/qehindex.htm

The Queen Elizabeth is one Montréal hotel that has set itself apart over the years. Its lobby, decorated with fine wood panelling, is magnificent. Visitors will find a number of shops on the main floor. Two of the hotel's floors, designated "Entrée Or," boast luxurious suites and are like a hotel within the hotel. Nu-

merous renovations were completed in 1996. The hotel is conveniently located in the heart of downtown, and its underground corridors provide easy access to the train station and the underground city.

Ritz Carlton Montréal
$215

⊙, ℜ

1228 Rue Sherbrooke Ouest
H3G 1H6

☎ *842-4212*
☎ *800-363-0366*
⇻ *842-4907*
www.ritz-carlton-montreal.com

The Ritz Carlton Montréal was inaugurated in 1912. Renovated over the years to continue offering its clientele exceptional comfort, it has managed to preserve its original elegance. The rooms are decorated with superb antique furniture. The marble bathrooms, moreover, add to the charm of this outstanding establishment. The Ritz has an excellent restaurant called Café de Paris (see p 188), which has a pleasant garden in summer (see Jardin du Ritz p 187).

Omni Montréal
$215

300 rooms

≈, ⊙, ℜ, ☀, ◠, ℜ, ♿

1050 Rue Sherbrooke Ouest
H3A 2R6

☎ *284-1110*
☎ *800-228-3000*
⇻ *845-3025*
www.omnihotels.com

One of the most renowned hotels in Montréal, the Omni Montréal offers comfortable, spacious accommodations. Nevertheless, the standard rooms are decorated in an unoriginal fashion and the bathrooms are small for such a prestigious establishment. The lobby, however, is large and elegant, and the hotel is famous for its restaurants. The outdoor pool is

Québec

heated and open year-round.

Bonaventure Hilton
$219
367 rooms
☼, ≈, ⊘, tv, ℜ
1 Place Bonaventure, H5A 1E4
☎878-2332
☎800-267-2575
≈878-3881
≈878-1442
Guests of the Bonaventure Hilton, located on the boundary between downtown and Old Montréal, enjoy a number of little extras, such as a massage service, that make this hotel the perfect place to relax in. The rooms are simply decorated in a simple manner, without a hint of extravagance, and the bathrooms are small. The hotel has a heated outdoor swimming pool, where guests can swim all year round, as well as a lovely garden and access to the underground city (see p 194).

Loews Hôtel Vogue
$329
126 rooms, 16 suites
≈, ⊛, ℝ, ⊘, ☼, ℜ
1425 Rue de la Montagne, H3G 1Z3
☎285-5555
☎800-465-6654
≈849-8903
www.loewshotels.com/vogue.html
At first sight, the Loews Hôtel Vogue, a glass and concrete building with no ornamentation, looks bare. The lobby, embellished with warm-coloured woodwork, gives a more accurate idea of the luxury and elegance of this establishment. The large rooms, with their confortable furniture, further attest to the hotel's elegance. Each room has a whirlpool bath and two suites have a sauna.

Plateau Mont-Royal

Auberge de la Fontaine
$154 bkfst incl.
21 rooms
⊛
1301 Rue Rachel Est, H2J 2K1
☎597-0166
≈597-0496
The stylish and carefully decorated Auberge de la Fontaine lies opposite lovely Parc Lafontaine. A feeling of calm and relaxation emanates from the rooms, all of which are nicely decorated. Guests are offered a complimentary snack during the day. All these attractive features have made this a popular place – so much so that it is best to make reservations.

Near the Airports

Mirabel Airport

Château de l'Aéroport-Mirabel
$115
≈, ⊘, ⊘, ℜ
12555 Rue Commerce, A4, J7N 1E3
☎476-1611
☎800-361-0924
≈476-0873
www.chateaumirabel.com
Directly accessible from Mirabel Airport, the Château de l'Aéroport-Mirabel was built to accommodate travellers with early morning flights. Unlike its downtown cousins, this hotel's high season is from November to May. The massage service is particularly appreciated by nervous flyers. The rooms are very functional and comfortable.

Dorval Airport

Best Western Hôtel International
$99
⊘, ⊛, △, ≈, ℜ
13000 Chemin Côte-de-Liesse
☎631-4811
☎800-361-2254
≈631-7305
Entirely renovated in 1996, the rooms in the Best Western Hôtel International are pleasant and affordable. The hotel also offers an interesting service: after spending the night here, guests can park their car here for up to a month, free of charge.

Hilton Montréal Aéroport
$149 bkfst incl.
482 rooms
⊘, ⊛, ᕧ, △, ℜ
12505 Côte-de-Liesse, H9P 1B7
☎631-2411
☎800-268-9275
≈631-0192
The Hilton Montréal Aéroport has pleasant rooms but its main advantage is its proximity to the airport.

Restaurants

Vieux-Montréal

Bonaparte
$$
opens at 7am for bkfst, noon for lunch and 5:30pm for dinner
443 Rue Saint-François-Xavier
☎844-4368
The varied menu of the French restaurant Bonaparte always includes some delicious surprises. The tables on the mezzanine offer a lovely view of Old Montréal.

Le Petit Moulinsart
$$
closed Sat noon and Sun
139 Rue St-Paul Ouest
☎843-7432
Le Petit Moulinsart is a
friendly Belgian bistro that
could easily pass for a
small museum devoted to
the characters of the Tintin
comic books by Georges
Rémi, a.k.a. Hergé. All
sorts of knick-knacks and
posters related to the
Tintin books decorate the
walls, menus and tables.
Service is friendly, but
slow. Besides the tradi-
tional dish of mussels and
French fries, don't miss
Colonel Sponz's sorbet and
Capitaine Haddock's salad.

Gibby's
$$$
closed at noon
298 Place d'Youville
☎282-1837
Gibby's is located in a
lovely, renovated old sta-
ble and its menu offers
generous servings of beef
or veal steaks served at
antique wooden tables set
around a glowing fire and
surrounded by low brick
and stone walls. In sum-
mer, patrons can eat com-
fortably outdoors in a large
inner courtyard. All in all,
an extraordinary decor,
which is reflected in the
rather high prices. Vegetar-
ians beware.

Claude Postel
$$$-$$$$
closed Sat noon and Sun
443 Rue Saint-Vincent
☎875-5067
Claude Postel enjoys an
established reputation in
the old part of town. An
extensive menu boasts
some true triumphs of
French cuisine that are
rather pricey; the *table
d'hôte* is just as tasty, and
much more reasonable.
The decor is simple and
refined.

The chef and owner also
runs a pastry shop next
door, so save some room
for dessert.

Maison Pierre-du-Calvet
$$$$
closed Sun and Mon
405 Rue Bonsecours
☎282-1725
Following a disagreement,
the Filles du Roi restaurant
closed its doors to reopen
under the name Maison
Pierre-du-Calvet. This jewel
among Montréal restau-
rants has given way to a
magnificent inn (see p 184)
boasting one of the best
dining rooms in the city.
The new establishment is
particularly recommended
for its delicious and imagi-
native French cuisine. Its
menu, based on game,
poultry, fish and beef,
changes every two weeks.
The elegant surroundings,
antiques, ornamental plants
and discrete service further
add to the pleasure of an
evening meal here.

Downtown

Ben's Delicatessen
$
900 Boulevard de Maisonneuve
Ouest
☎844-1000
At the beginning of the
century, a Lithuanian immi-
grant modified a recipe
from his native country to
suit the needs of workers,
and thus introduced the
smoked-meat sandwich to
Montréal, and in the pro-
cess created Ben's Delica-
tessen. Over the years, the
restaurant has become a
Montréal institution, attract-
ing a motley crowd from
7am to 3:30am. The worn,
Formica tables and photo-
graphs yellowed by time
give the restaurant an
austere appearance.

Brûlerie Saint-Denis
$
2100 Rue Stanley, in the Maison
Alcan
☎985-9159
Brûlerie Saint-Denis serves
the same delicious coffee
blends, simple meals and
sinful desserts as the other
two Brûleries. Though the
coffee is not roasted on
the premises, it does come
fresh from the roasters on
Saint-Denis (see also
p 190).

Le Commensal
$-$$
1204 McGill College Ave.
☎871-1480
Le Commensal is a buffet-
style restaurant. The food,
all vegetarian, is sold by
weight. Le Commensal is
open every day until
11pm. The inviting mod-
ern decor and big win-
dows looking out on the
downtown streets make it
a pleasant place to be.

Café du TNM
$$
84 Rue Ste-Catherine Ouest
☎866-8668
Café du TNM is a wonder-
ful addition to this some-
what rundown area. You
can enjoy a simple drink,
coffee or dessert in the
deconstructionist decor on
the ground floor, or a
good meal upstairs, where
the atmosphere is like a
Parisian *brasserie*. The
menu goes with the decor:
classic French bistro cui-
sine. Impeccable service,
attractive presentation and
flawless food – what more
could you ask for?

Jardin du Ritz
$$
1228 Rue Sherbrooke Ouest
☎842-4212
The Jardin du Ritz is the
perfect escape from the
summer heat and the in-
cessant downtown bustle.
Classic French cuisine is

Québec

featured on the menu, with tea served on a patio surrounded by flowers and greenery, next to the pond with its splashing ducks. Only open during the summer months, the Jardin is an extension of the hotel's other restaurant, Le Café de Paris (see below).

Café de Paris
$$$
1228 Sherbrooke Ouest
☎842-4212
Café de Paris is the renowned restaurant of the magnificent Ritz-Carlton Hotel (see p 185). Its sumptuous blue and ochre decor is refined and beautiful. The carefully thought-out menu offers delicious dishes.

Club Lounge 737
$$$
closed Sat and Sun noon
1 Place Ville-Marie
☎397-0737
Located on the 42nd floor of Place Ville-Marie, the Club Lounge 737 boasts large windows allowing for an unobstructed view of Montréal and its surroundings. Its buffet consists of a variety of French-inspired creations. Be warned that the prices here are as high as the restaurant is.

Julien
$$$
closed Sat and Sun
1191 Rue Union
☎871-1581
Julien is a Montréal classic, thanks largely to its *bavette à l'échalote* or steak with shallots, which is one of the best in the city. But it isn't just the *bavette* that attracts patrons, as each dish is more succulent than the last. For that matter, everything here is impeccable, from the service to the decor and even the wine list.

Katsura
$$$
2170 Rue de la Montagne
☎849-1172
At Katsura, located in the heart of downtown, visitors can savour refined Japanese cuisine. The main dining room is furnished with long tables, making this the perfect place for groups. Smaller, more intimate rooms are also available.

Les Caprices de Nicolas
$$$$
2071 rue Drummond
☎282-9790
Les Caprices de Nicolas is among Montréal's best restaurants. The food is fine, French and innovative to the last morsel. A special deal allows you to have a different glass of wine with each dish, for the price of a bottle of wine. The impeccable service is unpretentious, and the decor resembles an interior garden.

Shaughnessy Village

Chez la Mère Michel
$$$$
closed Sat noon, Sun, Mon noon
1209 Rue Guy
☎934-0473
Chez la Mère Michel is arguably one of Montreal's best restaurants. Inside the lovely old house on Guy Street lie three exquisitely decorated, intimate dining rooms. At the front, banquettes and chairs covered in richly printed fabrics welcome patrons to their elegantly laid tables, while in the back a cozy fireplace and profusion of plants set the mood. Market-fresh ingredients are combined with excellence by Chef Micheline to create delightful French regional specialties, as well as a changing five-course

seasonal *table d'hôte*. The service is friendly and attentive. The impressive wine cellar boasts some of the finest bottles in the city.

Westmount and the West End

Franni
$
closed Mon
5528 Rue Monkland
☎486-2033
Franni, a café decorated with woodwork, ceramic tiles and plants, is unfortunately too small for its many customers who flock here for the delicious cheesecakes.

Kaizen
$$$$
4120 Rue Ste-Catherine O.
☎932-5654
The best Japanese restaurant in Westmount, Kaizen serves all the classics from this land of the rising sun. The prices are high but the portions are gargantuan! The staff won't even mind if you share your plate.

Île Sainte-Hélène and Île Notre-Dame

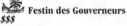 Festin des Gouverneurs
$$$
☎879-1141
Festin des Gouverneurs recreates feasts like those prepared in New France at the beginning of colonization. Characters in period costumes and traditional Québec dishes bring patrons back in time to these celebrations. The restaurant only serves groups and reservations are necessary.

Hélène-de-Champlain
$$$
closed noon
☎*395-2424*
On Île Sainte-Hélène, the restaurant Hélène-de-Champlain lies in an enchanting setting, without question one of the loveliest in Montréal. The large dining room, with its fireplace and view of the city and the river, is extremely pleasant. Each corner has its own unique charm, overlooking the ever-changing surrounding landscape. Though the restaurant does not serve the fanciest of gastronomic cuisine, the food is good. The service is courteous and attentive.

 Nuances
$$$$
every day 5:30pm to 11pm
Casino de Montréal, Île Notre-Dame
☎*392-2708*
☎*800-665-2274, ext 4322*
On the fifth floor of Montréal's Casino, Nuances is one of the best dining establishments in the city. Refined and imaginative cuisine is served in a decor rich in mahogany, brass, leather and views of the city's lights. Of particular note on the menu are the creamy lobster *brandade* in flaky pastry (*brandade crémeuse de homard en millefeuille*), brochette of grilled quail (*brochette de caille grillée*), roast cutlet of duck (*magret de canard rôti*), tenderloin of Québec lamb (*longe d'agneau du Québec*) and striped polenta with grilled tuna (*polenta rayée entourée d'une grillade mi-cuite de thon*). The delectable desserts are each presented exquisitely. The plush and classic ambiance of this restaurant is perfect for business meals and special occasions. The casino also has four less expensive restaurants: **Via Fortuna**

(*$$*), an Italian restaurant; **L'Impair** (*$*), a buffet; **La Bonne Carte** (*$$$*), a buffet with *à la carte* service and **L'Entre-Mise** (*$*), a snack bar.

Quartier Latin

La Paryse
$
302 Rue Ontario Est
☎*842-2040*
Tiny La Paryse is often crowded with students, for a very simple reason: it serves delicious hamburgers and home-made French fries in generous portions.

Le Pélerin
$
330 Rue Ontario Est
☎*845-0909*
Located near Rue Saint-Denis, Le Pélerin is a pleasant, unpretentious café. The wooden furniture, made to look like mahogany, and the works of modern art on exhibit create a friendly atmosphere that attracts a diverse clientele. This is the perfect place to grab a bite and chat with a friend. The service is attentive and friendly.

Zyng
$$
1748 Rue St-Denis
☎*284-2016*
This branch of the Toronto chain of friendly noodle and *dim sum* restaurants brings flair to this overly commercial part of St-Denis. The flavours of China, Japan, Thailand, Korea and Vietnam meet and mix here, creating very original dishes.

Plateau Mont-Royal

L'Anecdote
$
801 Rue Rachel Est
☎*526-7967*
L'Anecdote serves hamburgers and vegetarian club sandwiches made with quality ingredients. The place has a 1950s-style decor, with movie posters and old Coke ads on the walls.

Aux 2 Marie
$
4329 Rue Saint-Denis
☎*844-7246*
Typical Plateau residents hang out at the small chaming café Aux 2 Marie. Besides an impressive selection of coffees roasted on the premises, they also serve excellent and unpretentious meals at affordable prices. The new terrace upstairs is quite pleasant in the summer. Slow service.

Binerie Mont-Royal
$
367 Avenue Mont-Royal Est
☎*285-9078*
With its decor made up of four tables and a counter, the Binerie Mont-Royal looks like a modest little neighbourhood restaurant. It is known for its specialty, baked beans (*fèves au lard* or "*binnes*") and also as the backdrop of Yves Beauchemin's novel, *Le Matou* (*The Alley Cat*).

Québec

Brûlerie Saint-Denis
$
3967 Rue Saint-Denis
☎286-9158
Brûlerie Saint-Denis imports its coffees from all over the world and offers one of the widest selections in Montréal. The coffee is roasted on the premises, filling the place with a very distinctive aroma. The menu offers light meals and desserts. See also p 187.

 Chu Chai
$$
4088 Rue St-Denis
☎843-4194
Chu Chai dares to be innovative and you have to congratulate them for it. So many restaurants are just like so many others! Here, the Thai vegetarian menu they've come up with is quite a pastiche: vegetarian shrimp, vegetarian fish and even vegetarian beef and pork. The resemblance to the real thing is so extraordinary that you will spend the evening wondering how they do it! The chef affirms that they really do consist of vegetable-based products like seitan and wheat. The results are delicious and delight the mixed clientele that squeezes into the modest dining room or onto the terrace. They offer economical lunch specials.

Côté Soleil
$$
closed on Mon in winter
3979 Rue St-Denis
☎282-8037
Côté Soleil offers a different menu each day and will never disappoint. Here is good French cooking that is occasionally inventive and not expensive. It is probably the best place to eat in this area for the price. This restaurant has smiling, attentive staff, an attractive terrace on the street and decor that is low-keyed but inviting.

Fondue Mentale
$$
closed noon
4325 Rue Saint-Denis
☎499-1446
Fondue Mentale occupies a typical Plateau Mont-Royal old house with superb woodwork. As the restaurant's name suggests, fondue is the specialty here – and what a choice, each more appetizing than the last! The Swiss fondue with pink pepper is particularly delicious.

Ouzeri
$$
4690 Rue Saint-Denis
☎845-1336
Ouzeri set out on a mission to offer its clientele refined Mediterranean cuisine, and succeeded. The food is excellent, and the menu includes several surprises, such as vegetarian moussaka and scallops with melted cheese. With its high ceilings and long windows, this is a pleasant place, where you'll be tempted to linger on and on, especially when the Greek music sets your mind wandering.

Continental
$$-$$$
closed noon
4169 Saint-Denis
☎845-6842
The staging is very subtle at the Continental. Some evenings, the restaurant is positively charming, with its attentive, courteous staff, stylish clientele and updated 1950s-style decor. The varied menu includes a few surprises such as crispy oriental noodles. The cuisine is sublime at times and the presentation is always most carefully presented.

 Poco Piu
$$-$$$
closed Sun and Mon
4621 Rue Saint-Denis
☎843-8928
Upon entering Poco Piu you will be seduced by the plush yet relaxed atmosphere. The choice of dishes will certainly satisfy, all the while allowing a delicious voyage through the wonders of Italian cuisine.

 L'Express
$$$
3927 Rue Saint-Denis
☎845-5333
The yuppie gathering place during the mid-1980s, L'Express is still highly rated for its dining-car decor, lively Parisian bistro atmosphere, which few restaurants have managed to recreate, and consistently appealing menu. Over the years, this restaurant has developed a solid reputation.

Toqué
$$$$
3842 Rue Saint-Denis
☎499-2084
If you're looking for a new culinary experience, Toqué is without a doubt the place to go in Montréal. The chef, Normand Laprise, insists on having the freshest ingredients and manages the kitchen, where dishes are always prepared with great care and beautifully presented. Not to mention the desserts, which are veritable modern sculptures. The service is exceptional, the wine list good, the modern decor elegant, and the high prices do not seem to deter anyone. One of the most original dining establishments in Montréal.

Entertainment

Bars and Danceclubs

L'Air du Temps
194 Rue Saint-Paul Ouest
L'Air du Temps ranks among the most famous jazz bars in Montréal. Set in the heart of Old Montréal, it has a fantastic interior decorated with scores of antiques. As the place is often packed, it is necessary to arrive early to get a good seat. The cover charge varies according to the show. Call for information on upcoming acts.

Le Balattou
4372 Boulevard Saint-Laurent
Dark, smoky, jam-packed, hot, hectic and noisy, Le Balattou is without a doubt the most popular African nightclub in Montréal. On weekends, the cover charge is $7 (including one drink). Shows are presented only during the week, when the cost of admission varies.

Les Beaux Esprits
2073 Rue Saint-Denis
A bar with a modest decor, Les Beaux Esprits presents good jazz and blues shows.

Belmont sur le Boulevard
4483 Boulevard Saint-Laurent
A clientele composed mainly of junior executives crowds into the Belmont sur le Boulevard. On weekends, the place is literally overrun with customers. Cover charge Thursdays ($3), Fridays and Saturdays (4$).

Café Campus
57 Rue Prince Arthur
Obliged to move from its original location in front of the Université de Montréal, Café Campus has settled into a large place on Rue Prince Arthur. The decor is still quite plain. Good musicians frequently give shows here.

Di Salvio's
3519 Boulevard Saint-Laurent
Di Salvio's Art Deco interior and 1950s-style furniture create a unique, original setting. Patrons lucky enough to get picked from the line-up (it can be difficult to get in) dance to acid-jazz music.

Dogue
4177 Rue Saint-Denis
The Dogue is the ideal place to dance, dance, dance. The music, which ranges from Elvis classics to the latest Rage Against the Machine hit, gratifies a rather young, high-spirited crowd thirsting for cheap beer. There are two pool tables, which are a bit in the way, but keep the pool sharks entertained. The place is jam-packed seven days a week, so you are strongly advised to get there early.

Les Foufounes Électriques
87 Rue Sainte-Catherine Est
Foufounes Électriques is a fantastic, one-of-a-kind bar-discotheque pick-up joint. The best bar in Québec for dancing to alternative music, it attracts a motley crowd of young Montrealers, ranging from punks to medical students. The decor, consisting of graffiti and strange sculptures, is wacky, to say the least. Don't come here for a quiet night.

Thursday's
1449 Rue Crescent
Thursday's bar is very popular, especially among the city's English-speaking population. It is a favourite meeting place for business people and professionals.

Whisky Café
5800 Boulevard Saint-Laurent
The Whisky Café has been so conscientiously decorated that even the men's bathrooms are on their way to becoming a tourist attraction. The warm colours used in a modern setting, the tall columns covered with woodwork and pre-1950s-style chairs all create a sense of comfort and elegance. The clientele consists of well-off, well-bred gilded youth between the ages of 20 and 35.

The Rave Scene

If you like electrifying, pounding dancefloors, go to one of the city's after-hours clubs, which are always packed. The party atmosphere will leave you spinning for days! Eccentricity goes at these places, where dancing is the main attraction.

The crowd is generally young and friendly. Opening and closing hours vary (between 2am and 9am) from place to place. Since the sale of alcohol is prohibited after 3am, water, juice and smart drinks are served at after-hours clubs.

Here are some places where you can rave... at your own risk!

Back Street
1459 St-Alexandre

Blade
1296 Amherst

Daylight
1254 Rue Stanley (corner Ste-Catherine)

Red Lite
1955 Notre-Dame-de-Fatima, Laval

Sona
1439 Rue de Bleury

Québec

Stéréo
858 Rue Ste-Catherine Est

Gay and Lesbian Bars

Cabaret l'Entre-Peau
1115 Rue Sainte-Catherine Est
☎525-7566
The Cabaret l'Entre-Peau puts on transvestite shows. The place attracts a lively, mixed clientele.

Sisters
1333 Rue Sainte-Catherine Est
2nd floor
☎522-4717
Sisters is for lesbian and bi women. The latest mainstream hits get things moving and shaking on the dance floor.

Sky Pub
1474 Rue Ste-Catherine Est
☎529-6969
The most popular gay bar in Montréal, Sky Pub, has an elegant decor that is refined, soft and inviting. A profusion of wood and carefully chosen lighting make it a choice place, but the music is at times too loud and often banal. In the summer you can sit on the terrace and people-watch on Rue Sainte-Catherine, and when evening comes, you can always go upstairs where a younger crowd hangs out. At the beginning of the week, Sky Pub presents shows that often star Mado Lamothe and her Québec Travesti.

Unity
Thu to Sun 10pm to 3am
1400 Rue Montcalm
Unity, a large gay dance club, is popular with all ages, but its clientele is mostly male. It is spread over several different levels and has a mezzanine from which you can watch an entrancing light show and ravers and muscle queens dancing to techno music on the main

floor. One room upstairs is devoted to 1980s music and another to hip-hop. There is an immense rooftop terrace open on warm summer nights, from which you can see the Benson & Hedges International fireworks display.

Theatres

Place des Arts
260 Boulevard de Maisonneuve Ouest
Place-des-Arts métro station
☎285-4200
☎842-2112 *box office*
The complex contains five theatres: Salle Wilfrid-Pelletier, Théâtre Maisonneuve, Théâtre Jean-Duceppe, Théâtre du Café de la Place, and, since 1992, the Cinquième Salle. The **Orchestre Symphonique de Montréal** (*for subscription information call ☎849-0269, otherwise call the Place des Arts box office*) and **Grands Ballets Canadiens** (*for subscription information call ☎842-9951, otherwise call the Place des Arts box office*) both perform in this venerable hall.

The **Centaur Theatre** (*453 Rue Saint-François, ☎288-3161*) presents big English productions and is the main theatre for the anglophone community.

Shows at the **Spectrum** (*318 Rue Sainte-Catherine Ouest, ☎861-5851, Place-des-Arts métro station*) usually begin around 11pm. Count on at least $10 to get in. As with Club Soda, shows after 11pm are usually free during the Festival de Jazz.

Théâtre Saint-Denis
1594 Rue Saint-Denis
Berri-UQAM métro station
☎849-4211

Théâtre du Nouveau Monde
84 Rue Ste-Catherine Ouest
☎861-0563
See p 187

Ticket Sales

There are three major ticket agencies in Montréal that sell tickets for shows, concerts and other events over the telephone. Service charges, which vary according to the show, are added to the price of the ticket. Credit cards are accepted.

Admission
☎790-1245
☎800-361-4595

Telspec
☎790-2222

Billetterie Articulée
(an *Admission* ticket outlet)
☎844-2172

Information on the Arts

Info-Arts (Bell)
☎790-ARTS
This service's operators provide information on current cultural and artistic events in the city.

Movie Theatres

The following show films in French:

Complexe Desjardins
Rue Sainte-Catherine Ouest, between Jeanne-Mance and Saint-Urbain
Place-des-Arts métro station
☎849-3456

Le Parisien
480 Rue Sainte-Catherine Ouest
McGill métro station
☎866-3856

Quartier Latin
350 Rue Émery
☎849-4422

The following show films in English:

Égyptien
Cours Mont-Royal 1455 Rue Peel
Peel métro station
☎849-3456

Eaton Centre
705 Ste-Catherine Ouest
McGill métro station
☎985-5730

Le Faubourg
in Faubourg Ste-Catherine
1616 Ste-Catherine Ouest
Guy métro station

The Paramount
977 Rue Ste-Catherine Ouest.,
corner Metcalfe, next to Simons
Peel métro station
☎866-0111

The following are repertory theatres:

La Cinémathèque Québécoise
335 Boulevard de Maisonneuve Est
Berri-UQAM métro station
☎842-9763
La Cinémathèque Québécoise is a technologically advanced French theatre and the projection quality is always outstanding. Repertory and art films are shown here.

Ex-Centris
3536 Boulevard Saint-Laurent,
Saint-Laurent métro station and
Bus 55
☎847-2206
French and English
Ex-Centris is fast becoming a Montréal cultural institution. The brainchild of local media guru, Daniel Langlois, this theatre/café/architectural gem is host to numerous festivals and media events. Buying a ticket for one of the fantastic films screened here is a unique, televised experience!

Impérial
1430 Rue de Bleury
Place-des-Arts métro station
☎848-0300
This is the oldest and most beautiful movie theatre in Montréal. It shows second-run movies for a mere $3.

Cinéma du Parc
3575 Avenue du Parc
Place-des-Arts métro station, bus 80
☎287-7272
The Cinéma du Parc is *the* place to see international, indie and cult flicks. Pick up their detailed, informative schedule at any Montréal bar or café. Discounts for students and seniors.

Office National du Film (National Film Board)
1564 Rue Saint-Denis
☎496-6301
A *cinérobothèque* allows 100 people to watch NFB films at once. A robot, the only one like it in the world, loads each machine. The complex is dedicated to Québec and Canadian cinema.

You can also see large-screen productions at:

Le Cinéma Imax
Vieux-Port de Montréal, Rue de la Commune corner Boulevard Saint-Laurent
☎496-4629
Films are presented on a giant screen.

Festivals and Cultural Events

The **Tour de l'Île** takes place in June. The event can accommodate a maximum of 45,000 cyclists, who ride together for some 65km around the island of Montréal. Registration begins in April, and costs $21 for adults and half-price for children under 11 and senior citizens.

Registration forms are available at Canadian Tire stores (in Québec) and from **Tour de l'Île de Montréal** (*1251 Rue Rachel Est, H2J 2J9, ☎847-8356*).

June is marked by an international event that captivates a large number of fans from all over North America – the **Grand Prix Players du Canada** (*to reserve seats, call ☎350-0000*), which takes place at the Circuit Gilles Villeneuve on Île Notre-Dame during the second week of June. This is without question one of the most popular events of the summer. During these three days, it is possible to attend a variety of car races, including the roaring, spectacular Formula One competition.

In 1998, the **Concours International d'Art Pyrotechnique** (International Fireworks Competition) (*☎871-1881*) starts in mid-June and runs until mid-July. The world's top pyrotechnists present high-quality musical fireworks shows every Saturday in June and every Sunday in July. Montrealers crowd to the La Ronde amusement park (*tickets cost $28, $29 or $30; call ☎790-1245*), on the Pont Jacques-Cartier or alongside the river (both at no cost) to admire the spectacular plumes of fire that colour the sky above the city for over half an hour.

During the **Festival International de Jazz de Montréal** (*☎871-1881*), hundreds of shows set to the rhythm of jazz and its variations are presented on stages erected around Place des Arts. From June 29 to July 9, 2000, this part of the city and a fair number of theatres will be buzzing with activity.

Québec

The event offers people an opportunity to take to the streets and be carried away by the festive atmosphere of the fantastic, free outdoor shows that attract Montrealers and visitors in large numbers each year. You have to pay for indoor shows, except for late-night performances at the Spectrum or at Kola Note.

Humour and creativity are highlighted during the **Festival Juste pour Rire - Just for Laughs Festival** (☎*845-3155 or 790-HAHA*), which will be held from July 13 to 23, 2000. Theatres host comedians from a variety of countries for the occasion. Théâtre Saint-Denis presents short performances by a number of different comedians. Free outdoor shows are held on Rue St-Denis.

The **FrancoFolies** (☎*871-1881*) are organized to promote French-language music and song. From July 27 to August 5, 2000, artists from francophone countries (Europe, Africa, French Antilles, Québec and French Canada) will perform, providing spectators with a unique glimpse of the world's French musical talent.

During the last week of August, the **Festival International des Films du Monde** (World Film Festival; ☎*848-3883*) is held in various Montréal movie theatres. During this competition, films from different countries are presented to Montréal audiences. At the end of the competition, prizes are awarded to the most praiseworthy films. The best category is the *Grand Prix des Amériques*.

During the festival, films are shown from 9am to midnight, to the delight of movie-goers across the city.

Winter's cold does not preclude the festival spirit; it merely provides an opportunity to organize another festival in Montréal, this time to celebrate the pleasures and activities of this frosty season. The **Fête des Neiges** takes place on Île Notre-Dame, from late January to mid-February. Skating rinks and giant toboggans are available for the enjoyment of Montréal families. The ice-sculpture competition also attracts a number of curious onlookers.

Spectator Sports

Montréal has professional hockey and baseball teams and hosts international sporting events.

The **Molson Centre** (*1250 Rue de la Gauchetière,* ☎*989-2841*). From fall to spring, the famous Montreal Canadiens play hockey in the Centre Molson. There are 41 games during the regular season. The play-offs and finals follow, at the end of which the winning team walks away with the legendary Stanley Cup.

Spring signals the beginning of baseball season at the **Stade Olympique** (*4141 Avenue Pierre-de-Coubertin,* ☎*846-3976*). The Expos play against the different teams of the National Baseball League at the Olympic Stadium.

Casino

With 2,700 slot machines and 100 gaming tables (blackjack, roulette, baccarat, poker, etc.), the **Casino de Montréal** (*free admission, every day 24hrs, Île Sainte-Hélène métro station and Bus 167,* ☎*392-2746*) is without a doubt a major player in the city's nightlife. Following the addition of a new wing in 1996 in the former Québec pavilion, the casino is now one of the 10 biggest in the world in terms of its gaming equipment. A cabaret show, also added in 1996, has seen the likes of Liza Minelli, André-Philippe Gagnon and Jean-Pierre Ferland to name but a few, and has brought a new vitality to the place.

Shopping

The Underground City

The 1962 construction of Place Ville-Marie, with its underground shopping mall, marked the origins of what is known today as the underground city. The development of this "city under the city" was accelerated by the construction of the métro, which opened in 1966. Soon, most downtown businesses and office buildings, as well as a few hotels, were strategically linked to the underground pedestrian network and, by extension, to the métro.

Today, the underground city, now the largest in the world, has five distinct sections. The first is in the middle of of the Métro system, around the Berri-UQAM station, and is connected to the buildings of the Université du Québec à Montréal (UQAM), the Galeries Dupuis and the bus station. The second is located between the Place-des-Arts and Place-d'Armes stations, and is linked to Place des Arts, the Musée d'Art Contemporain, Complexe Desjardins, Complexe Guy Favreau and the Palais des Congrès, forming an exceptional cultural ensemble. The third, at the Square-Victoria station, serves the business centre. The fourth, which is the busiest and most important one, is identified with the McGill, Peel and Bonaventure stations. It encompasses the The Bay department store; the Promenades de la Cathédrale, Place Montréal Trust and Cours Mont-Royal shopping centres, as well as Place Bonaventure, 1000 de la Gauchetière, the train station and Place Ville-Marie. The fifth and final area is located in the commercial section around the Atwater station; it is linked to Westmount Square, Collège Dawson and Place Alexis Nihon.

Shopping Centres and Department Stores

Several downtown shopping centres and department stores offer a good selection of clothing by well-known fashion designers, including Jean-Claude Chacok, Cacharel, Guy Laroche, Lily Simon, Adrienne Vittadini, Mondi, Ralph Lauren, Versace, Armani, Calvin Klein, Tommy Hilfiger, Nautica, Nygard, DKNY and many others.

Holt Renfrew
1300 Rue Sherbrooke Ouest
☎*842-5111*

Ogilvy
1307 Rue Sainte-Catherine Ouest
☎*842-7711*

Place Montréal Trust
1600 Avenue McGill College
☎*843-8000*

Place Ville-Marie
5 Place Ville-Marie
☎*861-9393*

Westmount Square
4 Westmount Square
☎*932-0211*

The Bay
Square Phillips (on Rue Sainte-Catherine Ouest)
☎*281-4422*

Simons
677 Rue Ste-Catherine O.
☎*282-1840*

Sportswear and Outdoor Equipment

Those who are going on an expedition in the great outdoors should make their first stop at **La Cordée** (*2159 Rue Sainte-Catherine Est*, ☎524-1106).

For warm, fashionable clothing that is perfectly suited to the outdoors, see the creations at **Kanuk** (*485 Rue Rachel*, ☎527-4494)

Bookstores

General

Champigny
(French)
4380 Rue Saint-Denis
☎*844-2587*

Chapters
(French and English)
1171 Rue Sainte-Catherine Ouest
☎*849-8825*

Indigo
(French and English)
Place Montréal Trust
☎*281-5549*

Librairie Gallimard
(French)
3700 Boulevard Saint-Laurent
☎*499-2012*

Paragraphe Books and Café
(English)
2220 McGill College
☎*845-5811*

Librairie Renaud-Bray
(French)
5252 Chemin de la Côte-des-Neiges
☎*342-1515*
4301 Rue Saint-Denis
☎*499-3656*
5117 Avenue du Parc
☎*276-7651*

WH Smith
(French and English)
Place Ville-Marie
☎*861-1736*
Promenades de la Cathédrale
☎*289-8737*

Specialized

Librairie Allemande
(German books)
3488 Chemin de la Côte-des-Neiges
☎*933-1919*

Librairie Las Americas *(Spanish books)*
10 Rue Saint-Norbert
☎*844-5994*

Librairie l'Androgyne
(gay and feminist literature)
3636 Boulevard Saint-Laurent
☎*842-4765*

Librairie C.E.C. Michel Fortin
(education, languages)
3714 Rue Saint-Denis
☎*849-5719*

Librairie McGill
(academic and general)
3421 McTavish
☎*398-7444*

Québec

Librairie du Musée des Beaux-Arts
(art)
1368 Rue Sherbrooke Ouest
☎285-1600, ext 350

Librairie Olivieri
(contemporary art)
185 Rue Sainte-Catherine Ouest
☎847-6903

Librairie Olivieri
(foreign literature, art)
5200 Rue Gatineau
☎739-3639

Librairie Renaud-Bray
(children)
5219 Chemin de la Côte-des-Neiges
☎342-1515

Librairie Ulysse
(travel)
4176 Rue Saint-Denis
☎843-9447
560 Avenue du Président-Kennedy
☎843-7222

Music

Archambault Musique
500 Rue Sainte-Catherine Est
☎849-6201
175 Rue Sainte-Catherine Ouest
Place des Arts
☎281-0367

HMV
1020 Rue Sainte-Catherine Ouest
☎875-0765
Annexe at 1035 Rue Ste-Catherine
Ouest
☎987-1809
sale-priced merchandise

Sam the Record Man
399 Rue Sainte-Catherine Ouest
corner Rue Saint-Alexandre
☎281-9877

Québec Crafts

Craft shops, known as *boutiques d'artisanat* in French, offer an impressive selection of objects illustrating the work and specific themes dear to artisans from here and abroad.

Local crafts include Canadian, Aboriginal, as well as Québec works. Each year during the month of December, the ***Salon des Métiers d'Art du Québec*** (Québec Art and Crafts show) is held at Place Bonaventure (*901 Rue de la Gauchetière Ouest*). The show lasts about 10 days and provides Québec artists the opportunity to display and sell their work.

Throughout the year, it is also possible to purchase several beautifully crafted items by Québec artists at one of the **Le Rouet** boutiques (*136 Rue Saint-Paul Est*, ☎875-2333; *1500 Avenue McGill College in Place Montréal-Trust,* ☎843-5235). **Le Chariot** (*446, Place Jacques-Cartier,* ☎875-6134) offers a good selection of Aboriginal arts and crafts.

Guilde Canadienne des Métiers d'Arts (*2025 Rue Peel,* ☎849-6091) is a small boutique that sells Canadian and Quebecois art. It also has two small galleries that exhibit Inuit and First Nations art and crafts.

The **Galerie d'Objets d'Art du Marché Bonsecours** (*350 Rue St-Paul E.,* ☎878-2787) is another great place to buy Québec art.

Gifts and Gadgets

If you are looking for an original gift, the **Céramique** (*4201 Rue St-Denis,* ☎848-1119; *95, Rue de la Commune Est,* ☎868-1611) art-café gives you the chance to paint a clay object yourself while comfortably seated over a light meal or a drink. The experienced staff is there to help you. This is probably the most personalized gift you can get!

Boutique du Musée d'Art Contemporain (*185 Rue Sainte-Catherine Ouest,* ☎847-6226) and **Boutique du Musée des Beaux-Arts de Montréal** (*1390 Rue Sherbrooke Ouest,* ☎285-1600) have a whole store of splendid reproductions and other items: T-shirts, decorative objects and more. A great find for beautiful souvenirs.

At **Valet de Cœur** (*4408 Rue Saint-Denis,* ☎499-9970), you will find parlour games, puzzles, chess and checker boards among other things.

Southern Québec

This chapter includes two of Québec's tourist regions, namely Montérégie and the Eastern Townships.

The six hills in Montérégie–Mont Saint-Bruno, Mont Saint-Hilaire, Mont Yamaska, Mont Rigaud, Mont Saint-Grégoire and Mont Rougemont–are the only large hills in this flat region. The hills, which do not rise much over 500m, are spread out and were long considered ancient volcanoes. Actually, they are metamorphic rocks that did not break through the upper layer of the earth's crust, and became visible as the neighbouring land eroded over a long period of time.

The Montérégie area is a beautiful plain that's rich in history and agriculture. Located between Ontario, New England and the foothills of the Appalachians in the Eastern Townships (just south of Montréal) with many natural transportation routes such as the majestic Rivière Richelieu, the Montérégie has always played an important military and strategic role. The many fortifications that can now be visited in the area were once outposts that served to protect the col-

ony from the Iroquois, the British and the Americans respectively. It was also in Montérégie that the United States experienced its first military defeat, in 1812. The *Patriotes* and the British laterconfronted each other in Saint-Charles-sur-Richelieu and Saint-Denis, during the 1837 rebellion.

As for the Eastern Townships, this beautiful region is located in the Appalachian foothills in the southernmost part of Québec. The rich architectural heritage and mountainous countryside give Les Cantons d'Est (The Eastern Townships) a distinctive character remi-

niscent in many ways of New England. Picturesque villages marked by what is often typically Anglo-Saxon architecture lie nestled between mountains with rounded summits and lovely little valleys.

As may be gathered from many place names, such as Massawippi and Coaticook, this vast region was originally explored and inhabited by the Abenaki First Nation. When New France later came under English control and the United States declared its independence, many American colonists still loyal to the British monarchy (known as

Loyalists) settled in the Eastern Townships. Throughout the 19th century, these settlers were followed by waves of immigrants from the British Isles, mainly Ireland, and French colonists from the overpopulated St. Lawrence lowlands. Though the local population is now over 90% French-speaking, the area still bears obvious traces of its Anglo-Saxon past, most notably in its architecture. Many towns and villages are graced with majestic Anglican churches surrounded by beautiful 19th-century Victorian or vernacular American-style homes. The Townships are still home to a handful of prestigious English institutions, like Bishop's University in Lennoxville.

Finding Your Way Around

Ferries

Montérégie

St-Paul-de-l'île-aux-Noix – Île-aux-Noix
mid May to mid November
☎*(450) 291-5700*

St-Denis – St-Antoine-sur-Richelieu
mid-May to mid-Nov
☎*(450) 787-2759*

St-Marc-sur-Richelieu – St-Antoine-sur-Richelieu
mid-May to mid-Nov
☎*(450) 584-2813*

St-Roch-de-Richelieu – St-Ours
mid-May to mid-Nov
☎*(450) 785-2161*

Sorel – St-Ignace-de-Loyola
open all year
☎*(450) 743-3258*

Ferry Longueuil – Île Charron
mid-May to mid-Nov
☎*(450) 442-9575*

River shuttle Longueuil – Montréal
mid-May to mid-Nov
☎*(514) 281-8000*

Hudson – Oka
mid-May to mid-Nov
☎*(450) 458-4732*

Bus Stations

Montérégie

Saint-Jean-sur-Richelieu
600 Boulevard Pierre-Caisse
☎*(450) 359-6024*

Saint-Hyacinthe
1330 Rue Calixa-Lavallée
☎*(450) 778-6090*

Sorel
191 Rue du Roi
☎*(450) 743-4411*

Longueuil
(*bus terminal*)
1001 Rue de Sévigny
☎*(450) 670-3422*

Longueuil
STRSM (*Métro terminal, Longueuil station*)
100 Place-Charles-Lemoyne
☎*(450) 463-0131*

Eastern Townships

Bromont
624 Rue Shefford
(dépanneur Shefford)
☎*(450) 534-2116*

Sutton
28 Rue Principale (Esso station)
☎*(450) 538-2452*

Magog-Orford
67 Rue Sherbrooke (Terminus Café)
☎*(819) 843-4617*

Sherbrooke
20 Rue King Ouest
☎*(819) 569-3656*

Lac-Mégantic
6630 Rue Salaberry (Dépanneur 6630 Fatima)
☎*(819) 583-0112*

Practical Information

The area code for **Montérégie** is *450*, except for **Île Perrot**, which is *514*.

There are two area codes in the **Eastern Townships**; *819* and *450*.

Tourist Information

Montérégie

Association Touristique Régional de la Montérégie
11 Chemin Marieville, Rougemont
J0L 1M0
☎*(450) 469-0069*
☎*(514) 990-4600*
⇒*(450) 469-1139*
www.tourisme-monteregie.qc.ca

Saint-Jean-sur-Richelieu
315 Macdonald, suite 301, J3B 8J3
☎*359-9999*
⇒*359-0994*

Mont-Saint-Hilaire
1080 Chemin des Patriotes Nord
☎*536-0395*
☎*888-536-0395*
⇒*536-3147*

Saint-Hyacinthe
Parc des Patriotes, 2090 Rue Cherrier
☎*774-7276*
☎*800-849-7276*
⇒*774-9000*

Sorel
92 Chemin des Patriotes
☎746-9441
☎800-474-9441
≈780-5737

Longueuil
989 Rue Pierre-Dupuy
☎674-5555

Office du Tourisme de la Rive-Sud (convention bureau)
205 Chemin Chambly
☎670-7293
≈670-5887

Vaudreuil-Dorion
seasonal office
331 Rue Saint-Charles (maison Valois)
☎424-8620

Salaberry-de-Valleyfield
980 Boulevard Mgr-Langlois
☎377-7676

Sûroit Tourism Office
30 Avenue du Centenaire, office 126
☎377-7676
☎800-378-7648
≈377-3727

Eastern Townships

Tourisme Cantons de l'Est
20 Rue Don-Bosco S., Sherbrooke
J1L 1W4
☎(819) 820-2020
☎800-355-5755
≈(819) 566-4445
www.tourisme-cantons.qc.ca

Bromont
83 Boulevard Bromont, J0E 1L0
☎(450) 534-2006

Granby
650 Rue Principale, J2G 8L4
☎(450) 372-7273
☎800-567-7273

Rougemont
11 Chemin Marieville, J0L 1M0
☎(450) 674-5555

Magog-Orford
55 Rue Cabana, J1X 2C4
☎(819) 843-2744
☎800-267-2744

Sherbrooke
3010 Rue King Ouest, J1L 1Y7
☎(819) 821-1919
☎800-561-8331

Sutton
1049, 11-B Rue Principale Sud
CP 1049, J0E 2K0
☎(450) 538-8455
☎800-565-8455

Lac-Mégantic
3295 Rue Laval N., G6B 1A5
☎(819) 583-5515
☎800-363-5515

Exploring

Montérégie

★★
Chambly

The town of Chambly is located on a privileged site alongside the Richelieu. The river widens here to form the Bassin de Chambly at the end of the rapids, which once hindered navigation on the river and made the area a key element in New France's defence system.

In 1665, the Carignan-Salières regiment, under the command of Captain Jacques de Chambly, built the first pile fort to drive back the Iroquois who made frequent incursions into Montréal from the Mohawk River. In 1672, the captain was granted a seigneury in his name for services rendered to the colony.

The town that gradually formed around the fort flourished during the Anglo-American war of 1812-14 while a sizeable British garrison was stationed there. Then, in 1843, the Canal de

Chambly opened, allowing boats to bypass the Richelieu Rapids and thereby facilitating commerce between Canada and the United States. Many transportation and import-export companies opened in the area at this time. Today, Chambly is both a suburb of Montréal and a getaway and leisure spot.

Fort Chambly National Historic Site ★★★ (*$3.75; early Mar to mid-May, Wed to Sun 10am to 5pm; mid-May to mid-Jun, every day 9am to 5pm; mid-Jun to early Sep, every day 10am to 5pm; early Sep to mid-Oct, every day 10pm to 5pm, mid-Oct to end Nov Wed to Sun 10am to 5pm; 2 Rue Richelieu,* ☎658-1585). Also called Lieu Historique National du Fort Chambly, this is the largest remaining fortification of the French Regime. It was built between 1709 and 1711 according to plans drawn by engineer Josué Boisberthelot de Beaucours at the request of the Marquis of Vaudreuil. Defended by the *Compagnies Franches de la Marine*, the fort had to protect New France against a possible British invasion. It replaced the four pile forts that had occupied this site since 1665.

Saint-Paul-de-l'Île-aux-Noix

This village is known for its fort, built on Île aux Noix (literally: island of nuts) in the middle of the Richelieu. Farmer Pierre Joudernet was the first occupant of the island, paying his seigneurial rent in the form of a bag of nuts, hence the island's name. Towards the end of the French Regime, the island became strategically important because of its

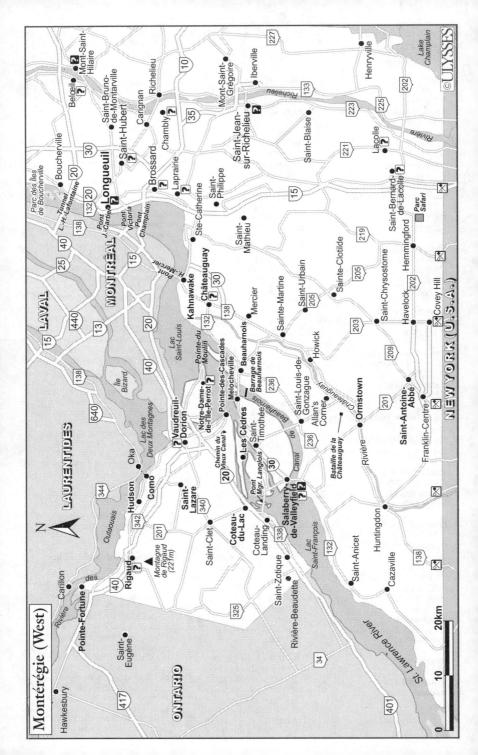

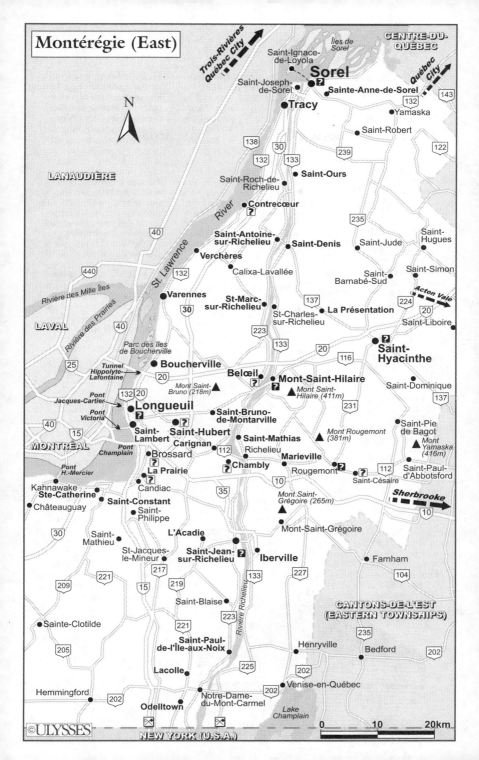

proximity to Lake Champlain and the American colonies. The French began to fortify the island in 1759 but had such poor resources that the fort was taken by the British without difficulty. In 1775, the island became the headquarters for the American revolutionary forces who attempted to invade Canada. Then, during the War of 1812-14, the reconstructed fort served as a base for the attack on Plattsburg (New York State) by the British.

Fort-Lennox National Historic Site ★★ (*$5.25; mid-May to late Jun, Mon to Fri 10am to 5pm, Sat and Sun 10am to 6pm; late Jun to early Sep, Mon to Sun 10am to 6pm; 1 61st Avenue, J0J 1G0, ☎291-5700*) is also called Lieu Historique National du Fort Lennox. Taking up two-thirds of Île aux Noix and significantly altering its face, Fort Lennox was built on the ruins of previous forts between 1819 and 1829 by the British, prompting the construction of Fort Montgomery by the Americans just south of the border. Behind the wall of earth and surrounded by large ditches are a powder keg, two warehouses, the guardhouse, the officers' residences, two barracks and 19 blockhouses. This charming cut-stone ensemble by engineer Gother Mann is a good example of the colonial neoclassical architecture style of the British Empire.

The two-storey **Blockhaus de Lacolle ★** (*free admission; late May to late Aug every day 9am to 5pm; early Sep to early Oct, Sat and Sun 9am to 5pm; 1 Rue Principale, ☎246-3227*), a squared wooden building with loopholes, is found at the southernmost point of the Saint-Paul-de-l'Île-aux-Noix municipality. It dates back to 1782, making it one of the oldest wooden structures in Montérégie. It is also one of the few buildings of this type to survive in Québec.

★
Mont-Saint-Hilaire

This small town, located at the foot of Mont Saint-Hilaire, was originally part of the seigneury of Rouville, granted to Jean-Baptiste Hertel in 1694. It remained in the hands of the Hertel family until 1844 when it was sold to Major Thomas Edmund Campbell, secretary to the British governor who ran an experimental farm that remained in operation until 1942.

Mont-Saint-Hilaire has two urban centres, one along the Richelieu where the parish church is located, and the other on the southeast side of the mountain which enjoys a mild microclimate and is home to orchards and maple groves.

Blockhaus de Lacolle

·Though recently scarred by the addition of parking lots and an ostentatious gate, the **Manoir Rouville-Campbell ★** (*125 Chemin des Patriotes Sud*) remains one of the most magnificent seigneurial residences in Québec. It was built in 1854 by British architect Frederick Lawford who also contributed to the interior decor of the Église de Saint-Hilaire. During the 1980s, the house and the stables were transformed into an inn (see p 214).

The façade of the **Église Saint-Hilaire ★★** (*260 Chemin des Patriotes Nord*) was originally supposed to have two towers topped with spires. As a result of internal arguments, only the bases of the towers were erected in 1830 and a steeple placed in the centre of the facade was later installed. The interior decor, done in the Gothic-Revival style, was completed between 1838 and 1928. The masterpiece of this interior is the work of painter Ozias Leduc (1864-1955) and was completed at the end of the 19th century.

★★
Saint-Hyacinthe

Saint-Hyacinthe's main attraction is the vitality of the city and its inhabitants. The city is divided into the upper part of town, which is more administrative, religious and middle-class, and the lower part of town, more working-class and commercial. Rarely in rural Québec have the liveliness of a town centre and the monuments that dominate its landscape been so successfully preserved as here. It is best to explore downtown Saint-Hyacinthe on foot.

The town also specializes in the construction of large pipe organs. The Casavant brothers set up their famous organ factory outside the city in 1879 (*900 Rue Girouard Est*). Approximately 15 electropneumatic organs are made here every year and are installed throughout the world by the house experts. Guided tours are sometimes organized. Guilbault-Thérien organbuilders have been building mechanical traction organs since 1946, according to French and German models of the 18th century (*2430 Rue Crevier*). Saint-Hyacinthe also has a music bookstore dedicated solely to the organ and the harpsichord (*Ex Arte, 12790 Rue Yamaska*).

The **Cathédrale Saint-Hyacinthe-le-Confesseur** ★ (*1900 Rue Girouard Ouest*) is a squat building despite its 50m-high spires. It was built in 1880 and modified in 1906 according to designs by Montréal architects Perrault and Venne. They contributed the Romanesque Revival style and interesting rococo interior that's reminiscent of some of the subway stations in Moscow.

La Présentation

The beautiful church in this modest village was built shortly after the La Présentation parish was created, following the division of part of Saint-Hyacinthe in 1804.

The **Église de La Présentation** ★★ (*551 Chemin de L'Église*) is unique among other temples built in Montérégie during the same era because of its finely sculpted stone facade, completed in 1819. Note the inscriptions written in Old French

above the entrances. The vast presbytery, hidden in the greenery as well as the modest sexton house complete this landscape typical of Québec rural parishes.

★
Saint-Denis

Throughout the 1830s, Saint-Denis was home to large political gatherings as well as the headquarters of the *Fils de la Liberté* (Sons of Freedom), a group of young French Canadians who wanted Lower Canada (Québec) to become an independent country. But even more importantly, Saint-Denis was the site of the only *Patriotes* victory over British forces during the 1837-38 rebellion. On November 23, 1837, General Gore's troops were forced to withdraw to Sorel after a fierce battle against the *Patriotes* who were poorly equipped but determined to defeat the enemy. The British troops took revenge a few weeks later, however, by surprising the inhabitants while they slept, pillaging and burning the houses, businesses and industries of Saint-Denis.

The town of Saint-Denis, founded in 1758, experienced an intense period of industrialization in the early 19th century. Canada's largest hat industry was located here, producing the famous beaver-pelt top hats worn by men throughout Europe and America. Other local industries in Saint-Denis included pottery and earthenware. The repression that followed the rebellion put an end to this economic expansion, and from then on the town became a small agricultural village.

A monument was unveiled in 1913 in **Parc des Patriotes** to honour the memory of the Saint-Denis *Patriotes*. It is located in the middle of the square that was known as Place Royale before becoming Place du Marché (a market place) and then a public park in the early 20th century.

The **Maison Nationale des Patriotes** ★ (*$4; May to Sep, every day 10am to 5pm; Nov, Tue to Fri 10am to 5pm; 610 Chemin des Patriotes, ☎787-3623*). To the south of the park stands a former stone inn built for Jean-Baptiste Mâsse in 1810. The building's irregular shape is characteristic of urban homes of the late 18th century: firebreak walls with corbels, veranda on the main floor, and optimum usage of the land. It is one of the rare examples of this type found outside of Montréal and Québec City.

★
Sainte-Anne-de-Sorel

This village is oriented more towards hunting and fishing than other communities in Montérégie because of its proximity to the Sorel islands. Writer Germaine Guèvremont (1893-1968), who lived on one of these islands, introduced this archipelago located in the middle of the St. Lawrence to the literary world in her novel *Le Survenant*.

The best way to explore the **Îles de Sorel** ★ is by taking one of the cruise boats that crosses the archipelago of approximately 20 islands (*two types of cruises are offered: Croisière des Îles de Sorel, 1665 Chemin du Chenal-du-Moine, and Excursions et Expéditions de*

Canots, ☎ *743-7227 or 888-701-7227).* The hour and a half-long cruises begin at the Chenal du Moine. This large waterway was named in the 17th century following the discovery of the frozen body of a Recollet monk (*moine*) who had been travelling from Trois-Rivières to Sorel along the channel (*chenal*).

The islands are an excellent place to observe aquatic birds, especially during the spring and fall. A few houses on piles with individual piers dot the flat landscape which offers views of the vast expanse of Lac Saint-Pierre downstream.

There are two restaurants at the end of the Île d'Embarras (accessible by car) that serve *gibelotte*, a fish fricassee typical of this region.

Saint-Constant

The **Musée Ferroviaire Canadien** ★★ (*$6; early May to early Sep, every day 9am to 5pm; early Sep to mid-Oct, Sat and Sun 9am to 5pm; 120 Rue Saint-Pierre,* ☎ *632-2410*) displays an impressive collection of railway memorabilia, locomotives, freight cars, and maintenance vehicles. The famous *Dorchester* locomotive, put into service in 1836 on the country's first railway between Saint-Jean-sur-Richelieu and La Prairie, is worth noting as are many luxurious 19th century passenger cars of that belonged to Canadian Pacific.

Also on display are foreign locomotives such as the powerful *Châteaubriand* from the SNCF (French Railway System), put into service in 1884.

★ La Prairie

The streets of Vieux-La Prairie ★★ have an urban character rarely found in Québec villages during the 19th century. Several houses were carefully restored after the Québec government declared the area an historical district in 1975. A stroll along Saint-Ignace, Sainte-Marie, Saint-Jacques and Saint-Georges streets reveals this distinctive flavour. Some of the wood houses are reminiscent of those once found in Montréal districts (*240 and 274 Rue Saint-Jacques*). Other homes draw their inspiration from French Regime architecture (two-sided roofs, firebreak walls, dormer windows), except for the fact that they are partially or totally built of brick instead of stone (*234 and 237 Rue Saint-Ignace, 166 Rue Saint-Georges*). Lastly, the stone house covered with wood at number 238 Rue Saint-Ignace is the only surviving testimony of the French Régime in Vieux-La Prairie.

★ Longueuil

Located across from Montréal, this city is the most populous in Montérégie. It once belonged to the Longueuil seigneury, granted to Charles Le Moyne (1624-1685) in 1657.

He headed a dynasty that played a key role in developing New France. Many of his 14 children are famous, such as: Pierre Le Moyne d'Iberville (1661-1706), first governor of Louisiana; Jean-Baptiste Le Moyne de Bienville (1680-1768), founder of New Orleans; and Antoine Le Moyne de Châteauguay (1683-1747), governor of Guyana.

The eldest son, Charles Le Moyne de Longueuil, inherited the seigneury upon the death of his father. Between 1685 and 1690, he had a fortified castle built on the site of the current Église Saint-Antoine-de-Padoue. The castle had four corner towers, a church and many wings. In 1700, Longueuil was raised to the rank of baron by Louis XIV, the only such case in the history of New France. The baron of Longueuil saw to the development of his land which continued to expand until it reached the banks of the Richelieu.

The site of the **Église Saint-Antoine-de-Padoue** ★★ (*Rue Saint-Charles, at the corner of Chemin de Chambly*) was once occupied by a 17th-century castle known as the Château de Longueuil. After being besieged by American rebels during the 1775 invasion, it was requisitioned by the British army. A fire broke out while a garrison was stationed here in 1792, destroying a good part of the building. In 1810, the ruins were used as a quarry during the building of a second Catholic church. A few years later, Rue Saint-Charles was built right through the rest of the site, forcing the complete destruction of this unique North American building.

Archaeological excavations took place during the 1970s, tracing the castle's exact site and unearthing part of its foundations that are visible to the east of the church.

The 1810 church was demolished in 1884 to make room for the present building, the largest church in Montérégie. The exterior is inspired by flamboyant Gothic art, but remains close to Victorian eclecticism.

Kahnawake

In 1667, the Jesuits set up a mission for the converted Iroquois at La Prairie. After moving four times, the mission settled permanently in Sault-Saint-Louis in 1716. The Saint-François-Xavier mission has now become Kahnawake, a name that means "where the rapids are." Over the years, Iroquois Mohawks from the state of New York joined the mission's first inhabitants so that English is now the first language on the reserve, even though most inhabitants still use the French names given to them by the Jesuits. In 1990, Mohawk Warriors demonstrated by blocking the Pont Mercier bridge for months in a show of support for the demands made by the Mohawks of Kanesatake (Oka). Tension between Québec authorities and the natives still exists in the area surrounding the reserve, but visitors need not worry as they are generally warmly welcomed in Kahnawake.

The **Enceinte**, **Musée** and **Église Saint-François-Xavier** ★★(*Main St.*), or the Saint-François-Xavier wall, museum and church. Villages and missions were required under the French Regime to surround themselves with fortifications. Very few of these walls have survived. The wall of the Kahnawake mission, still partially standing, is the kind of ruin rarely found north of Mexico. It was built in 1720 according to plans of the King's engineer, Gaspard Chaussegros de Léry, to protect the church and the Jesuit convent, built three years earlier. The guardroom, powder magazine and officers' residences (1754) are also still standing. From the platform behind the Jesuit convent, visitors can enjoy spectacular views of the seaway, Lachine and Montréal.

The church was modified in 1845 according to the plans of Jesuit Félix Martin and redecorated by Vincent Chartrand (1845-47) who also made some of the furniture. Guido Nincheri designed the polychromatic vaulted ceiling in the 20th century. Also found here is the tomb of Kateri Tekakwitha, a young Mohawk. The convent houses the museum of the Saint-François-Xavier mission where visitors can see some of the objects that belonged to the Jesuits who still led the parish. The village around the church offers one of the largest concentrations of rubble masonry homes in Québec. However, following the example of the fortified walls, these homes are not shown off to their full advantage. Many of them have been defaced, covered up with more modern materials or simply abandoned.

Châteauguay

The Châteauguay seigneury was granted to Charles Le Moyne in 1673.

He immediately had Château de Guay built on Île Saint-Bernard, at the mouth of the Rivière Châteauguay. One hundred years later, a village stood out around the Église Saint-Joachim. The roads and Boulevards that run along the river and Lac Saint-Louis are still dotted with pretty farmhouses built between 1780 and 1840 when the seigneury belonged to the Sœurs Grises (the Grey Nuns). The municipality has developed considerably since 1950, making it a large component of the Montréal suburbs.

When the first church in Châteauguay was built in 1735, it was the westernmost parish on the south shore of the St. Lawrence. Work on the present **Église Saint-Joachim** ★★ (*1 Boulevard Youville*) began in 1775 in order to more easily serve a growing number of parishioners. The **Hôtel de Ville** neighbours the church to the north. It is located in the former convent of the Congrégation de Notre-Dame (1886).

Salaberry-de-Valleyfield

This industrial city came into being in 1845 around a saw and paper mill purchased a few years later by the Montréal Cotton Company. This growing industry led to an era of prosperity in the late 19th century in Salaberry-de-Valleyfield, making it one of Québec's main cities at the time. The old commercial and institutional centre on Rue Victoria recalls this prosperous period and gives the city more of an urban atmosphere than Châteauguay whose population is higher. The city is cut in half by the old Canal de Beauharnois, in operation from 1845 to 1900 (not to be confused with the current Canal de Beauharnois located to the south of the city).

A diocese since 1892, Salaberry-de-Valleyfield was graced with the current **Cathédrale Sainte-Cécile ★** (*31 Rue de la Fabrique*) in 1934, following a fire in the previous church. The cathedral is a colossal piece of work. Architect Henri Labelle designed it in the late Gothic Revival style, narrower and closer to the historical models, added with elements of Art Deco. The facade is adorned with a statue of Sainte Cécile, patron saint of musicians, and the bronze entrance doors are decorated with many bas-reliefs done by Albert Gilles that depict the life of Jesus.

The **Battle of the Châteauguay National Historic Site ★** (*$3.25; late May to early Sep, every day 10am to noon, 1pm to 5pm; early Sep to late Oct, Sat and Sun 10am to noon, 1pm to 5pm; closed on holidays except Jul 1; 2371 Chemin Rivière-Châteauguay Nord, ☎829-2003*) is also called the Lieu Historique National de la Bataille de la Châteauguay. During the U.S. War of Independence, the Americans attempted over the winter of 1775-76 their first takeover of Canada, which became a British colony in 1760. They were forced back by the majority French population. In 1812-13, the Americans tried once again to take over Canada. This time, it was loyalty to the Crown of England and the decisive battle of Châteauguay that thwarted the Americans' attempt. In October 1813, the 2,000 troops of U.S. General Hampton

gathered at the border. They entered Canadian territory during the night along the Rivière Châteauguay. But Charles Michel d'Irumberry de Salaberry, seigneur of Chambly, was waiting for them along with 300 militiamen and a few dozen Aboriginals. On October 26, the battle began. Salaberry's tactics got the better of the Americans, who retreated, putting an end to a series of conflicts and inaugurating a lasting friendship between the two countries.

Hemmingford

Highway 15 leads to the town of Hemmingford near the U.S. border. **Parc Safari ★** (*$20; $68 per car; late May to mid-Sep, every day from 10am; 850 Rte. 202, ☎247-2727 or 800-465-8724*) is located here. The park is an interesting zoological garden where animals from Africa, Europe and America wander freely as visitors tour the grounds in their cars. You can tune your radio to the same station as the park to have an informative description of each animal, which makes the visit worthwhile. There's also an amusement park with many attractions such as merry-go-rounds, a wading pool for the little ones, restaurants and shops. A wonderful family outing.

Eastern Townships

★

The Wine Route

European visitors might consider it quite presumptuous to call the road between Dunham and Stanbridge East (*Rte. 202 W.*) the "Wine Route." But

the concentration of vineyards in this region is unique in the province, and Québec's attempts at wine-making have been so surprisingly successful that people have been swept away by their enthusiasm. There are no châteaux or distinguished old counts here, only growers who sometimes have to go as far as renting helicopters to save their vines from freezing. The rotor blades cause the air to circulate, preventing frost from forming on the ground during crucial periods in May.

The region is, however, blessed with a microclimate and soil favourable for grape growing (slate). The various wines are sold only at the vineyards where they are produced.

You can visit the **L'Orpailleur** (*1086 Rte. 202, J0E 1M0, Dunham, ☎450-295-2763, ≈450-295-3112*) winery whose products include a dry white wine and Apéridor, an apéritif similar to Pineau des Charentes.

The **Domaine des Côtes d'Ardoises** (*879 Rte. 202, Dunham, J0E 1M0, ☎450-295-2020*) is one of the few Québec vineyards that produces red wine.

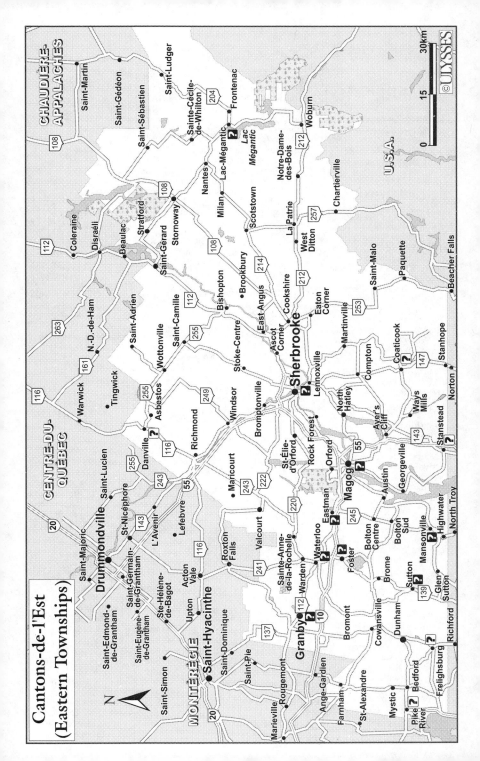

Here, as at other wineries, the owner will give you a warm welcome.

Les Blancs Coteaux
(*1046 Rte. 202, Dunham, JOE 1M0,* ☎*450-295-3503*) not only makes quality wine but also has a lovely craft shop.

Bromont

Developed in the 1960s, Bromont has become a favourite vacation area among Montréalers. It is renowned for its downhill ski resort, its sports facilities, and also for having hosted the 1976 Olympic equestrian competitions.

Visiting the **Musée du Chocolat** (*Jun to Oct, Mon to Fri 10am to 6pm, Sat and Sun 9am to 5:30pm, Nov to May, Tue to Fri 10am to 6pm, Sat and Sun 9am to 5:30pm; 679 Rue Shefford,* ☎*450-534-3893*) is a golden opportunity for gourmands with discriminating palates to indulge in sinfully delicious chocolate. The museum presents the history of chocolate since the arrival of the Spanish in South America, the process of changing cocoa beans into powder and a few art works featuring... chocolate, of course! If your taste buds become overly sated, you can purchase all kinds of delicious sweets made right on the premises. Light meals are also served here.

Valcourt

Bombardier was not the only mechanic in Québec to develop a motor vehicle for use on snow-covered surfaces. Residents had to come up with something, since many roads in the province were not cleared of snow until the beginning of the 1950s. As automobiles were, for all practical purposes, somewhat unreliable, people had to depend on the same means of transportation as their ancestors, namely the horse-drawn sleigh. Bombardier was the only individual, however, to succeed in making a profit from his invention, most notably because of a lucrative contract with the army during World War ll. Though the company later diversified and underwent considerable expansion, it never left the village of Valcourt – which is to this day the site of its head office.

The **Musée J.-Armand-Bombardier** ★ (*$5; every day 10am to 5pm, closed Mon early Sep to late Apr; 1001 Avenue Joseph-Armand-Bombardier;* ☎*450-532-5300*) is a museum that traces the development of the snowmobile, and explains how Bombardier's invention was marketed all over the world. Different prototypes are displayed along with a few examples of various snowmobiles produced since 1960. Group tours of the factory are also available.

Granby

A few kilometres from the verdant Parc de la Yamaska, Granby (the "princess of the Eastern Townships") basks in the fresh air of the surrounding countryside. In addition to its Victorian-style houses, this city boasts grand avenues and parks graced with fountains and sculptures. Transected by the Yamaska Nord River, it's also the point where the Montérégiade and Estriade bicycle trails converge. The city's youth and dynamism are reflected in its multiple festivals, notably the Festival International de la Chanson, an international song festival that has exposed a number of excellent performers to the French-speaking world.

Visitors to the **Granby Zoo** ★★ (*$19.95; early Jun to late Sep, every day 10am to 6pm, call for the rest of the Year; take Exit 68 or 74 from Hwy. 10 and follow the signs;* ☎*450-372-9113*) can see some 250 animal species from various different countries, in particular North America and Africa. This is an old-style zoo, so most of the animals are in cages and there are few areas where they can roam freely. It is nevertheless an interesting place to visit.

The **Parc de Récréation de la Yamaska**, see p 221.

The **Centre d'Interprétation de la Nature du Lac Boivin**, see p 222.

★★
Knowlton

Lac Brome ★, a circular body of water, is popular among windsurfers who can use a parking lot and a little beach on the side of the road near Knowlton. The duck from this lake is known for its flavour and is featured on the menus of local inns and restaurants when in season.

The **Musée Historique du Comté de Brome** ★ (*$3.50; mid-May to mid-Sep, Mon to Sat 10am to 4:30pm, Sun 11am to 4:30pm; 130 Rue Lakeside;* ☎*450-243-6782*), the historical museum of Brome County, occupies five Loyalist buildings and traces the lives and history of the region's inhabitants. In addition to the usual furniture and photographs, visitors can see a reconstructed general store, a

19th-century court of justice and, what's more unusual, a collection of military equipment, including a World War I airplane.

★
Sutton

Sutton, which is located at the base of the mountain of the same name, is one of the major winter resorts in the Eastern Townships. The area also has several well-designed golf courses. Among the local houses of worship, the Gothic Revival Anglican **Grace Church** (built out of stone in 1850) is the most noteworthy. Unfortunately, its steeple no longer has its pointed arch.

★★
Lac Memphrémagog

Lac Memphrémagog, which is 40km long and only 1 to 2 km wide, will remind some visitors of a Scottish loch. It even has its own equivalent of the Loch Ness monster, named "Memphre," sightings of which go back to 1798! The southern portion of the lake, which cannot be seen from Magog, is located in the United States. The name Memphrémagog, like Massawippi and Missisquoi, is an Abenaki word.

Sailing enthusiasts will be happy to learn that the lake is one of the best places in Québec to enjoy this sport.

★★
Saint-Benoît-du-Lac

This municipality consists solely of the estate of the **Abbaye de Saint-Benoît-du-Lac**, an abbey founded in 1913 by Benedictine

monks who were driven away from the Abbaye de Saint-Wandrille-de-Fontenelle in Normandy. Aside from the monastery, there are guest quarters, an abbey chapel and farm buildings. However, only the chapel and a few corridors are open to the public. Visitors will not want to miss the Gregorian chants sung at vespers at 5pm every day.

★
Magog

Equipped with more facilities than any other town between Granby and Sherbrooke, Magog has a lot to offer sports lovers. It is extremely well situated on the northern shore of Lac Memphrémagog but has unfortunately been subjected to unbridled development for several years now. The town's cultural scene is worth noting. Visitors can go to the theatre or the music complex, set in the natural mountain surroundings. The textile industry, once of great importance in the lives of local residents, has declined, giving way to tourism. Visitors will enjoy strolling down Rue Principale, which is lined with shops and restaurants.

The **Théâtre du Vieux-Clocher** see p 219.

The **Parc de Récréation du Mont-Orford** ★★ see p 212.

The **Centre d'Arts Orford** ★ see p 219.

★★
North Hatley

Attracted by North Hatley's enchanting countryside, wealthy American vacationers built luxurious villas here between 1890 and 1930. Most of these still line the northern part of Lac Massawippi, which, like Lac Memphrémagog, resembles a Scottish loch. Beautiful inns and gourmet restaurants add to the charm of the place, ensuring its reputation as a vacation spot of the utmost sophistication. In the centre of the village, visitors will notice the tiny Shingle-style **United Church**, which looks more Catholic than Protestant.

Manoir Hovey ★ (*Chemin Hovey*), a large villa built in 1900, was modelled on Mount Vernon, George Washington's home in Virginia. It used to be the summer residence of an American named Henry Atkinson, who entertained American artists and politicians here every summer. The house has since been converted into an inn.

Manoir Hovey

★ Lennoxville

This little town, whose population is still mainly English-speaking, is home to two prestigious English-language educational institutions; Bishop's University and Bishop's College. Established alongside the road linking Trois-Rivières to the U.S. border, the town was named after Charles Lennox (the fourth Duke of Richmond) who was governor of Upper and Lower Canada in 1818. Once off the main road (Rte. 143) explore the town's side streets to see the institutional buildings and lovely Second Empire and Queen Anne houses nestled in greenery.

Bishop's University ★ (*College Road*), one of three English-language universities in Québec, offers 1,300 students from all over Canada a personalized education in an enchanting setting. It was founded in 1843 through the efforts of a minister named Lucius Doolittle. Upon arriving at the university, visitors will see **McGreer Hall**, built in 1876 by architect James Nelson and later modified by Taylor and Gordon of Montréal to give it a medieval look. **St. Mark's Anglican Chapel**, which stands to its left, was rebuilt in 1891 after a fire. Its long, narrow interior has a lovely oak trim as well as stained-glass windows by Spence and Sons of Montréal.

★★ Sherbrooke (pop. 79,432)

Sherbrooke, the Eastern Townships' main urban centre, is nicknamed the Queen of the Eastern Townships. It spreads over a series of hills on both sides of the Rivière Saint-François, accentuating its disorderly appearance. The city nevertheless has a number of interesting buildings, the majority of which are located on the west bank. Sherbrooke's origins date back to the beginning of the 19th century. Like so many other villages in the region, it grew up around a mill and a small market. However, in 1823, it was designated as the site of a courthouse intended to serve the entire region which set it apart from the neighbouring communities. The arrival of the railroad here in 1852 as well as the downtown concentration of institutions, such as the head office of the Eastern Township Bank, led to the construction of prestigious Victorian edifices which transformed Sherbrooke's appearance. Today, the city is home to a large French-language university, founded in 1952 in order to counterbalance Bishop's University in Lennoxville. Despite the city's name, chosen in honour of Sir John Coape Sherbrooke, governor of British North America at the time it was founded, the city's population has been almost entirely French-speaking (95%) for a long time.

An important financial institution in the last century, now merged with the CIBC (Canadian Imperial Bank of Commerce), the former **Eastern Townships Bank** ★★ (*241 Rue Dufferin*) was established by the region's upper class who were unable to obtain financing for local projects from the banks in Montréal. Its Sherbrooke head office, erected in 1877, was designed by Montréal architect James Nelson who was involved at the time in building Bishop's University. It is considered the finest Second Empire building in Québec outside of Montréal and Québec City.

Following a donation from the Canadian Imperial Bank of Commerce (CIBC) and major renovations, the building now houses the **Musée des Beaux-Arts** (*$4; late Jun to early Sep, Tue to Sun 1pm to 5pm, Wed 1pm to 9pm; 241 Rue Dufferin, ☎819-821-2115*). Gérard Gendron's work, which greets visitors in the main hall, reflects the building's former tenants and its present vocation. Besides the museum's large collection of naive art, there are several works by local contemporary artists. Volunteers are available to answer questions on the exhibitions which usually change every two months.

Some of the loveliest houses in Sherbrooke are located on **Parc Mitchell** ★★. Adorned with a fountain by sculptor George Hill (1921), **Maison Morey** (*not open to visitors; 428 Rue Dufferin*), is an example of the bourgeois Victorian style favoured by merchants and industrialists from the British Isles and the United States. It was built in 1873 for Thomas Morey.

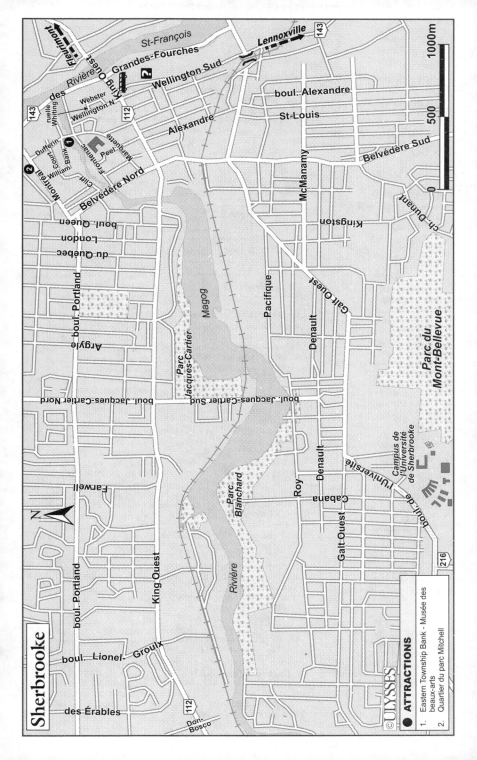

Sherbrooke

N

St-François
Fleurimont
Rivière O. bury
des Rivière O. bury
Grandes-Fourches
Wellington Sud
Lennoxville
143

boul. Alexandre
St-Louis
Belvédère Sud

ruelle Whiting
Webster
Wellington N.
143
112
Alexandre

Dufferin
Frontenac
Peel
Marquette
William court
Bank
Cliff
1
2
Montréal

Belvédère Nord

boul. Queen
London
du Québec

boul. Portland

Argyle
Magog
Parc Jacques-Cartier

boul. Jacques-Cartier Nord
boul. Jacques-Cartier Sud
boul. Jacques-Cartier

Pacifique
Denault
Galt Ouest

McManamy
Kingston

Parc du Mont-Bellevue

Farewell
Parc Blanchard
Rivière
Roy
Cabana
Denault

Campus de l'Université de Sherbrooke
l'Université
boul. de l'Université

boul. Portland
King Ouest
Groulx
boul. Lionel- Groulx

des Érables
112
Don- Bosco
Galt Ouest
216

1000m
500
0

© ULYSSE

ATTRACTIONS

1. Eastern Township Bank - Musée des beaux-arts
2. Quartier du parc Mitchell

Notre-Dame-des-Bois

Located in the heart of the Appalachians at an altitude of over 550m, this little community acts as a gateway to Mont Mégantic and its observatory as well as Mont Saint-Joseph and its sanctuary.

The **ASTROlab du Mont-Mégantic** ★★ (*from $10; mid-Jun to Sep, every day 10am to 6pm, 8pm to 11pm; late May to mid-Jun, Sat to Sun 11am to 5pm; early Sep to mid-Oct, Sat-Sun 11am to 5pm; 189 Route du Parc, ☎819-888-2941, astrolab.qc.ca*) is an interpretation centre on astronomy. The interactive museum's various rooms and multimedia show reveal the beginnings of astronomy with the latest technology. Lasting approximately 1hr 15min, a guided tour to the summit of Mont Mégantic walks visitors through the facilities. Famous for its observatory, Mont Mégantic was chosen for its strategic position between the Universities of Montreal and Laval as well as its distance from urban light sources. As the second-highest summit in the Eastern Townships, it stands at 1,105m. During the **Festival d'Astronomie Populaire du Mont Mégantic** (a local astronomy festival held the second week of July), astronomy buffs can observe the heavens through the most powerful telescope in eastern North America. Otherwise, the latter is only available to researchers. A new observatory with a 60cm telescope, however, is now open to the public. In summer, basic celestial mechanics workshops are also given.

A vast expanse of crystal-clear water stretching

17km, **Lac Mégantic** ★★ is teeming with all sorts of fish, especially trout, and attracts a good many vacationers eager to go fishing or simply enjoy the local beaches. Five municipalities around the lake, Lac-Mégantic being the most well-known, welcome visitors lured by the lovely mountainous countryside.

Parks

Montérégie

Centre de la Nature du Mont Saint-Hilaire ★★ (*$4; every day 8am until one hour before sundown; 422 Rue des Moulins, Mont-Saint-Hilaire, J3G 4S6, ☎467-1755*). Situated on the upper half of Mont Saint-Hilaire, this nature conservation centre is a former estate that brigadier Andrew Hamilton Gault passed on to Montréal's McGill University in 1958. Scientific research is conducted here and recreational activities (hiking, cross-country skiing) are permitted throughout the year on half of the estate which covers 11km². The Centre was also recognized as a Biosphere Reserve by UNESCO in 1978 for its mature forest that has remained virtually untouched over the centuries. An information centre on the formation of the Montérégie hills and a garden of indigenous plants can be found at the park's entrance.

Eastern Townships

The **Parc du Mont-Orford** ★★ (*C.P. 146, Magog, J1X 3W7; ☎819-843-6233*)

stretches over 58km² and includes – in addition to the mountain – the area around Lac Stukely. During the summer, visitors can enjoy the beach, the magnificent golf course (*$30 a round*), back-country campsites, and some 50km of hiking trails (the most beautiful path leads to Mont Chauve). The park also attracts winter sports lovers with its cross-country ski trails and 33 downhill ski runs (*$34 a day*).

The **Parc de la Gorge de Coaticook** ★★ (*$6; late Jun to early Sep, 9am to 8pm, early Sep to late Jun, 10am to 5pm, Sat and Sun 10am to 6pm; 135 Rue Michaud, Coaticook; ☎819-849-2331 or 888-524-6743, ⇔819-849-2459*) protects the part of the impressive 50m gorge created by the Rivière Coaticook. Trails wind across the entire area, enabling visitors to see the gorge from different angles. Cross the suspension bridge over the gorge, if you dare!

Known mainly for its famed observatory (see p 212), the **Parc de Conservation du Mont-Mégantic** (*$4; every day 9am to 5pm; no pets allowed; 189 Route du Parc, Notre-Dame-des-Bois, ☎819-888-2941*) covers an area of 58.8km². It displays the different types of mountainous vegetation characteristic of the Eastern Townships and contains the Mont St-Joseph and Mont Mégantic hills. Heavy infrastructure has not been able to disturb the tranquillity of this park whose goal is educational. Hikers and skiers can take advantage of the Park's interpretive trails, cabins, campsites and, if lucky, observe up to 125 species of migrating birds. Snowshoeing in winter and mountain-biking in summer.

Outdoor Activities

Hiking

Eastern Townships

The **Sentier de l'Estrie**
(☎*819-868-3889*) network
of trails winds over 150km
through the Chapman,
Kingsbury, Brompton,
Orford, Bolton, Glen, Echo
and Sutton areas. You can
obtain a topographical
guide of the trail and the
membership card necessary to walk it for $20.
Keep in mind that most of
the trail runs across private
property. The various
landowners have accorded
an exclusive right of way
to members.

Horseback Riding

Eastern Townships

The **Centre Équestre de
Bromont** (*100 Rue Laprairie*,
☎*450-534-3255*) hosted the
1976 Olympic equestrian
events for which a variety
of stables and rings, both
exterior and interior, were
built. Some of
these facilities
are now used
for riding
classes.

Downhill Skiing

Eastern Townships

The **Station de Ski Bromont**
(*$34; 150 Rue Champlain,
Bromont*, ☎*450-534-2200*)
has 23 runs, 20 of which
are lit until 11:30pm for
night-skiing. The mountain
has a vertical drop of over
400m.

Mont Sutton ★ (*$39; 671
Chemin Mapple, Sutton;*
☎*450-538-2545*) has 53
downhill ski runs and a
vertical drop of 460m. It is
known for its magnificent
glade runs.

Mont Orford ★ (*$33.75;
Magog,* ☎*819-843-6548*) is
among the prettiest ski
centres in Québec. It
boasts 40 trails.

Owl's Head ★ (*$30; Chemin
du Mont Owl's Head,
Mansonville,* ☎*450-292-3342
or 800-363-3342*) is one of
the most beautiful ski
resorts in the Eastern
Townships region, with
sweeping views of Lac
Memphrémagog and the
surrounding mountains.
There are 27 runs for skiers of all different levels.

Accommodations

Montérégie

Chambly

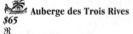
La Maison Ducharme
$100 bkfst incl.
≈
124 Rue Martel
☎*447-1220*
⇥*447-1018*
This pleasant B&B is in an
old 19th-century barracks
(see p 199), right near Fort
Chambly. Tastefully decorated, the house is steeped
in the antique luxury of
another era when people
took the time to make
every detail in their house
immaculate. A lovely English garden and pool add
nicely to this large property next to the Rivière
Richelieu rapids.

Saint-Jean-sur-Richelieu

Auberge des Trois Rives
$65
ℜ
297 Rue Richelieu, J3B 6Y3
☎*358-8077*
The Auberge des Trois
Rives is a pleasant B&B set
up in a rustic home. A
restaurant and a terrace
offer a pretty view of the
water. There are
10 modestly decorated but
comfortable rooms spread
over two floors. Take note
that prices may be higher
during the hot-air balloon
festival.

Québec

Mont-Saint-Hilaire

 Manoir Rouville Campbell
$150
≡, ≈, ℜ
125 Chemin des Patriotes
☎*446-6060*
☎*800-714-1214*
⇒*446-4878*
The Manoir Rouville Campbell has a mystical air about it. As you enter the manor, it's as though time has stopped or even gone back a century. This place, now 200 years old, has seen many chapters of Québec history unfold. It was converted into a luxury hotel in 1987 and is now owned by Québec comedian Yvon Deschamps. The dining room, bar and gardens overlooking the Richelieu complement this lordly manor.

Saint-Hyacinthe

Hotel Gouverneur Saint-Hyacinthe
$160
≡, ⊛, ≈, ⊘, △, ℜ
1200 Daniel-Johnson Ouest, J2S 7K7
☎*774-3810*
☎*800-363-0110*
⇒*774-6955*
In a building next to the highway, the Hotel Gouverneur Saint-Hyacinthe offers pretty rooms and many services to ensure its visitors a pleasant stay. Tennis and squash courts are available, and the peaceful lobby is decorated with plants and a fountain.

Saint-Marc-sur-Richelieu

 Hostellerie les Trois Tilleuls
$150
≡, ⊛, ℜ, ≈, tv, ℜ
290 Rue Richelieu J0L 2E0
☎*584-2231*
☎*800-263-2230*
⇒*584-3146*
The Hostellerie les Trois Tilleuls belongs to the prestigious Relais et Châteaux association. Built next to the Rivière Richelieu, it enjoys a tranquil rural setting. The name of the establishment comes from the three grand linden trees (called *tilleul* in French) which shade the property. The rooms are decorated with rustic furniture and each has a balcony overlooking the river. Outside, guests have access to gardens, a lookout and a heated pool.

Eastern Townships

Dunham

 Pom-Art B&B
$65
$80 bkfst incl.
sb/pb
677 Chemin Hudson
☎*(450) 295-3514*
☎*(888) 537-6627*
With its 0.5ha of land, the Pom-Art B&B, built in 1820, is a real gem. Denis and Lise offer guests a warm welcome, not to mention an exceptional breakfast where apples from the region figure prominently. An ideal abode in which to seek refuge after a tiring day on the slopes of Mont Sutton, located 15km away. Indeed, the most luxurious of the three rooms boasts a fireplace and a window looking out on the surrounding mountains.

Bromont

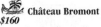 Château Bromont
$160
≈, ≡, ℜ, ✪, △, ⊛, ℜ
90 Stanstead, J0E 1L0
☎*(450) 534-3433*
☎*800- 304-3433*
⇒*(450) 534-0514*
Those looking for comfort can head to the Château Bromont where both the main rooms and the bedrooms are elegantly decorated with antique furniture. The property is located alongside Mont Bromont, providing skiers with easy access to the slopes.

Around Lac Brome

Auberge Joli Vent
$80 bkfst incl.
≈
667 Chemin Bondville, Foster J0E 1R0
☎*(450) 243-4272*
⇒*(450) 243-0202*
Auberge Joli Vent is a lovely inn with a pleasant setting, despite being alongside the road. The modestly furnished rooms have a rustic charm.

Knowlton

 Auberge Lakeview
$157.60 bkfst incl. Fri to Sun
$137 bkfst incl. Mon to Thu
⊛, ≈, ℜ, ⊗
50 Rue Victoria
☎*(450) 243-6183*
☎*800- 661-6183*
⇒*(450) 243-0602*
Ideally located near ski resorts and golf courses, the Auberge Lakeview offers a thoroughly Victorian atmosphere. Indeed, the 1986 renovations have restored some of the noble antiquity to this historic monument, built in the latter half of the 19th century. Rates for rooms, both comfortable and spacious, include the continental breakfast.

Sutton

Auberge La Paimpolaise
$47.50 bkfst incl.
≈, ⊛, ≈, ℜ
615 Maple, C.P. 548, J0E 2K0
☎*(450) 538-3213*
☎*800-263-3213*
⇄*(450) 538-3970*
Auberge La Paimpolaise inn near the ski slopes is set up in two separate buildings. The reception is in a small wooden, Swiss-chalet-style house, and the rooms are in a long concrete annex. The rooms are somewhat austere. This is a very plain hotel with a clientele consisting mainly of skiers.

Magog

Aux Jardins Champêtres
$70 sb
$90 pb, bkfst incl.
$126 ½b
1575 Chemin des Pères
☎*(819) 868-0665*
Surrounded by wild flowers and cats, Aux Jardins Champêtres recalls summers spent at grandma's. Located a few minutes from Magog and l'Abbaye St-Benoit-du-Lac, this B&B boasts comfortable rooms as well as a swimming pool. The welcoming little farm also owes its reputation to its excellent and varied country cooking.

Orford

Auberge La Grande Fugue
$18/pers.
May to Oct
3166 Chemin du Parc
☎*(819) 843-8595*
☎*800- 567-6155*
Situated near the Centre d'Arts d'Orford, the Auberge La Grande Fugue consists of a series of small cottages surrounded by nature. A communal kitchen is available to guests.

Manoir des Sables
$175
ℑ, K, ⊛, ≈, ℝ, ℜ, ⌂, ☉, ≈, tv
90 Avenue des Jardins
☎*(819) 847-4747*
☎*800-567-3514*
⇄*(819) 847-3519*
In the shadow of Mont Orford is the very opulent and modern Manoir des Sables. The hotel features a multitude of services and facilities such as indoor and outdoor swimming pools, an 18-hole golf course, tennis courts and a health spa. Several rooms boast fireplaces, and those on the top floor offer magnificent views of the lake and of the 60ha property. Rooms in the "Privilège" wing come with exemplary service and include continental breakfasts.

Village Mont-Orford
$245
≈, K
5015 Chemin du Parc, J1X 3W8
☎*(819) 847-2662*
☎*800-567-7315*
⇄*(819) 847-3635*
The Village Mont-Orford is comprised of several buildings, each containing a few lovely, fully equipped condos. Approximately 200m from there, a quadruple chair lift takes skiers up to Mont Orford's runs.

Ayer's Cliff

Auberge Ripplecove
$165
≈, ℑ, ⊛, ≈, ℜ
700 Rue Ripplecove
☎*(819) 838-4296*
☎*800- 668-4296*
⇄*(819) 838-5541*
Located on a natural, 6ha property facing Lac Massawippi, the Auberge Ripplecove is wonderfully peaceful. Its elegant Victorian-style dining room and tasteful guestrooms ensure comfort in unparalleled, intimate surroundings.

Moreover, the more luxurious rooms have their own fireplaces and whirlpool baths. A variety of outdoor activities are offered. The place becomes absolutely magical in winter.

North Hatley

Auberge Hatley
$130
≈, ⊛, ℑ, ≈, ℜ
Route 108, J0B 2C0
☎*(819) 842-2451*
⇄*(819) 842-2907*
The Auberge Hatley occupies a superb residence built in 1903. The spacious living room looking out on the lake is furnished with beautiful antiques. A vast garden surrounds the inn and its pool. A magical place to escape to.

Manoir Hovey
$170
⊛, ℑ, ☉, ≈, ℜ
575 Chemin Hovey, J0B 1C0
☎*(819) 842-2421*
☎*800-661-2421*
⇄*(819) 842-2248*
Built in 1900, the Manoir Hovey reflects the days when wealthy families spent their vacations in the beautiful country houses of the Townships. Converted into an inn 40 years ago (see p 209), it is still extremely comfortable. The 40 rooms are decorated with lovely antique furniture, and most offer a magnificent view of Lac Massawippi. The property retains much of its old, natural charm.

Sherbrooke

Le Vieux Presbytère
$65 bkfst incl.
1162 Blvd. Portland
☎*(819) 346-1665*
The largest town in the Eastern Townships has only three Bed and Breakfasts. The recently opened Le Vieux Presbytère has

Québec

five tastefully decorated rooms. Those who like antique furniture will be delighted with several of the owners' finds, not to mention the beautiful sitting room that welcomes guests on the ground floor. There is also a safe place to leave bicycles. Take note, however, that this Bed and Breakfast is open only during the summer months.

Delta Hotel
$156
≡, ⅃, ☉, ≈, ⊘, △, ℜ
2685 Rue King Ouest, J1L 1C1
☎*(819) 822-1989*
☎*800- 268-1133*
⊶*(819) 822-8990*
The pinkish Delta Hotel is also on the way into town. Recently built, it offers its guests a wide range of facilities, including an indoor pool, a whirlpool and an exercise room.

Restaurants

Montérégie

Chambly

Crêperie du Fort Chambly
$$-$$$
1717 Rue Bougogne
☎*447-7474*
The Crêperie du Fort Chambly, on the edge of Bassin de Chambly, occupies a wooden house that recalls the sea. They serve crêpes, of course, but also cheese fondues. Waterfront terrace and friendly service.

Saint-Jean-sur-Richelieu

 **Le Manneken Pis**
$
320 Rue Champlain
☎*348-3254*
With a name like that, Belgian waffles are sure to be nearby – and what delicious waffles they are and with such fine chocolate! The coffees, roasted on site, are also excellent. A pleasant terrace faces a little marina. They also serve bread with various spreads and salads.

 Chez Noeser
$$$
wine
236 Rue Champlain
☎*346-0811*
A few years ago, Denis and Ginette Noeser left Montréal and their Rue Saint-Denis restaurant to settle in Saint-Jean-sur-Richelieu. Their latest restaurant offers particularly courteous service and delicious classic French cuisine. There is a terrace during the summer months.

Saint-Hyacinthe

Chez Pépé
$$
1705 Rue Girouard Ouest
☎*773-8004*
and
Grillade Rose
$$
494 Rue Saint-Simon
☎*771-0069*
In Saint-Hyacinthe there are two restaurants that everyone knows about, and they both have the same owner. Although it's not *haute cuisine*, Chez Pépé and Grillade Rose both offer simple tasty meals in a pleasant decor and both places have terraces. Each restaurant is based on a different theme; Pépé's is Italian

and offers a selection of pastas, and Grillade Rose is Santa Fe-style with grill dishes and nachos.

Saint-Marc-sur-Richelieu

Hostellerie des Trois Tilleuls
$$$$
290 Rue Richelieu
☎*856-7787*
☎*800-263-2230*
The restaurant in the Hostellerie des Trois Tilleuls serves up some gems of fine French gastronomy. The artfully prepared menu offers traditional and sophisticated meals, and the dining room has a nice view of the river. The beautiful terrace is open to guests during the summer.

Eastern Townships

Dunham

L'Orpailleur
$-$$
Jun to late Oct
1086 Route 202
☎*(450) 295-3763*
The restaurant at the L'Orpailleur vineyard, open only in the summer, has a short but high-quality menu. A pleasant terrace looks out on the vineyard so guests can enjoy the lovely countryside while eating. The service is extremely friendly. Reservations necessary.

Granby

Ben la Bédaine
$
599 Rue Principale
☎*(450) 378-2921*
The name Ben la Bédaine, which means "Potbelly Ben," is certainly evocative. This place is a veritable shrine to French fries.

Maison de Chez Nous

$$$-$$$$
closed Mon and Tue
847 Rue Mountain
☎*(450) 372-2991*
The owner of Maison de Chez Nous gave up his wine cellar so that his customers, who may now bring their own wine, could save a little money. Furthermore, the menu offers the best and most refined Québec cuisine.

Cowansville

 McHaffy
$$$-$$$$
351 Rue Principale
☎*(450) 266-7700*
A must in the region, McHaffy, whose menu changes every two months, offers fine, international cuisine made with local ingredients and is accompanied by a Blancs Coteaux wine chosen by Alain Bélanger, one of Québec's best wine waiters. At lunch, patrons enjoy lighter meals on a pleasant terrace. Not to be missed is the duck festival, from mid-October to mid-November when chef Pierre Johnston creates excellent dishes for the occasion.

Bromont

 Les Délices de la Table
$$-$$$
641 Rue Shefford
☎*(450) 534-1646*
Les Délices de la Table is a small country-style caterer with bright yellow walls, lace curtains and tablecloths with floral and fruit motifs. It's the kind of place where you feel right at home as soon as you open the door. Sample some tasty dishes that are made with local products and are carefully prepared by the chef who is also the owner. Filled with regular customers, this tiny restaurant is becoming quite popular, so reservations are recommended.

Etrier Rest-O-Bar

$$$
closed Mon
547 Shefford
☎*(450) 534-3562*
The Etrier Rest-O-Bar serves excellent cuisine to an established clientele. The restaurant is located a short distance outside the city in a pleasant, though unsophisticated setting.

Sutton

Il Duetto

$$$-$$$$
every day from 5pm
227 Académie-Élie
☎*(450) 538-8239*
Il Duetto serves fine Italian cuisine in a quiet country setting in the hills around Sutton. The pasta is home-made and the main dishes are inspired by the regional cuisines of Italy. The five-course menu is a good sampling of the variety of Italian cooking.

Magog

La Grosse Pomme

$$
276 Principale Ouest
☎*(819) 843-9365*
La Grosse Pomme is a friendly restaurant serving good bistro-style food. In the evening, the ambiance is livened up by chatty patrons both young and old.

La Paimpolaise

$$-$$$
*open evenings only
closed Mon and Tue in winter*
Route 112
☎*(819) 843-1502*
Though it is located on a very busy street, La Paimpolaise still has character. A friendly restaurant in a charming little house, it serves a wide selection of crepes and other French dishes. This is without question one of the best places to eat in the city.

Orford

Les Jardins

$$$-$$$$
90 Avenue des Jardins
☎*(819) 847-4747*
☎*800- 567-3514*
⇌*(819) 847-3519*
With its modern decor, the restaurant at the Manoir des Sables, Les Jardins is somewhat lacking in character. Fortunately, its large windows look out on Mont Orford. The menu features gourmet cuisine, including a *"table estrienne,"* so guests can sample regional flavours.

Ayer's Cliff

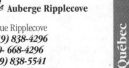 **Auberge Ripplecove**
$$$$
700 Rue Ripplecove
☎*(819) 838-4296*
☎*800- 668-4296*
⇌*(819) 838-5541*
Recognized as a four-diamond establishment, the restaurant of the Auberge Ripplecove offers fine gourmet cuisine of great distinction. Its Victorian atmosphere and elegant decor make it an excellent place for a romantic meal.

North Hatley

Pilsen

$$
55 Rue Principal
☎*(819) 842-2971*
Located inside a large house on the shores of Lac Massawippi, the Pilsen serves good, simple food, such as salads and hamburgers, in a warm, friendly atmosphere. Its attractive country decor gives it a very pleasant, old-fashioned character.

Auberge Hatley
$$$$
Route 108
☎*(819) 842-2451*
The restaurant at the Auberge Hatley, which has received numerous awards, is without question one of the region's best places to eat. The skillfully prepared gourmet meals will please even the most discerning palates. Not to mention that the dining room is beautifully decorated and offers a magnificent view of Lac Massawippi. Reservations necessary.

 Manoir Hovey
$$$$
575 Chemin Hovey
☎*(819) 842-2421*
Graced with antique furniture and a fireplace, the dining room of the Manoir Hovey has a quiet atmosphere which makes for a lovely evening. The cuisine, as refined as the Auberge Hatley's, has also earned a lot of praise.

Sherbrooke

Presse Boutique Café
$-$$
4 Rue Wellington Nord
☎*(819) 822-2133*
A laid-back clientele frequents the Presse Boutique Café. In addition to visual-art exhibitions and shows by local and other musicians, patrons can enjoy a wide variety of imported beers, a simple menu (salads, *croque-monsieur*, sandwiches, etc.) and vegetarian dishes. Moreover, two Internet stations are available (*$6/hr*, *$1/10min*).

Da Toni
$$$$
15 Belvédère Nord
☎*(819) 346-8441*
Located right in the heart of the new downtown area, the opulent Da Toni

has a well-established reputation. Indeed, for 25 years now, patrons have been enjoying its fine French and Italian cuisine, served with a wide selection of wines in a classic decor. The table d'hôte features five excellent, reasonably priced main courses. Though somewhat noisy, the terrace allows guests to enjoy a drink outside during the summer.

Notre-Dame-des-Bois

 Aux Berges de l'Aurore
$$$$
May to Oct, Tue to Sun 6pm to 9pm
Jul and Aug everyday
139 Route du Parc
☎*(819) 888-2715*
Located close to lush Mont Mégantic, the intimate and very charming Aux Berges de l'Aurore serves excellent Québec cuisine. Seasoned with wild herbs gathered in the surrounding countryside, its dishes are most original. From the very first bite, guests will appreciate why it received the *Mérite de la Fine Cuisine Estrienne* award!

Entertainment

Montérégie

Upton

Unique in North America, the concept of **La Dame de Coeur** (*late Jun to early Sep; 611 Rang de la Carrière*, ☎*549-5828*) is sure to fascinate young and old alike. Located in a magnificent historical site, the "Queen of Hearts" puts on terrific puppet shows complete with striking visual effects.

The outdoor theatre has an immense roof and pivoting seats that are heated on chilly evenings.

Saint-Jean-sur-Richelieu

The **Festival de Montgolfières** (☎*347-9555*, *www.montgolfieres.com*), a hot-air-balloon festival, fills the sky over Saint-Jean-sur-Richelieu with approximately 100 multicoloured hot-air balloons. Departures take place every day from 6am to 6pm, weather permitting. Exhibitions and shows make up some of the other activities that take place during the festival.

Valleyfield

In early July, Valleyfield hosts the **Régates Internationales de Valleyfield** (*$15 before Jun 24, $19.50 afterward*, ☎*371-6144 or 888-371-6144*). The competition involves several categories of hydroplane races, with speeds reaching 240km/h. The regattas always attract a large number of visitors.

Kahnawake

Various traditional Aboriginal events (dances, songs, etc.) are organized as a part of the **Pow Wow** (*second week in Jul;* ☎*638-9699*), held in Kahnawake every year during the second weekend of July. Most of the activities are held on Île Kateri Tekakwitha.

Eastern Townships

Sherbrooke

Au Vieux Quartier
252 Rue Dufferin
Located in the old downtown area, the pub Au

Vieux Quartier has a re-laxed ambiance. The place remains faithful to classic rock, as evidenced by photographs of various rock stars covering the walls. Moreover, every Sunday night, different local musicians perform here.

The Université de Sherbrooke's cultural centre houses the **Salle Maurice O'Bready**, (*2500 Boulevard Université, ☎819-820-1000*), where concerts, be they classical or rock, are presented

A former church converted into a concert hall, the **Vieux Clocher de Sherbrooke** (*1590 Galt Ouest, ☎819-822-2102*) now welcomes music lovers and entertainment-seekers. Taking on the same role as its predecessor in Magog, the new hall accommodates approximately 500 spectators. It offers "discovery-shows" featuring young Quebecers and well-established performers. Performance listings can be found in the Sherbrooke daily *La Tribune*.

Orford

The **Centre d'Arts Orford** (*3165 Chemin du Parc, ☎819-843-3981 or 800-567-6155*) provides advanced training courses to young musicians during summertime. An annual festival also takes place at the centre which is made up of several buildings designed in the 1960s by Paul-Marie Côté. The exhibition room that tops off the centre was originally the Man and Music (*l'Homme et la Musique*) pavilion at Expo '67, and was designed by Desgagné and Côté.

During the months of July and August, the **Festival Orford** (*3165 Chemin du Parc, ☎819-843-3981 or 888-310-3665, ≈819-843-7274*) offers a series of concerts featuring ensembles and world-famous virtuosos. Several excellent free concerts are also presented by young musicians who come here for the summer to hone their skills at the Centre d'Arts Orford. This high-calibre festival is an absolute must for all music lovers.

Magog

Located inside an old Protestant church built in 1887, the **Théâtre du Vieux-Clocher** (*64 Rue Merry Nord Magog-Orford; ☎819-847-0470*) staged many shows that later became very successful in both Québec and France. Those interested in attending a show should reserve their seats well in advance. The theatre is small, yet attractive.

A few days of festivities are organized as part of the **Traversée Internationale** (*$5; mid-Jul; ☎819-843-5000, ≈819-843-5621*), including performances by Québec theatrical artists, exhibits of all kinds and shows by folk singers. The highlight of the celebrations is the arrival of swimmers from Newport, USA. The 42km swim is undertaken by athletes considered among the best in the world.

Shopping

Montérégie

Iberville

Les Jardins de Versaille (*late Jun to late Dec, every day 9am to 5pm, mid Jan to late Jun, Wed to Sun; 399 Rang Versailles, Route 227, ☎346-6775*) specializes in beautiful dried-flower arrangements. Workshops are offered.

La Maison sous les Arbres (*2024 Route 133 Sud, ☎347-1639*). Imagine an art gallery set up in someone's house. You can shop for your bathroom articles in the bathroom, kitchen articles in the kitchen, and so on. Great for people who love to poke around in other people's houses.

Vignoble Dietrich-Jooss (*year round, Tue to Sun 9am to 6pm; 407 Grande Ligne, ☎347-6857*). Originally from Alsace, friendly owners Victor, Christiane and their daughter Stéphanie have owned this vineyard since 1986. Their wines have already earned many prizes in various prestigious competitions – 38 international medals to be precise. Connoisseurs consider the white *cuvé spécial* to be the most Alsatian in character. Wine tasting available.

Québec

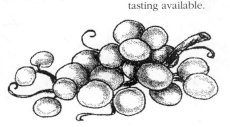

Eastern Townships

Rougemont

The **Cidrerie Michel Jodoin** (*every day; 1130 Rang de la Petite-Caroline,* ☎*450-469-2676*) is a family-run business that arguably sells the best cider in Québec. Michel Jodoin's studies in Champagne, Brittany and Normandy, along with the unique taste of Québec's variety of apples, have helped him to create a delicious brew. On site, you can visit the facilities and learn about the minimum two-year, oak-barrel aging process of these fine ciders. Tastings available.

Western Québec

This chapter includes the part of the province extending north and west of Montreal that corresponds to the tourist region of Lanaudière, the Laurentians and the Outaouais.

The Lanaudière region extends north of Montréal, from the plains of the St. Lawrence to the Laurentian plateau. Except for the part of the region engulfed in the urban sprawl of Montréal, Lanaudière is a peaceful area of lakes, rivers, farmland, wild forests and huge open spaces. It's a great place to kick back and try your hand at the various sports and activities the area has to offer like skiing, canoeing, snowmobile rides, hiking, hunting and fishing. As one of the first colonized areas in New France, your visit will most certainly also include a tour of the region's rich architectural heritage.

Continuing west you'll come to the most renowned resort area in Québec, the beautiful Laurentides region. Also called the Laurentians, it attracts a great many visitors all year round.

For generations now, people have been "going up north" to relax and enjoy the beauty of the Laurentian landscape. The lakes, mountains and forests provide a particularly fine setting for a variety of physical activities or outings. With the highest concentration of ski resorts in North America, skiing naturally gets top billing here when winter rolls around. The villages scattered at the foot of the mountains are both charming and friendly.

The southern part of the region, known as the Basses-Laurentides, was settled early on by French colonists who came here to cultivate the rich farmland. A number of local villages reveal this history through their architectural heritage. The settling of the Laurentian plateau, initiated by the now-legendary Curé Labelle, began much later toward the middle of the 19th century. The development of the Pays d'En Haut, or highlands, was part of an ambitious plan to colonize the outlying areas of Québec in an effort to counter the exodus of French Canadians to industrial towns in the northeastern United States. Given the poor soil, farming here was hardly profitable. Nevertheless,

Curé Labelle succeeded in founding about 20 villages and attracting a good number of French-Canadian colonists to the region.

Still farther west is the Outaouais region. Discovered early on by explorers and trappers, it was not settled by whites until the arrival of Loyalists from the United States in the early 19th century.

Forestry was long the region's main economic activity. Used in shipbuilding, red and white pine were particularly important to the timber industry. The logs were sent down the Ottawa River and the St. Lawrence to Québec City, where they were loaded onto ships headed for Great Britain. Forestry still plays an important role here, but service industries and government offices are also a major source of jobs – a situation resulting from the proximity of Canada's capital region.

Finding Your Way Around

Lanaudière

By Car

Highway 25 is the extension of Boulevard Pie-IX and leads towards Terrebonne, the first stop on this tour. It continues east to Assomption on Route 344. Next take Route 343 N. to Joliette and Route 158 West to Berthierville.

Bus Stations

Terrebonne
Galeries de Terrebonne

Joliette
250 Rue Richard (at the Point d'Arrêt restaurant)
☎(450) 759-1524

Repentigny
435 Boulevard Iberville (at the Hôtel de ville)
☎(450) 654-2315

Rawdon
3168 1re Avenue (at the Patate à Gogo)
☎(450) 834-2000

Saint-Donat
751 Rue Principale (Dépanneur Boni-Soir)
☎(819) 424-1361

Train Station

Joliette
380 Rue Champlain
☎800-363-5390

Laurentides (Laurentians)

By Car

From Montréal follow Highway 13 North. Take the exit for Route 344 West towards Saint-Eustache. This road continues to Oka. A ferry from Oka leads to Hudson (see p 198) in the Montérégie region. Or Highway 15 (the Autoroute des Laurentides) to Saint-Jérôme (Exit 43). Landmarks along the way include the imposing Collège de Sainte-Thérèse (1881) and its church, on the right, and the only General Motors automobile assembly plant in

Québec, on the left. A little farther, before Saint-Jérôme, is Mirabel Airport. Highway 15 and then Route 117 lead to Saint-Jovite. Mont-Tremblant is north of here on Route 327. Continue on the 117 to reach Labelle and Mont-Laurier.

Bus Station

Saint-Eustache
550 Arthur Sauvé
☎(450) 472-9911

Saint-Sauveur
166 Rue Principale, facing the municipal garage
Centrale Limocar
☎(450) 435-6767

Piedmont
760 Boulevard de Laurentides

Sainte-Adèle
1208 Rue Valiquette (Pharmacie Brunet)
☎(450) 229-6609

Mont-Tremblant
Chalet des Chutes
☎(819) 425-2738

Lac-Mercier
1950 Chemin Principal
☎(819) 425-8315

The Outaouais

By Car

From Montréal, there are two ways of to reach the starting point of the tour: one through the Ottawa River valley, and a faster way through Ontario.

1. Take Highway 13 North, then Route 344 West. Finally take Route 148 West toward Ottawa.

2. Take Highway 40 West, which becomes Route 17 West across the Ontario border. In Hawkesbury, cross the Ottawa River to return to Québec. Turn left on Route 148 West, toward Montebello and Ottawa.

Bus Stations

Montebello
570 Rue Notre-Dame
☎*(819)423-6900*

Hull
238 Boulevard Saint-Joseph
☎*(819)771-2442*

Ottawa (Ontario)
265 Catherine St.
☎*(613)-238-5900*

By Train

The small Hull-Chelsea-Wakefield steam train is a great way to see part of the rural Gatineau valley. The 32km trip takes approximately 5hrs and stops for two hours in Wakefield. In general, however, the best ways to explore the valley are by car or bicycle.

Practical Information

The **Lanaudière region** and the **southern part of the Laurentians region** use the *450* area code.

The **Outaouais** and the **northern part of the Laurentians region** use the *819* area code.

Tourist Information

Lanaudière

Tourisme Lanaudière
2643 Rue Queen, C.P. 1210
Rawdon, J0K 1S0
☎*843-2535*
☎*800-363-2788*
≈*834-8100*
tourisme-lanaudiere.qc.ca

Berthierville
760 Rue Gadoury
☎*836-1621*

Joliette
500 Rue Dollard
☎*759-5013*
☎*800-363-1775*

Terrebonne
1091 Boulevard Moody
☎*964-0681*

Rawdon
3588 Rue Metcalfe
☎*834-2282*

Saint-Donat
536 Rue Principale
☎*(819) 424-2883*

Laurentides (Laurantians)

Maison du Tourisme des Laurentides
14142 Rue de la Chapelle
Mirabel, J7J 2C8
☎*(450) 436-8532*
☎*800-561-6693*
≈*(450) 436-5309*

Saint-Eustache
600 Rue Dubois, J7P 5L2
☎*(450) 491-4444* (summer only)

Saint-Sauveur-des-Monts
Chemin Des Frênes
☎*(450) 229-3729*

Sainte-Adèle
1490 Rue Saint-Joseph
☎*(450) 229-3729*

Mont-Tremblant
1001 Montée Ryan
☎*(819) 425-2434*

Labelle
7404 Boulevard du Curé-Labelle
☎*(819) 686-2606*

Mont-Laurier
177 Boulevard Paquette
☎*(819) 623-4544*

The Outaouais

Association Touristique de l'Outaouais
103 Rue Laurier
Hull, J8X 3V8
☎*778-2222*
☎*800-265-7822*
≈*778-7758*
www.tourisme-outaouais.org

Montebello
502-A Rue Notre-Dame
☎*423-5602*

Hull
103 Rue Laurier
☎*778-2222*

Ottawa (Ontario)
90 Wellington Rd.
☎*(613) 239-5000*
☎*800-465-1867*

Maniwaki
156 Rue Principale Sud
☎*449-6627*

Exploring

Lanaudière

★★
Terrebonne

Located along the banks of the rushing Rivière des Mille-Îles, this municipality gets its name from the fertile soil (*terre* meaning earth, and *bonne* meaning good) from which it grew. Today it is included in the

Québec

ribbon of suburbia surrounding Montréal. Yet the old town, divided into an *haute-ville* and *basse-ville* (upper and lower town), has preserved some of its residential and commercial buildings. Terrebonne is probably the best place in Québec to get an idea of what a prosperous 19th-century seigneury was really like.

Île des Moulins ★★ (*free admission; late Jun to early Sep, every day 1pm to 9pm; at the end of Rue des Braves,* ☎471-0619) is an impressive concentration of mills and other pre-industrial equipment from the Terrebonne seigneury. Located in a park, most of the buildings have been renovated and now serve as community and administrative buildings. Upon entering, the first building on the left is the old flour mill (1846), then the saw mill (restored in 1986), which houses the municipal library. Next is the Centre d'Accueil et d'Interprétation de l'Île des Moulins (information centre) in what was once the seigneurial office. This cut stone building was constructed in 1848 according to plans by Pierre-Louis Morin.

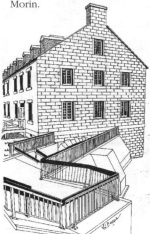

★
Joliette

At the beginning of the 19th century, the notary Barthélémy Joliette (1789-1850) opened up logging camps in the northern section of the Lavaltrie seigneury, which was at the time still undeveloped land. In 1823, he founded "his" town around the sawmills and called it "L'Industrie," a name synonymous with progress and prosperity. The settlement grew so rapidly that in just a few years it had eclipsed its two rivals, Berthier and L'Assomption. The town was renamed Joliette in 1864 in honour of its founder. Barthélémy Joliette completed many other ambitious projects, most notably the construction of the first railroad belonging to French Canadians and a bank where money bearing the Joliette-Lanaudière name was printed.

Père Wilfrid Corbeil c.s.v. founded the exceptional **Musée d'Art de Joliette** ★★ (*$4; late Jun to early Sep, Tue to Sun 11am to 5pm; rest of the year, Wed to Sun noon to 5pm; 145 Rue Wilfrid-Corbeil,* ☎756-0311) with works collected during the 1940s by the clerics of Saint-Viateur that show Québec's place in the world. This is the most important regional museum in Québec. Since 1976 it has been located in a rather menacing building on Rue Corbeil. On display are major pieces from Québec and Canadian artists like Marc-Aurèle de Foy Suzor-Côté, Jean-Paul Riopelle and Emily Carr as well as works by European and American artists like Henry Moore and Karel Appel. One section of the

museum is devoted to Québec religious art while another contains religious art from the Middle Ages and Renaissance periods with some excellent examples from France, Italy and Germany.

The Festival International de Lanaudière was begun by Père Fernand Lindsay c.s.v. Each year during the months of July and August, a variety of music concerts and opera singers are presented as part of the festival. In 1989 the 2,000-seat open-air **Amphithéâtre de Lanaudière** (*1575 Base-de-Roc,* ☎759-7636 or 800-561-4343) was constructed to increase the capacity and accessibility of the event. Until then, the festival was limited to the churches of the area. Artist Georges Dyens completed the interior design of the aisles and the exquisite sculptures.

★
Berthierville

The modest Autray Seigneury was conceded to Jean Bourdon, an engineer of the king of France, in 1637. The land corresponds to the sector Berthier-en-bas, or Berthierville, along the shores of the St. Lawrence. The more extensive Berthier Seigneury was conceded to Sieur de Berthier in 1672 before passing through several hands. It corresponds in part to Berthier-en-haut, or Berthier. In 1765 both these tracts of land were acquired by James Cuthbert, an aide-de-camp of General Wolfe during the battle of the Plains of Abraham in Québec City, as well as a friend of the Duke of Kent. He developed the land mainly for use as a vacation spot.

N

Lanaudière

0   10   20km

Réserve
Faunique
Rouge-
Matawin

Manouane
(environ 70km)

Réservoir
Taureau

Saint-Ignace-
du-Lac

Saint-Michel-
des-Saints

Lac
Kaiagamac

131

Réserve
Faunique
Mastigouche

Saint-Zénon

MAURICIE

Parc du
Mont-Tremblant

Lac
Lavigne

131

Lac des Îles

Saint-Alexis-
des-Monts

Saint-Donat

Lac
Archambault

Lac
Ouareau

Sainte-Émélie-
de-l'Énergie

Saint-Damien

Saint-Charles-
de-Mandeville

347

Lac
Maskinongé

Saint-
Didace

Saint-Édouard-
de-Maskinongé

Saint-Côme

131

Saint-Gabriel-
de-Brandon

347

Notre-Dame-
de-la-Merci

Saint-Jean-
de-Matha

348

Saint-Edmond

Québec

Sainte-Béatrix

Saint-Cléophase

Saint-
Barthélemy

138

Saint-Alphonse-
Rodriguez

337

Saint-Félix-
de-Valois

Saint-Norbert

Saint-
Mélanie

347

40

Entrelacs

125

Sainte-Marceline-
de-Kildare

131

Saint-Viateur

Saint-Cuthbert

329

Chertsey

Saint-Ambroise-
de-Kildare

Notre-Dame-
de-Lourdes

Berthierville

Île Dupas

Sainte-Marguerite-
du-Lac-Masson

341

Rawdon

Sainte-
Élisabeth

St-Ignace-
de-Loyola

125

Joliette

158

Sorel

132

335

341

Saint-Liguori

Saint-Thomas

Sainte-Agathe-
des-Monts

346

Crabtree

Saint-Paul-
de-Joliette

40

132

Ste-Victoire

Sainte-Julienne

Saint-Calixte

335

125

Saint-Jacques

Lanoraie

31

30

LAURENTIDES
(LAURENTIANS)

Saint-Esprit

Saint-Alexis

Saint-Gérard-
Majella

131

Saint-Ours

15

Laurentides

339

St-Roch-
de-l'Achigan

343

Lavaltrie

Contrecœur

Sainte-Sophie

125

L'Épiphanie

138

Saint-Louis

La Plaine

L'Assomption

Saint-Jérôme

25

Saint-Sulpice

132

30

158

15

335

337

Le Gardeur

138

Verchères

Mascouche

Repentigny

MONTÉRÉGIE

117

Terrebonne

640

344

Charlemagne

Lachenaie

25

40

30

© ULYSSES

Québec

The **Église
Sainte-Geneviève** ★★
(*780 Montcalm*) is a
Lanaudière treasure. Con-
structed in 1781, it is one
of the oldest churches in
the region. The interior's
Louis-XVI styling was de-
signed by Amable
Gauthier and Alexis

Millette between 1821 and
1830. Many elements in
the decor combine to
make this building truly
exceptional. The decor has
a richness rarely seen at
that time, comprising elements such as the original
high altar, crafted by Gilles
Bolvin in 1759, the shell-

shaped retable and the
diamond-pattern
ornamenting the vault.
There are also several
paintings, including one of
Sainte-Geneviève (a
French canvas from the
19th century hanging over
the high altar), and six

works by Louis Dulongré, painted in 1797.

Gilles Villeneuve, the championship race-car driver killed tragically during the qualifying trials for the 1982 Grand-Prix of Belgium, was from Berthierville. The **Musée Gilles-Villeneuve** (*$6; every day 9am to 5pm; 960 Avenue Gilles Villeneuve, ☎836-2714 or 800-639-0103, ≠836-3067*) is dedicated to the illustrious career of the Ferrari Formula 1 driver, his prizes, his souvenirs and his cars. In the last few years, Gilles' son Jacques has taken up where his father left off and become a top-ranked Formula 1 driver at the heart of the British Williams-Renault team. The museum now devotes a new section to the career of Jacques Villeneuve.

★
Rawdon

The other spot of interest in the vicinity is **Parc des Cascades** ★ (*$6 per car; mid-May to mid-Oct, every day; ☎834-4149*), which can be reached on Route 341, the extension of Boulevard Pontbriand. Located on the bank of Rivière Ouareau, which runs in lovely cascades over the rocky riverbed here, this park includes a picnic area where sunbathers stretch out during the hot summer months.

★
Saint-Donat

Minutes away from Mont-Tremblant, the small town of Saint-Donat extends east to the shores of Lac Ouareau. Saint-Donat, tucked between mountains reaching up to 900m and the shores of Lac Archambault, is also a

departure point for the **Parc du Mont-Tremblant** (see p 232).

Laurentides (Laurentians)

Saint-Jérôme

This administrative and industrial town is nicknamed "La Porte du Nord" (The Gateway to the North) because it marks the passage from the St. Lawrence valley into the mountainous region that stretches north of Montréal and Québec City. The Laurentians are one of the oldest mountain ranges on earth. Compressed by successive glaciations, the mountains are low, rounded, and composed of sandy soil. Colonization of this region began in the second half of the 19th century with Saint-Jérôme as the starting point.

The **Cathédrale de Saint-Jérôme** ★ (*free; every day 7:30am to 4:30pm; facing Parc Labelle, 355 Rue St-Georges, ☎432-9741*), a simple parish church when it was erected in 1899. It's now a large Roman-Byzantine-style edifice reflecting Saint-Jérôme's prestigious status as the "headquarters" of the colonization of the Laurentians. A bronze statue of Curé Labelle, sculpted by Alfred Laliberté, stands in front of the cathedral.

Saint-Jérôme is also the starting point of the **Parc Linéaire le P'tit Train du Nord** ★★. This extraordinary bike path, which becomes a cross-country ski trail in winter, stretches 200km, from Saint-Jérôme to Mont-Laurier along the same route once followed by the Laurentian railroad.

★
Saint-Sauveur-des-Monts

Located perhaps a little too close to Montréal, Saint-Sauveur-des-Monts has been over-developed in recent years. Condominiums, restaurants and art galleries have sprung up like mushrooms. Rue Principale is very busy and is the best place in the Laurentians to mingle with the crowds. This resort is a favourite among entertainers, who own luxurious secondary residences on the mountainside. The Église Saint-Sauveur is also very popular with engaged couples who have to put their names down on a long waiting list in order to be married there.

Station de Ski du Mont-Saint-Sauveur, see p 233.

Station de Ski du Mont-Habitant, see p 233.

★
Sainte-Adèle (pop. 7,800)

The Laurentians were nicknamed the Pays-d'En-Haut (the Highlands) by 19th-century colonists heading for these northern lands, far from the St. Lawrence Valley. Writer and journalist Claude-Henri Grignon, born in Sainte-Adèle in 1894, used the region as the setting for his books. His famous novel, *Un homme et son péché* (A Man and his Sin), depicts the wretchedness of life in the Laurentians back in those days. Grignon asked his

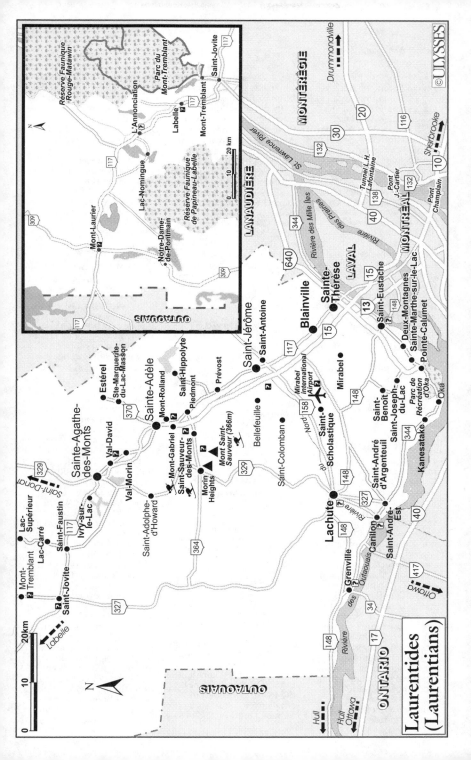

Laurentides (Laurentians)

good friend, architect Lucien Parent, to design the village church that graces Rue Principale to this day. On August 27, 1997, the villages of Mont-Rolland and Sainte-Adèle merged to form the new municipality of Sainte-Adèle.

Au Pays des Merveilles *($8; mid-Jun to late Aug, every day 10am to 6pm; late may to mid-Jun, weekends only; 3595 Chemin de la Savane,* ☎*229-3141)* is a small, modest amusement park that will appeal mainly to young children. Slides, a wading pool, a miniature golf course and maze. have all been laid out in a setting reminiscent of Alice's Adventures in Wonderland (*Alice au Pays des Merveilles* in French). At $8 per person (even for children), the admission charge is a bit steep.

Station de Ski du Chanteclerc, see p 233.

★
Ville d'Estérel

In Belgium, the name Empain is synonymous with financial success. Inheriting the family fortune in the early 20th century, Baron Louis Empain was an important builder just like his father, who was responsible for the construction of Heliopolis, a new section of Cairo (Egypt). During a trip to Canada in 1935, Baron Louis purchased Pointe Bleue, a strip of land that extends out into Lac Masson. In two years, from 1936 to 1938, he erected about 20 buildings on the site. They were all designed by Belgian architect Antoine Courtens to whom we also owe the Palais de la Folle Chanson and the facade of the

Église du Gésu in Brussels, as well as the Grande Poste in Kinshasa, Zaïre. Empain named this entire development **Domaine de l'Estérel**. The onset of World War II thwarted his plans, however, and the land was divided up after the war. In 1958, a portion was purchased by Québec businessman Fridolin Simard who began construction of the present **Hôtel L'Estérel** along Route 370. He then divided the rest of the property into lots. On these pieces of land, visitors will find lovely modern houses made of stone and wood designed by architect Roger D'Astou.

Val-David

Val David attracts visitors not only because it is located near the Laurentian ski resorts, but also for its craft shops where local artisans display their work. Composed of pretty houses, the village has managed to retain its own unique charm.

★
Sainte-Agathe-des-Monts

Set in the heart of the Laurentians, this is a business- and tourist-oriented town that sprang up around a sawmill in 1849. When the railway was introduced to the region in 1892, Sainte-Agathe-des-Monts became the first resort area in the Laurentians. Located at the meeting point of two movements of colonization (the Anglo-Saxon settling of the county of Argenteuil and the French-Canadian settling of Saint-Jérôme), the town succeeded in attracting wealthy vacationers. Lured by Lac des

Sables, they built several beautiful villas around the lake and near the Anglican church. The region was once deemed a first-class resort by important Jewish families of Montréal and New York. In 1909, the Jewish community founded Mount Sinai Sanitarium (the present building was erected in 1930) and built synagogues in Sainte-Agathe-des-Monts and Val-Morin in subsequent years.

★★★
Mont-Tremblant Resort

Some of the largest sports and tourist complexes in the Laurentians were built by wealthy American families with a passion for downhill skiing. They chose this region for the beauty of the landscape, the province's French charm and above all for the northern climate that makes for a longer ski season than in the United States. The Station de Ski du Mont-Tremblant was founded by Philadelphia millionaire Joseph Ryan in 1938. The resort is now owned by Intrawest, which also owns Whistler Resort in British Columbia. It has invested a considerable amount of money in Tremblant to put it on a par with the huge resorts of western Canada and the United States. At the height of the season, 74 trails (including several new ones) attract downhill skiers to Tremblant's slopes (914m). During the summer, the magnificent new golf course is just as popular. Not only does this place have the longest and most difficult vertical drops in the region, it also boasts a brand-new resort complex set in a cute little village of traditional

Quebecois-style buildings at the base of the mountain:

★
Mont-Tremblant Village

On the other side of Lac Tremblant lies the charming Mont-Tremblant Village (not to be confused with the resort area that Intrawest started developing in 1993). In a more authentic setting, visitors here will find attractive shops and restaurants as well as many other places to stay, including the famous Club Tremblant (see p 237).

The Outaouais

★
Montebello

The Outaouais region did not experience significant development under the French Regime. Located upstream from the Lachine Rapids, the area was not easily accessible by water. Until the early 19th century, it was thus left to hunters and trappers and the beginning of the forestry operations. The Petite-Nation seigneury, granted to Monseigneur de Laval in 1674, was the only attempt at colonization in this vast region. It was not until 1801 when the seigneury passed into the hands of notary Joseph Papineau that the town of Montebello was established. Papineau's son, Louis-Joseph Papineau (1786-1871), head of the French-Canadian nationalist movement in Montréal, inherited the Petite-Nation seigneury in 1817. Returning from an eight-year exile in the United States and France following the rebellion of 1837-38, he

was disillusioned and disappointed by the stand taken by the Catholic clergy during the rebellion. Papineau retired to Montebello where he built an impressive manor.

his father died and was refused a Catholic burial. Made from the funeral mask of the deceased, a bust of the elder Papineau by Napoléon Bourassa is one of the interesting objects found in the chapel.

Manoir Papineau

The **Manoir Louis-Joseph-Papineau ★★** *(suggested donation; late May to early Sep, every day 10am to 5pm; 500 Rue Notre-Dame, ☎423-6965)* was erected between 1846 and 1849 in the monumental neoclassical villa style. The house was designed by Louis Aubertin, a visiting French architect. The towers added in the 1850s give the house a medieval appearance. One of the towers houses a precious library that Papineau placed here to protect it from fire. The manoir has approximately 20 staterooms (through which visitors can now stroll) and features a rich Second Empire decor. It is located on lovely tree-shaded grounds and is owned by the Canadian Pacific hotel chain which also manages the nearby Château Montebello. A small wooden walkway leads to the **Chapelle Funéraire des Papineau** (1853) where 11 members of the family are buried. Note that this is an Anglican chapel. Papineau's son joined the Church of England when

The **Château Montebello ★★** *(392 Rue Notre-Dame; ☎423-6341)* is a large resort hotel on the Papineau estate. As the largest log building in the world, the hotel was erected in 1929 (Lawson and Little, architects) in a record 90 days. The impressive lobby has a central fireplace with six hearths, each facing one of the building's six wings.

Hull

Although the road leading into Hull is named after an important post-war town planner, the city is certainly not a model of enlightened urban development. Its architecture is very different from that of Ottawa, just across the river. Hull is a mixture of old factories, typical working-class houses, tall, modern government office buildings, and barren land awaiting future government expansion. The town was founded by American Loyalist Philemon Wright who introduced forestry operations to the Ottawa Valley.

Québec

Wood from the region was cut, made into rafts, floated to Québec City, and eventually used in the construction of ships for the British Navy. By 1850, Hull was an important wood-processing centre. For many generations the Eddy Company, which is based in the area, has sup-plied matches to the entire world. The modest wood-frame houses that line the streets of Hull are nick-named "matchboxes" be-cause they once housed many employees of the Eddy match factory, and because they have had more than their fair share of fires. In fact, Hull has burned so many times throughout its history that few of the town's historical buildings remain. The for-mer town hall and a beau-tiful Catholic church burned down in 1971 and 1972, respectively. While Ottawa has the reputation of being a quiet city, Hull is considered more of a

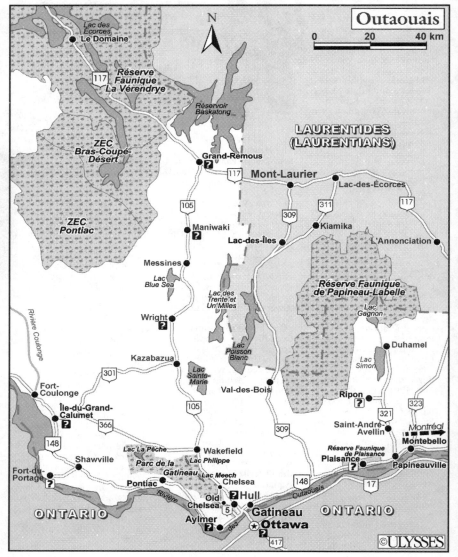

fun town, essentially because the legal drinking age is a year younger and the bars stay open later in Québec. It's not uncommon to see crowds of Ontarians along the **Promenade du Portage** on Saturday nights.

The **Canadian Museum of Civilization** ★★★ (*$8; early May to mid-Oct; $5 mid-Oct to late Apr; early May to mid-Oct every day 9am to 6pm; mid-Oct to late Apr, every day 9am to 5pm, closed Mon; 100 Rue Laurier,* ☎ *776-7000*) or the Musée Canadien des Civilisations. Many parks and museums were established along this section of the Québec-Ontario border as part of a large redevelopment program in the National Capital Region between 1983 and 1989. Hull became the site of the magnificent Canadian Museum of Civilization that is dedicated to the history of Canada's various cultural groups. If there is one museum that must be seen in Canada, this is the one. Douglas Cardinal of Alberta drew up the plans for the museum's two striking curved buildings, one housing the administrative offices and restoration laboratories, and the other the museum's collections. Their undulating design brings the rock formations of the Canadian Shield, shaped by wind and glaciers to mind.

From the grounds behind the museum, visitors have a beautiful view of the Ottawa River and Parliament Hill.

The Grande Gallerie (Great Hall) houses the most extensive collection of native totem poles in the world. Another collection brilliantly recreates different periods in Canadian history, from the arrival of the Vikings around AD 1000 to life in rural Ontario in the 19th century and French Acadia in the 17th century. Contemporary native art, as well as popular arts and traditional crafts, are also on display. In the Musée des Enfants (Children's Museum), young visitors choose a theme before being led through an extraordinary adventure. Screening rooms have been equipped with OMNIMAX technology, a new system developed by the creators of the large-screen IMAX. Most of the movies shown here deal with Canadian geography.

The **Casino de Hull** ★★ (*11am to 3am; 1 Boulevard du Casino,* ☎*800-665-2274 or 772-2100*) has an impressive location between two lakes: Leamy Lake, in the park of the same name; and Lac de la Carrière, which is in the basin of an old limestone quarry.

The theme of water is omnipresent all around the superb building, inaugurated in 1996. The magnificent walkway leading to the main entrance is dotted with towering fountains while the harbour has 20 slips for boaters. The gambling area, which covers 2,741m^2, includes 1,300 slot machines and 58 playing tables spread around a simulated tropical forest. Québec painter Jean-Paul Riopelle's famous 40m-long painting, *Hommage à Rosa Luxembourg* ★★★, dominates the room. The artist created this immense triptych in honour of Joan Mitchell, his partner of many years.

Parc de la Gatineau

Parc de la Gatineau ★ (see p 232) is the starting point for this tour. Established in 1934, the park is an area of rolling hills, lakes and rivers that measures more than 35,000ha.

The **Domaine Mackenzie-King** ★★ (*free admission, $6 for parking; mid-May to mid-Oct Mon to Fri 11am to 5pm, Sat and Sun 10am to 6pm; Rue Barnes in Kingsmere, Parc de la Gatineau,* ☎*613-239-5000 and 827-2020*). William Lyon Mackenzie King was Prime Minister of Canada from 1921 to 1930, and again from 1935 to 1948.

Québec

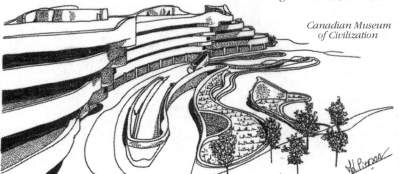

Canadian Museum of Civilization

With his love of art and horticulture rivalling his interest in politics, he was always happy to get away to his summer residence near Lac Kingsmere, which is today part of Parc de la Gatineau. The estate consists of two houses (of which one is now a charming tea room), a landscaped garden and follies (false ruins that were popular at the time). Unlike most follies, however, which were designed to imitate ruins, those on the Mackenzie-King estate are authentic building fragments. They were mostly taken from the original Canadian House of Parliament, destroyed by fire in 1916, and from Westminster Palace, damaged by German bombs in 1941.

Parks

Lanaudière

The **Réserve Faunique Rouge-Matawin** (*26km west of Saint-Michel-des-Saints;* ☎833-5530) is 1,394km² of greenery, through which flow about 450 lakes and waterways. It is home to an abundant and fertile wildlife. There is no lack of activities, from hiking, hunting, fishing, canoe-camping and wildberry-picking, to snowmobiling in the winter.

Laurentides (Laurentians)

The **Parc d'Oka and the Calvaire d'Oka** ★ (*2020 Chemin d'Oka,* ☎450-479-8337) encompasses about 45km of trails for hikers in the summer and cross-country skiers in the winter. Most of the trails lie south of Route 344, crisscrossing a relatively flat area. North of Route 344, two other trails lead to the top of the Colline d'Oka (168m) where visitors can drink in a view of the entire region. The longer trail (7.5km) ends at a panoramic viewing area while the shorter one (5.5km) guides visitors past the oldest stations-of-the-cross in the Americas. This calvary was set up by the Sulpicians back in 1740 in an effort to stimulate the faith of Aboriginals recently converted to Catholicism. Humble and dignified at the same time, the calvary is made up of four trapezoidal oratories and three rectangular chapels built of whitewashed stone. Now empty, these little buildings once housed wooden bas-reliefs depicting the Passion of Christ. The park also has campsites (*$16/day,* ☎450-479-8337) and an information centre.

Parc du Mont-Tremblant ★★ (*Chemin du Lac Tremblant,* ☎819-688-2281), created in 1894, was originally known as Parc de la Montagne Tremblante (Trembling Mountain Park) in reference to an Algonquian legend. It covers an area of 1,250km², encompassing the mountain, seven rivers and about 500 lakes. Opened in 1938, the ski resort has been welcoming skiers ever since. A day of skiing costs $44. The park also includes nine cross-country ski trails which stretch over 50km. The resort caters to sports enthusiasts all year round. Hiking buffs can explore up to 100km of trails here. Two of these-La Roche and La Corniche-have been rated among the most beautiful in Québec. The park also has bicycle paths, mountain bike circuits, and offers water sports like canoeing and windsurfing.

The Outaouais

Parc de la Gatineau ★ (*visitor centre is located in Chelsea, also accessible via Boulevard Taché in Hull,* ☎827-2020) is not far from downtown Hull. The 35,000ha park was founded during the Depression in 1934 to protect the forests from people looking for firewood. It is crossed by a 34km long road dotted with panoramic lookout points, including **Belvédère Champlain**, which offer superb views of the lakes, rivers and hills of the region. Outdoor activities can be enjoyed here throughout the year. Hiking and mountain biking trails are open during the summer. There are many lakes in the park, including Lac Meech that was the name of the Canadian constitutional agreement drawn up nearby but never ratified. Watersports such as windsurfing, canoeing and swimming are also very popular and the park rents small boats and camp sites. **Lusk Cave**, formed some 12,500 years ago by water flowing from melting glaciers, can be explored. During the winter, approximately 190km of cross-country skiing trails are maintained (*approx. $7 per day*). **Camp Fortune** (☎827-1717) has 17 downhill skiing runs, 13 are open at night. It costs $30 during the day and $20 at night.

Outdoor Activities

Rock-climbing

Laurentides
(Laurentians)

The **Val-David** area is renowned for its rock faces. A number of mountains here are fully equipped to accommodate climbers' needs: **Mont King**, **Mont Condor** and **Mont Césaire** are among the most popular. For more information, on equipment rentals or guide services, contact **Passe Montagne** (*1760 Montée 2e Rang, Val-David, J0T 2N0*, ☎*819-322-2123 or 800-465-2123*), a trail-blazing rock-climbing outfit in the Val-David region. Their team of experts offer excellent advice.

Cycling

Laurentides
(Laurentians)

The former railway line of the **P'tit Train du Nord** (*14142 de la Chapelle, Mirabel, J7J 3B9*, ☎*450-436-8532, 514-990-5625 in Montréal or 800-561-6673*, ≈*450-436-5309*) which carried Montréalers up north for many years, has been transformed into a superb 200km bike path from Saint-Jérôme to Mont-Laurier. It leads through a number of little villages where accommodations

and restaurants in all price ranges can be found.

Rafting

Laurentides
(Laurentians)

Thanks to the thrilling Rivière Rouge, the Laurentians offer excellent conditions for whitewater rafting – among the best in Canada, according to some experts. Of course, there is no better time to enjoy this activity than during the spring thaw. Rafting during this period can prove quite a challenge, however, so previous experience is recommended. The best season for novices is summer when the river is not too high and the weather is milder. For further information, contact **Nouveau Monde, Expéditions en Rivière** (*$89 per person; 100 Chemin de la Rivière Rouge, Calumet, J0V 1B0*, ☎*819-242-7238 or 800-361-5033*, ≈*819-242-0207*), which offers group outings every day.

Downhill Skiing

Laurentides
(Laurentians)

There are two ski resorts in the mountains around Piedmont; **Station Mont-Olympia** (*$31; 330 Chemin de la Montagne,* ☎*450-227-3523*) which has 21 slopes and a total vertical drop of 192m, and **Station du Mont-Avila** (*$31; Chemin Avila,* ☎*450-227-4671*) where visitors will find about

10 slopes, the longest of which is 1,050m.

A small mountain with a vertical drop of only 210m, **Mont Saint-Sauveur** (*$38; 350 Rue Saint Denis,* ☎*514-227-4671*) attracts lots of skiers because of its proximity to Montréal. It offers 26 downhill ski trails, a few of which are lit for night-skiing.

As Mont-Saint-Sauveur is often overcrowded, some might prefer the slopes of the neighbouring mountains, which have fewer trails but shorter lift lines. The **Station de Ski du Mont-Habitant** (*$29; 12 Boulevard des Skieurs,* ☎*450-227-2637*), with eight runs, is one of these.

We should also mention **Ski Morin-Heights** (*$31; Chemin Bennett,* ☎*450-227-2020*), which has 22 trails, 16 of which are lit for night-skiing; and the modest (eight trails) **L'Avalanche** (*$22; 1657 Chemin de l'Avalanche,* ☎*450-327-3232*) ski centre, located near Saint-Adolphe-d'Howard.

The Sainte-Adèle region also attracts skiers with its two good-sized ski resorts. The **Station de Ski du Mont-Gabriel** (*$31; 1501 Montée Gabriel, Ste-Adèle,* ☎*450-227-1100*) has 21 trails (10 lit for night-skiing) for skiers of all different levels. The handsome Chantecler tourist complex was built near the **Station de Ski du Chanteclerc** (*$25, 1474 Chemin Chanteclerc,* ☎*450-229-3555*), with 22 trails, including 13 that are lit in the evening.

In Val-Morin, skiers can head to **Belle Neige** (*$26; Rte. 117,* ☎*819-322-3311*), which has 14 trails of all different levels of diffi

Québec

culty. In the Val-David area, you'll find **Mont-Alta** (*$20; Rte. 117,* ☎*819-322-3206)* and the **Station de Ski Vallée-Bleue** (*$23; 1418 Chemin Vallée-Bleue,* ☎*819-322-3427),* with 22 and 16 trails, respectively.

The **Station de Ski Mont-Blanc** (*$32; Rte. 117,* ☎*819-688-2444 or 800-567-6715),* in Saint-Faustin, has 35 runs and the second-highest vertical drop in the Laurentians (300m).

Station de Ski Mont-Tremblant see p 232.

Gray Rocks (*$42,60; 525 Chemin Principal,* ☎*819-425-2771 or 800-567-6767)* is another resort in the region. It has about 20 trails, with a vertical drop of 191m (much lower than at Mont-Tremblant).

Accommodations

Lanaudière

Joliette

Château Joliette
$90
ℜ
450 Rue St-Thomas, J6E 3R1
☎*752-2525*
☎*800-361-0572*
≈*752-2520*
In a large red brick building by the river, the Château Joliette is the largest hotel in town. Though the long corridors are cold and bare, the modern rooms are large and comfortable.

Saint-Alphonse-Rodriguez

Auberge sur la Falaise
$118 bkfst incl.
≡, ⊛, ℜ, ⊘, ≈, ℜ, ⌂
324 Av. Du Lac Long Sud, J0K 1W0
☎*883-2269*
≈*883-0143*
Ten kilometres from the village of Saint-Alphonse-Rodriguez, after a long climb past peaceful Lac Long and into what seems like another world, is the marvellous Auberge sur la Falaise. Perched on a promontory, the inn dominates this serene landscape, reserving exceptional views for its guests. The 25 rooms in this modern building are luxurious, some of them with whirlpool baths and fireplaces. The hotel does double duty as a spa and offers many sports activities. Finally, the cuisine served in the dining room is among the best in the area (see p 238).

Saint-Jean-de-Matha

Auberge de la Montagne Coupée
$110
≡, ≈, ℜ, ⌂
1000 Rue de la Montagne-Coupée J0K 2S0
☎*886-3891*
☎*800-363-8614*
≈*886-5401*
www.montagnecoupée.com
Another exceptional establishment, Auberge de la Montagne Coupée appears after what seems like an interminable climb. Reward is at hand though in this immense white building with huge bay windows.

The hotel has 50 comfortable, modern rooms bathed in natural light, some of which have fireplaces. In the dining room and the lounge, large windows reveal a breathtaking panorama. The hotel has a remarkable restaurant as well as an equestrian centre and a summer theatre at the bottom of the grounds (see p 238).

Saint-Donat

Parc du Mont-Tremblant
$17
2951 Rte. 125 Nord, C.P. 1169 J0T 2C0
☎*819-424-7012*
≈*424-2086*
The Pimbina section of Parc du Mont-Tremblant, near Saint-Donat, accessible via Route 125, includes 341 campsites.

Manoir des Laurentides
$80
K, ℜ, ⊛, ≈
290 Rue Principale, J0T 2C0
☎*819-424-2121*
☎*800-567-6717*
≈*424-2621*
The Manoir des Laurentides, well located by the water's edge, offers good value for your money. The rooms in the three-storey main building are comfortable but boring, though each has its own balcony. There are also two rows of motel rooms that stretch to the lakefront and about 40 cottages equipped with kitchenettes. Since this spot is often quite lively, visitors who value peace and quiet should opt for motel rooms or cottages. A beach and a small marina at the water's edge are available to guests.

Laurentides (Laurentians)

Saint-Sauveur-des-Monts

Hôtel Châteaumont
$85
≈, tv, ℜ, ≈, ☉
50 Rue Principale, J0R 1R6
☎*(450) 227-1821*
≈*(450) 227-1483*
A beautiful row of fir trees graces the garden of the Hôtel Châteaumont, forming an attractive entranceway. The rooms have modern furnishings, and all but two are equipped with a fireplace, a real plus after a day of skiing.

Relais Saint-Denis
$145
≈, ☉, ℜ, ⊛, ≡, tv, ℜ
61 Rue Saint-Denis, J0R 1R4
☎*(450) 227-4766*
☎*888-997-4766*
≈*(450) 227-8504*
The long green and white building of the Relais Saint-Denis is modern-looking for a country inn. Fortunately, the attractively decorated rooms are more inviting. Behind the building is a pleasant garden with a swimming pool.

Sainte-Adèle

Le Chanteclerc
$100 bkfst incl.
$170 ½b
≈, ≡, tv, △, ☉
1474 Chemin duChanteclerc
J8B 1A2
☎*(450) 229-3555*
☎*800-223-0883*
≈*(450) 229-5593*
At Le Chanteclerc, whose name and emblem (a rooster) were inspired by Edmond Rostand's play, guests can enjoy a multitude of activities in an pristine lakeside setting at the foot of Mont Chanteclerc. The golf course is picturesque with mountains on either side. The sizeable sports complex and the handsome stone building with its 300 or so rooms attracts quite a crowd.

L'Eau à la Bouche
$195
≈, ≡, tv, ℜ
3003 Boulevard Sainte-Adèle
J0R 1L0
☎*(450) 229-2991*
☎*888-828-2991*
≈*(450) 229-7573*
A member of the prestigious Association des Relais et Châteaux, the hotel L'Eau à la Bouche is known for its excellent gourmet restaurant and extremely comfortable rooms. Don't be fooled by the building's rustic appearance; the rooms *are* elegantly furnished. The hotel itself dates from the mid-1980s and is set back from the road. It offers a splendid view of the ski slopes of Mont Chanteclerc. The restaurant is in a separate building. The complex is located on Route 117, a fair distance north of the village of Sainte-Adèle.

Ville d'Estérel

Hôtel l'Estérel
$120
≈, ☉, △, ℜ
39 Boulevard Fridolin-Simard
J0T 1E0
☎*(450) 228-2571*
☎*888-378-3735*
≈*(450) 228-4977*
At the Hôtel l'Estérel, a large complex located on the shores of Lac Masson, guests can enjoy a variety of water sports and diverse athletic activities such as tennis, golf and cross-country skiing. The accent is placed mainly on these activities while the rooms, although comfortable, are decorated in outmoded colours.

Val-Morin

Far Hills
$238
≈, △, ℜ
Far Hills
☎*514-990-4409*
☎*800-567-6636*
≈*(819) 322-1995*
Making the most of its extensive grounds, the Far Hills has an extremely peaceful country setting. Its clientele includes cross-country skiers, who come to enjoy over 100km of trails. Not only are the rooms adorable, but the hotel also has a very good restaurant.

Val-David

Chalet Beaumont
$19
K
1451 Beaumont, J0T 2N0
☎*(819) 322-1972*
☎*800-461-8585*
≈*(819) 322-3793*
from the bus stop, take Rue de l'Eglise across the village to Rue Beaumont and turn left; it's about a 2km walk
The Chalet Beaumont, located in a peaceful mountain setting, is one of only two youth hostels in the Laurentians. A log building with two fireplaces, it's a very appealing, comfortable place. The Chalet Beaumont is an excellent option for outdoor enthusiasts on a tight budget. It is wise to ask with whom you'll be sharing a room, since groups of young students often stay here on field trips to Val-David.

Auberge du Vieux Foyer
$164
⊛, ℜ, K, ℜ, ≈, ♿
3167 R.R. 1, J0T 2N0
☎*(819) 322-2686*
☎*800-567-8327*
≈*322-2687*
The comfortable Auberge du Vieux Foyer is ideal for

travellers looking for a peaceful getaway. The service is impeccable, the rooms are comfortable and the food is highly rated. Guests can borrow bicycles.

 La Sapinière
$270

≈, ≡, tv, ℑ, ℜ, ⅄

1244 Chemin de la Sapinière
J0T 2N0

☎ *(819) 322-2020*
☎ *800-567-6635*
⇌ *(819) 322-6510*

La Sapinière, in a rustic log building, is far from luxurious. The rooms have nevertheless been entirely renovated. The hotel is therefore a comfortable place to stop during a tour of the region, especially for its beautiful location.

Sainte-Agathe-des-Monts

Auberge La Saint-Venant
$86 bkfst incl.
K, pb, tv
234 Rue Saint-Venant, J8C 2Z7
☎ *(819) 326-7937*
☎ *800-697-7937*
☎ *(819) 326-4848*

The Auberge La Saint-Venant is one of the best-kept secrets in Sainte-Agathe. A big, beautiful, yellow house perched atop a hill, it has nine large, tastefully decorated rooms with big windows that allow lots of light to flood in. The service is friendly yet discreet.

Lac-Supérieur

Base de Plein Air le P'tit Bonheur
$153/pers.
sb for 2 nights
5 meals, activities and animation
ℜ
1400 Chemin du Lac Quenouille
Lac-Supérieur, J0T 1P0
☎ *(819) 326-4281*
⇌ *(819) 326-9516*

The Base de Plein Air le P'tit Bonheur is nothing less than an institution in the Laurentians. Once a children's summer camp, it now caters to families looking to take an "outdoor vacation." Set on a vast piece of property on the shores of a lake right in the heart of the forest, it has four buildings containing a total of nearly 450 beds, most in dormitories. About 20 of the beds are in separate rooms, each equipped with a private bathroom and able to accommodate up to four people. Of course, this is the perfect place to enjoy all sorts of outdoor activities: sailing, hiking, cross-country skiing, skating and more.

Mont-Tremblant Resort

Château Mont Tremblant
$129
◎, ≡, ≈, ℜ, △, ◎, tv
3045 Chemin Principal, J0T 1Z0
☎ *(819) 681-7000*
☎ *800-441-1414*
⇌ *(819) 681-7097*

Overlooking the village of Mont-Tremblant Resort, the Château Mont Tremblant is one of only two additions to have been made to the prestigious Canadian Pacific hotel chain in a century (the other being located in Whistler, British Columbia). This imposing 316-room hotel manages to

combine a genuine rustic warmth, well-suited to the surroundings, with all the comforts one expects from a top-flight establishment. It also houses a large convention centre and numerous conference rooms.

Manoir-Labelle Marriott Residence Inn
$195
≡, ≈, ℜ, ◎, tv, K
170 Chemin Curé-Deslauriers
J0T 1Z0
☎ *(819) 681-4000*
☎ *800-228-9290*
⇌ *(819) 681-4099*

The prestigious, international Marriot chain has also joined in the action at Tremblant, with its Manoir-Labelle Marriott Residence Inn, a large building located right at the start of the village. The place rents out studios and one- or two-bedroom apartments, each equipped with a kitchenette. Some units even have a fireplace.

Station Touristique du Mont-Tremblant
3005 Chemin Principal, J0T 1Z0
☎ *(819) 681-3000*
☎ *800-461-8711*
⇌ *(819) 681-5999*

The Station Touristique du Mont-Tremblant directly manages a whole assortment of lodgings. Visitors may rent a room or an apartment in the **Kandahar** (*$225;* ≡, ≈, △, tv, K) complex, located near a pond in the "Vieux-Tremblant" area, or in the luxurious **Deslauriers**, **Saint-Bernard** and **Johanssen** (*$225; tv, ≡, K*) complexes, which face onto Place Saint-Bernard. Families will be better off with a fully equipped condo in **La Chouette** (*$260*). These units are small but flooded with natural light. What's more, they offer excellent value for the money, making them an option well worth considering in this area.

Mont-Tremblant Village

Parc du Mont-Tremblant
$17
☎*(819) 688-2281*
There are nearly 600 campsites in the Diable sector of Parc du Mont-Tremblant. Restrooms and showers.

Auberge de Jeunesse Mont-Tremblant
$20
ℜ
2213 Chemin Principal
P.O. Box 1001, J0T 1Z0
☎*(819) 425-6008*
≈*(819) 425-3760*
The Auberge de Jeunesse Mont-Tremblant youth hostel opened in the fall of 1997. Formerly the L'Escapade hotel, it has 84 beds either in dormitories or private. The common areas include a kitchen, a café/bar/restaurant and a living room with a fireplace.

Hôtel Mont Tremblant
$71 bkfst incl.
sb/pb
1900 Chemin Principale, J0T 1Z0
☎*(819) 425-3232*
≈*(819) 425-9755*
On the first floor of the Hôtel Mont Tremblant, visitors will find a bar while on the second, there are modest but satisfactory rooms given the price and the location – all in the heart of the village, near the ski resort.

Auberge Gray Rocks
$140
≈, ≡, ℜ, △, ⊛, ⅋, K, ⊘, tv
525 Chemin Principal, J0T 1Z0
Rte. 327, J0T 2H0
☎*(819) 425-2771*
☎*800-567-6767*
≈*(819) 425-3006*
The Auberge Gray Rocks also offers a range of activities and facilities, aiming at satisfying vacationers' every desire. Particular care has been taken to provide guests with the widest range of activities possible.

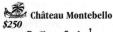 **Club Mont-Tremblant**
$200
≈, ≡, △, ⊘, tv, ℜ, &, K
121 Avenue Cuttle, J0T 1Z0
☎*(819) 425-2731*
☎*800-363-2314*
≈*(819) 425-9903*
At Club Mont-Tremblant, guests can rent either a very functional, well-equipped condo or a conventional room. The vast peaceful site is perfect for outdoorsy types (Parc du Mont-Tremblant is right nearby) as well as those who prefer to relax far from the city in a beautiful natural setting.

The Outaouais

Montebello

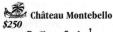 **Château Montebello**
$250
≡, ⊛, ⊘, ℜ, ≈, △, &
392 Rue Notre-Dame
☎*423-6341*
☎*800-441-1414*
≈*423-5283*
www.cphotels.ca
Christened the Château Montebello, this beautiful pine and cedar building stands next to Ottawa River. It's the largest log building in the world and is equipped with several facilities, including an indoor and outdoor swimming pool, squash courts and an exercise room.

Hull

Auberge de la Gare
$88 bkfst incl.
≡, ⊛
205 Boulevard St-Joseph, J8Y 3X3
☎*778-8085*
☎*800-361-6162*
≈*595-2021*
The Auberge de la Gare is a simple, conventional hotel that offers good value for your money. The service is both courteous and friendly and the rooms are clean and well-kept, albeit nondescript.

Gatineau Park

Parc de la Gatineau
$19
Camping du Lac Philippe
Rte. 366
☎*456-3016*
$15
Camping du Lac La Pêche
Rte. 366
☎*456-3016*
Without a doubt one of the most beautiful places in the area to camp, Parc de la Gatineau, has over 350 campsites that have everything for people wanting to sleep in the great outdoors. There are also facilities for recreational vehicles.

Restaurants

Lanaudière

Terrebonne

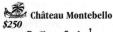 **L'Étang des Moulins**
$$$
closed Mon
888 Rue St-Louis
☎*471-4018*
L'Étang des Moulins occupies a magnificent stone house. The inventive French menu oozes refinement from the lobster Thermidore to the frog's legs in puff pastry. Without a doubt one of the best restaurants in Lanaudière.

Le Folichon
$$$-$$$$
closed Mon
804 Rue Saint-François-Xavier
☎*492-1863*
Le Folichon, which means playful and lighthearted, lives up to its name in the historic quarter of Terrebonne. In the summer, the shaded terrace is the best place to relax. The five-course *table d'hôte* menu has a solid reputation. Particularly tasty are the escargot and grilled duck. Impressive wine list.

Joliette

Antre Jean
$$$
closed Mon and Tue
385 St-Viateur
☎*450-756-0412*
Amongst the many fine restaurants, Autre Jean seems to be the unofficial favourite with the locals. French cuisine specialties, prepared as they are in France, are served as part of the table-d'hôte menu. The decor is warm and inviting along with an unpretentious atmosphere.

Saint-Alphonse-Rodriguez

 Auberge sur la Falaise
$$$-$$$$
324 Av. Du Lac Long Sud
☎*883-2269*
At the extraordinary Auberge sur la Falaise, meals are served in a setting of perfect tranquillity. Nestled in the deep forest, overlooking the calm surface of a lake, this establishment is the perfect retreat from the hectic pace of modern life (even if it is just for a meal). With a great deal of skill, the chef adapts French cuisine to Québec flavours – *médaillon de caribou aux bleuets du Lac* (caribou with

blueberries), loin of lamb, pike *mousseline*, and maple custard. The obvious choice for epicureans is the five-course gourmet menu – a memorable experience, indeed!

Saint-Jean-de-Matha

 Auberge de la Montagne Coupée
$$$$
1000 Chemin de la Montagne-Coupée
☎*886-3891*
Auberge de la Montagne Coupée, another spot famous for its peaceful setting, offers an exciting menu of innovative Québecois cuisine. The dining room is surrounded by two-storey bay windows that look out on an absolutely breathtaking scene. And this is just the beginning – the best part of the evening (the meal!) is yet to come. Imaginatively presented game dishes are enhanced by succulent treasures such as grain-fed poultry with leeks, Oka cheese in *dijonnaise* sauce and lamb with goat cheese. The service is attentive and the wine list is excellent. Very copious breakfasts are also served.

Saint-Donat

La Petite Michèle
$
327 Rue St-Donat
☎*819-424-3131*
La Petite Michèle is just the place for travellers looking for a good family restaurant. The atmosphere is relaxed, the service friendly and the menu traditional Québecois.

Maison Blanche
$$
515 Rue Principale
☎*819-424-2222*
The food is always delicious at the Maison

Blanche. The house specialty-a divine, juicy, rare steak-is known far and wide.

Auberge Havre du Parc
$$$-$$$$
2788 Rte. 125, Lac-Provost
☎*819-424-7686*
The Auberge Havre du Parc not only boasts an exceptionally peaceful setting but also has an excellent selection of French specialties.

Laurentides (Laurentians)

Saint-Jérôme

Le Jardin d'Agnès
$$-$$$
open Wed to Sat for dinner, Mon to Sat for lunch
401 Rue Laviolette
☎*(450) 431-2575*
Le Jardin d'Agnès is set up inside a pretty stone house overlooking the Rivière du Nord. Among the promising dishes are chicken breast with old-fashioned mustard and filet of lamb with basil cream. Waterfront terrace out back.

Saint-Sauveur-des-Monts

Le Chrysanthème
$$
open Wed and Thu 5pm, Fri to Sun noon
173 Rue Principale
☎*(450) 227-8888*
Le Chrysanthème has a beautiful, spacious outdoor seating area and is a wonderful place to dine on a fine summer evening. The restaurant serves authentic Chinese cuisine, making for a nice change of pace in this area.

Papa Luigi
$$-$$$
155 Rue Principale
☎*(450) 227-5311*
The menu at Papa Luigi is made up of – you guessed it – Italian specialties as well as seafood and grill dishes. Set up inside a lovely, blue, wooden house, this restaurant draws big crowds, especially on weekends. Reservations strongly recommended.

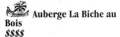 **Le Mousqueton**
$$-$$$
open from 5:30pm on
closed Sun and Mon
120 Rue Principale
☎*(450) 227-4330*
Nearby, on the other side of the street, you'll see the green house that is home to Le Mousqueton. Innovative, contemporary Québec cuisine is served here in a warm, unpretentious atmosphere. Game, fish and even ostrich appear on the menu.

Mont-Rolland

Auberge La Biche au Bois
$$$$
closed Mon
1806 Rte. 117
☎*(450) 229-8064*
The enchanting natural setting of the Auberge La Biche au Bois on the banks of the Rivière Simon is sure to whet your appetite. The menu is made up of Québec and French specialties like duck with Québec blueberries, veal Roquefort and smoked salmon with eggplant. Romantic ambiance.

Sainte-Adèle

La Scala
$$-$$$
closed Tue and Wed in winter
1241 Chemin Chanteclerc
☎*(450) 229-7453*
There are several small restaurants on the little road leading to the Chanteclerc. The most appealing is La Scala. Guests can sit in the cozy, inviting dining room or, weather permitting, outside on the shady terrace which offers a lovely view of Lac Rond. The menu is made up of Italian and French specialties. The lamb tenderloin is a tried and true favourite.

Clef des Champs
$$$-$$$$
closed Mon
875 Chemin Pierre-Péladeau
☎*(450) 229-2857*
The Clef des Champs serves French cuisine fit for even the most discerning palates. The warmly decorated dining room is just right for an intimate dinner for two. The wine cellar is excellent.

L'Eau à la Bouche
$$$$
3003 Boulevard Sainte-Adèle
☎*(450) 229-2991*
One of the finest restaurants not only in the Laurentians but in all of Québec can be found at the hotel L'Eau à la Bouche. Chef Anne Desjardins takes pride in outdoing herself day after day, serving her clientele outstanding French cuisine made with local ingredients. Her Abitibi trout, Atlantic salmon and Far North caribou all bear witness to her exceptional finesse. Two menus (one with three courses, the other with six) are offered each evening. Excellent wine cellar. An unforgettable gastronomic experience!

Sainte-Marguerite-du-Lac-Masson

 Bistro à Champlain
$$$$
closed Mon in summer
winter open Thu to Sun
75 Chemin Masson
☎*(450) 228-4988*
Don't be put off by the uninspired exterior of the Bistro à Champlain in Sainte-Marguerite-du-Lac-Masson. The place is actually one of the best restaurants in the Laurentians. It serves excellent *nouvelle cuisine* made with fresh local ingredients. The interior is extraordinary – a veritable art gallery where you can admire a number of paintings by Jean-Paul Riopelle, a close friend of the owners, as well as works by other artists like Joan Mitchell and Louise Prescott. The restaurant also boasts one of the province's most highly reputed wine cellars which may be toured by appointment. Everyone can sample some of the wines in this impressive stock since even the finest are available by the glass. Reservations strongly recommended.

Val-Morin

Hôtel Far Hills
$$$$
Rue Far Hills
☎*(819) 322-2014*
from Montréal
☎*990-4409*
The Hôtel Far Hills still has one of the finest restaurants in the Laurentians. The gourmet cuisine is positively world-class. Make sure to try the salmon *aux herbes folles du jardin* (with homegrown wild grasses), a sheer delight.

Québec

Val-David

La Sapinière
$$$$
1244 Chemin La Sapinière
☎ *(819) 322-2020*
The restaurant in La Sapinière (see p 236) has been striving for over 60 years now to concoct creative dishes inspired by the culinary repertoires of both Québec and France. Among the house specialties, the *lapereau* (young rabbit), *porcelet* (piglet) and the gingerbread are particularly noteworthy, and the *tarte au sucre à la crème* (sugar pie) is an absolute must. Very good wine list.

Sainte-Agathe-des-Monts

Le Havre des Poètes
$$
Mon to Fri 11:30 to 2pm
Fri and Sat 6pm on
55 Rue St-Vincent
☎ *(819) 326-8731*
At the restaurant Le Havre des Poètes, singers perform French and Québec classics. The food is well-rated but people come here mainly for the ambiance. Reservations for groups of 25 or more.

Chez Girard
$$-$$$
18 Rue Principale O.
☎ *(819) 326-0922*
At the restaurant Chez Girard, set back a little from the road and not far from Lac des Sables, guests can enjoy delicious French cuisine in an extremely pleasant setting. It has two floors, the first being the noisiest.

Sauvagine
$$$$
1592 Rte. 329 N.
☎ *(819) 326-7673*
Sauvagine is a French restaurant cleverly set up inside what used to be the chapel of a convent. Ex-tremely well thought-out, it is decorated with large pieces of period furniture.

Mont-Tremblant Resort

Aux Truffes
$$$$
every day 6pm to 10pm
3035 Chemin Principal, Place Saint-Bernard, in the Intrawest complex
open every day during high season 6pm-10pm
☎ *(819) 681-4544*
Aux Truffes is the best restaurant in the Mont-Tremblant Resort. In an inviting modern decor, guests dine on succulent nouvelle cuisine. Truffles, foie gras and game are among the predominant ingredients.

La Légende
$$$$
closed temporarily
Mont Tremblant
☎ *(819) 681-3000*
☎ *800-461-8711, ext. 5500*
La Légende is a gourmet restaurant located at the top of Mont Tremblant in the Grand-Manitou complex, which also has a cafeteria. Of course, the spectacular view of the area is the main attraction. Don't underestimate the restaurant's Québec cuisine, though: game, fish, veal, beef and pork are all prepared with a great deal of finesse here. Outdoor seating available. Note: The restaurant is currently under renovation and will reopen on November 19, 2000. For groups of 25 to 30 people only, reservations are required.

Mont-Tremblant Village

Club Tremblant
$$$-$$$$
Avenue Cuttles
☎ *(819) 425-2731*
The magnificent dining room of the Club Tremblant (see p 237) offers a panoramic view of the lake and Mont Tremblant. The chef prepares traditional French gastronomic cuisine. On Thursday and Saturday nights, the restaurant serves a lavish buffet. The Sunday brunch is also very popular. Reservations strongly recommended.

The Outaouais

Hull

Aux Quatre Jeudis
$
44 Rue Laval
☎ 771-9557
A pleasant café/restaurant/bar/gallery/movie theatre/terrace with a very laid-back atmosphere, Aux Quatre Jeudis is patronized by a young, slightly bohemian clientele. It shows movies, and its pretty terrace is very popular in the summertime.

The Casino has all the facilities for your gambling pleasures – two restaurants serve excellent meals away from all the betting: **Banco** (**$$**) offers a reasonably priced, quality buffet and various menu items; while the more chic and expensive **Baccara** (**$$$$**; *closed for lunch; 1 Boulevard du Casino*, ☎ 772-6210) has won itself a place among the best restaurants of the region. The set menu always consists of superb dishes that you can enjoy along with spectacular views of the lake. The well-stocked wine cellar and impeccable service round out this memorable culinary experience.

Café Henry Burger
$$$$
69 Laurier
☎777-5646
The stylish Café Henry Burger specializes in fine French cuisine. The menu changes according to the availability of the freshest ingredients and always offers dishes to please the most discerning palate. The restaurant has long maintained an excellent reputation.

Chelsea

L'Orée du Bois
$$$
open after 5:30pm
closed Sun and Mon in winter
15 Kingsmere Road, Old Chelsea
☎827-0332
It would be unheard of to visit the Outaouais without going to the Parc de la Gatineau – if only for a meal. L'Orée du Bois is set up inside a rustic house in the country. The crocheted curtains and wood and brick interior add to the ambiance. This is the kind of family business that you find all over France. For 17 years now, Manon has been welcoming guests and overseeing the dining rooms, while Guy focuses his expertise on the food. Guy has developed a French cuisine featuring ingredients from the various regions of Québec. The menu thus lists dishes made with wild mushrooms, fresh goat cheese, Lac Brome duck, venison and fish smoked on the premises, using maple wood. The prices are very reasonable and the portions generous. A pleasant evening is guaranteed!

Papineauville

La Table de Pierre Delahaye
$$$
closed Mon and Tue
247 Papineau
☎427-5027
La Table de Pierre Delahaye is worth a stop. Forget Montebello! This restaurant is sure to linger in your memory. It's run by a couple – Madame greets the guests and Monsieur takes care of the food. The welcome is always warm and cordial and the Norman-style cuisine succulent. If the thought of sweetbreads makes your mouth water, look no further. The rooms in this historic house (1880) are oozing with atmosphere. Parties of eight or more can even have a room all to themselves.

Entertainment

Bars and Danceclubs

Saint-Sauveur-des-Monts

Les Vieilles Portes
Rue Principale
The bar Les Vieilles Portes is a nice place to get together with friends for a drink. It has a pleasant outdoor terrace open during the summer.

Bentley's
235 Rue Principale
Bentley's is often full of young people who come here to have a drink before going out dancing.

Mont-Rolland

Bourbon Street
Rte. 117, Mont-Rolland
Bourbon Street hosts good live music and is frequented by a relatively young clientele.

Mont-Tremblant Resort

Petit Caribou
3005 Chemin Principal, C.P. 1014
☎(819) 681-4500
The Petit Caribou is a young, energetic bar that really fills up after a good day of skiing.

Hull

Everyone knows about the bars along the Promenade du Portage, including Ontarians who come here to top off the night when they've been out partying. The crowd is relatively young.

Aux Quatre Jeudis
44 Laval
For many years now, Aux Quatre Jeudis has been *the* place for the café crowd. It has lots of atmosphere and there's a big, attractive terrace to hang out on in the summer.

Le Bop
5 Aubry
☎777-3700
Le Bop is a pleasant little place in old Hull. You can kick off your evening with a reasonably priced, decent meal. The music ranges from techno and disco to soft rock and even a little hard rock.

Le Fou du Roi
253 Boulevard St-Joseph
Le Fou du Roi is where the 30-something crowd hangs out. There's a dance floor, and the windows open onto a little terrace in the summertime. This place is

Québec

also a popular after-work gathering place.

777
Marina
1 Boulevard du Casino
The Casino de Hull has two beautiful bars: the 777 and the Marina which serve no less than 70 Canadian microbrews.

Theatres

Sainte-Adèle

The **Pavillon des Arts de Sainte-Adèle** (*1364 Chemin Sainte-Marguerite*, ☎450-229-2586) is a 210-seat concert hall in a former chapel. Twenty-five classical concerts are presented here annually. Each is followed by a music lover's wine and cheese in the adjoining gallery.

Festivals and cultural events

Lanaudière

Joliette

The most important event on the regional calendar is the **Festival International de Lanaudière** (☎759-7636 or 800-561-4343). During the most beautiful weeks of the summer, dozens of classical, contemporary and popular music concerts are presented in the churches of the area and outdoors at the superb Amphithéâtre de Lanaudière.

Saint-Donat

When autumn arrives, the forests of the Saint-Donat-region turn into a multicoloured natural extravaganza. To celebrate this spectacular burst of colour, various family activities are organized during **Weekends des Couleurs** (*Sep and Oct;* ☎819-424-2833 or 888-783-6628).

Laurentides

The **Festival des Couleurs et des Arts St-Sauveur** (☎450-227-4671) takes place from mid-September to mid-October, when the landscape is ablaze with flamboyant colours. Countless family activities are organized in Saint-Sauveur, Sainte-Adèle, Sainte-Marguerite-du-Lac-Masson, Sainte-Adolphe-d'Howard, (*Bal d'Automne*, ☎819-327-3232), Sainte-Agathe and Mont-Tremblant to celebrate this time of the year.

Shopping

Laurentides (Laurentians)

Saint-Sauveur-des-Monts

Visitors will find all sorts of treasures at **La Petite École** (*153 Rue Principale*), ranging from Christmas decorations to dried flowers, not to mention kitchen utensils and beauty products.

Those in search of all kinds of souvenirs will find just what they're looking for at **L'Art du Souvenir** (*191A Rue Principale*).

The Outaouais

Hull

The **boutique of the Canadian Museum of Civilization** (*100 Rue Laurier*) is, in a way, part of the exhibit. Although the Canadian and native craft pieces aren't of the same quality as those exhibited at the museum, you'll find all sorts of reasonably priced treasures and lots of great little curios.

Québec City

Québec City ★★★ is a magical place whatever the season. Meandering through the winding streets on a winter evening is an enchanting experience: the snow sparkles under the light of the streetlamps and the whole city looks like a scene from *A Christmas Carol*.

Merry makers appear through the window panes of a restaurant, illuminated by the light dancing from the hearth, savouring hearty fare. They've come to join the carnival, or maybe they're setting off on an excursion to the ski slopes of Mont Sainte-Anne.

Québec City stands out as much for the stunning richness of its architectural heritage as for the beauty of its location. The Haute-Ville quarter covers a promontory more than 98m high, known as Cap Diamant, and juts out over the St. Lawrence River, which narrows here to a mere 1km. In fact, it is this narrowing of the river that gave the city its name: in Algonquian, *kebec* means "place where the river narrows." Affording an impregnable vantage point, the heights of Cap Diamant dominate the river and the surrounding countryside. From the inception of New France, this rocky peak played an important strategic role and was the site of major fortifications early on. Dubbed the "Gibraltar of North America," today Québec is the only walled city north of Mexico.

The cradle of New France, Québec is a city whose atmosphere and architecture are more reminiscent of Europe than of America. The stone houses that flank its narrow streets and the many spires of its churches and religious institutions evoke the France of the Old Regime. In addition, the old fortifications of Haute-Ville, the Parliament and the grandiose administrative buildings attest eloquently to the importance of Québec in the history of the country. Indeed, its historical and architectural richness are such that the city and its historic surroundings were recognized by UNESCO in 1985 as a World Heritage Site, the first in North America.

Finding Your Way Around

By Plane

Aéroport Jean-Lesage, though smaller than Montréal's airports, receives international flights.

Ridesharing

Rides are organized to Québec City with **Allo-Stop** (*655 Rue Saint-Jean*, ☎*522-3430*).

By Car

Québec City can be reached from Montréal along either shore of the St. Lawrence River. Highway 40 East runs along the north shore, becoming the 440 on the outskirts of Québec City and then Boulevard Charest once you get downtown. On the south shore, Highway 20 runs east until the Pierre-Laporte bridge. Across the bridge, Boulevard Laurier continues to Québec City, becoming Grande-Allée Est as you enter the downtown area.

Car Rental

Budget
Airport
☎*872-9885*

29 Côte du Palais
Vieux Québec
☎*692-3660*

Hertz
Airport
☎*871-1571*

580 Grande-Allée
Québec City
☎*647-4949*

44 Côte du Palais
Vieux-Québec
☎*694-1224*
≈*692-3713*

National
Airport
☎*871-1224*

295 Rue Saint-Paul
Québec City
☎*694-1727*
≈*694-2174*

By Bus

A network of bus routes covers the entire city. A $53 monthly pass allows unlimited travel. A single trip costs $2 (exact change only) or $1.70 with the purchase of tickets (sold at newspaper stands). Transfers, if needed, should be requested from the driver upon boarding. Take note that most bus routes are in operation between 6am and 12:30am. Fridays and Saturdays, there is additional "late-night" bus service for #800, #801, #7, #11 and #25; all leave from Place d'Youville at 3am. For more information: ☎*627-2511*.

Bus Station

320 Rue Abraham-Martin
Gare du Palais
☎*525-3000*

Train Station

450 Rue de la Gare-du-Palais
☎*800-835-3037*

By Ferry

The **ferry** (*$1.75; cars $4.75; 10 Rue des Traversiers*, ☎*644-3704*), from Lévis to Québec City takes 20min. As the schedule varies widely depending on the season, it is best to check crossing times when planning a trip.

Taxis

Taxi Coop
☎*525-5191*

Taxi Québec
☎*525-8123*

Practical Information

Area code: *418*

Tourist Information Office

Office du Tourisme et des Congrès de la Communauté Urbaine de Québec
835 Avenue Wilfrid-Laurier
G1R 2L3
☎*692-2471*
≈*692-1481*
www.quebec-region.cuq.qc.ca
Its opening hours are not very convenient, so stop by during normal business hours.

Maison du tourisme de Québec
12 Rue Sainte-Anne
(in front of the Château Frontenac)
G1R 3X2

Post Office

300 Rue Saint-Paul
☎*694-6176*

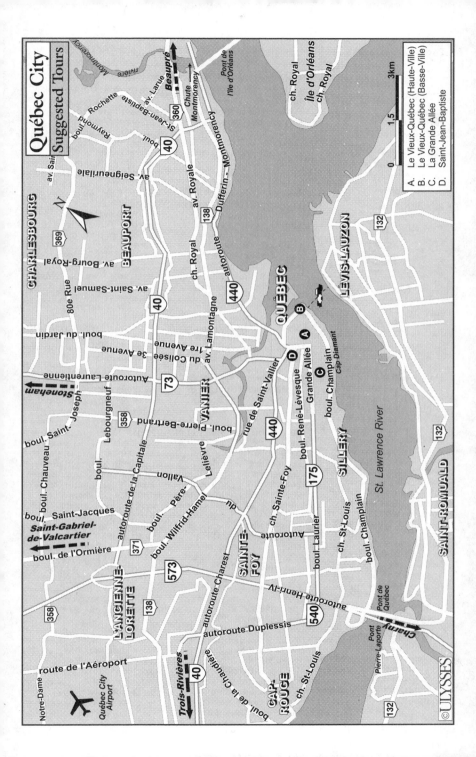

Banks

Banque Royale
700 Place d'Youville
☎ 692-6800

Caisse Populaire Desjardins du Vieux-Québec
19 Rue des Jardins
☎ 694-1774

Banque Nationale
1199 Rue St-Jean
☎ 647-6273

Exploring

★★★
Vieux-Québec

Haute-Ville, or upper town, covers the plateau atop Cap Diamant. As the administrative and institutional centre, it is adorned with convents, chapels and public buildings whose construction dates back, in some cases, to the 17th century. The walls of Haute-Ville, dominated by the citadel, surround this section of Vieux-Québec and give it the characteristic look of a fortress. These same walls long contained the development of the town, yielding a densely built-up bourgeois and aristocratic milieu. With time, the picturesque urban planning of the 19th century contributed to the present-day image of Québec City through the construction of such fantastical buildings as the Château Frontenac and the creation of such public spaces as Terrasse Dufferin, in the *belle époque* spirit.

Porte Saint-Louis *(at the beginning of the street of the same name)*. This gateway is the result of Québec City merchants' pressuring the government between 1870 and 1875 to tear down the wall surrounding the city. The Governor General of Canada at the time, Lord Dufferin, was opposed to the idea and instead put forward a plan drafted by Irishman William H. Lynn to showcase the walls while improving traffic circulation. The design he submitted exhibits a Victorian romanticism in its use of grand gateways that bring to mind images of medieval castles and horsemen. The pepper-box tower of Porte Saint-Louis, built in 1878, makes for a striking first impression upon arriving at downtown Québec City.

Lieu Historique National des Fortifications-de-Québec ★. Québec City's first wall was built of earth and wooden posts. It was erected on the west side of the city in 1693, according to the plans of engineer Dubois Berthelot de Beaucours, to protect Québec City from the Iroquois. Work on much stronger stone fortifications began in 1745, designed by engineer Chaussegros de Léry, when England and France entered a new era of conflict. However, the wall was unfinished when the city was seized by the British in 1759. The British saw to the completion of the project at the end of the 18th century. Some work began on the citadel in 1693 but the structure as we know it today was essentially built between 1820 and 1832. Nevertheless, the citadel is largely designed according to the Vauban principles from the 17th century, principles that suit the location admirably.

Walking along **Terrasse Dufferin ★★★**, overlooking the St. Lawrence, provides an interesting sensation compared to the pavement we are used to. It was built in 1879 at the request of the governor general of the time, Lord Dufferin. The boardwalk's open-air pavilions and ornate streetlamps were designed by Charles Baillargé and were inspired by the style of French urban architecture common under Napoleon III. Terrasse Dufferin is one of Québec City's most popular sights and is the preferred meeting place of young people. The view of the river, the south shore and Île d'Orléans is magnificent. During the winter months, a huge ice slide is set up at the western end of the boardwalk.

Château Frontenac ★★★ *(1 Rue des Carrières)*. The first half of the 19th century saw the emergence of Québec City's tourism industry when the romantic European style of the city began to attract growing numbers of American visitors. In 1890, the Canadian Pacific Railway company, under Cornelius Van Horne, decided to create a chain of distinguished hotels across Canada. The first of these hotels was the Château Frontenac, named in honour of one of the best-known governors of New France, Louis de Buade, Comte de Frontenac (1622-1698).

The Château Frontenac was built in stages. The first section was completed in 1893 and three sections were later added, the most important of these being the central tower (1923), the work of architects Edward and William Sutherland Maxwell.

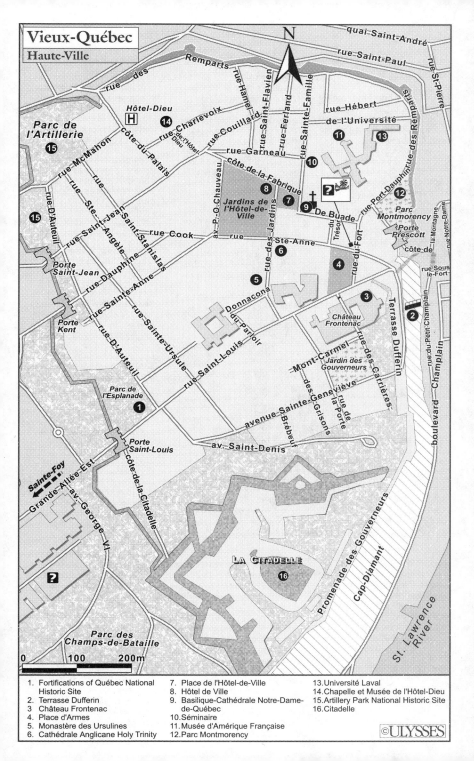

Vieux-Québec
Haute-Ville

N

quai-Saint-André

rue-Saint-Paul

Remparts

rue-des

Hôtel-Dieu **H**

14

rue-Charlevoix

rue-Hébert
de-l'Université

11

13

Parc de
l'Artillerie

15

côte-du-Palais

rue-de-l'Hôtel-Dieu

rue-Couillard

rue-Saint-Flavien

rue-Ferland

rue-Sainte-Famille

rue-Garneau

10

rue-McMahon

Ste-Jean

Saint-Stanislas

côte-de-la-Fabrique

av.-P.-O.-Chauveau

Jardins de
l'Hôtel-de-
Ville

8

7

9 De-Buade

rue-du-Trésor

rue-Port-Dauphin

rue-des-Remparts

12

Parc
Montmorency

15

rue-D'Auteuil

rue-Saint-Angèle

rue-Cook

rue-des-Jardins

rue

rue-des-Ste-Anne

6

rue-du-Fort

Porte
Prescott

côte-de-

Porte
Saint-Jean

rue-Dauphine

rue-Sainte-Anne

5

4

rue-Sous
le-Fort

Porte
Kent

rue-Sainte-Ursule

rue-D'Auteuil

Donnacona

du-Parloir

rue-Saint-Louis

Château
Frontenac

3

2

Terrasse Dufferin

rue-du-Petit-Champlain

rue-de-la-Montagne

rue-Notre-Dame

Parc de
l'Esplanade

1

Mont-Carmel

Jardin des
Gouverneurs

rue-des-Carrières

rue-de
la-Porte

des-Grisons

avenue-Sainte-Geneviève

rue-Saint-Denis

des-Gisons

Porte
Saint-Louis

côte-de-la-Citadelle

av.-Saint-Denis

avenue-Sainte-Brébeuf

boulevard-Champlain

Sainte-Foy

Grande-Allée-Est

av.-George-VI

2

LA CITADELLE

16

Promenade-des-Gouverneurs

Cap-Diamant

St. Lawrence River

Parc des
Champs-de-Bataille

0   100   200m

1. Fortifications of Québec National
   Historic Site
2. Terrasse Dufferin
3. Château Frontenac
4. Place d'Armes
5. Monastère des Ursulines
6. Cathédrale Anglicane Holy Trinity
7. Place de l'Hôtel-de-Ville
8. Hôtel de Ville
9. Basilique-Cathédrale Notre-Dame-
   de-Québec
10. Séminaire
11. Musée d'Amérique Française
12. Parc Montmorency
13. Université Laval
14. Chapelle et Musée de l'Hôtel-Dieu
15. Artillery Park National Historic Site
16. Citadelle

©ULYSSES

To appreciate the Château fully, go inside to the main hall, decorated in a style popular in 18th-century Parisian *hôtels particuliers*, and visit the Bar Maritime in the large main tower overlooking the river. The Château Frontenac has been the location of a number of important events in history. In 1944, the Québec Conference was held at the Château Frontenac. At this historic meeting, U.S. President Franklin D. Roosevelt, British Prime Minister Winston Churchill and Canadian Prime Minister Mackenzie King met to discuss the future of post-war Europe. On the way out of the courtyard is a stone with the inscription of the Order of Malta, dated 1647, the only remaining piece of Château Saint-Louis.

Château Frontenac

Until the construction of the citadel, **Place d'Armes** ★ was a military parade ground. It became a public square in 1832. In 1916, the *Monument de la Foi* (Monument of Faith) was erected in Place d'Armes to mark the tricentennial of the arrival of the Récollet religious order in Québec. Abbot Adolphe Garneau's statue rests on a base designed by David Ouellet.

Monastère des Ursulines ★★★ (*18 Rue Donnacona*). In 1535, Sainte Angèle Merici founded the first Ursuline community in Brescia, Italy. After the community had established itself in France, it became a cloistered order dedicated to teaching (1620). With the help of a benefactor, Madame de la Peltrie, the Ursulines arrived in Québec in 1639 and, in 1641, founded a monastery and convent where generations of young girls have received a good education. The Ursuline convent is the longest-running girls' school in North America. Only the museum and chapel, a small part of the huge Ursuline complex, where several dozen nuns still live, are open to the public.

The **Anglican Cathedral of the Holy Trinity ★★** (*31 Rue des Jardins*) was built following the British acquisition of Québec, when a small group of British administrators and military officers established themselves in Québec City. These men wanted to distinguish their presence through the construction of prestigious buildings with typically British designs. However, their small numbers resulted in the slow progress

of this vision until the beginning of the 19th century when work began on an Anglican cathedral designed by Majors Robe and Hall, two military engineers. The Palladian-style church was completed in 1804. This significant example of non-French architecture changed the look of the city. The church was the first Anglican cathedral built outside Britain and, in its elegant simplicity is a good example of British colonial architecture. The roof was made steeper in 1815 so that it would not be weighted down by snow.

Place de l'Hôtel-de-Ville ★, a small square, was the location of the Notre-Dame market in the 18th century. A monument in honour of Cardinal Taschereau, created by André Vermare, was erected here in 1923.

The American Romanesque Revival influence seen in the **Hôtel de Ville** (*2 Rue des Jardins*) stands out in a city where French and British traditions have always predominated in the construction of public buildings. The building was completed in 1895 following disagreements among the mayor and the city councillors as to a building plan. Sadly, a Jesuit college dating from 1666 was demolished to make room for the city hall. Under the pleasant gardens outside the building, where popular events are held in the summer, is an underground parking lot, a much needed addition in this city of narrow streets.

Cathédrale Catholique Notre-Dame-de-Québec ★★★ (*at the other end of Place de l'Hôtel-de-Ville*). The history of Québec City's cathedral underscores the problems faced by builders in New France and the determination of the Québécois in the face of the worst circumstances. The cathedral as it exists today is the result of numerous phases of construction and a number of tragedies that left the church in ruins on two occasions. The first church on this site was built in 1632 under the orders of Samuel de Champlain, who was buried nearby four years later. This wooden church was replaced in 1647 by Église Notre-Dame-de-la-Paix, a stone church in the shape of a Roman cross that would later serve as the model for many rural parish churches.

In 1674, New France was assigned its first bishop in residence, Monseigneur François-Xavier de Montmorency-Laval (1623-1708), who decided that this small church, after renovations befitting its status as the heart of such an enormous ministry, would become the seat of the Catholic Church in Québec. A grandiose plan was commissioned from architect Claude Baillif, which, despite personal financial contributions from Louis XIV, was eventually scaled down. Only the base of the west tower survives from this period. In 1742, the bishop had the church remodelled by engineer Gaspard Chaussegros de Léry, who is responsible for its present layout, featuring an extended nave illuminated from above. The cathedral resembles many urban churches built in France during the same period.

During the siege of Québec, in 1759, the cathedral was bombarded and reduced to ruins. It was not rebuilt until the status of Catholics in Québec was

settled by the British crown. The oldest Catholic parish north of Mexico was finally allowed to begin the reconstruction of its church in 1770, using the 1742 plans.

The work was directed by Jean Baillargé (1726-1805), a member of a well-known family of architects and craftsmen. This marked the beginning of the Baillargé family's extended, fervent involvement in the reconstruction and renovation of the church. In 1789, the decoration of the church interior was entrusted to Jean Baillargé's son François (1759-1830), who had recently returned from three years of studying architecture in Paris at the Académie Royale. He designed the chancel's beautiful gilt baldaquin with winged caryatids four years later. The high altar, the first in Québec designed to look like the facade of a Basilica, was put into place in 1797. The addition of baroque pews and a plaster vault created an interesting contrast. Upon completion, the spectacular interior emphasized the use of gilding, wood and white plasterwork according to typically Québécois traditions.

In 1843, Thomas Baillargé (1791-1859), the son of François, created the present neoclassical facade and attempted to put up a steeple on the east side of the church. Work on the steeple was halted at the halfway point when it was discovered that the 17th-century foundations were not strong enough. Charles Baillargé (1826-1906), Thomas Baillargé's cousin, designed the wrought-iron gate around the front square in 1858. Between 1920 and 1922, the church was carefully restored, but

just a few weeks after the work was completed, a fire seriously damaged the building. Raoul Chênevert and Maxime Roisin, who had already come to Québec from Paris to take on the reconstruction of the Basilica in Sainte-Anne-de-Beaupré, were put in charge of yet another restoration of the cathedral. In 1959, a mausoleum was put into place in the basement of the church. It holds the remains of Québec bishops and various governors (Frontenac, Vaudreuil, de Callière). In recent years, several masters' paintings hanging in the church have been stolen, leaving bare walls and an increased emphasis on ensuring the security of the remaining paintings, including the beautiful *Saint-Jérôme*, by Jacques-Louis David (1780), now at the Musée de l'Amérique Française (see below).

Séminaire de Québec ★★★
(*late Jun to late Aug, contact the museum for the schedule of guided tours; 1 Côte de la Fabrique, ☎692-3981*). During the 17th century, this religious complex was an oasis of European civilization in a rugged, hostile territory. To get an idea of how it must have appeared to students of the old day, go through the old gate (decorated with the seminary's coat of arms) and into the courtyard before proceeding through the opposite entryway to the reception desk.

The seminary was founded in 1663 by Monseigneur François de Laval, on orders from the Séminaire des Missions Étrangères de Paris (Seminary of Foreign Missions), with which it remained affiliated until 1763. As headquarters of the clergy throughout the colony, it was at the semi-

Québec

nary that future priests studied, parochial funds were administered and ministerial appointments were made. Louis XIV's Minister, Colbert, further required the seminary to establish a smaller school devoted to the conversion and education of Aboriginals.

Following the British Conquest and the subsequent banishing of the Jesuits, the seminary became a college devoted to classical education. It also served as housing for the bishop of Québec after his palace was destroyed by the invasion. In 1852, the seminary founded the Université Laval, the first French-language university in North America. Today, most of Laval's campus is located in Sainte-Foy. The vast collection of buildings of the seminary is home to a priests' residence facing the river, a private school and the Faculty of Architecture of Université Laval, which returned to its former location in 1987.

Musée de l'Amérique Française ★ (*$3; late Jun to early Sep, every day, 10am to 5pm; early Sep to late Jun, Tue to Sun, 10am to 5pm; 9 Rue de l'Université, ☎692-2843*) is a museum devoted to the history of French America. It contains a wealth of over 450,000 artifacts including silverware, paintings, oriental art and numismatics, as well as scientific instruments collected for educational purposes over the last three centuries by priests of the seminary. The museum occupies five floors of what used to be the residences of the Université Laval. The first Egyptian mummy brought to America is on view, as are several items that belonged to Monseigneur de Laval.

Parc Montmorency ★ was laid out in 1875 after the city walls were lowered along Rue des Remparts and the Governor General of Canada, Lord Dufferin, discovered the magnificent view from the promontory. George-Etienne Cartier, Prime Minister of the Dominion of Canada and one of the Fathers of Confederation, is honoured with a statue here, as are Louis Hébert, Guillaume Couillard and Marie Rollet, some of the original farmers of New France. These last three disembarked in 1617 and were granted the fiefdom of Sault-au-Matelot, on the future site of the seminary (1623). These attractive bronzes are the work of Montréal sculptor Alfred Laliberté.

The halls of the old **Université Laval ★** can be seen through a gap in the wall of the ramparts. Built in 1856 in the gardens of the seminary, they were completed in 1875 with the addition of an impressive mansard roof surmounted by three silver lanterns. When the spotlights shine on them at night, it creates the atmosphere of a royal gala.

The Augustinian nurses founded their first convent in Québec in Sillery. Uneasy about the Iroquois, they relocated to Québec City in 1642 and began construction of the present complex, the **Chapelle et Musée de l'Hôtel-Dieu ★★** (*32 Rue Charlevoix*), which includes a convent, a hospital and a chapel. Rebuilt several times, today's buildings date mostly from the 20th century. The oldest remaining part is the 1756 convent, built on the vaulted foundations from 1695, hidden behind the 1800 chapel. This chapel was erected using material

from various French buildings destroyed during the Seven Years' War. The stone was taken from the palace of the intendant, while its first ornaments came from the 17th-century Jesuit church. Today, only the iron balustrade of the bell tower bears witness to the original chapel. The present neoclassical facade was designed by Thomas Baillargé in 1839 after he completed the new interior in 1835. The nun's chancel can be seen to the right. Abbot Louis-Joseph Desjardins used the chapel as an auction house in 1817 and again in 1821, after he purchased the collection of a bankrupt Parisian banker who had amassed works confiscated from Paris churches during the French Revolution. *La Vision de Sainte-Thérèse d'Avila* (Saint Theresa of Avila's Vision), a work by François-Guillaume Ménageot that originally hung in the Carmel de Saint-Denis near Paris, can be seen in one of the side altars.

Musée des Augustines de l'Hôtel-Dieu (*free admission; Tue to Sat, 9:30am to noon and 1:30pm to 5pm; Sun 1:30pm to 5pm; 32 Rue Charlevoix, ☎692-2492, ≈692-2668*). This museum traces the history of the Augustinian community in New France through furniture, paintings and medical instruments. On display is the chest that contained the meagre belongings of the founders (pre-1639), as well as pieces from the Château Saint-Louis, the residence of the first governors under the French Regime, including portraits of Louis XIV and Cardinal Richelieu. Upon request, visitors can see the chapel and the vaulted cellars. The remains of Blessed Marie-Catherine de Saint-Augustin, the founder of the community in New France, are kept in an adjoining chapel, as is a beautiful gilded reliquary in the Louis XIV style, sculpted in 1717 by Noël Levasseur.

Artillery Park National Historic Site ★★ (*$3.25; hours vary according to the season; 2 Rue d'Auteuil, ☎648-4205, ≈648-2506*), also called Lieu Historique National du Parc-de-l'Artillerie, takes up part of an enormous military emplacement running alongside the walls of the city. The reception and information centre is located in the old foundry, where munitions were manufactured until 1964. On display is a fascinating model of Québec City built between 1795 and 1810 by military engineer Jean-Baptiste Duberger for strategic planning. The model has only recently been returned to Québec City from England, where it was sent in 1813. It is an unparalleled source of information on the layout of the city in the years following the British Conquest.

The walk continues with a visit to the **Dauphine redoubt**, a beautiful, white roughcast building near Rue McMahon. In 1712, military engineer Dubois Berthelot de Beaucours drafted plans for the redoubt, which was completed by Chaussegros de Léry in 1747. A redoubt is an independent fortified structure that serves as a retreat in case the troops are obliged to fall back. The redoubt was never really used for this purpose but rather as military barracks. Behind it can be seen several barracks and an old cartridge factory constructed by the British in the 19th century. The officer's barracks (1820),

which has been converted into a children's centre for heritage interpretation, makes a pleasant end to the visit.

Citadelle ★★★ (*at the far end of the Côte de la Citadelle*). Québec City's citadel represents three centuries of North American military history and is still in use. Since 1920, it has housed the Royal 22nd Regiment of the Canadian Army, a regiment distinguished for its bravery during World War II. Within the circumference of the enclosure are some 25 buildings, including the officer's mess, the hospital, the prison, and the official residence of the Governor General of Canada, as well as the first observatory in Canada. The citadel's history began in 1693, when Engineer Dubois Berthelot de Beaucours had the Cap Diamant redoubt built at the highest point of Québec City's defensive system, some 100m above the level of the river. This solid construction is included today inside the King's bastion.

Throughout the 18th century, French and then British engineers developed projects for a citadel that remained unfulfilled. Chaussegros de Léry's powderhouse of 1750, which now houses the Museum of the Royal 22nd Regiment, and the temporary excavation works to the west (1783) are the only works of any scope accomplished during this period. The citadel that appears today was built between 1820 and 1832 by Colonel Elias Walker Durnford. Dubbed the "Gibraltar of America," and built according to principles expounded by Vauban in the 17th century, the citadel has never borne the brunt of a single

cannonball, though it has acted as an important element of dissuasion.

Basse-Ville

Québec's port and commercial area is a narrow U-shaped piece of land wedged near the waters of the St. Lawrence. This area is sometimes called Basse-Ville (lower town) of Vieux-Québec for its location just at the foot of the Cap Diamant escarpment. The cradle of New France, Place Royale is where, in 1608, Samuel de Champlain (1567-1635) founded the settlement he called "Abitation" that would become Québec City. In the summer of 1759, three quarters of the city was badly damaged by British bombardment. It took 20 years to repair and rebuild the houses. In the 19th century, the construction of multiple embankments allowed the expansion of the town and the linking by road of the area around Place Royale with the area around the intendant's palace. The decline of the port at the beginning of the 20th century led to the gradual abandonment of Place Royale; restoration work began in 1959.

The **Funiculaire** (*$1/pers.; ☎692-1132*) began operating in November of 1879. It was put into place by entrepreneur W. A. Griffith to bring the lower and upper towns closer together. It is an outdoor elevator that obviates the need to take the Escalier Casse-Cou (see below), or to go around Côte de la Montagne. Due to an unfortunate accident that occurred in the summer of 1996, the funicular has

Québec

been completely over-hauled.

The **Escalier Casse-Cou** (*Côte de la Montagne*) (literally, "the break-neck strairway") has been here since 1682. Until the beginning of the 20th century, it had been made of planks that were in constant need of repair or replacement. At the foot of the stairway is **Rue du Petit-Champlain**, a narrow pedestrian street flanked by charming craft shops and pleasant cafés located in 17th-and 18th-century houses. Some of the houses at the foot of the cape were destroyed by rockslides prior to the reinforcement of the cliff in the 19th century.

Place Royale ★★★ is the most European quarter of any city in North America. It resembles a village in northwestern France. Place Royale is laden with symbolism, as it was on this very spot that New France was founded in 1608. After many unsuccessful attempts, this became the official departure point of French exploits in America. Under the French Regime, Place Royale was the only densely populated area in a vast and untamed colony. Today, it contains the most significant concentration of 17th-and 18th-century buildings in the Americas north of Mexico.

The square itself was laid out in 1673 by Governor Frontenac as a market. It took the place of the garden of Champlain's Abitation, a stronghold that went up in flames in 1682, along with the rest of Basse-Ville. In 1686, Intendant Jean Bochart de Champigny erected a bronze bust of Louis XIV in the middle of the

square, hence the name of the square, Place Royale.

In 1928, François Bokanowski, then the French Minister of Commerce and Communications, presented Québécois Athanase David with a bronze replica of the marble bust of Louis XIV in the Gallerie de Diane at Versailles to replace the missing statue. The bronze, by Alexis Rudier, was not displayed until 1931, for fear of offending England.

Small, unpretentious **Église Notre-Dame-des-Victoires** ★★ *(Every day, early May to mid-Oct, every day 9:30am to 4:30pm; rest of year, 10am to 4:30pm: closed for weddings, baptisms and funerals; 32 Rue Sous-le-Fort, ☎692-1650)* is the oldest church in Canada. Designed by Claude Baillif, it dates from 1688. It was built on the foundations of Champlain's Abitation, and incorporates some of its walls. Initially dedicated to the Baby Jesus, it was rechristened Notre-Dame-de-la-Victoire after Admiral Phipps' attack of 1690 failed. It was later renamed Notre-Dame-des-Victoires (the plural) in memory of the misfortune of British Admiral Walker, whose fleet ran aground on Île-aux-Oeufs during a storm in 1711. The bombardments of the conquest left nothing standing but the walls of the church, spoiling the lovely interior. The church was restored in 1766, but was not fully rebuilt until the current steeple was added in 1861.

The **Musée de la Civilisation** ★★ *($7; Tue free admission, except in summer; late Jun to early Sep, every day 10am to 7pm; early Sep to late Jun, Tue to Sun 10am to 5pm; 85 Rue Dalhousie, ☎643-2158)* is

housed in a building that was completed in 1988 and portrays the traditional architecture of Québec City with its stylized roof, dormer windows and a belltower similar to those of the surroundings. Moshe Safdie, the architect who also designed Montréal's revolutionary Habitat '67, Ottawa's National Gallery and Vancouver's Public Library, has created a sculptural building with a monumental exterior staircase at its centre. The lobby provides a charming view of Maison Estèbe and its wharf, while preserving a contemporary look that is underlined by Astri Reuch's sculpture, *La Débâcle*.

The 10 rooms of this "sociological" museum present a collection of everyday objects relating to the Québec culture of today and yesteryear. The random grouping of this extensive collection tends to overwhelm, so it is a good idea to select a few rooms that seem particularly interesting. Some of the more remarkable items are the Aboriginal artifacts, the large French Regime fishing craft unearthed during excavations for the museum itself, some highly ornate 19th-century horse-drawn hearses, and some Chinese objets d'art and pieces of furniture, including an imperial bed from the collection of the Jesuits.

Vieux-Port ★ (*160 Rue Dalhousie*). The old port is often criticized for being overly American in a city of European sensibility. It was refurbished by the Canadian government for the maritime celebration, "Québec 1534-1984," the 300-year anniversary of Jacques Cartier's discovery

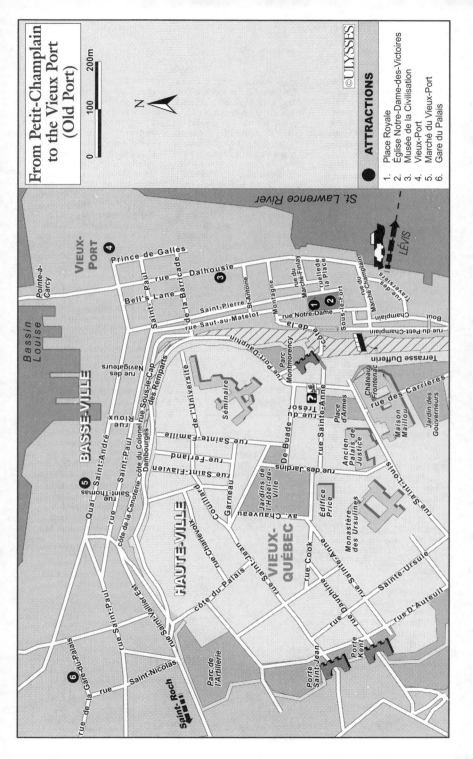

From Petit-Champlain to the Vieux Port (Old Port)

© ULYSSES

ATTRACTIONS

1. Place Royale
2. Église Notre-Dame-des-Victoires
3. Musée de la Civilisation
4. Vieux-Port
5. Marché du Vieux-Port
6. Gare du Palais

St. Lawrence River

LÉVIS

VIEUX-PORT

Pointe-à-Carcy

Bassin Louise

BASSE-VILLE

HAUTE-VILLE

VIEUX-QUÉBEC

Prince de Galles
Bell's Lane
rue de la Barricade
Saint-Paul
Dalhousie
rue Saut-au-Matelot
Saint-Pierre
St-Antoine
Montagne
rue Notre-Dame
rue du Marché-Finlay
ruelle de la Place
Sous-le-Fort
rue du Marché-Champlain
rue des Traversiers
Boul. Champlain
rue du Petit-Champlain
Terrasse Dufferin

rue des Navigateurs
rue Sous-le-Cap
côte de la Canoterie
Séminaire
rue de l'Université
rue Sainte-Famille
rue Ferland
rue Saint-Flavien
Parc Montmorency
rue du Port-Dauphin
côte de la Montagne
rue Sainte-Anne
rue du Trésor
Place d'Armes
De Buade
Château Frontenac
rue des Carrières
Maison Maillou
Jardin des Gouverneurs
Ancien Palais de Justice
rue des Jardins
rue Saint-Louis

Quai Saint-André
rue Saint-Thomas
rue Saint-Paul
rue Rioux
côte du Colonel Dambourgès
Couillard
Garneau
Jardins de l'Hôtel-de-Ville
av. Chauveau
Édifice Price
Monastère des Ursulines
rue Cook
rue Sainte-Anne
rue Dauphine
rue Sainte-Ursule
Sainte-Ursule
rue D'Auteuil

rue de la Gare-du-Palais
Saint-Roch
rue Saint-Nicolas
rue Saint-Paul Est
rue Saint-Vallier Est
Parc de l'Artillerie
côte du Palais
rue Saint-Jean
rue Saint-Jean
Porte Saint-Jean
Porte Kent

N

0   100   200m

of Québec. There are various metallic structures designed to enliven the promenade, at the end of which is the handsome **Édifice de la Douane** (1856), the old customs building, designed by William Thomas of Toronto. The entire port area between Place Royale and the entrance of **Bassin Louise** is known as **Pointe-à-Carcy**.

Marché du Vieux-Port ★ (*corner of Rue Saint-Thomas and Rue Saint-André*). Most of Québec City's public markets were shut down in the 1960s because they had become obsolete in an age of air-conditioned supermarkets and frozen food. However, people continued to want fruit and vegetables fresh from the farm, as well as contact with the farmers. Moreover, the market was one of the only non-aseptic places people could congregate. Thus, the markets gradually reappeared at the beginning of the 1980s. Marché du Vieux-Port was built in 1987 by the architectural partners Belzile, Brassard, Galienne and Lavoie. It is the successor to two other markets, Finlay and Champlain, which no longer exist. In the summer, the market is a pleasant place to stroll and take in the view of the Marina Bassin Louise at the edge of the market

For over 50 years, the citizens of Québec City clamoured for a train station worthy of their city. Canadian Pacific finally fulfilled their wish in 1915. Designed by New York architect Harry Edward Prindle in the same style as the Château Frontenac, the **Gare du Palais** ★ (*Rue de la Gare*) gives visitors a taste of the romance and charm that Québec City is known for. The 18m-high arrival hall that extends behind the giant window of the facade is bathed by sunlight passing through the leaded glass skylight of the roof. The Faïence tiles and multicoloured bricks of the walls lend a striking aspect to the whole. The station was closed for almost 10 years (from 1976 to 1985) at the time when railway companies were imitating airlines and moving their stations to the suburbs. Fortunately, it was re-opened, with great pomp, and now houses the bus and train stations. The building on the right is Raoul Chênevert's 1938 post office. It illustrates the persistence of the Château style of architecture that is so emblematic of the city.

Grande Allée

Grande Allée appears on 17th-century maps, but it was not built up until the first half of the 19th century, when the city grew beyond its walls. Grande Allée was originally a country road linking the town to Chemin du Roi and thereby to Montréal.

At that time, it was bordered by the large agricultural properties of the nobility and clergy of the French Regime. After the British Conquest, many of the domains were turned into country estates of English merchants who set their manors well back from the road. Then the neoclassical town spilled over into the area before the Victorian city had a chance to stamp the landscape with its distinctive style. Today's Grande Allée is the most pleasant route into the downtown area and the heart of extramural Haute-Ville. Despite the fact that it links the capital's various ministries, it is a lively street as many of the bourgeois houses that front onto it have been converted into restaurants and bars.

The **Hôtel du Parlement** ★★★ (*free admission; guided tours Mon to Fri, late Jun to early Sep, 9am and 4:30pm, Sat and Sun 10am to 4:30pm; early Sep to Jun, Mon to Fri, 9am to 4:30pm; at the corner of Dufferin and Grande Allée, ☎643-7239, ≈646-4271*) is known to the Québécois as l'Assemblée Nationale, the National Assembly. The seat of the government of Québec, this imposing building was erected between 1877 and 1886.

Hôtel du Parlement

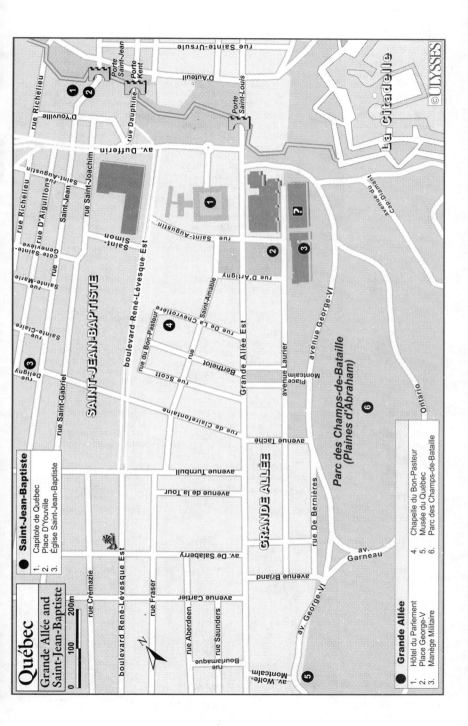

Québec

Grande Allée and Saint-Jean-Baptiste

0   100   200m

Saint-Jean-Baptiste
1. Capitole de Québec
2. Place D'Youville
3. Église Saint-Jean-Baptiste

Grande Allée
1. Hôtel du Parlement
2. Place George-V
3. Manège Militaire
4. Chapelle du Bon-Pasteur
5. Musée du Québec
6. Parc des Champs-de-Bataille

SAINT-JEAN-BAPTISTE

GRANDE ALLÉE

Parc des Champs-de-Bataille
(Plaines d'Abraham)

La Citadelle

© ULYSSES

rue Sainte-Ursule
rue Saint-Jean
Porte Saint-Jean
Porte Kent
Porte Dauphine
Porte Saint-Louis
D'Auteuil
rue Dauphine
av. Dufferin
D'Youville
rue Richelieu
rue Saint-Augustin
rue Richelieu
rue D'Aiguillon
Saint-Jean
rue Saint-Joachim
Côte Sainte-Geneviève
rue Sainte-Marie
Saint-Simon
rue Saint-Gabriel
rue Sainte-Claire
rue Béligny
rue Saint-Augustin
boulevard René-Lévesque Est
rue du Bon-Pasteur
rue De La Chevrotière
rue Scott
Berthelot
Saint-Amable
rue D'Artigny
Grande Allée Est
rue de Clairefontaine
avenue George-VI
avenue Laurier
Place Montcalm
avenue Taché
avenue Turnbull
avenue de la Tour
rue De Bernières
avenue Briand
av. Garneau
boulevard René-Lévesque Est
rue Crémazie
rue Fraser
av. De Salaberry
avenue Cartier
rue Aberdeen
rue Saunders
rue Bourdumaque
av. Wolfe-Montcalm
av. George-VI
Ontario

It has a lavish French Renaissance Revival exterior intended to reflect the unique cultural status of Québec in the North American context. Eugène-Étienne Taché (1836-1912) looked to the Louvre for his inspiration in both the plan of the quadrangular building and its decor. Originally destined to incorporate the two houses of parliament characteristic of the British system of government, as well as all of the ministries, it is today part of a group of buildings on either side of Grande Allée.

The numerous statues of the parliament's main facade constitute a sort of pantheon of Québec. The 22 bronzes of important figures in the history of the nation were cast by such well-known artists as Louis-Philippe Hébert and Alfred Laliberté. A raised inscription on the wall near the central passage identifies the statues. In front of the main entrance a bronze by Hébert entitled *La Halte dans la Forêt* (The Pause in the Forest) depicts an Aboriginal family. The work, which is meant to honour the original inhabitants of Québec, was displayed at Paris's World's Fair in 1889. *Le Pêcheur à la Nigog* (Fisherman at the Nigog), by the same artist, hangs in the niche by the fountain.

Place George V and the **Manège Militaire ★** (*opposite Parc Le Pigeonnier*). This expanse of lawn is used as a training area and parade ground by the military's equestrians. There are cannons and a statue in memory of the two soldiers who perished attempting to douse the flames of the 1889 fire in the suburb of Saint-Sauveur. Otherwise, the grounds serve mainly to

highlight the amusing Château-style facade of the Manège Militaire, the Military Riding Academy, built in 1888 and designed by Eugène-Étienne Taché, the architect of the Hôtel du Parlement.

Behind the austere facade of the Soeurs du Bon-Pasteur mother house, a community devoted to the education of abandoned and delinquent girls, is the charming, Baroque Revival style **Chapelle Historique Bon-Pasteur ★★** (*free admission; Jul and Aug, Tue to Sat, 1:30pm to 4:30pm; 1080 Rue de la Chevrotière, ☎648-9710, ≈641-1070*). Designed by Charles Baillargé in 1866, this tall, narrow chapel houses an authentic Baroque tabernacle dating from 1730. Pierre-Noël Levasseur's masterpiece of New France carving is surrounded by devotional miniatures hung on pilasters by the nuns.

The **Musée de Québec ★★★** (*$5.75; early Jun to early Sep, every day 10am to 5:45pm, Wed to 9:45pm; early Sep to late May, Tue to Sun 11am to 5:45pm, Wed to 8:45pm; Parc des Champs-de-Bataille, ☎644-6460, ≈646-3330*) was renovated and enlarged in 1992.

The older, west-facing building is on the right. Parallel to Avenue Wolfe-Montcalm, the entrance is dominated by a glass tower similar to that of the Musée de la Civilisation. The 1933 Classical Revival edifice is subterraneously linked with the old prison on the left. The latter has been cleverly restored to house exhibits, and has been rebaptized Édifice Ballairgé in honour of its architect. Some of the cells have been preserved.

A visit to this important museum is an introduction to the painting, sculpture and silverwork of Québec from the time of New France until today. The collections of religious art gathered from rural parishes of Québec are particularly interesting. Also on display are official documents, including the original surrender of Québec (1759). The museum frequently hosts temporary exhibits from the United States and Europe.

Parc des Champs-de-Bataille ★★ takes visitors back to July 1759: the British fleet, commanded by General Wolfe arrives in front of Québec City. The attack is launched almost immediately.

Musée de Québec

Rising from the Gulf of St. Lawrence, the Îles-de-la-Madeleine feature stunning landscapes with unusual shapes and warm colours. - *E. Dugas*

This exquisite architecture, typical of the French Regime, can still be found today within the province of Québec.
- *Guy Dagenais*

As soon as the waterways and lakes freeze over, the shacks go up, holes are drilled into the ice and ice fishing, called *pêche blanche*, begins.
- *P. Renaud*

Château Frontenac provides a fitting background to the warm fall colours that blend in perfectly with Québec's historic buildings. - *Y. Tessier*

The entrance to the Chinese Garden in Montréal's Jardin Botanique entices visitors to discover its many splendours. - *J. Pharand*

Almost 40,000 cannonballs crash down on the besieged city. As the season grows short, the British must come to a decision before they are surprised by French reinforcements or trapped in the December freeze-up. On the 13th of September, under the cover of night, British troops scale the Cap Diamant escarpment west of the fortifications. The ravines, which here and there cut into the otherwise uniform mass of the escarpment, allow them to climb and to remain hidden. By morning, the troops have taken position in the fields of **Abraham Martin**, hence the name of the battlefield and the park. The French are astonished, as they had anticipated a direct attack on the citadel. Their troops, with the aid of a few hundred Aboriginal warriors, throw themselves against the British. The generals of both sides are slain, and the battle draws to a close in bloody chaos. New France is lost!

The **Tours Martello** ★ (*$2; Jun to Sep, Sat and Sun noon to 5pm; late Jun to early Sep, every day 10am to 5pm, ☎648-4071*), two towers designed by the eponymous engineer, are characteristic of British defenses at the beginning of the 19th century. Tower number 1 (1808) is visible on the edge of Avenue Ontario; number 2 (1815) blends into the surrounding buildings on the corner of Avenue Laurier and Avenue Taché.

Saint-Jean-Baptiste

A student hangout complete with bars, theatres and boutiques, the Saint-Jean-Baptiste quarter is perched on a hillside between Haute-Ville and Basse-Ville. The profusion of pitched and mansard roofs is reminiscent of parts of the old city, but the orthogonal layout of the streets is quintessentially North American. Despite a terrible fire in 1845, this old Québec City suburb retains several examples of wooden constructions, forbidden inside the walls of the city.

At the beginning of the 20th century, Québec City was in dire need of a new auditorium, its Académie de Musique having burnt to the ground in March of 1900. With the help of private enterprises, the mayor looked for a new location. The Canadian government, owner of the fortifications, offered to furnish a strip of land along the walls of the city. While narrow, the lot grew wider as it grew deeper, making the construction of a fitting hall, the **Capitole** ★ (*972 Rue Saint-Jean, ☎694-4444*) possible. W. S. Painter, the ingenious Detroit architect already at work on the expansion of the Château Frontenac, devised a plan for a curved facade, giving the building a monumental air despite the restricted size of the lot. Inaugurated in 1903 as the Auditorium de Québec, the building is one of the most astonishing Beaux-Arts realizations in the country.

Place d'Youville is the public space at the entrance of the old section of town. Formerly an important market square, today it is a bustling crossroads and cultural forum. A recent redevelopment has given the square a large promenade area with trees and benches. The counterscarp wall, part of the fortifications removed in the 20th century, has been highlighted by the use of black granite blocks.

The Montcalm Market was levelled in 1932 to build a multifunctional space called the **Palais Montcalm** (*995 Place d'Youville*). Also known as the Monument National, this is the venue of choice for political rallies and demonstrations of all kinds. The auditorium has a sparse architecture, which draws on both neoclassical and Art-Deco schools.

The **Église Saint-Jean-Baptiste** ★ (*Rue Saint-Jean on the corner of Rue de Ligny*) stands out as Joseph Ferdinand Peachy's masterpiece. A disciple of French eclecticism, Peachy was an unconditional admirer of the Église de la Trinité in Paris. The resemblance here is striking, as much in the portico as in the interior. Completed in 1885, the building caused the bankruptcy of its architect, who was, unfortunately, held responsible for cracks that appeared in the facade during construction.

Parks

Parc des Champs-de-Bataille (see p 256), better known as the **Plains of Abraham**, is Québec City's undisputed park of parks. This immense green space covers about 100ha and stretches all the way to the Cap Diamant, which slopes down to the river. It is a magnificent place for local residents to enjoy all sorts of outdoor activities. Strollers and picnickers abound here during summer, but there is enough space for everyone to enjoy a little peace and quiet.

With its big trees and lawns, **Domaine Maizerets** (*free admission; 2000 Boulevard Montmorency*, ☎691-2385) is the perfect place for a leisurely stroll. Gardening buffs will love the arboretum and the landscaping; the Domaine also belongs to the "Jardins du Québec" organization. A number of historic buildings can also be found here, including the château that houses a small exhibition on the history of the estate. All sorts of outdoor activities can be enjoyed here in both summer and winter. Outdoor concerts, plays and conferences on ornithology and other subjects are held at the Domaine Maizerets year-round.

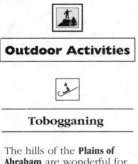

Outdoor Activities

Tobogganing

The hills of the **Plains of Abraham** are wonderful for sledding. Bundle up well and follow the kids pulling toboggans to find the best spots!

During winter, a hill is created on **Terrasse Dufferin**. You can glide down it comfortably seated on a toboggan. First purchase your tickets at the little stand in the middle of the terrace (*$1/ride; late Dec to mid-Mar, every day 11am to 11pm; 692-2955*), then grab a toboggan and climb to the top of the slide. Once you get

there, make sure to take a look around: the view is magnificent!

Accommodations

Hospitalité Canada Tours is a free telephone service operated by the Maison du Tourisme de Québec (12 Rue Ste-Anne, ☎800-665-1525, ≈393-8942). Depending on the kind of accommodations you're looking for, the staff will suggest various places belonging to the network and even make reservations for you.

Vieux-Québec

Centre Internationale de Séjour
$16 members
$48 double room
sb
19 Rue Sainte-Ursule, G1R 4E1
☎800-461-8585
☎694-0755
The Centre Internationale de Séjour is a youth hostel with 250 beds for young people during the summer months. The rooms can accommodate from two to eight people, the dormitories from 10 to 12, and there are also private double rooms.

Auberge de la Paix
$19 bkfst incl.
plus $2 for bedding if you don't have your own
sb, K
31 Rue Couillard, G1R 3T4
☎694-0735
Behind its lovely white facade in Vieux-Québec, Auberge de la Paix has a youth-hostel atmosphere. It has 59 beds in rooms that can accommodate from two to eight people, as well as a kitchenette and a living room. In summer, the pretty back

yard is all abloom. Children welcome!

Maison Acadienne
$77
⊛, ≡, K
43 Rue Sainte-Ursule, G1R 4E4
☎694-0280
☎800-463-0280
≈694-0458
A number of old houses on Rue Sainte-Ursule have been converted to hotels. Among these, Maison Acadienne is easily spotted by its large, white facade. The rooms are rather lacklustre, although some of them have been renovated.

 **Château Frontenac**
$375
ℜ, ≡, ♿, ⊛, ≈, ☺
1 Rue des Carrières, G1R 4P5
☎800-441-1414
☎692-3861
≈692-1751
The Château Frontenac is by far the most prestigious hotel in Québec City (see p 246). Its elegant entrance hall is decorated with wood panelling and warm colours. The reception, unfortunately, is often somewhat cooler. The rooms are decorated with classic refinement and are very comfortable. A new wing has recently been completed and, besides guest rooms, houses an indoor pool.

Basse-Ville

Hôtel Belley
$75
K
249 Rue Saint-Paul, G1K 3W5
☎692-1694
☎888-692-1694
≈692-1696
The pleasant Hôtel Belley stands opposite the market at the Vieux-Port. A hotel since 1877, this handsome building will leave you with fond memories for years to come. It has eight

simply decorated, cozy rooms, some with exposed brick walls, others with wooden beams and skylights. The ground floor is home to a bar called Taverne Belley, whose breakfasts and lunches, served in two lovely rooms, are very popular with locals. A number of extremely comfortable and attractively decorated lodgings, some with terraces, are also available in another house across the street. These may be rented by the night, the week or the month.

 The Priori
$145 bkfst incl.

⊛, ℜ
15 Rue du Saul-au-Matelot
G1K 3Y7
☎692-3992
☎800-351-3992
≈692-0883

The Priori is located on a quiet street in Basse-Ville. The building is very old but has been renovated in a very modern style. The decor successfully contrasts the old stone walls of the building with up-to-date furnishings. The appearance is striking and even the elevator is distinctive. The Priori is highly recommended.

Auberge Saint-Antoine
$219 bkfst incl.

⊛, ≡
10 Rue Saint-Antoine, G1K 4C9
☎692-2211
☎888-692-2211
≈692-1177

Auberge Saint-Antoine is located near the Musée de la Civilisation. This lovely hotel is divided into two buildings. The lobby is located in a tastefully renovated old stone building and is distinguished by exposed wooden beams, stone walls and a beautiful fireplace.

Each room is decorated according to a different theme and has its own unique charm.

Grande Allée

Hôtel Loews Le Concorde
$125

♿, ≡, ≈, ⊘, △, ℜ
1225 Place Montcalm, G1R 4W6
☎647-2222
☎800-463-5256
≈647-4710

Also just outside Vieux-Québec is the Hôtel Loews Le Concorde. It is part of the Loews hotel chain and has spacious, comfortable rooms with spectacular views of Québec City and the surrounding area. There is a revolving restaurant on top of the hotel.

Saint-Jean-Baptiste

Hôtel du Théâtre Capitole
$180

ℜ, ≡, ⊛
972 Rue Saint-Jean
☎694-4040
☎800-363-4040
≈694-1916

Adjoining the newly renovated theatre is the Hôtel du Théâtre Capitole. The hotel is located in the part of the building surrounding the theatre. While not luxurious, the rooms are amusing, the decor resembling a stage set. At the entrance is the restaurant Il Teatro (see p 370).

Restaurants

Vieux-Québec

Chez Temporel
$

25 Rue Couillard

At Chez Temporel all the food is prepared on the premises. Whether you opt for a butter croissant, a *croque-monsieur*, a salad or the special of the day, you can be sure that it will be fresh and tasty. To top it all off, the place serves some of the best espresso in town! The servers sometimes have more work than they can handle, but a touch of understanding on your part will be rewarded a hundred times over. Tucked away in a bend in little Rue Couillard, the two-storey Temporel has been welcoming people of all ages and stripes for over 20 years now. Open early in the morning to late at night.

Frères de la Côte
$$

1190 Rue Saint-Jean
☎692-5445

The Frères de la Côte serves delectable bistro fare, including pasta, grill, and thin-crust pizzas baked in a wood-burning oven and topped with fresh delicious ingredients. All-you-can-eat mussels and fries are offered on certain evenings. The atmosphere is lively and laid-back, and the place is often packed, which is only fitting here on bustling Rue Saint-Jean. Guests can take in the action outside through the restaurant's big windows.

Québec

Chez Livernois
$$-$$$
1200 Rue Saint-Jean
☎*694-0618*
Chez Livernois is a bistro located inside Maison Serge-Bruyère. It is named for photographer Jules Livernois, who set up his studio in this imposing 19th-century house in 1889. The excellent cuisine consists mainly of pasta and grill dishes, and the atmosphere is a bit more relaxed than at La Grande Table (see p 260).

 Élysée-Mandarin
$$$
65 Rue d'Auteuil
☎*692-0909*
The Élysée-Mandarin, which also boasts prime locations in Montréal and Paris, serves excellent Szechuan, Cantonese and Mandarin cuisine in a decor featuring a small indoor garden and Chinese sculptures and vases. The food is always succulent and the service, extremely courteous. If you are in a group, try the tasting menu: it would be a shame not to sample as many of the dishes as possible!

Le Saint-Amour
$$$
48 Rue Sainte-Ursule
☎*694-0667*
Chef and co-owner of Le Saint-Amour, Jean-Luc Boulay, creates succulent, innovative cuisine that is a feast for both the eyes and the palate. The desserts concocted in the *chocolaterie* on the second floor are positively divine. A truly gastronomic experience! To top it all off, the place is beautiful, comfortable and has a warm atmosphere. The solarium, open year-round and decorated with all sorts of flowers and other plants, brightens up the decor. On

fine summer days, its roof is removed, transforming it into a sun-drenched patio. Valet parking.

Aux Anciens Canadiens
$$$-$$$$
closed Christmas and New Year's Day at lunch
34 Rue Saint-Louis
☎*692-1627*
Located in one of the oldest houses in Québec City, the restaurant Aux Anciens Canadiens serves up-scale versions of traditional Québec specialities. Dishes include ham with maple syrup, pork and beans, and blueberry pie (Maison Jacquet, p 336).

Le Champlain
$$$$
1 Rue des Carrières
☎*692-3861*
Le Champlain is the Château Frontenac's restaurant. Needless to say, its decor is extremely luxurious, in keeping with the opulence of the rest of the hotel. The outstanding French cuisine also does justice to the Château's reputation. Chef Jean Soular, whose recipes have been published, endeavours to add an original touch to these classic dishes. Impeccable service provided by waiters in uniform.

La Grande Table
$$$$
closed at lunch
1200 Rue Saint-Jean
☎*694-0618*
La Grande Table, in Maison Serge-Bruyère, has a solid reputation that extends far beyond the walls of the old city. Located on the top floor of a historic house between Couillard and Garneau Streets, it serves gourmet French cuisine that delights both the eye and the palate. The attractive decor in-

cludes paintings by Québec artists. Valet parking.

Basse-Ville

Cochon Dingue
$$
46 Boulevard Champlain
☎*692-2013*
The Cochon Dingue is a charming café-bistro located between Boulevard Champlain and Rue du Petit-Champlain. Mirrors and a checkerboard floors make for a fun, attractive decor. The menu features bistro fare, such as *steak-frites* and *moules-frites* combos (steak and fries or mussels and fries). The desserts will send you into raptures. The Cochon Dingue has two other locations, one on the Grande Allée Tour (*46 Boulevard René-Lévesque Ouest,* ☎*523-2013*) and another in Sillery (*1326 Avenue Maguire,* ☎*684-2013*).

Café du Monde
$$-$$$
57 Rue Dalhousie
☎*692-4455*
Café du Monde is a large Parisian-style brasserie serving dishes one would expect from such a place, including steak tartar and *magret de canard* (duck filet). There is a singles bar at the entrance. The waiters, dressed in long aprons, are attentive.

Laurie Raphäel
$$$-$$$$
17 Rue Dalhousie
☎*692-4555*
The chef and co-owner of Laurie Raphäel, Daniel Vézina, was named the best chef in Québec in 1997. A book of his tempting recipes was published the same year. When creating his mouthwatering dishes, Vézina draws inspiration from culinary

traditions from all over the world, preparing giblets, seafood, meat, and other produce in innovative ways. It goes without saying, therefore, that the food at Laurie Raphaël is delicious! In May 1996 the restaurant moved into newer, more spacious quarters with a semi-circular exterior glass wall. The chic decor includes creamy white curtains, sand- and earth-tones and a few decorative, wrought-iron objects.

Grande Allée

Le Louis-Hébert
$$$
668 Grande Allée Est
☎525-7812
Le Louis-Hébert, a chic restaurant with a plush decor, serves French cuisine and delectable seafood. There is a solarium decked with greenery at the back. Courteous, attentive service.

L'Astral
$$$-$$$$
Hotel Loews Le Concorde
1225 Place Montcalm
☎647-2222
A revolving restaurant located at the top of one of the city's largest hotels, L'Astral serves excellent French food and provides a stunning view of the river, the Plains of Abraham, the Laurentians and the city. It takes about one hour for the restaurant to revolve completely. This is a particularly good place to go for Sunday brunch.

Saint-Jean-Baptiste

Il Teatro
$$$
972 Rue Saint-Jean
☎694-9996
Il Teatro, inside the magnificent Théâtre Capitole, serves excellent Italian

cuisine in a lovely dining room with a long bar at its far end and big, sparkling windows all around. The courteous service is on par with the delicious food. During summer, guests can dine in a small outdoor seating area sheltered from the hustle and bustle of Place d'Youville.

Entertainment

Bars and Danceclubs

Vieux-Québec

Le Chanteuteuil
1001 Rue Saint-Jean
Le Chanteuteuil, at the foot of the hill on Rue d'Auteuil, is a pleasant bistro. People spend hours here chatting away, seated at bench-tables around bottles of wine or beers.

Emprise
Hôtel Clarendon
57 Rue Sainte-Anne
Emprise is housed in the oldest hotel in the city (see p 354). This elegant bar is recommended to jazz fans. There is no cover charge.

La Fourmi Atomik
33 Rue d'Auteuil
Hidden away beneath Le d'Auteuil, La Fourmi Atomik is *the* underground bar in Québec City. There is a different musical theme every night, from break beat, punk rock, alternative and '80s new wave to the latest releases. During summer, the patio is always packed.

Saint-Alexandre
1087 Rue Saint-Jean
Saint-Alexandre is a typical English pub that serves 175 types of beer, 19 of

which are on tap. The decor is appealing and the ambiance pleasant.

Du Petit-Champlain au Vieux-Port

L'Innox
37 Rue Saint-André
L'Innox is a big place at the Vieux-Port that brews good beer and serves other drinks. Its lager, *blanche* (white) and *rousse* (red) beers are all as delicious as can be. There is also a small *économusée* on the premises.

Grande Allée

Chez Dagobert
600 Grande Allée Est
Chez Dagobert is a huge, popular nightclub located in an old stone house. There is always a crowd and no cover-charge.

Chez Maurice
575 Grande Allée Est
Chez Maurice, which occupies an old house on Grande Allée, is a big, chic, trendy danceclub. The place to go to see and be seen and dance to the latest hits. Chez Maurice hosts theme nights that include a very popular disco night. Inside, you'll also find a cigar room called **Chez Charlotte**, which truly merits the label *bar digestif* (cocktail lounge)!

Gay and Lesbian Clubs

L'Amour Sorcier
789 Côte Sainte-Geneviève
L'Amour Sorcier is a small bar in the Saint-Jean-Baptiste quarter. The atmosphere really heats up here sometimes. During summer, it has a pretty patio.

Ballon Rouge

811 Rue Saint-Jean
The gay nightclub Ballon
Rouge has an exclusively
male clientele. Each of its
several rooms has its own
particular ambience.

Drague

804 Rue St-Augustin
Drague is a large, loud,
smoky tavern for men
only.

Theatres and Performance Halls

The Québec City edition of
French-language magazine
Voir is distributed free of
charge and provides information on the main events
of the city.

Music

The **Orchestre Symphonique
de Québec**, Canada's oldest
symphony orchestra, per-
forms regularly at the
Grand Théâtre de Québec
(*269 Boulevard René-
Lévesque Ouest,* ☎*643-8131*),
where you can also catch
the **Opéra de Québec**.

Theatres

Grand Théâtre de Québec
269 Boulevard René Lévesque Est
☎*643-8131*
This theatre has two halls.

Le Palais Montcalm
995 Place d'Youville
☎*691-2399*
☎*670-9011*

Théâtre de la Bordée
1143 Rue Saint-Jean
☎*694-9631*

Théâtre Capitole de Québec
972 Rue Saint-Jean
☎*694-4444*

Le Périscope
2 Rue Crémazie Est
☎*529-2183*

Théâtre du Trident
at the Grand Théâtre de Québec
269 Boulevard René-Lévesque Ouest
☎*643-8131*

Movie Theatres

Cinéma de Paris
Place d'Youville
☎*694-0891*

Les Galeries
5401 Boulevard des Galeries
☎*628-2455*

Place Charest
500 Rue Dupont
☎*529-9745*

Festivals and Cultural Events

Carnaval de Québec
(☎*626-3716 or 888-737-
3789*), Québec City's winter carnival, takes place
annually during the first
two weeks of February. It
is an opportunity for visitors and residents of Québec City to celebrate the
beauty of winter. It is also
a good way to add a little
life to a cold winter that
often seems interminable.
Various activities are organized. Some of the most
popular include night-time
parades, canoe races over
the partially frozen
St. Lawrence River and the
international ice and snow
sculpture contests on the
Plains of Abraham and in
front of the carved ice
castle at Place du
Parlement. This can be a
bitterly cold period of the
year, so dressing very
warmly is essential.

The **Festival d'Été de Québec**
(☎*692-4540*) is generally
held for 10 days in early
July, when music, songs,
dancing and other kinds of
entertainment from all
over the world liven up
Québec City. The festival
has everything it takes to
be the city's most impor-

tant cultural event. The
outdoor shows are particularly popular.

Place du Parlement houses
the **Plein Art** (☎*694-0260*)
exhibit from late July to
early August. All kinds of
arts and crafts are dis-
played and sold.

People from the Québec
City region have been
enjoying themselves at
Expo-Québec (*Parc
d'ExpoCité,* ☎*691-7110*) every August for 50 years
now. This huge fair, com-
plete with an amusement
park, is held in front of the
Colisée for about 10 days
at the end of the month.

During Carnaval (see
above), the city hosts a
number of sporting events,
including the **Tournoi International de Hockey Pee-wee
de Québec** (☎*524-3311*).

Shopping

Bookstores

La Maison Anglaise
Place de la Cité, Sainte-Foy
☎*654-9523*
The best selection of
English books in Québec
City.

CDs and Cassettes

Sillons Le Disquaire
1149 Avenue Cartier
☎*524-8352*

Archambault
1095 Rue Saint-Jean
Vieux-Québec
☎*694-2088*

Craft Shops and Artisans' Studios

Atelier La Pomme
47 Rue Sous-le-Fort
☎*692-2875*
Leather goods.

Boutique Sachem
17 Rue Desjardins
☎*692-3056*
Aboriginal crafts.

Galerie-Boutique Métiers d'Art
29 Rue Notre-Dame
Place Royale
☎*694-0267*
Québec-made crafts.

Galerie d'Art Indien Cinq Nations
25½ Rue du Petit-Champlain
☎*692-3329*
Aboriginal crafts.

Les Trois Colombes
46 Rue Saint-Louis
☎*694-1114*
Handcrafted items and quality clothing.

L'Oiseau du Paradis
80 Rue du Petit-Champlain
☎*692-2679*
Paper and paper objects.

Pot-en-Ciel
27 Rue du Petit-Champlain
☎*692-1743*
Ceramics.

Verrerie d'Art Réjean Burns
156 Rue St-Paul
☎*694-0013*
Stained glass, lamps.

Verrerie La Mailloche
58 Rue Sous-le-Fort
Petit-Champlain
☎*694-0445*
Shop-made glass objects.

Jewellery and Decorative Arts

Lazuli
774 Rue Saint-Jean
☎*525-6528*

Origines
54 Côte de la Fabrique
Vieux-Québec
☎*694-9257*

Pierres Vives
23½ Rue du Petit-Champlain
☎*692-5566*

Louis Perrier Joaillier
48 Rue du Petit-Champlain
☎*692-4633*

R.Pierson

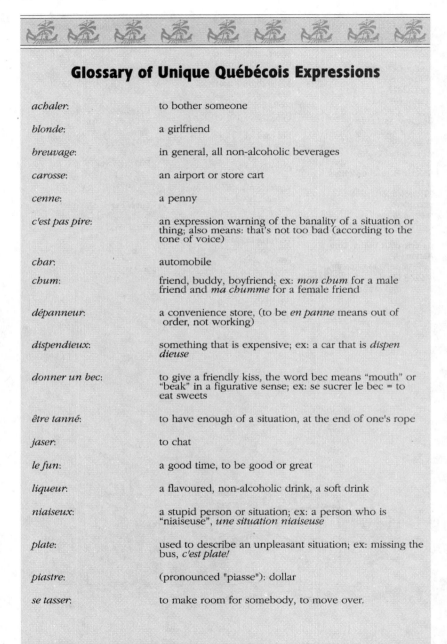

Glossary of Unique Québécois Expressions

achaler: to bother someone

blonde: a girlfriend

breuvage: in general, all non-alcoholic beverages

carosse: an airport or store cart

cenne: a penny

c'est pas pire: an expression warning of the banality of a situation or thing; also means: that's not too bad (according to the tone of voice)

char: automobile

chum: friend, buddy, boyfriend; ex: *mon chum* for a male friend and *ma chumme* for a female friend

dépanneur: a convenience store, (to be *en panne* means out of order, not working)

dispendieux: something that is expensive; ex: a car that is *dispen dieuse*

donner un bec: to give a friendly kiss, the word bec means "mouth" or "beak" in a figurative sense; ex: se sucrer le bec = to eat sweets

être tanné: to have enough of a situation, at the end of one's rope

jaser: to chat

le fun: a good time, to be good or great

liqueur: a flavoured, non-alcoholic drink, a soft drink

niaiseux: a stupid person or situation; ex: a person who is "niaiseuse", *une situation niaiseuse*

plate: used to describe an unpleasant situation; ex: missing the bus, *c'est plate!*

piastre: (pronounced "piasse"): dollar

se tasser: to make room for somebody, to move over.

The Area Around Québec City

This chapter includes the area immediately outside Québec City as well as the Charlevoix, Mauricie-Centre-du-Québec and Chaudière-Appalaches regions.

Under the French Regime, Québec City was the main urban centre of New France and the seat of the colonial administration. To supply produce to the city and its institutions, farms were introduced to the area in the middle of the 17th century. The farming region on the periphery of the city was the first populated rural zone in the St. Lawrence Valley. Traces of the first seigneuries granted to settlers in New France are still visible in this historically rich rural area. The farmhouses are the oldest of New France and the descendants of their first residents are now scattered across the American continent.

For years, artists have been captivated by the beauty of the Charlevoix region. From the town of Saint-Joachim to the mouth of the Rivière Saguenay, dramatic mountainous countryside contrasts sharply with the expansive open water of the St. Law-

rence. A scattering of charming villages and towns dot the coastline, dwarfed by mountains that fall away into the salt water of the river and steep-sided valleys. Away from the river, Charlevoix is a wild, rugged region where boreal forest sometimes gives way to taiga.

The old houses and churches found throughout the region are vestiges of Charlevoix's history as a French colony. In addition, the division of farmland in the area continues to reflect the seig-

neurial system of land grants used under the French Regime.

The rich architectural heritage and exceptional geography are complemented by a dazzling variety of flora and fauna. The Charlevoix region was named a "World Biosphere Reserve" in 1988 by UNESCO and is home to many fascinating animal and plant species. A number of whale species feed at the mouth of the Rivière Saguenay during the summer. In the spring and fall, hundreds of thousands of snow geese make migratory stops, creating a remarkable sight near Cap-Tourmente, farther west. Deep in the hinterland, the territory has all the properties of tundra, a remarkable occurrence at this latitude. This area is home to a variety of animal species such as the caribou

was the second city founded in New France (1634). First a fur-trading post, it became an industrial centre with the founding of the Saint-Maurice ironworks in 1730. Since the end of the 19th century, the exploitation of the surrounding forests has made Trois-

tion, the land is still divided according to the lines of the old seigneurial system. Finally, in the extreme south of the region lies the area known as "Centre-du-Québec." The gently rolling hills of this countryside herald the mountains of the Appalachians. There are interesting annual festivals in the area including an international music festival in Victoriaville and an international folklore festival in Drummondville.

and the large Arctic wolf. Charlevoix's plant life is rich in species unique to eastern Canada.

The Mauricie–Centre-du-Québec region is an amalgam of diverse regions on either side of the St. Lawrence. Located about halfway between Montréal and Québec City, this large region runs from north to south and includes terrain of the three types that make up the province: the Canadian Shield, the St. Lawrence plains, and part of the Appalachian mountain range.

The city of Trois-Rivières is generally considered the heart of this region. It

Rivières the hub of the provincial pulp and paper industry. Further up the Rivière Saint-Maurice, the towns of Shawinigan and Grand-Mère, also major industrial sites, serve as centres for the production of hydro-electric power and for the major industries that consume that power. To the north lies a vast untamed expanse of lakes, rivers and forest. This land of hunting and fishing also contains the magnificent Mauricie National Park, reserved for outdoor activities such as canoeing and camping.

To the south lie the rural zones on either side of the St. Lawrence. Opened up very early to coloniza-

The Chaudière-Appalaches region is made up of several small areas with very distinct geographical features. Located opposite Québec City on the south shore of the St. Lawrence, it stretches across a vast fertile plain before slowly climbing into the foothills of the Appalachian Mountains all the way to the American border. Originating in Lac Mégantic, the Rivière Chaudière runs through the centre of this region, then flows into the St. Lawrence across from Québec City.

A pretty pastoral landscape unfolds along the river between Leclercville and Saint-Roch-des-Aulnaies, an area occupied very early on by the French. There are attractive villages, including Saint-Jean-Port-Joli, an important provincial crafts centre. Out in the gulf, adventure awaits in the

Archipel de l'Île-aux-Grues.

Further south, the picturesque Beauce region extends along the banks of the Rivière Chaudière. The river rises dramatically in the spring, flooding some of the villages along its banks almost every year. That gave muddied local inhabitants the nickname "jarrets noirs" which translates somewhat inelegantly as "black hamstrings." The discovery of gold nuggets in the river bed attracted prospectors to the area in the middle of the 19th century. Farms have prospered in the rolling green hills of the Beauce for hundreds of years. Church steeples announce the presence of little villages scattered evenly across the local countryside. The Beauce region is also home to Québec's largest concentration of maple groves, making it the true realm of the *cabane à sucre* (sugar shack). The spring thaw gets the syrup flowing and signals the sugaring-off season. Local inhabitants, called Beaucerons, are also known for their sense of tradition and hospitality.

The asbestos region, located a little further west of the Rivière Chaudière, around Thetford Mines, has a fairly varied landscape punctuated with impressive open-cut-mines.

Finding Your Way Around

Québec City Region

By Car

From Québec City, take the Autoroute Dufferin-Montmorency (Highway 440) towards Beauport (Exit 24).

To go to Île d'Orléans from Québec, take Autoroute Dufferin-Montmorency (Highway 440) to the Pont de l'Île. Cross the river and turn right on Route 368, also called Chemin Royal, which circles the island.

By Bus

Sainte-Anne-de-Beaupré (*9687 boul. Ste-Anne, Irving, ☎827-5169*) is accessible by bus (*320 Rue Abrahahm-Martin, ☎525-3000*).

Sainte-Foy
3001 Chemin des Quatre-Bourgeois
☎650-0087

Public Transportation

Bus number 53 leaves from Place Jacques-Cartier (*$1.85, Rue du Roi, at the corner of Rue de la Couronne*) and drops visitors near the Chute Montmorency.

To reach Wendake from Québec City, take bus #801, the métrobus whose stops are clearly indicated (for example, at Place d'Youville). From the Charlesbourg terminus, take bus #72 to Wendake. The historic village of

Onhoüa Chetek8e is north of the reserve and accessible by taxi.

By Ferry

Sainte-Foy
3255 Chemin de la Gare (corner Chemin St-Louis)
☎800-835-3037

Charlevoix

By Car

To get to Charlevoix from Québec City, take Route 138, the main road in the region. After crossing a low-lying area close to the St. Lawrence, Route 138 veers into the rolling Charlevoix countryside. This area is the southwest extremity of the Laurentides mountains. The north side of the river valley is bordered by the Laurentides for hundreds of miles to the east. Île d'Orléans can be seen from here on clear days.

Bus Stations

Baie-Saint-Paul
2 Route de l'Équerre (Centre Commercial Le Village)
☎(418) 435-6569

Saint-Hilarion
354 Route 138
☎(418) 457-3855

Clermont
83 Boulevard Notre-Dame
☎(418) 439-3404

La Malbaie–Pointe-au-Pic
46 Ste-Catherine
☎(418) 665-2264

By Ferry

The car ferry to **Île aux Coudres** (*free;* ☎*418-438-2743*) leaves from Saint-Joseph-de-la-Rive. There is usually a half-hour wait before boarding during the summer months. The crossing takes approximately 15min. The 26km island tour takes about half a day. The roads that run along the river are ideal for bike rides. (They can be rented on the island).

Saint-Siméon:
The ferry (*$10.20, cars $26;* ☎*862-5094*) from Rivière-du-Loup travels to Saint-Siméon in 1hr, 5min.

Baie-Sainte-Catherine:
The ferry (*adults and cars free,* ☎*418-235-4395*) travels between Tadoussac and Baie-Sainte-Catherine in approximately 10min.

Mauricie–Centre-du-Québec

By Car

From Montréal, take Highway 40 (Félix Leclerc), followed by Highway 55 S. for a short while, and then turn onto Route 138 E. as far as Trois-Rivières.

Bus Stations

Trois-Rivières
275 St. Georges
☎*374-2944*

Grand-Mère
800 6e Avenue
☎*533-5565*

Shawinigan
1563 Boulevard Saint-Sacrement
☎*539-5144*

Victoriaville
64 Boulevard Carignan
☎*752-5400*

Drummondville
330 Rue Hériot
☎*477-2111*
☎*472-5252*

By Ferry

La Tuque
550 Rue Saint-Louis
☎*523-3257*

Shawinigan
1560 Chemin du CN
☎*537-9007*

Drummondville
263 Rue Lindsay
☎*472-5383*

Chaudière-Appalaches

By Car

From Montréal, take Highway 20 to Exit 253, then follow the 265 N. to Deschaillons, and turn right on Route 132 E. From Québec City, cross the river to take Route 132 in either direction.

Bus Stations

Lévis
5401 Boulevard Rive-Sud
☎*837-5805*

MontCentre-du-Québecmagny
5 Boulevard Taché Ouest
☎*248-3292*

Saint-Jean-Port-Joli
27 Avenue de Gaspé Est
☎*598-6808*

Saint-Georges
☎*228-4040*

Thetford Mines
127 Rue Saint-Alphonse Ouest
☎*335-5120*

Train Stations

Montmagny
4 Rue de la Station
☎*800-361-5390*

By Ferry

The ferry between Québec City and Lévis (*$1.75; car $5,* ☎*644-3704*) takes only 15min. The schedule is subject to change but there are frequent crossings.

The ferry to Île aux Grues, the **Grue des Îles** (*free;* ☎*248-3549*), leaves from the Montmagny dock and takes about 20min. The schedule varies with the tide.

The following companies also ferry people to Île aux Grues or to Grosse Île. The boats of **Taxi des Îles** (*Île aux Grues $10 one way; Grosse Île $32 round-trip, 4.5hrs*) is recognizable by the yellow and black colour scheme of its boats and frequently travel to the islands from the Montmagny dock. **Croisières Lachance** (*prices varies with different packages, cruises to Grosse-île and the Montmagny archepelago; 110 de la Marina, Berthier-sur-Mer, GOR 1EO,* ☎*259-2140 or 888-476-7734*), offers daily cruises from Berthier-sur-Mer.

Practical Information

The **Québec City, Charlevoix** and **Chaudière-Appalaches regions** use the *418* area code.

Mauricie–Centre-du-Québec uses *819*.

Tourist Information

Québec City region

Centre d'Information de l'Office du Tourisme et des Congrès de la Communauté Urbaine de Québec
835 Wilfred Laurier Avenue
Quebec, Quebec G1R 2L3
☎*649-2608*
⇒*522-0830*
www.quebecregion.com

Sainte-Anne-de-Beaupré
9310 Boulevard Ste-Anne
☎*827-5281*

Île d'Orléans
490 Côte du Pont, Saint-Pierre
☎*828-9411*

Deschambault
12 Rue des Pins
☎*286-3002*

Charlesbourg
7960 Boulevard Henri-Bourassa
☎*624-7720*

Charlevoix

Association Touristique de Charlevoix
630 Boulevard de Comporté
C.P. 275, La Malbaie, G5A 1T8
☎*665-4454*
☎*800-667-2276*
⇒*665-3811*

Baie-Saint-Paul:
444 Boulevard Mgr-de-Laval
(Belvédère Baie-Saint-Paul)
☎*435-4160*

Mauricie–Centre-du-Québec

Tourism Mauricie-Centre-du-Québec *Mon to Fri 8:30am to noon and 1pm to 4:30pm*
2775 Boulevard Jean XIII
Trois-Rivières Ouest, G8Z 4J2
☎*375-1222*
☎*(800) 567-7603*
⇒*375-0301*

Chambre de Commerce de Trois Rivieres
168 Rue Bonaventure, G9A 2B1
☎*375-9628*

Chambre de Commerce du Cap-de-la-Madeleine
170 Rue des Chenaux
☎*375-5346*

Chambre de Commerce de Victoriaville
122 Rue Aqueduc, P.C. 641
☎*758-6371*

Drummondville
1350 Rue Michaud
☎*477-5529*

Chambre de Commerce de Nicolet
30 Rue Notre-Dame
☎*293-4537*

Chaudière-Appalaches

Association Touristique Chaudière-Appalaches
800 Autoroute Jean-Lesage
St Nicolas, G7A 1C9
☎*831-4411*
☎*888-831-4411*
⇒*831-8442*
www.chaudapp.qc.ca

Lévis
5995 Rue St-Laurent
☎*838-6026*

Montmagny
45 Avenue du Quai, C.P. 71 G5V 3S3
☎*248-9196*
☎*800-463-5643*
⇒*248-1436*
www.montmagny.com

Saint-Jean-Port-Joli
7 Place de l'Église, G0R 3G0
☎*598-3747*
⇒*598-3085*

Saint-Georges
8585 Boulevard Lacroix, G5Y 1L3
☎*227-4642*
⇒*228-2255*

Thetford Mines
682 Rue Monfette Nord, G6G 7G9
☎*335-7141*
⇒*338-4984*
www.tourisme-amiante.qc.ca

Exploring

Québec City Region

Nestled between the St. Lawrence and the undeveloped wilderness of the Laurentian massif, this long, narrow strip of land is the ancestral home of many families whose roots go back to the beginning of the colony. It illustrates how the spread of the population was limited to the riverside in many regions of Québec and recalls the fragility of development in the era of New France.

The colony's first road, the Chemin du Roy (or king's road) was built under orders from Monseigneur de Laval during the 17th century. From Beauport to Saint-Joachim, it follows the Beaupré shore. A typical style characterized by a raised main floor covered in stucco, long balconies with intricately carved wood balusters and lace-curtained windows is repeated in houses along this road. Since about 1960, however, the suburbs of Québec City have gradually taken over the shore, marring the simple beauty of the area. Nevertheless, the Chemin du Roy is still an extremely pleasant route. Whether rounding a cape, making one last jaunt in the Laurentians, or exploring the plains of the St. Lawrence, this route offers magnificent views of the mountains, the fields, the river and Île d'Orléans.

Québec

★
Beauport

The large white house known as **Manoir Montmorency** (*2490 Avenue Royale,* ☎*663-3330*) was built in 1780 for British governor, Sir John Haldimand. At the end of the 18th century, the house became famous as the residence of the Duke of Kent, son of George III and father of Queen Victoria. The manor, which once housed a hotel, was severely damaged by fire in May 1993. It has been restored according to the original plans and now hosts an information centre, a few shops and a restaurant (see p 301), that offers exceptional view of the Montmorency Falls, the St. Lawrence and Île d'Orléans. The small Sainte-Marie chapel on the property and the gardens is open to the public.

The Manoir Montmorency is nestled in the **Parc de la Chute Montmorency** ★★ (*free admission, parking $7, cablecar $5 one-way $7 return; accessible all year; for opening hours and parking* ☎*663-2877, ≈663-1666, chutemontmorency.qc.c a*). , With its source in the Laurentians, the Rivière Montmorency flows along peacefully until it reaches a sudden 83m drop. It then tumbles into a void, creating one of the most impressive natural phenomena in Québec. At one and a half times the height of Niagara Falls, the Montmorency Falls flow at a rate that can reach 125,000 litres-per-second during the spring thaw. Samuel de Champlain, the founder of Qué-

bec City, was impressed by the falls and named them after the viceroy of New France, Charles, Duc de Montmorency. During the 19th century, the falls became a fashionable leisure area for the well-to-do of the region who would arrive in horse-drawn carriages or sleighs.

To take in this magnificent spectacle, a park has been set up, and a tour of the falls is possible. From the manor, follow the pretty cliff walk, location of the Baronne lookout. You'll soon reach two bridges – the Pont Au-dessus de la Chute and the Pont Au-dessus de la Faille – which pass the falls and the fault respectively, with spectacular views. Once in the park you'll find picnic tables and a playground. The bottom of the falls are reached by the 487-step panoramic staircase or the trail. The cable-car provides a relaxing and picturesque means of reaching the top. In winter, steam freezes into a cone of ice, called a sugar-loaf, making a good ice-wall that anyone feeling adventurous can climb.

The lower part of the park is also accessible by car, though a complicated detour is required: continue along Avenue Royale, turn right on Côte de l'Église, then right again on Highway 40. The parking lot is

on the right. To get back to Avenue Royale, take Boulevard Sainte-Anne west, Côte Saint-Grégoire and finally Boulevard des Chutes to the right.

★
Sainte-Anne-de-Beaupré

This long, narrow village is one of the largest pilgrimage sites in North America. In 1658, the first Catholic church on the site was dedicated to Saint Ann. Sailors from Brittany, who had prayed to the Virgin Mary's mother, were saved from drowning during a storm on the St. Lawrence. A great number of pilgrims soon began to visit the church. The second church, built in 1676, was replaced in 1872 by a huge temple that was destroyed by fire in 1922. Finally work began on the present basilica which stands at the centre of a virtual complex of chapels, monasteries and facilities as varied as they are unusual. They include the **Bureau des Bénédictions**, (blessings office) and the Cyclorama. Each year, Sainte-Anne-de-Beaupré welcomes more than a million pilgrims who stay in the hotels and visit the countless souvenir boutiques, of perhaps dubious taste, along Avenue Royale.

The **Basilique Sainte-Anne-de-Beaupré** ★★★ (*information counter is loctated near the entrance, early May to mid-Sep, every day 8:30am to 5pm; 10018 Avenue Royale,* ☎*827-3781, ≈827-8227*), towers over the small, metal-roofed wooden houses that line the winding road. It's surprising not only for its impressive size, but also for the feverish activity it inspires all summer long.

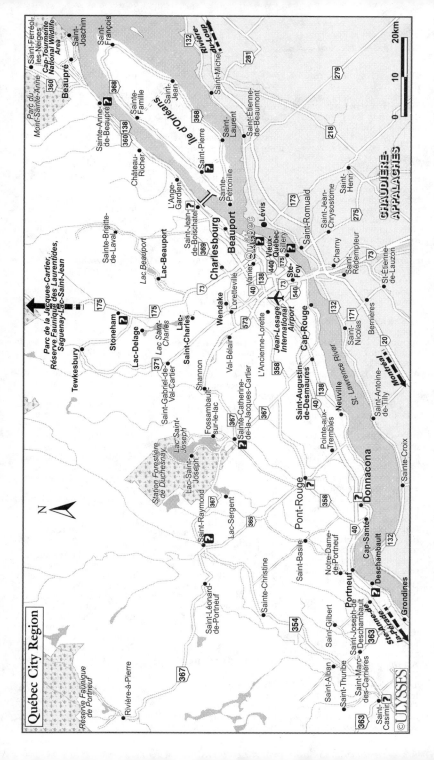

The church's granite exterior, which takes on a different colour depending on the ambient light, was designed in the French Romanesque Revival style by Parisian architect Maxime Roisin who was assisted by Quebecer Louis Napoléon Audet. Its spires rise 91m into the sky above the coast while the nave is 129m long and the transepts over 60m wide. The wooden statue gilded with copper sitting atop the church's facade was taken from the 1872 church. When the fire destroyed the former basilica, the statue stayed in place while everything collapsed around it.

The basilica's interior is divided into five naves supported by heavy columns with highly sculpted capitals. The vault of the main nave is adorned with sparkling mosaics designed by French artists Jean Gaudin and Auguste Labouret, recounting the life of Saint Anne. Labouret also created the magnificent stained glass found all along the perimeter of the basilica. The left transept contains an extraordinary statue of Saint Anne cradling Mary in her right arm. Her tiara reminds the visitor that she is the patron saint of Québec. In a beautiful reliquary in the background, visitors can admire the Great Relic, part of Saint Anne's forearm sent over from the San Paolo Fuori le Mura in Rome. Finally, follow the ambulatory around the choir to see the ten radiant chapels, built in the 1930s, whose polychromatic architecture is Art-Deco inspired.

The **Cyclorama de Jérusalem** ★★ (*$6; late Apr to late Oct every day 9am to 6pm, Jul and Aug every day 9am to 8pm, 8 Rue Régina, near the*

parking lot ☎*827-3101,* ⇔*827-8279*). This round building with oriental features houses a 360° panorama of Jerusalem on the day of the crucifixion. This immense *trompe l'œil* painting, measuring 14m by 100m, was created in Chicago around 1880 by French artist Paul Philippoteaux and his assistants. A specialist in panoramas, Philippoteaux produced a work of remarkable realism. It was first exhibited in Montréal before being moved to Sainte-Anne-de-Beaupré at the very end of the 19th century. Very few panoramas and cycloramas, so popular at the turn of the century, have survived to the present day.

The **Musée de Sainte Anne** ★ (*$5; Apr to mid-Oct, every day 10am to 5pm; Oct to Apr, Sat and Sun 10am to 5pm; 9803 Boulevard Ste-Anne,* ☎*827-6873,* ⇔*827-6870*) is dedicated to sacred art honouring the mother of the Virgin Mary. These interestingly diverse pieces were acquired over many years from the basilica but have only recently been put on display for the public. Sculptures, paintings, mosaics, stained-glass windows and goldworks are dedicated to the cult of Saint Anne as well as written works expressing prayers or thanks for favours obtained. The history of pilgrimages to Sainte-Anne-de-Beaupré is also explained. The exhibition is attractively presented and spread over two floors.

★★ Cap Tourmente

The pastoral and fertile land of Cap Tourmente is the eastern-most section of the St. Lawrence plain, before the mountains of

the Laurentian Massif reach the shores of the St. Lawrence. The colonization of this area at the beginning of the 17th century represented one of the first attempts to populate New France. Samuel de Champlain, the founder of Québec City, established a farm here in 1626, the ruins of which were recently unearthed. The land of Cap Tourmente was acquired by Monseigneur François de Laval in 1662, and cultivated by the Société des Sieurs de Caen. Soon the land passed into the hands of the Séminaire de Québec which eventually built a retreat for priests, a school, a summer camp and, most importantly, a huge farm that met the institution's dietary needs and brought in a substantial income. Following the British Conquest, the seminary moved the seat of its Beaupré seigneury to Cap Tourmente, leaving behind the ruins of the Château Richer. The **Château Bellevue** ★ was built between 1777 and 1781. This superb building is endowed with a neoclassical cutstone portal. The property's Saint-Louis-de-Gonsague Chapel (1780) is well hidden in the trees.

Île d'Orléans

Located in the middle of the St. Lawrence River downstream from Québec City, this 32km-by-5km island is famous for its old-world charm. Of all regions of Québec, the island is the most evocative of life in New France. When Jacques Cartier arrived in 1535, the island was covered in wild vines, which inspired its first name – Île Bacchus. However, it was soon renamed in homage to the Duc d'Orléans. With the exception of Sainte-Pétronille, the parishes on the island were established in the 17th century. The colonization of the entire island followed soon after. In 1970, the Quebec government designated Île d'Orléans as a historic district. The move was made in part to slow down the development that threatened to turn the island into yet another suburb of Québec City, as well as part of a widespread movement among Québécois to protect the roots of their French ancestry by preserving old churches and houses. Since 1936, the island has been linked to the mainland by a suspension bridge, the Pont de l'Île.

★★
Sainte-Pétronille

Paradoxically, Saint-Pétronille was the site of the first French settlement on Île d'Orléans and is also its most recent parish. In 1648, François de Chavigny de Berchereau and his wife Éléonore de Grandmaison established a farm and a Huron mission here. However, constant Iroquois attacks forced the colonists to move further east, to a spot facing Sainte-Anne-de-Beaupré. It was not until the middle of the 19th century that Sainte-Pétronille was consolidated as a village when its beautiful location began to attract numerous summer visitors. Anglophone merchants from Québec City built beautiful second homes here, many of which are still standing along the road.

★★
Saint-Jean

In the mid-19th century, Saint-Jean was the pre-ferred homebase of nautical pilots who made a living guiding ships through the difficult currents and rocks of the St.Lawrence. Some of their neoclassical or Second Empire houses remain along Chemin Royal. They provide evidence of the privileged place held by these seamen who were indispensable to the success of commercial navigation.

The most impressive manor from the French Regime still standing is in Saint-Jean. The **Manoir Mauvide-Genest ★★** was built in 1734 for Jean Mauvide, the Royal Doctor, and his wife, Marie-Anne Genest. This beautiful stone building has a rendering coat of white roughcast in the traditional Norman architectural style. The property officially became a seigneurial manor in the middle of the 18th century. Mauvide, having become rich doing business in the Caribbean, bought the southern half of the Île d'Orléans seigneury. The Manoir is currently under renovation and therefore closed to the public.

In 1926, Camille Pouliot, descendant of the Genest family, bought the manor house. He then restored it, adding a summer kitchen and a chapel. He later transformed the house into a museum, displaying furniture and objects from traditional daily life. Pouliot was one of the first people to be actively interested in Québec's heritage. The manor still has a museum on the second floor devoted to antique furniture and everyday objects while the main floor is taken up by a restaurant.

★
Saint-François

As the smallest village on Île d'Orléans, Saint-François retains many buildings from its past. However, some are far from the Chemin Royal and are therefore difficult to see from Route 368. The surrounding countryside is charming and offers several pleasant panoramic views of the river, Charlevoix and the coast. The famous wild vine that gave the island its first name, Île Bacchus, can also be found in Saint-François.

On the roadside, as you leave the village, there is an **observation tower ★★** that offers excellent views to the north and east. Visible are the Îles Madame et au Ruau which mark the meeting point of the fresh water of the St. Lawrence and the salt water of the gulf. Mont Sainte-Anne's ski slopes, Charlevoix on the north shore and the Côte-du-Sud seigneuries on the south shore can also be seen in the distance.

★
Sainte-Famille

The oldest parish on Île d'Orléans was founded by Monseigneur de Laval in 1666 to establish a settlement across the river from Sainte-Anne-de-Beaupré for colonists who had previously settled around Sainte-Pétronille. Sainte-Famille has retained many buildings from the French Regime. Among them is the town's famous church, one of the greatest accomplishments of religious architecture in New France and the oldest two-towered church in Québec.

Québec

Église Sainte-Famille

The beautiful **Église Sainte-Famille** ★★ (*3915 Chemin Royal*) was built between 1743 and 1747 to replace the original church built in 1669. Inspired by the Église des Jésuites in Québec City, which has since been destroyed, Father Dufrost de la Jemmerais ordered the construction of two towers with imperial roofs. This explains the single steeple sitting atop the gable. Other unusual elements such as five alcoves and a sun dial by the entrance (since destroyed) make the building even more original. In the 19th century, new statues were installed in the alcoves, and the imperial roofs gave way to two new steeples, bringing the number of steeples to three.

Though modified several times, the interior decor retains many interesting elements. Sainte-Famille was a wealthy parish in the 18th century, thus allowing the decoration of the church to begin as soon as the frame of the building was finished. In 1748, Gabriel Gosselin installed the first pulpit and in 1749 Pierre-Noël Levasseur completed construction of the present tabernacle of the high altar. Louis-Basile David, inspired by the Quévillon school, designed the beautiful coffered vault in 1812. Many paintings adorn the church, including: *La Sainte Famille* (The Holy Family) painted by Frère Luc during his stay in Canada in 1670; the *Dévotion au Sacré Coeur de Jésus* (Devotion to the Sacred Heart of Jesus, 1766); and *Le Christ en Croix* (Christ on the Cross) by François Baillargé (circa 1802). The church grounds offer a beautiful view of the coast.

Saint-Pierre

The most developed parish on Île d'Orléans had already lost some of its charm before the island was declared a historic site. Saint-Pierre is particularly important to the people of Québec as the home for many years of the renowned poet and singer Félix Leclerc (1914-1988). The singer and songwriter who penned *P'tit Bonheur* was the first musician to introduce Quebecois music to Europe. He is buried in the local cemetery.

With the exception of Sillery near Québec City, the towns and villages on this tour are all located along the Chemin du Roy, the first maintained road between Montréal and Québec City, built in 1734. Running along the St. Lawrence (some parts parallel to Route 138), and lined with beautiful 18th-century French-style houses, churches and windmills, this road is one of the most picturesque drives in Canada.

★★ Sillery

This well-to-do suburb of Québec City retains many traces of its varied history, influenced by the town's dramatic topography. There are actually two sections to Sillery: one at the base and the other at the top of a steep cliff that runs from Cap Diamant to Cap-Rouge. In 1637, the Jesuits built a mission in Sillery on the shores of the river with the idea of converting the Algonquins and Montagnais who came to fish in the coves upriver from Québec City. They named the fortified community for the mission's benefactor, Noël Brûlart de Sillery, an aristocrat who had recently been converted by Vincent de Paul.

By the following century, Sillery was already sought after for its beauty. The Jesuits converted their mission to a country house and the bishop of Samos built Sillery's first villa (1732). Following the British Conquest, it became the preferred town of administrators, military officers and British merchants, all of whom built themselves luxurious villas on the cliff in architectural styles then fashionable in England. The splendour of these homes and their vast English gardens were in stark contrast to the simple houses lived in by workers and clustered at the base of the cliff. The occupants of these houses worked in the shipyards where a fortune was being made building ships out of wood coming down the Outaouais region to supply the British navy during Napoleon's blockade that began in 1806. The shipyards, set up in Sillery's sheltered coves, had all disappeared before Boulevard Champlain, now running along the river's edge, was built in 1960.

The **Bois-de-Coulonge** ★ (*free admission; open every day; 1215 Chemin St. Louis,* ☎528-0773, ⇒528-0833) to the east borders Chemin Saint-Louis. This English park once surrounded the residence of the lieutenant-governor of Québec, the King or Queen's representative in Québec until the title was abolished in 1968. The stately home was destroyed in a fire in 1966 though some of its outbuildings have

survived, notably the guard's house and the stables. The Saint-Denys stream flows through the eastern end of the grounds at the bottom of a ravine. In 1759, British troops gained access to the Plains of Abraham, where a historic battle decided the future of New France, by climbing through this ravine. Bois de Coulonge, one of the Jardins du Québec, now has magnificent gardens and a well-arranged arboretum to walk through.

The **Maison des Jésuites de Sillery** ★★ (*suggested donation; closed Mon; Jun to Sep 11am to 5pm, Oct to May 1pm to 5pm; 2320 Chemin du Foulon,* ☎654-0259, ⇒684-0991), built of stone and covered with white plaster, occupies the former site of a Jesuit mission, a few ruins of which are still visible. In the 17th century, the mission included a fortified stone wall, a chapel, a priest's residence and Aboriginal housing. As European illnesses such as smallpox and measles devastated the indigenous population, the mission was transformed into a hospice in 1702. At the same time, work began on the present house, a building with imposing chimney stacks. In 1763, the house was rented to John Brookes and his wife, writer Frances Moore Brookes, who immortalized it as the setting for her novel, *The History of Emily Montague,* published in London in 1769. It was also during this time that the structure was lowered and the windows were made smaller in size, in the New England saltbox tradition. Covered with a catslide roof, the house now has two stories in front and one in back.

By 1824, the main building was being used as a brewery and the chapel had been torn down. The house was later converted into offices for various shipyards. In 1929, the Maison des Jésuites became one of the first three buildings designated as historic by the government of Québec. Since 1948, it has housed a museum that details the 350-year history of the property.

★
Neuville

A vein of limestone, traversing the region from Neuville to Grondines, has been tapped for the construction of prestigious buildings across the province since the French Regime. This explains the large number of rubblestone houses dotting the villages in the area. Today, most of the jobs related to the extraction and cutting of this grey stone are concentrated in the town of Saint-Marc-des-Carrières, west of Deschambault.

The village of Neuville was formerly part of the Pointe-aux-Trembles seigneury granted to the royal engineer Jean Bourdon in 1653. The houses of Neuville are built into the hills at varying elevations so that most of them have a view of the St. Lawrence. This terraced layout lends this section of the Chemin du Roy a certain charm.

Rue des Érables ★★ (*guided visits,,* ☎286-3002) has one of the largest concentrations of old stone houses outside Québec's large urban centres. This is explained by the abundance of the necessary raw material and the homeowners' desire to make use of the talents of local builders and stonemasons. No. 500 on Rue des Érables was built for Édouard Larue who acquired the Neuville seigneury in 1828. The huge house is representative of traditional rural Québec architecture with its raised stone foundation and gallery covered with flared eaves, running the whole length of the facade.

In 1696 the villagers undertook the construction of the simple **Église Saint-François-de-Sales** ★★ (*guided tours; Rue des Érables*). It was added to and altered during the following centuries, to the point where the original elements of the building have all but disappeared. A newer chancel was built in 1761, the nave was expanded in 1854, and finally, a new facade was added in 1915. The present church is the result of these transformations. The interior of the church houses an impressive piece of baroque art from the period of the French Regime: a wood baldaquin (richly ornamented canopy over the altar) ordered in 1695 for the chapel of the episcopal palace in Québec City.

★
Cap-Santé

The construction of the **Église Sainte-Famille** ★★ (*guides tours; ☎286-3002*) went on between 1754 and 1764 under the auspices of curate Joseph Filion, but was seriously disrupted by the British Conquest. In 1759, materials intended for the finishing touches on the building were requisitioned for the construction of Fort Jacques-Cartier. Nevertheless, the completed church, with its two steeples and its high nave lit

by two rows of windows, is an ambitious piece of work for its time, and was possibly the largest village church built under the French Regime. The three beautiful wooden statues placed in the alcoves of the facade in 1775 have miraculously survived Québec's harsh climate. The imitation cutstone done in wood covering the stone walls was added in the 19th century. Before stepping inside the church, be sure to visit the wooded cemetery and presbytery built by Thomas Baillargé in 1850.

Today the **Vieux Chemin** ★ (the old road) is nothing more than a simple road passing in front of the church, but it was once part of the Chemin du Roy that linked Montréal and Québec City. Numerous well-preserved 18th-century houses facing the river can still be seen along the road, making it one of the most picturesque drives in Canada.

★★
Deschambault

The charming tranquillity of this agricultural village on the banks of the St. Lawrence was a bit disturbed recently by the development of an aluminum smelter. Deschambault was founded thanks to the efforts of Seigneur Fleury de la Gorgendière who previously had a church built in nearby Cap Lauzon in 1720. Because the village has grown slowly, it retains its small-town charm.

The **Maison Deschambault** (*128 Route 138*) is visible at the end of a long tree-lined lane. The stone building equipped with fire-break walls was probably built in the late 18th

century. It was practically in ruins in 1936 when the Québec government, who owned the building at the time, undertook its restoration, a rarity in an era when many elements of Québec's heritage had already been lost. The building now houses a charming inn (see p 297), and a fine French restaurant (see p 301).

The **Vieux Presbytère** (*$1.50; Jun to Aug every day 9am to 5pm, May, Sep and Oct, Sat and Sun only, 10am to 5pm; 117 Rue Saint-Joseph, ☎286-6891*) occupies a prime location behind the church offering a beautiful panoramic view of the river and the south shore. The small presbytery building, set apart in the centre of a large lawn, was built in 1815 to replace the first presbytery dating from 1735. The foundations of the original building are visible near the entrance. In 1955, an antique dealer saved the presbytery from destruction, and then in 1970, a residents' association began using the building as an exhibition centre, demonstrating a dynamic community commitment to preserving its heritage.

★
Charlesbourg

The Notre-Dame-des-Anges seigneury was granted to the Jesuits in 1626, making it one of the first permanent settlements inhabited by Europeans in Canada. Despite this early settlement and original seigneurial design, few buildings built before the 19th century remain in Charlesbourg. The fragility of early buildings and the push to modernize are possible explanations for this void. Since 1950, Charlesbourg has become one of the main suburbs of

Vieux Presbytère

Québec City, and has lost much of its original character.

The **Église Saint-Charles-Borromée** ★★ (*135 80° Rue Ouest*) revolutionized the art of building in rural Québec. Architect Thomas Baillargé, influenced by the Palladian movement, showed particular innovation in the way he arranged the windows and doors of the facade to which he added a large pediment. Construction of the church began in 1828 and was uninterrupted. The original design has remained intact since. The magnificent interior decor by Baillargé was done in 1833.

★
Wendake

Forced off their land by the Iroquois in the 17th century, 300 Huron families moved to various places around Québec before settling in 1700 in Jeune-Lorette, known today as Wendake. Visitors will be charmed by the winding roads of the village in this native reserve located on the banks of the Rivière Saint-Charles. The museum and gift shop provide a lot of information on the culture of this peaceful and sedentary people.

The **Église Notre-Dame-de-Lorette** ★ (*140 Boulevard Bastien*), the Huron church, completed in 1730, is reminiscent of the first churches of New France. This humble building with a white plaster facade conceals unexpected treasures in its chancel and in the sacristy. Some of the objects on display were given to the Huron community by the Jesuits and come from the first chapel in Ancienne-Lorette (late 17th century). Among the works to be seen are several statues by Noël Levasseur, created between 1730 and 1740, an altar-facing depicting an Aboriginal village, by the Huron sculptor François Vincent (1790) and a beautiful *Vierge à l'Enfant* (Madonna and Child) sculpture, by a Parisian goldsmith (1717). In addition, the church has a reliquary made in 1676, chasubles from the 18th century and various liturgical objects by Paul Manis (circa 1715). However, the most interesting element is the small, Louis XIII-style gilded tabernacle on the high altar, sculpted by Levasseur in 1722.

The Huron village of **Onhoüa Chetek8e** (*$6; every day 9am to 5pm; 575 Rue Stanislas-Koska, ☎842-4308, ⇒842-3473*) is a replica of a Huron village from the time of early colonization. The traditional design includes wooden longhouses and fences. Visitors are given an introduction to the lifestyle and social organization of the ancient Huron nation. Various Aboriginal dishes are also served and worth a taste.

Charlevoix

The Charlevoix countryside could have been created for giants – the

Québec

villages tucked into bays or perched atop summits look like dollhouses left behind by a child. Rustic farmhouses and luxurious summer houses are scattered about, and some have been converted into inns. Although Charlevoix was one of the first regions in North America where tourism flourished, the area further inland is still a wilderness area of valleys and tranquil lakes.

★★
Baie-Saint-Paul

Charlevoix's undulating geography has proved a challenge to agricultural development. Under the French Regime, only a few attempts at colonisation

were made in this vast region that, along with parts of the Beaupré coast, was overseen by the Séminaire de Québec. Baie-Saint-Paul, at the mouth of the Rivière du Gouffre valley, was home to a few settlers.

Although Charlevoix has some of the planet's oldest rock formations, several major earthquakes have rocked the pastoral region since it was first colonized. The following description by Baptiste Plamondon, then vicar of Baie-Saint-Paul, appeared in the October 22, 1870 edition of the *Journal de Québec*:

"It was about half an hour before noon... a tremendous explosion stunned the population. Rather than simply tremble, the earth seemed to boil, such that it caused vertigo... The houses could have been on a volcano, the way they were tossed about. Water gushed fifteen feet into the air through cracks in the ground..."

A bend in the road reveals Baie-Saint-Paul in all its charm, and a slope leads to the heart of the village that has maintained a quaint small-town atmosphere. Set out on foot along the pleasant Rue Saint-Jean-Baptiste, Rue Saint-Joseph, and Rue Sainte-Anne where small wooden houses with man-

sard roofs now house boutiques and cafés. For over 100 years, Baie-Saint-Paul has attracted North American landscape artists, inspired by the mountains and a quality of light particular to Charlevoix. There are many art galleries and art centres in the area that display and sell beautiful Canadian paintings and sculptures.

A selection of paintings by Charlevoix artists is displayed in the modern building, the **Centre d'Art de Baie-Saint-Paul** ★ *(free admission; late Jun to early Sep, every day 9am to 7pm; early Sep to late Jun, every day*

9am to 5pm; 4 Rue Ambroise-Fafard, ☎435-3681, ⇋435-6269), designed in 1967 by architect Jacques DeBlois. A painting and sculpture symposium, where works by young artists are displayed, is held by the centre every August.

The **Centre d'Exposition de Baie-Saint-Paul** ★★ *($3; late Jun to early Sep, every day 9am to 7pm, early Sep to late Jun 9am to 5pm; 23 Rue Ambroise-Fafard,* ☎435-3681) is a museum and gallery completed in 1992 according to blueprints by architect Pierre Thibault. It houses travelling exhibits from around the world as well as the René Richard gallery where several paintings by this Swiss-born artist are on display (see below).

★
Saint-Joseph-de-la-Rive

The rhythm of life in this village on the St. Lawrence followed the rhythm of the river for many generations as the boats beached along the shore testify eloquently. In recent decades, however, tourism and handicrafts have replaced fishing and ship-building as the staples of the economy. East of the dock where the ferry to Île aux Coudres lands, a fine sandy beach tempts swimmers into the chilly saltwater. A little wooden building in front of the church is a reminder of the fragility of human endeavours within the immense marine landscape of Charlevoix.

The **Papeterie Saint-Gilles** ★ *(free admission; Jun to Dec, Mon to Fri 8am to 5pm, Sat and Sun 9am to 5pm; Jan to Mar, Sat 1pm to 5pm, Sun*

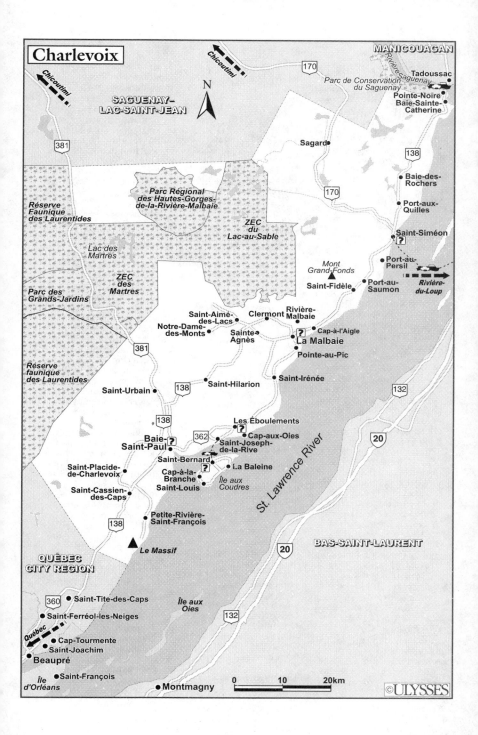

Manoir Richelieu

noon to 4pm; 304 Rue Félix-Antoine-Savard, ☎635-2430, ≈635-2613) is a traditional papermaking workshop founded in 1966 by priest and poet Félix-Antoine Savard (1896-1982, author of *Menaud Maître-Draveur*). He was assisted by Mark Donohue, a member of a famous Canadian pulp and paper dynasty. Museum guides explain the different stages involved in making paper using 17th century techniques. Saint-Gilles paper has a distinctive thick grain and flower or leaf patterns integrated into each piece, producing a high quality writing paper sold on site in various packages.

The **Exposition Maritime** ★★ (*$2; mid-May to mid-Jun and early Sep to mid-Oct, Mon to Fri 9am to 4pm, Sat to Sun 11am to 4pm, late Jun to Sep every day 9am to 5pm; 305 Place de l'Eglise*, ☎635-1131 or 635-2803, ≈635-2803), located in a shipyard, recaptures the golden era of the schooner. Visitors are welcome to climb aboard the boats on the premises.

★★
Île aux Coudres

Visitors are sometimes surprised to learn that a number of whale species live in the St. Lawrence. For several generations the economic livelihood of Île aux Coudres centred around whale hunting (mainly belugas) and whale blubber was melted to produce lamp oil. Ship building, mainly small craft, was also an important regional industry.

Île-aux-Coudres is the municipality that was formed when the villages of Saint-Bernard and Saint-Louis merged (*arrival and departure point on Île-aux-Coudres*). The ferry lands at the Quai de Saint-Bernard where the following tour of the island begins. The dock is the best place from which to contemplate the Charlevoix mountains. One of the last shipyards still in operation in the region can also be seen from here.

The **Musée Les Voitures d'Eau** ★ (*$4; mid-May to mid-Jun and mid-Sep to mid-Oct, Sat and Sun 10am to 5pm; mid-Jun to mid-Sep,* every day 10am to 6pm; Chemin des Coudriers, Île aux Coudres, ☎438-2208) presents exhibits dealing with the history, construction and navigation of the small craft once built in the region. The museum was founded in 1973 by Captain Éloi Perron who recovered the wreck of the schooner *Mont-Saint-Louis*, now on display.

The **Moulins Desgagné** ★★, or **Moulins de l'Isle-aux-Coudres** (*$2.75; mid-May to mid-Jun and late Aug to mid-Oct, every day 10am to 5pm; mid-Jun to late Aug, every day 9am to 6:30pm; 247 Chemin du Moulin, Île aux Coudres, ☎438-2184*). It is extremely rare to find a water mill and a windmill operating together. Indeed, the Saint-Louis mills are a unique pair in Québec. Erected in 1825 and 1836 respectively, the mills complement one another by alternately generating power according to prevailing climatic conditions. Along with a forge and milling house, the mills were restored by the Québec government, which also has established on-site information centres. The machinery necessary for operation is still in perfect condition and is now back at work grinding wheat and buckwheat into flour. Bread is made in an antique wood oven.

★
Les Éboulements

In 1663, a violent earthquake in the region caused a gigantic landslide. It's said that half a small mountain sank into the river. The village of les Éboulements is named after the event (*éboulements* means landslide in English).

★ Saint-Irénée

Saint-Irénée, or Saint-Irénée-les-Bains, as it was known during the Belle Époque, is the gateway to the part of Charlevoix usually considered the oldest vacation spot in North America. In the late 18th century, British sportsmen were the first Europeans to enjoy the pleasures of the simple life that the wild region had to offer. They were followed by wealthy Americans escaping the heat of summer in the United States. Wealthy English- and French-Canadian families also had summer houses with lovely gardens built for them in Charlevoix. Saint-Irénée is renowned for its picture-perfect landscapes and classical music festival.

★ La Malbaie– Pointe-au-Pic

On his way to Québec City in 1608, Samuel de Champlain anchored in a Charlevoix bay for the night. To his surprise, he awoke the next morning to find his fleet resting on land and not in water. Champlain learned that day what many navigators would come to learn as well. The water recedes a great distance in this region and will trap any boat not moored in deep enough water. In exasperation, he exclaimed *"Ah! La malle baye!"* (Old French which translates roughly to "Oh what a bad bay!"), inadvertently providing the name for many sites in the region. The towns of Pointe-au-Pic, La Malbaie, and Cap-à-l'Aigle now form a continuous web of streets and houses lining the bay.

The Malbaie seigneury passed through three owners before being seriously developed. Jean Bourdon received the land for services rendered to the French crown in 1653. Too busy with his job as prosecutor for the king, he invested nothing in it. The seigneury was then granted to Philippe Gaultier de Comporté in 1672. Following his death, it was sold by his family to merchants Hazeur and Soumande who harvested wood on the property for the construction of ships in France. The seigneury became crown property in 1724. Exceptionally, it was then granted, under English occupation to Captain John Nairne and Officer Malcolm Fraser in 1762 who began colonizing it.

Seigneurs Nairne and Fraser initiated a long-standing tradition of hospitality in Charlevoix. In their respective manors, they hosted friends and even strangers from Scotland and England. Following the example of these seigneurs, French Canadians began welcoming visitors from Montréal and Québec during the summer months. Eventually, larger inns had to be built to accommodate the increasing number of urban vacationers now arriving on steamships that moored at the dock in Pointe-au-Pic. Among the wealthy visitors was U.S. President Howard Taft and his family, who were very fond of Charlevoix.

In the early 20th century, a wave of wealthy Americans and English Canadians built summer houses along **Chemin des Falaises**, a street well worth exploring. The houses reflect popular architectural styles of the period, including the charming Shingle Style

characteristic of seaside resorts on the U.S. east coast, that's distinguished by a cedar shingle exterior. Another popular trend at the time was to build houses that resembled 17th-century French manor houses, complete with turrets and shuttered casement windows. Beginning in 1920, the architecture of summer residences started to incorporate traditional local building styles. La Malbaie architect Jean Charles Warren (1869-1929) became known for designing a style of rustic furniture inspired by local traditions and the English Arts and Crafts movement. Owning one of his creations became a must among summer residents. The most important and impressive building from the turn-of-the-century construction boom is the Manoir Richelieu, at the west end of Chemin des Falaises.

La Malbaie is now the regional administrative centre and, since its amalgamation with the neighbouring municipality of Pointe-au-Pic in 1995, has confirmed its position of strength within the region's tourist industry. It is henceforth officially known as "La Malbaie–Pointe-au-Pic".

The original wood building of the **Manoir Richelieu** ★ ★ (*181 Avenue Richelieu*), the only grand hotel in Charlevoix to survive, was built in 1899. Destroyed in a fire, it was replaced by the current cement building in 1929. The hotel was designed by architect John Smith Archibald in the Château Style. Many famous people have stayed at the hotel from Charlie Chaplin to the King of Siam and the Vanderbilts of New York City. The casino is a recon-

Québec

struction of the Château Ramezay in Montréal. Visitors not staying at the Manoir can nevertheless discreetly walk through its hallways, elegant salons and gardens overlooking the St. Lawrence.

The region's number-one attraction is the **Casino de Charlevoix** (183 Avenue Richelieu, ☎665-5300 or 800-665-2274, ≈665-5322), an attractively designed European-style casino located next to the Manoir Richelieu. Proper dress required.

Cap-à-l'Aigle

From Boulevard de Comporté in La Malbaie, visitors can catch a glimpse of a stately stone house sitting high on the Cap-à-l'Aigle escarpment. The building is the old manor house of the Malcolm Fraser seigneurs, a property also known as Mount Murray. It is matched to the east of Rivière Malbaie by the John Nairne seigneury, established west of the waterway and simply named Murray Bay in honour of James Murray, British Governor at the time. Cap-à-l'Aigle, whose tourism industry dates back to the 18th century, forms the heart of the Mount Murray seigneury.

Jardins aux Quatre Vents ★★ (*by appointment only, on the left hand side of Route 138*), on the grounds of the Cabot family estate, is one of the most beautiful private gardens in Québec. The garden is meticulously tended and expanded annually. Unfortunately, it is open to the public for only a few days every year. Strictly speaking, the gardens comprise 22 separate gardens, each one having its own theme.

For example, there is the Potager en Terrasses (terraced vegetable garden), the Jardin du Ravin (ravine garden), Les Cascades (waterfalls), and the Lac des Libellules (dragonfly lake). The Quatre Vents (four winds) garden began in 1928 with the planting of the Jardin Blanc (white garden) where all the flowers are, naturally, white as snow.

Mauricie–Centre-du-Québec

The Valley of the Rivière Saint-Maurice is located halfway between Montréal and Québec City on the north shore of the St. Lawrence River. As the cradle of Canada's first major industry, Mauricie has always been an industrial region. Its towns feature fine examples of architecture of the industrial revolution. Nevertheless, the vast countryside surrounding the towns remains primarily an area of mountain wilderness covered in dense forest, perfect for hunting, fishing, camping and hiking.

★★ Trois-Rivières

The look of the town, once similar to Vieux-Québec, was completely changed by a fire in June 1908. It now resembles more a town of the American Midwest. Often considered as simply a place to stop for a break between Montréal and Québec, Trois-Rivières is unfortunately underestimated by most tourists. However, it remains a city redolent of Old-World charm with its many cafés, restaurants and bars on Rue des Forgesas well as the terrace overlooking the St.

Lawrence. Halfway between Montréal and Québec City, this urban centre is home to 100,000 people.

Trois-Rivières is located at the confluence of the St. Lawrence and Saint-Maurice rivers where the latter divides into three branches, giving the town its name. It was founded in 1634 by Sieur de Laviolette. From the outset, the town was surrounded by a stone wall that now marks the city's historic area. In the 17th century, there were three regional governments in the St. Lawrence valley apart from the Governor of New France: that of Québec City, Montréal, and Trois-Rivières. More modest than its two sister cities, the latter boasted a population of a mere 600 and a total of 110 houses. The real boom took place in the middle of the 19th century with the advent of the pulp and paper industry. For a time, Trois-Rivières was the world's leading paper producer.

The **Cathédrale de l'Assomption** ★ (*Mon to Sat 7am to 11:30am and 2pm to 5:30pm, Sun 8:30am to 11:30am and 2pm to 5pm, reservations neccesary for groups; 362 Rue Bonaventure* ☎374-2409) was built in 1858 according to the plans of architect Victor Bourgeau, well known for the many churches he designed in the Montréal area. The cathedral's massive Gothic-Revival style is vaguely reminiscent of London's Westminster Abbey, also designed in the mid-19th century. Guido Nincheri's stained-glass windows, executed between 1923 and 1934, are certainly the most colourful element in what is otherwise an austere interior.

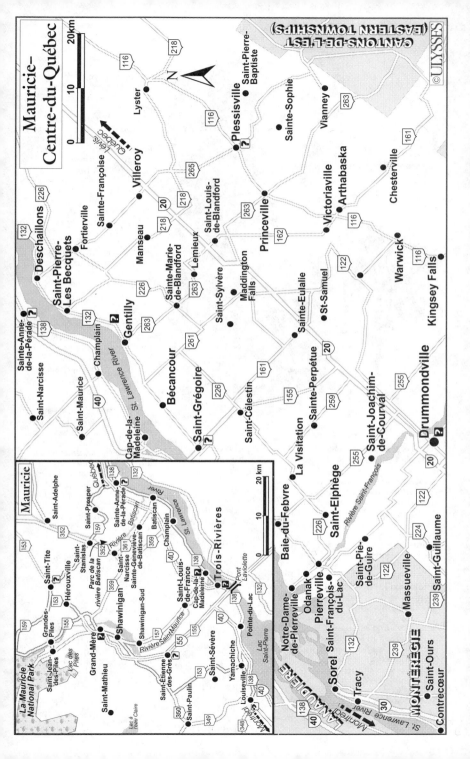

Mauricie—
Centre-du-Québec

Sanctuaire Notre-Dame-du-Cap

The **Forges du Saint-Maurice National Historic Site** ★★ (*$4; mid-May to mid-Oct, every day 9am to 5pm, group reservations necessary; 10000 Boulevard des Forges, ☎378-5116, ≈378-0887*) is also called Lieu Historique National Les Forges du Saint-Maurice. These iron-works began in 1730 when Louis XV granted permis-sion to François Poulin de Francheville to work the rich veins of iron-ore that lay under his land. The presence of dense wood lots (a source of charcoal), limestone, and a swift-run-ning waterway, favoured the production of iron. The workers of this first Canadian ironworks mostly came from Bur-gundy and Franche-Comté in France. They were kept busy making cannons for

the king and wood-burn-ing stoves for his subjects in New France.

After the British conquest (1760), the plant passed into the hands of the Brit-ish colonial government, which in turn ceded it to a private enterprise. The works were in use until 1883. At that time, the plant included the smelter and forges as well as the Grande Maison (the fore-man's house) at the centre of a worker's village. Fol-lowing the 1908 fire, the residents of Trois-Rivières recuperated the material necessary to rebuild their town from the forge, leav-ing only the foundations of most buildings. In 1973, Parks Canada acquired the site and rebuilt the fore-man's house to serve as an information centre. They

set up a second, very inter-esting centre on the site of the smelting forge.

The visit begins at the foreman's house, a huge white building said to have been inspired by the archi-tecture of Burgundy. Vari-ous aspects of life at the ironworks are presented, as are the products of the works. On the second floor is a model depicting the layout of the works in 1845. The model is used as the basis of a sound and light show after which the site can be perused by walking along various footpaths.

Cap-de-la-Madeleine

As the heartland of Cathol-icism in North America, Québec is home to a num-ber of major pilgrimage destinations visited every year by millions from all over the world.

The **Sanctuaire Notre-Dame-du-Cap** ★★ (*free admission, schedule varies depending on the season, guided visit for groups by appointment, from May to Oct, visitors can par-ticipate in the symbolic torch-flame walk in good weather; 626 Rue Notre-Dame, ☎374-2441, www.sanctuaire-ndc.ca*), a shrine under the auspices of the Oblate Missionaries of the Virgin Mary, is consecrated to the worship of the Virgin. The history of this sanctu-ary began in 1879 when it was decided a new parish church was needed in Cap-de-la-Madeleine. Be-ing the month of March, the stones for the new church had to be trans-ported from the south side of the river. Strangely, the river had not frozen over that winter.

Following the prayers and rosaries addressed to the statue of the Virgin pre

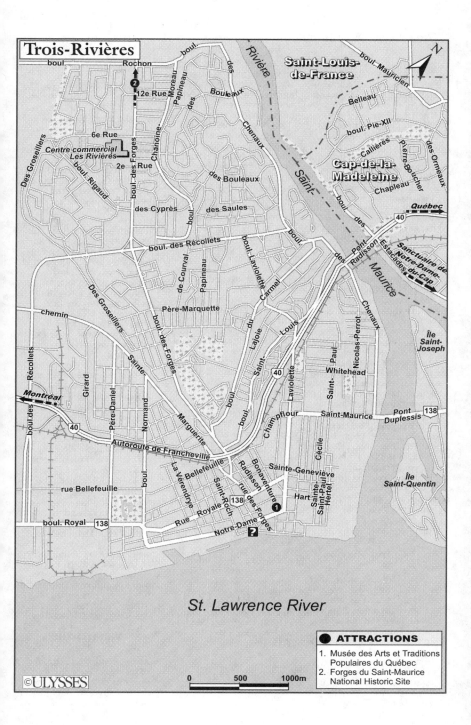

sented to the parish in 1854, an ice-bridge formed "as if by miracle," allowing the necessary stones to be transported in one week. The parish priest, Father Désilet, decided to preserve the old church and to turn it into a sanctuary devoted to the Virgin. Built between 1714 and 1717, the sanctuary is one of the oldest churches in Canada. Visitors meditate before the statue of the Virgin. In 1888, it is recounted that the statue opened its eyes in front of several witnesses.

Today, the miraculous ice-bridge is symbolized by the **Pont des Chapelets** (1924), visible in the garden of the sanctuary. A Stations of the Cross, a calvary, a holy sepulchre and a small lake complete this riverside garden. Surrounded by an expanse of asphalt and looking like something from the set of a Cecil B. DeMille movie is the enormous **Basilique Notre-Dame-du-Rosaire**. Work on the basilica was begun in 1955 by architect Adrien Dufresne, a disciple of Dom Bellot. The Dutch master glazier Jan Tillemans created three sets of windows depicting the history of the sanctuary, that of Canada, and the mysteries of the rosary.

★ Grand-Mère

The town was named after a rock bearing a strong resemblance to the profile of an old woman. Found on an island in the middle of the Saint-Maurice, the rock was transported piece by piece to a park in downtown Grand-Mère when the hydro-electric dam was constructed in 1913. The town and its neighbour Shawinigan are good examples of "com-

pany towns" where life revolves around one or two factories. Their presence extends to the residential patterns, the towns being divided into two distinct sections, one for management (mostly anglophone at first) and one for workers (almost exclusively francophone). The town features many well thought-out industrial buildings designed by talented architects brought in from outside the area.

Grand-Mère came into being at the end of the 19th century with the development of the forestry industry. Pulp and paper factories processed trees cut down in the logging camps of Haute-Mauricie. The town was developed in 1897 by the Laurentide Pulp and Paper Company, the property of John Foreman, Sir William Van Horne and Russell Alger, hero of the American Civil War. After the 1929 Stock Market Crash, the town's economy diversified and moved away from the pulp and paper industry that had helped it grow.

The **Église Catholique Saint-Paul de Grand-Mère ★** (*on the corner of 6ᵉ Avenue and 4ᵉ Rue*) has an false Italian-style facade put up in 1908. The colourful interior from the 1920s is adorned with both re-mounted paintings by Montréal artist Monty and a Guido Nincheri fresco depicting the apotheosis of St. Paul. The high altar, as well as the side altars, is marble. Behind the church is an Ursuline convent affiliated with the one in Trois-Rivières.

Shawinigan

In 1899, Shawinigan became the first city in Québec to be laid out according to the principles of urban planning, thanks to the powerful Shawinigan Water and Power Company that supplied electricity to all of Montréal. The name of this hilly town means "portage at the peak" in Algonquian. The town itself was hard hit by the recession of 1989-93 that left indelible marks on its urban landscape: abandoned factories, burnt-out buildings, empty lots and so on. Nevertheless, Shawinigan boasts many architecturally interesting buildings from the first third of the 20th century. Some of its residential streets resemble those of interwar English suburbs.

Inaugurated in the spring of 1997, the **Cité de l'Énergie** (*$14; early Jun 1 to Jun 25 10am to 5pm, Jun 26 to Sep 4 Mon to Sun 10am to 8pm, Sep 5 to Oct 15 Tue to Sun 10am to 5pm; 1000 Avenue Melville, G9N 6T9, ☎536-4992, 536-2982 or 800-383-2483*) promises to acquaint many a visitor, children and adults alike, with the history of industrial development in Québec in general and Mauricie in particular. The hub of this development is the town of Shawinigan, singled out by aluminum factories and electric companies at the beginning of the 20ᵗʰ century thanks to the strong currents in the Rivière Saint-Maurice and the 50m-high falls nearby.

Victoriaville

As the economic heartland of the area, Victoriaville owes its development to the forestry and steel industries. Named after Queen Victoria who reigned at the time of the town's establishment (1861), it now incorporates the surrounding municipalities of Arthabaska and Sainte-Victoire-d'Arthabaska.

Arthabaska ★, the southern portion of Victoriaville, means "place of bulrushes and reeds" in the native language. It has produced or welcomed more than its share of prominent figures in the worlds of art and politics. Its residential sectors have always boasted a refined architecture, notably in the European and American styles. The town is especially known for its Victorian houses, particularly those along Avenue Laurier Ouest. In 1859, Arthabaska became the judicial district of the township. Then followed the construction of the courthouse, the prison and the registry office that would make the fortune of the town. While Arthabaska was superseded by Victoriaville at the turn of the century and these buildings have now been demolished, it still retains a good part of its Belle Époque charm.

The **Maison Suzor-Côté** (*846 Boulevard Centre-du-Québec Sud*) is the birthplace of landscape painter Marc-Aurèle de Foy Suzor-Côté (1869-1937). His father had built the humble home 10 years earlier. One of Canada's foremost artists, Suzor-Côté began his career decorating churches, including Arthabaska's, before leaving to study at Paris's École des Beaux-Arts in 1891. After taking first prize at both the Julian and Colarossi academies, he worked in Paris before moving to Montréal in 1907. From then on, he returned annually to the family house, gradually turning it into a studio. His impressionist winter scenes and July sunsets are well-known. The house is still a private residence (*not open to the public*).

The **Musée Laurier** ★ (*$3.50; Jul to Aug, Mon to Fri 9am to 5pm, Sat and Sun 1pm to 5pm; Sep to Jun, Tue to Fri 9am to noon and 1pm to 5pm, Sat and Sun 1pm to 5pm; 16 Rue Laurier Ouest, ☎357-8655*) occupies the house of the first French-Canadian Prime Minister (1896 to 1911), Sir Wilfrid Laurier (1841-1919). Born in Saint-Lin in the Basses-Laurentides, Laurier moved to Arthabaska as soon as he finished his legal studies. Two admirers turned his house into a museum in 1929.

The ground floor rooms retain their Victorian furniture while the second floor is partly devoted to exhibits. Paintings and sculptures by Québéc artists encouraged by the Lauriers are on view throughout the house. Of particular interest are the portrait of Lady Laurier by Suzor-Côté and the bust of Sir Wilfrid Laurier by Alfred Laliberté.

Drummondville

Drummondville was founded in the wake of the War of 1812 by Frederick George Heriot who gave it the name of the British Governor of the time, Sir Gordon Drummond. The colony was at first a military outpost on the Rivière Saint-François but the building of mills and factories soon made it a major industrial centre.

The **Village Québécois d'Antan** ★ ★ (*$11; early Jun to early Sep, every day 10am to 6pm; Sep, every day 11am to 4pm; 1425 Rue Montplaisir, ☎478-1441*) traces 100 years of history. Some 70 colonial-era buildings have been reproduced to evoke the atmosphere of village life from 1810 to 1910. People in period costume make *ceintures fléchées* (v-design sashes), candles and bread. Many historical television shows are shot on location here.

The **Parc des Voltigeurs** ★ has recently been undergoing a facelift. The only heritage building between Montréal and Québec, which happens to be visible from Highway 20, lies in the southern part of the park. The **Manoir Trent**, built in 1848 for retired British Navy officer George Norris Trent, is not really a manor but a large farmhouse. It was acquired by the Compagnons de l'École Hotelière, a training school for hoteliers, which is also a reference centre that lets visitors sample its culinary attempts.

Québec

Chaudière-Appalaches

This tour is dotted with charming villages at regular intervals along the majestic St-Lawrence. It encompasses both the Rive-Sud of Québec City and the Côte-du-Sud (the southern shore and coast), gradually taking on a maritime flavour as the river widens. Visitors will enjoy stunning views of this vast stretch of water as its colour varies with the time of day and temperature as well as Île d'Orléans and the mountains of Charlevoix. The tour also features some of the loveliest examples of traditional architecture in Québec, including churches, seigneurial manors, mills and old houses, whose windows open onto vast open spaces. It is perhaps this region that best represents rural Québec.

★ Lotbinière

Granted to René-Louis Chartier de Lotbinière in 1672, the seigneury of Lotbinière is one of the few estates to have always remained in the hands of the same family. Since he had a seat on the Conseil Souverain (sovereign council), the first seigneur did not actually live on the premises. Nevertheless, he saw to it that the land and the village of Lotbinière were developed. At the heart of Lotbinière, which quickly became one of the most important villages in the region, visitors will find many old houses made of stone and wood. This area is now protected by the provincial government.

Along with its presbytery and former convent, the monumental **Église Saint-Louis ★★** (*7510 Rue Marie-Victorin*) provides a lovely setting from which to enjoy a view of the river. Set parallel to the St-

Lawrence, the present building is the fourth Catholic church to be built in the seigneury of Lotbinière. Designed by François Baillargé, it was begun in 1818. The spires as well as the crown of the facade are the result of modifications made in 1888. Its polychromatic exterior – white walls, blue steeples and red roof – creates a surprising (and very French) tricolour effect.

The church is a masterpiece of traditional religious art in Québec. Without question, the key piece is the neoclassical reredos shaped like a triumphal arch, sculpted by Thomas Baillargé in 1824. In the middle hang three paintings dating back to 1730, which are attributed to Frère François Brékenmacher, a Récollet monk from the Montréal monastery. The organ in the jube, originally intended for the Anglican cathedral in Québec City, was built in London by the Elliott Company in 1802.

Domaine Joly de Lotbinière

Too high for the Anglican church, it was put into storage before being acquired by Père Faucher, the parish priest, in 1846. A century later, it was restored and equipped for electric power by the Casavant Company of Saint-Hyacinthe.

Sainte-Croix

The Chartier de Lotbinière lineage dates back to the 11th century. In the service of French kings for many generations, the family preserved its contacts with the motherland even after establishing itself in Canada, despite the British conquest and the distance between the two lands. In 1828, Julie-Christine Chartier de Lotbinière married Pierre-Gustave Joly, a rich Huguenot merchant from Montréal. In 1840, Joly purchased a part of the Sainte-Croix land from the Québec City Ursulines to build a seigneurial manor there. It would come to be known as the Manoir de la Pointe Platon, or the Domaine Joly de Lotbinière.

Domaine Joly de Lotbinière ★★ (*$6; mid-Jun to Sep every day 10am to 7pm; mid-May to mid Jun and Sep to mid-Oct on weekends; Route de la Pointe-Platon,* ☎926-2462) is part of the Jardins de Québec association. The main attraction here is the superb setting on the banks of the St-Lawrence. It's especially worthwhile to take the footpaths to the beach to gaze out at the river, the slate cliffs and the opposite shore, where the Église de Cap Santé is visible. Numerous rare century-old trees, floral arrangements and an aviary adorn the grounds of the estate. There is also a boutique and café with a patio. Built in 1840 to overlook the river, the manor is designed as a villa with wraparound verandas.

Though the interior is disappointing, it does include a small exhibition on the family of the Marquis de Lotbinière. Visitors will learn, for example, that Henri-Gustave, the son of Pierre-Gustave Joly, was born in Épernay (France). He later became Premier of Québec (1878-79), federal Revenue Minister and finally Lieutenant-Governor of British Columbia. The Domaine Joly de Lotbinière came under the care of the provincial government in 1967 when the last seigneur, Edmond Joly de Lotbinière, had to vacate the premises.

★★
Lévis

Founded by Henry Caldwell in 1826, Lévis developed rapidly during the second half of the 19th century due to the introduction of the railroad (1854) and the establishment of several local shipyards supplied with wood by sawmills owned by the Price and Hamilton families. With no railway line on the north shore of the St-Lawrence at the time, some of Québec City's shipping activities were transferred to Lévis. Originally known as Ville d'Aubigny, Lévis was given its present name in 1861 in memory of Chevalier François de Lévis who defeated the British in the Battle of Sainte-Foy in 1760. The upper part of the city, consisting mostly of administrative buildings, offers some interesting views of Vieux-Québec that's located on the opposite side of the river. The very narrow lower part welcomes the trains and the ferry linking Lévis to the provincial capital. Lévis merged with its neighbour, **Lauzon**, in 1990.

Built during the stock market crash of 1929, the **Terrasse de Lévis** ★★ (*Rue William-Tremblay*) offers spectacular views of downtown Lévis and Québec City. From here, you can take in Vieux-Québec's Place Royale, located along the river, and the Château Frontenac and Haute-Ville above. A few modern skyscrapers stand out in the background, the tallest being the Édifice Marie-Guyart located on Québec City's Parliament Hill.

Maison Alphonse-Desjardins (*free admission; Mon to Fri 10am to noon and 1pm to 4:30pm, Sat and Sun noon to 5pm; 6 Rue du Mont-Marie,* ☎835-2090). Alphonse Desjardins (1854-1920) was a stubborn man. Eager for the advancement of the French-Canadian people, he struggled for many years to promote the concept of the *caisse populaire* (credit union), a cooperative financial institution controlled by its members, and by all the small investors who hold accounts there. In the family kitchen of his house on Rue Mont-Marie, Desjardins and his wife Dorimène conceived the idea and set up the first *caisse populaire*. At first, the Caisses Desjardins aroused suspicion, but eventually became an important economic lever. Today there are more than 1,200 branches across Québec with more than 5 million members.

The Gothic Revival house where the Desjardins lived for nearly 40 years was built in 1882. It was beau-

Québec

tifully restored on its 100th anniversary and converted into an information centre which focuses on Desjardins's career and achievements. Visitors can watch a video and see several restored rooms. The offices of the Société Historique Alphonse-Desjardins are located on the second floor.

Maison Alphonse-Desjardins

The **Fort No.1 at Pointe de Lévy National Historic Site** ★ (*$3; mid-May to mid-Jun, Sun to Fri 9am to 4pm; mid-Jun to late Aug, every day 10am to 5pm; early Sep to late Oct, Sun noon to 4pm; 41 Chemin du Gouvernement,* ☎*835-5182*) is also called the Lieu Historique National du Fort-Numéro-Un. Fearing a surprise attack from the Americans at the end of the Civil War, the British (and later Canadian) government built three separate forts in Lévis that were incorporated into Québec City's defence system. Only Fort No.1 remains intact.

Made of earth and stone, it illustrates the evolution of fortified structures in the 19th century when military techniques were advancing rapidly. Visitors will be particularly interested in the rifled bore (an imposing piece of artillery) as well as the vaulted pillboxes and the caponiers, masonry structures intended to protect the moat. The site also includes an exhibition on the history of the fort. Finally, from the top of the wall, visitors can enjoy a lovely view of Québec City and Île d'Orléans. A little further along are the remnants of **Fort de la Martinière** (*$2; May to Oct, every day 9am to 4pm; Nov to Apr, Mon to Fri 9am to 4pm; 9805 Boul. de la Rive-Sud,* ☎*833-6620*) which also offers an exhibition of various implements of war. The grounds have picnic areas.

Montmagny

The **Centre Éducatif des Migrations** ★ (*$6; late Apr to mid-Nov, every day 9:30am to 5:30pm; 53 Rue du Bassin-Nord,* ☎*248-4565*) is located on the Pointe-aux-Oies campsite. This information centre on bird migrations deals with the *sauvagine*, or snow goose. It also has a theatre presenting a sound and light show about the colonization of the region and the arrival of immigrants at Grosse-Île. The sound and light show is an excellent way to begin your visit to Grosse-Île. Though the link between these two

subjects seems somewhat tenuous, the exhibits and the show are extremely instructive.

Grosse Île and the Irish Memorial National Historic Site ★★ (*independent or guided visits; May to Oct; A catering service is available on site (at a higher cost). Instead, we suggest you bring your own lunch for a picnic by the shore where there are tables for visitors.* ☎*248-8888 or 800-463-6769*) is also called the Lieu Historique National de la Grosse-Île-et-le-Mémorial-des-Irlandais. An excursion to Grosse Île is to step back into the sad history of North American immigration. Fleeing epidemics and famine, Irish emigrants to Canada were particularly numerous from the 1830s to the 1850s. In order to limit the spread of cholera and typhus in the New World, authorities required transatlantic passengers to submit to a quarantine before allowing them to disembark at the port of Québec. Grosse Île was the logical location for this isolation camp, far enough from the mainland to sequester its residents effectively, but close enough to be convenient. On this "Quarantine Island", each immigrant was inspected with a fine-tooth comb. Travellers in good health stayed in "hotels" whose luxury depended on the class of the berths they had occupied on the ships. The sick were immediately hospitalized.

A total of four million immigrants from 42 different countries passed through the port of Québec between 1832 and 1937. It is impossible to ascertain how many of these spent time on Grosse Île but close to 7,000 people perished there. In 1847, the year of the Great Potato

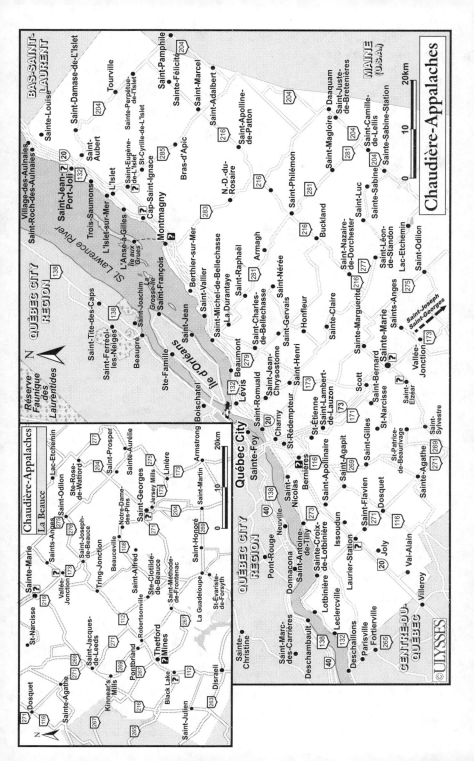

Chaudière-Appalaches

Famine, a major cause of Irish emigration, the typhus epidemic was particularly virulent and especially hard on Irish immigrants. Among the 7,000 deaths registered over 105 years, 5,434 were counted in this tragic year.

In memory of this sad year, people of Irish descent have made pilgrimages to Grosse Île every year since 1909. A Celtic cross stands on the island in memory of those who came here and those who unfortunately did not survive the experience. On March 17 1997, Saint Patrick's Day, Minister of Canadian Heritage Sheila Copps remembered the tragedy by renaming the site Grosse Île and the Irish Memorial National Historic Site.

The guided tour of Grosse Île, partly made on a small motorized train, reveals the island's natural beauty and its built structures. Among the 30 buildings still standing, a few are now open to the public. Open since the summer of 1997 and presently being restored, the disinfecting building informs visitors about Canadian technology at the end of the 19th century and gives them a glimpse inside a lazar house (a hospital for people with infectious diseases).

This is where victims of the 1847 typhoid epidemic were quarantined. These precious remnants of a tragic page in Canadian history give the place a particular allure. Thanks to the help of Parks Canada, history comes to life here. The barracks still stand, as does the imposing disinfection building, recently opened to the public for the first time. Together, these buildings recount a

page of the tragic history of this part of the continent.

Île aux Grues ★★ is the only island of the Isle-aux-Grues archipelago that is inhabited year round. It is an excellent spot for watching snow geese in the spring, for hunting in autumn, and for walking in summer. Locked in by ice during the winter, residents can only access the mainland by airplane. A few rural inns dot this 10km-long agricultural island. A bicycle trip through its golden wheat fields along the river is one of the more pleasant ways to explore the area. The island is also accessible by car thanks to the Grue des Îles ferry (see p 268). At the centre of the island is the village of **Saint-Antoine-de-l'Isle-aux-Grues** with its little church and its lovely houses. There is a craft shop, a cheese store that sells a delicious locally produced cheese, and a small museum that reveals past and present traditions of island life. To the east is the **Manoir Seigneurial McPherson-LeMoine** that was rebuilt for Louis Liénard Villemonde Beaujeu after the island was sacked by the British army in 1759. This attractive house, fronted by a long gallery, was the summer home of historian James McPherson-LeMoine at the end of the 19th century. Today, it is the haven of painter Jean-Paul Riopelle.

There is a small tourist information stand at the end of the dock that is staffed during the high season. If you plan to spend a few days on the island, bring enough cash since there is only one small bank on the island.

(It does'nt have an automatic teller machine).

★
L'Islet-sur-Mer

As its name ("Islet by the Sea") suggests, this village's activities are centred around the sea. Since the 18th century, local residents have been handing down the occupations of sailor and captain on the St. Lawrence from father to son. Some have even become highly skilled captains and explorers on distant seas. In 1677, Governor Frontenac granted the seigneury of L'Islet to two families – the Bélangers and the Couillards – who quickly developed their lands. They turned both L'Islet-sur-Mer, on the banks of the St-Lawrence, and L'Islet, farther inland, into prosperous communities that still play an important role in the region.

The wind coming off the sea is a gauge of the immensity of the nearby river. A good place to breathe this sea air is from the front step of the **Église Notre-Dame-de-Bonsecours** ★★ (*15 Rue des Pionniers Est, Route 132*). The present church, begun in 1768, is a large stone building with no transepts. Executed between 1782 and 1787, the interior decor reflects the teachings of the Académie Royale d'Architecture in Paris where the designer François Baillargé had recently been a student. Unlike earlier churches, the reredos consequently mimics the shape of the semicircular chancel, itself completely covered with gilded Louis-XV and Louis-XVI-style wood panelling. The coffered ceiling was added in the 19th century as were the spires on the steeples that were redone in 1882. The tabernacle was designed by Noël Levasseur and came from the original church in 1728. Above it hangs *L'Annonciation* (The Annunciation) painted by Abbé Aide-Créquy in 1776. The glass doors on the left open onto the former congregationist chapel that was added to the church in 1853. Occasional summer exhibitions with religious themes are put on there.

With objects related to fishing, ship models, an interpretive centre and two real ships, the **Musée Maritime Bernier** ★★ (*$9; mid-May to mid-Jun and mid-Sep to mid-Oct, every day 9am to 5pm; mid-Jun to early Sep, every day 9am to 6pm; the rest of the year, Tue to Fri, 10am to noon and 1pm to 4pm; 55 Rue des Pionniers Est, ☎247-5001*) recounts the maritime history of the St-Lawrence from the 17th century to the present day. Founded by the Association des Marins du Saint-Laurent, the institution occupies the former Couvent de l'Islet-sur-Mer (1877) and bears the name of one of the village's most illustrious citizens, Captain J. E. Bernier (1852-1934). Bernier was one of the first individuals to explore the Arctic, thus securing Canadian sovereignty in the Far North.

★
Saint-Jean-Port-Joli

Saint-Jean-Port-Joli has become synonymous with handicrafts, specifically wood carving. The origins of this tradition go back to the Bourgault family which made its living carving wood in the early 20th century. On the way into the town, Route 132 is lined with an impressive

number of shops where visitors can purchase a wooden pipe-smoking grandfather or knitting woman. A museum exhibits the finest pieces. Though the handicraft business is flourishing now more than ever, the village is also known for its church and for Philippe Aubert de Gaspé's novel *Les Anciens Canadiens* (Canadians of Old), written at the seigneurial manor.

The charming **Église Saint-Jean-Baptiste** ★★ (*2 Avenue de Gaspé Ouest*), built between 1779 and 1781, is recognizable by its bright red roof topped by two steeples and placed in a way altogether uncommon in Québec architecture: one in the front, the other in the back at the beginning of the apse. The church has a remarkable interior made of carved, gilded wood. Pierre Noël Levasseur's rocaille tabernacle, crowned with a wood shell supported by columns, comes from the original chapel and dates back to 1740. The side galleries, added to the nave in order to increase the number of pews, are also somewhat rare in Québec. Those in Saint-Jean-Port-Joli, dating back to 1845, are the only ones to have survived the waves of renovation and restoration of the past 40 years.

★★
Saint-Roch-des-Aulnaies

This pretty village on the banks of the St. Lawrence is actually made up of two neighbourhoods. The one around the church is called Saint-Roch-des-Aulnaies while the other, not far from the manor, is known as the Village des Aulnaies. The name

"Aulnaies" refers to the abundance of alder trees (*aulnes*) that grow along the Rivière Ferrée and powers the seigneurial mill. Nicolas Juchereau, the son of Jean Juchereau, Sieur de Maur from Perche, was granted the seigneury in 1656. Most of the old residences in Saint-Roch-des-Aulnaies are exceptionally large – a sign that local inhabitants enjoyed a certain degree of prosperity in the 19th century. The manor and its mill are located on the right after the bridge that spans the Rivière Ferrée.

Seigneurie des Aulnaies ★★ (*$6; late May to early Sep, every day 9am to 6pm; mid-May to mid-Oct; every day, 10am to 4pm; 525 Chemin de la Seigneurie, ☎354-2800*). The Dionne estate has been transformed into a fascinating information centre, focusing on the seigneurial era. Visitors are greeted in the former miller's house, converted into a shop and café. Its menu includes pancakes and muffins made with flour ground in the neighbouring mill, a large stone structure rebuilt in 1842 on the site of an older mill. Guided tours of the mill in operation enable visitors to understand its complex gearing system, set in motion by the Rivière Ferrée. Its main milling wheel is the largest in Québec.

A long staircase leads to the manor that stands on a promontory. Like the manor in Lotbinière, this looks more like a charming villa than an austere seigneurial residence. Interactive display units, set up in different rooms in the basement, provide a detailed explanation of the principles behind the seigneurial system and its im-

Québec

pact on the rural landscape of Québec. The more sober main floor contains reception rooms furnished according to 19th-century tastes.

Saint-Georges

Divided into Saint-Georges-Ouest and Saint-Georges-Est on either side of the Rivière Chaudière, this industrial capital of the Beauce region is reminiscent of a New England manufacturing town. A German-born merchant by the name of Georges Pfotzer is considered the true father of Saint-Georges. He took advantage of the opening of the Lévis-Jackman route in 1830 to launch the forest industry here. In the early 20th century, the Dionne Spinning Mill and various shoe manufacturers established themselves in the region, leading to a significant increase in population. Today, Saint-Georges is a sprawling city. Though the outskirts are somewhat grim, there are a few treasures nestled in the centre of town.

The **Église Saint-Georges ★★** (*1re Avenue, in Saint-Georges-Ouest*) stands on a promontory overlooking the Rivière Chaudière. Begun in 1900, it is unquestionably Québec City architect David Ouellet's masterpiece (built in collaboration with Pierre Lévesque). The art of the Belle Époque is beautifully represented here by the central steeple towering 75m and the magnificent three-level interior that has been lavishly sculpted and gilded. In front of the church stands an imposing statue entitled **Saint Georges Terrassant le Dragon** (*St. George Slaying the Dragon*). This is a fibreglass copy of the fragile original. Louis Jobin's original metal-covered wooden statue (1909) is now exhibited at the Musée du Québec in Québec City.

Thetford Mines

Asbestos is a strange ore with a whitish, fibrous appearance that is valued for its insulating properties and resistance to heat. It was discovered in the region in 1876, promoting the development of a portion of Québec that had previously been considered extremely remote. Large American and Canadian companies developed the mines in Asbestos, Black Lake and Thetford Mines (before the mines were nationalized in early 1980s), building industrial empires that made Québec one of the highest-ranking producers of asbestos in the world.

The **Musée Minéralogique et Minier de la Région de l'Amiante** (*$5; late Jun to early Sep, every day 9.30am to 5pm; early Mar to late Dec every day, 1pm to 5pm; 711 Boulevard Smith Sud, ☎335-2123*) houses superb collections of rocks and minerals from all over the world, including samples of asbestos taken from 25 different countries. There are also exhibits explaining the development of the mines and the different characteristics of rocks and minerals found in Québec.

Mine Tours ★★ (*$10; mid-Jun to early Sep, every day at 1:30pm; Jul 1:30pm and 10:30am; 682 Rue Mofette N., ☎335-7141 or 335-6511*) provide a unique opportunity to see an asbestos mine in operation. In addition to visiting extraction sites and going down into an open-cut mine, partici-

pants can attend an information session on asbestos-based products.

Parks

Québec City Region

The **Mont Sainte-Anne ★** (*2000 Boulevard Beaupré, C.P. 400, Beaupré, G0A 1E0, ☎827-4561, ≈827-3121, www.mont-sainte-anne.com*) cover 77km² and includes 800m-high Mont Sainte-Anne, one of the most beautiful downhill-ski sites in Québec (see p 296). Various other outdoor activities are possible. The park has 200km of mountain-bike trails that become 200km of cross-country trails in winter. Access to both is $5 per day. Sports equipment can also be rented on site. There are a few hotels close to the ski hill and the park.

The **Cap-Tourmente National Wildlife Area ★★** (*570 Chemin du Cap-Tourmente, Saint-Joachim, Apr to Oct, ☎827-4591, Nov to Apr, ☎827-3776, ≈827-6225*) is located on pastoral, fertile land. Each spring and autumn its sandbars are visited by countless snow geese who stop to gather strength for their long migration. The reserve also has birdwatching facilities and naturalists on hand to answer your questions about the 250 species of birds and 45 species of mammals that you might encounter on the hiking and walking trails that traverse the park.

Throughout the year, hordes of visitors come to

Parc de la Jacques-Cartier ★★ (*Route 175 Nord, ☎848-3169 or 644-8844 off-season*), located in the Réserve Faunique des Laurentides 40km north of Quebec City. The area is called Vallée de la Jacques-Cartier after the river of the same name that runs through it, winding between steep hills. Benefitting from the microclimate caused by the river being hemmed in on bothsides, the site is suitable for a number of outdoor activities. The flora and fauna are abundant and diverse. The winding and well laid-out paths sometimes lead to interesting surprises like a moose and its offspring foraging for food in a marsh. Before heading out to discover all the riches the site has to offer, you can get information at the nature centre's reception area. Campsites, chalets and equipment are all available to rent (see "Outdoor Activities" section).

south. Hikes led by naturalists are organized throughout the summer. Caribou have been spotted on some of the trails. The park's Mont du Lac des Cygnes (Swan Lake Mountain) trail is among the most beautiful in Québec. Visitors can also go on canoe-camping trips.

Parc des Hautes-Gorges-de-la-Rivière-Malbaie ★★ (*early Jun to mid-Oct, every day 9am to 5pm; from Baie-Saint-Paul, take Route 138 to Saint-Aimé-des-Lacs, 123-B Rue Principale, ☎439-4402, ⇄439-3735*), which covers over 233km² of land, was created to protect the area from commercial exploitation. Over 800 million years ago, a crack in the earth's crust formed the magnificent gorges after which the park is named. Later the terrain was shaped by glaciers. The park features an incredible diversity of vegetation ranging from maple stands to alpine tundra. The rock faces, some of which are 800m high, tower over the river and are used for rock-climbing. The best known climb, "Pomme d'Or," is a 350m-high expert-level trail.

Other park activities include snowmobiling, hiking (the Acropole trail is particularly scenic), and canoe-camping. The park's rental centre has mountain bikes and canoes. **River boat cruises** (*$20; duration: 1hr 30min, ☎439-4402, ⇄439-3735*) are also offered. A trip down the river is the best way to truly appreciate the park.

Mauricie–Centre-du-Québec

The **Mauricie National Park** ★ (*$3.50 per person for one day, $8 per family; Grand-Mère; ☎538-3232*) is also known as Parc National de La Mauricie. It was created in 1970 to preserve a part of the Laurentians. It's the perfect setting for outdoor activities such as canoeing, hiking, mountain biking, snowshoeing and cross-country skiing. Hidden among the woods are several lakes and rivers as well as natural wonders of all kinds. Visitors can stay in dormitories year-round for $21 per person. Reservations can be made at ☎537-4555.

Outdoor Activities

Rafting

Québec City Region

In spring and summer, the Rivière Jacques-Cartier gives adventurers a good run for their money. Two longstanding companies offer well-supervised rafting expeditions with all the necessary equipment. At **Village Vacances Valcartier** (*1860 Boulevard Valcartier, St-Gabriel-de-Valcartier, ☎844-2200 or 888-384-5524, www.valcartier.com*), they promise lots of excitement on an 8km ride. With **Excursions Jacques-Cartier** (*978 Av. Jacques-Cartier Nord, Tewkesbury, ☎848-7238, ⇄848-5687*), you can also experience

---

Charlevoix

Located at the eastern edge of the Réserve Faunique des Laurentides, the **Parc des Grands-Jardins** ★★ (*4 Place de l'Église, Baie-St-Paul, ☎846-2057 or 435-3101, ⇄435-5297*) is rich in flora and fauna characteristic of taiga and tundra – a very unusual occurrence this far

some very exciting runs. Rafting excursions are also offered on the Rivière Batiscan in the **Réserve Faunique de Portneuf.**

Downhill Skiing

Québec City Region

Mont-Sainte-Anne (*$45 per day; Mon 9am to 4pm, Tue to Fri 9am to 10pm, Sat 8:30am to 10pm, Sun 8:30pm to 4pm; 2000 Boulevard Beau Pré, C.P. 400, Beaupré, G0A 1E0, ☎827-4561, ☎827-3121, www.mont-sainte-anne.com*) is one of the biggest ski resorts in Québec. Among the 51 runs, some reach 625m in height and 14 are lit for night skiing. It's also a delight for snowboarders. Rather than buying a regular ticket, you can buy a pass worth a certain number of points that are valid for two years. Points are deducted each time you take the lift. Equipment rentals are also available (*skiing $25/day, snowboarding $35/day*).

The **Station Touristique Stoneham** (*$39; Stoneham, ☎848-2411 or 800-463-6888*) welcomes visitors year-round. In the winter there are 25 runs, 16 of which are lit. For cross-country skiers there are 30km of maintained trails that are at the disposal of hikers, mountain-bikers and horseback riders in the summer.

Charlevoix

Le Massif (*$32.75; 1350 rue Principale, C.P. 47 Petite-Rivière-St François, ☎632-5876, www.lemassif.com*) is one of the finest ski centres in Québec. At 770m, it has the highest slopes in eastern Canada and receives abundant snow each winter that is enhanced with artificial snow to create ideal ski conditions. Although it is constantly being modernized, the ski centre still blends into the natural surroundings. And what nature! The mountain, which rises almost up from the river, has a breathtaking view from the summit. Three ski lifts, one of which is a quadruple, take skiers to the 20 different runs ranging from intermediate to advanced levels. At the bottom of the slopes are a bar and a cafeteria that serves good food at reasonable prices.

Parc Régional du Mont Grand-Fonds ★ (*$26; 1000 Chemin des Loisirs, La Malbaie, ☎665-0095*) has 13 355m runs. The longest one is 2,500m.

Ice-fishing

Mauricie–Centre-du-Québec

From December to February, thousands of of **ice-fishing** fans converge on the Rivière Sainte-Anne to fish for tomcod. The river is covered with fishing huts in the winter. These can be rented along with the necessary equipment from the Comité de Gestion de la Rivière Sainte-Anne, the river's management committee (*Ste-Anne-de-la-Pérade, ☎418-325-2475*). The price is $15/pers. per day (maximum four per cabin), and $18 on weekends.

Accommodations

Québec City Region

Château-Richer

Auberge Baker
$65 sb
$89 pb, bkfst incl.
ℑ, ⊛, ℜ, K
8790 Avenue Royale, G0A 1N0
☎*666-5509*
⇒*824-4412*
For over 50 years, The Auberge Baker has existed in this hundred-year-old Côte-de-Beaupré house. Its stone walls, low ceilings, wood floors and wide-frame windows enchant visitors. The five bedrooms are on the dimly-lit upper floor but there are also a kitchenette, a bathroom and an adjoining terrace on the same floor. The rooms are meticulously decorated in authentic fashion and furnished with antiques. They serve delicious food.

Beaupré (Mont Sainte-Anne)

Hôtel Val des Neiges
$90
$160 ½b
≈, ⊙, △, ℜ, ⊛, ℑ
201 Val des Neiges, G0A 1E0
☎*827-5711*
☎*800-554-6005*
⇒*827-5997*
Many chalets have recently been built around the base of the Mont Sainte-Anne in newly developed areas. Among these is the Hôtel Val des Neiges. The decor is rustic and the rooms are comfortable. The complex also includes small, well-equipped condos. Cruise packages are also offered.

La Camarine
$105
$113 and up, ½b
≡, ⊛, ℑ, ⊛
10947 Sainte-Anne, G0A 1E0
☎*827-5703*
☎*800-567-3939*
⇒*827-5430*
La Camarine faces the Saint Lawrence River. This charming high-quality inn has 30 rooms. The decor successfully combines the rustic feel of the house with the more modern wooden furniture. This is a delightful spot.

Île d'Orléans

On Île d'Orléans, there are about 50 bed and breakfasts! A list can be obtained from the tourist office. There are also a few guesthouses with solid reputations and a campground. Therefore, there are plenty of options for getting the most out of your stay on this enchanting island.

Le Vieux-Presbytère
$60-75 bkfst incl.
$110-145 ½b
pb/sb, ℜ
1247 Avenue Monseigneur-d'Esgly St-Pierre, G0A 4E0
☎*828-9723*
☎*888-282-9723*
⇒*828-2189*
Le Vieux-Presbytère guesthouse is in fact located in an old presbytery just behind the village church. The structure is predominantly made out of wood and stone. Low ceilings with wide beams, wide-frame windows and antiques such as woven bed-covers and braided rugs take you back to the era of New France. The dining room and the lounge are inviting. This is a tranquil spot with rustic charm.

Le Canard Huppé
$125 bkfst incl.
$175 ½b
≡, ℜ
2198 Chemin Royal, St-Laurent G0A 3Z0
☎*828-2292*
☎*800-838-2292*
⇒*828-0966*
Le Canard Huppé has enjoyed a very good reputation over the last few years. Their eight, clean, comfortable, country-style rooms are scattered with wooden ducks. The restaurant is also just as renowned and appealing (see p 301). The service is conscientious, and the surrounding beautiful.

Deschambault

Maison Deschambault
$125 bkfst incl.
$175 ½b
ℜ
128 Chemin du Roy, G0A 1S0
☎*286-3386*
⇒*286-4064*
Maison Deschmbault offers five luxurious rooms, decorated with flower patterns and pastel colours. There are also a small bar, a dining room that serves fine cuisine (see p 301), a conference room, a massage service all in an enchanting old manor house (see p 276). In this peaceful setting, relaxing is no trouble at all.

Charlevoix

Baie-Saint-Paul

Parc des Grands-Jardins
$14-$20
4 Place de l'Eglise, Baie-St-Paul
☎*800-665-6527*
The Parc des Grands-Jardins rents out small cottages and shelters This park is a popular place for fishing so if you want to stay here during summer,

Québec

you'll have to reserve early.

Auberge de Jeunesse Le Balcon Vert
$15
Route 362, G0A 1S0
☎*435-5587*
One of the least expensive places to stay in town is the Auberge de Jeunesse Le Balcon Vert. This youth hostel offers small chalets that sleep four people, as well as campsites. It's only open during the summer.

Le Genévrier campground
$20
Route 138, at the Baie-Saint-Paul exit, G0A 1B0
☎*435-6520*
Le Genévrier campground is a vast recreational-tourist complex in perfect harmony with its natural environment. Campers of all persuasions are sure to find what they are looking for here. The campground offers 450 sites, mostly on forested land, for all types of lodging and shelter from the biggest motorhomes to tents for wilderness camping. Several fully equipped, modern and comfortable cottages are situated by the river or lake. In summer, two more rustic but fully equipped log cabins with bedding and showers are also for rent. Every day, an extensive program of sports and leisure activities is offered. Hiking and mountain-biking trails along the river.

Auberge La Maison Otis
$180 ½b
≈, △, ℜ
23 Rue St-Jean-Baptiste, G3Z 1M0
☎*435-2255*
☎*800-267-2254*
≈*435-2464*
Auberge La Maison Otis has a slick ambiance, is tastefully decorated and serves divine food. The old section has small, snug rooms with bunk-beds

whereas the rooms in the new section are large and cozy. Located in the heart of the city, this former bank is an example of classic Québec architecture.

Île aux Coudres

Cap-aux-Pierres Hotel
$75
≈, ℜ
246 Route Principale, La Baleine G0A 2A0
☎*438-2711*
☎*888-554-6003*
≈*438-2127*
A long building with several skylights, the Cap-aux-Pierres Hotel offers pleasant rustic rooms.

Saint-Irénée

Auberge des Sablons
$184 ½b
sb/pb
ℜ
223 Chemin Les Bains, G0T 1V0
☎*452-3240*
☎*800-267-3594*
≈*452-3240*
The charming Auberge des Sablons is a pretty white house with blue shutters, located in a peaceful spot next to Domaine Forget. The rooms are pleasant but not all have private bathrooms.

La Malbaie–Pointe-au-Pic

Auberge Les Trois Canards et Motels
$95-$225
ℜ, ≈, △
49 Côte Belleveue, G0T 1M0
☎*665-3761 or 800-461-3761*
≈*665-4727*
The Auberge Les Trois Canards et Motels has a magnificent view of the entire region. The inn offers nine rooms, each warmly decorated with a fireplace, thick carpets, and a whirlpool. The motel rooms are not as nice

but still offer a great view of the water.

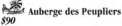 **Manoir Richelieu**
$299
≈, K, ℜ
181 Avenue Richelieu, G0T 1M0
☎*665-4431*
☎*800-463-2613*
≈*665-3093*
A veritable institution in Quebec, the Manoir Richelieu is a distinguished establishment that is still the choice holiday resort in Québec. What's more, $140 million were spent to renovate and expand the facility in 1999. Perched on a point overhanging the river, the century-old building is adorned with turrets, gables and a sloped roof. This jewel of Norman architecture has 405 rooms, of which 35 are suites. Some rooms are a little small but all are comfortable. There are numerous boutiques on the main floor as well as an underground passageway to the casino. Its refurbished decor includes works by local artists whose creations are featured in the rooms, restaurant (see p 302), health café and conference rooms. The woodwork, wrought iron and ceramics blend beautifully together.

Cap-à-l'Aigle

Auberge des Peupliers
$90
△, ℜ
381 Saint-Raphaël G0T 1S0
☎*665-4423*
≈*665-3179*
The Auberge des Peupliers sits on a hillside overlooking the St. Lawrence. The rooms are decorated with wooden furniture that creates a warm, charming atmosphere. The inn also has pleasant, quiet living rooms.

La Pinsonnière
$275 ½b
○, ≈, ⊙, ℜ
124 Saint-Raphaël, GOT 180
☎*665-4431*
☎*800-387-4431*
≈*665-7156*
The luxurious La Pinsonnière features a wonderful location on a headland overhanging the river. The rooms are tastefully decorated and each is different from the next. This is a very pleasant hotel with a very popular restaurant.

Mauricie–Centre-du-Québec

Trois-Rivières

Auberge de Jeunesse la Flotille
$19 or $16.50 for members for dormitories
$36.40 or $33 for members for private rooms
497 Rue Radisson, G9A 2C7
☎*378-8010*
The Auberge de Jeunesse la Flotille is a pretty little youth hostel close to Trois-Rivière's nightlife. There are some 40 beds in the summer season and 10 less in the winter.

Hôtel Delta
$93
≈, ⊙, ○, ℜ
1620 Notre-Dame, G9A 6E5
☎*376-1991*
≈*372-5975*
The high tower of the Hôtel Delta is easy to spot next to the downtown area. The rooms are spacious, and the hotel also has sports facilities.

Grand-Mère

Auberge Le Florès
$70-$90
tv, ≈, ≡, ℜ
4291 50ᵉ Avenue, G9T 6S5
☎*538-9340*
≈*538-1884*
The Auberge Le Florès is a superb period house. Though not spectacular, the rooms are quite comfortable.

Shawinigan

Auberge l'Escapade
$49-$145
⊛, ♿, ℜ; ℜ
3383 Rue Garnier, G9N 6R4
☎*539-6911*
☎*539-7669*
A well-kept place on the way into town, the Auberge l'Escapade has several different personalities. The choice of accommodations here ranges from basic, inexpensive rooms (*$53*) to luxurious rooms decorated with period furniture (*$145*). In between the two, there are pretty, comfortable rooms that offer good value for the money (*$63-$80*). What's more, the restaurant serves tasty food.

Saint-Alexis-des-Monts

Hôtel Sacacomie
$139
4000 Rang Sacacomie, J0K 1V0
☎*265-4444*
☎*888-265-4414*
≈*265-4445*
The Hôtel Sacacomie is a magnificent establishment with log cabins nestled in the middle of the forest near the Mastigouche reserve. Overhanging the majestic Lac Sacacomie, the facility has an idyllic location with a beach nearby. There's a great range of activities all year round.

Pointe-du-Lac

🌴 **Auberge du Lac Saint-Pierre**
$85-$154
ℜ, ≈, ≡, ⊛, ○, ⊙
1911 Rue Notre-Dame
CP 10, G0X 1Z0
☎*377-5961*
☎*371-5579*
☎*888-377-5971*
www.aubergelacst-pierre.com/introang.html
The Auberge du Lac Saint-Pierre is located in Pointe-de-Lac, a small village at the north end of Lac Saint-Pierre (actually just a widening in the St. Lawrence). The flora and fauna that make their home in and around the "lake" are characteristic of marshy areas. Perched atop a promontory that slopes down to the shore, this large inn boasts an outstanding location. It has comfortable modern rooms, some of which have a mezzanine for the beds, leaving more space in the main room. The dining room serves excellent food (see p 303). There are bicycles on hand if you feel like exploring the area. Take advantage of them!

Drummondville

Motel Blanchette
$50
⊛
225 Boulevard St-Joseph Ouest
J2E 1A9
☎*477-1222*
☎*800-567-3823*
≈*478-8706*
The Motel Blanchette has a good location and pretty, reasonably priced rooms. The Motel has been recently renovated.

Québec

Victoriaville

Le Suzor
$57.95-$69.95
$152.95 for a suite
1000 Boulevard Jutras
G6S 1E4
☎*357-1000*
⇌*357-5000*
www.hotelsuzor.com
The modern Le Suzor
hotel is in a quiet part of
town. The pleasant, spa-
cious rooms have new
furniture.

Chaudière-Appalaches

Saint-Antoine-de-Tilly

Manoir de Tilly
$115 bkfst incl.
◔, ⊛, ♻, ℑ, ℜ
3854 Chemin de Tilly, C.P. 28
G0S 2C0
☎*886-2407*
☎*888-862-6647*
⇌*886-2595*
Manoir de Tilly is an historic home that dates from
1788. The guestrooms are
not, however, in the older
part of the building, but
rather in a modern wing
that nonetheless offers all
of the comfort and peace
one could desire. Each
room has a fireplace and a
beautiful view. The service
is attentive and the dining
room offers fine cuisine
(see p 303). The inn also
has a gym and conference
rooms.

Beaumont

Manoir de Beaumont
$100 bkfst incl.
≈
485 Route du Fleuve, G0R 1C0
☎*833-5635*
⇌*833-7891*
Perched high on a hill and
surrounded by trees, the
Manoir de Beaumont of-
fers bed-and-breakfast
accommodations in perfect
calm and comfort. Its five

rooms are attractively decorated in period style,
matching the house itself.
A large, sunny living room
and a swimming pool are
at guests' disposal.

Montmagny

Manoir des Érables
$99
⊛, ≈, ⊛, ♻, ℑ, ≡
220 Boulevard Taché E., G5V 1G5
☎*248-0100*
☎*800-563-0200*
⇌*248-9507*
The Manoir des Érables is
an old, English-style seigneurial abode. The opu-
lence of its period decor
and the warm, personal
welcome make guests feel
like royalty. The rooms are
beautiful and comfortable
and many have fireplaces.
On the ground floor, there
is pleasant cigar lounge
decorated with hunting
trophies where guests can
choose from a wide variety
of scotches and cigars.
There is also a dining
room and a bistro
(see p 304), both of which
serve excellent cuisine.
Also available are motel
rooms under the maples,
set off from the hotel, and
a few rooms in a lodge
that is just as inviting as
the manor itself.

Saint-Eugène de l'Islet

Auberge des Glacis
$82/pers.
½b; ℜ
46 Route Tortue, G0R 1X0
☎*247-7486*
☎*(877) 245-2247*
⇌*247-7182*
www.aubergedesglacis.com
The Auberge des Glacis
has a special charm about
it, set in an old seigneurial
mill at the end of a tree-
lined lane. Each of the
comfortable rooms has a
name and its own unique
decor. Delicious French
cuisine is featured in the

dining room (see p 304).
The stone walls and wood-
framed windows of the
mill have been preserved
as part of the finery of the
establishment whose prop-
erty includes a lake, bird-
watching trails, a small
terrace, and, of course, the
river. This is an especially
peaceful spot that's perfect
for relaxation.

Saint-Jean-Port-Joli

Maison de L'Ermitage
$58 bkfst incl.
56 Rue de l'Hermitage, G0R 3G0
☎*598-7553*
⇌*598-7667*
The inn at Maison de
L'Ermitage is located in an
old, red-and-white house
with four corner towers
and a wraparound porch
with a view of the river. It
offers five cozy rooms and
a tasty breakfast. The
house is full of sunny
spots furnished for reading
and relaxing and its yard
slopes down to the river.
The annual sculpture festival is held just next door.

Saint-Georges

Auberge-Motel Benedict-Ar-
nold
$69
≈, ≡, ℜ, ⊛
18255 Boulevard. Lacroix, G5Y 5B8
☎*228-5558*
☎*800-463-5057*
⇌*227-2941*
Auberge-Motel Benedict-
Arnold has been a well-
known stopover near the
United States border for
many generations. The inn
has over 50 rooms, each of
them decorated with pri-
vacy in mind. Motel rooms
are also available. Two
dining rooms offer quality
fare. The staff is very
obliging.

Restaurants

Québec City Region

Beauport

 Manoir Montmorency
$$$
2490 Avenue Royale
☎663-3330
The Manoir Montmorency (see p 270) enjoys from a superb location above the Montmorency Falls. From the dining room surrounded by bay windows, there is an absolutely magnificent view of the falls, the river and Île d'Orléans. Fine French cuisine, prepared with the best products in the region, is served in pleasant surroundings. A wonderful experience for the view and the food! The entrance fee to the Parc de la Chute Montmorency (where the restaurant is located) and the parking fees are waived upon presentation of your receipt or by mentioning your reservation.

Beaupré
(Mont Sainte-Anne)

 La Camarine
$$$$
10947 Sainte-Anne
☎827-5703
La Camarine also houses an excellent restaurant that serves Québec nouvelle cuisine. The dining room is peaceful with a simple decor. The innovative dishes are a feast for the senses. In the basement of the inn is another small restaurant, the Bistro that offers the same menu and prices but it is only open in the winter. Equipped with a fireplace,

it's a cozy spot for an après-ski and is open in the evening for drinks.

Île d'Orléans

 La Goéliche
$$$-$$$$
22 Chemin du Quai, Ste-Pétronille
☎828-2248
The dining room at La Goéliche has lost its splendour. It's still pleasant though and you can still get one of the most beautiful views of Québec City. Fine French cuisine is served here: stuffed quail, nuggets of lamb and saddle of hare.

Canard Huppé
$$$-$$$$
2198 Chemin Royal, St-Laurent
☎828-2292
The dining room of the Canard Huppé serves fine regional cuisine. Prepared with fresh ingredients that abound in the area– island specialties such as duck, trout and maple products– these little dishes will delight the most demanding of palates. Although the room is somewhat dark (with forest green being the predominant colour) the country decor is, on the whole, pleasant.

Sainte-Foy

 La Fenouillère
$$$-$$$$
3100 Chemin St-Louis
☎653-3886
At La Fenouillère, the menu of refined and creative French cuisine promises a succulent dining experience. This restaurant is also proud to possess one of the best wine cellars in Québec. The decor is simple and comfortable.

 Michelangelo
$$$-$$$$
3111 Chemin Saint-Louis
☎651-6262
The Michelangelo serves fine Italian cuisine that both smells and tastes wonderful. The classically decorated dining room, although busy, is warm and intimate. The courteous and attentive service adds to the pleasure of the food.

Deschambault

Bistro Clan Destin
$$
109 Rue de l'Eglise
☎286-6647
Just in front of the village church is the Bistro Clan Destin with its lovely flowered decor. The menu is varied and good daily specials are served.

 Maison Deschambault Inn
$$$
128 Route 138
☎286-3386
≈286-4711
The restaurant in the Maison Deschambault Inn is well-known for its excellent menu which consists mainly of fine French cuisine as well as various specialties of the region. The setting is particularly enchanting (see p 276).

Wendake

 Nek8arre
$$-$$$
9am to 5pm and evenings with reservation
575 Rue Stanislas-Kosca
☎842-4308
≈842-3473
At the Huron Village of Onhoüa Chetek8e, (see p 277), there is a pleasant restaurant whose name means "the meal is ready to serve." Nek8arre introduces you to traditional Huron cooking. On the

Québec

menu there are wonderful dishes such as clay trout, caribou or venison *brochettes* with mushrooms accompanied by wild rice and corn. The wooden tables have little embedded texts explaining the eating habits of Aboriginal cultures. Numerous objects scattered here and there will arouse your curiosity and luckily the waitresses act as part-time "ethnologists", answering your questions. All this in a pleasant atmosphere. The entry fee to the village will be waived if you are only going to the restaurant.

Charlevoix

Baie-Saint-Paul

Le Mouton Noir
$
43 Rue Sainte-Anne
☎435-3075
The country decor of the Mouton Noir restaurant was recently renovated, causing it to lose a bit of its charm. While the restaurant has a good reputation, the food can be a little unimaginative. Nevertheless, it is a pleasant place with a view of the river.

La Maison Otis
$$$$
23 Rue Saint-Jean-Baptiste
☎435-2255
The finest and most sophisticated of cuisines is featured at La Maison Otis. It has developed an avant-garde gourmet menu where regional flavours adopt new accents and compositions. Guests are treated to a delightful culinary experience and a relaxing evening in the inviting decor of the oldest part of the inn that used to be a bank. The service is impeccable and several ingredients on the menu

are home-made. Fine selection of wines.

Saint-Joseph-de-la-Rive

La Maison Sous les Pins
$$$-$$$$
352 Rue F.-A.-Savard
☎635-2583
The warm and intimate dining rooms of the inn La Mason Sous les Pins can accommodate about 20 guests. They come here to discover the refined aromas emanating from a medley of regional and French dishes with an emphasis on local ingredients. Friendly reception and romantic ambiance. Non-smoking.

Île aux Coudres

La Mer Veille
$$-$$$
Pointe de Islet, west side of the island
☎438-2149
La Mer Veille is a very popular restaurant that serves light meals and an appealing table-d'hôte.

Saint-Irénée

Auberge des Sablons
$$$$
223 Chemin Les Bains
☎452-3594
Charm, romance and good taste combine with culinary quality at the Auberge des Sablons, ensuring a delightful dining experience. Guests here can savour excellent French cuisine while admiring the ocean from the terrace or dining room.

La Malbaie–Pointe-au-Pic

Auberge des Trois Canards
$$$$
49 Côte Bellevue
☎665-3761
☎800-461-3761
The chefs at the Auberge des Trois Canards have always been daring and inventive in integrating local ingredients or game with their refined cuisine. Invariably succeeding with panache, they have endowed the restaurant with an enviable nationwide reputation. The service is outstanding and the staff is genuinely cordial and knowledgeable about the dishes served. Good wine list.

Manoir Richelieu
181 Avenue Richelieu
☎665-3703
☎888-294-0111
Renovations have completely transformed Manoir Richelieu (see p 298). It now has several new restaurants and bistros, two of which deserve honourable mention. Le Saint-Laurent (**$$$$**) offers a delicious table d'hôte and buffet all day long. Don't miss its Sunday brunch. The brand-new Le Charlevoix (**$$$$**) restaurant is located in the expanded part of the hotel (which forms a rotunda) in the same magnificent atrium with a breath-taking view of the river. It serves creative, gourmet cuisine inspired by local products.

Cap-à-l'Aigle

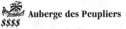
Auberge des Peupliers
$$$$
381 Rue Saint-Raphaël
☎665-4423 *or* 888-282-3743
The Auberge des Peupliers has many wonderful surprises in store for its guests

that are the fruits of its chef's fertile imagination and audacity. Patrons have only to abandon themselves to these intoxicating French and regional flavours that's sure to delight any palate.

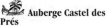 **La Pinsonnière**
$$$$
124 Rue Saint-Raphaël
☎665-4431
☎800-387-4431
The food at La Pinsonnière has long been considered the height of gastronomic refinement in Charlevoix. Despite increasingly fierce competition, it's still worthy of the title in many respects. La Pinsonnière offers a very upscale, classic gourmet menu that should be savoured at leisure. The wine cellar remains the best-stocked in the region and one of the finest in Québec.

Mauricie–Centre-du-Québec

Trois-Rivières

Auberge Castel des Prés
5800 Boulevard Royal
☎375-4921
The Auberge Castel des Prés has two different restaurants: **L'Étiquette** (*$$*) serves bistro-style cuisine and **Chez Claude (Castel des Prés)** (*$$-$$$*) offers traditional French cuisine, making it an excellent choice in this area. The chef has won a number of culinary awards. The menu includes pasta, meat and fish dishes with rich, flavourful sauces. In warm weather, guests can enjoy a sheltered outdoor terrace cooled by summer breezes.

Pointe-du-Lac

Auberge du Lac Saint-Pierre
$$$-$$$$
1911 Route 138
☎377-5971
☎888-377-5971
If you go to the Auberge du Lac Saint-Pierre (see p 299) for dinner, start your evening with a short walk on the shore to work up an appetite, or perhaps have an apéritif on the terrace with its view of the river. While the modern decor of the dining room is a bit cold, there's nothing bland about the presentation of the dishes, much less their flavour. The menu, made up of French and Québec cuisine, includes trout, salmon, lamb and pheasant that are all artfully prepared. Reservations required.

Bécancour

Auberge Godefroy
$$$-$$$$
17575 Boulevard Bécancour
☎233-2200
☎800-361-1620
The spacious dining room of the Auberge Godefroy looks out onto the river. The delicious French cuisine varies from classic to original creations made with regional produce. Succulent desserts!

Victoriaville

Plus Bar
$-$$
192 Boulevard Des Sud
☎758-9927
Plus Bar serves a splendid *poutine* (French fries with gravy and curd cheese) that's deemed one of these best in these parts. You can savour this magnificent "culinary" creation while taking in the latest sporting events on a big-

screen TV. Watch out: the "plus" size portion might be a little more "plus" than you're expecting!

Drummondville

Le Globe-Trotter
$$
600 Boulevard Saint-Joseph
☎478-4141
☎800-567-0995
The restaurant of the hotel Le Dauphin, Le Globe-Trotter serves international cuisine. The helpings are large and there is also an "all you can eat" option. The decor is a little bleak but the atmosphere is nice and relaxed.

Chaudière-Appalaches

Saint-Antoine-de-Tilly

 Manoir de Tilly
$$$$
3854 Chemin de Tilly
☎886-2407
The restaurant of Manoir de Tilly serves refined French cuisine based on local products such as lamb and duck or, for more imaginative dishes, ostrich and deer. The renovated dining room preserves not even a hint of the historic building but is pleasant nonetheless. Here, diners savour carefully prepared and finely presented dishes that are complemented by the view through the large windows on the north wall.

Lévis

Piazzeta
$$
5410 Boulevard de la Rive-Sud
☎835-5545
Lévis is home to a branch of the popular Piazzeta restaurant chain. This one is unfortunately located in

a rather commercial setting along Route 132 with none of the charm of Vieux-Lévis. Nonetheless, the ambiance is pleasant. Delicious, creatively garnished thin-crust pizza and tasty side dishes such as prosciutto and melon are served.

Montmagny

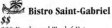

Bistro Saint-Gabriel
$$
220 Boulevard Taché Est
☎248-0100
Bistro Saint-Gabriel occupies the basement of the Manoir des Érables (see p 300). Made of very large stones, the old walls and the low ceiling confer a very unique atmosphere on the spot. During the summer, meals are served in the open air on a terrace where fish and meat are grilled before your eyes.

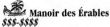

Manoir des Érables
$$$-$$$$
220 Boulevard Taché E.
☎248-0100
The dining room of Manoir des Érables (see p 300) features fish and game. Goose, sturgeon, burbot, lamb and pheasant are lovingly prepared in traditional French style. Served in the inn's magnificent dining room, these local foods enchant guests who can dine in the warm glow of a fireplace in the fall and winter. One of the finest restaurants in the region.

Saint-Eugène-de-l'Islet

Auberge des Glacis
$$$-$$$$
46 Route Tortue
☎247-7486
Auberge des Glacis serves fine French cuisine that is likely to become one of

the best memories of any trip! The dining room, set in a historic mill (see p 300), is bright and pleasantly laid out. Diners savour meat and fish dishes as easy on the eyes as they are on the taste buds. The restaurant also serves a light lunch that may be enjoyed on a riverside terrace.

L'Islet-sur-Mer

La Paysanne
$$$
497 Rue des Pionniers E.
☎247-7276
The restaurant La Paysanne is set right on the riverbank and offers a spectacular view of the St. Lawrence and the north shore. The fine French cuisine plays on regional flavours and is attractively presented.

St-Jean-Port-Joli

Coureuse des Grèves
$$
300 Route de l'Église
☎598-9111
Coureuse des Grèves is a friendly restaurant-café in a very attractive old house named after a seafarers' legend. They serve asty light meals such as spinach squares served with celeriac salad. In summer, diners take advantage of a large sheltered patio. This is a popular spot,and the service is business-like but courteous. The upstairs bar is also quite a draw in the evening.

Saint-Georges

La Table du Père Nature
$$$
10735 1ʳᵉ Avenue
☎227-0888
La Table du Père Nature is definitely one of the best restaurants in town. Guests enjoy innovative French cuisine prepared with skill

and sophistication. Just reading the menu is enough to make your mouth water. The restaurant occasionally serves game.

Entertainment

Festivals and Cultural Events

Charlevoix

The **Symposium de la nouvelle peinture au Canada** (**☎435-3681**) is held annually in Baie-Saint-Paul. Throughout the month of August, visitors can admire huge works based on a suggested theme and created here by approximately 15 artists from Québec, Canada and abroad.

Mauricie– Centre-du-Québec

The **Festival de Musique Actuelle de Victoriaville** (**☎758-9451,** *www.fimav.qc.ca*) takes place each year in May. This festival is an exploration of new musical forms. Of course, this event won't appeal to everyone but it is an adventure for musicians and spectators alike.

Chaudière-Appalaches

In the fall, snow geese leave the northern breeding grounds where they have spent the summer and head south toward milder climates. On the way, they stop on the banks of the St. Lawrence River, especially in spots that provide abundant food for them like the sand bars of Montmagny. These feathery visitors are the perfect excuse to celebrate the **Festival de l'Oie Blanche** (*10 days in October*, ☎*248-3954, puissanceinternet.com/festival*), which features all sorts of activities related to watching and learning about these beautiful migrating birds.

Casino

Charlevoix

The **Casino de Charlevoix** (*183 Avenue Richelieu,* ☎*665-5300 or 800-665-2274, www.casinos.quebec.com*), in Pointe-au-Pic, next to the Manoir Richelieu, is a European-style casino. Formal dress required.

Shopping

Québec City Region

Île d'Orléans has a handful of craft shops, antique dealers and cabinet-making studios. One of these, the **Corporation des Artisans de l'île** (☎*828-2519*), is located in the Saint-Pierre church. There are also about half-a-dozen art galleries on the island, many in the village of Saint-Jean.

The shop of the **Forge à Pique-Assaut** (*2200 Chemin Royal, St-Laurent,* ☎*828-9300*) sells various forged-metal objects from candleholders to furniture as well as other crafts.

Charlevoix

Baie-Saint-Paul

Baie-Saint-Paul is particularly noteworthy for its **art galleries**. There is a little of everything here as each shop has its own specialty. These include oils, pastels, watercolours, etchings – paintings by big names and the latest artists, originals and reproductions, sculpture and poetry. Whatever your heart desires! Take an enjoyable stroll along Rue St-Jean-Baptiste and the neighbouring streets where you'll find countless beautiful galleries staffed by friendly and chatty art dealers.

Saint-Joseph-de-la-Rive

The wonderful paper made at the **Papeterie Saint-Gilles** (*304 Rue Félix-Antoine-Savard,* ☎*635-2430*) is sold on the premises. The quality of the cotton paper is remarkable. Some is decorated with maple or fern leaves. You can also purchase a collection of narratives, stories and Québec songs printed on these fine sheets.

Chaudière-Appalaches

Saint-Jean-Port-Joli

Saint-Jean-Port-Joli is renowned for its crafts and many of its shops sell the work of local artisans. If this sort of shopping interests you, this town has much to offer. There are also a few second-hand stores here to the delight of treasure hunters, many of them along Route 132.

Boutique Jacques-Bourgault, (*326 Avenue de Gaspé Ouest*), between Musée des Anciens Canadiens and Maison Médard-Bourgaut, sells contemporary and religious art.

Artisanat Chamard (*mid-Mar to late Dec, 8am to 5pm; in summer, every day 8am to 9pm; 601 Avenue de Gaspé Est,* ☎*598-3425*), whose fine reputation dates back nearly half a century, sells woven goods and ceramics as well as Aboriginal art.

Eastern Québec

This chapter covers a vast region that includes the tourist regions of Bas-Saint-Laurent, Gaspésie, Îles-de-la-Madeleine, Saguenay–Lac-St-Jean, Manicouagan and Duplessis.

The picturesque Bas-Saint-Laurent region extends east along the St. Lawrence River from the little town of La Pocatière to the village of Sainte-Luce and south to the borders of the United States and New Brunswick. Besides the particularly fertile agricultural land next to the river, much of the Bas-Saint-Laurent is composed of farming and forestry development areas covering gently rolling hills sparkling with lakes and streams.

The shores of the vast Gaspé peninsula are washed by the waters of Baie des Chaleurs, the St. Lawrence River and the Gulf of St. Lawrence. Many Quebecers cherish unforgettable memories of their travels in this mythical land in the easternmost part of Québec. People dream of touring Gaspésie and discovering its magnificent coastal landscape, where the Monts Chic-

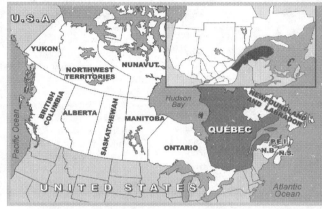

Chocs plunge abruptly into the cold waters of the St. Lawrence. They dream of going all the way to the famous Rocher Percé, heading out to sea toward Île Bonaventure, visiting the extraordinary Forillon National Park, and then slowly returning along Baie des Chaleurs and through the valley of Rivière Matapédia in the hinterland.

This beautiful part of Québec, with its strikingly picturesque scenery, is inhabited by friendly, fascinating people who still rely mainly on the sea for their living. The majority of Gaspesians live in small villages along the coast, leaving the centre of

the peninsula covered with dense Boreal forest. The highest peak in southern Québec lies here in the part of the Appalachians known as the Chic-Chocs.

The word *Gaspé* means "land's end" in the language of the Micmacs, who have been living in this region for thousands of years. Despite its isolation, the peninsula has attracted fishermen from many different places over the centuries, particularly Acadians driven from their lands by the English in 1755. Its population is now primarily francophone.

Gaspésie's main attractions are its rugged,

mountainous landscapes and the Gulf of St. Lawrence, which is so huge that it might as well be the ocean. The coastline is studded with a string of fishing villages, leaving the interior devoid of towns and roads, much as it was when Jacques Cartier arrived in 1534.

The Îles-de-la-Madeleine (sometimes referred to in English as the Magdalen Islands) rise from the middle of the Gulf of St. Lawrence more than 200km from the Gaspé Peninsula. They constitute a 65km-long archipelago of about a dozen islands, many connected to one another by long sand dunes. Swept by winds from the open sea, these small islands offer superb and colourful scenery. The golden dunes and the long wild beaches blend with the red sandstone cliffs and the blue sea. Villages with brightly painted houses, lighthouses and harbours add the finishing touches to the islands' beautiful scenery.

The 15,000 *Madelinots* (as residents are called) have always earned their livelihood from the sea. They continue to do so today by fishing for crab, bottom-feeding fish, mackerel and lobster. The population, mostly of French origin, live on seven islands of the archipelago: Île de la Grande Entrée, Grosse Île, Île aux

Loups, Île du Havre aux Maisons, Île du Cap aux Meules, Île du Havre Aubert and Île de d'Entrée. Only Île d'Entrée, where a few families of Scottish ancestry live, is not linked by land to the rest of the archipelago.

Lac Saint-Jean is a veritable inland sea with a diameter of over 35km; from it flows the Rivière Saguenay, the location of the southernmost fjord in the world.

In a way, these two impressive bodies of water form the backbone of this magnificent region. Moving swiftly toward the St. Lawrence River, the Rivière Saguenay flows through a rugged landscape studded with cliffs and mountains. Aboard a cruise ship or from the banks of the river, visitors can enjoy a series of gorgeous panoramic views of this untouched natural setting. The Saguenay is navigable, as far as Chicoutimi, and governed by the eternal rhythm of the tides. Its rich marine animal life includes various species of whale in the summer. In the heart of the region, visitors will find the bustling city of Chicoutimi, the main urban centre in this part of Québec. The region's first settlers came here in the 19th century, attracted by the beautiful fertile plains and excellent farmland around the lake. The hard life of these pioneers, who

were farmers in the summer and lumberjacks in the winter, was immortalized in Louis Hémon's novel *Maria Chapdelaine*. Sweet, delicious blueberries abound in the area and have made the region of Lac Saint-Jean famous. The fruit is so closely identified with the region that Quebecers all over the province have adopted the term *bleuets*, blueberries, as an affectionate nickname for the local inhabitants. Residents of both the Saguenay and Lac Saint-Jean regions are renowned for their friendliness and spirit.

The Manicouagan region borders the St. Lawrence for some 300km, extends north into the Laurentian plateau to include the Monts Groulx and the Réservoir Manicouagan. It's joined to the Duplessis region, forming what is called the Côte Nord or north shore. Covered by thick Boreal forest, Manicouagan also has an extensive river system that powers the eight generating stations of the Manic-Outardes hydroelectric complex.

Duplessis is a vast, remote region bordered to the south for almost 1,000km by the Gulf of St. Lawrence and to the north by Labrador. Its small population of francophones, anglophones and Montagnais is concentrated along the St. Lawrence coast and in a few inland mining towns. The region is far from any large urban centres, and its economy has always been based on natural resources. Aboriginals have lived in the region for thousands of years. In the 16th century, Basque and Breton fishers and whalers set up seasonal posts in the region. Today, the important economic activities are fishing, forestry, and iron and titanium mining. Additional jobs are provided by a large aluminum smelter that was built in Sept-Îles to take advantage of the availability of hydroelectricity.

Finding Your Way Around

Bas-Saint-Laurent

By Car

Turn off Highway 20 and take Route 132 East. Highways 232, 185 and 289 run through the Bas-St-Laurent, taking you to the heart of this region to its spectacular forests and valleys.

Bus Stations

Rivière-du-Loup
83 Boulevard Cartier
☎ *(418) 862-4884*

Rimouski
90 Rue Leonidas
☎ *723-4923*

Train Stations

La Pocatière
95 Rue Principale
☎ *800-361-5390*

Rimouski
57 de l'Évêché Est
☎ *800-361-5390*

Rivière-du-Loup
615 Rue Lafontaine
☎ *800-361-5390*

Trois-Pistoles
231 Rue de la Gare
☎ *800-361-5390*

By Ferry

Rivière-du-Loup
Cost: $10.20, car $25
Duration: 1hr
☎ *(418) 862-5094*
☎ *(514) 849-4466*
(from Montréal)
☎ *(418) 638-2856*
(from St-Siméon)
Links Rivière-du-Loup and Saint-Siméon in Charlevoix.

Isle-Verte
La Richardière ferries
($5, car $20, May to Nov,
☎ *418-989-2843*) ferries passengers from Isle-Verte to Notre-Dame-des-Sept-Douleurs. If you don't have a car, you can take a taxi-boat (*$6.50;*
☎ *418-898-2199*).

Trois-Pistoles
A ferry runs between Trois-Pistoles and Les Escoumins (*$10, car $26;*
☎ *418-233-2202*). The crossing takes 90min and, if you're lucky, you might see some whales. Reserve in advance for summer.

Gaspésie

Bus Stations

Matane
750 Avenue du Phare Ouest
(Irving station)
☎ *562-1177*

Saint-Anne-des-Monts
90 Boulevard Sainte-Anne
☎ *763-3321*

Gaspé
20 Rue Adams
☎ *368-1888*

Percé
Ultramar, Anse-à-Beaufils
☎ *782-5417*

Bonaventure
118 Rue Grand Pré
(Motel Grand-Pré)
☎ *534-2053*

Carleton
561 Rue Perron
☎ *364-7000*

Amqui
3 Boulevard Saint-Benoit
☎ *629-4898*

Train Stations

Gaspé
3 Boulevard Marina
☎ *368-4313*

Percé
44 L'Anse au Beaufils
☎ *800- 361-5390*

Bonaventure
217 Rue de la Gare
☎ *800-361-5390*

Carleton
116 Rue de la Gare
☎ *800-361-5390*

Matapédia
10 Rue MacDonnell
☎ *800-361-5390*

Québec

By Ferry

Baie-Comeau - Matane
(*$11.50, cars $27.50;*
☎*562-2500*) the crossing
takes 2hrs 30min. The
schedule varies from year
to year so be sure to check
when planning your trip.
Reservations are a good
idea during summer.

Godbout - Matane (*$11.50,
cars $27.50;* ☎*562-2500*) the
crossing takes 2hrs 30min.
Reservations are a good
idea during summer.

Miguasha - Dalhousie
(*$1, cars $12, mid-Jun to
early Sep, on the hour as of
8am in Dalhousie and
6:30am in Miguasha,*
☎*794-2792*). The crossing
take 15min and saves you
about 70km of driving.

Îles-de-la-Madeleine

By Car

Of the seven inhabited
islands of the Îles-de-la-
Madeleine, six are linked
together by Route 199. The
proposed tour takes visi-
tors to each island to discover some of their hidden
treasures.

The seventh island, Île
d'Éntrée, is only accessible
by boat and is a trip in
itself. The **S.P. Bonaventure**
(☎ *986-5705*) boat leaves
the Cap-aux-Meules pier
from Monday to Saturday,
and the trip takes approximately 1hr.

Car rentals are available
for visitors who want to
drive around the islands.

Cap-aux-Meules Honda
1090 Rue La Vernière
☎*(418) 986-4085*
They also rent motorcy-
cles.

Tilden
Airport
☎*(418) 969-2590*

By Plane

Air Canada (☎*888-247-2262*)
offers daily flights to the
Îles-de-la-Madeleine. Most
flights make stopovers in
Québec City, Mont-Joli or
Gaspé, so count on a 4hr
trip. Considerable price
reductions can be found
by booking well in ad-
vance.

By Ferry

Traversier Le Madeleine
(*$35, car $67, motorcycle
$23.50, bicycle $8.25;*
☎*418-986-3278 or
888-986-3278, ≈986-5101,
www.ilesdelamadeleine.-
com/ctma*) leaves from
Souris (Prince Edward
Island) and reaches Cap-
aux-Meules in about 5hrs.
Try to reserve in advance
if possible If not, arrive at
the pier a few hours be-
fore departure, or to be
extra sure, go to Souris the
day before your departure
and reserve seats. Ask for
the ferry-crossing sche-
dule, as it changes from
one season to the next.

The cargo and passenger
vessel **CTMA Voyageur** (*$500
one-way in high season,
includes meals;*
☎*418-986-6600*) leaves the
port of Montréal every
Sunday and sails down the
St-Laurent to the Îles-de-la-
Madeleine; the boat can
take about 15 people and
the trip takes 48hrs.

By Bicycle

Without a doubt, bikes are
the best way to get around
on the islands. Here is
bike rental outfit:

Le Pédalier
365 Chemin Principal, Cap-aux-
Meules
☎*(418) 986-2965*

Saguenay–
Lac-Saint-Jean

By Car

From Québec City, take
Route 138 E. to Saint-Si-
méon. Turn left on to
Route 170, which passes
through the village of
Sagard on its way to the
Parc du Saguenay. This
road continues onto Chi-
coutimi. It is possible and
even recommended to
combine this tour with a
tour of the Charlevoix
region, farther south (see
p 277).

Bus Stations

Chicoutimi
**Autobus Tremblay et Trem-
blay**
55 Rue Racine E.
☎*(418) 543-1403*

Jonquière
Autocar Jasmin
2249 Rue Saint-Hubert
☎*(418) 547-2167*

Alma
430 Rue du Sacré-Cœur (Coq-Rôti
restaurant)
☎*(418) 662-5441*

Train Stations

Hébertville
15 Rue Saint-Louis
☎*800-361-5390*

Jonquière
2439 Rue Saint-Dominique
☎*800-361-5390*

Chambord
78 Rue de la Gare
☎*800-361-5390*

Manicouagan

By Car

From Beauport (near Québec), take Route 138, which runs along the north shore of the St. Lawrence River, to Natashquan in Duplessis. At Baie-Sainte-Catherine, a ferry crosses the Rivière Saguenay to Tadoussac. To follow the Manicouagan tour, continue on Route 138: You can't go wrong – there is only one highway!

Bus Stations

Tadoussac
443 Rue Bateau-Passeur (Petro-Canada Station)
☎*(418) 235-4653*

Bergeronnes
138 Rte. 138 (Irving Station)
☎*(418) 232-6330*

Baie-Comeau
212 Boulevard LaSalle
☎*(418) 296-6921*

By Ferry

Except for the Baie-Ste-Catherine – Tadoussac ferry, it is better to reserve a spot a few days in advance in the summer.

Tadoussac
The ferry ride from Baie Sainte-Catherine to Tadoussac (*free,* ☎*418-235-4395*) takes only 10min. The schedule varies greatly from one season to the next, so make sure to double-check the times before planning a trip.

Baie-Comeau
The ferry ride from Baie-Comeau to Matane (*$11.50, cars $27.50, motorcycles $20.65,* ☎*562-2500 or 877-562-6560, ⇌560-8013*) takes 2hrs 30min.

Godbout
The ferry ride from Godbout to Matane, in Gaspésie (*$11.50, cars, $27.50, motorcycles $20.65;* ☎*562-2500 or 877-562-6560, ⇌560-8013*) takes 2hrs 30min.

Les Escoumins
There is a ferry from Trois-Pistoles to Les Escoumins (*$26, car $25;* ☎*233-2202 from Les Escoumins and 851-4676 from Trois Pistoles*) that lasts 1hr 30min.

Duplessis

By Car

Route 138 provides access to much of this region before ending at Havre-Saint-Pierre.

In 1996, Route 138 was extend to reach Natashquan. However, during the summer, only hydroplanes and weekly supply boats from Havre-Saint-Pierre link the inhabitants of the scattered villages farther east to the rest of Québec. In the winter, snow and ice provide a natural route for snowmobiles between villages. The following tour will be particularly interesting to those who really love the outdoors and want to get away from the hustle and bustle of the city.

By Plane

Canadian Regional (☎*800-665-1177 in Canada;* ☎*800-426-7000 in the U.S.*) serves Port-Menier on île d'Anticosti, via Havre St. Pierre. There are usually three flights per week.

During the summer and during the Christmas season, **Air Satellite** (☎*589-8923 or 800-463-8512*) offers daily flights from Rimouski, Sept-Îles, Baie-Comeau, Havre-Saint-Pierre and Longue-Pointe-de-Mingan.

Confortair (☎*968-4660*) offers charter flights to île d'Anticosti.

In the summer, **Air Schefferville** (☎*800-361-8620 or 393-3333*) offers direct flights from Montréal to Schefferville.

Bus Stations

Sept-Îles
126 Rue Monseigneur Blanche
☎*962-2126*

Havre-Saint-Pierre
1130 Rue de l'Escale
☎*538-2033*

Natashquan
183 Chemin d'En Haut (Auberge La Cache)
☎*726-3347*

By Train

QNS&L
☎*962-9411*
The train links Sept-Îles to Schefferville and runs three times a week in summer and twice a week in winter. The trip lasts from 10 to 12hrs and crosses the Canadian Shield to the outlying tundra.

By Boat

The **Relais Nordik inc.** cargo boat (*rate varies according to the destination; Apr to Jan;* ☎*723-8787 or 800-463-0680 from outside area code 418*) leaves from Sept-Îles and travels to Port-Menier, Havre-Saint-Pierre, Natashquan, Kegaska, La Romaine, Harrington Harbour, Tête-à-la-Baleine, La Tabatière, Saint-Augustin, Vieux-Fort and Blanc-Sablon. There is only one departure a week, so check the schedule before planning a trip.

Québec

Practical Information

Area code: **418**

Tourist Information

Bas-Saint-Laurent

Association Touristique du Bas-St-Laurent
148 Rue Fraser, Rivière-du-Loup
G5R 1C8
☎*867-3015*
☎*800-563-5268*
≈*867-3245*
www.tourismebas-st-laurent.com

Rivière-du-Loup
189 Rue Hôtel-de-Ville
☎*862-1981*

Saint-Fabien
33, Route 132 Ouest G0L 2Z0
☎*869-3333*

Rimouski
50 Rue St-Germain Ouest G5L 4B5
☎*723-2322*
☎*800-746-6875*

Gaspésie

Association Touristique de la Gaspésie
357 Route de la Mer, Sainte-Flavie
G0J 2L0
☎*775-2223*
☎*800-463-0323*
≈*775-2234*
www.tourisme.gaspesie.com

Sainte-Flavie
357 Route de la Mer, G0J 2L0
☎*775-2223*
≈*775-2234*

Matane
968 Avenue du Phare Ouest
G4W 3P5
☎*562-1065*

Gaspé
27 Boulevard York Est
☎*368-6335*

Percé
142 Route 132 Ouest
☎*782-5448*

Carleton
629 Boulevard Perron, G0C 1J0
☎*364-3544*

Pointe-à-la-Croix
1830 Rue Principale G0C 1L0
☎*788-5670*

Îles-de-la-Madeleine

Association Touristique des Îles-de-la-Madeleine
128 Chemin Débarcadère, Cap-aux-Meules
☎*986-2245*
≈*986-2327*
www.ilesdelamadeleine.com
mailing address: C.P. 1028, Cap-aux-Meules, G0B 1B0

Saguenay– Lac-Saint-Jean

Association Touristique du Saguenay - Lac-Saint-Jean
198 Rue Racine E., Bureau 210
Chicoutimi, G7H 1R9
☎*543-9778*
☎*800-463-9651*
≈*543-1805*

La Baie
1171 7e Avenue, G7B 1S8
☎*697-5050*

Chicoutimi
295 Rue Racine E.
☎800-463-6565

Jonquière
2665 Boulevard du Royaume
G7S 5B8
☎*548-4004*
☎*800-561-9196*
≈*548-7348*

Alma
1385 Chemin de la Marina
☎*668-3016*
☎*888-289-3016*

Saint-Félicien
1209 Boulevard du Sacré-Cœur
C.P. 7, G8K 2R3
☎*679-9888*
≈*679-0562*

Manicouagan

Association Touristique Régionale de Manicouagan
337 Boulevard Lasalle, suite 304
Baie Comeau, G4Z 2Z1
☎*294-2876*
☎*888-463-5319*
≈*294-2345*

Tadoussac
197 Rue des Pionniers, G0T 2A0
☎*235-4744*
≈*294-2345*

Baie-Comeau
2630 Boulevard Laflèche
☎*589-3610*

Duplessis

Association Touristique Régionale de Duplessis
312 Avenue Brochu, Sept-Îles
G4R 2W6
☎*962-0808*
☎*888-463-0808*
≈*962-6518*
www.tourismecote-nord.com

Sept-Îles
Corporation touristique de Sept-Île
1401, Boulevard Laure Ouest
G4R 4K1
☎*962-1238*
☎*888-880-1238*
≈*968-0022*
www.vitrine.net/ctsi/index.html
CTSI@globetrotter.net

Havre-Saint-Pierre
Seasonal
957 Rue de la Berge
☎*538-2512*

Natashquan
33 Allée des Galets
☎*726-3756*

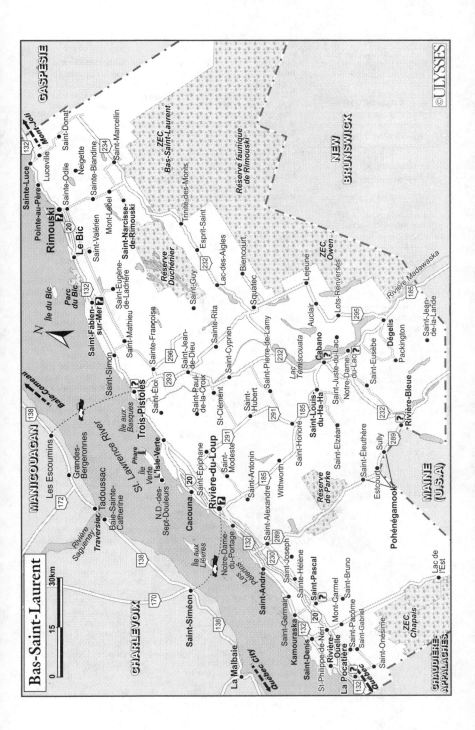

Bas-Saint-Laurent

© ULYSSES

Exploring

Bas-Saint-Laurent

★★

Kamouraska

On January 31, 1839, the young Seigneur of Kamouraska, Achille Taché, was murdered by a former friend, Doctor Holmes. The Seigneur's wife had plotted with Holmes, her lover, to do in her husband and flee to distant lands. The incident inspired Anne Hébert's novel *Kamouraska*, which was made into a film by prominent Québécois director Claude Jutra. The novel, and later the film, brought a level of fame to the village. Kamouraska, an Algonquin word meaning "bulrushes by the water," earned a place in the colourful history of rural Québec. For many years, the village was the eastern-most trading post on the Côte-du-Sud. Kamouraska stands on several ranges of rocky hillocks that provide a striking contrast to the adjacent coastal plain. The unusual rugged terrain is a remnant of ancient mountains long worn down by glaciers and typical of the area.

★

Rivière-du-Loup

Rivière-du-Loup, set on several ranges of rolling hills, has become one of the most important towns in the Bas-Saint-Laurent region. Its strategic loca-

tion made it a marine communication centre for the Atlantic, the St. Lawrence, Lac Témiscouata and the St. John River in New Brunswick. Later, it was an important railway centre when the town was the eastern terminus of the Canadian train network. Rivière-du-Loup is the turn-off point for the road to New Brunswick and is linked by ferry to Saint-Siméon on the north shore of the river.

Manoir Fraser ★ *($3.50; late Jun to mid-Oct, every day 10am to 5pm; 32 Rue Fraser, ☎867-3906).* The Rivière du Loup seigneury was granted to a wealthy Québec merchant named Charles Aubert de la Chesnaye in 1673. It later passed through several owners, all of whom showed little interest in the remote region. The house, originally built for Timothy Donahue in 1830, became the Fraser family residence in 1835. In 1888, it was modified to suit contemporary tastes by Québec architect Georges-Émile Tanguay.

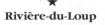

The house was renovated in June 1997 with the help of local residents. It is now open to the public with guided tours, as well as a multimedia presentation of an official dinner of the time.

Église Saint-Patrice ★ *(121 Rue Lafontaine)* was rebuilt in 1883 on the site of an earlier church erected in 1855. It houses several treasures, including a representation of the Stations of the Cross designed by Charles Huot, stained-glass windows created by the Castle company (1901) and statues by Louis Jobin. Rue de la Cour, in front of the church, leads to the **Palais de Justice** *(33 Rue de la Cour)*, the courthouse constructed in 1882 by architect Pierre Gauvreau. A number of judges and lawyers built beautiful houses on the shady streets nearby.

The **Musée du Bas-Saint-Laurent** ★ *($3.50; every day 1pm to 5pm; early Sep to late Jun, Mon and Wed 6pm to 9pm; 300 Rue Saint-Pierre, ☎862-7547)* displays objects characteristic of the region and holds contemporary art exhibits (these are often more interesting). The building itself, made of concrete, is a perfect example of ugly modern architecture.

★

Isle-Verte

The village of Isle-Verte was once an important centre of activity in the Bas-Saint-Laurent region. Several buildings remain from this period. Meanwhile, life in the surrounding countryside follows a traditional pattern that keeps time with the continuing rhythm of the tides. Just offshore lies Île Verte, the island named by the explorer Jacques Cartier who, upon spotting the lush island, exclaimed *"Quelle île verte!"*, literally "What a green island!".

Though 12km long, only 40 people live on Île Verte

Its isolation and constant winds have discouraged many would-be colonists over the years. Basque fishermen (Île aux Basques lies nearby), however, made use of the island from very early on. French missionaries were also a presence on the island. They were there to convert the Malecite Aboriginals who came to the island every year to trade and fish. Around 1920, the island enjoyed an economic boom when the region became a source of a type of sea moss that was dried and used to stuff mattresses and carriage seats.

Visitors to the island have the opportunity to watch sturgeon and herring being salted in little smokehouses, taste excellent local lamb, watch beluga and blue whales and photograph the waterfowl, black ducks and herons. The **Lighthouse** ★★ *($6; mid-May to mid-Oct, every day 10am to 5pm; Route du Phare, ☎898-2730, members.tripod.com/ileverte)*, or *phare*, located on the eastern tip of the island, is the oldest on the St. Lawrence (built in 1806). Five generations of the Lindsay family tended the lighthouse from 1827 to 1964. From the top of the tower, the view can seem almost endless.

Trois-Pistoles

According to legend, a French sailor passing through the region in the 17th century dropped his silver tumbler, worth three pistols, in the nearby river, giving the river its unusual name. The name was adopted by the small industrial town that sprang up next to the river.

When the colossal **Église Notre-Dame-des-Neiges** ★★ *(mid-May to mid-Sep, every day 9am to 4pm; mid-Oct to mid-May, 1pm to 5pm; 30 Rue Notre-Dame Est, ☎851-4949)* was built in 1887, the citizens of Trois-Pistoles believed their church would soon be named the cathedral of the diocese. This explains the size and splendour of the building, topped by three silver steeples. The honour eventually fell to the Rimouski church (the masterpiece of architect David Ouellet) to the great dismay of the congregation of Notre-Dame-des-Neiges. An Ottawa canon by the name of Georges Bouillon decorated the elaborate Roman Byzantine interior.

★★
Saint-Fabien-sur-Mer and Le Bic

The landscape suddenly becomes more rugged, giving visitors a taste of the Gaspé region further east. In Saint-Fabien-sur-Mer, a line of cottages is wedged between the beach and a 200m-high cliff. An octagonally-shaped barn built around 1888 is located inland in the village of Saint-Fabien. This type of farm building originated in the United States and, while interesting, proved relatively impractical and enjoyed limited popularity in Québec.

★
Rimouski

At the end of the 17th century, a French merchant named René Lepage, originally from Auxerre, France, undertook the monumental task of clearing the Rimouski seigneury. The land thus became the easternmost area on the Gulf of St. Lawrence to be colonized under the French regime. In 1919, the Abitibi-Price company opened a factory here, turning the town into an important wood-processing centre. Today, Rimouski is considered the administrative capital of eastern Québec, and prides itself for being on the cutting edge of the arts. Rimouski means "land of the moose" in Micmac.

The **Canyon des Portes de l'Enfer** *($5; mid-May to late Oct, every day 9:30am to 5pm; Saint-Narcisse-de-Rimouski, 5.6km along a dirt road, ☎735-6063)* is a fascinating natural spectacle, especially in winter. Literally the "gates of hell," this canyon starts at the 18m Grand Saut falls and stretches nearly 5km on either side of the Rivière

Québec

Rimouski, with cliffs reaching as high as 90m in places. Guided boat tours are conducted in the canyon.

Pointe-au-Père

Musée de la Mer and the **Pointe-au-Père Lighthouse National Historic Sight ★★** (*$5.50; mid-Jun to late Aug, every day 9am to 6pm; Sep to mid-Oct, every day 10am to 5pm; 1034 Rue du Phare Ouest, ☎ 724-6214*) is also known as the Lieu Nationale Historique du Phare-Pointe-au-Père. It was off the shores of Pointe-au-Père that the *Empress of Ireland* sank in 1914, claiming the lives of 1,012 people. The Musée de la Mer houses a fascinating collection of objects recovered from the wreck and provides a detailed account of the tragedy. The nearby lighthouse, which is open to the public, marks the exact spot where the river officially becomes the Gulf of St. Lawrence.

Gaspésie

★
Grand-Métis

Grand-Métis is blessed with a micro-climate that once attracted wealthy summer visitors to the area and also made it possible for horticulturist Elsie Reford to plant a landscape garden here. The garden is now the town's main attraction, containing a number of species of trees and flowers that cannot be found anywhere else at this latitude in North America. The word "Métis" is derived from the Malecite name for the area, "Mitis" meaning "little poplar."

The **Jardins de Métis ★★** (*$8; early Jun to late Aug, every day 8:30am to 6:30pm; Sep and Oct, every day 8:30am to 5pm; 200 Route 132, ☎ 775-2221, ≈ 775-6201*). In 1927, Elsie Stephen Meighen Reford inherited an estate from her uncle, Lord Mount Stephen, who had made his fortune by investing in the Canadian Pacific transcontinental railroad. The following year, she began laying out a landscape garden that she maintained and expanded until her death in 1954. Seven years later, the government of Québec purchased the estate and opened it to the public. The garden is divided into eight distinct ornamental sections – the Floral Massif, the Rock Garden, the Rhododendron Garden, the Royal Walkway, the Primrose Garden, the Crab Apple Garden, the *Muret* (low wall) overlooking Baie de Mitis, and the Underbrush, which contains a collection of indigenous plants. The mosquitoes are voracious here, so don't forget your insect repellent.

The **Musée de la Villa Historique Reford ★★** (*Jun to mid-Sep, every day 9am to 5pm; in the Jardins de Métis, ☎ 775-3165*), a 37-room villa set in the midst of the Jardins de Métis, offers a glimpse of what life was like for turn-of-the-century Métissiens. Visitors can tour a number of rooms, the servants' quarters, the chapel, the general store, the school and the doctor's office. There is also a restaurant and gift shop.

Matane

The main attraction in Matane, whose name means "Beaver Pond" in Micmac, is the salmon and the famous local shrimp

that are celebrated at an annual festival. The town is the region's administrative centre and economic mainspring due to its diversified industry based on fishing, lumber, cement-making, oil refining and shipping. During World War II, German submarines came all the way to the town pier.

★
Gaspé

It was here that Jacques Cartier claimed Canada for King Francis I of France in early July 1534. However, it was not until the beginning of the 18th century that the first fishing post was established in Gaspé, and the town itself did not develop until the end of that century. Throughout the 19th century, the lives of an entire population of poorly-educated, destitute French-Canadian and Acadian fishermen were regulated by the large fishing companies run by the merchants from the island of Jersey. During World War II, Gaspé prepared to become the Royal Navy's main base in the event of a German invasion of Great Britain that explains why there are a few military installations around the bay. Today, Gaspé is the most important town on the peninsula, as well as the region's administrative centre. The city follows the waterfront in a narrow ribbon of development.

In 1977, upon the initiative of the local historical society, the **Musée de la Gaspésie ★★** (*$3.50; late Jun to early Sep, every day 8:30am to 8:30pm; early Sep to mid-Jun, Tue to Fri 9am to 5pm, Sat and Sun noon to 5pm; 80 Boulevard Gaspé, ☎ 368-1534, ≈ 368-1535*) was erected on Pointe Jacques Cartier, overlooking Baie

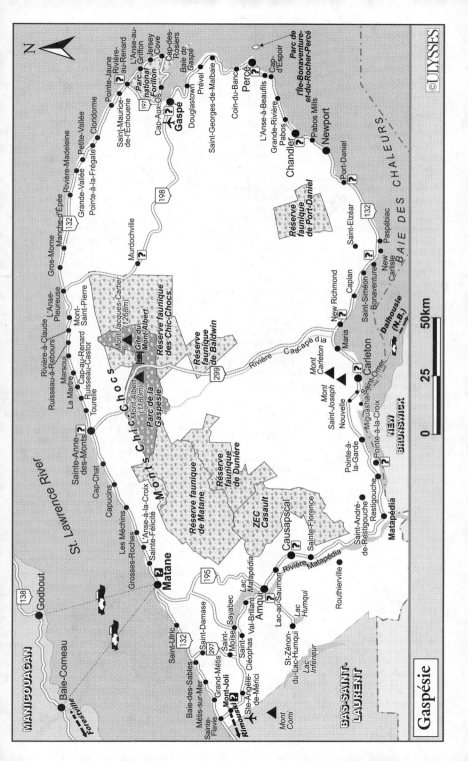

Gaspésie

© ULYSSES

de Gaspé. A museum of history and popular tradition, it houses a permanent exhibit entitled *Un Peuple de la Mer* (A People of the Sea), tracing life in Gaspésie from the first Aboriginal inhabitants, members of the Micmac tribe, all the way up to the present day. Temporary exhibits are also featured at the museum.

Cathédrale du Christ-Roi ★ (*20 Rue de la Cathédrale*), the only wooden cathedral in North America, has a contemporary design characteristic of Californian "shed" architecture, which is foreign to the east coast of the continent. Designed by Montréal architect Gérard Notebaert, it was erected in 1968 on the foundations of an earlier basilica, which was begun in 1932 to commemorate the 400th anniversary of Jacques Cartier's arrival in Canada. But it was never completed due to a lack of funds. The interior is bathed in soft light from a lovely stained glass window by Claude Théberge who made it with antique glass. Visitors will also find a fresco showing Jacques Cartier taking possession of Canada. The fresco was received as a gift from France in 1934.

★★
Percé

A famous tourist destination, Percé lies in a beautiful setting that has unfortunately been somewhat marred by the booming hotel industry. The majestic scenery features several natural phenomena, the most important being the famous Rocher Percé, which is to Québec what the Sugar Loaf is to Brazil. Since the beginning of the 20th century, artists have been flocking to Percé

every summer, charmed by the beautiful landscapes and the local inhabitants.

Upon arriving in Percé, visitors are greeted by the arresting sight of the famous **Rocher Percé ★★★**, a wall of rock measuring 400m in length and 88m in height at its tallest point. Its name, which translates as pierced rock, comes from the two entirely natural arched openings at its base. Only one of these openings remains today, since the eastern part of the rock collapsed in the mid-19th century. At low tide, starting from Plage du Mont Joli, it is possible to walk around the rock and admire the majestic surroundings and the thousands of fossils trapped in the limestone (*inquire about the time of day and duration of the tides beforehand*).

At the Percé docks, there are many boats that take people out to **Parc de l'Île Bonaventure ★★** (see p 331). During the high season, there are frequent departures from 8am to 5pm. The crossing often includes a short ride around the island and Rocher Percé so that passengers can get a good look at the park's natural attractions. Most of these outfits allow you to spend as long as you want on the island and come back on any of their boats, which travel back and forth regularly between the island and the mainland.

The **Centre d'interprétation de Percé** (*free admission; early Jun to mid-Oct, every day 9am to 5pm*) shows a short film on the history of Île Bonaventure and the gannets that nest there. Visitors will also find an exhibition area, saltwater aquariums and two short footpaths. Finally, there is a shop run by local birdwatchers that sells books and souvenirs.

Paspébiac

This little industrial town used to be the headquarters of the Robin company, which specialized in processing and exporting cod. The business was founded in 1766 by Charles Robin, a merchant from the island of Jersey, and then expanded to several spots along the coast of Gaspésie and even along the Côte-Nord. In 1791, Robin added a shipyard to his facilities in Paspébiac to build vessels to transport fish to Europe. Around 1840, the company began to face fierce competition from an enterprise owned by John LeBoutillier, one of Robin's former employees. Then, the failure of the Bank of Jersey in 1886 had a severe impact on fishing enterprises in Gaspésie, which never regained their former power.

The **Site Historique du Banc-de-Paspébiac** ★★ (*$5; late May to mid-Jun, every day 9am to 5pm; mid-Jun to mid-Sep, every day 9am to 6pm; mid-Sep to early Oct, every day 9am to 5pm; 3e Rue, Route du Quai, ☎752-6229*). A *banc* is a strip of sand and gravel used for drying fish. Paspébiac's *banc*, along with the town's deep, well-protected natural port, lent itself to the development of a fishing industry. In 1964, there were still some 70 buildings from the Robin and LeBoutillier companies on the *banc*. That year, however, most of them were destroyed by a fire. The eight surviving buildings have been carefully restored in this historic site and are open to the public.

★
Carleton

Carleton, like Bonaventure, is a stronghold of Acadian culture in Québec, and a seaside resort with a lovely sandy beach washed by calm waters that are warmer than elsewhere in Gaspésie. They account for the name of the bay (*chaleur* means warmth). The mountains rising up behind the town give it a distinctive character. Carleton was founded in 1756 by Acadian refugees who were joined by deportees returning from exile. Originally known as Tracadièche, the little town was renamed in the 19th century by the British elite in honour of Sir Guy Carleton, Canada's third governor.

Nouvelle

Palaeontology buffs will surely be interested in **Parc de Miguasha** ★★ (*free admission; early Jun to mid-Oct, every day 9am to 6pm; 231 Miguasha Ouest,*

Nouvelle, ☎794-2475), recently named a UNESCO World Heritage Site, and the second-largest fossil site in the world. The park's **palaeontology museum** displays fossils discovered in the surrounding cliffs, which formed the bottom of a lagoon 370 million years ago. The information centre houses a permanent collection of many interesting specimens. In the laboratory visitors can learn the methods used to remove fossils from the rock and identify them. The park also has an amphitheatre that is used for audiovisual presentations.

West of Miguasha, Baie des Chaleurs narrows considerably as it approaches the mouth of the Rivière Restigouche, which flows into it.

Îles-de-la-Madeleine

★
Île du Cap aux Meules

Our tour begins on Île du Cap aux Meules since it is the archipelago's most populated island as well as the docking point for all the ferries (Cap-aux-Meules). Home to the region's major infrastructures, (hospital, high school, CÉGEP), this island is the centre of local economic activity. This activity does not take away from the island's charm, however, with its brightly painted houses that some say allow sailors to see their homes from the sea.

A climb to the top of the **Butte du Vent** ★★ reveals a superb panorama of the island and the gulf.

The beautiful **Chemin de Gros-Cap** ★★, south of Cap-aux-Meules, runs along the Baie de Plaisance and offers breathtaking scenery. If possible, stop at the **Pêcherie Gros-Cap**, where the employees can be seen at work in this fish-processing plant.

For a long time, **Étang-du-Nord** was home to almost half the population of the Îles-de-la-Madeleine and constituted the largest fishing village. With the foundation of Cap-aux-Meules (1959) and Fatima (1954), however, it lost a significant part of its population, and now only has just over 3,000 inhabitants. The municipality, with its beautiful port, welcomes many visitors every year who come to take advantage of the region's tranquillity and natural beauty.

North of Étang-du-Nord, visitors can take in the splendid view by walking along the magnificent **Falaises de la Belle Anse** ★★. The violent waves crashing relentlessly along the coast are an impressive sight from the top of this rocky escarpment.

Québec

Seals

★★★
Île du Havre Aubert

The beautiful Île du Havre Aubert, dotted with beaches, hills and forests, has managed to keep its picturesque charm. From early on it was home to various colonies. Even today, buildings testify to these early colonial years. Prior to this, it was populated by Micmac communities, from which relics have been discovered.

Havre-Aubert, the first stop on the island, stretches along the sea and benefits from a large bay ideal for fishing. Apart from the magnificent scenery, the most interesting attraction is without a doubt the **La Grave ★★★** area. It has developed along a pebbly beach and gets its charm from the traditional cedar-shingled houses. It lies at the heart of a lively area, and is home to several cultural events. Boutiques and cafés line the streets, which are always enjoyable, even in bad weather. The few buildings along the sea were originally stores and warehouses that received the fish caught by locals.

For anyone interested in the fascinating world of marine life, the **Aquarium des Îles-de-la-Madeleine ★** (*$4; early Jun to late Aug, every day 10am to 6pm, early Sep to mid-Oct, every day 10am to 5pm; P.O. box 146, 982 Route 199, La Grave, ☎937-2277*) is a real treat. Here visitors can observe (and even touch) many different marine species

such as lobsters, crabs, sea urchins, eels, a ray, as well as a multitude of other fish and crustaceans. The second floor has more of an educational atmosphere with exhibits explaining the various fishing techniques used by the islands' fishers throughout the years.

The **Musée de la Mer ★** (*$3.50; late Jun to late Aug, Mon to Fri 9am to 6pm, Sat to Sun 10am to 6pm; late Aug to late Jun, Mon to Fri 9am to noon and 1pm to 5pm, Sat to Sun 1pm to 5pm; Pointe Shea, at the end of Highway 199, ☎937-5711*) recounts the history of the populating of the islands as well as the relationship that links the Madelinots' to the sea. Visitors also have the opportunity to explore the world of fishing and navigation, as well as discover some of the myths and legends that surround the sea.

Sandy Hook Dune ★★★ (see p 332)

The road that runs along the sea between the Pointe à Marichite and the Étang-des-Caps offers a magnificent **view ★★** of the Gulf of St. Lawrence. From the small village of **L'Étang-des-Caps**, the small Île Corps Mort is visible in the distance on clear days.

Île du Havre aux Maisons

Île du Havre aux Maisons ★★ is characterized by its bare landscape and

its small, attractive villages with pretty little houses scattered along the winding roads. The steep cliffs at the southern end of the island overlook the gulf and offer a fascinating view of this immense stretch of water. The Dune du Nord and the Dune du Sud are two long strips of sand found at both extremities of the island and are home to beautiful beaches. In the centre of the town, also named **Havre-aux-Maisons**, stand the Vieux Couvent (old convent) and the presbytery. The town is also the island's main centre of activity.

La Méduse ★ (*37 Chemin de la Carrière, Havre-aux-Maisons, ☎969-4245*) glass-blowing factory opens its doors to visitors, allowing them to see the glass-blowers and work. Next to the workshop is a small boutique that displays the items made there.

The scenic Chemin de la Pointe-Basse crosses the south of the island along the Baie de Plaisance and offers beautiful views. A small path along the road, between the Cap à Adrien and the Cap à Alfred, descends towards the sea, revealing the charming natural haven of Pointe-Basse.

Grosse Île

The rocky coasts of **Grosse Île** have caused numerous shipwrecks, whose survivors have settled here. A good number of these accidental colonists were Scottish and approximately 500 of them still live here today. Most earn their living from fishing and agriculture, while some also work in the Seleine saltworks, which opened in 1983.

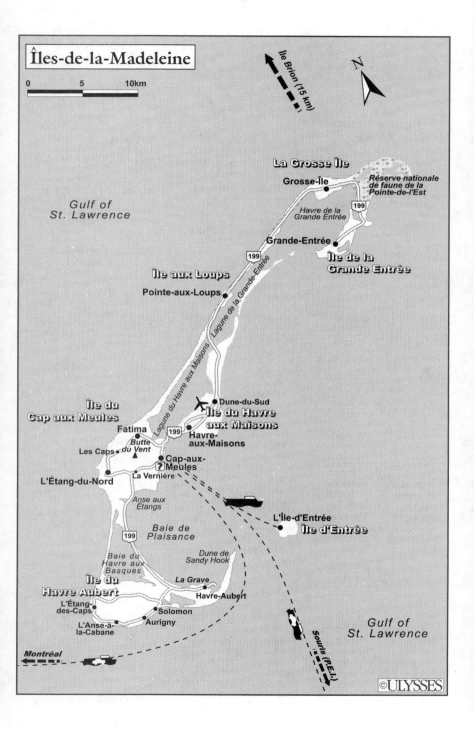

Highway 199 continues until the **Pointe-de-l'Est National Wildlife Area** ★ (see below).

★
Île de la Grande Entrée

Île de la Grande Entrée, colonized in 1870, was the last of the Îles-de-la-Madeleine to be inhabited. Upon arriving, cross Pointe Old-Harry to check out a striking view of the gulf. This tip of the island was named in honour of Harry Clark, who was the area's only inhabitant for many years. The island's main town, **Grande-Entrée**, has an active port that serves as a departure point for many brightly painted fishing boats, usually for lobster fishing.

The **Old Harry School** (*Jun to Aug, Mon to Fri 8am to noon and 1pm to 4pm; 787 Chemin Principal, ☎985-2116*) is a reproduction of an old-fashioned schoolhouse. A quick tour includes old photos and paraphernalia.

To know more about the lives of seals, visit the **Centre d'interprétation du phoque** ★ (*Jun to Aug, every day 11am to 6pm; 377 Route 199; ☎985-2833*) where various exhibits explain the lifestyle of these mammals.

★★
Île d'Entrée

Île d'Entrée differs from the rest of the islands not only because of its geographic location (it is the only inhabited island that is not linked to the others), but also because of its population of some 200 residents, all of Scottish descent. This small community lives

almost entirely from the sea and has managed to settle on this land despite the waves and the wind. The island has its own infrastructure to meets the needs of its residents (electricity, roads, and telephone). An incredible serenity prevails here.

Saguenay– Lac-Saint-Jean

★
Rivière-Éternité

With a poetic name that translates as Eternity River, how could anyone resist being carried away by the stunning beauty of the Saguenay, especially because Rivière-Éternité is the gateway to **Parc du Saguenay** ★★★ (p 332) and the marvelous **Parc Marin du Saguenay–St-Laurent** ★★★ (p 509), where whales can be observed in their natural habitat.

On the first of the three cliffs that form Cap Trinité is a statue of the Virgin Mary, christened **Notre-Dame-du-Saguenay**. Carved out of pine by Louis Jobin, it was placed here in 1881 in thanks for a favour granted to a travelling salesman who was saved from certain death when he fell near the cape. The statue is tall enough (8.5m) to be clearly visible from the deck of ships coming up the river.

★
La Baie

La Baie is an industrial town occupying a beautiful site at the far end of the Baie des Ha! Ha!, which is old French for *impasse* (dead-end). The colourful term "Ha!Ha!" was supposedly employed

by the region's first explorers, who headed into the bay thinking it was a river. The town of La Baie is the result of the 1976 merging of three adjacent municipalities (Bagotville, Port-Alfred and Grande-Baie). The latter was founded in 1838 by the Société des Vingt-et-Un, making it the oldest of the three. At La Baie, the Saguenay is still influenced by the salt-water tides, giving the town a maritime feel. La Baie also has a large **sea port**, which is open to the public.

Musée du Fjord ★ (*$4; late Jun to early Sep, Mon to Fri 9am to 6pm, Sat and Sun 10am to 6pm; early Sep to late Jun, Mon to Fri 8:30am to noon and 1:30pm to 5pm; Sat and Sun 10am to 5pm; 3346 Boulevard de la Grande-Baie S., ☎697-5077, ☎697-5079*). The Société des Vingt-et-Un was founded in La Malbaie (Charlevoix) in 1837 with the secret aim of finding new farmlands to ease overcrowding on the banks of the St. Lawrence. Under the pretext of cutting wood for the Hudson's Bay Company, the Société cleared the land around a number of coves along the Saguenay and settled men, women and children there.

On June 11, 1838, Thomas Simard's schooner, with the first settlers on board, set anchor in the Baie des Ha! Ha! The colonists disembarked and, under the supervision of Alexis Tremblay, built the region's very first wood cabin (4m x 6m), thus marking the birth of the present town of La Baie. The Musée du Fjord houses an interesting permanent exhibition, describing the settling of the Saguenay region from an ethnographic angle. Temporary art and science exhibits are

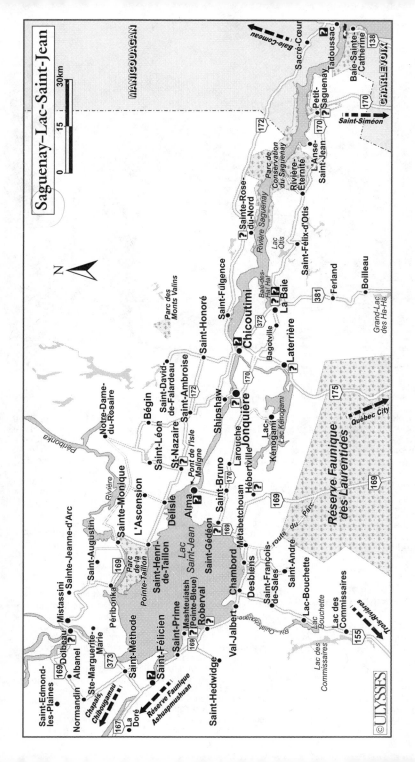

Saguenay–Lac-Saint-Jean

MANICOUAGAN

CHARLEVOIX

Baie-Comeau

Sacré-Cœur

Tadoussac
Baie-Sainte-
Catherine 138

Saguenay
Petit-
Saguenay

170

Saint-Siméon

172

L'Anse-
Saint-Jean

170
170

Parc de
Conservation
du Saguenay

Rivière-
Éternité

Saint-Félix-d'Otis

Sainte-Rose-
du-Nord

Lac
Otis

Ferland

Boilleau

Rivière Saguenay

Grand-Lac
des Ha!Ha!

Parc des
Monts Valins

Saint-Fulgence

381

Chicoutimi

Baie-des-
Ha! Ha!

La Baie

Saint-Honoré

372

Bagotville

Laterrière

Saint-David-
de-Falardeau

Saint-Ambroise

170

Bégin

172

Saint-Léon

Shipshaw

Jonquière
Larouche
Hébertville

Lac-
Kénogami
(Lac Kénogami)

Notre-Dame-
du-Rosaire

St-Nazaire

Pont de l'Isle
Maligne

170
169

Réserve Faunique
des Laurentides

175

Québec City

169

Sainte-Monique

Rivière

Péribonka

L'Ascension

Delisle

Alma

Saint-Bruno

Métabetchouan

169

route du Parc

Saint-Augustin

Saint-Henri-
de-Taillon

Parc
de la
Pointe-Taillon

Sainte-Jeanne-d'Arc

Lac
Saint-Jean

Saint-Gédéon

169

Chambord

Desbiens

Saint-François-
de-Sales

Saint-André

Mistassini

Dolbeau

169

Albanel

Saint-Méthode

Saint-Prime

Roberval

Val-Jalbert

Lac-Bouchette

Lac
Bouchette

Normandin

169

Ste-Marguerite-
Marie

373

Saint-Félicien

169 (Pointe-Bleue)
Mashteuiatsh

Saint-Edmond-
les-Plaines

Chapais,
Chibougamau

La
Doré

167

Réserve Faunique
Ashuapmushuan

Saint-Hedwidge

Lac des
Commissaires

Lac des
Commissaires

155

Trois-Rivières

© ULYSSES

N

0   15   30km

Péribonka

Pulperie de Chicoutimi

also presented here each year.

At the **Palais Municipal** ★ (*$28.5; early Jul to mid-Aug, at 8pm; 591 5e Rue,* ☎888-873-3333*), visitors can see *La Fabuleuse Histoire d'un Royaume*, an elaborate historical pageant similar to those presented in some provincial French towns. Bringing this colourful extravaganza to life involves over 200 actors and 1,400 costumes, along with animals, carriages, lighting effects and sets.

★
Chicoutimi

In the language of the Montagnais, "Chicoutimi" means "there where it is deep." That refers to the waters of the Saguenay, navigable as far as this city, the most important urban area in the entire Saguenay–Lac-Saint-Jean region. For over 1,000 years, nomadic Aboriginal peoples used this spot for meetings, festivities and trade. Starting in 1676, Chicoutimi became one of the most important fur-trading posts in New France. The post remained active up until the mid-19th century, when two industrialists, Peter McLeod and William Price, opened a sawmill nearby (1842). This finally enabled the development of a real town on the site, graced with the presence of three powerful rivers: the Moulin, the Chicoutimi and the Saguenay.

Religious and institutional buildings are predominant in downtown Chicoutimi. Its main commercial thoroughfare is Rue Racine. Very little remained of the 19th-century Victorian town after most of Chicoutimi was destroyed by a raging fire in 1912. The rest has been "modernized" or stripped of its character over the past 30 years. Along the streets, visitors will notice shop signs bearing typical Saguenay names like Tremblay and Claveau, as well as English-sounding names like Harvey and Blackburn. This indicates a phenomenon found only in this part of the country: the assimilation of English-speaking families into French-speaking society.

At the turn of the 20th century, several large-scale French-Canadian enterprises were established in the Saguenay–Lac-Saint-Jean region, the largest being the pulp mills in Val-Jalbert and Chicoutimi. The **Pulperie de Chicoutimi** ★★ (*$7; mid-Jun to early Sep, every day, 9am to 6am; Jul, every day 9am to 8pm; 300 Rue Dubuc,* ☎698-3100, ⬛698-3158*) was founded in 1896 by Dominique Guay and then expanded several times by the powerful North American Pulp and Paper Company, directed by Alfred Dubuc. For 20 years, the company was the largest mechanical manufacturer of pulp and paper in Canada, supplying the French, American and British markets. This vast industrial complex, built alongside the turbulent Rivière Chicoutimi, included four pulp mills equipped with turbines and digesters, two hydroelectric stations, a smelter, a repair shop and a railway platform. The decline of pulp prices in 1921 and the crash of 1929 led to the closing of the pulp mill. It remained abandoned until 1980. In the meantime, most of the buildings were ravaged by fire, which, if nothing else, showed the strength of their thick stone walls.

Since 1996, the whole complex has become a gigantic museum covering an area of over 1ha. In addition to stopping in at the Maison-Musée du Peintre Arthur-Villeneuve, visitors can go on a 12-stop self-guided tour of the site and take in a thematic exhibition.

Jonquière

In 1847, the Société des Défricheurs (meaning land-clearers) du Saguenay received authorization to set up business alongside Rivière aux Sables. The name Jonquière was chosen in memory of one of the governors of New France, the Marquis de Jonquière. The town's early history is marked by the story of Marguerite Belley of La Malbaie, who escorted three of her sons to Jonquière on horseback to prevent them from being tempted to emigrate to the United States. In 1870, the territory between Jonquière and Saint-Félicien, in the Lac-Saint-Jean region, was destroyed by a major forest fire. It took

over 40 years for the region to recover. Today, Jonquière is regarded as an essentially modern town whose economic mainspring is the Alcan aluminum smelter.

This multinational company owns several factories in the Saguenay–Lac-Saint-Jean region, replacing the Price brothers and their wood empire as the largest local employer. The towns of Arvida and Kénogami merged with Jonquière in 1975, forming a city large enough to rival nearby Chicoutimi. Jonquière is known for its industrial tours.

The **Centrale Hydroélectrique de Shipshaw** ★★ (*free tour; Jun to Aug, Mon to Fri 1:30pm and 3pm; 1471 Route du Pont, ☎699-1547*), which began operating in 1931, is a striking example of Art-Deco architecture. It supplies electricity to the local aluminum smelters.

Val-Jalbert

The **Village Historique de Val-Jalbert** ★★ (*$10; early Apr to mid-Jun and late Aug to late Dec, every day 9am to 5pm; mid-Jun to late Aug, every day 9am to 7pm; Route 169, C.P. 307; ☎275-3132 or 888-675-3132, ≈275-5875*) began in 1901 when an industrialist by the name of Damase Jalbert built a pulp mill at the foot of the Rivière Ouiatchouane falls. The enterprise prospered quickly, becoming the most important industrial company run entirely by French Canadians. The drop in pulp prices in 1921, followed by the shift to artificial pulp in the manufacture of paper, forced the mill to close down in 1927 at which point the village was completely deserted by its inhabitants.

Val-Jalbert is a rich slice of North America's industrial heritage. Part of the village still looks like a ghost town, while the rest has been carefully restored to provide visitors with accommodations and an extremely informative interpretation centre. Various viewing areas, linked by a gondola (*$3.25*), have been built to enable visitors to appreciate fully the surroundings. There is a campground beside the village and accommodations are available in some of the restored houses.

Saint-Félicien

At the **Zoo Sauvage de Saint-Félicien** ★★ (*$17; mid-Oct to late Oct and early May to mid-May, by reservation only; mid-May to late May, every day 9am to 5pm; early Jun to late Aug, every day 9am to 6pm; early Sep to mid-Oct, every day 9am to 5pm; early Nov to late Apr, walking access Mon to Fri, special hours (tours by train) during the winter; ☎679-0543 or 800-667-5687, ≈679-3647*), visitors can observe various species of Québec's indigenous wildlife in their natural habitat. What makes this zoo unusual is that the animals are not in cages. They roam about freely, while visitors tour the zoo in small, screened buses. A lumber camp, a fur-trading post, a Montagnais encampment, and a settler's farm have all been reconstructed, and along with the authentic buildings onsite, add a historical feel to this unique zoo.

★
Péribonka

Louis Hémon was born in Brest (France) in 1880. After attending the Lycée Louis-LeGrand in Paris, he obtained his law degree from the Sorbonne. In 1903, he settled in London where he started his career as a writer. His adventurous spirit eventually led him to Canada. He first lived in Québec City, then in Montréal, where he met some investors who wanted to build a railroad in the northern part of the Lac-Saint-Jean region. He headed off to scout out a location but became fascinated instead by the local inhabitants' daily life. In June 1912, he met Samuel Bédard, who invited him to his home in Péribonka. Hémon helped out on the farm, secretly recording his impressions of the trip in a notebook. These impressions later formed the basis of his masterpiece, the novel *Maria Chapdelaine*.

Hémon did not, however, have time to enjoy his novel's tremendous success. On July 8, 1913, he was hit by a train while walking on the railroad tracks near Chapleau, Ontario, and died a few minutes later in the arms of his travelling companions. *Maria Chapdelaine* was serialized in *Le Temps* in Paris, then published as a novel by Grasset in 1916, and finally translated into several languages. No other work of literature has done so much to make Québec known abroad. The novel was even adapted three times for the screen: by Jean Duvivier in 1934 (with Madeleine Renaud and Jean Gabin), Marc Allégret in 1949 (with Michèle Morgan in the title role) and Gilles Carle in 1983 (with Carole Laure in the title role). Péribonka is a charming village that serves as the starting point for the swimming race, the Traversée Internationale du Lac Saint-Jean.

Musée Louis-Hémon ★★
(*$5.50; Jun to Sep, every day 9am to 5pm; Sep to Jun, Mon to Fri 9am to 4pm; 700 Route 169, ☎374-2177, ≈374-2516*) is located in the house where Louis Hémon spent the summer of 1912 with Samuel Bédard and his wife Eva (née Bouchard). It is still visible alongside Route 169 and is one of a few rare examples of colonial homes in the Lac-Saint-Jean region to have survived the improvements in the local standard of living.

The extremely modest house that inspired Hémon was built in 1903. Since it was converted into a museum in 1938, its furnishings have remained intact, and are still laid out in their original positions in the humble rooms. A large postmodern building was erected nearby in order to house Hémon's personal belongings, as well as various souvenirs of the villagers who inspired his work and memorabilia relating to the success of *Maria Chapdelaine*.

Alma

This industrial town lies along the edge of the Lac-Saint-Jean region. It is home to a large aluminum smelter and a paper mill, all surrounded by working- and middle-class neighbourhoods. Parc Falaise serves as a reminder that Alma has been the twin town of Falaise, Normandy since 1969.

Tours of the facilities of the **Papeterie Alma ★** (*Jun 22 to early Sep, Tue and Thu*

9.30am to 1.30pm; 1100 Rue Melançon, ☎668-9400, ext. 9348) are also offered. The tour includes a visit to the pulp department and the machine room, as well as an explanation of the manufacturing process.

Manicouagan

★★
Tadoussac

In 1600, eight years before Québec City was founded, Tadoussac was established as a trading post. It was chosen for its strategic location at the mouth of the Saguenay river. Tadoussac was the first permanent white settlement north of Mexico. In 1615, the Récollet religious order established a mission that operated until the mid-19th century. The town's tourism trade received a boost in 1864 when the original Tadoussac Hotel was built to better accommodate the growing number of visitors coming to the area to enjoy the sea air and breathtaking landscape. Although the town is old by North American standards, it has a look of impermanence, as if a strong wind could sweep the entire town away.

Dominating the town, the **Hôtel Tadoussac ★** (*165 Rue du Bord-de-l'Eau, ☎235-4421*) is to this community what the Château Frontenac is to Québec City: its symbol and landmark. The current hotel was built between 1942 and 1949 by the Canada Steamship Lines, following the destruction of the first hotel. Reminiscent of the resort hotels built in New England during the second half of the 19th century, Hôtel Tadoussac is long

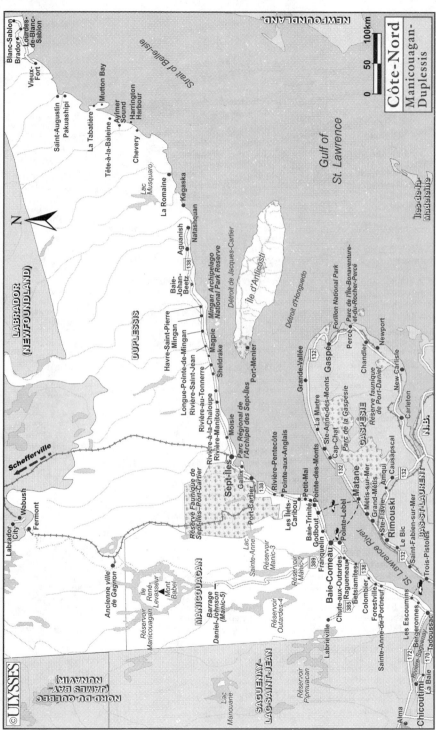

Côte-Nord
Manicouagan-
Duplessis

Barrage Daniel-Johnson

and low and its weathered wood-siding exterior contrasts sharply with the bright red roof. The polished wood panelling and antique furniture that characterize the interior decor reflect traditional rural French-Canadian tastes.

The **Centre d'Interprétation des Mammifères Marins ★** (*$5.50; mid-May to late Oct, every day noon to 5pm, late Jun to late Sep, every day 9am to 8pm; 108 Rue de la Cale-Sèche, ☎235-4701*) is an information centre that was created to educate people about the whales that migrate to the region every summer. The centre features skeletons of various sea mammals, video presentations, and an aquarium with specimens of fish species that live in the St. Lawrence. Naturalists are on hand to answer questions.

The **Dunes de Sable** (sand dunes) and the **Maison des Dunes ★** are located approximately 5km north of Tadoussac. The dunes were formed thousands of years ago as glaciers receded. Although the government now protects the dunes, it is still possible to ski on them at certain times. For information and equipment rental, contact the youth hostel or the **Centre d'interprétation des Dunes de Sable** (*free admis-*

sion; *May to Oct, every day 9am to 7pm; Chemin du Moulin-à-Baude, ☎235-4238*). Turn right onto Rue des Pionniers from Route 138. The dunes are 3.5km farther on. The Maison des Dunes parking lot is located 5.8km past the turnoff from Route 138.

Baie-Comeau

In 1936, Colonel Robert McCormick, publisher and senior editor of *The Chicago Tribune*, no longer wanted to be dependant upon foreign paper-making companies. He chose to build his own paper factory in Baie-Comeau, sparking the transformation of a quiet village into a bustling mill. Over the years, other large companies were attracted to Baie-Comeau by the abundance and low cost of local hydro-electric power. The young town is named after Napoléon Comeau (1845-1923), famed trapper, geologist and naturalist of the Côte-Nord.

The **Centrales Manic 2 et Manic 5 (Barrage Daniel-Johnson) ★★★** (*free admission; every day: Manic 2, 9am, 11am, 1.30pm and 3.30pm; Manic 5, 9am, 11am, 1:30pm and 3:30pm; 135 Boulevard Comeau, ☎294-3923*), the generating stations and dam, are located on the Rivière

Manicouagan. A 30min drive through the beautiful Canadian Shield landscape leads to the first dam of the complex Manic 2, the largest hollow-joint gravity dam in the world. A guided tour of the dam brings visitors inside the imposing structure. A 3hr drive further north leads to the more impressive Manic 5 and the Daniel-Johnson dam. Built in 1968, the dam is named after a Québec premier who died on the morning the dam was officially declared completed. With a 214m central arch and measuring 1,314m in length, it is the largest multiple-arch structure in the world. The dam regulates the water supply to the generating stations of the Manic-Outardes complex. Visitors can walk to the foot of the dam as well as to the top where there is a magnificent view of the Vallée de la Manicouagan and the reservoir, which measures 2,000km^2

Duplessis

Sept-Îles

This town, which extends along the vast Baie de Sept-Îles (45km^2), is the administrative centre of the Côte Nord. A fur-trading post under the French Regime, Sept-Îles experienced an industrial boom in the early 20th century sparked by the development of the forestry industry. By about 1950, Sept-Îles had become an important relay point in the transport of iron and coal – resources extracted from the Schefferville and Fermont mines and sent to

Sept-Îles by railroad. The town's deep-water port is ice-free during the winter and ranks second in Canada after Montréal in terms of tonnage handled annually. Sept-Îles is named after the archipelago of seven islands in the entrance to the bay. The town is a good starting point for exploring the northern regions of Labrador and Nord-du-Québec.

The **Vieux-Poste** ★ (*$3.25; late Jun to late Aug, every day 9am to 5pm; Boulevard des Montagnais, ☎968-2070*) is a reconstruction of the important Sept-Îles fur-trading post established during the French Regime. Based on archaeological excavations and documents from the period, the compound appears as it would have in the mid-18th century. It's complete with a chapel, stores, houses and protective wooden fences. Montagnais culture is explored through exhibits and, according to season, various outdoor activities.

The **Musée Régional de la Côte-Nord** ★ (*$3.25; late Jun to Labour Day, every day 9am to 5pm; rest of the year, Mon to Fri 9am to noon, 1pm to 5pm, Sat and Sun 1pm to 5pm; 500 Boulevard Laure, ☎968-2070*) displays some 40,000 objects of anthropological and artistic importance found during the many archaeological digs carried out along the Côte-Nord. It also features stuffed wildlife, Aboriginal objects and contemporary artistic works (paintings, sculptures and photographs) from various regions of Québec.

★
Havre-Saint-Pierre

This small picturesque town was founded in 1857 by fishermen from the Îles-de-la-Madeleine. In 1948, following the discovery of large titanium deposits 43km inland, the town's economy was transformed overnight by the QIT-Feret-Titarle company. It became an active industrial centre and port. Since the opening of the Mingan Archipelago National Park Reserve in 1983, Havre-Saint-Pierre has also developed a significant tourism industry. The town is an excellent starting point for visitors who want to explore the Îles de Mingan and the large Île d'Anticosti.

The **Centre Culturel et d'interprétation de Havre-St-Pierre** ★ (*$2; late Jun to early Sep, every day 10am to 10pm; 957 Rue de la Berge, ☎538-2512 or 538-2512*) is an information centre in the Clark family's former general store, which has been skilfully restored. Local history is recounted with an exhibit and slide show.

Centre d'Accueil et d'interprétation, Réserve du Parc National de l'Archipel-de-Mingan (*free admission; mid-Jun to late Aug, every day 10am to 5:30pm; 975 Rue de l'Escale, ☎538-3285*) is the information centre for the Mingan Archipelago park. Here visitors will find a photo exhibit as well as all the information they will need concerning the flora, fauna and geology of the Mingan islands.

★★
Île d'Anticosti

The presence of Aboriginals on Île d'Anticosti goes back many years. The Montagnais made sporadic visits to the island but the harsh climate discouraged permanent settlement. In 1542, Basque fishers named the island "Anti Costa," which roughly means "anti-coast," or "after travelling all this way across the Atlantic, we still haven't reached the mainland!" In 1679, Louis Jolliet was given the island by the king of France for leading important expeditions into the middle of the North American continent. Jolliet's efforts to settle Anticosti were limited by the island's isolation, poor soil and high winds. To make matters much worse, British troops returning from a failed bid to take Québec City in 1690 were shipwrecked on the island and slaughtered most of the settlers living there. Anticosti is feared by sailors because more than 400 ships have run aground here since the 17th century.

In 1895, Île d'Anticosti became the exclusive property of Henri Menier, a French chocolate tycoon. The "Cocoa Baron" introduced white-tailed deer and foxes to the island to create a personal hunting preserve. In addition, he established the villages of Baie-Sainte-Claire (later abandoned) and Port-Menier, now the only settlement on the island. Menier governed the island like an absolute monarch reigning over his subjects. He established forestry operations on the island and commissioned a cod-fishing fleet. In 1926, his heirs sold Anticosti to a consortium of Canadian forestry companies named Wayagamack that continued operations until 1974 when the island was sold to the Québec government and became a wildlife reserve. Not until 1983 were residents given the right to purchase land and houses on the island. Anticosti, still unexplored in parts, holds many surprises, such as the **Grotte à**

Québec

la Patate cave (see p 333), discovered in 1982.

Port-Menier

Port-Menier, where the ferry from Havre-Saint-Pierre docks, is the only inhabited village on the island, with a population of 340. Most village houses were built during the Menier era, giving the village a certain architectural uniformity. Foundations of the **Château Menier** (1899), an elaborate wooden villa built in the American shingle-style tradition, can be seen from Route de Baie-Sainte-Claire. When the villagers could not adequately maintain the spectacular estate, they set fire to it in 1954, reducing an irreplaceable historical building to ashes. In **Baie-Sainte-Claire**, visitors can see the remains of a lime kiln built in 1897, the only vestige of the short-lived village that once stood on this site.

Baie-Johan-Beetz

Originally known as "Piastrebaie" due to its location at the mouth of the Rivière Piashti, this village was renamed after the learned Belgian naturalist Johan Beetz in 1918. Piastrebaie was founded around 1860 by Joseph Tanguay, who, along with his wife Marguerite Murdock, earned a living here fishing salmon. Over the following years, a number of immigrants from the Îles-de-la-Madeleine arrived. These included the Bourque, Loyseau, Desjardins and Devost families, whose descendants still live mainly on hunting and fishing.

Maison Johan-Beetz ★ (*$3; mid-May to mid-Jun 9am to 6pm, mid-Jun to mid-Jul 9am to 5pm, mid-Jul to mid-Oct 9am to 6pm, every day, reser-*

vations recommended; ☎*539-0137, 15 Rue Johan-Beetz).* Johan Beetz was born in 1874 at the Oudenhouven castle in Brabant, Belgium. Grief-stricken over the death of his fiancée, he wanted to take off for the Congo but a friend convinced him to emigrate to Canada instead. A hunting and fishing fanatic, he visited the Côte-Nord, and soon set up residence there. In 1898, he married a Canadian and built this charming Second-Empire-style house, which can be visited by appointment. Beetz painted lovely still-lifes on the doors inside. In 1903, he became something of a pioneer in the fur industry when he started breeding animals for their pelts, which he sold to the Maison Revillon in Paris.

Johan Beetz contributed greatly to his neighbours' quality of life. Thanks to his university studies, he had learned the rudiments of medicine and became the man of science in whom the villagers placed their trust. Equipped with books and makeshift instruments, he treated the ills of the inhabitants of the Côte-Nord as best as he could. He even managed to save the village from Spanish influenza with a skilfully monitored quarantine. If you ask the elderly people here to tell you about Monsieur Beetz, you'll hear nothing but praise.

★ Natashquan

Withits wooden houses buffeted by the wind, this small fishing village is where the famous poet and songwriter Gilles Vigneault was born in 1928. Many of his songs describe the people and scenery of the Côte-Nord. He periodically returns to Natashquan for inspiration and still owns a house here. In the Montagnais language, Natashquan means "place where bears are hunted." The neighbouring village of Pointe-Parent is inhabited by Montagnais.

Blanc-Sablon

This isolated region was visited as early as the 16th century by Basque and Portuguese fishers. They established camps where they melted seal blubber and salted cod before shipping it to Europe. It has been suggested that Vikings, who are known to have established a settlement on the nearby island of Newfoundland, might have set up a village near Blanc-Sablon around the year AD 1000. However, archaeological digs have only just begun. Brador, a fishing camp used by French fishers from Courtemanche, has recently been reconstructed.

Blanc-Sablon is only 4km from Labrador, a large, mostly arctic territory. Much of Labrador was once part of the province of Québec, but it is now the mainland half of the province of Newfoundland. It is accessible by road from Blanc-Sablon. The former British colony of Newfoundland did not become a part of Canada until 1949. A ferry links Blanc-Sablon and the island of Newfoundland.

Parks

Bas-Saint-Laurent

Parc du Bic ★★ (*free admission; closed to cars in winter; for a schedule of summer activities, contact reception,* ☎*869-3502*) is an area of 33km² and features a jumble of coves, jutting shoreline, promontories, hills, escarpments and marshes, as well as deep bays teeming with a wide variety of plant and animal life. The park is a good place for hiking, cross-country skiing and mountain biking and also has an information centre (*Jun to mid-Oct every day 9am to 5pm*).

Gaspésie

Parc de la Gaspésie ★★★ (*free admission; early Jun to early Sep, every day 8am to 8pm; early Sep to mid-Sep, every day 8am to 5pm; 124 1re Avenue Ouest,* ☎*763-7811*) covers an area of 800km², and encompasses the famous Monts Chic-Chocs. It was established in 1937, in an effort to heighten public awareness regarding nature conservation in the Gaspésie. The park is composed of conservation zones devoted to the protection of the region's natural riches and an a-

mbient zone made up of a network of roads, trails and lodgings. The Chic-Chocs form the northernmost section of the Appalachian Mountains. They stretch over 90km from Matane to the foot of Mont Albert. The McGerrigle Mountains lie perpendicular to the Chic-Chocs, covering an area of 100km². The park's trails run through three levels of terrain, leading all the way to the summits of the four highest mountains in the area: Mont Jacques-Cartier, Mont Richardson, Mont Albert and Mont Xalibu. This is the only place in Québec where white-tailed deer (in the rich vegetation of the first level), moose (in the boreal forest) and caribou (in the tundra, at the top of the mountains) co-exist. Hikers are required to register before setting out.

The motto of **Forillon National Park ★★★** (*$3.75; year round, every day 8am to noon and 1pm to 4:30pm; 122 Boulevard Gaspé;* ☎*368-5505*) is "harmony between man, land and sea." Many an outdoor enthusiast dreams about this series of forests, mountains and cliff-lined shores all crisscrossed by hiking trails. Home to a fairly wide range of animals, this national park abounds in foxes, bears, moose, porcupines and other mammals. Over 200 species of birds live here, including herring gulls, cormorants, finches, larks and gannets. Depending on the season, visitors might catch a glimpse of whales or seals from the paths along the coast. A variety of rare plants also lie hidden away in Forillon National Park, contributing to a greater understanding of the soil in which they grow. Visitors will find not

only natural surroundings here in the park, but also traces of human activity. This vast area (245 km²) once included four little villages. The 200 families inhabiting them were relocated, but not without a fight, when the park was established in 1970. The buildings of the greatest ethnological interest were kept and restored. These included the 10 or so **Maisons de Grande-Grave**, the **Phare de Cap-Gaspé** (the lighthouse), the **former Protestant Church** of Petit-Gaspé and the **Fort Péninsule**, part of the fortifications erected during World War II to protect Canada from attacks by German submarines.

Particularly notable buildings in Grande-Grave, originally populated by Anglo-Norman immigrants from the Island of Jersey in the English Channel, include the **Magasin Hyman** (1845). The store's interior has been carefully reconstructed to evoke the early 20th century, while the **Ferme Blanchette** at the seaside could easily grace a postcard. All of these are either fully or partly open to the public.

At **Parc de l'Île Bonaventure ★★** (*transportation fee, but free admission to the island itself; early Jun to late Jun 8:15am to 4pm, late Jun to late Sep 8:15am to 5pm, late Sep to mid-Oct 9:15am to 4pm; 4 Rue du Quai,* ☎*782-2240,* ⌨*782-2241*), visitors will find large bird colonies, as well as numerous footpaths lined with rustic houses. The trails range from 2.8 to 4.9km in length and cover a total of 15km. Due to the aridity of the surroundings, visitors don't have to fear stinging insects on the island. There is also no water along the trails so be sure to bring a canteen. All trails end at an impressive bird sanctuary, where some 200,000 birds, including about 55,000 gannets, form a wildlife exhibition.

Îles-de-la-Madeleine

The eastern tip of Grosse Île, made up of dunes and beaches, is home to the diverse bird life that is characteristic of these islands. It is one of the best sites for spotting various species, such as the rare piping plover (that only nests on the islands), the northern pintail, the betted kingfisher, the atlantic puffin and the horned lark. Take care not to damage the nesting sites (generally clearly marked). This entire zone is protected by the **Pointe-de-l'Est National Wildlife Area ★**, also known as the Réserve Nationale de Faune de la Pointe-de-l'Est.

The **Plage de l'Hôpital**, located along the Dune du Nord, is a good place to go for a dip and watch the seals. There is also a shipwreck here. It should be noted that the currents become dangerous toward Pointe-aux-Loups. The Anse de l'Hôpital, Cap de l'Hôpital, Plage de l'Hôpital and Étang-de-l'Hôpital are all named after a boat that came into the cove (*anse*) carrying passengers suffering from a contagious illness (typhus). The boat was quarantined and only doctors and nurses were allowed on board.

Like a long strip of sand stretching into the gulf, **Sandy Hook Dune ★★★** is several kilometres long and its beach is among the nicest on the islands. This spot is a favourite with nudists, who come to swim in complete tranquility.

The **Plage de l'Ouest ★** stretches from the northwest part of Île du Havre Aubert to the southwest part of Île du Cap aux Meules. Perfect for swimming and shell collecting, it is renowned for its magnificent sunsets.

The **plage de la Dune du Sud ★** offers several kilometres of beach that is great for swimming

One of the most beautiful beaches of the islands, the **Plage de la Grande Échouerie ★★**, stretches for about 10km in the Pointe-de-l'Est wildlife area.

Saguenay– Lac-Saint-Jean

The **Parc du Saguenay ★★★** (*3415 Boulevard de la Grande Baie South, La Baie, G7B 1G3, accessible from Route 170, ☎544-7388, ≈697-1550*) extends across a portion of the shores of the Rivière Saguenay. It stretches from the banks of the estuary (located in the Manicouagan tourist region) to Sainte-Rose-du-Nord. In this area, steep cliffs plunge into the river, creating a magnificent landscape. The park has about 100km of hiking trails, providing visitors with an excellent opportunity to explore this fascinating region up close. A few of the more noteworthy trails include a short, relatively easy one along the banks of the Saguenay (1.7km), the Sentier de la Statue, which stretches 3.5km and includes a difficult uphill climb and the superb, 25km Sentier des Caps that takes three days (registration required). During winter, the trails are used for cross-country skiing. Accommodation in the form of campsites and shelters is available.

Manicouagan

The **Parc Marin du Saguenay–Saint-Laurent ★★★** (*182 Rue de l'Eglise, Tadoussac, ☎235-4703 or 800-463-6769*) features the Fjord du Saguenay, the southern-most fjord in the world, and was created to protect the area's exceptional aquatic wildlife. Carved out of the glaciers, the fjord is 276m deep near Cap Éternité, and just 10m deep at the mouth. The distinctive geography in the fjord, created by glacial deposits, includes a basin where fauna and flora indigenous to the Arctic can be found. The top 20m of water in the Saguenay is fresh and its temperature varies between 15°C and 18°C, whereas the deeper water is saline and maintains a temperature of approximately 1.5°C. This environment, a remainder of the ancient Goldthwait sea, supports wildlife such as the arctic shark and the beluga, creatures otherwise seen further north.

A number of whale species frequent the region to feed on the marine organisms that proliferate here due to the constant oxygenation in the water. One of these, the blue whale, reaches lengths of 30m and is the largest mammal in the world. Seals and occasionally dolphins can be seen in the park as well.

From early on, European fishers took advantage of

the abundance of marine life with the result that some species were overhunted. Today, visitors can venture out on the river to observe the whales at close range. However, strict rules have been set to protect the animals from being mistreated, and boats must maintain a certain distance.

Duplessis

The **Parc Régional de l'Archipel des Sept-Îles** ★★ is made up of several islands: Petite Boule, Grande Boule, Dequen, Manowin, Corossol, Grande Basque and Petite Basque. There is also an abundance of cod in the area, making fishing a popular activity. Trails and campsites have been set up on Île Grande Basque. For cruises around the archipelago, see p 335.

A series of islands and islets stretching over a 95km-long area, the **Mingan Archipelago National Park Reserve** ★★ (*Havre-St-Pierre*, ☎*538-3331 or 538-3285*) is also called the Réserve de Parc National de l'Archipel-de-Mingan. It boasts incredible natural riches. The islands are characterized by distinctive rock formations made up of very soft stratified limestone that has been sculpted by the waves. The formations are composed of marine sediment that was swept into the area some 250 million years ago from equatorial regions before being washed up on land and covered by a mantle of ice several kilometres thick. As the ice melted some 7,000 years ago, the islands re-emerged with their impressive stone monoliths. In addition to this fascinating element,

the marine environment encouraged the development of varied and unusual plant life. Approximately 200 species of birds nest here, including the Atlantic puffin, the gannet, and the Arctic tern. The river is also home to several whale species, including the blue whale.

There are two **visitor information centres**, one in Longue-Pointe-de-Mingan (*625 Rue du Centre*, ☎*949-2126*) and the other in Havre-Saint-Pierre (*975 Rue de l'Escale*, ☎*538-3285*). Both are open only in the summer. There are campsites on the island. Some of the islands have hiking trails.

In addition to natural attractions, the park also contains the vestiges of a very old Aboriginal settlement, dating back over 4,000 years. Montagnais from the village of Mingan were the first to visit this spot regularly to hunt for whales and gather berries.

Apart from the Viking explorers, who are known to have visited the island of Newfoundland, the first Europeans to set foot on Canadian soil are believed to have been Basque and Breton whale hunters who left evidence of their presence on Mingan islands. Archeologists have found remnants of the circular ovens made of stone and red tile (16th century) that they used to melt the whale blubber before exporting it to Europe where it was used to make candles. In 1679, Frenchmen Louis Jolliet and Jacques de Lalande purchased the archipelago for use as a fur-trading post and cod-salting site. The related installations were destroyed by the British during the Conquest (1760).

Measuring 222km in length and 56km in width, the **Réserve Faunique de l'Île d'Anticosti** ★★ is big enough to accommodate a number of activities including hunting, walking, swimming and fishing. The island has belonged to the Québec government since 1974, but was not open to hikers until 1986. The reserve is very popular among hunters and is known for its white-tailed deer. Contributing to the magnificent scenery are breathtaking panoramas, long beaches, waterfalls, caves, cliffs, and rivers.

It is possible to visit the reserve and its many natural attractions by car, provided that your vehicle is in good shape, but you'll need a few days. Sixty-five kilometres from Port-Menier, you'll find a waterfall called **Chute Kalimazoo** (*Île d'Anticosti*). A little farther lies **Baie-MacDonald**, named after Peter Mac-Donald, a fisher from Nova Scotia, who lived here as a hermit for a number of years. It is said that after falling ill and being treated in Baie-Sainte-Catherine, he walked nearly 120km in showshoes to get back home. The bay is a magnificent spot, trimmed with a long strip of fine sand. If you continue on the road that runs alongside these magnificent beaches, you'll come to **Pointe Carleton**, whose lighthouse dates from 1918. Nearby, you can see the wreckage of the **M.V. Wilcox**, a minesweeper that ran aground in 1954.

About 12km from Pointe Carleton, you'll find the road leading to the **Caverne de la Rivière à la Patate**. If your car has four-wheel drive, you can follow the road for 2km, then you'll

Québec

have to walk two more. This cave, which stretches nearly 625m, was discovered in 1981 and examined by a team of geographers in 1982.

The **Chute and Canyon de la Vauréal** ★★ are two of the major natural sites on Île Anticosti. The waterfall (*chute*) flows into the canyon from a height of 70m, offering a truly breathtaking spectacle. You can take a short (1hr) hike along the river and inside the canyon, to the base of the falls. This will give you a chance to see some magnificent grey limestone cliffs streaked with red and green shale. If you continue 10km on the main road, you'll come to the turn-off for **Baie de la Tour** ★★, which lies another 14km away. You'll find a long beach there with majestic limestone cliffs rising up behind it.

Outdoor Activities

Cruises and Whale-watching

Bas-Saint-Laurent

The **Excursions du Littoral** (*$30; Jun to Oct, every day 9am or 1pm; 518 Route du Fleuve, Notre-Dame-du-Portage,* ☎*862-1366*) offers visitors a chance to observe grey seals and migratory birds near the Îles Pélerins during a 3hr cruise.

The **Duvetnor** (*early Jun to mid-Sep, every day; 200 Rue Hayward, Rivière-du-Loup,*

☎*867-1660*) company offers a variety of cruises. You can visit the Îles du Bas-Saint-Laurent and see black guillemots, eider ducks and razorbills. The cruises start at the Rivière-du-Loup marina and last anywhere from 1.5 to 8hrs, depending on your destination. You can even stay overnight in a lighthouse on one of the islands (see p 336).

The **Croisières Navimex** (*$35; Jul to Oct, departures at 9am, 1pm and 5pm, Exit 507 off the 20, 200 Rue Hayward, Rivière-du-Loup,* ☎*867-3361*) take passengers on whale-watching cruises aboard the *Cavalier des Mers*. You'll get to see belugas, lesser rorquals and maybe even a blue whale. Make sure to bring some warm clothing. The cruises last about 3.5hrs.

The **Excursions ALIBI-TOURS** to the Îles du Bic (*$25; Jun to Oct; Parc du Bic marina,* ☎*736-5232*) lets visitors explore the islets, cliffs and reefs of the Bic. During this 2hr cruise, you'll see lots of birds, as well as grey and common seals.

Écomertours Nord-Sud (*606 des Ardennes, Rimouski, G5L 3M3,* ☎*724-6227 or 888-724-8687*) offer a variety of packages that showcase the river and the islands, dotting it as far as the Gulf of St. Lawrence and the Basse-Côte-Nord. The boat used for these cruises, which range in length from two to eight days, is called the *Écho des Mers* (Echo of the Seas). It can carry up to 49 passengers and about 15 crew members and has comfortable cabins. These "ecotours" are led by specialists whose aim is to familiarize passengers with the region's flora and fauna. If you go all the way to the

Basse-Côte-Nord, you'll get the chance to meet the locals. The company also offers more adventurous kayaking and scuba-diving packages. The cruises start at the Rimouski Est dock.

Gaspésie

Les Agences Touristiques de Gaspé Inc. (*$17; mid-Jun to mid-Sep; at the Cap-des-Rosiers harbour, Forillon National Park,* ☎*892-5629*) takes passengers out on the *Félix-Leclerc* to see a seal colony and the birds that nest in the cliffs. A guide is present on all cruises, which last nearly 2hrs. If you're lucky, you might even see some whales. Make sure to dress warmly, as the wind is often very cold. The departure schedule varies greatly depending on the date, so call beforehand.

Observation Littoral Percé (*$31 for a 2:30pm to 3pm excursion, Jun to Oct; near the Hôtel Normandie; Route 132, Percé,* ☎*782-5359*) hosts whale-watching excursions. With a little luck, you might also meet up with a school of white dolphins. Don't expect to see whale tails like those in photographs. Usually, only the whale's back is visible and often the animal is far away. The companies that organize these excursions must adhere to strict laws and have to pay large fines if they don't keep their distance. The outings start early in the morning and last two to 3hrs. Make sure to bundle up and wear a good windbreaker.

Îles-de-la-Madeleine

A boat ride on the *Le Ponton III* of the **Excursions de la Lagune** (*$20; daily departures in the summer at 11am,*

2pm, and 6pm; Île du Havre aux Maisons, ☎969-2088) is an exciting 2hr trip on the waves, during which visitors can observe the sea floor and occasionally some shellfish through the boat's glass bottom.

The schooner **La Gaspésienne 26** (*$40; Mon-Sat during the tourist season; La Grave marina, Île du Havre Aubert, ☎937-2213*) is one of a handful of the 50 *Gaspésiennes* to have been restored. A veritable floating work of art, this schooner will carry you off to contemplate the sea in absolute peace and quiet. There are two cruises per day, each 4hrs long.

Saguenay–Lac-Saint-Jean

The cruise-company **La Marjolaine** (*$30; Boulevard Saguenay, C.P. 203, Port de Chicoutimi, G7H 587, ☎543-7630 or 800-363-7248, ⇒693-1701*) organizes cruises on the Saguenay, one of the most enjoyable ways to take in the spectacular view of the fjord. The ship sets out from Chicoutimi, en route to Sainte-Rose-du-Nord. Passengers return by bus, except during June and September when the return trip is by boat. Each cruise lasts an entire day. It is also possible to take the trip in the opposite direction, from Sainte-Rose-du-Nord to Chicoutimi.

Manicouagan

Many agencies near the dock organize boat trips onto the river:

Croisières AML (*$34; mid-May to late Oct, 3 departures a day; 175 Rue des Pionniers Tadoussac, Departure from the Pier of Tadoussac and from Baie Sainte-Catherine*

☎235-4262), offers whale-watching trips in large, comfortable boats that accommodate up to 300 people. The expedition lasts approximately 3hrs, with a selection of large, comfortable boats or rubber dinghies, which are very safe. Nature guides accompany the passengers. Departures are from the Tadoussac and Baie-Sainte-Catherine piers. Whale-watching excursions as well as cruises on the Saguenay.

Croisières Famille Dufour (*$35, May to Oct, 3 departures a day; 165 Rue du Bord-de-L'eau, Tadoussac; ☎235-4421, or 800-463-5250*) offers excursions on large, comfortable boats such as the wonderful Famille-Dufour II catamaran. If you want to be closer to the action, the company also has a few large, powerful dinghies. Whale-watching excursions as well as cruises on the Saguenay are offered and have nature guides on board.

The **Croisières Neptune** (*$30; mid-May to mid-Oct; 9am, 11:30am, 2pm and 4:30pm; 507 Rue du Boisé, C.P. 194, Bergeronnes, G0T 1G0, ☎232-6716 or 232-6768*) whisks thrill-seekers into the heart of the fjord aboard 8m long, well-equipped rubber dingies to watch the magnificent sea mammals frolicking about.

Captain Gérard Morneau (*$25; Jun 1 to Oct 15, every day 11am; other times may be arranged; 3hrs; 539 Route 138, C.P. 435, Les Escoumins, G0T 1K0, ☎233-2771 or 800-921-2771*), who has over 20 years of experience under his belt, favours a friendly, relaxed approach aboard his 10m boat, the *Aiglefin*. He seeks out common rorquals and

blue whales in their feeding grounds east of Les Escoumins.

The Ross clan of Les Escoumins truly deserve the title **Les Pionniers des Baleines** (*$27; mid-May to mid-Oct; 3 Departures a day; 2.5hr cruise; 42 Rue des Pilotes, Les Escoumins, ☎233-3274 or 233-2727, ⇒233-3338*), or the "whale pioneers," the name of their whale-watching outfit. It now has two inflatable dinghies, each able to accommodate 12 passengers.

The **Gîte du Phare de Pointe-des-Monts** (*$20; mid-May to mid-Oct, 2 Departures a day; 2hr cruise, 1684 Boulevard Joliet, Baie-Comeau, G5C 1P8; ☎939-2332 or 589-8408 during the low season*) organizes several fascinating excursions that are a wonderful way to wind up a stay in this extraordinary place. Aboard a rubber dinghy or a small fishing boat, passengers can contemplate the seascape at the beginning of the Gulf of St. Lawrence and observe the sea mammals that live there.

Duplessis

The **Tournée des îles** (*$20; 140 Boulevard Laure Ouest, Sept-Îles, ☎968-1818 or 962-1238*), a 3hr cruise through the Archipel des Sept-Îles, offers a glimpse of the rich marine life of the St. Lawrence that is home to many kinds of aquatic mammals, particularly whales. The boat goes to Île Corossol, a large bird sanctuary.

For whale-lovers, the most wonderful experience the Côte-Nord has to offer is to set out with the biologists of the **Station de Recherche des Iles de Mingan** (*$70/person; 124 Rue du*

Bord-de-la-Mer, Longue-Pointe, ☎*949-2845,* ⇌*948-1131*) for a close encounter with some **humpback whales**. Seated aboard 7m **dinghies**, passengers take part in a day of research that involves identifying the animals by the markings under their tails. Biopsies are also occasionally carried out and useful data is compiled. These outings are not recommended, however, for anyone prone to seasickness, as they start at the research station at 7am and last a minimum of 6hrs (sometimes much longer) in turbulent waters.

Accommodations

Bas-Saint-Laurent

Kamouraska

Motel Cap Blanc
$53
K, tv, 🐾
300 Avenue Morel, G0L 1M0
☎*492-2919*
The Motel Cap Blanc has simple, comfortable rooms with lovely views of the river. Pets are allowed.

Saint-André

 La Solaillerie
$54 bkfst incl.
$89 bkfst incl.
pb/sb, ℜ
112 Rue Principale, G0L 2H0
☎*493-2914*
A large house dating from the late 19th century, La Solaillerie has a magnificent white facade and a big wraparound porch on the second storey. Inside, the sumptuous decor evokes the era in which the house was built. The five guestrooms are cozy, comfortable and tastefully decorated in classic "old inn" tradition. One even has a canopy bed! Each room has a sink and a claw-footed bathtub and offers a lovely view of the river. There are plans to construct another building with six additional rooms. As far as the food is concerned, gourmets can expect some delightful surprises (see p 342).

Rivière-du-Loup

Auberge de Jeunesse Internationale
$19 bkfst incl.
46 Rue Hôtel-de-Ville, G5R 1L5
☎*862-7566*
☎*800-461-8585*
The Auberge de Jeunesse Internationale in Rivière-du-Loup is a youth hostel that offers the most affordable accommodation in town. The rooms are dorm-style and simple but clean.

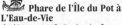 **Auberge de la Pointe**
closed mid-Oct to early May
$80
≈, △, ⊘, ℜ, tv, ✪
10 Boulevard Cartier, G5R 3Y7
☎*862-3514*
☎*800-463-1222*
⇌*862-1882*
The Auberge de la Pointe is particularly well-located. In addition to comfortable rooms, guests can indulge in a hydrotherapy, algotherapy or massage-therapy session and enjoy spectacular sunsets from the balcony. There is also a summer theatre.

Îles du Pot à L'Eau-de-Vie

 Phare de l'Île du Pot à L'Eau-de-Vie
$140/pers., ¹/₂b Cruise incl.
200 Rue Hayward, Rivière-du-Loup
G5R 3Y9
☎*867-1660*
☎*877-867-1660*
⇌*867-3639*
The Phare de l'Île du Pat à L'Eau-de-Vie is a lighthouse on an island in the middle of the St. Lawrence that exposes its white facade and red roof to the four winds. Owned by Duvetnor, a non-profit organization dedicated to protecting birds, the Pot à L'Eau-de-Vie archipelago is swarming with water birds. Duvetnor offers package rates that include accommodations, meals and a cruise on the river with a naturalist guide. The lighthouse, over a century old, has been carefully restored. It has three cozy guestrooms and delicious food. If you're looking for a peaceful atmosphere, this is the place to stay.

Trois-Pistoles

Motel Trois-Pistoles
$50
≡, 🐾, ℜ, tv
64 Route 132 Ouest, G0L 4K0
☎*851-2563*
The Motel Trois-Pistoles has 32 comfortable rooms, some affording a lovely view of the river. The sunsets from this spot are absolutely magnificent.

Le Bic

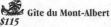

Auberge du Mange Grenouille
$55 sb bkfst incl.
$80 pb bkfst incl.
ℜ
148 Rue Sainte-Cécile, G0L 1S0
☎736-5656
The nine-room Auberge du Mange Grenouille has a good reputation in Québec and beyond. Guests are warmly welcomed, served succulent food, and stay in 15 cozy rooms decorated with antiques. The Inn also hosts murder-mystery parties.

Rimouski

Hôtel Rimouski
$85
≈, ≡, ℜ, ☉, tv, ⴠ
225 Boulevard René-Lepage Est
G5L 1P2
☎725-5000
☎800-463-0755
⇄725-5725
The Hôtel Rimouski has a unique design Its big staircase and long swimming pool in the lobby will appeal to many visitors. Children under 18 can stay in their parents' room for free.

Pointe-au-Père

Auberge La Marée Douce
$65 bkfst incl., $135 ½b
ℜ
1329 Boulevard Sainte-Anne
G5R 8X7
☎722-0822
⇄736-5167
The Auberge La Marée Douce is a riverside inn located in Pointe-au-Père, near the Musée de la Mer. Built in 1860, it has comfortable rooms, each with its own decor.

Gaspésie

Matane

Auberge La Seigneurie
$70 bkfst incl.
sb/pb
621 Rue Saint-Jérôme, G4W 3M9
☎562-0021
☎(877) 783-4466
⇄562-4455
Visitors will find the perfect place to relax at the confluence of the St. Lawrence and Matane rivers. Auberge La Seigneurie is an inn with comfortable rooms, located on the former site of the Fraser seigneury.

Riôtel Matane
$99
ℜ, ≡, ⊛, ≈, ◠, ☉
250 Avenue du Phare E., G4W 3N4
☎566-2651
☎800-463-7468
⇄562-7365
The Riôtel Matane makes a charming first impression. Upon their arrival, visitors will notice the care that has been taken to make the place both attractive and comfortable. The wooden spiral staircase and leather armchairs are just a hint of what is to come. On their way through the restaurant and bar, guests will enjoy an exquisite view of the St. Lawrence. The rooms on the 3rd floor are among the newest in the hotel, which also has a tennis court and a golf course.

Parc de la Gaspésie

There are a number of different **campgrounds** (*$17; mid-Jun to late Sep*) in Parc de la Gaspésie, as well as 19 **cabins** (*$69*) that can accommodate four, six or eight people (☎763-2288 or 888-270-4483, ⇄763-7803).

Gîte du Mont-Albert
$115
ℜ, K, ≈, ◠
☎763-2288
☎888 270-4483
⇄763-7803
For panoramic views, head to the Gîte du Mont-Albert, located in Parc de la Gaspésie. The building is U-shaped, so each comfortable room offers a sweeping view of Mont Albert and Mont McGerrigle.

Forillon National Park

There are four campgrounds in the park, with a total of 368 sites. To reserve one, dial ☎368-6050 (*early Jun to mid-Oct, Forillon National Park, 122 Blvd. De Gaspé, Gaspé, G4X 1A9*). Only half the sites may be reserved and for the rest, the park follows a first-come, first-served policy. The **Camping Des-Rosiers** (*$16; Secteur Nord*), a partially wooded area by the sea, has 155 tent and RV sites (*42 with electricity; $18*). The **Camping Bon-Ami** (*$16; Secteur Sud*) has 135 tent and RV sites on a wooded stretch of land covered with fine gravel.

Gaspé

Residence hall of the CÉGEP de la Gaspésie et des Îles
$22
K
94 Rue Jacques-Cartier, G4X 2P6
☎368-2749
www.cgaspesie.qc.ca
The residence hall of the CÉGEP de la Gaspésie et des Îles rents out its rooms between June 15 and August 15. Guests are provided with a kitchenette, bedding, towels and dishes.

Québec

Quality Inn
$105
≡, ⊛, ℜ
178 Rue de la Reine, G4X 1T6
☎ *368-3355*
☎ *800- 462-3355*
≈ *368-1702*
Quality Inn is downtown,
next to a shopping centre.
The rooms are pleasant
and comfortable.

Percé

Camping du Gargantua
$16
222 Route des Failles
☎ *782-2852*
The Camping du Gargan-
tua is definitely the most
beautiful campground in
the Percé area. It offers a
view not only of Rocher
Percé and the ocean, but
also of the verdant sur-
rounding mountains.

Auberge du Gargantua
$50
ℜ
Jun to mid-Oct
222 Route des Failles, G0C 2L0
☎ *782-2852*
≈ *782-5229*
L'Auberge du Gargantua
has been looking out over
Percé from atop its pro-
montory for 30 years now
and is well-known to
anyone familiar with the
Gaspé peninsula. Its res-
taurant is one of the best
in the region, and its location and view are unfor-
gettable. The small, motel-
style rooms are simply
decorated but comfortable.

La Normandie
$60
✖, ℜ
open early May to mid-Oct
221 Route 132 Ouest, G0C 2L0
☎ *782-2112*
☎ *888 463-0820*
≈ *782-2337*
The hotel-motel La Nor-
mandie has a well- esta-
blished reputation in Percé. During the high sea-

son, this luxury establishment is full most of the time. Both the restaurant
and the rooms offer a view
of the famous Rocher Per-
cé.

Paspébiac

 Auberge du Parc
$79
Feb to Nov
△, ℜ, ⊙, ≈
68 Boulevard Gerard -D.-Levesque
G0C 2K0
☎ *752-3355*
☎ *800-463-0890*
≈ *752-6406*
The Auberge du Parc oc-
cupies a 19th-century
manor erected by the
Robin company. It stands
in the midst of a wooded
area, providing a perfect
place to relax. Whirlpools,
body wraps, therapeutic
massages, acupressure and
a saltwater pool enhance
the stay.

New Carlisle

**Maison du Juge
Thompson**
$70 bkfst incl.
sp/pb
Jul and Aug
105 Gérard-D-Lévesque
☎ *752-6308*
There is a pretty room
waiting for you at the
Maison du Juge Thompson
a lovely old villa dating
from 1844. It's complete
with walking paths and a
beautiful period garden.
You can relax and admire
the sea from the veranda.
The tasty English-style
breakfasts are an added
bonus.

Carleton

Aqua-Mer Thalasso
$1293.50 for seven days
⊙, ≈
868 blvd. Perron, G0C 1J0
☎ *364-7055*
☎ *800- 463-0867*
≈ *364-7351*
The Aqua-Mer Thalasso,
located in an enchanting
setting, offers a number of
week-long packages that
include treatments, meals
and return transportation
from Charlo airport in New
Brunswick.

Pointe-à-la-Garde

**Auberge de Jeunesse and
Château Bahia**
$36 bkfst incl.
ℜ
summer only
152 Boulevard Perron, G0C 2M0
☎ *788-2048*
≈ *788-2048*
Auberge de Jeunesse and
Château Bahia are set back
from the road, halfway
between Carleton and
Matapédia. This youth
hostel is a great place to
relax. During the high
season, the clientele
consists mainly of Euro-
peans. Guests are offered
high-quality regional dishes such as fresh salmon
and maple-flavoured ham
(all at modest prices) and
may sleep either in the
hostel or in the château
behind it.

Îles-de-la-Madeleine

Île du Cap aux Meules

Le Barachois campground
$15 +taxes
Fatima
☎ *986-6065*
☎ *986-5678*
Le Barachois campground
can accommodate tents or
campers in its 80 wind-
sheltered sites. Located in
the middle of a small wooded area along the sea, it

has a peaceful atmosphere.

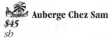 **Auberge Chez Sam**
$45
sb
1767 Chemin de L'Etang- du-Nord
L'Étang-du-Nord, G0B 1E0
☎*986-5780*
The very warm welcome
at the Auberge chez Sam
will quickly make guests
feel et home. The place
has five attractive well-
kept rooms.

**Auberge Maison du
Cap-Vert**
$49 bkfst incl.
year round
202 Chemin L'Aucoin, P.O.
Box 521
Fatima, G0B 1K0
☎*986-5331*
The Maison du Cap-Vert is
a family inn with five absolutely charming rooms
with comfy beds and a
unique decor. This place
has made a name for itself
in just a short period of
time. With its delicious, all-
you-can-eat breakfasts, it is
definitely a good deal.

Château Madelinot
$109
ℜ, ≈, ℝ, ⊗, ⌂
323 Highway 199, C.P.44, G0B 1B0
☎*986-3695*
☎*800- 661-4537*
⇄*986-6437*
Visitors might first be surprised to find that the Château Madelinot is not a
château, but rather a large
house. But the comfortable
rooms and superb view of
the sea make it easy to get
over the disappointment.
The place offers many
services including a saltwater spa and a large
swimming pool, and is
without a doubt the most
well-known accommoda-
tion on the islands.

Île du Havre Aubert

Plage du Golfe campground
$16
535 Chemin du Bassin, G0S 1A0
☎*937-5115*
☎*937-5224*
⇄*937-5115*
The Plage du Golfe cam-
ground has more than 70
sites, some of which ac-
commodate trailers.

La Marée Haute
$75 bkfst incl.
sb/pb
ℜ
25 Chemin des Fumoirs, G0B 1J0
☎/⇄*937-2492*
Located close to La Grave,
La Marée Haute is a lovely
little inn where guests
receive an extremely warm
welcome. The rooms are
cozy and attractively decorated. One of the owners
also cooks. You won't
regret trying one of these
lovingly and meticulously
prepared dishes. The view
from the inn is absolutely
ravishing!

Havre Sur Mer
$105 bkfst incl.
ℜ
1197 Chemin du Bassin, L'île-du-
Havre-Aubert, G0B 1A0
☎*937-5675*
⇄*937-2540*
The Havre Sur Mer, near
the cliff's edge, enjoys a
magnificent location. The
rooms have a communal
terrace from which every-
body can enjoy the beautiful view. The inn is furnished with antiques and
attracts many visitors. If
you are interested in
staying here, it is best to
make reservations in ad-
vance.

Île du Havre aux Maisons

Au Vieux Couvent
$55
ℜ
292 Highway 199, Havre-aux-
Maisons, G0B 1K0
☎*969-2233*
⇄*969-4693*
Au Vieux Couvent was
built during World War I,
serving first as a convent,
and then as a school. It
has since been converted
into a quaint hotel with
approximately 10 rooms,
some of which (the corner
rooms) have a nice view
of the sea.

La P'tite Baie
$55-$70
187 Highway 199, Havre-aux-
Maisons G0B 1E0
auberge.petitebaie@sympatico.ca
Set up in a charming
100-year-old house, the
P'tite Baie is made of wood and enjoys a warm and
comfortable atmosphere.
The impeccable rooms at
this inn offer a superb
view of the surrounding
area.

Île de la Grande Entrée

**Grande-Entrée campground of
the Club Vacances "Les Îles"**
$12
Grande-Entrée, G0B 1H0
☎*985-2833*
☎*888-537-4537*
⇄*985-2226*
Grande-Entrée camp-
ground of the Club Vacan-
ces "Les Îles" has 40 sites,
eight of which are set up
for trailers. A dormitory is
available for visitors on
rainy days.

Club Vacances "Les Îles"
$150-165 all included
377 Grande-Entrée G0B 1H0
☎*985-2833*
☎*888-537-4537*
www.clubiles.qc.ca
In addition to offering
comfortable rooms, the

Québec

Club Vacances "Les Îles" organizes several activities and excursions so that visitors can discover the area's natural riches. Guests can also partake of their meals in the cafeteria, where they are served generous portions.

Île d'Entrée

Chez McLean
$45 bkfst incl.
G0B 1C0
☎*986-4541*
There are very few accommodation options on this island. You can stay, however, with the local inhabitants at Chez McLean. This house was built over 60 years ago and has managed to keep its character of yesteryear.

Saguenay–Lac-St-Jean

La Baie

La Maison de la Rivière
$70
ℜ, ⊛
9122 Chemin de la Batture
G7B 3P6
☎*544-2912*
☎*800-363-2078*
≈*544-2912*
La Maison de la Rivière lies in an enchanting setting, surrounded by beautiful greenery. Its peaceful atmosphere makes it a daydreamers' paradise. Guests are warmly received. Unique, specialized packages are offered that focus on regional and native gastronomy, wild plants, the outdoors, cultural activities, romanticism and alternative medicine. Guide service. Comfortable, tastefully decorated rooms are designated by names taken from nature, rather than by numbers.

Ten of them have private balconies with stunning views of the fjord. Modern architecture with an ecological slant.

L'Auberge des Battures
$90/$120
6295 Boulevard de la Grande-Baie
Sud, G7B 3P6
☎*544-8234*
☎*800-668-8234*
≈*544-4351*
L'Auberge des Battures not only offers a spectacular view of La Baie des Ha! Ha!, but also has wonderful accommodations and refined cuisine.

Auberge des 21
$110
☉, ⊛, ≈, ℜ, tv
621 Rue Mars, G78 4N1
☎*697-2121*
☎*800-363-7298*
≈*544-3360*
The charming Auberge des 21 offers magnificent, recently renovated rooms at reasonable prices with view of the Baie des Ha! Ha!. In addition to comfortable rooms, a health club helps travellers to relax as much as possible.

Chicoutimi

Hôtel des Gouverneurs
$110
≈, ℜ, ≡, tv
1303 Boulevard Talbot, G7H 4Cl
☎*549-6244*
☎*888-910-1111*
≈*549-55227*
Located in the heart of town, the Hôtel des Gouverneurs is a meeting place frequented by businesspeople looking for rooms with all the modern conveniences.

Jonquière

Hôtel Holiday Inn Saguenay
$120
≈, ≡, ℜ, ☉, tv
2675 Boulevard du Royaume
G7S 5B8
☎*548-3124*
☎*800-363-3124*
≈*548-1638*
Though outside the centre of town, the Hôtel Holiday Inn Saguenay is nevertheless very well located on the road between Jonquière and Chicoutimi and has pleasant rooms.

Val-Jalbert

This ghost town has an outstanding **campground** (*$17.50;* ☎*275-3132*). A vast stretch of land that is dotted with beautiful natural sites that will delight fans of rustic camping.

Lodgings and hotel rooms are available in the historic village (*$70.77;* ☎*275-3132*).

Saint-Félicien

Camping de St-Félicien
$20
≈
☎*679-1719*
As may be gathered from its name, the Camping de St-Félicien is located beside the zoo, so you might be awakened by animal noises at night. It occupies a large piece of land, and is equipped with all the necessary facilities.

Hôtel du Jardin
$99
⊛, ≈, ≡, ℜ, ◌, tv
1400 Boulevard du Jardin, G8K 2N8
☎*679-8422*
☎*800-463-4927*
≈*679-4459*
The Hôtel du Jardin offers standard rooms near the zoo.

Péribonka

Auberge de l'Île-du-Repos
$18/pers. in dormitory
105 Route Île-du-Repos, G0W 2G0
☎347-5649
☎800-461-8585
⇒347-4810
Alone on an island, the Auberge de l'Île-du-Repos offers a fascinating cultural programme and beautiful surroungings that stimulate conversation.

Alma

Complexe Touristique de la Dam-en-Terre
$118/4 ppl.
1385 Chemin de la Marina, G8B 5W1
☎668-4599
☎888-289-3016
The Complexe Touristique de la Dam-en-Terre rents out well designed cottages with a beautiful view of Lac Saint-Jean. Campers can opt for the more economical campsites.

Manicouagan

Tadoussac

Camping Tadoussac
$18
428 Rue du Bateau-Passeur G0T 1A0
☎235-4501
No place offers a more stunning panoramic view than Camping Tadoussac that looks out over the bay and the village.

Maison Majorique
$16
158 Rue du Bateau-Passeur G0T 2A0
☎235-4372
☎800-461-8585
⇒235-4608
The Maison Majorique is Tadoussac's youth hostel. It has dormitories, private rooms, even campsites in summer, and offers a whole variety of outdoor activities as well as reaso-nably priced cafeteria meals.

 Hôtel Tadoussac
$80
closed in winter
ℜ
165 Rue du Bord-del'Eau, G0T 2A0
☎235-4421
☎800-561-0718
⇒235-4607
Located by the river, the Hôtel Tadoussac resembles a late 19th-century manor house and is distinguished by its bright red roof. The hotel, made famous as the backdrop for the movie Hotel New Hampshire, is not as comfortable as one might expect.

Baie-Comeau

La Caravelle
$56
ℵ, ≈, ℜ
202 Boulevard LaSalle, G4Z 2L6
☎296-4986
☎800-469-4986
⇒296-4622
Anyone who visits Baie-Comeau regularly knows about La Caravelle, a hotel-motel that looks out over the town from atop a hill. It has 70 renovated rooms, a number of which are available at low rates. Some rooms are equipped with a water bed and some with a fireplace.

Le Petit Château
$78 bkfst incl.
ℜ
2370 Boulevard Laflèche, G5C 1E4
☎295-3100
☎295-3225
What, you might ask, is that splendid house in its own little Garden of Eden right in the middle of town? Le Petit Château, a bed and breakfast, has a simple, country atmos-phere but is nonetheless inviting.

Godbout

Aux Berges
$45 sb
$55 pb bkfst incl.
K, ℜ
180 Rue Pascal-Comeau, G0H 1G0
☎568-7748
⇒568-7833
Any way you look at it, Aux Berges is one of the best bed and breakfasts on the Côte-Nord. The rooms are simple and the place is far from luxurious. But the graciousness of the hosts, the tourist services available to guests and the sophisticated regional cuisine make all the diffe-rence. This is a place to kick back and relax in the heart of a fascinating village. Aux Berges also rents out log cabins, located near the main building.

Duplessis

Sept-Îles

Camping Sauvage de l'Ile Grande-Basque
$7
Jul to mid-Sep
Corporation Touristique de Sept-Îles, 1401 Boulevard Laure Ouest G4R 4K1
☎962-1238
☎968-1818 (summer)
☎968-0022
Many city-dwellers dream of camping on an unspoi-led island in the peaceful wilderness. The Camping Sauvage de l'Ile Grande-Basque can make such dreams a reality in the magnificent setting of the Baie de Sept-Îles. This island is the closest to the shore, making it a good stopping place for kaya-kers and canoeists. Firepits and firewood available. No drinking water.

Québec

Havre-Saint-Pierre

Auberge de la Minganie
$15
K
May to Oct
Route 138, G0G 1P0
☎ *538-2944*
The friendly Auberge de la Minganie youth hostel is located on the outskirts of town, beside the Mingan Archipelago National Park Reserve. Visitors arriving by bus can ask the driver to let them off here. Many cultural and outdoor activities are offered.

Hôtel-Motel du Havre
$62
ℜ, K
970 Boulevard de l'Escale, G0G 1P0
☎ *538-2800*
☎ *888-797-2800*
☎ *538-3438*
You can't miss the Hôtel-Motel du Havre, located at the intersection of the main road and Rue de l'Escale, which runs through town to the docks. This place is definitely the big hotel in town. Though some rooms have benefited from recent attempts at renovation, others remain drab and a bit depressing. Friendly service.

Île d'Anticosti

Auberge Au Vieux Menier
$17.50/pers. in the dormitory
$35 bkfst incl. in the B&B
Jun to Sep
sb, ℜ
Box 112, Port-Menier, G0G 2Y0
☎ *535-0111*
The Auberge Au Vieux Menier falls somewhere between a bed and breakfast and a youth hostel. Located on the site of the former Saint-Georges farm. Exhibitions. Low rates.

Auberge Port-Menier
$66
ℜ, ctv
Box 160, Port-Menier, G0G 2Y0
☎ *535-0122*
☎ *535-0204*
⇔ *535-0204*
The Auberge Port-Menier, a venerable institution on the island, offers clean rooms and excellent food in a modest setting. The lobby is decorated with magnificent wooden reliefs from the Château Meunier. The inn serves as the starting point for a number of guided tours. Bicycle rentals.

Baie-Johan-Beetz

 Maison Johan-Beetz
$50 bkfst incl.
15 Johan-Beetz
☎ *539-0157*
The historic Maison Johan-Beetz is a truly exceptional hotel and a veritable monument decorated with Beetz's own artwork. The rooms are basic yet comfortable.

Natashquan

Auberge La Cache
$85
183 Chemin d'En Haut, G0G 2E0
☎ *726-3347*
⇔ *726-3508*
The Auberge La Cache has about 10 pleasant rooms.

Restaurants

Bas-Saint-Laurent

Saint-André

La Solaillerie
$$$-$$$$
112 Rue Principale
☎ *493-2914*
The dining room at La Solaillerie has been carefully decorated to highlight the historic character of the old house in which it is located. In this inviting setting, guests savour excellent cuisine lovingly prepared and served by the owners of the inn. Drawing his inspiration from a French culinary repertoire, the chef uses fresh regional ingredients like quail, lamb and fresh and smoked salmon to create new dishes according to his fancy.

Rivière-du-Loup

Saint-Patrice
$$-$$$
169 Rue Fraser
☎ *862-9895*
The Saint-Patrice is one of the best restaurants in town. Fish, seafood, rabbit and lamb are the specialities.

Le Novello
$$
Another restaurant at the same address, Le Novello serves pasta and thin-crust pizza in a bistro setting.

La Terrasse and La Distinction
$$
171 Rue Fraser
☎ *862-6927*
The restaurants in the Hôtel Lévesque –
La Terrasse and La Distinc-

tion – serve a variety of delicious Italian dishes, as well as smoked salmon prepared according to a traditional method in the hotel's smokehouse.

Trois-Pistoles

L'Ensolleillé
$-$$
138 Rue Notre-Dame Ouest
☎*851-2889*
The vegetarian café/restaurant L'Ensolleillé has a very simple à-la-carte menu. The three-course lunch and dinner menus are a good deal.

Michalie
$$
55 Rue Notre-Dame Est
☎*851-4011*
Michalie is a charming little restaurant serving some of the best regional cuisine, as well as gourmet Italian food.

Saint-Fabien

 Auberge Saint-Simon
$$$
18 Rue Principale
☎*738-2971*
In the warm, traditional atmosphere of the Auberge Saint-Simon, guests will enjoy another excellent Bas-Saint-Laurent dining experience. Rabbit, lamb, halibut and seafood are paired with fresh vegetables grown in the restaurant's garden.

Le Bic

Auberge du Mange Grenouille
$$$-$$$$
148 Sainte-Cécile
☎*736-5656*
The Auberge du Mange Grenouille is one of the best restaurants in the Bas-Saint-Laurent. Once a general store, it's decorated with old furniture carefully chosen to com-

plement the architecture. Guests are offered a choice of six daily tables d'hôte that include fowl, lamb and fish dishes. Everything served here is delicious and the service is always attentive.

Rimouski

Café-Bistro Le Saint-Louis
$$-$$$
97 Rue St-Louis
☎*723-7979*
The Café-Bistro Le Saint-Louis looks just like its Parisian cousins and is filled with all the same aromas. It offers a large selection of imported beer and microbrews. The menu, which changes daily, is delicious and the dishes are served in a pleasant atmosphere.

Serge Pouly
$$-$$$$
284 Rue Saint-Germain Est
☎*723-3038*
Serge Pouly serves game, seafood, steak and French specialties. The relaxed atmosphere and attentive service make this the perfect place for an intimate dinner for two.

Gaspésie

Grand-Métis

Les Ateliers Plein Soleil
$-$$
Jardins de Métis
Les Ateliers Plein Soleil takes pride in making sure everything is perfect: the waiters and waitresses, dressed in period clothing, are attentive; the decor is picturesque and the Métis and Québécois cuisine is served in generous portions.

Métis-sur-Mer

 Au Coin de la Baie
$$$$
1140 Route 132
☎*936-3855*
Au coin de la Baie is open between the end of June and the end of August. Here, visitors can treat themselves to smoked salmon royale and "cedar" sorbet. The wine list is excellent.

Matane

Vieux Rafiot
$$-$$$
1415 Avenue du Phare, alongside Route 132
☎*562-8080*
The Vieux Rafiot attracts lots of visitors to its incredible dining room, which is divided into three sections by partitions with portholes and decorated with paintings by local artists. In addition to the novel decor, guests can enjoy a variety of delicious dishes.

Parc de la Gaspésie

 Gîte du Mont-Albert
$$$$
☎*762-2288*
The Gîte du Mont-Albert offers innovative seafood dishes that are definitely worth a try. During the Game Festival in September you can sample more unusual meats like guinea hen, bison and partridge.

Gaspé

Brise-Brise
$-$$
2 Côte Cartier, Place Jacques-Cartier
☎*368-1456*
The bistro/bar Brise-Brise is probably the nicest café in Gaspé. The menu includes sausages, seafood, salads and sandwiches. The place also features an assortment of beer and

Québec

coffee, an enjoyable happy hour, live shows all summer long, and dancing late into the evening.

Fort Prével

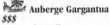 **Fort Prével**
$$$-$$$$
2053 Boulevard Douglas
☎*368-2281*
☎*888 377-3835*
At Fort Prével, guests are plunged into an historic atmosphere and get to savour delicious French and Québec cuisine. These skilfully prepared and elegantly presented dishes are served in a huge dining room. The menu includes fish and seafood, of course, as well as all sorts of specialties that will satisfy any gourmet.

Percé

 Auberge Gargantua
$$$
222 Rue des Failles
☎*782-2852*
The decor of the Auberge Gargantua is reminiscent of the French countryside where the owners were born. The dining room offers a splendid view of the surrounding mountains, so be sure to arrive early enough to enjoy it. The dishes are all gargantuan and delicious, and usually include an appetizer of periwinkle, a plate of raw vegetables, and soup. Guests choose their main dish from a long list, ranging from salmon to snow crab and a selection of game.

 La Normandie
$$$-$$$$
221 Route 132 Ouest
☎*782-2112*
Regarded by many as one of the best restaurants in Percé, La Normandie ser-

ves delicious food in an altogether charming spot. Diners rave about the *feuilleté de homard au champagne* (lobster in puff pastry with champagne) and the *pétoncles à l'ail* (scallops with garlic). The restaurant also features an extensive wine list.

 Auberge à Percé
$$$$
1 Promenade du Bord de Mer
☎*782-5055*
☎*888- 782-5055*
Though there are lots of restaurants in Percé, few fall into the gourmet category. The exception is the Auberge à Percé which serves divinely prepared scallops, lobster, fish and red meat. The restaurant's charming building seems tailor-made for the beautiful setting.

Bonaventure

Café Acadien
$$-$$$
early Jun to mid-Sep
168 Rue Beaubassin
☎*534-4276*
Le Café Acadien serves good food in a charming setting. Open throughout the summer season, this place is very popular with locals and tourists alike, which might explain why the prices are a little high.

Carleton

 La Seigneurie
$$-$$$
482 Boulevard Perron
☎*364-3355*
The restaurant in the Hôtel-Motel Baie Bleue, La Seigneurie, serves a wide variety of delicious dishes based on game, fish and seafood. The view from the dining room is superb.

Îles-de-la-Madeleine

Île du Cap aux Meules

P'tit Café
$$
☎*986-2130*
Le P'tit Café in the Château Madelinot serves Sunday brunch from 10am to 1:30pm. Those with a taste for novelty can order seafood, red meat or chicken cooked on a hot stone. The menu includes a large selection of appetizers, soups and charbroiled dishes. In addition to a view of the sea, the decor is enhanced by temporary exhibitions by artists from the islands and elsewhere in Québec.

La Table des Roy
$$$$
Jun to mid-Sep from 6pm, closed Sun
La Vernière
☎*986-3004*
Since 1978, La Table des Roy has offered refined cuisine to delight every visitor's tastebuds. Prepared in a multitude of ways, the tempting menu features seafood, such as grilled scallops and lobster with *coralline* sauce. The dining room is charming and adds a particular style to this excellent restaurant that also offers dishes adorned with edible flowers and plants of the islands. It is advised to reserve in advance.

Île du Havre Aubert

Café de la Grave
$$-$$$
early May to early Oct 8:30am to 3pm
Havre-Aubert
☎*937-5765*
Decorated like an old general store, the Café de la Grave has a very pleasant atmosphere. When

the weather is bad, you can spend hours here chatting. In addition to muffins, croissants and a wide variety of coffees, the menu offers healthy and sometimes unusual dishes, such as *pâté de loup marin*, which are always good. This café is delightfully welcoming and will leave you with lasting memories.

La Saline
$$-$$$
1009 Route 199
☎937-2230
A former salting shed in La Grave, La Saline serves excellent regional cuisine. *Loup-marin*, cod, mussels, shrimp and other saltwater treats appear on the menu. Guests also have a splendid view of the sea.

La Marée Haute
$$$$
25 Chemin des Fumoirs
☎937-2492
The chef and co-owner of La Marée Haute knows how to bring out the best in fish and seafood. In this pretty inn, you can sample sea perch, shark or mackerel while drinking in the magnificent view. You can taste the ocean in these dishes, whose expertly enhanced flavour will send you into raptures. The menu also includes a few equally well-prepared meat dishes and some succulent desserts.

Île du Havre aux Maisons

 **La P'tite Baie**
$$$
year round
187 Route 199
☎969-4073
La P'tite Baie serves well-prepared grill, seafood and fish, as well as a number of beef, pork and chicken dishes. *Loup-marin* is served here in season. In addition to the à-la-carte

menu, there is a table-d'hôte with a choice of two main dishes. The service is courteous and a great deal of care has gone into the decor.

La Moulière
$$$
8am to 10pm
292 Highway 199
☎969-2233
There are two restaurants in the Hôtel Au Vieux Couvent (see p 339). La Moulière, located on the main floor, occupies a large room that formerly served as a chapel. It serves excellent dishes in a lively atmosphere. **Rest-O-Bar** (*$$*) is found on the same floor, in the former parlour that extends onto a terrace overlooking the sea. Hamburgers and mussels are among the dishes served in this restaurant, which is as popular as La Moulière.

Grosse Île

Chez B&J
$$
year round
243 Route 199
☎985-2926
Chez B&J serves fresh scallops, halibut, lobster salad and fresh fish.

Île de la Grande Entrée

Délice de la Mer
$$
early Jun to Sep 9am to 8pm
907 Route 199, Quai de Grande-Entrée
☎985-2364
The Délice de la Mer specializes in simply prepared seafood dishes. The lobster is delicious. Affordable prices and home-made desserts.

Saguenay–Lac-St-Jean

La Baie

 **Le Doyen**
$$$$
Auberge des 21, 621 Rue Mars
☎544-9316
With its succulent game dishes, the restaurant Le Doyen boasts one of the region's best menus. The dining room commands a remarkable, sweeping view of the Baie des Ha! Ha! The Sunday brunch is excellent. Run by renowned chef Marcel Bouchard, who has won numerous regional, national and international awards, Le Doyen is making a tangible contribution to the evolution and refinement of regional Québec cuisine.

 **La Maison de la Rivière**
$$$$
9122 Chemin de la Batture
☎544-2912
The head chef at La Maison de la Rivière has developed a menu focussed on Aboriginal traditions, regional dishes and international cuisine. This superb inn lies in an extremely pleasant setting, featuring a lovely view of the fjord.

Chicoutimi

La Cuisine
$$
387 Rue Racine Est
☎698-2822
The scent of freshly ground coffee permeates the air at La Cuisine. We especially recommend the steak tartare, mussels, rabbit, sweetbreads and *steak-frites* (steak and fries).

Le Privilège
$$$-$$$$
1623 Boulevard St-Jean-Baptiste
☎698-6262
Le Privilège ranks among the finest restaurants in the region. A feast for the senses can be found in this picturesque 100-year-old house. Intuitive cuisine with market-fresh ingredients for a lucky few at a time. Friendly and relaxed ambiance and service. Reservations required.

Jonquière

Chez Pachon
$$$
1904 Rue Perron
☎542-3568
The Chez Pachon restaurant, an institution in the town of Chicoutimi, moved to Jonquière in August 1999. It now occupies the magnificent heritage home of the Price brothers situated in a wonderful countryside setting. Its chef, who is already famous in the region, concocts a gourmet extravaganza of French-style cuisine with regional flavours. His specialities include *Cassoulet de Carcassonne* (a casserole dish from southwestern France), *confit de magret et foie de canard* (magret duck breast and liver confit), fillet and loin of lamb, calf sweetbreads, as well as fish and seafood. Dinner only. Reservations required.

 L'Amandier
$$$$
5219 Chemin Saint-André
☎542-5395
L'Amandier has an astonishing dining room decorated with carved plaster and an overabundance of woodwork. The restaurant serves regional cuisine made with fresh ingredients.

Somewhat removed from town, it is not easy to find. Reservations required. Good food is joined here by a unique ambiance well-suited to dining among friends. The inviting decor and the hosts' hospitality create a festive mood.

Le Bergerac
$$$-$$$$
closed on Sun and Mon
3919 Rue Saint-Jean
☎542-6263
One of the finest restaurants in Jonquière, Le Bergerac has developed an excellent repertoire of dishes. Lunchtime menu du jour and evening table d'hôte.

Saint-Félicien

Hôtel du Jardin
$$-$$$$
1400 Boulevard du Jardin, G8K 2N8
☎679-8422
The fine regional cuisine served at the Hôtel du Jardin is never disappointing.

Alma

Bar Restaurant Chez Mario Tremblay
$$-$$$
534 Collard Ouest
☎668-6431
People don't come to the Bar Restaurant Chez Mario Tremblay to enjoy the meal of their life. They are attracted by the owner's reputation as a hockey player and coach, which earned him the nickname "*le bleuet bionique*" (the bionic blueberry). This brasserie-style restaurant is a popular gathering place for hockey fans.

Manicouagan

Tadoussac

La Bolée
$$-$$$
164 Rue Morin
☎235-4750
Try the restaurant La Bolée for simple but tasty meals like stuffed crepes. It is also a good place to come later in the evening for a drink. There is a bakery below the restaurant.

Café du Fjord
$$
152 Rue du Bateau-Passeur
☎235-4626
The Café du Fjord is located in an uninteresting-looking house but it is very popular. A seafood buffet is offered for lunch and nights are livened up with shows or with dance music.

Bergeronnes

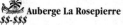 **Auberge La Rosepierre**
$$-$$$
66 Rue Principale
☎232-6543
An inn with a unique charm about it, the Auberge La Rosepierre has a tastefully decorated dining room with a table d'hôte featuring regional flavours and cooking methods. Naturally, fish and seafood dishes occupy a large part of the menu and are always prepared with flair.

Baie-Comeau

Les 3 Barils
$$
200 Boulevard LaSalle
☎296-3681
Les 3 Barils is an unpretentious place serving simple fare.

Le Manoir
$$-$$$
8 Rue Cabot, G4Z 1L8
☎296-3391
The hotel restaurant at Le Manoir has a well-established reputation. In an extremely inviting and luxurious decor, guests dine on expertly prepared cuisine worthy of the most elaborate praise. A meeting place for business-people and industrialists, it will also appeal to tourists, who will enjoy the unique view of the bay and the holiday atmosphere that pervades the outdoor seating area. Outstanding wine list.

Pointe-des-Monts

Restaurant du Fort de Pointe-des-Monts
$$$
Route du Vieux Fort
☎939-2332
The Restaurant du Fort de Pointe-des-Monts, located in a quiet little bay, has a menu consisting mainly of fresh seafood dishes. The cuisine is excellent and the service impeccable.

Duplessis

Sept-Îles

Café du Port
$$
495 Avenue Brochu
☎962-9311
The charming Café du Port prepares simple and delicious dishes and is one of the area's most popular restaurants.

Havre-Saint-Pierre

Chez Julie
$-$$
1023 Rue Dulcinée
☎538-3070
Chez Julie has an excellent reputation for seafood. The coffee shop decor,

complete with vinyl seat covers, does not seem to discourage the customers, who flock to the restaurant for seafood and smoked-salmon pizzas.

Île d'Anticosti

Auberge Place de l'Île
Box 47, Port-Menier, G0G 2Y0
☎535-0279
Auberge Place de l'Île offers excellent family-style cuisine with a different lunch menu every day. Located in the heart of town, the inn has seven clean, comfortable rooms.

Pointe-Carleton
$-$$
SÉPAQ
The dining room of the Pointe-Carleton is the best and most pleasant place to eat on the island. Whether you're sitting in the bright dining room or outside on the terrace, the view is spectacular and the cuisine succulent. A different specialty is featured every evening. If you happen to come on a "Bacchante" night (fisher's platter), don't miss it.

Natashquan

Auberge La Cache
$$$
6:30am to 10am and 6pm to 8:30pm
183 Chemin d'En Haut
☎726-3347
A good meal can be had at the Auberge La Cache that features meat and seafood dishes.

Entertainment

Festivals and Cultural Events

Bas-Saint-Laurent

The **Carrousel International du Film de Rimouski** (☎722-0103, ≈724-9504) is a film festival for the younger generation. It takes place the third week of September and lasts for seven days, during which about 40 movies are shown. The screenings are held at the Centre Civique in the afternoon and evening.

Gaspésie

Matane's famous shrimp is prized by seafood-lovers far beyond Gaspésie. The **Festival de la Crevette** (☎562-0404) is held in its honour each year at the end of June.

Îles-de-la-Madeleine

The **Concours des Châteaux de Sable** (Sand Castle Contest) takes place annually in August on the Havre-Aubert beach. Participants work for hours to build the best sand castle. Visitors wanting to put their talent to the test can register by calling Artisans du Sable at ☎937-2917.

Saguenay–Lac-St-Jean

The **Carnaval-Souvenir de Chicoutimi** (*mid-Feb*; ☎543-4438) celebrates the customs of winter in days gone by with period costumes and traditional activities.

Québec

Since 1955, the last week in July has been devoted to the **Traversée Internationale du Lac Saint-Jean** (☎*275-2851*). Swimmers cover the 40km between Péribonka and Roberval in 8hrs, with some even making the return trip in 18hrs.

Shopping

Bas-Saint-Laurent

La Samare (*84 Rue St-Germain Ouest, Rimouski,* ☎*723-0242*) has a large array of articles made of fish skin, as well as a wide selection of carvings, vases and other objects – all handcrafted by Inuit artisans.

Gaspésie

Grand-Métis

Les Ateliers Plein Soleil (*every day 9am to 6:30pm; Jardins de Métis,* ☎*775-3165*), a group of artisans from Grand-Métis, runs the Maison Reford. They make all sorts of hand-woven tablecloths, doilies and napkins that can be purchased in their shop along with herbs, locally produced honey and homemade tomato ketchup.

Percé

Thanks to its central location, you can't miss the Place du Quai, a cluster of over 30 shops and restaurants, as well as a laundromat and an S.A.Q. (liquor store).

Îles-de-la-Madeleine

Les Artisans du Sable (*P.O. Box 336, La Grave, Havre-Aubert,* ☎*937-2917,* ≠*937-2129*) sell several sand items made according to a special technique used only by Madelinot artisans. These items, which vary from decorations to lampshades, are wonderful souvenirs of the islands. You can also learn more about sand here.

You can buy lovely stone pieces (most made from alabaster) at the two **Madelipierre** (*70 Chemin Principal, Cap-aux-Meules;* ☎*986-6949*) boutiques located on the islands.

Saguenay–Lac-Saint-Jean

Blueberry Patches

Here in the land where three blueberries can just about fill a pie, you might want to check out one of the following blueberry patches:

Bleuetière Au Gros Bleuet
226 Rang 2, 3km from Falardeau
☎*673-4558*

Bleuetière de Saint-François-de-Sales Chemin du Moulin
15km west of the village of Saint-François-de-Sales
☎*348-6642*

Ontario

Often the first image that comes to mind when thinking of Ontario is the Great Lakes, those tremendous expanses of fresh water surrounded by the untamed abundance of nature.

Another obvious image invokes vast, fertile fields dotted with farmhouses charmingly adorned with balconies, shutters and flowers. Finally, there are those tiny hamlets with their splendid dwellings that in many cases have reigned over their surroundings for more than a century and a half; and those towns with a priceless architectural heritage, silent witnesses to the prosperity of Canada's richest province. Rural Ontario certainly has plenty to delight romantic souls looking for tranquillity and a glimpse of the past, but this province also has an eminently modern, urban face. After all, it encompasses Toronto, Canada's biggest city, and Ottawa, its federal capital.

With a land mass of 1,068,000km² (412,400mi²), Ontario is the second largest Canadian province in terms of surface area, behind only Québec. It is bordered to the east by Québec, to the west by Manitoba, to the north by Hudson Bay, and to the south by the United States. Part of its southern boundary is delineated by the 49th parallel, with the rest formed by lakes Superior, Huron, Erie and Ontario, and, furthest east, by the St. Lawrence River. These waterways allow easy access to much of Ontario and in the past set the basis for settlement of the province.

The Canadian Shield stretches in a semi-circle around Hudson Bay from Québec right into the Northwest Territories and covers a big chunk of Ontario. Formed in the pre-Cambrian period, this vast expanse of rock has endured the ravages of time, scraped bare by glaciers, which gave way to river and lake beds as well as to hills that are almost never more than 100m high. While the forests covering these lands have spurred prosperous industries, it is the subsoil that holds much of the wealth, with impressive deposits of gold, silver, nickel and other minerals. Very sparsely populated, the Canadian Shield is mostly covered by forest, which changes according to latitude.

Ontario prides itself on having four of the five Great Lakes (Ontario, Erie, Huron and Superior) form its southern and southwestern boundaries. (Lake Michigan, the fifth of the Great Lakes, lies entirely within the United States.) Besides the Great Lakes and St. Lawrence River, Ontario has about 400,000 other lakes and rivers, which have played a defining role in the history of the province. They were a source of essential food to the First Nations and provided the main access into the territory.

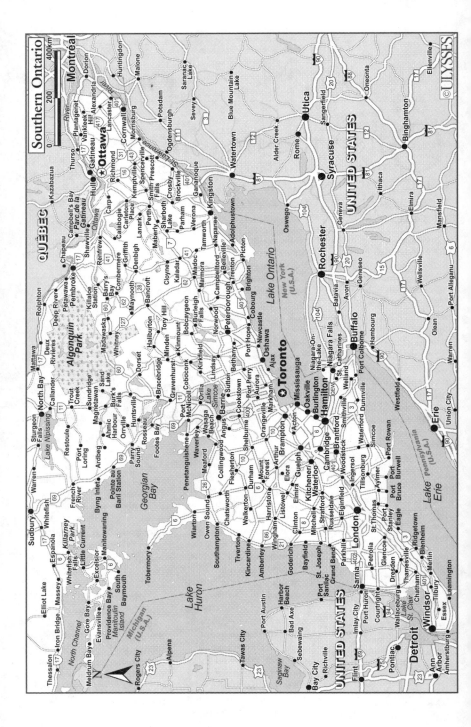

Southern Ontario

Ottawa

Who would have
thought that, less than 200 years ago, at the confluence of the Ottawa and Rideau rivers, in the heart of a dense forest, a city would develop that would become the capital of Canada?

The history of Ottawa goes back to the days after the War of 1812, during which British forces in Canada were pitted against American troops. The British colonial authorities recognized the importance of protecting the navigable waters of the St. Lawrence between the newly built towns along the river, in particular those between Montréal and Kingston. Defending this waterway was not a simple matter. Over a sizable distance, one shore lay on the Canadian side and the other on the American side. A canal between the Ottawa River and Kingston that would bypass the St. Lawrence between the present-day cities of Ottawa and Kingston was proposed as a solution. This strategic military decision was the impetus for the founding of Ottawa.

An early agricultural settlement led by

Philmeon Wright had begun on the site of what is today Hull, on the Québec side of the border, around the year 1800. Construction of the canal began in 1826 under the supervision of Lieutenant-Colonel By. A tiny hamlet developed with the workers brought in to build the canal and the managers brought to oversee the construction. It was called Bytown after the lieutenant-colonel.

It took seven years to complete the canal. In 1832, a little village was built at the confluence of the Ottawa River and the Rideau Canal. The town flourished, mostly because many people found work

as wood-cutters in the dense forest surrounding it..

Two very distinct areas developed on each side of the canal: the upper town, on the west side where the more affluent inhabitants had sumptuous dwellings built; and the lower town, on the east side, that became home to the town's poorer residents (mostly French and Irish, both predominantly Catholic). There was rivalry and tension between these two groups and Bytown's first years were tumultuous ones. The 19th century profoundly transformed this small city of just a few thousand souls.

Kingston was the capital of United Canada between 1841 and 1844. But its proximity to the United States worried the authorities who feared eventual attacks on this important, yet vulnerable colonial administrative centre. They sought another site for the capital, with Toronto, Québec City, Montréal and Bytown. Though it was gritty and violent, Bytown had a lot to recommend it. It was located at the boundary between Upper and Lower Canada, had an equally English-speaking and French-speaking population, and the British government owned ideal land for the construction of governmental buildings. In 1857, Bytown was chosen as the capital of United Canada and then became known as Ottawa. It remained capital with the signing of the British North America Act in 1867 and has kept the title ever since.

Forestry allowed the town and the surrounding region to prosper in the 19th century but this industry went into decline during the 20th century. At the same time, however, its status as national capital enabled it to attract the burgeoning federal civil service, which became the principal local employer. A city plan was adopted at the turn of the 20th century to beautify the area. But Ottawa wasn't transformed until 1937and took

the grand appearance it has today when French architect and town planner Jacques Greber was appointed to develop a new layout for the city centre. Today, the elegant buildings of Parliament Hill and the broad avenues lined with splendid Victorian dwellings bear witness to the success of this plan that brought Ottawa among the ranks of Canada's most beautiful cities.

Finding Your Way Around

By Car

An excellent system of highways and expressways makes Ottawa easy to reach from many points in Ontario and Quebec.

From Toronto, follow Highway 7 which crosses Peterborough and goes directly to Ottawa. It's also possible to drive along the St. Lawrence, taking Highway 401 to Prescott and, then, Highway 16 to Ottawa.

From Montréal, take Highway 40 and then the 417, getting off at the Nicholas Street. exit to reach the downtown area.

By Bus

Both expensive and inexpensive buses cover most of Canada. Except for public transportation, there is no government-run service. Several compa-

nies service the country: Gray Coach, Greyhound and Voyageur Colonial all serve the Ontario region.

Going to Ottawa by bus is usually the least expensive option. Moreover, bus service from Montréal and Toronto is both rapid and punctual, with frequent departures.

Ottawa Bus Station
265 Catherine Street
☎238-5900

From the bus station, you can get to the downtown area by bus (OC Transpo 4) or by car via Kent or Bank Streets.

By Train

VIA Rail transports passengers between the various Canadian provinces and serves several cities in southern and northern Ontario. This is without a doubt the most pleasant way of travelling from Montreal or Toronto to the capital. You will thus be treated to a comfortable ride while being waited on hand-and-foot.

The Ottawa train station is located a dozen minutes by car from the downtown area and is served by a good road network and public transport.

Ottawa Train Station
200 Tremblay Road
☎244-8289

To get there by car, take the eastbound 417. The station is located a short distance past Riverside Drive. If you go by public transportation, take the OC Transpo's bus no. 95 that runs from the station to downtown, stopping right near Parliament Hill. A ticket costs $1.85.

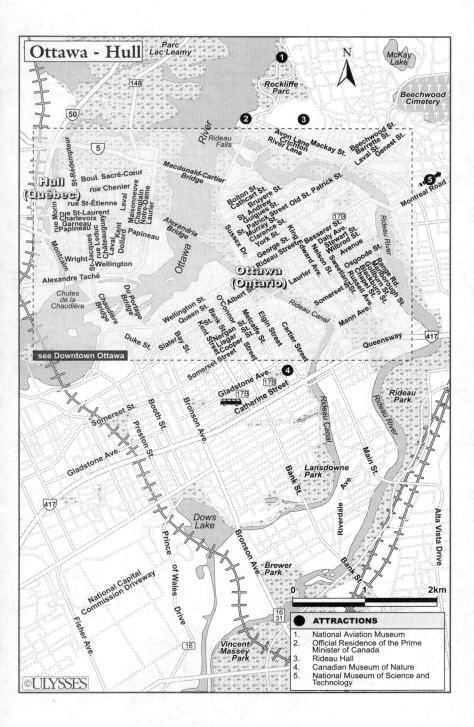

You can also take a taxi from the station. The ride downtown should cost you under $10.

By Plane

Macdonald-Cartier Airport

Ottawa's international airport (*50 Airport Dr.,* ☎*998-5213,* ≈*954-2136*) is small but welcomes several flights a day from other Canadian cities and different countries. It is located about twenty minutes from downtown and easily reached by car (there are a number of car-rental companies here), by taxi or by bus (OC Transpo no.96).

Practical Information

Area code: *613*

Tourist Information

A brand new tourist information office has just opened its doors a stone's throw from Parliament Hill. Brochures, information, hotel-room reservation that you could possibly need are available here.

Capital Call Centre
Late May to early Sep every day, 8:30am to 9pm rest of the year, every day, 9am to 5pm
90 Wellington St.
☎*239-5000 or 800-465-1867*

You can also obtain a great deal of additional tourist-related information by checking out various websites. Here are a few:

www.capcan.ca
www.ottawakiosk.com
www.tourottawa.org

Exploring

The Rideau Canal is the heart of Ottawa in two senses. The very foundation of the city was spurred by the construction of the canal. Geographically, the canal is the dividing line between the eastern part of the city, called Lower Town, and the western part, known as Upper Town. The first tour described in this chapter runs the length of this crucial waterway and presents the main attractions along its shores. The next two tours –Upper Town and Lower Town– reveal the beautiful architectural achievements that transformed Ottawa's image at the turn of the century.

The Rideau Canal

Ottawa's existence is in part a result of the British-American War of 1812 during which British authorities realized the extent of the vulnerability of the St. Lawrence River, the vital link between Montreal and the Great Lakes. Once the conflict ended, the British began to devise plans defend the

waterway. They concluded that a canal linking the south bank of the Ottawa River, at the village of Wrightown, to the city of Kingston would provide the security they desired.

The **Bytown Museum** ★ (*$2; mid-May to end of Nov, Mon to Sat 10am to 5pm, Sun 1pm to 5pm; next to the locks,* ☎*234-4570*) was built at the foot of Barrack Hill, just next to the locks, in 1827. This stone house is the oldest edifice in the city and still encloses the Intendance, which houses various exhibitions inside.

The **Rideau Canal** snakes through the city to the great delight of people who come for a breath of fresh air in the urban mêlé. In the summer, its banks offer parkland dotted with picnic tables, as well as paths alongside the canal for pedestrians and cyclists. Once the canal is frozen over, in the winter, it is transformed into a vast skating rink that crosses the city. There's a small lodge facing the National Arts Centre where skaters can don their blades and warm up.

The **National Arts Centre** (*53 Elgin St., between Confederation Square and the Rideau Canal,* ☎*996-5051*) on the west bank of the canal, occupies the former location of Ottawa's 19th-century city hall that was destroyed by fire. It was built between 1964 and 1967 by Montreal architects Affleck, Desbarats, Dimakopoulos, Lebensol and Sise.

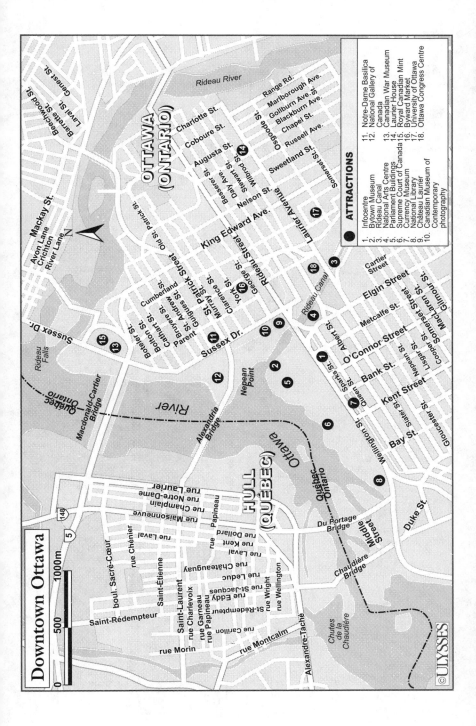

Downtown Ottawa

0   500   1000m

ATTRACTIONS

1. Infocentre
2. Bytown Museum
3. Rideau Canal
4. National Arts Centre
5. Parliament Buildings
6. Supreme Court of Canada
7. Currency Museum
8. National Library
9. Château Laurier
10. Canadian Museum of Contemporary photography
11. Notre-Dame Basilica
12. National Gallery of Canada
13. Canadian War Museum
14. Laurier House
15. Royal Canadian Mint
16. Byward Market
17. University of Ottawa
18. Ottawa Congress Centre

Rideau River

OTTAWA (ONTARIO)

Beechwood St.
Barrette St.
Laval St.
Genest St.

Charlotte St.
Cobourg St.
Augusta St.

Range Rd.
Marlborough Ave.
Gollburn Ave. st.
Blackburn Ave.
Chapel St.
Russell Ave.
Sweetland St.

Osgoode St.
Wilbrod St.
Stewart St.
Daly Ave.
Nelson St.
Besserer St.

Somerset St.

Mackay St.
Avon Lane
Crichton
River Lane

King Edward Ave.

Laurier Avenue

Sussex Dr.

Old St. Patrick St.

Cumberland St.
Boteler St.
Bruyère St.
St. Andrew St.
Guigues Ave.
St. Patrick St.
Murray St.
Clarence St.
York St.
George St.
Rideau Street

Parent
Cathcart St.

Rideau Canal

Cartier Street
Elgin Street
Metcalfe St.
O'Connor Street
Bank St.
Kent Street
Bay St.

Gilmour St.
MacLaren St.
Cooper St.

Sparks St.
Queen St.
Albert St.
Slater St.
Nepean St.
Lisgar St.

Gloucester St.

Sussex Dr.

Rideau Falls

Nepean Point

Macdonald-Cartier Bridge

Alexandra Bridge

Ottawa River

Québec Ontario

Québec Ontario

Wellington St.

Du Portage Bridge

HULL (QUÉBEC)

rue Laurier
rue Notre-Dame
rue Champlain
rue Maisonneuve
rue Laval
rue Chénier

boul. Sacré-Cœur
Saint-Étienne
Saint-Laurent
rue Charlevoix
rue Garneau
rue Papineau
rue Eddy
rue St-Rédempteur

Papineau
rue Kent
rue Laval
rue Châteauguay
rue Leduc
rue St-Jacques
rue Wright
rue Wellington

Saint-Rédempteur
rue Morin

rue Carillon
rue Montcalm

Alexandre-Taché

Chutes de la Chaudière

Chaudière Bridge

Middle Street

Duke St.

148
5

Rideau Falls

© ULYSSES

Excellent concerts and plays are presented here throughout the year (see p 366), while the advantages of the centre's canal-side location are amplified in summertime by pleasant patios.

Upper Town

From Bytown's very beginnings, the beautiful west bank of the Rideau Canal was a magnet to the well-to-do English Protestant families who were migrating to the fledgling city. Upper Town, the city's upper-class neighbourhood (if the nascent community could be called a city in those days), became ever more attractive over the years as new houses sprang up to accommodate newly arriving families. The area entered its heyday around the 1860s when Ottawa was chosen as the national capital and the magnificent federal Parliament Buildings were erected on the summit of Barrack Hill. That summit then belonged to the British Crown and is still capped by the impressive sight of these government buildings. Within about fifty years, the broad avenues of Upper Town were trimmed with exquisite Victorian buildings by a construction boom in part triggered by the neighbourhood's new prominence.

The half-day tour of this neighbourhood begins at the Parliament Buildings and visits some of the most beautiful buildings in the city.

The **Parliament Buildings** ★★★ (*information on activities, ☎239-5000 or 800-465-1867*) truly dominate Ottawa. The summit of the hill is topped by three buildings spread over a 200-square-metre garden. The Centre Block contains the House of Commons and the Senate – the two chambers of the federal government (see further below). The two other buildings –East Block and West Block enclose various administrative offices.

When Ottawa was designated the capital of the Province of Canada in 1857, city authorities realized that these splendid buildings would have to be built since, as there was no appropriate edifice in which to accommodate parliament. When a call was held for sender Thomas Fuller and Chilion Jones's plans for a neo-Gothic building won the contract. The deadlines imposed on the designers were very tight and construction began before all of the inevitable kinks in a project of this scale could be worked out. The impressive budget of 250,000 pounds sterling that had been allotted for the project was surpassed barely one year later. When authorities were accused of mismanaging public funds, the work on the building was interrupted. Three years passed before a Royal Commission of Inquiry into the affair recommended that construction resume. In 1866, the first session of Parliament was held in thestill unfinished building, .

Although the construction of Centre Block was riddled with problems, the overall project's final result is justifiably the pride of the Ottawa's citizens. Three splendid neo-Gothic buildings dominate the horizon of the city, which, up until the erection of the Parliament Buildings, had been a conglomeration of modest wood houses.

Just 40 years later, on February 3, 1916, a terrible fire broke out in Centre Block, destroying the rooms of the west wing before spreading to those of the east wing. The magnificent edifice was entirely consumed by flame, with the exception of the Library of Parliament. It was spared thanks to the quick wits of a clerk who closed the thick iron doors that separated it from the rest of the building. The library –a splendid, 16-sided neo-Gothic building covered by a lantern-shaped roof – may still be visited today. Its interior is richly decorated in white-pine woodwork and comprises a large reading room lit by lancet windows on each of its sides as well as small alcoves that enclose part of the library collection. Its centre is occupied by a white-marble statue of Queen Victoria that was sculpted by Marshall Wood in 1871.

Guided tours of **Centre Block** (*free; late May to early Sep, Mon to Fri 9am to 7:40pm, Sat and Sun 9am to 4:40pm; Sep to May, every day 9am to 4:40pm*) visit the interior of the building, including the west wing where visitors are treated to an up-close look at the House of Commons. Members of Parliament elected through universal suffrage hold debates and adopt federal laws.

In the east wing of the building, these guided tours pause at the large room that houses the Senate. The government appointed members of the federal legislature's upper chamber are responsible for studying and approving laws adopted by the House of Commons.

In addition to these two rooms, the guided tours visit the **Library of Parliament** as well as the **Peace Tower** where you can see the white-marble Memorial Chamber.

Since the earliest days of its construction, Centre Block has been flanked on either side by East Block and West Block, the work of Thomas Stent and Augustus Laver. East Block, a beautiful composition of asymmetrical elevations, is made of cut stone in shades that range from cream to ochre and is embellished by towers, chimneys, pinnacles, lancet windows, gargoyles and various sculptures. Originally built to house the Canadian civil service, it now encloses the offices of senators and members of Parliament. A guided tour is offered and highlights a few rooms that have been restored to their 19th-century appearances.

The Office of the Governor General and the Chamber of the Privy Council are also located here. West Block is used exclusively for the offices of Members of Parliament and is not open to the public.

Parliament is also the scene of numerous events, notably the **changing of the guard**, which takes place every day from late June to late August at 10am, when you can see soldiers parading in their ceremonial garb. A **sound and light show** (*free admission; mid-May to mid-Jun, 9:30pm and 10:30pm*) presents the history of Canada.

Continuing along Wellington Street, another Canadian institution comes into view: the **Supreme Court of Canada** ★ (*guided tours available; corner of Wellington St. and Kent St., ☎995-5361*). This Art Deco building was conceived by architect Ernest Cormier who began its construction in 1939. Only one modification was brought to its original plans which favoured a flat roof. The Public Works Department, which still favoured the Château style, required that the roof be altered to give it its current appearance (or it may have been requested by Prime Minister Mackenzie King). The tremendous interior space created by this peaked roof is now occupied by the court's library.

At the end of Wellington Street stand the buildings of the **National Library and Archives of Canada** (*395 Wellington St.*) which contain an impressive collection of documents dealing with Canada as well as Canadian publications. Temporary exhibitions are also presented here.

The considerable changes that Ottawa underwent in the second half of the 19th century had repercussions on the development of its commercial arteries. From the town's very beginnings, two sections have vied for the status of business centre: the surroundings of the Byward Market in Lower Town, and **Sparks Street** in Upper Town. Great effort was expended by local residents and shopkeepers to embellish Sparks Street. Thanks to them, this elegant road of five- and six-storey buildings was one of the very first to be paved with asphalt, have streetcars and be illuminated by street lamps. In those days it was known as the "Broadway" of Ottawa. Its commercial role never ebbed, and today it offers a beautiful pedestrian mall between Kent and Elgin Streets that is especially pleasant in the summertime when its concentration of pretty shops attracts crowds of patrons and browsers.

The first stop on Sparks Street is a visit to the **Currency Museum** ★ (*$2; Tue to Sat 10:30am to 5pm, Sun 1pm to 5pm; 245 Sparks St., ☎782-8914*), which is located inside the Bank of Canada by the rear entrance. The exhibition is spread over eight rooms and retraces the history of the creation of currency.

Lower Town

In the early days of Bytown, the poorly irrigated land on the east bank of the canal was unappealing to newcomers.

Ontario

Supreme Court

Irrigation work was carried out in 1827, making it more attractive, and gradually it was populated but not by the well-to-do. Labourers looking for affordable housing established themselves here, and French and Irish workers, mostly Catholic, made up the majority in this neighbourhood. Conditions were difficult; skirmishes between the Irish and the French, who were often competing for the same jobs, were frequent and life in the neighbourhood was not always rosy. Few traces remain of these first difficult years in Lower Town. The buildings of the era, most of which were made of wood, rarely resisted the wear of the years. A few scattered here and there mostly reflect the French origins of neighbourhood residents. Left by the wayside in the second half of the 19th century, the neighbourhood was left out of the building boom that overtook Upper Town. Here, there are very few of the neo-Gothic constructions that were so popular in that period. At the beginning of the 20th century, Sussex Drive, which delimits the western edge of the neighbourhood, was embellished by the construction of magnificent Château-style buildings.

Then, over the course of this century, other buildings, including the very beautiful National Gallery of Canada, perfected the image of this elegant artery.

Wellington Street spans the canal, becoming Rideau Street on this bank where it is lined with a multitude of shops that are fun to browse in for a spell.

The first building on the tour is the unmistakable and imposing **Château Laurier ★★** (*1 Rideau St.*), on the shore of the Rideau Canal, that has been one of the most prestigious hotels in the city since the day it opened its doors (see p 363). Ross and MacFarland were hired in 1908 to complete the blueprints. They favoured the Château style to keep with the look of the other Canadian Pacific hotels. They built an elegant, romantically alluring hotel of relatively bare stone façades topped by pointed copper roofs, turrets and dormers. No detail was overlooked in making this a hotel of the highest quality. The interior decoration, which can be admired in the lobby, is sumptuous. The very first guest to register, in 1912, was none other than Sir Wilfrid Laurier, then Prime Minister, who

had strongly supported the creation of the railroad and in whose honour the hotel was named.

Nearly is the **Canadian Museum of Contemporary Photography** (*free admission; May to Sep, Mon and Tue, Fri and Sun 11am to 5pm, Wed 4pm to 8pm, Thu 11am to 8pm; Sep to Apr, Wed and Thu 11am to 8pm, Fri to Sun 11am to 5pm; 1 Rideau Canal, ☎990-8257, ⩵990-6542*), which has a collection containing more than 158,000 images created from the photographic resources of the National Film Board of Canada.

In 1841, **Notre Dame Basilica ★★** (*Sussex Dr. at the corner of Saint Patrick St.*), topped by two elegant steeples, was built to serve Catholics in Lower Town, French-speakers as well as the English-speaking Irish. In the choir stall, you will notice the presence of Saint John the Baptist and of Saint Patrick. This is the oldest church in the city. Its magnificent choir stall of finely worked wood and statues of the prophets and evangelists by Louis-Philippe Hébert are still in perfect condition.

The **National Gallery of Canada ★★★** (*free admission to the permanent collection; Jun to early Oct, every day 10am to 6pm; Oct to late May, Wed to Sun 10am to 5pm, Tue 10am to 8pm; 380 Sussex Dr., ☎990-1985*), with its collection of 45,000 works of art, 1,200 of which are on display, offers a fabulous trip through the art history of Canada and elsewhere.

This modern glass, granite and concrete building, rises above the Ottawa

River, a masterpiece by architect Moshe Safdie, it's easily identified by its harmonious tower, covered with glass triangles, recalling the shape of the parliamentary library visible in the distance.

The first rooms of the museum on the ground floor, are devoted to the works of Canadian and American artists. Fifteen of these rooms trace the evolution of Canadian artistic movements.

The following rooms present important works by artists who made their mark in the early 20th century. Space is also given to artists who gained renown by creating painting techniques and exploiting themes that were particular to them, including British Columbian artist Emily Carr (*Indian Hut, Queen Charlotte Islands*). You can also contemplate canvasses by great 20th-century Québec painters, notably Alfred Pellan (*On the Beach*), Jean-Paul Riopelle (*Pavane*), Jean-Paul Lemieux (*The Visit*), and Paul-Émile Borduas (*Leeward of the Island*).

The ground floor also includes Inuit art galleries that merit special attention. With about 160 sculptures and 200 prints, they provide an occasion to admire several masterpieces of Inuit art. Among them are *The Enchanted Owl* by Kenojuak and the beautiful sculpture *Man and Woman Seated with a Child*.

The museum also houses an impressive collection of American and European works. Works of the great masters are presented in chronological order, and in the course of your visit you can contemplate cre-

ations by many famous painters.

The string of rooms on the ground floor surrounds a very unique gallery that houses an under-appreciated work: the beautiful interior of the **Chapelle du Couvent Notre-Dame-du-Sacré-Coeur**, designed by Georges Bouillon in 1887-1888. When the convent was demolished in 1972, the structure of the chapel was taken apart piece by piece and preserved. A few years later, a room was specially laid out in the National Gallery to accommodate it. Its splendid choir and its wooden, fan-shaped vaults and cast-iron columns may still be admired here.

The entrance to the **Canadian War Museum** ★ (*$3.50; May to mid-Oct, every day 9:30am to 5pm, Thu to 8pm; mid-Oct to May, closed Mon; 330 Sussex Dr., ☎776-8600 or 800-555-5621*) is impossible to miss, what with a tank sitting on the lawn in front. The museum was laid out in a beautiful building designed at the beginning of the century by David Ewart to house the National Archives. The exhibitions are spread over three stories and retrace the history of the Canadian Army from its very first battles in the early days of colonization to its participation in the momentous wars that have marked the 20th century.

Just next door to the Canadian War Museum is the building that houses the **Royal Canadian Mint** ★ (*$2; Mon to Fri 9am to 4pm, Sat and Sun 10am to 5pm; 320 Sussex Dr., ☎993-8990*), conceived by Ewart in 1905-1908. Common Canadian coins were once struck here, but today the mint produces only silver,

gold and platinum collector's pieces. The entire process may be seen here: the selection and cutting of precious metals; the striking of the coins and the quality control procedure. It is best to visit during the week when it is possible to see the coins being made through large bay windows. Tours are offered on the weekend, but in the absence of workers the whole process has to be imagined.

One of Ottawa's liveliest places, the **Byward Market** ★★ (*around York and George streets*) is a pleasant open-air market where various merchants gather to sell fruits, vegetables, flowers and all sorts of other knick-knacks and treasures. All around, and on the neighbouring streets, there are many shops, restaurants, bars and cafés, some with pretty outdoor terraces. On fine summer days, the area is at its most lively with crowds of people out for a stroll or a little shopping. On sunny summer days, the market is bustling with relaxed crowds strolling around and shoppers seeking out special ingredients.

Laurier House ★ (*$2.25; Apr to Sep, Tue to Sat 9am to 5pm, Sun 2pm to 5pm; Oct to Mar, Tue to Sat 10am to 5pm, Sun 2pm to 5pm; 335 Laurier Ave. E., ☎992-8142*), a delightful residence built in 1878, belonged to Sir Wilfrid Laurier. Elected Prime Minister of Canada in 1896, that year his party, the Liberal Party of Canada, offered him this house. Laurier was the first French-Canadian Prime Minister holding that post post until 1911. He lived in this house until his death in 1919.

Ontario

Later, Lady Laurier gave it to William Lyon Mackenzie King who succeeded her husband as Liberal leader. When King died in 1950, the house was bequeathed to the government as part of Canada's heritage. Visiting it today, you can explore several rooms decorated according to King's tastes and a few others decorated with the Laurier family's furniture.

Ottawa University, previously known as Ottawa College, was originally run by a religious order and served the Catholic communities of Ottawa. The university is now a renowned educational institution. Its campus is bordered by Laurier Avenue, Nicholas Street and King Edward Avenue.

The **Ottawa Congress Centre**, located on the shore of the canal, hosts various events throughout the year.

Outside of Downtown

Ottawa has several other tourist attractions worth mentioning. Although they lie outside of downtown, they are not far and are easy to reach.

Past the Royal Canadian Mint, Sussex Drive runs along the eastern bank of the Ottawa River to a posh section of the city. A series of magnificent homes appears next, but number 24 should catch your eye. It is an immense stone house surrounded by a beautiful garden – the

Official Residence of the Prime Minister of Canada. Built in 1867 for businessman Joseph Currier, it became the home of Canadian prime ministers in 1949. For obvious reasons, it is not open to the public.

Chateau Laurier

Not far from 24 Sussex Drive another splendid residence crops up, surrounded by a pleasant and huge garden that covers 40 hectares: **Rideau Hall** ★★ (*free; schedule varies; 1 Sussex Dr.,* ☎998-7113). This is the official residence of Canada's Governor General, the representative of the Queen of England, Elizabeth II. It is a sumptuous Regency-style home that was built in 1838 for Thomas McKay, the designer of the entrance to the Rideau Canal. In 1865, the government rented the building to accommodate the governor general of the day, Lord Monck, and then bought the property in 1868. Since then, many modifications have been made to the original building.

A vast and pleasant garden surrounds the house where you can linger about. Guided tours are offered during the summer of the five rooms open to the public.

Across from Rideau Hall is a very pleasant green space, **Rockcliffe Park** ★. This pretty garden is especially beautiful in the springtime, when thousands of flowers bloom here. There is also a belvedere with a wonderful **view** ★ of the river with Québec on the other side.

Visitors are immediately impressed upon entering the **National Aviation Museum** ★★★ (*$5; May to Sep, every day 9am to 5pm; Sep to May, Tue to Sun 10am to 5pm; Rockliffe Airport,* ☎993-2010 or 1-800-463-2038) by the unique atmosphere of this huge, wonderfully laid-out building. The fascinating exhibition housed here and culled from the museum's beautiful collection of airplanes thoroughly brings to light the dazzling, rapid-fire evolution that so far is just under 100 years old. Eight themes are explored: the era of pioneers, the First World War, bush piloting, airlines, the British Commonwealth training plan, the Second World War, air and sea forces, and the era of jet planes.

The **Canadian Museum of Nature** ★ (*$5; closed monday in winter; May to Sep, every day 9:30am to 5pm, Thu to 8pm; Sep to May, every day 10am to 5pm, Thu to 8pm; corner of McLeod St.*

and Metcalfe St.,
☎566-4700), in a huge, recently renovated three-story building, houses many small exhibitions on various facets of nature. Myriad themes, including geology, the formation of the planet, animals of pre-historic Canada, indige-nous mammals and birds of Canada, and the fantas-tic world of insects and of plant life, are presented in a fascinating manner.

The **National Museum of Sci-ence and Technology** ★★ (*$6; May to Sep, every day 9am to 6pm, Fri to 9pm; Sep to Apr, Tue to Sun 9am to 5pm; 1867 St. Laurent Blvd.,* ☎991-3044) offers a pleas-ant opportunity to enter the world of science and technology – a universe that may seem too com-plex at first glance to some. The appeal of this museum is not based on any particular exhibition but rather on its panoply of interactive presentations on various subjects. For example, computer sci-ence is tackled in an exhi-bition entitled "Connexions". About 500 computers are dis-played, illustrating the ex-traordinary technological leaps and bounds that the field has made in just 50 years. Another exhibition, "Love, Leisure and Laun-dry," recounts the evolu-tion of the multitude of little tools used in our daily lives – like lamps, toilets and iceboxes – that have greatly contributed to our improved standard of living. Other fascinating topics, such as transporta-tion and printing, are also dealt with. Through games, explanatory panels and models of all sorts, visitors to the museum gain a better understand-ing of how the world works and have fun at the same time.

Outdoor Activities

Cycling

The Ottawa region is crisscrossed by no fewer than 150 kilometres of pathways that are very pleasant to meander on foot or by bicycle. Whether you opt for an outing along the Rideau Canal, on the Rockliffe promenade or along the Ottawa River, you will benefit the pleasant land-scapes, from peace and quiet and, above all, from trails that are very well laid out for cycling. On Sunday mornings from late May to early September, cyclists are in seventh heaven since these routes are closed to automobile traffic. Maps of Ottawa's bicycle and walking paths are available at the capital Infocentre.

Bicycle Rental

Cyco's
5 Hawthorne Ave.
☎567-8180

Dow's Lake Pavilion
☎232-1001

Skating

Imagine lacing on a pair of skates and gliding uninter-rupted over 8 kilometres of ice. Every winter, as soon as the **Rideau Canal** has frozen over in late December or early Janu-ary, the canal is trans-formed into a vast skating

rink, one of the longest in the world. The ice surface is cleared and maintained for the pleasure of skaters of all ages. There is a heated cabin just a few steps from the National Arts Centre where skaters can lace up out of the cold.

Dow's Lake also has a heated lodge in which to don your skates, warm up and have a bite to eat.

Ice Conditions
☎239-5234

Accommodations

Since it has many pleasant and comfortable hotels, inns and Bed & Breakfasts,you won't have any trouble finding a place to stay in Ottawa. With a wide range of amenities. Prices are generally higher during the week than on weekends because many business travellers visit the city.

Upper Town

Doral Inn
$69
K, tv
486 Albert St.
K1R 5B5
☎230-8055
The Doral Inn is set up in a lovely Victorian house and contains about forty rooms. Alongside the hall are two small lounges appointed with second-hand furniture, giving them an antiquated look that will appeal to some. The rooms are simply furnished and offer decent comfort for the price. All are equipped with private bathrooms and some also have kitchenettes. Rooms

Ontario

can be rented for the day, the week, or the month.

Albert House
$80 bkfst incl.
tv
478 Albert St.
K1R 5B5
☎*236-4479*
Next door, the Albert House is also located in an appealing residence. There are only 17 rooms, giving it a pleasant family atmosphere. Each of the rooms is perfectly maintained and decorated with care.

Lord Elgin Hotel
$90
ℜ, ⅃
100 Elgin St.
K1P 5K8
☎*235-3333* or *800-267-4298*
≈*235-3223*
The Lord Elgin Hotel is among those untimely Ottawa institutions. Very few pieces of furniture, however, have managed to conserve any traces of its past save for the lobby that still has a pretty centre light and an antique mobile hanging from the ceiling. The rooms are large and decorated with modern furnishings that may fail to lend the charm of yesteryear but nonetheless make for a pleasant stay.

Delta
$105
≈, ℜ, △, ⊘
361 Queen St., K1R 7S9
☎*238-6000*
≈*238-2290*
As you enter the Delta you will immediately notice the efforts made to create a more intimate atmosphere than at the standard downtown chain hotel. The spacious rooms are attractively furnished in mahogany that will please even

the most exacting guests. The pool with a water slide is an added bonus if you are travelling with children.

Sheraton
$119
≈, ℜ, △, ⊘, ⅃
150 Albert St., K1P 5G2
☎*238-1500* or *800-489-8333*
≈*235-2723*
Some prefer older establishments filled with antiques and an elegant decor. Still others opt for modern styling and the utmost in service. Those who fit into the latter category will appreciate the very modern Sheraton with its conference halls, large rooms with offices, telephones with voice-mail, hair dryers and fitness centre with a pool, a sauna and a whirlpool.

Carmichael Inn & Spa
134$ bkfst incl.
ℜ
46 Cartier St., K2P 1J3
☎*236-4667*
≈*563-7529*
Set in an imposing old house, the Carmichael Inn & Spa is part of Ottawa's heritage. This non-smoking establishment has 11 rooms, decorated with antiques and fitted with queen-size beds.

Lower Town

For low-priced accommodations during the summer, **Ottawa University** (*85 University St.,* ☎*562-5771,* ≈*562-5157*) and **Carleton University** (*1125 Colonel By Promenade,* ☎*520-5611,* ≈*520-3952*) rent basic but adequate rooms in the residence halls.

Youth Hostel
$17 for members
$21 dormitories
$37/room
K
75 Nicholas St., K1N 7B9
☎*235-2595*
Right next to the Rideau Centre, in the middle of everything, you will see an imposing building that once housed the city's prison. Entirely remodelled, it now houses a youth hostel. In addition to dormitories and three rooms, the hostel has a fully-equipped communal kitchen.

McGee Inn
$68 bkfst incl. and sb
$78 bkfst incl. and pb
⊛, ≈
185 Daly Ave., K1N 6E8
☎*237-6089*
The Sandy Hill district is full of charming Victorian houses. If you would like to stay in one but cannot afford the luxury, the McGee Inn is a good choice. This red-brick house, erected in 1886, still has its original character. Admittedly, the rooms are simply decorated, but they are tasteful nonetheless. Moreover, the place is well-kept and all the rooms are air conditioned.

Olde Bytown Bed and Breakfast
$79 bkfst incl.
pb, sb
459 Laurier Ave. E., K1N 6R4
☎*565-7939*
≈*565-7981*
Located in a quiet neighbourhood and affording a superb view of Strathcona Park, the Olde Bytown Bed and Breakfast is a choice place for those who appreciate the cachet of turn-of-the-century Victorian houses. The B & B's every room is meticulously kept and graced with beautiful antiques, flowered wallpaper and old artifacts. There are seven

wonderfully cosy rooms in which guests could easily spend hours daydreaming.

Auberge King Edward
$80
525 King Edward Ave., K1N 7N3
☎*565-6700*
The Auberge King Edward is set up in a very beautiful house dating from the beginning of the century. In keeping with the period of the building, all the rooms are graced with antiques and myriad old curios. This somewhat cluttered decor has undeniable charm and imparts an atmosphere of calm and well-being to the establishment. The inn boasts two charming living rooms as well as three exceedingly well-kept bedrooms (one with a private bathroom).

Novotel
$105
ℜ, ≈, ⌂, ☉
33 Nicholas St., K1N 9M7
☎*230-3033 or 800-NOVOTEL*
⇌*230-7865*
With its dark blue foyer trimmed with steel and wood, the Novotel stands apart from the city's Victorian hotels. This modernity is not without refinement despite the fact that some will describe it as cold. The rooms are somewhat warmer with their dark colours pleasantly adorning the spacious quarters. All have a rather large bathroom.

Westin Hotel
$135
≈, ℜ, ⌂, ◉, ☉, &, ✻
11 Colonel By Dr.
☎*560-7000*
⇌*569-2013*
The Westin Hotel has what may be the most enviable location in Ottawa, facing the Rideau Canal, opposite the National Arts Centre and right in the heart of all the commotion. It is part of the complex that includes the Rideau Centre shopping mall and the Ottawa Convention Centre. Rooms are very spacious and extremely comfortable, offering magnificent views of the canal. The hotel has a very good restaurant, Daly's (excellent atmosphere, interesting and refined cuisine), and even a happening night club. Very good weekend packages are usually available.

Château Laurier
$169
≈; ⌂; &
1 Rideau St., Ottawa K1N 8S7
☎*241-1414 or 800-441-1414*
⇌*562-7030*
The opulence and luxury of the Château Laurier (see p 360), part of the Canadian Pacific hotel chain, will appeal to those who like to rave about beautiful things. Upon entering the hotel, visitors will be swept away by the decor: wainscotted walls, cornices, bas reliefs and antiques. The lobby itself gives an idea of the comfort and elegance of the rooms, all stocked with wooden furnishings, plush couches and comfortable beds. Undeniably pleasant, the rooms combine one-time elegance with today's comforts. Two very good restaurants and a sports centre with a lovely Art Deco swimming pool add to the place's overall appeal.

Restaurants

The city of Ottawa has many kinds of restaurants. Whether you prefer steak or roast beef, fish or French, Italian, Asian or other specialties, the city's restaurants are sure to meet your expectations.

Many are open for both lunch and dinner. Keep in mind, however, that satisfying your hunger after 11pm can prove difficult.

This chapter offers you a selection of a few good restaurants in the city. If you would like more information on Ottawa's restaurants: *www.dine.net*.

The Rideau Canal

Ritz on the Canal
$$
375 Queen Elizabeth Dr.
at Fifth Ave.
☎*238-8998*
The menu at the Ritz on the Canal differs somewhat from those of its sister establishments (see further below) in that it also features "gourmet" pizzas baked in a wood-burning oven. This restaurant is particularly appreciated in summer on account of its outstanding setting and huge terrace facing a part of the canal that resembles a bay. No smoking.

Café of the National Arts Centre
$$$
53 Elgin St.
☎*594-5127*
The Café of the National Arts Centre offers an unbeatable view of the teeming activity on the Rideau Canal with boats in the summer and skaters in the winter. During the summer months, meals are served on a comfortable, well-designed terrace. Beyond a doubt, this is one of the most pleasant outdoor terraces in town. Refined Canadian cooking is offered with the chef making inventive use of quality products from various regions of Canada. Grilled Atlantic salmon is a specialty. Not to be missed are the wonderful desserts. Prices are on the high side,

Ontario

however, unless a fixed-price menu is offered, which is unfortunately rare.

Upper Town

D'Arcy McGee
$$
44 Sparks St.
☎230-4433
If there is one place in Ottawa in which to enjoy a good meal in an unparalleled ambiance, it is definitely the D'Arcy McGee. This typical Irish pub, located a stone's throw from Parliament Hill, is the haunt par excellence of civil servants. Extremely warm and frequented by a clientele of all ages, it has become one of the city's absolute musts.

Ritz
$$
274 Elgin St.
☎235-7027
Elgin Street is home to an institution known to just about everyone in town: the Ritz. Waiting is almost obligatory at this Italian restaurant which does not accept reservations. Its pasta dishes are deservedly renowned. Fortunately, this restaurant now has younger siblings. The **Ritz Uptown** (*226 Nepean,* **☎238-8752**) is inside an old house and reservations are accepted.

Le Métro
$$$
315 Somerset St. W.
☎230-8123
Le Métro is undoubtedly one of the best eating spots in town. The *escargots* with roquefort in pastry are a true joy as are the steak tartare or simple beef fillet with *béarnaise* sauce. The opulent, harmonious decor, the quiet atmosphere and the big, comfortable leather chairs

assure you a relaxing and delicious evening.

Chez Jean-Pierre
$$$
210 Somerset St. W.
☎235-9711
A little to the east toward Elgin Street, Chez Jean-Pierre does not have the most inviting of façades, and the interior decor is not its strong point. But these are things you can live with since it's known for the fine French cuisine and the solid service. This is a restaurant where quality is a long-time tradition.

Friday's
$$$
150 Elgin St.
☎237-5353
A feeling of well-being will sweep over you as soon as you walk into Friday's which occupies a magnificent Victorian house built in 1875. The place is irresistible with its large antique-decorated rooms, its big wooden tables and its high-backed chairs, which exude old-fashioned charm. Its rooms have been transformed into dining rooms where a relaxing atmosphere prevails. If the decor doesn't win you over, the succulent roast surely will. Of course, with all this going for it, Friday's has a devout following so reservations are recommended.

Lower Town

Rideau Street

MarcheLino Mövenpick
$
Rideau St., at Sussex Dr.
☎569-4934
Having a good meal in a shopping centre may seem illusory... And yet, MarcheLino Mövenpick, in the Rideau Centre, attracts crowds of happy diners. The restaurant's recipe for

success is simple: a large dining-room, attractively decorated with plants and wooden tables, and delicious, quickly-prepared dishes from fresh, quality ingredients. In this lively place, everyone is free to stroll about, choosing their dishes from one of the various stations. Sushi, salads, pasta, quiches and all sorts of other dishes sure to please the most demanding palates are prepared before your eyes.

Santé
$$$
45 Rideau St.
☎241-7113
Located on the second floor of a building facing the Rideau Centre, Santé is easy to miss, so keep your eyes peeled. Its Californian, Thai and Caribbean specialties are true delights, especially the Bangkok noodles. This spot is an oasis of quiet repose with big bay windows opening onto some of the city's main attractions. Save room for something from the tempting dessert list. Attentive service.

Around Byward Market

Although the surroundings of the Byward Market form the area most visited by tourists and locals alike, there are disappointingly few worthwhile restaurants. On the other hand, if you have sudden pangs of hunger or thirst, this is the place to be, especially in the summer. There are a number of friendly outdoor cafés and plenty of pedestrian traffic. In short, it is lively and very pleasant.

Beaver Tails
87 George St. corner William St.
☎241-1230
Your sweet tooth will want to sample Beaver Tails. Do

not be alarmed! These are merely delicious treats made from sugared deep-fried dough, something of a cross between a doughnut and a cookie.

Memories
$
7 Clarence St.
☎*241-1882*
Memories is almost always packed. Why? Because almost everyone in Ottawa comes to try the many desserts that have made its reputation. The selection of cakes and pies of all sorts is so impressive that it can be hard to choose. But the greatest temptation may fall on the delicious, oversized portions of apple pie. Light meals (interesting soups, sandwiches, salads) are also available. The coffee is good.

Blue Cactus
$-$$
2 Byward Market
☎*241-7061*
Blue Cactus is a Tex-Mex restaurant with the usual megacocktails, *nachos* (try the very filling Blue Cactus *nachos*), *fajitas* and so on. The atmosphere at this spot, which is popular with young people, may be a little too lively for some.

Clair de lune
$-$$
81B Clarence St.
☎*241-2200*
For years now, Clair de lune has been delighting diners with its laid-back ambiance as well as its menu which features good, simple dishes.

Casablanca
$$
41 Clarence St.
☎*789-7855*
If you want to discover the flavours of Morocco, head to Casablanca whose tasty dishes offer a wonderful opportunity to sample

unique flavours and aromas.

Mama Grazzi's
$$
25 George St.
☎*241-8656*
Set in a small, delightful space where you will feel at home almost immediately, Mama Grazzi's also boasts original, delicious and delightful Italian cooking.

Ritz
$$
89 Clarence St.
☎*789-9797*
If you like the cuisine at the Ritz, there is a second one near Byward Market.

Café Crêpe de France
$$
76 Murray St.
The Café Crêpe de France is worth a visit for its Breton-style crepes, its salads or for its weekend brunch. The setting is congenial, with exposed brick, red-and-white-checked tablecloths, and subdued lighting. Big bay windows let in plenty of daylight. In the summer, you can dine on the pretty little outdoor terrace. Besides crepes, different full-course meals are offered each day, but they aren't as good. This is an ideal spot for a light lunch or for a dessert crepe in the evening.

The Fish Market
$$-$$$
54 York St.
☎*241-3474*
The Fish Market is an Ottawa institution, set up on the edge of the Byward Market. The restaurant is decorated with nets, buoys and other objects related to fishing. That's only right and proper in an establishment specializing in fish, shellfish and seafood which is always impeccably fresh. Downstairs, two other dining rooms meet

other culinary needs. **Coasters**, whose large picture windows look out on the bustling market, is just as pleasant. Dishes here are less sophisticated (fish n' chips) and more moderately priced, but quite good. The third room, **Vineyards**, is the place to go if all you want is a drink (good selection of wine by the glass) and a bite to eat. Shows are sometimes featured here.

Domus Café
$$$
85 Murray St.
☎*241-6007*
Domus Café is undoubtedly one of the best restaurants in Ottawa. The food is refined and innovative, made with the freshest of ingredients. Its success is derived from original combinations of international flavours. Recipes are drawn from the many cookbooks sold at the adjacent store. The menu changes every day, but some of the most popular items keep reappearing. While choice is never exhaustive, the selection is interesting enough to make it difficult to decide. The desserts, limited to a choice of four or five, are some of the best in Ottawa. The wine list includes excellent Californian wines, some available by the glass. And finally, try the Sunday brunch. It is divine and well worth the wait (reservations are not accepted for brunch).

Would a jaunt to the Château Laurier strike your fancy? If you go in for this kind of treat but do not wish to squander a fortune on a single meal, head to **Wilfrid's** (*$$; 1 Rideau St.,* ☎*241-1414*) come lunch time. You will thus be regaled with a warm dining room, comfortable armchairs, an unobstructed

Ontario

view of the Rideau Canal and a delicious but affordable lunch (*à-la-carte* dishes are around $10). The dinner menu is more refined and more expensive (*$$$-$$$$*). Coming here for breakfast is also very pleasant, but will cost you at least $10. On Sundays, **Zoe's** is the place to go for a delicious brunch (*$22.95*) served in a quiet and elegant ambiance.

Entertainment

Ottawa has never been famous for its nightlife. Though its streets are often deserted after 11pm, you can enjoy the rest of your night by knowing a few of its secrets. In addition to the warm pubs and lively bars, mostly set up along Elgin Street and around Byward Market, the city has a flourishing cultural life. Excellent shows are presented at the National Arts Centre, where the city's various theatre companies perform. Finally, entertaining festivals are organized throughout the year.

Bars and Danceclubs

Until just a few years ago, many Ottawans would finish off the night in Hull, where bars were open until 3am. Since April 1996, however, the two cities have adopted the same closing hours, so that bars in both Ottawa and Hull now close at 2am. Whatever your preference, you will find enjoyable bars on either side of the Ottawa River.

Near downtown Ottawa, there are several bars and pubs along Elgin Street, that is quite lively in the evening.

Maxwell's
340 Elgin St.
☎*232-5771*
Maxwell's, upstairs from a restaurant, is popular with trendy youth. In the summer, there are tables on a large balcony facing the lively street.

D'Arcy McGee
44 Sparks St.
The D'Arcy McGee can pride itself on being the only real Irish pub in Ottawa. The interior was completely built in Ireland, then transported to Ottawa where it was reconstructed piece by piece. Extremely warm, decorated with woodwork, stained-glass windows and scores of marvellous knick-knacks, the place is always full. Concerts are presented here on certain evenings. Good selection of beers on tap.

Yuk Yuk's
Wed to Sat
88 Albert St.
☎*236-5233*
Yuk Yuk's is part of a chain offering comedy shows, some of them actually quite funny. This is an interesting alternative to a conventional bar. No smoking on Thursdays.

The area around the Byward Market is home to several bars, many of them clustered along George and York streets.

Vineyard's Wine Bar Bistro
54 York St.
☎*241-4270*
Vineyard's Wine Bar Bistro is a friendly, congenial little bar where you can enjoy wine, beer and cheese. Musicians often perform here with jazz at the top of the list.

Hard Rock Café
73 York St.
☎*241-2442*
Part of the well-known chain, Ottawa's Hard Rock Café is a carbon copy of its sister establishments with blaring rock music and electric guitars adorning the walls.

Heart and Crown
67 Clarence St.
Though lacking the character of the D'Arcy McGee, the Heart and Crown is another fashionable Irish pub in the capital. Relaxed ambiance and good selection of beers.

Earl of Sussex
431 Sussex Dr.
☎*562-5544*
Ottawa just wouldn't be right without an English pub: so the Earl of Sussex was thus set up here. Warm decor, beer on tap and fish & chips on the menu is only fitting in this type of establishment.

Zoe's
1 Rideau St.
If spending hours in a smoky club with a mixed crowd dancing to deafening music is not your thing, the chic Zoe's in the Château Laurier might be the place to go. Everything here is calm and comfy from the delightfully soft music to the cozy armchairs.

Festivals and Cultural Activities

The **National Arts Centre** (*53 Elgin St.*, ☎*996-5051*, ≈*996-9578*) is Ottawa's cultural headquarters with an opera house and two theatres where top-notch performances are offered year-round.

Winterlude (in February) no longer needs an introduction. Its reputation is well established in Canada. For 10 days in early February, all sorts of winter festivities are held on what is billed as the world's longest skating rink.

The **Tulip Festival** is held in May during the Victoria Day long weekend. The city is then abloom with thousands of tulips bestowed by the Netherlands to thank Canada for taking in Queen Wilhemina during the Second World War. Shows and activities of all kinds take placein various parts of the city, including Confederation Park and Dow's Lake.

The **Festival Canada** (☎996-5051) takes place in July. Culture holds pride of place for four weeks as 70 dance, jazz and opera performances are presented at the National Arts Centre.

Shopping

Upper Town

Sparks Street, a long pedestrian thoroughfare lined with trees, benches and lovely shops, makes for a very pleasant little stroll. On rainy days, you can browse indoors at the **240 Sparks** shopping centre which comprises several attractive boutiques.

Sparks Street, between Elgin and O'Connor Streets, is a good place to shop for Canadian-made handicrafts. The first among many such shops is the **Snow Goose** (*83 Sparks St.*, ☎232-2213) that boasts

a wide selection of creations by Inuit and First Nations artisans, including sculptures and engravings. The shop also carries an abundance of leather and fur accessories, notably mocassins, gloves and hats.

A stone's throw away, **Canada's Four Corners** (*93 Sparks St.*, ☎233-2322) also sells Aboriginal handicrafts. However, you'll have to rummage through all the assorted junk and plastic objects just to find a good-quality item.

Canada Books (*Sparks St.*) has a fine selection of Canadian books whether it be literature, arts, photography or other topics.

If you couldn't find what you're looking for at Canada Books, you can check out the incredible selection at **Smithbooks** across the street. In addition to a wide selection on Canada, there are books on many other subjects as well as novels and travel guidebooks.

Lower Town

The shopping mall *par excellence* in the capital, the **Rideau Centre** (*50 Rideau St.*), with some 200 shops including Eaton, is where you'll find it all.

For window shopping and some interesting finds, nothing beats a stroll around the **Byward Market**. All year round, there are handicraft stalls on two floors of the central pavilion. In the summer, fruit and vegetable producers set up shop here. It is a pleasant spot to shop or merely to linger.

The museum shop at the **National Gallery of Canada**

(*380 Sussex Dr.*) is just the place for those who like to rummage for hours through a mind-boggling amount of reproductions, be they posters, jewellery or decorative objects. In addition to these quality copies, the boutique boasts an amazing collection of art books as well as works by Aboriginal and other artisans and sculptors.

Part of the huge chain of bookshops, Ottawa's **Chapters** (*47 Rideau St., at Sussex Dr.*, ☎241-0073) features an incredible selection of books for all tastes in both English and French.

Librairie du Soleil (*321 Dalhousie St.*, ☎241-6999) is the only French bookstore in the capital.

Window-shopping on Bank Street

In fine weather, after exploring Sparks Street, turn onto Bank Street, another of Ottawa's pleasant main thoroughfares. As you walk along some parts of the street are a little dull, but overall it will not fail to charm you. It boasts two distinct commercial sections: one around Somerset Street and a second one south of Queensway.

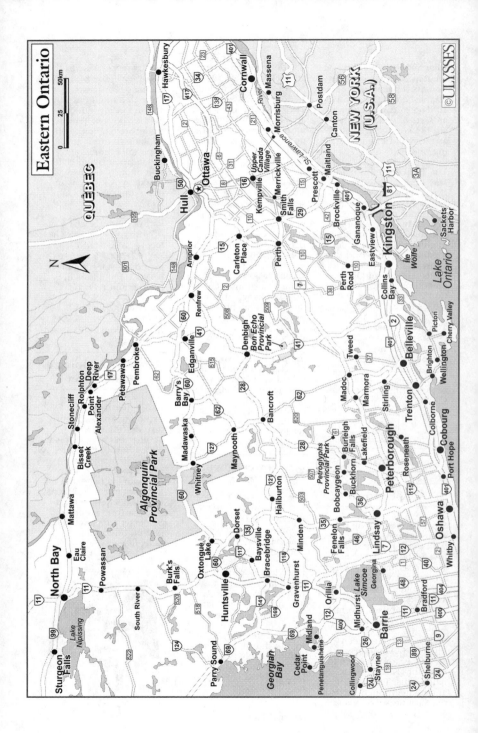

Eastern Ontario

Southeastern Ontario

Southeastern Ontario,
a rich plain between the St. Lawrence River and the Canadian Shield, has always been a favourable place for human habitation.

Aboriginal peoples were drawn here by the fertile land and abundant supply of fresh water, while French colonists were attracted by the region's strategic location along the lucrative fur route. Later, Loyalists arriving from the newly independent United States chose to establish their new villages in these vast spaces. This hospitable region has been welcoming new inhabitants ever since. Some villages, such as Kingston, have since developed into lovely cities, while others preserved their old-fashioned character, becoming popular vacation spots.

Finding Your Way Around

By Car

From the Québec border, Highway 401 runs all the way to Oshawa, in the Toronto area. If you have more time, however, we recommend Route 2, which runs alongside the St. Lawrence, leading through lovely pastoral scenery and offering some magnificent views. It runs through or near all the stops on this tour (Cornwall, Morrisburg, Prescott, Brockville, Gananoque and Kingston).

Visitors starting out from Ottawa can take the 417 and then the 138 to Cornwall.

Bus Stations

There is bus service to every little town along this tour.

Cornwall
120 Tolgate Rd. W.
☎(613) 932-9511

Kingston
121 Counter St.
☎(613) 542-5044
Belleville
45 Dundas St. E.
corner of Pinnacle St.
☎(613) 962-9544

Oshawa
47 Bond St. W.
☎(905) 723-2241

Train Stations

The train through the Montreal-Windsor corridor runs alongside part of the area covered by this tour, so visitors can easily reach Cornwall, Kingston and Oshawa by train.

Cornwall
Station St.

Kingston
800 Counter St.
☎544-5600

Oshawa
Thornton St.

Practical Information

The **area code** is *613*, except for Oshawa, which is *905*.

Tourist Information

Central Ontario Association
Gateway Country
539 Bancroft K0L 1C0
☎*(613) 332-1513*
☎*800-461-1912*
⇒*332-2119*

Eastern Ontario Travel Association
P.O Box 99 Merrickville
K0G 1N0
☎*659-4300 or 800-567-3278*
⇒*269-4885*

Prince Edward County Chamber of Tourism and Commerce
PO Box 50
Picton, K0K 2T0
☎*476-2421 or 800-640-4717*
⇒*476-7461*
www.pec.on.ca

Exploring

The shores of the St. Lawrence River were among the very first parts of Ontario to be colonized on the Great Lakes route. As early as the 17th century, a number of French forts were built here, most notably Fort Frontenac (1673), on the site now occupied by Kingston. Long before any forts were erected, however, Iroquoian tribes (Hurons and Iroquois) fought over the borders of this vast territory, delimited by the southern part of the St. Lawrence River and the shores of the Great Lakes. This tour will guide you alongside the majestic St. Lawrence, which meets Lake Ontario at Kingston. In addition to picturesque towns like Kingston, this tour features a visit to Upper Canada Village, a reconstructed pioneer village that will transport you 100 years back in time and outstanding natural sites like the Thousand Islands.

Cornwall

In 1784, in the wake of the American Revolution, a number of Scots left the United States and settled on the shores of the St. Lawrence River, where they founded Cornwall. This rather grim-looking industrial city is now the largest Ontarian town on the St. Lawrence. Located on the Quebec border, it is populated by both English- and French-speakers. The pulp and paper industry, hydroelectric dams and the cotton industry form the backbone of the local economy, but have never brought the town any real prosperity. Some particularly gloomy sectors and an uninteresting industrial zone ring the nondescript downtown area made up of uninspiring buildings. A bridge links Cornwall to New York State For many, Cornwall is just a place to pass through on their way somewhere else.

If you do decide to spend some time in Cornwall, however, there are a few interesting tourist attractions, including the **Inverarden Regency Cottage Museum** *(free admission; Apr to Nov, Tue to Sat 11am to 5pm, Sun 2pm to 5pm; Montreal Rd., east of Boundary, ☎938-9585).* This magnificent house, erected in 1816 for fur merchant John McDonald, is one of the finest examples of Regency architecture in Ontario. It has no fewer than 14 rooms, all decorated with lovely period furniture. The museum's splendid garden, which looks out onto the St. Lawrence, is an exquisite place to stroll about on a fine summer day.

The little **United Counties Museum in the Wood House** *(free admission; Apr to Nov, Tue to Sat 11am to 5pm, Sun 1pm to 5pm; 731 Second St. W., ☎932-2381),* better known locally as the Wood House Museum, displays a number of paintings by Canadian artists, as well as various everyday objects from the early days of colonization, including toys and tools.

Just outside of Cornwall is **Cornwall Island**, a Saint-Régis First Nations reserve.

Morrisburg

Morrisburg would be just another little town if it weren't for the proximity Upper Canada Village – a remarkable tourist attraction consisting of houses from eight little villages that were flooded when the water level of the river was raised during the construction of the St. Lawrence Seaway. The houses were moved to Crysler Farm Battlefield Park, where they now make up a fascinating historical reproduction of a 19th-century community. The park also has a small monument commemorating the Canadian victory over American troops in the War of 1812.

Upper Canada Village

With 35 buildings, **Upper Canada Village** *($12.75; May to Oct, every day 9:30am to 5pm; Crysler Farm Battlefield Park, 11km east of Morrisburg, on Rte. 2, ☎543-3735 or 800-437-2233)* is an outstanding reconstruction of the type of village found in this part of Canada back in the 1860s. The place has a remarkably authentic feel about it and you will be continually surprised by the extraordinary attention to detail that went into building it. A sawmill, a general store, a farm, a doctor's house... nothing is missing in this village, which you can explore on foot or by horse-drawn cart. To top off this almost idyllic tableau, the "villagers" are costumed guides able to answer all your questions. Their carefully designed outfits reflect both their trade and social class. You can spend several hours exploring Upper Canada Village and watching the various inhabitants go about their business (running the sawmill, working on the farm and using the flour mill).

Prescott

For many years, Prescott occupied a key location on the St. Lawrence Seaway. The rapids at this point on the river prevented boats from going any farther, forcing them to unload their merchandise here. A fort was thus built to defend the area. Today, this charming little town still has an active port, since it has the only deep-water harbour between Montreal and Kingston.

Most people, however, come here to see the fort.

In 1838-1839, **Fort Wellington** ★ *($3; May to Sep, every day 10am to 5pm; head east on Route 2, ☎925-2896)* was erected on the site of an earlier military structure built during the Canadian-American War of 1812. With its massive stone walls and blockhouse, the fort was designed to protect the seaway. It remained in use until the 1920s, and has since been restored and opened to the public, complete with guides to liven up the atmosphere.

Brockville

Brockville boasts a number of splendid buildings, including the Johnston District Courthouse, which bear witness to the golden era of the Loyalists. From the late 18th century when it was founded up until the beginning of the 20th, Brockville, like many other towns along the St. Lawrence, enjoyed a long period of opulence, reflected in its magnificent residences.

In the centre of town, **Court House Square** is one of the most attractive architectural masterpieces that reflects the opulence of the past. It is surrounded by magnificent stone buildings, most notably the **Johnston District Courthouse** (now the United Counties of Leeds and Grenville). A fine example of the Palladian style, the courthouse was built between 1745 and 1841.

If you like old stone buildings, you will be charmed by **Fulford Place National Historic Site** *($4; summer Wed to Sun from 11am to 3:15pm, winter Sat and Sun from 11am to 3:15pm; 287 King St. E., ☎498-3003)*. This splendid Edwardian manor has organized tours. Furnished with period pieces, it takes you back to another era.

★★

The Thousand Islands

Islands, islands and still more islands... the Thousand Islands, which actually number 1,865, boast some remarkably beautiful scenery. The Cataraquis First Nation, who inhabited this region before the colonists arrived, called it "The Garden of the Great Spirit." While exploring the area, you will discover all sorts of islands. They range from tiny islets (two trees and 2.5m² of land are the minimum requirements for an island to be categorized as such) to large islands adorned with opulent houses.

A cruise on the St. Lawrence is an extremely pleasant way to enjoy a close look at this veritable maze of islands, some of which are especially interesting. In addition to taking in the fascinating scenery, you can actually visit some of the islands, such as Gordon Island, the smallest national park in Canada, and Heart Island, home of Boldt Castle. Don't forget, however, that the latter is in U.S. territory so European passengers must show their passport before disembarking there.

Visitors can choose from a number of Thousand Islands cruises, all of which set out from the Gananoque and Kingston marinas (see p 378).

Ontario

Ivy Lea

The Ivy Lea Bridge crosses over the Thousand Islands into New York State, allowing you to stop at Hill Island, if you like. The island is home to the **Skydeck** (*$3.95; Jun to Aug, 8:30am to sunset, May, Sep and Oct every day 9am to 6pm; ☎659-2335*), a 120m-high observation tower which commands an outstanding **view ★★** of the region's myriad islands.

Gananoque

Upon entering Gananoque, you will be greeted by a long commercial artery lined with scores of fast-food restaurants and motels. The place is not especially inviting, but it does serve as a departure point for cruises in the Thousand Islands region and several lovely houses from the last century line its waterfront.

Kingston

In 1673, the Comte de Frontenac sent René-Robert Cavelier de La Salle up the St. Lawrence River to scout out the perfect location for a trading post. La Salle chose to erect a fort, Fort Frontenac, at the point where the river meets Lake Ontario. The site was a strategic one, since it was located along the route taken by both explorers and *coureurs des bois* (trappers). From that point on, the French began to develop lucrative commercial ties with Aboriginal peoples. They remained in the region for nearly a century, until 1758, when the fort was captured by the English

under Colonel Bradstreet, putting an end to French colonization in the area.

After the English conquest, the area was abandoned until 1783 when Loyalists arriving from the United States founded Kingston here. As a stopping point on the Great Lakes Route, the town enjoyed renewed prosperity. Fort Henry was built to protect the area during the War of 1812. Kingston gradually became larger and larger, and was even the capital of Upper and Lower Canada for a few years (1841-1844). Due to its proximity to the U.S. border and the fear of an American invasion, however, it lost the title to Montreal, which only held it itself until 1849, when Ottawa was finally named capital.

A number of magnificent Victorian buildings bear witness to the city's glorious past as do several large military schools – most importantly the Royal Military College and the National Defense College. Furthermore, Kingston lies on the shores of Lake Ontario and has an extremely attractive downtown area, that bustles with life when the weather is fine. We have outlined a walking tour to help you explore this town, one of Eastern Ontario's jewels.

Fort Henry ★★ (*$10.50; May to Sep, every day 10am to 5pm; Rte. 2, ☎800-437-2233*) was built between 1832 and 1837 on a promontory overlooking Lake Ontario to protect Upper Canada in the event of an American invasion. This large military post was never attacked, however, and was abandoned after the 1870's, when an invasion no longer seemed likely. Later, in the 1930's,

the building underwent renovations.

At the entrance, you will be greeted by guides in period costume who will tell you about life at the fort during the 19th century. You will also have a chance to attend shooting drills performed by the Fort Henry Guard, whose uniforms are similar to those worn by English soldiers in 1867. This is definitely the most memorable part of the visit. After watching these demonstrations, you can tour the barracks, whose rooms still contain 19th-century furnishings and tools, offering a good idea of what daily life was like here back then. Finally, you can spend some time admiring the museum's fine collection of 19th-century English military equipment.

The Royal Military College is visible on nearby Point Frederick. Not far from there is the Frederick Tower, a Martello tower dating from 1846, that houses the **Royal Military College of Canada Museum** (*free admission; late Jun to early Sep, every day 10am to 5pm; ☎541-6000, ext. 6664*). There you can learn about the history of the college and the first military conflicts to take place in this region. This stone tower with thick walls (the section facing Lake Ontario is 15m wide) is the largest of the six Martello towers built in the 19th century to protect Kingston.

Kingston's era of prosperity during the 1840s and 1850s corresponds to the apogee of neoclassicism in Canada. It is therefore not surprising to find a significant collection of buildings in this style, the majority of which are of grey limestone extracted from local quarries. This is the case

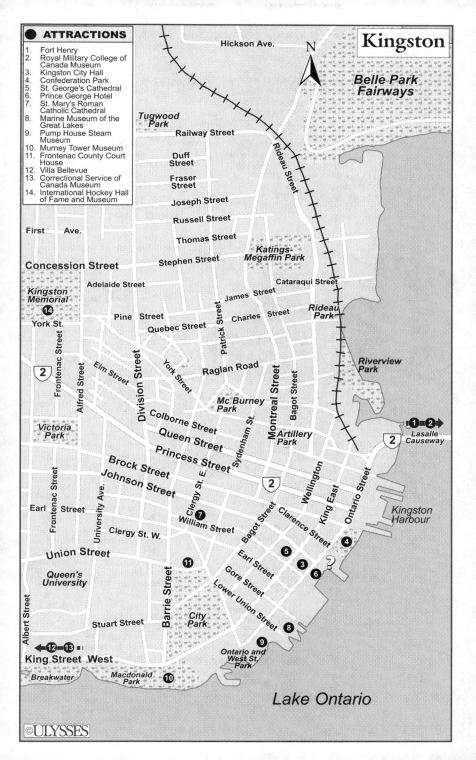

Kingston

ATTRACTIONS

1. Fort Henry
2. Royal Military College of Canada Museum
3. Kingston City Hall
4. Confederation Park
5. St. George's Cathedral
6. Prince George Hotel
7. St. Mary's Roman Catholic Cathedral
8. Marine Museum of the Great Lakes
9. Pump House Steam Museum
10. Murney Tower Museum
11. Frontenac County Court House
12. Villa Bellevue
13. Correctional Service of Canada Museum
14. International Hockey Hall of Fame and Museum

Hickson Ave.

Belle Park Fairways

Tugwood Park

Railway Street

Duff Street

Fraser Street

Joseph Street

Russell Street

Thomas Street

Stephen Street

Katings-Megaffin Park

Rideau Street

Cataraqui Street

First Ave.

Concession Street

Kingston Memorial

York St.

Adelaide Street

Pine Street

Quebec Street

James Street

Charles Street

Rideau Park

Riverview Park

2

Frontenac Street

Alfred Street

Elm Street

Division Street

York Street

Patrick Street

Raglan Road

Mc Burney Park

Montreal Street

Bagot Street

Victoria Park

Colborne Street

Queen Street

Princess Street

Sydenham St.

Artillery Park

Lasalle Causeway

2

Brock Street

Johnson Street

Frontenac Street

University Ave.

Earl Street

Clergy St. W.

Clergy St. E.

William Street

2

Wellington

King East

Ontario Street

Kingston Harbour

1 2

Union Street

Queen's University

Barrie Street

Bagot Street

Clarence Street

Earl Street

Gore Street

Lower Union Street

5

3

6

4

?

Albert Street

Stuart Street

City Park

8

King Street West

12 13

Breakwater

Macdonald Park

10

Ontario and West St. Park

9

Lake Ontario

©ULYSSES

with Kingston's **City Hall** ★
(216 Ontario St.). This vast
building was constructed
between 1842 and 1844
when the town was the
seat of government for
United Canada. Following
the decision to move the
colonial capital to Mon-
treal, the town councillors
graciously, though unsuc-
cessfully, offered the government this city hall in
the hopes that it might
change its mind.

City Hall

City Hall overlooks the
water and is reminiscent of
the grand public buildings
of Dublin, Ireland. The
Council Room and Ontario
Hall on the second floor
have what are considered
the most beautiful interior
neoclassical decors in
Canada.

Confederation Park lies Just
opposite City Hall, on the
banks of the Cataraqui
River. This vast stretch of
greenery is a perfect place
for a stroll. Right beside
the park, you'll find the
tourist office, where you
can catch the **Confederation
Tour Train** *($8; mid-May to
Sep, 10am to 7pm)*, a small
train that runs through the
old parts of Kingston.

Cruises to the Thousand
Islands set out from the
marina by the park (see
p 378).

Keep walking on **Ontario
Street**, Kingston's major

downtown artery, which is
lined with all sorts of little
shops and restaurants with
pretty terraces. You'll
come first to the Prince
George Hotel whose origi-
nal section was built in
1809. Two additions were
added later and the building as it stands now was
completed in 1867. It was
further renovated and
transformed into a hotel in
1978.

St. George's Cathedral is the
seat of the Anglican bishopric of Kingston. De-
signed by Thomas Rogers,
this lovely neoclassical
building was completed in
1825. The portico, tower
and clock were added in
1846, while the cupola
dates from 1891. On the
same block, the former
post office and **customs
house** are reminiscent of
the 17th-century England
of Inigo Jones. These two
edifices were built in 1856
by Montreal architects
Hopkins, Lawford and
Nelson.

At the beginning of the
19th century, the Catholic
bishopric of Kingston covered all of Upper Canada
(Ontario). In 1843, **St.
Mary's Roman Catholic Cathedral** ★ *(corner of Johnson
and Clergy Sts.)* was built so
that the bishopric would
have a worthy house of
worship. The 60m-high

neo-Gothic tower was
added in 1887.

You will eventually come
to two little museums lo-
cated almost side by side.
The first, the **Marine Museum of the Great Lakes**
*($3.95; Mon to Fri 10am to
5pm, open all week from Jun
to early Sep; 55 Ontario St.,
☎542-2261)*, deals with the
history of navigation on
the Great Lakes, from 1678
on. Moored in front of the
museum is the *Alexander
Henry*, an icebreaker that
has been converted into
an inn (see p 379).

The second museum, the
Pump House Steam Museum
*(early Jun to early Sep; 55
Ontario St., ☎542-2261)* is a
fully restored pumping
station containing different
models of steam pumps,
as well as other machinery
dating from 1849. These
huge pumps were one of
the most important sources
of energy in the 19th century.

Martello towers, invented
by the engineer of the
same name, were a com-
mon part of the British
defense system in the early
19th century. The Murney
Tower, located in **Macdonald Park**, was erected in
1846 to defend the port.
This squat stone tower
now houses the **Murney
Tower Museum** *($2; May to
Sep every day 10am to 5pm;
at the corner of King St. and
Barrie St., ☎544-9925)*,
which displays an assort-
ment of 19th-century military articles.

Built entirely of local sandstone, the **Frontenac County
Court House** ★, designed
by Edward Horsey, is a
fine example of the neo-
classical architecture of the
mid-19th century. It was
originally supposed to be
the Parliament building but
was never used for that

purpose. The huge fountain in front of it was erected in 1903.

The Court House looks out onto a pleasant park that is flanked by a few magnificent Victorian houses.

The handsome stone buildings of Queen's University lie to the west. There are two museums on campus, the most noteworthy being the **Agnes Etherington Arts Centre ★** *(free admission; Tue to Fri 10am to 5pm, Sat and Sun 1pm to 5pm; ☎533-6767)*, located in its namesake's former home, built in the 19th century. It contains all sorts of lovely objects, including beautiful collections of African and Inuit art, making it a delightful place to visit.

The second museum, the **Miller Museum of Geology and Mineralogy** *(free admission; Mon to Fri 9am to 5pm; at the corner of Union St. and Division St., ☎545-6767)* displays a collection of minerals, rocks and fossils.

When it was built back in the 1840s, **Bellevue House ★** *($2.75; Jun to Sep, every day 9am to 6pm; Apr to May and Sep to Oct, every day 10am to 5pm; 35 Centre St., ☎545-8666)* was the subject of much discussion. Its Tuscan-style architecture, being somewhat novel at the time, earned it a variety of nicknames, including "the pagoda." In 1848 and 1849, it was the family residence of John A. Macdonald, Canada's first prime minister (1867-1873). Upon entering the house, you will discover a splendid interior adorned with furniture dating from the time when Macdonald lived here. You can visit the elegant dining room and the bedroom, where Macdonald's ailing

wife lay confined to her bed, and enjoy a stroll in the pretty garden surrounding the house.

We inevitably approach the **Correctional Service of Canada Museum ★** *(free admission; late May to early Sep, Wed to Fri 9am to 4pm, Sat to Sun 10am to 4pm; 555 King St. W., ☎530-3122)* with a bit of scepticism. What could such a museum contain? However, the museum achieves its objective of providing an insight into several aspects of incarceration. In order to demystify a world that too remains obscure in the minds of the general population, several aspects of prison life are addressed. This includes the work carried out by some inmates who can do small jobs while staying in prison, and a display of some of the various weapons that prisoners have managed to create. The museum also shows changes in attitudes towards correctional services and presents the different kinds of corporal punishment to which prisoners could be subjected up until 1968. Perhaps the most captivating section is the one that displays the evolution of the prisoner's cell from a tiny dungeon that was used in the last century to the small room of today that is arranged more "ergonomically." The visit also encourages reflection on the role of correctional services in our society.

Bellevue House

Hockey fans won't want to miss the **International Hockey Hall of Fame** *($2; Jul to early Sep, Mon to Fri 10am to 5pm, Sun noon to 5pm; at the corner of York and Alfred)*. It displays photographs and pieces of equipment, thus showing how the sport has evolved over the years. It is located a short distance from downtown Kingston.

Wolfe Island

South of Kingston, you can take a free ferry to Wolfe Island, an undeveloped stretch of land with a single hamlet, Marysville. Route 95 runs across the island and another ferry carries passengers to the United States.

Quinte's Isle

Quinte's Isle abounds in lovely pastoral scenes, which you'll discover as you round a bend in the road or explore the shores of the island. With its peaceful hamlets, vast fertile fields and long sandy beaches, Quinte's Isle is sure to appeal to city-dwellers in search of beautiful natural landscapes. Although large numbers of visitors come here to savour the bucolic atmosphere in summer, the island has not become touristy. It is crisscrossed by a few roads, which are perfect for cycling.

Ontario

Belleville

Pleasantly situated at the mouth of the Moïra river on the Bay of Quinte, Belleville was founded by Loyalists who fled from the United States in 1784. It grew steadily throughout the 19th century, gradually transforming itself into the pretty city with attractive homes that we know today. Its lovely residential areas are perfect for strolls. The main attraction, however, is the marina on the bay where there are many summertime activities, the most important of which is the Waterfront Festival, which turns the marina into a veritable fairground of outdoor activities. There is a picturesque promenade from which you can see the pretty little boats bobbing on the waves. Quinte's Isle is easily reached from Belleville.

The city has preserved many of its heritage buildings, most notably the **Glanmore Historic Site** (*$3; Jun to Aug, Tue to Sun 10am to 4:30pm; Sep to May, Tue to Sun 1pm to 4:30pm; 257 Bridge St. E., ☎962-2329*). Located in an elegant building built in 1883 in the Second Empire style, all of its rooms have been renovated and adorned with lovely Victorian furnishings. The walls and ceilings have also been richly decorated. On the second floor, you will find several small exhibits, including a collection of lamps. The basement contains a reconstructed general store and servant's room, offering a glimpse of what everyday life was like in 19th-century Belleville.

Trenton

The **Trent-Severn Waterway** starts here in Trenton. In summer, visitors in all kinds of boats crowd to the marina to set off on an excursion on the waterways that crisscross the centre of the province all the way to Georgian Bay.

Cobourg

Cobourg lies in the heart of the countryside on the shores of Lake Ontario. At first glance, it looks like a simple little town. On your way through, however, you will discover some impressive buildings that bear witness to a prosperous past. Cobourg's port was one of the busiest in the region, and flour mills, sawmills and car factories fueled the local economy. One of the most noteworthy of these elegant edifices is the majestic, Palladian-style **town hall ★** (*Victoria Hall, 55 King St. W.*), designed by architect Kivas Tully in 1860. During these years, Ontario's towns underwent a period of growth, and needed larger municipal buildings. Huge sums of money were allocated for the construction of these new buildings.

In fact, townspeople seem to take as much civic pride in the amount spent on the projects as in the city halls themselves. With this background knowledge, it becomes easier to understand why a relatively small community would have such an imposing town hall! This large building houses the provincial courts, a concert hall and an art gallery whose exhibits include handicrafts and paintings by Canadian artists. A few steps away stands **St. Peter's Church**, a lovely example of Gothic Revival architecture that was begun in 1851.

Port Hope

It is easy to be enchanted by Port Hope's charming town centre, with its string of more than forty craft and antique shops. The village dates back to 1788, when Peter Smith settled here. A few years later, in 1793, he was followed by a group of Loyalists, who actually founded the town. A few beautiful old buildings bear witness to the past, including **St. Mark's Church** (erected in 1822) and some pretty houses built in the different architectural styles that were fashionable in Ontario in the 19th century.

Cobourg City Hall

These treasures of brick and stone have been painstakingly restored in the last several decades. The town now has some of the prettiest and best preserved buildings in the region.

Oshawa

Oshawa, the last town on this tour, lies about 50km from Toronto, whose presence is already tangible. This town has flourished as a result of its automobile industry, which was launched at the beginning of the century. Since Robert McLaughlin began manufacturing cars here, it has become the most highly developed in Ontario. When General Motors purchased his plant, he became director of the company's Canadian division. GM has since been the town's largest employer.

Like many industrial towns in North America, Oshawa is a drab-looking place. It does, however, have a few interesting attractions, most related to McLaughlin and the automobile industry.

The **Robert McLaughlin Gallery** ★ *(free admission; Tue, Wed and Fri 10am to 5pm; Thu until 9pm, Sat and Sun noon to 4pm; 72 Queen St., ☎905-576-3000)* displays some lovely paintings by contemporary Canadian artists, including abstract pieces by members of the Painters Eleven, who made a name for themselves in the 1950s. These artists' technique was to paint quickly, drawing only on the inspiration of the moment to infuse their work with a feeling of intensity.

You can step into the world of automobiles at the **Canadian Automotive Museum** ★ *($5; Mon to Fri 9am to 5pm, Sat and Sun 10am to 6pm; 99 Simcoe St. S., ☎905-576-1222)*, a very nondescript building containing over 60 antique cars.

The **Oshawa Community Museum** *($2; Jul and Aug noon to 5pm, Sun 1pm to 5pm, Sep to Jun Mon to Fri noon to 4pm, Sun 1pm to 5pm, closed Sat year-round; Simcoe St. S, in Lakeview Park, ☎905-436-7624)* consists of three historic little houses once owned by the Robinson, Henry and Guy families respectively. It presents several small exhibits, including one on electricity.

If you only have time to see one attraction in Oshawa, head straight to **Parkwood Estate** ★★ *($6; Jun to Sep Tue to Sun 10:30am to 4:30pm, Sep to May Tue to Sun 1:30pm to 4pm; 270 Simcoe St. N., ☎433-4311)*, the sumptuous former residence of R.S. McLaughlin. The house stands in the midst of a magnificent garden featuring a harmonious combination of stately trees, hedges and verdant stretches of lawn, crowned by a lovely fountain. The outstanding garden is an indication of the opulence of the house itself, whose 55 beautifully decorated rooms make for a captivating visit.

Parks

The Parks of the St. Lawrence ★★ *(R.R. 1, Morrisburg, K0C 1X0, ☎613-543-3704)* are a group of tourist attractions, including historic sites such as Upper Canada Village (see p 371), Fort Henry (see p 372) and the beautiful **St. Lawrence Islands National Park** ★★, whose 23 islands and countless islets lie strewn across a distance of 80km, from Gananoque to Lancaster. These islands are actually the crests of mountains that were submerged when the glaciers receded and the St. Lawrence River was formed. Their vegetation is very distinctive, featuring species usually found either much further north or south. As you pass from one island to the next, you might be surprised by the diversity of the plant-life that makes for a patchwork of remarkable settings.

Most of the islands have been adapted with tourists in mind. Like those along the **Long Sault Parkway**, some are accessible by car while others only by boat. Picnic areas, beaches (Crysler Beach) and campgrounds (Ivy Lea and Mallorytown) are scattered here and there, so visitors can enjoy a variety of outdoor activities while exploring the fascinating natural surroundings. For further information, stop by the **park headquarters** in Mallorytown.

Route 2 and the Thousand Islands Parkway run alongside the river, offering some magnificent views of the St. Lawrence and the islands. Some of the islands have hiking trails that are very pleasant to walk along. If you are pressed for time and don't want to go onto the islands, you can explore the banks of the St. Lawrence by taking the Mainland Nature Trail that starts at the park headquarters in Mallorytown. Finally, if you prefer cycling to canoeing, go for a ride on the beautiful bike path that runs alongside the Thousand Islands Promenade.

Sandbanks Provincial Park ★ *(R.R. 1, Picton, K0K 2T0, ☎613-393-3319)*, on the southwest shore of Lake Ontario, has sand dunes and a magnificent beach, making it a hit with vacationers looking for a place to catch some sun and enjoy the water on hot summer days.

Outdoor Activities

Cruises

Following the St. Lawrence

The **Thousand Islands** region is the perfect place for a pleasant trip on the St. Lawrence. Cruises from **Gananoque** and **Kingston** offer a chance to take in some lovely scenery. Boats also leave from **Brockville**.

From Gananoque

Gananoque Boat Line ☎*(613) 382-2144* ☎*(613) 382-2146* *3hr cruise: $16*

From Kingston

Island Queen ☎*(613) 549-5544* *3hr cruise: $18* *90min cruise: $12.50*

Accommodations

Cornwall

Vincent Massey Street and Brookdale Avenue, both lined with hotels and small motels, are located close to the entrance to town. The local inns have sacrificed old-fashion charm for modern comfort but it is easy to find decent accommodation. The **Ramada Inn** *($80; ≡, ≈, △, ⊛, ; 805 Brookdale, K6J 4P3, ☎933-8000 or 800-272-6232 ⇒933-3392)*, **Best Western** *($99; ≡, ≈, ℜ, △, ⊛, ; 1515 Vincent-Massey, K6H 5R6, ☎932-0451 or 800-528-1234, ⇒938-5479)* and the **Comfort Inn** *($109; ≡; 1755 Vincent-Massey, K6H 5R6, ☎932-7786 or 800-4CHOICE, ⇒938-3476)* are noteworthy for their wide range of amenities.

Morrisburg

Upper Canada Migratory Bird Sanctuary Nature Awareness Campsite *$17.75- $22* ☎*543-3704 or 537-2024* ⇒*543-2847* At the Upper Canada Migratory Bird Sanctuary Nature Awareness Campsite, which is part of the **Parks of the St. Lawrence**, fifty campsites have been laid out in a lovely natural setting.

You can also camp at one of the other campgrounds in the **Parks of the St. Law-**

rence *(☎800-437-2233)* that are beautifully situated on the banks of the river. For reservations:

Glengarry ☎*347-2595*

Mille Roches Woodlands and McLaren ☎*534-8202*

Riversite/Cedar ☎*543-3287*

Ivy Lea ☎*659-3507*

Gananoque

Victoria Rose Inn *$80-180* 279 King St. W., K7G 2G7 ☎*382-3368* When entering Gananoque by the highway, you'll find yourself on the main street lined with mundane fast-food restaurants. Press on towards the river, however, and you'll discover two delightful inns. The Victoria Rose Inn, located in a magnificent Victorian residence, has nine spacious and inviting rooms.

Trinity House Inn *$90-150 bkfst incl.* 90 Stone St. S., K7G 1Z8 ☎*382-8383* ⇒*382-1599* *www.trinityinn.com* Another option is the Trinity House Inn that is located in an elegant brick house built in 1859. Its historic charm has not been lost because it has been renovated with great care. The rooms blend the elegance of another era (antique furniture decorate the rooms) with the comforts of today. An attractive terrace, a pleasant sitting room and a pretty garden will also make your stay here enjoyable.

Kingston

Kingston International Hostel
$
329 Johnson, K7L 5C8
⇌*531-8237*
The Kingston International Hostel, located close to the downtown area, welcomes visitors in both summer and winter. Fewer beds are available during winter.

Alexander Henry
$42 sb
$65 pb
May to Oct
55 Ontario St., K7L 2Y2
☎*542-2261*
⇌*542-0043*
The Alexander Henry, which you are sure to have noticed on your way past the Maritime Museum, is a restored icebreaker that has been converted into a very unusual inn. Don't expect a luxurious room. People stay here for the experience more than the comfort.

Queen's University
$47 bkfst incl.
Jean Royce Hall, K7M 2B9
☎*(613) 545-2550*
You can also find inexpensive accommodation at the residence halls of Queen's University, which rents out a few rooms during summer.

Queen's Inn
$89 to $139
125 Brock, K7L 1S1
☎*546-0429*
The downtown Queen's Inn, a 19th-century stone house with a restaurant on the ground floor, offers pleasant accommodations. Although they're well-kept, the rooms are decorated with imitation wood furniture, so they don't have the old-fashioned charm that visitors might hope to find.

Kingston boasts some magnificent 19th-century houses that have been carefully restored over the years. Several have been converted into inns that manage to combine charm and comfort. You will have little trouble tracking down a few of these masterpieces of Victorian architecture in the area around downtown Kingston.

The Secret Garden
$95, bkfst incl.
≡
73 Sydenham St., K7l 3H3
☎*531-9884*
⇌*531-9502*
www.the-secret-garden.com
A magnificent historic house converted into a bed and breakfast nearby, The Secret Garden has beautiful stained glass windows and attractive flower arrangements inside where the charming decorative objects placed here and there create a welcoming atmosphere. There are only four rooms but each one is furnished with antiques and decorated differently to keep the feeling of a family setting.

Hochelaga Inn
$145 bkfst incl.
25 Sydenham St. S., K7L 3G9
☎*549-5534*
⇌*549-5534*
The beautifully maintained Hochelaga Inn is a fine example of the city's establishments. Built in the 1880's, this superb redbrick house has an ornately decorated green and white facade with a pretty turret and a large balcony. It offers a peaceful atmosphere and 23 tastefully decorated rooms furnished with lovely antiques.

Holiday Inn
$135-165
≡, ≈, ℜ, ◐, ⊛
1 Princess St., K7L 1A1
☎*549-8400 or 800-465-4329*
⇌*549-2014*
The Holiday Inn is a large, rather uninspiring modern building but features an outstanding location right at the edge of Lake Ontario. The comfortable rooms offer a lovely view of the water and all the comings and goings at the Kingston marina.

Quinte's Isle

There are a number of charming places to stay on Quinte's Isle, including some lovely B&Bs set in the heart of the countryside and a few well-maintained campgrounds.

Picton

Waring House
$105 bkfst incl.
R.R. 8, K0K 2T0
☎*476-7492*
⇌*476-6648*
Just outside of Picton, you will notice a lovely stone house surrounded by a large garden. While Waring House is over 100 years old, it has, of course, undergone quite a few renovations during this time. It is now a beautiful B&B with a restaurant that serves delicious meals (see p 381). Inside, everything has been done to make this an elegant place to stay: some of the finest cuisine in the area, a courteous welcome, and tastefully decorated rooms, with handsome antique furniture.

Ontario

Belleville

Clarion Inn
$109
≡, ℛ
211 Pinnacle St., K8N 3A7
☎962-4531 or 800-CLARION
⇄966-5894
A big red-brick building set in the heart of Belleville, the Clarion Inn is somewhat massive-looking. The inn mainly has suites. Each of the 50 suites is originally furnished according to a different theme (Ethos Suite, Northern Lights Suite).

Ramada Inn on the Bay
$100
≡, ≈, ℛ, ○
11 Bay Bridge Rd., K8N 4Z1
☎968-3411
⇄968-2235
Another place to keep in mind is the Ramada Inn on the Bay, pleasantly located on the banks of the Moira River and with comfortable rooms.

Cobourg

Woodlawn Inn
$100 bkfst incl.
420 Division St., K9A 3R9
☎372-2235
⇄372-4673
www.woodlawninn.com
At first sight, the Woodlawn Inn might not seem too appealing because of the busy the street on which it is located. However, this red-brick house is surrounded by a magnificent garden, which minimizes the noise. Built in 1835, the place has been carefully renovated. Its 16 rooms are tastefully decorated and impeccably well maintained. This classy establishment also has a restaurant (see p 381)

Oshawa

Travelodge
$85
≡, ≈, ⊛
940 Champlain Ave., L17 7A6
☎905-436-9500 or 800-578-7878
⇄436-9544
Being an industrial town, Oshawa is hardly a vacation spot. Visitors can nevertheless find comfortable accommodation at the Travelodge.

Restaurants

Cornwall

There are a number of fast-food restaurants on Vincent-Massey Street, including a Saint-Hubert, which specializes in barbecue chicken.

The Gemini Café
$
241 Pitt St.
☎936-9440
If you are staying in town for a while, you can opt for something a little more interesting than fast food. The Gemini Café has a daily menu listing a variety of tasty dishes.

Gananoque

At first glance, Gananaque seems to have only fast food restaurants. As you go further into town, however, you will discover charming establishments serving good food. There are two inns where visitors can eat well and enjoy themselves. The restaurant of the **Victoria Rose Inn** *($$-$$$; 279 King St. W.,* ☎382-3368) is open all day long and serves delightful

meals. If you want to eat in a very beautiful environment, **Trinity House Inn** *($$$; 90 Stone St. S.,* ☎382-8383) has a mouth-watering dinner menu.

Kingston

Sleepless Goat Café
$
91 Princess St.
☎545-9646
The Sleepless Goat Café is an altogether charming place to take a break from bustling Ontario Street while savouring a delicious cup of coffee and a slice of cheesecake.

Curry Village
$$
169A Princess St.
☎542-5010
Kingston has everything for Indian food lovers. Try Curry Village, whose curry and tandoori dishes have won over more than one fan. Some say it is the best Indian restaurant in town. It is up to you to decide.

Stoney's
$$
189 Ontario St.
☎545-9424
Ontario Street runs alongside the lake and a number of restaurants have set up terraces here to take advantage of the lovely view. Stoney's has probably one of the prettiest terraces of all. At lunchtime, it is a highly coveted spot from which to observe the nonstop activity on the street while enjoying a slice of quiche or a salad.

Café Max
$$
39 Brock St.
at the corner of King
☎547-2233
The Café Max offers an inexpensive nightly table d'hote, with a choice of soup or Caesar salad, a main course such as

Tandoori chicken served with pasta, and coffee. The food is honest and always served in generous portions, making the place extremely popular with the local residents who willingly line up for a table on Saturday nights.

Chez Piggy
$$
68 Princess St.
☎ 549-7673
To enter Chez Piggy, you must first pass through a small inner courtyard, where you will see the terrace and the lovely 19th-century stone buildings that house the restaurant. These superb buildings have been tastefully renovated, and Chez Piggy has long been a favourite of Kingston residents, who readily line up for a delicious meal, both at lunchtime, when the restaurant serves simple fare like quiche and salads, and at dinnertime, when the menu is more sophisticated, listing a variety of dishes, notably chicken and lamb.

Le Caveau
$$-$$$
354 King St. E.
☎ 547-1617
Le Caveau occupies the main floor and the basement, both with a limited number of tables. The brick walls and woodwork create a warm, cozy atmosphere in which you can savour delicious meals prepared with a dash of originality. Standard items such as filet mignon with cognac sauce and tuna fish steak with pink pepper sauce are always on the menu, and will not leave you disappointed. The restaurant also has good selection of wines sold by the glass.

Quinte's Isle

Picton

Waring House
$$$
R.R. 8
☎ 476-7492
The Waring House, a superb 19th-century house, is both a pretty inn and a pleasant restaurant. The dining room has big picture windows looking out onto the neighbouring fields, providing a serene atmosphere in which to enjoy your meal. The menu features dishes made with local ingredients, including fresh fish right from the lake. Classics like Beef Wellington are also listed.

Bloomfield

Mrs Dickenson's
$
55 Main St.
☎ 393-3356
Mrs Dickenson's is a Bloomfield institution that will delight hungry travellers. This café is open only during the day and serves simple sandwiches and succulent desserts. A perfect place to unwind.

Belleville

Limestone Café
$$
184 Front St.
☎ 966-3406
You will probably have noticed the lovely Limestone Café as you walk along the town's main street. Inside, stone walls give the dining room a nice touch. Here, you can enjoy a good meal in a pleasant environment. The menu features European dishes.

Cobourg

Casey's
$$
1 Strathy Rd.
☎ (905) 372-9784
If you can't stand the thought of eating French fries again, go to Casey's that serves good grilled meats with vegetables on the side.

Woodlawn Inn
$$$
420 Division St.
☎ (905) 372-2235
For an excellent meal that is not exorbitantly priced, head to the Woodlawn Inn. The Victorian decor is a little excessive, but warm and welcoming nonetheless and will no doubt win you over. The refined menu lists delicious dishes that will tingle your tastebuds.

Oshawa

Cultures
$
Simcoe St.
corner of Athol St.
☎ (905) 728-5356
For a good, healthy meal, head to Cultures, which serves flavourful sandwiches and salads.

Fazio
$$-$$$
33 Simcoe St.
☎ 571-3042
If you prefer a heartier meal, Fazio is the place for you. This restaurant dishes up simple yet tasty Italian fare in a somewhat impersonal dining room.

Ontario

Entertainment

Kingston

The **Grand Theatre**
(218 Princess St., ☎530-2050)
is the hub of cultural
activity in Kingston, presenting plays and classical
music concerts.

Kingston Brewery Co.
34 Clarence St.
☎542-4978
At the end of the day, the
terrace of the Kingston
Brewery Co. is the perfect
place to drink a cold beer
and chat with friends.

Royal Oak
331 King E.
☎542-3339
The Royal Oak, a British-
style pub, is very popular
with university students. It
has a good selection of
imported beer on tap.

Toucan-Kirkpatricks
76 Princess St.
☎544-1966
Toucan-Kirkpatricks,
located right nearby, has a
similar clientele and sometimes hosts live music.

Shopping

Gananoque

Newly built on the shores
of Lake Ontario, the **Historic 1000 Islands Village**
(Water St.) has the most
beautiful setting. With
several stores selling a
range of articles such as
souvenirs, mementos and
books, it is a great place to
shop.

Kingston

Downtown Kingston
centres around Ontario
Street, with Brock and
Princess as secondary
arteries. If you hunt
around a little, you're sure
to find a few little treasures here.

For a small gift or handicrafts, check out the **Olden
Green** and **Corner Store**,
*(corner of Princess St. and
Ontario St.)*, which have
some lovely items.

As you walk down King
Street, keep an eye out for
the pretty storefronts of
Metalwork, which has a
fantastic selection of jewellery, and **La Cache** *(208
Princess St., ☎544-0905)*,
one of a chain of charming
shops found all over
Canada that sells clothing,
bed linens and other articles. Brock Street boasts
some of Kingston's petti-
est storefronts, many
seemingly right out of
another era. **Cooke's**, a typical turn-of-the-century
general store, is perfectly
charming. It sells specialty
foods like Rogers choco-
lates from Victoria (British
Columbia) and delicious
preserves.

Kingston now has a great
bookstore, **Indigo Books,
Music & Café**
*(259 Princess St.,
☎546-7650)*, where you
can browse and read in a
comfortable environment.
There is also a café.

Central Ontario

The lands on both sides of the St. Lawrence were among the first to be colonized by Loyalists fleeing the newly independent United States.

They settled on a small strip of land; forests to the north were unsuitable for agriculture and farming, and thus only little hamlets developed. Today, human presence is scarce, and forests of broad-leafed and coniferous trees crisscrossed by lakes and rivers set the backdrop for this region.

Finding Your Way Around

By Car

The Kawartha Lakes

This tour begins at Peterborough, situated mid-way between Ottawa and Toronto and consequently easily accessible. The Haliburton Higlands are to the east of this area.

From **Ottawa**: take Route 7.

From **Toronto**: Take Highway 2, then Highway 115 which goes to Peterborough.

The Muskoka Lakes

Take Highway 400 from Toronto to Barrie, then pick up Highway 11.

By Bus

The Kawartha Lakes and the Haliburton Highlands

Peterborough
Simcoe St.
corner of George St.
☎ *(705) 743-1590*

The Muskoka Lakes

Barrie
15 Maple Ave.

Orillia
150 Front St.
☎ *(705) 326-4101*

Gravenhurst
On Second St.
☎ *(705) 687-2301*

Huntsville
At the corner of Main and Centre.

Georgian Bay

Owen Sound
1020 Third Ave. E.
☎ *(519) 376-5375*

Collingwood
70 Hurontario
☎ *(705) 445-4231*

By Train

The Muskoka Lakes

The train to North Bay passes through this region, stopping in Barrie and Orillia.

Barrie
15 Maple Ave.
☎*(705) 728-5571*

Orillia
150 Front St.
☎*(705) 326-4101*

Gravenhurst
150A Second St.
☎*(705) 687-2301*

Huntsville
At the corner of Main and Centre

Practical Information

Area Code: *705*, except for Owen Sound: *519*.

The Kawartha Lakes

Kawarta Lakes Tourism Peterborough
175 George St. N.
Peterborough, ON, K9J 3G6
☎*(705) 742-2201*
☎*800-461-6424*
⇌*742-2494*
www.quidnovis.com/tourism.

The Muskoka Lakes

This region has been geared towards tourism since 1876, when vacationers started coming here to enjoy the peaceful natural setting of Kawatha, whose Aboriginal name means "Land of Shining Water." Kawatha has since become Kawartha, but has managed to retain its unique character, having successfully combined the beauty of a still unspoiled natural setting with the comfort of a few charming little villages where visitors can dine and sleep. Many pleasure-boaters pass through this region on the Trent-Severn Waterway,

making for some fascinating activity around the locks.

Hunnia Tourism Association
Simcoe County Building
Midhurst, ON, L0L 1X0
☎*(705) 726-8502*
⇌*(705) 726-3991*
www.county.simcoe.on.ca

Georgian Bay

Georgian Triangle Tourist Association
601 First St.
Collingwood, L9Y 4L2
☎*(705) 445-7722*
⇌*(705) 444-6158*
www.georgiantriangle.org

Exploring

The Kawartha Lakes and the Haliburton Highlands

Peterborough

In 1825, Governor Peter Robinson led 2,000 Irish immigrants to the site of present-day Peterborough, on the shores of Little Lake and the Otonabee River, and founded the town that still bears his first name. Peterborough itself is a rather gloomy-looking place, which serves as a stopping point for motorists travelling between Ottawa and Toronto. Visitors using the Trent-Severn Waterway, however, will see the town in a more attractive light, since it has three locks, including an amazing **hydraulic lift lock ★**, an elevator dating back to 1904, which still lifts boats some 20m above water so that they can continue on to Georgian Bay. Peterborough is also

the home of **Trent University**.

One of the city's charming little museums is the **Canadian Canoe Museum ★** *(910 Monaghan Rd.,* ☎*705-748-9153)*, which has a wonderful collection of kayaks and canoes. The canoe, so central to the life of Aboriginal People and the first colonists, is one of the hallmarks of Canadian history. The exhibits show the evolution of canoe-making, from traditional bark canoes to modern ones. Of course, the museum also inevitably touches on the fur trade and the history of the country in general.

If you have a little time to spare, you can visit **Hutchison House Museum** *($2; May to Dec, Tue to Sun 1pm to 5pm; Jan to Mar, Mon to Fri 1pm to 5pm; 270 Brock St., K9H 2P9,* ☎*705-743-9710)*, the former home and office of Peterborough's first resident doctor. Now restored, it contains some mementos of the city's early days.

Centennial Museum *(free admission; Mon to Fri 9am to 5pm, Sat and Sun noon to 5pm; 300 Hunter St. E., west of the locks, PO Box 143, K9J 6Y5,* ☎*705-743-5180,* ⇌*705-743-2614)* traces the history of the city, from the beginning of colonization to the 20th century, with particular emphasis on the difficult life of its early immigrants.

Lakefield

Lakefield lies at the point where the Otonabee River flows into Lake Katchenawooka, the first lake on the Trent-Severn Waterway. The river's tumultuous waterfalls are now controlled by a lock. Lakefield's only attraction

In the Plateau Mont-Royal, the streets are lined with duplexes and triplexes whose apartments can only be accessed by amusingly contorted exterior staircases.
- *E. Dugas*

Sunset over Vancouver, a prosperous modern city.
- *Walter Bibikow*

Canadian-style excessiveness: the Toronto metropolis with its skyscrapers and most famous building, the CN Tower. - *Tibor Bognár*

Guardian of Canadian democracy, the Ottawa Parliament lies on the shore of the Rideau Canal. - *P. Quittemelle*

Along the Outaouais River, the Ottawa Valley has more than its share of beautiful flower-lined houses, as do many of Ontario's other regions. - *Paul Jensen*

is its charming town centre, made up of pretty little red brick houses.

★
Petroglyphs Provincial Park

The Ojibwa who once lived in this region left behind scores of petroglyphs carved in white marble. They used these symbols to tell their children the story of life. **Petroglyphs Provincial Park** *(Woodview, K0L 3E0,* ☎ *705-877-2552)* was founded in order to protect these testimonies to the Ojibwa past, which are five to 10 centuries old. Visitors can admire a few of the 900 petroglyphs found in the park, which are now sheltered by a large building.

★
Bobcaygeon

After passing through Peterborough, the road winds through a dense, seemingly uninhabited forest interspersed with peaceful hamlets. Bobcaygeon is one of these picturesque little villages, whose quaint downtown is sure to charm you. It also has the first lock to be built on the canal (1883), surrounded by a pleasant park shaded by large trees and benches from which you can watch the boats pass by.

★
The Haliburton Highlands

East of the Kawartha Lakes, the verdant plains of the St. Lawrence gradually give way to a dense forest, and then hills and rocky escarpments, offering a glimpse of the landscape that characterizes the Canadian Shield to the

north. Some 600 lakes and rivers lie strewn across this territory, which attracts fans of outdoor activities like canoeing in the summer and skiing in the winter. The region is also scattered with a handful of peaceful hamlets like **Minden** and **Haliburton**, each of which has restaurants and hotels.

The region's highlight, **Algonquin Provincial Park** ★★★ (see p 389) stretches north of here. It has waterways for canoeing, hiking trails and cross-country ski trails.

★★
The Muskoka Lakes

For nearly a century now, the lovely Muskoka Lakes region has been attracting vacationers, who come here for the charming villages and unobtrusive but well-developed tourist infrastructure. This tour will take you from Toronto to Barrie and Orillia, and then farther north, into the Muskoka Lakes region, from Gravenhurst to Huntsville.

Barrie

Outside the greater Toronto area, the highway continues north along Lake Simcoe. It skirts round Kempenfelt Bay, which stretches westward like a long arm of the sea, at the end of which lies Barrie, the most populous town in the region. Although the outskirts of Barrie can seem somewhat stark at first sight, you will be pleasantly surprised by the downtown area, which is attractively located alongside the bay.

Those fond of water sports can head to **Centennial**

Park, whose lovely sandy beach is often packed on hot summer days.

The **Simcoe County Museum** *($4; Mon to Sat 9am to 4:30 pm, Sun 1pm to 4:30pm; R.R.2, Mingesing,* ☎ *705-728-3721)*, located some 8km north of town, offers a survey of local history, starting with the region's first inhabitants and continuing up to the 20th century. The reconstruction of an 1840s commercial street is by far the most interesting of the major displays.

★
Orillia

The site of present-day Orillia, located at the meeting point of Lakes Simcoe and Couchiching, was inhabited by the Ojibwa First Nation for many years. Around 1838, they were driven out of the region by European colonists, at which point an urban area began to develop. Surrounded by woods and water, it was naturally geared toward the forest industry and agriculture. Then, toward the end of the 19th century, another lucrative industry began to flourish here: tourism. Ever since, visitors have been flocking to Orillia, lured by its attractive location on the shores of Lake Couchiching. The town also became known through the writings of Stephen Leacock (1869-1944), who lived here.

In 1908, Stephen Leacock purchased a plot of land on Lake Couchiching and had a magnificent house built. At the **Stephen Leacock Museum** ★ *($7; Jun to Sep, every day 10am to 5pm, Sep to Jun, Mon to Fri 10am to 5pm; located just off Hwy. 12B, follow Forest Ave. N. to museum Dr., 50 Museum*

Ontario

Dr., ☎ *705-329-1908,* ≈ *705-326-5578,* *www.transdata.ca/~leacock),* now open to the public, visitors can see where the author wrote some of his works and even examine a few of the actual manuscripts. The rooms are decorated with period furniture.

Leacock taught history and economics at McGill University (Montréal), but is known primarily for his literary output, characterized by wit and irony. *Sunshine Sketches of a Little Town* will be of particular interest to visitors, since the stories take place in the fictional town of Mariposa, later revealed to be the town of Orillia.

Stretched along Lake Couchiching, near the marina, is a beautiful **park** ★ with a promenade, a few benches and a small beach. The *Island Princess*, which docks at the marina, takes visitors on cruises on the lake.

★
Gravenhurst

Gravenhurst was once a modest lumberjack village. Like the neighbouring towns, however, it has been reaping the benefits of the public's infatuation with this region since the late 19th century. Visitors began coming here for the lovely natural setting and built the beautiful Victorian homes that still grace the streets. As the gateway to the Muskoka Lakes region, Gravenhurst welcomes throngs of summer visitors attracted by its peaceful atmosphere and air of days gone by. Gravenhurst lies on the shores of Lake Muskoka, short cruises of the lake aboard the *R.M.S. Segwun* are offered (see p 391).

Gravenhurst was the birthplace of the eminent Canadian doctor Norman Bethune. To learn more about his accomplishments, stop by **Bethune Memorial House** *($2.50; mid-May to Oct, every day 10am to 5pm, Nov to Apr Mon to Fri 10am to 5pm; 235 John St. N.,* ☎ *705-687-4261, ont_bethune@pch.qc.ca),* where he grew up. Here, you'll find articles relating to different aspects of his life, as well as some of the technical innovations for which he was responsible, including the mobile blood transfusion unit.

Bracebridge

Located on the banks of the Muskoka River, Bracebridge is a very pretty town graced with elegant houses and attractive shops and centred around a magnificent park shaded by stately trees. At the edge of town, the Muskoka River empties into Lake Muskoka. Visitors are well served here, as the charming streets are lined with comfortable hotels and B&Bs.

★
Huntsville

Huntsville is a picturesque town located at the meeting point of Vernon and Fairy Lakes. In order to make the most of the setting, the downtown area has been laid out on the shores of both lakes, which are linked by a small bridge. On one side, you can browse through charming shops, while on the other, you can enjoy lunch on one of several attractive waterfront terraces. The town has a few decent places to stay, but most visitors opt for the su-

perb hotel complexes in the surrounding countryside.

The **Muskoka Pioneer Village** *($7; mid-May to Jun and Sep Sat and Sun 10am to 4pm, Jul and Aug every day 10am to 4pm; Brunel Rd.,* ☎ *705-789-7576)* is a reconstruction of an early 19th century village. It is made up of about a dozen little buildings, including a smithy, an inn and a general store, where the local settlers' daily life is re-enacted.

Georgian Bay

Bruce Peninsula extends into Lake Huron, forming one side of magnificent Georgian Bay, whose shores are dotted with vacation spots. This tour will take you through a few of the region's prettiest villages and into the heart of what was once Huronia.

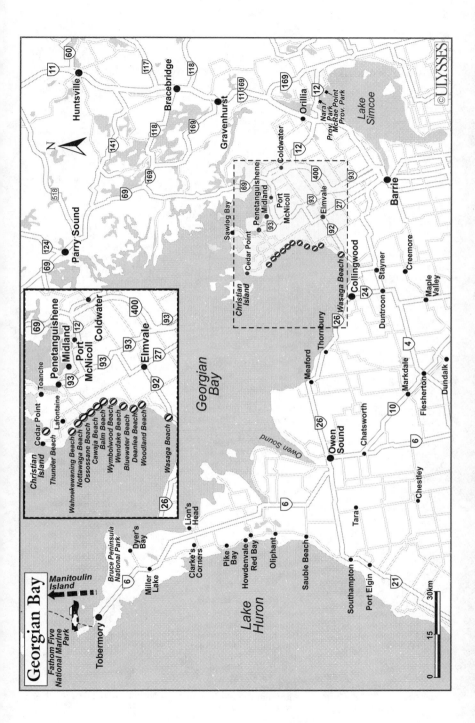

★★
Bruce Peninsula

The Bruce Peninsula, the continuation of the Niagara Escarpment, extends into Lake Huron, rising up here and there to form islands, most importantly Manitoulin Island. This ridge is as high as 100m in some places, making for some remarkably beautiful scenery that you can enjoy during an outing in one of the parks that protects this unique area (see p 390).

Tobermory

Tobermory lies at the tip of the peninsula. Although the village itself is rather ordinary, it attracts large numbers of visitors because of its location. Not only is it the point of departure for outings to Fathom Five National Marine Park (see p 390) and the ferry ride to Manitoulin Island aboard the *Chi-Cheemaun*, it also marks the end of the Bruce Trail (see p 390, 437).

Owen Sound

Formerly known as Sydenham, this little town was renamed after Admiral Owen, who made the first hydrographic studies of Georgian Bay, thus making it safer for boats to sail on the Great Lakes. Although Owen Sound is located alongside this magnificent body of water, with its lovely scenery, a number of factories have been built along part of the shoreline, giving some sections of town a gloomy look.

For a stroll through a pleasant stretch of greenery, go to **Harrisson Park ★**, which has picnic tables, a restaurant and a number of ponds with ducks and wild geese paddling about in them.

Owen Sound is also known as the birthplace and childhood home of the great Canadian landscape painter Tom Thomson (1877-1917). The **Tom Thomson Art Gallery ★** *(donations welcome; Mon to Sat 10am to 5pm, Sun noon to 5pm; 840 First Ave. W., ☎519-376-1932)* is devoted to this artist, whose magnificent paintings reveal a highly personal interpretation of the Canadian wilderness, particularly the Canadian Shield. The museum displays a fine collection of his paintings, as well as a number of works by other Canadian painters, including members of the Group of Seven.

★
Collingwood

Collingwood, also located on the shores of Georgian Bay, was an important shipbuilding centre at the beginning of the 20th century. When that industry started to decline, the town managed to capitalize on its location near the Blue Mountains and lovely beaches on the bay, and develop a prosperous tourist industry. This little town now has everything a vacationer could ask for – pretty shops, a comfortable inn and good restaurants.

★★

Wasaga Beach

Magnificent Wasaga Beach, a strip of sand stretching about 14km along Georgian Bay, is a virtual paradise for vacationers looking for places to enjoy water sports. Although there are some lovely summer homes along the beach, part of it has unfortunately been overdeveloped, so a jumble of cheap-looking souvenir shops and unattractive motels detracts somewhat from the beauty of the landscape. This area is nonetheless a good place to have fun, and is popular with a younger crowd.

The **Nancy Island Historic Site** *(Moseley St.)* tells the story of the *HMS Nancy*, a sailing ship that went down in the bay in 1814 during the War of 1812. In addition to seeing the wreckage of the ship, visitors will learn about 19th-century fur-traders and their way of life.

★★

Midland

Now a peaceful little town, Midland once lay at the heart of Huronia, just a few kilometres from the site where the fearsome Iroquois martyrized and killed many Hurons and Jesuit priests who had come here to convert them to Christianity. Thanks to several fascinating historical reconstructions, visitors can relive the colony's early days.

The **Huronia Museum and Indian Village** *(6$, 549 Little Lake Park,☎705-526-2844, georgianbaytourism.on.ca)* nevertheless offers an introduction to Huron society, complete with a reconstructed village.

You can board the *Miss Midland ($14; town dock, ☎705-526-0161)* for a cruise in the bay, for a magnificent view of the 30,000 Islands.

Standing by the side of the highway is the **Martyr's Shrine** *(Hwy. 12, near Sainte-Marie)*, a Catholic sanctuary dedicated to the first Canadian martyrs, including Jean de Brébeuf, Gabriel Lalemant and Antoine Daniel. The fascinating historic site Sainte Marie Among the Hurons lies on the opposite side of the road.

Sainte-Marie Among the Hurons ★★ *($9.75; May to Oct every day 10am to 5pm; Hwy. 12.5km east of Midland, ☎705-526-7838, www.saintemarieamongtheHurons.on.ca).* When colonists first arrived here, the Georgian Bay region was inhabited by Hurons, who were among the first Aboriginal peoples nations in Ontario to come into contact with Europeans (Étienne Brûlé came here around 1610). The Huronsand the French got along so well that Jesuit missionaries came to the region in 1620 to try to convert them to Christianity and founded a mission here in 1639. Their efforts had profound repercussions on Huron society: it split into two groups – those who had been converted and those who hadn't. The resulting disputes upset the social structure. In addition, many Hurons fell victim to illnesses brought over by the Euro-

peans (influenza, small-pox, etc.), further destabilizing their society.

The Hurons were thus in a weakened state when it came time to fight the Iroquois, who were determined to take control of the fur trade. In 1648, the Iroquois attacked the mission, captured, tortured and killed Jesuit missionaries Jean de Brébeuf, Antoine Daniel and Gabriel Lalemant, and massacred the Hurons. In 1649, the last Hurons and Jesuits abandoned the mission and fled to Quebec City.

Sainte-Marie Among the Hurons is an exact replica of the mission as it appeared in the 1630s. The site includes the village, its longhouses and the various tools used by the Hurons. Guides in period dress (Jesuit priests, colonists, Hurons) offer an idea of what daily life was like here. After touring the mission, you can further increase your knowledge of Huron society by visiting the museum located on the premises.

Wye Marsh Wildlife Centre (see p 391).

Parks

The Kawartha Lakes and the Haliburton Highlands

Algonquin Provincial Park ★★★ *(10$/car; PO Box 219, Whitney, K0J 2M0, ☎705-633-5572or 888-ONT-PARK, ≈705-633-5581, www.algonquinpark.on.ca)* was created in 1893, thus protecting 7,700km² of Ontario's territory from the forest industry. This vast stretch of wilderness boasts some fantastic scenery, which has charmed many a visitor. Back in 1912, it was a source of inspiration for Canadian painter Tom Thomson, whose presence will linger here forever, since he not only created his most beautiful works in the park, but also died here mysteriously in 1917. Shortly after, following in Thomson's footsteps, the Canadian landscape painters known as the Group of Seven came here in search of subject matter.

For over a century, Algonquin Park has been captivating outdoor enthusiasts, who are drawn here by the shimmering lakes with their small population of loons, the rivers that wind around the bases of rocky cliffs, the forest of maples, birches and conifers, the clearings covered with blueberry bushes, and the varied animal life that includes beavers, racoons, deer, moose and black bears. As you set out by foot or by canoe into the heart of this untamed wilderness, you will be embarking on one of the most enchanting journeys imaginable.

Only one road (Route 60, which is 56km long), starting in Pembroke and leading as far as Huntsville, runs through the southern part of the park. The information office is located along the way. You can only go deeper into the wilderness on foot, skis or by canoe. The park obviously attracts a lot of visitors, and a limited number of people are allowed access to certain sites. It is therefore advisable to make reservations.

The **Algonquin Visitor Centre** *(at Km 43)* was opened in 1993 as a reception area for visitors to the park. It has a bookstore with brochures on the park's flora and fauna, as well as maps of hiking trails and canoeing routes crisscrossing the park. There is also a small exhibition presenting the history of this region's people and animals and a restaurant.

A few kilometres from the East Gate, the old Visitor Centre has been transformed into the **Algonquin Logging Museum** which relates the history of logging in this region. As well as looking at the exhibition, you can follow a 1.5km path leading into the forest. This hike is interspersed with 19 points of interest including a woodcutter's cabin and a dam, both made of logs.

Georgian Bay

Bruce Peninsula National Park ★★ *(PO Box 189, Tobermory, NOH 2R0,* ☎519-596-2233)* covers a large portion of the 80km peninsula that stretches into Lake Huron, forming part of the shoreline of Georgian Bay. Within this vast park, there are tracts of private property as well as stretches of untouched wilderness where you can find a mixed forest and unusual flowers, including about 40 different kinds of orchids. The animal life is no less fascinating; the park is home to deer, beavers, the dangerous massasauga (a venomous snake), and as many as 170 species of birds. You can venture into the heart of the park on one of a number of hiking trails, including the **Bruce Trail** and the Cyprus Lake trails. Visitors also have access to beaches (on Cyprus Lake and Dorcas Bay) and campsites.

A series of islands, 19 in all, trails off the tip of the Bruce Peninsula; these are actually the last peaks of the Niagara Escarpment. These limestone masses have been eroded over the years, and now form odd-looking rocky pillars, the best known and most strangely shaped of all being Flowerpot Island. **Fathom Five National Marine Park ★★** *(PO Box 189, Tobermory, NOH 2R0,* ☎519-596-2233)* encompasses this entire area.

All these rocky islets are completely wild, except for Flowerpot Island, where campsites and paths have been cleared. Hidden around them lie the wrecks of a number of ships that went down in the sometimes treacherous waters of Lake Huron in the late 19th and early 20th centuries. You can take part in a scuba-diving excursion or go for a ride on a glass-bottomed boat to view these sunken ships.

The scenery around the 30,000 islands that dot Georgian Bay is typical of the Canadian Shield, featuring twisted pines and bare rocks of the same type that inspired Tom Thomson and the Group of Seven. In fact, many people have been enchanted by the landscapes here, including wealthy vacationers who began purchasing the islands one by one until 1929, when the **Georgian Bay Islands National Park ★** *(PO Box 28, Honey Harbour, POE 1E0,* ☎705-756-2415, http://parkscanada.pch.gc.ca/gbi)* was created in order to keep 59 of these in the public domain. These unspoiled areas are only accessible by boat; if you don't have one, you can take a water taxi from Honey Harbour or one of the private boats that set out from the marinas of coastal towns like Penetanguishene and Midland. The only campsites and hiking trails you'll find are on Beausoleil Island. No matter where you go, however, always make sure to bring along sufficient food and water.

Outdoor Activities

Hiking

Georgian Bay

One hiking trail follows the railroad from Collingwood to Meaford-Heberg; in the winter, it becomes a cross-country ski trail. The 32km **Georgian Trail** runs along the Niagara Escarpment.

Bird-watching

The dual purpose of the **Wye Marsh Wildlife Centre ★** (*$6; late May to Sep every day 10am to 6pm, until 4pm during the rest of the year; Hwy. 12, near Sainte Marie Among the Hurons,* ☎ *705-526-7809, www.wyemarsh.com*) is to protect the marshes in this area and increase public awareness of the importance, and fragility, of this fascinating world. There are trails through the woods and the swamps so that visitors can observe all sorts of birds, including chickadees. Some of them get along particularly well with human beings and will not hesitate to eat seeds out of your hand.

Cruises

The Kawartha Lakes and the Haliburton Highlands

The **Trent-Severn Waterway** stretches 386km and offers a unique and enjoyable way of exploring the Ontario landscape. For further information or to plan a trip:
Trent-Severn Waterway
PO Box 567, Peterborough, K9J 6Z6
☎ (705) 742-9267

If you don't have a boat but would like to spend a few hours on the Waterway, you can take a cruise from Lindsay or Fenelon Falls:

Skylark VIII Boat Tours
$15
Wellington St.
Lindsay
☎ (705) 324-8335

Fenelon Falls Cruise
$14
Tickets available on Oak Street
☎ (705) 887-9313

The Muskoka Lakes

In Gravenhurst, you can set out to discover some of the beautiful scenery of the Muskoka Lakes on a real 19th-century steamboat (reservations recommended), the **R.M.S. Segwun** (*$15,75; Town Pier,* ☎ *705-687-6667).*

Georgian Bay

A cruise around the Georgian Bay Islands (from Midland, Penetanguishene or Parry Sound) is a wonderful opportunity to get a taste of magnificent scenery:

PCML Cruises
town dock
☎ *(705) 526-0161*

Georgian Queen Cruises
town dock
☎ *(705) 549-7795*
☎ *800-506-2628*

Island Queen
town dock
☎ *(705) 746-2311*
☎ *800-506-2628*

Downhill Skiing

For downhill skiing, the place to go is the **Blue Mountain Resort** *(R.R.3, Collingwood, L9Y 3Z2,* ☎ *705-445-0231),* which has the highest vertical drop in the region (219m). Some of the trails are open for night skiing as well.

A number of shops in the area sell, rent and repair equipment, so you'll have no trouble finding everything you need.

Accommodations

The Kawartha Lakes and the Haliburton Highlands

Peterborough

Trent University
$
310 London St., K9J 7B8
☎ *(705) 748-1260*
During summer vacation, visitors looking for inexpensive accommodation can stay in the residence halls at Trent University.

Ontario

Holiday Inn
$129

≡, ≈, ℜ, ⊛, ◌, ᕕ, ⚞

50 George St., N., K9J 3G5

☎(705) 743-1144

☎800-465-4329

⇆(705) 740-6557 or 740-6559

www.holiday.inn.com

Peterborough's Holiday Inn is easy to find since it is located right at the edge of town. This big hotel is fully equipped to accommodate families and has two swimming pools.

Bobcaygeon

Bobcaygeon Inn
$80

≡, ℜ

31 Main St., K0M 1A0

☎738-5433

The building now known as the Bobcaygeon Inn has been accommodating visitors since the 1920s. Although it has been renovated, its attractively decorated rooms still have an old-fashioned charm about them. The place also boasts an outstanding location, right at the edge of the water.

Fenelon Falls

Eganridge Inn & Country Club
$170 bkfst incl.

ℜ, ≡

R.R. 3, K0M 1N0

☎/⇆(705) 738-5111

www.eganridge.com

Set right in the country, Eganridge Inn & Country Club is the ideal place for nature-lovers who are looking for rustic yet comfortable lodgings. Set up in a wonderful house built in 1837, its renovated rooms combine antique charm with modern comfort. Its antique-style furniture makes for a charming setting. It is surrounded by an absolutely beautiful garden with a view of sparkling Sturgeon Lake. A golf course and a delicious Swiss restaurant are on the premises. You can also stay in one of the very comfortable chalets whose rustic decor is simply charming. Fixed prices including golf are available.

Haliburton

Domaine of Killien
$335 ½b

from Haliburton take Hwy. 118 west to Country Rd. 19; continue for 10 km to Carrol Rd.

PO Box 810
Haliburton, K0M 1S0

☎(705) 457-1100

⇆(705) 457-3853

www.domainofkillien.on.ca

The Domaine of Killien is *the* place. This establishment has 12 spacious rooms in a large house or in charming cabins. All are attractively decorated with woodwork. The tranquil atmosphere is perfect for leaving the worries and stresses of city life far behind, and the exquisite garden of over 2,000ha has a vast array of well-maintained hiking and cross-country skiing trails. There is also a wonderful French restaurant on the premises.

Algonquin Provincial Park

Highway 60 crosses the southern part of the park for 56km where there are no less than eight camping areas. They are set up for visitors who want to discover the beauty of nature without having to travel far into the park for several days. This is a great place for family excursions; some of the areas have more than 250 sites with electricity, while other smaller ones have camping in the wild. Whatever your preference, you will definitely be thrilled. You can make reservations (☎705-

633-5538, ⇆705-633-5581, *www.algonquinpark.on.ca*).

Arowhon Pines
$175 fb

P0A 1B0

winter ☎(416) 483-4393

summer ☎(705) 633-5661

⇆(416) 483-4429

Imagine spending the night in the heart of Algonquin Park's forest, far from the crush of the city at the Arowhon Pines hotel. You will slip into sweet slumber in a rustic decor that is just as inviting as big-city luxury hotels. Destined to become one of those special memories you will cherish long after returning to the bustle of the regular day-to-day.

The Muskoka Lakes

Orillia

Lakeside Inn
$75

86 Creighton St.

L3V 1B2

☎(705) 325-2514

⇆329-2084

www.incyedge.com/lakeside

The Lakeside Inn is more like a motel than a charming inn, but its location on the banks of Lake Couchiching makes it a pleasant place to stay.

Gravenhurst

Muskoka Sands Inn
$199

≡, ≈, ℜ, ⊛, ◌, ᕕ

Muskoka Beach Rd.

☎(705) 687-2233

☎800-461-0236

⇆(705) 687-7474

The Muskoka Sands Inn lies in a very peaceful setting outside of Gravenhurst, on the shores of Lake Muskoka. The cabins and buildings containing the rooms are scattered across its extensive grounds. Guests will also find lots to do here, since the complex has a beach, swimming pools and tennis courts.

Bracebridge

Muskoka Riverside Inn
$129
≡, ℜ, △, ₭
300 Ecclestone Dr.
☎*(705) 645-8775*
☎*800-461-4474*
⇔*(705) 645-8455*
On your way into town, you'll pass the Muskoka Riverside Inn, a large, uninspiring place that nonetheless meets modern standards of comfort and even has a few bowling lanes.

Inn at the Falls
$130
≈, ℜ
1 Dominion St., P1L 1R6
☎*(705) 645-2245*
⇔*645-5093*
www.innatthefalls.net
The more elegant Inn at the Falls offers antique-furnished rooms. It is made up of several old houses, each more charming than the last, and all face onto a quiet little street that leads to the Muskoka River, near the falls.

Huntsville

The most attractive places to stay, however, are located in a small valley a few kilometres outside of town. Take Route 60 to Route 3, which will take you to a vast stretch of greenery punctuated by large hotel complexes.

Grandview
$187
≡, ≈, ℜ, △, ₭
939 Hwy. 60, P1H 1Z4
☎*(705) 789-4417*
☎*800-461-4454*
⇔*(705) 789-6882*
The elegant Grandview was once a private resi-

dence. It has since been converted into a magnificent hotel complex where everything has been designed to ensure guests' satisfaction. The charmingly decorated rooms and varied choice of activities, ranging from golf to walks in the woods, make a stay here both fun and relaxing.

Deerhurst
$209
≡, ≈, ℜ, △, ₭
1235 Deerhurst Dr., P1H 2E8
☎*(705) 789-6411*
☎*800-461-4393*
⇔*(705) 789-2431*
The Deerhurst hotel complex lies on the shores of Peninsula Lake, in an outstanding natural setting where you can savour clean air and a tranquil atmosphere. The complex is made up of three-storey buildings with extremely comfortable rooms, some of which are equipped with kitchenettes and fireplaces. To ensure that guests are entertained as well as comfortably lodged, all sorts of activities are planned.

Georgian Bay

Owen Sound

Best Western Inn on the Bay
$115
ℜ, ₭
1800 Second Ave. E., N4K 2S7
☎*(519) 371-9200*
⇔*(519) 371-6740*
The Best Western Inn on the Bay stands at the far end of a dreary-looking industrial area, overlooking the waters of Owen Sound. The building has been cleverly designed so that every room has a lovely view of the bay. This place boasts the most attractive setting in town, and is therefore often full on weekends.

Collingwood

Blue Mountain Auberge
$20
R.R.3, L9Y 3Z2
☎*(705) 445-1497*
⇔*(705) 444-1497*
There are several places to stay at the foot of the Blue Mountains, the least expensive being the Blue Mountain Auberge, whose no-frills dormitories are decent for the price. Some rooms are also available (*$80 to $120*).

Blue Mountain Inn
$165
≈, ℜ, △, ₭, ⊖, ₭
R.R.3, L9Y 3Z2
☎*(705) 445-0231*
⇔*(705) 444-5619*
The Blue Mountain Inn complex boasts a prime location for skiing, right at the foot of the slopes. The comfortable rooms are located inside a long building, which is a bit too modern-looking for the setting. There are also apartments with kitchenettes. Ski packages available.

Beild House Inn
$399 fb for 2 nights
64 Third St.,L9Y 1K5
☎*(705) 444-1522*
☎*888-322-3453*
⇔*(705) 444-2394*
www.beildhouse.com
In the centre of town, the magnificent Beild House Inn, with its pretty brick facade is easy to spot. Surrounded by a splendid garden shaded by majestic trees, it has 16 rooms, all extremely appealing and elegant.

Wasaga Beach

All sorts of nondescript, charmless motels lie close to the beach. For more peace and quiet, we recommend staying in one of the neighbouring towns instead.

Lakeview Motel
$65
44 Mosley St., L0L 2P0
☎*429-5155*
On Mosley Street, the
Lakeview Motel is one
possibility, but don't expect a very warm welcome
from the owner. The place
does have the advantage
of a beach-side location,
however.

Restaurants

The Kawartha Lakes and the Haliburton Highlands

Peterborough

Häaselton
394 George St.
☎*(705) 741-5456*
Häaselton is not far from
the Eaton Centre, which
literally dominates down-
town Peterborough. You
can relax for a spell with a
nice cappuccino or have
lunch.

The Gazebo
$-$$
summer only
150 George St. N.
☎*(705) 743-1144*
The Gazebo is a pleasant
place to have a meal.
Located in the Holiday
Inn, it is situated at the
poolside at the edge of
Little Lake. Grill dishes are
featured on the menu,
which also lists simple
meals that are bound to
satisfy the whole family.

Bobcaygeon

Big Tomato
$-$$
Bobcaygeon Inn
31 Main St.
☎*738-5433*
The Big Tomato is a great
place for pizza, hamburg-
ers and pasta. This place is
not fancy: the decor is
ordinary (plastic table-
cloths, a window facing
the water), but has a
beach-holiday atmosphere
and a view of the locks.

Fenelon Falls

Eganridge
$$$
R.R. 3
☎*738-5111*
The restaurant at the
Eganridge hotel has a
fabulous location and
promises a memorable
gastronomic experience.
Its relaxing atmosphere is
enhanced by big bay win-
dows that open onto a
garden and Sturgeon Lake.
The cuisine has French,
Mediterranean and Califor-
nian flavours, and changes
according to the season to
ensure that the ingredients
are always of the highest
quality. If your budget
allows it, do not miss this
feast!

Algonquin Provincial Park

Arowhon Pines
$$$$
summer only
☎*(705) 633-5661*
The Arowhon Pines restau-
rant boasts an exceptional
setting next to one of
Algonquin Park's many
lakes. The only thing that
might interrupt your meal
as you contemplate the
enchanting surroundings,
is the echo of the forest.
Besides the cozy fireplace
in the centre of the dining
room, you will savour an
excellent cuisine prepared
with the freshest of ingre-
dients.

The Muskoka Lakes

Barrie

Weber's
$
11 Victoria St.
☎*(705) 734-9800*
Weber's is a local burger
institution that is sure to
satisfy ravenous and mild
hunger attacks.

Tara
$$
128 Dunlop St. E.
☎*(705) 737-1821*
Tara, located downtown,
serves up delicious Indian
food. All the effort is concentrated on the excellent
cuisine, such that the unin-
spired decor is soon for-
gotten.

Orillia

Weber's
$
16 Front St. N.
☎*(705) 326-1919*
Weber's is a local road-
side institution at the edge
of town, where you can
enjoy a good char-broiled
burger.

Frankie's
$$
83 Mississaga St. W.
☎*(705) 327-5404*
Frankie's, a lovely restau-
rant with a relaxed atmo-
sphere serves delicious,
innovative Italian cuisine
with fresh ingredients.

Bracebridge

Muskokan
$
at the corner of Kimberley
and Manitoba St.
In fine weather, the terrace
at the Muskokan is defi-
nitely one of the most
pleasant places in the area
for lunch. Seated in the

delightful shade offered by stately trees and parasols, you can start off your day with a good, simple meal.

Inn at the Falls
$$$$
17 Dominion St.
☎*(705) 645-2245*
The well-located restaurant at the Inn at the Falls boasts a beautiful view of the Muskoka River. Comfortably seated in the elegant dining room, you can enjoy this magnificent setting while savouring such irresistible dishes as beef tournedos in a chanterelle sauce and grilled swordfish. Although each dish is more delicious than the last, try to save some room for dessert – you'll be glad you did.

Huntsville

The banks of the Muskoka River, with its wooden terrace and string of restaurants, whose main attraction is their idyllic location, is the perfect spot for a noontime meal. **Blackburn's Landing** *($)* serves simple fare like hamburgers, pasta and salads, as does the **Pasta & Grill** *($, 7 John St.* ☎*(705) 789-1635)*, next door.

Georgian Bay

Owen Sound

Inn on the Bay
$-$$
1800 Second Ave. E.
☎*(519) 371-9200*
The Inn on the Bay is perfect for breakfast and a glorious sunrise over the water.

Norma Jean
$-$$
243 Eight St. E.
☎*(519) 376-2232*
Norma Jean is a pleasant little restaurant whose walls are adorned with posters and statuettes of Marilyn Monroe. The perfect place to go for a bite with friends, it has quite a strong following, no doubt drawn by the tasty burgers, salads and beef dishes.

Collingwood

Christopher
$$-$$$
167 Pine St.
☎*(705) 445-7117*
Christopher is sure to catch your eye, as it occupies a magnificent house built in 1902 as a wedding present. It has lost none of its character over the years, and is perfectly suited to an intimate meal at lunchtime *($-$$)*, when quiche and pasta dishes are served, or in the evening, when the menu is more elaborate.

Shopping

The Muskoka Lakes

Orillia
Rama Moccasin & Craft Shop
R.R. 6
☎*(705) 325-5041*
On your way through the Rama reserve, you'll pass by the Rama Moccasin & Craft Shop, which is typical of the stores found on native reserves. Don't be put off by the building's wacky appearance (the parking lot is adorned with wooden bears and tepees); the place sells lovely crafts, including Ojibwa moccasins, *mukluks*, Inuit and Iroquois carvings, prints and all sorts of jewellery.

Georgian Bay

Collingwood

Clerkson's
94 Pine St.
☎*(705) 445-2212*
At Clerkson's, set up inside a big, beautiful house, you can treat yourself to some handicrafts, decorative objects or perhaps even a piece of antique-style furniture.

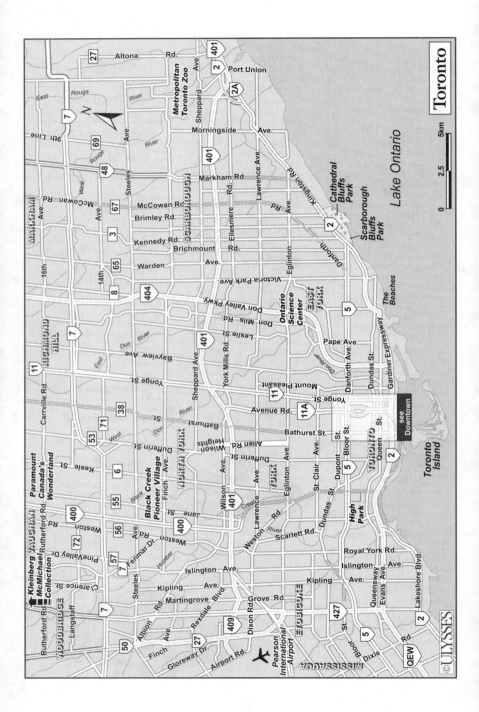

Toronto

Toronto

The first European
to discover Lake Ontario and to set foot on the ground that would become the largest city in Canada was Étienne Brûlé, a French explorer sent by Samuel de Champlain.

Brûlé's expedition took place in 1615, at the beginning of the French colonization of North America. Like many of his predecessors, Brûlé was in search of a navigable route across the continent to the riches of the Orient.

The French established a fur-trading post in 1720. About 30 years later, the British built a fort in an attempt to counter competition from their commercial rivals. The French ultimately burned their Fort Rouillé in 1759 as they beat a hasty retreat from advancing British troops.

To make the most of the potential of this excellent site, the British purchased it in 1787 from the Mississauga natives for 1,700 pounds sterling. John Graves Simcoe, the first governor of Upper Canada, in need of a capital for the new province that was well-protected

and far enough from the U.S. border to avoid political invasion, chose this site in 1793. A small fort called York was built, and the area's new status as the capital attracted a few colonists. The 700 people that had settled here by 1812 succeeded in pushing back the Americans, who had declared war on Britain the year before, but not before the town was seized for a few days and then destroyed.

In 1834, the city was incorporated and re-named Toronto. Its population was 9,000 at the time. During the 19th century, Toronto underwent

rapid expansion, particularly from 1850-1860 with the construction of the railway between Montréal and New York.

At the beginning of the 20th century, Toronto gained a reputation that it couldn't seem to shake. It became known as "Toronto the Good" ; rather fitting, especially after the 1906 legislation on the "Lord's Day" which forbade the city's residents from working on Sunday.

Toronto's growth over the last 20 years has redefined the city, both on a literal and figurative level. Figuratively, in the sense that nowhere else in Canada are there as many different ethnic communities, a characteristic that distinguishes the city from the rest of Ontario and also from the Toronto of old. Toronto is not only the financial centre of Canada, but also the heart of culture in English-speaking Canada. The city was redefined literally on January 1, 1998, when the new Megacity of Toronto officially came into existence. Despite wide anti-amalgamation protests and a No-win in a referendum that came out against the proposal, the six municipalities (Scarborough, North York, York, East York, Etobicoke and Toronto), which each had their own council along with a metropolitan government, are now joined and form one huge city; a city that is bigger than any American city except New York, Los Angeles and Chicago, and that has about 2.3 million people. The "Vote No to Megacity" movement feared that the amalgation would destroy the fibre and individuality of their cities, something that remains to be seen.

Finding Your Way Around

The grid-system of Toronto's streets makes it easy to get around. Yonge (pronounced *young*) Street

is the main north-south artery and it divides the city into east and west. Street addresses that have the suffix "East" or "E." lie east of Yonge and vice versa; 299 Queen St. W. is therefore a few blocks west of Yonge. Toronto's downtown is generally considered to be the area south of Bloor, between Spadina and Jarvis.

By Car

Most people arriving by car from east or west will enter Toronto on Highway 401, which crosses the northern part of the city. Coming from the west, take Highway 427 south to the Queen Elizabeth Way (QEW), continue east to the Gardiner Expressway, and exit at York, Bay or Yonge Streets for downtown. Coming from the east, the quickest way to reach downtown is on the 401 then the Don Valley Parkway; continue to the Gardiner Expressway, then exit at York, Bay or Yonge Streets. Those coming from the United States will follow the shores of Lake Ontario on the QEW to the Gardiner Expressway. Keep in kind that rush-hour traffic can be very heavy on Toronto's highways, especially on the Don Valley Parkway.

Car Rentals

Avis
Hudson Bay Centre
at Yonge and Bloor
☎*964-2051*

Budget
141 Bay St.
☎*364-7104 or 363-1111*

Hertz
128 Richmond St. E.
☎*363-9022*

Thrifty
134 Jarvis
☎*868-0350*

National
40 Dundas St. W.
☎*591-8414*

By Plane

Lester B. Pearson International Airport (☎*247-7678*) is Canada's biggest and busiest airport. Fifty airlines fly into one of three terminals here. The airport is 27km from downtown Toronto. By car, take Highway 427 South to Queen Elizabeth Way and follow it to the Gardiner Expressway. Take the York, Yonge or Bay exit for downtown. The **Airport Express** (*$13,75 one way, $23,65 return,* ☎*800-387-6787 or 905-564-6333*) bus goes from the airport to various city hotels.

Toronto City Centre Airport (☎*203-6945 or 868-6942*) is located on Hanlan's Point, one of the Toronto Islands. Short-haul commuter flights use this airport. It is accessible by special ferry at the foot of Bathurst Street.

By Train

Union station
corner of Front and Bat Sts.
☎*366-8411*
All VIA trains arrive at Union Station.

By Bus

Greyhound Lines of Canada
downtown at 610 Bay St.
☎*367-8747*

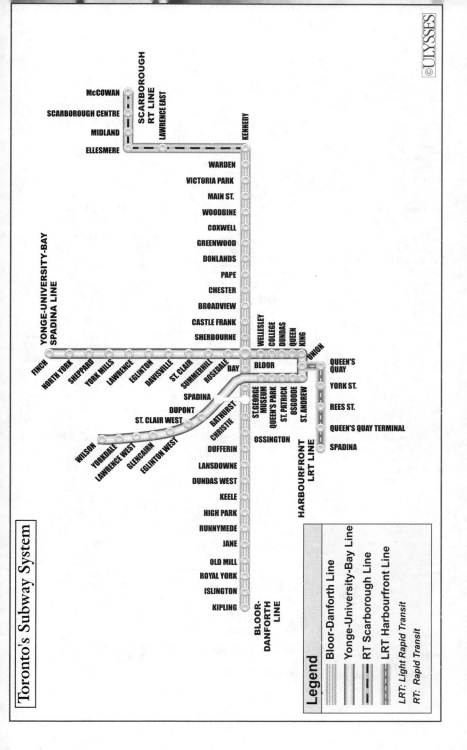

Toronto's Subway System

©ULYSSES

Legend

	Bloor-Danforth Line
	Yonge-University-Bay Line
	RT Scarborough Line
	LRT Harbourfront Line

LRT: Light Rapid Transit

RT: Rapid Transit

Public Transportation

Toronto's public transportation system is run by the **Toronto Transit Commission**, or **TTC** (*www.ttc.ca*). It includes a subway, buses and streetcars. There are three subway lines and the Harbourfront LRT. Buses and streetcars run along the city's major arteries. You can transfer between buses, streetcars and subways without paying another fare, but you will need a transfer, so always take one, just in case. Pick up a copy of the *Ride Guide*, as well. It points out most of the major attractions and how to reach them by public transportation.

A single **fare** is $2 for adults, $1,40 for students (you must have a TTC student card) and seniors, and $0.50 for children under 12. Five adult tickets, or tokens, cost $8.50, 8 student or senior tickets or tokens cost $9, and 10 child tickets or tokens cost $4. If you plan on taking several trips in one day, buy a Day Pass for $7, which entitles you to unlimited travel on that day. Sundays are really economical, since one Day Pass can be used by two adults, or by a family (two adults and four children, or one adult and five children). A monthly pass costs $88,50 for adults and $75 for students and seniors.

For route and schedule information call ☎*393-(INFO) 4636*; for fare and general information call ☎*393-(TONE) 8663*.

On Foot

Toronto's underground city, called the **PATH**, is one of the largest in the country. It weaves its way under the streets from Union Station on Front Street all the way to the Atrium on Bay at Dundas Street. The perfect escape for those cold winter days, it provides access to shops and restaurants.

Practical Information

The Greater Toronto Area is covered by two **area codes**, 416 and 905. The City of Toronto uses *416* and nearby cities like Mississauga and Markham, as well as those further afield, use *905*. Calls within a zone are local and do not require the area code. Some calls between these two zones are also local, though they require the area code. Long distance calls must be preceded by a *1*. Numbers listed in this guide are located within the 416 area code unless otherwise indicated.

Tourist Information Offices

Tourism Toronto
Queen's Quay Terminal
207 Queen's Quay
Suite 590, M5J 1A7
☎*203-2500 or 800-363-1990*

Ontario Travel Centre
Year-round
Mon -Fri 10am to 9pm
Sat 10am to 5pm
Sun noon to 5pm
lower level of the Eaton Centre
at Queen and Yonge Sts.
☎*800-668-2746 or 314-0944*

This office is more accessible than the Tourism Toronto office.

Foreign Exchange

Thomas Cook Foreign Exchange
9 Bloor St. W.
☎*923-6872*

Post Office

General Information
☎*979-8822*

Main Post Offices
36 Adelaide St. E.
or 1117 Queen St. W.

Exploring

★★★

The Waterfront

Being near a major body of water often determines the location of a city, and Toronto is no exception. For many years, however, the city of Toronto neglected its waterfront. The Gardiner Expressway, the old railway lines and the numerous warehouses that disfigured the shore of Lake Ontario offered little attraction for residents. Fortunately, efforts were made to revive this area, and it is now home to luxury hotels, many shops, and numerous cafés bustling with activity.

Harbourfront Centre ★ (*free admission, 410 Queen's Quay W.;* ☎*973-4000 or 973-3000 for information on special events*) is a good example of the changes on Toronto's waterfront. It can be easily reached by the Union Station trolley

Toronto Downtown

© ULYSSES

0   0,5   1km

1. Harbourfront Centre
2. Toronto's Waterfront Museum
3. Queen's Quay Terminal
4. Toronto Island
5. Skydome
6. CN Tower
7. Air Canada Centre
8. Fort York
9. Ontario Place
10. Princess of Wales Theatre
11. Royal Alexandra
12. Roy Thompson Hall
13. Sun Life Tower
14. First Canadian Place
15. Toronto-Dominion Centre
16. Bank of Nova Scotia
17. National Club Building
18. Bank of Commerce Building
19. Toronto Dominion Bank
20. Number 15
21. Original Toronto Stock Exchange
22. Royal Bank Plaza
23. Union Station
24. Royal York Hotel
25. BCE Place
26. Hockey Hall of Fame
27. Gooderham Building
28. St. Lawrence Hall
29. St. James Cathedral
30. King Edward Hotel
31. The Bay
32. Elgin and Wintergarden Theatres
33. Pantages Theatre
34 Old City Hall
35. New City Hall
36. Nathan Philip Square
37. City TV and MuchMusic
38. Kensington Market
39. Art Gallery of Ontario
40. The Grange
41. ProvincialParliament
42. University of Toronto
43. Bata Shoe Museum
44. Royal Ontario Museum
45. Gardiner Museum of Ceramic Art
46. Park Plaza Hotel
47. Yorkville Public Library
48. Firehall No. 10
49. Village of Yorkville Park

Subway Line
Subway Station

running west toward Spadina Avenue. Since the federal government purchased 40ha (100 acres) of land along the shores of Lake Ontario, dilapidated old factories and warehouses have been renovated, turning this into one of Toronto's most exciting areas. Apart from the pretty little cafés and the numerous shops, a variety of shows and cultural events also help make this the pride of Torontonians.

The Pier: Toronto's Waterfront Museum *($8.50; closed Jan-Feb, every day 10am to 6pm; 245 Queen's Quay W., ☎338-PIER)* is the city's newest cultural heritage attraction. Located in a restored 1930 shipping warehouse, The Pier replaces and far surpasses the old Marine Museum. Young visitors will find steam whistles to pull, along with the Discovery Gallery set up inside the hull of a ship. Other fascinating displays include those on Toronto's changing shoreline and harbour, Lake-Ontario ship-wrecks and historic battles and a simulated race against famous oarsman Ned Hanlan. Visitors can also watch artisans constructing traditional wooden boats, and even sign up for a course. Finally, you can take one of these boats out for a tour of the harbour. The short waterfront walking tours offered in summer are also interesting.

A few steps away, at the foot of York Street, is **Queen's Quay Terminal** ★★★ *(207 Queen's Quay W.)*, where boats leave for trips around the bay and the Toronto Islands. This former warehouse has been completely renovated and modified to house a dance theatre, as well as

about 100 restaurants and shops.

At the foot of Bay Street, a ferry transports passengers back and forth to the **Toronto Islands Park** ★★★. The dock is just behind the Harbour Castle Westin Hotel. The Toronto Islands are the ideal spot to relax, catch a little sun, go for a bike ride, or in-line skate, take a stroll, or go for a swim.

The **SkyDome** ★★ *(guided tour $9.50; every day 9am to 4pm; tour schedules may vary depending on events; 1 Blue Jay Way, Suite 3000, ☎341-2770)*, the pride of Toronto, is the first sports stadium in the world with a fully retractable roof. In poor weather, four panels mounted on rails come together in 20min, despite their 11,000 tonnes, to form the SkyDome's roof. Since opening in 1989, this remarkable building has been home to the American Baseball League's Toronto Blue Jays and to the Canadian Football League's Toronto Argonauts. Daily 30min guided tours on SkyDome's technical aspects are offered *(☎341-2770)*.

The **CN Tower** ★★★ *(observation deck $16: every day, summer 10am to midnight, autumn 9am to 11pm, winter 10am to 10pm; Q-Zar, Simulator Theatre, Virtual World: every day, summer 10am to 10pm, autumn Sun to Thu, 10am to 8pm; Fri-Sat, 10am to 10pm; winter Sun to Thu 11am to 8pm, Fri-Sat 11am to 10pm; Front St.W., ☎360-8500)*.

No doubt the most easily recognizable building in Toronto, the CN Tower dominates the city from a height of 553.33m (1,815 feet), making it the highest observation tower in the world. Originally built by the Canadian National Railway company to help transmit radio and TV signals past the numerous downtown buildings, it has become one of the city's main attractions. To avoid long lines, go early in the morning or late in the day, especially in the summer and on weekends. If the day is overcast, it is best to postpone your visit.

The foot of the tower offers numerous activities. You can also reach the observation deck in an elevator that lifts you off the ground floor at a speed of 6m per second, equivalent to the takeoff of a jet aircraft. Located 335.25m up and set on four levels, the observation deck is the tower's focal point. The view from the top is splendid. On a clear day, you can see over a distance of 160km and even make out Niagara Falls. Because its height, you may feel the tower sway in the wind. This is perfectly normal and actually makes the structure safer.

Air Canada Centre *(40 Bay St.)* is the new home of the National Hockey League's Toronto Maple Leafs and the National Basketball Association's Toronto Raptors. This brand new arena can seat up to 20,000 people!

Builders were so intent to make sure fans had a good view of the game that televisions were installed in each of the bathrooms!

It was on the shores of Lake Ontario, at **Fort York** *($4.75; summer, Mon to Fri 10am to 5pm, Sat and Sun noon to 5pm; rest of the year, Tue to Fri 10am to 4pm, Sat and Sun noon to 5pm)* that Toronto came into being. Built in 1783 by Governor John Graves Simcoe in response to a looming U.S. threat, Fort York was destroyed by U.S. invaders in 1813 and rebuilt soon afterward. As relations with the United States improved rapidly, the front gradually lost its purpose. In the 1930s, the city of Toronto renovated it extensively to turn it into a tourist attraction. Now, Fort York is the site of the largest Canadian collection of buildings dating from the War of 1812. A visit includes a tour of the barracks, which are furnished as they were when they housed officers and soldiers, as well as a small museum with a short informative video on the history of the fort. In the summer, guides in period dress perform military manoeuvres.

Ontario Place ★ *(free admission except during special events; day passes offer unlimited access to various attractions except for bungee-jumping and windsurfing; May to Sep, Mon to Sat 10:30am to midnight, Sun 10:30am to 11pm; Cinesphere open year-round; 955 Lakeshore Blvd. W., ☎314-9900; from late May to early September, a bus service links Union Station with Ontario Place).* Designed by Eberhard Zeidler, Ontario Place consists of three islands joined by bridges. Five structures are suspended several metres

above the water and bustle with activities. An enormous white sphere stands out from the other buildings; inside is the **Cinesphere**, an **IMAX cinema** *(☎965-7722)* with an impressive six-storey-high movie screen.

Ontario Place has a marina with a capacity for about 300 boats, centred around the ***HMCS Haida***, a World War II destroyer. If you have children, head to the **Children's Village**, with its playgrounds, pool, waterslides, waterguns, bumper-boats, Nintendo centre, LEGO creative centre, cinema and other attractions. The not-so-young will appreciate the **Forum**, an outdoor amphitheatre with musical shows every evening.

The Theatre and Financial Districts

Start at the corner of King and John. The stretch of King Street from here to Simcoe Street is also known as Mirvish Walkway, after the father-and-son duo of discount-store magnates who refurbished the area by saving the Royal Alex from the wrecking ball and by filling in the empty warehouses with restaurants for hungry theatre-goers.

The spanking new **Princess of Wales Theatre** *(300 King St. W., ☎872-1212)* was built in 1993 expressly for the musical *Miss Saigon.* Though no tours are offered, it is worth taking a peek inside to see the minimalist moon and star decor of the lobby.

Continue to **The Royal Alexandra** ★★ *(260 King St.*

W., ☎872-3333). Between these two theatres, plastered on the walls of Ed Mirvish's various food emporiums, is a collection of newspaper articles attesting to the entrepreneur's various exploits. The Royal Alexandra was named after the king's consort, and is now popularly known as the Royal Alex. Its rich Edwardian styling and Art Nouveau decor with plush red velvet, gold brocade and green marble were restored in the 1960s by Ed Mirvish himself.

Across the street rises **Roy Thompson Hall** ★★★ *(45min guided tours Mon to Sat 12:30pm; $4; 60 Simcoe St., ☎593-4822),* one of the most distinctive buildings in Toronto's cityscape. The space-age about 3,700m^2 mirrored-glass exterior was designed by Canada's Arthur Erickson and gets mixed reviews, having been compared to an upside-down mushroom and a ballerina's tutu. The interior, however, is another story, boasting striking luminosity, a glamorous lobby and exceptional acoustics that the resident Toronto Symphony and Mendelssohn Choir make beautiful use of.

A large courtyard lies west of Roy Thompson Hall, bordered to the west by **Metro Hall** (facing the Princess of Wales), and to the south by Simcoe Place (the large square building to the left) and the **CBC Broadcast Centre** (the tall building to the right).

Continue into the heart of Toronto, to its **financial district**, where money makes many local residents run themselves ragged and is the leading preoccupation. The district stretches from Adelaide Street to the north to Front Street to the

Ontario

south, and between University Avenue to the west and Yonge Street to the east.

Historically, high finance in Toronto has always been centred in this area. It all started at the intersection of Yonge and Wellington in the mid-1800s, when the only form of advertising available to financial organizations was architecture. Image was everything in those days, and the impression of solidity and permanence was achieved through majestic entrance halls, cornices, porticoes and the like. By the early 1900s, the hub had shifted north to King and Yonge, and the sleek Art Deco style was in vogue. As the district expanded to the west, skyscrapers were built right up against the road on Bay Street, creating a northern version of the Wall Street canyon. In the last three decades, the steel and glass towers became the centrepieces of vast windswept courtyards. More recently, these concrete parks have come in direct competition with the ever-expanding underground walkway system known as the PATH. The debate continues as to the merits of these impersonal tunnels, which shuttle office workers to and from.

As you walk east along King Street, the first steel ang glass tower is the **Sun Life Tower** ★ *(150-200 King St. W.)*, standing opposite St. Andrew's Church at the corner of Simcoe and King Streets. At the northeast corner of York and King stands the august-marble tower known as **First Canadian Place** ★★. Though its stark exterior and squat base are not very appealing, the interior commercial space is bright and

airy. The **Toronto Stock Exchange** ★★ *(free admission; Mon to Fri 9:30am to 4pm, guided tours at 2pm; 130 King St.,* ☎*947-4670)* is the heart of Canadian high finance. Stock Market Place at the TSE is located on the ground floor of the Exchange Tower, in the reception area. This is one of the more interesting stops in the district, as you can watch the action on the trading floor from an observation gallery.

Halfway between York and Bay, the **Standard Life** and **Royal Trust** buildings stand on the south side of King Street next to the impressive **Toronto-Dominion Centre** ★★ *(55 King St. W.)*, on the southwest corner of King and Bay. The work of famous modernist Ludwig Mies van der Rohe, it was the first International-style skyscraper built in Toronto in the mid-1960s.

At the northeast corner of King and Bay is the Art-Deco **Bank of Nova Scotia** ★ *(44 King St. W.)*. A few more gems lie up Bay Street, notably the **National Club Building** *(303 Bay St.)*, the **Bank of Montreal** *(302 Bay St.)* and the **Canada Permanent Building** *(320 Bay St.)* with its splendid Art Deco lobby.

Back on King Street, the **Bank of Commerce Building** ★★★ *(25 King St. W.)* is considered by many to be the best bank building and office tower in Toronto's financial district. Enter the immense banking hall to view the roseate stone, gilt mouldings and blue-coffered barrel vault. To the east, on the corner of King and Bay, is the **"Old" Bank of Commerce Building**, which for many years was the tallest build-

ing in the British Commonwealth. In between and facing Bay Street is **Commerce Court** *(243 Bay St.)*, which encompasses the two aforementioned buildings and a slick skyscraper built in the early 1970s.

The **Toronto Dominion Bank** ★★★ *(55 King St. W.)* lies on the southwest corner of King and Yonge. Its interior is a feast for the eyes. A central staircase leads down to the vault, touted as the largest in Canada when it was built, while another, even more formal staircase on the right leads up to the main banking hall.

At number 15 Wellington Street is the oldest building on this tour. Originally the Commercial Bank of Midland District (1845), then the Merchant's Bank, it is now simply known as **Number 15** ★★, or depending who you talk to, Marché Mövenpick (see p 417). Make your way to Bay. About halfway up the block towards King Street, on the east side, is the **Original Toronto Stock Exchange** ★★★ *(234 Bay St.)* the city's most typically Art Deco building. The 22,5m stone frieze above the door mixes irony and humour as only a Canadian stock exchange building could. Located in the magnificently restored interior, the **Design Exchange** *($5; Tue to Fri 10am to 6pm, Sat and Sun noon to 5pm;* ☎*216-2160)* features exhibits of international and national designers.

The lavish and imposing **Royal Bank Plaza** ★★★ *(200 Bay St.)* is below Wellington. The gold enriched mirrored exterior is like a breath of fresh air amidst the sober white-collar demeanour of Toronto's financial district, especially at twilight. The gold also acts as an insulator!

Front Street and St. Lawrence

It was in the rectangular area formed by George, Berkley, Adelaide and Front streets that Commander John Graves Simcoe of the British army founded the town of York in 1793. Today it is better known as Toronto. This part of the city, close to Lake Ontario, was the business centre of the growing city for many years. At the end of the 19th century, economic activity slowly moved toward what is today known as the financial district, leaving behind a partially deserted area. Like Harbourfront, the St. Lawrence neighbourhood has undergone major renovations over the last couple decades, financed by the federal, provincial and municipal governments. Today, a cheerful mixture of 19th- and 20th-century architecture characterizes an area where the city's various socioeconomic groups converge.

Union Station ★★ *(65-75 Front St. W.)* ranks first among Canadian railway stations for its size and magnificence. It was built in the spirit of great U.S. railway terminals, with columns and coffered ceilings inspired by the basilicas of ancient Rome. Work on the station began in 1915 but was only completed only in 1927. This was one of the masterpieces of Montréal architects Ross and Macdonald. Its facade on Front

Street stretches over 250m, concealing the port and Lake Ontario in the background.

The **Royal York Hotel** ★★ *(100 Front St. W.)* is a worthy introduction to downtown Toronto for anyone arriving by train at Union Station. Its message to new arrivals is clear: the Queen City is indeed a major metropolis that will play second fiddle to none. This hotel, the biggest in the Canadian Pacific chain, has more than 1,500 rooms on 25 floors. Like the station, it was designed by Montréal architects Ross and Macdonald. Here, the château style of the railway hotels is combined with Lombard and Venetian elements (see also p 415).

Enter **BCE Place** ★★★ by the courtyard located east of the Canada Trust Tower. BCE Place stretches from Bay Street to Yonge Street and is made up of twin towers linked by a magnificent five-storey glass atrium supported by enormous white metal ribs. This bright and airy space is a delightful place to rest for a few moments or grab a bite to eat. There are fast-food counters on the lower level, or for something unique, head instead to the **Marché Mövenpick** (see p 417), a unique blend of restaurant and market.

BCE Place also encloses the entrance to the famous **Hockey Hall of Fame** ★ *($12; summer, Mon to Sat 9:30am to 6pm, Sun 10am to 6pm; rest of the year, Mon to Fri 10am to 5pm, Sat 9:30am to 6pm, Sun 10:30am to 5:30pm; 30 Yonge St., ☎360-7735)*, a veritable paradise for hockey fans. Do not miss the Bell Great Hall, at the centre of which is the original Stanley Cup, North America's oldest professional sports trophy, donated by Lord Stanley of Preston in 1893. Other highlights include a reconstitution of the Montréal Canadiens' dressing room as well as some of hockey's most exciting moments on video.

At the corner of Yonge and Front Streets is the old **Bank of Montreal Building** ★★. The Hockey Hall of Fame is actually located in this building, though the only entrance is through BCE Place. Built in 1886 by architects Darling and Curry, the Bank of Montreal building is one of the oldest 19th-century structures still standing in Toronto. Designed during a prosperous and optimistic period, its architecture conveys a sense of power and invulnerability typical of the era, with imposing masonry, splendid porticoes and gigantic windows.

Hockey Hall of Fame

A little further east along Front Street beyond Berczy Park is the amusing *trompe l'oeil* fresco painted on the back of the **Gooderham Building** ★ *(49 Wellington St.)*. This mural, created by Derek Besant in 1980, has become a well-known sight in Toronto. Contrary to popular belief, it does not portray the windows of the Gooderham Building but rather the facade of the Perkins Building, located across the street at 41-43 Front Street East. The Gooderham is often called the Flatiron Building because of its triangular structure that recalls the shape of its famous and more recent New York namesake.

Look back in the direction from which you came and contemplate the interesting vista of the Flatiron Building framed by the office towers of the financial district and the CN Tower. Across Front Street, the gleaming facades that now house shops and cafes are merely those of simple warehouses.

At the corner of Jarvis Street is the **St. Lawrence Market** ★★ *(91 Front St. E.)*. Built in 1844, it housed the city hall until 1904, the year Henry Bowyer Lane converted it into a public market. Expanded in 1978, St. Lawrence Market is famed today for the fresh fruits and vegetables, fish, meats, sausages and cheeses sold inside. Actually, this giant red-brick building completely envelops the former city hall, which is still perceptible in the facade. The best time to go is on Saturday, when the fish is freshest and local farmers arrive at 5am to sell their products across the street at the **Farmer's Market**.

St. Lawrence Hall ★ *(151 King St. E.)* was Toronto's community centre in the latter half of the 19th century. This Victorian structure was built to present concerts and balls. Among the celebrities who performed here were Jenny Lind, Andelina Patti, Tom Thumb and P.T. Barnum. For several years, St. Lawrence Hall was also home to the National Ballet of Canada.

Lovely **St. James Park**, a 19th-century garden with a fountain and annual flower beds, lies a few steps to the west. Seated on one of its many benches, you can contemplate Toronto's first Anglican cathedral, **St. James Cathedral** ★★ at the corner of Church and King Streets. Built in 1819, it was destroyed in the 1849 fire that levelled part of the city. The St. James Cathedral you see today was built on the ruins of its predecessor. It has the highest steeple in all of Canada and the second highest in North America, after St. Patrick's Cathedral in New York. The interior is far more elaborate than its sober, yellow-brick Gothic exterior suggests.

The splendid **King Edward Hotel** ★★ *(37 King St. E.)* (see p 415), between Church Street and Leader Lane, was designed in 1903 by E.J. Lennox, architect of the Old City Hall (see p 407), Massey Hall (see p 419) and Casa Loma (see p 412). With its Edwardian style, its wonderful mock marble columns on the ground floor and its magnificent dining rooms, the King Edward was one of Toronto's most luxurious hotels for nearly 60 years, until, with the decline of the surrounding area, it fell into disrepair. Splendid Café Victoria (see

p 417) ultimately saved the hotel from destruction.

Queen West, Kensington and Chinatown

This tour starts at the corner of Yonge and Queen Streets where Queen West begins. **The Bay** department store occupies the southwest corner and the whole south side of Queen all the way to Bay. The stunning Art Deco entrance at Richmond and Yonge was added in 1928.

Head north on Yonge Street. On the left is the exterior of the six-storey shopping mecca, the Eaton Centre ; on the right you'll soon come upon two more of Toronto's majestic theatres, the Elgin and Wintergarden and the Pantages.

The **Elgin and Wintergarden Theatres** ★★ *(1hr tours, $4; Thu 5pm, Sat 11am; 189 Yonge St.)* form the last operating double-decker theatre complex in the world. Opened in 1914 as vaudeville theatres, the Elgin downstairs was very opulent, while the Wintergarden upstairs was one of the first "atmospheric theatres," with trellised walls and columns disguised as tree trunks supporting a ceiling of real leaves. After a stint as a movie house, these landmarks were restored by the Ontario Heritage Centre and again serve as live theatre venues.

Once the biggest vaudeville house in the British Empire, the **Pantages Theatre** *(1hr tours Mon, Tue and Fri 11:30am, Sat 10:30am;*

$4; 263 Yonge St., ☎*364-4100)* went through many reincarnations as a picture palace and then a six-theatre movie house, before it was finally restored to its original splendour in 1988-89. It is perhaps best-known as the home of Andrew Lloyd Webber's *Phantom of the Opera.*

Even if you have no desire to go shopping, at least take a peek inside the **Eaton Centre ★★**, which runs along Yonge Street between Queen and Dundas. And if you do need something, by all means linger in this glass-roofed arcade, which a few sparrows have decided is more pleasant than outside. Here, so-called streets have been stacked five-storeys high and lined with benches and trees. Look up and you will see Michael Snow's exquisite flock of fibreglass Canada geese, called *Step Flight*, suspended over the Galleria. Framed by two 30-storey skyscrapers and two subway stations (Dundas and Queen Stations) and occupying 557 400m², the Eaton Centre contains more than 320 stores and restaurants, 2 indoor parking lots and a 17-theatre cinema complex.

Once you've had your fill of shopping, exit the Eaton Centre via Trinity Square, at the northwest corner of the mall.

The **Church of the Holy Trinity ★★** (1847), the **Rectory** (1861) and the **Scadding House** (1857) are some of Toronto's oldest landmarks, and the original plans for the Eaton Centre called for their demolition. Fortunately, enough people objected and the huge

mall was built around the building trio, leaving a pleasant space amidst the concrete.

Head down James Street towards the back of **Old City Hall ★★** *(60 Queen St. W.)* designed by E.J. Lennox in 1889. As you make your way around the building towards the front on Queen Street, look up at the eaves, below which the architect carved the letters "E J LENNOX ARCHITECT" to ensure that his name would be remembered. Lennox won a contest to design the building, but the city councillors denied his request to engrave his name on a cornerstone. In retaliation, he had carved disfigured versions of their faces above the front steps so that they would have to look on their gargoyle-like selves every day! By the time all these insulting personal touches were revealed, it was too late to do anything about them.

Old City Hall

In 1965, the municipal administration of Toronto moved out of its Victorian city hall and into **New City Hall ★★** *(100 Queen St. W.)*, a modernist masterpiece that quickly gained a certain notoriety and became so symbolic of Toronto as the CN Tower. Once again, a contest was held to choose the city's most avant-garde architect and this time the winner was Finn Viljo Revell, a

master of Scandinavian post-war rationalist thinking. Its two curved towers of unequal length are like two hands protecting the saucer-shaped structure that houses the Council Room.

Nathan Phillips Square ★, a vast public space in front of New City Hall, is named after the mayor of Toronto, who blessed the city with many new facilities in the early 1960s. A large pool of water straddled by three arches is transformed into a skating rink in the winter. Nearby stands *"The Archer"*, by Henry Moore, and the Peace Garden.

Make your way along Queen Street West. Lined with trendy shops, cafés and bars for most of its length, it is also the home of **CityTV** and **MuchMusic** *(299 Queen St. W.)*, "the nation's music station."

The former Wesley Building was built for a publishing company in 1913-15, and note grotesque readers and scribes adorn its facade. In the Speakers' Corner video booth you can laud or criticize any cause you like, and maybe even end up on national television.

Take the time to stroll along **Queen West ★★** and admire the hip and modern boutiques. There are even a few interesting architectural highlights, as most of these shops occupy late-19th-century buildings.

Now you can head north on Spadina. The five blocks between Queen and Dundas might not look like much, but they contain some of the best bargains in town, from designer clothes to designer food, from evening wear to kitchenware. At the intersection of Spadina and Dundas, you will find yourself in the heart of Toronto's **Chinatown ★ ★ ★**. The community radiates from this point north to College Street, south to Queen and east to Bay, and is the largest Chinatown in North America. The neighbourhood actually began around Elizabeth Street where New City Hall now stands. It gradually moved west to Spadina, though remnants of it remain all along Dundas. The best time to explore the fascinating tea shops, herbalists and Chinese grocers is on Sunday, when sounds of Cantonese pop music, mounds of fresh vegetables, racks of roasted duck and smells of ginseng transport you to another world. Sunday is also the day when most Chinese families head out for brunch, though they call it dim sum, and it is quite different from bacon and eggs!

Before straying too far along Dundas, check out **Kensington Market ★ ★**,

located along Kensington Street. This bazaar epitomizes Toronto's multi-ethnicity. It began as a primarily Eastern European market, but is now a wonderful mingling of Jewish, Portuguese, Asian and Caribbean culture. The lower half of Kensington is mostly vintage clothing shops, while the upper portion boasts international grocers peddling fresh and tasty morsels from all over the world. Perfect for picnic fixings!

Whether you decide on a picnic or dim sum, make sure to save time for an edifying afternoon at the Art Gallery of Ontario and The Grange.

The Art Museum of Toronto was founded in 1900, but was without a permanent home until 1913, when The Grange (see below) was bequeathed to the museum. A new building was added in 1918, and the first exhibition of Canada's renowned Group of Seven was held in 1920 at what was by then known as the Art Gallery of Toronto. A significant chapter in Canada's and Toronto's cultural histories was thus written. In 1966, the museum received provincial support and was officially rebaptized the **Art Gallery of Ontario ★ ★ ★** *(admission is on a pay-what-you-can basis, $5 per person is suggested; special exhibitions are priced individually; May to Oct, Tue and Thu to Sun 10am to 5:30pm, Wed 10am to 10pm, Oct to May, Wed 10am to 10pm, Thu to Sun 10am to 5:30pm; 317 Dundas St. W., ☎979-6648).* Successive

renovations and additions over the years have all tried to reinvent the AGO, by introducing new elements in place of old ones. Exhibits feature contemporary art and Inuit sculptures, and the beautiful Tanenbaum Sculpture Atrium exposes a facade of The Grange. The Henry Moore Sculpture Centre is one of the museum's greatest treasures. The Canadian historical and contemporary collections contain major pieces by such artists like Cornelius Krieghoff, Michael Snow, Emily Carr, Jean-Paul Riopelle, Tom Thomson and the Group of Seven – Frederick Varley, Lawren Harris, Franklin Carmichael, A. Y. Jackson, Arthur Lismer, J. E. H. MacDonald and Frank H. Johnson. The museum also boasts masterpieces by Rembrandt, Van Dyck, Reynolds, Renoir, Picasso, Rodin, Degas and Matisse, to name a few.

Adjacent to the Art Gallery of Ontario stands its original home, **The Grange ★** *(admission included with AGO ticket; May to Oct, Tue and Thu to Sun noon to 4pm, Wed noon to 9pm; Oct to May, Wed noon to 9pm, Thu to Sat noon to 4pm; Grange Park, south of the AGO, ☎977-0414 or 979-6648).* The Georgian-style residence was built in 1817-18 by D'Arcy Boulton Jr., a member of Toronto's ruling elite, the much-reviled Family Compact. The city of Toronto was barely 30 years old at the time, yet by 1837, the year of Mackenzie's rebellion, The Grange had become the virtual seat of political power and thus symbolized the oppressive colonial regime in Upper Canada. The house was willed to the Art Museum of Toronto in 1910. It was restored to its 1830s grandeur and the whole house was opened to the public in 1973. This aristocrat's house, with its grand circular staircase and fascinating servants' quarters, was one of Toronto's first brickwork buildings.

End your day with a hearty meal on Baldwin Street, in Chinatown's residential area. The block to the east of McCaul harbours some fantastic little restaurants.

Around Queen's Park

Each of the 10 provinces has its own legislative assembly. Ontario's is located in the **Provincial Parliament** ★★ *(1 Queen's Park)*, at the centre of Queen's Park in the middle of University Avenue. The red sandstone building (1886-1892) was designed in the Richardsonian neoRomanesque style by architect Richard A. Waite of Buffalo, who is also responsible for several other Canadian buildings, including the old headquarters of the Grand Trunk Railway on McGill Street in Montréal.

The 40 or so buildings of the **University of Toronto** ★★ *(between Spadina Rd. to the west, Queen's Park Cres. to the east, College St. to the south and Bloor to the north)* dot a vast and verdant English-style campus. Granted a charter in 1827, the institution didn't really get going until the construction of its first building in 1845 which is no longer standing. Today, the University of Toronto is considered one of the most important in North America.

The oldest building on campus is **University College** *(15 Kings College Circle)*, built in 1859 by architects Cumberland and Storm. The result is a picturesque neo-Romanesque ensemble with remarkably detailed stone carvings.

Philosopher's Walk ★ is a winding road that heads north from Hoskins. The Taddle Creek once flowed where the philosopher now walks to the wafting sounds of music students practising their scales at the **Royal Conservatory of Music** *(273 Bloor St.)*. A contemplative stroll next to the newly planted oak trees leads to the Alexandra Gates (which originally stood at Bloor and Queen's Park).

Bloor and Yorkville

This tour covers the area around Bloor and Yorkville, two names that are now synonymous with expensive, upscale and trendy. The tour has a little something for everyone, including some of Toronto's finest museums and best shopping.

The area north and west of Bloor and Bedford was once the Village of Yorkville, which was incorporated in 1853 and existed as a separate town until 1883 when it was annexed to the city of Toronto. The first signs of the area's trend-setting status appeared in the postwar era, as the 19th-century residences were transformed into coffeehouses and shops Yorkville became the focus of Canada's folk music scene in the 1960s. The gentrification

of the area took off in the 1970s and 1980s and multi-purpose complexes and high rises have sought to make optimal use of now outrageously expensive rental properties on Bloor Street.

Start at the corner of St. George and Bloor Streets, just a few steps from the St. George subway station. This corner is at the extreme southwest of The Annex (see p 412), an area containing many wonderfully preserved 19th-century homes.

The new home of the **Bata Shoe Museum** ★★ *($6; Tue to Sat 10am to 5pm, Thu until 8pm, Sun noon to 5pm; 327 Bloor St. W., ☎979-7799)* is a whimsical start to a serious tour of the museums and a great place to get a few ideas before you hit the shops! The first museum of its kind in North America, it holds 10,000 shoes and provides an extraordinary perspective on the world's cultures. The new building was designed by architect Raymond Moriyama to look like a shoe box, and the oxidized copper along the edge of the roof is meant to suggest a lid resting on top. Some of the more memorable pieces of footwear on display include the space boots of Apollo astronauts, geisha platform sandals and a pair of patent-leather beauties that once belonged to Elvis Presley.

Ontario

The **Royal Ontario Museum** ★★★ *($10; Mon to Sat 10am to 6pm, Tue 10am to 8pm, Sun 11am to 6pm; 100 Queen's Park, ☎586-5549 or 586-5551; Museum subway; parking is expensive)* is actually two museums in one since admission to the ROM, as it is called, also includes admission to the George R. Gardiner Museum of Ceramic Art (see below). Canada's largest public museum, as well as a research facility, the ROM preserves some six million treasures of art, archaeology and natural science. After extensive renovation, restoration and the opening of new galleries, the ROM can now display these priceless treasures using techniques that protect them from decay. Upon entering the impressive free-Romanesque-style building, your eyes are drawn up to the Venetian glass ceiling that depicts a mosaic of cultures. The ceiling is the only part of the museum that was not built using materials from Ontario. Continuing into the museum, your eyes are drawn up once again by the towering totem poles flanking the lobby, one of which is 24m tall, and whose top is just 15cm shy of the ceiling! With exhibits on Romans and Nubians, Chinese art and antiquities including a Ming tomb, and everything from bats to dinosaurs, your first stop should be at the Mankind Discovering Gallery, where the layout and workings of the ROM are explained.

On the east side of Queen's Park Avenue, the **George R. Gardiner Museum of Ceramic Art** ★★★ *(5 $, free first Tues of the month; Mon to Sat 10am to 5pm, Tue until 8pm, Sun 11am to 5pm; 111 Queen's Park,*

☎586-8080) boasts a striking collection of porcelain and pottery. Four galleries span history from the pre-Colombian Mayans and Olmecs to European treasures of the last 500 years.

The luxurious **Park Plaza Hotel** *(4 Avenue Rd.)*, built in 1926, stands at the northwest corner of Avenue and Bloor. The rough stone walls, sweeping slate roof and belfry of the **Church of the Redeemer** *(162 Bloor Ste. W.)* occupy the northeast corner of Bloor and Avenue.

The stretch of Bloor Street from Queen's Park Avenue Road to Yonge is a collection of modern office buildings, shopping malls and ultra-chic boutiques and galleries such as Holt Renfrew, Chanel, Hermès, Tiffany's and Hugo Boss. According to some, Bloor Street is Toronto's Fifth Avenue, so make your way along it as quickly or as leisurely as you wish.

Heading west along Yorkville, you'll come to the grand **Yorkville Public Library** *(22 Yorkville Ave.)* built in 1907 and remodelled in 1978. The bold porticoed entrance still dominates the facade just as it did when this library served the village of Yorkville.

Right next door is the old **Firehall No. 10** ★ *(34 Yorkville Ave.)*, built in 1876 and then reconstructed (except for the tower, used to dry fire hoses) in 1889-90. This red- and yellow-brick house is still in use. The coat of arms on the tower was salvaged from the town hall; the symbols on it represent the vocations of the town's first councillors: a beer barrel for the brewer, a plane for the

carpenter, a brick mould for the builder, an anvil for the blacksmith and a bull's head for the butcher.

An exceptional collection of galleries, shops and cafés line Yorkville, Hazelton and Cumberland. More architectural gems, too numerous to list, are on Hazelton Avenue. These have all been faithfully restored, some to the extent that they look like new buildings; nevertheless, the results are aesthetically pleasing and worth a look.

One block south is Cumberland Street, with fancy boutiques and galleries on one side, and the **Village of Yorkville Park** ★★ on the other. This urban park, which lies over a subway station, is an uncommon mix of urban ecology, local history and regional identity. It is divided into 13 zones, each representing a different part of the province's geography. The huge boulder toward the centre is native Canadian Shield granite.

Toronto: City of Neighbourhoods

Many people view Toronto as a bastion of Anglo-Saxon culture, as Canada's financial hub or as the home to the Blue Jays and the CN Tower, but few realize that it is also a city of tremendously diverse neighbourhoods. While some areas are defined by their architectural extravagance or lack thereof, a perhaps more interesting handful are defined by the people who live there. Toronto's ethnic diversity is a marvel; with some 70 nationalities and more than 100 languages, the city is emblematic of the Canadian mosaic, and restaurant-goers are all the happier for it!

Chinatown

Toronto's best-known ethnic neighbourhood is Chinatown (see p 408). There are actually six Chinatowns in greater Toronto, but the most exciting and vibrant is probably the one between University, Spadina, Queen and College. During the day, fresh vegetables line the sidewalks around the intersection of Spadina and Dundas, the area's core, while at night, the bright yellow and red lights are reminiscent of Hong Kong. Picturesque, adjacent **Kensington Market** is often associated with Chinatown. The vintage clothing stores and specialty food shops from Europe, the Caribbean, the Middle East and Asia are definite must-sees.

Little Italy

Italians make up the city's largest ethnic group, and their spiritual home is Little Italy, located on College Street near Bathurst, where trattorias and boutiques add a bit of the Mediterranean to this Canadian metropolis. The neighbourhood extends to **Corso Italia** on St. Clair Avenue, west of Bathurst. This vibrant mix of traditional shops and designer Italian boutiques is a marvellous spot for a real cappuccino or Italian gelato.

Greektown

Greektown is also known as **The Danforth** after the street that runs through it. Greektown is perhaps a misnomer anyway since the community is now home to Italians, Greeks,

East Indians, Latin Americans and Chinese. The Greeks still dominate, however, when it comes to restaurants, and Greektown, with its late-night fruit markets, specialty food shops, taverns and summer cafés, is a real culinary experience.

Little Poland

Between the Lakeshore and Dundas Street West, Roncesvalles Avenue is known as Little Poland, a pleasant area of grand trees and stately Victorian buildings. This is where you can catch an Eastern European film or savour traditional home-made cabbage rolls and pirogies at one of the many cafés.

Portugal Village

The traditional *azulejos* (ceramic tiles) and a glass of port will make you think you are in Portugal when you visit the area around Dundas Street West, Ossington Avenue, Augusta Avenue and College Street, known as Portugal Village. Bakeries here sell some of the best bread in town, while cheese stores, fish markets and lace and crochet shops occupy every other corner.

Little India

Little India is a collection of spice shops, clothing stores, restaurants and movie houses along Gerrard Street, east of Greenwood Avenue. These establishments are frequented by Toronto's East Indian community, which is now spread throughout the city.

Caribbean Village

The area around Bathurst Street north of Bloor Street is the commercial district known as the Caribbean Village. Great food shops sell delicious treats, including savoury patties (pastry turnovers with spicy meat fillings) and *roti* (flat bread with meat, fish or vegetable filling) of the islands.

Gay Village

Toronto has the largest population of gays and lesbians in Canada, and is a surprisingly welcoming place considering the city's occasionally stodgy reputation. The Gay Village is centred around the corner of Church and Wellesley Streets. Another popular hangout is Hanlan's Point on the Toronto Islands.

Rosedale

Both of Toronto's most distinguished and affluent neighbourhoods lie just north of the downtown area. The first one, Rosedale, is bound by Yonge Street to the west, the Don Valley parkway to the east, Bloor Street to the south and St. Clair Avenue to the north. Rosedale began as the estate of Sheriff William Jarvis, and was so named by his wife Mary after the wild roses that once abounded here. The

Ontario

wild roses and the original house overlooking the ravine are now gone, replaced by a collection of curved streets lined with exquisite residences representing quite a variety of architectural styles. Rosedale was once considered too far from town, but today its natural ravine setting is one of its major assets. Some of the prettiest residences lie on South Drive, Meredith Crescent, Crescent Road, Chestnut Park Road, Elm Avenue and Maple Avenue.

Forest Hill

North of St. Clair Avenue, the second posh area, known as Forest Hill, begins. It extends north to Eglinton, east to Avenue Road and west to Bathurst Street. The former village of Forest Hill was incorporated into the city of Toronto in 1968. Perhaps in keeping with its name, one of the village's first bylaws back in the 1920s was that a tree be planted on every lot. This haven of greenery is home to some of the city's finest dwellings; many of the loveliest grace Old Forest Hill Road. The community is also home to one of the country's most prestigious private schools, Upper Canada College, which has produced such luminaries as authors Stephen Leacock and Robertson Davies.

Cabbagetown

Cabbagetown was once described as the "biggest Anglo-Saxon slum" and was for many years an area to be avoided. It has been transformed in recent years, however, and is now a prime example of gentrification in Toronto. Its name originated with Irish immigrants who ar-

rived here in the mid-19th century and grew cabbages right on their front lawns. Cabbagetown's residential area lies around Parliament Street (its commercial artery), and extends east to the Don Valley, and between Gerrard and Bloor Streets. It contains majestic trees and small, quaint Victorian homes, many of which have historic markers. Winchester, Carlton, Spruce and Metcalfe Streets are all lined with these charming gems.

The Annex

Extending north and west of the intersection of Bloor Street and Avenue Road to Dupont and Bathurst Streets is an area that was annexed by the city of Toronto in 1887, and is now appropriately called The Annex. As this was a planned suburb, a certain architectural homogeneity prevails; even the unique gables, turrets and cornices are all lined up at an equal distance from the street. Take a stroll along Huron Street, Lowther Avenue and Madison Avenue to get a true feel for the Annex's architectural character, which residents have long fought to preserve. Save a few ugly apartment high-rises along St. George Street, their efforts have been successful.

Torontonians are sometimes known for their reserve, modesty and discretion. Of course there are exceptions to every rule, and one of these is certainly **Casa Loma ★ ★** (*$9; every day 9:30am to 5pm, last admission at 4pm; 1 Austin Terrace,* ☎*923-1171*), an immense Scottish castle with 98 rooms built in 1914 for Sir Henry Mill Pellatt (1859-1939), the eccentric colo-

nel who made his fortune by investing in electricity and transportation companies. Pellatt owned, among other things, the tramways of São Paolo, Brazil! His palatial residence, designed by E.J. Lennox, the architect of Toronto's Old City Hall, includes a vast ballroom that can hold up to 500 guests and has a pipe organ, as well as a library with 100,000 volumes and an underground cellar. The self-guided tour leads through various secret passages and "lost" rooms. Great views of downtown Toronto can be had from the towers.

To the east of Casa Loma, at the top of the Davenport hill and accessible by the Baldwin Steps, is **Spadina ★** (*$5; Jun to Dec, Mon to Fri 9:30am to 5pm, Sat and Sun noon to 5pm; Jan to May, Tue to Fri 9:30am to 4pm, Sat and Sun noon to 5pm; 285 Spadina Rd.,* ☎*392-6910*), another house-turned museum of Toronto's high society. This one is smaller but just as splendid if you want to get a taste of Canadian Art Nouveau. The grounds include a solarium overflowing with lush greenery and a charming Victorian garden, in bloom from May to September. The residence has been renovated several times and features glassed-in overhangs that offered its owners panoramic views of the surroundings that Aboriginals called *Espanidong,* and the English *Spadina* (pronounced *Spadeena*).

The Beaches

Last but not least, there is The Beaches (Toronto really does have everything!). This is perhaps Toronto's most charming neighbourhood, for obvious reasons – sun, sand, a beach-side boardwalk, classic clapboard and shingle cottages and the open water all lie just a streetcar ride away from the hectic pace of downtown. Bound by Kingston Road, the old Greenwood Raceway grounds, Victoria Park Avenue and Lake Ontario, The Beaches is more than just a neighbourhood; it is a way of life. Weary travellers will revel in the chance to sunbathe on the hot sand, take a quick dip in the refreshing water and, as the sun sets, do some window-shopping and lounge about on a pretty patio.

Other Sights

Ontario Science Centre ★★★ *($10; every day 10am to 5pm, 770 Don Mills Rd., ☎429-4100, www.osc.on.ca).* Since its opening on September 27, 1969, the Science Centre has welcomed over 30 million visitors, young and old alike. Designed by architect Raymond Moriyama, it houses 650 different expositions. The best thing about the centre is its many hands-on exhibits and experiments. One of the biggest crowd-pleasers is the electricity ball that makes your hair stand on end. The brand new OMNIMAX theatre, which is an improved version of the IMAX, seats 320 people under an enormous 24m-wide dome with a powerful hi-fidelity sound system.

For an enjoyable change of scenery within 30min of downtown Toronto, head to the **Toronto Metropolitan Zoo ★★** *($12; Meadowvale Rd. West Hill, Scarborough, follow Hwy. 401 to exit 389, then take Meadowvale Dr. ☎392-5900,*

www.torontozoo.com), where you can see some 4,000 animals from the four corners of the world and take advantage of this lovely 300ha park. The African pavilion is particularly interesting. Canadian wildlife is also well represented, and several species that have adapted to the local climate roam free in large enclosures.

The first one of its kind in the country, **Paramount Canada's Wonderland** *(Pay One Price Passport: guests aged 7-59 $39.99; May, Sep and Oct, Sat and Sun 10am to 8pm; Jun to Labour Day, every day 10am to 10pm; 9580 Jane St., Vaughan, ☎905-832-7000, Rutherford exit from Hwy. 400 and follow the signs, or Yorkdale or York Mills subway then take special GO express bus)* is the answer if you have a day to spare and children to please. Gut-wrenching rides include the Vortex, the only suspended roller coaster in Canada, and the renowned Days of Thunder, which puts you behind the driver's seat for a simulated stock-car race. The park also features a waterpark called Splash Works with 16 rides and slides, and live shows at the new Kingswood Theatre *(☎905-832-8131).* The restaurant facilities may not be to everyone's liking, so pack a lunch.

The **McMichael Collection ★★★** *($7; mid-Oct to May, Tue to Sun 10am to 4pm, May to mid-Oct, every day 10am to 5pm; 10365 Islington Ave., Kleinsburg, Ontario, ☎905-893-1211)* houses one of Canada's most magnificent collections of Canadian and Aboriginal art, and draws many visitors to the peaceful hamlet of Kleinberg on the outskirts of Greater Toronto. A magnificent stone and log

house built in the 1950s for the McMichaels is home to the collection. Art-lovers from the start, their initial collection of paintings by Canadian masters are the mainstay of the museum's present collection. Large and bright galleries present an impressive retrospective of the works of Tom Thomson as well as of the Group of Seven, those artists who strove to reproduce and interpret Ontario's wilderness from their own perspective. Inuit and First Nations art is also well represented, notably the work of Ojibwa painter Norval Morrisseau, who created his own "pictographic" style.

Parks

High Park *(for information ☎392-1111),* located in the western part of the city and bound by Bloor Street to the north, the Queensway to the south, Parkside Drive to the east and Ellis Avenue to the west, is Toronto's Central Park. It is accessible both by subway (Keele or High Park stations) and streetcar (College or Queen). The city's largest park, High Park features tennis courts, playgrounds, bike paths and nature trails; skating and fishing on Grenadier Pond; rare flora; wildlife indigenous to the area and animal paddocks where buffaloes, llamas and sheep are kept; a beach on Lake Ontario; a swimming pool and finally historic Colborne Lodge and the Howard Tomb and Monument. "Shakespeare Under the Stars" is one of the park's most popular sum-

Ontario

mer attractions (*park information :* ☎*392-1111*).

Scarborough Heights Park and **Cathedral Bluffs Park** command breathtaking views of Lake Ontario from atop the scenic bluffs, while **Bluffer's Park** offers scenic and spacious beaches and picnic areas.

Toronto Islands Park (*year-round; Metro Parks general information* ☎*392-8186; ferry return fares $4; schedule: May to Sep, first departure 8am then every 30 min or 15 min during peak hours, last ferry to the city from Hanlan's Point is at 9:30pm, from Centre Island 11:45pm, from Ward's Island 11:30pm; call for departure times for rest of the year* ☎*392-8193; to reserve picnic sites for large groups* ☎*392-8188)* lies on a group of 17 islands collectively known as the Toronto Islands, a short, 8min ferry ride from Toronto Harbour. Three ferries, each departing from the Mainland Ferry Terminal at the foot of Bay Street, service the three biggest islands, Hanlan's Point, Centre Island and Ward's Island; bridges connect the other islands that are occupied by private homes, yacht clubs and an airport. Bicycles are permitted on all of the ferries, except sometimes the Centre Island ferry, which gets very crowded on weekends. Bikes can be rented at Hanlan's Point and at the pier, while canoes, rowboats and pedalboats can be rented on Long Pond east of Manitou Bridge.

Outdoor Activities

Cycling

The **Martin Goodman Trail**, a 22km jogging and cycling path, follows the shore of Lake Ontario from the mouth of the Humber River west of the city centre, past Ontario Place and Queen's Quay to the Balmy Beach Club in The Beaches. Call ☎*367-2000* for a map of the trail.

Toronto Island Bicycle Rental *$5/hr tandem $10* Centre Island ☎*203-0009*

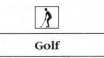

Skating

There are several enchanting places to go **ice-skating** in the city. These include the rink in front of New City Hall, Grenadier Pond in High Park and York Quay at Harbourfront. For information on city rinks call ☎*392-1111*.

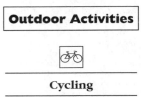

Golf

There are five municipal **golf** courses (two executive and three regulation), which operate on a first-come first-serve basis.

For something more challenging, take a little jaunt

out to Oakville, to the **Glen Abbey Golf Club** (*green fees and cart $145, discount rates in off-season and on weekends after 2pm $85;* ☎*905-844-1800)*. This spectacular course was the first designed by Jack Nicklaus. The rates are high, but it's a real thrill to play where the pros tee off. This is the home of the Canadian Open Championship.

Accommodations

The Waterfront

SkyDome Hotel *$209-$529* ≡, ℜ, ≈, ⊘, pb, ◊, tv, &, ✕ 1 Blue Jays Way, M5V 1J4 ☎*341-7100 or 800-228-9290* ⇌*341-5090 or 341-5091* The SkyDome Hotel has 346 rooms with panoramic views, 70 of which overlook the inside of the stadium. The latter cost more, but what a view! You have a choice of restaurants and a bar that also offers a view of the playing field. The modern rooms are adequate but nothing special. Valet and room service are available day and night.

Radisson Plaza Hotel Admiral *$279* ≡, ⊛, ≈, pb, & 249 Queen's Quay W., M5J 2N5 ☎*203-3333 or 800-333-3333* ⇌*203-3100* If you like the sea, you will feel at home at the Radisson Plaza Hotel Admiral. The decor of this charming hotel has a seafaring motif, with rooms that give guests the impression they are aboard a cruise ship. The view of the bay from the fifth-floor pool is quite spectacular.

Regular shuttle service is offered between the hotel and the downtown area.

Westin Harbour Castle
$295
≡, ≈, ℜ, ☺, pb, ◯, tv, ♿, ⚡
1 Harbour Square, M5J 1A6
☎ *869-1600 or 800-228-3000*
↪ *869-0573*
The Westin Harbour Castle used to be part of the Hilton hotel chain. In 1987, Westin and Hilton decided to swap their respective Toronto hotels. Located on the shore of Lake Ontario, in a calm and peaceful spot, the Westin Harbour Castle is just a few steps from Harbourfront Centre and the ferry to the Toronto Islands. To help guests reach the downtown area, the hotel offers a free shuttle service; it also lies on a streetcar line.

The Theatre and Financial Districts

Strathcona Hotel
$129
≡
60 York St., M5J 1S8
☎ *363-3321 or 800-268-8304*
↪ *363-4679*
For a pleasant hotel located in the heart of downtown, just a few steps from the Royal York Hotel and a short walk from the waterfront, head to the Strathcona Hotel.

Front Street and St. Lawrence

French Novotel
$260
≡, ⊛, ℜ, ☺, pb, ◯, tv
45 The Esplanade, M5E 1W2
☎ *367-8900 or 800-668-6835*
↪ *360-8285*
The French Novotel enjoys an ideal Toronto location, just minutes from the Harbourfront, the St. Lawrence and Hummingbird

centres, and Union Station. Comfort is assured at this hotel, except perhaps for the rooms facing The Esplanade, whose peace and quiet may be disturbed by noise from the outdoor bars.

Royal Meridien King Edward Hotel
$290
≡, ℜ, ☺, pb, tv, ♿, ⚡
37 King St. E., M5C 1E9
☎ *863-9700 or 800-225-5843*
↪ *367-5515*
Built in 1903, the Royal Meridien King Edward Hotel is the oldest hotel in Toronto and still one of the most attractive. Rooms at this very elegant establishment each have their own character but do not, unfortunately, offer much in terms of views. The magnificent lobby and the two ballrooms make up for this, though. Airport buses stop here regularly.

Royal York Hotel
$179-$299
≡, ≈, ☺, pb, ◯, tv
100 Front St. W., M5J 1E3
☎ *863-6333 or 800-828-7447*
☎ *800-441-1414*
With its renovated guest rooms, its 34 banquet rooms (each decorated differently), and its 10 restaurants, it is easy to understand why the Royal York Hotel is one of Toronto's most popular hotels. The impressive, sumptuously decorated lobby is an indication of the elegance of the rooms.

Queen West, Kensington and Chinatown

Bond Place Hotel
$109
≡, ℜ, tv
65 Dundas St. E., M5B 2G8
☎ *362-6061 or 800-268-9390*
↪ *360-6406*
The Bond Place Hotel is undoubtedly the best located hotel for enjoying the city beat and for mixing with the varied throng at the corner of Dundas and Yonge Streets.

Toronto Marriott Eaton Centre
$229
≡, ≈, ℜ, ⊛, ◯, ☺, pb, tv, ♿
525 Bay St., M5G 2L2
☎ *597-9200 or 800-905-0667*
↪ *598-9211*
If you prefer to have everything under the same roof, the brand-new Toronto Marriott Eaton Centre will fit the bill. Linked to the famous Eaton Centre, a shoppers' mecca and one of the city's attractions (see p 407), the Marriott has huge, well-equipped rooms (they even have irons and ironing boards). If you wish to relax, there are two ground-floor lounges, one with pool tables and televisions.

Around Queen's Park

Hostelling International
members $18.85
non-members $23.13
K, tv, ℜ
76 Church St., M5B 1Y7
☎ *971-4440 or 800-668-4487*
↪ *971-4088*
Hostelling International, open day and night, offers 175 beds in semi-private rooms or dormitories at very affordable prices. There is a television lounge, a laundromat, a kitchen and a restaurant with a pool table and dart

Ontario

board, as well as an outdoor terrace.

Bloor and Yorkville

Inter-Continental Toronto
$375
≡, ≈, ℜ, ☉, pb, ○, tv, ♿
220 Bloor St. W., M5S 1T8
☎ *960-5200 or 800-267-0010*
⇝ *920-8269*
Just a few steps from the Royal Ontario Museum (see p 410) and from Yorkville Street, the Inter-Continental Toronto is sure to win you over with its vast, tastefully decorated rooms and its exemplary service.

Four Seasons Hotel Toronto
$385
≡, ⊛, ≈, ℜ, ☉, pb, tv, ♿
21 Avenue Rd., M5R 2G1
☎ *964-0411 or 800-268-6282*
⇝ *964-2301*
If you are looking for top-of-the-line luxury accommodations, the Four Seasons Hotel Toronto is one of the most highly rated hotels in North America. This complex lives up to its reputation, with impeccable service and beautiful rooms. It also has a gorgeous ballroom with Persian carpets and crystal chandeliers. The hotel restaurant, Truffle, with Uffizi sculptures of two wild boars at the entrance, will satisfy your tastebuds with some of the best food in Toronto.

Neighbourhoods

Annex

Global Guest House
$62 sb, $72 pb
no smoking, ≡
9 Spadina Rd., M5R 2S9
☎ *923-4004*
⇝ *923-1208*
Global Guest House is a popular, inexpensive and ecologically sound alterna-

tive, ideally located just north of Bloor Street. The nine rooms are all spotless and simply decorated.

Lowther House
$75 sb
$100 pb, bkfst incl.
tv, ≡
72 Lowther Ave., M5R 1C8
☎ *323-1589 or 800-265-4158*
⇝ *962-7005*
Lowther House is a charming, beautifully restored Victorian mansion in the heart of the Annex and just minutes from many of the city's best sights. A double whirlpool bath, sun room, fireplace, claw-footed tub and delicious Belgian waffles are just some of the treats that await visitors at this home away from home.

High Park

Marigold Hostel
$22.35 bkfst incl.
2011 Dundas St. W., M6R 1W7
☎ *536-8824 after 7pm*
⇝ *533-4402*
An alternative to the big, expensive hotels, the Marigold Hostel is a charming little hotel that is often filled with young travellers and students who prefer to save a bit of cash and will forego a private bathroom.

Near the Airport

Sheraton Gateway Hotel at Terminal Three
$99-$245
≡, ⊛, ℜ, ☉, pb, tv, ♿
AMF, PO Box 3000, Mississauga
L5P 1C4
☎ *(905) 672-7000*
☎ *800-565-0010*
⇝ *(905) 672-7100*
The Sheraton Gateway Hotel at Terminal Three, linked directly to Toronto's Pearson International Airport, is the best located hotel for in-transit passengers. It has 474 attractively decorated, fully soundproof rooms with pan-

oramic views of the airport and the city.

Best Western Carlton Place Hotel
$190
≡, ⊛, ≈, ℜ, ○, tv, pb, ♿
33 Carlson Court, Etobicoke
M9W 6H5
☎ *675-1234 or 800-528-1234*
⇝ *675-3436*
If you want to be close to the airport, the Best Western Carlton Place Hotel offers decent, comfortable rooms at reasonable prices.

Restaurants

The Waterfront

Wayne Gretzky's
$$
99 Blue Jays Way
☎ *979-PUCK*
Wayne Gretzky's is a sports bar par excellence, complete with the great-one's sweaters, trophies and skates. Burgers, all taste-tested by Wayne himself, and a good selection of pastas round out the regular pub fare on the menu.

360
$$$$
CN Tower
301 Front St. W.
☎ *362-5411*
Imagine having a meal with all of Toronto at your feet. This is what awaits you atop the CN Tower, at the 360 revolving restaurant, which offers good food as well as one of the finest views in town.

The Theatre and Financial Districts

Marché Mövenpick
$$-$$$
in BCE Place
☎*366-8986*
At the Marché Mövenpick, you can choose from a tasty array of dishes each more tempting than the last, and prepared right before your eyes. After finally deciding on your meal, you may face the problem of finding a table, for this spot is very popular (see further below).

Acqua
$$$
BCE Place
10 Front St. W.
☎*368-7171*
As its name suggest, the decorative theme at Acqua is water. While observing this fine and rather unusual decor, you will enjoy succulent dishes drawn from Mediterranean and California culinary traditions.

Mövenpick Restaurant
$$
165 York St.
☎*366-0558*
Mövenpick Restaurant serves the same delicious Swiss specialties as the Marché (see further above) but with table service and without the hectic cafeteria ambiance.

Fenice
$$$-$$$$
319 King St. W.
☎*585-2377*
Fenice invites you to enjoy delicious Italian dishes prepared with fresh ingredients, and to delight in a warm atmosphere with soothing classical music in the background.

Front Street and St. Lawrence

C'est What
$$
67 Front St. E.
☎*867-9499*
A wonderful medley of cuisines is served into the wee hours at this before- and after-theatre stop. The exciting menu features exotic salads and original sandwiches. The ambiance is almost pub-like, with cozy chairs, board games and mood music that runs from folk to jazz.

Le Papillon
$$-$$$
16 Church St.
☎*363-0838*
You are sure to be satisfied at Le Papillon; the menu offers a tempting variety of dishes combining the delicacies of French and Québécois cuisines. The crêpes are especially good.

Café Victoria
$$$-$$$$
King Edward Hotel
37 King St. E.
☎*863-4125*
Café Victoria is enchanting with its classically decorated dining room and intimate, symmetrically placed tables. The meal, a veritable feast ending with a delicious dessert, is sure to be memorable.

The Senator
$$$$
closed *Mon*
249 Victoria
☎*364-7517*
The Senator has survived the recent explosion of the Toronto restaurant scene and still serves one of the best steaks in town in a classy, refined setting.

Queen West, Kensington and Chinatown

Future Bakery
$
739 Queen St. W.
☎*504-8700*
Future Bakery is a lofty café where the air is infused with the wonderful aromas of baking bread and brewing coffee. You can stop in for picnic fixings, stay for a piece of one of the sumptuous cakes or pies, or for a hearty meal of varenyky, cabbage rolls and borscht. You can even settle in with a good book and a coffee for hours on end!

Swatow
$
309 Spadina
☎*977-0601*
Swatow is a no-fuss eatery with an extensive menu that is guaranteed to satisfy your palate. There is nothing fancy about this place, but you can't beat it for its genuine Cantonese cooking served up fast and good, just like in China.

La Hacienda
$-$$
640 Queen St. W.
☎*703-3377*
La Hacienda, a charming restaurant with a retro decor recalling the 1960s, offers a menu consisting mostly of Mexican dishes, many of which will satisfy vegetarian gourmets.

Bamboo
$$
312 Queen St. W.
☎*593-5771*
Queen Street West is one of Toronto's liveliest streets after dark, and the Bamboo restaurant is one of the most colourful spots around. To reach the dining rooms, you have to squeeze through a narrow

Ontario

passageway linking the "temple" to the street. You can then choose between a two-level outdoor terrace or one of two indoor dining rooms. This one-of-a-kind restaurant, with food spanning Caribbean, Malay, Thai and Indonesian flavours, also offers reggae and salsa shows.

Margaritas Fiesta Room
$$
14 Baldwin St.
☎977-5525
Margaritas Fiesta Room provides quite an escape with its infectious Latin music and its tasty dishes including Toronto's best nachos and delicious guacamole. This piece of Mexico will transport you far from the rush of urban Toronto.

Left Bank
$$-$$$
567 Queen St. W.
☎504-1626
A cavernous and austere decor, exquisite presentation, attitude, mood lighting and an interesting interpretation of southwestern cuisine: pretty much sums up the dining experience at Left Bank.

Peter Pan
$$$
373 Queen St. W.
☎593-0917
Peter Pan offers a beautiful 1930s decor, as well as delicious and imaginative dishes. Pastas, pizzas and fish take on an original look here. Service is courteous.

The Bodega
$$$
30 Baldwin St.
☎977-1287
The Bodega serves resolutely gastronomic French dishes made with the freshest of ingredients. The wall coverings, lace trim and the music that wafts through the dining room

help create an authentic French atmosphere.

Around Queen's Park

Kalendar's Koffee House
$
546 College St.
☎923-4138
The relaxed setting at Kalendar's Koffee House is ideal for an intimate tête-à-tête over coffee and cake, or a light lunch. The menu lists an array of interesting sandwiches and simple dishes.

College Street Bar
$$
574 College St.
☎533-2417
The friendly College Street Bar boasts a tasty Mediterranean menu and lively environment. This hot spot is frequented by a young crowd, most of whom just stop in to have drinks and soak up the atmosphere.

Barberian's
$$$$
7 Elm St.
☎597-0335
There is nothing quite like a tender-grilled sirloin steak from Barberian's. Steak dominates the menu here, which may seem a little scanty to anyone hoping for other choices. It is best to reserve in advance.

Bloor and Yorkville

Flo's Diner
$
10 Bellair St.
☎961-4333
Among the chic stores in the Yorkville district, you might be surprised to discover a traditional diner. Like most establishments of this type, Flo's Diner is a good spot for hamburgers. In the summer, there is a rooftop terrace.

Jacques L'Omelette
$$-$$$
126-A Cumberland Ave.
☎961-1893
It is really worth taking the trouble to find Jacques L'Omelette, also called Jacques Bistro du Parc. This charming little spot is located upstairs in a fine Yorkville house. The very friendly French owner offers simple but high-quality food. The fresh Atlantic salmon and the spinach salad are among the pleasant surprises on the menu.

Bistro 990
$$$$
990 Bay St.
☎921-9990
The Bistro 990 is quite simply one of the best places to eat in Toronto. Delicious *nouvelle cuisine* items are offered in a Mediterranean setting, with outstanding preparations of lamb, salmon and duck.

Neighbourhoods

The Annex

Kensington Kitchen
$$$
124 Harbord St.
☎961-3404
At the Kensington Kitchen, you can enjoy Mediterranean dishes while seated comfortably in a pretty New Age dining room. This is a good spot on fine summer days, when you can enjoy the same specialties on the rooftop terrace.

Le Paradis
$$-$$$
166 Bedford Rd.
☎921-0995
Le Paradis serves authentic French bistro cuisine – at authentic bistro prices. The decor is simple and the service reserved, but a devoted following and the

delicious cooking make it
a must.

The Beaches

Whitlock's
$$
1961 Queen St. E.
☎*691-8784*
Whitlock's is a longstand-
ing tradition at the Beach.
Located in a lovely old
building, the atmosphere is
casual and unpretentious.
The menu is varied and
down-to-earth. It typifies
the real "Beach," as com-
pared to the glitz and
trendiness of what some
like to call the "Beaches."

Entertainment

Bars and Nightclubs

Big Bop
651 Queen St. W.
☎*504-6699*
The Big Bop is packed
every night on weekends
with a young crowd (the
capacity is 800 people!),
who let loose to oldies on
the first floor and rock 'n'
roll, dance and house
upstairs. The decor is
eclectic to say the least.
This is a major meat mar-
ket for young adults.

Whiskey Saigon
250 Richmond St. W.
☎*593-4646*
Whiskey Saigon is one of
Toronto's consummate
dance halls. Retro, rap,
reggae and rock all have
their place here.

Brunswick House
481 Bloor St. W.
☎*964-2242*
Toronto's most popular
student hangout is the
Brunswick House. Big-
screen televisions, shuffle-
board, billiard tables, lots

of beer and a character
named Rockin' Irene are
the mainstays in this his-
torical building, the oldest
party spot in town. Jazz
and blues create a more
mellow atmosphere at
Albert's Hall upstairs.

Gay Bars

Woody's
467 Church St.
☎*972-0887*
Woody's is a popular
meeting place for gay
men. Set in the heart of
the gay village, the atmo-
sphere is casual and
friendly.

Boots
592 Sherbourne
☎*921-0665*
Boots is a popular and
intense dance bar fre-
quented by a gay and
straight clientele. Theme
nights include fetish nights
and other intriguing possi-
bilities.

Theatres

The Toronto Symphony
Orchestra and Toronto
Mendelssohn Choir both
perform in the exceptional
acoustic space of **Roy
Thompson Hall** (*60 Simcoe
St.,* ☎*593-4828*).

For **theatre**, **ballet** and **opera**
look into the offerings at
the following theatres:

Royal Alexandra
360 King St. W.
☎*872-3333*

Princess of Wales Theatre
300 King St. W.
☎*872-1212*

Pantages Theatre
263 Yonge St.
☎*872-3333*

Théâtre Français de Toronto
231 Queen's Quay W.
☎*534-6604*

Young People's Theatre
165 Front St. E.
☎*862-2222*

Massey Hall
178 Victoria St.
☎*593-4828*

Hummingbird Centre
1 Front St. E.
☎*872-2262*

Canadian Opera Company
239 Front St.
☎*363-8231*

For popular music
concerts:

SkyDome
1 Blue Jay Way
☎*963-3513*

Air Canada Centre
☎*872-5000*

Tickets for these and other
shows are available
through:

Ticketmaster
☎*870-8000*

Spectator Sports

The National Hockey
League's Toronto Maple
Leafs just moved into their
new digs at the Air Canada
Centre, where they will
play from November to
April. The play-offs follow
the regular season and last
right into June.

The Toronto Raptors of the
National Basketball Associ-
ation (NBA) also play at
the new Air Canada Cen-
tre.

The Toronto Blue Jays of
the American Baseball
League and the Toronto
Argonauts of Canadian
Football League (CFL) both
play at the SkyDome.

The Molson Indy car races
(☎*260-9800*) take place in
mid-July.

Ontario

Festivals and Cultural Events

Benson & Hedges International Fireworks Festival
Mid-Jun through Jul
☎442-3667

Du Maurier Downtown Jazz
late Jun
☎928-2033

The **Caribana** Caribbean festival, from late July to beginning of August, features the largest parade in Canada – it lasts 12hrs!

Canadian National Exhibition
late Aug to early Sept
☎393-6000

Toronto's **International Film Festival** (☎967-7371, *for tickets: Film Festival Box Office,* ☎968-FILM) at the beginning of September is becoming a truly star-studded event.

Shopping

Downtown Toronto is a shoppers' paradise; from big designers to discount bonanzas, there is certainly a store that has what you are looking for.

Shopping Areas and Malls

Kensington Market *(on Kensington St., north of Dundas St. W.),* vintage clothing and international foods.

Queen's Quay Terminal
(207 Queen's Quay) gift shops in Harbourfront.

Eaton Centre
Yonge, between Queen and Dundas St.
Huge shopping complex

Bloor Street and Yorkville Avenue are both lined with exclusive shops and boutiques including **Holt Renfrew** *(50 Bloor St. W.,* ☎922-2333) and **Hazelton Lanes** *(Hazelton, near Yorkville).*

Honest Ed's
581 Bloor St. W.
at the corner of Bathurst St.
☎537-1574
Garish yet delightful in all its neon splendour, Honest Ed's discount store opened for business more than 40 years ago, and is a Toronto institution. It is the flagship enterprise of philanthropist Ed Mirvish, the man behind the historic Royal Alexandra and The Princess of Wales Theatres.

General Bookstores

World's Biggest Bookstore
20 Edward St.
☎977-7009

Chapter's
110 Bloor St. W.
☎920-9299

Specialized Bookstores

Open Air Books and Maps
(travel)
25 Toronto St.
☎363-0719

Maison de Presse Internationale
(newspapers)
124-126 Yorkville Ave.
☎928-2328

Ulysses Travel Bookshop
(travel)
101 Yorkville Ave.
☎323-3609

Antiques

Harbourfront Antique Market
390 Queen Quay W.
☎260-2626

Antiques – Michel Taschereau
176 Cumberland St.
☎923-3020

Aboriginal Art

Arctic Canada
125 Yorkville, Queen's Quay Terminal
☎203-7889

The Guild Shop
118 Cumberland St.
☎921-1721

Southwestern Ontario

Southwestern Ontario was once inhabited only by the Huron, Erie, Petun and Neutral First Nations, and was highly coveted by the Iroquois, whose territory lay south of Lake Erie.

Once Europeans began arriving here, the situation erupted into a bloody war, which was at its worst between 1645 and 1655, when the Iroquois, armed with guns, attacked the other First Nations. By the end of the conflict, all but a handful of the tens of thousands of Hurons, Eries, Petuns and Neutrals living in the region had been wiped out, and the victorious Iroquois took over the territory. They did not stay for long, however; in the following years, other Nations, primarily the Mississaugas, succeeded in recapturing the land and in driving the Iroquois back to their original territory. Although their numbers had been diminished by armed conflicts and illnesses (influenza, smallpox, etc.) brought over by the Europeans, the First Nations remained in control of southwestern Ontario until the end of the 18th century, when the English began colonizing the region. Although relatively few Aboriginal people live in the area today, numerous tourist sites have been established in an effort to familiarize visitors with the culture of those who once inhabited this part of the province.

Most of the colonists were farmers who worked the fertile soil, gradually turning the region into Ontario's granary. Due to the unique microclimate on the shores of Lake Erie, they were able to plant vineyards and orchards as well. The population grew gradually, and lovely towns like London, Kitchener-Waterloo, Windsor and Hamilton developed. Finally, southwestern Ontario is also home to one of the natural wonders of the world, Niagara Falls.

Finding Your Way Around

By Car

Mennonite Country

From Toronto: Take Highway 401 to Kitchener-Waterloo.

Hamilton and Surroundings

From Toronto: Take the Queen Elizabeth Way (QEW).

The Wine Route

From Toronto: Take the Queen Elizabeth Way (QEW), which leads to Hamilton and St. Catharines.

London and Surroundings

From Toronto: Head west on Highway 2, which leads to London via Brantford.

The Far Southwest

From Toronto: Take the 401 West towards Chatham, then pick up the 40, which leads to the 3, the starting point of the tour.

Train Stations

Mennonite Country

Kitchener-Waterloo
126 Weber St.

Stratford
101 Shakespeare St.

Hamilton and Surrondings

Hamilton
1199 Waterdown Rd.
☎800-361-1235

London and Surroundings

Brantford
5 Wadworth St.

London
197 York

The Far Southwest

Windsor
298 Walker Rd.
☎800-361-1235

Sarnia
125 Green St.

Bus Stations

Mennonite Country

Kitchener-Waterloo
15 Charles St.
☎(519) 741-2600

Stratford
101 Shakespeare St.
☎(519) 271-7870

Hamilton and Surroundings

Hamilton
36 Hunter St.
☎800-387-7045

The Wine Route

St. Catharines
7 Carlisle St.

In summer, there is daily bus service between Niagara-on-the-Lake and both St. Catharines and Niagara Falls. If you don't have a car, the only way to get to Niagara-on-the-Lake during the rest of the year is by taxi.

Niagara Falls
4555 Erie Ave.
☎(905) 357-2133

London and Surroundings

Brantford
64 Darling St.
☎(519) 756-5011

London
101 York
☎(519) 434-3245

The Far Southwest

Windsor
44 University St. E.
☎(519) 254-7575

Sarnia
461 Campbell St.
☎(519) 344-2211

Practical Information

Area Codes: **519**, except for Hamilton and Niagara Falls: **905**.

Tourist Information Offices

Southern Ontario Tourism Organization
180 Greenwich St., Brantford, N3S 2X6
☎756-3230 or 800-267-3399
⇌756-3231

Southwestern Ontario Travel Association
4023 Meadowbrook Drive Suite 113, London, N6L 1E7
☎652-1391 or 800-661-6804
⇌652-0533

Exploring

Mennonite Country

This tour will lead you on the trail of the Mennonites, the first communities to colonize southwestern Ontario. These farmers, who came here from the United States to work the region's fertile land, were followed by other settlers, mostly of English, Scottish and German descent, who founded lovely towns.

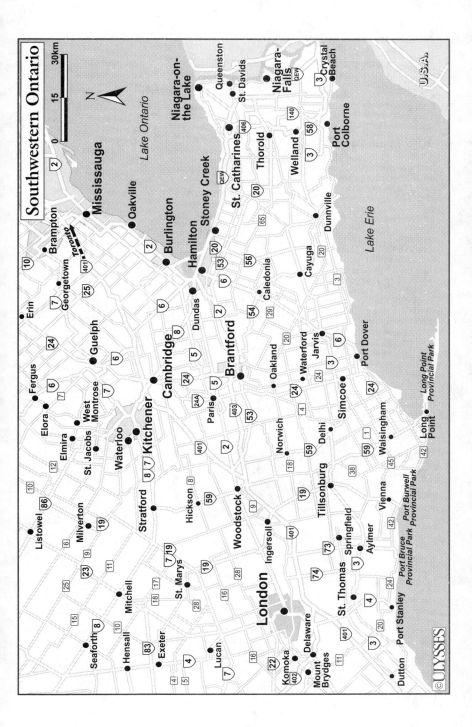

Despite all the years that have gone by, people here have managed to preserve some of their ancestors' traditions.

★★
Kitchener-Waterloo

In the wake of the American Revolution, those individuals who had declined to fight alongside the American troops were persecuted. The Mennonites, who had refused to take up arms for religious reasons, thus decided to emigrate to Ontario, where they could purchase fertile land at low prices. This first wave of immigrants arrived at the very end of the 18th century. Other colonists, mainly of German origin, also settled in the region, founding towns like Kitchener. Even today, a good part of the population of Kitchener-Waterloo is of German descent. In fact, every year the city hosts the largest Oktoberfest outside Germany.

Originally, Kitchener and Waterloo were simply neighbouring towns, but as they both grew, they merged into one large urban area and were officially joined. Kitchener-Waterloo thus has two downtown areas, one on King Street, near Erb Street East (Waterloo) and the other along King Street West, around Queen Street (Kitchener). However, there are places where the two towns still seem like

separate entities rather than a united whole. Kitchener-Waterloo is a pleasant city with several noteworthy tourist attractions.

Right near the Seagram Museum is the **Canadian Clay and Glass Gallery** ★ *(Erb St.)*, which houses several collections of ceramic and glass objects, including one donated by the Indusmin silica company. Also on display are a number of works by Canadian artists like Denise Bélanger-Taylor, Irene Frolic, Joe Fafard and Sadashi Inuzuka. The museum has occupied the present building, designed by Vancouver architects John and Patricia Patkau, since 1993.

City Hall stands at the corner of King and Queen, along with a shopping arcade known as Market Square, where the local **Farmer's Market** is held every Saturday morning (see p 445).

A visit to the **Joseph Schneider Haus** *($2,25; May to Sep, Wed to Sat 10am to 5pm, Sun 1pm to 5pm, closed for 6 weeks after Christmas; 466 Queen St. S., ☎742-7752),* the former home of a German Mennonite, will give you an idea how simply 19th-century Mennonites lived. Guides on the premises explain the rustic, austere lifestyle of members of this community.

Next, you will come to the **Kitchener-Waterloo Art Gallery** *(donations welcome; Tue, Wed, Fri and Sat 10am to 5pm, Thu 10am to 9pm, Sun 1pm to 5pm; 101 Queen St. N., Kitchener ☎579-5860),* whose collection, spread over seven rooms, is quite modest on the whole. Most of the works exhibited are paintings by contemporary artists. The gallery regularly hosts temporary exhibitions as well.

The **Woodside National Historic Site** ★ *($2.50; May to Dec, every day 9am to 5pm; 528 Wellington St. N., ☎571-5684).* William Lyon Mackenzie King, Prime Minister of Canada from 1921 to 1930 and from 1935 to 1948, lived here between the ages of five and 11. After touring the house, which has been restored and refurnished to look just as it did when Mackenzie lived here, you can take a stroll around the magnificent wooded grounds.

★
St. Jacobs

The charm of St. Jacobs, or Jacobstettel, as it used to be called, is in its main street, which is lined with craft shops whose windows alone are fascinating enough to capture your attention for hours. This Mennonite village, which has managed to preserve its old-time appearance, is overrun year-round by visitors lured here by the pretty shops and the peaceful atmosphere pervading the streets.

Those interested in learning more about the Mennonites can go to the **Visitors Centre** *($3; May to Oct, Mon to Fri 11am to 5pm, Sat 10am to 5pm, Sun 1:30pm to 5pm; Nov to Apr, Sat 11am to*

4:30pm, Sun 2pm to 4:30pm; 33 King St., ☎664-3518), which presents a half-hour film on the subject.

Twice a week, local farmers gather at the **St. Jacobs Farmer's Market** to sell farm produce and handicrafts. Not only is this a picturesque scene, but it's also the perfect opportunity to purchase some delicious local foodstuffs.

Elora

Elora was founded in 1832 on the banks of the Grand River, on a site suitable for a mill. This magnificent stone structure has since been converted into a charming inn that serves as a focal point for the local tourist industry. It is surrounded by shops in little stone houses, where you can purchase all sorts of knick-knacks.

Guelph

Scottish novelist John Galt, known for his works on Lord Byron, made several trips to Upper Canada for the Canada Company. He even lived here from 1826 to 1829, at which time he founded the town of Guelph (1827) on the shores of the Speed River.
To create a pleasant environment, he incorporated large parks and wide arteries into the town's design, something highly unusual in those days. Today, this dynamic city is known for its university, the **University of Guelph**, whose magnificent buildings are located south of the Speed River.

The **MacDonald Stewart Arts Centre** ★ (358 Gordon St., ☎837-0010), located on the university campus, has a lovely collection of Canadian and Inuit art, which is displayed in spacious, well laid-out rooms and complemented by informative written commentaries.

On the winding streets of downtown Guelph, you'll find several interesting commercial and public edifices, including **Guelph City Hall** ★ (59 Carden St.), which looks out onto a small public square. This elegant neo-Renaissance style building, designed by architect William Thomas, was erected in 1857.

An imposing church, **Our Lady of the Immaculate Conception** ★★, towers over City Hall. In the 19th century, most parishioners of Ontario's Catholic churches were Irish immigrants who had fled the potato famine and French Canadians who had come here from Québec in search of a brighter future. This church is the masterpiece of Irish architect Joseph Connolly, and owes its existence to an enterprising French-Canadian priest by the name of Father Hamel.

Since the families of the local communities were larger than average, the place had to be big. Its construction lasted from 1876 to 1926. Connolly opted for the Gothic Revival style of the cathedral of Cologne in Germany. The only part of the church that truly reflects a Germanic influence, however, is the upper apse at the back of the building, which is surrounded by numerous apsidioles.

Stratford

Tom Patterson, a shopkeeper with a passion for Shakespeare, came up with the idea of starting a Shakespeare festival (see p 444) here in 1951. Then a modest hamlet, Stratford has since become an enchanting little town, where crowds of visitors flock each year to see the plays and enjoy the charming setting. Its downtown area is very attractive, and splendid **Queen's Park** ★★ lies stretched along the banks of the Avon, where ducks, swans and barnacle geese paddle about. The park is also home to the **Festival Theatre**, where some of the plays are presented.

Our Lady of the Immaculate Conception

Ontario

Stratford

★
St. Marys

St. Marys, nicknamed Stonetown, is home to a number of magnificent old buildings that bear witness to its prosperous past. A few of these, including the **town hall**, built in 1891 of stone from the local quarries, are located along Church Street, in the centre of town. A little farther along, the **Opera House** is sure to catch your eye. Erected in 1879 by James Elliott, it originally had shops on the ground floor, with a theatre above, and was later converted into a mill. Since its renovation, it has housed shops and private apartments.

Hamilton and Surroundings

There are two large cities to the west of Lake Ontario: Toronto and Hamilton. The stretch of road leading through Toronto's suburbs and Hamilton's industrial outskirts is not very appealing, but you can't avoid it if you want to go to Niagara Falls. There are, however, a few noteworthy attractions along the way, including the Royal Botanical Gardens in Hamilton.

Burlington

The westernmost shore of Lake Ontario is occupied by Burlington to the north and Hamilton to the south. Set side by side and linked by Beach Boulevard, these two cities could almost be considered a single urban area. Burlington, the less populous of the two, is a peaceful residential town with little to offer in terms of tourist attractions, except perhaps for the little **Joseph Brant Museum** *($2.75; Tue to Fri 1am to 4pm, Sun 1pm to 4pm, closed Sat and Mon; 1240 North Shore E. Blvd.,* ☎*905-634-3556),* the last home of the Mohawk chief for which it is named.

★
Hamilton

Up until the arrival of the first colonists, who did not begin settling this area until the end of the 18th century, the site now occupied by Hamilton was the focal point of a conflict among First Nations. The Iroquois had virtually wiped out the Neutrals who had first inhabited the area. In turn, however, the Iroquois were driven out by white colonists. In 1815, George Hamilton drew up the plans for the

city. Hamilton flourished in the 20th century, thanks to the steel, automobile and home-appliance industries, among others. These industries left their mark on the city, whose surrounding landscape is vast, stark and dreary.

Hamilton is nonetheless pleasantly located on Lake Ontario, whose shores are lined with lovely parks, including **Bayfront Park** and **Dundurn Park** where you can enjoy a stroll or a bike ride, relax on a bench or at a picnic table, and watch the lively activity at the marina. Along with the residential neighbourhood on the hillside with its superb Victorian homes, this is definitely the prettiest part of town. Downtown Hamilton and its surroundings, along King Street, are not particularly attractive places to explore on foot, except for **Hess Village** ★, a cluster of elegant houses, shops and restaurants.

There are, however, a few interesting places to visit including the **Art Gallery of Hamilton** ★ *(free; Thu 11am to 9pm, Tue-Sun 11pm to 5pm; 123 King St. W.,* ☎*905-527-6610).* Open since 1914, it houses paintings, prints and other works of art. Its collection of contemporary art is particularly rich, and makes for some fascinating viewing. Unfortunately, however, the written commentary accompanying the pieces can be a bit vague.

The classically inspired, Georgian-style **Whitehern** *($3.50; Tue to Sun 1pm to 4pm; 41 Jackson St. E.,* ☎*905-546-2018)* was erected in the late 1840s. In 1852, one Dr. McQueston purchased it, and the splendid house remained in his family's

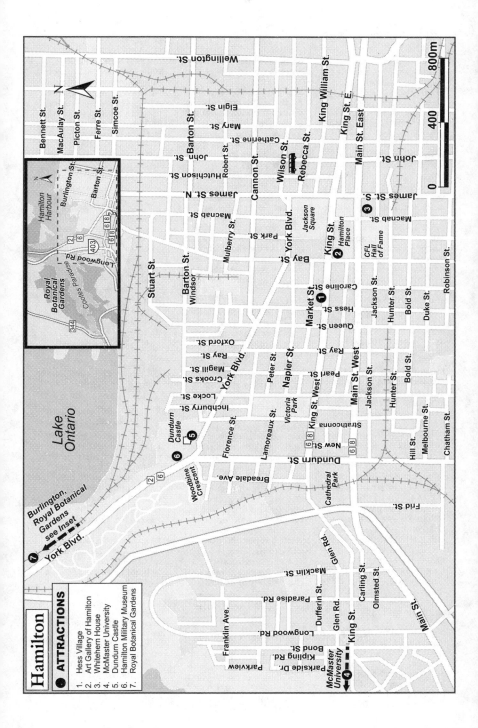

Hamilton

● ATTRACTIONS

1. Hess Village
2. Art Gallery of Hamilton
3. Whitehern House
4. McMaster University
5. Dundurn Castle
6. Hamilton Military Museum
7. Royal Botanical Gardens

Lake Ontario

Burlington, Royal Botanical Gardens see Inset

York Blvd.

Hamilton Harbour

Royal Botanical Gardens

Coote's Paradise

Longwood Rd.

Burlington St.

Barton St.

McMaster University

Parkside Dr.
Parkview
Franklin Ave.
Kipling Rd.
Bond St.
Longwood Rd.
Dufferin St.
Glen Rd.
Paradise Rd.
King St.
Macklin St.
Carling St.
Olmsted St.
Main St.

Frid St.
Cathedral Park
Breadale Ave.
Woodbine Crescent

Dundurn St.
New St.
King St. West
Strathconna
Main St. West
Jackson St.
Hunter St.
Bold St.
Hill St.
Melbourne St.
Chatham St.

Florence St.
Lamoreaux St.
Victoria Park
Peter St.
Napier St.
Pearl St.
Ray St.
Oxford St.
Inchbury St.
Locke St.
Crooks St.
Magill St.
Ray St.

Barton St.
Windsor
Stuart St.
Mulberry St.
Park St.
York Blvd.
Macnab St.
James St. N.
Hutchison St.
Robert St.
John St.
Barton St.
Cannon St.
Catherine St.
Mary St.
Elgin St.
Wellington St.

Bennett St.
MacAulay St.
Picton St.
Ferre St.
Simcoe St.

N

Jackson Square
Hamilton Place
Market St.
Hess St.
Queen St.
Caroline St.
Bay St.
York Blvd.
King St.
Wilson St.
Rebecca St.
King William St.
King St. E.
Main St. East
John St.
James St. S.
Macnab St.
CFL Hall of Fame
Jackson St.
Hunter St.
Bold St.
Duke St.
Robinson St.

0   400   800m

possession until 1968. Now open to the public, it has been restored to its original state, complete with period furnishings, and thus reflects the tastes of a prosperous 19th century family.

Founded in Toronto in the mid-19th century, **McMaster University** moved to Hamilton in 1928. The following year, construction was begun on **University Hall** ★, a lovely building similar to those found on the campuses of Oxford and Cambridge in England. Its facade is adorned with numerous gargoyles and masks symbolizing the various disciplines taught at the university.

Hamilton's most interesting attractions are hidden away outside the downtown area.

Dundurn Castle ★★ *($7, late May to early Sep, every day 10am to 4:30pm; noon to 4pm during the rest of the year, closed Mon until Victoria Day; 610 York Blvd.* ☎*905-546-2872),* generally viewed as the jewel of Hamilton, truly deserves to be called a castle. Its dimensions are impressive and its architecture is a skilful blend of English Palladianism and the Italian Renaissance style characteristic of Tuscan villas. It was built in 1835 for Sir Allan MacNab, Prime Minister of the United Provinces of Canada from 1854 to 1856. Restored, furnished and decorated as it was back in 1855, this castle, with its 35 opulent rooms, reveals a great deal about upper-class life in the 19th century. The former servants' quarters in the basement are perhaps the most fascinating rooms of all, since they offer an idea of how difficult life was for those

without which the castle wouldn't have functioned.

Another, smaller building on the castle grounds houses the **Hamilton Military Museum** *($2; Jun to Sep every day 11am to 5pm, Sep to Jun, Sun noon to 5pm, Tue to Sat 11am to 5pm, closed Mon; ☎905-546-4974).* Here, you will find a collection of the various uniforms worn by Canadian soldiers over the years.

You can enjoy a unique outing just a step away from downtown Hamilton, at the **Royal Botanical Gardens** ★★ *($7; every day 9:30am to 6pm; Plains Rd., at the intersection of Hwy. 6 and Hwy. 403; ☎905-527-1158),* where you can stroll about amidst luxuriant flowers and explore wonderfully preserved natural habitats. A large section of the park, which covers some 1,000ha in all, is known as "Cootes Paradise," a stretch of marshes and wooded ravines crisscrossed by footpaths. In addition to this untouched area, you will find a variety of gardens, including a rose garden, the largest lilac garden in the world and a rock garden, where thousands of flowers bloom in the spring. The Royal Botanical Gardens are enchanting year-round; in the winter, when the outdoor gardens are bare, you can visit the greenhouses, where various flower shows are presented.

The Wine Route

This tour covers the region to the west of the Niagara River along the U.S. border. Control over this area was once crucial as far as shipping on Lakes Ontario and Superior was concerned, and

the two forts that were built to protect it still stand on either side of the river. Nowadays, however, the region is best known for its wineries and orchards, and for the extraordinary Niagara Falls, which has continued to amaze people of all ages and inspire lovers and daredevils for decades.

St. Catharines

St. Catharines flourished with the construction of the Welland Canal. There have been four of these canals in all, the first of which was dug in 1829 and the last, still in use, in 1932. The Welland Canal, which links Lakes Ontario and Lake Erie, was designed to surmount a natural obstacle, the 99.5m Niagara Escarpment, which would otherwise be impassable. Forty-two kilometres long and equipped with eight locks, the canal enables ships to travel from St. Catharines to Port Colborne. There are viewing areas all along it, the most interesting being the **Lock 3 Viewing Complex** ★ *(free admission; the canal is closed to ships from Dec to Mar; take the*

Glendale Avenue exit from the QEW and follow the signs, ☎905-684-2361) in St. Catharines, where visitors can watch ships go through the lock from a large observation deck. At the neighbouring **St. Catharines Museum** (*$3; summer, every day 9am to 9pm; rest of the year, Mon to Fri 9am to 5pm; ☎905-984-8880)*, you can learn about the history of the canal and see a short documentary that explains how the lock works.

★★
Niagara-on-the-Lake

The history of Niagara-on-the-Lake dates back to the late 18th century, when the town, then known as Newark, was the capital of Upper Canada (1791 to 1796). Nothing remains of that time, however, for the town was burned during the War of 1812, which pitted the British colonies against the United States. After the U.S. invasion, the town was rebuilt, and graced with elegant English-style homes, which have been beautifully preserved and still give this community at the mouth of the Niagara River a great deal of charm. Some of these houses have been converted into elegant inns that welcome visitors to the celebrated Shaw Festival (see p 445), or those who are simply lured here by the town's English atmosphere.

After the American Revolution, the British abandoned Fort Niagara, which stands on the east side of the Niagara River. To protect their remaining colonies, however, they decided to build another fort. Between 1797 and 1799, Fort George was erected on the west side of the river. Within a few years, the two countries were fighting again. In 1812, war broke out, and the Niagara-on-the-Lake region, which shared a border with the United States, was in the eye of the storm. Fort George was captured, then destroyed in 1813, only to be rebuilt in 1815.

At the **Fort George National Historic Park ★** (*$6; Jul and Aug, every day 10am to 5pm; mid-May through Jun and Sep and Oct, every day 9:30am to 4:30pm; Nov to Mar, Mon to Fri 9am to 4pm; Apr to mid-May, every day 9:30am to 4:30pm; Niagara Parkway S., ☎905-468-4257)*, you can tour the officer's quarters, the guard rooms, the barracks and other parts of the restored fort.

There are a number of vineyards in the Niagara-on-the-Lake region, set amidst large, striped fields all along the side of the highway. Some of these offer tours.

Queenston

A pretty hamlet on the banks of the Niagara River, Queenston consists of a few little houses and verdant gardens. It is best known as the former home of Laura Secord.

Farther south, you'll reach the foot of Queenston Heights. If you're feeling energetic, you can climb the steps to the statue of Isaac Brock, a British general who died in this area during the War of 1812, while leading his men to victory. You will also enjoy a splendid **view ★** of the region.

A few kilometres before Niagara Falls, lie the **Niagara Parks Botanical Gardens** (*Niagara Pkwy., ☎877-642-7275, www.niagaraparks.com)*, a horticulture school whose beautifully kept gardens are open to the public.

Niagara Falls

The striking spectacle of Niagara Falls has been attracting crowds of visitors for many years, a trend supposedly started when Napoleon's brother came here with his young wife. Right beside the falls, the town of the same name is entirely devoted to tourism, and its downtown area is a series of nondescript motels, uninteresting museums and fast-food restaurants, accented by scores of colourful signs. These places have sprung up in a chaotic manner, and no one seems to have given a second thought to aesthetics. There's no denying that the Niagara Falls are a natural treasure, but the town has no real attractions except maybe for the casino.

Niagara Falls ★★★ was created some 10,000 years ago, when the glaciers receded, clearing the Niagara Escarpment and diverting the waters of Lake Erie into Lake Ontario. This natural formation is remarkably beautiful, with two falls, one on either side of the border. The American Falls are 64m-high and 305m-wide, with a flow of 14 million litres per minute, while Canada's Horseshoe Falls, named for their shape, are 54m-high and 675m-wide, with a flow of 155 million litres of water per minute. The rocky shelf of the falls is made of soft stone, and it was receding at a rate of one metre per year until some of the water was diverted to nearby hydroelectric power stations.

Ontario

The rate of erosion is now about 30cm per year.

It would be hard not to be impressed by the sight of all that raging water crashing down into the gulf with a thundering roar. This seemingly untameable natural force has been a source of inspiration to many a visitor. In the early 20th century, a few daring souls tried to demonstrate their bravery by going over the falls in a barrel or walking over them on a tightrope, resulting in several deaths. In 1912, such stunts were outlawed.

Victoria Park ★ was created in 1885, in order to protect the natural setting around the falls from unbridled commercial development. This beautiful green space alongside the river is scored with hiking and cross-country ski trails.

There are **observation decks** ★★★ in front of the falls, which can also be viewed from countless other angles:

The *Maid of the Mist* ★ ($10.65; May to Oct, departures every 30min; 5920 River Rd., ☎905-358-5781) takes passengers to the foot of the falls, which make the boat seem very small indeed. Protected by a raincoat, which will prevent you from getting drenched during the outing, you can view the American side of the falls and then the Canadian side, right from the middle of the horseshoe.

If you climb to the top of the **Skylon Tower** ($7.95; every day from 8am to 1am; 5200 Robinson St., ☎356-2651), you can view the falls ★★ at your feet, a truly unique and memorable sight. You can enjoy a similar view from the **Minolta Tower** ($6.95; every

day from 8:30am on; 6732 Oakes Prom., ☎356-1501).

The **Spanish Aero Car** ($5.50; year round, weather permitting, 9am to 9pm; Niagara Pkwy., ☎905-356-2241) offers a bird's-eye view of the falls from a height of 76.2m.

For a closer look at the falls, head to the **Table Rock Panoramic Tunnels** ($6.50; every day starting at 9am; Victoria Park, ☎905-358-3268), which lead behind the Canadian side.

How about soaring through the air over the falls? You can do just that thanks to **Niagara Helicopter** ($85; every day from 9am on, weather permitting; 3731 Victoria Ave., ☎905-357-5672).

An **elevator** transports visitors all the way down to the rapids (Great Gorge Adventure $5; year-round, weather permitting from 9am on; 4330 River Rd., ☎905-374-1221).

Niagara has countless museums, some of little interest. A number of them are located in the downtown area known as Clifton Hill.

If you have a little time to spare, visit the **Niagara Falls Museum** ($6.75; May to Sep, every day 9am to 10pm, Oct to Apr, 10am to 5pm; 5651 River Rd.), whose collection ranges from Egyptian mummies to souvenirs of daredevils who have tried to conquer the falls.

The **IMAX Theatre** ($7.50; May to Oct every day; 6170 Buchanan Ave., ☎905-374-4629) shows a giant-screen film on the falls.

If you'd like to forget about the falls for a little while and watch some

performing sea-lions, dolphins and whales instead, head to **Marineland** ($27.95; Apr to Oct, 10am to 5pm; Jul and Aug, 9am to 6pm; 7657 Portage Rd., ☎905-356-9565). The little zoo and carousels are sure to be a hit with the kids.

London and Surroundings

A major centre of Iroquois culture in Ontario, the London area boasts fascinating tourist attractions that enable visitors to learn about Iroquois history, customs and traditions. Over 150 years ago, the Iroquois began sharing this territory with English colonists, who were lured here by the fertile land. Once a modest hamlet, London now has a rich architectural heritage that makes it one of the loveliest towns in the region.

Brantford

This rather gloomy-looking town was named after Joseph Brant, whose Mohawk name was Thayendanegea. Its downtown area appears to have been abandoned by the local shopkeepers. Anyway, people come here to learn more about Iroquois culture, not for the buildings.

In the 17th century, the Iroquois Confederacy known as the Five Nations managed to wipe out the Nations living in southwestern Ontario and take over their land. In the late 1800s, however, the Mississaugas drove the Iroquois back to their original territory south of the Great Lakes.

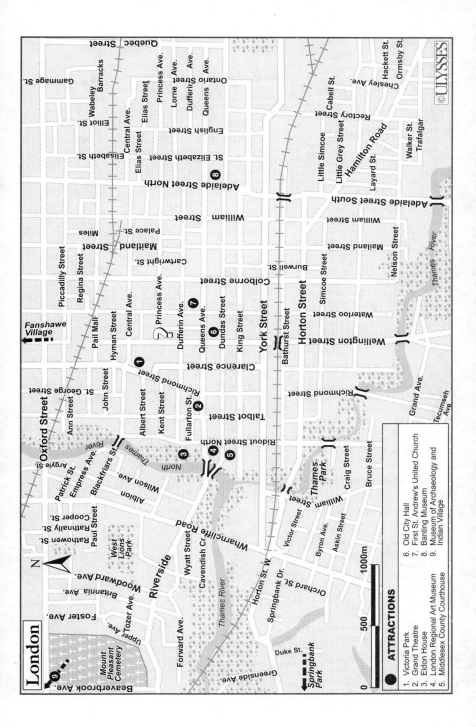

London

N

© ULYSSES

ATTRACTIONS

1. Victoria Park
2. Grand Theatre
3. Eldon House
4. London Regional Art Museum
5. Middlesex County Courthouse
6. Old City Hall
7. First St. Andrew's United Church
8. Banting Museum
9. Museum of Archaeology and Indian Village

0   500   1000m

Fanshawe Village

Springbank Park

Quebec Street

Gammage St.

Barracks

Wabeley St.

Elliot St.

Elias Street

Elias Street

Central Ave.

Elias Street

St. Elizabeth Street

Elisabeth St.

English Street

Princess Ave.

Lorne Ave.

Dufferin Ave.

Ontario Street

Queens Ave.

Adelaide Street North ❽

Hackett St.

Ormsby St.

Chesley Ave.

Cabell St.

Rectory Street

Little Grey Street

Little Simcoe

Hamilton Road

Layard St.

Walker St.

Trafalgar

William Street

Adelaide Street South

William Street

Maitland Street

Nelson Street

Thames River

Miles

Palace St.

Maitland Street

Cartwright St.

Colborne Street

Burwell St.

Simcoe Street

Piccadilly Street

Regina Street

Princess Ave. ❼

Dufferin Ave.

Queens Ave. ❻

Dundas Street

York Street

Bathurst Street

Waterloo Street

Horton Street

Wellington Street

Pall Mall

Hyman Street

Central Ave.

King Street

Richmond Street

Clarence Street

❶

St. George Street

John Street

Richmond Street

Fullarton St.

Talbot Street

❷

Oxford Street

Ann Street

Albert Street

Kent Street

Ridout Street North

Grand Ave.

Tecumseh Ave.

Argyle St.

Patrick St.

Empress Ave.

Blackfriars St.

Thames River

North

❸

❹

❺

Bruce Street

Craig Street

Thames Park

William Street

Victor Street

Byron Ave.

Askin Street

Cooper St.

Paul Street

Rathnally St.

Rathowen St.

West Lions Park

Albion Ave.

Wilson Ave.

Wharncliffe Road

Cavendish Cr.

Wyatt Street

Riverside

Forward Ave.

Thames River

Horton St. W.

Orchard St.

Springbank Dr.

Duke St.

Greenside Ave.

Woodward Ave.

Britannia Ave.

Foster Ave.

Tozer Ave.

Upper Ave.

Mount Pleasant Cemetery

Beaverbrook Ave. ❾

During the American Revolution, the Six Nations (the Tuscaroras had since joined the other five), based in the northeastern United States, declared themselves neutral, with the exception of a few warriors, like Joseph Brant, who fought alongside the British. Nevertheless, in the wake of the English defeat, all of the Iroquois had to leave the United States. As a gesture of thanks for the Iroquois's assistance during the war, Great Britain granted them 202,350ha of land along the Grand River. Two thousand Iroquois thus returned to the region, and 450 of them settled on the site now occupied by Brantford. In 1841, British colonists purchased back part of the land and took up residence here.

At the edge of town, you will see a small white church known as the **Royal Chapel of the Mohawks ★**, the oldest Protestant church in Ontario. It was erected by King George III to thank the Iroquois for their assistance during the American Revolution.

The **Woodland Cultural Centre ★** *($4; Mon to Fri 8:30am to 4pm, Sat and Sun 10am to 5pm; 184 Mohawk St., ☎759-2650, ext. 241)* traces the history of the Six Nations. Articles on display include tools, clothing, wampum (traditional belts) and handicrafts. A short visit here is a pleasant way to learn about Iroquois customs and traditions.

Alexander Graham Bell was born in Edinburgh, Scotland in 1847 and moved to Brantford with his parents in 1870. The **Bell Homestead** *($2.75; Tue to Sun 9:30am to 4:30pm; 94 Tutela Heights, ☎756-6220)*, where he lived from 1870 to 1881, is open to the public. It is decorated the same way it was in those years and houses a number of Bell's inventions.

To learn more about the colonization of this region, head to the **Brant County Museum and Archives** *($2; Wed to Fri 9am to 5pm, Sat 1pm to 4pm, Jul to Aug Sun 1pm to 4pm; 57 Charlotte St., ☎752-2483)*, which displays various tools and other articles that belonged to the early settlers. The museum is particularly informative in regards to Mohawk Chief Joseph Brant (1742-1807).

★★
London

The industrious Colonel John Graves Simcoe, the first Lieutenant-Governor of Upper Canada, played an important role in the development of the young British colony. It was he who decided to divide the present-day London region into townships. His plan also included the founding of London itself (1793), which was supposed to become the capital of Upper Canada, but never did. He also lured farmers here from the United States by selling them fertile land at low prices. These so-called "Eleventh Hour Loyalists," who arrived after 1791, included a number of Quakers and Mennonites (especially in the Kitchener-Waterloo area).

Unlike most towns that experience a period of slow, steady growth before any prestigious public buildings are erected, London sprang to life immediately with the construction of an impressive government edifice known as the **Middlesex County Building** *(399 Ridout St. N.)* on a previously undeveloped piece of land that had been scouted out in the late 18th century as a potential site for a large town. This picturesque building was begun in 1828, and the town grew up around it over the following years. London is home to a number of other magnificent 19th-century buildings, the most beautiful of which are included in the following walking tour.

The tour starts at **Victoria Park**, a large, beautiful stretch of greenery in the heart of town. After the Rebellion of 1837, the British troops who had been sent to London set up their quarters here. When they left in 1868, the town took over the land and turned it into a magnificent park.

At the corner of Richmond and Fullarton, you will see the **Grand Theatre** *(471 Richmond St., ☎672-8800)*, erected in 1901 on the site of the Masonic Temple and the Grand Opera House, which burned down in 1900. Since 1982, the building has undergone major renovations, and visitors can now take in a play here.

On the banks of the Thames River is the elegant white **Eldon House ★** *($3; Tue to Sun noon to 5pm; 481 Ridout St. N., ☎672-4580)*, the oldest private residence in London. Built for the Harris family in 1834, it is still decorated with 19th-century furnishings and is now open to the public.. On Ridout Street, you will find a number of other lovely homes dating back to the town's first few years.

If you keep heading south on Ridout, you'll come to the **London Regional Art and Historical Museums** (*free admission; Tue to Sun noon to 5pm; 421 Ridout St. N., ☎672-4580*), a large, rather unusual-looking building designed by architect Moriyama. It is shaped like a cross, with big picture windows that let in a lot of natural light. The art collection consists primarily of works by Canadian painters, while the second-floor rooms are devoted to an exhibit on the history of London.

London, England has the Thames and the Tower; London, Canada, the Thames and the **Middlesex County Courthouse ★** (*399 Ridout St. N.*). This former courthouse has a prison whose Gothic Revival architecture is reminiscent of a medieval castle with crenelated towers.

The Middlesex County Courthouse is a solid brick building covered with stucco made to look like freestone. Like Montreal's Notre-Dame Basilica, built around the same time, it is an excellent example of the first attempts at architectural historicism in Canada. In the case of the courthouse, medieval accents have been added to a fundamentally neoclassical building.

The central tower, added in 1878, was modelled after the tower of the Canadian Parliament in Ottawa.

Nineteenth-century Canadian and American courthouses were usually inspired by ancient Greek and Roman architecture. The more medieval style of the Middlesex County Courthouse can be explained by the association

between the building and the name of the town in which it is located, as well as by the building's dominant presence in a community once governed by citizens from rural Scotland, where traditional clan leaders lived in medieval castles enshrouded in the Highland mists.

At the corner of Wellington stands the **Old City Hall**, a neoclassical building erected in 1918 and enlarged by T.C. McBride in 1927.

Located in the midst of a pleasant stretch of greenery, the **First St. Andrew's United Church ★** (*350 Queens Ave.*) was originally built for one of London's many Presbyterian communities. A brick building erected between 1868 and 1871, it has all the traditional Gothic Revival elements typical of Protestant churches, including ogival openings and a steeple topped by a spire. Inside, the nave has an austere, exposed wooden skeleton. Nearby, you'll find the Neo-Renaissance manse, the former residence of the minister, Reverend Doctor.

As you continue along Waterloo Street, take the time to admire the magnificent Victorian homes dating from the 19th and early 20th centuries.

If you have a little time to spare, you can take Dundas all the way to Adelaide Street instead of turning onto Waterloo. This will give you a chance to see the little **Banting Museum** (*$3; Tue to Sat noon to 4pm; 442 Adelaide N., ☎673-1752*), devoted to the life and achievements of celebrated doctor Frederick Grant Banting (1891-

1941), who, along with Scottish doctor John Macleod, won the Nobel Prize in medicine in 1923 for discovering insulin.

After passing through a peaceful residential neighbourhood, you'll reach the **Museum of Indian Archaeology ★** (*$3.50; museum: summer, Mon to Sat 10am to 5pm; autumn, Wed to Sun 10am to 4:30pm; winter, Sat and Sun 1pm to 4pm, village: May to Aug, 10am to 5pm; 1600 Attawandaron Rd., ☎473-1360*), which focuses on the archaeological excavations that revealed traces of Aboriginal dating back to well over 10,000 years. Through a survey of this research, the museum teaches visitors about the history, way of life and traditions of the First Nations. Outside, you'll find a reconstructed Iroquois village, complete with a longhouse.

The Far Southwest

This tour covers the strip of land flanked by Lakes Erie and St. Clair. Located alongside the United States, its proximity has had a profound influence on the history of the region. Not only has the area often been the theatre of British-American conflicts, but it was also through here that many black slaves fled to Canada. The American influence is still very evident in this region, and some towns, like Windsor, live very much in the shadow of their imposing neighbour.

Kingsville

Each year, Kingsville is visited by crowds of barnacle geese that stop here during their migratory flight. This phenomenon can be traced back to one

Ontario

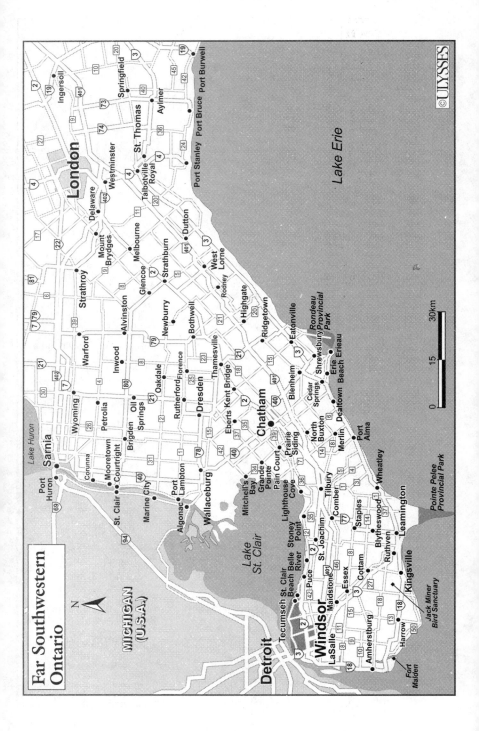

Far Southwestern Ontario

N

MICHIGAN (U.S.A.)

Lake Huron

Lake St. Clair

Lake Erie

Detroit

London

Sarnia

Windsor

© ULYSSES

0   15   30km

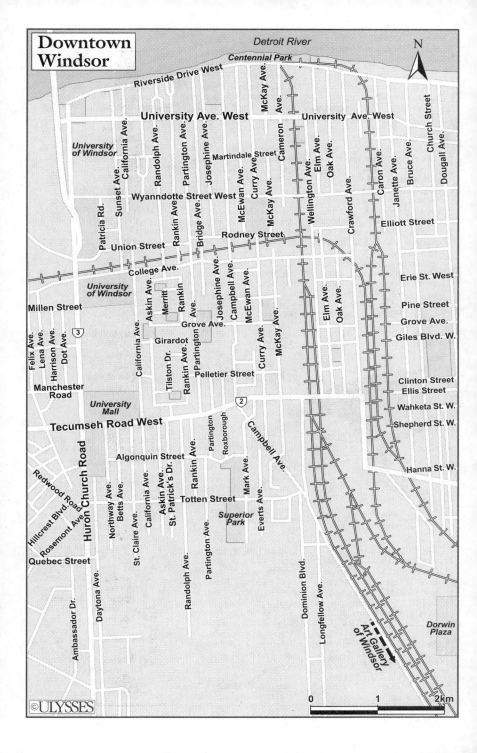

Downtown Windsor

Detroit River

Centennial Park

Riverside Drive West

University of Windsor

University Ave. West

University Ave. West

Patricia Rd.

Sunset Ave.

California Ave.

Randolph Ave.

Partington Ave.

Josephine Ave.

Martindale Street

McEwan Ave.

Curry Ave.

McKay Ave.

Cameron Ave.

Wellington Ave.

Elm Ave.

Oak Ave.

Crawford Ave.

Caron Ave.

Janette Ave.

Bruce Ave.

Church Street

Dougall Ave.

Wyanndotte Street West

Rankin Ave.

Bridge Ave.

Rodney Street

Elliott Street

Union Street

College Ave.

Millen Street

University of Windsor

Askin Ave.

Merritt

Rankin Ave.

Josephine Ave.

Campbell Ave.

McEwan Ave.

Curry Ave.

McKay Ave.

Elm Ave.

Oak Ave.

Erie St. West

Pine Street

Grove Ave.

Giles Blvd. W.

California Ave.

Grove Ave.

Girardot

Tilston Dr.

Rankin Ave.

Partington

Pelletier Street

Clinton Street

Ellis Street

Wahketa St. W.

Shepherd St. W.

Felix Ave.

Lena Ave.

Harrison Ave.

Dot Ave.

Manchester Road

University Mall

Tecumseh Road West

Partington

Roxborough

Campbell Ave.

Mark Ave.

Everts Ave.

Hanna St. W.

Redwood Road

Huron Church Road

Algonquin Street

Northway Ave.

Betts Ave.

California Ave.

Askin Ave.

St. Patrick's Dr.

Rankin Ave.

Totten Street

Partington Ave.

Superior Park

Hillcrest Blvd

Rosemont Ave.

Quebec Street

Daytona Ave.

St. Claire Ave.

Randolph Ave.

Dominion Blvd.

Longfellow Ave.

Art Gallery of Windsor

Dorwin Plaza

Ambassador Dr.

©ULYSSES

0   1   2km

Jack Miner, who began trying to attract these graceful winged creatures to his property in 1904. His efforts were successful, and this area became one of the first in Canada to be set aside for birds; it was designated a national bird sanctuary in 1917. Today, **Jack Miner's Bird Sanctuary** ★ *(free admission; Mon to Sat 9am to 5pm; north of Kingsville, west of Division Rd., ☎977-289-8328, www.jackminer.com)* is still open to the public, and you can go there to observe the wild geese. Open year-round, it attracts large numbers of birds in late March and from the end of October through November.

★
Amherstburg

The little town of Amherstburg, located at the mouth of the Detroit River, played an important role in local history when British troops were posted here at **Fort Malden** ★ *($2.50; May to Oct, every day 10am to 5pm; Nov to Apr, Sun to Fri 1pm to 5pm, closed Sat; 100 Laird Ave., ☎736-5416)* during the War of 1812, with orders to protect the English colonies in this area. Unfortunately, they were no match for the enemy forces, which succeeded in capturing the

fort and destroying part of it. After being returned to Canada in 1815, it was reconstructed, and still stands guard over the river – symbolically, at least.

The **North American Black Historical Museum** *($4.50; mid-Apr to late Oct, Wed to Fri 10am to 5pm, Sat and Sun 1pm to 5pm; 277 King St., ☎736-5434, www.Blackhistoricalmuseum .com)* was built in memory of the black slaves who fled to Canada from the United States. It tells the sad epic tale of the men and women who were taken by force from Africa and brought to America to work on plantations. Visitors will also learn about the underground railway slaves used to reach Canada.

★
Windsor

Some people say that Windsor's greatest attraction is the Detroit skyline on the horizon. This is not simply a snide remark; Detroit, which stands on the opposite shore of the river of the same name, really does have something magical about it when viewed from here.

At the end of the 17th century, the French decided to set up a small trading post on the banks of the Detroit River. Due to their friendly relations with local Aboriginal peoples the fort prospered. When France lost its American colonies to the British in 1763, however, the settlement was abandoned.

Later, in 1834, the English began settling the east bank of the river, founding a village named Sandwich, which later became

Windsor. The town enjoyed its first period of prosperity with the construction of the Welland Canal, which enabled boats to sail into Lake Erie, and then with the arrival of the railway. It wasn't until the beginning of the 20th century, however, that the town really flourished; its population grew from 21,000 inhabitants in 1908 to 105,000 in 1928. This boom was largely due to the local automobile industry. Today, this industrial city has a rather depressing downtown area. There are a few pleasant spots, however, especially along the river, where a number of parks have been laid out. These include the magnificent **Coventry Gardens** ★ *(Riverside Dr., at the corner of Pillette Rd.)*, adorned with beautiful flowers and the **Fountain of Peace**. Windsor also has a **casino** (see p 445).

If you are only staying in Windsor for a little while and can only visit one attraction, make it the **Art Gallery of Windsor** ★★ *(free admission; Tue to Sat 10am to 5pm, Sun noon to 5pm; 3100 Howard Ave., ☎969-4494)*, which has an amazingly rich collection of true masterpieces by great Canadian artists. These magnificent paintings and sculptures are complemented by clear, detailed written commentary on various facets of Canadian art. The museum also boasts a superb collection of Aboriginal art.

Willistead Manor *($4; open 1st and 3rd Sun in winter, every Sun and Wed July to Aug; call ahead 1899 Niagara St., ☎253-2365)*, a splendid Tudor-style house built for Edward Walker, son of distiller Hiram Walker, is one of the city's loveliest examples of early 20th-century architecture. Its opulent rooms are elegantly decorated with furnishings from the 1900s. If you'd like to spend a day outdoors without leaving Windsor, go to the **Ojibwe Park and Nature Centre** *(free admission 10am to 5pm daily;* ☎*966-5852)*, where you'll find nature trails crisscrossing the forest and the vast, tall-grass prairie.

Sarnia

Sarnia is a rather dreary town whose outskirts have a futuristic look because of the area's thriving petrochemical industry. Fortunately, the parks along Lake Huron and the St. Clair River make it easy to forget about the factories, which are no doubt useful but disfigure the landscape.

Parks and Beaches

The Far Southwest

At the southwestern tip of Ontario, a finger of land known as Point Pelee stretches into Lake Erie; this is the southernmost part of Canadian territory. Surrounded by marshes, this point is home to a variety of wildlife. Birds are particularly plentiful, especially in the spring and the fall, when a number of migratory species stop here. The area has been set aside as **Point Pelee National Park ★★** *(from Leamington, take Hwy. 33; R.R.1, N8H 3V4,* ☎*519-322-2365,* ⩰*322-1277)*, which has some pleasant hiking trails.

As an added attraction, there are long wooden docks that lead deep into marshes, making it possible to observe some of the nearly 350 species of birds found here in their natural environment. In September, monarch season, the park is filled with these orange and black butterflies. There are several beaches on Point Pelee as well.

Outdoor Activities

Hiking

In addition to hiking trails in the provincial and national parks, various other trails wind their way through southwestern Ontario, covering distances of several kilometres. **Hike Ontario** *(1185 Eglinton Ave. E., North York, M3C 3C6,* ☎*416-426-7362)*, the association that maintains these trails, can provide you with heaps of information.

The **Bruce Trail** is definitely the best known of all these trails, since it is the oldest and longest. It runs along the Niagara Escarpment, starting at Niagara Falls and ending at Tobermory, some 736km away. This trip obviously can't be made in a day and requires considerable preparation, but some wonderful surprises await hikers along the way. From Niagara, the trail follows the shoreline of Lake Ontario to Hamilton, heads north to

Collingwood, then crisscrosses through fields to Owen Sound. From there, it leads out onto the Bruce Peninsula, running alongside the cliffs and affording some spectacular views. For more information, contact:

Bruce Trail Association
P.O. Box 857, Hamilton
ON, L8N 3N9
☎*(905) 529-6821*
www.brucetrail.org

Cycling

The quiet, charming country roads on the southwest peninsula are perfect for cycling. You can enjoy a ride through the fields in the St. Jacobs area, tour the local vineyards or follow the shoreline of Lake Huron. In most towns, you'll have no trouble finding a bike shop for any necessary repairs.

The Wine Route

Niagara Bicycle Touring *(tours start at the Pillar & Post Hotel* ☎*905-468-1300)* arranges 3h bike trips through the Niagara-on-the-Lake region.

A road reserved for cyclists and pedestrians runs along the Niagara River (and the Niagara Parkway) from Niagara-on-the-Lake to Fort Erie, a distance of about 40km. Cyclists of all levels can enjoy this pleasant, peaceful ride.

Ontario

Bird-watching

Mennonite Country

The **Kortright Waterfowl Park** *($2; Mar to Oct Sat and Sun 9am to 5pm; 8km north of Hwy. 401; take Exit 195 and follow the signs, ☎824-6729)* is both a wilderness preserve and a research centre. This lovely, well laid-out area is a birder's paradise, with nearly 100 species to spot.

The Far Southwest

Large numbers of migratory birds stop alongside Lake Erie to gather their strength before setting out across this huge body of water and, as a result, outstanding bird-watching areas dot the shoreline.

Jack Miner's Bird Sanctuary *(north of Kingsville, west of Division Rd., ☎733-4034)* was created in 1904 to protect certain species of birds, particularly ducks and barnacle geese, which come here in large numbers.

Point Pelee National Park is another outstanding place to observe all sorts of birds – as many as 350 different species during the migration seasons. It is laid out so that visitors can see as many birds as possible, with trails leading into the forest and wooden docks crisscrossing the marshes.

Accommodations

Mennonite Country

Kitchener-Waterloo

There are several full comfort hotels in town, but if you're looking for a charming inn, the neighbouring villages have more to offer.

Walper Terrace Hotel
$89 bkfst incl.
ℜ, ⚿
1 King St. W., N2G 1A1
☎745-4321
The nearby Walper Terrace Hotel, by contrast, is a handsome building dating back to 1893, whose charms are perhaps a bit outdated. Although not as luxurious as the more modern hotels, it is nevertheless comfortable.

Sheraton
$99
≈, ⊛, △, ⚿, ⚲
105 King St. E., N2G 3W9
☎744-4141
≈578-6889
The Sheraton, located alongside Market Square, is unquestionably one of the most elegant places to stay in town. A modern hotel complex, it has spacious rooms and all the amenities. Large picture windows in the lobby look out onto a magnificent indoor swimming pool.

St. Jacobs

Countryside Manor
$70 bkfst incl.
39 Henri St., N0B 2N0
☎664-2622
The Countryside Manor is one of those places you'll want to come back to. The owners are friendly, and you'll feel right at home in the pleasant rooms of their charming little house. The breakfasts, both copious and delicious, are equally memorable.

Benjamin's Inn
$95 bkfst incl.
ℜ
17 King St., St. Jacobs, N0B 2N0
☎664-3731
Benjamin's Inn is a pretty building that has stood in the centre of town for over a century; it has been renovated in order to accommodate visitors. The rooms are furnished with antiques, and have a cozy charm that adds to the pleasure of being on vacation.

Jacobstettel Guest House
$125 bkfst incl.
ℜ
126 Isabella, N0B 2N0
☎664-2208
Stately trees adorn the garden of the Jacobstettel Guest House, a splendid Victorian house with about a dozen charming rooms, all decorated with antiques.

Elora

Elora Mill Country Inn
$150 bkfst incl.
77 Mill St. W., N0B 1S0
☎846-5356
≈846-9180
The stone mill by the falls around which the town of Elora grew is now the splendid Elora Mill Country Inn. The place still plays a central role in the community, for its excellent reputation has long been attracting visitors,

who come here for the tastefully decorated rooms and succulent cuisine.

Stratford

During the finest months of the year, when the Shakespeare festival is in full swing, the local hotels are often full. Fortunately, there are plenty of attractive B&Bs in town. You can reserve a room in many of these places through the Stratford Festival Accommodation Bureau (P.O. Box 520, Stratford, N5A 6V2, ☎273-1600 or 800-567-1600, ≈273-6173).

You might try your luck at one of the following B&Bs, which are all pleasant and centrally located:

Victorian Inn
$110
≈, ℜ, ☺, ൽ
10 Romeo St., N5A 5M7
☎271-2030
Despite its name, there's nothing very Victorian about the Victorian Inn, a big, nondescript white-brick building. It does, however, boast a superb view of the Avon River, as well as luxurious rooms and sports facilities.

On peaceful Church Street, the magnificent yellow brick **Stone Maiden Inn** ($130; 123 Church St., ☎271-7129) and the more modest but nonetheless charming **Maples of Stratford** ($85 to 95 sb; 220 Church, ☎273-0810) are two possibilities.

Bentley's Inn
$145
ℜ
99 Ontario St., N5A 3H1
☎271-1121
≈272-1853
Bentley's Inn, located in the heart of downtown Stratford, is a lovely brick building dating back to the

beginning of the 20th century. The rooms are well-kept and have an old-fashioned charm about them. This may not be the height of luxury, but it's still quite pleasant.

St. Marys

Westover Inn
$125
≈, ℜ
300 Thomas St., N4X 1B1
☎284-2977 or 800-COTTAGE
≈284-4043
www.westoverinn.com
Bentley's Inn, a true haven of peace, lies in a positively breathtaking setting in the heart of the countryside, surrounded by stately trees. If the location isn't enough to win your heart over completely, you're sure to be enchanted by the bright rooms, with their big windows and antique furnishings.

Hamilton and Surroundings

Hamilton

Hamilton has surprisingly few hotels and motels for a city of its size. The options are essentially limited to big chain hotels, which lack character, but are nonetheless quite comfortable. If you're on a tight budget and don't mind staying in a generic motel, you might be better off in Burlington.

Admiral Inn
$95
ℜ
149 Dundurn St. N.
☎(905) 529-2311
≈(905) 529-9100
The Admiral Inn has comfortable, modern rooms that are fairly typical of this kind of hotel, located on the way into the city. Its facade, on the other

hand, is more unique, with lots of picture windows, and as a result the lobby and restaurant are wonderfully bright and sunny.

Those who would rather stay downtown can choose from one of two Hamilton mainstays. The old **Howard Johnson Plaza Hotel** ($99; ≈, ℜ, ⌂, ⊛, ൽ, ☇; 112 King St. E., L8N 1A8, ☎905-546-8111, ≈905-546-8144) looks as if it has seen better days, but the rooms are nonetheless pleasant. If its old-fashioned look puts you off, head to the nearby **Ramada Hotel** ($99;≈, ⌂, ⊛, ൽ, ☇; 150 King St. E., ☎905-528-3451 or 800-228-2828, ≈522-2281), whose more modern looking architecture and lobby might be more your style.

The Wine Route

Niagara-on-the-Lake

If you have money to spare, you can really spoil yourself in Niagara-on-the-Lake, which has scores of top-notch inns. Visitors on a tight budget will have a harder time finding a place to stay, however.

One of the local B&Bs is a popular solution, especially at an affordable $60 or so per night for two people. For a complete list, write to:

B&B Association
P.O. Box 1515
Niagara-on-the-Lake
Ontario, L0S 1J0
☎(416) 468-4263

Moffat Inn
$89
ℜ
60 Picton St., L0S 1J0
☎(905) 468-4116
The Moffat Inn, located near the centre of town, is a charming little white

Ontario

building adorned with green shutters. It has about 20 well-kept rooms, some with an attractive fireplace.

Pillar and Post Inn
$220
≈, ☉, ℜ, ◉, △, ዿ
48 John St., L0S 1J0
☎*(905) 468-2123*
⇄*(905) 468-3551*
The vast, enchanting lobby of the Pillar and Post Inn boasts plants, antiques and big skylights. The hushed atmosphere will make you feel like staying here for hours. This is just a fore-taste of what you'll find in the rooms: beautiful wooden furniture, arm-chairs with floral patterns and even, in some cases, a fireplace. The place also has a gym, which can make a stay here that much more relaxing.

Queens Landing Inn
$220
≈, ℜ, ◉, △, ዿ
155 Byron St., L0S 1J0
☎*(905) 468-2195*
☎*800-361-6645*
⇄*(905) 468-2227*
With its wide facade adorned with four white columns, the Queens Landing Inn is somewhat ostentatious, but nonethe-less elegant, standing there proudly alongside the Ni-agara River. It has 137 large, tastefully decorated rooms, each with a whirl-pool bath and a fireplace. A first-class hotel by any standard.

Prince of Wales
$275
≈, ℜ, △, ◉, ዿ
6 Picton St., L0S 1J0
☎*(905) 468-3246*
☎*800-263-2452*
⇄*(905) 468-5521*
A real local institution, the Prince of Wales stands at the end of Queen Street, a commercial artery. This superb building, erected in 1864, has managed to re-tain its charm over the

years. In spite of its age, it remains extremely elegant, from its richly decorated sitting and dining rooms to its comfortable guest rooms. The place is being renovated in 1999.

Niagara Falls

Niagara Falls, southwest-ern Ontario's tourist mecca, has at least a hun-dred hotels, most mem-bers of big North Amer-ican chains, as well as a host of B&Bs. The local hotels are packed over summer vacation but empty during the low season, which is therefore a good time for bargain rates.

Youth Hostel
$21/person
4549 Cataract Ave., L2E 3M7
☎*(905) 357-0770*
The most inexpensive place in town is without question the Youth Hostel, an excellent option for visitors who are watching their pennies.

If you drive along the river before coming into town, you will pass a series of hotels offering modern standards of com-fort and a lovely view of the rapids. The **Comfort Inn** *($229; ≈, ℜ, ✷; 4009 River Rd. L2E 3E5,* ☎*905-356-0131,* ⇄*905-356-3306),* the **Days Inn** *($170; ≈, ℜ, ◉, △; 4029 River Rd., L2E 3E5,* ☎*905-356-6666 or 800-263-2543,* ⇄*905-356-1800)* and the **Best Western Fireside** *($225; ≈, ℜ, △; 4067 River Rd., L2E 3E4,* ☎*905-374-2027 or 800-661-7032,* ⇄*774-7746),* all in a row, have similar rooms, although those in the Fallsview (see further below) are equipped with gas-burning fireplaces.

Travelodge
$129
≈, ℜ, △
5234 Ferry St., L2G 1R5
☎*(905) 374-7771*
☎*800-578-7878*
Other hotels are near all the action without being right in the middle of it, thus offering the advan-tage of being located on a somewhat quieter street than Clifton Hill. The Travelodge and the **Quality Hotel** *($189; ≈, ℜ, △; 5257 Ferry Lane, L2G 1R6,* ☎*(905) 356-2842)* both have clean, even pleasant rooms.

Sheraton Fallsview Hotel
$159
6755 Oakes St., L2G 3W7
☎*(905) 374-1077*
⇄*(905) 374-6224*
At the very end of Oakes Street stands the beautiful Sheraton Fallsview Hotel, which definitely has the best location of all. Each of the rooms offers unim-peded views of the falls.

Old Stone Inn
$189
≈, ℜ, ◉
5425 Robinson St., L2G 7L6
☎*(905) 357-1234*
☎*800-263-6208*
⇄*(905) 357-9299*
www.oldstoneinn.on.ca
The Old Stone Inn is one of the few hotels in Niag-ara Falls with a little char-acter. The lobby and the restaurant are located in-side an old mill dating from 1904; the rooms, quite comfortable, in a more recent wing.

Days Inn Overlooking The Falls
$249
6361 Buchanan Ave., L2G 3V9
☎*(905) 357-7377*
The finest hotels stand at the top of the hill over-looking the falls, enabling guests to enjoy a beautiful view. They also offer the added advantage of a peaceful location, set away from the downtown area.

The Days Inn Overlooking The Falls has 239 comfortable rooms, the more expensive of which have views of the falls.

London and Surroundings

London

Rose House B&B
$50 sb
$65 pb
526 Dufferin, N6B 2A2
☎433-9978
For lodgings right near downtown London, yet with the peace and quiet of a residential neighbourhood, head to the Rose House B&B, which has pretty, well-kept rooms. If the place is full, you can try one of the other 20 or so B&Bs in town. A complete listing is available at the tourist office *(300 Dufferin Ave., ☎432-2211)*.

If you prefer a hotel but don't want to spend a fortune, try Wellington Street, outside the downtown area, which is lined with modern hotels with somewhat impersonal but nonetheless decent rooms. These include a **Days Inn** *($110; ≈; 1100 Wellington, N6E 1M2, ☎681-1240)* and the **Best Western Lamplighter** *($110; 591 Wellington, N6C 4R3, ☎681-7151, ⇄681-3271)*.

Idlewyld Inn
$120
36 Grand Ave., N6C 1K8
☎433-2891
The Idlewyld Inn, a splendid 19th-century house, has nothing in common with modern hotels. It has been renovated over the years, but has managed to retain its old-time charm. There are 27 rooms, each with its own unique decor.

Delta London Armouries
$135
≈, ℜ, ⊛, ◌, 🐕
325 Dundas, N6B 1T9
☎679-6111 or 800-668-9999
⇄679-3957
One of the top-notch hotels in town, the Delta London Armouries, is a converted armory topped by a tall glass tower. Although somewhat surprising at first sight, the combination is nonetheless harmonious. The rooms, furthermore, are impeccable.

The Far Southwest

Windsor

Windsor has neither a B&B association nor a youth hostel, so it can be hard to find an inexpensive place to stay in town. There are, however, a few average hotels with fairly reasonable rates, especially during the low season. Most of these are located on Huron Church Drive, a busy street with little to recommend it.

Holiday Inn
$115
⊛, ◌, ♿
1855 Huron Church Dr., N9C 2L6
☎966-1200
⇄966-2521
Closer to the downtown area, a stone's throw from the bridge to the United States, the Holiday Inn has pretty rooms with all the comforts and offers a wide range of amenities, including a pleasant restaurant and an indoor swimming pool. Good rates are available during the low season if you reserve three days in advance.

Hilton
$160
ℜ, ≈
277 Riverside Dr. W., N9A 5K4
☎973-5555 or 800-445-8667
⇄973-1600
A handsome brick and glass building, the Hilton boasts an excellent location by the riverside, steps away from the casino and downtown Windsor.

Quality Suites
$184
🐕, K
250 Dougall Ave., N9A 7C6
☎977-9707 or 800-668-4200
⇄977-6404
If you'd like to have your own kitchenette, try the Quality Suites, whose modern rooms are not very cozy but extremely well kept. Not far from the downtown area.

Restaurants

Mennonite Country

Kitchener-Waterloo

To make it easier for you to locate the following restaurants, we have specified whether each one is located in Kitchener or Waterloo.

Harmony Lunch
$
90 King St. N., Waterloo
☎886-4721
The facade of the Harmony Lunch looks as if it hasn't been touched since the place opened almost 50 years ago. Although this little restaurant looks rather uninviting at first, its "ham"burgers (literally made of ham) have won it a loyal clientele.

Ontario

Kings Bridge Crossing
$$
77 King St. N., Waterloo
☎886-1130
The dining room of the
Kings Bridge Crossing is
extremely cozy, with its
comfortable armchairs,
wallpaper and woodwork
– just the kind of atmo-
sphere that complements a
good meal. The menu lists
simple dishes like pasta,
roast beef and hamburg-
ers.

Golf's Steak House
$$$
598 Lancaster W., Kitchener
☎579-4050
If you're in the mood for
the kind of tender, juicy
steak that is a hallmark of
American cuisine, head to
Golf's Steak House. The
dining rooms are attrac-
tively decorated, and a
meal includes a steak (try
the New York Sirloin),
unlimited salad from the
salad bar and the soup of
the day.

St. Jacobs

Stone Crock
$$
41 King St.
☎664-2286
The Stone Crock, a Men-
nonite restaurant, has a
modest dining room and a
pleasant family atmo-
sphere. The setup is sim-
ple: an all-you-can-eat,
full-course meal including
soup, salad bar, a choice
of three main dishes (roast
turkey, fried chicken or
spareribs) and dessert for
$13.95 per person.

Benjamin's Inn
$$-$$$
17 King
☎664-3731
There's something capti-
vating about the atmo-
sphere at Benjamin's Inn,
and once you've taken a
seat in the dining room,
you'll feel like staying

there for hours. Perhaps
it's the rustic charm of the
place, or the lovely fire-
place. Or maybe it's the
meal itself, made up of a
succession of delicious
dishes. Whatever the rea-
son, you're sure to have a
wonderful time here.

Elora

Desert Rose Café
$
Metcalfe St.
The unpretentious Desert
Rose Café is the perfect
place for a lunchtime
snack, like a piece of
quiche or a salad, or sim-
ply to treat yourself to a
delicious dessert in the
afternoon. The carrot cake
and the butter tarts are
especially worthy.

La Cachette
$$$
13 Mill St. E.
☎846-8346
La Cachette, a little gem of
a French restaurant, is
situated alongside the
river in a pretty house
with two charming little
dining rooms – one on the
main floor, for smokers,
and the other on the sec-
ond floor, for non-smok-
ers. The menu is even
more appealing than the
decor, listing succulent
dishes like duck cutlet
with apples and calvados
and grilled lamb with
herbes de Provence. In
summer, you can enjoy
your meal outside, by the
riverside, comfortably
seated on the terrace.

River Mill Inn
$$$-$$$$
77 Mill St. W.
☎846-5356
Residents of Elora are truly
spoiled when it comes to
good restaurants. In addi-
tion to La Cachette, there's
the River Mill Inn, where
you can enjoy a delicious
meal in a dining room
with a lovely view of the

falls. The mouth-watering
menu lists a variety of
dishes, such as
Chateaubriand and lamb
with a cheese filling.

Guelph

There are all sorts of
charming places to enjoy a
delicious meal in Guelph,
which prides itself on
having over 100 restau-
rants. The following are a
few of the finest and most
pleasant ones on town.

Bookshelf Café
$
41 Quebec St.
☎821-3333
The aptly named Book-
shelf Café, located at the
back of a bookstore, is a
cozy little spot with big
picture windows, a re-
laxed, youthful atmo-
sphere and an appetizing
menu.

Woolwich Arms Pub
$-$$
176 Woolwich St.
☎836-2875
The Woolwich Arms Pub
is known for its delicious
"specialty burgers" and
attractive terrace, which is
a pleasant place to eat on
a fine summer day.

Georgian Creed's
$$-$$$
16 Douglas St.
☎837-2692
The Georgian Creed's,
hidden away on a quiet
street a few steps from
downtown Guelph, has a
beautiful decor and serves
delicious dishes that are
sure to satisfy your palate.

Stratford

Down the Street
$-$$
Ontario St.
With its wooden benches,
wrought-iron tables and
artists' drawings on the
walls, Down the Street is
more like a friendly café

where people come to chat than a restaurant. It does have an appetizing menu, however, listing simple, tasty dishes like chicken linguine and Santa Fe Spicy Grilled Cheese.

The Church
$$
at the corner of Waterloo and Brunswick
☎273-3424

The Church, a century-old converted church, has a unique ambiance that is truly irresistible. Add to that its delicious cuisine, and you've got the perfect recipe for a wonderful evening.

Fellini's
$$
107 Ontario St.
☎271-3333

Fellini's is a terrific, unpretentious restaurant decorated with checkerboard tablecloths. The menu lists a variety of pasta dishes, offering a good opportunity to sample some succulent Italian specialties.

Hamilton and Surroundings

Hamilton

Toby
$
King St., on Jackson Sq.

You'll have no trouble finding a place to eat downtown on King Street, which is lined with fast-food restaurants. One option is Toby, known for its big, tasty burgers.

Sundried Tomatoes
$$
at the corner of St. John and Main St. E.
☎(905) 522-3155

For something a little more sophisticated, you can try the classier Sundried Tomatoes. The extremely pleasant dining room is spacious enough so that

guests have plenty of elbow room. This place will appeal particularly to those with a penchant for oysters, which have top billing on the menu.

The Wine Route

St. Catharines

Beantrees
$
204 St. Paul St.
☎(905) 682-3357

The little bistro Beantrees must have the most eclectic clientele in St. Catharines. This is a perfect place for lunch, and manages to attract students looking for a place to chat and while away the time; business people, who stop in for a quick bite and shoppers lured inside by the impressive selection of tea.

Niagara-on-the-Lake

The Oban
160 Front St.
☎(905) 468-2165

The dining rooms at The Oban occupy a good part of the ground floor of a magnificent house. Some of the tables are set on a long veranda with big picture windows, and it is in this section of the restaurant (**$$$-$$$$**) that you can sample some of the succulent dishes that have conquered both the hearts and the palates of so many people. Another room inside (**$$**), is more of a pub, with pictures covering the walls, antique furniture, all sorts of knick-knacks, a piano and a fireplace. Seated in a captain's chair or on a love seat, plate on your knees or on a coffee table, you'll feel a bit like you're in your own living room. The menu lists simple dishes, such as chicken

cacciatore and fried shrimp.

Prince of Wales
6 Picton St.
☎(905) 468-3245

The elegant Prince of Wales has two dining rooms. The first (**$$$$**) and more ritzy of the two, has a refined menu and is harmoniously decorated with antiques. The second (**$$**) has a more relaxed atmosphere, a pub-style decor and a simple menu that's perfect for lunch, with selections like chicken fingers and salads.

Niagara Falls

Clifton Hill is lined with fast-food restaurants, which are devoid of charm, but will suit your needs if you're simply looking for a quick bite.

Tony's Place
$
5467 Victoria Ave.

For ribs or roast chicken, visit Tony's Place.

Old Stone Inn
$$-$$$
5425 Robinson St.
☎(905) 357-1234

For a refined meal, try the restaurant at the Old Stone Inn, where you'll find a lovely dining room in a building dating back to the turn of the century. The menu lists an excellent selection of specialties from a number of different countries.

Skylon Tower
$$$-$$$$
5200 Robinson St.
☎(905) 356-2651

Finally, if your top priority is a view of the falls, your best bet is the restaurant in the Skylon Tower. The menu features fish and meat dishes. Of course, you pay for the view, but what a view it is!

Ontario

London and Surroundings

London

Mario's
$
428 Clarence
☎*433-4044*
Mario's offers an appealing combination of spareribs and jazz.

Jewel of India
$$
390 Richmond
☎*434-9268*
The modest-looking Jewel of India deserves its name, for it truly is a little jewel as far as Indian cuisine is concerned, complete with curries, Tandouris and *nan* bread. Not to mention that you can enjoy a real little feast here without spending a fortune.

Marienbad
$$$
122 Carling St.
☎*679-9940*
The Marienbad has managed to keep up a good reputation over the years, attracting guests with its filling but tasty goulashes and *schnitzels*.

The Far Southwest

Kingsville

Vintage Goose
$$$
24 Main St.
The charming little Vintage Goose is without a doubt the most pleasant restaurant in town, with its appetizing menu and lovely dining room adorned with all sorts of knick-knacks and statuettes and containing a handful of wooden tables with pretty flowered tablecloths.

Windsor

Old Fish Market
$$
156 Chatham St. W.
☎*253-3474*
The Old Fish Market is decorated in an original manner with fishing nets, buoys, anchors and other such paraphernalia.

This nautical atmosphere will help put you in the mood for one of the poached, grilled or fried fish dishes on the menu, which are all served in generous portions.

Plunkette Bistro
$$-$$$
28 Chatham St. E.
☎*252-3111*
The orange columns on the facade of the Plunkette Bistro look somewhat out of place in this part of town. Nevertheless, the menu features simple but tasty pasta and beef dishes.

Entertainment

Mennonite Country

Kitchener-Waterloo

Kings Bridge Crossing
77 King N.
Waterloo
☎*886-1130*
At the end of the day, people flock to the Kings Bridge Crossing for a

good meal, then top off the evening with a drink. If you don't want to eat here, have a seat in the bar section. The place features live music on certain nights.

The **Oktoberfest**, the largest festival of its kind outside Germany, serves as a reminder that a good part of the local population is of German descent. It is a major event in this region, during which all sorts of activities are organized; stalls selling sausages, sauerkraut and beer are set up and a festive atmosphere prevails.

Stratford

Down the Street
Ontario St.
Down the Street is both a pleasant little restaurant and pub with a good selection of draft beer. Its unpretentious atmosphere makes for a great place to chat.

During the **Stratford Festival**, which takes place every year from May to November, various Shakespearean plays and other classics are presented. The festival is so popular that the town has no fewer than three theatres, the **Festival Theatre** (*55 Queen St.*), the **Avon Theatre** (*99 Downie*) and the **Tom Patterson Theatre** (*Lakeside Dr.*).

To reserve seats or obtain information on the festival calendar, call or write to:

Stratford Festival Box Office
PO Box 520, Stratford
ON, N5A 6V2
☎*273-1600*
☎*800-567-1600*
⇌*273-6173*

Hamilton and its Surroundings

Hamilton

Gown and Gavel
Hess St.
The Gown and Gavel, which occupies one of the lovely Victorian houses in Hess Village, is something of a local institution and has a steady student clientele.

The Wine Route

Niagara-on-the-Lake

The Oban
160 Front St.
☎ *(905) 468-2165*
The Oban is *the* place in town for a drink with friends, or even alone, ensconced in a comfortable armchair by the fireplace.

The internationally renowned **Shaw Festival** *($22-$65, reservations* ☎*905-468-2153 or 800-511-7429,* ≈*905-468-3804,* *www.shaufest.com/shaw.html)* has been held every year since 1962. From April to October, visitors can take in various plays by George Bernard Shaw at one of the three theatres in town, the **Festival Theatre**, the **Court House Theatre** or the **Royal George Theatre**.

Niagara Falls

Visitors to Niagara Falls who feel lucky and who are looking for a bit of a distraction can now find it at the **Niagara Falls Casino** *(5705 Falls Ave.,* ☎*905-374-5964 or* *888-946-3255,* ≈*905-374-5998)*. Spacious and housed in a beautiful modern building, it includes black-jack tables

and baccara as well as many slot-machines, and is sure to please all kinds of players.

London and its Surroundings

London

Aeolian Hall hosts year-round concerts by the **London Symphony Orchestra**. For reservations, call ☎**679-8778**.

The town also has some wonderful playhouses, including the **Grand Theatre** *(471 Richmond St.,* ☎*672-8800)*, where plays are presented year-round.

The Far Southwest

Windsor

Windsor is proud of its casinos. The **Casino** *(337 Riverside Dr. W.,* ☎*258-7878)* is housed in a charmless building It is located on the shores of the Detroit River, opposite the United States, and Americans make up the bulk of its clientele. Business is so good that another, even bigger casino opened in 1997.

Shopping

Mennonite Country

Kitchener-Waterloo

Market Square, located at the corner of King and Queen Streets, looks like your average shopping mall, but the place really comes alive every Satur-

day morning when the local **Farmer's Market** is held here. On the ground floor, you'll find all sorts of handicrafts, quilts, knitted goods and clothing; in the basement, a variety of foodstuffs, including honey, preserves, sausages, bread, cheese, etc.

St. Jacobs

St. Jacobs is full of **craft shops**, each one more enticing than the last. Rather than tell you where to go, we'll leave you the pleasure of poking around this maze of little stores on your own.

The local **Farmer's Market** *(Hwy. 17, at the west edge of town)*, where handicrafts, foodstuffs and livestock are sold, is a show like no other.

Guelph

There are some charming little shops on Quebec Street, including the **Bookshelf Café**, a restaurant and bookstore, and the **Maison de Madeleine**, where you can purchase unique and pretty decorative items for your home.

Stratford

You'll find some wonderful Aboriginal art (sculptures and prints) at **Indigena** *(151 Downie St.)*.

Finally, if you're looking for a souvenir of the festival, make sure to stop by the **Theatre Store** *(96 Downie St.)*.

The Wine Route

Niagara-on-the-Lake

Downtown Niagara-on-the-Lake is home to all

sorts of enticing shops, and a visit here wouldn't be complete without a little browsing.

J.W. Outfitters *(Queen St.)* looks like a simple souvenir shop, but inside you'll find terrific T-shirts and lovely posters of Aboriginal art.

Greaves *(Queen St.)* specializes in jellies, jams and marmalades, all of which are delicious.

For an unforgettable tasty treat, stop by **Maple Leaf Fudge** *(Queen St.)*.

London and Surroundings

Brantford

The little shop in the **Woodland Cultural Centre** *(184 Mohawk St.)* has a good selection of Aboriginal crafts, books and posters.

London

As far as Aboriginal art is concerned, **Innuit** *(201 Queen Ave., ☎672-7770)* is definitely one of the loveliest galleries in this part of the province. Inside, you'll find sculptures and lithographs by artists from all over Canada. A feast for the imagination, even if you can't afford to buy anything.

Novacks Travel Bookstore *(211 King St., ☎434-2282)* has a vast array of travel guides and outdoor equipment.

The Far Southwest

Windsor

Downtown Windsor is located along Ouellette Avenue, which is lined with all sorts of shops. The Art Gallery of Windsor shop, **AGW**, has a lovely and unique selection of merchandise. There are two branches, one at 500 Ouellette Avenue and the other at the museum *(310 Howard Ave.)*.

Northern Ontario

N orth of the 46th
parallel lies a vast, untamed stretch of land
dominated by forests, lakes and rivers.

It was by exploring these rivers that Europeans first penetrated deep into this wilderness and discovered two virtual inland seas, Lakes Huron and Superior. They also encountered Aboriginal peoples who survived on hunting and fishing and soon developed an interest in a luxury product in great demand in the Old World: fur. In the 17th century, the Europeans decided to set up trading posts so that they could do business with the northern Aboriginal groups who were masters in the art of hunting.

It wasn't until the 19th century, however, that these first settlements, which were scattered all over the territory, began to grow into small towns. The villages in Northern Ontario remained small and few in number even though a wave of French-speaking immigrants, many of whom were poor, began to settle in the region in the early 20th century after rich mineral deposits were discovered here,

Northern Ontario is bounded to the south by the Mattawa River and Lakes Huron and Superior. Its irregular landscape features a forest of leafy trees and conifers punctuated by rocky escarpments (typical of the Canadian Shield) to the south, and a boreal forest farther north. A tiny portion of the territory, in the extreme north, is tundra, distinguished by its sparse vegetation.

Finding Your Way Around

The territory covered in this chapter is vast, and its roads might cover dozens of kilometres before reaching a village. Driving is the best means of transportation here, although many towns and villages are served by buses. The train also goes to North Bay, Sudbury and a number of other towns farther north.

By Car

The 17 is the only highway that stretches all the way across northern Ontario. It starts in Ottawa and runs through North Bay, Sudbury, Sault Ste. Marie, Wawa and Thunder Bay, all the way to Kenora, on the Manitoba border.

If you are coming from Toronto, take the 440 to Barrie and then the 11 to North Bay.

By Bus

You can easily get from one town to another by bus, but it might seem like a long ride because there are frequent stops along the way.

Bus stations

Mattawa
Pine St., at the Shell service station

North Bay
100 Station Rd.
☎*(705) 495-4200*

Sudbury
854 Notre Dame Ave.
☎*(705) 524-9900*

Sault Ste. Marie
73 Brock St.
☎*(705) 949-4711*

Thunder Bay
815 Fort William Rd.
☎*(807) 345-2194*

Kenora
610 Lakeview Dr.
☎*(807) 468-7172*

By Train

A railway connects Toronto and North Bay: a second one runs along Georgian Bay, and goes from Toronto to White River via Sudbury.

North Bay
100 Station St.
☎*(705) 495-4200*

Sudbury
233 Elgin St., downtown
☎*800-361-1235*

Or, if you are arriving from Toronto or western Québec:
2750 Boul. LaSalle E.

By Ferry

If you are coming from the southern part of the province, you can reach Manitoulin Island aboard the ferry **Chi-Cheemaun** *(car $24.50, adults $11.20;* ☎*800-265-3163)*, which links Tobermory (at the northern tip of the Bruce Peninsula) to South Baymouth from spring to fall. The crossing takes 1hr 45 min. Reservations are accepted, but to keep them you must arrive 1 hr before boarding.

Summer Schedule

Tobermory-South Baymouth
7am, 11:20am, 3:40pm, 8pm

South Naymouth-Tobermory
9:10am, 1:30pm, 5:50pm, 10pm

Spring and Autumn Schedule

Tobermory-South Baymouth
8:50am, 1:30pm, 6:10pm (Fri only)

South Naymouth-Tobermory
11:10am, 3:50pm, 8:15pm (Fri only)

If you are coming from northern Ontario on Highway 17, you can get to the Island by taking Highway 6, which runs from Espanola to Little Current.

Practical Information

Area code **705**, except for **Pembroke 613** and the **Thunder Bay** and **Kenora** area **807**.

Tourist Information Offices

Almaquin Nipissing Travel Association
at the corner of Seymour St. and Hwy. 11, P.O. Box 351 North Bay P1B 8H5
☎*(705) 474-6634*
☎*800-387-0516*

Rainbow Country Travel Association 2726 Whippoorwill Ave. Sudbury, P36 1E9
☎*(705) 522-0104*
☎*800-465-6655*
≈*(705) 522-3132*

Algoma Kinniwabi Travel Association
553 Queen St. East Suite 1 Sault Ste. Marie, P6A 2A4
☎*(705) 254-4293*
☎*800-263-2546*

North of Superior Tourism
1119 Victoria Ave., Thunder Bay P7C 1B7
☎*(807) 626-9420*
☎*800-265-3951*

Ontario's Sunset Country Travel Association
102 Main Street, 2nd floor, ste. 201 P.O. Box 647M, Kenora, P9N 3X6
☎*(807) 468-5853*
☎*800-665-7567*

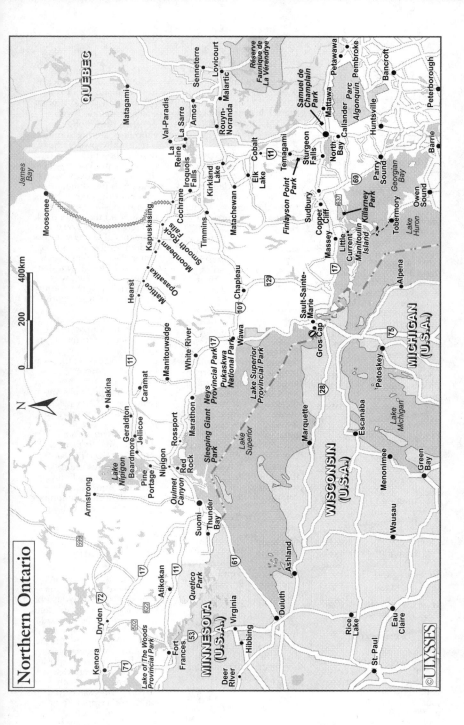

Northern Ontario

Exploring

On the Trail of the First Explorers

In 1615, French explorers Samuel de Champlain and Étienne Brûlé along with a crew of Hurons sailed up the Ottawa River, crossed Lake Nipissing and continued to Huronia, at the edge of Georgian Bay (Lake Huron). The French remained on friendly terms with the Hurons for the next two decades, during which time they travelled quite frequently to this region, thus familiarizing themselves with the entire area all the way to Lake Superior. Nevertheless, colonization was a slow process, and no real settlements – neither French nor English – were established here for several decades.

This route through the middle of Northern Ontario nonetheless played a major role in the province's early history, for it enabled the *coureurs des bois* (trappers) to develop lucrative trading relations with the Aboriginal people. This tour follows the trail of these first explorers, through the towns of North Bay, Sudbury, Sault Ste. Marie and Thunder Bay.

From Ottawa, take Highway 17 to Thunder Bay.

Pembroke

Pembroke, a rather nondescript town located on the banks of the Ottawa River, is the first stop on your journey north. Its main attraction is the river flowing alongside it, especially the rapids, which are popular with rafting buffs (see p 456).

Samuel de Champlain Park ★ *(Hwy. 17, between Mattawa and North Bay,* ☎ *705-744-2276)* lies along the banks of the Mattawa River, which early colonists used as a fur-trading route to travel deeper into Ontario, toward the Great Lakes. In memory of these explorers, the **Voyageur Museum** houses a small collection of objects related to their way of life, including an interesting replica of the kind of birch-bark canoe they used.

Most sports activities revolve around the Mattawa River, which is the nerve centre of the park. Visitors interested in hiking through the forest will find trails leading to the river and running alongside it for a fair distance, while those who know a bit about canoeing can paddle to their heart's content, either for a short trip or for a real adventure of several days. Backcountry campsites have been cleared throughout the park, which also has three campgrounds.

North Bay

Upon arriving in North Bay, you will be greeted by long, uninspiring boulevards lined with motels and large shopping centres. These streets, however, are not representative of this northern city, which boasts some lovely homes and a picturesque downtown area (Main Street between Cassell's and Fisher) that is unfortunately fighting a losing battle against local malls. The beauty of this town lies in its simplicity, its spruce little houses with their well-kept gardens, and above all in its location on magnificent Lake Nipissing. A pleasant **promenade** ★ studded with benches runs along the shoreline. During summer, a peaceful crowd gathers here at the end of the day to savour the last rays of the sun as it slowly disappears into the shimmering waters of the lake. Visitors who so desire can take a cruise from the town dock to French River. Local inhabitants also enjoy access to another lovely body of water, Trout Lake, which lies east of town. Not that long ago, this lake was coveted as cottage country by local well-to-do families.

Beside the tourist office, you'll see the former home of the Dionne family, a modest log house that was moved here from Callander. It now houses the **Dionne Quintuplet Museum** *(Adult $2.25, child $1.50; May to Oct every day from 9am to 5pm; Jul and Aug from 9am to 7pm; P.O. Box 747, Seymour St., P1B 8J8,* ☎ *(705)472-8480)*, which displays photographs of Cecile, Emily, Yvonne, Annette and Marie, as well as a number of their personal belongings.

★ Sudbury

Although a few trading posts were set up in this region in the early days of colonization, it wasn't until the arrival of the railroad in 1883 that Sudbury truly began to thrive. When the railroad was being built, the largest nickel deposits in the world were discovered here, along with sizeable deposits of uranium and copper, thus ushering in a period of major development for the town. The metals came from the Sudbury basin, which was probably created by the impact of a meteorite. To this day, mining plays an important role in the local economy.

The source of Sudbury's prosperity is apparent all over town. Verdant, leafy forests give way to barren, almost lunar landscapes. Over the past few years, all sorts of measures have been taken to restore some of the local greenery, but the traces left by the mining industry seem to be indelible. The town is therefore not particularly charming. Fortunately, some interesting projects have been launched to compensate for the drab scenery, and attractions such as Science North are well worth a visit.

Science North ★ ★ *($15; Jun to early Sep, 9am to 6pm; May and Oct, 9am to 5pm; Nov to Apr, 10am to 4pm; 100 Ramsey Lake, ☎(705)522-3701, 800-461-4898, www.sciencenorth.on.ca)* is an unusual-looking building shaped like a giant snowflake. Its architecture is appropriate, since its goal is to familiarize the public with the mysteries of science and nature. Inside, visitors will find a whole range of small-scale, thematic exhibitions, short films and interactive and educational games intended to make often complex scientific information easy to understand. Themes such as the biosphere, the atmosphere and the geosphere are explored in a manner that will satisfy the curiosity of both the young and the not so young. The top-floor laboratories are open to all, offering a unique opportunity to experiment with a variety of natural and scientific phenomena.

The centre also has an **IMAX** *($8)* theatre, which presents strikingly realistic films.

To top it all off, Science North boasts a lovely setting on Lake Ramsey, and a pleasant park has been laid out along the shore. Wooden footbridges run through a swampy area, offering visitors a chance to take a stroll through tall grasses inhabited by scores of birds and other little animals. Finally, you can set out on a lake cruise aboard the **Cortina** *($7.95)*.

Next to the mine, you'll see a giant nickel, a reminder that these 5¢ coins were once made with local nickel.

The **Path of Discovery** *(begins at Science North, ☎800-461-4898)*, a guided tour of the town and its surrounding area, enables visitors to learn about the geological history of the Sudbury basin. It also leads to the Inco Mine, one of the largest nickel producers in the world.

A few small museums display various everyday objects from the early 20th century. These places will appeal to visitors interested in local culture, but don't expect to find any treasures. It is always wise to call before stopping by.

The **Copper Cliff Museum** *(free admission; Jun to Aug, 11am to 4pm; at the corner of Balsam and Power)* displays a wide array of typical tools found in a miner's shack at the beginning of the century.

At the **Flour Mill Museum** *(free admission; Jun to Aug, Tue to Fri 10am to 4pm, Sun 1pm to 4pm; Saint Charles St)*, you can see the different machines used by

turn-of-the-century settlers and learn about their daily lives.

You can also visit the **Laurentian University Museum and Arts Centre** *(contributions welcomed; Tue to Sun noon to 5pm; corner of Nelson and St. John St.)*, set up in the former home of W.J. Bell, a timber magnate.

★★
Killarney Provincial Park

To get to the little town of Killarney, take Highway 63, which runs alongside lovely **Killarney Park** ★ ★ *(☎(705) 287-2800)*. This vast stretch of untouched wilderness extends into Georgian Bay and is strewn with scores of crystal-clear rivers and lakes, making it a canoeist's paradise. Exploring the park offers a chance to discover the magical landscapes that characterize the Canadian Shield, where lakes and rivers and birch and pine forests meet the cliffs of the La Cloche Mountains. The park has something for everyone, whether you want to canoe down a river with stretches of turbulent water or prefer to hike or ski along a trail through the woods. The sites at the campground are equipped with electricity, and a number of other spots have been cleared for wilderness camping. You can rent all the necessary equipment for a canoe trip in the little village of Killarney.

★
Manitoulin Island

Manitoulin Island has been inhabited by Aboriginal people for centuries –

Ontario

nearly 100 of them, according to archaeological excavations. Their presence here has not been continuous, however; in the 1700s, for reasons that are still unclear, local Aboriginal decided to leave the island and settle farther south. Over a century later, in the 1820s, Aboriginal groups were again settled on the island as more and more colonists began settling in southern Ontario. For years, only a handful of natives lived on this huge territory, one of the largest freshwater islands in the world, with an area 1,600km². Little by little, however, Manitoulin Island began to attract English colonists, and in the 19th century, Aboriginals had to negotiate with British authorities about sharing their land.

The Aboriginal presence is quite evident on the island, with Odawa, Potawotami and Ojibwa scattered across the territory. Many villages and lakes also bear Aboriginal names, such as Sheguiandah, Manitowaning and Mindemoya, which can be traced back to legends that still haunt these areas. The name Manitoulin itself refers to one such legend, according to which the island is the land of the great spirit **Gitchi Manitou**.

A peaceful island with charming little villages, picturesque hamlets and over a hundred lakes, this place will delight visitors looking for rural areas and tranquil natural surroundings, but has little to offer big-city goers. With its long, white-sand beaches, hiking trails and waters abounding in fish, it is a veritable playground for outdoorsy types.

★★
Sault Ste. Marie

The Ojibwa used to call this site Batawing in reference to its location on the banks of St. Mary's River, which forms a series of tumultuous waterfalls between Lake Huron and Lake Superior. The falls (*saults*) also prompted Jacques Marquette, a Jesuit priest, to name the mission he founded here Sainte-Marie du Sault. Its strategic location at the juncture of two of the Great Lakes made it an important supply stop for fur-traders, but up until 1840, it was essentially used to store merchandise. With the opening of the Bruce Mine in the 1850s, the town truly began to flourish.

Today, life in Sault Ste. Marie centres around the iron, steel and wood industries, as well as shipping, since large numbers of vessels pass through the local locks every day. You can watch these immense ships going through the locks from an attractive promenade along St. Mary's River. This park also attracts a lot of birds, especially barnacle geese. For a closer look at the lock mechanisms, take a tour with **Locks Tour Canada** (*$17; Roberta Bondar Dock*, ☎(705)253-9850).

The canal was built to bypass the rapids that lie between Lake Huron and Lake Superior, thus allowing boats to travel from one to the other. Construction was begun in 1895. With time, however, the canal became too narrow for boats to pass

through and needed to be reconditioned. In the process, it was altered to allow the passage of cruise ships as well. Also, the canal's banks were landscaped to create a park called the **Sault Canal National Historic Site**, which has 2km of well-maintained trails.

Sault Ste. Marie, or "the Soo," as it is popularly known, is a delightful place. A lovely, peaceful city with long, tree-shaded streets lined with opulent, old-fashioned houses, it has a unique charm and is no doubt one of the most attractive towns in Northern Ontario. Aside from its lovely downtown area and residential neighbourhoods, which you can explore at your leisure, it has a few interesting tourist attractions and is the starting point for a magnificent excursion to the Agawa Canyon.

The historical retrospective at the **Sault Ste. Marie Museum** (*$2; Oct To May, Tues to Sat 10am to 5pm, Sun 1pm to 4:30pm, June to Sept. Mon to Sun; 690 Queen St. E.,* ☎(705)759-7278) offers visitors a chance to step back 10,000 years in time. It begins with the first Aboriginals to inhabit the region and continues to the 20th century.

Among other things, visitors will find a reconstructed wigwam and a collection of everyday objects from early colonial times. These articles are not particularly valuable, but the place is nonetheless quite interesting.

The pretty stone **Ermatinger House** ★ *($2; Jun to Sep, every day 10am to 5pm; mid-Apr to May, Mon to Fri 10am to 5pm; Oct and Nov, 1pm to 5pm; 831 Queen St. E., ☎(705)759-5443)* was erected in 1824 by a wealthy fur trader named Charles Oakes Ermatinger as a gift for his Ojibwa wife. Built before the town developed, it is the oldest house in northwestern Ontario. Upon entering the house, which is decorated with antiques, you will be greeted by guides in period dress, creating the impression that you are reliving a bygone era.

The **Algoma Art Gallery** *(donation appreciated; Mon to Sat 9am to 5pm, Sep to Dec, Sat. 1pm to 4pm; 10 East St., www.artgalleryofalgoma.on.ca ☎(705)949-9067)* has two rooms containing works by artists from Canada and elsewhere. The collection is small, but some of the paintings are beautiful. The gallery also presents temporary exhibits.

Roberta Bondar Park was laid out on the shores of St. Mary's River, near downtown, as a tribute to Canada's first female astronaut, a native of Sault Ste. Marie. Its gigantic tent (1,347m²) is used for all sorts of events in both summer and winter, including the Winter Carnival.

At the end of Bay Street, you can't miss the big hangar that houses **The Canadian Bushplane Heritage Cen-**tre *($5; May to sept, 9am to 9pm, Oct to April, 10am to 4pm; 50 Pim St., ☎(705)945-6242, www.bushplane.com)*. Several bush planes are on display, most notably the Beaver, a sturdy craft used in the exploration of Canada's remote regions. However, bush planes are not the only models on display: airplanes used to fight forest fires are also featured. You can see these machines up close and even climb into some to gain a better understanding of what goes into flying an airplane.

The **Great Lakes Forestry Centre** *(free admission; Jul, Mon to Fri 10am to 4pm; 1219 Queen St. E., ☎(705)759-5740 ext. 2222)*, the largest centre of its kind in Canada, studies the development of Canadian forests. You can visit the greenhouses and laboratories where the research is carried out to find out more about the country's natural riches. Reservations are required.

Bellevue Park stretches alongside St. Mary's River east of town. It is very popular with local residents, who come here to stroll about and look at the bison, deer and other animals in the little **zoo**. The park also attracts large numbers of barnacle geese, who honk up a storm, detracting somewhat from the peacefulness of the setting.

For a memorable outing in the heart of the Northern Ontario wilderness, climb aboard the Algoma train for a visit to the **Agawa Canyon Park** ★★★ *($54; May to Sep, every day 8am; Jan to Mar, Sat and Sun 8am; the station is located in the Station Mall, ☎(705)946-7300, 800-242-9287)*. Comfortably seated in a charming little period train, you will wind through the forest, passing along hillsides and riverbanks and taking in some strikingly beautiful scenery that changes with the seasons, from an intense green in summer to orange and red hues in fall and finally, a dazzling white in winter. The train departs early in the morning and travels through the woods for over 3hrs before reaching its destination in the heart of the forest. Passengers then have 2hrs to stroll about, visit the falls or climb the hills. Afterward, you will head back to town with your head full of images of majestic landscapes. Reservations are recommended, particularly in the fall.

Wawa

Large numbers of barnacle geese (wild geese) flock to this region every year to nest, The whole sky can be filled with the birds as they pass overhead on their migratory journey. In fact, the town took its name from these wild geese, called "Wawa" in Ojibwa. A 9m-high statue of a wild goose is erected in the town as a tribute to these seasonal visitors. It also commemorates the inauguration of the Trans-Canada Highway in 1960.

Nipigon

A trading post was set up here at the mouth of the Nipigon River in 1678, making this the first site on the north shore of Lake Superior to be colonized by the French. Nipigon is located near a fascinating natural attraction, **Red Rock** ★, a series of 200m-high red cliffs whose colour indicates the presence of hematite.

★★
Ouimet Canyon

This breathtaking canyon, which is 107m deep and about 150m wide, can be viewed from two thrilling wooden lookouts. Stunted arctic flora is all that can survive in the perpetually cold temperature at the bottom of the canyon and along its steep sides.

★★
Thunder Bay

Aboriginals settled in the Thunder Bay region over 10,000 years ago. When the first Europeans arrived in the area, Ojibwa people were still living here. They never left this territory and still make up a significant portion of the population.

Judging this to be a strategic site, the French founded (Fort) Caministiquoyan here in 1679 to make it easier for merchants to trade in this region. The development of Northern Ontario was a slow process, however, and it wasn't until 1803, with the establishment of the Fort William Company, that people of European descent began settling permanently in this region. The fort soon became the hub of the fur trade, and travellers came here all the way from Montréal to purchase furs from trappers. This naturally had a positive impact on the region's growth, since more and more colonists began taking up residence here. During the 19th century, Fort William and Port Arthur developed side by side. They finally joined in 1970 to form Thunder Bay. Because of the way it was founded, the town still has two downtown areas; the southern centre is located around Victoria

and Brodie Streets, and the northern centre, between Algoma, Water and Keskus Streets.

Located about 100km from Manitoba, Thunder Bay is the last sizeable town in western Ontario. It is a unique place, boasting all the advantages of a modern, dynamic and multicultural city, yet located just a short distance from stretches of untouched wilderness that you can explore on foot, by canoe or on skis.

Thunder Bay lies on the shores of magnificent Lake Superior, to which it owes some of its prosperity. Its port, the last stop for ships on the St. Lawrence Seaway, is one of the busiest in Canada. If you go to the **port**, you will not only find some gigantic ships, but also 15 grain elevators used for storage, dotting the surrounding area for several kilometres. The biggest one of all is the Saskatchewan **Wheat Pool Terminal**. You can see a small part of the port by strolling along the promenade near the marina, behind the tourist office.

The promenade around the marina is very pretty, but for a closer look at the impressive ships or to view the port from another angle, take a seat aboard the **MV Welcome ★** (*$12.50; 10am departure from the marina; ☎807-344-2512*), which takes passengers on a tour of the marina, then follows the Kaministkwia River through town to Fort William. This pleasant excursion takes 2 hrs (one-way), with passengers returning to the marina by bus.

Old Fort William ★★ (*$10; mid-May to mid-Oct; half-hour guided tours available;*

on Hwy. 61, Broadway Ave. S., ☎807-577-2327) is a fascinating reconstruction of original Fort William as it appeared in the early 19th century. The world's largest reconstruction of a fur-trading post, it is an enchanting place to visit. The fort is made up of about 40 buildings, where guides in period dress (trappers, merchants and Ojibwa Indians) recreate everyday life in the 1800s, transporting visitors two centuries back in time.

The **Thunder Bay Museum** (*$5; 425 East Donald St., ☎807-623-0801*) displays a wide variety of objects related to local history, including articles used by early settlers, military and medical instruments and a collection of Aboriginal artifacts. It offers an excellent opportunity to learn more about the daily life of the First Nations peoples and first colonists to inhabit this region.

The **Thunder Bay Art Gallery** (*$2; Tue to Thu noon to 8pm, Fri to Sun noon to 5pm, closed Mon; on the campus of Confederation College; 1080 Keewatin St., ☎807-577-6427*) has some interesting Aboriginal works.

At the eastern edge of town, a **statue of Terry Fox** serves as a tribute to the courage of that young Canadian hero. Suffering from cancer, to which he had already lost a leg, Fox set off on a "Marathon of Hope" across Canada to raise money for research against the disease. He started in Newfoundland and made it across part of Canada, but had to stop here.

Centennial Park stretches along Lake Boulevard at the northeast edge of town; pretty trails follow the water and run through the woods. This is a pleasant place for the whole family, with picnic areas and a replica of a 1910 logging camp. Canoes and pedalboats can be rented at the lovely beach nearby.

Whole families go to **Chippewa Park** *(south of Hwy. 61B)*, located alongside Lake Superior, for picnics or to ride the carousels in the amusement park. Camping.

The 183m-high **Mount McKay Lookout** ★, stands next to Thunder Bay in the heart of the Fort William Ojibwa reserve. From the top, you can enjoy a magnificent view of the town and its surrounding area. Aboriginal crafts are sold here as well.

Ontario is rich in **amethyst**, the official stone of the province. The deposits in the Thunder Bay region were formed several million years ago by the intrusion of a boiling, silica-rich liquid into the granite here. As it cooled, the liquid formed crystals of this semi-precious stone, a type of quartz. You can tour the **Thunder Bay Amethyst Mine Panorama** *($3; mid-May to Oct 10am to 7pm; 58km east of Thunder Bay, East Loon Rd.; 807-622-6908)* and even rent tools so that you can chip off a few pieces for yourself.

You can also visit the **agate mine** *(take Hwy. 17 east, then Hwy. 527 north, ☎807-683-3595)*, the only one of its kind in Canada. You can tour the facilities and even mine your own agate.

Kenora

Kenora is located at the western edge of Ontario, a few kilometres from the Manitoba border. In the 19th century, both provinces tried to lay claim to this part of the territory. Ontario won out, and was officially granted the land in 1892. Kenora wasn't actually founded until 1905, with the union of three small municipalities, Keewatin, Norman and Rat Portage.

Deer

Its name was formed by combining the first two letters of these three names (Ke-No-Ra). The Kenora region is rich in natural resources, especially wood. The pulp and paper industry is thus the mainstay of the local economy. The local lakes and forests have also led to the development of another prosperous industry, tourism. This is a true paradise for fishing and hunting, not to mention lovely excursions in the great outdoors on the shores of Lake of the Woods.

Parks

Highway 17 runs through **Lake Superior Provincial Park** ★★ *(after Sault Ste. Marie on Hwy. 17, ☎705-856-2284)*, which covers some 80km of Lake Superior shoreline. A vast expanse of greenery, it boasts several magnificent beaches, as well as hiking trails that lead deep into the heart of the forest that blankets part of its territory. The park also contains petroglyphs carved by Ojibwa Indians over 9,000 years ago; the best place to see them is on Agawa Rock. Several other hiking trails wind through the park, sometimes revealing traces of the Ojibwa who lived here long ago. Also, fishing buffs will be pleased to know that fishing is allowed in the park's rivers and lakes, which abound with trout and pike.

Those wishing to spend a few days in the park can set up camp at the Agawa Bay or Interior campground *(reservations: P.O. Box 267, P0S 1K0, ☎888-668-7275)*.

Aside from a few extremely beautiful hiking trails, no road leads through **Pukaskwa National Park** ★ *(take the 17 to Rte. 627, a few kilometres before Marathon; ☎807-229-0801 ext. 242)*, which is still more or less untouched. Some of these lead to stunning panoramas, among them the magnificent nearly 60-km-long **Coastal Hiking Trail** ★★. The park covers 1,878 km² and is scored with rivers that are perfect for canoeing and kayaking. The park also protects a vast stretch of boreal forest. The cold temperatures generated by the lake affect the vegetation here; spruce is predominant in some areas, while only alpine species are able to survive in others. For some interesting information on the local vegetation, stop by the **Hattie Cove Interpretive Centre**, which is the starting point for a number of canoe routes. Camping.

Neys Provincial Park ★ *(take Hwy. 17, then follow the signs that appear a few kilometres past Marathon, ☎807-229-1624)* covers a small area that might seem quite ordinary at first glance. However, it has one of the prettiest beaches in northern Ontario and a herd of caribou.

Right near Thunder Bay, on Lake Superior, **Sleeping Giant Park** ★ *(take Hwy. 17 then turn onto Rte. 587)* protects a rocky peninsula that was supposedly created by none other than Nanibijou, the "Great Spirit" of the Ojibwa. Legend has it that Nanibijou showed the Ojibwa the location of a rich silver mine in order to reward them for their loyalty. He insisted, however, that the existence of the mine remain a secret from the white man; otherwise he would turn into stone and let them all perish. Unfortunately, the secret leaked out. All the men were swallowed up by the waters of Lake Superior, and Nanibijou fell asleep and metamorphosed into a rocky headland, hence the name of the peninsula. Whether you believe the legend or not, there really is a silver mine here. Located about 40km from

Thunder Bay, the park is an excellent place to enjoy the region's striking natural beauty. Its trails lead through enchanting landscapes and offer some splendid **views** ★★ of the lake. The park also has some extremely pleasant beaches that are occasionally overrun by local townspeople on hot summer days. Visitors are welcome to camp here. In winter, when the area is blanketed with snow, about 40km of cross-country trails crisscross this magnificent territory.

Kakabeka Falls Provincial Park *(from Thunder Bay, take Hwy. 17, ☎807-473-9231 or 800-667-8386)* is located about 20km west of Thunder Bay. The park was created to protect the impressive Kakabeka Falls, which cascade 39m into the Kaministiquia River. *Coureurs de bois* knew about the falls, which presented a grave obstacle in their westward travels, forcing them to portage their canoes and all their goods. Needless to say, this was an arduous process, made even more difficult by the river's steep, rocky banks. You can still view these turbulent falls, which are now harnessed for a hydroelectric project. Apart from the falls themselves, the park has hiking and crosscountry ski trails, picnic areas and campsites.

Quetico Provincial Park *(take Hwy. 11 from Shabaqua Corners, ☎807-597-2735 or 807-597-4602)* covers a huge expanse of land along the Minnesota border. Its countless lakes and rivers have made it a big favourite with Ontarian canoeists. It is crisscrossed by nearly 1,500km of canoe routes along which

you can encounter a variety of animal species. There are also a number of hiking trails for those who prefer walking. Canoes can be rented at **Quetico North Tourist Services**: *P.O. Box 100, Atikokan, P0T 1C0, ☎807-929-3561.*

Lake of the Woods Provincial Park ★ *(take Hwy. 71 from Bergland, south of Kenora, then pick up the 600, ☎807-488-5531)* encompasses the magnificent lake after which it was named. This vast stretch of water has 105,000km of shoreline and attracts some remarkable avian species. With a little luck, you might spot a group of white pelicans or a majestic bald eagle. If the mood strikes you, you can take a walk on one of the many hiking trails along the shore or set out on the water to see a few of the 15,000 islands that stud the lake.

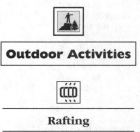

Outdoor Activities

Rafting

In the **Pembroke** area, thrill-seekers can brave the turbulent waters of the Ottawa and Petawawa Rivers aboard a rubber raft. The ride is especially exciting during the spring thaw, when the waters are at their highest. Rafting excursions are organized by a number of different outfits, including:

Esprit Rafting Adventures
P.O. Box 463, K8A 6X7
☎*(819) 683-3241*
≈*(819) 683-3641*

River Run
P.O. Box 179 Beachburg K0J 1C0
☎*(613) 646-2501*
☎*800-267-8504*

Wilderness Tour
P.O. Box 89, Beachburg K0J 1C0
☎*(613) 646-2291*
☎*800- 267-9166*

Hunting and Fishing

Salmon, trout, perch and muskie are just a few of the fish you can catch in the lakes and rivers of Northern Ontario. Some places are especially renowned, including Lake Nipissing and Trout Lake, in **North Bay**, as well as several other parks and reserves in northern Ontario.

Manitoulin Island is also very popular for fishing, since some good catches, including salmon, can be made off its shores.

A few parks in Northern Ontario also have something to offer hunting fans. Black bear, deer and moose are a few of the animals hunters can hope to bag, depending on the region. Some parts of northern Ontario, including the **Kenora** area, are reputed to be good for hunting.

Of course, permits are required for both hunting and fishing. To apply for one, or to obtain information regarding regulations, contact:

Ontario Ministry of Natural Resources
Information Centre, MacDonald Building, Office M1-73, 900 Bay Street, Toronto, M7A 2C1
☎*(416) 314-1177 (fishing)*
☎*(416) 314-2225 (hunting)*

Snowmobiling

A network of about 33,000km of snowmobile trails winds its way across the immense territory of Northern Ontario. These interconnected trails, enable snowmobilers to travel from town to town, reach small villages and ride through the snow-covered forest, all the while enjoying the majestic scenery around them. To plan a snowmobile trip or to obtain further information, call ☎*800-263-7533 or 800-263-2546.*

Accommodations

On the Trail of the First Explorers

North Bay

You'll have no trouble finding a place to stay in North Bay, which is the largest town in the region and has all sorts of hotels and motels.

Travelodge
$95 bkfst incl.
≡, 🐾, ♿
718 Lakeshore Dr., P1A 2G4
☎*(705) 472-7171 or 888-483-6887*
≈*(705) 472-8276*
The hotels and motels lining Lakeshore Drive are perfect for visitors who have a car and are planning to spend a few days in town. One good choice is the Travelodge. Its well-kept rooms have a certain charm about them and it's located just steps away

from the beaches on Lake Nipissing.

Sunset Motel Park and Cottages
$99
⊛, ◯, ℜ
641 Lakeshore Dr., P1A 2E9
☎*(705)472-8370*
☎*800-463-8370*
≈*(705)476-5647*
The nearby Sunset Motel Park and Cottages has charmingly decorated rooms and little cottages with fireplaces, making for a cozy atmosphere. It is also located just a stone's throw away from Lake Nipissing and Sunset Beach.

Days Inn
$100
≡, ◯
255 McIntyre St. W., P1B 2Y9
☎*(705) 474-4770*
The Days Inn is one of the few hotels in downtown North Bay. The building looks somewhat austere, but the rooms are perfectly adequate.

Sudbury

There is no youth hostel or charming B&B in Sudbury, but several international hotel chains are represented here, so comfortable accommodation is readily available.

Fairbanks Provincial Park
$20
follow Hwy. 144 for 55km
☎*(705) 965-2702*
You can pitch you tent at the Fairbanks Provincial Park campground, not far from town.

Laurantian University
$30/person
Ramsey Lake Rd.
☎*(705) 675-4814*
During the summer, you can rent a room at the residences of Laurantian University. The level of comfort is basic, of course,

Ontario

but quite decent for the price.

Sheraton
$81
≡, ≈, △, ⊛, ℜ, ⅅ
1696 Regent St., P3E 3Z8
☎ *(705) 522-3000*
☎ *800-461-4822*
⇌ *(705) 522-8067*
Right nearby stands the Sheraton, a renowned establishment with lovely rooms and all sorts of amenities, including a pool and a sauna.

Travelway Inn
$82
≡, ℜ
1200 Paris St., P3E 3A1
☎ *(705) 522-1122*
☎ *800-461-4883*
⇌ *(705) 522-3877*
In the same part of town as the Travelodge, Travelway Inn has clean, comfortable and pleasant rooms.

Venture Inn
$95
≡, ℜ
1956 Regent St., P3E 3Z9
☎ *(705) 522-7600*
☎ *888-483-6887*
⇌ *(705) 522-7648*
Another option is to stay in one of the hotels along Regent Street. You won't find any charming inns here, but some of the places have decent rooms. One of these is the Venture Inn, which is located near the highway, making it a convenient place to stop for the night.

Travelodge
$112
≡, ≈, ⊛, ⅅ, ✖
1401 Paris St., P3E 3B6
☎ *(705) 522-1100*
☎ *800-578-7878*
⇌ *(705) 522-1668*
The various hotels near the Science North complex each seem to be trying to outdo the other by offering as many amenities as possible and attractive modern rooms. The Travelodge

offers package deals including accommodation and tickets to Science North. Guests also enjoy the use of an indoor swimming pool.

Manitoulin Island

There aren't any big hotel complexes on Manitoulin Island, nor are any major North American chains represented here. You will find a number of B&Bs and campgrounds, however.

Little Current

Hawkberry Motel
$78
≡
P.O. Box 123, P0P 1K0
☎ *(705) 368-3388*
⇌ *(705) 368-3824*
On the outskirts of Little Current, the Hawkberry Motel consists of a number of long brick buildings with a red roof, whose aesthetic shortcomings must be overlooked. Inside, however, are large rooms with desks, hair dryers, large areas for your luggage and spacious bathrooms: in short, everything you need for a comfortable stay. The rooms are decent despite their lack of charm.

Gore Bay

Queen's Inn
$70
19 Water St., P0P 1H0
☎ *(705) 282-0665*
The Gore Bay marina is the site of laid-back activity, especially at the end of the day when the boats arrive at the docks. If you enjoy being near the water and a convivial atmosphere, stay at the Queen's Inn. This establishment occupies a splendid house facing the bay. Dating back to 1880, it has been renovated, preserving its

historic charm. The five well-maintained rooms are elegantly furnished, and overall the place is enchanting.

Sault Ste. Marie

Algonquin Hotel
$28, $21.25 for Hostelling International members
864 Queen St. E., P6A 2B4
☎ *(705) 253-2311*
There are a few inexpensive places to stay in town. One of the cheapest is the Algonquin Hotel, which is that much more of a bargain, since the modest rooms are well-kept, and the place is conveniently located near the bus terminal.

Brockwell Chambers
$75 bkfst incl.
183 Brock St., P6A 3B8
☎ / ⇌ *(705) 949-1076*
Brockwell Chambers is probably the most charming place to stay in Sault Ste. Marie. This B&B is located in a very pretty turn-of-the-century house. Its three rooms have been carefully renovated and are attractively decorated with antique furnishings. All the rooms are large and have their own bathrooms, providing privacy. Breakfast is served in an elegant dining room. This establishment is near downtown on a pleasant tree-lined street. Non-smoking environment.

Bay Front Quality Inn
$114
≡, ≈, ℜ, △, ⊛
180 Bay St. E., P6A 6S2
☎ *(705) 945-9264*
☎ *800-228-5151*
⇌ *(705) 945-9766*
The Bay Front Quality Inn is located near downtown and has a view of St. Mary's River. Although the decor is a little faded, the rooms are perfectly comfortable.

Holiday Inn
$114
≡, ≈, ℜ, △, ☉, ♿, 🐎
208 St. Mary's River Dr., P6A 5V4
☎ *(705) 949-0611 or 800-HOLIDAY*
≈ *(705) 945-6973*
The Holiday Inn underwent major renovations in 1998 to restore its former charm. It is now one of the best places to stay in town because of its pleasant interior and above all its location on the St. Mary's River. You can see the swimming pool from the lobby, the restaurant and the piano bar which, like some of the rooms, offer a view of the river.

Thunder Bay

The last major town in northern Ontario, Thunder Bay is a lovely place with a wide range of accommodations.

Longhouse Village
$16
R.R.13, 1594 Lakeshore Dr., P7B 5E4
☎ *(807) 983-2042*
Located in a delightfully peaceful setting, the Longhouse Village is actually a youth hostel with dormitories – the perfect place for visitors looking for a friendly atmosphere. If you have a tent, you can pitch it on one of the campsites ($16) instead.

Lakehead University
$30/two people
$20/person
955 Oliver Rd., P7B 5E1
☎ *(807) 343-8612*
During the summer, you can stay in the residences of Lakehead University.

Best Western Nor'Westers
$99
◔, ≈
R.R. 4, 2080 Hwy. 61, P7C 4Z2
☎ *(807) 473-9123 or 888-473-2378*
www.nor-wester_tb.com
The Best Western Nor'Westers is another good place to stay if you're looking for modern comfort. Its many amenities include an exercise room, a pool and rooms with fireplaces.

White Fox Inn
$129 bkst incl.
1345 Mountain Rd.
☎ *(807) 577-FOXX*
☎ *800-603-FOXX*
www.whitefox.com
The White Fox Inn is one of those B&Bs that you will remember for a long time. A relaxing atmosphere pervades the rooms, each of which is tastefully decorated with a different theme.

The Valhalla Inn
$129
1 Valhalla Inn Rd. P7E 6J1
☎ *(807) 577-1121*
☎ *800-964-1121*
≈ *(807) 475-4723*
The Valhalla Inn is one of the finest establishments in town. Travellers will delight in the lovely, spacious and newly renovated rooms. There is also a sports centre.

Kenora

Comfort Inn
$88
1230 Hwy. 17, P9N 3W8
☎ *(807) 468-8845*
☎ *800-228-5150*
The Comfort Inn is a convenient place to stay, with comfortable rooms for the price.

Restaurants

On the Trail of the First Explorers

North Bay

Old Chief
$$
May to Sept
Government Dock
☎ *(705) 495-1444*
Nothing quite beats taking in the tranquil waters of Lake Nipissing while dining aboard the boat Old Chief. This vessel has been anchored in North Bay since it was replaced by a more modern craft and was completely renovated and converted into a restaurant that specializes in fish dishes.

Churchill's
$$$
631 Lakeshore Dr.
☎ *(705) 476-7777*
If you're looking for something a little dressier, Churchill's is just the place. It serves what just may be the best prime rib in town.

Kabuki House
$$$
349 Main St. W.
☎ *(705) 495-0999*
The Kabuki House is a charmingly decorated little place that serves succulent Japanese specialties like *sukiyaki* in a romantic atmosphere. A delicious change from the usual burgers and fries.

Sudbury

Cooke House
$
65 Elm St.
☎ *(705) 673-9274*
The Cooke House has a very plain decor, but

Ontario

serves good family-style fare.

Vesta Pasta
$$
49 Elgin
☎(705) 674-4010
A modest-looking little house in downtown Sudbury, Vesta Pasta is one of those charming places that are such a pleasure to discover. Not only does it have an adorable dining room, but it also serves delectable Italian cuisine. You can't go wrong on the menu; the veal and pasta dishes are all masterfully prepared.

Manitoulin Island
Little Current

Old English Pantry
$
13 Water St.
Little Current
☎(705) 368-3341
The Old English Pantry is a relaxed, inviting place to linger over a cup of tea and scones.

Anchor Inn Hotel
$$
1 Water St.
☎(705) 368-2023
The Anchor Inn Hotel serves quite simply prepared meals, but fresh fish dishes figure prominently on the menu. Although the food is good, the decor is quite plain. However, the terrace is quite pleasant.

Sault Ste. Marie

Smart
$
473 Queen St.
☎(705) 949-8484
Smart is a charming little restaurant with big bay windows. Its interior consists of a few tables and some antique furniture. The warm and friendly atmosphere makes this the perfect place to go for

lunch and to try some of the delicious sandwiches and salads made with fresh ingredients.

Lone Star Cafe
$$
360 Great Northern Rd.
☎(705) 945-7610
The Lone Star Cafe is a real landmark in the Soo, with its big plastic cactuses, rubber iguanas and many photos on the walls. This cute restaurant serves Tex-Mex food like quesadillas and fajitas. The friendly ambiance and generous portions make dining here a pleasant experience.

Thymely Manner
$$$-$$$$
531 Albert St.
☎(705) 759-3262
The Thymely Manner is one of the finest dining establishments in town. Its red brick building is tastefully decorated, and the dining room is perfect for a romantic evening out. The menu will delight the most exacting gourmands, and Italian specialties, like seafood pasta or salmon with herbs, appear on the daily menu. The service is very attentive.

Thunder Bay

Hoito Restaurant
$$
314 Bay St.
☎(807) 345-6323
The Hoito Restaurant is well-known in Thunder Bay for its delicious, innovative cuisine. What makes the menu unique is an ingenious blend of Finnish and Canadian culinary traditions. The crepes on the breakfast menu are truly delectable.

Armando Fine Italian Cuisine
$$$
28 North Cumberland
☎(807) 344-5833
The atmosphere at some restaurants is so romantic that you can't help but have a lovely evening. This is true of Armando Fine Italian Cuisine, the perfect place to savour excellent Italian cuisine to the soothing sounds of violin music.

Harrington Court
$$$
170 North Algoma St.
☎(807) 345-2600
Harrington Court is located in an old, meticulously restored house with the perfect atmosphere for a delicious meal.

White Fox Inn
$$$-$$$$
take Hwy. 61
to 1345 Mountain Rd.
☎(807) 577-FOXX
The restaurant at the White Fox Inn, located just outside town, is worth the detour. Guests enjoy excellent food and a refined atmosphere, and the wine list will satisfy even the most demanding connoisseurs.

Entertainment

On the Trail of the First Explorers

North Bay

Arts Centre
at the corner of Main and Wyld
The Arts Centre often hosts entertaining shows.

Old Chief
Government Dock
The patio of the Old Chief bar is a lovely place to have a drink on warm

summer nights, especially in the early evening when you can watch the sun set over the lake.

Sudbury

Sudbury Theatre Centre
170 Shaughnessy
☎*(705) 674-8381*
The Sudbury Theatre Centre presents plays and comedy all year round.

Pat and Mario
1463 LaSalle
☎*(705) 560-2500*
Pat and Mario is known for its Italian cuisine, but its bar also attracts quite a crowd in the evening, and is a good place for a fun night out.

Manitoulin Island

Many Aboriginal families gather at the Wikemigong reserve for the **Pow Wow** that takes place at the beginning of August and includes many ceremonies and dances.

Sault Ste. Marie

You can find out all about the various cultural activities in town by phoning the **Arts Council of Sault-Sainte-Marie** *(☎(705) 945-9756)*. For tickets to various events, go to **Station Mall** *(293 Bay St., ☎(705) 945-5323)*.

Lone Star Cafe
$$
360 Great Northern Rd.
☎*(705) 945-7610*
Apart from serving excellent meals, the Lone Star Cafe is a great place to meet friends for an evening out.

Thunder Bay

Quality shows are presented at the **Thunder Bay Community Auditorium** *(450 Beverly St., ☎(807) 684-4444 or 800-463-8817)*.

Port Arthur Brasserie and Brew Pub
901 Red River Rd.
☎*(807) 767-4415*
The Port Arthur Brasserie and Brew Pub is a pleasant place with an interesting selection of imported beers. Things pick up considerably during the summer when everyone heads outside on to the pretty terrace.

Shopping

On the Trail of the First Explorers

North Bay

North Western
440 Wyld
North Western sells lovely Aboriginal handicrafts.

Manitoulin Island

Sheguiandah

The **Ten Mile Point Trading Post** *(1651 84th Ave. SW, Sheguiandah)* has a large selection of beautiful Aboriginal handicrafts. Mocassins, jewellery, sculptures and engravings are just some of the items sold here. If this is your kind of place, it is definitely worth stopping in.

Sault Ste. Marie

The train for Agawa Canyon Park leaves from the parking lot of the **Station Mall** *(293 Bay St.)* shopping centre where you can find various interesting shops like **Loon Nest**, which sells handicrafts and souvenirs.

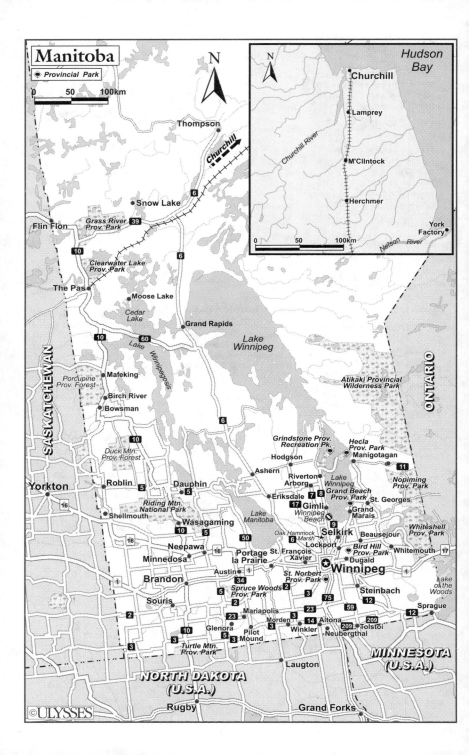

Manitoba

Mention the word

Manitoba and two images swiftly come to mind: professional hockey's Winnipeg Jets, who don't even reside here anymore, and polar bears – which definitely do.

The popular impression of Manitoba seems to be that it is mostly a place for passing through. But in fact, visitors have been coming to Manitoba – and staying – for more than a century. They have swelled its capital city of Winnipeg into Canada's fourth-largest city and created a surprising mix of immigrant culture more diverse than anywhere else between Vancouver and Toronto.

In the beginning, the province was occupied by several Aboriginal groups who gave the province its name. Manitou was a highly revered spirit among the First Nations who lived there, and the rapids of Lake Manitoba were believed to be his voice.

Once the English and French arrived, however, the story of Manitoba swiftly became the story of a running feud between two rival fur-trading companies: the English-owned Hudson's Bay Company and the French-Indian North West Company that emerged later and, for a time was a successful competitor.

The French-Canadian explorer Pierre de la Vérendrye made quite a mark on the region's fur trade. La Vérendrye was the first European to penetrate the grasslands of Manitoba. His trading posts established populations in what would eventually become the communities of Dauphin, The Pas, Selkirk and Portage la Prairie. This French influ-

ence is still evident today. In fact, the eastern Winnipeg suburb of St. Boniface, which was a separate city before it was amalgamated in 1972, is the largest French settlement in Canada outside of Québec.

The Metis made up a considerable part of this French-speaking population. The descendants of French trappers and Aboriginal people, the French-speaking, Catholic Metis lived on the Red and Assiniboine Rivers, in settlements that were annexed to Canada in 1869. Fearing for their language, education, land and religious rights, they were led by Louis Riel in their pursuit of responsible government for the territory. What little they had was slowly being taken away, leading settlers, both white and Metis, to set up their own provisional government. The outrage over the trial and execution of Ontarian Orangeman Thomas Scott for defying the authority of the said government forced Riel into exile in the United States. He did return to Canada, to Saskatchewan this time, to continue his fight and lead the Northwest Rebellion. Riel, the man who might have been the first premier of Manitoba, was executed for treason in 1885 and has been seen as a martyr by many ever since.

There are also considerable Ukrainian and Mennonite influences in Manitoba as well as a sizeable population of Icelandic immigrants. The beginning of the latter influx can be precisely dated. In 1875 a string of volcanic eruptions drove Icelanders to North America in search of another home. Many of them settled in the Interlake district, on the shores of lakes Winnipeg and Manitoba, where they traded in their skills at saltwater fishing for the taking of whitefish. Manitobans have gone to great lengths to preserve all these immigrants' stories, keeping their history alive through numerous museums and historic parks.

It is certainly true that the southern portion of the province is flat, levelled by great glaciers during the most recent Ice Age. Where thousands of square kilometres of uninterrupted tallgrass prairie once rolled under the press of the wind, colourful fields of hard wheat, flax, canola and sunflowers thrive today. In wet areas, pocket marshes teeming with resident and migrating waterfowl replace the fields.

But whatever Manitoba lacks in varied topography it makes up for with its fertile farmland and immense lakes that are home to countless birds. In fact, only about 40% of the province is flat. The rest is comprised of hills and waterways carved out of the Canadian Shield, a mass of hard ancient rock surrounding Hudson Bay that surfaces most obviously here and in northern Ontario. This land is shot through with deep pine forests, cliffs, and lakes. It's not unusual to see elk, caribou and bears in this rugged landscape.

In the sparsely populated Far North, tundra becomes predominant and the wildlife grows more spectacular still, with the singular light of the luminous Subartic summers, white whales and polar bears.

Finding Your Way Around

By Plane

Winnipeg International Airport is situated surprisingly close to the downtown area, only about 5km away.

Two major airlines handle traffic from both coasts: **Air Canada** (☎943-9361) and **Canadian Airlines** (☎632-1250) are both located in the airport.

By Bus

Greyhound Canada (☎800-661-8747) runs to the major towns and cities. In Winnipeg, the terminal is located at the corner of Portage Avenue and Colony Street.

By Train

VIA Rail's (☎800-561-8630 *from western Canada*) cross-country Canadian service passes through the province, usually stopping in Winnipeg around 5pm (westbound) or 12:50pm (eastbound); if the train is on time, it can be an excellent way to arrive in Winnipeg before dinner. Winnipeg's grand **Union Station** (*132 Main St.*), located right in the centre of downtown at the major intersection of Broadway and Main Street, is the largest station in Manitoba and the usual stopping point.

Smaller stations are located in Brandon, Portage la Prairie and other towns roughly parallel to the Trans-Canada Highway.

Public Transportation

Winnipeg Transit (☎986-5054), located in an underground facility at the corner of Portage and Main, runs a decent bus system around the city. Rides cost $1.55, slightly less if purchased in bulk-ticket blocks.

The city also maintains a transit information line (☎986-5700).

Taxis

Unicity (☎947-6611) is the main taxi company in Winnipeg.

Practical Information

Area Code: *204.*

Tourist Information

Winnipeg Tourism
279 Portage Ave., Winnipeg
☎*(800) 665-0204*
☎*943-1970*
www.tourism.winnipeg.mb.ca
Winnipeg Tourism runs a year-round information centre that is open week-days all year and seven days a week during the summer months.

Manitoba Travel Ideas Centre
Travel Manitoba, 24 Forks Market Rd., Winnipeg, R3C 3H8
☎*(800) 665-0040*
☎*945-3777*
www.travelmanitoba.com
The Manitoba Ideas Centre, beside The Forks Market, is open year round and has longer hours. In other parts of the province, tourism office hours vary a great deal, but the larger ones are open year round.

Post Office

The main **post office** (*266 Graham Ave.,* ☎*987-5054*) is located right downtown.

Safety

Manitoba is generally safe, although much of downtown Winnipeg becomes deserted after dark. Some caution is thus advised. The city's police department maintains 17 stations in six districts around the city: dial *911* for emergencies. There is also a **Royal Canadian Mounted Police** detachment (*1091 Portage Ave.,* ☎*983-5420*) in the city.

The **Canadian Automobile Association** maintains offices in the province's most populous areas, offering roadside assistance and information to members. Its offices are located at:

Winnipeg

870 Empress St.
☎*987-6161*

501 St. Anne's Rd.
☎*987-6201*

1353 McPhillips St.
☎*987-6226*

Brandon

20-1300 18th St.
☎*727-1394*

Altona

61 Second Ave. NE
☎*324-8474*

Climate

Summers are warm and dry. Winter, however, can bring dangerously low temperatures and blinding snowstorms. Temperatures can plunge to below -30°C, with the windchill and it can feel even colder. Thus, you should take the necessary precautions, especially if you are planning to drive outside of town in the winter. For updated weather forecast information in Winnipeg, call ☎*983-2050.*

Exploring

Downtown Winnipeg

Manitoba boasts the largest city in the prairies. Winnipeg, a bona fide metropolis of more than 700,000, rises improbably from the plains at the convergence of three rivers and is the likely starting point for most visitors' journeys around the province.

The city was settled by a Scotsman named Thomas Douglas, fifth Earl of Selkirk, as a 187,000km^2 settlement called the Red River Colony (a monument at the end of Alexander Avenue marks the exact spot). Douglas was an

Manitoba

emissary of the Hudson's Bay Company.

All roads in Winnipeg seem to lead to **The Forks** ★★ (*behind Union Station, corner of Mark St. And Broadway Ave.*), which have always been a focal point in the province. This fertile confluence of the Red and Assiniboine rivers was the original camping ground of the region's Aboriginal peoples, and later the base camp for the North West Company, the area's original fur-trapping concern. The company's headquarters (*77 Main St.*) still stand across a busy street from the original site. Today, however, The Forks is synonymous with the covered market of the same name.

Inside, dozens of stalls house purveyors of everything from fresh fish, candy and East-Indian food to frozen yogurt and handmade jewellery. There's even a fortune teller.

The riverwalk takes you on a lovely stroll along the banks of the Red River, and gives you a superb view of Saint Boniface, including its famous basilica, that lies just on the other side. There is a small marina that rents canoes and pedal-boats in the summer, and lots of green spaces perfect for a picnic. Many events take place on the plaza just outside the market, in the summer as well as winter, and several restaurants have terraces here, that are extremely pleasant on hot summer nights.

In the adjacent Johnson Terminal, a former rail station, the city's tourism office dispenses plenty of useful information. The **Manitoba Travel Idea**

Centre ★ is short on information but long on inspiration, especially for kids, who love the intriguing (if strangely juxtaposed) dioramas. The Terminal also contains more stores and coffee shops.

In the same complex but a different building is the **Manitoba Children's Museum** ★★★ (*$4; 45 Forks Market Rd.,* ☎*956-5437*), the only children's museum in western Canada. The building was once a railway facility, containing an engine house and train repair shops as well as a blacksmith's shop. Today, there's a whimsical hand at work, creating such displays as a fully functioning television studio and a diesel engine from the 1950s. Sports fans will be interested in the "Goals for Kids" display, commemorating the now-defunct Winnipeg Jets hockey team with various memorabilia.

The most recent addition to The Forks are the CanWest Global ballpark and the Manitoba Theatre For Young People, an imaginatively designed building on Forks Market Road. Inquire within about their family-oriented activities.

Adjacent to The Forks complex and facing downtown sits **Union Station** ★ (*132 Main St.*), designed by the same team of architects that designed Grand Central Station in New York City. The station was built during Winnipeg's golden age when the city was considered the "Gateway to the West," and thus an important economic centre. Today, its impressive grandeur seems a little out of place. The station features a huge dome plas-

tered inside in pink and white and pierced with arching half-moon windows. The walls are covered with the famous local Tyndall limestone.

It is only a few blocks west up Assiniboine Street or along the river to Manitoba's **Legislative Building** ★★★ (*free admission, Jul to Sep every day, 9am to 6pm, Oct to Jun Mon to Fri by appointment; 450 Broadway,* ☎*945-5813*). This is where the province's parliamentary business is taken care of. It's an impressive property that's full of interesting touches like limestone walls embedded with fossils, two bronze bisons, a bust of Cartier and more. Up top, the dome is capped with the 4m-tall **Golden Boy**, a French sculpture of a boy carrying a sheaf of wheat underneath one arm and extending a torch toward the sky with the other. Guided tours in French and English are available throughout the day during the summer. Behind "the Leg" are landscaped gardens containing a fountain and a statue of Louis Riel. The original and more controversial sculpture of this Metis leader now stands across the river, behind St. Boniface College.

Just down Assiniboine Avenue, **Dalnavert** ★ (*$4; closed Mon and Fri, Jun to Aug noon to 4:30pm, Sep to Dec and Mar to May noon to 4:30pm, Jan and Feb Sat and Sun noon to 4:30; 61 Carlton St.,* ☎*943-2835*) is an old brick Queen-Anne-Revival-style home built for Sir Hugh John Macdonald, son of former Prime Minister John A. Macdonald, and former premier of Manitoba. Its interest lies mainly in its period furnishings, and in the fact

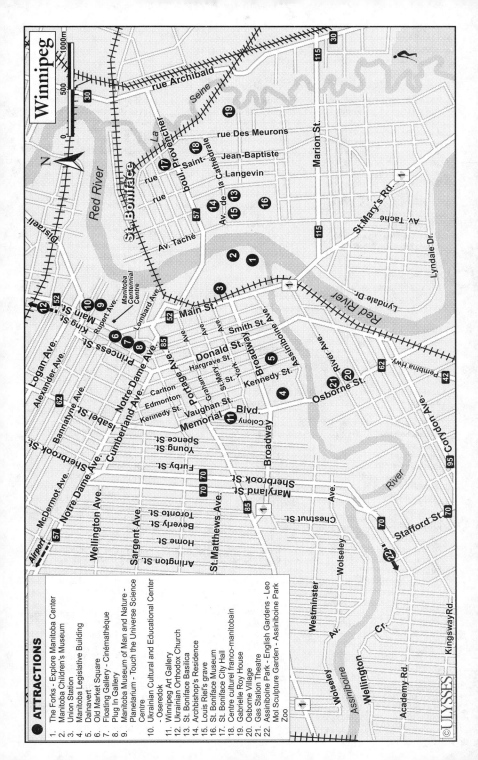

Winnipeg

ATTRACTIONS

1. The Forks - Explore Manitoba Center
2. Manitoba Children's Museum
3. Union Station
4. Manitoba Legislative Building
5. Dalnavert
6. Old Market Square
7. Floating Gallery - Cinémathèque
8. Plug In Gallery
9. Manitoba Museum of Man and Nature - Planetarium - Touch the Universe Science Centre
10. Ukrainian Cultural and Educational Center - Oseredok
11. Winnipeg Art Gallery
12. Ukrainian Orthodox Church
13. St. Boniface Basilica
14. Archbishop's Residence
15. Louis Riel's grave
16. St. Boniface Museum
17. St. Boniface City Hall
18. Centre culturel franco-manitobain
19. Gabrielle Roy House
20. Osborne Village
21. Gas Station Theatre
22. Assiniboine Park - English Gardens - Leo Mol Sculpture Garden - Assiniboine Park Zoo

© ULYSSES

that it was among the very first homes in the city to be built with such amenities as indoor plumbing.

The best way to get acquainted with downtown Winnipeg's history and architecture is to take one of the **Exchange District Walking Tours** (*Closed Mon, May to Sep every hour 10am to 3pm, depart from Old Market Square; $5;* ☎*942-6716,* ⇌*943-8741; exchbiz@mb.sympatico.ca*). The tours are 1.5 to 2 hours long.

The **Exchange District** ★★★, close to downtown, northwest of Portage and Main, is Winnipeg's former warehouse district. Today the smart industrial buildings have been given fresh coats of paint and new occupants, such as print shops, bookstores, theatre companies and the like have moved in.

The district surrounds **Old Market Square**, a small park with a stage for outdoor performances. The Fringe Festival (see p 486) is one of the events that makes use of this urban greenspace each year.

Some of the most striking buildings can be found by walking in the area of Albert Street and Notre Dame Avenue. The **Paris Building** (*269 Portage Ave.*) features many architectural flourishes such as scrolls, urns, Cupid figurines and other ornamental terra cotta work. The nearby **Birks Building**, across Portage (*at Smith St. and Portage Ave.*) displays an Egyptian mosaic.

Around the corner, away from the busy traffic of Portage Avenue, the **Alexander Block** (*78-86 Albert St.*) was the first Edwar-

dian-style construction in the neighbourhood and the only residence built here in that style. It was once a businessman's home. Finally, a few paces up Albert, the spectacular **Notre Dame Chambers** (*213 Notre Dame Ave.*), also known as the Electric Railway Chambers Building, is a terra cotta building with arches along the top, that's lit up brightly at night with some 6,000 white lights.

The Exchange District is also home to a number of small, independent galleries that specialize in contemporary art. Among these, the **Floating Gallery** (*218-100 Arthur St.;* ☎*942-8183*) is notable for its photograph exhibits. The gallery is located right on Old Market Square in the Artspace building that also houses the **Cinematheque**, a venue for independent films. You can always find truly avant-garde multimedia installations in the no-frills warehouse space at the **Plug In Gallery** (*286 McDermot Ave.,* ☎*942-1043, www.plugin.mb.ca*), only a few blocks away.

The city's finest museums are also very close to the Exchange District. Located within a complex of science attractions in the same downtown building, the **Manitoba Museum of Man and Nature** ★★★ (*$5; mid-May to early Sep 10am to 6pm; rest of the year, Tue to Fri 10am to 4pm, Sat, Sun, Mon and holidays 10am to 5pm; 190 Rupert Ave.,* ☎*956-2830*), is Winnipeg's showcase museum, a tour-de-force emphasizing Manitoba's natural and social history. Separate galleries teach the visitor about the province's geology, grasslands ecology, Arctic ecology – a polar bear diorama is the star here – and Aboriginal history. Other

special exhibit rooms describe the voyage of the English ship the **Nonsuch** (that established the Hudson's Bay Company's presence in western Canada in 1670) with a replica of the ship which visitors can board to explore the cabins and deck as well as the construction of the railroad to the far northern Manitoba port town of Churchill.

The tour ends with a very popular and well-designed two-storey recreation of late-1800s downtown Winnipeg, including a cobbler, chapel, movie theatre and much more. Museum officials are excited about a new display slated to open in May 2000, showcasing an impressive number of Hudson's Bay Company items. But even before it arrives, this museum is still a must-see. Other attractions on the lower floor of the same building include a **Planetarium** (*$4; Tue to Fri 3pm Sat to Sun 11am to 4pm; high season, every day, 11am to 6pm,* ☎*943-3139*) and the **Touch the Universe Science Centre** (*same hours as museum; $4*), where visitors can learn about science and technology through "hands-on" activities. It is especially popular with children.

Nearby, the **Ukrainian Cultural and Educational Centre** ★★ (*free; Tue to Sat 10am to 4pm, Sun 2pm to 5pm; 184 Alexander Ave. E.,* ☎*942-0218*), also known as **Oseredok**, houses a number of Ukrainian-related services and exhibits under one roof, including a library, art gallery, gift shop and outreach program offices. The museum, located on the fifth floor, shows typical Ukrainian-decorated Easter eggs and other folk arts such as carving and embroidery.

Housed in a striking triangular building of pale limestone, the **Winnipeg Art Gallery** ★★ (*$4, every day 11am to 5pm; free admission Wed 11am to 9pm; Winter closed Mon; 300 Memorial Blvd.,* ☎ *786-6641*) is best known for its vast collection of Inuit art and sculptures. Founded in 1912, the museum boasts everything from 16th-century Flemish tapestry to modern art. It is particularly strong on Canadian artists, decorative porcelains and silver, and collections acquired from the Federal Department of Indian and Northern Affairs and the Hudson's Bay Company. Aboriginal works are displayed in changing exhibits on the mezzanine level. There is an interesting gift shop as well as a pleasant rooftop restaurant with a terrace, open only at lunch.

In the city's north end, on north Main Street, the **Ukrainian Orthodox Church** ★★ is one of the city's most distinctive landmarks, decked in handsome burgundy and gold paint and possessing the trademark Ukrainian dome.

St. Boniface

Just across the Red River in St. Boniface, the distinctive ruins of the **St. Boniface Cathedral** ★★★ (*190 Ave. de la Cathédrale*) are a must-see. The walls are all that remain of the church, which burned in 1968, but are still very impressive. This was actually the fourth cathedral to stand on this spot. No wonder it remains a kind of shrine for Canada's largest French-speaking population outside of Quebec.

The giant circular opening in the stone once contained a giant roseate stained-glass window. The beautiful **Archbishop's residence** (*141 Ave. de la Cathédrale*) right next door is one of the oldest remaining stone buildings in western Canada.

In the cemetery in front of the basilica, **Louis Riel's grave** is marked by a simple red stone that belies the renown of the man who lies beneath it. Other stones on the lawn mark the graves of French settlers and Metis, including Chief One Arrow. There's also a glorious view of the river and the city skyline from this vantage point.

Behind the cathedral stands the silver-domed **St. Boniface College** (*200 Ave. de la Cathédrale*), established in the 1800s. A sculpture of Louis Riel stands at its northern entrance.

Next door to the cathedral, the **St. Boniface Museum** ★★ (*$2; Jul to Sep Mon to Fri 9am to 5pm, Sat 10am to 4pm, Sun 10am to 8pm, closed weekends Oct to Jun; 494 Tache Ave., St. Boniface;* ☎ *237-4500*) was built as a convent in 1846 and tells a number of fascinating stories about the city's French roots. It's the oldest building in Winnipeg and its largest log structure. Of particular note is the tale of the four Grey Nuns (*Les Soeurs Grises*) who founded the convent. They travelled some 2,400km by canoe from Montréal, taking nearly two full months to complete the arduous journey.

Other highlights in the museum include holy-water vessels, church objects and western Canada's oldest statue, a papier mâché Virgin Mary, decked in a

blue shawl. It was crafted by the artistic Sister Lagrave, one of the original Grey Nuns.

Strolling north along the river brings you to the Provencher Bridge where you can stop for a snack at the crêperie located right in the middle of the bridge (the former gatehouse). The bridge leads onto Provencher Boulevard, the main shopping and entertainment area in St. Boniface, that's lined with some interesting shops and locales. The old **St. Boniface City Hall** (*219 Provencher Blvd.*) and the modern **Centre Culturel Franco-manitobain** (*340 Provencher Blvd.*) are located on this street.

Fans of Gabrielle Roy can see the house in which she grew up and where several of her works, including one of her most famous novels *Rue Deschambault*, are set. Distinguished by a commemorative plaque, the **Gabrielle Roy House** at 375 Rue Deschambault cannot be toured since it's a private home.

East of St. Boniface, on the edge of the city, sits the ultra-modern **Royal Canadian Mint** ★ (*May to Aug Mon to Fri, 9am to 4pm; Sep to Apr Mon to Fri 10am to 2pm; 520 Lagimodière Blvd.,* ☎ *257-3359*) where all of Canada's circulation coinage is minted. Tours and observation areas give insight into the process.

Greater Winnipeg

South of the Assiniboine River but easily accessible from Memorial Boulevard by crossing the Osborne Bridge, **Osborne Village** is considered by some the city's hippest address with its trendy shops and restaurants. People come here to browse or meet for coffee, or to take in one of the varied shows at the **Gas Station Theatre** (*454 River Ave.*, ☎*284-9477*) that hosts everything from live theatre to music, contemporary dance and improv comedy.

Assiniboine Park ★★

(☎*986-6921*) is a popular walking and cycling destination. Its extensive tree-lined paths wind along the river of the same name, and are surrounded by wide open lawns where families come to picnic or play frisbee. During the winter, you can skate to piped music on the **Duck Pond** or use the cross-country ski trails.

The park's **English Gardens** are a wonderful surprise when in bloom: colourful carpets of daisies, marigolds, begonias, and more artfully arranged beneath dark, shaggy columns of spruce trees. This garden blends almost seamlessly into the **Leo Mol Sculpture Garden ★★**, an adjacent area containing the works of a single sculptor. Mol, a Ukrainian who immigrated to the city in 1949, has created whimsical bears, deer and nude bathers among other forms. A glass-walled **gallery** (*free; early Jun to late Sep noon to 8pm*, ☎*986-6531*) displays hundreds more pieces of his work while a reflecting pool catches the grace of several posed figures. Mol's studio, moved to a new home just behind the gallery, can also be viewed.

The park's most popular feature is the **Assiniboine Park Zoo ★★★** (*$3; every-day 10am to 4pm, in summer until sundown;* ☎*986-6921*). More than

1,300 animals live here, including Russian lynx, a polar bear, kangaroo, snowy and great horned owls. The zoo even imported residents like the *vicuña* (similar to the lama) and Siberian tigers. A statue of "Winnie-the-Bear" on the zoo grounds honours the famous Pooh's origins as a bear cub. Purchased by a Winnipeg soldier in Ontario the cub was carried to England where author A.A. Milne saw it and brought its story to a worldwide audience of children.

The **Prairie Dog Central** (*$13; Jul and Aug Sat and Sun 11am and 3pm, Sep Sun only; 0.5 km north of Inkster Blvd. on Prairie Dog Trail,* ☎*780-7328 to reserve or 453-8796 for info*) is a vintage steam train dating back to circa 1900 that welcomes visitors aboard for a unique 2.5hr excursion to Warren, northwest of Winnipeg.

Living Prairie Museum, in a suburb west of downtown, is said to contain the last significant pocket of tallgrass prairie in Canada. If so, these 12ha are a stark testament to the loss of the once vast prairie.

This is a rather small plot surrounded by an airfield, a school and housing developments, making it hard to imagine the wide open plains. However, the adjacent **nature centre ★** (*free entry; Jul and Aug every day 10am to 5pm; 2795 Ness Ave.,* ☎*832-0167*) does an adequate job of explaining and recapturing what once existed here. An annual festival, in August, draws further attention to this ecosystem.

Southwest of downtown, the **Fort Whyte Nature Centre ★★** (*$4; Jun to Oct Mon to Tue 9am to 5pm, Wed to Fri 9am to 9pm, Sat and Sun 10am to 9pm; Nov to May Mon to Fri 9am to 5pm, Sat and Sun 10am to 5pm; 1961 McCreary Rd.,* ☎*989-8355*) is a pocket of wilderness that's a bit more vital. Its animal life includes foxes and muskrats as well as a number of birds. An interpretive centre on the premises features an aquarium, a demonstration beehive and other exhibits designed with children in mind.

Tiny **Riel House ★★** (*suggested donation $2; mid-May to early Sep every day 10am to 6pm; 330 River Rd., just south of Bishop Grandin Blvd., St. Vital;* ☎*257-1783*) is set on a narrow river lot along the Red River. This building was home to famous Metis leader Louis Riel (see p 25) and his family for several years and belonged to his descendants until 1969. Riel's body lay in state here after he was executed for treason in 1885. In addition to its connection with Riel, the museum paints a vivid picture of what life was like for the Metis in the Red River Settlement. Guided tours are available.

The **St. Norbert Farmers Market** (*late Jun to Thanksgiving Sat 8am to 3pm, Jul and Aug Wed 3pm to dusk;* ☎*275-8349*) is just south of the perimeter, on the east side of Pembina Highway. During the summer, people come from all over southern Manitoba to sell their products at the outdoor stalls. Locally grown fruits and vegetables, home-made bread and baking, plants, crafts and traditional Mennonite farmer's sausage are all sold here.

Eastern Manitoba

Dugald

Just east of Winnipeg, in the small town of Dugald, is the **Dugald Costume Museum** ★ (*$4; Jun to Aug 10am to 5pm, May and Sep Wed to Fri 10am to 5pm, Sat and Sun noon to 5pm; $4; at the intersection of Hwy. 15 and Dugald Rd.,* ☎*853-2166,* ⬜*853-2077*), the first of its kind in Canada. A 35,000-piece collection of costumes dating back to 1765 is displayed in tableaus, housed in an 1886 pioneer home. Special exhibits illustrate aspects of costume; one recent exhibit, for instance, explained the long history of the silk trade. The museum somehow has also acquired some of Queen Elizabeth I's linen napkins dating from the late 16th century.

Oak Hammock

Birds are the most satisfied visitors to **Oak Hammock Marsh and Conservation Centre** ★★ (*$3.75; May to Sep every day 10am to 8pm, Oct to Apr every day 10am to 4:30pm, head north on Hwy. 8, then east on Hwy. 67,* ☎*467-3300*), a protected wetland (once farmland) a few kilometres north of downtown Winnipeg. Among the annual arrivals are Canada geese, ducks and more than 250 other species. Mammals also like the park and all are visible while walking the centre's boardwalks (constructed so as not to disturb the marsh) and dikes. Special guided tours and canoe excursions are also available.

An excellent **interpretive centre** ★ on site explains the value of the wetland and allows visitors to see it via remote-controlled cameras installed in the marsh. The Canadian headquarters of Ducks Unlimited is also located here.

Red River Heritage Road

From Route 9 heading north, the **Red River Heritage Road** ★★ makes a nice meander off the beaten track. This territory once formed the heart of Thomas Douglas's "lower settlement" of Hudson's Bay Company charges. The dirt heritage road is beautifully laid out along the river banks and is well-marked with historic sites. It passes a number of old limestone buildings, including the William Scott farmhouse and the **Captain Kennedy Museum and Tea House** ★★ (*free admission; Mon to Sat 11am to 4:30pm, Sun 11am to 6pm;* ☎*334-2498*). It was built by trader Captain William Kennedy in 1866 with three restored period rooms, English gardens and a superb view of the river. There is a pleasant restaurant where you can have a lovely English-style tea with scones.

Near the end of the road, the **St. Andrews-on-the-Red Anglican Church** ★★★ is the oldest stone church in western Canada still being used for public worship. It is handsome with massive stone walls and typical English pointed windows – the stained glass was supposedly shipped in molasses from England to protect it from breaking. Inside, benches are still lined with the original buffalo hide.

Just south of the church, **St. Andrews Rectory** ★★ (☎*334-6405 or 785-6050*), a striking little building that is now a national historic park. Signs on the grounds tell the story and interpreters are available during summertime to discuss the rectory's function.

Selkirk

On Route 9A, Selkirk, a small river town marked by a giant green fish, is home to several important attractions. **Lower Fort Garry** ★ (*$5.50; mid-May to early Sep, 10am to 6pm; PO 37, off Hwy. 9, just south of Selkirk,* ☎*785-6050*), just south of town, is a recreated trading post. It recalls the former importance of this post, built to replace the original Fort Garry in Winnipeg after it was carried away by flood waters. Exhibits include a recreated doctor's office, powder magazine, Aboriginal encampment and blacksmith's shop. The main attraction, however, is the big stone house at the centre of the property, constructed for the governor of the Hudson's Bay Company. It displays many interesting artifacts, including housewares and an old piano transported here by canoe from Montréal. Costumed characters interact with visitors while baking, trading and otherwise acting out their roles.

Several bridges across the Red River provide good views of the surrounding landscape. Downtown, hugging the river, lies **Selkirk Park** (see p 478). The world's largest Red River Ox Cart (6.5m high and 13.7m long) stands here. The **Marine Museum of Manitoba** ★ ★ (*$3.50; May to Sep every day 9am to 5pm; 490 Evelyn St., ☎482-7761*) occupies six ships – including Manitoba's oldest steamship – at the park entrance. An actual lighthouse that once stood on Lake Winnipeg is also located here.

St. Peter's Dynevor Church ★ sits just across the Red River, and has a lovely view of it. The stone church, built in 1854, is a reminder of the first agricultural colony in western Canada. It employed a combination of missionaries and First Nations. **Chief Peguis** is buried in the churchyard as are other settlers of the colony.

North of Selkirk on Route 9, the **Little Britain Church** ★ is one of just five surviving Red River Settlement stone churches that remain standing in the province. It was constructed between 1872 and 1874.

Lockport

East of town, in Lockport at the foot of the large bridge, a park is home to the **Kenosewun Centre** (*free admission; mid-May to mid-Sep 11am to 6:30pm; ☎757-2902*). The name means "there are many fishes" in the Cree language. The centre displays Aboriginal horticultural artifacts and material on the history of the town and offers tourist

information. Pathways lead to the St. Andrews lock and dam.

Driving northeast from Selkirk, you will reach a series of beautiful white sandy beaches. As some of the province's finest, they include Winnipeg Beach (see p 478) and Camp Morton.

Gimli

Situated on the shores of Lake Winnipeg, Gimli is still the heart of Manitoba's Icelandic population. A Viking statue welcomes visitors to the centre of town. The town was once the capital of a sovereign republic known as New Iceland. A maritime ambiance still pervades the streets, though today it is mainly sailboats and windsurfers that set out from the marina and beach. The history of the town's fishing industry and the lake's geological formation are recounted at the **Lake Winnipeg Visitor Centre** (*at the harbour, ☎642-7974.*)

The region's Icelandic heritage is commemorated with an annual festival and is also on display at the **New Icelandic Heritage Museum** (*☎642-7974*) that's scheduled to open at its new location at the Betel Waterfront Centre in the late summer of 2000. The museum will recount the history of the first Icelandic settlers to arrive on the shores of Lake Winnipeg with the collection including interesting historical artifacts. In the meantime, a small temporary exhibit on the Vikings may be viewed at Gimli's school (*free admission; 2nd floor, 62 Second Ave*).

Around Lake Winnipeg

On the eastern side of Lake Winnipeg, Route 59 passes through resort towns located on some of the province's best beaches. **Grand Beach** ★★★, **Grand Marais** and **Victoria Beach** ★ are the places to go during the summer for stunning white sand. Turning southeast again on Route 11, angling toward the Ontario border, the province's seemingly endless flatlands suddenly drop away and are replaced by rocks, rushing rivers and trees. As the road proceeds east, the towns become increasingly woodsy while the fishing, canoeing and hiking become truly spectacular.

Pinawa is known for a paper mill and a festival celebrating paper, hydroelectric power and fish while **Lac du Bonnet** is home to an underground nuclear research facility. A string of increasingly remote provincial parks compete for the attention of the traveller seeking off-the-beaten track Manitoba.

Southern Manitoba

Directly south of Winnipeg, between the city and the United States border, lies the Pembina Valley – the province's Mennonite country. The drive is absolutely flat and the endless fields are interrupted only by the leafy oases of towns such as **Altona**. The town is famous for its fields of sunflowers and an annual festival that celebrates them (see p 486).

Steinbach

Southeast of Winnipeg, Steinbach is the largest town in the region and features the popular **Mennonite Heritage Village ★★** (*$5; Jul to Aug Mon to Sat 10am to 7pm, Sun noon to 5pm; May, Jun, Sep Mon to Sat 10am to 5pm, Sun noon to 5pm; Oct to May by appointment only, interpretive centre weekdays 10am to 4pm; Hwy. 12, ☎326-9661*). A 16ha village is laid out in the traditional pattern. The buildings focus on the lives of Mennonites, people of Dutch origin who emigrated to the province from Russia in 1874. Attractions include : a restaurant offering authentic Mennonite food (plums and meat are featured); a general store selling such goods as stone-ground flour and old-fashioned candy; sod and log houses; an interpretative building; exhibition galleries, and a windmill with 20m-high sails.

Mariopolis

In Mariopolis, an unusually beautiful church reminds visitors of the strong French and Belgian culture in the province. **Our Lady of the Assumption Roman Catholic Church ★★★** combines careful brickwork with a striking steeple whose alternating bands of black and white draw the eye upward to a simple cross.

Morden

Morden, another Mennonite stronghold, is known for its attractive agricultural research facility and streets of graceful fieldstone mansions. Various local tour operators will point out the homes for a small fee. The **Morden and District Museum ★** (*$2; Jun to Aug every day 1pm to 5pm; Sep to*

May Wed to Sun 1pm to 5pm; 111B Gilmour Ave., ☎822-3406*) displays a good collection of prehistoric marine fossils, reminders of the vast inland sea that once covered North America. Also in town, the **Agriculture Canada Research Station** (*Mon to Fri 8am to 5pm; ☎822-4471*) has impressive ornamental gardens.

Winkler

A bit farther east on Route 14, Winkler is home to the unusual **Pembina Thresherman's Museum ★** (*$3; closed in winter; Mon to Fri 9am to 5pm, Sat and Sun 1pm to 5pm; ☎325-7497*), filled with tools and machines from another era.

Neubergthal

Just southeast of Altona, Neubergthal is one of the province's best-preserved Mennonite towns. It has a distinctive layout (just one long street lined with houses) and equally distinctive architecture, featuring thatched roofing and barns connected to houses.

Tolstoi

Just east of the small town of Tolstoi on Route 209, a 128ha **patch of tallgrass prairie ★★** (*☎945-7775*) is maintained by the Manitoba Naturalists Society. This is the largest remaining tract of this kind being protected in Canada.

Central Manitoba

Two main Routes pass across central Manitoba. The **Trans-Canada Highway** (*1*) is the faster of the two. Whule less visually rewarding, it does pass

through the major population centres of Brandon and Portage La Prairie. The **Yellowhead Highway** (*16*) is a somewhat more scenic journey.

St. François-Xavier

Taking the Trans-Canada west from Winnipeg, it's not far to St. François-Xavier, a solidly French-Canadian village featuring two of Manitoba's most interesting restaurants as well as an intriguing Cree legend of a white horse. This is the oldest Metis settlement in the province, established in 1820 by **Cuthbert Grant**. Legendary for his acumen at hunting buffalo, Grant is buried inside the town's Roman Catholic church. The picturesque setting along a bow of the Assiniboine River makes this an excellent destination for a short excursion out of the city.

From here, **Route 26** makes a short scenic detour along the tree-lined Assiniboine River, once home to a string of trapping posts.

Portage La Prairie

A little farther west lies Portage La Prairie (pop. 20,000), founded in 1738 by French-Canadian explorer Pierre Gaultier de la Vérendrye as a resting stop on the riverine canoe journey to Lake Manitoba. The town's most interesting natural attraction is the crescent-shaped lake, a cutoff bow of the Assiniboine River that nearly encircles the entire downtown.

Island Park ★ sits inside that crescent, providing beautiful tree-shaded picnic spots by the water. It also hosts several attractions, including a golf

Manitoba

course, playground, deer and waterfowl sanctuary (watch for the Canada geese), fairgrounds and a "you-pick" strawberry farm. Canoeing is excellent here. Good relief from the heat and glare of driving.

The limestone **city hall** ★★, a former post office right on the main street, was designed by the same architect who planned Canada's first Parliament Buildings. It is surprisingly ornate and has been declared a federal historic site.

Fort la Reine Museum and Pioneer Village ★★★ *($3; May to mid-Sep Mon to Fri 9am to 6pm, Sat to Sun 10am to 6pm; at Hwys. 26 and 1A, ☎857-3259)* is not, in fact, a fort, but rather an eclectic mix of old prairie buildings set on a small lot just east of town. This is not to say that it's not worth a visit. Its small size makes the museum more manageable and the varied collection is often surprising. Finery such as mink stoles and gramophones tells of the aspirations of the people who once lived in this small prairie city. Forming a stark contrast to the wash tubs, well-worn highchairs and rusted gas pumps found elsewhere in the museum, they give an excellent sense of the typical life of the average settler. It includes everything from a small trading post, trapper's cabin, school, church and barn to weathered houses like those prairie travellers see standing abandoned and on the verge of collapse in the flat, endless landscape.

Perhaps the museum's most remarkable piece is the luxurious and well-equipped railway car specially fitted for William Van Horne of the Cana-

dian Pacific Railway who traveled in it while overseeing the construction of the rail line. Next to it is one of the humble cabooses which are fast disappearing from the ends of trains across Canada. Children especially will enjoy climbing into the lookout dome of this relic from the past!

Austin

The highway west then passes through more fields and towns, reminders of the richness of the local farmland. A short distance south of the one-street town of Austin, the **Manitoba Agricultural Museum** ★ *($5; mid-May to early Oct every day 9am to 5pm; Box 10, R0H 0C0, ☎637-2354, ≈637-2395)* is particularly strong on farm equipment and old vehicles; John Deere tractors, implements and ancient snowmobiles are typical of the collection, which is the largest operating vintage farm machinery in Canada. An old prairie schoolhouse, train station, general store and amateur radio museum have also been moved here to add atmosphere.

Every summer, the **Thresherman's Reunion and Stampede** brings the place alive with farm contests and a race between a turtle and an old-fashioned tractor. (Sometimes the turtle wins!).

Glenboro

A detour 40km south of the Trans-Canada takes you to **Glenboro**, gateway to Spruce Woods Provincial Park (see p 479) And home to **Grund Church** ★, the oldest Icelandic Lutheran church in Canada. Manitoba's last remaining

cable ferry still crosses the Assiniboine River here.

Brandon

Brandon (pop. 40,000) is Manitoba's second-largest city, a city so tied to the fortunes of the surrounding wheatfields that wheat is still grown experimentally right near the centre of town. Many gracious Victorian homes stand in the residential area just south of downtown. The handsome 1911 **Central Fire Station** ★ *(637 Princess Ave)* and neoclassical **Courthouse** *(Princess Ave. and 11th St.)* Are both on Princess Avenue, one of the city's main streets.

Turn right on 18th Street to reach the **Daly House Museum** ★★ *($2; Mon to Sat 10am to 5pm, Sun noon to 5pm; 122-18th St., ☎727-1722)*. It's the best place to get a feel for Brandon's history. Once home to Brandon's mayor, the house today includes a grocery store, recreated City Council chamber and research centre. A little farther is the attractive campus of **Brandon University**.

Heading north along 18th Street leads you to Grand Valley Road which takes you to the **Experimental Research Farm** ★★ *(every day 8am to 4:30pm; Gran Valley Rd., ☎7267650)* whose scenic grounds and striking modern glass building are set in an idyllic location with a view of the valley. Guided tours are available Tuesdays and Thursdays at 1:30pm and 3:30pm.

Finally, there's an interesting aircraft museum housed in Hangar No. 1 of the city airport on the northern outskirts of

Brandon. The **Common-wealth Air Training Plan Museum** ★ (*$3; May to Sep, Mon to Sun 10am to 4pm, Oct to Apr 1pm to 4pm; Box 3, R.R. 5, Brandon,* ☎ *727-2444*) features vintage planes from WWII Royal Canadian Air Force training schools that were held here. Some of the more interesting articles include a restored vintage flight simulator, memorials, official telegrams announcing casualties and losses and biographies of flyers.

Souris

Southwest of Brandon, Souris is known for its **swinging suspension bridge** ★, Canada's longest at 177m. The bridge was constructed at the turn of the century and restored after a 1976 flood swept it away. The adjacent **Hillcrest Museum** (*$2; Jun Sun 2pm to 5pm; Jul to early Sep every day 10am to 6pm;* ☎ *483-2008 or 483-3138*) preserves items of local historical interest.

Neepawa

Another choice for touring central Manitoba is the Yellowhead Highway (16). Lying to the west of Winnipeg, Neepawa touts itself as "Manitoba's Loveliest Town." This is no idle boast, especially in lily season when this pretty little town blooms. The oldest operating courthouse in Manitoba is here as is the **Margaret Laurence Home** (*$2; May 1 to Aug Mon to Fri 10am to 5pm, weekends noon to 6pm, Sep to Oct every day noon to 5pm; 312 First Ave.,* ☎ *476-3612*), dedicated to the beloved author who was born here. Laurence's typewriter and furniture are the highlights.

Minnedosa

Minnedosa, a tiny town to the west, surprises with its Czecho-slavakian population. A series of prairie potholes, glacier-made depressions in the earth that later filled with rainwater, lie south of town on Route 262 and provide optimum conditions for waterfowl such as drake, mallards and teal. Continuing north of Minnedosa on the same route, the road enters a valley good for spotting white-tailed deer. A wildlife viewing tower provides even better opportunities to do so.

Dauphin

Just north of the Yellowhead, Dauphin is transformed into the famous **Selo Ukrainia** ("Ukrainian Village") during the **National Ukrainian Festival** (see p 486) each summer. The event draws thousands to the town in late July.

Also in Dauphin, the **Fort Dauphin Museum** ★ (*$3; May to Sep Mon to Fri 9am to 5pm, also on weekends Jul and Aug; 140 Jackson St.,* ☎ *638-6630*) recreates one of the area's French-run NorthWest Company trading posts, showcasing fur trapping and other pioneer activities. The displays and buildings include a trapper's cabin, blacksmith's shop, one-room rural schoolhouse, Anglican church and the trading post. There's even a birchbark canoe made entirely from natural materials and a collection of fossils such as a bison horn, mammoth tusk and an ancient canine skull.

Northern Manitoba

The Pas

The so-called Woods and Water Route shows another side of Manitoba. The Pas, home to a large Aboriginal population, hosts an important annual gathering of trappers and has an exceedingly clear lake. Most visitors head for the **Sam Waller Museum** ★★ (*$2; mid-May to Aug Mon to Sat 10am to 7pm, Sun noon to 5pm; Sep to mid-May every day 1pm to 5pm; 306 Fischer Ave.,* ☎ *623-3802*). Built in 1916 and occupying the town's former courthouse, it covers local natural and cultural history based on the eclectic collection of Sam Waller. Walking tours are offered.

A wall of **Christ Church** ★★ (*Edwards Ave.,* ☎ *623-2119*) is inscribed with the Ten Commandments in the Cree language. The church was built in 1840 by Henry Budd who was the first Aboriginal in Canada ordained to the Anglican ministry. It still retains some furnishings fashioned by ships' carpenters and brought here during an 1847 expedition.

Flin Flon

Flin Flon is Canada's most whimsically named municipality and greets visitors with a jumble of streets climbing the rocky hills. Located mostly in Manitoba with a smaller part spilling over into Saskatchewan, Flin Flon is the most important mining centre in this part of the country and has grown to become the province's sixth-largest city.

Manitoba

Flin Flon was named by a group of gold prospectors in 1915 who found a copy of the mass-market science fiction paperback of the same name during a northern Manitoba portage. Later, on a lakeshore near here, they staked a mining claim and named it for the book's main character, Josiah Flintabbatey Flonatin, or "Flinty" to locals. Thus, the green 7.5m-tall **Josiah Flintabbatey Flonatin statue** presides over the city's entrance. It was designed for the city by the renowned American cartoonist Al Capp.

Polar Bear

A walk around town reveals old boomtown-era hotels, bright red headframes indicating mine shafts, and historic redwood cabins. Of all these historic sites, though, the **Flin Flon Station Museum** ★★ (*$2; mid-May to early Sept every day 11am to 7pm;* ☎687-2946) might be the best. It has a small collection of local mining artifacts, including a diving suit and helmet for underwater prospecting, a Linn tractor, a train sweeper and an ore car. The collection also includes a stuffed 9kg lake trout that was caught near here.

Churchill

Special arrangements are required to reach the far north of Manitoba. Isolated and cold, Churchill nevertheless beguiles travellers with its remoteness and stunning wildlife. The place is also important historically, having helped the English first establish a foothold in Manitoba. They chose the site because of a superb natural harbour so it's fitting that the town's dominant feature today is a huge **grain elevator** beside the docks.

The townsite is also located right in the middle of the migratory path of the area's **polar bear** population, – a mixed blessing for the town's inhabitants. While these majestic animals attract visitors from around the world to this remote spot every autumn, they also wander right into town occasionally, posing a potential risk to anyone who crosses their path. In addition to the bears, people also come here. They come to see caribou, seals, birds and especially white **beluga whales** in summer. And there is always the possibility of an astonishing display of the aurora borealis, or northern lights.

The **Visitor Reception Centre**, in Bayport Plaza, orients visitors with an overview of the fur posts and forts. **Fort Prince of Wales** ★★ (*$5; Box 127, R0B 0E0,* ☎675-8863, ≈675-2026), an enormous, diamond-shaped stone battlement located at the mouth of the Churchill River, is historically interesting. After four decades of steady construction by the English, it was surrendered to Canadian forces without a fight. The fort can only be reached by boat or helicopter. During the summer, park staff lead interpretive tours of the site.

Sloop's Cove National Historic Site ★★
(☎675-8863), 4km upstream from the fort, is a natural harbour that provided safe haven for huge wooden sailing ships at least as far back as 1689. When the Hudson's Bay Company set up shop here, its sloops were moored to these rocks with iron rings. Some of the rocks still bear inscriptions from the men posted such as explorer Samuel Hearne who presided over the company in its heyday. Like Fort Prince of Wales, the site can only be reached by boat or helicopter.

Across the river, **Cape Merry National Historic Site** ★ (☎675-8863) preserves a gunpowder magazine, the only remnant of a battery built here back in 1746. It is reached via the Centennial Parkway.

The **Eskimo Museum** ★★★ (*free admission; summer Mon 1pm to 5pm, Tue to Sat 9am to noon and 1pm to 5pm; winter Mon and Sat 1pm to 4:30pm, Tue to Fri 10:30am to 4:30 pm, Sat 1am to 4:30pm; 242 La Vérendrye Ave., R0B 0E0,* ☎675-2030) maintains one of the world's pre-eminent collections of Inuit artifacts. Founded in 1944 by the local Roman Catholic Diocese, it contains artifacts dating from as far back as 1700BC. A set of ornately carved walrus tusks is among its most impressive pieces.

The **Northern Studies Centre** (*Launch Rd.*, ☎675-2307), 25km east of Churchill proper, is located in a former rocket test-range. Today, students come here to study the northern lights, Arctic ecology, botany, meteorology, geology and more. Guided tours are available for $5. It is best to call ahead.

York Factory National Historic Site ★★★ (*Box 127, R0B 0E0*, ☎675-8863, ⌐675-2026), 240km southeast of Churchill, is what remains of the Hudson Bay Company fur-trade post that first established the English in western Canada. A wooden depot built in 1832 still stands here, and there are ruins of a stone gunpowder magazine and a cemetery with markers dating back to the 1700s. However, access can only be gained by charter plane or canoe. Some guided tours are also offered in summer through Parks Canada.

Finally, there are the spectacular **polar bears** ★★★, easily Churchill's premier attraction. Autumn is the time to observe them, and the only way is as part of a guided tour. There are at least a dozen operators in Churchill The options include:

North Star Tours and Travel Agency (*Box 520, Churchill*, ☎800-665-0690 or 675-2629; ⌐675-2852). Mark Ingebrigtson leads natural history – and sometimes Aboriginal culture – package tours along the shores of Hudson Bay.

Tundra Buggy Tours (*Box 662, Churchill*, ☎800-544-5049 or 675-2121; ⌐675-2877). Len and Beverly Smith lead polar bear safaris in both English and French. Vehicles are specially outfitted to accommodate photographers.

Seal River Heritage Lodge (*Box 1034, Churchill*, ☎800-665-0476 or 675-8875; ⌐675-2386). Mike Reimer runs ecotours out of a remote wilderness lodge in the north country. Sights include caribou, polar bears, beluga whales and seals.

Caribou

Parks

Greater Winnipeg

Birds Hill Provincial Park, just north of Winnipeg, sits on a gentle rise deposited by retreating glaciers. It makes for easy and popular cross-country skiing. In summer, visitors bike and hike the park's trails (one of which is wheelchair-accessible) to view prairie wildflowers – including several species of rare orchid – or head for a small beach. The park is also the site of the city's annual folk-music extravaganza (see p 486).

Grand Beach Provincial Park is the most popular beach in Manitoba, hands down. Situated on Lake Winnipeg's eastern shore, it consists of lovely white sand and grassy 8m-high dunes that seem to have been lifted directly from Cape Cod. As a bonus, the beach is wheelchair-accessible. Three self-guiding trails wind through the park – Spirit Rock Trail, Wild Wings Trail and the Ancient Beach Trail – enlightening beach goers before they slap on the sunblock. This is also a good spot for windsurfing. There are full tourist facilities here, including a restaurant, campground and outdoor amphitheatre for concerts. A golf course lies just outside the park.

St. Norbert Provincial Park (*free, mid-May to Sep, Thu to Mon, 10:30am to 5:30pm; 40 Turnbull Dr.*, ☎269-5377) is a 6.8ha, south-Winnipeg complex of buildings, a former Metis and then

Manitoba

French-Canadian settlement at the juncture of the Red and La Salle rivers. The restored gambrel-roofed Bohémier farmhouse and two other homes are on display as well as a self-guided trail.

Eastern Manitoba

Winnipeg Beach Provincial Recreational Park ★★ (☎389-2752) has long been a favourite summer getaway for Winnipeg residents. Besides the well-known beach and a boardwalk, the park's grounds also include a marina, campground and bay that's a favourite with windsurfers.

Whiteshell Provincial Park ★★★ (*from Winnipeg, take Hwy. 1 east to Falcon Lake or West Hawk Lake; or, farther north, take Provincial Rd. 307 to Seven Sisters Falls, or Hwy. 44 to Rennie, www.whiteshell.mb.ca*) is one Manitoba's largest and best. Occupying some 2,500km², it is rich in lakes, rapids, waterfalls, fish and birds. There's something for everyone: **Alf Hole Goose Sanctuary** ★ (☎369-5470) is among the best places in the province to see Canada geese, especially during migration; the rocks at **Bannock Point** ★, laid out by local First Nations to resemble the forms of snakes, fish, turtles and birds, are of archaeological interest; the cliffs of **Lily Pond** ★ are 3.75 billion years old. This is also the location of the province's deepest lake. That's popular with scuba divers. **Hiking** is also good in Whiteshell. Hikes include: the Forester's Footsteps Trail, an easy walk through jackpine forest and then up a granite ridge, the Pine Point Trail,

which is suited for cross-country skiing in winter; and the White Pine trail. A **Visitor Centre** and the **Whiteshell Natural History Museum** (*free, May to Sep every day 9am to 5pm, ☎348-2846, www.whiteshell.mb.ca*) help orient travellers and explain the park's ecology, geology and wildlife.

Nopiming Provincial Park (*from Winnipeg, take Hwy. 59 north to Hwy. 44; continue east along Hwy. 11, before turning onto Provincial Rd. 313 north and finally taking Provincial Rd. 315 east to Bird Lake, which lies just south of the park*) shows a whole different side of Manitoba – a place of huge granite outcrops and hundreds of lakes. The surprising presence of woodland caribou here is an added bonus as are the fly-in and drive-in **fishing lodges** scattered through the park. "Nopiming" is an Anishinabe (Ojibwa and Cree) word meaning "entrance to the wilderness."

Atikaki Provincial Wilderness Park ★★★ (*from Winnipeg, take Hwy. 59 N, then turn onto Provincial Rd. 304*), in the east of the province along the Ontario border, consists of a 400,000ha hodgepodge of cliffs, rock formations, pristine lakes and cascading rivers. It is, however, extremely difficult to get to, requiring a canoe, floatplane or a hike of several days to reach its interior. A result, it contains the most unspoiled wilderness in the province's major parklands. Among the highlights are a series of rock murals painted by Aboriginals and a 20m waterfall well suited for whitewater canoeing. As Atikaki means "country of the caribou," moose and

caribou sightings are quite possible.

Hecla Provincial Park ★★ (*from Winnipeg, take Hwy. 8 North along Lake Winnipeg to Gull Harbour, ☎279-2056*) is a beautiful and interesting park, combining lake ecology with dramatic island geology and the colours and creatures of the forest. Interpretive programs take place year-round and there's a tower for viewing and photographing wildlife. The park's **Hecla Village** ★ adds a short trail with points of historical interest relating to Icelandic culture and architecture and a **heritage home museum** ★★ (*Thurs to Mon 11am to 5pm*), a restored 1920s home. Adjacent **Grindstone Provincial Park** ★★ is still being developed, and therein lies its beauty: it is not nearly as busy as Hecla.

East of Lake Winnipeg, the **Narcisse Wildlife Management Area** on Route 17 becomes wildly popular late each April when thousands of resident red-sided garter snakes emerge from their limestone dens to participate in a visceral mating ritual.

Selkirk Park, a riverside park in downtown Selkirk, has lots of recreational opportunities. There are campgrounds, boat-launching pads and an outdoor swimming pool. Snowshoeing and ice fishing are possible in winter. In spring and summer, the park is home to a bird sanctuary with an observation deck for viewing Canada geese and other birds.

Central Manitoba

Grand Valley Provincial Recreation Park ★ (*just west of Brandon on Hwy. 1*) is best known for the **Stott Site ★★**, a designated provincial heritage site. Bones and artifacts from at least 1,200 years ago have been discovered here. A bison enclosure and camp has been reconstructed.

North of Portage La Prairie on the shore of Lake Manitoba, lies the 18,000ha **Delta Marsh**, one of the largest waterfowl staging marshes in North America, stretching 8km along the lake and a great place to bring binoculars. At Delta Beach, a waterfowl and wetlands research station studies ecological questions in a natural environment.

Approximately 23km south of Roblin, the **Frank Skinner Arboretum Trail** commemorates the work of Dr. Frank Leith Skinner, a famous Canadian horticulturist. This farm served as Skinner's laboratory for breeding new strains of plants. Visitors can walk atop a former dike, visit Skinner's greenhouse, and walk the Wild Willow Trail.

Western Manitoba

The "Spirit Sands," a desert landscape of immense sand dunes in **Spruce Woods Provincial Park ★★** (*take the Trans-Canada Hwy. 1 west to Carberry, then take Hwy. 5 south; from May to Sep ☎827-2543, from Sep to May ☎834-3223*), never fails to take visitors by surprise. Self-guided trails take hikers through the dunes and the surrounding spruce forests and prairie

and to the "Devil's Punch Bowl," an unusual pond created by underground streams. Campgrounds and a sandy beach for swimming make this large park popular in the summer.

Turtle Mountain National Park ★★ (*from Brandon, travel 100km on Hwy. 10 South until you reach the park*), composed of compacted coal and glacial deposits, rises more than 250m above the surrounding prairie land. Explorer La Vérendrye called it the "blue jewel of the plains" and its gentle hills lend themselves to mountain biking, horseback riding and hiking. There is also, of course, a considerable population of the beautiful painted turtles that give the mountain its name. Camping is available at three lakes here.

Riding Mountain National Park ★★★ (*☎800-707-8480 or 848-7275*) rises majestically from the plains with aspen-covered slopes that are habitats for wild animals such as elk, moose, deer, wolves and lynx. The largest black bear ever seen in North America was killed here by a poacher in 1992, and bison are contained within a large **bison enclosure ★★** near Lake Audy. Route 10, running north-south, passes directly through the heart of the park and past the shores of its most beautiful lakes. The 12m-high wooden Agassiz lookout tower here gives a superb view of the surrounding territory. The remains of an old sawmill also fall within park boundaries and does a series of geological formations called beach ridges – former edges of a giant lake.

The local Aboriginal people own and operate a traditional **Anishinabe Village** (*Southquill Camp; ☎204-925-2030, ⬆204-925-2027; www.uredco.com; On site May 15 to Spr 15; ☎/⬆204-848-2815*) in the park that offers visitors the opportiunity to learn about Anishinabe culture. The camp features tipi accommodation and campsites, walking tours, traditional teachings, performances and local crafts.

Route 19 begins in the centre of the park and travels a switchback path up (or down) the park's steepest ridge. The naturalist Grey Owl, an Englishman who passed himself off as an Aboriginal person, lived here for six months, giving talks along with his two tamed beavers (he spent most of his time in Prince Albert National Park p 503). His remote **cabin ★** is located 17km up a hiking trail off Route 19. More than 400km of trails have been cleared at Riding Mountain National Park, including : the North Escarpment Loop, best for views; Whitewater Lake, giving a history of the prisoner-of-war camp that was once here; and the Strathclair Trail, formerly a fur trappers' route through the wooded hills. The park is also dotted with a number of pristine lakes superb for swimming. The sand beach at Wasagaming on **Clear Lake ★★** is a hub of activity. There is also a superb **golf course**.

Duck Mountain Provincial Park ★★★ (*from Dauphin, take Hwy. 5 West, then Provincial Rd. 366 North*) rises in long hills near the Manitoba-Saskatchewan border. Forests, meadows and lakes appear where the land has wrinkled upward in the Manitoba Escarpment formation. This is the home of **Baldy Mountain ★★**, the highest mountain in the province at 831m (there is also a tower at the top to get a still better view). It also features six hiking trails and a lake so clear that he bottom, 10m below, can be seen from its surface.

Northern Manitoba

At **Clearwater Lake Provincial Park ★** (*from The Pas, take Hwy. 10 North to Provincial Hwy. 287, then head east to the park*), the lake water is so clear that the bottom is visible 11m below the surface, making it one of the clearest lakes in the world. It is well known for its lake trout and northern pike. Also interesting is a series of enormous limestone slabs on the south shore. Known as "the caves," they splintered off from the nearby cliffs and can be reached by a trail.

The newly-created Wapusk National Park lies within the **Cape Churchill Wildlife Management Area ★★**. Together with the **Cape Tatnam Wildlife Management Area ★★** it takes in the coastline of Hudson Bay from Churchill to the Ontario border – a tremendous stretch of wild country that totals nearly 2.4 million hectares of land. They harbour polar bears, woodland caribou and many more birds and animals. They are accessible only by plane.

The region of **Grass River Provincial Park ★★** (*from Flin Flon, take Hwy. 10 South, turn left onto Hwy. 39 which takes you to the park*) was used by the Aboriginal peoples for thousands of years and then explored

anew by the English. Countless islands and some 150 lakes interrupt the river. A Karst spring, which gushes from a rock cliff, is one of the park's most fascinating sites.

Outdoor Activities

Birdwatching

Eastern Manitoba

The **Netley Marsh Provincial Recreational Park ★** (*Rte. 320, 16km north of Selkirk*) is one of the most frequented spots in the country for migrating birds and said to be one of the most important waterfowl nesting areas in North America. At least 18 species of ducks and geese flock here each autumn to feed before heading south for the long winter.

Northern Manitoba

Bird Cove ★, 16km east of Churchill, might be the area's best spot for observing the hundreds of bird species that pass through here, including possibly the rare Ross Gull. The wreck of the Ithaca, which sank in a storm on its way to Montreal in 1961 with a load of nickel ore, sits at the western tip of the cove.

For addresses of polar bear-observation outfitters see p 477.

Water Sports

Eastern Manitoba

Gimli's best rental agency for water and land sports is **H2O Beach and Adventure Sports** (☎642-9781), located right on the sandy beach of **Lake Winnipeg**. It rents bicycles, in-line skates, sailboats, kayaks, beach volleyballs, windsurfing equipment and just about everything else one could want or need.

It's purely manufactured fun but **Skinner's Wet 'n' Wild Waterslide Park** (☎757-2623) in Lockport keeps drawing crowds anyway. The attraction contains four big waterslides, two smaller slides, a giant hot tub, mini-golf, batting cages and lots more. It's impossible to miss the complex, situated at the west end of the Lockport bridge.

Accommodations

Bed and Breakfast of Manitoba (☎661-0300, *www.bedandbreakfast.mb.ca* coordinates reservations for approximately 70-member B&Bs throughout the province.

The Manitoba Country Vacations Association (☎/≈667-3526, *www.countryvacations.mb.ca* in Winnipeg, provides a similar service but a different experience. It books rooms at farms or other rural vacation destinations.

Downtown Winnipeg

Guest House International Hostel
$14-$34
sb, ≡
168 Maryland St., R3G 1L3
☎772-1272
⇨772-4117
This is a quirky old house in a residential neighbourhood very close to downtown Winnipeg. However, be cautious when walking in this area at night. Walls feature art by Aboriginal children and there are all kinds of rooming options. A game room in the somewhat crowded basement adds appeal and the price is right.

Ivey House International Hostel
$14 members, $18 non-members
sb, tv, K
210 Maryland St., R3G 1L6
☎772-3022
⇨784-1133
This extremely friendly and well-run Hostelling International-member facility is situated close to downtown (and very close to the other hostel). A classy operation, featuring a big kitchen, great staff and rooms that sometimes include desks.

Casa Antigua
$50
sb
209 Chestnut St.
☎775-9708
This quiet and reasonably priced bed and breakfast, in a residential neighbourhood near the two hostels, was built in 1906 and is furnished with lovely antiques. Both English and Spanish are spoken here, and three bedrooms – all with a shared bathroom – are offered.

Ramada Marlborough
$89
⊘, P, ✈, tv, ≡, ℜ
331 Smith St., R3B 2G9
☎(800) 667-7666
☎942-6411
⇨942-2017
With its central location and beautiful facade, the Ramada Marlborough makes a stunning first impression. While the sophisticated style is carried through in the hotel's wood-panelled dining room and the pleasant breakfast room, the guestrooms don't quite measure up, tending to be somewhat gloomy and cramped. Nevertheless, the place is comfortable.

Hotel Fort Garry
$119
tv, ≡, △, ℜ, ≈, ⊛, ⊘
222 Broadway, R3C 0R3
☎(800) 665-8088
☎942-8251
⇨956-2351
One of the most recognizable hotels on the city's skyline, this big-shouldered, neo-Gothic building was built by the Canadian National Railway in 1913. The impressive lobby and function rooms welcome guests in high style, though the rooms themselves are somewhat disappointing for a hotel of this calibre. The place is currently undergoing extensive renovations that are to be completed by 2003.

The Radisson Winnipeg
$89-$119
✈, ⅋, tv, ≡, ℜ, ≈, △, ⊛
288 Portage Ave., R3C 0B8
☎(800) 268-1133
☎956-0400
⇨947-1129
Smack in the downtown business district, this posh hotel features an haute-cuisine restaurant, childcare services and laundry service. Elegantly remodelled, the tastefully deco-

rated rooms offer every comfort and excellent views. Very friendly and professional service make this one of the best places to stay.

Place Louis-Riel All-Suite Hotel
$100 studio, $110 one bedroom
tv, ≡, K, ℜ
190 Smith St., R3C 1JB
☎947-6961
⇨947-3029
Every unit in this downtown high-rise is a suite, comprising several rooms and usually a kitchenette. Sixteen of the suites have two bedrooms. Ideal for longer visits.

Crowne Plaza Winnipeg Downtown
$99-$150
tv, ⅋, P, ≡, K, ℜ, ≈, ⊛, △
350 St. Mary Ave., R3C 3J2
☎942-0551
☎(800) 2CROWNE
⇨943-8702
This centrally located hotel comes with all the frills: four restaurants, a dry cleaning service, a beautiful pool, a recreation area and an attractive lobby. It even offers aerobic classes!

The Lombard
$89-$119
tv, ⅋, ⊘, ✈, ≡, ℜ, ≈, △, ⊛, K
2 Lombard Place, R3B 0Y3
☎957-1350
☎(800) 441-1414
⇨956-1791
Under new ownership – it was formerly in the Westin chain – this landmark is among the top posh digs in the city. It's where the Rolling Stones stay when they're in town though they sometimes get bumped by business conventions. Located at the busy and famous corner of Portage and Main.

Manitoba

St. Boniface

Gîte de la Cathédrale Bed and Breakfast
$50, bkfst
⊗, P, sb
581 Rue Langevin, St. Boniface
☎233-7792
Gîte de la Cathédrale Bed and Breakfast is located right across from Provencher Park in old St. Boniface. Five pleasant, flowery bedrooms are available. All are air-conditioned. Hostess Jacqueline Bernier's traditional French-Canadian breakfast may include pancakes with maple syrup, an omelette, or delicious French toast, served at a beautifully set table. Service is in French and very friendly.

Eastern Manitoba

Selkirk

Daerwood Motor Inn
$65
tv, P, ♣, ♿, ≡
162 Main St., R1A 1R3
☎482-7722
☎(800) 930-3888
≈482-8655
The Daerwood Motor Inn offers reasonably priced accommodations in central Selkirk, not far from several important local attractions. Rooms with kitchen units cost only $5 extra, and videocassette players are also available for an extra charge.

Riverton

Gull Harbour Resort
$90
♿, P, tv, ≡, ℜ, ≈, ⊛, △, ⊘
Box 1000, B0C 2R0
☎279-2041
☎(800) 267-6700
≈279-2000
A beautiful resort on the tip of an island. This con-

vention centre is especially well known for the golf courses nearby as well as the natural scenery of Hecla and Grindstone parks. It's also located close to the Hecla Island Heritage Home Museum.

Gimli

Lakeview Resort
$86
tv, K, ♿, ♣, P, ≡, ℜ, ≈, △
10 Centre St.
☎(800) 456-4000
☎642-8565
≈642-4400
The Lakeview Resort is right on the harbour in Gimli. Guests can choose a country-style suite or a room overlooking either the small town or the large lake from which the town derives most of its business. Breaking with the tradition of impersonal rooms in most big hotel chains, rooms here feature quilts, a fresh scent, hardwood floors and in-room mini bars ther's also a cozy fireplace in the lobby. Each room has a balcony.

Southern Manitoba

Winkler

Winkler Inn
$70
tv, ≡, ♣, ♿, ℜ, ≈, ⊛
851 Main St., R6W 4B1
☎(800) 829-4920
☎325-4381
≈325-9656
The fertile Pembina Valley draws visitors to Winkler, and the Winkler Inn accommodates them with a wide variety of amenities, including queen-sized beds and a view of the pool. A bar, restaurant, pool, and 10-person hot tub are also on site.

Central Manitoba

Wasagaming

New Chalet
$70
tv, P, ≈, ≡, ♿
CP 100, Wasagaming, R0J 2H0
☎848-2892
The New Chalet is open year-round and offers some of the best accommodations in the area. Pleasant and newly renovated, this well-kept establishment is centrally situated and offers guests the use of its outdoor swimming pool. It should be noted that since the hotel lies within park boundaries, guests must pay the park admission fee.

Lake Audy

Riding Mountain Guest Ranch
$75 per person, fb
sb
Box 11, 20km west of Clear Lake on Hwy. 354, R0J 0Z0
☎848-2265
One of the better guest ranch experiences in the province. Host Jim Irwin takes groups or individuals into his three-and-a-half storey ranch house, leading bison-viewing tours and serving meals in a dining room. Special touches here include a billiard table, a hot tub overlooking the fields, air conditioning in summer and a wood-heated sauna in winter. The ranch is quite close to Riding Mountain National Park, and the property also includes groomed trails for cross-country skiing and tobogganing. Irwin specializes in hosting group events. Minimum two-day stay. Reservations are recommended.

Roblin

Harvest Moon Inn
$64 bkfst incl.
tv, K, ☂, ≡
25 Commercial Dr., R0L 1P0
☎937-3701
☎888-377-3399
≈937-3701
The Harvest Moon Inn is a
new all-suite hotel with
lots of room. Each suite
includes a microwave,
refrigerator, television and
videocassette recorder. A
small selection of free
movies is available at the
front desk. As a bonus, the
family that runs the business is full of fishing advice and interesting stories
about their travels.

Brandon

Comfort Inn by Journey's End
$78
tv, ≡, P, ☂
925 Middleton Ave., R7C 1A8
☎727-6232
☎(800) 228-5150
≈727-2246
The Comfort Inn offers
super rooms and profes-
sional management right
on the Trans-Canada Fa-
cade north of downtown
Brandon. Rooms here
feature work tables and
sofas a bonus for business
travellers. The only draw-
back is the place's popu-
larity since it's often
booked up months in
advance.

Northern Manitoba

Churchill

Northern Lights Lodge
$88
tv, ☂, ℜ
Box 70, R0B 0E0
☎675-2403
≈675-2011
This northern outpost
caters to those in search of
the polar bears who can
usually be seen frolicking
on the shores of Hudson

Bay. The inn is only open
from June until November,
and there is a restaurant
on premises.

Polar Inn
$100
tv
15 Franklin St., R0B 0E0
☎675-8878
≈675-2647
The presence of polar
bears has inspired a whole
slew of motels and inns in
Churchill, including this
one. Rooms have been
recently updated and in-
clude all modern amenities
like telephones and televisions. Mountain-bike rentals are a real bonus for
outdoor types and shop-
pers will find the on-site
gift shop pleasant.

Restaurants

Downtown Winnipeg

Rogue's Gallery and Coffeehouse
$
closed Mon
432 Assiniboine Ave.
☎947-0652
www.roguesgallery.mb.ca
Rogue's Gallery and
Coffeehouse occupies a
large, rambling house on
the river where young, hip
Winnipeggers come for a
coffee or a bite to eat.
Works by local artists hang
on the brightly coloured
walls. The limited but
diverse menu of dishes
ranging from Italian
chicken or pasta to rotis
and falafel can be sampled
in the various eclectically
furnished rooms of this
two-storey building or on
the pretty summer patio.
There is no table service.

Alycia's
$
559 Cathedral Ave.
☎582-8789
This is likely the most
popular of Winnipeg's
half-dozen or so Ukrainian
eateries. "It sticks with
you," say customers of the
food here. Indeed, the
place is well-known
around town for thick
soups, hearty perogies,
cabbage rolls and other
warming fare. Red creamy
sodas and decorations,
such as Ukrainian Easter
eggs and pictures of the
Pope, add to the festive
mood. The owners also
run a deli next door that
offers takeout meats and
side dishes.

Le Café Jardin
$
lunch only
340 Provencher Ave.
☎233-9515
Attached to the
Franco-Manitoban Cultural
Centre, this café serves
French-Canadian cuisine as
well as light meals and
pastries baked on-site. The
outdoor terrace is popular
in summertime.

Nucci's Gelati
$
643 Corydon Ave.
☎475-8765
On a hot summer night,
this ice cream parlour is
the place to be. Don't be
put off by the long line-up.
The 30 flavours of deli-
cious home-made gelato
are well worth the wait!
The huge servings will
keep you cool as you stroll
along Winnipeg's Italian
strip that comes alive with
a festive atmosphere at
night.

Blue Note Café
$-$$
875 Portage Ave.
☎774-2189
A local hangout where you
can chow down on bur-
gers, chili and other bar

food. Groovy jazz plays on the sound system each night until about 9pm when a local musical act takes the stage. There's history here, too. The original location, downtown on Main Street, was where music star Neil Young and Canadian heroes Crash Test Dummies both got their starts.

Carlos & Murphy's
$$
129 Osborne Ave.
☎284-3510
Right beside the Tap & Grill (see below), this small, dark restaurant has a real frontier feel to it. Rough wooden beams are nailed to the wall in the pattern of a sunset, and saddles and other western gear decorate the interior. The Tex-Mex food comes in large portions and is good with a lime Margarita or a Mexican beer.

Da Mamma Mia Ristorante
$$
631 Corydon Ave.
☎453-9210
One of the many Italian restaurants on Corydon Avenue, this one is worth visiting for its patio, fringed with basil and other herbs destined for the restaurant's kitchen. The terrace has the *de rigueur* colourful umbrellas, checkered tablecloths, and even a small fountain. The interior, on the other hand, is quite dark and has an ornate gilded and slightly kitschy decor. So come here on a warm, sunny day. Simple meals of pasta, pizza and salad are served.

Elephant and Castle
$$
350 St. Mary Ave.
☎942-5555
Located in the lobby of the well-appointed Holiday Inn Crown Centre, this handsome English-style pub serves up the expected fare: turkey pot pie, bangers and mash, fish and chips, soups and sandwiches. The food is tasty and served with a smile. The dessert selection is especially good, including mousse, sherry trifle, deep-dish apple crisp, home-made pies and more. There's also a full bar selection.

Tap & Grill
$$
closed Sun
137 Osborne St.
☎284-7455
Located in the trendy Osborne Village, this restaurant has a relaxed Mediterranean atmosphere. Wicker chairs, shutters and ceramic tile floors create a cool, southern interior. There is an outdoor terrace in the back, surrounded by trellises and plants. It's an idyllic and very popular spot in the summertime. The menu includes meat dishes, seafood, pasta and a selection of fresh salads. Lemon, garlic and sun-dried tomatoes are the dominant flavours.

Hy's Steak Loft
$$$
216 Kennedy St.
☎942-1000
The brick-warehouse appearance of this downtown institution is quite deceiving. It's one of those places where smoky backroom deals are forged over Alberta prime rib. Politicians and other bigshots head for the wood-panelled steak room to watch the beef char-grilled to order on an open grill right before their eyes. Those with real clout ask for one of the Loft's private dining rooms and discuss changes in insurance laws or whatever else needs to be arranged out of the public's earshot. There's also a smoking room and lounge on the premises that's good for relaxing before and after the big meal.

Orlando's Seafood Grill
$$$
709 Corydon Ave.
☎477-5899
For something a little more upscale, try this elegant Portuguese restaurant with a contemporary indoor decor and a charming deck patio. It is known for its expertly prepared fish dishes such as, on occasion, delicacies like shark. Attentive and knowledgeable service.

The Velvet Glove
$$$$
2 Lombard Ave.
☎985-6255
Located in the prestigious Lombard Hotel, this restaurant caters to Winnipeg's high rollers. Entrees might include choices of the chef's latest creations in beef, seafood or lamb. Whatever's cooking, though, all meals begin with a simple soup and salad.

Eastern Manitoba

Gimli

Seagull's Restaurant
$-$$$
10 Centre St.
☎642-4145
This restaurant's biggest draw is its patio located right on the beach. Items like battered fish and gyros are served in a large dining room and you can try some Icelandic Vinetarta for dessert. Although there is nothing special about this place, it's the best sit-down restaurant in town.

Central Manitoba

Brandon

Humpty's
$
Hwy. 1
☎ *729-1902*
This restaurant, located in a gas station on a Brandon service road running parallel to the Trans-Canada, serves up solid stick-to-your-ribs food such as burgers, eggs and lots of filling sandwiches. Locals swear by it.

Casteleyn Cappuccino Bar
$
closed Sun
908 Rosser Ave.
☎ *727-2820*
This place is an oasis on the prairie, well worth a detour to Brandon. The Belgian Casteleyn family has been making hand-dipped chocolates here for seven years. Recently, they opened a bright new space and added gelato, Italian sodas and a cappuccino bar. This place is more of a coffeehouse than a restaurant but there's a tasty selection of meat and vegetable focaccia sandwiches each day. Other dessert options include Grand Marnier truffles, amaretto cheesecake and peach chocolate gateau. A wonderful lunch or snack experience.

Over the Moon
$$
934 Rosser Ave.
☎ *727-1448*
Several noteworthy restaurants can be found on Rosser Avenue between 9th and 10th Sts. Among these, Over the Moon serves appetizing pastas and fusion fare in its contemporary dining room or on the lovely patio with hanging geraniums.

St.François-Xavier

The Nun's Kitchen
$$
1033 Hwy. 26
☎ *864-2300*
Located in – what else – a former convent, this restaurant serves good food in a little French village outside of Winnipeg. Entrees include buffalo, quiche, chicken, ribs and the like. Prices are surprisingly reasonable. The sunny dining room has lovely views of the surrounding countryside.

The Medicine Rock Café
$$$
990 Hwy. 26, St. Francis-Xavier
☎ *864-2451*
Located in a large, new log building with comfortable booths and lots of windows, this place features one of the most interesting menus in the province. Dishes include ostrich, emu, boar and rabbit. Reservations are recommended as this restaurant is often crowded.

Shellmouth

The Church Caffe
$$
Box 15; head north 25km from Russel on Hwy. 83, 10km west on Hwy. 482 and north again on Hwy. 549
☎ *564-2626*
Housed in a former United Church, this place serves Austrian dinners in a scintillating lakeside location. It takes a bit of searching to find it but the reward is a selection of beef, pork and turkey entrees that come with soup and salad. The restaurant won the Flavour of Rural Manitoba Award in 1995.

Wasagaming

T.R. McKoy's Italian Restaurant
$-$$
on Wasagaming St.
☎ *848-4653*
This is an unexpected gem, serving well-prepared pasta, pizza and grill dishes in a friendly and relaxed ambiance.

Entertainment

Winnipeg

Bars and Pubs

King's Head Pub
120 King St.
☎ *957-7710*
This might be Winnipeg's best bar. Located in the Exchange District, it features lots of imported beers and a wide selection of scotch, plus darts and pool. Food is also available.

Toad in the Hole
112 Osborne St.
☎ *284-7201*
In funky Osborne Village, this is a good pub with plenty of pints of various imported brews. Darts and pool are available here also.

Cultural Events

Royal Winnipeg Ballet
380 Graham Ave.
☎ *(800) 667-4792*
☎ *956-2792*
The Royal Winnipeg Ballet is Canada's best-known dance company, housed in its own performance building right downtown. The ballet company won a gold medal at the International Ballet Competition.

Manitoba

In addition to regular performances, it sometimes hosts tours of its facility.

The Winnipeg Fringe Festival

(*held in Jul;* ☎*956-1340, fringe@mtc.mb.ca*) is one of the largest theatre festivals of its kind, featuring a mix of local talent and international groups who perform in various small downtown venues. Real discoveries are to be made among the wide variety of shows that range from family entertainment to experimental works. Free outdoor performances are held at Old Market Square (see p 468) throughout the festival.

Folkorama (☎*800-665-0234 or 982-6210*), Winnipeg's huge annual summer bash, lasts two weeks each August and covers a lot of ground. Representatives of the city's many cultures – French, Ukrainian, Hungarian, Chinese, Japanese and East Indian to name a few – cook the food, sing the songs and dance the dances of their homelands in the many pavilions that spring up around the city for this event.

Some 30,000 folkies converge on **Bird's Hill Park** (p 477) for one fun-filled weekend each July to sing, dance, or simply enjoy the **Winnipeg Folk Festival** (☎*231-0096*), one of North America's finest festivals of its kind. The extravaganza draws talented musicians from around the world to play on outdoor stages for enthusiastic crowds of all ages.

Gaming

Club Regent
1425 Regent Ave. W.
☎*957-2700*
Palm trees and waterfalls set a Caribbean theme for the Club Regent casino. The emphasis here is on electronic gaming: bingo, poker and Keno. There are also slot machines here.

St. Boniface

The **Festival du Voyageur** (*768 Ave. Taché, St. Boniface;* ☎*237-7692; voyageur@festivalvoyageur.mb.ca*) is a giant annual street party in St. Boniface each February, celebrating winter and the voyageurs who settled the province. Action at the big outdoor pavilion includes sled-dog races, snow sculptures and children's activities while musical performers entertain the crowds at night.

The **Cercle Molière** (*340 Provencher Blvd. and 825 Rue St-Joseph;* ☎*233-8055*) is Canada's oldest permanent theatre company, staging three major productions and the smaller "série Café-Théâtre" every year. Performances are in French.

Eastern Manitoba

Gimli

Islendingadagurinn (the Icelandic Festival of Manitoba) takes place during three days in late August, celebrating the local heritage from that far-off land right in downtown Gimli. The festival includes a parade, music, poetry, Icelandic food and more.

Southern Manitoba

Altona

The **Manitoba Sunflower Festival** celebrates the tall yellow flower for three days each July in Altona with Mennonite foods, parades, dancing in the street and the like.

Morris

The **Morris Stampede and Exhibition** turns Morris, an otherwise slowpoke town, into rodeo central for five days in early July. It is Canada's second-largest rodeo (after Calgary), and features chuckwagon and chariot races, an agricultural fair, and (of course) bullriding and other rodeo contests.

Central Manitoba

Dauphin

The hugely popular **National Ukrainian Festival** (*119 Main St. S., Dauphin;* ☎*638-5645;* ≈*638-5851*) takes place in Dauphin for three days each mid-summer, beginning on a Friday morning. Heritage village festivities include a bread-baking competition, embroidery contests, an Easter-egg decorating competition, folk arts, lots of dancing and a beer garden.

Brandon

The whole town of Brandon puckers up for the **International Pickle Festival**, held downtown each September. Besides the obvious pickle-tastings, attractions include expanded musical stages, classic car shows, kickboxing contests, and a full slate of children's events such as the "Oodles of Onions Contest." Truly quirky, but nevertheless a real slice of small- town prairie life.

Portage La Prarie

In Portage La Prairie, the annual **Strawberry Festival** draws visitors from all over the province. Held in

mid-July, it features lots of
street dances, entertainment and a flea market in
addition to strawberry
treats.

Northern Manitoba

The Pas

The **Northern Manitoba
Trappers' Festival** in The Pas
runs for five days each
February. Festivities here
include a famous sled-dog
race.

Shopping

Winnipeg

Shopping is concentrated
in the downtown area.
The Eaton Centre, Hudson's Bay Company and
the North West Company
are within a few blocks of
each other. They are
connected by a series of
covered elevated walkways that are especially
appreciated in wintertime.
The library and other
buildings are also linked
via these "skywalks."

Winnipeg's **Hudson's Bay
Company** (*Portage Ave. and
Memorial Blvd.*) was once
the flagship of the illustrious chain, founded as a
trading company in 1610.
Now a modern department
store, it still sells the original Hudson's Bay Blankets
and other unique merchandise.

Eaton Place (*downtown at
234 Donald St.*), has more
than 100 shops connected
by the walkways. **Portage
Place** is another downtown
mall spanning three
blocks. It contains
160 shops or so, an IMAX
theatre and an in-house
theatre company. **Polo
Park**, (*1485 Portage Ave., on
the way to the airport*), contains more than 180 shops
and leans toward upscale
department stores. Among
other stores downtown,
The **Bayat Gallery**
(*163 Stafford St.,
☎888-88INUIT or 475-5873*)
is particularly interesting as
the city's best of Inuit art
gallery.

Osborne Village has a number of great little boutiques
that should not be left
unexplored. Jewellery,
paperware, gifts, clothes,
cookingware and more
can be found in shops
along Osborne Street between River and
Stradbrook Avenue.

Toad Hall (*54 Arthur St.;
☎956-2195 or 888-333-
TOAD*) is a place that most
children can only dream
of. Shelves brimming with
quality toys – both contemporary and traditional,
line the walls of this store.
It has a whimsical atmosphere that will transport
children and adults alike
into the magical realms of
the imagination. Everything from complete handmade Czech puppet theatres to electric train sets,
colourful kites and magic
sets are sold.

McNally Robinson (*1120
Grant Ave.; ☎475-0483,
info@mcnallyrobinson.ca*) is
by far the best bookstore
in the city. It has a huge
selection in every field
with special emphasis on
prairie writing. A spiral
staircase winds around a
massive tree trunk, leading
to the children's section on
the second floor. Its restaurant, Café au Livre,
serves light lunches and
desserts.

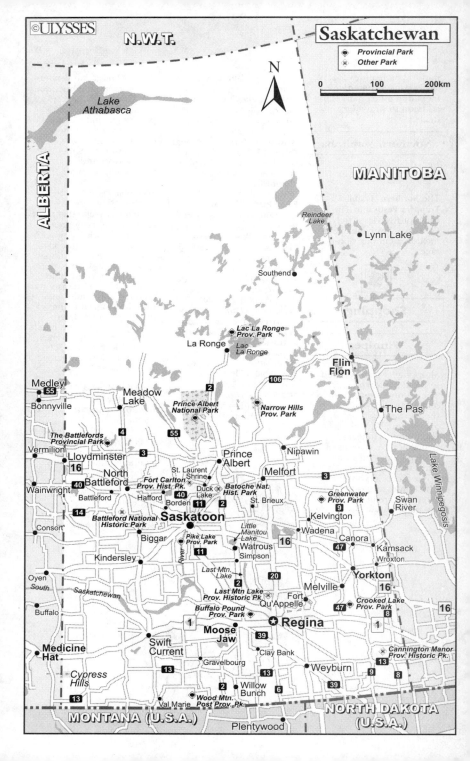

Saskatchewan

In the popular imagination, Saskatchewan is but one continuous wheat field – a place with little topography or cultural diversity.

And the traveller passing through parts of southern Saskatchewan in late summer can hardly be forgiven for thinking otherwise. After all, this is Canada's breadbasket, producing a full 60% of the nation's wheat in acres of golden fields that literally stretch to the horizon.

It is for this reason that the place is usually portrayed as nothing more than a cold monotonous patch of grassland between the lakes of Manitoba and the mountains of Alberta. And it's true! The entire province is subject to such bitterly cold winters that "plug-ins" – electric connections that keep a car battery warm overnight – are standard at a good hotel.

However, a little probing reveals a much richer identity than the stereotype indicates. The spectacular Qu'Appelle Valley cuts across two-thirds of the province, slicing into the level plain with deep glacial creases running down to the river. Venture to Saskatchewan's two major cities and surprising architectural touches are revealed. In other areas, a preponderance of Eastern European churches crop up – painted church domes rising from the prairie like delicately painted Easter eggs, testifying to the province's solid Ukrainian influence.

Farther north, the prairies abruptly give way to foothills and then genuine mountains, woods and lakes. They make it a bit less surprising to learn that there is more forest here – in fact, half a province worth – than farmland. All of the major rivers in the province flow east into Manitoba, eventually emptying into Hudson Bay.

Saskatchewan's First Nations include the Assiniboine and the Blackfoot. Later, the Cree took on the most active role, pushing aggressively westward to satisfy traders' voracious appetite for furs. Later, Sitting Bull came to southern Saskatchewan after routing General Custer of the United States Army at Little Big Horn. Eventually, most First Nations' land in the province was sold or ceded to the government by treaty. But there are still more Aboriginal reserves here than anywhere else in Canada.

L ouis Riel and the Metis, descendants of French voyageurs and Aboriginal people, made a significant mark on prairie history here in the hills and valleys of Saskatchewan. In 1884, after fighting for the rights of the Metis and being exiled to the United States, Riel was called up by the settlers of present-day Saskatchewan (then part of the vast Northwest Territories). Riel's small band, fighting for provincial status for Saskatchewan and better treatment of Aboriginals and Metis, defeated Dominion troops in several early skirmishes. But Riel never wanted a military conflict, hoping rather for negotiation.

T he Canadians, led by MacDonald, waited for the victory that seemed inevitable. They outnumbered Riel's force – especially since a new coast-to-coast railroad was now capable of quickly bringing reinforcements. The Metis were finally defeated at Batoche in the last armed conflict on Canadian soil. While Riel was hanged as a traitor, he is still a hero in some quarters of the province for his unswerving determination to retain his people's sovereignty. Saskatchewan joined Confederation in 1905.

S ince Riel's time, few other individuals have made such a personal mark on the province, save John Diefenbaker. Growing up in a tiny homestead near the Saskatchewan River, he rose from the post of a country lawyer to become Prime Minister of Canada in the early 1960s. His law office, boyhood home, adult home and university office are all well-visited attractions. A lake also bears his name. Popular folk singer Joni Mitchell (born Joan Anderson) is probably the most famous contemporary daughter of the province. Having spent her formative years in Saskatoon, she is still known to drop by and sing an occasional set in a local club there.

G enerally speaking, however, time still moves slowly in Saskatchewan. Today, farmers are diversifying and growing such crops as flax. While the mining of potash and the damming of rivers provide steady jobs, wheat and oil continue to power the economy. The province's two major cities both contain just over 200,000 residents and strive to fill the short summer with festivities. Regina is the elegant capital, so English that it appears never to have left the Crown. Saskatoon features a large university and a thriving cultural scene as well as proximity to many

of the province's natural attractions.

Finding Your Way Around

By Plane

The province's two largest airports are located in Regina and Saskatoon. Several major carriers serve the province, shuttling to and from Calgary, Toronto, Vancouver and other Canadian cities.

Air Canada's offices in Regina (☎525-4711) and Saskatoon (☎652-4181) are both located at the city airport.

Canadian Regional Airlines also has offices in Regina (☎569-2307) and in Saskatoon (☎800-665-1177), both located at the airport.

To get to **Saskatoon's John G. Diefenbaker Airport**, head about 7km directly north of the city. A chain of motels marks the approach. It is about a $12 taxi ride from downtown.

Regina Airport lies just southwest of the city, about 5km away. A cab ride costs about $10.

By Bus

Greyhound Canada (☎800-661-8747) serves the province's major destinations. In Regina, the bus depot (☎787-3340) is located at 2041 Hamilton St. In Saskatoon, the depot (☎933-8000) is at 50 23rd St. E, corner of Pacific Avenue.

The **Saskatchewan Transportation Company** also serves lesser-visited parts of the province. In Regina, STC buses (☎787-3340) depart from the same depot at 2041 Hamilton Street In Saskatoon, call ☎933-8000 to reach the company.

By Train

VIA Rail's (☎800-561-8630 *from western Canada*) cross-country Canadian service passes through the province during the night, making a stop here difficult, although not impossible. Coming from the east, for example, the thrice-weekly train stops in Saskatoon at 2:40am. Eastbound trains pass through at 2:45am.

The Saskatoon station (☎800-561-8630), located in the extreme southwest of the city at Cassino Avenue and Chappell Drive, is the largest station and the usual point of embarking or disembarking in Saskatchewan. The cross-country train no longer runs through Regina. Smaller stations exist at Watrous and Biggar, stopping only on passenger request.

There is no train service to Regina.

Public Transportation

Regina Transit (*333 Winnipeg St.,* ☎777-7433) serves the capital city and offers discounts if you buy a booklet of tickets.

Saskatoon Transit (☎975-3100) operates buses around that city.

Taxis

Capital Cab (☎791-2225) operates throughout Regina. In Saskatoon, try **Radio Cabs** (☎242-1221).

Practical Information

Area Code: **306**.

Tourist Information Offices

Tourism Saskatchewan (☎800-667-7191, *www.sasktourism.com*) can be reached year-round. Provincial tourism information centres, scattered around the province on major highways, are only open during the summers. The lone exception is the centre in downtown Regina (*1900 Albert St.,* ☎787-2300) which remains open all year.

Local tourism office hours vary a great deal, but the larger ones are open year-round.

Tourism Regina (*Trans-Canada Hwy. 1,* ☎789-5099 or 800-661-5099) is way out on the eastern fringe of the city, impossible to reach except by driving. It is well-stocked and friendly. It is open all day on weekdays year-round, and all day on weekends from May through August.

Tourism Saskatoon (*#6-305 Idylwyld Dr. N.,* ☎242-1206 or 800-567-2444) is located downtown and remains open weekdays all year. In summer months, it is open on weekends as well.

Post Offices

Regina
2200 Saskatchewan Dr.

Saskatoon
at the corner of Fourth Ave, N and 23rd St. E

Safety

The province is quite safe, even in its few urban areas. In case of mishaps, the **Regina Police Station** (*1717 Osler St.,* ☎777-6500) and **Saskatoon Police Station** (*130 Fourth Ave. N,* ☎975-8300) are the places to call. There is also a **Royal Canadian Mounted Police** (*1721 Eighth St. E,* ☎975-5173) detachment in Saskatoon and Regina (*1601 Dewdney Ave. W, same telephone no.*)

The **Canadian Automobile Association** maintains offices in the province's most populous areas, offering roadside assistance and information to members. In Regina, offices are located at 200 Albert St. N (☎791-4321), 208 University Park Dr. (☎791-4323) and at 3806 Albert St. (☎791-4322); in Saskatoon, they are located at 204-3929 Eighth St. E (☎668-3770) and 321 Fourth Ave. N (☎668-3737).

Other offices are located in Moose Jaw (*80 Caribou St. W,* ☎693-5195); North Battleford (*2002-100th St.,* ☎445-9451); Prince Albert (*68-13th St. W,* ☎764-6818); Swift Current (*15 Dufferin St. W,* ☎773-3193); Weyburn (*110 Souris Ave.,* ☎842-6651); and Yorkton (*159 Broadway St. E,* ☎783-6536).

Climate

Summers are generally warm and dry with a great deal of sunshine. Winter, however, can bring dangerously low temperatures and blinding snowstorms; Temperatures can plunge to below -30°C, with the windchill making it feel even colder. Travellers should take the appropriate precautions.

For updated weather forecast information in Regina, call ☎780-5744; in Saskatoon, call ☎975-4266.

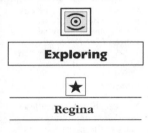

Exploring

★

Regina

Though it's hard to see from downtown, the **Wascana Centre ★★★** is a huge green space – reputedly the largest urban park in North America; even larger than New York City's Central Park. It's the logical spot from which to begin exploring the city.

This nearly 400ha complex includes a lake, a university, bridges, lawns, gardens, a convention centre and even a bird sanctuary. Walking trails and bike paths wind throughout, and there are ample parking and well-kept public washrooms.

A particularly interesting local institution here is **Speaker's Corner ★★**, a podium on the lakeshore where opinions may be proffered to the public. This is a serious podium, with the gas lamps and birches coming from England.

Saskatchewan's cruciform **Legislative Building ★★★** (*free admission; May to Sep every day 8am to 9pm; Oct to Apr every day 8am to 5pm; Albert St. and Legislative Dr.,* ☎787-5358), facing Wascana Lake and landscaped gardens and lawns, may be Canada's most impressive provincial capital building. Its huge dome rises above the city. At the entrance, the fountain is one of a pair from London's Trafalgar Square (the other is now in Ottawa).

Inside, ministers transact the business of the province. In session, it's possible to sit in on the legislative machinations.

An Aboriginal heritage gallery and architectural flourishes such as a rotunda also occupy the building. Guided tours leave every half-hour from the front reception desk.

Wascana Waterfowl Park ★ is home to swans, pelicans and geese. Some migrate while others live here year-round. The small size of the pond allows visitors to get quite close to many of the birds.

The **John Diefenbaker Homestead ★★** (*May to Sep every day 9am to 6pm;* ☎522-3661) commemorates Diefen-baker, who grew up in northern Saskatchewan and served as Prime Minister of Canada. The homestead – which Diefenbaker actually helped his father build when he was just 10 years old – includes original family furnishings. A second, smaller building on the property belonged to Diefenbaker's uncle.

The **MacKenzie Art Gallery ★** (*free admission; every day 11am to 6pm; Wed and Thu until 10pm; 3475 Albert St.,* ☎522-4242), located in the Wascana Centre at the corner of Albert Street and 23rd Avenue, showcases travelling exhibitions and a permanent collection. The gallery, funded by the bequest of a local attorney, includes a painted bronze statue of John Diefenbaker standing on a chair.

Legislative Building

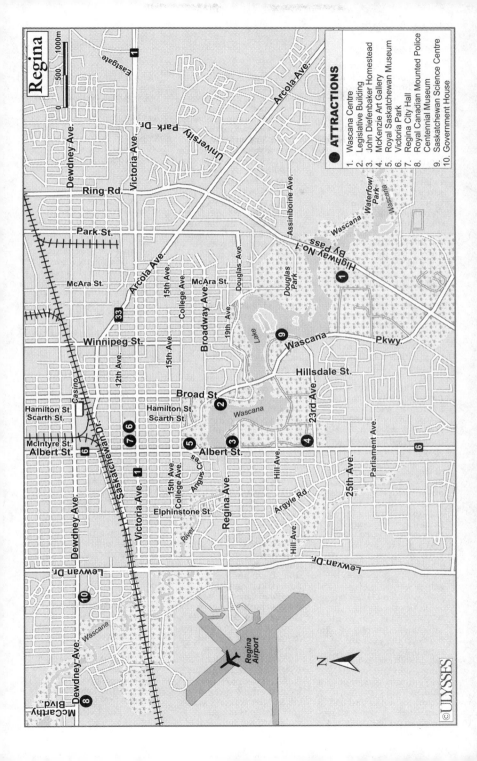

Regina

0 500 1000m

ATTRACTIONS

1. Wascana Centre
2. Legislative Building
3. John Diefenbaker Homestead
4. McKenzie Art Gallery
5. Royal Saskatchewan Museum
6. Victoria Park
7. Regina City Hall
8. Royal Canadian Mounted Police Centennial Museum
9. Saskatchewan Science Centre
10. Government House

© ULYSSES

Moving across the Prince Albert Bridge toward downtown, the **Royal Saskatchewan Museum** ★ (*free admission; every day 9am to 4:30pm; College Ave. and Albert St.*, ☎ *787-2815*) occupies a nice corner of parkland. This is Regina's natural history museum. The exhibits are heavy on sandbox-style dioramas of dinosaurs accompanied by stentorian voice-overs, and there's more Saskatchewan geology here than a visitor could ever want or need to know. Still, this is the best place in town to see aboriginal Canadian artifacts and hear recorded Aboriginal voices. An impressive selection of black-and-white photographs of native leaders, along with videotape of some dances and ceremonies, makes a fitting closing to the walk.

A few blocks north of the museum, toward downtown, you will come across lovely **Victoria Park** ★★★. It's an outstanding urban green space, the best on the prairies, right in the centre of Regina with a fantastic view of downtown's modern skyscrapers. A series of pathways radiate like spokes of a wheel outward from the war memorial at the centre. Spruce trees add a lovely contrast to the grass and gardens.

Nearby, Regina's **city hall** ★★ (*free admission; Mon to Fri 8am to 4:30pm; 2476 Victoria Ave.*, ☎ *777-7305*) is also worth a look while downtown. The lights on the roof are designed to resemble a queen's crown at night. Tours, which must be booked in advance, offer a glimpse of the council chambers, foyer and forum. There is also a souvenir shop on the premises.

Scarth Street is downtown's pedestrian mall that ends at a large forgettable shopping centre called the Cornwall Centre. Just a few doors before the centre, the **Regina Plains Museum** ★★ (*$2; Apr to Sep every day 10am to 4pm; Oct to Mar every day 10am to Fri 10am to 4pm; 1801 Scarth St.*, ☎ *780-9435*) is a bit hard to find but worth the trip. Located four floors up in the same downtown building that houses the Globe Theatre, this stop makes a good introduction to life on the plains.

The museum contains the obligatory recreations of a plains chapel, schoolhouse, bedroom and post office. More interesting are a small display describing the migrations of Aboriginal people through the province; an elegant glass sculpture of a wheatfield; a display on Louis Riel's trial; period surveyor's tools that were used to carve up the prairie (on paper, at least); and an old police mug book containing criminals' photographs. The cons' offenses, described in cursive handwriting as "cheating at cards," "resident of a bawdy house," and the like, make for entertaining reading.

The only two major sites requiring a drive are just a few minutes west of downtown and nearly adjacent to each other. The **Royal Canadian Mounted Police Centennial Museum** ★★★ (*free admission; Jun to Sep 15 every day 8am to 6:45pm; Sep 15 to May every day 10am to 4:45pm; Dewdney Ave. W,* ☎ *780-5838*) is a popular, well laid-out attraction located on the grounds of the RCMP's training academy. Exhibits at this walk-through museum

include many rifles, redserge uniforms and other police artifacts dating from the formation of the R.C.M.P. force in 1873 to keep order and quell bootleggers in the Canadian Northwest. The story of the force's creation, its march west across the prairies (their inaugural 3,200km walk from Montréal) and eventual relocation to the Regina post are all traced in detail here.

The museum is obviously strong on military items from all historical period. As a bonus, it also contains some truly interesting material relating to the darker side of the pioneers' resettling of the west: First Nations land treaties, a buffalo skin incised with victories, Sitting Bull's rifle case, a buffalo skull paired with an ironic quote about the native buffalo hunt, the personal effects of Louis Riel, and so forth.

Government House ★ (*free admission; Tue to Sun, 1pm to 4pm; 4607 Dewdney Ave. W.*, ☎ *787-5773*), near the RCMP training grounds, has been home to some of the province's highest officials since the late 19th century. While it is still the private home of Saskatchewan's lieutenant governor, tours are offered. On some summer weekend afternoons, the staff also serves tea.

The **Saskatchewan Science Centre** ★ (*at Winnipeg St. and Wascana Dr., Wascana Centre,* ☎ *800-667-6300 or 352-5811*) is best known for its 17m IMAX cinema with sound on all sides. Another section of the museum, the **Powerhouse of Discovery** (*$6.50*), presents exhibits and live talks.

Southern Saskatchewan

The Trans-Canada Highway runs east to west through southern Saskatchewan, crossing wheatfields and the occasional town. East of Regina, it gives no hint of the spectacular vista that lies just a few kilometres to the north, in the Qu'Appelle Valley that runs parallel to it at this point. West of Regina the land is perfectly flat. This is the scenery for which Saskatchewan is best known, making humans feel, as the popular saying goes, like a fly on a plate.

★★★
Qu'Appelle River Valley

The Fort Qu'Appelle River Valley makes for a surprising detour. The river has cut a little valley in the otherwise flat countryside. **Route 247** (*north of the Trans-Canada between Whitewood and Grenfell*), barely known by tourists, runs along the river as it dips through the brown and green hills. It passes **Round Lake ★★** and then **Crooked Lake Provincial Park ★★**, which has beautiful lakes for swimming, fishing and sightseeing. A string of tiny tree-shaded resort towns provides campgrounds and the odd country store.

Continuing along the very poorly maintained Route 22 takes you to a worthwhile, if isolated, destination: the **Motherwell Homestead National Historic Site ★★** (*$4; summer every day 10am to 6pm; Box 247, Abernethy, ☎333-2116, ☎333-2210*). This impressive Victorian fieldstone house with gingerbread trim was built by W.R. Motherwell, who was famous for developing innovative dryland farming techniques at the turn of the century. The property, which more or less amounts to an estate, does not lack for anything. The grounds encompass a tennis court, croquet lawn, arbours, a herb garden and barnyard. The interior of the house is just as astonishing an example of high living in the midst of deserted prairie. Visitors can tour the house and grounds and are even invited to help with the farm chores. There is a food concession stand on the premises.

At a bend in the valley, where the river feeds into a series of lakes, the small town of **Fort Qu'Appelle** charms visitors with its setting – tucked among hills – as well as a smattering of historic sites. The tourist information centre is situated inside a former train station. A former Hudson's Bay Company log cabin, for which the town is named, is now a small **museum ★** (*$2; early June to late Aug 10am to 5pm; Bay Ave. and Third St., ☎332-6443 or 332-4319*). The fort was the site of a historic treaty ceding vast tracts of First Nation lands in Saskatchewan to the Canadian government.

Moose Jaw

Moose Jaw (pop. 30,000), a former bootlegging capital during US prohibition years, sprouts up in the flatlands west of Regina and offers visitors a glimpse into little-known aspects of the province's past. While it is now a sleepy little town where the parking meters still accept nickels, impressive bank buildings and the ornate city hall attest to its more glamorous past.

The **Western Development Museum's Transportation Museum ★** (*$5;every day 9am to 6pm; Jan to Mar Mon closed; 50 Diefenbaker Dr., ☎693-5989*), in a somewhat forlorn location north of downtown, serves up the history of Canadian transportation – everything from canoes, Red River carts and pack horses to vintage rail cars, automobiles and airplanes. A narrow-gauge railway runs behind the museum on weekends and holidays from late May to Labour Day. Also popular is the **Snowbirds Gallery** that is devoted to Canada's national aerobatic team. The jet planes' artful manoeuvres come to life on a big movie screen in the flight simulator, in the museum's cinema (*$1.50*).

Crescent Park ★, just east of downtown, on the banks of the Moose Jaw River, is a pleasant place for a short walk beneath trees and over a picturesque bridge. The secret underground passages of Moose Jaw were but a rumour until a car plunged through the pavement and wound up 4m below street level in what are now referred to as the **Tunnels of Little Chicago ★★★** (*$7; 108 Main St. N., ☎693-5261*). Today, a guided tour takes visitors through a small portion of the vast hidden network. Interpreters explain how they were built by the Chinese labourers who had come to work on the railway and decided to go "underground," in this case literally, when Canada went back on its promise to grant them citizenship once the task was completed. Later, the passages were used as hideouts of a different kind as bootlegging operations were set up here and gangsters from as far away as Chicago slipped into town, evading the long arm of the law.

It is said that the illustrious Al Capone himself made appearances here when the heat became too strong south of the border. The tour evokes both the abysmal living conditions endured by the Chinese in these dark, cramped quarters and the scintillating era of speakeasies and corruption. While the adjacent museum is less interesting, the tour of the tunnels is an excellent way to become immersed in the history of this once-electrifying town.

Claybank

Southeast of Moose Jaw, on Highway 339, is little Claybank and its historic **Claybank Brick Plant ★** (*$3; Jul to Aug Sat and Sun 10am to 4pm; ☎306-868-4774*). Operated from 1914 until 1989, the plant was one of Canada's two major plants of this kind during that time. Its bricks were used in buildings such as Quebec City's Chateau Frontenac. The complex of high chimneys and dome-like kilns can be toured by arrangement. There is also a tea room on the premises.

Gravelbourg

Southwest of Moose Jaw, a 115km detour off the Trans-Canada down Routes 2 and then 43, Gravelbourg is the acknowledged centre of French culture in Saskatchewan. A French-Canadian cultural centre and dance troupe both make their homes here. Most prominent among downtown buildings is the **Cathédrale**

Notre-Dame de l'Assomption ★★ (*free admission; every day 9am to 5pm, guided tours Jul and Aug, $2; ☎648-3322*). Built in 1918, the church is a historic property and features wonderful interior murals painted by Charles Maillard, its founding pastor, over a 10-year period.

Nearby, on Fifth Avenue East, the **Musée de Gravelbourg ★** (*Jul and Aug 1pm to 5pm, 5th Ave. E., ☎648-3301*) preserves mementoes from the original French-speaking settlers of the region, including the missionary Father L.P. Gravel for whom the town is named.

Other Sights

Nearby, **Wood Mountain Post Provincial Historic Park ★★** (*donation; Jun to mid-Aug everyday 10am to 5pm; ☎694-3659*), a former Mountie post, is interesting particularly for its association with the Sioux chief Sitting Bull and his people. Sitting Bull came here in the spring of 1877 after defeating the United States Army at the battle of Little Big Horn. As many as 5,000 Sioux were already hiding in the surrounding hills.

The chief quickly forged a friendship with police Major James Walsh. But political pressure from both the Canadian and United States governments replaced Walsh with another officer who began a siege against the Sioux. The two buildings here, staffed with interpreters, recount the story in more detail.

Sitting Bull's former camp is located near the village of Willow Bunch in **Jean-Louis Legare Park ★**.

A Metis trader, Legare supplied food to the Sioux during their exile and also provisioned them for their long march back to the United States in 1881.

Approximately 40km north of Regina on Route 20 is **Last Mountain House Provincial Park ★** (*free admission; Jul to Sep, ☎787-2080*), a small yet interesting recreation of a short-lived Hudson's Bay Company fur post. Built of wood and local white clay, the post was established near a buffalo herd in the adjacent river valley in 1869. However, the buffalo moved west the following year and never returned.

Today the windswept park's displays include a fur press, trading store, icehouse for preserving meat, bunkhouse quarters for trappers and the more spacious officers' quarters. During the summer, park interpreters are on hand to recreate the experience.

Saskatoon

Set on the banks of the South Saskatchewan River, Saskatoon is Saskatchewan's hip address. Home to a large university and a world leader in agricultural biotechnology, the city also offers a host of outdoor activities and cultural events year-round. They include a jazz festival, fringe and folk festivals, and the famous Shakespeare on the Saskatchewan theatre series. Once a major stop on the trans-Canadian rail network, the downtown still has some impressive buildings from that era.

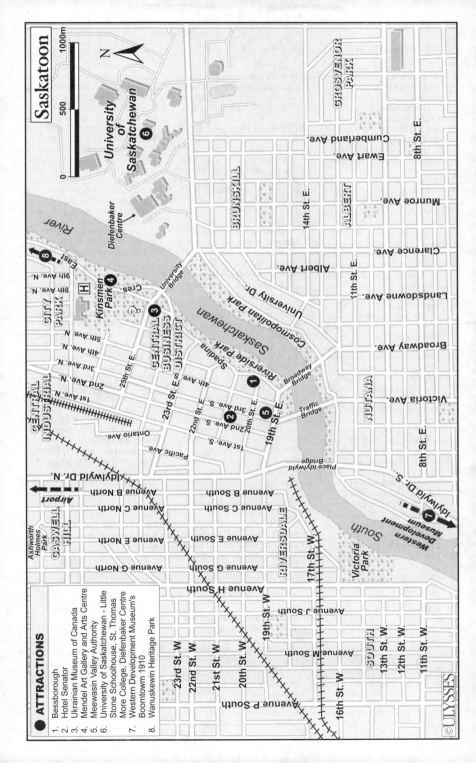

Saskatoon

N

0   500   1000m

University of Saskatchewan
⑥

River

Diefenbaker Centre

University Bridge

GROSVENOR PARK

Cumberland Ave.
8th St. E.

Ewart Ave.

BRUNSKILL

14th St. E.

Munroe Ave.

ALBERT

Clarence Ave.

Albert Ave.
11th St. E.

Landsdowne Ave.

Broadway Ave.

NUTANA

Victoria Ave.

8th St. E.

Cres.
Cosmopolitan Park
University Dr.

Saskatchewan

Riverside Park

Broadway Bridge

CENTRAL INDUSTRIAL

Idylwild Dr. N.

Airport

CITY PARK
9th Ave. N. *East*
8th Ave. N.
⑧
Kinsmen Park ④ 🅷

5th Ave. N.
4th Ave. N.
3rd Ave. N.
2nd Ave. N.
1st Ave. N.
25th St.

③
CENTRAL BUSINESS DISTRICT

23rd St. E.

Spadina

4th Ave. S. E.
3rd Ave. S. E.
②

22nd St. S.
2nd Ave. S.
1st Ave. S.
Ontario Ave.
Pacific Ave.

①

20th St. E.
19th St. E.
⑤
Traffic Bridge

Place Idylwild Bridge

Ashworth Holmes Park

GASWELL HILL

Avenue B North
Avenue C North
Avenue E North
Avenue G North
Avenue H South

Avenue B South
Avenue C South
Avenue E South
Avenue G South

RIVERSDALE

17th St. W.

19th St. W.

Avenue J South
Avenue M South

SOUTH

Victoria Park

Western Development Museum

⑦
Idylwild Dr. S.
8th St. E.

23rd St. W
22nd St. W
21st St. W
20th St. W

16th St. W.

Avenue P South

13th St. W.
12th St. W.
11th St. W.

© ULYSSES

● ATTRACTIONS

1. Bessborough
2. Hotel Senator
3. Ukrainian Museum of Canada
4. Mendel Art Gallery and Arts Centre
5. Meewasin Valley Authority
6. University of Saskatchewan - Little Stone Schoolhouse, St. Thomas More College, Diefenbaker Centre
7. Western Development Museum's Boomtown 1910
8. Wanuskewin Heritage Park

Among the city's most striking buildings is the castle-like railway hotel, the **Bessborough**. It was built by relief workers during the depression era as were the graceful arched bridges that span the river from downtown.

While the Bessborough is Saskatoon's best-known hotel, the **Hotel Senator** (*243 21st St. E.*) is its oldest. Built in 1908 as the Flanagan Hotel, it boasted such extravagances as steam heating, hot and cold running water, and a telephone in each room. Although the Senator can no longer be considered a luxury hotel by any stretch of the imagination, some of its former glory is still in evidence. The marble pillar at the foot of the staircase, the wood-panelled dining room with its original chandelier, and the marble floor of the lobby all recall a more prosperous era in the hotel's history.

Saskatoon's most interesting commercial street is **Broadway Avenue**, south of the river. Located downtown, **Second Avenue** is lined with small shops selling everything from CDs and LPs to books, pottery and international crafts. It intersects with **21st Street East**, which boasts the major banks, a few slightly more upscale shops, and some attractive older storefronts including the Art Deco facade of the former Eaton's department store (now housing an Army Navy and Surplus store).

At the corner of 21st Street East and First Ave. is an interesting sculpture commemorating a chance meeting of two of the most prominent figures in Canadian history. It depicts Sir Wilfrid Laurier buying a newspaper from a young John Diefenbaker, circa 1910.

Historical sites are harder to find. The city is, in fact, rather short on cultural attractions. Nearly all of the good ones are concentrated downtown along the river. It's possible to see everything of note in a single busy day.

The **Ukrainian Museum of Canada** ★ ★ (*$2; Tue to Sat 10am to 5pm, Sun 1pm to 5pm; 910 Spadina Cr. E, ☎244-3800*) is a surprisingly good history lesson beneath a small roof. Through a series of walk-through rooms, the museum uses texts and simple articles to describe the Ukrainian people's Eastern European origins and persecution, their migration to North America, their settlement of the prairies, and their subsequent endurance as a people. Highlights among the displays include a large section on the deep religious significance of the beautiful art of *pysanka* (Easter-egg decoration), a careful explanation of the distinctively domed Ukrainian churches and a delineation of where and why the Ukrainians settled where they did. Some intricate ornamental breads and examples of *rozpys* – the decorative painting of furnishings, walls and doors – are also nice touches.

The **Mendel Art Gallery and Arts Centre** ★ ★ ★ (*free admission; summer every day 9am to 9pm, winter every day noon to 9pm; 950 Spadina Cr. E, ☎975-7610*) is the province's best art museum. Its exhibits rotate quite regularly, and whether drawn from the permanent collection or just on loan, they're always interesting. Concurrently showing might be American James Walsh's astonishingly thick acrylics in one gallery, several different multimedia installations occupying another and a collection of modern prints, paintings and other media works by First Nations artists sprinkled throughout. The museum also contains such amenities as a children's room, coffee shop, a good gift shop and a small yet lovely conservatory.

A footpath from the back of the centre leads down to the river, hooking up with an extensive network of trails running north and south along both river banks. The **Meewasin Valley trails** ★ ★ (*www.lights.com/meewasin*) extend more than 50km along the river, a joy for cyclists and walkers. The valley's other amenities include an outdoor skating rink and an urban grassland reserve. The **Meewasin Valley Authority headquarters** ★ (*402 Third Ave. S, ☎665-6888*) provide an introduction to the river and the city.

Southeast, across the river, lies the large and pretty **University of Saskatchewan** ★ ★ campus. Several attractions of historic interest are found here, though some are only open during the summer when school is out of session. Especially quaint is the **Little Stone Schoolhouse** ★ (*☎966-8384*), Saskatoon's first schoolhouse, dating from 1887. The **St. Thomas More College chapel** ★ (*☎966-8900*) is worth a look for its mural by Canadian artist William Kurelek, and the university **observatory** (*☎966-6429*) opens to the public Saturday evenings.

Also not to be missed, the **Diefenbaker Centre** ★ (*$2; Mon to Fri 9:30am to 4:30pm, Tue and Thr 9:30am to 8pm, Sun 12:30pm to 5pm; ☎966-8384*) preserves many of Diefenbaker's personal papers and effects His gravestone is located nearby on the university campus. Other displays include replicas of the former Prime Minister's office and Privy Council chamber. Splendidly located with a view of the river and the downtown, the centre is also famous for housing what is probably the most renowned piece of furniture in the province: a simple maple desk that once belonged to John A. Macdonald, the man considered the Father of Canadian confederation.

On the outskirts of town sits the **Western Development Museum's Boomtown 1910** ★ (*$5; every day 9am to 5pm; 2610 Lorne Ave. S., ☎931-1910*). It reconstructs a typical western mining town's main street in movie-set fashion, with more than 30 buildings making up the complex. Like many of the province's museums, its exhibits lean toward agricultural equipment and farm implements. Also outside the city, about 4km away, is **Valley Road**, an agricultural drive leading to a number of fruit, vegetable and herb farms in the area.

Finally, a 10min drive to the north leads to the wonderful **Wanuskewin Heritage Park** ★★★ (*$6; May to Sep every day 9am to 9pm; Oct to Apr everyday 9am to 5pm; ☎931-6767*), perhaps the best native museum in the prairies. The area around Saskatoon was settled continuously for thousands of years before the first white settlers arrived. A river valley just

north of the city was long used as a "buffalo jump" where local Aboriginal peoples hunted and established winter camps. Now the property is open to the public as a series of archaeological sites – ancient tipi rings and a medicine wheel, for instance, are within walking distance. An indoor museum and interpretive centre dealing with the history of First Nations people can also be found here.

"A people without history is like wind in the buffalo grass," says a panel in the museum, which does indeed throw much light onto the Aboriginal peoples of the Plains. The differences among Cree, Dene, Lakota, Dakota and Assiniboine are carefully explained in one display, and their recorded voices can be heard by pressing a button. Other rooms in the centre host art exhibits and slide shows, talks and conferences, and an Aboriginal foods café. Ongoing archaeological research is also conducted on the grounds.

Yellowhead Highway

Yorkton

Yorkton would be rather uninteresting but for the **Western Development Museum's "Story of People" museum** ★★ (*$5; May to Sep every day 9am to 6pm; Hwy. 16, ☎783-8361*). It traces the history of the various immigrant populations that have made the province as colourful as it is.

Yorkton is also the site of western Canada's first brick Ukrainian church. **St. Mary's Ukrainian Catholic Church** ★★ (*155 Catherine St., ☎783-4594*), built in 1914, is topped with a

distinctive 21m-high cathedral dome. The dome was painted in 1939-41 by Steven Meush and is considered one of the most beautiful on the continent. Inside, there is beautiful icon work by Ihor Suhacev. If the church is not open, visitors can ask at the adjacent rectory for a look inside. The church also hosts an annual "Vid Pust" (Pilgrimage Day) celebration each June.

Veregin

Approximately 50km north off the Yellowhead, Veregin houses the **National Doukhobour Heritage Village** ★★ (*$3; mid-May to mid-Sep every day 10am to 6pm; mid-Sep to mid-May Mon to Fri, 10am to 4pm; ☎542-4441*). It's an 11-building complex that throws light on one of the province's most intriguing immigrant groups. The Doukhobours came to Saskatchewan in 1899 and established a short-lived community here, eschewing meat, alcohol and tobacco in favour of an agrarian existence. While they soon moved further west, this museum preserves the original prayer home and machinery shop. Also on display are a brick oven, bath house, agricultural equipment and blacksmith's shop.

Canora

Just 25km west of Veregin, Canora welcomes travellers with a 7.6m statue in Slavic dress. A tourist booth operates next to the statue from June until September to orient visitors to local attractions. This little village is also home to a fine restored **Ukrainian Orthodox Heritage Church** ★ (*Jun to mid-Sep every day 8am to 6pm; 710 Main St., ☎563-5662*) Built in 1928, the church displays Kiev architecture and stained glass. Visitors can obtain a key next door at 720 Main St. when the church isn't open.

Wroxton

Wroxton is some distance from the Yellowhead – 35km north – but it's interesting for its two Ukrainian churches on opposite ends of the village. Both domes are visible just north of the main highway and can be reached by driving along one of the town's several dirt roads.

Around Wadena

In the Wadena area, **Big Quill Lake** and various other marshes on both sides of the Yellowhead offer good opportunities to view birds. The advocacy group Ducks Unlimited helps preserve many of these lands and interprets them for the general public. **Little Quill Lake Heritage Marsh** ★, best reached from Highway 35, was designated an international shorebird reserve in 1994 and is open year-round. This marsh hosts more than 800,000 migrating and resident shorebirds each year. Visitors can hike, learn from interpretive signs and climb an observation tower.

St. Brieux

St. Brieux features a little **museum** ★ (*mid-May to Aug everyday 10am to 4pm; 300 Barbier Dr., ☎275-2229*) in a former Roman Catholic rectory. It contains artifacts of early settlers from Quebec, France and Hungary. Tours here are conducted in both English and French.

Muenster

Continuing west, also near the Yellowhead, the small town of Muenster is notable for a beautiful twin-towered cathedral and adjoining monastery. **St. Peter's Cathedral** ★★ (*free; Mar to Dec 9am to 9pm; closed Jan and Feb, ☎682-5484*), built in 1910, features paintings by Berthold Imhoff, a German-born count who later moved to St. Walburg, Saskatchewan, and became an artist. Approximately 80 life-sized figures grace the cathedral with saints and religious scenes making up the interior. **St. Peter's Abbey** ★★ (*March 1 to Dec 31, 8am to dusk, ☎682-1777*) gives a sense of what the monastic life is like. A self-guided tour reveals the abbey's farm, gardens, print shop and so on. It's also possible to sleep a night in the monastery for a small donation.

★
Little Manitou Lake

For centuries, travellers have been making a trip to Little Manitou Lake to "take the waters." This lake is so high in natural mineral salts that a person swimming can't sink. In fact, the water is even saltier here than in the Dead Sea, or in any ocean on Earth. The salts are reputed to have restorative powers. That's why a strange little tourist town has sprung up around the lake, itself oddly placed among barren hills.

Borden

Borden, the boyhood home of John Diefenbaker – his house has been moved to downtown Regina – is interesting as a

stop because you can tour a local **United Grain Growers (UGG) grain elevator** ★ (*every day 8am to 5pm; ☎997-2010*) year-round. Guests are requested to phone ahead, however, to arrange these tours.

The Battlefords

Battleford (pop. 4,000), former capital of the Northwest Territories, was once important but is today overshadowed by its twin city of North Battleford across the Saskatchewan River. As usual, railway politics decided the fate of the twin towns. **Fort Battleford National Historic Site** (*$4; mid-May to mid-Oct every day 9am to 5pm; ☎937-2621*) recalls the original impetus for the townsite – a Mountie post – complete with four restored period buildings. The barracks house contains additional displays of historical interest explained by guides in period police costume.

North Battleford (pop. 14,000) is often visited for the **Western Development Museum's Heritage Farm and Village** ★ (*$5; May to mid-Sep every day 8:30am to 6:30pm; the rest of the year Tue to Sun 1pm to 5pm, ☎445-8033*), a mostly agricultural museum featuring plenty of period farm machinery.

The town is also famous as home to artist Allan Sapp. The **Allan Sapp Gallery** ★ (*free admission; May to Sep every day 1pm to 5pm; Oct to May Wed to Sun 1pm to 5pm; ☎445-1760*) showcases the work of the prairies' best-known and loved Aboriginal artist. Sapp's paintings, recollections of Aboriginal life from a half-century ago hang in the important museums of Canada and are displayed and sold here. Located on the ground floor of a restored Carnegie library, the gallery also contains hundreds of works by Sapp's mentor Allan Gonor.

West Central Saskatchewan

Poundmaker Trail

Route 40, also called Poundmaker Trail, is the former stronghold of the Poundmaker Cree Nation. **Cut Knife** features what is said to be Canada's largest tomahawk, a suspended sculpture of wood and fiberglass whose fir handle is more than 16m long and supports a six-tonne blade. The surrounding park contains the obligatory small museum. The legendary **Chief Poundmaker's** (*www.wbm.ca/wilderness/pou ndmake*) grave is also in town on the Cree Reserve. It is a testament to a man who favoured peace over war and surrendered his force of natives to the Mounties rather than continue to shed blood.

Hafford

Just northeast of Saskatoon, near the village of Hafford, the **Redberry Project Highway 40** ★ (☎549-2400) maintains one of the province's best waterfowl projects in a federal migratory bird sanctuary on Redberry Lake. Their motto is "we have friends in wet places," and the specialty here is pelicans. More than 1000 American white pelicans nest on the lake's New Tern Island. It's just one of 14 colonies of these birds in Saskatchewan. Boat tours are also avail-

able that cost about $15 for approximately 1.5hrs.

Prince Albert

Prince Albert (pop. 39,000), the oldest city in the province, is a gateway in more ways than one. It is the largest town near **Prince Albert Provincial Park** ★★★ (☎663-4512), the site of a huge mill that converts the northern forests into pulp and paper, and the source of three Canadian Prime Ministers (see p 503). Though the town began as a fur post for Northwestern explorer Peter Pond in 1776, the town as it exists today was established nearly a full century later by the Reverend James Nisbet as a mission for local Cree.

The **Diefenbaker House Museum** (*free admission; mid-May to early Aug Mon to Sat 10am to 6pm, Sun 10am to 9pm; 246 19th St. W., ☎953-4863*) is probably the most famous stop in town. It contains many of the former Canadian Prime Minister's personal effects and furnishings, and describes his relationship to the city.

The **Prince Albert Historical Museum** (*$1; River St. and Central Ave.; mid-May to early Aug Mon to Sat 10am to 6pm, Sun10am to 9pm; ☎764-2992*) brings local history into focus, beginning with native and fur-trader culture from the mid-1800s. There is also a second-floor tearoom with a balcony overlooking the North Saskatchewan River.

Several other museums in Prince Albert are also worth a look. The **Evolution of Education Museum** (*free admission; mid-May to early Sep every day 10am to 8pm; ☎953-4385*) is located in a

former one-room schoolhouse, and the **Rotary Museum of Police and Corrections** (*free admission; mid-May to Sep 10am to 8pm; ☎922-3313*) is inside a former North West Mounted Police guardhouse. It includes a fascinating display of weapons fashioned by prisoners trying to break out of provincial jails.

Around Duck Lake

Southwest of Prince Albert, **Duck Lake** was the site of one of the most famous events in Saskatchewan history: the battle between Louis Riel and his band of Metis and the North West Police. The **Duck Lake Regional Interpretive Centre** ★★ (*$4; 5 Anderson Ave.; mid-May to early Sep every day 10am to 5:30pm; ☎467-2057*) describes the events as they unfolded and displays artifacts from the Metis Resistance campaign. You can also climb a viewing tower of the battlefield grounds. A series of painted outdoor murals welcome the visitor.

About 25km west of Duck Lake, **Fort Carlton Provincial Historic Park** ★★ (*$2.50; mid-May to early Sep; every day 10am to 6pm; ☎467-4512*) dates from 1810. It's another in the string of Hudson's Bay Company posts in Saskatchewan. An important land treaty was also signed here. Today the site consists of a reconstructed stockade and buildings. Interpretive staff lead tours and explain how the fort was a Mountie post until the Battle of Duck Lake. Just outside the fort, a Plains Cree encampment – three tipis furnished in typical late-19th-century fashion – give a sense of what and how the Aboriginal peoples traded with the English. The objects in these tipis include robes, skins, pipes, weapons and other ceremonial objects.

St. Laurent

St. Laurent Shrine ★ (*May 1 to Aug 31; ☎467-2212*) makes for an enjoyable side trip in the area. Built in 1874 as an Order of the Oblate mission right on the South Saskatchewan River, it's quite similar to the Our Lady of Lourdes shrine in France. Sunday services are held at 4pm during July and August. Annual pilgrimages also take place during those months. The tradition dates back to 1893, when one of Brother Guillet's leg miraculously healed after he prayed to the shrine.

Batoche National Historic Park ★★★ (*$4; May 18 to Oct 14 9am to 5pm; ☎423-6227*) is where Riel's story came to its end in March of 1885. The site, a peaceful agricultural valley where the Metis had settled after moving westwards, became capital of the Metis resistance when Riel challenged the Canadian government. Today, a walking path, museum and interpretive staff guide visitors through the remains of the village of Batoche, including the restored St. Antoine de Padoue church and rectory. There are also trenches and rifle pits used by the Mountie forces during their four-day siege of Batoche.

Parks

Southern Saskatchewan

Buffalo Pound Provincial Park ★ (*☎694-3659*), 23km northeast of Moose Jaw, presents a variety of recreational choices, including most popularly a chance to view grazing bison. A number of hiking trails wind through the dips and rises of the Qu'Appelle Valley: the trail tells the story of the Charles Nicolle Homestead, a stone dwelling built in 1930; another proceeds through a marsh; and yet another traverses the junction of two rivers, an area rich with such wildlife as painted turtles, deer and great blue herons. The river is also a popular beach and boating destination.

Bison

Cannington Manor Provincial Historic Park ★ (*free admission; May to Sep 10am to 6pm; ☎577-2131*) recounts a short-lived experiment by the Englishman Captain Edward Pierce who tried to form a utopian colony based on agriculture here. And for a while it worked – colonists spent a combi-

nation of days working the fields and diversions such as fox hunts, cricket, horse races and afternoon tea, but he experiment did not survive. The manor features period antiques and farm tools used on the site. Six other buildings – some original, some reconstructed – complete the park.

Last Mountain Lake National Wildlife Area ★★ (*free admission; May 1 to Oct 31; ☎836-2022*), occupying the northern end of the lake with the same name, is believed to be the oldest bird sanctuary on the North American continent. More than 250 species of bird touch down here during their annual migrations south, including the spectacular whooping crane. These migrations are most spectacular during spring (mid-May) and fall (September). Visitors either choose to follow a scripted tour by car or climb the observation tower and take the two hiking trails on foot. The preserve is best reached by turning east off Highway 2 at the town of Simpson, then following signs to the lakeshore. There is talk that the site's administrators may soon begin charging a fee to visit the preserve.

Grasslands National Park ★★ (*year-round; between Val Marie and Kill-deer, south of Hwy. 18; ☎298-2257*) was the first representative portion of original mixed-grass prairie set aside in North America. Among the variety of habitats represented here are grasslands, buttes, badlands and the Frenchman River Valley. Spectacular views can be seen from some of the butte tops while the wildlife includes the rare swift fox, pronghorn antelopes and golden eagles. Most interesting, though, is the unique **prairie dog town ★★**, where colonies of black-tailed prairie dogs still live in their natural environment. Guided hikes are given from the park office in Val Marie on summer Sundays. While wilderness camping is permitted in the park, but permission must be obtained from private landowners to access certain parts of it.

Pike Lake Park ★ (☎933-6966), a small recreational park about 30km southwest of Saskatoon, is a popular day trip for residents of Saskatchewan's largest city. The terrain here includes lawns shaded by aspen, ash and birch trees, a good beach and lots of wildlife. Watersports facilities include a pool, waterslide and canoes for hire. Hiking trails, tennis courts, golf and mini-golf are also available here.

The Yellowhead Highway

Cumberland House Provincial Historic Park ★★★ (☎888-2077), on an island in the North Saskatchewan River near the Manitoba border, was quite important historically: it was the first Hudson's Bay Company fur post in western Canada. Later, it served as a port for steamboat traffic along the river. An 1890s-era powderhouse and part of a sternwheeler paddleboat are all that remain, but it's still a fascinating stop.

Duck Mountain Provincial Park ★★ (☎542-5500) sits 25km east of Kamsack,

right on the Manitoba border. Open year-round, the park completely surrounds popular Madge Lake. The mountain itself rises 240m above the surrounding terrain that's covered with aspens. Full recreational facilities are here, including a campground, mini-golf course, fishing gear and beach. A lodge within park grounds provides accommodations.

The Battlefords Provincial Park ★ (☎386-2212) is considered one of the recreational jewels of the province. Its location on the northeast shore of Jackfish Lake provides easy access to fishing and sailing. Equipment is available for these watersports. There are also a golf course and mini-golf course on premises as well as a store and year-round resort-style accommodations.

Greenwater Lake Provincial Park ★ (☎278-2972) is on Highway 38, north of Kelvington in the province's eastern Porcupine Forest. There is a marina with boat rentals and fishing gear in the summer as well as tennis, golf, and horseback-riding facilities. In winter, the park becomes a destination for cross-country skiers. Nice log cabins are also available for rent.

West-Central Saskatchewan

Prince Albert National Park ★★★ (☎663-4522), encompassing 400,000ha, is one of Saskatchewan's finest parks. Entering from the south entrance on Route 263, you will pass through grassland and fields, then aspen parklands and finally forests.

Waskesiu Lake is the park area's largest and most popular body of water, and is where most of the services, beaches and activities are located. Farther off the beaten track, the park is noted for several good canoe routes and hiking trails that provide access to bird and plant life. Bird enthusiasts, for instance, come to glimpse Canada's second-largest colony of American white pelican, who nest on Lavallee Lake. Wolves, elk and buffalo also live here. Hikers often choose to explore Boundary Bog Trail. It penetrates the park's muskeg territory and includes carnivorous pitcher plants and dwarf stands of larch more than a century old as well as the Treebeard Trail that winds through tall, aromatic groves of balsam fir and white spruce.

The park is most famous, however, for wise old Archibald Bellaney, an Englishman who came here in 1931, took the name of Grey Owl, and lived on a remote lake. **Grey Owl's Cabin ★**, a one-room log cabin on Ajawaan Lake, can only be reached by boat, canoe or on foot via a 20km trail during summer. Grey Owl lived here for seven years. Tours are available from park staff.

Lac La Ronge Provincial Park ★★★ (☎800-772-4064 or 425-4244) lies just north of Prince Albert Park on Route 2, providing similar scenery – and more of it – than its more well-known neighbour. It's the province's largest provincial park. There are more than 100 lakes including enormous Lac La Ronge that is dotted with what are said to be more than

1,000 islands. Cliffs, rock paintings and sand beaches can also be found in the park.

Additionally, Lac La Ronge Park contains one of the province's showcase historic sites, the **Holy Trinity Anglican Church Historic Site ★★★**. As Saskatchewan's oldest standing building, it's an enormous structure in an oddly remote location. Built in the late 1850s from local wood, then completed with stained-glass windows shipped from England, the church was part of the historic Stanley Mission.

Narrow Hills Provincial Park ★★ (☎426-2622) lies just to the east of Prince Albert Park, although there is no direct connecting route. It can only be reached by a series of roads. It is famous for its eskers (the long, narrow glacially deposited hills that give the park its name) and more than 25 bodies of water that harbour a number of species of game fish. One esker is topped by a fire tower, and its main building includes a small museum.

Scenic **Anglin Lake ★★**, southwest of Prince Albert Park, has at least one particularly distinguishing feature: it harbours the continent's largest nesting loon population.

Loon

Accommodations

Regina

Turgeon International Hostel
$18
K, tv, sb, ⊗
2310 McIntyre St., S4P 2S2
☎*800-467-8357*
☎*791-8165*
⇌*721-2667*
A great value for the guest who enjoys interacting with other travellers, this friendly hostel provides dorm rooms, a family room with space for five and a room for groups. The house once belonged to William Turgeon, an Acadian from New Brunswick who came to Regina and ran a successful law practice for many years. It was later purchased by Hostelling International and moved on a flatbed trailer.

With the Royal Saskatchewan Museum visible at the end of the street, its location is superb and the family room is a super bargain. There's also a huge self-catering kitchen, delightful travel library, airy television room and great manager. The neighbourhood is also within walking distance of all the city's major attractions and restaurants. The office is closed during the day, however, and the facility closes completely during January.

Crescent House
$50 bkfst incl.
sb
180 Angus Cr.
☎*352-5995*
cheryl.mogg@dlcwest.com
Crescent House is a Bed and Breakfast located on a crescent-shaped street just minutes on foot from most of Regina's major attractions. Special touches include a fireplace, three friendly terrier dogs, and a backyard shaded by 17m ash and elm trees.

Country Inns & Suites
room $76
suites $91 bkfst incl.
tv, ≡, K, ✖, P
3321 Eastgate Bay, S4Z 1A4
☎*800-456-4000*
☎*789-9117*
⇌*789-3010*
This hotel chain strives to offer a more homey atmosphere than most chain. Rooms are done up with brass beds and duvets resembling quilts. Most rooms have mini-bars on the honour system. All guests receive free newspapers and can make free local calls. Suites also come with a sitting room, sofa bed and microwave – continental breakfast is included. Located just off Highway 1, at the eastern edge of town.

Chelton Suites Hotel
$79-$125
tv, ≡, ⊘, ℝ, K, ✖, P
1907-11th Ave., S4P 0J2
☎*800-667-9922*
☎*569-4600*
⇌*569-3531*
The Chelton Suites Hotel rents out attractive and very spacious suites that come fully equipped with kitchenettes, desks and couches – everything you could need for a longer stay. The attractive red brick building and large windows give it a distinctive look.

Sands Resort and Hotel
$85
tv, ≈, ℜ, ✳, ≈, △, ☉
1818 Victoria Ave., S4P 0R1
☎800-667-6500
☎569-1666
≈352-6339
The Sands Resort and Hotel was in the process of becoming a Ramada resort at the time of our visit. Extensive renovations make this centrally located hotel one of the most attractive places to stay in Regina. Additional perks include suites with whirlpools and all the amenities expected of an upscale hotel.

Travelodge
$91
⊛, *tv*, ≈, ℜ, ≈, ☉
4177 Albert St. S, S4S 3R6
☎800-578-7878
☎586-3443
≈586-9311
Unlike many other hotels in this chain, Regina's Travelodge has a unique character: a California theme pervades the building, from the attractive pastel lobby with its glitzy chandelier to the fake rocks and greenery in the pool area. While the rooms provide exceptional comfort, the Hollywood-themed restaurant is sure to be a hit with the kids and star(let)s-in-the-making.

Delta Regina Hotel
$119
P, ⅄, ℝ, ✳, ⊛, △
The Delta Regina Hotel offers guests luxurious accommodations, right near downtown. The rooms have a muted yet stylish decor, and most offer fine views of the city. The friendly and professional service, complete list of amenities, attractive pool area and overall elegance combine to pamper business travellers and vacationers alike.

Regina Inn Hotel and Convention Centre
$139
tv, ≈, ℜ, ⊛, ☉; ✳ ⅄
1975 Broad St., S4P 1Y2
☎525-6767
☎800-667-8162
≈525-3630
Another centrally located luxury hotel, its amenities include a dinner theatre, suites with whirlpools, a health club and winter plug-ins. Guests can choose from four on-site restaurants and lounges catering to fine or casual diners. All rooms have balconies.

Hotel Saskatchewan-Radisson Plaza
$134-$144
tv, ≈, ℜ, △, ☉, ⊛
2125 Victoria Ave., S4P 0S3
☎800-333-3333
☎522-7691
≈522-8988
This hotel's fabulous location along one side of pretty Victoria Park, facing the city skyline, is only the beginning of the luxury that makes it Regina's crown jewel of accommodations. Built in 1927 by the Canadian Pacific Railroad, the hotel features such decorative notes as a chandelier from the Imperial Palace in St. Petersburg. More touches were added during a $28-million renovation in the early 1990s. There's also the original barbershop, a health club, massage therapists and an elegant dining room. How classy is it? Queen Elizabeth and Richard Chamberlain stay here whenever they're in town – not at the same time, of course – in the $995-per-night Royal Suite where a special device heats towels as occupants bubble in the tub and the windows are fitted with bulletproof glass. It's 3,000 square feet of luxury and history.

Southern Saskatchewan

Swift Current

Heritage Inn Bed and Breakfast
$50
sb
Hwy. 4 bypass to Waker Rd., Box 1301
☎773-6305
≈773-0135
Archaeologists and equine enthusiasts like this small Bed and Breakfast for its horses and Swift Current Petroglyph complex – both located on the property. There are two rooms containing queen-size beds, and a family-style room with a set of bunks and a single bed.

Fort Qu'Appelle

Company House Bed and Breakfast
$50-60 bkfst incl.
sb/ac
Box 159, 172 Company Ave., S0G 1S0
☎332-6333
chbbt@sk.sympatico.ca
The Company House Bed and Breakfast is in a turn-of-the-century home with three attractive guest rooms and fully renovated bathrooms. Guests can relax by the beautiful fireplace in the living room or in the wicker chairs on the porch. Friendly hosts Jill and Jerry Whiting are happy to share their knowledge and enthusiasm for the surrounding region with guests. Reservations recommended.

Saskatchewan

Country Squire Inn
$65
tv, 🐾, P, ≡, ℜ
Hwy. 10, S0G 1S0
☎332-5603
≈332-6708
Probably the best afford-
able hotel-motel in the
Fort Qu'Appelle Valley.
Big clean rooms, cheerful
help and a good restaurant
(see p 509) all add up to
an enjoyable experience.
Short hiking trails beginning behind the place
climb to the top of sur-
rounding hills. There's also
a lounge, a bar and
"offsales" – on-premises
sale of beer.

Moose Jaw

Temple Gardens Mineral Spa Hotel and Resort
$89
tv, ≡, ℜ, ≈, ⌂, ☺
24 Fairford St. E., Moose Jaw
☎800-718-7727
☎694-5055
≈694-8310
This resort, tucked improbably down a sidestreet off
Moose Jaw's slow-moving
main drag, offers true
luxuries to the dusty prairie traveller. The big open
lobby gives a hint of
what's to come. Regular
hotel rooms here are
roomy enough with big
sofas. But the 25 full suites
are the real hit: king-sized
beds, cotton robes, tables,
enormous walk-in bath-
rooms and a two-person
mineral water whirlpools
create a romantic experi-
ence in each. Furthermore,
all resort guests have free
access to the resort's
fourth-floor, 2000m² pool
of mineral water. There is
also a small health club
featuring Nautilus ma-
chines and treadmills, a
poolside café and a restaurant.

Saskatoon

Patricia Hotel Hostel
*$12 members, $17 non-mem-
bers*
sb, ℝ
345 Second Ave. N., S7K 2B8
☎242-8861
≈664-1119
For hostel prices, visitors
get very basic accommo-
dations in a hotel that has
frankly seen better days.
The advantage here is the
low, low price and the
location close to down-
town. However, there are
no kitchen facilities or
special touches, save a
local bar beneath the dorm
rooms. Rooms are very
basic with two bunkbeds
and shared washrooms.
Some single rooms are
available, however. These
are in slightly better condition and all have a television and private bathroom
(*$30 per person, $34 for two*).

Ramblin' Rose Bed and Break-fast
$45, bkst
sb/pb, tv, ☺
Box 46, R.R. 3, S7K 3J6
☎668-4582
Located south of
Saskatoon, near popular
Pike Lake Provincial Park,
this cedar home offers two
private suites with private
baths and two with shared
baths. Extras are plentiful –
a whirlpool, tv/vcr, video
and book library among
them. Pets are welcome
here, and guests are also
welcome to hike any of
several nature trails on the
property. While the rooms
are comfortable, you
should try to book one on
the main floor, rather than
in the semi-basement.

🌴Brighton House Bed and Breakfast
$45 bkfst incl.
sb/pb, tv, ☺
1308 Fifth Ave. N, S7K 2S2
☎664-3278
≈664-6822
brighton.house@eudoramail.com
The Brighton House Bed
and Breakfast is in a lovely
white clapboard house
with blue and pink trim,
located outside the down-
town area and surrounded
by a well-tended garden.
All the rooms are delightfully furnished with floral
prints and antiques. The
"honeymoon suite" comes
with a private bathroom
and sun porch. Hosts Barb
and Lynne are sure to
make you feel right at
home. Extra touches in-
clude the family suite on
the top floor, which pro-
vides ample space for children to play, and the outdoor hot tub and croquet
set that are at guests' disposal.

Imperial 400
$59-$67
🐾, tv, K, ≡, ℜ, ≈, ☺
610 Idylwyld Dr. N, S7L 0Z2
☎800-781-2268
☎244-2901
≈244-6063
This 176-room motel fea-
tures an indoor recreation
complex with a whirlpool
and (leaky) water-slide,
and in-house movies, mak-
ing it a good deal for families. Even more attractive
are kitchenettes in some
rooms. There is also a
restaurant on premises.

Radisson Hotel Saskatoon
$84-$119
tv, ≡, ℜ, ≈, ⌂, ☺, ♿, ☺
405-20th St. E, S7K 6X6
☎800-333-3333
☎665-3322
≈665-5531
This elegant and newly
renovated high-rise luxury
hotel caters to everyone.
There are three executive
floors and six meeting
rooms, not to mention

waterslides, a sauna, whirlpool and gym. Its location right on the South Saskatchewan River means good access to outdoor recreation. It includes 14 deluxe suites complete with a bar and an extra telephone connection and modem hook-up for your computer.

Delta Bessborough
$109
tv, ≡, ℜ, ≈, △, ⊛, ⊘
601 Spadina Cr. E, S7K 3G8
☎*244-5521*
⇄*653-2458*
One of Saskatoon's most distinguishing landmarks, the Delta Bessborough is a former CN hotel in the *faux* French *château* style with many turrets and gables. While the renovated lobby and restaurant don't do justice to the grand old edifice, the rooms are comfortable, if somewhat dark, and have retained such luxurious touches as the original bathroom fixtures and deep ceramic tubs. Modern conveniences such as in-room coffee makers, voicemail and hairdryers have, of course, been added. The elegant ballrooms and extensive river property are among Saskatoon's most prized sites for all kinds of functions and receptions.

Saskatoon Inn
$109-129
≡, *tv*, ≈, ⊛, ⎣
2002 Airport Dr., S2L 6M4
☎*800-667-8789*
☎*242-1440*
⇄*224-2779*
Conveniently located right by the airport, the Saskatoon Inn offers spacious, attractive rooms with all the comforts and conveniences. It also has a unique recreation area with a swimming pool and ping-pong table set amid a profusion of greenery traversed by winding walkways. The adjoining restaurant and lounge elaborate on the tropical theme, providing a sort of indoor oasis that is especially welcome in the dead of a northern Saskatchewan winter!

Sheraton Cavalier
$119-$129
tv, ≡, ℜ, ≈, △, ⊛, ⎣, ⊘, △
621 Spadina Cr. E, S7K 3G9
☎*800-325-3535*
☎*652-6770*
⇄*244-1739*
Beautifully set on the river, the Sheraton Cavalier is a glamorous hotel with a sophisticated contemporary style. The rooms have all the comforts and conveniences, and the friendly and efficient service ensures a pleasant stay. The hotel's amenities include two indoor waterslides, a ballroom, a cigar lounge and mountain bike rentals.

The Yellowhead Highway

Manitou Beach

Manitou Springs Resort
$79
tv, ≡, ⊛, ⊘
MacLachlan Ave., S0K 4T0
☎*800-667-7672*
☎*946-2233*
⇄*946-2554*
An old and well-known resort in western Canada, this facility is famous for its three pools of heated mineral water drawn from Little Manitou Lake. Other services at the resort include massage therapy, reflexology, and a fitness centre.

West Central Saskatchewan

North Battleford

Battlefords Inn
$54
tv, ≡, ℜ, ≈, △
11212 Railway Ave. E, S9A 2R7
☎*800-691-6076*
☎*445-1515*
⇄*445-1541*
Known for spacious rooms, this inn provides king- and queen-size beds, free local phone calls and free in-room coffee. Meals can be taken in the on-site restaurant, and alcohol can be purchased in the licensed beverage room.

Prince Albert

South Hill Inn
$65
tv, ≡, ℜ, ⊛
3245 Second Ave. W, S6V 5G1
☎*800-363-4466*
☎*922-1333*
⇄*763-6408*
Highlights of this conveniently located inn include big comfortable rooms, televisions with the option of in-house movies and free coffee. There is also a licensed restaurant on the premises.

Restaurants

Regina

Magellan's Global Coffee House
$
1800 College Ave.
☎*789-0009*
magellan@magellanscafe.com
A coffee place in a remodelled fieldstone house at the edge of Wascana Park, Magellan's Global Coffee House is where the up-

wardly mobile congregate for their java fix.

Bushwakker
$-$$
closed Sun
2206 Dewdney Ave.
☎359-7276
A fun brewpub on the edge of an industrial area. Locals don't think twice about motoring over here to try the latest batch of Harvest Ale or some other concoction, buffered by a fancy hamburger or other typical bar fare. The bar also offers offsales (small and very large bottles of the brewery's beer) in addition to the usual taps.

Heliotrope
$-$$
2204 McIntyre St.
☎569-3373
Heliotrope is the only vegetarian restaurant in Saskatchewan, and quite possibly one of the best in all Canada. The chairs and tables in this brick house are cozy. While a fireplace keeps things warm during the winter, in the summer there's a great outdoor patio. Entrees are expertly handled – everything from lunches of falafel, vegetables and burgers to dinners of Moroccan stew, Thai curries and *gado gado*. Dessert is a real stunner with in-season fruit cheesecake and home-made gelato that consists only of fresh fruit and water.

Brown Sugar
$$
closed Sun
1941 Scarth St.
☎359-7355
A Caribbean eatery in the middle of the prairies? Absolutely. This blue-trimmed place, decorated in Caribbean prints, delivers authentic rotis (meat-filled pastry pockets), jerk chicken and dishes like fish cutter (fish on a bun) as well as ackee and salt fish that are otherwise impossible to find in western Canada. There's also a great selection of imported Caribbean soft drinks and home-made libations such as ginger beer, mauby, sorrel and banana cow to consider. The meal isn't over until the knockout tropical ice cream has been tasted.

Cathedral Village Free House
$$
2062 Albert St.
☎359-1661
Filling contemporary fare from all over the map – a concept that doesn't always work, but satisfies much of the time. Lunch might consist of straightforward buffalo burgers, salads, stir-fried vegetables, wood-fired oven pizza and the like. Dinner leans toward pasta and other Italian dishes. The place gets extra points for having eight beers on tap. The crowd here is young and hip despite the stodgy name, possibly explaining the erratic service. At least the location is central and the decor, with bold colours and tiled floor, is welcoming.

Neo Japonica
$$
2167 Hamilton St.
☎359-7669
The all-around most charming restaurant in Regina, Neo Japonica serves exquisite Japanese cuisine in a small, unassuming house with an inviting decor. The food's artistic presentation is matched only by its expert preparation. If you order the special plate, you can sample the teriyaki chicken, vegetable and shrimp tempura, nigri sushi and Japanese tea for under $10. Homemade green tea and ginger ice cream are the perfect finale for any meal.

Danbry's
$$-$$$
1925 Victoria Ave.
☎525-8777
⇌525-3635
Danbry's successfully blends the luxurious historic character of one of Canada's oldest private clubs, which used to be located here, with contemporary style. From the wood-panelled main dining room to private dining rooms, a lounge and cigar lounge, care has been taken to maintain an atmosphere of comfort and sophistication. The menu features such delicacies as grilled salmon and asparagus salad with dijon dressing and roasted duck with sour cherry sauce. The service is exceptionally friendly.

Orleans
$$$
1907 11th Ave.
☎525-3636
A dash of Cajun cuisine on a busy downtown street, you'll find a sampling of the dishes that make the real New Orleans a mouthwatering destination: jambalaya, gumbo and *étouffée* are all on the menu. Unfortunately, the original recipes have been somewhat altered to cater to North American tastes. However, the special dijon sauce (not listed on the menu – ask your server) and live jazz on Wednesdays make this place worthwhile.

Southern Saskatchewan

Fort Qu'Appelle

The Country Squire
$$
Hwy. 10
☎*332-5603*
☞*332-6708*
Attached to the inn of the same name, this restaurant serves tasty, hearty portions in a convivial atmosphere. Locals often drop by for a bite of grilled salmon, burgers (choose from elk, bison, hamburger or ostrich!), salad or fish and chips.

Caronport

The Pilgrim
$-$$
7am to 11pm
Trans-Canada Hwy. 1
☎*756-3335*
Yet another restaurant in a gas station, this one is located in the small town of Caronport, just west of Moose Jaw. This place serves family fare and a salad bar. Its reputation for hearty prairie cooking and a 60-item salad and soup bar is solid.

Saskatoon

The Original Bulk Cheese Warehouse
732 Broadway Ave.
☎*652-8008*
The Original Bulk Cheese Warehouse is the place to load up on picnic provisions like from samosas, quiche, salads, fresh shrimp cocktails and desserts. Of course, it also offers an impressive selection of cheeses, including a local buffalo mozzarella.

Chocolatier Bernard Callebaut
$
125 Second Ave. N.
☎*652-0909*
Right in the centre of downtown Saskatoon, a small Canadian chain based in Calgary serves up artful cream chocolates and bars of baking chocolate made of all-natural ingredients. A special treat here are the hand-dipped chocolate ice cream bars that are delicious beyond words, and only a few dollars apiece.

Broadway Café
$
814 Broadway Ave.
☎*652-8244*
This restaurant is located right in the heart of Saskatoon's hippest district. However, that's a bit misleading. This is merely a diner that serves up burgers, eggs and the like to swarms of locals. The snappy service is cheerful but a bit off-putting out here in laid-back Saskatchewan. Daring entrées should definitely be avoided. Diners will also want to note that the owner does not accept credit cards. Nevertheless, an authentic local experience.

Emily's Jazz
$
616 10th St. E
☎*664-1953*
Emily's Jazz, just off Broadway, is a small, inviting neighbourhood café with pretty blue walls and mismatched wooden furniture. Enjoy delicious homemade food such as borscht (Ukrainian beet soup), perogies and healthy sandwiches in a homey atmosphere. The melt-in-your-mouth flapper pie is sensational! The service is very friendly, and live jazz is played here on some nights.

Michel's Montreal Smoked Meats
$
closed Sun
101-129 Second Ave. N
☎*384-6664*
Fortuitously placed right next to Saskatoon's Belgian chocolate shop, this enterprising French-Canadian eatery tries to match Montréal quality from 3,000km away – and nearly succeeds. While the peppery smoked meat, stuffed between two slices of rye bread and embellished with generous squirts of mustard, doesn't have quite the bite of its Québec counterpart, it's still very good. Other great touches include homemade sour pickles, a very basic (and therefore good and crunchy) coleslaw, and black-cherry cola and spruce beer imported from Quebec.

Wanuskewin Café
$
R.R 4
☎*931-6767*
Located in the native heritage park of the same name, just north of Saskatoon, this little café offers a good quick sampling of native-style cookery. Entrées aren't large here but they are tasty. The fare ranges from a warming, hearty cup of bison stew with a side of bannock (bread) to bison with wild rice. Dessert offerings include pastries featuring the tart local Saskatoon berry while the line of First Nation soft drinks – bottled by an Aboriginal-owned company – are among the beverages offered.

Berry Barn
$-$$
830 Valley Rd.
☎*978-9797*
Located approximately 10km south of the city, the Berry Barn makes for a

pleasant excursion to the country. Saskatoon berry bushes line the parking lot, hinting at the delights to come: berry pies, waffles, syrup and tea accompany hearty meals of perogies and farmer's sausage. The rustic pine-finished dining room has a great view of the river. After your meal, you can browse in the gift shop for still more berry products or pick some berries yourself at the you-pick farm. Reservations recommended.

Genesis
$-$$
901D 22nd St. W., Saskatoon
☎*244-5516*
Widely acclaimed as Saskatoon's best healthy food, the menu leans toward Chinese food and macrobiotic cooking. Dim sum (dumplings) is available at lunchtime.

Mykonos
$$-$$$
416-21st St. E.
☎*244-2499*
Mykonos serves the usual kebabs, seafood, lamb and moussaka, but the overall flavour is not exactly authentic. The formal dining room has a maritime décor that is attractive, though, like the food, is not exactly Greek. Overpriced, but still one of the better restaurants in town. The friendly service adds to the dining experience.

Saskatoon Station Place
$$-$$$
221 South Idylwyld Dr.
☎*244-7777*
Saskatoon Station Place draws guests with its railway motif: plush dining cars with mahogany trim surround a mock train station. While the Belle Epoque reigns supreme in the decor, the restaurant service and menu are more family-style. Dishes cover

the basics of burgers, steak and pasta. Still, it's a good choice for an evening out. Be sure to stop in at the lounge for a pre-dinner drink.

Tarragon's Restaurant
$$$
closed Mon
119 Third Ave. S.
☎*664-3599*
Tarragon's is Saskatoon's most lauded restaurant. Owner and chef David Powell concocts such delights as Alaskan King Crab, Gazpacho and Gulf Shrimp Provençale for guests to enjoy in the spacious, multi-level dining room.

West Central Saskatchewan

North Battleford

DaVinci's Ristorante Italiano
$$
1001 Hwy. 16
☎*446-4700*
Even Leonardo himself might be surprised that the menu here is not exclusively Italian as the name suggests. Traditional Louisiana flavours and continental European dishes are also served.

Prince Albert

Amy's on Second
$$
2990 Second Ave.
☎*763-1515*
Fresh ingredients and a healthy approach to cooking make this restaurant a popular switch from the many local fast-food joints. Salads are made to order and come with homemade soups. Also featured are steak, chicken and pasta dishes.

Entertainment

Regina

The **Buffalo Days** festival occupies one week each summer, usually beginning in late July and lasting into early August. Festivities kick off with a Sunday picnic in lovely Wascana Park. From there, it's on to a raft of shows and, eventually, fireworks.

Southern Saskatchewan

Saskatoon

Most of the pubs and clubs in Saskatoon are concentrated along Second Avenue South.

The **SaskTel Saskatchewan Jazz Festival** (☎*652-1421*) brings world-class jazz, gospel and world music to Saskatoon's riverbanks for 11 days each June. Musicians range from international stars to local artists. Some performances are held in the Delta Bessborough Gardens, adjacent to the landmark hotel.

The **Great Northern River Roar** is either an abomination or a great time, depending on your opinion of powerboats tearing up and down the river. Either way, there's no avoiding these races when they arrive in Saskatoon each July. Some 60,000 spectators are said to watch as the powerboats charge around courses at speeds that can reach 225km/h.

Shopping

Regina

Shopping is concentrated downtown, with the **Scarth Street Mall** as the usual starting point. All the major stores are nearby.

Saskatoon

Shopping in Saskatoon is easy, with several downtown malls and streets dedicated to the activity. Perhaps the most popular area is the **Bayside Mall** (*225 Second Ave. N*), next to and including The Bay department store. The **Midtown Plaza,** on First Avenue South between 22nd St. E and 20th St. E, is another good option. **Second Avenue South** is the place to go for all the pubs, clubs and street life.

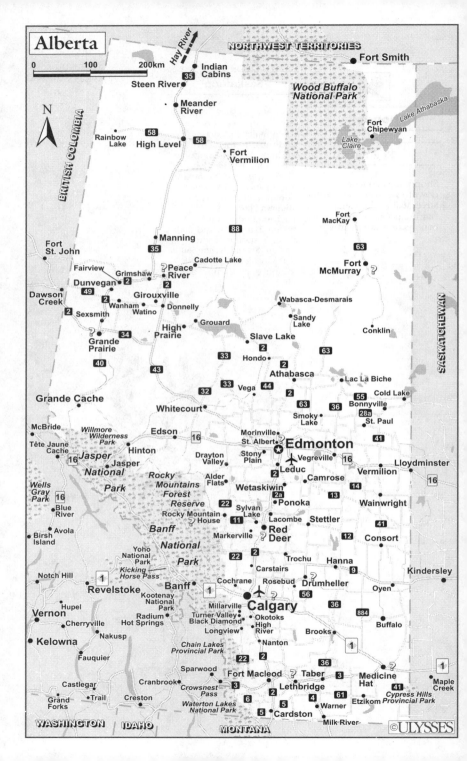

Freshly cut bundles of hay dot Prairie fields, with the Rockies rising up in the distance.
- *Troy & Mary Parlee*

Tight rows of barley sheaves dancing in the wind in one of the Prairies' numerous fields.
- *Anne Gardon*

Like other western provincial capitals, Edmonton boasts a magnificent parliament.
- *Troy & Mary Parlee*

Dawn gently breaks the mist over Pacific Rim National Park as the ocean washes over its dense forests and beaches. - *Sean O'Neill*

On this windy, snowy ice field, the king of the North catches a few rays.
- *Rosing Mauritius*

Set against the mountains and glaciers of Bylot Island, a symbol of the Catholic presence in Pond Inlet, Nunavut.
- *Jacqueline Grekin*

Alberta begins
on the eastern slopes of the Rocky Mountains and extends eastward into the vast Canadian prairies.

This province prospered as a result of the oil boom of the 1970s, which sealed the destiny of its two largest cities, Edmonton, the provincial capital in the north, and Calgary its flourishing southern metropolis. While Edmonton's claim to fame is its gigantic shopping mall, this boomtown also has a sophisticated atmosphere and a thriving arts community. Calgary, best known for its world-famous Stampede, is a city of concrete and steel and a western city through and through.

The fabulous chain of mountains, the Rocky Mountains, run diagonally southeast – northwest along the border between Alberta and British Columbia and into the Yukon territory. This vast region, which stretches more that 22,000km², is known the world over for its natural beauty and welcomes some six million visitors each year.

The vast expanses and sometimes desert-like conditions you'll traverse while making your way from west to east in Southern Alberta are in stark contrast to the looming, snow-capped Rocky Mountains. Neat rows of wheat and other grains, perfectly round bales of hay, and the occasional grain elevator are about the extent of the relief across the slow-rolling terrain of this part of the province.

Southern Alberta boasts some of the best sights and scenery of the whole province, from Waterton Lakes National Park and the mining towns of Crowsnest Pass to the historic Aboriginal gathering place at Head-Smashed-In Buffalo Jump, and the edge of the endless prairies.

This section also takes you to Central Alberta, a land that was once the realm of the dinosaurs. Dinosaurs thrived along the shores of this subtropical sea and along the rivers that emptied into it. They lived here for millions of years, until about 70 million years ago. Today, the region is a good place to dig for a dinosaur bone or two. The landscape, known as the Badlands, also includes hoodoos, mesas and gorges.

Calgary and Southern Alberta

C algary may well be a thriving metropolis of concrete and steel, but it's still a western city through and through.

S et against the Rocky Mountains to the west and prairie ranchlands to the east, this young, prosperous city flourished during the oil booms of the 1940's, 1950's and 1970's but its nickname, Cowtown, tells a different story. Before the oil, there were cowboys and gentlemen, and Calgary originally grew thanks to a handful of wealthy ranching families.

W hen departing Calgary, it is difficult to resist the pull of the Rocky Mountains and head south. However, southern Alberta boasts some of the best sights and scenery of the whole province, from Waterton Lakes National Park and the mining towns of Crowsnest Pass to the historic native gathering place at Head-Smashed-In Buffalo Jump, and the edge of the endless prairies.

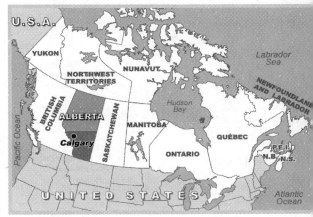

Finding Your Way Around

By Car

The majority of Calgary's streets are numbered, and the city is divided into four quadrants, NE, NW, SE and SW. This may seem extremely unimaginative on the part of city-planners but it makes it easy for just about anyone to find their way around. Avenues run east-west and streets run north-south. **Centre Street** divides the city between east and west while the Bow River is the dividing line between north and south. The Trans-Canada Highway runs through the city, where it is known as 16th Avenue North. Many of the major arteries through the city have much more imaginative names. Not only are they not numbered but they are called trails – an appellation that reflects their original use. These are **Macleod Trail**, which runs south from downtown (ultimately leading to Fort Macleod, hence its name); **Deerfoot Trail** which runs north-south through the city and is part of Highway 2; and **Crowchild Trail** which heads northwest and joins **Bow Trail** before becoming Highway 1A.

Calgary's "Motel Village" is located along 16th Avenue NW between 18th Street NW and 22nd Street NW.

Car Rentals

National Car Rental
Airport
☎*(403) 221-1692*
Northeast
2335 78th Ave. NE
☎*(403) 250-1396*
Southeast
114 Fifth Ave. SE
☎*(403) 263-6386*

Budget
Airport
☎*(403) 226-1550*
Downtown
140 Sixth Ave. SE
☎*(403) 226-0000*
☎*(800) 267-0505*

Avis
Airport
☎*(403) 221-1700*
Downtown
211 Sixth Ave. SW
☎*(403) 269-6166*
☎*(800) TRY-AVIS*

Thrifty
Airport
☎*(403) 221-1961*
Downtown
123 Fifth Ave. SE
☎*(403)262-4400*
☎*(800) 367-2277*

By Plane

Calgary International Airport is located northeast of downtown Calgary. It is Canada's fourth-largest airport and houses a whole slew of facilities and services. It features restaurants, an information centre, hotel courtesy phones, major car rental counters, currency exchange and a bus tour operator.

Air Canada, Canadian Airlines International, American Airlines, Delta Airlines, Northwest Airlines, United Airlines and K.L.M. all have regular flights to the airport. Regional companies (Air B.C. and Canadian Regional) also serve Calgary International.

There is a shuttle from the Calgary airport to the major downtown hotels; the **Airporter** (☎*403-531-3909*) charges $8.50 one-way and 15$ return, while a taxi will run about $25.

By Train

Via does not service Calgary. The train passes through Edmonton, however, and there is a bus connection between the two cities.

The only rail service from Calgary is offered by **Great Canadian Railtour Company Ltd. - Rocky Mountain Railtours**. See p ? for more information.

By Bus

Calgary Greyhound Bus Depot
877 Greyhound Way SW, off 16th St.

☎*(403) 265-9111*
☎*(800) 661-8747*
Services: restaurant, lockers, tourist information.

Brewster Transportation and Tours offers coach service from Calgary to Banff departing from Calgary International Airport. For information call ☎*(403) 221-8242* or *800-661-1152*, or visit their web site at *www.brewster.ca*.

Southern Alberta

Lethbridge Greyhound Bus Depot
411 Fifth St. S
☎*327-1551*
services: restaurant, lockers.

Medicine Hat Greyhound Bus Depot
557 Second St. SE
☎*527-4418*

Public Transit

Public transit in Calgary consists of an extensive bus network and a light-rail transit system known as the **C-Train**. There are three C-Train routes: the Anderson C-Train follows Macleod Trail south to Anderson Road; the Whitehorn C-Train heads northeast out of the city; and the Brentwood C-Train runs along Seventh Avenue and then heads northwest. The C-Train is free in the downtown core. You can transfer from a bus to a C-Train. Tickets are $1.60 for a single trip or $5.50 for a day pass. For bus information, call **Calgary Transit** at ☎*262-1000*. You can tell them where you are and where you want to go and they'll gladly explain how to do it.

By Foot

A system of interconnected enclosed walkways links many of Calgary's downtown sights, shops and hotels. Known as the **+15**, it is located 15 feet above the ground. The malls along Seventh Avenue SW are all connected as are the Calgary Tower, Glenbow Museum and Palliser Hotel.

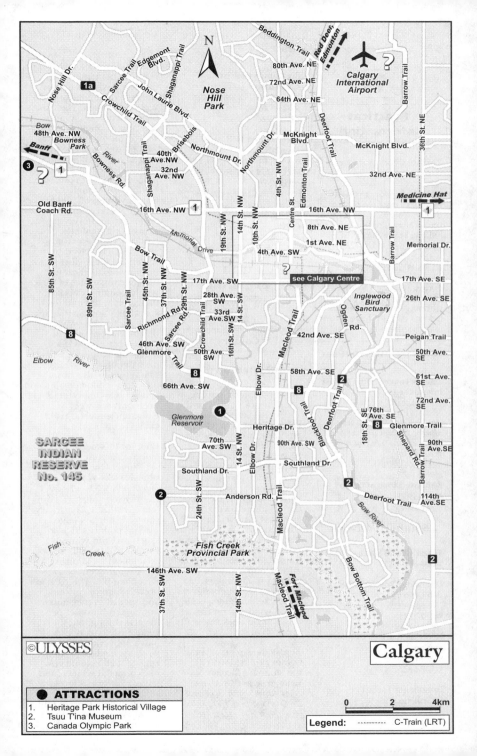

Calgary

ATTRACTIONS

1. Heritage Park Historical Village
2. Tsuu T'ina Museum
3. Canada Olympic Park

| 0 | 2 | 4km |

Legend: ---------- C-Train (LRT)

©ULYSSES

SARCEE INDIAN RESERVE No. 145

Nose Hill Park

Calgary International Airport

see Calgary Centre

Inglewood Bird Sanctuary

Glenmore Reservoir

Fish Creek Provincial Park

Bowness Park

Streets and Roads:

Nose Hill Dr., Sarcee Trail, Edgemont Blvd., John Laurie Blvd., Shaganappi Trail, Crowchild Trail, Beddington Trail, Red Deer/Edmonton, Barrow Trail, 80th Ave. NE, 72nd Ave. NE, 64th Ave. NE, McKnight Blvd., 36th St. NE, Bow River, 48th Ave. NW, Banff, Brisebois, Shaganappi Trail, Bowness Rd., 40th Ave. NW, 32nd Ave. NW, Northmount Dr., Northmount Dr., 4th St. NW, Centre St., Edmonton Trail, Deerfoot Trail, McKnight Blvd., 32nd Ave. NE, Old Banff Coach Rd., Memorial Drive, 16th Ave. NW, 19th St. NW, 14th St. NW, 10th St. NW, 16th Ave. NW, 8th Ave. NE, 1st Ave. NE, Medicine Hat, Memorial Dr., Barrow Trail, 85th St. SW, Bow Trail, 45th St. NW, 37th St. NW, 29th St. NW, 28th Ave. SW, 4th Ave. SW, 17th Ave. SW, 17th Ave. SE, 26th Ave. SE, 89th St. SW, Sarcee Trail, Richmond Rd., Sarcee Rd., Crowchild Trail, 33rd Ave. SW, 14th St. SW, 16th St. SW, Macleod Trail, 42nd Ave. SE, Ogden Rd., Peigan Trail, 50th Ave. SE, 46th Ave. SW, Glenmore Trail, 50th Ave. SW, 58th Ave. SE, 61st Ave. SE, 72nd Ave. SE, Elbow River, 66th Ave. SW, Elbow Dr., Blackfoot Trail, Deerfoot Trail, 18th St. SE, 76th Ave. SE, Glenmore Trail, 90th Ave. SE, Heritage Dr., 70th Ave. SW, 90th Ave. SW, Shepard Rd., Barrow Trail, 114th Ave. SE, Southland Dr., Southland Dr., 24th St. SW, Anderson Rd., Macleod Trail, Fish Creek, 146th Ave. SW, 37th St. SW, 14th St. NW, Fort Macleod/Macleod Trail, Bow Bottom Trail, Bow River, Deerfoot Trail

Practical Information

The area code for **Calgary** is **403**.

Information on everything from road conditions to movie listings to provincial parks is available from the **Talking Yellow Pages**. In Calgary call ☎**521-5222**. A series of recorded messages is accessible by dialling specific codes. The codes are listed in the front of the yellow pages phone book. Telephone booths usually have a telephone book.

Tourist Information

Calgary Tower Centre Tourist Information
Centre St. and Ninth Ave. SW
Mid-May to early Sep, every day 8:30am to 5pm; winter, Mon to Fri 8:30am to 5pm, Sat and Sun 9:30am to 5pm
☎*263-8510*
☎*800-661-1678*

B&B Association of Calgary
☎*543-3900*
≈*543-3901*

Southern Alberta

Travel Alberta South
☎*800-661-1222*

Lethbridge Tourist Information Centre
2805 Scenic Dr.
☎*320-1222*

Medicine Hat Tourist Information
8 Gehring Rd. SE
☎*527-6422*

Drumheller Tourist Information
60 First Ave. W
☎*823-1331*

Big Country Tourist Association
170 Centre St., #28 Drumheller
☎*823-5885*
≈*823-7942*

High Country B&B Association
Box 772, Turner Valley, T0L 2A0
☎*933-4174 or 888-933-4183*
≈*933-2870*
(*covers the area southwest of Calgary, from Priddis to Waterton Lakes National Park*)

Exploring

Calgary

Downtown

We recommend starting your tour of Calgary at the 190m, 762-step, 55-storey **Calgary Tower** ★★ (*$6.15; every day, summer 7:30am to 11pm, winter 8am to 10pm; Ninth Ave, corner of Centre St SW,* ☎*266-7171*). The city's most famous landmark not only offers a breathtaking view of the city, including the ski-jump towers at Canada Olympic Park, the Saddledome and the Canadian Rockies through high-power telescopes. It also houses the city's tourist information centre, a revolving restaurant and a bar. Photographers should take note that the specially tinted windows on the observation deck make for great photos.

Across the street, at the corner of First Street SE, is the stunning **Glenbow Museum** ★★★ (*$8; Mon to Wed 9am to 5pm, Thu and Fri 9am to 9pm; 130 Ninth Ave. SE,* ☎*268-4100*). Three

floors of permanent and travelling exhibits chronicle the exciting history of Western Canada. The displays include contemporary and Aboriginal art as well as an overview of the various stages of the settling of the West from the First Nations to the first pioneers, the fur trade, the North West Mounted Police, ranching, oil and agriculture. Photographs, costumes and everyday items bring to life the hardships and extraordinary obstacles faced by settlers. There is also an extensive exhibit on the Aboriginal peoples of the whole country. Check out the genuine tipi and the sparkling minerals that are both part of the province's diverse history. A great permanent exhibit documents the stories of warriors throughout the ages. The museum also hosts travelling exhibitions. Free gallery tours are offered once or twice weekly. Great museum shop and café.

Built for the medal presentation ceremonies of the '88 Winter Olympics, the **Olympic Plaza** ★★★ (*205 Eighth Ave. SE*) is a fine example of Calgary's potential realized. This lovely square features a large wading pool (used as a skating rink in winter) surrounded by pillars and columns in an arrangement reminiscent of a Greek temple. The park is now the site of concerts and special events, and is frequented by street performers throughout the year. It is also a popular lunch spot with office workers. Each pillar in the Legacy Wall commemorates a medal winner, and the paving bricks are inscribed with the names of people who supported the Olympics by purchasing bricks for $19.88 each!

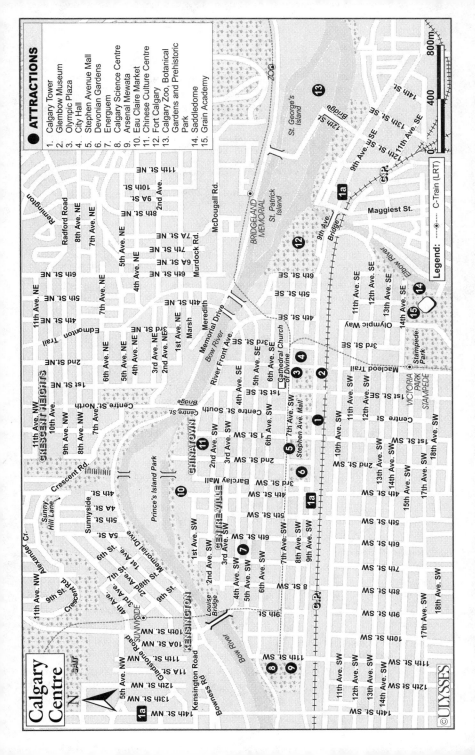

Calgary Centre

N

● ATTRACTIONS

1. Calgary Tower
2. Glenbow Museum
3. Olympic Plaza
4. City Hall
5. Stephen Avenue Mall
6. Devonian Gardens
7. Energuem
8. Calgary Science Centre
9. Arsenal Mewata
10. Eau Claire Market
11. Chinese Culture Centre
12. Fort Calgary
13. Calgary Zoo, Botanical Gardens and Prehistoric Park
14. Saddledome
15. Grain Academy

Legend: ------ C-Train (LRT)

© ULYSSES

0   400   800m

Across from the Olympic Plaza is **City Hall** (*Second St. SE, corner of Macleod Tr.*), one of few surviving examples of the monumental civic halls that went up during the Prairies boom. It was built in 1911 and still houses a few offices.

The **Stephen Avenue Mall** (*Eighth Ave between First St. SE and Sixth St. SW*) is an excellent example not only of Calgary's potential but also of the contrasts that characterize this cowtown metropolis. The mall is part vibrant pedestrian meeting place, part wasteland and unsavoury hangout. It may have fountains, benches, cobblestone, restaurants and shops, but it also has more than its share of boarded-up storefronts and cheap souvenir and T-shirt shops. The beautiful sandstone buildings that line the Avenue are certainly a testament to better and different times, as are the businesses they house, including an old-fashioned shoe hospital and several western outfitters. One of these buildings is the **Alberta Hotel**, a busy place in pre-prohibition days. Other buildings house trendy cafés and art galleries as the street once again becomes a meeting place for lawyers, doctors and the who's who of Calgary – just as it was at the beginning of the century.

Interconnected malls line the street west of First Street SW, including the Scotia Centre, TD Square, Bankers Hall, Eaton Centre and Holt Renfrew. Though this type of commercialism might not appeal to everyone, hidden within TD Square is a unique attraction — Alberta's largest

indoor garden, **Devonian Gardens** ★★ (*free admission, donations accepted; every day 9am to 9pm; 317 Seventh Ave. SW, between Second and Third Sts. SW, Level 4, TD Square, ☎268-3888*). For a tranquil break from shopping, head upstairs, where 1ha of greenery and blossoms await. Stroll along garden paths high above the concrete and steel and enjoy the art exhibitions and performances that are often presented here.

At the **Energeum** ★ (*free admission; summer, Sun to Fri 10:30am to 4:30pm; rest of year, Mon to Fri 10:30am to 4:30pm; Energy Resources Building, 640 Fifth Ave. SW, ☎297-4293*) you can learn all about Alberta's number one resource – energy. Whether it is oil, natural gas, oil sands, coal or hydroelectricity, everything from pipelines to rigs to oil sands plants is explained through hands-on exhibits and computer games.

Across the street is the Renaissance Revival **McDougall Centre**, a government building that was declared a historic site in 1982.

Public Art

The peculiar looking concrete building on 11th Street SW is **The Calgary Science Centre** ★★★ (*$9; every day 10am to 4pm; 701 11th St. SW, ☎221-3700*), a wonderful museum that children will love. Hands-on displays and multi-media machines cover a whole slew of interesting topics. The museum boasts a planetarium, an observatory, a science hall and two theatres that showcase mystery plays and special-effects shows. The recently completed 220-seat domed theatre features an exceptional sound system, all the better to explore the wonders of the scientific world.

Along the Bow

Kensington is a hip area that is hard to pin down. To get a true sense of the alternative attitude that pervades the coffee shops, bookstores and boutiques, explore Kensington Road between 10th and 14th Streets NW.

The recently built **Eau Claire Market** ★★ (*Mon to Wed 10am to 6pm, Thu and Fri 10am to 9pm, Sat 10am to 6pm, Sun 10am to 5pm; next to the Bow River and Prince's Island Park, ☎264-6450*) is part of a general initiative in Calgary to keep people downtown after hours. The large warehouse-like building houses specialty food shops that sell fresh fruit, vegetables, fish, meats, bagels and baked goods. There are also neat gift shops with local and imported arts and crafts, clothing stores, a great bookstore, fast-food and fine restaurants, a movie theatre and a 300-seat **IMAX** (*☎974-4600*) theatre.

Calgary's **Chinese Cultural Centre** ★★ (*$2; every day 9am to 9pm; 197 First St. SW,* ☎262-5071) is the largest of its kind in Canada. Craftsmen were brought in from China to design the building whose central dome is patterned after the Temple of Heaven in Beijing. The highlight of the intricate tile-work is a glistening golden dragon. The centre houses a gift shop, a museum, a gallery and a restaurant.

Calgary's small **Chinatown** lies around Centre Street. Although it only has about 2,000 residents, the street names written in Chinese characters and the sidewalk stands selling durian, ginseng, lychees and tangerines all help to create a wonderful feeling of stepping into another world. The markets and restaurants here are run by descendants of Chinese immigrants who came west to work on the railroads in the 1880s.

Fort Calgary ★★★ (*$5; May to mid-Oct every day 9am to 5pm; 750 Ninth Ave. SE,* ☎290-1875) was built as part of the March West that brought the North West Mounted Police to the Canadian west to stop the whisky trade. Arriving at the confluence of the Bow and Elbow rivers in 1875, "F" Troop chose to set up camp here either because it was the only spot with clean water or because it was halfway between Fort Macleod and Fort Saskatchewan. Nothing remains of the original Fort Calgary. The structures and outline of the foundations on the site today are part of an ongoing project of excavation and discovery undertaken mostly by volunteers. In

fact, the fort will never be completely rebuilt since that would interfere with archaeological work underway. An excellent interpretive centre includes great hands-on displays (the signs actually say "please touch"), woodworking demonstrations and the chance to try on the famous, scarlet Mountie uniform. Friendly guides in period costume provide tours.

The **Calgary Zoo, Botanical Gardens and Prehistoric Park** ★★ (*$9.50 summer, $8 winter; May to Sep, every day 9am to 6pm; Sep to May, every day 9am to 4pm; St. George's Island, 1300 Zoo Rd. NE,* ☎232-9300 or 232-9372) is the second largest zoo in Canada. Opened in 1920, it is known for its realistic re-creations of natural habitats that are now home to over 300 species of animals and 10,000 plants and trees. Exhibits are organized by continent and include tropical birds, Siberian tigers, snow leopards and polar bears as well as animals indigenous to this area. The Prehistoric Park recreates the world of dinosaurs with 27 full-size replicas set amidst plants and rock formations from prehistoric Alberta.

tracks between Ninth and 10th Avenues.

The Stampede grounds are used year-round for a variety of activities. The aptly named **Saddledome** has the world's largest cable-suspended roof and is a giant testimony to the city's cowboy roots. Apparently, there was some controversy over its name, though it is hard to imagine what else they could have called it! It is home to the city's National Hockey League team, the Calgary Flames, and is also used for concerts, conventions and sporting events. The figure skating and ice-hockey events of the 1988 Olympics were held here. Tours are available (☎777-1375). Also on the park grounds is the **Grain Academy** ★ (*free admission; year-round Mon to Fri 10am to 4pm; Apr to Sep, Mon to Sat noon to 4pm; on the +15 level of the Round-Up Centre,* ☎263-4594), which traces the history of grain farming and features a working railway and grain elevator. Finally, thoroughbred and harness racing take place on the grounds year-round and there is also a casino.

Saddledome

Alberta

Southeast and Southwest

This tour explores Calgary immediately south of downtown. For the purposes of this guide, we will delineate by the CPR

Heritage Park Historical Village ★★ (*$11, May to Sep every day, Sep to Oct weekends and holidays only; 1900 Heritage Dr. SW,* ☎259-1900) is a 26ha park on the Glenbow Reservoir. Step back in time as you stroll through a real 1910 town of historic houses decorated with period furniture, wooden sidewalks, a working blacksmith, a tipi, an old schoolhouse, a post office, a divine candy store and the Gilbert and Jay Bakery, known for its sourdough bread. Staff in period dress play piano in the houses and take on the role of suffragettes speaking out for women's equality in the Wainwright Hotel. Other areas in the park recreate an 1880s settlement, a fur trading post, a ranch, a farm and the coming of the railroad. Not only is this a magical place for children, with rides in a steam engine and a paddlewheeler on the reservoir, but it is also a relaxing place to escape the city and enjoy a picnic.

The **Tsuu T'Ina Museum** ★ (*donation; Mon to Fri 8am to 4pm; 3700 Anderson Rd. SW, ☎238-2677*) commemorates the history of the Tsuu T'Ina First nation, who are Sarcee. Tsuu T'Ina means "great number of people" in their language. Nearly wiped out several times in the 1800s by diseases brought by Europeans, the Tsuu T'Ina were shuffled around reserves for many years. But they persevered and were eventually awarded their reserve on the outskirts of Calgary in 1881. They held on to the land, spurning pressure to sell it. Some of the pieces on display were donated by Calgary families who used to trade with the Tsuu T'Ina whose reserve lies immediately to the west of the museum. Other items, including a tipi and two headdresses from the 1930s, were retrieved from the Provincial Museum in Edmonton.

Northeast and Northwest

North of the Bow River, the biggest draw in the Northwest is Canada Olympic Park. In the Northeast there isn't much besides the airport.

Canada Olympic Park ★★★ (*museum $7, tours $10; summer every day 9am to 10pm, winter every day 9am to 6pm; on 16th Ave. NW, ☎247-5452*), or COP, built for the 1988 Winter Olympic Games, lies on the western outskirts of Calgary. This was the site of the ski-jumping, bobsleigh, luge, freestyle skiing and disabled events during the games. It is now a world-class facility for training and competition. Artificial snow keeps the downhill ski slopes busy in the winter. The park also offers tours year-round and the chance to try the luge in the summertime (*$13 for one ride, $22 for two*) or the bobsleigh in the winter, or view summer ski-jumping.

Visitors to COP have the choice of seven different guided tour packages ranging from a self-guided walking booklet to the Grand Olympic Tour for $10, which includes a guided bus tour, chair-lift ride, the Olympic Hall of Fame and the tower. It is worth taking the bus up to the observation deck of the 90m ski jump tower visible from all over the city. You'll learn about the refrigeration system, which can make 1,250 tonnes of snow and ice in 24hrs, the infamous Jamaican bobsleigh team, the 90- and 70m- towers and the plastic-surface landing material used in the summer.

If you do decide to take the bus, sit on the left for a better view of the towers and tracks. The **Naturbahn Teahouse** (*☎247-5465*) is located in the former starthouse for the luge. Delicious treats and a scrumptious Sunday brunch are served, but be sure to make reservations. The **Olympic Hall of Fame and Museum** (*$3.75; mid-May to Sep every day 8am to 9pm, call ahead for winter hours; ☎247-5452*) is North America's largest museum devoted to the Olympics. The whole history of the games is presented with exhibits, videos, costumes, memorabilia and a bobsleigh and ski-jump simulator. You'll find a tourist information office and a gift shop near the entrance.

Southern Alberta

Okotoks

Okotoks is the largest city between Calgary and Lethbridge. It is also home to several antique and craft shops. The **Ginger Tea Room and Gift Shop** (*43 Riverside Dr., ☎938-2907*) is a Victorian mansion where afternoon tea is served on weekdays and two floors of collectibles and crafts can be admired or purchased (see "Restaurants" section, p. 531). A walking tour map is available at the tourist office (*53 N. Railway St., ☎938-3204*) and includes several historic buildings which date from when the town was a rest stop along the Macleod Trail between Fort Calgary and Fort Macleod.

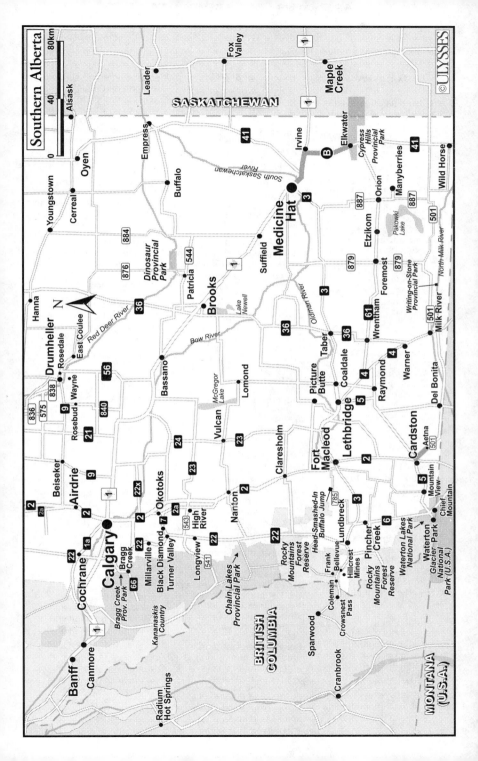

Longview

The **Bar U Ranch National Historic Site ★★** (*$6; mid May to mid-Oct, every day 10am to 6pm; winter, call for group reservations; Longview, Alberta, ☎395-2212 or 800-568-4996*) opened in the summer of 1995 and commemorates the contribution of ranching to the development of Canada. It is one of four ranches that once covered almost all of Alberta, and until recently was still a working ranch. Now, people are able to wander freely around the ranch and observe ranching operations on a scaled-down, demonstration level. "Bar U" refers to the symbol branded on cattle from this ranch. A beautiful new visitors' centre features an interpretive display on breeds of cattle, the roundup, branding and what exactly a quirt is. A 15min video on the Mighty Bar U conveys the romance of the cowboy way of life and also explains how the native grasslands and Chinook winds unique to Alberta have been a perpetual cornerstone of ranching. The centre also houses a gift shop and a restaurant where you can savour an authentic buffalo burger.

Chain Lakes Provincial Park ★ (see Parks section, p. 528) is the only real attraction along this stretch of Highway. It sits between the Rocky Mountains and the Porcupine Hills in a transition zone of spring-fed lakes. There is a campground. Further south, the splendid pale yellow grasslands, dotted occasionally by deep blue lakes, roll up into the distant Rocky Mountains. There is an otherworldly look about the mountains looming on the horizon.

★★★
Waterton Lakes National Park

Waterton Lakes National Park, along with Glacier National Park in Montana, is part of the world's first International Peace Park. With stunning scenery, an exceptional choice of outdoor activities and varied wildlife, Waterton is not to be missed. Its main attraction, however, is its ambience. Many say it is like Banff and Jasper of 20 years ago, before the crowds and the mass commercialism. Waterton Townsite is home to restaurants, bars, shops, grocery stores, laundry facilities, a post office and hotels. There is also a marina from which lake cruises depart. Things slow down considerably in the winter, though the cross-country skiing is outstanding. For more information see the Parks section, p 528.

★
Cardston

Cardston is a prosperous-looking town nestled in the rolling foothills where the grasslands begin to give way to fields of wheat and the yellow glow of canola. The town was established by Mormon pioneers fleeing religious persecution in Utah. Their move here marked one of the last great covered-wagon migrations of the 19th century. Cardston might not seem like much of a tourist town, but it is home to one of the most impressive monuments and one of the most unique museums in Alberta. The monument is the **Mormon Temple** (*free admission; every day 9am to 9pm; 348 Third St. W., ☎653-1696*) that seems a tad out of place rising from the prairie. This truly majestic edifice took 10 years to construct and was the first temple built by the church outside the United States. The marble comes from Italy and the granite was quarried in Nelson, B.C. When it came time to do renovations recently, a problem arose because there was no granite left in Nelson. Luckily, several blocks were found in a farmer's field nearby, having been left there in storage when the temple was built. Only Mormons in good standing may enter the temple itself, but the photographs and video presented at the visitors' centre should satisfy your curiosity. A walk on the beautiful grounds adjacent to the temple is also highly recommended.

The unique museum is the **Remington-Alberta Carriage Centre ★★★** (*$6.50; mid-May to early Sep, every day 9am to 8pm; Sep to May, every day 9am to 5pm; 623 Main St., ☎653-5139*), opened in 1993. "A museum on carriages?", you may ask. The subject matter may seem narrow, but this museum is definitely worth a visit. Forty-nine of the approximately 260 carriages were donated by Mr. Don Remington of Cardston on the condition that the Alberta government build an interpretive centre in which to display them. The wonderfully restored carriages and enthusiastic, dedicated staff at this magnificent facility make this exhibit first-rate.

Take a guided tour through the 1,675m^2 display gallery where town mock-ups and animated street scenes provide the backdrop for the collection – one of the best in the world among elite carriage facilities. The interesting film *Wheels of Change* tells the story of this once huge industry that was all but dead by 1922. Visitors can also learn how to drive a carriage, watch the restoration work in progress, take a carriage ride and have an old-fashioned picture taken.

★

Fort Macleod

The town of Fort Macleod centres around the fort of the same name that was first set up by the North West Mounted Police in an effort to stop the whisky trade. Troops were sent to raid Fort Whoop-Up (see p 526) in 1874, but got lost along the way. By the time they got to Whoop-Up, the traders had fled. They continued west to this spot by the Oldman River and established a permanent outpost. The original settlement was on an island 3km east of the present town, but persistent flooding forced its relocation in 1882. The fort as it stands now was reconstructed in 1956-1957 as a museum. The **Fort Museum** ★ (*$4.50; May and Jun, every day 9am to 5pm; Jul to Sep 9am to 8:30pm; Sep to mid-Oct, every day 9am to 5pm; mid-Oct to Dec 23 and Mar to May, weekdays 10am to 4pm; 219 25th St. at Third Ave., ☎553-4703*) houses exhibits of pioneer life at the time of the settlement, dioramas of the fort, tombstones from the cemetery and an interesting section of artifacts and photographs of the Plains Blood and Peigan tribes. A Mounted Patrol performs a musical ride four times a day in July and August.

Fort Macleod's downtown area is very representative of a significant period in history.

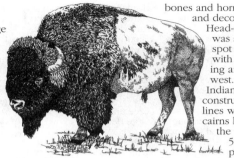

Most of the buildings were erected between 1897 and 1914, except the Kanouse cabin that lies inside the fort walls and dates from much earlier.

Walking-tour pamphlets are available at the tourist office. The tour includes such notable edifices as the **Empress Theatre**, which retains its original pressed-metal ceiling panels, stage and dressing rooms (complete with graffiti from 1913). Movies are still shown here, despite a ghost who occasionally gets upset with the way things are run. The **Silver Grill**, an old saloon across the street, has its original bar and bullet-pierced mirror while the sandstone **Queen's Hotel** still rents rooms (reservations are not recommended!)

The arrival of the horse in the mid-1700s signalled the end of a traditional way of hunting buffalo among Plains Indians. For 5,700 years before this, the Plains Indians had depended on **Head-Smashed-In Buffalo Jump ★★★** (*$6.50; May to Sep, every day 9am to 7pm; Sep to May, every day 9am to 5pm; 15km northwest of Fort Macleod on Hwy. 785, ☎553-2731*). From it they got meat: fresh and dried for pemmican; hides for tipis, clothing and moccasins; and

bones and horns for tools and decorations. Head-Smashed-In was an ideal spot for a jump, with a vast grazing area to the west. The Plains Indians would construct drive lines with stone cairns leading to the cliff. Some 500 people participated in the yearly hunt. Men dressed in buffalo-calf robes and wolf skins lured the herd towards the precipice. Upon reaching the cliff, the leading buffalo were forced over the edge by the momentum of the stampeding herd behind them. The herd was not actually chased over the cliff, but rather fear in the herd led to a stampede. The area remains much as it was thousands of years ago, though the distance from the cliff to the ground drastically changed as the bones of butchered bison piled up, as much as 10m deep in some places.

Today, the jump is the best preserved buffalo jump in North America and a UNESCO World Heritage Site. Many assume that the name comes from the crushed skulls of the buffalo, but it actually refers to a Peigan legend of a young brave who went under the jump to watch the buffalo topple in front of him. The kill was exceptionally good that particular day, and he was crushed by the animals. When his people were butchering the buffalos after the kill, they discovered the brave with his head smashed in – hence the name.

The interpretive centre, built into the cliff, comprises five levels and is visited from the top down. Start off by following the trail along the top of the cliff for a spectacular view of the plain and the Calderwood Jump to the left. Marmots can be seen sunning themselves on the rocks below and generally contemplating the scene. Continuing through the centre, you'll learn about Napi, the mythical creator of people according to the Blackfoot. The centre leads through Napi's world, the people and their routines, the buffalo, the hunt, the contact of cultures and European settlement. An excellent film entitled *In Search of the Buffalo* is presented every 30min. The tour ends with an archaeological exhibit of the excavation work at the site. Back outside the centre you can follow a trail to the butchering site. The annual Buffalo Days celebrations take place here in July. The centre has a great gift shop and a small cafeteria that serves buffalo burgers.

★★
Lethbridge

Lethbridge, known affectionately by locals as "downtown L.A.," is Alberta's third largest city and a pleasant urban oasis on the heart of the prairies. Steeped in history, the city boasts an extensive park system, pretty tree-lined streets, interesting sights and a diverse cultural community. You're as likely to meet ranchers as business people, Hutterites or Mormons on the streets of L.A.

Indian Battle Park ★★, in the Oldman River valley in the heart of town, is where Lethbridge's history comes alive. It is the site of Fort Whoop-Up, once the setting of a terrible battle. On October 25, 1870, Cree, displaced by European settlers into Blackfoot territory, attacked a band of Blood Blackfoot camped on the banks of the Oldman River. In the ensuing battle, the Blood were aided by a group of nearby Peigan Blackfoot, and by the end some 300 Cree and 50 Blackfoot were dead.

A year earlier, American whisky traders had moved into southern Alberta from Fort Benton, Montana. Since it was illegal to sell alcohol to Aboriginal People in the United States, the traders headed north into Canada where there was no law enforcement. They set up Fort Hamilton nearby, at the confluence of the St. Mary's and Oldman rivers, which became the headquarters of American activity in southern Alberta and Saskatchewan. This activity involved the trading of a particularly lethal brew which was passed off as whisky to the Aboriginal People. Besides whisky, this firewater may have also contained fortified grain alcohol, red pepper, chewing tobacco, Jamaican ginger and black molasses.

When fire destroyed the original fort, a second, called **Fort Whoop-Up ★★**, was built to continue the trading of whisky and guns for buffalo hides and robes. Fort Whoop-Up was the first and most notorious of 44 whisky-trading posts. The American encroachment on Canadian territory, the illicit trading demoralizing Aboriginal People, and news of the Cypress Hills massacre (see p. 405) prompted the Canadian government to form the North West Mounted Police. Led by scout Jerry Potts, the Mounties, under the command of Colonel Macleod, arrived at Fort Whoop-Up in October of 1874. Word of their arrival preceded them, however, and the place was empty by the time they arrived. A cairn marks the site of this fort. The reconstructed fort houses an interesting **interpretive centre** (*$2.50; summer, Mon to Sat 10am to 6pm, Sun noon to 5pm; winter, Tue to Fri 10am to 4pm, Sun 1pm to 4pm; Indian Battle Park, ☎329-0444*) where visitors can experience the exciting days of the whisky trade. You can also taste fresh bannock, a round, flat Scottish cake made from barley and oatmeal and cooked on a griddle. Guides in period costume offer tours.

Paths weave their way through five traditional Japanese gardens at the **Nikka Yuko Japanese Garden ★★** (*$4; mid-May to end of Jun, every day 9am to 5pm; Jul and Aug every day 9am to 9pm; Sep, every day 9am to 5pm; Seventh Ave. S and Mayor Magrath Dr., ☎328-3511*). These aren't bright, flowery gardens, but simple arrangements of green shrubs, sand and rocks in the style of a true Japanese garden — perfect for quiet contemplation. Created by renowned Japanese garden designer Dr. Tadashi Kudo of the Osaka Prefecture University in Japan, Nikka Yuko was built in 1967 as a centennial project and a symbol of Japanese and Canadian friendship (*Nikka Yuko* actually means friendship). The bell at the gardens symbolizes this friendship, and when it is rung, good things are supposed to happen simultaneously in both countries.

Across the Prairie to Medicine Hat

The prairies roll on and on as far as the eye can see along this stretch of highway surrounded by golden fields that are empty but for the occasional hamlet, grain elevator or abandoned farmhouse. Towns were set up every 16km because that was how far a farmer could haul his grain. As you drive this road, you will come upon what was once the town of Nemiskam, about 16km out of Foremost. Another 16km down the road is Etzikom. With fewer than 100 inhabitants these days, Etzikom's days may be numbered. For a look at the way things used to be, and a chance to stretch your legs, stop in at the **Etzikom Museum ★** (*donation; May to Sep, Mon to Sat 10am to 5pm, Sun noon to 6pm; Etzikom, ☎666-3737, 666-3792 or 666-3915*). Local museums like this can be found throughout Alberta, but this is one of the best of its kind and makes for a pleasant stop off the highway. Located in the Etzikom School, the museum houses a wonderful recreation of the Main Street of a typical town, complete with barber shop, general store and hotel. Outside is the Windpower Interpretive Centre, a collection of windmills including one from Martha's Vineyard, Massachusetts, U.S.A.

★
Medicine Hat

Rudyard Kipling once called Medicine Hat "a city with all hell for a basement," referring to the town's location above some of western Canada's largest natural gas fields. Medicine Hat prospered because of this natural resource that now supplies a thriving petro-chemical industry. Clay deposits nearby also left their mark on the city, contributing to the city's once thriving pottery industry. Medicine Hat, like many towns in Alberta, features several parks. As for its name, legend has it that a great battle between the Cree and the Blackfoot took place here. During the battle, the Cree medicine man deserted his people. While fleeing across the river, he lost his headdress in mid-stream. Believing this to be a bad omen, the Cree abandoned the fight and were massacred by the Blackfoot. The battle site was called Saamis, which means medicine man's hat. When the Mounties arrived years later, the name was translated and shortened to Medicine Hat.

The **Saamis Tipi** is the world's tallest tipi. It was constructed for the 1988 Calgary Winter Olympics, and then purchased by a Medicine Hat businessman following the Games. The tipi symbolizes the First Nations way of life, based on spirituality, the circle of life, family and the sacred home.

You'll probably have seen the pamphlets for the **Great Wall of China**. This is not a replica of the real thing, but quite literally a wall of china produced by the potteries of Medicine Hat from 1912 to 1988. Though many of the pieces on display are priceless collector's items, the best part of the **Clay Interpretive Centre ★★** (*$3; summer 9am to 5:30pm, winter 8am to 4:30pm; ☎529-1070*) is the tour of the old Medalta plant and kilns. Medalta once supplied the fine china for all Canadian Pacific hotels. Today, workers' clothes and personal effects remain in the plant which closed down unexpectedly in 1989. Medalta Potteries, Medicine Hat Potteries, Alberta Potteries and Hycroft China established Medicine Hat's reputation as an important pottery centre. Tour guides lead visitors through the plant and explain the intricate and labour-intensive work that went into each piece. The tour ends with a fascinating visit inside one of the six beehive kilns outside.

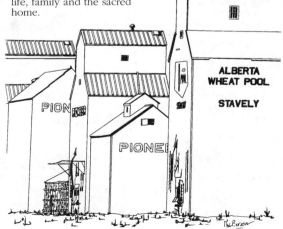

ALBERTA WHEAT POOL

STAVELY

Alberta

Historic Walking Tour pamphlets are available at the information office for those interested in exploring the turn-of-the-century architecture of Medicine Hat's downtown core.

Parks

Southern Alberta

Waterton Lakes National Park ★★★ *(per car for one day: groups $8, $4; camping from $10 to $23; for information call ☎859-5133 or write Waterton Lakes National Park, c/o Superintendent, Waterton Park, Alberta, TOK 2M0. Note that reservations are not accepted for campgrounds.)* is located right on the US-Canadian border and forms one half of the world's first International Peace Park. (The other half is Glacier National Park, Montana). Waterton boasts some of the best scenery in the province and is well worth the detour required to visit it. Characterized by a chain of deep glacial lakes and upside-down mountains with irregularly shaped summits, this area where the peaks meet the prairies offers wonderful hiking, cross-country skiing, camping and wildlife-viewing opportunities.

The unique geology of the area is formed by 1.5-billion-year-old sedimentary rock from the Rockies that was dumped on the 60-million-year-old shale of the prairie during the last ice age. Hardly any transition zone exists between these two regions that are home to abundant and varied wildlife, where species from a prairie habitat mix with those of

sub-alpine and alpine regions (some 800 varieties of plants and 250 species of birds). One thing to remember, and you will be reminded of it as you enter the park, is that wild animals here are just that — wild. While they may appear tame, they are unpredictable and potentially dangerous. Visitors are responsible for their own safety.

There is one park entrance accessible from Highway 6 or 5. On your way in from Highway 6, you will come upon a **buffalo paddock** shortly before the park gate. A small herd lives here and can be viewed by visitors from their cars along a loop road through the paddock. These beasts are truly magnificent, especially framed against the looming mountains of the park. Fees must be paid at the gate and information is available at the information centre a short distance inside the park beyond the gate. Park staff can provide information on camping, wildlife-viewing and the various outdoor activities that can be enjoyed here, including hiking, cross-country skiing, golf, horseback riding, boating and swimming. The park's trademark **Prince of Wales Hotel** (see p. 530) was built in 1926-1927 by Louis Hill, head of the Great Northern Railway, to accommodate American tourists that the railway transported by bus from Montana to Jasper. (Today, the majority of

visitors to the park are still American).

As you approach **Writing-on-Stone Provincial Park ★★** *(free admission; park office ☎647-2364)*, located only about 10km from the U.S. border, you'll notice the carved out valley of the Milk River and in the distance the Sweetgrass Hills rising up in the state of Montana. The Milk River lies in a wide, green valley with strange rock formations and steep sandstone cliffs. Formed by iron-rich layers of sandstone that protect the softer underlying layers, the hoodoos appear like strange mushroom-shaped formations. Along with the cliffs, they were believed to house the powerful spirits of all things in the world, attracting Aboriginal people to this sacred place as many as 3,000 years ago.

Writing-on-Stone Provincial Park protects more rock art — petroglyphs (rock carvings) and pictographs (rock paintings) — than any other place on the North American plains. Dating of the rock art is difficult and based solely on styles of drawing and tell-tale objects. For example, horses and guns imply that the drawings continued into the 18th and 19th centuries.

The majority of the rock art sites are located in the larger part of the provincial park which is an archaeological preserve. Access is provided only through scheduled interpretive tours. For this reason it is extremely important to call the park's **natu-**

ralist office (☎647-2364)
ahead of time to find out
when the tours are head-
ing out. They are given
daily from mid-May to
early September, and free
tickets, limited in number,
are required. These may
be obtained from the naturalist office one hour before the tour begins. Wildlife checklists and fact
sheets are also available at
the naturalist office.

The park boasts an excel-
lent campground (inquire
at park office regarding
fees). Visitors also have
the opportunity to practise
a whole slew of outdoor
activities, including hiking
and canoeing. It's a convenient place to start or end
a canoe trip along the Milk
River.

Outdoor Activities

Canoeing and Rafting

The Milk River is a great
spot to explore by canoe.
With hot summer tempera-
tures, you can possibly
spot antelope, mule deer,
white-tailed deer, coyotes,
badger, beaver and
cottontail rabbits as well as
several bird species, Set in
arid southern Alberta, this
river is the only one in
Alberta that drains into the
Gulf of Mexico. Canoes
can be rented in
Lethbridge.

Milk River Raft Tours (*Box
396 Milk River, Alberta,
T0K 1M0*, ☎647-3586)
organizes rafting trips
along the river in the
vicinity of Writing-on-
Stone Provincial Park.

Trips last from 2 to 6hrs,
cost between $20 and $40
and can include lunch and
hikes through the coulees.

Accommodations

Calgary

There are often two rates
for Calgary hotels and
motels: a Stampede rate
and a rest-of-the-year rate.
The difference between
the two can be substantial
in some cases.

Downtown

Calgary International Hostel
$16 members
$20 non-members
520 Seventh Ave. SE, T2G 0J6
☎269-8239
⇒283-6503
The Calgary International
Hostel can accommodate
up to 114 people in
dormitory-style rooms.
Two family rooms are also
available in winter. Guests
have access to laundry and
kitchen facilities, as well as
to a game room and a
snack bar. The hostel is
advantageously located
two blocks east of City
Hall and Olympic Plaza.
Reservations are
recommended.

**Inglewood Bed & Break-
fast**
$70-$95
1006 Eighth Ave. SE, T2G 0M4
☎/⇒262-6570
One of the most charming
places recommended by
the Bed & Breakfast Asso-
ciation of Calgary is the
Inglewood Bed & Break-
fast. Not far from down-
town, this lovely Victorian
house is also close to the
Bow River's pathway

system. Breakfast is pre-
pared by Chef Valinda.

Prince Royal Inn
$120-$155
ℜ, ◊, ⊘, tv, K
618 Fifth Ave. SW, T2P 0M7
☎263-0520
☎800-661-1592
⇒298-4888
The weekly, corporate and
group rates of the all-suite
Prince Royal Inn make this
perhaps the least expen-
sive hotel accommodation
right downtown. The fully
equipped kitchens also
help keep costs down.

Calgary Marriott Hotel
$149-$179
ℜ, ≈, ≡, ⊛, ◊, ⊘, tv, ✗, ⅗
110 Ninth Ave. SE, T2G 5A6
☎266-7331
☎800-228-9290
⇒262-8442
The business-class Calgary
Mariott Hotel is one of the
biggest of the downtown
hotels. Its spacious rooms
are decorated with warm
colours and comfortable
furnishings.

The Palliser
$289-$368
ℜ, ≡, ⊛, ◊, ⊘, tv, ✗, ⅗
133 Ninth Ave. SW, T2P 2M3
☎262-1234
☎800-441-1414
⇒260-1260
The Palliser offers distinguished, classic accommo-
dations in true Canadian
Pacific style. Built in 1914,
the hotel's lofty lobby (restored in 1997) retains its
original marble staircase,
solid-brass doors and su-
perb chandelier. While the
rooms are a bit small, they
have high ceilings and are
magnificently decorated in
classic styles.

Northeast and Northwest

An inexpensive accommo-
dation option, only available in summer, is to stay

at the residences of the
University of Calgary
(*$20/person in the dormito-
ries, $32/room and $50/suite;
3330 24th Ave. NW, Calgary,
☎220-3203*).

Pointe Inn
$80
ℜ, ≡, *tv*, 🐾
1808 19th St. NE, T2E 4Y3
☎*291-4681*
☎*800-661-8164*
⇌*291-4576*
Travellers just passing
through or who have early
or late flight connections
to make should consider
the convenience and rea-
sonable prices of the
Pointe Inn. From their
fresh appearance, you can
tell that the rooms were
recently renovated (1998).
Laundry facilities.

Calgary's **Motel Village** is
quite something: car-rental
offices, countless chain
motels and hotels, fast-
food and family-style restaurants and the Banff
Trail C-Train stop. The
majority of the hotels and
motels look the same, but
the more expensive ones
are usually newer and
offer more facilities. Most
places charge considerably
higher rates during Stam-
pede Week.
The Red Carpet Motor Hotel
$49-$89
≡, ℝ, *tv*, 🐾
4635 16th Ave. NW, T3B 0M7
☎*286-5111*
⇌*247-9239*
The Red Carpet Motor
Hotel is one of the best
values in Motel Village.
Some suites have small
refrigerators.

Highlander Hotel
$59-$149
ℜ, ≡, ≈, *tv*, 🐾
1818 16th Ave., T2M 0L8
☎*289-1961*
☎*800-661-9564*
⇌*289-3901*
The Scottish decor of the
Highlander Hotel is a nice
change from the typically

drab motel experience.
Close to services and a
shopping mall. Airport
shuttle service available.

🏝️**Econo Lodge**
$89
ℜ, ≡, ≈, *K*, *tv*, 🐾
2231 Banff Tr. NW, T2M 4L2
☎*289-1921*
⇌*282-2149*
Not to be confused with
the other hotel of (almost)
the same name above, the
Econo Lodge is a good
place for families. Children
will enjoy the outdoor
pool and playground
while the laundry facilities
and large units with kitchenettes are very practical.
The Louisiana family res-
taurant serves inexpensive
Cajun and Creole food.

Holiday Inn Express
$95
≡, ≈, ◉, △, ⊘, *tv*, 🐾
2227 Banff Tr. NW, T2M 4L2
☎*289-6600*
☎*800-HOLIDAY*
⇌*289-6767*
The Holiday Inn Express
offers quality accommoda-
tions at affordable prices.
Rooms are furnished with
king- and queen-size beds,
and a complimentary con-
tinental breakfast is served.

Southern Alberta

Waterton Townsite

Things slow down consid-
erably during the winter
months when many hotels
and motels close and oth-
ers offer winter rates and
packages.

The Northland Lodge
$50
sb/pb, ℝ
on Evergreen Ave. Waterton Lakes
National Park, T0K 2M0
☎*859-2353*
Open from mid-May to
mid-October, The North-
land Lodge is a converted
house with nine cosy

rooms. Some rooms have
balconies and barbecues.

The Kilmorey Lodge
$86
♿, ℜ, *K*
117 Evergreen Ave. Box 100,
Waterton Lakes National Park
T0K 2M0
☎*859-2334*
⇌*859-2342*
The Kilmorey Lodge is
open year-round. It is ideally located overlooking
Emerald Bay, and many
rooms have great views.
Antiques and duvets con-
tribute to the old-fash-
ioned, homey feel. Two
wheelchair-accessible
suites have recently been
added. The Kilmorey also
boasts one of Waterton's
finest restaurants, the
Lamp Post Dining Room
(see p 533).

🏝️ **Prince of Wales Hotel**
$175-$190
economy room
$347 suite
ℜ
Waterton Lakes National Park,
T0K 2M0
☎*859-2231*
☎*(602) 207-6000*
⇌*859-2630*
reservations:
☎*236-3400*
The venerable Prince of
Wales Hotel, open from
mid-May until the end of
September, is definitely the
grandest place to stay in
Waterton. It features bell-
hops in kilts and high tea
in Valerie's Tea Room, not
to mention the unbeatable
view. The lobby and
rooms are all adorned with
original wood panelling.
The rooms are actually
quite small and unspectac-
ular, however, with tiny
bathrooms and a rustic
feel. Those on the third
floor and higher have balconies. Try to request a
room facing the lake,
which is, after all, the reason people stay here.
Things will certainly
change here if the rumours

about expanding the Prince of Wales are true (see p 528).

Lethbridge

 Art Deco Heritage House B&B
$50 bkfst incl.
sb
1115 Eighth Ave. S, T1J 1P7
☎ *328-3824*
↪ *328-9011*
Built in 1937, the Art Deco Heritage House B&B is located on one of Lethbridge's pretty tree-lined residential streets, only a few minutes' walk from downtown. The guest rooms are uniquely decorated in accordance with the design of the house and include many of the house's original features. This house is an Alberta Provincial Historic Resource.

Days Inn
$64-$67 bkfst. incl.
≡, ⊛, K, ≈, ☺, tv, ✖, ᗰ
100 Third Ave. S, T1J 4L2
☎ *327-6000*
☎ *(800) 661-8085* ↪ *320-2070*
Days Inn is the best motel choice downtown. The typical motel-style rooms are non-descript, but modern and clean. A free continental breakfast is served. Coin laundry available. You can also take advantage of the brand-new pool.

Lethbridge Lodge Hotel
$119-$139
≡, ≈, ℜ, ⊛, tv, ✖
320 Scenic Dr., T1J 4B4
☎ *328-1123*
☎ *(800) 661-1232*
↪ *328-0002*
The best hotel accommodation in Lethbridge is found at the Lethbridge Lodge Hotel overlooking the river valley.

The comfortable rooms, decorated in warm and pleasant colours, seem almost luxurious when you consider the reasonable price. The rooms surround an interior tropical courtyard where small footbridges lead from the pool to the lounge and Anton's Restaurant (see p 533).

Medicine Hat

 The Sunny Holme B&B
$65 bkfst incl.
271 1st St. SE, T1A 0A3 ☎ *526-5846*
Besides the one central hotel, there is actually another, very pleasant place to stay that is close to downtown, along pretty First Street SE. The Sunny Holme B&B is in a grand western Georgian house with a Victorian interior. The three rooms are decorated in the arts and crafts style, and each has its own bathroom. A large leafy lot surrounds the house. Sourdough pancakes are just one of the breakfast possibilities. Be sure to call ahead.

Best Western Inn
$99
ℜ, ☺, ≡, ≈, ◇, ⊛, K, tv, ✖;
1051 Ross Glen Dr.
☎ *529-2222*
↪ *529-1538*
For about the same price, you can stay along the motel strip at the Best Western Inn. The surroundings may not be as pleasant, but the facilities and rooms are more modern. Guests have access to an indoor pool and laundry facilities, and can benefit (hopefully) from the only casino in town.

Restaurants

Calgary

Downtown

Schwartzie's Bagel Noshery
$
Eighth Ave. SW
☎ *296-1353*
If you don't think you'll last until dinner, grab a bagel to go from Schwartzie's Bagel Noshery. Imagine the most typical and the most original bagels you can and they probably have one. You can also eat in; the interior is inviting and comfortable.

 Drinkwaters Grill
$$
237 Eighth Ave. SE
☎ *264-9494*
As the new kid on the block when it comes to steakhouses in Calgary, its self-billing as "contemporary" is appropriate. The huge sky-blue-coloured columns, modern tableaux, classic dark wooden chairs and upholstered banquettes are appealing. On the menu, there is everything from thin-crust pizza to spinach and strawberry salad, Chilean sea bass and, of course, a range of very acceptable sirloins, strips and other fine cuts, each with original accompaniments. They have theatre specials and a Happy Hour from 3:30pm to 7pm, Monday to Friday.

The Silver Dragon
$$
106 Third Ave. SE
☎ *264-5326*
This is one of the best of the many Chinese restaurants in Chinatown. The staff is particularly friendly

Alberta

and the dumplings particularly tasty.

Caesar's Steakhouse
$$$$
512 Fourth Ave. SW
☎264-1222
and 10816 Macleod Tr. S
☎278-3930
While it's one of Calgary's most popular spots to dig into a big juicy steak, they also serve good seafood. The elegant decor features Roman columns and soft lighting.

Hy's
$$$$
316 Fourth Ave. SW
☎263-2222
Hy's, around since 1955, is the other favourite for steaks. The main dishes are just slightly less expensive than Caesar's and the atmosphere is a bit more relaxed, thanks to wood panelling. Reservations are recommended.

The Rimrock Room
$$$$
In the Palliser Hotel, 133 Ninth Ave. SW
☎262-1234
The Palliser Hotel's Rimrock Room serves a fantastic Sunday brunch and of course healthy portions of prime Alberta beef. The Palliser's classic surroundings and fine food coalesce into one of Calgary's most elegant dining experiences.

Along the Bow

 **Good Earth Café**
$
at Eau Claire Market, 200 Barclay Parade SW
☎237-8684
Good Earth Café is a wonderful coffee shop with tasty wholesome goodies all made from scratch. Besides being a choice spot for lunch, this is also a good source of picnic fixings.

Deane House Restaurant
$$
year-round, Wed to Sun 11am to 2pm
806 Ninth Ave. SE, just across the bridge from Fort Calgary
☎269-7747
The Historic Deane House Restaurant is a pleasant tearoom located in the house of former RCMP commanding officer Richard Burton Deane. Soups and salads figure prominently on the menu.

Stromboli Inn
$$
1147 Kensington Cresc. NW
☎283-1166
The Stromboli offers unpretentious service and ambiance and classic Italian cuisine. Locals recommend it for its pizza though the menu also includes handmade gnocchi, plump ravioli and a delicious veal gorgonzola.

 Buchanan's
$$$
738 Third Ave. SW
☎261-4646
Buchanan's gets the nod not only for its innovative steaks and chops in blue cheese sauce, but also for its excellent wine list (fine choices by the glass) and impressive selection of single malt scotches. This is a power-lunch favourite of Calgary's business crowd.

Southeast and Southwest

 Nellie's Kitchen
$
17th Ave. SW between Seventh and Sixth St. SW
Everything is made from scratch at the informal Nellie's Kitchen, a neat little rendez-vous for lunch and people-watching.

 Kremlin
$$
2004 Fourth St. SW
☎228-6068
This tiny restaurant serves Russian "love food" that you will fall in love with. The hearty borscht with herb bread is a real deal. Or maybe you'll go for the perogies with their filling of the day or the oh-so-tender tenderloin with rosemary, red wine and honey. For dessert, who could say no to perogies filled with Saskatoon berries and topped with orange brandy cream sauce? The decor is eclectic, cosy and perfect for "love food."

Passage To India
$$
1325 Ninth Ave. SE
☎ 263-4440
The owner of Passage To India left India 30 years ago to come to Canada and brought his secret recipes along in his luggage. He recently left his job as a civil servant to devote himself full time to his culinary passion. The great variety of impressive dishes on the menu will definitely satisfy lovers of Indian cuisine, such as beef, chicken and vegetables. Even the wine and beer come from India.

Entre Nous
$$-$$$
2206 Fourth St. SW
☎228-5525
Entre Nous, which means between us, boasts a friendly and intimate bistro atmosphere, perfect for savouring some good French food. Special attention to detail, from the hand-selected ingredients to the *table d'hôte* menu, make for a memorable dining experience. Reservations recommended.

Cannery Row
$$$
317 10th Ave. SW
☎*269-8889*
Cannery Row serves this landlocked city's best seafood. An oyster bar and casual atmosphere is intended to make you feel like you're by the sea, and it works. Fresh halibut, salmon and swordfish are prepared in a variety of ways. **McQueen's Upstairs** (*$$$; upstairs,* ☎*269-4722*) has a similar seafood-ori-.ented menu but is slightly more upscale.

The Inn on Lake Bonavista
$$$$
747 Lake Bonavista Dr. SE
☎*271-6711*
This is one of Calgary's finest dining rooms with fine menu selections like filet mignon and Châteaubriand that are complemented by fine views over the lake.

Northeast and Northwest

Mamma's Ristorante
$$$
320 16th St., NW
☎*276-9744*
Mamma's has been serving Italian cuisine to Calgarians for more than 20 years. The ambiance and menu offerings are both equally refined, the latter including homemade pasta, veal and seafood dishes.

Southern Alberta

Waterton

The Lamp Post Dining Room
$$$
in Kilmorey Lodge
☎*859-2334*
The Lamp Post offers what some argue is the best dining in Waterton. The traditional charm, coupled with award-winning food

and relatively reasonable prices definitely make it one of the best.

Garden Court Dining Room
$$$$
☎*859-2231*
The atmosphere at the Garden Court Dining Room in the Prince of Wales Hotel is unbeatable. This formal dining room serves a complete menu and daily specials that often include delicious seafood or pasta. Reservations are not accepted. There, you can also enjoy an equally elegant ambience and a stunning view out the **Windsor Lounge** and **Valerie's Tea Room** where afternoon tea and continental breakfast are both served.

Lethbridge

O'Sho Japanese Restaurant *$*
1219 Third Ave. S
☎*327-8382*
For a change from Alberta beef, try the O'Sho Japanese Restaurant where classic Japanese fare is enjoyed in traditional style from low tables set in partitioned rooms.

The Penny Coffee House
$
Ninth St. S, between Fifth and Sixth Ave. S
Located next to B. Maccabee's bookseller, The Penny Coffee House is the perfect place to enjoy a good book. Don't worry if you haven't got one since there is plenty of interesting reading material on the walls. This café serves delicious hearty soups and chilis, filling sandwiches, a wonderful cheese and tomato scone, sodas and of course a great cup of Java.

Anton's
$$$$
Lethbridge Lodge
☎*328-1123*
The Lethbridge Lodge is home to Anton's, the city's finest restaurant. The pasta dishes are particularly well received (as is the setting) in the hotel's tropical indoor courtyard. Reservations are recommended.

Medicine Hat

The City Bakery
$
Fifth Ave. SW, between Third and Fourth St. SW
☎*527-2800*
The City Bakery bakes up wonderful fresh breads and New York bagels.

Rustler's
$
901 Eighth St. SW
☎*526-8004*
Rustler's is another spot that transports you back to the lawless wild west. The restaurant even boasts a blood-stained card table preserved under glass for all to gawk at! The menu features steaks, chicken, ribs, pasta and several Mexican dishes. Breakfasts are particularly busy and copious.

Entertainment

Calgary

Avenue is a monthly publications that lists what's going on throughout Calgary, including live acts around town and theatre offerings. It is available free of charge throughout the city. **The Calgary Mirror** and **ffwd** are free news and entertainment weeklies.

Alberta

Bars and Nightclubs

Things have changed since the heyday of **Electric Avenue** (*11th Avenue SW*). The downtown core is picking up as are 12th Avenue and 17th Avenue. **Senor Frog's** and **Crazy Horse** are popular with young professionals, with dance tunes at the former and classic rock and roll at the latter. **The Republic** (*219 17th Ave. SW, ☎244-1884*) and **The Warehouse** (*733 10th Ave. SW, ☎264-0535*) offer more "alternative" alternative.

The cocktail craze has hit Calgary. The best places to lounge and sip martinis are the **Auburn Saloon** (*200 Eighth Ave. SW, ☎290-1012*), the **Embassy** (*516C Ninth Ave., ☎213-3970*), **Quincy's** (*609 Seventh Ave. SW, ☎264-1000*), which also has cigars, and finally **Diva** (*1154 Kensington Cresc., ☎270-3739*), in Kensington.

Boystown (*213 10th Ave. SW, ☎265-2028*) attracts a gay crowd, while **The 318** and **Victoria's Restaurant** (*17th Ave. at Second St. SW*), both located in the same building, cater to mixed crowds. **Rook's** is a relaxed bar with great 25¢ chicken wings and a mostly lesbian clientele.

Kaos Jazz Bar (*718 17th Ave. SW, ☎228-9997*) is a popular jazz club with live shows Thursday to Saturday. This is also a fun café with an interesting menu.

If you're itchin' to two-step, then you're in luck. Calgary has two great country bars. At **The Ranchman's** (*9615 Macleod Tr. SW, ☎253-1100*), the horseshoe-shaped dance floor is the scene of two-step lessons on Tuesdays

and line-dancing lessons on Wednesdays. It's packed the rest of the week. The **Rockin' Horse Saloon** (*7400 Macleod Tr. SE, ☎255-4646*) is where the real cowboys and cowgirls hang out. For some two-stepping downtown head to **Cowboy's** (*826 Fifth St. SW, ☎265-0699*).

Cultural Activities

Alberta Theatre Projects (*☎294-7475*) is an excellent troupe that performs great contemporary plays.

Those in need of some culture may want to inquire about performances of the **Calgary Opera** (*☎262-7286*), the **Calgary Philharmonic Orchestra** (*☎571-0270*) and the **Alberta Ballet** (*☎245-2274*).

Calgary has an **IMAX** theatre in the Eau-Claire Market (*☎974-IMAX or 974-4700*).

Uptown Screen (*612 Eighth Ave., ☎265-0120*) shows foreign films in an old revamped theatre downtown. First-run movies can be seen at movie theatres throughout the city. Pick up a newspaper for schedules and locations, or call the **Talking Yellow Pages** (*☎521-5222*) (see p 518).

Festivals and Events

The **Calgary Exhibition and Stampede** is deservedly called the "Greatest Show on Earth." It began in 1912 when many people expected that the wheat industry would eventually supercede the cattle industry and was only intended to be a one-time showcase for traditional cowboy skills. Of course the cattle

industry has thrived, and the show has been a huge success ever since.

Every July, around 100,000 people descend on Stampede Park for the extravaganza. It begins with a parade, which starts at Sixth Avenue SE and Second Street SE at 9am. However, be sure to get there early (by 7am) if you want to see anything. The main attraction is of course the rodeo where cowboys and cowgirls show off their skills.

The trials take place every afternoon at 1:30pm with the big final being held on the last weekend. Reserved seats for this event sell out quickly and you are better off ordering tickets in advance if you have your heart set on seeing the big event. There are also chuck-wagon races with heats for the Rangeland Derby held every evening at 8pm and the final on the last weekend. Downtown's **Olympic Plaza** is transformed into **Rope Square** where free breakfast is served every morning from the backs of chuck wagons. Festivities continue throughout the day in the Plaza. Back at Stampede Park, an "Indian Village" and agricultural fair are among the exhibits to explore. Evening performances often showcase some of the biggest stars in country music. A gate admission fee of $8 is charged and allows access to all live entertainment except for shows at the Saddledome, where tickets must be purchased in advance. For information on the good rodeo seats, write to **Calgary Exhibition and Stampede** (*Box 1060, Station M, Calgary, Alberta, T2P 2L8, or call ☎261-0101 ☎800-661-1260*)

The **Calgary International Jazz Festival** (☎233-2628) takes place the last week of June. The **International Native Arts Festival** (☎233-0022) and **Afrikadey** (☎283-7119) both take place the third week of August, and highlight entertainment and art from a variety of cultures from all over the world. The **Calgary Winter Festival** (☎543-5480) takes place in late January or February.

Spectator Sports

The Canadian Football League's **Calgary Stampeders** play their home games in **McMahon Stadium** (*1817 Crowchild Tr. NW,* ☎289-0205 ☎800-667-FANS) from July to November. The National Hockey League's **Calgary Flames** play at the **Olympic Saddledome** (*17th Ave. and Second St. SE,* ☎777-4646 or 777-2177) from October to April.

Southern Alberta

Fort Macleod

Main Street's **Empress Theatre** (*235 24th St.,* ☎553-4404 or 800-540-9229) is an original theatre from 1912. In fact, it's one of the oldest theatres in the province. It presents popular films throughout the year. Depending on the time of year, musical concerts, plays and conferences alternate with various film programs.

Every year in mid-July, the **Annual Pow-Wow** is held at Head-Smashed-In Buffalo Jump. A large tipi is set up on the grounds where visitors can see traditional native dancing and sample

some native food. For information call ☎553-2731.

Shopping

Calgary

The **Eaton Centre, TD Square, Scotia Centre** and **The Bay** department stores line Eighth Avenue SW, as does a collection of swanky upscale shops including **Holt Renfrew** and the boutiques in **Penny Lane Hall**.

The **Eau-Claire Market** is a wonderful spot to pick up just about anything. Imported goods, including Peruvian sweaters and southwestern-style decorating items, are all sold right next to fresh fish and produce. **Sandpiper Books** (also located on 10th Avenue) on the upper level is a marvellous bookshop with a good collection of books on Alberta.

Not only are **Kensington Avenue** and the surrounding streets a pleasant place to stroll, but the area is also full of interesting specialty shops that are worth a look. One of these is **Heartland Country Store** (*940 Second Ave. NW*) which sells beautiful pottery. There is a collection of shops, cafés and galleries along 17th Avenue SW, with a distinctly upbeat atmosphere. Along Ninth Avenue SE, east of the Elbow River, in Inglewood, gentrified houses now contain antique shops and cafés.

To make sure you fit in, the **Alberta Boot Co.** (*614 10th Ave. SW*) is the place to outfit yourself for the Stampede, with boots in all sizes and styles.

The kingdom of records, cassettes and movies in Calgary is called **Recordland** (*1204 Ninth Ave. SE, near 11th St. SE*). They have every style of music here-- and at unbeatable prices: three CDs for just $25!

Mountain Equipment Co-op (*830 10th Ave. SW,* ☎269-2420) is a co-operative that is essentially open only to its members. However, it only costs $5 to join and is well worth it. High-quality camping and outdoor equipment, clothing and accessories are sold at very reasonable prices.

Arnold Churgin Shoes (*221 Eighth Ave. SW,* ☎262-3366 *and at the Chinook Centre, Macleod Tr. at Glenmore Tr.,* ☎258-1818) sells high-quality women's shoes at reasonable prices and offers excellent service – a must for those with a weakness for footwear!

Callebaut Chocolates (*1313 First St. SE,* ☎265-5777) makes delicious Belgian chocolates right here in Calgary. They are available throughout the city, but at the head office in the Southeast you can see them being made.

Central Alberta and Edmonton

Central Alberta

encompasses a vast swath of the province that includes the Red Deer River Valley, the foothills, the Rocky Mountains Forest Reserve and the heartland.

A region that holds an inestimable amount of natural resources, forestry, farming and oil drive the economy of this region, as does tourism that has been boosted by the occasional discovery of a dinosaur bone or two.

Edmonton, the capital of the province, is easily accessible from anywhere in Central Alberta and has an unusually sophisticated atmosphere with fine restaurants and a thriving arts community. Edmonton has become the technological, service and supply centre of Alberta.

Finding Your Way Around

By Car

Edmonton's streets are numbered; the avenues run east-west and the streets run north-south. The major arteries include: **Calgary Trail**, which runs north into the city (northbound it is also known as 103rd Street and southbound as 104th Street); **Whitemud Drive** runs east-west, lying south of the city centre providing access to West Edmonton Mall, Fort Edmonton Park and the Valley Zoo; **Jasper Avenue** runs east-west through downtown where 101st Avenue would naturally fall; and Highway 16, the Yellowhead Highway, crosses the city north of downtown, providing access to points in the tour of northern Alberta

Car Rentals

Budget

Airport
☎ *(780) 448-2000*
Downtown
10016 106th Street
☎ *(780) 448-2001*

Hertz

Airport
☎ *(780) 890-4565*
Downtown
☎ *(780) 423-3431*

Tilden

Airport
☎ *(780) 890-7232*
Downtown
☎ *(780) 422-6097*

Avis

Airport
☎*(780)890-7596*
Downtown
Sheraton Hotel, 10235 101st St.
☎*(780) 448-0066*

Discount

Downtown
Hotel Macdonald, 9925 Jasper Ave.
☎*(780) 448-3892*

Thrifty

Airport
☎*(780) 890-4555*
Downtown
10036 102nd St.
☎*(780) 428-8555*

By Plane

Edmonton International Airport is located south of the city centre. It offers many services and facilities, including restaurants, an information centre, hotel courtesy phones, major car-rental counters, currency exchange and a bus tour operator.

Air Canada, Canadian Airlines International, American Airlines, Delta Airlines, Northwest Airlines, United Airlines and Lufthansa all have regular flights to the airport. Regional companies (Air B.C. and Canadian Regional) fly in and out of the municipal airport, located north of the city.

The **Sky Shuttle** (☎ *780-465-8515*) travels to downtown hotels and to Edmonton's municipal airport. It passes every 20min on weekends and every 30min during the week. The trip is $11 one-way and $18 return.

A taxi from the airport to downtown costs about $30.

By Bus

Central Alberta

Drumheller Greyhound Bus Depot
308 Center St.
☎*(403) 823-7566*
Services: restaurant, tourist information.

Edmonton

Edmonton Greyhound Bus Depot
10324 103rd St.
☎*(780) 413-8747*
☎*(780) 420-2440*
☎*800-661-8747*
Services: restaurant, lockers.

Edmonton South Greyhound Bus Depot
5723 104th St., 2 blocks north of Whitemud Freeway on Calgary Trail
☎*(780) 433-1919*

By Train

Via Rail's transcontinental railway passenger service makes a stop in Edmonton three times a week, continuing west to Jasper and Vancouver or east to Saskatoon and beyond. The new VIA train station is at 12360 121st Street, about 15min from downtown.

Public Transit

Edmonton's public transit also combines buses and a light-rail transit system. The LRT runs east-west along Jasper Avenue, south to the university and then north to 139th Street. With only 10 stops, the train runs underground and in the city centre. The LRT is free between Churchill and Grandin stops on weekdays from 9am to 3pm and Saturdays from 9am to 6pm. Fares are $1.60 for adults and a day pass is $4.75. Route and schedule information is available by calling ☎*(780) 496-1611*.

By Foot

Edmonton's downtown core has its own system of walkways known as the pedway system. It lies below and above ground and at street level. It seems complicated at first, though is very well indicated and easy to negotiate once you have picked up a map at the tourist information centre.

Practical Information

The area Code for **Calgary and surroundings** is *403*, while **Edmonton and surroundings** is *780*

Information on everything from road conditions to movie listings to provincial parks is available from the Talking Yellow Pages. In Edmonton, call ☎*780-493-9000*. A series of recorded messages is accessible by dialling specific codes. The codes are listed in the front of the yellow pages phone books that are usually found in phone booths.

Tourist Information

Central Alberta

Drumheller Tourist Information
at the corner of Riverside Dr. and 1st St. W
☎*(403) 823-1331*

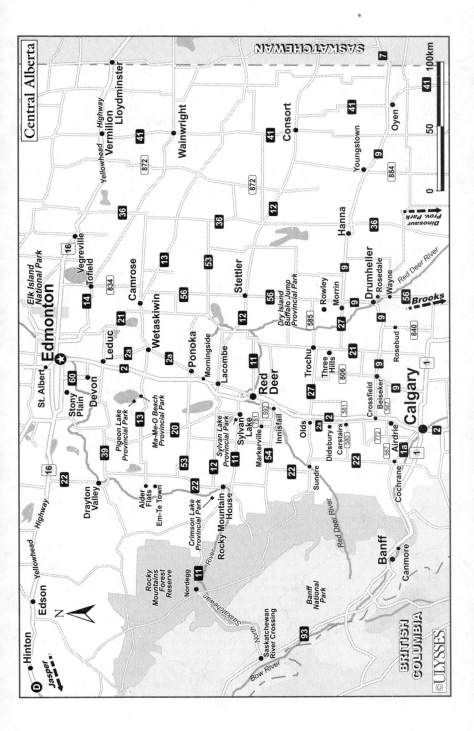

Central Alberta

**Big Country
Tourist Association**
170 Centre St., #28, Box 2308,
Drumheller, T0J 0Y0
☎*(403) 823-5885*
⌐*(403) 823-7942*

Red Deer Tourist Information
25 Riverview Park
☎*(403) 346-0180*
☎*800-215-8946*

Rocky Mountain House
tourist information in a trailer
north of town on Hwy. 11
summer only
☎*(403) 845-2414*

Chamber of Commerce
In Town Hall
year round
☎*(403) 845-5450*

Edmonton

**Edmonton Tourism Civic
Centre**
1 Sir Winston Churchill Square;
also in Gateway Park,
south of downtown on Calgary Trail
(Hwy. 2)
☎*(780) 496-8423*
☎*800-463-4667*

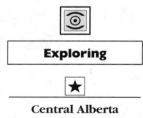

Exploring

★

Central Alberta

Where the Red Deer River
Valley now lies was once
the coastal region of a vast
inland sea. The climate
probably resembled that of
the Florida Everglades and
was an ideal habitat for
dinosaurs. After the extinction of the dinosaurs, ice
covered the land. As the
ice retreated 10,000 years
ago, it carved out deep
trenches in the prairie.
This and subsequent
erosion have uncovered
dinosaur bones and
shaped the fabulously

interesting landscape of
hoodoos and coulees
you'll see on this Dinosaur
odyssey.

Brooks

Brooks began as a railway
stop in the 1880s, and
soon developed a major
irrigation system. The
**Brooks Aqueduct National and
Provincial Historic Site** (*$2;
mid-May to Sep, every day
10am to 6pm; 3km southeast
of Brooks,* ☎*403-362-4451*)
began operating in the
spring of 1915. At the time
it was the longest concrete
structure (3.2km) of its
kind in the world. It was a
vital part of the irrigation
of southeastern Alberta for
65 years.

South of Brooks on High-
way 873 is **Kinbrook Provincial Park ★** and Lake Newell. The wildlife observation possibilities here are
excellent. See Parks, p 548.

★★★
Dinosaur Provincial
Park

The town of Brooks is also
a great jumping-off point
for Dinosaur Provincial
Park that was declared a
UNESCO World Heritage
Site in 1979. The park's
landscape consists of Badlands, called mauvaises
terres by French explorers
because there was neither
food nor beavers there.

These eerie Badlands con-
tain fossil beds of international significance where
over 300 complete skele-
tons have been found.
Glacial meltwater carved
out the Badlands from the
soft bedrock, revealing
hills laden with dinosaur
bones. Wind and rain
erosion continues today,
providing a glimpse of
how this landscape of

hoodoos, mesas and
gorges was formed.

There are two self-guided
trails and a loop road. The
best way to see the park,
however, is to follow a
guided-tour into the re-
stricted nature preserve,
though this requires a bit
of planning. Unless you
plan to arrive early, it is
extremely important to call
ahead for the times of the
tours to make sure you are
there in time to reserve a
spot (see Parks, p 549).
Visitors can tour the **Field
Station of the Tyrell
Museum ★** (see p 549 for
fee and schedule informa-
tion) for an introduction to
the excavation of dinosaur
bones, and then head off
on their own adventure.

★★★
Drumheller

The main attractions in
Drumheller are located
along the Dinosaur Trail
and East Coulee Drive: the
Royal Tyrell Museum of
Palaeontology, the Bleriot
Ferry, the Rosedale Sus-
pension Bridge, the Hoo-
doos, East Coulee, the
Atlas Coal Mine and the
Last Chance Saloon. Ero-
sion in the Red Deer River
Valley has uncovered
dinosaur bones and
shaped the fabulously
interesting landscape of
hoodoos and coulees
found in Drumheller. Be-
sides the bones, early
settlers discovered coal.
Agriculture and the oil and
gas industries now drive
the local economy.

The Dinosaur Trail runs
along both sides of the
Red Deer River. The first
stop on Highway 838 (the
North Dinosaur Trail) is
the **Homestead Antique Museum** (*$3; mid-May to mid-
Oct, every day 9am to 5pm;
Jul and Aug, every day 9am
to 8pm;* ☎*403-823-2600,*

www.tyrellmuseum.com). It features a collection of 4,000 items from the days of the early settlers, but it is not the highlight of the tour. That honour falls on the **Royal Tyrell Museum of Palaeontology** ★★★ (*$6.50; mid-May to Sep every day 9am to 9pm; Oct to mid-May, Tue to Sun 10am to 5pm; 6km west of Drumheller on Hwy. 838,* ☎*403-823-7707 or* ☎*888-440-4240).* This mammoth museum contains over 80,000 specimens, including 50 full-size dinosaur skeletons. There are hands-on exhibits and computers, fibre-optics and audio-visual presentations. The Royal Tyrell is also a major research centre where visitors can watch scientists cleaning bones and preparing specimens for display. There is certainly a lot to thrill younger travellers here. However, the wealth of information to absorb can be a bit overwhelming. Special new displays are always being set up. You can participate in the **Day Dig** (*$85, children 10 to 15 $55, includes lunch, snacks, transportation and admission to the museum, reservations required; mid-May to late Jun, Sat and Sun, late Jun to end of Aug every day),* which offers an opportunity to visit a dinosaur quarry and excavate fossils yourself, or the **Dig Watch** (*$12, children 7 to 17 $8, under 7 free, families $30; daily departures from the museum at 10am, noon, 2pm),* a 90min guided tour to an actual working excavation site, where you'll see a dig in progress. Call ahead for tour times.

The next stop is the world's largest **Little Church**, which can accommodate "10,000 people, but only 6 at a time." The seven-by-eleven-foot house of worship, opened in 1958, seems to have been more popular with vandals than the devout and was rebuilt in 1990.

★★★
Hoodoo Trail/East Coulee Drive

Once back in Drumheller, get on East Coulee Drive (also called the Hoodoo Trail) which heads southeast along the Red Deer River. The town of **Rosedale** originally stood on the other side of the river next to the Star Mine. The suspension bridge across the Red Deer looks flimsy, but is said to be safe for those who want to venture across. Take a detour to cross the 11 bridges to get to **Wayne**. The bridges are perhaps the best part, as the main attraction in town, the Rosedeer Hotel with its **Last Chance Saloon**, leaves something to be desired. Rooms are available for rent at $15/night, but settle for a beer and some nostalgia instead. You can also have a good steak cooked up on the grill. The fourth floor is closed because legend has it that the spirit of a murderer from the early 1900s still wanders there.

About halfway between Rosedale and East Coulee, you'll see some of the most spectacular **hoodoos** ★★★ in southern Alberta. These strange mushroom-shaped formations result when the softer underlying sandstone erodes. **East Coulee**, a town that almost disappeared, was once home to 3,000 people but only 200 residents remain. The **East Coulee School Museum** (*$2.15; summer, every day 9am to 6pm; winter, closed Sat and Sun;* ☎*403-822-3970)* occupies a 1930s school house. A small tea room and galleryare found inside. Although the Atlas Coal Mine ceased operations in 1955, the **Atlas Coal Mine Museum** (*$3; May to Oct, every day 9am to 6pm;* ☎*403-822-2220)* keeps the place alive to this day across the river from town. The last standing tipple (a device for emptying coal from mine cars) in Canada stands among the mine buildings that you can explore on your own or as part of a guided tour. The colourful owner of the Wildhorse Saloon, in front of the mine, was instrumental in saving the School Museum and the Atlas Coal Mine. Don't drink anything that's not bottled in this place.

Rocky Mountain House

Despite its evocative name, Rocky Mountain House is not a picturesque log cabin in the woods but rather a gateway town into the majestic Rocky Mountains. The town, known locally as Rocky, is home to just under 6,000 people and represents a transition zone between the aspen parkland and the mountains. The exceptional setting is certainly one of the town's major attractions which otherwise offers the gamut of services – hotels, gas stations and restaurants. Just outside Rocky lies the town's namesake, Rocky Mountain House National Historic Site, along with a wealth of outdoor possibilities. They include river trips in voyageur canoes and fishing, hiking and cross-country skiing at Crimson Lake Provincial Park.

Alberta

The **Rocky Mountain House National Historic Park** ★★ (*$2.25; May to Sep, every day 10am to 6pm, call for winter hours; 4.8km southwest of Rocky on Hwy. 11A, ☎845-2412*) is Alberta's only National Historic Park and the site of four known historic sites. Rocky Mountain House is interesting because it exemplifies, perhaps better than any other trading post, the inextricable link between the fur trade and the discovery and exploration of Canada.

Two rival forts were set up here in 1799: Rocky Mountain House by the North West Company and Acton House by the Hudson's Bay Company. Both companies were lured by the possibility of establishing lucrative trade with the Kootenay First Nation, west of the Rockies. It was only after the merging of the Hudson's Bay Company and the North West Company in 1821 that the area was called Rocky Mountain House.

Trade with the Kootenay never did materialize. In fact, except for a brief period of trade with the Blackfoot in the 1820s, the fort never prospered and actually closed down. It was then rebuilt on several occasions. It closed for good in 1875 after the North West Mounted Police made the area to the south safe for trading. The Hudson's Bay Company thus set up a post in the vicinity of Calgary. As an interesting aside, the Hudson's Bay Company (today the cross-Canada department store The Bay) makes more money on its real estate holdings than on its retail operations.

The visitors centre presents a most informative exhibit on the fur-trading days at Rocky Mountain House. You can take a look at the clothing of the Plains Indians and how it changed with the arrival of fur traders as well as artifacts and testimonies of early explorers. Visitors can also choose to view one of several excellent National Film Board documentaries. Two interpretive trails lead through the site to listening posts (in English and French) along the swift-flowing North Saskatchewan River. Stops include a buffalo paddock and demonstration sites where tea is brewed and a York Boat, once used by Hudson's Bay Company traders, is displayed. (The North West Company traders preferred the birchbark canoe, even though it was much slower). All that remains of the last fort are two chimneys.

Rocky Mountain House was also a base for exploration. David Thompson, an explorer, surveyor and geographer for the North West Company, played an integral role in the North West Company's search for a route through the Rockies to the Pacific. He was based at Rocky Mountain House for a time. Ultimately beaten by the Americans in his pursuit, he travelled 88,000km during his years in the fur trade, filling in the map of Western Canada along the way.

Alder Flats

Alder Flats itself is of little interest to visitors. A few kilometres south, however, is another town that is full of attractions, a place ironically called **Em-Te Town**. Here you'll find a saloon, jailhouse, harness shop, schoolhouse, church and emporium, located in a pretty setting at the end of a gravel road. Built from scratch in 1978, this is a neat place to experience life the way it was in the old west with trail rides and home-cooked meals at the Lost Woman Hotel. However, some may find the whole experience a bit contrived. In addition to the attractions, there are campsites and cabins for rent as well as a restaurant.

★★★
David Thompson Highway

The drive west from Rocky Mountain House runs along the edge of the Rocky Mountain Forest Reserve. Stunning views of the Rocky Mountains line the horizon. Highway 11, the David Thompson Highway, continues west from Rocky Mountain House up into the Aspen Parkland and on into Banff National Park (see p 559). The town of **Nordegg** lies at the halfway point of the highway. In addition to an interesting museum, the Nordegg Museum, the town offers access to great fishing, the Forestry Trunk Road and camping and is also home to the Shunda Creek Hostel (see p 550). The only services available west of Nordegg before the Highway 93 are at the David Thompson Resort (see p 550).

★
Red Deer

Red Deer, a city of 60,000 people, began as a stopover for early commercial travellers along the Calgary-Edmonton Trail. Red Deer is an erroneous translation of *Waskasoo* which means elk in Cree. Since the shores of the river were frequented by elk, Scottish settlers thought that the animals resembled red deer found in Scotland. During the Riel Rebellion of 1885, the Canadian militia built Fort Normandeau at this site. The post was later occupied by the North West Mounted Police. The railway, agriculture, oil and gas all contributed to the growth of Red Deer, at one point the fastest growing city in Canada.

Red Deer is another Alberta city whose extensive park system is one of its greatest attractions. The **Waskasoo Park System** weaves its way throughout the city and through the Red Deer River valley with walking and cycling trails. The information centre is located at **Heritage Ranch** (*25 Riverview Park, at the end of Cronquist Dr.,* ☎*403-346-0180*) on the western edge of town. Take the 32nd Street Exit from Highway 2, left on 60th Street and left on Cronquist Drive. Heritage Ranch also features, among other things, an equestrian centre, picnic shelters and access to trails in the park system.

Fort Normandeau ★ (*free; late May to end of Jun, every day 10am to 6pm; Jul to early Sep, every day noon to 8pm;* ☎*403-347-2010 or 403-347-7550*) is located west of Highway 2 along 32nd Street. The fort as it stands today is a replica of the original. A stopping house next to the fort was fortified and enclosed in palisade walls by the **Carabiniers de Mont Royal** under Lieutenant J.E. Bédard Normandeau who anticipated an attack by the Cree during the Louis Riel Rebellion of 1885. The fort was never attacked. An interpretive centre next to the fort describes Ab-

original, Metis and European settlement of the area. Visitors can see wool being spun, and rope, soap, candles and ice cream being made.

★
Wetaskiwin

The city of Wetaskiwin is home to one of the finest museums in the province. Like the Remington-Alberta Carriage Centre in Cardston (see p 524), the Reynolds-Alberta Museum proves again that there is more to Alberta than Calgary, Edmonton and the Rockies. Though there isn't much to see in Wetaskiwin besides the Reynolds-Alberta and the Aviation Hall of Fame, this pleasant city has an interesting main street, and respectable restaurants and hotels.

The **Reynolds-Alberta Museum** ★★★ (*$6.50; Late Jun to early Sep, 9am to 7pm; Sep to Jun, Tue to Sun 9am to 5pm; west of Wetaskiwin on Hwy. 13,* ☎*780-361-1351 or 800-661-4726*) celebrates the "spirit of the machine" and is a wonderful place to explore. Interactive programs for children bring everything alive. A top-notch collection of restored automobiles, trucks, bicycles, tractors and related machinery is on display.

Among the vintage cars is one of about 470 Model J Duesenberg Phaeton Royales. This one-of-a-kind automobile cost $20,000 when it was purchased in 1929. Visitors to the museum will also learn how a grain elevator works, and can observe the goings-on in the restoration workshop through a large picture window. Tours of the warehouse, where over 800 pieces are

waiting to be restored, are offered twice daily (*$1, call ahead for times, sign up at front desk*). Pre-booked 1hr guided tours are also available.

Edmonton

Edmonton seems to suffer from an image problem, and undeservedly so. People have trouble getting past the boomtown atmosphere and the huge mall! Admittedly it is a boomtown since it grew out of the wealth of the natural resources that surround it. But this city of new money has more than made good with an attractive downtown core, a park system and cultural facilities, including theatres and many festivals (see p 555). With all this going for it, though, the city's biggest attraction still seems to be its gargantuan shopping mall. You be the judge!

Downtown and North of the North Saskatchewan River

Begin your tour of Edmonton with a visit to the **Tourist Information Centre** (*Mon to Fri 8am to 5pm*) located in the **Civic Centre** (*1 Sir Winston Churchill Square*). The hours may not be very practical, but the staff is very friendly and helpful. While there, pick up a *Ride Guide* to figure out the public transportation system. The impressive City Hall is the centrepiece of the **Edmonton Civic Centre**, a complex that occupies six city blocks and includes the Centennial Library, the Edmonton Art Gallery, Sir Winston Churchill Square, the Law Courts Building, the Convention Centre and

Alberta

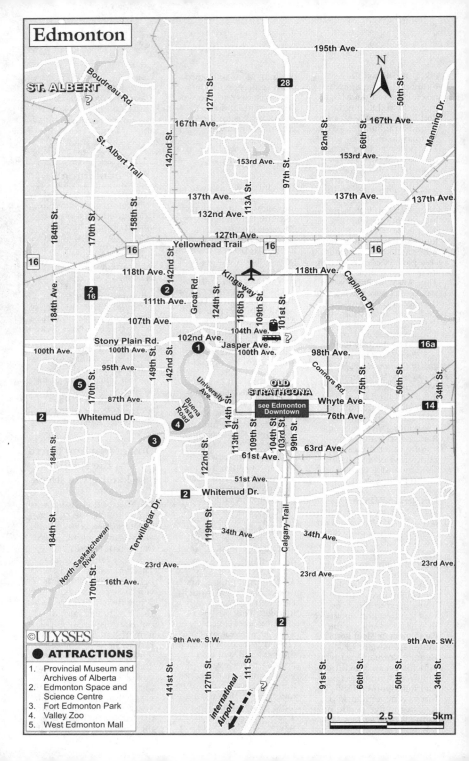

Edmonton

ST. ALBERT

Boudreau Rd.

195th Ave.

28

St. Albert Trail

167th Ave.

167th Ave.

153rd Ave.

153rd Ave.

137th Ave.

137th Ave.

137th Ave.

132nd Ave.

127th Ave.

Yellowhead Trail

16

16

16

118th Ave.

118th Ave.

Kingsway

Capilano Dr.

111th Ave.

Groat Rd.

107th Ave.

Stony Plain Rd.

102nd Ave.

100th Ave.

100th Ave.

Jasper Ave.

98th Ave.

16a

100th Ave.

95th Ave.

OLD STRATHCONA

87th Ave.

University Ave.

Whyte Ave.

Whitemud Dr.

see Edmonton Downtown

76th Ave.

16

Buena Vista Road

Connors Rd.

14

North Saskatchewan River

61st Ave.

63rd Ave.

51st Ave.

Whitemud Dr.

Terwillegar Dr.

34th Ave.

34th Ave.

23rd Ave.

23rd Ave.

23rd Ave.

16th Ave.

2

9th Ave. S.W.

9th Ave. SW.

©ULYSSES

International Airport

● ATTRACTIONS

1. Provincial Museum and Archives of Alberta
2. Edmonton Space and Science Centre
3. Fort Edmonton Park
4. Valley Zoo
5. West Edmonton Mall

0   2.5   5km

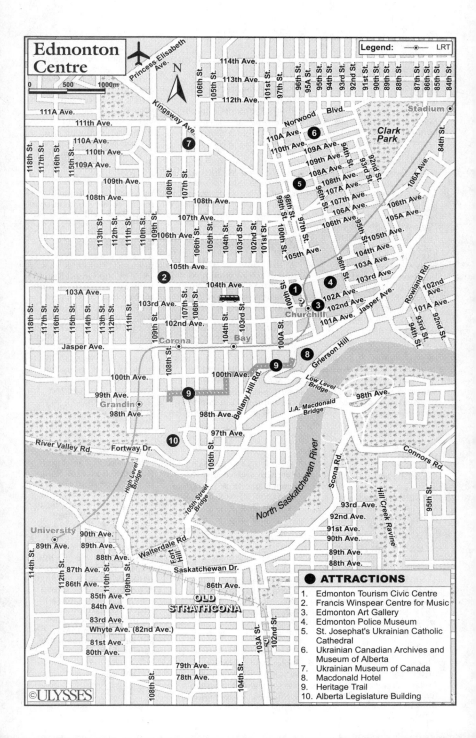

Edmonton Centre

Legend: ———●——— LRT

0   500   1000m

ATTRACTIONS

1. Edmonton Tourism Civic Centre
2. Francis Winspear Centre for Music
3. Edmonton Art Gallery
4. Edmonton Police Museum
5. St. Josephat's Ukrainian Catholic Cathedral
6. Ukrainian Canadian Archives and Museum of Alberta
7. Ukrainian Museum of Canada
8. Macdonald Hotel
9. Heritage Trail
10. Alberta Legislature Building

©ULYSSES

the Citadel Theatre. With its impressive eight-storey glass pyramid, City Hall opened in 1992 on the site of the old city hall.

While City Hall may be the centrepiece of the Civic Centre, its biggest star these days is certainly the brand new **Francis Winspear Centre for Music** ★ ★ (*4 Sir Winston Churchill Square*), which will hopefully bring some life back to Edmonton's fading urban core. Built with a $6 million gift from Edmonton businessman Francis Winspear, the 1,900-seat hall is faced with Manitoba tyndall limestone to match City Hall and brick to match the neighbouring Stan Milner Library. The Edmonton Symphony Orchestra now makes its home here.

On the eastern side of Sir Winston Churchill Square lies the **Edmonton Art Gallery** ★ ★ (*$3, free Thu pm; Mon to Wed 10:30am to 5pm, Thu and Fri 10:30am to 8pm, Sat and Sun 11am to 5pm; ☎780-422-6223*). Admission is free when the museum can find sponsorship. Fine art by local, Canadian and international artists is unfortunately a bit lost in this drab building. But a new curator and plans for exciting new shows promise to breathe new life into the gallery. Still, it's worth checking out.

The **Edmonton Police Museum** ★ (*free admission; Mon to Sat 9am to 3pm; 9620 103A Ave., ☎780-421-2274*) is a bit of a change from your typical museum excursion as it traces law enforcement in Alberta's history. Located on the second floor of the Police Service Headquarters, it houses displays of uniforms, handcuffs, jail

cells and the force's former furry mascot!

The stretch of 97th Street from 105th to 108th Avenue is Edmonton's original Chinatown with plenty of shops and restaurants. Along 107th Avenue, from 95th Street to 116th Street, is an area known as the Avenue of Nations. Shops and restaurants there represent a variety of cultures from Asia, Europe and the Americas. Rickshaws provide transportation during the summer months.

At the corner of 97th Street and 108th Avenue is **St. Josephat's Ukrainian Catholic Cathedral** ★. Among Edmonton's several Ukrainian churches, this is the most elaborate and is worth a stop for its lovely decor and artwork. One block to the east, 96th Street is recognized in *Ripley's Believe It or Not* as the street with the highest concentration of churches (16). It is appropriately known as Church Street.

Head east to 96th Street then north to 110th Avenue to the **Ukrainian Canadian Archives and Museum ofAlberta** ★ (*donation; Tue to Fri 10am to 5pm, Sat noon to 5pm; 9543 110th Ave., ☎780-424-7580*), which houses one of the largest displays of Ukrainian archives in Canada. The lives of Ukrainian pioneers around the turn of the century are chronicled through artifacts and photographs. About 10 blocks to the west, the smaller **Ukrainian Museum of Canada** ★ (*free admission; Jun to Aug, Mon to Fri 9am to 4pm, winter by appt; 10611 110th Ave., ☎780-483-5932*) displays a collection of Ukrainian costumes, Easter eggs, and household items.

Head south on 95th Street to 102nd Avenue to Edmonton's new **Chinatown**, the focal point of which is the Chinatown Gate at 97th Street. The gate is also a symbol of the friendship between Edmonton and its sister city Harbin in China. Roll the ball in the lion's mouth for good luck.

In true Canadian Pacific tradition, the Chateau-style **Hotel Macdonald** ★ ★ is Edmonton's ritziest place to stay (see p 551) and was for many years the place to see and be seen in Edmonton. Completed in 1915 by the Grand Trunk Railway, it was designed by Montréal architects Ross and MacFarlane. The wrecker's ball came close to falling in 1983 when the hotel closed. A $28-million restoration, however, brought the Macdonald back in all its splendour. If you aren't staying here, at least pop in to use the facilities, or better yet, enjoy a drink overlooking the river from the hotel's suave bar, The Library.

The next stop on the tour is the Alberta Legislature Building. It is a fair walk to get there from the Hotel Macdonald, but nevertheless a pleasant one, along the tree-lined **Heritage Trail** ★ ★ ★. This historic fur-traders' route from Old Town to the site of Old Fort Edmonton is a 30min walk that follows the river bank for most of its length. A red brick sidewalk, antique light standards and street signs will keep you on the right track. The river views along Macdonald Drive are remarkable, especially at sunset.

Legislative Building

The 16-storey vaulted dome of the Edwardian **Alberta Legislature Building** ★★ (*mid-May to early Sep weekdays 9am to 5pm, weekends 9am to 5pm; Sep to May weekdays 9am to 4:30pm, weekends noon to 5pm; Nov to Feb closed Sat, Guided tours every hour on the hour in the morning and every 30min in the evening; 107th St. at 97th Ave., ☎780-427-7362*) is a landmark in Edmonton's skyline. Sandstone from Calgary, marble from Québec, Pennsylvania and Italy, and mahogany from Belize were used to build the seat of Alberta government in 1912. At the time, the Legislature stood next to the original Fort Edmonton, but today it is surrounded by gardens and fountains. Be sure to visit the government greenhouses on the south grounds. Tours begin at the Interpretive Centre where Alberta's and Canada's parliamentary tradition is explained.

Old Strathcona and South of the North Saskatchewan River

Old Strathcona ★★★, once a city independent of Edmonton, Strathcona was founded when the Calgary and Edmonton Railway

Company's rail line ended here in 1891. Brick buildings from that era still remain in this historic district which is the best-preserved in Edmonton. While the area north of the North Saskatchewan River is clean, crisp and new with the unfinished feel of a boom town, south of the river, in Old Strathcona, a sense of character is much more tangible. An artistic, cosmopolitan and historic atmosphere prevails there. Walking tour brochures are available from the **Old Strathcona Foundation** (*Mon to Fri 8:30am to 4:30pm; 10324 Whyte Ave., suite 401, ☎780-433-5866*).

The four glass-pyramid greenhouses of the **Muttart Conservatory** ★★★ (*$4.50; Mon to Fri 9am to 6pm, Sat and Sun 11am to 6pm; 9626 96A St., off 98 Ave., ☎780-496-8755*) are another of the landmarks of Edmonton's skyline. Flourishing beneath three of these pyramids are floral displays of arid, temperate and tropical climates, respectively. Every month a new, vivid floral display is put together under the fourth pyramid. The conservatory is accessible from bus #51 south on 100th Street.

About 6km west as the crow flies, north of the river, is the **Provincial Museum and Archives of Alberta** ★★ (*$6.50; every day 9am to 5pm; 12845 102 Ave., ☎780-453-9100, www.pma.edmonton.ab.ca*). The natural and human history of Alberta is traced from the Cretaceous period and through the Ice Age to the pictographs of the province's earliest Aboriginal peoples. The merging of their cultures and those of the early explorers and pioneers is explained in the native display. The habitat gallery reproduces Alberta's four natural regions while the Bug Room is abuzz with exotic live insects. Travelling exhibits complement the permanent collection. The displays are a bit dated, but nonetheless provide an interesting overview of the world of contrasts that is Alberta.

Government House ★ (*Sun 1pm to 5pm; free guided tours every half-hour ☎780-427-2281*), the former residence of Alberta's lieutenant-governor, is located beside the Provincial Museum. The three-storey sandstone mansion features the original library and oak-panelling along with newly renovated conference rooms. Take bus #1 along Jasper Avenue, or bus #116 along 102 Avenue.

Also north of the river is the **Edmonton Space and Science Centre** ★ (*$7; mid-Jun to Sep every day 10am to 6pm; Sep to mid-Jun, Tue to Sun 10am 6pm; 11211 142nd St., ☎780-451-3344*). All sorts of out-of-this-world stuff is sure to keep the young and old busy. You can embark on a simulated space mission at the Challenger Centre or create music on a giant piano. The Margeret Ziedler Star Theatre presents multimedia shows. An IMAX theatre is also on site (see p 555).

In the North Saskatchewan River Valley, off Whitemud and Fox Drives, lies **Fort Edmonton Park** ★★★ (*$7; May and Jun, Mon to Fri 10am to 4pm, Sat and Sun 10am to 6pm; Jul to Aug, every day 10am to 6pm; over Christmas for sleigh rides; ☎780-496-8787*). This is Canada's largest historic park and home to an authentic reconstruction of Fort Edmonton as it stood in 1846. Four historic villages recreate different periods at the fort: the fur-trading era at the fort itself; the settlement era on 1885 Street; the municipal era on 1905 Street; and the metropolitan era on 1920 Street. Period buildings, period dress, period automobiles and period shops, including a bazaar, a general store, a saloon and a bakery, will bring you back in time.

Reed's Bazaar and Tea Room serves a "proper" English tea with scones from 12:30pm to 5pm. Theme programs for children are put on Saturday afternoons. Admission is free after 4:30pm, but

don't arrive any later in order to catch the last train to the fort. Take note that you'll be tight for time if you choose this frugal option, so it depends how much you want to see.

Across the river is the **Valley Zoo** ★ (*$5.25, lower rate in winter; May to Jun every day 9:30am to 6pm; Jul and Aug until 8pm; Sep to mid-Oct weekdays 9:30am to 4pm, weekends 9:30am to 6pm; winter every day 9:30am to 4pm; at the end of Buena Vista Rd., corner 134th St., ☎496-6911*), a great place for kids. It apparently began with a story-book theme but has since grown to include an African veldt and winter quarters which permit it to stay open for that season. The residents include Siberian tigers and white-handed gibbons along with more indigenous species. Kids enjoy run-of-the-mill pony rides and more exotic camel rides.

Last, but certainly not least, is Edmonton's pride and joy the **West Edmonton Mall** ★★★ (*87th Ave. between 170th St. and 178th St.*). You may scoff to hear that some visitors come to Edmonton and never leave the West Edmonton Mall. Then you may swear that you won't give in to the hype and visit it, but these reasons alone are enough to go, if only to say you've been.

There are real submarines at the Deep-Sea Adventure; dolphin shows; underwater caverns and barrier reefs; the largest indoor amusement park; a National Hockey League-size rink where you can watch the Edmonton Oilers practise; an 18-hole golf course; a waterpark complete with wave pool, waterslides, rapids, bungee

jumping and whirlpools; a casino, bingo room and North America's largest billiard hall; fine dining on Bourbon Street; a life-size, hand-carved and painted replica of Columbus' flagship, the *Santa Maria*; replicas of England's crown jewels; a solid ivory pagoda; bronze sculptures; and fabulous fountains, including one fashioned after a fountain at the Palace of Versailles. Finally, the Fantasyland Hotel (see p 552) is a lodging that truly lives up to its name... and, oh yeah, we almost forgot, there are also some 800 shops and services – this is a mall after all. It seems it is possible to come and never leave! Even though it is a shopping mall, the West Edmonton Mall simply has to be seen and therefore merits its three stars!

Parks

Central Alberta

★

Kinbrook Island Provincial Park

The shores of Lake Newell, the largest artificial lake in the province, are home to over 250 species of birds and fowl. Colonies of double-crested cormorants and American white pelicans occupy several of the protected islands on the lake. The best wildlife viewing is from the eastern shore. There are also walking trails through nearby Kinbrook Marsh. For information and reservations: ☎*403-362-2962*.

★★★
Dinosaur Provincial Park

Dinosaur Provincial Park offers amateur palaeontologists the opportunity to walk through the land of the dinosaurs. Declared a UNESCO World Heritage Site in 1979, this nature preserve harbours a wealth of information on these formidable former inhabitants of the planet. Today, the park is also home to more than 35 species of animals.

The small museum at the **Field Station of the Tyrell Museum** (*$4.50; mid-May to early Sep, every day 9am to 9pm; Sep to May, Mon to Fri, 8:15am to 4:30pm; ☎403-378-4342 or 403-378-4344* for bus tour reservations), the loop road and the two self-guided trails (the **Cottonwood Flats Trail** and the **Badlands Trail**) will give you a summary introduction to the park. Two exposed skeletons left where they were discovered can be viewed. The best way to see the park, however, is on one of the guided tours into the restricted nature preserve that makes up most of the park. The 90min **Badlands Bus Tour** leads into the heart of the preserve for unforgettable scenery, skeletons and wildlife; the **Centrosaurus Bone Bed Hike** and **Fossil Safari Hike** offer close-up looks at excavation sites. Tickets for all of these tours go on sale at 8:30am the day of the event at the field station and space is limited. Arrive early in July and August. To avoid missing out, visitors are strongly advised to call ahead to find out when the tours leave.

The park also features campgrounds and a Dinosaur Service Centre with laundry, showers, picnic and food.

The cabin of John Ware, an ex-slave from Texas who became a well-respected Albertan cattle rancher, lies near the campground.

★★
Elk Island National Park

The magnificent **Elk Island National Park** (*$4; open year-round; park administration and warden Mon to Fri 8am to 4pm, ☎780-992-2950; camping ☎998-3161*) preserves part of the Beaver Hills area as it was before the arrival of settlers when Sarcee and Plains Cree hunted and trapped in these lands. The arrival of settlers endangered beaver, elk and bison populations, prompting local residents and conservationists to petition the government to set aside an elk reserve in 1906.

Coyote

The plains bison that live in the park actually ended up there by accident. They escaped from a herd placed there temporarily while a fence at Buffalo National Park (see p 669) in Wainwright, Alberta was being completed. The plains bison herd that inhabits the park began with those 50 escaped bison.

Elk Island is also home to a small herd of rare wood bison, North America's largest mammal. In 1940, pure wood buffalo were thought to be extinct, but by sheer luck a herd of about 200 wood buffalo were discovered in a remote part of the park in 1957. Part of that herd was sent to a fenced sanctuary in the Northwest Territories.

Today the smaller plains bison are found north of Highway 16 while the wood bison live south of the highway. While touring the park, remember that you are in bison country and that these animals are wild. Though they may look docile, they are dangerous, unpredictable and may charge without warning. So stay in your vehicle and keep a safe distance (50 to 75m).

Elk Island became a national park in 1930 and is now a 195km^2 sanctuary for 44 kinds of mammals, including moose, elk, deer, lynx, beaver and coyote. The park offers some of the best wildlife viewing in the province. It is crossed by major migratory fly ways; be on the look-out for trumpeter swans in the fall.

The park office at the South Gate, just north of Highway 16, can provide information on the two campgrounds, wildlife viewing and the 12 trails that run through the park, making for great hiking and cross-country skiing. Fishing and boating can be enjoyed on Astotin Lake, and the park even boasts a nine-hole golf course.

Alberta

Accommodations

Central Alberta

There are campsites at **Kinbrook Island Provincial Park** (☎403-362-2962) as well as at **Dinosaur Provincial Park** (☎403-378-3700). The latter has more facilities, including a snack bar, showers and a laundry.

Brooks

Douglas Country Inn
$77 bkfst incl.
ℜ, ≡, pb
Box 463, T1R 1B5
☎(403) 362-2873
≈(404) 362-2100
The Douglas Country Inn is 6.5km north of town on Hwy. 873. A casual country atmosphere is achieved in each of the seven beautifully appointed rooms and throughout the rest of the inn. The only television is in the small TV room, which is rarely used. Enjoy your complimentary sherry by the fire in the sitting room. The special occasion room ($99) boasts a divine Japanese soaker tub with a view.

Drumheller

Alexandra International Hostel
members $15
non-members $20
30 Railway Ave. N, T0J 0Y0
☎(403) 823-6337
≈(403) 823-5327
A converted downtown hotel now houses the Alexandra International Hostel. It opened in 1991 after renovations and is independently operated in cooperation with Hostelling International.

Most dorm rooms have eight beds, though there are some with fewer, and several even have private bathrooms. There are kitchen and laundry facilities on the premises as well as all sorts of information brochures and a mountain-bike rental service.

Heartwood Manor
$79-$150
®, ≡, tv, ⚹, &
320 Railway Ave. E, T0J 0Y4
☎(403) 823-6495
☎888-823-6495
≈(403) 823-4935
By far the prettiest place to stay in town is the Heartwood Manor, a bed and breakfast in a restored heritage building, where a striking use of colour creates a cosy and luxurious atmosphere. Nine of the ten rooms have whirlpool baths and five even boast fireplaces. A spacious cottage and a two-bedroom suite are also available. Yummy home-made fruit syrups are served with the pancake breakfast. French and English spoken.

Rocky Mountain House

Voyageur Motel
$58
≡, K, ℝ, tv
on Hwy. 11 S, Box 1376, T0M 1T0
☎(403) 845-3381
☎888-845-3569
≈(403) 845-6166
The Voyageur is a practical choice with spacious, clean rooms, each equipped with a refrigerator. Kitchenettes are also available for a surcharge. Each room also has a VCR.

Walking Eagle Motor Inn
$75, cabins $35
≡, ℜ, tv, bar, fridge
on Hwy. 11, Box 1317, T0M 1T0
☎(403) 845-2804
≈(403) 845-3685
The log exterior of the Walking Eagle Motor Inn encloses 63 clean and large rooms decorated in keeping with the hotel's name. The hotel owes its attractive appearance to a complete renovation and paint-job. In addition, a brand new 35-room motel ($80) was built right next door. There's a microwave and refrigerator in each one of the clean – but rather drab – rooms.

Nordegg

Shunda Creek Hostel
members $14
non-members $19
west of Nordegg, 3km north of Hwy. 11, on Shunda Creek Recreation Area Rd.
☎/≈(403) 721-2140
Set against the stunning backdrop of the Rocky Mountains in David Thompson Country, the Shunda Creek Hostel is surrounded by countless opportunities for outdoor activities. The two-storey lodge encloses kitchen and laundry facilities, a common area with a fireplace and 10 rooms able to accommodate a total of 48 people. It also adjoins an outdoor hot tub. Hiking, mountain biking, fishing, canoeing, cross-country skiing and ice-climbing are possible nearby.

David Thompson Resort
$70
pb, ≡, ≈
☎(403) 721-2103
This is more of a motel and RV park than a resort, but regardless it is the only accommodation between Nordegg and Highway 93, the Icefields Parkway, and you can't beat the

scenery. The resort rents bicycles and can organize helicopter tours of the area.

Red Deer

Many conventions are held in Red Deer, and as a result weekend rates in the many hotels are often less expensive.

McIntosh Tea House Bed and Breakfast
$65
pb
4631 50th St., T4N 1X1
☎*(403) 346-1622*
This is the former home of the great grandson of the creator of the McIntosh apple. Each of the three upstairs rooms of the red-brick historic Victorian is decorated with antiques. Guests can enjoy a game of apple checkers in the private parlour. Tea and coffee are served in the evening and a full breakfast in the morning.

Wetaskiwin

The Rose Country Inn
$55
≡, ℜ, ℝ, K, bar, tv
4820 56th St., T9A 2G5
☎*(780) 352-3600*
⇆*(780) 352-2127*
Close to the Reynolds-Alberta Museum, on 56th Street, the Rose Country Inn is one of the best deals in town. Each of the recently renovated rooms has a refrigerator and microwave oven.

Edmonton

Downtown

Edmonton International Hostel
members $15
non-members $20
≡
10422 91st St., T5H 1S6
☎*(780) 988-6836*
⇆*(780) 988-8698*
This hostel is located close to the bus terminal, in a questionable area, so take care. The usual hostel facilities, including laundry machines, common kitchen and a common room with a fireplace are rounded out by a small food store and bike rentals.

The Edmonton House Suite Hotel
$140-$195
ℜ, K, ≈, △, tv, ☉, 🐕
10205 100th Ave., T5J 4B5
☎*(780) 420-4000*
☎*800-661-6562*
⇆*(780) 420-4008*
The Edmonton House is actually an apartment-hotel with suites that boast kitchens and balconies. This is one of the better apartment-hotel options in town. Reservations are recommended.

Hotel MacDonald
$249-$295
≡, ℜ, ≈, ⊛, △, ☉, tv, bar, 🐕
10065 100th St., T5J 0N6
☎*(780) 424-5181*
☎*800-441-1414*
⇆*(780) 424-8017*
www.cphotels.com
Edmonton's grand chateau-style Hotel MacDonald is stunning. Classic styling from the guest rooms to the dining rooms make this an exquisite place to stay.

A variety of weekend packages are available, including golf packages and romantic getaways. Call for details.

West of Downtown

West Harvest Inn
$72-$79
≡, ℜ, ⊛, tv
17803 Stony Plain Rd., T5S 1B4
☎*(780) 484-8000*
☎*800-661-6993*
⇆*(780) 486-6060*
The West Harvest Inn is the other inexpensive choice within striking distance of the mall. This hotel is relatively quiet and receives quite a few business travellers.

Best Western Westwood Inn
$79
≡, △, ☉, ≈, ℜ, tv
18035 Stony Plain Rd., T5S 1B2
☎*(780) 483-7770*
☎*800-557-4767*
☎*800-528-1234*
⇆*(780) 486-1769*
The Best Western Westwood Inn is also close to the mall. The rooms are more expensive here but they are also much larger and noticeably more comfortable and more pleasantly decorated.

Edmonton West Travelodge
$79-$89
≈, ≡, ⊛, tv, 🐕
18320 Stony Plain Rd., T5S 1A7
☎*(780) 483-6031*
☎*800-578-7878*
⇆*(780) 484-2358*
For those who want to be close to the shopping but aren't necessarily big spenders, the Edmonton West Travelodge is one of two relatively inexpensive hotels located close to the West Edmonton Mall. The rooms were recently redone and there is a big indoor pool.

Alberta

Fantasyland Hotel & Resort
$165
☺, ☜, ≡, ℜ, ☻, △, *tv, bar*
17700 87th Ave., T5T 4V4
☎ *(780) 444-3000*
☎ *800-661-6454*
≈ *(780) 444-3294*
www.fantasylandhotel.com
Travellers on a shopping vacation will certainly want to be as close to the West Edmonton Mall as possible, making the Fantasyland Hotel & Resort the obvious choice. Of course, you might also choose to stay here just for the sheer delight of spending the night under African or Arabian skies or in the back of a pick-up truck!

Old Strathcona and South of the North Saskatchewan River

Southbend Motel
$44
K, tv, ☜
5130 Calgary Tr. Northbound
T6H 2H4
☎ *(780) 434-1418*
≈ *(780) 435-1525*
For a very reasonable rate, guests can stay at the Southbend Motel, where rooms are admittedly a bit dated, and for no extra charge use all the facilities at the Best Western Cedar Park Inn next door (see below). These include a pool, a sauna and an exercise room.

The Best Western Cedar Park Inn
$104-$149
≡, ℜ, ≈, △, ☺, *tv,* ☜
5116 Calgary Tr. Northbound
☎ *(780) 434-7411*
☎ *800-661-9461*
☎ *800-528-1234*
≈ *(780) 437-4836*
The Cedar Park Inn is a large hotel with 190 equally spacious rooms. Some of these are called theme rooms ($150), which essentially means there is a hot-tub for two, a king-size bed, a living room and a fancier decor. Weekend and family rates are available, and there is a courtesy limo service to the airports or the West Edmonton Mall.

Restaurants

Central Alberta

Brooks

Peggy Sue's Diner
$
603 Second St. W
Peggy Sue's is a neat little family-run eatery. Smoked meat, burgers, great fries and delicious mud pie can be eaten in or taken out.

Drumheller

Yavis Family Restaurant
$$
249 Third Ave.
☎ *(403) 823-8317*
This restaurant has been around for years. The interior is fairly non-descript, and so is the menu. The selections are nonetheless pretty good, especially the great big breakfasts.

Sizzling House
$$
160 Centre St.
☎ *(780) 823-8098*
The Sizzling House serves up tasty Thai cooking, and is recommended by locals. A good place for lunch, the service is quick and friendly.

Cochrane

Home Quarter Restaurant & Pie Shoppe
$$
216 First St. W
☎ *(780) 932-2111*
Cochrane's friendly Home Quarter Restaurant is the home of the ever-popular Rancher's Special breakfast with eggs, bacon and sausage. Home-made pies are available all day long to eat in or take out. The lunch and dinner menu includes filet mignon and chicken parmesan.

Red Deer

City Roast Coffee
$
4940 50th St.
☎ *(403) 347-0893*
The City Roast serves hearty soup, sandwich lunches and good coffee. The walls are decorated with posters announcing local art shows and events.

Wetaskiwin

The MacEachern Tea House & Restaurant
$-$$
Mon to Sat until 4:30pm, Jul and Aug also open Sun 10am to 4pm
4719 50th Ave.
☎ *352-8308*
Home to specialty coffees and over 20 teas. The menu boasts hearty home-made soups and chowders as well as sandwiches and salads.

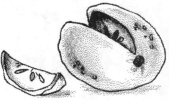

Edmonton

Downtown

Cheesecake Café Bakery Restaurant
$
17011 100th Ave.
☎*(780) 486-0440*
10390 51st Ave.
☎*(780) 437-5011*
A huge variety of cheesecakes – need we say more?

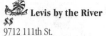 **Levis by the River**
$$
9712 111th St.
☎*(780) 482-6402*
Levis is located in a converted house overlooking the North Saskatchewan River Valley. Innovative and delicious dishes are served in its several small dining rooms and, in the summer, you can enjoy great views and spectacular sunsets on the terrace. Service can be slow if they are really busy, but the chocolate pecan pie on the dessert menu is worth the wait!

The **West Edmonton Mall's** Bourbon Street harbours a collection of moderately priced restaurants. **Café Orleans** (*$$*; ☎ *780-444-2202*) serves Cajun and Creole specialties; **Sherlock Holmes** (*$$*; ☎ *780-444-1752*) serves typical English pub grub; **Albert's Family Restaurant** (*$*; ☎ *780-444-1179*) serves Montréal-style smoked meat; the **Modern Art Café** (*$-$$*; ☎ *780-444-2233*) is a new-world bistro with pizzas, pasta and steaks (the art, the furniture) is for sale.

Bistro Praha
$$$
10168 100A St.
☎*(780) 424-4218*
Edmonton's first European bistro, Bistro Praha is very popular and charges in accordance. Favourites like cabbage soup, Wiener schnitzel, filet mignon, tortes and strudels are served in a refined but comfortable setting.

 La Bohème
$$$
6427 112th Ave.
☎*(780) 474-5693*
La Bohème is set in the splendidly restored Gibbard Building. A delicious variety of classic yet original French appetizers and entrées are enjoyed in a romantic setting complete with a cozy fire. Bed and breakfast accommodation is also offered upstairs.

Claude's on the River
$$$$
9797 Jasper Ave.
☎*(780) 429-2900*
This is one of Edmonton's finest restaurants. An exceptional river-valley view, menu offerings like Australian rack of lamb in a provençale crust and other distinguished French dishes, as well as an extensive wine list explain why.

Hy's Steakloft
$$$$
10013 101A Ave.
☎*(780) 424-4444*
Like its Calgary counterpart, Hy's Steakloft serves up juicy Alberta steaks done to perfection. Chicken and pasta dishes round out the menu. A beautiful skylight is the centrepiece of the restaurant's classy decor.

Old Strathcona and South of the North Saskatchewan River

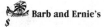 **Barb and Ernie's**
$
9906 72nd Ave.
☎*(780) 433-3242*
This is an exceptionally popular diner-style restaurant with good food, good prices and a friendly, unpretentious ambience. Breakfast is a particularly busy time, so expect to have to wait a bit for a table in the morning. You can always come later, however, since breakfast is served until 4pm.

Block 1912
$
10361 Whyte Ave.
☎*(780) 433-6575*
Block 1912 is a European café that won an award for its effort to beautify the Strathcona area. The interior is like a living room, with an eclectic mix of tables, chairs and sofas. Lasagna is one of the simple menu's best offerings. Soothing music and a relaxed mood are conducive to a chat with friends or the enjoyment of a good book.

 Café La Gare
$
10308A 81st Ave.
☎*(780) 439-2969*
Among the many cafés in Old Strathcona, the Café La Gare seems to be the place to be. Outdoor chairs and tables are reminiscent of a Parisian café. The only food available are bagels and scones. An intriguing intellectual atmosphere prevails.

Alberta

 **Packrat Louie Kitchen & Bar**
$$
10335 83rd Ave.
☎(780) 433-0123
A good selection of wines and a nice atmosphere are mixed with interesting music. The menu offerings are varied and generally well prepared.

Turtle Creek
$$
8404 109th St.
☎(780) 433-4202
Turtle Creek is an Edmonton favourite for several reasons, not the least of which are its California wines and relaxed ambiance. The dishes follow the latest trends in Californian and fusion cuisine very well, though a little predictably. The weekend brunch is a good deal. Free indoor parking.

 **The Unheard of Restaurant**
$$$$
9602 82nd Ave.
☎(780) 432-0480
The name fits and it doesn't. This restaurant is no longer unheard of, yet it is an exception to Edmonton's dining norm. Recently expanded, it offers both à la carte and table d'hôte menus. While the menu changes every two weeks, it usually features fresh game in the fall and chicken or beef the rest of the year. Inventive vegetarian dishes are also available. The food is exquisite and refined. Reservations are required.

Entertainment

Edmonton

Vue Weekly is a free news and entertainment weekly that outlines what's on throughout the city.

Bars and Nightlife

Barry T's on 104th Street is a sports pub that attracts a young crowd with a mix of country and popular music. **Club Malibu** at 10310 85th Avenue attracts crowds of young professionals. **The Thunderdome** is another hot spot with top-name rock'n'roll acts. There is always something happening at the **Sidetrack Cafe** (*10333 112th St., ☎780-421-1326*) resto-bar with its mix of comedy, rock and jazz acts.

The **Sherlock Holmes** (*10012 101A Ave., ☎780-426-7784*) has an impressive choice of British and Irish ales on tap. The relaxed atmosphere seems to attract a mixed crowd. The **Yardbird Suite** (*10203 86th Ave., ☎780-432-0428*) is the home base of the local Jazz Society, with live performances every night of the week. A small admission fee is charged. **Blues on Whyte** (*10329 82nd Ave., ☎780-439-5058*) showcases live acts.

The Rebar (*10551 Whyte Ave., ☎780-433-3600*) is an exquisitely decorated bar that often welcomes techno musicians. Many DJs as well as alternative music groups file through here every week.

The Roost (*10345 104th St., ☎780-426-3150*) is one of the few gay bars in Edmonton.

Well known as Edmonton's premiere country bar, the **Cook County Saloon** (*8010 103rd St., ☎780-432-2665*) offers lessons for amateur line-dancers and a mechanical bull for those closet cowboys looking for a wild eight seconds.

Cultural Activities

The **Citadel Theatre** is a huge facility with five theatres inside. A variety of shows are put on from children's theatre to experimental and major productions. For information contact the box office at *☎780-426-4811 or 780-425-1820*.

The **Northern Light Theatre** (*☎780-471-1586*) stages innovative and interesting works.

For some more classical culture, check out the offerings of the **Edmonton Opera** (*☎780-429-1000*), the **Edmonton Symphony Orchestra** (*in the Francis Winspear Centre for Music, box office ☎780-428-1414*) and the **Alberta Ballet** (*☎780-428-6839*).

First-run movies are shown throughout the city. For locations and schedules, pick up a newspaper or call the **Talking Yellow Pages** *☎780-493-9000* (see p 538).

The new cinema megacomplex **Silver City** (*West Edmonton Mall; ☎780-444-1242*) opened its doors in May 1999. The 12 comfortable, modern theatres offer all the latest predictable Hollywood productions. There is also an IMAX.

More spectacular cinematic events occur at the giant **IMAX** (*$8; 11211 142nd St.,* ☎ *780-451-3344*) theatre at the **Edmonton Space and Science Centre** (see p 548).

Calendar of Events

Edmonton is touted as a city of festivals, and **Edmonton's Klondike Days** is possibly the city's biggest event. During the Yukon gold-rush, gold diggers were attracted to the "All-Canadian Route," which departed from here. The route proved almost impassable and none of the prospectors made it to the Yukon before the rush was over. This tenuous link to the gold rush is, nevertheless, reason enough for Edmontonians to celebrate for 10 days in July. Starting the third Thursday in July, festivities, parades, bathtub road races, sourdough raft races and a casino bring the city to life. Every morning, free pancake breakfasts are served throughout the city. For information call ☎ *780-423-2822*.

Other festival highlights include the **Jazz City International Festival** (☎ *780-432-7166*) that takes place during the last week in June.

In late June and early July, **The Works: A Visual Arts Celebration** (☎ *780-426-2122*) sees art exhibits take to the streets. The **Edmonton Heritage Festival** (☎ *780-488-3378*) features international singing and dancing during the first week in August. The **Edmonton Folk Music Festival** (☎ *780-429-1899*) takes place the second week in August and tickets are recommended. The **Fringe Theatre Festival** (☎ *780-448-9000*) is one of North America's largest alternative-theatre events. It takes place throughout Old Strathcona starting the second Friday in August for ten days. The **Dreamspeakers Festival** (☎*451-5033*) at the end of May celebrates native arts and culture.

Shopping

Edmonton

Besides the obvious, the **West Edmonton Mall** (see "Exploring," p 548) and its 800 shops and services located at 87th Avenue and 170th Street, there are regular malls scattered north, south and west of the city centre.

Downtown, the **Eaton Centre** and **The Bay** boast the usual department store offerings.

Old Strathcona makes for a much more pleasant shopping experience with some funky specialty shops, bookstores and women's clothing stores along **Whyte Avenue** (*82nd Avenue*), including **Avenue Clothing Co.** and **Etzio**, and along 104th Street. **Strathcona Square** (*8150 105th St.*) is located in an old converted post office and boasts a bright assortment of cafés and boutiques all set in a cheery market atmosphere. The **Treasure Barrel** (*8216 104th St.*) is like a permanent craft fair showcasing arts and crafts of all kinds and for all tastes.

High Street at 124th Street (*124th St. and 125th St. between 102nd Ave. and 109th Ave.*) is an outdoor shopping arcade with galleries, cafés and shops located in a pretty residential area.

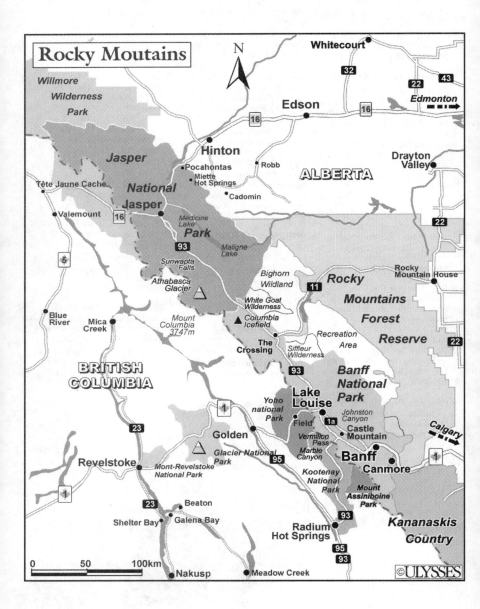

Rocky Moutains

N

Willmore
Wilderness
Park

Whitecourt

32

22 43

Edmonton

Edson

16

Hinton

Jasper

Pocahontas
Miette
Hot Springs

Robb

Drayton
Valley

ALBERTA

Tête Jaune Cache

National

Jasper

Cadomin

Valemount 16

Medicine
Lake

93

Sunwapta
Falls

Maligne
Lake

Park

Bighorn
Wildland

Rocky

Rocky
Mountain House

5

Athabasca
Glacier

White Goat
Wilderness

11

Mountains

Blue
River

Mica
Creek

Mount
Columbia
3747m

Columbia
Icefield

Recreation
Area

Forest

Reserve

22

The
Crossing

Siffleur
Wilderness

BRITISH
COLUMBIA

93

Banff

Lake
Louise

National
Park

Calgary

Yoho
national
Park

Field

Johnston
Canyon

1a

23

1

Golden

Vermilion
Pass

Castle
Mountain

Revelstoke

Mont-Revelstoke
National Park

Glacier National
Park

95

Marble
Canyon

Banff

Canmore

1

Kootenay
National
Park

Mount
Assiniboine
Park

1

23

Beaton

Shelter Bay

Galena Bay

93

Kananaskis
Country

Radium
Hot Springs

0   50   100km

Nakusp

Meadow Creek

95

93

©ULYSSES

The Rocky Mountains

I n Canada, the term
"Rockies" designates a chain of high Pacific mountains reaching elevations of between 3,000 and 4,000m.

These mountains consist of crystalline and metamorphous rock that has been thrust upwards by collision between the Pacific tectonic plate and the North American continental plate, and then later carved out and eroded by glaciers. The mountain chain runs northwesterly along the border between Alberta and British Columbia, and extends to the Yukon territory. This vast region, which stretches more than 22,000km², is known the world over for its natural beauty and welcomes some six million visitors each year. Exceptional mountain scenery, wild rivers sure to thrill white-water rafting enthusiasts, still lakes whose waters vary from emerald green to turquoise blue, parks abounding in all sorts of wildlife, world-renowned ski centres and quality resort hotels all come together to make for an unforgettable vacation.

Finding Your Way Around

By Plane

Most people fly into the airports in Calgary, Edmonton or Vancouver and then drive to the national and provincial parks.

By Car

For information on road conditions in Banff, you can call **Environment Canada** (☎403-762-2088) or the **Banff warden's office** (☎403-762-1450); in Jasper, call the weather service (☎403-852-3185) or the

Alberta Motor Association *(Jun to Aug, ☎403-852-4444; year-round, ☎800-222-4357)*, which you can also call for roadside assistance. For Yoho National Park, call the **tourist office** *(summer, ☎250-343-5324; winter, ☎250-343-6432)* and for Kootenay National Park, the **park office** *(☎250-347-9615)*.

This kind of information is also available at national-park entrance gates and in all local offices of Parks Canada.

By Bus

Banff National Park

The **Bus Station** *(☎403-762-6767 or 800-661-8747)*, located on the way into Banff on Mount Norquay Road, at the corner of Gopher Road, is used by **Greyhound** (☎*800-661-8747*) and **Brewster Transportation and Tours** (☎ *403-762-6735*). The latter company takes care of local transportation and organizes trips to the icefields and Jasper.

Jasper National Park

The **Greyhound Bus Station** (☎ *403-852-3926*) is located on Connaught Drive, right in the middle of Jasper. **Heritage Cabs** (☎ *403-852-5558*) serves the area.

By Train

Banff National Park

The **Rocky Mountaineer Train Station** is right next to the bus station on Railway Drive.

Jasper National Park

Via
☎*800-561-8630*
The train station is located next to the Greyhound bus terminal.

Practical Information

The parks in the Rocky Mountains straddle two Canadian provinces, Alberta and British Columbia, which have different area codes.

The area code is **403** for Alberta, except for **Jasper**, which is **780**.

The area code for British Columbia is **250**.

Parks Canada Offices

Information about the different parks and regions is available through the offices of Parks Canada and the tourist information offices.

Banff
224 Banff Ave., Box 900
Banff, AB, T0L 0C0
☎*(403) 762-1550*
⇒*(403) 762-3229*

Lake Louise
☎*(403) 522-2822*
⇒*(403) 522-1212*

Jasper
500 Connaught Drive, Box 10
Jasper, AB, T0E 1E0
☎*(780) 852-6220*
⇒*(780) 852-5601*

Radium Hot Springs
Kootenay National Park
Box 220, Radium Hot Springs
BC, V0A 1M0
☎*(250) 347-9615*

Tourist Information

Banff National Park and The Icefields Parkway

On your way in from Highway 1A, you'll pass the **Alberta Visitor Information Centre** (☎*800-661-8888*) at the western edge of Canmore, at Dead Man's Flats.

Banff Visitor Centre
224 Banff Ave., Box 900
Banff, AB, T0L 0C0
☎*(403) 762-8421*
☎*(403) 762-0270*
⇒*(403) 762-8163*

Banff National Park
224 Banff Ave., Box 900
Banff, AB, T0L 0C0
☎*(403) 762-1550*
⇒*(403) 762-1551*

Lake Louise Visitor Information Centre
☎*(403) 522-3833*

Jasper National Park

Jasper Tourism and Chamber of Commerce
Box 98, 632 Connaught Dr.
Jasper, AB, T0E 1E0
☎*(780) 852-3858*
⇒*(780) 852-4932*

Parks Canada
500 Connaught Dr.
Box 10, Jasper, AB, T0E 1E0
☎*(780) 852-6220*
⇒*(780) 852-5601*

Kootenay and Yoho National Parks

Kootenay National Park
Box 220, Radium Hot Springs
BC, V0A 1M0
☎*(250) 347-9615*

Golden and District Chamber of Commerce and Travel Information Centre
located in the centre of town
☎*(250) 344-7125*

Field
every day 9am to 6pm
at the entrance to town
☎*(250) 343-6324*

Kananaskis Country

Kananaskis Country Head Office
Suite 100, 3115 12th St. NE
Calgary, AB, T2E 7J2
☎*(403) 297-3362*

Tourism Canmore Kananaskis
801 Eighth St., Canmore
T1W 2B3
☎*678-1295*
⇒*678-1296*
www.canmorekananaskis.com

**Bow Valley Provincial
Park Office**
Located near the town of Seeby
☎ *(403) 673-3663*

**Peter Lougheed Provincial
Park
Visitor Information Centre**
Located 3.6 km from
Kananaskis Trail (Hwy 40)
☎ *(403) 591-6344*

Barrier Lake
Information Centre
☎ *(403) 673-3985*

**Elbow Valley
Information Centre**
☎ (403) 949-4261

Exploring

★★★

Banff National Park

The history of the **Canadian
Pacific** railway is inextrica-
bly linked to that of the
national parks of the
Rocky Mountains. In No-
vember 1883, three work-
men abandoned the rail-
way construction site in
the Bow Valley and
headed towards Banff in
search of gold. When they
reached Sulphur Mountain,
however, brothers William
and Tom McCardell and
Frank McCabe discovered
sulphur hot springs in-
stead. They took a concession in order to turn a
profit with the springs, but
were unable to counter the
various land-rights dis-
putes that followed.

The series of events drew
the attention of the federal
government, which sent
out an agent to control the
concession. The renown of
these hot springs had
already spread from rail-
way workers to the vice-

president of Canadian
Pacific, who came here in
1885 and declared that the
springs were certainly
worth a million dollars.
Realizing the enormous
economic potential of the
Sulphur Mountain hot
springs, which were al-
ready known as **Cave and
Basin**, the federal government quickly purchased
the rights to the conces-
sion from the three work-
ers and consolidated its
property rights on the site
by creating a nature re-
serve the same year. Two
years later, in 1887, the
reserve became the first
national park in Canada
and was named Rockies
Park, and then Banff Na-
tional Park. In those days
there was no need to pro-
tect the still abundant
wildlife, and the mindset
of government was not yet
preoccupied with the preservation of natural areas.
On the contrary, the gov-
ernment's main concern
was to find an economi-
cally exploitable site with
which to replenish state
coffers, in need of a boost
after the construction of
the railroad. To comple-
ment the springs which
were already in vogue that
wealthy tourists in search
of spa treatments, tourist
facilities and luxury hotels
were built. Thus was born
the town of Banff, today a
world-class tourist mecca.

A bit farther along Banff
Avenue, stop in at the
**Natural History
Museum** ★ *($3; every day;
Sep and May 10am to 8pm;
Jul and Aug 10am to 10pm;
Oct to Apr 10am to 6pm;
112 Banff Ave.,
☎ 403-762-1558).* This museum traces the history of
the Rockies and displays
various rocks, fossils and
dinosaur tracks, as well as
several plant species that
you're likely to encounter
while hiking.

The **Whyte Museum of the
Canadian Rockies** ★★★
*($4; mid-May to Mid-Oct,
every day 10am to 6pm; winter, Tue to Sun 1pm to 5pm,
Thu 1pm to 9pm; 111 Bear
St., ☎ 403-762-2291)* relates
the history of the Canadian
Rockies. You'll discover
archaeological findings
from ancient Kootenay
and Stoney First Nation
settlements, including
clothing, tools and jewellery. Museum-goers will
also learn the history of
certain local heros and
famous explorers like Bill
Peyto, as well as that of
the railway and the town
of Banff. Personal objects
and clothing that once
belonged to notable local
figures are exhibited. The
museum also houses a
painting gallery and extensive archives, in case you
want to know more about
the region. Right next to
the Whyte Museum is the
Banff Public Library *(Mon,
Wed, Fri and Sat 11am to
6pm, Tue and Thu 11am to
9pm, Sun 1pm to 5pm; at the
corner of Bear and Buffalo
Sts., ☎ 403-762-2661).*

Cave and Basin ★★★
*($2.25; Jun to Aug, every day
9am to 6pm; Sep to May
9:30am to 5pm; at the end of
Cave Ave., ☎ 403-762-1556)*
is now a national historic
site. These springs were
the origin of the vast network of Canadian national
parks (see p 559). How-
ever, despite extremely
costly renovations to the
basins in 1984, the pool
has been closed for secu-
rity reasons since 1992.
The sulphur content of the
water actually deteriorates
the cement, and the pool's
paving is badly damaged
in some places. You can
still visit the cave into
which three Canadian Pa-
cific workers descended in
search of the springs, and
smell the distinctive odour
of sulphurous gas, caused

**The Rocky
Mountains**

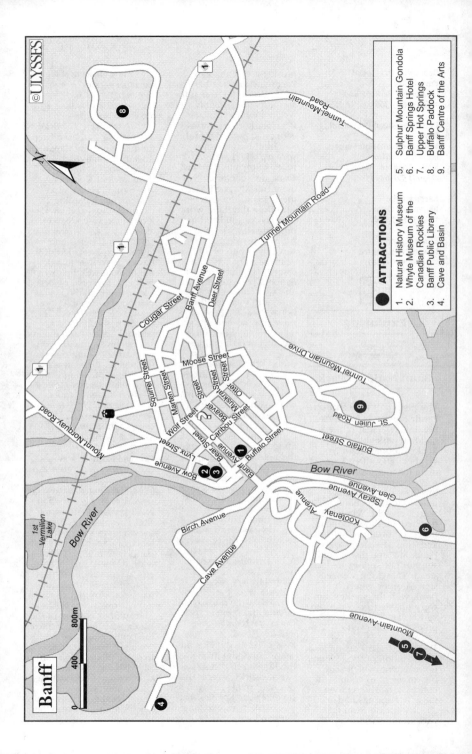

Banff

ATTRACTIONS

1. Natural History Museum
2. Whyte Museum of the Canadian Rockies
3. Banff Public Library
4. Cave and Basin
5. Sulphur Mountain Gondola
6. Banff Springs Hotel
7. Upper Hot Springs
8. Buffalo Paddock
9. Banff Centre of the Arts

©ULYSSES

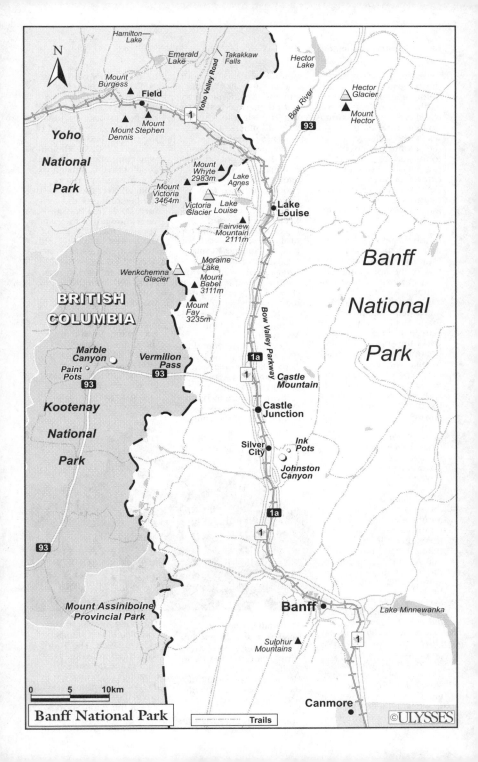

N

Hamilton
Lake
Emerald
Lake
Takakkaw
Falls
Hector Lake
Mount
Burgess
Field
Yoho Valley Road
Bow River
93
Hector
Glacier
Mount
Hector
Mount Stephen
Mount
Dennis

Yoho

National

Park

1

Mount
Whyte
2983m
Lake
Agnes
Mount
Victoria
3464m
Victoria
Glacier
Lake
Louise
**Lake
Louise**
Fairview
Mountain
2111m

Banff

Moraine
Lake
Mount
Babel
3111m
Wenkchemna
Glacier
Mount
Fay
3235m

National

**BRITISH
COLUMBIA**

Marble
Canyon
Vermilion
Pass
93
Paint
Pots
93
Bow Valley Parkway
1a
1
Castle
Mountain

Park

Kootenay

National

Castle
Junction
Silver
City
Ink
Pots
Johnston
Canyon

Park

1a
1

Mount Assiniboine
Provincial Park

Banff
Lake Minnewanka
1

Sulphur
Mountains

1

0   5   10km

Banff National Park

Canmore

Trails

©ULYSSES

by bacteria that oxydize the sulphates in the water before it spurts out of the earth. The original basin is still there, but swimming is no longer permitted. If you watch the water, you'll see the sulphur gas bubbling to the surface, while at the bottom of the basin you can see depressions appearing in the sand caused by this same gas (this is most obvious in the centre of the basin).

In the theatre you can take in a short film on Banff National Park and the history of the hot springs and their purchase by the government for only $900. You'll learn that the McCardell brothers and Frank McCabe were not actually the first to discover the springs – Assiniboine Indians were already familiar with their therapeutic powers. European explorers had also already spoken of them. However, the three Canadian Pacific workers, knowing a good thing when they saw it, were the first to try to gain exclusive rights over the springs and the government simply followed suit.

If you want to experience the sensation of Sulphur Mountain's waters (how rapturous it is to soak in them after a long day of hiking!), head up Mountain Avenue, at the foot of the mountain, to the hot spring facilities of **Upper Hot Spring ★★★** *($7 for access to the pool; $32 for the whirlpool thermal baths and basins; bathing suit and towel rentals available; every day 10am to 10pm, call ahead to verify schedule and fees; up from Mountain Ave., ☎ 403-762-1515).* The establishment includes a hot water bath (40°C) for soaking and a warm pool (27°C) for swimming. If

you have at least an hour and are at least 17 years old, then by all means try out the thermal baths. This is a Turkish bath that consists of immersion in hot water followed by aromatherapy treatment. You then lay out on a bed and are ensconced in sheets and blankets. The soothing effect is truly divine.

If you haven't got the energy to hike up to the top of the mountain, you can take the **Sulphur Mountain Gondola** *($14; open until sundown; at the end of Mountain Ave., at the far end edge of the Upper Hot Springs parking lot,* ☎ *403-762-2523).* The panoramic view of Banff, Mount Rundle, the Bow Valley, the Aylmer and the Cascade Mountains is superb. The gondola starts out at an altitude of 1,583m and climbs to 2,281m. Be sure to bring along warm clothes, as it can be cold at the summit.

tourists who would soon be flocking to the hot springs. Construction began in 1887, and the hotel opened its doors in June 1888. Although the cost of the project had already reached $250,000, the railway company launched a promotional campaign to attract wealthy visitors from all over the world. By the beginning of the century, Banff had become so well known that the Banff Springs Hotel was one of the busiest hotels in North America. More space was needed, so a new wing was built in 1903. It was separated from the original building by a small wooden bridge in case of fire. A year later a tower was built at the end of each wing. Even though this immense hotel welcomed 22,000 guests in 1911, the facilities again proved too small for the ever-increasing demand. Construction was thus begun on a central tower.

Banff Springs Hotel

The **Banff Springs Hotel ★★★** is also worth a look. After visiting the springs at Cave and Basin, William Cornelius Van Horne, vice-president of the Canadian Pacific railway company, decided to have a sumptuous hotel built to accommodate the

The building was finally completed as it stands today in 1928. The Tudor-style interior layout, as well as the tapestries, paintings and furniture in the common rooms, are all original. If you decide to stay at the Banff Springs Hotel (see p 574) you may run into the ghost of Sam

McAuley, the bellboy who helps guests who have lost their keys, or that of the unlucky young bride who died on her wedding day by falling down the stairs; her ghost supposedly haunts the corridors.

The **Banff Centre of the Arts** *(between St. Julien Rd. and Tunnel Mountain Dr.,* ☎*403-762-6300 or 403-762-6281)* was founded in 1933. More commonly known as the Banff Centre since 1978, this renowned cultural centre hosts the **Banff Festival of the Arts** each August. The festival attracts numerous artists and involves presentations of dance, opera, jazz and theatre. The centre also offers courses in classical and jazz ballet, theatre, music, photography and pottery. Finally, each year the centre organizes an international mountain film festival. There is a sports centre inside the complex as well.

Around Banff

The **Buffalo Paddock** ★★ *(free admission; May to Oct; to get there, head towards Lake Minnewanka, then take the Trans-Canada Highway towards Lake Louise; the entrance lies 1km farther, on the right)* provides an interesting opportunity, if you're lucky, to admire these majestic creatures up close. It is important, however, to stay in your car, even if you want to take photographs, as these animals can be very unpredictable and the slightest provocation may cause them to charge. This paddock was originally built by a group of wealthy Banff residents, that was planning to make it into a zoo. Since the whole idea of a zoo is not in keeping with the spirit of national

parks, the plains bison were sent off by train to be liberated in Wood Buffalo National Park, in northern Alberta and the southwest part of the Northwest Territories. They were replaced by wood buffalo that had migrated into the area and had to be protected from diseases that were killing off their species.

Twenty-two kilometres long and 2km, **Lake Minnewanka** ★★ is now the biggest lake in Banff National Park, but this expanse of water is not completely natural. Its name means "lake of the water spirit." These days it is one of the few lakes in the park where motor boats are permitted. Originally, the area was occupied by Stoney First Nation encampments. Because of the difficulties involved with diving in alpine waters and the scattering of vestiges that can be seen here, this lake is popular with scuba divers. Guided walks are given Tuesdays, Thursdays and Saturdays at 2pm. Besides taking a guided boat-tour with **Cruise and Tour Devil's Gap** *($26; Lake Minnewanka Boat Tours, Box 2189, Dept B, Banff,* ☎ *403-762-3473,* ⌨*403-762-2800)*, you can fish on the lake if you obtain the appropriate permit from Parks Canada, and skating is possible in the winter. A 16-kilometre hiking trail leads to the far end of the lake. At the **Aylmer Lookout Viewpoint** you will probably spot some of the mountain goats who frequent the area.

★★
Bow Valley Parkway

To get from Banff to Lake Louise, take the Bow Valley Parkway (Hwy 1A), which is a much more picturesque route than the Trans-Canada. About 140 million years ago, mountains emerged from an ancient sea as a result of pressure from the earth's strata. Flowing from the mountains, the Bow River was born, littering the plains to the east with sediment. Forty million years later, the foothills rose from the plains and threatened to prevent the river from following its course. However, even when rocks got in its path, the river managed to continue its route, sweeping away the rocky debris. This continual erosion resulted in the formation of a steep-sided V-shaped valley.

The abandoned town of **Silver City** lies further up the Bow Valley Parkway, on the left. Silver, copper and lead were discovered in the area in 1883. Prospectors arrived two years later, but the mineral deposits were quickly exhausted and ultimately the town was abandoned. In its glory days, this little city had some 175 buildings and several hotels, but just vestiges of these remain.

★★★
Lake Louise

Jewel of the Canadian Rockies, Lake Louise is known the world over thanks to its small, still, emerald-green lake. Few natural sites in Canada can boast as much success: this little place welcomes an average of about six million visitors a year.

The Rocky Mountains

Today, you can reach the lake by car, but finding a place to park here can be a real challenge. Stroll quietly around the lake or climb the mountain along the network of little trails radiating out from the lake's shore for a magnificent view of the Victoria Glacier, the lake and the glacial valley. Reaching **Lake Agnes** requires extra effort, but the **view ★★★** of **Victoria** (3,464m), **White** (2,983m), **Fairview** (2,111m), **Babel** (3,111m) and **Fay** (3,235m) **Mountains** is well worth the exertion.

If you aren't up to such a climb, you can always take the **Lake Louise Gondola**, which is open from 9am to 9pm and transports you to an altitude of 2,089m in just 10min.

Though the present-day **Chateau Lake Louise ★★** has nothing to do with the original construction, it remains an attraction in itself. This vast Canadian Pacific Hotel can accommodate 700 visitors. Besides restaurants, the hotel houses a small shopping arcade with boutiques selling all kinds of souvenirs.

Moraine Lake

When heading to Lake Louise, you will come to a turnoff for Moraine Lake on the left. This narrow, winding road weaves its way along the mountain for about 10km before reaching Moraine Lake, which was immortalized on the old Canadian $20 bill. Though much smaller than Lake Louise, Moraine Lake is no less spectacular. The lake often remains frozen until the month of June and is inaccessible in the winter,.

★
Canmore

This quiet little town of about 6,000 experienced its finest hour during the 1988 Winter Olympics. The cross-country, nordic combined and biathlon events were held here, along with the disabled cross-country skiing demonstration event. Since the games, the facilities at the **Canmore Nordic Centre** (*every day; from the centre of town head up Main St., turn right on Eighth Ave. and right to cross the Bow River. Turn left and head up Rundle Dr., then turn left again on Sister Dr. Take Spray Lake Rd. to the right and continue straight. The parking lot of the centre is located further up on the right, ☎ 403-678-2400*) have been used for other international events like the World Cup of Skiing in 1995. In summer the cross-country trails become walking and mountain-biking trails. Dogs are permitted between April 11 and October 30 if they are on a leash. Bears are common in the region in the summer, so be extra careful.

Marvellously situated at the entrance to Banff National Park and at the gateway to Kananaskis Country, Canmore welcomes many visitors each year, yet it is often easier to find accommodations here than in Banff. Nevertheless, it is a good idea to reserve your room well in advance.

The **Canmore Recreation Centre** (*every day 6am to 10pm; 1900 Eighth Ave., ☎ 403-678-5597, ≈ 678-6661*) organizes all sorts of summer activities for children. The facilities include a municipal pool, a sports centre and an exercise centre.

The Icefields Parkway

The route through the icefields follows Highway 93 from Lake Louise for 230km to the Continental Divide, which is covered by glaciers, before ending up in Jasper. This wide, well-paved road is one of the busiest in the Rockies during the summer, with a speed limit of 90km per hour. It runs through some incredibly majestic scenery.

The **Hector Lake ★★** lookout on the left, 17km from Lake Louise, offers a great view of both the lake and Mount Hector. The lake is fed by meltwater from the Balfour Glacier and the Waputik Icefields.

One kilometre before **Mosquito Creek**, you can clearly see the Crowfoot Glacier from the road. Photographs reproduced on information panels by the road show just how much the glacier has melted in recent years. A bit further along you can stop to take in the magnificent view of Bow Lake, and then visit little **Num-Ti-Jah Lodge** ("Num-Ti-Jah" is a Stony Plain name that means "pine marten"), built in 1922 by a mountain guide named Jimmy Simpson. At the time, there was no road leading this far, and all the building materials had to be hauled in on horseback. One of Simpson's descendants has since converted the place into a hotel and cleared a road for guests. Since all the tour buses stop here, the administration of the Num-Ti-Jah Lodge (see p 577) has decided in an effort to protect the privacy of its clientele, that only people with reservations for the night should be permitted to enter the building. It is therefore preferable to limit your tour to the outside of the chalet; otherwise you may receive a rather gruff welcome.

At the intersection of Highway 93 and 11, called **The Crossing**, you'll find a few souvenir shops, a hotel and some restaurants. Make sure your gas tank is full since there are no other gas stations before Jasper. This region was once inhabited by Kootenays who were forced to the western slopes by Peigans armed with guns, thanks to white merchants from the southeastern Rockies. Fearing that the Kootenay would eventually arm themselves, the Peigans blocked the way of white explorers who were attempting to cross the pass, and thus kept their enemies completely isolated.

The **Castleguard Cave** is located 117km from Jasper. A network of underwater caves, the longest in Canada, extends over 20km under the Columbia Icefield. Because of frequent flooding and the inherent dangers of spelunking, you must have authorization from Parks Canada to enter the caves.

The **Parker Ridge** ★★ trail, just 3km farther, makes for a wonderful outing. About 2.5km long, it leads up to the ridge, where, if you're lucky, you may spot some mountain goats. It also offers a great view of the Saskatchewan Glacier. Both the vegetation and the temperature change as you pass from the subalpine to the alpine zone. Warm clothing and a pair of gloves are a good idea.

At the **Sunwapta Pass** you can admire the grandiose scenery that marks the dividing line between Banff and Jasper National Parks. At 2,035m, this is the highest pass along the Icefields Parkway, after Bow Summit.

The **Athabasca Glacier** ★★★ and the **Columbia Icefield** are the focal points of the icefields tour. At the Athabasca Glacier, information panels show the impressive retreat of the glacier over the years. Those who wish to explore the ice on foot should beware of crevasses, which can be up to 40m deep. There are 30,000 on the Athabasca Glacier, some hidden under thin layers of snow or ice. Those without sufficient experience climbing on glaciers or lacking the proper equipment are better off with a ticket aboard the **Snowcoach Tour** *($30; May to mid-Oct, every day; tickets sold at the Brewster counter, near the tourist information centre,* ☎ *403-852-3332).* These specially equipped buses take people out onto the glacier.

The **Stutfield Glacier** ★★ lookout provides a view of one of the six

huge glaciers fed by the Columbia Icefield, which continues 1km into the valley.

Seventeen kilometres further, heading to Jasper, you'll come to an area called the **Mineral Lick**, where mountain goats often come to lick the mineral-rich soil.

The trail leading to the 25-m-high **Athabasca Falls** ★★, located 7km farther along, takes about 1hr to hike. The concrete structure built there is an unfortunate addition to the natural surroundings, but heavy traffic in the area would have otherwise destroyed the fragile vegetation. Furthermore, some careless individuals have had accidents because they got too close to the edge of the canyon. Travellers are therefore reminded not to go beyond the barriers; doing so could be fatal.

Jasper National Park

★★
Jasper and Surroundings

The town of Jasper takes its name from an old fur-trading post, founded in 1811 by William Henry of the North West Company. Jasper is a small town of just 4,000 residents which owes its tourist development to its location and the train station built here in 1911. When the Icefields Parkway was opened in 1940, the number of visitors who wanted to discover the region's majestic scenery grew continuously. Although this area is a major tourist draw, Jasper remains a decidedly

The Rocky Mountains

more tranquil and less commercial spot than Banff. This doesn't prevent hotel prices from being just as exorbitant as elsewhere in the Rockies, however.

The **Jasper-Yellowhead Museum and Archives** ★ *(free admission; mid-May to early Sep, every day 10am to 9pm; early Sep to mid-Oct, every day 10am to 5pm; winter, Thu to Sun 10am to 5pm; 400 Pyramid Lake Rd., facing the Aquatic Centre,* ☎ *780-852-3013)* tells the story of the region's earliest First Nations inhabitants, as well as mountain guides and other legendary characters from this area.

Mount Edith Cavell ★★★ is 3,363m high. To get there, take the southern exit for Jasper and follow the signs for the Marmot ski hill. Turn right, then left, and you'll come to a narrow road, that leads to one of the most lofty summits in the area. The road snakes through the forest for about 20km before coming to a parking lot. Several hiking trails have been cleared to allow visitors to enjoy a better view of this majestic mountain, as well as its suspended glacier, the **Angel Glacier**.

The mountain is named after Edith Louisa Cavell, a British nurse who became known during World War I for her refusal to leave her post near Brussels so that she could continue caring for the wounded in two camps. Arrested for spying by the Germans and accused of helping Allied prisoners escape, she was shot on October 12, 1915. To commemorate this woman's exceptional courage, the government of Canada named the most impressive mountain in the

Athabasca Valley after the martyred nurse. Mount Edith Cavell had previously been known by many other names. Aboriginal people called it "the white ghost," while travellers who used it as a reference point called it "the mountain of the Great Crossing," then "the Duke," "Mount Fitzhugh" and finally "Mount Geikie." No name had stuck, however, until the government decided to call it Mount Edith Cavell.

In just a few minutes, the **Jasper Tramway** ★★ *($16; mid-Apr to late Oct; take the southern exit for Jasper and follow the signs for Mount Whistler,* ☎ *780-852-3093)* whisks you up some 2,277m and deposits you on the northern face of **Mount Whistler**. You'll find a restaurant and souvenir shop at the arrival point, while a small trail covers the last few metres up to the summit (2,470m). The view is outstanding.

The road to Maligne Lake follows the valley of the river of the same name for 46km. Because of the tight curves of this winding road and the many animals that cross it, the speed limit is 60km/h. Before reaching the lake, the road passes one of the most beautiful resorts in Canada, the **Jasper Park Lodge**, run by Canadian Pacific. You can have a picnic, go boating or take a swim in one of the two pretty little lakes, **Agnes** and **Edith**, right next to this facility. Ten thousand years ago, as the glacier was retreating from this valley, two immense blocks of ice broke free and remained in place amidst the moraines and other debris left by the glaciers. As they melted they formed these two

small lakes. Lake Agnes has a beach.

Maligne Canyon ★★★ lies at the beginning of Maligne Road. Hiking trails have been cleared so that visitors may admire this spectacular narrow gorge abounding with waterfalls, fossils and potholes sculpted by the turbulent waters. Several bridges span the canyon. The first offers a view of the falls; the second, of the effect of ice on rock; and the third, of the deepest point (51m) of the gorge.

Maligne Lake ★★ is one of the prettiest lakes in the Rockies. Water activities like boating, fishing and canoeing are possible here, and a short trail runs along part of the shore. The chalet on the shore houses a souvenir shop, a restaurant-café and the offices of a tour company that organizes trips to little **Spirit Island**, the ideal vantage point for admiring the surrounding mountain tops.

The road that heads north to Edmonton crosses the entire Athabasca Valley. A large herd of moose grazes in this part of the valley, and the animals can often be spotted between the intersection of Maligne Road and the old town of Pocahontas, near Miette Hot Springs.

By continuing on the road to Hinton, you'll soon reach the hottest springs in all of the parks in the Rockies, **Miette Hot Springs**. The sulphurous water gushes forth at 57°C and has to be cooled down to 39°C for the baths. A paved path follows Sulphur Stream past the water purification station to the old pool, built out of logs in 1938; the trail finally

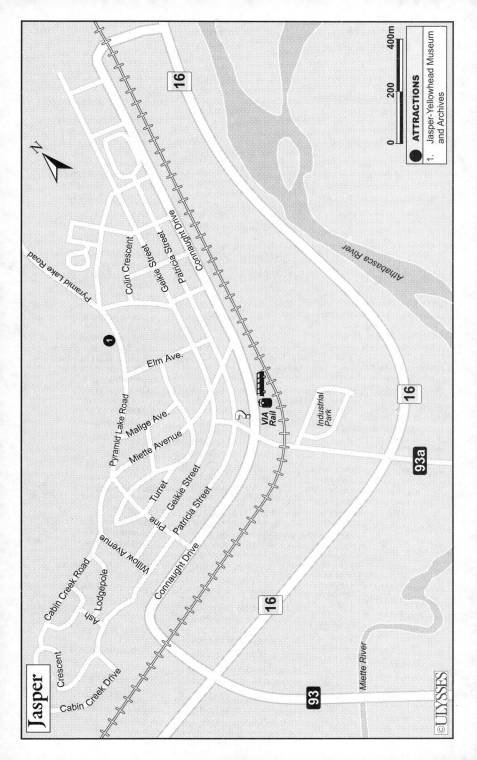

Jasper

Pyramid Lake Road

Colin Crescent
Gelkie Street
Patricia Street
Connaught Drive

Elm Ave.

Pyramid Lake Road

Malige Ave.
Miette Avenue

Turret
Pine
Geikie Street
Patricia Street

Cabin Creek Road
Ash
Lodgepole
Willow Avenue

Crescent

Cabin Creek Drive

Connaught Drive

VIA Rail

Industrial Park

Athabasca River

Miette River

16

16

16

93a

93

N

ATTRACTIONS

1. Jasper-Yellowhead Museum and Archives

0   200   400m

©ULYSSES

ends at one of three hot springs beside the stream. Several hiking trails have been cleared in the area for those who wish to explore the back country and admire the splendid scenery.

Kootenay and Yoho National Parks

★★
Kootenay National Park

Although less popular with the public than Banff and Jasper, Kootenay National Park nevertheless boasts beautiful, majestic landscapes and is just as interesting to visit as its more touristy neighbours. It contains two large valleys, the humid Vermillion River Valley and the drier Kootenay River Valley; the contrast is striking. The park owes its existence to a bold attempt to lay a road between the Windermere region and the province of Alberta. In 1905, Randolphe Bruce, a businessman from the town of Invermere who became lieutenant governor of British Columbia, decided to turn a profit with the local orchards. To do so he needed to lay a road between isolated Windermere and markets to the east. Bruce was so influential that construction began in 1911. A number of obstacles arose, and the audacious project soon proved too costly for the province to finance alone. As a result, the 22km of road, born of a bitter struggle between humans and nature, led nowhere, and the enterprise was abandoned. Refusing to admit defeat, Bruce turned to the federal government, which

agreed to help in return for the property alongside the road; thus was born Kootenay National Park in 1922.

Vermillion Pass, at the entrance of Kootenay Park, marks the Continental Divide; from this point on, rivers in Banff Park and points east flow to the east, while those in Kootenay Park flow west and empty into the Pacific.

A few kilometres farther lies **Marble Canyon ★★**, along with a tourist office where visitors can see a short film on the history of the park. Marble Canyon is very narrow, but you'll find a lovely waterfall at the end of the trail there. Several bridges span the gorge, and the erosion caused by torrential waters makes for some amazing scenery. Five hundred metres to the right, past the canyon, you'll find a trail leading to the famous **Paint Pots ★★**. These ochre deposits are created by subterranean springs that cause iron oxide to rise to the surface. Aboriginal people used this substance as paint. They would clean the ochre, mix it with water, and mould it into little loaves, that they would bake in a fire. They would then grind it into a fine powder and mix it with fish oil. They could use the final product to paint their bodies or decorate their tipis and clothing. According to the Aboriginals, a great animal spirit and a thunder spirit lived in the streams. Sometimes they would hear a melody coming from here, other times battle songs; to them, this meant that the spirits were speaking to them. To Aboriginals, ochre was the symbol of spirits, legends and important customs, while the first non-Aborigi-

nal to come here saw it as an opportunity to make money. At the beginning of the century, the ochre was extracted by hand and then sent to Calgary to be used as a colouring for paint. You can still see a few remnants of this era, including machines, tools and even a few piles of ochre, which were left behind when the area was made into a national park and all work here came to a halt.

One of the best places in the park for elk- and moose-watching is the **Animal Lick**, a mineral-rich salt marsh. The best time to go is early in the morning or at dusk. Viewing areas have been laid out along the road so that you can admire the scenery. The view is particularly lovely from the **Kootenay Valley Viewpoint ★★**, located at the park exit.

Radium Hot Springs

Located at the entrance to the park, this little town is surprisingly nondescript. You can, however, take a dip in the pool at the **Radium Hot Pools ★★** *($5; at the entrance to Kootenay Park, ☎ 250-347-9485)*, whose warm waters are renowned for their therapeutic virtues. Whether or not you believe these claims, which have yet to be backed by any medical evidence, a soak in these 45°C non-sulphurous waters is definitely very relaxing.

Yoho National Park

As in all the other parks in the Rockies, you must pay an entrance fee *($5 for one day, $35 a year)* if you wish to stay here. This fee does not apply if you are simply passing through the park.

A little further along, you'll find another trail leading to the **hoodoos**, natural rock formations created by erosion. The trail, which starts at the Hoodoo Creek campground, is very steep but only 3.2km long and offers an excellent view of the hoodoos.

Hiking to **Emerald Lake ★★** has become a tradition here in Yoho National Park. A short trail (5.2km) takes you around the lake. You can then visit **Hamilton Falls**. Picnic areas have been laid out near the lake. Thanks to a small canoe-rental outfit, you can also enjoy some time on the water. There is a small souvenir shop beside the boat-launching ramp.

The park's tourist office is located in Field, 33km east of the park entrance. During summer, visitors can learn more about the Yoho Valley by taking part in any number of interpretive activities. There are 400km of hiking trails leading through the valley deep into the heart of the region. Maps of these trails, as well as of those reserved for mountain bikes, are available at the **tourist office** *(Jul and Aug, every day 8:30am to 7pm; rest of year 9am to 7pm; on the way into town,* ☎*250-343-6783)* in **Field**. You can also purchase a topographical map of the park for $13. If you plan on staying more than a day here, you must register at the Parks Canada office, located in the same place. You can climb some of the mountains, but a special permit is required to scale Mount Stephen because

fossils have been discovered along the way.

Kananaskis Country

When Captain John Palliser led a British scientific expedition here from 1857 and 1860, the numerous lakes and rivers he found led him to christen the region Kananaskis, which means "gathering of the waters." Located 90km from Calgary, this region covers more than 4,000km², including the **Bow Valley**, **Bragg Creek** and **Peter Lougheed** provincial parks. Because of its proximity to Calgary, its beautiful scenery and the huge variety of outdoor activities that can be enjoyed here, it soon became one of the most popular destinations in the province, first with Albertans and then with visitors from all over the world.

Kananaskis Country has a great deal to offer in any season. During summer, it is a veritable paradise for outdoor enthusiasts, who can play both golf and tennis here, or go horseback riding, mountain biking, kayaking, river rafting, fishing or hiking. With its 250km of paved roads and 460km of marked trails, this region is easier to explore than any

other in Alberta. In winter, the trails are used for cross-country skiing and snowmobiling. Visitors can also go downhill skiing at Fortress Mountain or at Nakiska, speed down the toboggan runs, go skating on one of the region's many lakes or try dogsledding. Maps pertaining to these activities are available at the **Barrier Lake Information Centre** *(summer, every day 8:30am to 6pm, except Fri 8:30am to 7pm; autumn, Mon to Thu 9am to 4pm, Fri to Sun 9am to 6pm; winter every day 9am to 4pm; on Hwy. 40 near Barrier Lake,* ☎ *403-673-3985)*, where you'll also find the torch from the Calgary Olympics. It was carried all over Canada for three months, and then used to light the Olympic flame in Calgary on February 13, 1988. Eight events (downhill, slalom and giant slalom) were held in the Kananaskis region, on Mount Allan, in Nakiska.

The **Nakiska Ski Resort** *(near Kananaskis Village,* ☎ *403-591-7777)* was designed specifically for the Olympic Games, at the same time as the Kananaskis Village hotel complex. It boasts topnotch, modern facilities and excellent runs.

Kananaskis Village consists mainly of a central square surrounded by three luxurious hotels. It was designed to be the leading resort in this region. Its construction was funded by the Alberta Heritage Savings Trust and a number of private investors. The village was officially opened on December 20, 1987. It has a post office, located beside the **tourist information centre** *(summer, every day 9am to 9pm; winter, Mon to Fri 9am to 5pm)*, as well as a sauna and a hot tub *($2; every day 9am to 8:30pm)*, both of which are open to the general public. The Kananaskis Hotel houses a shopping arcade complete with souvenir and clothing shops, cafés and restaurants.

The tourist office in **Peter Lougheed Provincial Park** *(near the two Kananaskis Lakes)* features an interactive presentation that provides information on local flora, fauna, geography, geology and climatic phenomena. Mount Lougheed and the park were named after two well-known members of the Lougheed family. Born in Ontario, the honorable Sir James Lougheed (1854-1925) became a very prominent lawyer in both his home province and in Alberta, particularly in Calgary, where he was Canadian Pacific's legal advisor. He was named to the senate in 1889, led the Conservative Party from 1906 to 1921 and finally became a minister. The park owes its existence to his grandson, the honorable Peter Lougheed (1928-), who was elected Premier of Alberta on August 30, 1971. You can pick up a listing of the numerous interpretive programs offered here at the tourist office.

Outdoor Activities

Mountain Biking

Mountain bikes are permitted on certain trails. Always keep in mind that there might be people or bears around each bend. We also recommend limiting your speed on downhill stretches.

Banff National Park

You can rent a bicycle at many Banff hotels. In addition, there are some specialists, such as : **Bactrax** *(from $5/hr or $16/day; every day 8am to 8pm; Ptarmigan Inn, 339 Banff Ave.,* ☎ *403-762-8177)*; **Cycling the Rockies** *($50;* ☎ *403-678-6770)* organizes mountain-bike trips in the Banff area (each package includes a bicycle, a helmet, transportation to the point of departure, refreshments and the services of a guide).

Jasper National Park

The Jasper area is crisscrossed by bike trails.

A 9km trail leads from the parking lot opposite the Jasper Aquatic Centre to **Mina Lake and Riley Lake**. The pitch is fairly steep until you reach the firebreak road leading to Cabin Lake. Cross this road and continue to Mina Lake. Three and a half kilometres farther, another trail branches off toward Riley Lake. To return to Jasper, take Pyramid Lake Road.

The **Saturday Night Lake Loop** starts at the Cabin Creek West parking lot and climbs gently for 24.6km, offering a view of the Miette and Athabasca Valleys. Past Caledonia Lake, it winds through the forest to the High Lakes, where the grade becomes steeper. It then leads to Saturday Night Lake and Cabin Lake. From there, follow the firebreak road to Pyramid Lake Road, which will take you back to Jasper.

The **Athabasca River Trail** (25km) starts at the Old Fort Point parking lot, near Jasper Park Lodge. For the first 10km of the trail after the lodge's golf course, you will have to climb some fairly steep slopes, especially as you approach the Maligne Canyon. Bicycles are forbidden between the first and fifth bridges of the canyon trail, so you have to take Maligne Road for this part of the trip. After the fifth bridge, turn left and ride alongside the Athabasca River on trail 7. If you don't want to go back the way you came, take Highway 16.

Like the Athabasca River Trail, the **Valley of the Five Lakes Trail** and the **Wabasso Lake Trail** both start at the Old Fort Point parking lot. Trails 1, 1A and 9 begin here. The trip, which covers 11.2km, is quite easy up until the first lake in the valley, although a few spots are a bit rocky. At the first lake, the trail splits in two; take the path on the left, since it offers the best view of the lakes. The two trails merge into one again near a pond at the turn-off for Wabasso Lake. Pick up Highway 93, unless you want to go to Wabasso Lake, in which case you have to take trail 9 (19.3km), to the left of the pond. Head back to Jasper on the Icefields Parkway.

You have to drive to the parking lot at Celestine Lake, which marks the beginning of the trail (48km). A gravel road leads to the **Snake Indian Falls**, 22km away. About 1km farther, the road turns into a small trail that leads to Rock Lake.

Mountain Bike Rentals

Freewheel Cycle rents out quality mountain bikes and does repair *(618 Patricia St., Jasper,* ☎ *780-852-3898).*

At **On-Line Sport & Tackle** you'll find bikes, helmets and maps of bike paths *($18 per day; 600 Patricia St., Jasper,* ☎ *780-852-3630).*

Trail Sports
Canmore Nordic Center
☎ *(780) 678-6764*

Rafting

The rivers running through the Rockies have a lot to offer thrill-seekers. Whether it's your first time out or you already have some rafting experience, you'll find all sorts of interesting challenges here.

The most popular places to go rafting in the Banff area are **Kicking Horse River** and **Lower Canyon**. A few words of advice: wear a bathing suit and closed running shoes that you don't mind getting wet, dress very warmly (heavy wool and a windbreaker) and bring along a towel and a change of clothes for the end of the day.

Banff, Kootenay and Yoho National Parks

Hydra River Guides
$75 plus tax
209 Bear St., Box 778
Banff, T0L 0C0
☎*(403)760-9154*
☎*800-684-888*
≈*(403)760-3196*
Hydra River Guides offers day trips in Upper Canyon on Kicking Horse River.

Wild Water Adventures
full- and half-day packages
$109 and $67 respectively
(taxes not included)
Lake Louise and Banff
☎*(403)522-2211*
☎*800-647-4444*

Rocky Mountain Raft Tours
Box 1771
Banff, T0L 0C0
☎*(403)762-3632*

Glacier Raft Company
$85 per day
$49 for half a day
Banff, Alberta
☎*(403)762-4347*
Golden, BC
☎*(250)344-6521*
The Glacier Raft Company organizes trips down the Kicking Horse River. There is a special rate *($99, tax included)* for the **Kicking Horse Challenge**, which is a slightly wilder ride than the others.

Kootenay River Runners
$75-$300
Box 81, Edgewater
BC, V0A 1E0
☎*(250)347-9210*
☎*800-599-4399*
108 Banff Ave., Banff
☎*(403)762-5385*
Kootenay River Runners also has a branch in Banff, at the corner of Caribou and Bear Streets.

Rocky Mountain Rafting
$49 and up
Box 1767, Golden
BC, V0A 1H0
☎*(250)344-6979*
☎*800-808-RAFT*
Rocky Mountain Rafting, located in the Best Western, arranges trips down the Kicking Horse River.

Jasper National Park

Whitewater Rafting
Box 362
Jasper, T0E 1E0
☎*(780)852-RAFT*
☎*800-557-RAFT*
≈*(780) 852-3623*
Whitewater Rafting has a counter in **Jasper Park Lodge** *(*☎ *780-852-3301),* and another at the **Avalanche Esso** gas station *(702 Connaught Dr.,* ☎ *780-852-4FUN).* This company organizes trips down the Athabasca, Maligne and Sunwapta Rivers.

Maligne River Adventures
$59 and up
626 Connaught Dr.
Box 280, Jasper
T0E 1E0
☎*(780)852-3370*
In addition to other excursions, Maligne River Adventures offers an interesting three-day trip down the Kakwa River for $450 *(May and Jun).* Some experience is required, since these are class IV rapids, and are thus rather difficult to negotiate.

Two outfits offer trips for novices and children who would like to try rafting on slower-moving rapids: **Jasper Raft Tours** *($39, children $20; Box 398, Jasper, T0E 1E0,* ☎ *780-852-3613,* ≈ *780-852-3923)* and **Mount Robson Adventure Holidays** *($40 and up; children $15 and up Box 687, Valemount, BC, Mount Robson Provincial Park, V0E 2Z0,* ☎ *250-566-4368,* ≈*250-566-4351),* which also has a branch in Jasper *(604 Connaught Dr.)*.

Downhill Skiing

Banff National Park

Banff Mount Norquay
$39 full-day pass
on Norquay Rd.
Box 219, Banff, AB, T0L 0C0
☎*(403)762-4421*
Banff Mount Norquay was one of the first ski resorts in North America. It takes just 10min to drive here from downtown Banff. The resort has both a ski school and a rental shop. Call ahead for ski conditions.

Sunshine Village
$47 full-day
8km west of Banff
Box 1510
Banff, AB, T0L 0C0
☎*(403)760-6500*
☎*800-661-1676*
Sunshine Village is a beautiful ski resort located at an altitude of 2,700m on the Continental Divide between the provinces of Alberta and British Columbia. Because this resort is located above the tree line, it gets lots of sun. Call (403)277-SNOW for ski conditions. Ski rentals available.

Lake Louise
$51 per day
Box 5
Lake Louise, AB
T0L 1E0
☎*(403)522-3555*
Lake Louise has the largest ski resort in Canada, covering four mountainsides and offering skiers over 50 different runs. Both downhill and cross-country equipment are available for rent here. For ski conditions, call *(403)244-6665*.

Jasper National Park

Marmot Basin
$42 full day
take Hwy. 93 toward Banff then turn right on 93A
Box 1300
Jasper, AB, T0E 1E0
☎*(780)852-3816*
☎*(780) 488-5909 for ski conditions*
Marmot Basin is located about 20min by car from downtown Jasper. Ski rentals available.

Kootenay and Yoho National Parks

Kimberley Ski Resort
$35 full day
Box 40, Kimberley, BC
V1A 2Y5
☎*(250)427-4881*
☎*800-667-0871*
The Kimberley Ski Resort is the only real attraction in Kimberley, an amazing little Bavarian village. It has some decent trails that are perfect for family skiing.

Whitetooth
$32 per day
Box 1925, Golden, BC
V0A 1H0
Although Whitetooth is relatively small, it gets bigger every year. It has a few good, well-maintained runs.

Kananaskis Country

Nakiska
$40 day
P.O. Box 1988
Kananaskis Village, AB
T0L 2H0
☎*(403)591-7777*
☎*229-3288 for ski conditions*
Nakiska hosted the men's and women's downhill, slalom and combination events during the 1988 Winter Olympics. Like Kananaskis Village, it was built specifically for that purpose and boasts an excellent, modern infrastructure and top-notch

trails. Downhill and cross-country equipment are both available for rent here .

Fortress Mountain
$55 day
take Hwy. 40 past Kananaskis Village and turn right at Fortress Junction
suite 505
1550 Eighth St. SW, Calgary, AB
T2R 1K1
☎*(403)256-8473*
☎*(403)244-6665*
☎*244-4909 for ski conditions*
Fortress Mountain, located on the Continental Divide at the edge of Peter Lougheed Provincial Park, is less popular than Nakiska but nevertheless has some very interesting runs.

Cross-country Skiing

There are countless cross-country trails in the parks of the Rockies, whose tourist information offices distribute maps of the major trails around the towns of Banff and Jasper and the village of Lake Louise.

Canmore Nordic Centre
1988 Olympic Way, ste. 100
Canmore, AB, T1W 2T6
☎*(403)678-2400*
≈*(403)678-5696*
The Canmore Nordic Centre, which hosted the cross-country events of the 1988 Winter Olympics, deserves special mention for its magnificent trail network.

Mountain Climbing

Banff National Park

Yamnuska
200, 58-103 Bow Valley Trail
Canmore
☎*(403)678-4164*
✉*(403)678-4450*
www.yamnuska.com
Yamnuska is both the
name of the climbing
school and the name of
the first mountain you see
as you leave Calgary. The
school offers a range of
climbing courses, from
glacier climbing, to mountain survival-training, to
anything that has to do
with mountaineering in
general, whether by foot,
skis or snow board. It's the
most renowned school of
its kind in the country, and
its professionalism is impeccable.

Alpine Club of Canada
Indian Flats Rd.
4.5km east of Canmore
☎*(403) 678-3200*
✉*(403) 678-3224*
The Alpine Club of Canada
offers a wide range of
expeditions, from the first
great climb, to an easy
afternoon climb. The pos-
sibilities are endless, and
the prices accommodate
all budgets. One of the ⌐
most interesting excursions
involves passing the night
in one of many huts be-
longing to the association.

Jasper National Park

Peter Amann of the **Mountain Guiding and Schools**
offers mountaineering
lessons for novices and
experienced climbers alike
*(from $150 for 2 days; Box
1495, Jasper, AB, T0E 1E0,
☎/✉ 780-852-3237,
mann@incentre.net).*

Accommodations

Banff National Park

Banff

A list of private homes that
receive paying guests is
provided at the tourist
information office located
at 224 Banff Avenue. You
may obtain this list by
writing to the following
address:

**Banff-Lake Louise
Tourist Office**
P.O. Box 900
Banff, AB, T0L 0C0
☎*(403) 762-8421*
☎*(403) 762-0270*
✉*(403) 762-8163*

It is impossible to reserve
a campsite in advance in
the park, which has a
policy of first come, first
served. If you are leading
a fairly large group, contact the Parks Canada
offices in Banff.

Campsites generally cost
between $13 and $16,
according to the location
and the facilities at the
site. We advise you to
arrive early to choose your
spot. In high season, the
Banff campgrounds are
literally overrun with
hordes of tourists. It is
forbidden to pitch your
tent outside the area set
aside for this purpose.
Camping at unauthorized
sites is strictly prohibited,
for safety reasons and also
to preserve the natural
environment of the park.

Tunnel Mountain 1 and 2
toilets, showers, ☎
on Tunnel Mountain Rd
near the Banff Youth Hostel
Tunnel Mountain 1 and 2
has about 840 spaces for
trailers and tents.

Two Jack Lake Campgrounds
$13-$16
toilets, ☎
take the road going
to Lake Minnewanka
then head toward Two Jack Lake
☎*(403)762-1759*
The two Two Jack Lake
Campgrounds are located
on either side of the road
that runs alongside Two
Jack Lake. There are showers at the campground
near the water. The other
campground, deeper in
the forest, offers a more
basic level of comfort. It is
easier to find spaces at
these two campgrounds
than at those in Banff.

**Banff International Youth
Hostel**
$20 members
$29 non-members
on Tunnel Mountain Rd.
Box 1358, Banff, AB
T0L 0C0
☎*(403)762-4122*
☎*(403) 237-8282 in Calgary*
Banff International Youth
Hostel remains the cheap-
est solution, but it is often
full. It is essential to reserve well in advance to
arrive early. This friendly
youth hostel is only about
a 20min walk from the
centre of town. It offers a
warm welcome, and the
desk staff will be pleased
to help you organize river
rafting and other outdoor
activities.

Holiday Lodge
$67 bkfst incl.
311 Marten St.
Box 904, Banff, AB, T0L 0C0
☎*(403)762-3648*
✉*(403)762-8813*
Holiday Lodge has five
clean and relatively com-
fortable rooms and two
cabins. This old restored
house, located in the centre of town, offers good
and copious breakfasts.

Inns of Banff, Swiss Village and Rundle Manor
$80-$215
tv

600 Banff Ave.
Box 1077, Banff
AB, T0L 0C0
☎*(403)762-4581*
☎*800-661-1272*
⇌*762-2434*
These three hotels are really one big hotel with a common reservation service. Depending on your budget, you have the choice of three distinct buildings. Inns of Banff, the most luxurious, has 180 very spacious rooms, each facing a small terrace. The Swiss Village has a little more character and fits the setting much better. The rooms, however are a bit expensive at $150 and are less comfortable. Finally, Rundle Manor is the most rustic of the three but is short on charm. The Rundle's units have small kitchens, living rooms and one or two separate bedrooms. This is a safe bet for family travellers. Guests at the Rundle Manor and Swiss Village have access to the facilities of the Inns of Banff.

Rundle Stone Lodge
$95-$190
&, P, *tv*, ≈, ⊛

537 Banff Ave., Box 489
Banff, AB, T0L 0C0
☎*(403)762-2201*
☎*800-661-8630*
⇌*762-4501*
Rundle Stone Lodge occupies a handsome building along Banff's main street. In the part of the building located along Banff Avenue, the rooms are attractive and spacious, each with a balcony. Some also have whirlpool baths. The hotel offers its guests a covered, heated parking area in the winter. Rooms for travellers with disabilities are available on the ground floor.

Tannanhof Pension
$95-$165 bkfst incl.
✗

121 Cave Ave., Box 1914
Banff, AB, T0L 0C0
☎*(403)762-4636*
⇌*(403) 760-2484*
Tannanhof Pension has eight rooms and two suites located in a big, lovely house. Some rooms have cable television and private baths, while others share a bathroom. Each of the two suites has a bathroom with tub and shower, a fireplace and a sofa-bed for two extra people. Breakfast is German-style with a choice of four dishes.

Traveller's Inn
$95-$195
&, P, *tv*, △, ⊛

401 Banff Ave., Box 1017
Banff, AB, T0L 0C0
☎*(403)762-4401*
☎*800- 661-0227*
⇌*(403)-762-5905*
Most rooms at the hotel have small balconies that offer fine mountain views. Rooms are simply decorated, big and cosy. The hotel has a small restaurant that serves breakfast, as well as heated underground parking, an advantage in the winter. During the ski season, guests have the use of lockers for skis and boots, as well as a small store for the rental and repair of winter sports equipment.

High Country Inn
$125
△, P, *tv*, ≈, ⊛
heated underground

419 Banff Ave., Box 700
Banff, AB, T0L 0C0
☎*(403)762-2236*
☎*800-661-1244*
⇌*(403) 762-5084*
Located on Banff's main drag, this inn has big, comfortable, spacious rooms with balconies. Furnishings are very ordinary, however, and detract from the beauty of the

setting.

Banff Rocky Mountain Resort
$150-$230
tv, ⊛, ≈. ☺
squash courts, massage room, tennis courts
at the entrance to the town along Banff Ave.
Box 100, Banff, AB, T0L 0C0
☎*(403)762-5531*
☎*800-661-9563*
⇌*(403)762-5166*
Banff Rocky Mountain Resort is an ideal spot for families. The delightful little chalets are warm and very well equipped. On the ground floor is a bathroom with shower, a very functional kitchen facing a living room and dining room with a fireplace while upstairs are two bedrooms and another bathroom. These apartments also have small private terraces. Near the main building are picnic and barbecue areas as well as lounge chairs where you can lie in the sun.

Banff Springs Hotel
$240-$520
⊛, ☺, ≈, △, &, ✗, *tv*, ℜ, ≈, *bar*
Spray Ave., Box 960
Banff, AB, T0L 0C0
☎*(403)762-2211*
☎*800-441-1414*
⇌*(403) 762-4447*
Banff Springs Hotel is the largest hotel in Banff. Overlooking the town, this five-star hotel, part of the Canadian Pacific chain, offers 770 luxurious rooms in an atmosphere reminiscent of an old Scottish castle. The hotel was designed by architect Price, to whom is also credited Windsor Station in Montréal and the Château Frontenac in Québec City. Besides the typical turn-of-the-century chateau style, old-fashioned furnishings and superb views from every window, the hotel offers its guests bowling, tennis courts, a pool, a

sauna, a large whirlpool bath, and a massage room. You can also stroll and shop in the more than 50 shops in the hotel. Golfers will be delighted to find a superb 27-hole course, designed by architect Stanley Thompson, on the grounds.

Between Banff and Lake Louise

Johnston Canyon Resort
$98-$240
🏖, pb
from Banff, take the Trans-Canada Hwy. to the Bow Valley exit then take Hwy. 1A the Bow Valley Parkway
Box 875, Banff, AB, T0L 0C0
☎(403)762-2971
⇌(403) 762-0868
Johnston Canyon Resort is a group of small log cabins right in the middle of the forest. The absolute calm makes for a pleasant retreat. Some cabins offer a basic level of comfort, while others are fully equipped and have kitchens, sitting rooms and fireplaces. The largest cabin can accommodate four people comfortably. There is also a small grocery store offering a basic range of products.

Near Silver City

Castle Mountain Youth Hostel
$20 for members
$24 for non-members
27km from Banff on Hwy. 1A at the Castle Junction crossroads across from Castle Mountain Village for reservations, call the Banff reservations office
☎(403)762-4122
⇌(403) 762-3441
Castle Mountain Youth Hostel occupies a small building with two dormitories and a common room set around a big fireplace. The atmosphere is very pleasant, and the manager, who is from Québec, will

be happy to advise you on hikes in the area.

Lake Louise

Canadian Alpine Centre
$21-$31 per person
🐑, △, sb
on Village Rd., Box 115
Lake Louise, AB, T0L 1E0
☎(403)522-2200
⇌(403)522-2253
The Canadian Alpine Centre is a youth hostel offering rooms with two, four or six beds. Although fairly expensive, it is much more comfortable than other youth hostels. Guests have access to a laundry room, a common kitchen, a library, and the little **Bill Peyto's Café**. The hostel is equipped to receive travellers with disabilities. A piece of advice: reserve well in advance.

Lake Louise Inn
$143-$264
🐑, tv, ≈, ℜ
210 Village Rd., Box 209
Lake Louise, AB, T0L 1E0
☎(403)522-3791
☎800-661-9237
⇌(403) 522-2018
Lake Louise Inn is located in the village of Lake Louise. The hotel offers very comfortable, warmly decorated rooms.

Deer Lodge
$160-$210
ℜ, ⊛
near the lake
on the right before reaching the Chateau Lake Louise
Box 100
Lake Louise, AB, T0L 1E0
☎(403)522-3747
⇌(403) 522-3883
Deer Lodge is a very handsome and comfortable hotel. Rooms are spacious and tastefully decorated. The atmosphere is very pleasant.

Moraine Lake Lodge
$320-$395
⚱, ℜ
Box 70
Lake Louise, AB, T0L 1E0
☎(403)522-3733
⇌(403) 522-3719
Jun to Sep
☎(250)985-7456
Oct to May
⇌(250)985-7479
Moraine Lake Lodge is located at the edge of Lake Moraine. Rooms do not have phones or televisions. The setting is magnificent but packed with tourists at all times, detracting from its tranquillity.

Chateau Lake Louise
$329-$490
⚱, tv, ≈, ℜ, △
Lake Louise, AB, T0L 1E0
☎(403)522-3511
⇌522-3834
Chateau Lake Louise is one of the best-known hotels in the region. Built originally in 1890, the hotel burned to the ground in 1892 and was rebuilt the following year. Another fire devastated parts of it in 1924. Since then, it has been expanded and embellished almost continuously. Today, this vast hotel, which belongs to the Canadian Pacific chain, has 511 rooms with space for more than 1,300 guests, and a staff of nearly 725 to look after your every need. Perched by the turquoise waters of Lake Louise, facing the Victoria Glacier, the hotel boasts a divine setting.

Canmore

Restwell Trailer Park
$18
across Hwy 1A and the railway line near Policeman Creek
☎(403)678-5111
Restwell Trailer Park has 247 spaces for trailers and tents. Electricity, toilets, showers and water are available.

The Rocky Mountains

Ambleside Lodge
$65-$105
non-smokers only
123A Rundle Dr.
Canmore, AB, T1W 2L6
☎ *(403)678-3976*
⇌ *(403) 678-3916*
Ambleside Lodge welcomes you to a larg, handsome residence in the style of a Savoyard chalet just a few minutes from the centre of town. The comfortable common room is graced with a beautiful fireplace. Some rooms have private baths.

Lady MacDonald Country Inn
$80-$175
&, *tv*
Bow Valley Trail, Box 2128
Canmore, AB, T0L 0M0
☎ *(403)678-3665*
☎ *800-567-3919*
⇌ *(403) 678-9714*
Lady MacDonald Country Inn is a magnificent little inn established in a very pretty house. Eleven elegantly decorated rooms are placed at guests' disposal. Some rooms have been specially equipped to receive travellers with disabilities; others are spread over two floors to welcome families of four. The superb "Three Sisters Room" offers a magnificent view of the Rundle Range and Three Sisters mountains, as well as a fireplace and a whirlpool bath.

Rocky Mountain Ski Lodge
$100-$220
K, tv
1711 Mountain Ave., Box 8070
Canmore, AB, T1W 2T8
☎ *(403)678-5445*
☎ *800-665-6111*
⇌ *(403) 678-6484*
Rocky Mountain Ski Lodge faces a pleasant little garden. Rooms are clean and spacious. Units with livingrooms, fireplaces, and fully equipped kitchens start at $120.

The Creek House
$195 or
$2,100- $2,800/week for 4 people
701 Mallard Alley
☎ *678-2463*
☎ *888-678-6100*
⇌ *(403) 678-8721*
www.creekhouse.com
The Creek House is one of the most beautiful places to spend the night in Canmore and all of the Rockies. Gail and Greg bought and completely renovated this old house on the edge of the Bow River, from where you can see Cascade Mountain (3,000m). The decor of the rooms is impeccable. An artist made some magnificent murals, such as the one in the stairwell. At the end of 1999, Greg added the final touch – a rooftop jacuzzi!

The Icefields Parkway

Between Lake Louise and the Icefields Parkway

Rampart Creek Youth Hostel
$10 per person for members
$14 for non-members
closed Oct to Dec
near the campground
of the same name on Hwy 93
☎ *(780)762-4122*
Rampart Creek Youth Hostel comes off as a little rustic, but it is very well situated for hikers and cyclists visiting the glaciers.

Wilcox Creek Campground Columbia Icefield Campground
$10
$3 extra to make a wood fire
a few kilometres from the Columbia Icefield
These two campgrounds are equipped with the basics. You have to register yourself.

Waterfowl Lake Campground
$13
$3 extra to make a wood fire
above Lake Mistaya
just after the Mount Chephren lookout
As everywhere in the parks, it is first come, first served. Reservations are not possible unless you are a group. If that is the case, call the Parks Canada offices in Banff.

Athabasca Falls Youth Hostel
$15 per person for members
$19 for non-members
32km south of Jasper
☎ *(780) 852-3215*
In keeping with the rustic decor, this hostel has no running water, but it does have electricity and a kitchen. It is situated next to Athabasca Falls. Cyclists and hikers will appreciate this hostel's great location.

Hilda Creek Youth Hostel
$15 per person for members
$19 for non-members
closed Oct to Dec
just before the entrance
to Jasper National Park
☎ *(780) 762-4122*
or the Calgary reservations centre
☎ *(780) 237-8282*
This is a genuine mountain refuge, with no running water or electricity. This spot is heartily recommended for hikers because of its proximity to the finest hiking areas around the Athabasca Glacier. Information is available here, and the staff will be happy to indicate the must-sees. The welcome is friendly, and the scenery will take your breath away.

Rampart Creek Campground
$15 members
$19 non-members
$3 extra to make a wood fire
a few kilometres from the intersection
of Hwys. 11 and 93
The entrance to the campground is unguarded. You must register yourself and

leave the payment for your stay in an envelope.

The Crossing
$95
⌂, ℜ, tv, ⊛, cafeteria, pub
at the crossroads of Hwys 93 and 11, 80km from Lake Louise
Box 333, Lake Louise, AB
T0L 1E0
☎(780) 761-7000
⇒(780) 761-7006
The Crossing is a good place to stop along the Icefields Parkway.

Num-Ti-Jah Lodge
$125-$180
pb
on the shore of Bow Lake about 35km from Lake Louise
☎(780) 522-2167
⇒(780) 522-2425
Num-Ti-Jah Lodge was built by Jimmy Simpson, a famous mountain guide and trapper from the region. Jimmy Simpson's two daughters also have a place in the history of the Rockies. Peg and Mary became world-class figure skaters and made numerous tours of Canada and the United States. The name Num-Ti-Jah comes from a Stoney Plain word for pine marten. The spot is popular with tourists, for Bow Lake is one of the most beautiful in the region.

Jasper National Park

Jasper

Athabasca Hotel
$85-$135
sb/pb, ℜ, bar, tv
Box 1420, Jasper, AB
T0E 1E0
☎(780) 852-3386
☎800-563-9859
⇒(780) 852-4955
The Athabasca Hotel is located right in the centre of Jasper, facing the Via Rail station and the Brewster and Greyhound bus terminal. Decorated in old English style, the

rooms are appealing but not very big. The least expensive are near a central bathroom, but the others have their own facilities. Neither flashy nor luxurious, this hotel is quite adequate, and the rooms are pleasant. This is the cheapest place to stay in Jasper, so you'll have to reserve in advance. The hotel does not have an elevator.

Marmot Lodge
$85-$170
♿, ✻, tv, ≈, ℜ, K, ⊛
on Connaught Dr.
at the Jasper exit, toward Edmonton
Box 1200, Jasper, AB, T0E 1E0
☎(780) 852-4471
☎800-661-6521
⇒(780) 852-3280
Marmot Lodge offers very attractive rooms at what are considered reasonable prices in Jasper. The rooms are decorated in bright colours and old photographs hang on the walls, for a change from the normal decor. A terrace with tables has been set up in front of the pool, a good spot for sunbathing. The decor, the friendly staff and the scenery all contribute to making this hotel a very pleasant place. It provides the best quality-to-price ratio in town.

Jasper Inn
$96-$400
tv, ℜ, ≈, K, ⊛, ℝ
98 Geikie St., Box 879
Jasper, AB, T0E 1E0
☎(780) 852-4461
☎800-661-1933
⇒852-5916
Jasper Inn offers spacious, attractive, comfortable rooms, some of them equipped with kitchenettes.

Jasper Park Lodge
$169-$419
♿, ✻, ≈, ℜ, ℝ, tv, ☺, ⊛, ⌂
Box 40, Jasper, AB, T0E 1E0
☎(780) 852-3301
☎800-441-1414
⇒852-5107
Jasper Park Lodge constitutes beyond a doubt the most beautiful hotel complex in the whole Jasper area. Now part of the Canadian Pacific chain, the Jasper Park Lodge has attractive, spacious, comfortable rooms. It was built in 1921 by the Grand Trunk Railway Company to compete with Canadian Pacific's Banff Springs Hotel. The staff is very professional, attentive and friendly. A whole range of activities ise organized for guests. These include horseback riding and river rafting. You will also find one of the finest golf courses in Canada, several tennis courts, a big pool, a sports centre, and canoes, sailboards and bicycles for rent in the summer, plus ski equipment in the winter. Several hiking trails crisscross the site, among them a very pleasant 3.8km trail alongside Lake Beauvert. Whether you're staying in a room in the main building or in a small chalet, you are assured of comfort and tranquillity.

Each year Jasper Park Lodge organizes theme events, and hotel guests are invited to participate. Some weekends may be dedicated to the mountains and relaxation, with yoga and aerobics classes as well as water gymnastics and visits to the sauna; while another weekend may be set aside for the wine tastings of Beaujolais Nouveau; other activities are organized for New Year's. Ask for the activities leaflet for more information.

The Rocky Mountains

Outside Jasper

Whistler Campground
$15-$22
open May 5 to Oct 10
2.5km south of Jasper
take Hwy. 93
then turn on the road leading to the Whistler Mountain ski lift taking the first left for the campground
Whistler Campground has 781 sites facilities for both trailers and tents. Water, showers and electricity are available. You can also find firewood on the site. The maximum stay at the campsite is 15 days. To reserve, call the Parks Canada office in Jasper (see p 558).

Jasper's three youth hostels are located outside the town.

Jasper International Youth Hostel
$15 per person for members
$20 per person for non-members
7km west of Jasper or the Skytram rd.
☎(403)852-3215
Jasper International Youth Hostel is quite a comfortable establishment. It is a few minutes' walk from the summer gondola that goes to the top of Whistler Mountain, where there is a superb view over the Athabasca Valley. Reserve well in advance.

Maligne Canyon Youth Hostel
$15 per person for members
$19 per person for non-members
closed Wed in winter
11km east of Jasper
on the Maligne Lake road
☎(403) 852-3215
Maligne Canyon Youth Hostel is the ideal spot for anyone who likes hiking and other outdoor activities. The Skyline hiking trail begins right near the hostel, leading experienced hikers through Alpine scenery. The hike takes two or three days, but the superb view over the Jasper valley is a good reward for your efforts. Also located near the hostel, the Maligne River canyon offers some fine rapids and waterfalls both of which make excellent photo opportunities. Do not hesitate to talk with the manager of the hostel: he is an expert on local fauna and conducts research for Jasper National Park.

Mount Edith Cavell Youth Hostel
$15 per person for members
$19 per person for non-members
26km south of Jasper
take Hwy. 93A and then go 13 km up the curvy road leading to Mount Edith Cavell
☎(403) 852-3215
Mount Edith Cavell Youth Hostel is a genuine high mountain refuge, without water or electricity. It is built on one of the most beautiful mountains in the area, Mount Edith Cavell. Take warm clothing and a good sleeping bag, for you are in a high mountain area, and the temperatures are unpredictable. If you enjoy tranquillity and beautiful walks, you will be in paradise here.

Pine Bungalow Cabins
$75-$100
&, K
on Hwy. 16
near the Jasper golf course
Box 7, Jasper, AB, T0E 1E0
☎(403)852-3491
≈852-3432
Pine Bungalow Cabins fit the category of a motel. The cabins are fully equipped, and some even have fireplaces, but furnishings are very modest and in rather poor taste. All the same, it is one of Jasper's cheapest places to stay.

Jasper House
$80-$168
tv, K, ℜ
a few kilometres south of Jasper on Icefields Parkway at the foot of Mount Whistler
Box 817, Jasper, AB, T0E 1E0
☎(403) 852-4535
≈852-5335
Jasper House consists of a group of little chalet-style log houses built along the Athabasca River. Comfortable and quiet, the rooms are large and well equipped.

Pyramid Lake Resort
$89-$189
summer only
&, tv, ℜ
on the shore of Pyramid Lake
5km from Jasper
take Pyramid Lake Rd.
to Jasper and follow the signs to Lake Patricia and Pyramid Lake
Box 388, Jasper, AB, T0E 1E0
☎(403) 852-4900
☎(403) 852-3536
≈(403) 852-7007
Pyramid Lake Resort offers simple but comfortable rooms facing Pyramid Lake, where you can enjoy your favourite nautical activities. Rentals of motorboats, canoes, and waterskis are available at the hotel.

Miette Hot Springs

Miette Hot Spring Bungalows
$5-$80
K, ℜ
next to the Miette Hot Springs
Jasper East, Box 907, Jasper, AB, T0E 1E0
☎(403) 866-3750
☎(4030 866-3760, *in the off-season*
☎(403) 852-4039
≈(403) 866-2214
Miette Hot Spring Bungalows offers accommodations in bungalows and a motel. The motel rooms are rather ordinary, but those in the bungalows offer good quality.

Outside Hinton

Overlander Mountain Lodge
$100-$150
ℜ
2km to the left after leaving
Jasper National Park toward Hinton
Box 6118, Hinton, AB, T7V 1X5
☎*(403) 866-2330*
⇄*(403) 866-2332*
The Overlander Mountain
Lodge has several charm-
ing cabins. This establishment's location in a much
calmer area than the out-
skirts of Jasper, and the
exquisite surrounding
scenery make it a particularly pleasant place. This
place stands out from the
majority of motel-style
establishments in this
town. Reservations should
be made far in advance, as
Hinton is a common alter-
native to lodging in Jasper.

Kootenay and Yoho
National Parks

From Castle Junction
to Radium Hot
Springs

Kootenay Park Lodge
$74-$92 per cabin
mid-May to late Sep
🛒, ℜ, ℝ
on Hwy. 93 heading south
42km from Castle Junction
Box 1390, Banff, AB, T0L 0C0
☎*(403)762-9196*
in the off-season, phone Calgary
☎/⇄ *(403)283-7482*
Kootenay Park Lodge rents
10 small log cabins cling-
ing to the steep slopes of
the mountains of Kootenay
National Park. On site you
will find a small store
offering sandwiches and
everyday items. The res-
taurant is open only from
8am to 10am, noon to 2pm
and 6pm to 8:30pm.

Radium Hot Springs

Surprisingly, accommoda-
tions in Radium Hot

Springs consist essentially
of very ordinary motel
rooms. All along the
town's main drag you will
find motel fronts that rival
each other in ugliness. The
region is popular with
visitors, however, so here
are a few suggestions.

Misty River Lodge
$55-$75
🛒, ≈, *tv, K*
5036 Hwy 93, Box 363
Radium Hot Springs, BC, V0A 1M0
☎*(250)347-9912*
⇄*(250)347-9397*
Misty River Lodge is the
only exception to the
"ugly-motel" rule in Ra-
dium Hot Springs. The
rooms offer a decent level
of comfort. The bathrooms
are spacious and very
clean. Without a doubt,
the best motel in town.

The Chalet
$95
🛒, ☉, △, *tv,* ⊛
Box 456, Radium Hot Springs
BC, V0A 1M0
☎*(250)347-9305*
⇄*347-9306*
The Chalet offers modestly
furnished but comfortable
rooms, some of which
have balconies. Perched
above the little town of
Radium Hot Springs, this
big Savoy chalet-style
house offers an interesting
view of the valley below.

Fairmont Hot Springs

🌴 **Fairmont Hot Springs**
Resort
$139
🛒, ≈, ℜ, *tv,* ℝ, ⊛, △, ℜ
on Hwy. 93-95
near the Fairmont ski hills
Box 10, Fairmont Hot Springs
BC, V0B 1L0
☎*(250)345-6311*
☎*800-663-4979*
⇄*(250) 345-6616*
Fairmont Hot Springs Re-
sort is a wonderfully laid
out, magnificent hotel
complex offering special
spa, ski and golf packages.

Hotel guests can also take
advantage of tennis courts
and a two superb 18-hole
golf course. Guests have
unlimited access to the hot
springs. This establishment
also has a vast adjacent
campground *($15-$35)*.

Yoho National Park

Emerald Lake Lodge
$165-$275
Box 10, Field, V0A 1G0
☎*(250) 343-6321*
☎*(800)663-6336*
⇄*(250) 343-6724*
Emerald Lake Lodge, in
Yoho National Park, was
built by Canadian Pacific
in the 1890s and today is
an exquisite mountain
hideaway. The central
lodge, built of hand-hewn
timber is the hub of activity, while guests stay in
one of 24 cabins. Each
room features a fieldstone
fireplace, willow-branch
chairs, a down duvet, a
private balcony and terrific
lake views. Just 40km from
Lake Louise.

Golden and
Surroundings

McLaren Lodge
$70 bkfst incl.
above Hwy. 95 leaving Golden
toward Yoho National Park
Box 2586, Golden, BC
V0A 1H0
☎*(250)344-6133*
⇄*(250) 344-7650*
McLaren Lodge is an interesting spot in Golden for
nature-lovers. The owners
of this little hotel organize
river rafting excursions.
Rooms are rather small
and have a pleasant old-
fashioned air. This spot
has the best quality-to-
price ratio in Golden.

The Rocky
Mountains

Prestige Inn
$110
☂, ☕, K, ⚅, tv, ≈, ℜ, ⊘
1049 Trans-Canada Hwy
Box 9, Golden, BC, V0A 1H0
☎(250)344-7990
⇔(250) 344-7902
Prestige Inn is Golden's best hotel. Rooms are quite spacious, and bathrooms are well equipped.

Kananaskis Country

Mount Kidd RV Park
$19-$30
☂, ☕, *toilets, showers, laundromat,* ⌂
on Hwy. 40, a few kilometres south of Kananaskis Village
☎(403)591-7700
Mount Kidd RV Park has a surprising set-up. Located at the edge of the river in a forested area, it is definitely the most pleasant campground in the region. Guests also have the use of tennis courts or can head off on any of the many hiking trails in the area. Be sure to reserve ahead (groups especially) at this popular spot.

Kananaskis Village

Ribbon Creek Youth Hostel
$15 per person for members
$19 per person for non-members
along the road leading to the central square of Kananaskis Village
T0L 2H0
☎(403)762-4122
Ribbon Creek Youth Hostel is a pleasant little hostel that is almost always crowded. Do not wait to the last minute to reserve, or you will be disappointed. The common room, in front of the fireplace, is a pleasant spot to recover from the day's activities.

Kananaskis Inn Best Western
$160-$180
☕, tv, K, ⌂, ⚅, ≈, ℜ
on the central square of Kananaskis Village, T0L 2H0
☎(403) 591-7500
☎800-528-1234
⇔(403) 591-7633
Kananaskis Inn Best Western has 95 comfortable, pleasantly furnished rooms. The atmosphere at this hotel is quite agreeable, and the staff is friendly. However, the lobby is often besieged by visitors searching for souvenir shops or tea rooms.

Restaurants

Banff National Park

Banff

The restaurant at the Caribou Lodge, **The Keg**, serves American breakfasts and buffet-style food.

Joe BTFSPLK's
$
221 Banff Ave.
facing the tourist information centre
☎(403)762-5529
Joe BTFSPLK's (pronounced bi-tif-spliks) is a small restaurant with 1950s decor and good hamburgers. You'll learn that Joe BTFSPLK was a strange comic book character who walked around with a cloud above his head causing disasters wherever he went. It seems the only way today to avoid annoyances (such as spending too much money) may be to come to this little restaurant, very popular with locals for the burgers, fries, salads, chicken fingers and milkshakes. The restaurant also serves breakfasts for under $6.

Grizzly House
$$
every day 11:30am to midnight
207 Banff Ave.
☎(403)762-4055
Grizzly House specializes in big, tender, juicy steaks. The western decor is a bit corny, but your attention will quickly be diverted by your delicious meal.

 **Korean Restaurant**
$$
every day from 11:30am to 10pm
upstairs at Cascade Plaza
317 Banff Ave.
☎(403)762-8862
For anyone who has never tried Korean cuisine, here is a good chance to discover fine, deliciously prepared food. The staff will be happy to advise you in your selections.

Ticino
$$
5:30pm to 10:30pm
415 Banff Ave.
☎(403)762-3848
Ticino serves pretty good Italian cuisine as well as fondues. The decor is very ordinary, and the music tends to be too loud.

Caboose
$$$
every day 5pm to 10pm
corner of Elk St. and Lynx St.
☎(403)762-3622
☎(403)762-2102
Caboose is one of Banff's better eateries. The fish dishes, trout or salmon, are excellent, or you may prefer the lobster with steak, American style, or perhaps the crab. This place is a favourite with regular visitors.

 Le Beaujolais
$$$$
every day
212 Buffalo St.
☎(403)762-2712
Le Beaujolais prepares excellent French cuisine.

The dining room is very elegant and the staff is highly attentive. British Columbia salmon, baked with Pernod, is a true delicacy. The best food in Banff.

Lake Louise

 Moraine Lake Lodge
$$
every day
at the edge of Morraine Lake
☎ *(403)522-3733*
The Moraine Lake Lodge has a restaurant where you can enjoy good meals while contemplating the superb view over the lake and the Ten Peaks that stretch before your eyes.

Edelweiss Dining Room
$$$
every day
Chateau Lake Louise
☎ *(403)522-3511*
The Edelweiss Dining Room offers delicious French cuisine in very elegant surroundings with a view over the lake. Reservations are recommended.

Post Hotel
$$$
at the edge of the Pipestone River near the youth hostel
☎ *(403)522-3989*
Post Hotel houses an excellent restaurant recognized by the Relais et Châteaux association. Reservations are necessary, because this is one of the best dining rooms in Lake Louise. The setting of the hotel is enchanting.

Canmore

Nutter's
$
every day
900 Railway Ave.
☎ *(403)678-3335*
Nutter's is the best spot to find the fixings for sandwiches or other snacks for your back-country hikes. You will find a large selection of energizing or natural foods to take out, or you can eat in at the small tables near the windows.

Chez François
$$
adjacent to the Best Western Green Gables Inn
Hwy 1A
☎ *(403)678-6111*
Chez François is probably the best place to eat in Canmore. The chef, who comes from Québec, offers excellent French cuisine and a warm atmosphere in his restaurant.

Sinclairs
$$
every day
637 8th St.
☎ *(403)678-5370*
Sinclairs offers good food in a warm ambiance enhanced by a fireplace. Reservations are recommended in high season, when the restaurant is often full. The restaurant also offers an excellent selection of teas, a rarity around here.

The Icefields Parkway

The Crossing
$-$$
every day
at the junction of Hwys 93 and 11
80km from Lake Louise
☎ *(403)761-7000*
The Crossing houses a fairly large cafeteria with light meals where just about every traveller seems to stop. As a result, it is very crowded, with long line-ups.

Num-Ti-Jah Lodge
$-$$
every day
at the edge of Bow Lake
about 35km from Lake Louise
☎ *(403)522-2167*
The café at the Num-Ti-Jah Lodge serves sandwiches, muffins and cakes. You can warm up in this little café with tea or other hot beverages. This spot is popular with tourists and is often crowded.

Jasper National Park

Jasper

Coco's Café
$
every day
608 Patricia St.
☎ *(780)852-4550*
Coco's Café is a little spot that serves bagels, sandwiches and cheesecake.

Soft Rock Internet Cafe
$
633 Connaught Dr.
☎ *(780) 852-5850*
The Soft Rock Internet Cafe is much more than simply a place to send a few E-mails. It serves up enormous breakfasts all day long.

Jasper Inn Restaurant
$$
every day
Jasper Inn, 98 Geikie St.
☎ *(780) 852-3232*
Jasper Inn Restaurant serves up excellent fish and seafood. This is a very popular spot.

Tokyo Tom's Restaurant
$$
every day
410 Connaught Dr.
☎ *(780) 852-3780*
Tokyo Tom's Restaurant serves tasty Japanese food. The sukiyaki is excellent, but the gloomy decor is not.

 **Beauvert Dining Room**
$$$
every day
in Jasper Park Lodge
at the northern approach to Jasper
☎ *(780) 852-3301*
Beauvert Dining Room is a rather fancy restaurant. The French cuisine on offer is excellent. One of

the best restaurants in Jasper.

Outside Jasper

Pyramid Lake Resort
$
summer only, every day
at the edge of Pyramid Lake
5km from Jasper
take Pyramid Lake Rd. to Jasper
and follow the signs to Lake Patricia
and Pyramid Lake
☎*(780) 852-4900*
The restaurant of the Pyramid Lake Resort serves simple meals. The cuisine is good and unpretentious.

Hinton and Surroundings

Greentree Café
$
every day 5:30am to 11pm
in the Greentree Motor Lodge
☎*(780) 865-3321*
Greentree Café prepares delicious, copious breakfasts at unbeatable prices.

Ranchers
$
every day
in the Hill Shopping Centre
☎*(780) 865-4116*
A busy sopt, Ranchers prepares all sorts of pizzas.

Fireside Dining Room
$$
every day
in the Greentree Motor Lodge
☎*(780) 865-3321*
Fireside Dining Room is the best and most attractive restaurant in Hinton.

Overlander Mountain Lodge
$$$
every day
in the Overlander Mountain Lodge
2km past the toll booths
leaving Jasper National Park
heading toward Hinton
head left toward the hotel
☎*(780) 866-2330*
The Overlander Mountain Lodge's attractive restaurant serves excellent food. The menu changes daily, but if you have the oppor-

tunity, give in to temptation and savour the rainbow trout stuffed with crab and shrimp and covered with *béarnaise* sauce.

Kootenay and Yoho National Parks

Kootenay Park Lodge Restaurant
$
mid-May to late Sep
every day 8am to 10am
noon to 2pm and 6pm to
8:30pm
on Hwy 93 heading south
42 km from Castle Junction
☎*(403)762-9196*
Kootenay Park Lodge Restaurant offers light meals in simple surroundings. Isolated amidst grandiose scenery, you may want to finish your meal with a stroll through the surrounding countryside.

Radium Hot Springs and Surroundings

Fairmont Hot Springs Resort
$$
every day
on Hwy. 93-95
near the Fairmont ski hill
☎*(250)345-6311*
The restaurant at the Fairmont Hot Springs Resort will satisfy the most demanding customers. Its healthy food is excellent, and the decor is pleasant.

Golden

Prestige Inn
$$
every day
1049 Trans-Canada Hwy
☎*(250)344-7661*
The restaurant at the Prestige Inn encompasses the best of traditional cuisine in Golden.

Kananaskis Country

Chief Chiniki
$
every day
on Hwy 21, at Morley
☎*(403)881-3748*
Chief Chiniki offers typical North American dishes at reasonable prices. The staff is very friendly and attentive.

Mount Engadine Lodge
$$
Spray Lakes Rd.
☎*(403)678-2880*
Mount Engadine Lodge offers an interesting table d'hôte. The European-style cuisine is delicious.

L'Escapade
$$$
in the Hotel Kananaskis
☎*(403)591-7711*
L'Escapade is the hotel's French restaurant. Attractively decorated with red carpeting, comfortable armchairs and bay windows, this spot exudes warmth, all the better to linger over the excellent cuisine.

Entertainment

Bars and Danceclubs

Banff National Park

Banff

Rose and Crown
202 Banff Ave.
☎*(403)762-2121*
The Rose and Crown combines the western motif with classic English pub decor. There is a dance floor, and live bands often play here. You can also try your hand at a game of darts or pool.

Wild Bill's Legendary Saloon

upstairs at 201 Banff Ave.

☎(403)762-0333

If you prefer kicking up your heels in a real "western" setting, pull on your jeans and cowboy boots, grab your Stetson and saddle up for Wild Bill's Legendary Saloon. With a bit of luck, a friendly cowboy/girl may just show you how to dance the two-step.

The Buffalo Paddock Lounge and Pub

124 Banff Ave.

☎(403)762-3331

The Buffalo Paddock Lounge and Pub is a huge, slightly noisy bar in the basement of the Mount Royal Hotel.

Lake Louise

Charlie Two's Pub

Village Rd.

☎(403) 522-3791

The charming little Charlie Two's Pub is located in the Lake Louise Inn. This is a pleasant spot to have a drink and listen to some music. Simple dishes are also served.

Glacier Saloon

Chateau Lake Louise

☎(403)522-3511

The Glacier Saloon generally attracts a young, dancing crowd.

Jasper National Park

Jasper

Nick's Bar

Juniper St. between Connaught Dr. and Geikie St.

☎(780) 852-4966

Nick's Bar shows acrobatic skiing movies on a large screen – the stuff of dreams for those who wish they could tear down the slopes on two skis. A few light dishes are also served here. A pianist provides the musical entertainment some evenings.

Buckles Saloon

at the west end of Connaught Dr.

☎(780) 852-7074

Country music fans can do some two-stepping at Buckles Saloon. The decor is in keeping with Canada's wild west. You can dine on beer, hamburgers and sandwiches.

Shopping

Banff National Park

Banff

Banff's main drag is lined with souvenir shops, sports stores and clothing stores of all kinds. When it comes to shopping, the landscape is dotted with jewellery, souvenirs, essentials, sporting goods and T-shirts.

The **Hudson's Bay Company** *(125 Banff Ave.,* ☎*403-762-5525)* is owned by the oldest clothing manufacturer in Canada, established in 1670, and still sells clothes, souvenirs, cosmetics and much more.

The Shirt Company *(200 Banff Ave.,* ☎*403-762-2624)*, as its name suggest, sells T-shirts for all tastes and sizes.

Monod Sports *(129 Banff Ave.,* ☎*403-762-4571)* is the place for all of your outdoor needs. You'll find a good selection of hiking boots, all sorts of camping accessories as well as clothing.

The **Chocolaterie Bernard Callebaut** *(Charles Reid Mall, 127 Banff Ave.)* is a favourite of Belgian chocolate lovers.

The truffles are excellent.

The **Wine Store** *(in the basement of 302 Caribou St.,* ☎*403-762-3528)* is the place *par excellence* for a good bottle of wine.

Lake Louise and Surroundings

Moraine Lake Trading *(Moraine Lake Lodge,* ☎*403-522-3733)* is a small boutique where you'll find pieces of Aboriginal artwork.

Woodruff and Blum Booksellers *(Samson Mall, Lake Louise,* ☎*403-522-3842,* ⧉*522-2536)* has an excellent selection of both souvenir photography books and practical books on hiking trails in the region, rock-climbing, fishing and canoeing. It also sells postcards, compact discs, posters and topographical maps.

Jasper National Park

Jasper

Maligne Lake Books *(Beauvert Promenade, Jasper Park Lodge,* ☎*780-852-4779)* sells beautiful books of photography, newspapers and novels.

Exposures Keith Allen Photography *(Building 54, Stan Wright Industrial Park,* ☎*780-852-5325)* does custom framing and has a large stock of black-and-white and colour photographs of the area dating from the 1940s on, including unedited shots of Marilyn Monroe from the making of *River of No Return,* which was filmed in Jasper.

The Liquor Hut *(Patricia St. and Hazel Ave.,* ☎ *780-852-3152)* stocks a fine selection of wines and spirits.

Surroundings of Jasper

The **Sunwapta Falls Resort Gift Shop** *(53km south of Jasper, on the Icefields Parkway,* ☎ *780-852-4852)* sells Aboriginal artwork like blankets, moccasins and soapstone carvings. The jewellery section of the boutique includes jade, lapis-lazuli and "ammolite" pieces.

British Columbia

The sons of the French explorer La Vérendrye did not set eyes on the Rocky Mountains until the end of the 18th century, and England's George Vancouver only explored the Pacific coast and Columbia River in the last decade of the same century.

Carved out by countless fjords and dotted with hundreds of islands, British Columbia's jagged coastline is 7,000km long, not counting the shores of the islands. The largest of these is Vancouver Island, about the size of the Netherlands and home to the provincial capital, Victoria. Despite its name, the city of Vancouver is not on the island but rather lies across the Strait of Juan de Fuca, on the mainland. The Queen Charlotte Islands lie to the north. The maritime nature of the province is foremost in many minds, but in actuality three quarters of the province lie an average of more than 930m above sea level, and a 3,000m-high barrier of mountains is visible from the coast. A succession of mountain ranges stretches from west to east, all the way to the famous Rocky Mountains, whose summits reach up to 4,000m. This chain was named for its bare, rocky eastern slopes.

Despite the limited extent of the plains in British Columbia, 60% of the province's territory is covered by forest. The forest growing along the coast, on the Queen Charlotte Islands and on the west coast of Vancouver Island is so lush that it is referred to as temperate rain forest, the counterpart of the tropical rain forest. Douglas firs and western red cedars abound, as does the Sitka spruce. The Douglas fir can grow to up to 90m in height and 4.5m in diameter. This forest receives up to 4,000mm of rain per year and many of its trees are more than 1,000 years old, though most of the ancient Douglas firs were cut down in the last century. Much higher and drier, the province's interior is home to vast pine, spruce and hemlock forests.

Warmed by the Japanese current, the waters of the Pacific maintain a higher temperature than those of the Atlantic, which are cooled by the Labrador current. As a result, this region features very distinctive marine life, such as sea otters and sea lions.

British Columbia

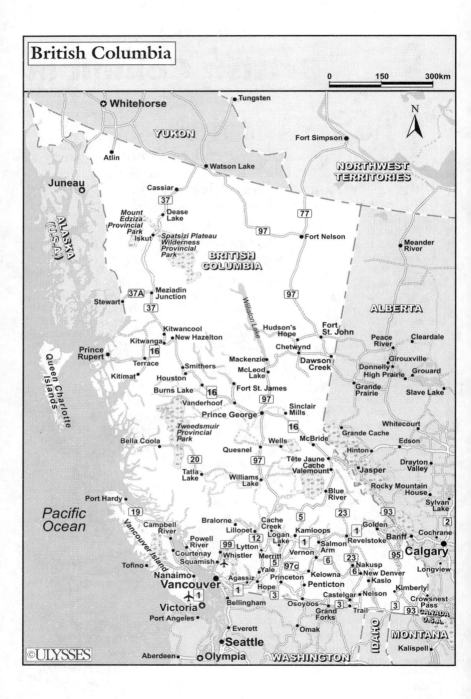

©ULYSSES

Southern British Columbia

This region, bordering the United States, is characterized by a blend of the urban and the undeveloped.

The Vancouver area, for example, resembles a big American city, though it is set against a backdrop of green mountains and blue sea. Here, you will find both wilderness and civilization.

The Okanagan Valley is home to countless orchards and some of the best wineries in the province. As one majestic landscape succeeds another, your eyes will be dazzled by the sea, the everlasting snows and the spring colours that appear very early in this region.

Communing with nature is a memorable experience of any trip in southern British Columbia. The waters that wash the deserted beaches beckon you to relax and let your mind wander. Stately trees stand guard over tranquil areas untouched by the forestry industry. Dotted with national and provincial parks, which lie stretched across the loveliest parts of the province, this region has an ex-

tremely varied landscape, with everything from perpetual snows and desert valleys to rivers teeming with fish.

Finding Your Way Around

By Car

Every highway in southern British Columbia is more spectacular than the last. One of these is the Trans-Canada which runs east-west across mountains, rivers, canyons and desert valleys.

Although the traffic is always fairly heavy, the Trans-Canada, provides an easy route eastward out of Vancouver, . The road leads to Calgary, running along the Fraser River, the Thompson River and Lake Shuswap at different points along the way. Another option is to take Highway 7 (the continuation of Broadway Ave.) out of downtown Vancouver along the north bank of the Fraser River. If you're pressed for time, you can take the newly opened Coquihalla Highway that runs between Hope and Kamloops. This is a toll highway, the only one in the province.

What's more, it is not as attractive as the others.

The spectacular Sea to Sky Highway (99) will take you up into northern British Columbia. Simply cross the Lions Gate Bridge and follow the signs for Whistler and Squamish.

By Ferry

To reach the Sunshine Coast, you must take a ferry from the coast or Vancouver Island.

BC Ferries
1112 Fort St.
Victoria, V8V 4V2
Victoria:
☎*(250) 386-3431*
☎*(888) 223-3779*
from Saltery Bay:
☎*487-9333*
Powell River:
☎*485-2943*

Practical Information

Area Code: **604** in the **Lower Mainland** (*Vancouver and suburbs*), **250** in the **rest of the province** (*north of Whistler, east of Hope, the islands*)

Tourist Information

Tourism Association of Southwestern B.C.
204-1755 West Broadway, Vancouver, BC V6J 4S5
☎*(604) 739-9011*
☎*(800) 667-3306*

Whistler Travel InfoCentre
2097 Lake Placid Rd.
☎*(604) 932-5528*

High Country Tourism Association
1-1490 Pearson Pl., BC V1S 1J9
☎*(250) 372-7770*
☎*(800) 567-2275*   ι

Kootenay Country Tourist Association
610 Railway St., Nelson, BC V1L 1H4
☎*(250) 352-6033*

Exploring

★★

The Sunshine Coast

Most people get to the Sunshine Coast by boat. There are no roads linking Vancouver to these resort towns. The daily comings and goings are dictated by the ferry schedule. As a result, the mentality here is completely different. The towns that have grown up along this coast benefit from the sea and what it yields. The Sunshine Coast runs along the Strait of Georgia, and is surrounded by Desolation Sound to the north, the Coast Mountains to the east and Howe Sound further south.

Langdale

It takes 40min to reach Langdale, a small port city at the southern tip of the Sunshine Coast. Ferries shuttle back and forth several times a day, but you have to arrive at the Horseshoe Bay terminal at least an hour early for some weekend departures. **Horseshoe Bay** lies 20km northwest of Vancouver. With **BC Ferries** (*information: 7am to 10pm*; **Vancouver**: ☎*888-223-3779*; **Victoria**: ☎*250-386-3431*), you can save up to 15% on the

price of your ticket if you return by way of Vancouver Island instead of opting for a round-trip. Ask for the Sunshine Coast Circlepac.

★

Gibsons

Visitors to Gibsons are sure to recognize the site of *The Beachcombers*, a Canadian Broadcasting Corporation (CBC) television series that was shot here for close to 20 years and broadcast in over 40 countries. On the way from Langdale to Gibsons, stop off at **Molly's Reach** to take a look at the photographs of the actors from the popular television show and to explore the little shops and restaurants along **Molly's Lane ★**. Gibsons, more recently, became Castle Rock for the film *Needful Things*, based on a Steven King novel.

A visit to the **Sunshine Coast Maritime Museum ★** (*at the end of Molly's Lane*, ☎*886-4114*) is a must. You will be greeted by a charming woman who will inspire you with her passion for the local marine life.

The Sunshine Coast has been developed in a thin strip alongside the forest. The area abounds in plant and animal life — orchids and wild roses, deer and black bears. River otters and beavers can be found near the coast while sealions and seals swim about further offshore.

★

Powell River

Powell River, an important waterfront town, boasts magnificent sunsets over Vancouver Island and the

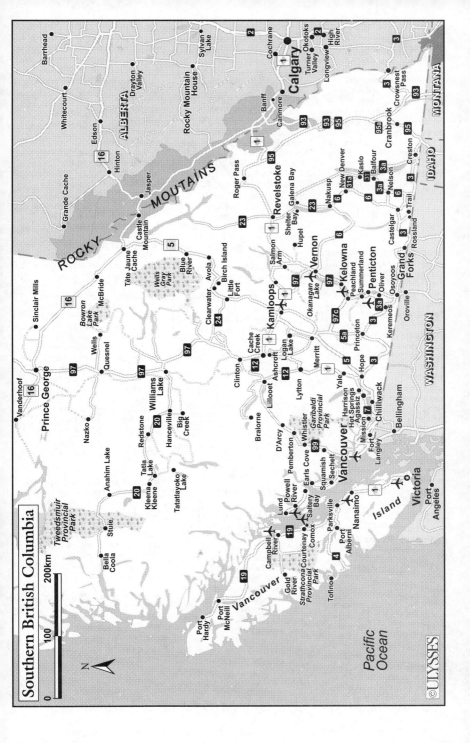

Southern British Columbia

islands in the Strait of Georgia. The spotlight is on outdoor activities in this region since the temperate climate is conducive to year-round fun and games. Forestry plays an important role in the local economy, but visitors come here for the lakes, the woods, the wildlife and the views.

★★
Lund

Lund, located at the beginning (or the end, depending on which direction you're heading) of Highway 101, is the gateway to marvellous **Desolation Sound ★★**, a marine life sanctuary easily accessible by canoe or kayak. The town port is magnificent with its old hotel, its adjoining shops and its wooden promenade, which skirts round the bay. Imagine a typical fishing village and your harbour will undoubtedly be filled with the fishing boats moored here. In terms of activities, there is much to choose from here from fishing and whale-watching trips to snorkelling and kayaking.

Fraser River Loop

Squamish

Located at the north end of Howe Sound, Squamish owes its existence to the forest industry that still helps support the local economy. You can see the forestry workers in action in the woods, at the sawmill or in the sorting yard where gigantic machines put blocks of wood in place. At the entrance from Squamish, you'll be intrigued by the big, black

rock face known as The Wall that descends steeply to the edge of the road. If you like rock climbing, you can tackle it with a guide. The **Soo Coalition for Sustainable Forests ★** *(4hr walk in the woods $30; dryland sort tour, $14 for two people; mill tour $14 for two people with own car, $24 without car; reservations required;* ☎*604-892-9766)* is an organization that works toward preserving both the forest and the jobs related to the industry. It arranges tours of the forest and the lumber yard to educate the public on this subject.

The historic **Royal Hudson Steam Train** *($45 round-trip; Jun to Sep, Wed to Sun; 10am departure from North Vancouver; 1311 W. First St.; it is also possible to come back by boat; for $78;* ☎*604-688-7246 or 800-663-8238)* runs between North Vancouver and Squamish, following the coastline and offering unimpeded views of the island and of the snow-capped peaks of the Coast Mountains.

★★
Whistler

Whistler has grown and become an important location not only for people who live there on a permanent basis, but also for the development of tourism. Besides the big hotels, more and more condominiums are being built and stores have multiplied. To allow visitors to get around more easily, a shuttle service around the village has been set up. Of course, the shops are mostly geared towards tourists but many are also for residents. There are shopping centres and large grocery stores. This encourages people to buy condos as secondary residences which benefits Whistler's economy.

Whistler attracts skiers, golfers, hikers, sailors and snowboarders from all over the world. An impressive hotel complex graces the little village at the foot of Blackcomb and Whistler mountains. Other amenities at this internationally renowned resort include restaurants, shops, sports facilities and a convention centre. Whistler is popular in summer and winter alike with each season offering its own assortment of activities.

In the early 1960s, a group of adventurers wanted this area to host the 1968 Winter Olympics and created Garibaldi Park for that purpose. Although their hopes for the Olympics did not come through, they did not give up on the idea of turning the valley into a huge ski resort. The population of Whistler increased tenfold in 20 years, and in the year 1993 alone over a million people enjoyed the outdoors here.

Whistler receives, on average, nearly 1000cm of snow each year, and the temperature hovers around -5°C during the winter months. For details about the host of activities available here, refer to the "Outdoor Activities" section (see p 597).

Whistler hosts all sorts of events throughout the year, including a men's World Cup downhill competition, World Cup acrobatic skiing, gay skiers' week and a jazz festival.

Take the time to walk through the hotel village at the foot of the mountains and soak up the festive, relaxed atmosphere. Everything has its price here, and enjoying yourself can be quite expensive.

Outside of the little village, at the edge of the Whistler area, lies Function Junction, a small-scale industrial centre.

Yale

Three major historical events contributed to the development of Yale: the growth of the fur trade, the gold rush and the construction of the railway. The town also marks the beginning of the Fraser Canyon, so buckle your seatbelts and keep your eyes wide open.

The **Alexandria Bridge** spans the Fraser at a striking point along the river that's only accessible by foot. The bridge is no longer part of the road system, but you can enjoy some splendid views of the Fraser from its promenade. A sign alongside the Trans-Canada Highway shows the way.

Hell's Gate ★ (*$10;* ☎*604-867-9277*) owes its name to Simon Fraser, the first European to navigate this river. For a while, even the salmon had trouble making their way through this gorge that had narrowed as a result of major landslides. The current was so strong that the fish couldn't swim upriver to spawn. To solve the problem, a pass was cleared. A cablecar will take you down to the water's edge, 152m below.

★
Hope

Hope, located at the confluence of the Coquihalla, Fraser and Nicolum Rivers, marks the gateway to the Fraser Canyon. The Hud-

son's Bay Company established a fur-trading post named Fort Hope on this site in 1848. 10 years later, prospectors lured by the discovery of gold would stock up on supplies here.

★
Harrison Hot Springs

The Harrison Hot Springs are located at the southern end of Harrison Lake. The Coast Salish First Nation used to come to here to soak in the warm mineral water that supposedly has curative powers. Gold prospectors discovered the springs in 1858. When a storm on Lake Harrison forced them to return to shore they happened to step into the warm water. The lake is surrounded by successive mountains peaks that stand out against the sky, making for a spectacular setting.

The indoor **Harrison Hot Springs Public Pool ★** (*$8.50; May to Nov, every day 8am to 9pm; Dec to Apr, Sun to Thu 8am to 9pm, Fri and Sat 8am to 10pm; at the intersection of Hot Springs Rd. and Lilloet Ave.,* ☎*604-796-2244*) offers access to the springs. In addition to running the public pool, the Harrison Hotel has acquired rights to the springs. Every year in September and October, sand-castle enthusiasts flock to the beaches on Harrison Lake with impressive results. The road, which runs alongside the lake, leads to Sasquatch Provincial Park.

Mission Xa:ytem Long House Interpretive Centre (*3km east of Mission; donations welcomed,* ☎*820-9725*). This First Nations archaeological site was discovered in 1990. Xa:ytem (pronounced

HAY-tum) is an Aboriginal word designating a boulder on a plateau on the Fraser River. According to geologists, the rock was deposited there by shifting glaciers. The Sto:lo First Nation, who have inhabited this region for more than 4,000 years, explain the boulder's presence by saying that it is what became of three chiefs who had committed a sin. Hundreds of relics have been found in this area, including tools and weapons made of stone. These articles are displayed in the centre which has Sto:lo guides.

Fort Langley

Fort Langley National Historic Site ★ (*$5; every day 10am to 5pm; Exit 66 North of the Trans-Canada, towards Fort Langley, at the intersection of Mavis and Royal Sts.;* ☎*888-4424*). Fort Langley was erected in 1827, 4km downriver from its present location on the south bank of the Fraser. It was moved in 1839 only to be ravaged by fire the following year. The Hudson's Bay Company used the fort to store furs that were shipped out to Europe.

The Thompson River as far as Revelstoke

Ashcroft

Ashcroft lies a few kilometres east of Highway 1. In 1860, gold prospectors heading north set out from here. You can go back to the Trans-Canada 1 East and make your way to Kamloops, passing through Cache Creek on the way in order to skirt Kamloops Lake and see the ginseng fields (see below). We recommend taking Highway 97C to Logan Lake and the Copper Valley mine. As you make your way through a magnificent desert valley, you'll see the Sundance Guest Ranch (see p 601 for details on staying there) that looks out over the Thompson River. Ever since the 1950s, this ranch has been sending visitors off on horseback rides across thousands of hectares of fields. Like most ranches in the region, it was once the home of stockbreeders.

Copper Valley ★★ (*May to Sep Mon to Fri 9:30am and 12:30pm, Sat and Sun 9:30am, 12:30pm and 3:30pm; tours last 2hrs 30min; ☎250-523-2443*). Copper Valley is one of the largest open-cut copper mines in the world. The industrial machinery and the equipment used to transport the ore are gigantic. Though you can't tour the mine, you'll notice its lunar landscape from the highway.

Kamloops

Kamloops (pop. 68,500), the capital of inland British Columbia, is a major stopover point. The local economy is driven chiefly by the forestry and tourism industries with mining and stock-breeding playing subsidiary roles.

West of Kamloops, ginseng crops lie hidden in fields beneath big pieces of black cloth. Large farms produce this root, which is highly coveted by Asians for the health benefits it is supposed to procure. The variety grown here, known as American ginseng, was discovered in eastern Canada several hundred years ago by Aboriginal people who made potions

with it. At the **Sunmore Company** (*925 McGill Place, ☎250-374-3017*), you can drop in and learn about ginseng farming in North America and how local methods differ from those employed in Asia.

Another activity that underlines the importance of the rivers in British Columbia is a cruise aboard the *Wanda-Sue* that sails along the Thompson River through bare mountains. Aboriginals, trappers, gold prospectors, lumberjacks and railway workers all travelled by boat before the railway lines and roads were laid here. The **Wanda-Sue** ★ sets out from the Old Kamloops Yacht Club (*$11.50; Apr to Sep; the trip lasts 2hrs; 1140 River St., near Tenth Ave., ☎250-374-7447*).

★★
Revelstoke

The history of Revelstoke is closely linked to the construction of the transcontinental railway. Many Italians came here to apply their expertise in building tunnels. To this day, the town's 9,000 residents rely mainly on the railroad for their income. Tourism and the production of electricity also play important roles in the economy of this magnificent town.

Revelstoke is a century-old town that has managed to retain its charm. Numerous Queen Anne, Victorian, Art Deco and neoclassical buildings here bear witness to days gone by. Pick up a copy of the **Heritage Walking & Driving Tour** ★ at the Revelstoke Museum (see below) or at the **Travel InfoCentre** (*204 Campbell Ave., ☎250-837-5345*).

The **Revelstoke Railway Museum** ★ (*$7; Jul and Aug every day 9am to 8pm; Dec to Mar by appt.; call ahead for spring and autumn hours; 719 Track St., ☎250-837-6060*) focuses on the construction of the railway across the Rockies and the history of Revelstoke. The exhibit features old objects, photos from the local archives and, most importantly, a 1940s locomotive and a company director's personal railway car, built in 1929.

At the **Revelstoke Dam** ★ (*free admission; May to Jun 9am to 5pm; Jun to Sep 8am to 8pm; Sep and Oct 9am to 5pm; closed Nov to May although group visits are permitted during the low season; take Hwy. 23 North, ☎250-837-6211*), you can learn about the production of hydroelectricity and visit a number of rooms, as well as the dam itself, an impressive concrete structure.

Revelstoke is a crossroads between the Rockies and the Kootenays, to the south. If you plan on continuing east to Alberta, stay on the Trans-Canada to Golden, Field and Lake Louise (see The Rocky Mountains, p 557). We recommend driving down into the Kootenays that are lesser known than the Rockies, but equally fascinating. Before heading south, however, continue until you reach **Rogers Pass** ★★, named after the engineer who discovered it in 1881. This valley was originally supposed to serve as a passage between the east and the west. But after a number of catastrophes, during which avalanches claimed the lives of hundreds of people, the Canadian Pacific railway company decided to build a tunnel instead. At the **Rogers Pass Centre ★** (☎ *250-814-5233*), located an hour from Revelstoke in Glacier National Park, visitors can learn about the epic history of the railway. A trail that runs along the former tracks will take you past the ruins of a railway station destroyed in an avalanche.

Okanagan-Similkameen

All sorts of natural treasures await discovery in this part of British Columbia. With its stretches of water and blanket of fruit trees, the Okanagan Valley, which runs north-south, is one of the most beautiful areas in the province. Okanagan wines have won a number of prizes. The orchards feed a good portion of the country, and the lakes and mountains are a dream come true for sporty types. The climate is conducive to a wide variety of activities: the winters, mild in town and snowy in the mountains, can be enjoyed by all. In the spring, the fruit trees are in bloom, while in summer and fall, a day of fruit-picking is often followed by a dip in one of the many lakes.

Princeton

American researchers come to the **Princeton Museum and Archives ★** (*Jul and Aug, every day 9am to 6pm; Sep to Jun, Mon to Fri 1pm to 5pm; Margaret Stoneberg, curator,* ☎ *295-7588, home* ☎ *295-3362*) to study its impressive collection of fossils. You'll get caught up in curator Margaret Stoneberg's enthusiasm as

she tells you about the pieces and how they bear witness to the region's history. Due to underfunding, the fossils pile up without being properly displayed, but it is nevertheless amazing to see how much the museum holds.

The **Maverick Cattle Drives Ltd.** (*$125, reservations required; lunch, morning and afternoon outings, cattle driving;* ☎ *250-295-6243 or 295-3753*) welcomes visitors who want to experience life on a ranch. You'll find yourself on the back of a horse, riding in the warm summer breeze across fields of wheat, taking in the view of the nearby glaciers. This wonderful experience also involves carrying out a number of tasks on the ranch. At the end of the day, all the cowboys get together at the saloon.

Osoyoos

Osoyoos lies at the bottom of the valley, flanked on one side by Osoyoos Lake and on the other by verdant slopes decked with vineyards and orchards. It is located a few kilometres from the U.S. border in an arid climate more reminiscent of an American desert, or even southern Italy, than a Canadian town. The main attraction here is the exceptionally warm lake, where you can enjoy a variety of water sports during summer.

★★★
The Wine Route

The wine route runs through the vast Okanagan region. North of Osoyoos and south of Oliver, you'll come across the **Domaine Combret ★** (*32057-131st Rd. 13, Oliver,* ☎ *250-498-8878,*

☎ *498-8879*). In 1995, the *Office International de la Vigne et du Vin*, based in Burgundy, France, awarded this French-owned vineyard the highest international distinction for its Chardonnay. Its Reisling also won a prize in 1995. You must call beforehand for a tour of the premises since the wine growers spend a good part of the day outside among the vines during the grape-picking season. Originally from the south of France, the Combrets come from a long line of vinters. Robert Combret first visited the Okanagan Valley in the 1950s, returning in the early 1990s. His son Olivier runs the family business now. Stop by and enjoy a sample some of his wine.

★
Penticton

Penticton lies between Okanagan Lake to the north and Skaha Lake to the south. The town has nearly 30,000 inhabitants and boasts a dry, temperate climate. Tourism is the mainspring of Penticton's economy. The area's First Nations named the site *Pen-tak-tin*, meaning "the place where you stay forever." A beach lined with trees and a pedestrian walkway run along the north end of town. The dry landscape, outlined by the curves of the sandy shoreline, contrasts with the vineyards and orchards. People come to Penticton for the outdoor activities, fine dining and local *joie de vivre*.

A visit to an orchard is a must, especially in the heart of summer during the fruit-picking season. Not only is the fruit plentiful, but more importantly

British Columbia

it's delicious. From July to late September, the region is covered with fruit trees bursting with scent and colour. The **Dickinson Family Farm** (*turn left onto Jones Flat Rd. from Hwy. 97 North, then right onto Bentley Rd. 19208,* ☎*250-494-0300*) invites visitors to stroll through its rows of fruit trees. You can purchase fruit (such as apples and pears) and fruit-based products on the premises. For a real treat, try the peach butter and the freshly pressed apple juice. Head out of Penticton on Lakeshore Drive and take the 97 North toward Summerland.

An outing in the mountains along the former route of the **Kettle Valley Railway ★★** offers another perspective of the Okanagan Valley. Laid at the turn of the century, these tracks connected Nelson in the east to Hope in the west, thus providing a link between the hinterland where tonnes of ore were being extracted, and the coast. Mother Nature was a major obstacle throughout the railway's short existence. Fallen debris, avalanches and snowstorms made the tracks impossible to use, and the line was abandoned. The $20 million cost of building the railway was never recovered.

You can follow the tracks on foot or by bicycle. The railway runs through Penticton on either shore of Okanagan Lake, and the terrain is relatively flat, making for a pleasant outing. The directions, however, are not very clear. Start on Main Street in downtown Penticton, and follow the signs for Naramata Road, then turn right onto MacMillan. At this point, the signs seem

to disappear but take the main road; as soon as its name becomes Chute Lake. Keep right and then turn right again on Smethurst Road and keep going until you reach the end. You can either leave your car in town or drive the first 6km (at your own risk) – pedestrians and cyclists have priority. You'll enjoy a direct view of Okanagan Lake along the way.

After 4.8km, you'll pass through a small tunnel. Make noise as you walk to drive off any rattlesnakes, black bears or cougars. On the west shore, in Summerland, a part of the track is now used by a steam engine. Head toward Summer-land on Highway 97 North, turn left on Solly Road and follow the signs for the **West Summerland Station of the Kettle Valley Steam Railway** (*May to Oct;* ☎*250-494-8422,* ⇌*494-8452*). Maps for both areas are available at the Penticton tourist office on Lakeshore Drive.

★
Kelowna

Kelowna is the heart and mind of the Okanagan Valley. It was here that a French Oblate by the name of Father Charles Pandosy set up the first Catholic mission in the hinterland of British Columbia in 1859. He introduced apple and grape growing into the Okanagan Valley and was thus largely responsible for its becoming a major fruit-producing region.

The **Father Pandosy Mission** (*May to early Oct, every day; on Benvoulin Rd., at the corner of Casorso Rd.,* ☎*250-860-8369*), which has been listed as a provincial his-

toric site since 1983, includes a church and a number of farm buildings.

Located on the shores of Okanagan Lake, Kelowna boasts several waterfront parks. One of these is **Knox Mountain Park** where you'll find a magnificent viewing area. You might even catch a glimpse of Ogopogo. To get to the park, take Ellis Street north out of downtown.

It takes about 20min to reach the first metal bridge that stretches across the **Myra Canyon ★★**. If you enjoy walking, you'll love this excursion. The local **Chamber of Commerce** (*544 Harvey Ave.,* ☎*861-1515*) or the **Okanagan-Similkameen Tourism Association** (*1332 Water St.,* ☎*860-5999*) can help you plan outings that take several days. Cyclists can pedal about to their heart's content while the more adventurous can spend a day riding to Penticton.

Almost all the wine produced in British Columbia comes from the Okanagan region (see The Wine Route, p 593). Over the past few years, local wines have won a number of international prizes. There are three vineyards along Lakeshore Road, south of Kelowna, including the **Cedar Creek Winery** (*5445 Lakeshore Rd.,* ☎*250-764-8866,* ⇌*250-764-2603*). Like its competitors in the region, it produces much more white wine than red. It is located on a pretty hill surrounded by vines and looking out onto Okanagan Lake. A free tour of the premises will give you a chance to sample some of the wines – the chardonnay is particularly noteworthy. You can also purchase a few bottles while you're there.

Vernon

Get back on the 97 North and continue on to Vernon which is set amidst three lakes. The town started out modestly in the 1860s, when Cornelius O'Keefe established a ranch here. The northern part of Vernon is an important stockbreeding area. Stop by the **Historic O'Keefe Ranch** (*every day May to Oct; 12km north of Vernon on Hwy. 97, ☎250-542-7868*) where you'll find the original ranch house, wooden church and ranching equipment. Forestry and agriculture play greater economic roles here than in Kelowna and Penticton where tourism is more important.

Kootenay Country

Located off the beaten tourist track, this region is a gold mine for visitors with a taste for mountains, lakes, history and chance encounters. Once again, the landscape is one of the major attractions – this is British Columbia, after all! Because this region is underappreciated, it remains virtually unspoiled, making it that much more interesting to explore.

Located in the southeast part of the province, the Kootenays are a series of mountains (the Rockies, the Purcells, the Selkirks and the Monashees) stretching from the north to the south. The great Columbia River runs through this region, creating the vast body of water known as Arrow Lake on its way. Natural resources such as forests and mines

have played a major role in the region's development. A number of towns bear witness to the different stages in the Kootenays' history.

New Denver

New Denver was the gateway to silver country at the turn of the century when there was an abundant supply of the metal in this region. The history of that era is presented at the **Silvery Slocan Museum** (*Jul to Sep, every day 10am to 4pm; at the corner of Sixth St. and Marine Dr., ☎250-358-2201*). When Canada declared war on Japan during the Second World War, Japanese residents of British Columbia were interned in camps in a number of towns in this region, including New Denver and Sandon. To learn more about their experience, stop in at the **Nikkei Internment Memorial Centre** (*$4; May to Oct, every day 9:30am to 5pm; by appt. during winter; 306 Josephine St., ☎250-358-7288*).

★★
Sandon

At the turn of the century, 5,000 people lived and worked in Sandon. By 1930, the price of silver had dropped and the mine had been exhausted, prompting an exodus from the town. During World War II, Sandon became an internment centre for Japanese who had been living on the coast. Shortly after the war, it became a ghost town once again, and a number of buildings were destroyed by fire and floods. Today, visitors can admire what remains of a number of old buildings as well as the first hydroelectric power plant constructed in the Canadian

West which still produces electricity.

Kaslo

Kaslo was built on the hills on the west shore of Kootenay Lake during the heyday of silver mining. A walk along the waterfront and a visit to the town hall will give you a glimpse of how beautiful the setting is. At the beginning of the century, people used to come here by paddle-boat. For nearly 60 years, until 1957, the SS Moyie shuttled passengers back and forth across Kootenay Lake for Canadian Pacific. The boat has since been transformed into a museum.

At **Ainsworth Hot Springs** ★ (*$6; swimsuit and towel rentals available; ☎229-4212*), which is located in an enchanting setting along the shore to the south, bathers can alternate between very cold and very warm water. The swimming pool overlooks Kootenay Lake and the valley is brilliant at sunset. The U-shaped cave studded with stalactites, the humidity and the almost total absence of light will transport you to another world. The temperature rises as you near the springs at the back of the cave, reaching as high as 40°C.

★★
Nelson

Make sure to park your car as soon as possible and explore this magnificent town on foot. Located at the southern end of the West Arm of Kootenay Lake, Nelson lies on the west flank of the Selkirk Mountains. In 1887, during the silver boom, miners set up camp here and worked together to build hotels, homes and public facilities. Numerous buildings now bear witness to the town's prosperous past. Nelson has managed to continue its economic growth today thanks to light industry, tourism and the civil service.

The Travel InfoCentre distributes two small pamphlets that will guide you through over 350 historic buildings. The town's elegant architecture makes walking about here a real pleasure. Classical, Queen Anne and Victorian buildings proudly line the streets. The stained-glass windows of the **Nelson Congregational Church** ★ (*at the corner of Stanley and Silica Streets*), the Chateau-style **town hall** ★ (*502 Vernon St.*), the group of buildings on **Baker Street** and above all the Italian-style **fire station** ★ (*919 Ward St.*) are eloquent reminders of the opulence of the silver mining era.

Its lovely architecture is not the only thing that sets Nelson apart from other inland towns in British Columbia. You will also find a number of art galleries here, many of which are integrated into restaurants, so you can contemplate works of art while looking over the menu. This setup is known as the **Artwalk** which enables artists to exhibit their work in participating businesses each year. For further information, contact the **West Kootenay Regional Arts Council** (*☎250-352-2402*).

Castlegar

Castlegar, which lies at the confluence of the Columbia and Kootenay Rivers, has no downtown area. While crossing the bridge in the direction of the airport, you'll see a suspended bridge built by the Doukhobors. Turn left for a closer look.

Back on the highway, go uphill, then turn right to reach the **Doukhobor Museum** ★ (*$3; May to Sep every day 9am to 5pm, ☎250-365-6622*). Fleeing persecution in Russia, the Doukhobors emigrated to Canada in 1898. They wanted to live according to their own rules rather than those of the State. For example, they were against participation in any war. They established communities on the prairies and farmed the land, adhering to their traditional way of life and gradually developing towns and setting up industries. One group, led by Piotr Verigin, left the prairies for British Columbia and took up residence in the Castlegar area. After the economic crisis of 1929 and the death of Verigin, the community diminished. But their descendants have taken up the task of telling visitors about their ancestors.

★ Rossland

Rossland is a picturesque little turn-of-the-century town that thrived during the gold rush and has managed to retain its charm. Located inside the crater of a former volcano, at an altitude of 1,023m above sea level, it attracts skiers and people who simply enjoy being in the mountains. Nancy Greene Provincial Park, named after the 1968 Olympic ski champion and Rossland native, boasts several majestic peaks. Red Mountain, renowned for its high-quality powder, is a world-class resort. Skier Kerrin Lee-Gartner, who won a gold medal in the 1992 Olympic Games, is also from Rossland.

All of the gold was mined from this region long before these Olympic skiers arrived. In 1890, a prospector discovered a large vein of gold here. The news spread and hundreds of adventurers came to try their luck, resulting in a gold rush. Numerous hotels, offices and theatres were built, and Rossland flourished. Then came the crash of 1929 that the town hard. That same year, a major fire destroyed part of the downtown area.

Rossland was on the decline. When the famous **Le Roi** mine closed down, the future did not look bright. Visitors can learn about the history of the gold rush at the **Le Roi mine** ★ and the **Rossland Historical Museum** (*$10 for mine tour and museum, $5 for museum; mid-May to mid-Sep, every day 9am to 5pm; at the intersection of the 3B and the 22; take Columbia Ave. east of the downtown area, ☎250-362-7722*), which features an audiovisual presentation and a collection of objects from that era. The **Ski Hall of Fame**, located in the same building, highlights the careers of Nancy Greene and Kerrin Lee-Gartner.

Parks

The Sunshine Coast

Desolation Sound Marine Park ★★ (*north of Lund, accessible by boat; campsites, hiking, kayaking, swimming, fishing, scuba diving, potable water, toilets; B.C. Parks at*

Tenedos Bay, Sechelt Area Supervisor, ☎604-885-9019) is popular with ocean lovers who come here to observe the animal life inhabiting these warm waters. More and more people are coming here to go sea kayaking, something that even novices can enjoy.

Fraser River Loop

Vast **Garibaldi Provincial Park ★★** *(information Garibaldi/Sunshine District, Brackendale; 10km north of Squamish, ☎604-898-3678)*, which covers 195,000ha, is extremely popular with hikers during summertime. Highway 99 runs along the west side of the park, offering access to the various trails.

The Thompson River as Far as Revelstoke

You can explore the woods on scores of paths in **Mount Revelstoke ★★** and **Glacier ★★ National Parks** *(for maps, information and regulations, contact Parks Canada in Revelstoke, ☎250- 837-7500)*. The level of difficulty varies. Some trails run past centuries-old trees or lead to the tops of mountains, affording splendid panoramic views.

Okanagan-Similkameen

Manning Provincial Park ★★ *(tourist information: summer, every day 8:30am to 4:30pm; winter, Mon to Fri 8:30am to 4:30pm; ☎250-840-8836)* is located on the boundary of the southwestern part of the province and the huge Oka-nagan-Similkameen region. It lies 225km from Vancouver, making it a popular get-

away for city-dwellers in search of vast green spaces.

Cathedral Provincial Park ★★ *(No dogs, no mountain bikes; for detailed maps and information, contact the BC Parks District Manager, Box 399, Summerland, B.C. V0H 1Z0, ☎250- 494-6500)* is located 30km southwest of Keremeos, in the southern part of the province, right alongside the U.S. border. There are two distinct kinds of vegetation here – the temperate forest and the plant growth characteristic of the arid Okanagan region. At low altitudes, Douglas firs dominate the landscape, giving way to spruce and heather higher up. Deer, mountain goats and wild sheep sometimes venture out near the turquoise-coloured lakes.

Kootenay Country

Kokanee Glacier Provincial Park ★★ *(contact the BC Parks Kootenay District Area Office for maps; Nelson, ☎250-825-3500)* has about 10 hiking trails of average difficulty that require a total of about 4hrs of walking. The park, which looks out over two lakes (Kootenay and Slocan), is accessible from a number of different places.

This is also the park where Michel Trudeau, the youngest son of former Canadian Prime Minister, Pierre Trudeau, drowned during a skiing excursion on November 13, 1998. Michel Trudeau, an experienced skier and guide, was swept 40m into Lake Kootenay by an avalanche.

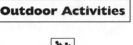

Outdoor Activities

Hiking

The Sunshine Coast

Inland Lake Park, located 12km north of Powell River, has been specially designed to enable people in wheelchairs to enjoy nature. The lake is 13km in circumference. Campsites have been laid out, and a few log houses are reserved for people with limited mobility. The picnic tables and swimming docks have been built with wheelchair-users in mind. The premier of British Columbia awarded the forest ministry a medal for the layout of this park.

Fraser River Loop

Except for the built-up area around Whistler, **Garibaldi Provincial Park** *(information Garibaldi/Sunshine District, Brackendale; 10km north of Squamish, ☎604-898-3678)* is a huge stretch of untouched wilderness. Hiking here is a magical experience, especially when you reach Garibaldi Lake whose turquoise waters contrast with the blue of the glacier in the back-

British Columbia

ground. The trails cover long distances, so you have to bring along food as well as clothing for different temperatures.

A series of hiking trails runs all the way up **Whistler Mountain** (☎604-932-3434) and **Blackcomb Mountain** (☎604-932-3141). From atop Whistler, you can see Black Tusk, a black sugarloaf 2315m high.

The Thompson River as Far as Revelstoke

There are opportunities for all sorts of walks and hikes for all levels around Kamloops. Excursions can last from 1 to 7hrs. The hike up **Mount Peter and Paul** follows a somewhat difficult route but the view from the summit is ample reward for the 7hrs of walking. You have to call the Indian Band Office (☎828-9700) to get authorization to go through the Aboriginal reserve. The **Paul Lake Provincial Park** trail takes you to Paul Lake Road. It's an easy and pleasant walk that takes between 1.5 and 2hrs.

At **Mount Revelstoke National Park★★** (*$4; permit required for entry into the park; outside Revelstoke, east of the bridge on the Trans-Canada, InfoLine ☎250-837-7500*), you have to drive 24km up to the summit of the mountain where you'll find a trail and a number of picnic areas.

There are a number of trails in **Glacier National Park** (*east of Revelstoke; for maps, information and regulations, contact Parks Canada in Revelstoke, ☎250-837-7500*), which enable you to view flourishing plant and animal life up close. There are varying levels of difficulty. Some trails run past centuries-old trees or climb to the tops of mountains, offering views of the neighbouring peaks.

Okanagan-Similkameen

Manning Provincial Park (*tourist information, summer, every day 8:30am to 4:30pm; winter, Mon to Fri 8:30am to 4:30pm; ☎250-840-8836*) is located on the boundary of the southwestern part of the province and the huge Oka-nagan-Similkameen region. It is popular with Vancouverites in search of vast green spaces. The magnificent mountains and valleys are crisscrossed by hiking trails.

The entrance to **Cathedral Provincial Park** (*for detailed maps and information, **BC Parks District Manager**, Box 399, Summerland, B.C. V0H 1Z0, ☎250-494-6500; no dogs, no mountain bikes*) is located near Kere-meos, on Highway 3. Some of the trails here extend more than 15km, and require a day of hiking, on average. At the summit, the trails are shorter and crisscross hilly terrain teeming with plant and animal life. You can ride to the top in an all-purpose vehicle. To reserve a seat, call the **Cathedral Lakes Lodge** (*☎888-255-4453*).

For a hike that takes only an hour but is incredibly beautiful, go to **Kalamalka Provincial Park**, a few kilometres from Vernon. The short trail leads right up to a little hill that steeply drops off into wonderful Kalamalka Lake.

Kootenay Country

Kokanee Glacier Provincial Park (*for maps, contact the BC Parks Kootenay District Area Office, Nelson, ☎250-825-3500*) has about 10 hiking trails of average difficulty for a total of about 4hrs of walking. The Woodbury Creek Trail, which takes less than 2hrs to cover, leads to Sunset Lake via Ainsworth Hot Springs.

Skiing

Fraser River Loop

With an annual snowfall of 9m and a 1,600m vertical drop, the Whistler ski resort is considered one of the best in North America. There are two mountains to choose from: **Whistler Mountain** and **Blackcomb Mountain** (*hotel reservations, ☎604-932-4222; from Vancouver, ☎685-3650; from the U.S., ☎800-634-9622*). The skiing here is extraordinary, and the facilities ultramodern – but mind your budget! You will understand why prices are so high upon seeing hordes of Japanese and American tourists monopolize the hotels and intermediate ski runs.

Whistler and Blackcomb Mountains together make up the largest skiing area in Canada. These world-class, twin ski play-

grounds are blessed with heavy snowfalls and boast enough hotels to house a city's entire population. This top-of- the-range ski metropolis also offers the possibility of gliding through pristine powder and, weather permitting, you will find yourself swooshing through an incredibly beautiful alpine landscape.

Whistler Mountain (*$51; from Vancouver, Hwy. 99 heading north for 130km, information ☎932-3434, ski conditions ☎932-4191*) is the elder of the two resorts. Experts, powderhounds and skijumpers will all flock to Peak Chair, the chair lift that leads to the top of Whistler Mountain. From its summit, diehard skiers and snowboarders have access to a ski area composed of blue (intermediate) and expert (black-diamond and double-diamond) trails, covered in deep fleecy snow.

Blackcomb Mountain (*$48; in Whistler; from Vancouver, Hwy. 99 heading north for 130km; 4545 Blackcomb Way, Whistler, B.C., V0N 1B4; information ☎932-3141, ski conditions ☎932-4211*) is the "stalwart" skiing mecca of ski buffs in North America. For years now, a fierce debate has been waged by skiers over which of the two mountains (Whistler or Black-comb) is the best. One thing is certain, Black-comb wins first place for its vertical drop of 1,609m. Check out the glacier at Blackcomb – it is truly magnificent!

If you're looking for a thrill, you can hop aboard a helicopter and set off for vast stretches of virgin powder. Contact **Whistler Heli-Skiing Ltd.** (*$450, three*

rides up, lunch, guide; ☎604-932-4105, ≈938-1225).

Mountain Heli Sports (*4340 Sundial Cr., Whistler, ☎604-932-2070*) is a very versatile agency, offering not only flights over mountains and Vancouver, but heli-skiing as well.

Tyax Heli-Skiing (*Box 849, Whistler, V0N 1B0, ☎604-932-7007*) is a very well-known agency in Whistler for heli-skiing.

The Thompson River as Far as Revelstoke

Albeit smaller than Whistler, the **Sun Peaks** (*day pass $44; 45min north of Kamloops, on Todd Mountain; ☎250-578-7222*) resort has recently undergone major renovations and now offers new equipment and accommodations.

Olympic champion Nancy Greene welcomes visitors to **Sun Peaks Resort** where they offer complete ski programs. (*45min NE of Kamloops, 3150 Creekside Way, ste. 50, Sun Peaks, B.C., V0E 1Z1, ☎800- 807-3257*).

Located 6km south of downtown on Airport Way, **Mount Mackenzie Ski** (*Revelstoke ☎250-837-5268*) is a family resort renowned for its high-quality powder. It is also fully equipped with ski lifts, dining facilities, a ski school and an equipment rental centre.

Mount Revelstoke National Park (*☎250-837-7500*) (see Parks, p 596, or Hiking, p 597) covers an immense stretch of virgin snow set against a backdrop of white peaks. This is a good place for cross-country skiing, since a number of longer trails have been laid out with shelters.

The immense skiing area at **Glacier National Park** (*☎837-7500*) (see "Parks", p 596) is perfect for those in search of adventure and quality powder. Because of the steep slopes and risk of avalanches, visitors are required to obtain a permit in order to ski here.

Heli-skiing and cat-skiing are available in this region. They attract a large number of skiers in search of unexplored terrain, far from ski lifts and artificial snow. This region receives record snowfall. In fact, Environment Canada has set up a centre here to measure the levels of precipitation. A number of outfits, including **Cat Powder Skiing Inc.** (*☎837-9489*) and **Selkirk Tangiers Heli-Skiing Ltd.** (*☎800- 663-7080 or 837-5378*), offer package deals.

Okanagan-Similkameen

The Okanagan valley is one of the places where you can ski in the morning and play golf in the afternoon. For skiing, **Silver Star** (*$41; ☎542-0224 or 800-663-4431, ≈558-6090, www.silverstarmtn.com*) is a mountain situated less than 30min from Vernon. It offers 84 runs and gets more than 6m of snow annually.

You can go downhill skiing all over this region. The major resorts are the **Apex Resort** near Penticton, **Big White Ski Resort** and the **Silver Star Mountain Resort** near Kelowna.

Skiing in the Okanagan, which already has a good reputation, is now enjoying a new boom with the creation of **Big White Ski Resort** (*☎800- 663-2772*). The Schumann family has invested $45 million in the site that was already very attractive and deemed acceptable for fine skiing. With 5 to 6m of snow falling here every year, the powder on these slopes doesn't need to be made artificially.

Everyone in the family appreciates winter skiing and snowboarding. Two hours from Kelowna and 1hr from Penticton, **Mont Baldy** has been offering affordable skiing on pleasant powder-covered slopes for 25 years.

Kootenay Country

Kokanee Glacier is a provincial park located 21km northeast of Nelson on Highway 3A. The road is gravel for 16 of the 21km and is not maintained in winter, when the only way to reach the park is on cross-country skis or by helicopter. Visitors are strongly advised to obtain specialized equipment for this type of excursion. The Slocan Chief Cabin can accommodate up to 12 people, but you have to make reservations through the **BC Parks Kootenay District Area Office** (*Nelson*, ☎250-825-3500).

Ski Whitewater lies a few minutes south of Nelson on Highway 6. This resort is the perfect place to spend a day skiing, whether you're an expert or just starting out.

Red Mountain, located 5min from Rossland, is one of the main centres of economic activity in this region. While miners used to work the mountain, today, it's a playground for skiers. Granite Mountain, renowned for its deep, fluffy powder, is also part of this resort. Opposite Red Mountain, **BlackJack**

Cross Country Trails consists of 50km of cross-country ski trails of all different levels of difficulty. **Red Mountain Resorts Inc**. (*☎362-7384, ski conditions ☎362- 5500, reservations ☎800-663-0105*).

Accommodations

The Sunshine Coast

Gibsons

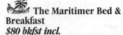 **The Maritimer Bed & Breakfast**
$80 bkfst incl.
tv, children 12 and over, no smoking
521 S. Fletcher Rd.
☎886-0664
Run by Gerry and Noreen Tretick, The Maritimer Bed and Breakfast overlooks the town and the marina. The charming scenery, friendly hosts and cozy atmosphere are sure to please. A private suite in the attic includes a sundeck. On the ground floor, there is a large room decorated with antique furniture and works of art by Noreen – a beautiful quilt graces one of the walls. Served on a terrace looking right out onto the bay, breakfast includes a shrimp omelette. After all, this is the seashore.

Powell River

Beacon Bed & Breakfast
$95-$125 bkfst incl.
&, no smoking, ⊗, children 12 and over
3750 Marine Ave.
☎485-5563
≈485-9450
Your hosts, Shirley and Roger Randall, will make you feel right at home. What's more, they will

take great pleasure in telling you all about their part of the country. The Beacon faces west and looks out onto the sea, so you can enjoy the sunset while taking a bath, no less! The simply laid-out rooms each have fully equipped bathrooms. Breakfast includes a special treat – blueberry pancakes.

The Coast Town Centre Hotel
$95-$115
ℜ, 🐾, P, ⊛, tv
4660 Joyce Ave.
☎485-3000
☎800-663-1144
≈485-3031
The Coast Town Centre is near Town Centre Mall, a large shopping centre in the heart of Powell River. The rooms are impeccable and spacious, and the hotel is equipped with a fitness centre. They also organize salmon-fishing excursions.

The Beach Gardens Resort & Marina
$99
tv, ≈, △, ℝ, P, ℜ, 🐾
7074 Westminster Ave.
☎485-6267
☎800-663-7070
≈485-2343
All the rooms are on the water's edge and offer spectacular views of the coast. At the restaurant you can savour some of their excellent West Coast cuisine. An indoor pool and a fitness centre top off the list of facilities. Afterwards, you can go for a drink in the Canoe Room pub. The resort also has a liquor store.

Lund

Lund Hotel
$69-$85
tv, ℜ
at the end of Hwy. 101
☎483-2400
A relaxing atmosphere prevails at the century-old Lund Hotel, which opens

onto the bay. The peaceful location and view of the boats coming and going more than compensate for the motel-style rooms.

Fraser River Loop

Whistler

Shoestring Lodge
$50-$65 for a room
$21 for a shared room
tv, ℜ, P
1km north of the village
to the right on Nancy Greene Dr.
☎*932-3338*
≈*932-8347*
The Shoestring Lodge is one of the least expensive places to stay in Whistler. Its low rates make it very popular, so reservations are imperative. The rooms include beds, televisions and small bathrooms. The decor is as neutral as can be. The youthful atmosphere will make you feel as if you're at a university summer camp where the students just want to have fun, and that's pretty much what this place is. The pub is known for its excellent evening entertainment (see p 606).

Chalet Beau Sejour
summer $80
winter $105 bkfst incl.
®, *shuttle, no smoking*
7414 Ambassador Cr.
White Gold Estate
☎*938-4966*
≈*938-6296*
The Chalet Beau Sejour, run by Sue and Hal, is a big, inviting house set on a mountainside. You can take in a lovely view of the valley and the mountains while eating the copious breakfast that Sue loves to prepare. A tour guide, she knows the region like the back of her hand. Don't hesitate to ask her what to see and do.

Listel Whistler Hotel
$99-$199
♿, 🐾, *tv*, ≈, ®, △, ℜ
4121 Village Green
☎*932-1133*
Vancouver
☎*688-5634*
☎*800-663-5472*
≈*932-8383*
The Listel Whistler Hotel is located in the heart of the village, so you don't have to look far to find some place to eat or entertain yourself. The simple layout of the rooms makes for a comfortable stay.

Canadian Pacific Chateau Whistler Resort
$129-$529
☺, 🐾, ♿, *tv*, ≈, ®, △, ℜ
4599 Chateau Blvd.
☎*938-8000*
☎*800-606-8244*
☎*800-441-1414*
≈*938-2099*
The luxurious Canadian Pacific Chateau Whistler Resort lies at the foot of the slopes of Blackcomb Mountain. It resembles a smaller version of Whistler Village, fully equipped to meet all your dining and entertainment needs and to ensure that your stay is a relaxing one.

Harrison Hot Springs

Sasquatch Provincial Park
$10 for four people
177 wooded lots
beach, playground, boat-launching ramp
cash only
Cultus Lake
☎*824-2300*
☎*796-3107*
At Sasquatch Provincial Park, you choose your own campsite and a park employee passes by to collect payment. Hidden in the mountains near Harrison Lake, this park has three campgrounds that welcome nature lovers every year. According to a Coast Salish legend, the Sasquatch is half-man,

half-beast and lives in the woods. To this day, some Aboriginal people claim to have seen the creature around Harrison Lake.

Harrison Heritage House and Kottage
$60-$130 bkfst incl.
no smoking
312 Lillooet Ave.
☎*796-9552*
Jo-Anne and Dennis Sandve will give you a warm welcome at their pretty house, located one street away from the beach and the public pool. Jo-Anne makes her own preserves. Certain rooms have whirlpools and fireplaces.

Harrison Hot Springs Hotel
$114-$200
🐾, ♿, ≈, ℜ, △
100 Esplanade
☎*(604) 796-2244*
☎*(800) 663-2266*
≈*796-3682*
The Harrison Hot Springs Hotel offers the benefits of the lake and the mountain. It is also the only hotel with access to the mineral springs making it a fun place where visitors get a sense of well-being. Outdoor heated pools, golf, dancing, children's playground and more.

The Thompson River as Far as Revelstoke

Ashcroft

Sundance Guest Ranch
$80-$185 per person
fb, horseback riding twice a day (cowboy boots required, rentals available)
≈, *tennis, tv*
Highland Valley Rd.
Box 489, V0K 1A0
☎*(250) 453-2422*
Run by former clients, the Sundance Guest Ranch will take you back to a bygone era when cowboys

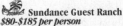
British Columbia

roamed freely on horse-back across as yet unexplored regions. The cost covers a stay of at least one day. Guests have access to a living room where they can bring their drinks. There is a separate living room just for children.

Kamloops

Best Western Kamloops Towne Lodge
$89-$138
≈, ⊛, △, ⊙, ℜ, ⴜ
1250 Rogers Way
☎*(250) 828-6660*
in western North America
☎*800-665-6674*
⇌*828-6698*
Located right near the Trans-Canada Highway on the way into town, the Best Western Kamloops Towne Lodge is a very comfortable, classic-style hotel that offers some splendid views of Kamloops and the Thompson River. You can also enjoy the scenery from one of the nearby motels, which vary only in price.

 **Sun Peaks Resort**
$90-$169
ℜ
45min NE of Kamloops
3150 Creekside Way, Ste. 50
Sun Peaks., V0E 1Z1
☎*800-807-3257*
⇌*(250) 578-7843*
Sun Peaks Resort is open all year and provides all the comforts. In the winter you can ski with Olympic champion Nancy Greene. There are, however, a number of other activities like swimming in the outdoor heated pool, snowmobile excursions, or the Christmas torch run. Families are welcome and young children can stay at the hotel and ski for free. There are plenty of summer activities, including golf and mountain biking. The complex also has a

variety of dining establishments.

Revelstoke

 **Revelstoke Youth Hostel**
$15-$19
K, sb
400 Second St. W.
☎*837-4050*
⇌*837-6410*
www.hostels.bc.ca
The Revelstoke Youth Hostel was completely renovated a short while ago. It is now a cheery and very comfortable facility, conveniently located in the centre of town. Free Internet access. Ski-accommodation packages starting from only $20/day!

 **Piano Keep Bed & Breakfast**
$80-$100 bkfst incl.
no smoking, ≡
815 MacKenzie Ave.
☎/⇌*(250) 837-2120*
The Piano Keep Bed & Breakfast is an imposing Edwardian house set in the midst of a garden. Host Vern Enyedy welcomes his guests in a charming setting featuring pianos from different eras. Both a collector and a music lover, Vern will gladly demonstrate his musical skill.

Best Western Wayside Inn
$89-$109
≡, 🏍, ⴜ, tv, ≈, ⊛, △, ℜ
1901 Laforme Blvd.
☎*(250) 837-6161*
in B.C. and Alberta
☎*800-663-5307*
☎*800-528-1234*
⇌*837-5460*
The Best Western Wayside Inn, on the north side of the Trans-Canada, is not only close to everything, but offers the added attraction of a pastoral setting with views of Revelstoke and the Columbia River.

Okanagan-Similkameen

Cathedral Provincial Park

 **Cathedral Lakes Lodge**
$99-$199
for reservations :
☎*888-255-4453*
administration :
☎*(250) 226-7560*
⇌*226-7528*
S4C8 Slocan Park, V0G 2E0
Cathedral Lakes Lodge has 10 rooms and six small cottages. The road to the top of the mountain is only open to the lodge's all-terrain vehicle, so you have to leave your car on Ashnola River Road in the lodge's base camp. If you go by foot, it will take you more than 6hrs to reach the lodge. Do not forget to reserve your seat in the vehicle. Turn left 4.8km west of Keremeos, cross over the covered bridge and drive along Ashnola River Road for 20.8km. If you plan on taking the bus, you have to call the lodge ahead of time to make arrangements for someone to pick you up. All this might seem complicated. But once you reach the top, you're sure to be enchanted by the mountain goats, marmots and flowers, not to mention glaciers stretching as far as the eye can see. Canoes and rowboats are available and the logge has a fireplace and a bar.

Southwest of Penticton

Olde Osprey Inn, Bed & Breakfast
$75-$100 bkfst incl.
sb, ✿, no smoking
Sheep Creek Rd.
☎/✆(250) 497-7134
This magnificent log house was built by George Mullen, who astutely chose a site on a mountainside with an unimpeded view of Yellow Lake and the surrounding area. Joy Whitley, for her part, makes sure your stay is as comfortable as possible. She is a painter, and some of her work is on display here. Joy's daughter, furthermore, is a musician. This amiable family knows how to put their guests at ease. The occasional osprey flies by at which point everything comes to a halt as all eyes turn skyward.

Osoyoos

Lake Osoyoos Guest House
$105 bkfst incl.
waterfront, K, cash only
5809 Oleander Dr.
☎(250) 495-3297
☎800-671-8711
✆495-5310
At the Lake Osoyoos Guest House, Sofia Grasso cooks up breakfast in her huge kitchen while guests sip freshly squeezed juice at the edge of Osoyoos Lake. Guests have use of a pedalboat to enjoy the lake and the changing colours of the valley as the day wears on.

Summerland

The Illahie Beach
$16-$20
170 campsites, free showers, laundry, pay phone, convenience store, beach
north of Penticton on Hwy. 97
☎494-0800
The Illahie Beach campground welcomes vacationers from April to October. The beaches and views of the Okanagan Valley make for a heavenly setting.

Kootenay Country

Ainsworth Hot Springs

Ainsworth Hot Springs Resort
$66-$86
⅃, ≈, tv, ℜ, no smoking, ⌂, in the caves, naturally warm water and ice-cold ≈
Hwy. 31
☎(250) 229-4212
☎800-668-1171
✆229-5600
The Ainsworth Hot Springs Resort is part of the facilities surrounding the caves. Guests have free access to the caves, and can get passes for friends.

Nelson

Inn the Garden Bed & Breakfast
$60-$70 bkfst incl.
sb/pb, adults only, P, no smoking
408 Victoria St.
☎(250) 352-3226
✆352-3284
This charming Victorian house, renovated by owners Lynda Stevens and Jerry Van Veen, lies steps away from the main street.

They also have a 3-bedroom cottage. The couple's warm welcome will make your stay in Nelson that much more pleasant. As one of their passions, they'll happily tell you about the town's architectural heritage.

The Heritage Inn
$69-$89 bkfst incl.
tv, ℜ, ⅃
422 Vernon St.
☎(250) 352-5331
✆352-5214
The Heritage Inn was established in 1898 when the Hume brothers decided to build a grand hotel. Over the years, the building has been modified with each new owner. In 1980, major renovations breathed new life into the old place. The library is worth visiting. With its woodwork and fireplace, it has all the elements necessary to create a pleasant atmosphere. The walls of the rooms and corridors are covered with photographs capturing the highlights of Nelson's history.

Rossland

Ram's Head Inn
$65-$85 bkfst incl.
⊛, ⌂, no smoking
at the foot of the slopes
on Red Mountain Rd.
Box 636, V0G 1Y0
☎(250) 362-9577
✆362-5681
An inviting house owned by Tauna and Greg Butler, the Ram's Head Inn feels like a home away from home. The fireplace, woodwork, simple decor and pleasant smells wafting out of the kitchen create a pleasant, informal atmosphere.

British Columbia

Restaurants

The Sunshine Coast

Powell River

Beach Gardens Resort Hotel
$$-$$$
7074 Westminster Ave.
☎*485-6267*
☎*800-663-7070*
The dining room at the
Beach Gardens Resort
Hotel looks out onto the
Malaspina Strait. The menu
lists divine seafood dishes
flavoured with Okanagan
wines.

Fraser River Loop

Whistler

Black's Pub & Restaurant
$
below Whistler and Blackcomb
Mountains
☎*932-6408 or 932-6945*
Black's Pub & Restaurant
serves breakfast, lunch and
dinner for the whole fam-
ily in a friendly atmo-
sphere. The views are
exceptional and it has one
of the best beer selections
in Whistler.

 Città Bistro
$
every day 11am to 1am
Whistler Village Square
☎*932-4177*
Located in the heart of the
village, Città Bistro has an
elaborate menu with selections ranging from salads
to pita pizzas. This is the
perfect place to sample
one of the local beers. In
both winter and summer, a
pleasant mix of locals and
tourists makes for an ex-
tremely inviting atmo-
sphere.

 Pika's
$
*Dec to Apr, 7:30am to
3:30pm*
at the top of the Whistler Village
Gondola
☎*932-3434*
If you want to be among
the first to ski the slopes in
the morning, head to
Pika's for breakfast. It is
worth getting up early the
day after a storm.

Thai One On
$$
every day, dinner
in the Le Chamois hotel
at the foot of the Blackcomb Moun-
tain slopes
☎*932-4822*
As may be gathered by its
name, Thai One On serves
Thai food with its wonder-
ful blend of coconut milk
and hot peppers.

Harrison Hot Springs

 Black Forest Restaurant
$-$$
180 Esplanade Ave.
☎*796-9343*
The Black Forest Restau-
rant is an Alsatian-style
restaurant with flowery
windows. The food, in-
cluding schnitzel,
Chateaubriand and fresh
pasta, has a European
flavour. They also serve
B.C. salmon. The wine list
is extensive. It's open year
round in the evening, but
only for breakfast in the
summer.

Kitami
$$
318 Hot Springs Rd.
☎*796-2728*
Kitami is a Japanese res-
taurant that invites you to
enjoy a meal in one of
their Tatami Rooms or at
the sushi bar.

Harrison Hot Spring Hotel
$$-$$$
100 Esplanade
☎*800-663-2266*
The restaurant at the Harri-
son Hot Spring Hotel of-
fers dinners that are a gas-
tronomical delight accom-
panied by music and danc-
ing. They serve meats and
fish.

The Thompson River
as Far as Revelstoke

Kamloops

Internet Café
$
462 Victoria
☎*828-7889*
Internet Café, whose motto
is «the world is at your
fingertips,» invites you to
check your messages, play
the lottery or surf the In-
ternet while enjoying a
salad or hamburger. The
atmosphere is friendly and,
if needed, the staff will
help you on the computer.

Grass Roots Tea House
$$
May to Sep
lunch 11:30am to 2:30pm
tea 2pm to 4pm
*dinner 6:30pm (one service,
reserve by 2pm)*
*reservations required during
winter*
262 Lorne St.
☎*(250) 374-9890*
Located in Riverside Park,
the Grass Roots Tea House
is a charming place sur-
rounded by trees where
you can enjoy a cup of
ginseng tea. Reservations
are required for dinner,
and the menu varies de-
pending on what day of
the week it is.

 Déjà Vu
$$$
Tue to Sat 5pm to 10pm
172 Battle St.
☎*374-3227*
Déjà Vu serves West Coast
and French cuisine featur-

ing an imaginative blend of fruit and seafood.

Revelstoke

Frontier Restaurant
$
every day 5am to midnight
near the tourist office
at the intersection of the Trans-Canada Hwy. and the 23
☎*(250) 837-5119*
At the Frontier Restaurant, you can put away a big breakfast in a typically western setting.

Black Forest
$$-$$$
5min west of Revelstoke
on the Trans-Canada
☎*(250) 837-3495*
The Black Forest is a Bavarian-style restaurant that serves Canadian and European cuisine. Top billing on the menu goes to cheese and fish. The setting and view of Mount Albert are enchanting.

Okanagan-Similkameen

Penticton

Hog's Breath Coffee Co.
$
every day
202 Main St.
☎*(250) 493-7800*
The Hog's Breath is the perfect place to start off your day with a good cup of coffee, and even more importantly, some peach muffins (in season): you'll love them! If you're looking for outdoors destinations, the owner, Mike Barrett, will gladly offer some suggestions.

Salty's Beach House
$-$$
1000 Lakeshore Dr.
☎*(250) 493-5001*
Seafood fans will find their favourite foods at Salty's Beach House. Make sure to come here at lunchtime

so you can enjoy the view of Okanagan Lake from the terrace. The pirate-ship decor gives the place a festive atmosphere.

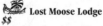 Lost Moose Lodge
$$
8min from the centre of Penticton
Beaverdell Rd.
☎*490-0526*
Lost Moose Lodge offers music, spectacular views and good barbecued food. It was restaurant of the year in 1996.

Theo's Restaurant
$$-$$$
687 Main St.
☎*(250) 492-4019*
Fine Greek cuisine and a relaxed atmosphere make for a pleasant meal at this extremely popular spot.

Granny Bogners Restaurant
$$$
302 Eckhardt Ave. W.
☎*(250) 493-2711*
This magnificent Tudor house was built in 1912 for a local doctor. In 1976, Hans and Angela Strobel converted it into a restaurant where they serve fine French cuisine made with local produce.

Kelowna

Joey Tomato's Kitchen
$-$$
every day
300-2475 Hwy. 97 N
at the intersection of Hwy. 33
☎*(250) 860-8999*
Joey Tomato's Kitchen is located near a large boulevard in a neighbourhood of shopping malls. The people who run this place have created a pleasant atmosphere. With its plants, parasols and little Italian car, that makes will keep your attention. The dining room is also extremely attractive – a large space brightened up by cans of food and bottles of

oil, making you feel as if you're, well, in Joey's kitchen. And the pasta! Be sure to try the fettucine with salmon and tomatoes: it's a real treat.

 The Yamas Taverna
$-$$
1630 Ellis St.
downtown
☎*763-5823*
The Yamas Taverna is a Greek restaurant *par excellence*. White and blue, and abundantly flowered, this restaurant assures clients an excellent evening with a Meditteranean flavour. Voted as "Best New Restaurant" and "Best Meal for the Money," you won't be disappointed, especially on Saturday nights when they feature belly dancing.

Kootenay Country

Nelson

El Zocalo Mexican Café
$$
802 Baker St.
☎*(250) 352-7223*
The successful El Zocalo Mexican Café occupies a Mexican-style building and features live Mexican music. Guests enjoy delicious, traditional Mexican cuisine in a fiesta-like atmosphere.

All Seasons Café
$$-$$$
every day
lunch 11:30am to 2:30pm
dinner 5pm to 10pm
Sun brunch 10am to 3pm
closed for lunch in winter
620 Herridge Lane, behind Baker St.
☎*(250) 352-0101*
The All Seasons Café is not to be missed. It lies hidden beneath the trees, so its terrace is bathed in shade. The soups might surprise you a bit – apple and broccoli (in season) is one example. The menu is determined by the season and what's available in the

British Columbia

area, with lots of space accorded to the fine wines of British Columbia. The friendly, efficient service, elegant decor and quality cuisine make for an altogether satisfying meal. The walls are adorned with works of art.

Rossland

Mountain Gypsy Cafe
$$
2167 Washington St.
☎*362-3342*
Mountain Gypsy Cafe offers a unique variety of eclectic dishes from couscous to chicken. The prices are very reasonable.

Olive Oyl's
$$-$$$
2067 Columbia
☎*263-5322*
Olive Oyl's cuisine is best described as contemporary or fusion cuisine, combining several different culinary trends. Its offerings include pasta, pizza and enormous brunches that are all meticulously prepared and presented.

Entertainment

Bars and Danceclubs

Fraser River Loop

Boot Pub
Whistler
1km north of the village on the right, on Nancy Greene Dr.
☎*932-3338*
At the Boot Pub, located in the Shoestring Lodge hotel, live musicians play R&B to an enthusiastic clientele.

Tommy Africa's
Gateway Dr., Whistler
☎*932-6090*
Young reggae fans get together at Tommy Africa's. Line-ups are common due to its popularity.

Shopping

Fraser River Loop

Whistler

Outside the little village, at the edge of the Whistler region, lies Function Junction, a small industrial area of sorts. You won't find just any industries here, however!

Whistler Brewery *(free admission; Alpha Lake Rd., Function Junction, south of Whistler Creekside,* ☎*932-6185)*. This microbrewery distributes its products locally, and they are extremely popular. You just might learn the recipe for their beer while touring the facilities.

Blackcomb Cold Beer & Wine Store *(across from The Chateau Whistler Inn,* ☎*932-9795)* has a large selection of B.C. wines. Helpful and courteous staff.

Kelty Expedition Gear *(Function Junction,* ☎*932-6381)* sells and rents anything you might need for outdoor activities as well as guitars to liven up an evening around the bonfire.

The Grove Gallery *(Delta Whistler Resort,* ☎*932-3517)* offers landscapes of Whistler and the mountains.

Whistler Inuit Gallery *(Canadian Pacific Chateau,* ☎*938-3366)* exhibits very attractive wood, bone, marble and bronze pieces by Aboriginal sculptors.

Harrison Hot Springs

Curiosities *(160 Lillooet Ave.,* ☎*796-9431)*, as the name suggests, sells souvenirs, toys for children, T-shirts and other vacation clothing.

A Question of Balance *(880 Hot Springs Rd.,* ☎*796-9622)* is an art gallery created by Canadian craftspeople. The knitting, sewing, ceramics and blown glass are beautiful and interesting.

Harrison Watersports *(6069 Rockwell Dr., behind the Rivtow Office, on Harrison Lake,* ☎*604- 796-3513 or 795-6775)* rents Jet Skis and organizes rides.

Crafts & Things Market *(*☎*796-2084)*. From March to November, Harrison Hot Springs hosts a number of markets. Call for dates and times.

The Thompson River as Far as Revelstoke

Kamloops

Farmer's Markets *(Saturdays, 200 block-St Paul St.; Wed at the corner of Third Ave. and Victoria St.)*. Delightful food markets are organized from May to October.

Okanagan-Similkameen

Kelowna

The **Far West Factory Outlet** *(230-2469 Rte. 97,* ☎*860-9010)* sells comfortable, light clothing by major brand names.

Valhalla Pure Outfitters *(453 Bernard Ave., downtown,* ☎*763-9696)* is a popular local manufacturer that specializes in clothing.

Mosaïc Books *(1420 St. Paul St., downtown,* ☎*736-4418)* carries a good selection of maps for excursions and books.

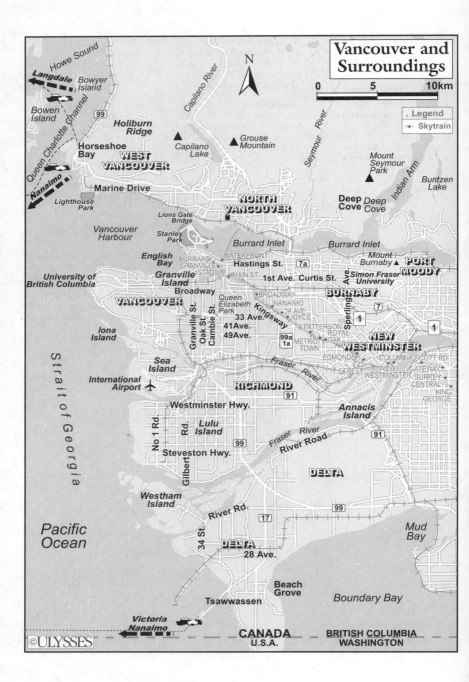

Vancouver and Surroundings

0   5   10km

. Legend
Skytrain

Howe Sound

Langdale

Bowyer Island

Bowen Island

99

Horseshoe Bay

Holiburn Ridge

WEST VANCOUVER

Capilano River

▲ Capilano Lake

▲ Grouse Mountain

Seymour River

Mount Seymour Park ▲

Buntzen Lake

Queen Charlotte Channel

Nanaimo

Lighthouse Park

Marine Drive

NORTH VANCOUVER

Deep Cove   Deep Cove

Indian Arm

Vancouver Harbour

Stanley Park

Lions Gate Bridge

Burrard Inlet

Burrard Inlet

Mount Burnaby ▲

PORT MOODY

English Bay

BURRARD GRANVILLE STADIUM

WATERFRONT

Hastings St.

7a

Simon Fraser University

Granville Island

MAIN ST.

1st Ave. Curtis St.

Ave.

BURNABY

University of British Columbia

VANCOUVER

Broadway

BROADWAY

Queen Elizabeth Park

Kingsway

NANAIMO
28 AVE.
JOYCE

Sperling

Simon Fraser University

Granville St.

Oak St.

Cambie St.

33 Ave.
41Ave.
49Ave.

99a
1a

PATTERSON
ROYAL
OAK

NEW WESTMINSTER

1

1

Iona Island

METRO TOWN

EDMONDS

COLUMBIA SCOTT RD.
STREET
NEW
WESTMINSTER

GATEWAY
SURREY
CENTRAL

KING
GEORGE

Sea Island

Fraser River

International Airport ✈

RICHMOND

91

Westminster Hwy.

Annacis Island

91

No 1 Rd.

Gilbert Rd.

Lulu Island

99

Steveston Hwy.

Fraser River

River Road

DELTA

S
t
r
a
i
t

o
f

G
e
o
r
g
i
a

Pacific Ocean

Westham Island

River Rd.

34 St.

17

99

Mud Bay

DELTA

28 Ave.

Beach Grove

Boundary Bay

Victoria Nanaimo 🚗

Tsawwassen

CANADA
U.S.A.

BRITISH COLUMBIA
WASHINGTON

©ULYSSES

Vancouver and Surroundings

Vancouver is truly a new city, one framed by the mighty elements of sea and mountains.

As part of one of the most isolated reaches on the planet for many years, the city has over the last 100 years developed close ties with the nations of the largest ocean on Earth.

Vancouver is one of the most multicultural metropolises of the Pacific Rim. Its history is tied to the development of British Columbia's natural resources. Most residents were lured here by the magnificent setting and the climate which is remarkably mild in a country known for its bitter winters and stifling summers. Vancouver, where Asia meets America, is a city well worth discovering.

Finding Your Way Around

By Car

Vancouver

Vancouver is accessible by the **Trans-Canada Highway 1**, which runs east-west. This national highway links all of the major Canadian cities. It has no tolls and passes through some spectacular scenery.

Coming from Alberta you will pass through the Rocky Mountains, desert regions and a breathtaking canyon.

The city is generally reached from the east by taking the "Downtown" exit from the TransCanada. If you are coming from the United States or from Victoria by ferry, you will enter the city on Highway 99 North. In this case expect it to take about 30min to reach downtown.

By Plane

Vancouver International Airport

Vancouver International Airport is located 15km from downtown. Besides the regular airport services (duty-free shops, cafeterias, restaurants), you will also find an exchange office. Several car-rental companies also have offices in the airport. It takes about 30min to get downtown by car or bus. A taxi or limousine will cost you about $25-$30. To reach downtown by public transit, take bus #100 for downtown and points east and bus #404 or #406 for Richmond, Delta and points south.

Take note: even if you have already paid various taxes included in the purchase price of your ticket, Vancouver International Airport charges every passenger an Airport Improvement Fee (AIF). The fee is $5 for flights within B.C. and to the Yukon, $10 for flights elsewhere in North America, and $15 for overseas flights. Credit cards are accepted, and most in-transit passengers are exempted.

By Train

Trains from the United States and Eastern Canada arrive at new intermodal **Pacific Central Station** (*Via Rail Canada, 1150 Station St., ☎800-561-8630*) where you can also connect to buses or the Skytrain. The cross-country Via train, **The Canadian** arrives in Vancouver three times a week from Eastern Canada.

BC Rail (*1311 West First St., North Vancouver, ☎984-5246*) trains travel the northern west coast. Schedules vary depending on the seasons.

During the summer, the **Great Canadian Railtour Company Ltd.** offers **Rocky Mountain Railtours** (*$725 per person, $670 per person double occupancy; ☎606-7200 or 800-665-7245, ≠606-7520*) between Calgary and Vancouver.

There is daily service aboard **Amtrak's Mount Baker International** from Seattle, Washington. The trip takes 3hrs and follows a scenic route. For reservations or information call Amtrak US Rail at **☎800-USA-RAIL** or **☎800-872-7245** (toll-free in North America).

By Ferry

Vancouver

Two ferry ports serve the greater Vancouver area for travellers coming from other regions in the province. Horseshoe Bay, to the northwest, is the terminal for ferries to Nanaimo (crossing time 90min), Bowen Island and the Mainland Sunshine Coast. Tsawwassen, to the south, is the terminal for ferries to Victoria (Swartz Bay crossing time 95min), Nanaimo (crossing time 2hrs) and the Southern Gulf Islands. Both terminals are about 30min from downtown. For information on these routes contact **BC Ferries** (*☎250-386-3431*).

The ferry between Granville Island and the Hornby Street dock runs from 7am to 8pm. For information contact **Granville Island Ferries**

(*☎684-7781*) or **Aquabus Ferries** (*☎689-5858*).

The Gulf Islands

BC Ferries carries passengers between Vancouver Island (Swartz Bay or Nanaimo) and the mainland (Horseshoe Bay or Tsawwassen), between Tsawwassen and the Gulf Islands (*reservations required for cars*), between Vancouver Island and the Gulf Islands, and between Quadra Island and Cortes Island. If you are travelling by car, it is a good idea to make reservations in the summertime, or to arrive quite early, to avoid a wait. *For reservations and sailing times call ☎(888) 223-3779 in B.C., or (250) 386-3431 outside the province.*

By Bus

Vancouver

Greyhound Lines of Canada Pacific Central Station 1150 Station St.
☎482-8747
☎800-661-8747

Public Transit

Vancouver

BC Transit bus route maps are available from the **Vancouver Travel InfoCentre** (*200 Burrard St., ☎683-2000*) or from the BC Transit offices in Surrey (*13401 108th Ave., 5th floor, Surrey, B.C., ☎800-903-4731 or 540-3450*). BC Transit also includes a rail transit system and a marine bus. The **Skytrain** runs east from the downtown area to Burnaby, New Westminster and Surrey. These automatic trains run from 5am to 1am all week, except

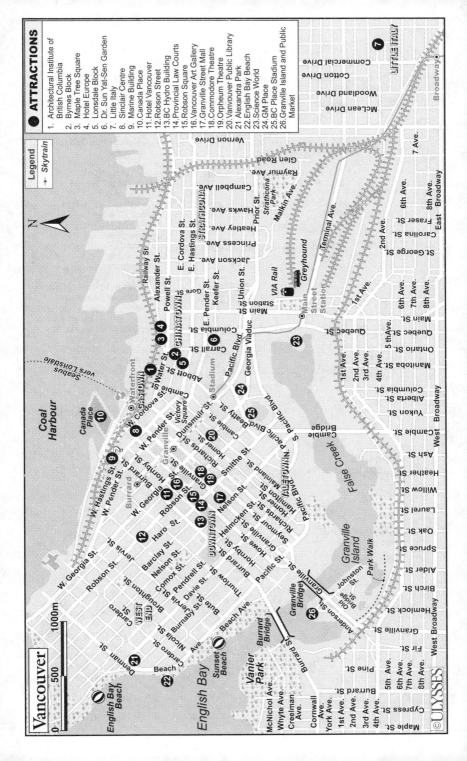

Vancouver

0 · 500 · 1000m

Legend
🚈 Skytrain

ATTRACTIONS

1. Architectural Institute of British Columbia
2. Byrnes Block
3. Maple Tree Square
4. Hotel Europe
5. Lonsdale Block
6. Dr. Sun Yat-Sen Garden
7. Little Italy
8. Sinclair Centre
9. Marine Building
10. Canada Place
11. Hotel Vancouver
12. Robson Street
13. BC Hydro Building
14. Provincial Law Courts
15. Robson Square
16. Vancouver Art Gallery
17. Granville Street Mall
18. Commodore Theatre
19. Orpheum Theatre
20. Vancouver Public Library
21. Alexandra Park
22. English Bay Beach
23. Science World
24. GM Place
25. BC Place Stadium
26. Granville Island and Public Market

© ULYSSES

Sundays when they start at 9am. The **Seabus** shuttles runs frequently between Burrard Inlet and North Vancouver.

Tickets and passes are available for **BC Transit**, including Skytrain and Seabus tickets from the coin-operated machines at some stops, in some convenience stores or by calling ☎**261-5100** or **521-0400**.

The fares are the same whether you are travelling on a BC Transit bus, the Skytrain or the Seabus. A single ticket generally costs $1.50 for adults and $0.75 for seniors, children and students (must have BC Transit GoCard), except at peak hours (Mon to Fri before 9:30am and 3pm to 6:30pm) when the system is divided into three zones. It costs $1.50 for travel within one zone, $2.25 within two zones and $3 within three zones.

Practical Information

Area Code: *604*

Tourist Information

Vancouver

The **Tourism Vancouver Tourist Info Centre** *(May to Sep, every day 8am to 6pm; Sep to May, Mon to Fri 8:30am to 5pm, Sat 9am to 5pm; Plaza Level, Waterfront Centre, 200 Burrard St., V6C 3L6, ☎683-2000, ≈682-6839, www.tourism-vancouver.org)* provides brochures and information on sights and accommodations for the city as well as for the province.

The Gulf Islands

Salt Spring Island Travel InfoCentre
year-round
121 Lower Ganges Rd., Box 111 Ganges, V8K 2T1
☎*537-5252*

Galiano Island Travel InfoCentre
seasonal
Sturdies Bay, Box 73, Galiano
V0N 1P0
☎*539-2233*

Gabriola Island Tourist Office
Box 249, V0R 1X0
☎*247-9332*

Exploring

★★★

Vancouver

★
Gastown

Just a few steps from downtown, Gastown is best discovered on foot. The area dates back to 1867 when John Deighton, known as Gassy Jack, opened a saloon for the employees of a neighbouring sawmill. Gastown was destroyed by fire in 1886. However, this catastrophe did not deter the city's pioneers who rebuilt from the ashes and started anew the development of their city that was incorporated several months later.

Along Water Street, you will see the steep roofs of **Gaslight Square** *(131 Water St.)*, a shopping centre laid out around a pretty inner court (Henriquez and Todd, 1975). Nearby are the offices of the **Architectural Institute of British**

Columbia ★*(free; summer Wed to Sun, Sep to May weekends only, 440 Cambie St., Suite 100, schedule and programme, ☎683-8588)*, which offers guided tours of Vancouver during the summertime.

The intersection of Water and Carrall Streets is one of the liveliest parts of Gastown. Long **Byrnes Block** *(2 Water St.)*, on the southwest corner, was one of the first buildings to be erected after the terrible fire of 1886. It was built on the site of Gassy Jack's saloon : a statue of the celebrated barkeep graces tiny **Maple Tree Square**. The thick cornice on the brick building is typical of commercial buildings of the Victorian era. Rising in front is the former **Hotel Europe** *(4 Powell St.)*, a triangular building erected in 1908 by a Canadian hotel-keeper of Italian descent.

Lonsdale Block *(8-28 W. Cordova St.)*, built in 1889, is one of the most remarkable buildings on this street which is undergoing a beautiful renaissance with the recent opening of several shops and cafés.

★★
Chinatown and East Vancouver

This tour starts at the intersection of Carall and East Pender. On East Pender Street, the scene changes radically. The colour and atmosphere of public markets, plus a strong Chinese presence, bring this street to life. The 1858 Gold Rush in the hinterland drew Chinese from San Francisco and Hong Kong; and railway construction brought thousands more Chinese to British Columbia in 1878. This community resisted many hard blows that might have ended its presence in the province. At the beginning of the 20th century, the Canadian government imposed a heavy tax on new Chinese immigrants, and then banned Chinese immigration altogether from 1923 to 1947. Today, the local Chinese community is growing rapidly due to the massive influx of immigrants from Hong Kong, making Vancouver's Chinatown one of the largest in all of North America.

It is well worth stopping in at the **Dr. Sun Yat-Sen Garden** ★ *(every day 10am to 7:30pm; 578 Carrall St., ☎689-7133)*, behind the traditional portal of the **Chinese Cultural Centre** at 50 East Pender St. Built in 1986 by Chinese artists from Suzhou, this garden is the only example outside Asia of landscape architecture from the Ming Dynasty (1368-1644). The 1.2ha green space is surrounded by high walls that create a virtual oasis of peace in the middle of bustling Chinatown. It is worth noting that Dr. Sun Yat-Sen (1866-1925), considered the father of modern China, visited Vancouver in 1911 in order to raise money for his newly founded Kuomintang ("People's Party").

The next part of town you'll pass through is known as **Little Italy**, but is also home to Vancouverites of Portuguese, Spanish, Jamaican and South American descent. In the early 20th century, the Commercial Drive area became the city's first suburb, with middle-class residents building small, single-family homes with wooden siding here. The first Chinese and Slavic immigrants moved into the neighbourhood during World War I, and another wave of immigrants, chiefly Italian, arrived at the end of World War II.

★★
Downtown

The **Sinclair Centre** ★ *(701 W. Hastings St.)* is a group of government offices. Occupying a former post office, its annexes are connected to one another by covered passageways lined with shops. The main building, dating from 1909, is considered to be one of the finest examples of the neo-baroque style in Canada.

Sinclair Centre

The **Marine Building** ★★ *(355 Burrard St.)*, which faces straight down West Hastings Street, is a fine example of the Art Deco style, that is characterized by vertical lines, staggered recesses, geometric ornamentation and the absence of a cornice at the top of the structure. Erected in 1929, the building lives up to its name, in part because it is lavishly decorated with nautical motifs and also because its occupants are ship-owners and shipping companies. Its facade features terra cotta panels depicting the history of shipping and the discovery of the Pacific coast.

Take Burrard Street toward the water to reach **Canada Place** ★★ *(999 Canada Place)*, which occupies one of the piers along the harbour and looks like a giant sailboat ready to set out across the waves. This multi-purpose complex, served as the Canadian pavilion at Expo '86, and is home to the city's Convention Centre, the harbour station where ocean liners dock, the luxurious Pan Pacific Hotel (see p 662) and an Imax theatre. Take a walk on the "deck" and drink in the magnificent panoramic view of Burrard Inlet, the port and the snow-capped mountains.

The imposing **Hotel Vancouver** ★ *(900 W. Georgia St.)*, a veritable monument to the Canadian railway companies that built it between 1928 and 1939, stands at the corner of West Georgia Street. For many years, its high copper roof served as the principal symbol of Vancouver abroad. Like all major Canadian cities, Vancouver had to have a Château-style hotel. Make sure to take a look at the gargoyles near the top and the bas-reliefs at the entrance that depict an ocean liner and a moving locomotive.

Turn left on Thurlow Street and left again on **Robson Street** ★ which is lined with fashionable boutiques, elaborately decorated restaurants and West Coast-style cafés. People sit at tables outside, enjoying the fine weather and watching the motley crowds stroll by. In the mid-20th century, a small German community settled around Robson Street, dubbing it Robsonstrasse, a nickname it bears to this day.

The former **B.C. Hydro Building** ★ *(970 Burrard St.)*, at the corner of Nelson and Burrard, was once the head office of the province's hydroelectric company. In 1993, it was converted into a 242-unit co-op and renamed The Electra. Designed in 1955 by local architects Thompson, Berwick and Pratt, it is considered to be one of the most sophisticated skyscrapers of that era in all of North America. The ground floor is adorned with a mural and a mosaic in shades of grey, blue and green, executed by artist B.C. Binning.

The **Vancouver Art Gallery** ★ *($10; May 3 to Oct 9, Mon to Wed 10am to 6pm, Thu 10am to 9pm, Fri 10am to 6pm, Sat 10am to 5pm, Sun and holidays noon to 5pm, closed Mon and Tue during winter; 750 Hornby St., ☎662-4700)*, located north of Robson Square, occupies the former Provincial Law Courts. This big, neoclassical-style building was erected in 1908 according to a design by British architect Francis Mawson Rattenbury. (His other credits include the British Columbia Legislative Assembly and the Empress Hotel, both located in Victoria, on Vancouver Island). Later, Rattenbury returned to his native country and was killed by his wife's lover. The museum's collection includes a number of paintings by Emily Carr (1871-1945), a major Canadian painter whose pri-

mary subjects were the Aboriginal peoples and landscapes of the West Coast.

Turn right on West Georgia Street, then right again to get to **Granville Street Mall** ★, the street of cinemas, theatres, nightclubs and retail stores. Its busy sidewalks are hopping 24hrs a day.

Stroll along the Granville Street Mall heading south towards Theatre Row. You'll pass the **Commodore Theatre** *(870 Granville St.)* and the **Orpheum Theatre** ★ *(649 Cambie St., free tour upon reservation ☎665-3050)*. Behind the latter's narrow facade, barely 8m wide, a long corridor opens onto a 2,800-seat Spanish-style Renaissance Revival theatre.

Vancouver Library

At the corner of Robson Street is a curious building that is somewhat reminiscent of Rome's Coliseum. It is the **Vancouver Public Library** ★★ *(free admission; year-round, Mon and Tue 10am to 9pm, Wed to Sat 10am to 6pm; Oct to Apr, Sun 1pm to 5pm, closed*

Sun in the summer; free tours can be arranged, ☎331-4041; 350 W. Georgia St., ☎331-3600). This brand-new building is the work of Montréal architect Moshe Safdie, known for his Habitat '67 in Montréal and the National Art Gallery in Ottawa.

★

West End

Excluding Vancouver Island, farther west, the West End is the end of the line, the final destination of that quest for a better life that thousands of city-dwellers from eastern Canada have embarked upon for generations. Despite all its concrete skyscrapers, the West End has a laid-back atmosphere, influenced both by the immensity of the Pacific and the wisdom of the Orient.

Head west on Davie Street, then left on Bidwell Street to reach **Alexandra Park** ★, which forms a point south of Burnaby Street. This luxuriant park also offers a splendid view of **English Bay Beach** ★★ *(along the shore between Chilco and Bidwell Sts.)* whose fine sands are crowded during the summer.

Head east on Robson Street to the **Robson Public Market** ★ *(1610 Robson, at the corner of Cardero)*, a bustling indoor market with a long glass roof. You'll find everything here from live crabs and fresh pasta to local handicrafts. You can also eat here, as dishes from all over the world are served on the top floor. A pleasure for both the palate and the eyes!

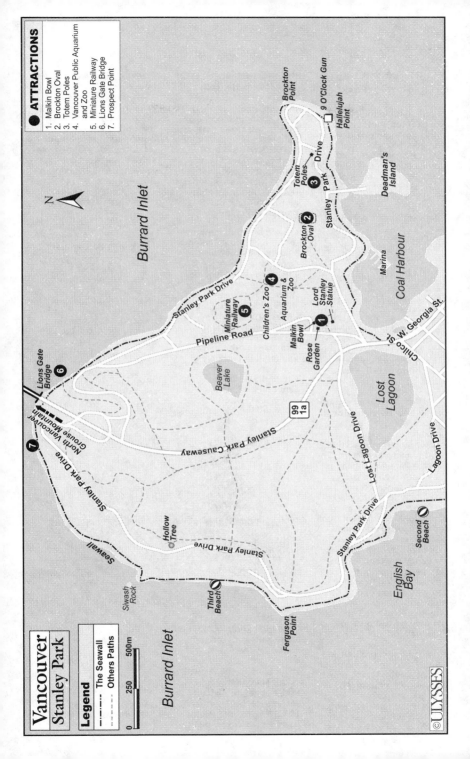

Vancouver
Stanley Park

Legend

— The Seawall
-·-·- Others Paths

|0   250   500m|

© ULYSSES

ATTRACTIONS

1. Malkin Bowl
2. Brockton Oval
3. Totem Poles
4. Vancouver Public Aquarium and Zoo
5. Miniature Railway
6. Lions Gate Bridge
7. Prospect Point

N

Burrard Inlet

Burrard Inlet

Stanley Park Drive

Lions Gate Bridge

North Vancouver
Grouse Mountain

Stanley Park Causeway

99
1a

Pipeline Road

Miniature Railway

Children's Zoo

Aquarium & Zoo

Malkin Bowl

Rose Garden

Lord Stanley Statue

Brockton Oval

Totem Poles Drive

Brockton Point

9 O'Clock Gun

Hallelujah Point

Stanley Park

Deadman's Island

Marina

Coal Harbour

W. Georgia St.

Chilco St.

Lost Lagoon

Lost Lagoon Drive

Lagoon Drive

Second Beach

English Bay

Ferguson Point

Third Beach

Siwash Rock

Seawall

Stanley Park Drive

Prospect Point

Beaver Lake

Hollow Tree

Stanley Park Drive

★★★
Stanley Park

Lord Stanley, the same person for whom ice hockey's Stanley Cup was named, founded Stanley Park on a romantic impulse back in the 19th century when he was Canada's Governor General (1888-1893). Stanley Park lies on an elevated peninsula stretching into the Georgia Strait, and encompasses 405ha of flowering gardens, dense woodlands and lookouts offering views of the sea and the mountains. Obviously Vancouver's many skyscrapers have not prevented the city from maintaining close ties with the nearby wilderness. Some species are held in captivity, but many others roam free – sometimes even venturing into the West End.

A 10km waterfront promenade known as the **Seawall** runs around the park, enabling pedestrians to drink in every bit of the stunning scenery here. The **Stanley Park Scenic Drive** is the equivalent of the Seawall for motorists. The best way to explore Stanley Park, however, is by bicycle. You can rent one from **Stanely Park Rentals** (*corner of West Georgia and Denman,* ☎688-5141) (see p 620). Another way to discover some of the park's hidden treasures is to walk along one of the many footpaths crisscrossing the territory. There are numerous rest areas along the way.

You'll be greeted by the sight of scores of gleaming yachts in the Vancouver marina with the downtown skyline in the background. This is the most developed portion of the park where you'll find the **Malkin Bowl**,

the **Brockton Oval** and most importantly, the **Totem Poles ★**. They're vivid reminders that was a sizeable Aboriginal population on the peninsula barely 150 years ago. The **9 O'Clock Gun** goes off every day at 9pm on Brockton Point (it is best not to be too close when it does). This shot used to alert fishermen that it was time to come in.

On the left is the entrance to the renowned **Vancouver Aquarium Marine Science Centre ★★★** (*$13; Jul and Aug, every day 9:30am to 7pm; Sep to Jun, every day 10am to 5:30pm;* ☎659-3474), which has the undeniable advantage of being located near the ocean. It displays representatives of the marine animal life of the West Coast and the Pacific as a whole, including magnificent killer whales, belugas, dolphins, seals and exotic fish.

The zoo at the back is home to sea lions and polar bears, among other creatures. The nearby **Miniature Railway** is a real hit with kids.

Head back to the Seawall under **Lions Gate Bridge ★★**, an elegant suspension bridge built in 1938. It spans the First Narrows, linking the afflu-

ent suburb of West Vancouver to the centre of town. **Prospect Point ★★★**, to the west, offers a general view of the bridge whose steel pillars stand 135m high. Next, the Seawall passes **Third Beach ★**, one of the most pleasant beaches in the region.

Other attractions

Head over to **Science World ★** (*$11.75 or $14.75 with movie; 1455 Quebec St.,* ☎443-7440), the big silver ball at the end of False Creek. Architect Bruno Freschi designed the 14-storey building as a welcome centre for visitors to Expo '86. It was the only pavilion built to remain in place after the big event. The sphere representing the Earth has supplanted the tower as the quintessential symbol of these fairs since Expo '67 in Montréal.

Vancouver's sphere contains an Omnimax theatre that presents films on a giant, dome-shaped screen. The rest of the building is now occupied by a museum that explores the secrets of science from all different angles.

During the summer of 1986, the vast stretch of unused land along the north shore of False Creek was occupied by dozens of showy pavilions with visitors crowding around them. Visible on the other side of an access road, **GM Place** *(Pacific Blvd. at the corner of Abbott,* ☎*899-7400)* is a 20,000-seat amphitheatre that was completed in 1995 and now hosts the home games of the local hockey and basketball teams, the Vancouver Canucks and Grizzlies respectively. Its big brother, **BC Place Stadium** *(777 Pacific Blvd. N.,* ☎*669-2300, 661-7373 or 661-2122,* ≈*661-3412)* stands to the south. Its 60,000 seats are highly coveted by fans of Canadian football who come here to cheer on the B.C. Lions. Big trade fairs and rock concerts are also held in the stadium.

Follow Pacific Boulevard under Granville Bridge, then turn left on Hornby Street and right on Beach Avenue. The False Creek ferry docks are nearby; catch a ferry for **Granville Island** and its **public market** ★ ★. You'll notice the vaguely Art Deco pillars of the Burrard Street Bridge (1930). In 1977, this artificial island, created in 1914 and once used for industrial purposes, saw its warehouses and factories transformed into a major recreational and commercial centre. The area has since come to life thanks to a revitalization project. A public market, many shops and all sorts of restaurants, plus theatres and artists' studios, are all part of Granville Island.

Van Dusen Botanical Gardens ★ ★ *(summer $5.50, winter $2.75; every day, summer 10am to nightfall, call for exact schedule; Apr and Sep 10am to 6pm;*

Oct to Mar 10am to 4pm; free guided tours every day, 1pm, 2pm and 3pm; 5251 Oak St., ☎*878-9274).* Since Vancouver is so blessed by Mother Nature, a number of lovely gardens have been planted in the area. These botanical gardens boasts plant species from all over the world. When the rhododendrons are in bloom (late May), the garden deserves another star. At the far end is a housing co-op that blends in so perfectly with the greenery that it looks like a gigantic ornamental sculpture (McCarter, Nairne and Associates, 1976).

Farther east on 33rd Avenue is another magnificent green space: **Queen Elizabeth Park** ★ ★ *(corner of 33rd Ave. and Cambie St.),* laid out around the **Bloedel Floral Conservatory** *($3.50; Apr to Sep, Mon to Fri 9am to 8pm, Sat and Sun 10am to 9pm; Oct to Mar, every day 10am to 5pm; at the top of Queen Elizabeth Park,* ☎*257-8570).* The latter, shaped like an overturned glass saucer, houses exotic plants and birds. The Bloedel company, which sponsored the conservatory, is the principal lumber company in British Columbia. This park's rhododendron bushes also merit a visit in springtime. Finally, the outdoor gardens offer a spectacular view of the city, English Bay and the surrounding mountains.

Keep right, and immediately after going down the roadway leading off the bridge, take a right on Chestnut Street to get to **Vanier Park** which is home to three museums. The **Vancouver Museum** ★ ★ *($8; Jul and Aug, every day 10am to 5pm; Sep to June closed Mon; 1100 Chestnut St., in Vanier Park,* ☎ *736-4431)*

forms its centrepiece. This museum, whose dome resembles the head-dress worn by the coastal Salish First Nation, presents exhibitions on the history of the different peoples who have inhabited the region.

On the same spot is the **Pacific Space Centre** *($12.50; presentations Tue to Sun 2:30pm and 8pm, extra shows Sat and Sun 1pm and 4pm;* ☎ *738-7827),* which houses the H.R. MacMillan Planetarium and relates the creation of our universe. It has a telescope through which you can admire the stars. The **Maritime Museum** *($6; May to Oct, every day 10am to 5pm; Nov to Apr closed Mon; 1905 Ogden Ave.,* ☎*257-8300)* completes the trio of institutions in Vanier Park. Being a major seaport, it is only natural that Vancouver should have its own maritime museum. The key attraction is the *Saint-Roch,* the first boat to circle North America by navigating the Panamá Canal and the Northwest Passage.

The tour continues onto the grounds of the **University of British Columbia** ★, or UBC. The university was created by the provincial government in 1908. But it was not until 1925 that the campus opened its doors on this lovely site on Point Grey. An architectural contest had been organized for the site layout, but the First World War halted construction work. It took a student demonstration denouncing government inaction in this matter to get the buildings completed. Only the library and the science building were executed according to the original plans. **Set Foot for UBC** *(May to Aug, free tours organized by students,* ☎*822-TOUR).*

British Columbia

To this day, the UBC campus is constantly expanding, so don't be surprised by its somewhat heterogeneous appearance. There are, however, a few gems including the **Museum of Anthropology** ★★★ *($6, free admission Tue 5pm to 9pm; in the summer, every day 10am to 5pm, in the winter closed Mon and Dec 25 and 26; 6393 NW Marine Dr.; from downtown, take bus #4 UBC or bus #10 UBC;* ☎*822-3825)* which is not to be missed both for the quality of Aboriginal artwork displayed here, including totem poles, and for the architecture of Arthur Erickson. Big concrete beams and columns imitate the shapes of traditional Aboriginal houses, beneath which have been erected immense totem poles gathered from former Aboriginal villages along the coast and on the islands. Wooden sculptures and various works of art form part of the permanent exhibition.

The Gulf Islands

Each of these islands is a different place to commune with nature and enjoy a little seclusion, far from traffic jams. Time is measured here according to the arrival and departure of the ferries. A convivial atmosphere prevails on these little havens of peace, especially at the end of the day when visitors and islanders mingle at the pub. Surprises await you on each trip — an island straight out of your dreams, perhaps, or the sight of a seal swimming under your kayak — moments that will become lifelong memories.

The Gulf Islands consist of some 200 islands scattered across the Strait of Georgia between the eastern shore of Vancouver Island and the west coast, near the San Juan Islands (U.S.A.).

★
Salt Spring Island

Salt Spring is the largest and most populous of the Gulf Islands. Aboriginals used to come here during summer to catch shellfish, hunt fowl and gather plants. In 1859, the first Europeans settled on the island and began establishing farms and small businesses here. Today, many artists have chosen Salt Spring as their home and place of work. When they aren't practising their art on the street, they welcome the public into their studios. As Vancouver Island is just a short trip from Salt Spring, some residents work in Victoria. The town of Ganges is the commercial hub of the island. A promenade runs alongside its harbour, past a number of shops and through two marinas.

★★
Galiano Island

With just over a tenth of the population of Salt Spring, this island is a quiet, picturesque place. It was named after Dionisio Galiano, the Spanish explorer who first sailed these waters. About 30km long and over 2km wide, Galiano faces northwest on one end and southeast on the other. Its shores afford some lovely views and are dotted with shell beaches.

Galiano Planet Revival Festival of Music (☎539-5778) presents Aboriginal dance performances and a varied repertoire of folk, jazz and funk performed by local artists.

★
Mayne Island

Mayne Island, Galiano's neighbour to the south, is a quiet place inhabited mainly by retirees. The limited number of tourists makes for a peaceful atmosphere while the relatively flat terrain is a cyclist's dream. In the mid-19th century during the gold rush, miners heading from Victoria to the Fraser River used to stop here before crossing the Strait of Georgia, hence the name Miners Bay. The first Europeans to settle on the island grew apples here, and their vast orchards have survived to this day. A few local buildings bear witness to the arrival of the pioneers. The **St. Mary Magdalene** ★ (*Georgina Point Rd.*) church, built entirely of wood in 1897, merits a visit. Take the opportunity to see the stained-glass windows on Sunday when the church is open for Mass.

The **Active Pass Lighthouse** ★ (*every day 1pm to 3pm; Georgina Point Rd.,* ☎539-5286) has been guiding sailors through these waters since 1885. The original structure, however, was replaced by a new tower in 1940 that was in turn replaced in 1969. The place is easy to get to and is indicated on most maps of the region.

★
Saturna Island

Saturna is possibly the most isolated and least accessible island of all the Gulf Islands. Its residents, who number around 300, are determined to keep it that way. Saturna has very

limited facilities, and only two restaurants. Don't let this deter you. Nature lovers will be fascinated by the island's **unusual flora and fauna**, like, for example, the **giant mushrooms** that grow around **Mount Warburton**.

Saturna's annual **Canada Day** celebration (*Jul 1*) is a huge lamb roast. It's the island's biggest gathering of the year.

★
Pender Islands

North and South Pender are the second most populated islands after Salt Spring and are joined together by a wooden bridge. They are fairly well equipped for tourists. Visitors come primarily to cycle or to lounge on the beaches. **Mount Normand** has a good reputation among walkers. From the summit there's an exceptional view of the **San Juan Islands**. The laid-back, bohemian atmosphere is immediately apparent upon arriving, what with all the natural food stores and organic farms. Every Saturday, from May to October, the Driftwood Centre hosts a very colourful **farmer's market** where you'll find good fresh produce.

★★
Quadra Island

Quadra Island has about 4,000 residents. In the summer the number doubles with the influx of tourists drawn here by its exceptional reputation for salmon fishing. Quadra is covered almost entirely by forests. Locals are proud of the lack of crime on their island; politeness and a friendly smile are of the utmost importance.

Quadra, like Cortes, is in the northern gulf and is one of the Discovery Islands. It can be reached by a ferry from Campbell River to **Quathiaski Cove** in less than 10min. Once on the island, be sure to visit the **Kwatkiutl Museum** (*every day 10am to 6pm; ☎285-3733*). This excellent museum of Aboriginal art presents relics that recount the lives of the island's first inhabitants. It is easily the most beautiful museum in the region. **Cape Mudge Lighthouse**, built in 1898, is nearby. Along the beach at the southern tip of the island, **petroglyphs**, drawn by Aboriginals 1000 years ago are revealed at low tide.

On the way to **Heriot Bay**, a small town in the northeast part of the island, you will come across the small BC Ferries terminal. This is where you catch the ferry to Cortes Island. Not far from the dock is the lovely little Rebecca Spit Marine Provincial Park.

★
Cortes Island

Cortes Island is located north of the Strait of Georgia, a few nautical miles from Desolation Sound and 45min from Quadra Island by ferry. The ferry ride alone, if the weather is nice, is worth the trip. Once on the island, you will soon realize that services for tourists are very limited.

People come here to commune with nature: clear **lagoons** rich in aquatic life, deep **forests** and fine-sand **beaches**. It's a paradise for sea kayaking, cycling and all sorts of excursions. Cortes Island is approximately 25km long and 13km wide. The north end is wild and uninhabited. On the south end, you'll find restaurants, hotels and grocery stores.

Parks and Beaches

The Gulf Islands

Mount Maxwell Provincial Park ★ (*Salt Spring Island, from Fulford-Ganges Rd., take Cranberry Rd., then Mount Maxwell Rd. all the way to the end, ☎391-2300*) lies on a mountainside. The lookout is easily accessible, and the view of Vancouver Island and the islands to the south is worth the trip.

Montague Harbour Maritime Park ★★ (*on the west side of Galiano Island, 10km from the ferry terminal, ☎391-2300*) is a top-notch park featuring a lagoon, a shell beach and an equipped campground. The view of the sunset from the north beach will send you off into a reverie.

Bluffs Park ★ (*Galiano Island, take Bluff Dr. from Georgeson Bay Rd. or Burrill Rd.*) offers a view from

British Columbia

above of aptly named Active Pass, where ferries heading for Swartz Bay (Victoria) and Tsawwassen (Vancouver) cross paths.

The **Bennet Bay beach** is a very pleasant spot – the best place on Mayne Island to take a walk.

Among the pleasant routes on the Pender Islands, the one that leads from **Mount Normand** to **Beaumont Provincial Park** is undoubtedly the most interesting. Picnic tables and campsites are available in the park, around the beach, so visitors can spend the night.

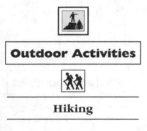

Outdoor Activities

Hiking

Vancouver

Stanley Park is definitely the best place to go hiking in Vancouver with over 50km of trails through forest and greenery along the sea- and lakeshores, including the **Seawall**, an outstanding 8km trail flanked by giant trees.

If you like gardens and are heading through Chinatown, you won't need a pair of hiking boots to visit the **Dr. Sun Yat-Sen Classical Chinese Garden** (☎689-7133) whose little bridges and trails will guide you through a realm of peace and serenity (see p 613).

Mountain hiking can be done on one of the peaks near the city centre. **Cypress Provincial Park** (☎924-2200) north of the municipality of West Van-

couver, has several hiking trails.

The hike up **Grouse Mountain ★★★** (☎984-0661) is not particularly difficult. But the incline is as steep as 25° in places, so you have to be in good shape. It takes about 2hrs to cover the 3km trail, that starts at the parking lot for the cable car. The view of the city from the top of the mountain is fantastic. If you are too tired to hike back down, take the cable car for the modest sum of $5.

Mount Seymour Provincial Park (☎986-2261) is another good hiking locale, offering two different views of the region. To the east is Indian Arm, a large arm of the sea extending into the valley.

A little farther east in this marvellous mountain range on the north shore, magnificent **Lynn Headwaters Park ★★★** is scored with forest trails. It is best known for its footbridge that stretches across an 80m-deep gorge. Definitely not for the faint of heart! To get there, take Highway 1 from North Vancouver to the Lynn Valley Road exit follow the signs and then turn right on Peters Road.

A 15min **ferry** (BC Ferry, ☎250-386-3431) ride from Horseshoe Bay transports you to **Bowen Island ★★★** (☎947-2216) where hiking trails lead through a lush forest. Although you'll feel as if you're at the other end of the world, downtown Vancouver is only 5km away as the crow flies.

The Gulf Islands

Llama Lakes Trekking (Box 414, Quathiaski Cove, Quadra Island V0P 1N0, ☎285-2413, ≈285-2473) offers guided hiking and camping trips. Food and camping equipment are supplied. If you don't have a vehicle, Llama Lakes Trekking will come and pick you up at the ferry dock in Quathiaski Cove or Heriot Bay, and take you to the trail. You can choose one-day to five-day hiking packages.

Cycling

Vancouver

The region has a multitude of trails for mountain biking. Just head to one of the mountains north of the city. A pleasant 8km ride runs along the Seawall in Stanley Park. Bicycle rentals are available at **Spokes Bicycle Rental** (1798 West Georgia St., corner of Denman, ☎688-5141). Outside Vancouver, you can go cycling in the Fraser Valley, near farms or along secondary roads.

Canoeing and Kayaking

Vancouver

Those who prefer running white water on canoes or kayaks can contact one of the following agencies, which organize expeditions and will equip you from head to toe: **Whitewater Kayaking Association of B.C.** (1367 Broadway, Van-

couver, V6H 4A9,
☎222-1577), or **Canadian
Adventure Tours** (Box 929,
Whistler, V0N 1B0,
☎938-0727), a good place
if you're passing through
Whistler.

Canadian River Expeditions
(301-3524 W. 16th Ave.,
Vancouver, V6R 3C1,
☎938-6651) allows you to
plan an expedition from
Vancouver.

Sea To Sky Trails
(105C-11831 80th Ave.,
Delta, V4C 7X6, ☎594-7701)
is a small adventure travel
agency located in a suburb
south of Vancouver .

The Gulf Islands

T'ai Li Lodge (Cortes Bay,
Cortes Island, ☎935- 6749) is
a marine-adventure centre
across from the park at
Desolation Sound. You
can learn to sail and sea
kayak in fantastic sur-
roundings with naturalist
guides. A package with
accommodation is also
available.

**Canadian Gulf Islands Cata-
maran Cruises** ($39; 4hr
cruise, snack included;
Montague Harbour, Galiano
Island, ☎539-2930) offer
2hr guided sea-kayak tours
for $25.

The crew of White Raven
organizes kayak excur-
sions for $20. For about
2hrs, you sail off to ex-
plore the surrounding
islands. The White Raven's
port of registry is at the
pier on Fourth Street.

Even though you can
reach the Broken Islands
archipelago easily from
Bamfield, kayak excur-
sions from Ucluelet can
also be arranged with
Majestic Ocean Kayaking
(☎726-2868).

Downhill Skiing

Vancouver

What makes Vancouver a
truly magical place is the
combination of sea and
mountains. The cold sea-
son is no exception as
residents desert the
beaches and seaside paths
to crowd the ski hills
which are literally sus-
pended over the city.
There are four ski resorts
close to the city: **Mount
Seymour** ($26; 1700 Mount
Seymour Rd., North Vancouver, V7G 1L3; Upper Level
Hwy. heading east, Deep Cove
Exit, information ☎986-2261,
ski conditions ☎718-7771,
☎/≈986-2267), a family
resort with beginner trails,
situated east of North
Vancouver above Deep
Cove; **Grouse Mountain** ($28,
night skiing $20; 6400 Nancy
Greene Way, North Vancou-
ver, ☎984-0661, ski conditions ☎986-6262, ski school
☎980-9311), a small resort
accessible by cable car that
offers an unobstructed
view of Vancouver that is
as magnificent by day as it
is by night; **Cypress Bowl**
($35, night skiing $23; from
North Vancouver, take
TransCanada Highway 1,
heading west for 16km, then
follow road signs. Information
and ski conditions
☎926-5612), a resort for
the most avid skiers, also
offers magnificent views
of Howe Sound and of the
city.

Another option is the vil-
lage-style **Hemlock Valley
Resort** ($32, night skiing $11;
Hwy. 1 heading east,
Agassizou Harrisson Hot
Springs Exit, ☎797-4411, ski
conditions ☎520-6222,
≈797-4440, accommodation
reservations ☎797-4444).

Situated at the eastern tip
of Vancouver's urban area
in the heart of the Cascade
Mountains, this resort offers an abundance of snow
and a spectacular view of
Mount Baker in the United
States.

As soon as enough snow
blankets the slope, in late
November or early Decem-
ber, these four ski resorts
are open every day until
late at night, thanks to
powerful neon lighting. It
should be noted, however,
that the first three resorts
do not provide accommo-
dation.

Of course there are also
Whistler and Black-comb,
two great hills easily accessible from Vancouver, see
p 598.

Accommodations

Vancouver is a big city
with lodgings for all tastes
and budgets. All accom-
modations shown here are
well located, within walking distance of bus stops
and, in most cases, in or
near the downtown area.
**Super Natural British Colum-
bia** (☎800-663-6000) can
make reservations for you.

Vancouver

Downtown

Vancouver Downtown YHA
$19 members
$23 non-members
1114 Burnaby St.
V6E 1P1
☎**684-4565**
≈684-4540
Vancouver Downtown
YHA is a big hostel (239
beds) right downtown at
the corner of Thurlow.

British Columbia

Common kitchen and tv room; coin-laundry.

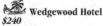 **Wedgewood Hotel**
$240
☺, △, ≡, ℜ
845 Hornby St., V6Z 1V2
☎689-7777
☎800-663-0666
⇒668-3074
The Wedgewood Hotel is small enough to have retained some character and style – in particular the lovely lobby complete with shiny brass accents, cosy fireplace and distinguished art – and large enough to offer a certain measure of privacy and professionalism. This is a popular option for business trips and romantic weekend getaways.

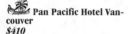 **Pan Pacific Hotel Vancouver**
$410
≡, ☺, ☺, tv, ≈, △, P, ℜ, &, ☒
300-999 Canada Place
☎662-8111
in Canada:
☎800-663-1515
in the US:
☎800-937-1515
⇒685-8690
The luxurious Pan Pacific Hotel Vancouver is located in Canada Place, on the shore of Burrard Inlet facing North Vancouver, with a good view of port activities. The hotel has 506 rooms, and its lobby, with its marble decor, 20m-high ceilings and panoramic view of the ocean, is magnificent.

West End

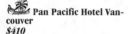 **Sylvia Hotel**
$115
tv, K, ℜ, ☒, P
1154 Gilford Street
☎681-9321
Located just a few steps from English Bay, this charming old hotel built in the early 1900s, offers unspoiled views and has

118 simple rooms. People come for the atmosphere, but also for food and drink at the end of the day. For those on lower budgets, rooms without views are offered at lower rates. The manager of this ivy-covered hotel is a Frenchman who is fully and justifiably dedicated to his establishment. Request a southwest-facing room (one facing English Bay) to benefit from magical sunsets over the bay.

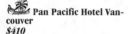 **West End Guest House Bed & Breakfast**
$150 bkfst incl.
P, ⊗
no children under 12
1362 Haro St.
☎681-2889
⇒688-8812
westendguesthouse.com
This magnificent inn set in a turn-of-the-century Victorian house is well situated near a park and near Robson Street. Evan Penner is your host. A minimum two-day stay may apply. The West End Guest House has an excellent reputation. (Nearby, at 1415 Barclay St., is Roedde House, built in Victorian-Edwardian style in 1893. It was designed by none other than the architect Francis Rattenbury who also created the Vancouver Art Gallery, the legislature building in Victoria, and the Empress Hotel.)

Landmark Hotel
$200
tv, ☺, ☺, ℜ, △, ≈, &
1400 Robson St.
☎687-0511
☎800-830-6144
⇒687-2801
The Landmark Hotel truly is a landmark with its 40 floors and its revolving resto-bar at the top. The view is fascinating and quite an experience!

 Sutton Place Hotel
$265-$415
☺, ☺, ≈, △, ℝ, ℜ, &
845 Burrard St.
☎682-5511
☎800-961-7555
⇒682-5513
The Sutton Place Hotel, formerly the Meridien, offers 397 rooms and the full range of five-star services normally provided by the top hotel chains. The European decor has been maintained. If you are a chocolate lover, don't miss the chocolate buffet served on Fridays.

Other Areas

The Globetrotter's Inn
$18 sb
45$ pb
tv
170 West Esplanade
North Vancouver
☎988-2082
⇒987-8389
The Globetrotter's Inn, in the heart of North Vancouver near the Seabus and the shops of Marine Drive and the Quay Market, is very affordable. Hostel-style dorm rooms are also available!

Canyon Court Motel
$110
tv, ≡, ≈
1748 Capilano Rd.
North Vancouver
☎/⇒988-3181
The Canyon Court Motel is located right next to the Capilano Suspension Bridge, the Lion's Gate Bridge and the Trans-Canada Highway. It is very comfortable and not too expensive.

 Summit View
$110-$150 bkfst incl.
tv, P, ℜ
5501 Cliffridge Pl.
☎990-1089
⇒987-7167
To get here from the Lions Gate Bridge, head toward North Vancouver, turn

right on Marine Drive, then, turn left on Capilano Road at the first intersection, right on Prospect Road, left on Cliffridge Avenue and finally left on Cliffridge Place. To get here from the Second Narrows Bridge, take Highway 1 west and exit onto Capilano Road, then continue as above.

Each room has its own character. In the elegant dining room, breakfast and dinner are prepared to order, according to your tastes or diet. Rock-climbing, skiing, fishing, canoeing, swimming and tennis are all possible nearby. The management offers bicycles to help you discover the wonders of the area. Low-season rates are considerably less expensive here.

Pillow Porridge Guest House
$85-$135 bkfst incl.
tv, ℝ, K,
2859 Manitoba St.
☎*879-8977*
⇄*897-8966*
www.pillow.net
The Pillow Porridge Guest House is a residence dating back to 1910, and the decor and ambience attest to it. These complete apartments with kitchens are pleasant and comfortable. Close to a number of ethnically diverse restaurants.

William House
$95-$190 bkfst incl.
tv
2050 W. 18th Ave.
☎/⇄*731-2760*
whouse@direct.ca
William House is a beautiful, completely restored country house, in the old area of Shaughnessy, a few minutes from downtown. Luxury suites and rooms offer a pleasantly calm, comfortable environment. The large garden and yard provide havens from all the noise of the

city. Well suited to business people. Prices are negotiable depending on the season and the length of your stay.

The Gulf Islands

Galiano Island

 **La Berengerie**
$60 bkfst incl.
sb, ℜ
Montague Harbour Rd. Galiano
☎*539-5392*
At La Berengerie, which has four rooms, guests enjoy a relaxing atmosphere in the woods. Huguette Benger has been running the place since 1983. Originally from the south of France, Madame Benger came to Galiano on a vacation and decided to stay. Take the time to chat with her and she'll be delighted to tell you all about the island. Breakfast is served in a large dining room. La Berengerie is closed from November to March.

Salt Spring Island

The Summerhill Guest House
$100-$125 bkfst incl.
209 Chu-An Dr.
☎*537-2727*
⇄537-4301
The Summerhill Guest House has been completely renovated. The interesting combination of landings and terraces lets in the sunlight and allows for some beautiful views of the Sansum Narrows. The breakfast is unusual and absolutely delicious. You'll feel right at home here.

Mayne Island

 **The Root Seller Inn**
$80 bkfst incl.
children 6 and over
sb, no smoking
478 Village Bay Rd. ☎*539-2621*
⇄*539-2411*
The Root Seller Inn lies hidden behind the flowers and trees lovingly planted by the charming Joan Drummond who has been welcoming guests to the island for over 30 years. It all started at the Springwater Hotel in 1960 when she and her husband, having just arrived on the island, opened a hotel. Since 1983, Joan has been receiving guests in her home and showing them the island. The big wooden Cape Cod-style house can accommodate eight people in three large rooms. It lies near Mariners Bay so guests can contemplate the scenery and watch the ferries on their way through Active Pass from the balcony.

Saturna Island

 **The East Point Resort**
$77-$104
P
187 East Point Rd.
☎*539-2975*
The East Point Resort provides natural surroundings with exclusive access to a smooth sandy beach. Visitors can choose from six small, luxurious and attractively decorated cottages.

Restaurants

Vancouver

Gastown

Water Street Café
$
*closes at 10pm weekdays
11pm weekends*
300 Water St.
☎*689-2832*
A handsome bistro with big windows facing Gastown. Tables are decorated with pretty lanterns, and service is friendly. The menu centres around pastas prepared in creative ways.

Top of Vancouver
$$$
*Sunday brunch buffet for
$26.95
every day 11:30am to 2:30pm
and 5pm to 10pm
except Sun brunch at 11am*
555 W. Hastings St.
☎*669-2220*
This restaurant is located atop Harbour Centre (the elevator is free for restaurant patrons). It revolves once an hour, giving diners a city tour from high in the air while they eat. Classic West Coast cuisine is served here.

Chinatown and East Vancouver

Waa Zuu Bee Café
$
every day 11:30am to 1am
1622 Commercial Dr.
☎*253-5299*
The Waa Zuu Bee Café is great and inexpensive. The innovative cuisine combined with the "natural-techno-italo-bizarre" decor are full of surprises. The pasta dishes are always interesting.

Sun Sui Wah Seafood Restaurant
$$
every day
3888 Main St., at Third Ave.
☎*872-8822*
Authentic Chinese food, lobster, crayfish, crab, oysters and, of course, Peking duck.

Cannery Seafood Restaurant
$$$
until 10pm
2205 Commissioner St.
☎*254-9606*
The Cannery Seafood Restaurant is one of the best places in town for seafood. It is located in the East End in a renovated, century-old warehouse. The view of the sea is fantastic.

Downtown

 **Bacchus Restaurant**
$$
Wedgewood Hotel
845 Hornby St.
☎*689-7777*
A lovely, intimate decor, an ambience enhanced by piano music and a cuisine cooked up by an award-winning chef make this restaurant popular with its downtown clientele.

Tsunami Sushi
$$
238-1025 Robson St.
☎*687-8744, unit 238*
Tsunami Sushi has a revolving sushi bar, much like those in Japan, from which patrons can choose specialties at will. Excellent quality for the price. Its huge, sunny terrace overlooks Robson Street.

 Il Giardino
$$$
1382 Hornby St.
☎*669-2422*
This popular restaurant has a renowned reputation for its attractive Italian-style decor, charming patio, inspired dishes with

local and European accents and its vast selection of Italian pasta. Always crowded. Warm, friendly ambience.

 **Le Crocodile**
$$$-$$$$
909 Burrard St.
entry by Smithe St.
☎*669-4298*
This establishment is the beacon of French cuisine in Vancouver, as much for the quality of its food as for its service, its decor and its wine list. Lovers of great French cuisine will be spoiled by the choice of red meats and the delicacies from the sea. The salmon tartare is a must – you *are* on the Pacific coast after all!

Lumière
$$$$
closed Mon
2551 W. Broadway Ave.
☎*739-8185*
Lumière is a favourite with Vancouver residents, especially chefs. The simple, white interior allows the food to shine, and shine it does. The fresh, local ingredients used in each dish make for creative and honest but very refined cuisine. One winning choice is veal tenderloin with braised turnip lasagna topped off by lemon tarts or chocolate truffles.

West End and Stanley Park

 True Confections
$
until 1am
866 Denman St.
☎*682-1292*
True Confections is a dessert place par excellence that serves huge slices of cake. Be sure to try the divine Belgian dark-chocolate torte.

Ohana Sushi
$-$$
1414 W. Broadway
☎732-0112
This chain of Japanese restaurants offers excellent dishes at reasonable prices. Service is efficient and pleasant. A fine Asian experience.

Liliget
$$
every day
1724 Davie St.
☎681-7044
Liliget is a First Nations restaurant that offers authentic Aboriginal-style food: salmon grilled on a wood fire, smoked oysters, grilled seaweed and roasted wild duck. Worth exploring.

 Raku
$$
838 Thurlow St., north of Robson
☎685-8817
A wealthy young Japanese clientele meets here and fits right in. It has the atmosphere of a noisy bar, but it is an ideal spot to begin a promising evening. The sushi and grilled meats are recommended.

 C
$$$
1600 Howe St.
≈605-8263
This Chinese restaurant, whose name evokes the sea, is the talk of the town, and for good reason. The chef has returned from Southeast Asia with innovative and unique recipes. Served on the stroke of 12, the C-style Dim Sum is a real delight. Titbits of fish marinated in tea and a touch of caviar, vol-au-vents with chanterelles, curry shrimp with coconut milk, and the list goes on... All quite simply exquisite. Desserts are equally extraordinary. For those who dare, the crème brûlée with blue

cheese is an unforgettable experience. This restaurant is an absolute must.

 Le Café de Paris
$$$
751 Denman St.
☎687-1418
The speciality of Le Café de Paris is its *cassoulet* (a stew originating from southwestern France). Many other dishes are inspired from different regions of France. The fries that accompany every dish are excellent. Good wine and prompt service.

The Fish House in Stanley Park
$$$
until 10:30pm
8901 Stanley Park Dr.
☎681-7275
The Fish House in Stanley Park is located in a Victorian house right in the heart of the park and just a few steps from the Seawall. Fine seafood and fish dishes are served in a lovely, opulent decor.

Teahouse Restaurant
$$$
until 10pm
along the Seawall
7501 Stanley park Dr.
☎669-3281
The Teahouse Restaurant serves delicious food and affords stunning views of English Bay from Stanley Park. Call ahead for reservations and for precise directions as it can be tricky to find.

 L'Hermitage
$$$-$$$$
every day
1025 Robson St., Suite 115
☎689-3237
The chef-owner Hervé Martin is an artist when it comes to French cuisine who will tell you stories from his days as the chef of the Belgian Royal Court. Wines from his native region of Burgundy accom-

pany the finest of dishes, each prepared carefully and with panache. The decor is chic and the service exemplary. The terrace, set back from Robson, is lovely in the summertime.

Other Areas

Bridges Bistro
$
until 11:30pm
1696 Durenleau St.
Granville Island
☎687-4400
≈687-0352
The Bridges Bistro boasts one of the prettiest terraces in Vancouver, right by the water in the middle of Granville Island's pleasure-boat harbour. The food and setting are decidedly West Coast.

Naam
$
open 24hrs
2724 W. 4th Ave.
☎738-7151
The Naam blends live music with vegetarian meals. This little restaurant has a warm atmosphere, friendly service, and is frequented by a young clientele.

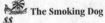 **The Smoking Dog**
$$
1889 W. First Ave.
☎736-8811
The Smoking Dog has a warm, lively atmosphere, lovely decor and reasonable prices for its carefully prepared *table d'hôte*. Exquisite steak, copious salads and creative daily specials. The fries that accompany every dish are golden brown on the outside and tender on the inside. Jean-Claude, the owner, is a friendly *Marseillais*.

Raku Kushiyaki Restaurant
$$-$$$
closed Mon
4422 W. 10th Ave.
☎*222-8188*

The young chefs of this little restaurant prepare local cuisine served with oriental aesthetic rules in mind. That will help you discover their art. Take a meal for two to appreciate the spirit of this *nouvelle cuisine* which encourages the sharing of meals among guests. The portions may seem small, but you still come away satisfied. Ingredients are chosen according to the seasons. For example, wild mushrooms are served accented with garlic, green bell peppers, butter, soya sauce and lime juice. This dish may seem simple, and it is, but the taste of the food is not masked by mediocre sauces. The meat and fish are also treated with subtlety.

The Gulf Islands

Galiano Island

 La Berengerie
$$
open only in the evening
Montague Harbour Rd.
☎*539-5392*

La Berengerie has a four-course menu with a choice of fish or meat. The dining room, located on the ground floor of a bed and breakfast, is furnished with antiques. Candlelight makes the atmosphere that much more inviting. Owner Huguette Benger prepares the delicious meals herself. During the day, her son's restaurant, **La Bohème**, serves vegetarian dishes on the terrace overlooking the garden.

Salt Spring Island

 **Alfresco Waterfront Restaurant**
$$
Grace Point Sq.
Ganges
☎*537-5979*

Alfresco Waterfront Restaurant is an Italian restaurant with good soups, seafood and excellent duck and lamb dishes.

Seacourt Gourmet Restaurant
$$
108 Fulford St. , Ganges

The Seacourt is a very good restaurant that serves international cuisine with a spicy touch. The fish is excellent but the real musts are the authentic caesar salad and the succulent crepes suzette. These two dishes are prepared right in front of you. An excellent place.

Quadra Island

 **Tsa-Kwa-Luten Lodge**
$
May to Sep every day
Lighthouse, Quadra Island
☎*285-2042*
reservations recommended

The site is truly spectacular, providing an unobstructed view of Discovery Passage. It's not unusual to see eagles flying over the restaurant. Regional specialties with a native influence are served here : try the excellent salmon ham burger. The wine list is extensive. In the summer, you can enjoy some barbecued salmon on the big outdoor terrace.

April Point Lodge & Fishing Resort
$$-$$$
903 April Point Rd.
☎*285-2222*
☎*888-334-3474*

For breakfast, lunch and dinner, the restaurant at this impressive resort serves meals that easily meet gourmets' high expectations. The wine list is equally impressive.

Cortes Island

 The Old Floathouse Restaurant
$
summer every day 11am to 2pm and 6pm to 10pm
Whaletown
follow the signs from the ferry terminal Gorge Harbour Marina Resort ☎*935-6631*
in winter
☎*935-6433*

The Old Floathouse Restaurant is one of the rare good restaurants on the island. It also benefits from a superb location on a magnificent property.

Entertainment

Vancouver

ARTS Hotline (☎*684-ARTS*) will inform you about all the shows (dance, theatre, music, cinema and literature) in the city.

The Georgia Straight
(☎*730-7000*). This weekly paper is published every Thursday and distributed free at many spots in Vancouver. You will find all the necessary information on coming shows and cultural events. This paper is read religiously each week by many Vancouverites and has acquired a good reputation.

For information on jazz shows in Vancouver, call the **Jazz Hotline** (☎*682-0706*).

To book tickets for cultural or sporting events, try the following:

Ticketmaster
☎280-4444

Arts Line
☎280-3311 *(for tickets only)*

Sports Line
☎280-4400

Bars and Danceclubs

Gastown

Blarney Stone
216 Carrall St.
☎687-4322
The Blarney Stone is the spot for authentic Irish jigs and reels. The ambience is frenetic, with people dancing everywhere, on the tables, on the chairs... A must-see!

Richard's on Richards
1036 Richard St.
☎687-6794
Richard's on Richards is an institution in Vancouver. People of all ages flock to this chic spot to see and be seen. Theme nights. A must try.

The Purple Onion Cabaret
every day
15 Water St., 3rd floor
☎602-9442
The Purple Onion Cabaret is the mecca of upbeat jazz in Vancouver with entertainment provided by a disc-jockey or live bands. Cover charge of $5 during the week and $7 on weekends. Wednesdays are dedicated to Latin jazz while on Fridays and Saturdays there's live jazz near the bar and "disco-funk" on the dance floor.

Downtown

Babalu
654 Nelson St.
at Granville St.
☎605-4343
is a lounge-style bar. It's the ideal spot to sip a cocktail while enjoying a little Frank Sinatra and a cigar. There is also dancing to jazzy rhythms. Cover charge of $3.

Chameleon Urban Lounge
every day
801 W. Georgia St.
☎669-0806
This excellent little downtown club is often packed on weekends, but it is calm during the week. Don't miss their trip-hop nights on Wednesdays, Afro-Cuban and Latin music on Thursdays, and Acid Jazz on Saturdays. Warning: get there early to avoid lineups. The cover charge is $5 on Fridays and Saturdays.

Gay and Lesbian Bars

Celebrities
free admission
1022 Davie St.
☎689-3180
Celebrities is definitely the best-known gay bar in Vancouver. Straights also come here for the music. Drag queens make conspicuous appearances, especially on Wednesdays, during the female impersonators night. Packed on weekends.

Charlie's Lounge
455 Abbott St.
☎685-7777
Charlie's Lounge is a relaxed bar with an elegant gay clientele, located on the ground floor of an old hotel. Opens at 4pm on Mondays and Tuesdays and at 3pm from Wednesday to Saturday. Sundays, they serve brunch from 11am to 2pm. Musical improv sessions in the afternoon and retro dance music at night.

Lotus Club
455 Abbott St.
☎685-7777
The Lotus Club is the only bar in Vancouver reserved exclusively for women. It's located in the same hotel as Charlie's Lounge and Chuck's Pub, on the ground floor.

Cultural Activities

Theatres

Art's Club Theatre
(1585 Johnston, ☎687-1644)
is a steadfast institution on the Vancouver theatre scene. Located on the waterfront on Granville Island, this theatre presents contemporary works with social themes. Audience members often get together in the theatre's bar after the plays.

The **Firehall Arts Centre**
(280 E. Cordova St.,
☎689-0926), in the east-central part of the city, has a very good reputation and, like Art's Club Theatre, presents contemporary plays dealing with social themes. Worth a visit.

The **Ford Centre for the Performing Arts** *(777 Homer St.,*
☎280-2222) is an immense, big-budget theatre that presents international mega-productions.

The **Queen Elizabeth Theatre**
(Hamilton St., at Georgia St.,
☎665-3050), a large hall with 2,000 seats, presents musicals and variety shows and is also the main performance space for the Vancouver Opera.

The **Vancouver Opera**
(845 Cambie St., ☎682-2871)
performs at the Queen Elizabeth Theatre (see above) because Vancouver is one of the major cities in

British Columbia

the world that doesn't have an opera house. The address here is for the administrative office which provides program information.

The old **Vogue Theatre** (*918 Granville*, ☎*331-7900*), renovated not long ago, follows the trend in Vancouver of presenting all types of shows: theatre, comedy, music and even film. The programming varies.

The Gulf Islands

Bars and Danceclubs

The Hummingbird Pub
$
every day until 12:30am
47 Sturdies Bay Rd. Galiano Island
☎*539-5472*
This is a friendly place where tourists and locals mingle over a good beer and a plate of fries.

Shopping

Vancouver

Markets

Robson Market (*Robson St. at Cardero*) has it all and then some: vegetables; fresh fish, some of it cleaned out; stands with fruit salads; meats, sausages and ham; pastries and other baked goods; a counter for Alsatian and German specialties; flowers and plants; vitamins and natural products; natural medicine clinic; hair salon; small restaurants upstairs. The market is covered, but well lit.

Granville Island Market (*9am to 6pm; Granville Island*) is Vancouver's best-known and most popular market. It is an immense commercial area surrounded by water with a fairground atmosphere. Good food, some of it prepared; fresh, good-quality vegetables, some of it organic; fresh fish and meat; wholesome breads; fast-food counters; andpleasant shops selling jewellery, clothing and equipment for water sports and outdoor activities. Take a day to look, sample and wander. Parking is hard to find on the street but there are two indoor parking (*fee*) lots nearby.

Bookstores

Little Sisters Book and Art Emporium (*every day 10am to 11pm; 1238 Davie St.*, ☎*669-1753 or 800-567-1662*) is the only gay bookshop in Western Canada. It offers gay literature as well as essays on homosexuality, feminism and related topics. It is also a vast bazaar, with products that include humorous greeting cards. With the support of several Canadian literary figures, this bookshop has been fighting Canada Customs which arbitrarily blocks the importation of certain publications. Books by recognized and respected authors such as Marcel Proust have been seized by Canada Customs, which has taken on the role of censor. Some of the same titles bound for regular bookshops have mysteriously escaped seizure by Canada Customs, leading to questions about discrimination.

Aboriginal Arts and Crafts

The **Inuit Gallery of Vancouver** (*345 Water St.*, ☎*688-7323*) sells some magnificent pieces of Aboriginal art from Canada's Far North and the Queen Charlotte Islands.

Khot-La-Cha (*270 Whonoak St., North Vancouver*, ☎*987-3339*). One block from Marine Drive and McGuire Street. Beautiful sculptures by First Nation's artists of the Salish Coast.

Leona Lattimer (*1590 W. 2nd Ave., west of Granville Island*, ☎*732-4556*) is a lovely gallery where you can admire some fine Aboriginal art, or, if you like, purchase a piece. Quality jewellery and prints. Expensive.

The Gulf Islands

Salt Spring Island

Mouat's Home Hardware (*106 Fulford Rd., Ganges, Salt Spring Island*, ☎*537-5551*) is well stocked with all the necessary supplies for camping and outdoor activities.

The **Ganges Village Market** (*374 Lower Ganges Rd., Ganges, Salt Spring Island*) sells all kinds of groceries. There's also a bakery and a delicatessen.

Everlasting Summer (*194 MacLennan Dr., Salt Spring Island*, ☎*653-9418*) specializes in dried-flower bouquets and aromatic plant cultivation. Don't miss the beautiful, romantic rose garden where weddings are often held.

Pender Islands

Try **Southridge Farms Country Store** (*Pender Islands,* ☎*229-2051*) for organic fruits and vegetables.

Mayne Island

If you need supplies or equipment for camping or hiking, stop in at **Miners Trading Post** (*Mayne Island,* ☎*539- 2214*), in the town of **Fernhill**. To get good organic fruits and vegetables, go to the **Mayne Open Market** (*Mayne Island,* ☎*539-5024*), called MOM by local residents. You can also pick up venison or beef for a tasty barbecue at the **Arbutus Deer Farm** (☎*539-2301*).

Quadra Island

Heriot Bay Consignment Shop (*West Rd., not far from the ferry dock, Quadra Island,* ☎*285-3217*). You'll find absolutely everything at the Heriot Bay Consignment Shop and have a lot of fun in this second-hand store.

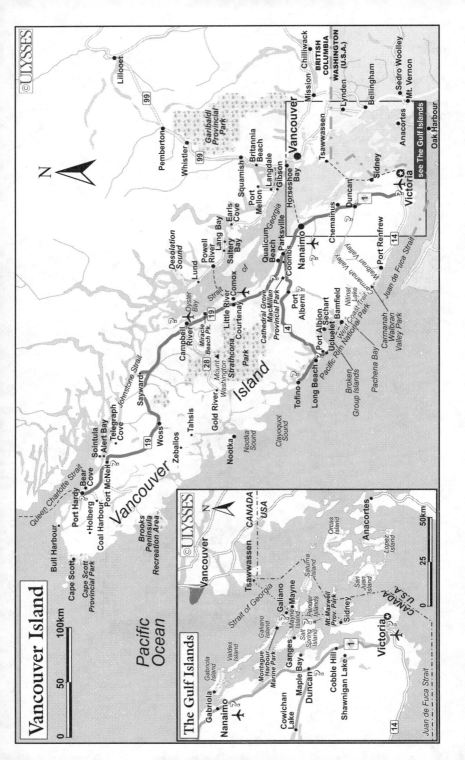

Victoria and Vancouver Island

Vast Vancouver Island stretches over 500km along the West Coast, with its southern tip facing the Olympic Mountains in Washington State (U.S.A.).

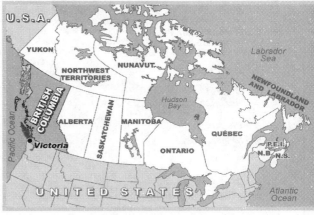

The island is split into two distinct regions by a chain of mountains that divides the north from the south. The sea has sculpted the west side, creating big, deep fjords while the shoreline on the east side is much more continuous. Most of the towns and villages on the island lie either on the east coast or along the Strait of Georgia where the Gulf Islands are located. One of those towns is the very British and beautiful Victoria, the province's capital.

Finding Your Way Around

By Plane

Victoria International Airport (☎953-7500) is located north of Victoria on the Saanich Peninsula, a half-hour's drive from downtown on Highway 17.

By Ferry

You can reach Victoria by car by taking a BC Ferry from Tsawwassen, located south of Vancouver on the coast. This ferry (*BC Ferry Corporation; in the summer, every day on the hour from 7am to 10pm; in the winter, every day every other hour from 7am to 9pm;* ☎*888-223-3779 in B.C. or 250-386-3431 from outside the province*) will drop you off at the Sydney terminal in Swartz Bay. From there, take Highway 17 South to Victoria (*see Tour D: The Saanich Peninsula,*).

BC Ferries also offers transportation to Victoria from the east coast of Vancouver Island. The ferry sets out from the Horseshoe Bay terminal, northwest of Vancouver, and takes passengers to Nanaimo. From there, follow the signs for the Trans-Canada Highway 1 South, which leads to Victoria, 113km away.

By Bus

Island Coach Lines
700 Douglas St.,
Victoria V8W 2B3
☎*(250)385-4411*
☎*388-5248*
This company offers transportation from Nanaimo to Port Alberni, Ucluelet and Tofino, on the west coast of Vancouver Island.

Pacific Coach Lines
700 Douglas St.,
Victoria V8W 1B1
☎*385-4411*
Pacific Coach Lines oper-
ates from downtown Van-
couver to downtown
Victoria in conjunction
with BC Ferries. These
buses also serve the Gulf
Islands.

By Public Transportation

Victoria

Public transportation in the
greater Victoria area is
provided by **BC Transit**
(☎*382-6161*).

Practical Information

Area Code: **250**

Tourist Information

For any information re-
garding Victoria and its
surroundings, contact:

**The Victoria Travel Informa-
tion Centre**
every day 9am to nightfall
812 Wharf St., V8W 1T3
☎*953-2033*

**Saanich Peninsula Chamber of
Commerce**
9768 3rd St., Sidney
☎*656-0525*

Exploring

★★ Victoria

Downtown Victoria is
cramped which can make
parking somewhat diffi-
cult. There are a number
of public lots where you
can pay to park your car,
including a very inexpen-
sive one on View Street,
between Douglas and
Blanshard, at the edge of
Old Town (on weekdays
and holidays, the cost is $2
for the day).

Any tour of Victoria starts
at the port, which was the
main point of access into
the city for decades. Back
in the era of tall ships, the
merchant marine operating
on the Pacific Ocean used
to stop here to pick up
goods destined for Eng-
land. Once the railway
reached the coast, how-
ever, the merchandise was
transported across Canada
by train, thus reducing the
amount of time required to
reach the east side of the
continent. From that point
on, the merchant marine
only provided a sea link to
Asia.

Bastion Square marks the
former site of Fort Victoria,
constructed by the Hud-
son's Bay Company in
1843 with the help of
hundreds of native people.
Twenty years later, the fort
was demolished to make
way for the city. Today, ·
the site is occupied by
public buildings like the
**Maritime Museum of British
Columbia** (*$5; every day
9:30am to 4:30pm; 28 Bas-
tion Sq.*, ☎*385-4222*).

From the days when tall
ships sidled up alongside
one another in the harbour
up until the present time,
it highlights great moments
in the history of sailing.

Walk down Bastion
Square, turn right on
Wharf Street, then head up
the north side of Johnson
Street. Go into **Market
Square ★**, which is sur-
rounded by shops facing
onto the street. This place
gets very lively during the
jazz, blues and theatre
festivals and on the
Chinese New Year.

Chinatown ★ (*west of Government Street, between
Fisgard and Pandora*) is full
of brightly coloured shops
and its sidewalks are decorated with geometric pat-
terns that form a Chinese
character meaning "good
fortune." At one time,
there were over 150 busi-
nesses in Chinatown as
well as three schools, five
temples, two churches and
a hospital. On your way
through this neighbour-
hood, you'll come across
the Tong Ji Men arch on
Fisgard Street – a symbol
of the spirit of cooperation
between the Chinese and
Canadian communities.
Fan Tan Alley ★, which
runs north-south (*south of
Fisgard St.*), is supposedly
the narrowest street in
Victoria. People used to
come here to buy opium
until 1908 when the fed-
eral government banned
the sale of the drug.

Craigdarroch Castle ★
(*$7.50; summer every day
9am to 7pm; winter every day
10am to 4:30pm; 1050 Joan
Cr.*, ☎*592-5323*) stands at
the east end of the down-
town area. It was built in
1890 for Robert Dunsmuir
who made a fortune in the
coal-mining business.

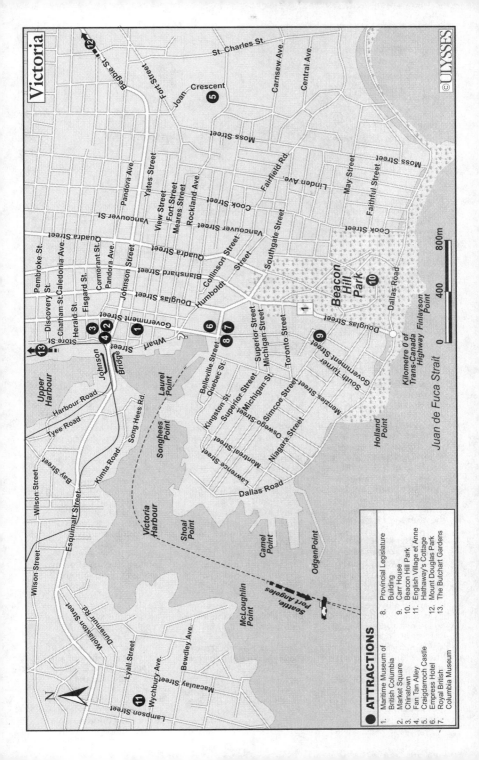

Victoria

ATTRACTIONS

1. Maritime Museum of British Columbia
2. Market Square
3. Chinatown
4. Fan Tan Alley
5. Craigdarroch Castle
6. Empress Hotel
7. Royal British Columbia Museum
8. Provincial Legislature Building
9. Carr House
10. Beacon Hill Park
11. English Village et Anne Hathaway's Cottage
12. Mount Douglas Park
13. The Butchart Gardens

© ULYSSES

Empress Hotel

He died before it was completed, but his widow and three children went on to live here. What makes this building interesting, aside from its dimensions, is its decorative woodwork and the view from the fifth floor of the tower. This residence is indicative of the opulent lifestyle enjoyed by the wealthy around the turn of the century.

The Empress Hotel ★★ (*behind the port of Victoria,* ☎*384-8111*) was built in 1905 for the Canadian Pacific railway company. It was designed by Francis Rattenbury in the Chateau style, just like the Chateau Frontenac in Québec City, only more modern and less romantic. As you enter through the main entrance and cross the lobby, let yourself be transported back to the 1920s when influential people found their way into the guest books.

Above all, make sure to stop by the Empress for afternoon tea (see p 641).

Head south on Douglas Street, then turn right on Belleville to reach the **Royal British Columbia Museum ★★** (*$9.65; every day 9am to 5pm; 675 Belleville St.,* ☎*800-661-5411 or 387-3701, message* ☎*387-3014*) where you can learn about the history of the city and the various peoples that have inhabited the province. The centrepieces of the collection are a reproduction of Captain Vancouver's ship and a Kwa-gulth First-Nation house. The museum also hosts some interesting temporary exhibitions.

The design for the **Provincial Legislature Buildings ★** (*free tours*) was chosen by way of a competition. The winner was architect Francis Rattenbury, who was then just 25 years old.

He went on to design many other public and privately-owned buildings.

Take Government Street south to Simcoe Street, and you will find yourself in the Carr family's neighbourhood. Built of wood, **Carr House ★** (*$5.35; mid-May to mid-Oct every day 10am to 5pm; 207 Government St.,* ☎*383-5843*) was erected in 1864 for the family of Richard Carr. After the American gold rush, the Carrs, who had been living in California, returned to England and then came back to North America to set up residence in Victoria. Mr. Carr made a fortune in real estate and owned many pieces of land – both developed and undeveloped – in this residential area. He died in 1888, having outlived his wife by two years. Emily Carr, the renowned painter, was only 17 at the time. Shortly after, she went first to San Francisco, then London and finally to Paris to study art. She returned to British Columbia around 1910 and began teaching art to the children of Vancouver. She eventually went back to Victoria and followed in her father's footsteps, entering the real-estate business. She also began travelling more along the coast in order to paint, producing her greatest works in the 1930s.

cent from here. For a reminder of exactly where you are in relation to the rest of Canada, Km 0 of the Trans-Canada Highway lies at the south end of Douglas Street.

lands, the Straits of Georgia and Juan de Fuca as well as the snow-capped peaks along the Canadian and U.S. coast. The colours of the sea and the mountains are most vibrant early in the morning and at the end of the day.

The Butchart Gardens ★★
(*$15.75 high season, $6 low season; every day 9am, summer until 10:30pm, winter until 5pm; Hwy. 17 N, 800 Benvenuto Ave., ☎652-4422*), which cover 26ha, were founded by the family of the same name in 1904. A wide array of flowers, shrubs and trees flourish in this unique space. Maps are available at the entrance. Fireworks light up the sky during July and August, and outdoor concerts are held here Monday to Saturday evenings from June to September.

Carr House

A unique painter and a reclusive woman, Emily Carr is now recognized across Canada as a great artist who left her stamp on the art world. Be sure to visit the Vancouver Art Gallery (see p 614) to learn more about her art since the main focus here is her private life. Carr House also distributes maps of the neighbourhood showing where the family lived at various times.

One of these places was **Beacon Hill Park ★** (*between Douglas and Cook Streets, facing the Juan de Fuca Strait*), a peaceful spot where Emily Carr spent many happy days drawing. A public park laid out in 1890, it features a number of trails leading through fields of wildflowers and landscaped sections. The view of the strait and the Olympic Mountains in neighbouring Washington State is positively magnifi-

English Village and **Anne Hathaway's Cottage ★**
(*$7.50; summer every day 9am to 7pm; winter every day 10am to 6:15pm during winter; 429 Lampson St., ☎388-4353*) lie west of downtown Victoria. Cross the Johnson Street Bridge, and after the sixth traffic light, turn left on Lampson Street. The Munro Bus, which you can catch at the corner of Douglas and Yates Streets, stops at the entrance. This little bit of England is a reconstruction of the birthplace of William Shakespeare and the home of his wife Anne Hathaway. A stroll among these buildings will take you back in time. Try to make it for afternoon tea at the Old England Inn.

At the entrance to **Mount Douglas Park ★★**, turn left on Cedar Hill Road, then right in order to reach the lookout which offers a 360° view of the gulf is-

From Victoria to the West Coast Trail

Head north on Government Street, which turns into Highway 1A (Old Island Highway) and follow the signs for Sooke. At Colwood, take Highway 14, which becomes Sooke Road near Port Renfrew. You'll pass through the suburbs west of town when you get to Sooke, which lies about 30km from Victoria. At the 17 Mile House restaurant, turn left onto Gillespie Road. This will take you into **East Sooke Park ★** where hiking trails lead through the wild vegetation by the sea. This is a perfect place for a family outing.

Head back to the 14 and turn left toward Port Renfrew. The highway runs alongside beaches and bays. The farther you get from Victoria, the more twists and turns there are

British Columbia

in the road. The terrain is mountainous and the views are spectacular. As you continue west on the 14, you'll notice a change in the landscape; forestry is still an important source of revenue for the province, and the large valleys in this region have been clear-cut.

Port Renfrew

Port Renfrew is a starting point for the **West Coast Trail ★★★**. This 75km trek is geared towards experienced, intrepid hikers prepared to face unstable weather conditions and widely varied terrain; in fact, it is considered one of the most difficult hiking trails in North America.

The Rest of the Island

Duncan

The **Native Heritage Centre ★★** (*$10; May to Oct every day; in winter every day 9:30am to 5pm; 200 Cowichan Way, Box 20038, ☎746-8119, ≈746-9854*), located in Duncan, was founded by the Cowichan First Nation in 1987. It has become a major tourist attraction over the last few years. The centre enables the Cowichan people to introduce others to their culture through interpretive activities and shows as well as handicraft and art exhibitions. The tour is detailed and most interesting; a beautiful: well-made film, imbued with the spirit of the community, will enthral viewers.

Located near the Trans-Canada Highway and the Cowichan River, the centre is composed of several reconstructions of traditional

structures, a restaurant, a café, a gallery and souvenir shop, and a historical interpretive centre that offers a totem-sculpture workshop. The art gallery sells only high quality hand-made articles such as baskets, drums, jewellery, knitwear, original or limited edition prints, soapstone sculptures, dolls, blankets, books and wood sculptures inspired by Salish, Nuu Cha Nulth (West Coast) and Kwagulth motifs.

Nanaimo

Nanaimo is an important town because of its link to the coast where ferries pick up hundreds of tourists headed for this region. Across the Strait of Georgia, it lies 35km from Vancouver and 1hr30min from Victoria by way of the Trans-Canada. Vacationers heading for the northern part of Vancouver Island or for Long Beach, to the west, pass through Nanaimo. This town is much more than just a stopover point, however; its seaport is graced with a pleasant promenade. Furthermore, visitors can easily catch a ferry to **Newcastle Island ★** and **Protection Island ★** to use the outdoor facilities and take in the view of Nanaimo. You can see all the local attractions, including old Nanaimo, on a walking tour.

The Bastion ★ (*Jul and Aug, every day 9am to 5pm*) was built by the Hudson's Bay Company in 1853 in order to protect the new trading post and the local residents. Its construction was supervised by two Quebecers, Jean-Baptiste Fortier and Leon Labine, both employees of the

company. The Bastion never came under attack and was abandoned when the company left in 1862. It was later used as a prison, and has served as a gathering place and a museum since 1910.

Port Alberni

Like many towns in British Columbia, Port Alberni owes its existence to the forest industry, fishing and trade. Its harbour is linked to the Pacific by a large canal, putting the town at an advantage as far as shipping is concerned. Port Alberni is also the gateway to the west coast of Vancouver Island. When you reach the top of the mountains surrounding Mount Arrowsmith, at an altitude of nearly 2,000m, you're almost at Port Alberni. Until recently, the range of activities in Port Alberni has been rather limited, but two new attractions have recently been added.

Keep left as you enter Port Alberni. Take Port Alberni Highway to Third Avenue, turn left on Argyle Street and then right toward the harbour. The **Harbour Quay** is a pleasant place to have a cup of coffee and inquire about which boats can take you to Pacific Rim National Park for the day. In the middle of the public square, you'll see a fountain adorned with granite sculptures showing the life cycle of the salmon.

The **M.V. Lady Rose** (*$15-$40; year-round, Bamfield: Tue, Thu, Fri and Sat 8am, during summer, Tue, Thu, Sat 8am in winter; Ucluelet and Broken Group Islands: Mon, Wed, Fri 8am; Harbour Quay, ☎723-8313 or 800-663-7192*) offers year-round transportation between Port Alberni and Bamfield, at the north end of the West Coast Trail. During summer, the **Frances Barkley** carries passengers to and from Ucluelet and the Broken Group Islands, south of Long Beach. All sorts of discoveries await you on these trips so make sure to bring along a camera, a pair of binoculars and a raincoat.

★
Ucluelet

Located at the south end of Long Beach, Ucluelet is a charming town whose main street is lined with old wooden houses. In the past, the only way to get here was by boat. The local economy is based on fishing and tourism. Over 200 species of birds can be found around Ucluelet. Migrating grey whales swim in the coves and near the beaches here between the months of March to May, making whale-watching one of the main attractions on the west coast.

At the south end of the village, in **He Tin Kis Park ★★**, there is a wooden walkway leading through a small temperate rainforest beside Terrace Beach. This short walk will help you appreciate the beauty of this type of vegetation. The **Amphitrite Point Lighthouse ★** has stood on the shore since 1908. In those days, this area was known as the "cemetery of the Pacific" because so many ships had run up onto the reefs here. The wreckage of one tall ship still lies at the bottom of the sea near the point. The Canadian Coast Guard has a shipping checkpoint offshore (*guided tours available during summer*).

★
Tofino

Tofino, situated at the northwest end of Long Beach, is a lively town where the many visitors chat about sunsets and the outdoors. Spanish explorers Galiano and Valdes, who discovered this coast in the summer of 1792, named the place after Vincente Tofino, their hydrography professor.

This town is also an artists' colony. The local painters and sculptors draw much of their inspiration from the unspoiled landscape of the west coast. The **House of Himwitsa ★**(see p. 643) (*at the end of the main street, near the port*) displays works by Aboriginal artists.

Campbell River

Campbell River is a choice destination for fans of salmon fishing. This sport can be enjoyed here year-round, and five varieties of salmon frequent the local waters. When you get to town, take the time to go to **The Museum at Campbell River ★** (*mid-May to Sep Mon to Sat 10am to 5pm, Sun noon to 5pm; winter Tue to Sun noon to 5pm; 470 Island Highway, opposite Sequoia Park, Fifth Ave., ☎287-3103*). It's interesting not only for its elegant architecture but also for its exhibits on Aboriginals and pioneers. Its collection includes a number of artifacts from Campbell River's early days. Furthermore, a significant part of the museum is devoted to Aboriginal engravings, sculpture and jewellery.

On your way into the centre of town, stop for a walk along **Discovery Pier ★** (*Government Wharf*), from which you

can admire the Strait of Georgia and the Coast Mountains. At the end, turn right and walk down Shoppers Row where you can purchase souvenirs, food or basic necessities. The Travel InfoCentre is located on this street as well.

★★
Telegraph Cove

This little paradise set back from the eastern shore of Vancouver Island was once the end point of a telegraph line that ran along the coast, hence the name. Later, a wealthy family set up a sawmill on land they had purchased around the little bay. From that point on, time has stopped. The little houses have been preserved, and the boardwalk alongside the bay is punctuated with commemorative plaques explaining the major stages in the village's history. Today, vacationers come here to go fishing, scuba diving and whale-watching. If you're lucky, you might catch a glimpse of a seal, an otter or even a whale from the boardwalk.

★★
Alert Bay

At the **U'mista Cultural Centre ★** (*$5; year-round Mon to Fri 9am to 5pm, noon to 5pm, and Sat and Sun during summer; Alert Bay, ☎974-5403*), you can learn about the Potlatch ("to give") ceremony through the history of the U'mista Aboriginal community. Missionaries tried to ban the ceremony. There was even a law forbidding members of the community from dancing, preparing objects for distribution or making public speeches. The ceremony

British Columbia

was then held in secret and during bad weather when the whites couldn't get to the island. A lovely collection of masks and jewellery adorns the walls. Don't miss the **Native Burial Grounds** and the **Memorial Totems ★★** which testify to the richness of this art.

Port Hardy

Port Hardy, a town of fishers and forest workers, is located at the northeast end of Vancouver Island. There is a wealth of animal life in this region, both in the water and on the land. If you aren't interested in going fishing or whale-watching, treat yourself to a walk through the forest in Cape Scott Park. Visitors en route to Prince Rupert and the Queen Charlotte Islands board the ferry in Port Hardy (*$80 return*).

The **Copper Maker ★** (*free admission; Mon to Sat 9am to 5pm; 114 Copper Way, Fort Rupert, on the outskirts of Port Hardy*, ☎*949-8491*) is an Aboriginal art gallery and studio where you'll find totem poles several metres high. Some are in the process of being made while others are waiting to be delivered to buyers. Take the time to watch the artists at work and ask them about the symbolism behind their drawings and sculptures.

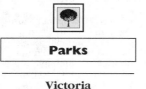

Parks

Victoria

Goldstream Provincial Park ★★★ (*20min from Victoria by Hwy. 1; BC Parks,* ☎*391-2300*) is one of the

major parks in the Victoria area. Picture 600-year-old Douglas firs lining hiking trails leading to Mount Finlayson and past magnificent waterfalls. In November, nature lovers come here to watch *coho, chinook* and *chum* salmon make their final voyage, spawn and die in Goldstream River. The fish are easy to see as the water is crystal clear. Not to be missed.

The Rest of the Island

Pacific Rim National Park, Long Beach Section ★★★ (*Long Beach information centre, Hwy. 4,* ☎*726-4212*) This park is trimmed with kilometres of deserted beaches running alongside temperate rain forests. The beaches, hiking trails and various facilities are clearly indicated and easy to reach. The setting is enchanting, relaxing and stimulating at once as well as being accessible year-round. The beaches are popular with surfing buffs, and **Live to Surf** (*1180 Pacific Rim Hwy., Tofino,* ☎*725-4464*) rents out surfboards and wetsuits.

Strathcona Park ★★ (*swimming, hiking, fishing and 161 campsites; 59km west of Campbell River on Hwy. 28,* ☎*954-4600*) is the oldest provincial park in British Columbia and the largest on Vancouver Island. Its 210,000ha of forest and fresh water abound in natural treasures, including huge Douglas firs over 90m high. It is here that you will find the Golden Hinde, the highest peak on Vancouver Island. It measures 2,220m.

Cape Scott Provincial Park ★★ (*67km northwest of Port Hardy on Holberg Rd.; register at Port Hardy Cham-*

ber of Commerce, ☎*949-7622; for all other information, BC Parks,* ☎*954-4600*) encompasses 15,070ha of temperate rain forest. Scott was a merchant from Bombay, India who financed all sorts of commercial expeditions. Many ships have run aground on this coast, and a lighthouse was erected in 1960 to guide sailors safely along their way. Sandy beaches cover two-thirds of the 64km stretch of waterfront. On the hilly terrain further inland, you'll find various species of giant trees such as red cedars and pines. This remote part of Vancouver Island receives up to 500mm of rainfall annually, and is frequently hit by storms. It is best to visit during summertime.

Outdoor Activities

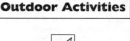

Fishing

Victoria

Victoria Harbour Charter (*50 Wharf St.,* ☎*381-5050*) hosts salmon-fishing excursions aboard a fully equipped 9m yacht. Thrills guaranteed.

Scuba Diving

Lured by the colourful underwater scenery and rich marine life, hundreds of divers flock to the eastern shore of Vancouver Island each year. The Nanaimo region is a wonderful place for this type of sightseeing. **Sundown Diving Charters** (*22 Esplanade, Nanaimo, V9R 4Y7,* ☎*753-1880 or 888-773-3483,* ≈*753-6445*).

Whale-watching

Island West Resort (*140 Bay St.,* ☎*726-7515*) as well as **Quest Charters** (*Boat Basin,* ☎*726-7532*) are two of the companies that offer whale-watching excursions departing from Ucluelet.

Chinook Charters (*$50; 450 Campbell St., Box 501, Tofino, V0R 2Z0,* ☎*725-3431 or 800-665-3646*) will take you out to sea to observe grey whales at close range. The best time to go is in March and April when there are large numbers of these sea mammals in the area.

Robson Bight Charters (*$70; Jun to Oct 9:30am; Sayward,* ☎*282-3833 or 800-658-0022*) arranges whale-watching tours in the Johnstone Strait. Each year, killer whales use this area as a sort of training ground for the new members of their families. A sight to remember.

Accommodations

Victoria

The YHA Victoria Hostel
$16 members, $20 non-members, some private rooms
sb, K
516 Yates St.
☎*385-4511*
≈*385-3232*
This stone and brick building with 108 beds is located in Old Town, right near the harbour. Members take precedence in youth hostels so it can be difficult for non-members to get a bed, especially during the high season.

🌴 **Swans Hotel Pub & Café**
$119-$179
ℝ, ℜ, tv
506 Pandora Ave.
☎*361-3310*
☎*800-668-SWAN*
≈*361-3491*
Without question, the undeniably charming Swans Hotel Pub & Café is one of the best places to stay in Victoria, especially if you're travelling in a group. The rooms are actually luxury apartments that can accommodate several people. Guests will find "real" works of art on the walls, plants, big-screen TVs and a pretty, inviting decor.

Dating back to the late 19th century, the hotel is located right in the heart of Old Town, steps away from Chinatown and the Inner Harbour. On the ground floor you will find a fun pub that serves what locals claim to be the best beer in North America and an excellent restaurant known for its fresh oysters.

🌴 **Canadian Pacific Empress Hotel**
$135-$305
✕, ᕕ, ≈, ⊛, ☉, △, tv, ℜ
721 Government St.
☎*384-8111*
☎*800-441-1414*
≈*381-4334*
The Empress is located on the Inner Harbour, adjacent to the museums and the interesting public and commercial areas. Designed by architect Francis Rattenbury, this luxurious 475-room hotel offers a relaxing atmosphere and a Chateau-style setting. A new wing has been added to the original quintessentially Victorian building without detracting from its legendary charm. Visitors stop here for tea or simply to admire the ivy-covered facade.

🌴 **Beaconsfield Inn**
$200-$259 bkfst incl.
P
998 Humboldt St.
☎*384-4044*
☎*888-884-4044*
≈*384-4052*
Located in the heart of Victoria, the Beaconsfield Inn is listed as a historic monument and combines luxury and sophistication. Guests can enjoy afternoon tea or a glass of sherry in the library and feast on a memorable breakfast. Expensive but British ambiance guaranteed.

The Haterleigh Heritage Inn
$202-$287 bkfst incl.
pb, ⊛, P
243 Kingston St.
☎*384-9995*
⇌*384-1935*
This old house, dating from 1901, has been lovingly restored with great attention to detail. A rich past lives on in its coloured glass windows and antique furnishings. The rooms are beautifully decorated and equipped with whirlpool baths and huge beds with goose-down comforters. Reputed to be the most romantic B&B in Victoria.

From Victoria to the West Coast Trail

Port Renfrew Hotel
$35
✘, sb
at the end of Hwy. 14, Port Renfrew
☎*647-5541*
⇌*647-5594*
The Port Renfrew Hotel is located on the village pier where hikers set out for the West Coast Trail. The rustic rooms are sure to please hikers longing for a dry place to sleep. There are laundry facilities on the premises as well as a pub that serves hot meals.

Traveller's Inn on Douglas Street
$90 bkfst incl.
≡, K, tv, P
710 Queens Ave., Victoria
☎*388-6641*
☎*370-1000*
☎*888-753-3774*
⇌*360-1190*
This soberly decorated inn is a renovated building with 36 rooms. Basic services are available, but there are no telephones in the rooms.

The Rest of the Island

Nanaimo

The Jingle Pot Bed & Breakfast
$75-$85 bkfst incl.
⌂, ≡, tv
4321 Jingle Pot Rd. V9T 5P4
☎*758-5149*
Run by a sailor named Captain Ivan, The Jingle Pot Bed & Breakfast has two rooms that have been fitted out in a luxurious fashion to ensure that guests enjoy a pleasant stay. If you're planning on going boating, the captain can give you some good advice.

Long Lake Inn
$95-$119
☉, tv, P
4700 North Island Hwy   ☎*758-1144*

☎*(800) 565-1144* ⇌*758-5832*
Enjoy a relaxing stay on the shores of Long Lake, north of Nanaimo. All rooms face the water, and guests have access to a private beach as well as a fitness centre. Only a stone's throw from BC Ferries' Departure Bay harbour.

Ucluelet

The Ucluelet Campground
$21-$31
100 sites, toilets, showers, ✘, ⛄
260 Seaplane Base Rd. ☎*726-4355*
Located within walking distance of Ucluelet. Reservations required.

The Canadian Princess Resort
$65-$75
sb/pb
Peninsula Rd.
☎*726-7771*
☎*(800) 663-7090*
⇌*726-7121*
This is a ship that sailed the waters along the coast

for nearly 40 years, and is now permanently moored at the Ucluelet pier. It has 26 rooms which are small and don't have a lot of extras, but offer a pleasant nautical atmosphere.

Tofino

The Tin-Wis Best Western
$90-$140
tv, ℜ, ⅊
1119 Pacific Rim Hwy.
☎*725-4445*
☎*(800) 528-1234*
⇌*725-4447*
The Tin-Wis Best Western is a large hotel run by Tla-O-Qui-Aht First Nations people. It offers all the comforts you would expect from a Best Western. The plants and wooden decorative elements blend harmoniously with the immediate surroundings, but the place is oversized (56 rooms).

Chesterman's Beach Bed & Breakfast
$125-$150 bkfst incl.
1345 Chesterman's Beach Rd.
☎/⇌*725-3726*
Picture a house on a beach lined with lush vegetation with the setting sun reflecting off the water. That's what awaits you at the heavenly Chesterman's Beach Bed & Breakfast. A simple walk on the beach every day is all you need to enjoy a satisfying vacation here. Three rooms are available.

Qualicum Beach

The Quatna Manor Bed & Breakfast
$75-$90 bkfst incl.
sb/pb, no smoking
512 Quatna Rd.
☎*752-6685*
⇌*752-8385*
The Quatna Manor Bed & Breakfast is definitely a place to keep in mind. The friendly reception from

hosts Bill and Betty will make your stay at their Tudor-style home that much more pleasant. A hearty breakfast is served in the dining room. Bill is retired from the air force. His job required a great deal of travelling, and his stories make for memorable breakfast conversation.

Campbell River

Edgewater Motel
$45-$60
🖈, K, tv
4073 South Island Hwy. near Oyster Bay
☎/≈923-5421
As its name suggests, the pretty little Edgewater Motel is located on the waterfront. The rooms are decent for the price, and you can prepare meals in them — a real plus if you're on a tight budget.

Telegraph Cove

The Telegraph Cove Resorts
$23 for a campsite for two adults, water, electricity ; $89-$155 for a cabin for 2 to 8 people
K, 🖈
☎928-3131
☎(800) 200-4665
≈928-3105
The Telegraph Cove Resorts welcome visitors from May to October. The campground, equipped with basic facilities, is somewhat bare but the view of the bay makes up for that. The cabins blend into the picturesque setting. The service is friendly, and you'll feel as if you're at some sort of summer camp. If you have to spend a few days in the northern part of the island, Telegraph Cove is a thoroughly pleasant place to visit.

Port Hardy

The Seagate Hotel
$90-$95
tv, ℜ
8600 Granville St.
☎949-6348
≈949-6347
The Seagate Hotel is located a stone's throw from the town pier. All of the rooms are sparingly decorated, and the view makes those facing the port much more attractive.

The Gulf Islands are covered with **bed and breakfasts** of all types. Though these places are generally quite expensive, you are unlikely to hear any complaints from the guests.

Restaurants

Victoria

Garrick's Head Pub
$
Bastion Square, on View St.
☎384-6835
The sunny terrace at Garrick's Head Pub, located on a pedestrian street, is a pleasant place to get together over a local beer. While the space may be limited inside, there is a giant-screen TV for sports fans.

The Snug
$
1175 Beach Dr.
☎598-4556
Oak Bay Beach Hotel's pub, the Snug, serves local beer and light meals. A quiet, well-kept place, it attracts a rather mature clientele.

Spinnakers Brew Pub & Restaurant
$
every day from 7am to 11pm
308 Catherine St.
☎386-2739
Spinnaker's serves beer and food in a laid-back setting with the house specialties listed on big blackboards. The terrace is very well positioned, beckoning guests to kick back and relax. This place radiates a festive, convivial atmosphere.

Empress Hotel's Bengal Lounge
$$
721 Government St.
☎384-8111
Recapturing the atmosphere of the British Empire of Queen Victoria, the beautiful Empress Hotel's Bengal Lounge serves a curry buffet featuring Indian specialties. The place is tastefully decorated with Eastern furniture, and guests have lots of elbow room.

Canadian Pacific Empress Hotel
$$-$$$
behind the port, 721 Government St.
☎384-8111
Tea-lovers get together in the Empress Hotel Canadian Pacific for tea with scones served with different kinds of jam. If you've got a big appetite, stop in for High Tea, which comes complete with cucumber and cream cheese sandwiches. This tradition supposedly originated during the reign of Queen Victoria, when the Duchess of Bedford, who tended to feel faint in the late afternoon, began fortifying herself with tea and little cakes and sandwiches. The old wood floors, comfortable furniture, giant teapots and courteous service make for an altogether satisfying experience.

Pablo
$$$
from 5pm on
225 Quebec St.
☎ *388-4255*
Contrary to what you might think, Pablo is a French restaurant, though paella is available upon request. Located near the port in an elegant Victorian house. Good but a bit expensive.

From Victoria to the West Coast Trail

17 Mile House
$
5126 Sooke Rd., Sooke
☎ *642-5942*
Located right before the entrance to Sooke Harbour Park, the 17 Mile House serves light meals in a cozy setting. The thoroughly laid-back atmosphere here makes this just the place to quench your thirst after a day of walking along the waterfront in Sooke.

Sooke Harbour House
$$$-$$$$
every day 3:30pm, dinner only
1528 Whiffen Spit Rd.
☎ *642-3421*
The Sooke Harbour House has been praised to the skies by people from all over the world. The Philips's gourmet cuisine has seduced thousands of palates. The hosts settle for nothing but the best and are masters when it comes to preparing local produce. The dining room, set up inside a country house, offers a view of Sooke Harbour. Enjoy the classic ambiance as you take your seat and look over the menu. Prepared in the West Coast Style, the dishes reveal Japanese and French influences. Vegetarian dishes are available. See also p 133.

The Rest of the Island

Nanaimo

 **Dinghy Dock Pub**
$
11am to 11pm, midnight Fri and Sat
no. 8 Pirate's Plank Protection Island
☎ *753-2373*
At this floating pub, attached to the Protection Island pier, you can enjoy a good local beer while observing the comings and goings in the Nanaimo harbour. The fish & chips are succulent. To get to the island, take the ferry from Commercial Inlet (*every hour from 9:10am to 11:10pm, midnight Fri and Sat*).

Javawocky Coffee House
$
8-90 Front St.
Pioneer Waterfront Plaza
☎ *753-1688*
Located on the seawall, the Javawocky Coffee House serves a wide assortment of coffee and light meals and offers a view of the Nanaimo port and the crowd strolling about there.

Ucluelet

Matterson House
$
1682 Peninsula Rd.
☎ *726-2200*
People come to the Matterson House, located on the main street, all day long in one of the oldest homes in Ucluelet. Don't hesitate to order salmon here – it's very fresh.

Long Beach

 Wickaninnish Restaurant
$-$$
11am to 9:30pm
at the bottom of Wick Rd.
☎ *726-7706*
Set on a big rock overlooking the beach, the Wickaninnish Restaurant offers a spectacular view of the Pacific Ocean. The menu is made up of seafood dishes. The pasta with smoked salmon is particularily tasty. Whatever you choose, your meal will be that much better accompanied by a glass of British Columbian white wine.

Tofino

Schooner Restaurant
$$$
331 Campbell St.
☎ *725-3444*
The Schooner Restaurant is a classic. It serves seafood and British Columbian wines. An inviting place, it has been decorated to look like a ship's hold and deck. The soft lighting creates a relaxing comfortable atmosphere.

Campbell River

The Seasons Bistro
$
6:30am to 2pm and 5:30pm to 10pm
261 Island Hwy.
☎ *286-1131*
The Seasons Bistro has an original menu featuring seafood pasta and pheasant with passionfruit. This place attracts both locals and tourists, and jazz lovers in particular.

Sayward

 The Cable Cafe
$
☎*282-3343*
The Cable Cafe offers simple, quality meals at reasonable prices. This is a fun place, with walls made of coiled cables.

Port Hardy

The Seagate Hotel Restaurant
$
open at 6:30am
8600 Granville St. ☎*949-6348*
The Seagate Hotel Restaurant has a wide-ranging menu. While enjoying a view of the harbour, you will dine alongside local residents, including fishers fresh from a day at sea.

Entertainment

Victoria

The Sticky Wicket Pub
919 Douglas St., Strathcona Hotel
☎*383-7137*
The Sticky Wicket Pub is located inside the Strathcona Hotel, just behind the Empress. This place attracts people of all ages and serves good beer. In nice weather, everyone heads up to the roof for some fun in the sun and a game of volleyball. At Legends Nightclub, also in the Strathcona, a clientele of all different ages dances to rock, R&B and jazz.

Uforia's
cover charge
1208 Wharf St.
☎*381-2331*
Uforia's attracts a fairly stylish crowd. People come here to party and kick up their heels on the dance floor.

Jazz

The **Victoria Jazz Society** (☎*388-4423*, ⚏*388-4407*) can provide you with information on local jazz and blues shows. The Victoria Jazz Festival takes place from late June to mid-July.

Shopping

Victoria

With its stained-glass windows and 8m ceilings, **Munro's** (*1108 Government St.*, ☎*382-2464*) is reputed to be the most beautiful bookstore in Canada. Good selection of Canadian, English and American books.

It is worth stopping in at **Rogers' Chocolates** (*913 Government St.*, ☎*384-7021*) to see the shop's lovely early 20th century decor and a pair of Art Nouveau lamps from Italy. Victoria Creams, available in a wide variety of flavours, are the specialty of the house.

The Rest of the Island

Ucluelet

The **Du Quaii Gallery** (*1971 Peninsula Rd.*, ☎*726-7223*) exhibits Aboriginal art. It is worth the trip just to see the building which looks like a Longhouse (a traditional Aboriginal cedar building).

Tofino

The House of Himwitsa (*300 Main St.* ☎*725-2017*) is an art gallery that displays drawings, paintings, sculptures and silver and gold jewellery. Ask about the legends referred to in these pieces and the symbolism employed by the artists.

Port Hardy

The **Copper Maker** (*every day; 112 Copper Way, Fort Rupert*, ☎*949-8491*) displays the works of a number of Aboriginal artists. Masks, pottery and symbolic jewellery can all be purchased here. These articles might seem expensive, but the prices are lower than in the bigger cities.

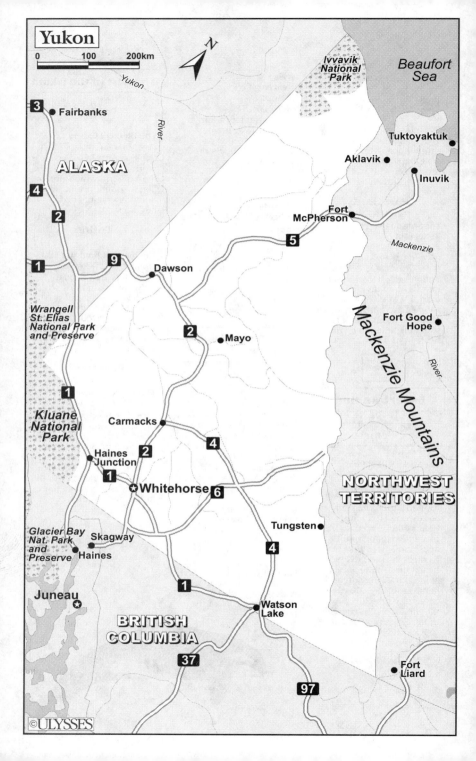

The Yukon

F ar to the north, above
British Columbia, is a region where glaciers lie nestled between high peaks.

H ere, the great Yukon River originates in the inland Tagish Lake, and seems to take sly pleasure in turning its back on the sea, heading north before forking off to the west, into Alaska. Fed by waters from many tributaries along the way, it finally flows into Bering Strait after travelling almost 3,200km. Aboriginals called it the "great river," or *Yukon*.

Geography

The Yukon River's name was later given to the Canadian territory over 480,00km² in size, making it twice as big as the United Kingdom. Its shape somewhat resembles a right-angle triangle, the sides of which are formed by the borders of Alaska on the west, the Northwest Territories to the north and east and British Columbia to the south. The northern-most tip of the triangle is on the Beaufort Sea, in the Arctic Ocean. Yukon Terri-tory is characterized by many mountain chains, starting with the St. Elias Mountains in the south-west. This extension of the Coastal Mountains includes Mount Logan whose peak reaches an altitude of 6,050m, making it the highest in Canada. To the east, the Mackenzie Moun-tains rise majestically. Be-tween the two, the land is flatter, especially in the southern Yukon. Almost 60% of the land is wooded, though the den-sity of the forest and the size of the trees diminish towards the north.

The Yukon climate is very similar to that of the Northwest Territories. Be-cause of its latitude, it ex-periences the same ex-treme conditions. Dawson is a perfect example of this. Here, a beautiful sum-mer day can contain 20 hours of sunlight with temperatures reaching 35°C. Conversely, a winter night can also last 20 hours with the ther-mometer dropping to -50°C. During the three summer months, the aver-age temperature is 21°C.

The average winter tem-perature ranges from -15°C to -27°C, depending on whether you are in the southern or central area. Because of the barrier created by the St. Elias Mountains, the Yukon does not benefit from the warm air currents of the Pacific. On the other hand, it doesn't get the heavy rain either. Dressing for such a climate is a tricky matter that requires partic-ular care, as you have to protect against both chil-blain and sunburn. Sun-glasses are a must, espe-cially in the spring when the bright sun reflects off the snow and is that much more intense.

Since the nights are so short, it's difficult to see the aurora borealis during the spring and summer. On the other hand, the sunrises and sunsets can last for many hours at this time of year. The most striking shades of red fill the sky and lend a rosy tinge to the already impressive landscape.

Human Settlement

Approximately 35,500 people live in the Yukon, mostly in the southern part of the territory. The Aboriginal community is comprised of about 7,000 people. English is the most common language, and French is spoken by about 9% of the population. Over 23,000 Yukonites live in the capital, Whitehorse. The three other major towns in the territory (1,500 to 3,000 residents) are Dawson, Watson Lake and Faro. The rest of the Population is dispersed among some 20 towns and hamlets, some of which are no more than a cluster of buildings. While the Yukon is a territory under Ottawa's jurisdiction, its local government handles most of its domestic affairs. Police services are provided by the Royal Canadian Mounted Police (RCMP).

The Yukon's modern history begins in 1825 when John Franklin explored its north shore. The Hudson's Bay Company proceeded to set up fur-trading Posts around 1840. Canada affirmed its sovereignty over the territory in 1895, sending in an RCMP detachment just in time to keep the Americans from doing likewise. The Gold Rush began in 1896, following the discovery of gold in the Klondike. This led to a demographic boom that lasted until 1904. Once the frenzy subsided, however, the total Population

dropped to under 5,000 inhabitants until the construction of the Alaska highway in 1942. The development of transPortation routes over land soon led to a drop in the amount of activity on the Yukon River. Thus, Dawson ceased to be the capital, and Whitehorse became increasingly developed as more and more services were introduced. Since the 1960s, so many mining towns have either been established or developed that the Population of the Yukon is now growing twice as fast as that of Canada on the whole.

The Yukon's first economic activity was fur trading. Indeed, muskrat, lynx, marten and beaver, among others, continue to be trapped today. Except in the southeastern part of the territory, there are few forests that can be profitably used for timber. Furthermore, the short growing season doesn't allow for any commercial agriculture, and cultivation is limited to domestic vegetable gardens. Despite the ups and downs inherent to the mining industry, the exploitation of minerals generates the most economic activity in the region. Lead, zinc, silver and, of course, gold are all mined here. And finally, close to 175,000 tourists visit the Yukon every year, leaving behind hundreds of millions of dollars in revenue.

Finding Your Way Around

By Plane

The Whitehorse Airport receives flights from Juneau and Fairbanks, Alaska. Generally, however, visitors from the south pass through Vancouver International AirPort on the way to Whitehorse. Canada's two major airlines offer flights in Boeing 737s. Flight time: 2hrs 20 minutes.

Almost all communities in the Yukon have a landing strip, no matter how rarely they are frequented. Various aircraft can also land on lakes, snowfields and glaciers. Four regional airlines assure regular links with the Yukon's main centres, and sometimes with Alaska as well. They are **Air North** *(P.O. Box 4998, Whitehorse, Y1A 4S2, ☎867-668-2228 or 800-764-0407; they offer a ticket for a limited period of time that is valid for all their destinations)*, **Alkan Air** *(P.O. Box 4008, Whitehorse, Y1A 3S9, ☎867-668-2107)*, **NWT Air** *(Ste. 02-13, Air Terminal Building, Whitehorse, Y1A 3E4, ☎800-661-0789)* and **First Air** *(P.O. Box 100, Yellowknife, N.W.T., X1A 2N1, ☎867-873-4461)*.

For more remote destinations, you can also charter a plane, hydroplane or helicopter to fly to almost any part of the Yukon. You can also take a tour of particular regions from the air. This service is not cheap, however: a 3hr excursion flight in a bush plane can easily cost $125 per person, and a helicopter is even more expensive.

Here are a few addresses:

Air North, Alkan Air, Action Aviation
P.O. Box 5898, Whitehorse, Y1A 5L6

Almon Landair
200-307 Jarvis St., Whitehorse Y1A 2H3
☎ *(867) 667-7790*
This company offers services in different languages and one- or two-week air-caravanning expeditions where you to travel in a small airplane that you rent for a certain period of time, and camp along the way)

Blacksheep Aviation
P.O. Box 4087, Whitehorse, Y1A 3S9
☎ *(867) 668-7761*

Bonanza Aviation
P.O. Box 284, Dawson City, Y0B 1G0
☎ *(867) 993-6904*

Heli-Dynamics
P.O. Box 4280, Whitehorse, Y1A 3T3
☎ *668-3536*

Northern Lights Air
P.O. Box 7, Watson lake, Y0A 1C0
☎ *(867) 536-2231*

By Car

You can get to the Yukon from the south by taking the Alaska Highway, which starts at Dawson Creek, a small town in British Columbia not far from the Alberta border. It's now a paved road with gas stations, food and lodgings at intervals ranging from 32 to 80km. From Canada's west coast, a second road from Prince Rupert heads inland through the mountains. This is the Stewart-Cassiar Highway, which joins the Alaska Highway just after it enters the Yukon. Before heading off on this route

it's imPortant to plan the trip carefully since there are few service areas along its 752km. On the other hand, the scenery is spectacular, especially at Stikine River Valley and Dease Lake.

You can also get to the Yukon from Inuvik, in the Northwest Territories at the mouth of the Mackenzie River, on the Arctic Ocean. This area is linked to Dawson by the Dempster Highway. Be warned that the name is somewhat misleading: Dempster "Highway" is actually a 663km-long unpaved dirt road. Furthermore, there are only two communities between Inuvik and Dawson.

Several roads connect the Yukon to Alaska. The main ones run from Anchorage, Fairbanks, Shagway and Haines. The quickest way to get to the Yukon is from the last two towns. Skagway is where gold-seekers crossed the mountains to get to Whitehorse and then Dawson.

The two main Yukon routes, the Alaska and Klondike Highways, are paved. Some main roads aren't, but are treated to reduce the amount of dust. Most roads, however, are neither paved nor treated. Take note that many roads, paved and unpaved alike, are not open year-round so it's best to get information from the **Yukon Road RePort** *(☎867-667-8215)* before heading out. Regardless of the type of vehicle, driving on Yukon roads requires that you take precautions and that you conform to a certain etiquette: the comfort and safety of passengers depend on it. The rules of the road are described in more detail in the chapter on the North-

west Territories (see p 659).

Many visitors decide to rent a vehicle once they've arrived, either in Alaska, British Columbia or Alberta. Some agencies in the south allow you to leave the vehicle in Whitehorse. Take note that Canadian residents are not allowed to enter Canada in a vehicle rented in the United States. Some agencies let you switch vehicles at the border.

In the Yukon, you can rent a car in Whitehorse, Watson Lake, Dawson and Faro. Other kinds of vehicles can be rented in Whitehorse as well. These include vans and recreational vehicles, which allow you to head out on long journeys on your own. Travelling by car is probably one of the best ways to really take advantage of the Yukon's wide open spaces, since you can stop wherever and whenever you want and stay as long as you want. The territorial government and some private businesses have set up campsites along the way.

By Bus

Buses are another option if you are coming from the south. Comfortable and air-conditioned, they run from Vancouver or Edmonton to Whitehorse.

Greyhound Lines of Canada
2191 Second Ave.
Whitehorse, Y1A 3T8
☎ *(867) 667-2223*

Gold City Tours
in the summer
P.O. Box 960
Dawson, Y0B 1G0
☎ *867-993-5175*

Yukon

By Train

A railway connection between Skagway and White Pass at the United States border was established in 1898, and continues to operate to this day. There is a bus connection from White Pass to Whitehorse. Contact **White Pass & Yukon Route Railway** *(P.O. Box 435, Skagway, Alaska, 99840, USA,* ☎*907-983-2217, or 800-343-7373, www.whitepassrailroad.com)* for more information. The train trip is only 45km long but passes through the mountains, where the change in elevation is over 850m. Whether you take it to get to Whitehorse or just take a return trip, it's definitely worthwhile.

By Boat

A ferry links Belling-ham, Washington and Prince Rupert, British Columbia to Alaska's main Ports. If you want to bring a vehicle, it's undoubtedly the most pleasant way to get to the Yukon while enjoying the unique coastal scenery. Contact **Alaska Marine Highway** *(P.O. Box 25535, Juneau, Alaska 99802-5535, USA* ☎*907-465-3941 or 800-642-0066)* for more information.

The Yukon's waterways, particularly the Yukon River, have been the main travel routes in the territory for over a century. There was even a time when steamships regularly stirred the waters between Dawson and Yellowknife with their paddle wheels. Today, the Yukon River still takes many passengers between the two cities, some in canoes, some in Zodiaks and others in heavier craft. There are also a number of other rivers in the territory for water-sPorts enthusiasts, and it is quite easy to rent a boat. You can do so at **Klondike Recreational Rentals** *(107 Copper Rd., P.O. Box 5156, Whitehorse, Y1A 2Z6,* ☎*867-668-2200 or 800-665-4755),* **Kanoe People** *(P.O. Box 5152, Whitehorse, Y1A 4S3,* ☎*867-668-4899; they also rent camping equipment and mountain bikes and offer guided excursions and trans-Portation),* **Prospect Yukon Wilderness & Watercraft Trips** *(P.O. Box 5323, Whitehorse, Y1A 4Z2,* ☎*867-667-4837),* **RRR Yukon Trail of '98 Goldrush Tours** *(P.O. Box 5254, Whitehorse, Y1A 4Z1,* ☎*867-633-4767)* or **Up North Boat & Canoe Rentals** *(86 Wickstrom Rd., P.O. Box 5418, Whitehorse, Y1A 5H4,* ☎*867-667-7905).*

Practical Information

Area code: **867**

Tourist Information Offices

The Yukon has six establishments called Visitor Reception Centres, or VRCs, that provide information to tourists. They are open from mid-May to mid-September and provide general information as well as specific information on the region and special exhibitions.

Whitehorse
☎*667-3084*

Dawson
☎*993-5566*

Watson Lake
☎*536-7469*

Beaver Creek
☎*862-7321*

Carcross
☎*821-4431*

Haines Junction
☎*634-2345*

Safety and Emergencies

In an area as sparsely Populated as the Yukon, the availability of immediate medical or Police services varies greatly depending on where you are.

Dawson
☎*993-4444 or 993-5555*

Haines Junction
☎*634-4444 or 634-5555*

Watson Lake
☎*536-4444 or 536-5555*

You can call **Whitehorse** Police and health services for free from anywhere in the territory *(*☎*667-3333 or 667-5555).*

Exploring

Whitehorse

The little city of Whitehorse is the capital and administrative centre of the Yukon and lies on the west side of the Yukon River, right at the foot of the plateau on which the airPort is located and across which the Alaska Highway now runs. The city has started to spread over to the east shore of the river, which is spanned by the Robert Campbell Bridge.

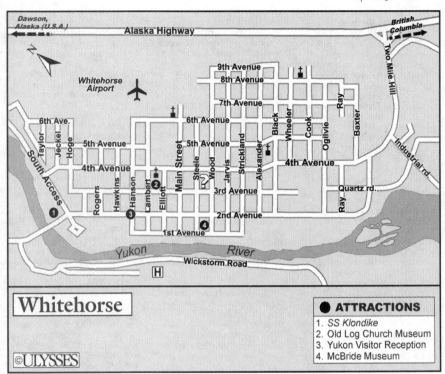

Whitehorse

ATTRACTIONS

1. SS Klondike
2. Old Log Church Museum
3. Yukon Visitor Reception
4. McBride Museum

©ULYSSES

Whitehorse is located at the natural upstream terminus on the Yukon River, which is why people people settled here in the first place. Gold prospectors travelling to the Klondike by way of Alaska had a hard time crossing the Whitehorse and Miles Canyon rapids with loaded canoes. The most prudent way to proceed was to reach the shore and then Portage the gear. Before long, a small train was shuttling back and forth alongside the rapids. Whitehorse was founded at the upstream end of the line. Once it was directly connected to the Alaskan shore by rail, the town grew quickly. Gold prospectors would stop here before transferring their merchandise onto boats or sleighs, depending on the season. Finally, in 1942,

the U.S. government decided to build the Alaska Highway. Whitehorse was clearly destined to become one of the main bases for the Canadian Portion of the construction. In 1953, it replaced Dawson as the capital of the territory.

The **Yukon Visitor Reception** *(100 Hanson St., at Second Ave.,* ☎667-3084*)* offers travellers arriving by air all sorts of general information on the entire territory and can answer questions about the capital. It presents a slide show on the national parks and historic sites.

The Yukon is celebrating the first century of its short history. The year 1995 marked the centennial of the arrival of the RCMP; 1997 was the year of trans-Portation and 1998, of

course, commemorates the Gold Rush.

Right near the bridge over the Yukon River is the *S.S. Klondike National Historic Site* *($3; Room 205-300, Main St., Y1A 2B5,* ☎667-4511 *during summer, or 667-3910).* The S.S. Klondike was a steamer built in 1929 to travel up and down the river between Whitehorse and Dawson; it sank in 1936. Rebuilt in 1937, it now houses a museum.

The best way to see the city is to go on one of the guided tours offered by the **Yukon Historical & Museums Association** *(Whitehorse Heritage Buildings Walking Tours, Jun to Aug; Donnenworth House, 3126 Third Ave., Po Box 4357, Y1A 3T5,* ☎667-4704*).*

Yukon

The **Yukon Gardens** *(P.O. Box 5059, Y1A 4S3, ☎668-7972)*, open from April to September, has paths, a miniature farm, a miniature golf course and a shop.

Constructed one room at a time, the **McBride Museum** *($4, summer every day 10am to 6pm, winter Thu to Sat noon to 4pm; First Ave. and Woods St., P.O. Box 4037, Y1A 3S9 ☎667-2709)* is open from mid-May to mid-September and by apPointment during the rest of the year. Devoted to the social and natural history of the Yukon, its collection includes objects from the Gold Rush days, trapping equipment, Aboriginal artifacts and photographs. A separate collection of stuffed and mounted animals provides a clear idea of the wildlife inhabiting the territory. The tour continues outside the log building where there are vehicles and machines used in the Yukon since non-Aboriginal people started settling here, as well as a former telegraph office and a period cabin once owned by Sam McGee.

The city's history is also visible in its most noteworthy buildings. At the corner of Third Avenue and Elliot Street, for example, the **Old Log Church Museum** *($2.50, May to Labour Day, closed winter; 303 Elliot St.; Jun to Sep, reduced hours the rest of the year; ☎668-2555)* houses a collection of objects related to the ancestral traditions of the Aboriginal peoples and to the major activities carried out in the territory since Europeans started settling here. Visitors will also learn about a bishop who ate his boots, a tale that inspired a scene in Charlie Chaplin's film *The Gold Rush*.

The headquarters of the territorial government, the resolutely modern **Administration Building** *(Second Ave.)*, is equally interesting. In addition to the local government, the edifice houses a collection of Aboriginal crafts and works by renowned Canadian artists, all owned by the territory.

The Administration Building isn't the only place in Whitehorse where the art world is represented. Right on Yukon Place, the **Yukon Arts Centre** is a magnificent building containing the largest art gallery in the territory, as well as a theatre. An outdoor amphitheatre completes the facilities.

At the **Yukon TransPortation Museum** *(Km 1473, Alaska Hwy., P.O. Box 5867, Y1A 5L6, ☎668-4792, ≈633-5547)*, right near the airPort on the Alaska Highway, you can discover the imPortance of the dogsled, relive the golden age of aviation and learn about the roads that opened up the territory.

Next to the TransPortation Museum, the **Yukon Beringia Interpretive Centre** *(6$; Km 1473, Alaska Hwy.; mid-May to mid-Sep 8am to 8pm, Sun 1pm to 5pm rest of the year, ☎667-5340, www.touryukon.com)* is an archaeology and palaeontology museum devoted chiefly to the last ice age, when the Yukon and Alaska were still linked to Asia by a land bridge called Beringia. The permanent exhibition includes a film, kiosks equipped with computers and the remains of various prehistoric animals, such as the mammoth, the giant bison, the giant beaver (weighing in at 170kg!), the giant bear and the sabre-toothed

cat. The museum also has displays on the first waves of Aboriginal peoples to migrate to the Yukon.

Though somewhat tamed by a hydroelectric dam, the waters of the Yukon River around Miles City and the Whitehorse rapids (upstream from Whitehorse) are still a sight worth seeing. This part of the river flows through a gorge hemmed in by strangely sculpted basalt cliffs for more than 1km. You can drive there, fly over the area in a helicopter *(Trans-North Helicopters, AirPort Hangar "C", Y1A 3E4, ☎633-4767)* or take a guided river cruise aboard the *MV Schwatka (P.O. Box 4001, Y1A 3S9, ☎668-4716)*. Lookouts, viewPoints and a footbridge have been laid out for visitors on the shore. Traces of Canyon City, one of the first communities established in the area, are still visible 2km from the Whitehorse bridge.

Each year, from late July through August, quinnat (or Chinook) salmon swim up the Whitehorse River, nearing the end of a journey that began in the open seas, over 3,000km away. A salmon ladder has been built to enable them to cross the dam and to return to and spawn in the exact sPot where they were born. You can watch this epic struggle when they migrate.

Dawson

On August 16, 1896, two members of the Tagish First Nation, Skookum Jim and Dawson Charlie, were prospecting in Rabbit Creek with an American friend by the name of George Carmack. Gold had already been found in the Yukon River, and this wasn't the first time the three friends had tried their luck. What they ended up finding near the **Klondike River**, however, was beyond their wildest dreams. There was gold – lots of it. The prospectors renamed "their" creek Bonanza Creek and staked their claim the next day, August 17, a date that remains in the collective memory of Yukon residents. Over the years, the bed of the Klondike and its tributaries gave forth the present-day equivalent of $1 billion worth of the yellow metal, making many people rich. It was also the site of the last and perhaps the greatest epic of the West: the great Gold Rush. Gold fever brought tens of thousands of dreamers to the north.

Jos Ladue came up with a completely different way to make his fortune. He decided to found the town of Dawson at the confluence of the Klondike and Yukon Rivers, at the foot of the nearly 900m-high **Midnight Dome**. Plots of land were snatched up for astronomical sums. Dawson grew rapidly; over 30,000 people were living here before the end of the century. It was the largest town in North America west of Winnipeg and north of Seattle. The finest cuisine, best wines and most beautiful merchandise were all available here – provided you could pay the price. In those days, everything in Dawson cost a fortune. People often paid their bills with nuggets of gold. In the good-time capital of North America, whiskey flowed like water but order prevailed, as the RCMP sent a detachment to the town and these Police officers were the only people allowed to bear arms.

As of 1904, however, the surface dePosits were exhausted, and the prospectors had to make room for big companies with the heavy equipment necessary to continue mining the area. The town would have died when these companies left in the 1960s if tourists hadn't started flocking here.

Today, Dawson has nearly 1,000 residents in winter and many more in summer. It is a town that lives on tourism and the memory of its golden days. Most of the local attractions are only accessible in warm weather. The place still has wooden sidewalks, unpaved roads and western facades. In preparation for the centennial of the Gold Rush, the federal government provided the funds to restore those buildings threatening to collapse and preserve the others.

The first thing to do upon arriving in Dawson is to stop by the **Visitors Reception Centre** *(Front and King St.,* ☎*993-5566)*, a reconstruction of a store from the Gold Rush era. This is the perfect introduction to Dawson: people come here to eat, drink, play and dance just like they did back in 1898. The centre can provide you with all the information you'll need for a pleasant stay in town and offers guided walking tours up to four times a day during summer.

There are several different ways to explore the town and its surroundings. **Gold City Tours** *(Front St., across from the boat called "Keno"; P.O. Box 960, YOB 1GO,* ☎*993-5175,* ≈*993-5261)* offers personalized guided bus tours. The itinerary

includes the town itself, the rivers, the gold mines and a trip up the Midnight Dome (the view is splendid in clear weather). Another option is to take a steamship cruise, which includes a meal; contact **Pleasure Island Restaurant & Yukon River Cruise** *(P.O. Box 859, YOB 1GO)*.

There are a number of noteworthy buildings in town. On Third Avenue, for example, there are **Harrington's Store** *(at Princess St.)*, which houses a collection of photographs; the **Palace Grand Theatre**, a reconstruction of an earlier building dating from 1899, which visitors can tour with a guide; and the **1901 Post Office**, still in operation today.

The guided tour of **Fort Herchmer** is also worthwhile. This is where the Mounties were garrisoned. You can see the jail cells, the stables and the officers' and privates' quarters.

A town like this naturally has to have a museum. The **Dawson City Museum & Historical Society** *($4; Jun to Sep 10am to 6pm; Main St. at 5th Ave., YOB 1GO,* ☎*993-5291,* ≈*993-5839, dcmuseum@yknet.yk.ca)* displays objects related to the Gold Rush and other aspects of local history, as well as prehistoric bones. A significant part of the collection is also devoted to Hän First nation. In addition, the museum houses a library, assorted presentations and a shop. Guided tours available.

Dawson is also the town of Poet **Robert Service** (1874-1958). Wherever you go in the territory, it seems that there is always someone quoting his work. In Dawson, you can visit his cabin on Eighth Avenue, where public readings of his poems are held. **Jack London's** cabin has been reconstructed next door (the original was 75km away). London was an American who became famous for his tales of the Far North. *The Call of the Wild* and *White Fang* are among his best-known works.

Of course, anyone who visits Dawson will want to see the Klondike and its two main goldbearing tributaries, Bonanza and Eldorado Creeks. You can take a road tour of the major sites. At Km 10 of Bonanza Creek Road, you can try your luck in gold-seeking at **Claim 33** *(P.O. Box 933, Y0B 1G0, ☎993-5804)*. A little farther along, on the same road, **Dredge No.4 Heritage Place** is the best possible illustration of the industrial exploitation that followed the Gold Rush. It is the largest dredge in North America.

Watson Lake

Founded by a trapper who settled here in 1898, Watson Lake is the Canadian gateway to the Yukon. The town lies just north of the British Columbia border. Its major growth period began in 1942, when it became a base camp for the construction of the Alaska Highway. Ever since, it has had all the services necessary for tourists, whether they are on their way to Whitehorse or want to enjoy one of many outdoor activities offered in the hinterland.

The **Alaska Highway Interpretive Centre** *(at the corner of Robert Campbell St. and the Alaska Hwy., ☎536-7469)* is Watson Lake Visitor's Reception Centre. It has a permanent exhibition on

the huge challenges involved in laying the highway.

Another interesting attraction commemorates the construction of the Alaska Highway. In 1942, Carl K. Lindley, a soldier and member of the construction team, was feeling homesick. To help shake off the feeling, he put up a sign showing the direction and distance to Danville, Illinois. Many others followed suit, and today there are over 30,000 signs in the **Watson Lake SignPosts Forest**.

From Dawson to Inuvik

Renting an RV and road-tripping across the Yukon is the perfect adventure if you like to drive. You can pick up a camper in Whitehorse, then take the **Klondike Highway** to Dawson where the real journey begins on the **Dempster Highway**, which goes all the way to Inuvik, in the Northwest Territories. The trip is punctuated by panoramas, interpretive centres and Aboriginal communities, and you can stop and admire the landscape or go on a hike whenever you please. If you take the trip in May or October, there is a good chance that you'll cross paths with migrating caribou. From Inuvik, you can take a plane to **Herschel Island**, north of the Yukon. Now a territorial park, the island has long been an important stopping place for inhabitants of the Far North. Traces of prehistoric Aboriginal communities and the docks where American whalers used to berth can be found here.

Parks

The Yukon is an unspoiled and bountiful wilderness, with many forests, tundra, mountains, glaciers, lakes and rivers. It is no surprise, therefore, that many people – local residents and visitors alike – enjoy skiing, canoeing, rafting, snowshoeing, mountain-climbing, hiking, horseback riding, fishing, hunting and mountain biking here. Venturing into the wilderness does call for a certain amount of caution, however, as well as the utmost respect for the environment and the need to keep it clean. It is particularly important to bring along enough food and clothing. Carrying a firearm for protection is generally permitted. Hunting and fishing are regulated, though, so make sure that you have the required permits before setting out. To help outdoor enthusiasts take full advantage of all the territory has to offer, the **Wilderness Tourism Association of the Yukon** *(P.O. Box 3960, Whitehorse, Y1A 3M6)* provides pertinent, up-to-date information on all sorts of services.

The federal government has turned the Canadian portion of the St. Elias Mountains into one of the loveliest parks in the country. **Kluane National Park** *(P.O. Box 5495, Haines Junction, Y0B 1L0, ☎634-2329)*, boasts **Mount Logan**, the highest summit in Canada, as well as the largest non-polar glaciers in the world. Park headquarters are in Haines Junction, at the local Visitor's Reception Centre. Kluane National Park is laced with trails. You can join a group outing or plan a solo trip; one option is to be dropped off by helicopter (the Visitor's Centre is the best place to make the necessary arrangements). Make sure to bring along a pair of binoculars to observe the wildlife. Before entering Kluane National Park, you must register and pay park fees. It is also strongly recommended to make sure that your information is up to date.

Outdoor Activities

Hiking

The most famous hike in the Yukon starts in Alaska and ends in British Columbia. The **Chilkoot Trail** follows the route taken by most gold prospectors across the mountains to the inland lakes that empty into the Yukon River. In the early days, prospectors would bring along everything they'd need to survive for a year – some 800kg of gear, which they had to carry themselves or find someone else to carry for them. Their goal was to reach **Bennett Lake** by fall and spend the winter there. Come spring, they would follow the lake, then the river to Dawson. Many died because they fell behind schedule, had an accident or were simply unlucky. The trail starts 16kg from Skagway, in Dyea, where hikers have to register. Before setting out, make sure to plan your trip well by contacting **Canadian Heritage, Parks**

Canada *(300 Main St., Room 205, Whitehorse, Y1A 2B5, ☎667-3910)*. The hike takes three to five days, leads through three former tent villages and has information panels and vestiges from the Gold Rush all along it. Bear in mind that the climate in the mountains can fluctuate drastically, even in July.

Less ambitious hikers can opt for one of the trails around the territory's major urban centres. Moreover, it is easy to rent a horse or a bike anywhere in the Yukon if you want to go for a short ride or on an excursion of a few days.

Yukon Conservation Association
302 Hawkins St.
P.O. Box 4163, Y1A 3T3
☎668-5678
The Yukon Conservation Association organizes group hikes during the summer. These outings are a good opportunity to learn more about the local geology and wildlife.

Canoeing, Rafting and Kayaking

Canoeing down the Yukon between Whitehorse and Dawson is a wonderful 10- to 14-day journey, most of which takes place on a long, quiet river. Some parts of the course are particularly interesting. A very long canyon frames the river for about 50km at the edge of Laberge Lake. Vestiges of the Gold Rush remain on the river banks. After the village of Carmacks are the **Five Finger Rapids**, which are easily crossed by canoe. The **Fort Selkirk** trading Post awaits canoeists

further along and Dawson is the final destination. If Possible, make a Point of timing your arrival here with one of the many events held in town during the summer.

Other waterways also have whirlPools, rapids and exciting descents for fans of rafting, kayaking and even canoeing. Engaging the services of an enterprise specializing in this type of expedition is recommended, as every river holds particular difficulties. The **Alsek River** (class IV) runs through Kluane Park from Haines Junction and lets you pass alongside the Lowell glacier. This 30m-high wall of ice accompanies paddlers for 13km! You can also go down the **Tatsenshini River** (class III-IV) from Dalton Post, south of Haines Junction. Renowned for its rocky landscapes, the river runs toward British Columbia, where it meets up with the Alsek River. Finally, at the northern tip of the territory, the **Firth River** (class IV) rushes through the tundra before it joins the Beaufort Sea. It flows through the heart of **Ivvavik National Park**, a preserve where the Inuit still live according to ancestral ways.

Golf

Whitehorse

Mountain-View 18-hole Golf Course
Off Range Road
P.O. Box 5883
Y1A 5L6
☎633-6020
Outside of town, the Mountain-View 18-hole Golf Course awaits golfing

enthusiasts from May 1 to September 30.

Hunting and Fishing

Hunting and fishing occupy a special place in Yukon culture. Mountain goats, bears, caribou and moose are special trophies for the hunter, much like a good-sized salmon or Arctic char can be to a fishing buff. There are dozens of different package deals to suit everyone's tastes and budgets, from deluxe outfitters to riverside campsites. As a general rule, the best hunting and fishing spots are only accessible by plane or helicopter. Most outfitters provide transportation and invaluable information on lawful hunting and fishing.

Dogsledding

From December to March, visitors have the unique opportunity to experience a dogsled ride. Whitehorse boasts a number of outfitters who can provide you with the necessary training to become true "mushers." You can then embark on a tour, generally lasting one to seven days, with rather rustic shelters along the way.

Adventure Packages

Air North flies travellers all over the Yukon and Alaska with its Douglas DC3s or DC4s and Piper Navajos. The crew is professional and friendly. Call ☎*800-764-0407* free of charge, or ☎*668-2228*.

Up North Boat and Canoe Rentals
May to Sep
Whitehorse
☎*667-7905*
Up North Boat and Canoe Rentals rents boats, canoes, kayaks and waterproof travel bags and organizes a multitude of outings and expeditions. The enterprise provides transportation by air, sea or land, and offers one- to 19-day excursions, including fishing trips, for one person or more. Some excursions require experience. Prices are affordable, but vary depending on the activity. Call ahead to find out the exact cost of the expedition you wish to undertake, as the enterprise has a wide variety of options.

Tatsenshini Expediting
1062 Alder St.
Whitehorse, Y1A 3W8
☎*633-2742*
⬚*633-6184*
www.tatsenshiniyukon.com
Tatsenshini Expediting is a highly respected adventure outfitter in the Yukon, organizing 11-day inflatable raft expeditions on the legendary waters of the Tatsenshini and Alsek Rivers. This trip is considered the "most beautiful in the world" in terms of scenery. Tours go through magnificent **Kluane National Park** and end in **Dry Bay**, amidst icebergs and glaciers.

Kanoe People Yukon Wilderness Outfitters
P.O. Box 5152
Whitehorse, Y1A 4S3
☎*668-4899*
⬚*668-4891*
Kanoe People Yukon Wilderness Outfitters is an excellent place to rent river and lake canoes and organize your own memorable excursions. Large groups can rent the Voyager Canoe, a 10m canoe (*$160/day*) that can accommodate eight to 16 people.

The following enterprises offer non-guided tours:

Wild & Woolly Yukon Survival Course
Po Box 92
Y0A 1B0
☎*390-2682*
Wild & Woolly Yukon Survival Course teaches useful things like how to orientate yourself using a topographical map and how to recognize grizzly, moose, wolf and other animal tracks. You will also learn defence tactics in case of a bear attack. Among the techniques taught here are standard ones (canoeing, recognizing edible and medicinal plants, hiking with a topographical map and compass, maintenance and sharpening of axes, using a knife, etc.), as well as traditional Aboriginal ones (starting a fire by rubbing two pieces of wood together, rope- and basket-making, using stone implements, building rudimentary shelters, etc.). This training will provide you with the means and confidence to tackle the Yukon's wild spaces.

Arctic Trails (*125 Copper Rd., Whitehorse, Y1A 2Z7,* ☎*668-2776*) rents aluminium boats, rubber dinghies, all-terrain vehicles and snowmobiles.

Accommodations

Whitehorse

Robert Service Campground
☎**668-6678 or 668-3721**
⇰**667-6334**
The Robert Service Campground is located on the banks of the Yukon River, 3min by car or 20min walking distance from downtown Whitehorse. All 48 campsites are pleasantly wooded and equipped with a picnic table and barbecue grill (the wood is free). A small grocery store and hot showers are also on hand. A good choice.

Wild Treats Vacation Properties
P.O. Box 9150
29 Wann Rd., Y1A 4A2
☎**633-3322**
Wild Treats Vacation Properties specializes in renting apartments and houses throughout the Yukon. Offering everything from log cabins to vast residences, Wild Treats will help you find whatever you need.

AirPort Chalet
$63 to $85
tv, ℜ, P
Mile 916 Alaska Hwy.
right across from the airPort
☎**668-2166**
The Airport Chalet has all the services for a family vacation. Located right near museums, it offers interesting activities and spacious hotel or motel rooms. Prices are reasonable, but it is best to call ahead to inquire about seasonal rates. Full hook-up RV sites are available. The establishment also has a family restaurant that serves fresh food (see p 657).

Four Seasons Bed & Breakfast
$75 to $85 bkfst incl.
&
18 Tagish Rd.
☎**667-2161**
Located 5min walking distance from downtown, the Four Seasons Bed & Breakfast has a family atmosphere and spacious rooms with all the amenities. The decor reflects the North of days gone by. Room service is provided within 15min of your call, and videos, music and books are at your disposal. The inn also organizes guided tours and customized excursions, depending on your needs. Suitable for families and business travellers alike. Open year-round. The inn only accepts cash and traveller's cheques.

Birch Street Bed & Breakfast
$75 to $85 bkfst incl.
pb, sb, ≈, ⌂
1501 Birch St.
Porter Creek
5min by car from downtown
☎**633-5625**
⇰**633-5660**
The Birch Street Bed & Breakfast is set in a quiet spot with a view of the valley. Hearty, home-made breakfasts are served by a cozy fire in the pleasant living room. Suitable for both business travellers and families. Open year-round.

Westmark Klondike Inn
$89 to $129
closed winter
tv, ℜ, P
2288 Second Ave.
☎**668-4747**
☎**800-544-0970**
⇰**667-7639**
The Westmark Klondike Inn has approximately 100 fully renovated and very comfortable rooms. Good American southwest cooking is on the menu at the hotel's **Arizona Charlie's Restaurant**, and smaller dishes are available in the cafeteria. You can also go for a drink at the Sternwheeler Lounge.

High Country Inn
$99
⊛, ⊘, *tv, ≈, &, ℜ, P*
4051 Fourth Ave.
☎**667-4471**
www.highcountryinn.yk.ca
The High Country Inn is said to be Whitehorse's top hotel, with 110 rooms affording a view of the magnificent landscape and a friendly staff to greet you. The inn provides free shuttle service (or limo, on request) from the airport. Moreover, the establishment is easily accessible to travellers with disabilities and provides all the comforts: pool, sauna, whirlpool baths, exercise room, free coffee in rooms and restaurant that makes the best pancakes in the North (see p 657).

Westmark Whitehorse
$129
tv, ℜ, P
Po Box 4250
Y1A 3T3
☎**668-4700**
☎**800-544-0970**
⇰**668-2789**
The Westmark Whitehorse is one of the most luxurious hotels in town, with 181 rooms and the biggest convention facility in the Yukon. The establishment has a restaurant offering fine cuisine (see p 657), as well as a friendly bar, the Village Spring Lounge.

Haines Junction

Dalton Trail Lodge
$120 fb
$1,500 to $1,700 for the week-long adventure package
ℜ
☎**634-2099**
www.daltontrail.com
The Dalton Trail Lodge is owned by an adventure-tour operator. Though situated deep in the coun-

try, near beautiful Dezadeash Lake, close to superb Kluane National Park, the lodge offers all the possible luxuries, with lovely, fully equipped rooms, a very good Swiss restaurant and a library where you can relax with a book by the fire while sipping a cocktail. During the day, you can go horseback riding or enjoy a guided tour of the park. Excursions of several days are also offered, with overnight stays in comfortable shelters. This is also a fisher's paradise, since the lake boasts hundreds of trout weighing in at 20kg. A little farther away, king, coho and sockeye salmon await you. In fact, organizers guarantee a spectacular catch only a helicopter ride away!

Alaska Highway (Km 1717)

Cottonwood Park Campground
Km 1717
Alaska Hwy.
6km from Sheep Mountain
Visitor's Centre
☎634-2739
Located in Kluane National Park, the Cottonwood Park Campground attracts those who enjoy sports of all kinds, from cyclists, walkers, fishing enthusiasts, hunters of mountain goats and other wild animals (on that note, do not forget your binoculars) to RV-travellers. Rates include use of all the amenities and attractions on the grounds, which include miniature golf. A family restaurant serves home-made dishes, and a souvenir shop offers a host of gift ideas.

Beaver Creek

Westmark Inn Beaver Creek
$89 to $129
tv, ℜ, P
Mile 1202, Alaska Hwy.
☎800-544-0970
≈862-7902
The Westmark Inn Beaver Creek is a standard roadside hotel of considerable size for these northern regions. In pioneer times, transport cafés such as this one provided both meals and a place to sleep. The Westmark Inn Beaver Creek's atmosphere manages to keep this spirit alive. The establishment boasts 174 very comfortable rooms. Don't miss the "musical dinner" at the Rendez-Vous, where a buffet is served.

Atlin Lake

The Hitching Post
$85 to $100
Km 38 Atlin Road Mobile 2M5177
White Mountain Channel
≈660-4429
mailing address
RR 1, Site 20, Comp. 182
Whitehorse, Y1A 4Z6
If you enjoy adventure and wild scenery, The Hitching Post has it all on the shores of Atlin Lake. Campsites and lovely little wood cabins await you here. Boats and canoes are available for fishing buffs, and horseback riding is organized. Reservations are strongly advised.

Dawson

Dawson Peaks Resort
$35 to $80/night
according to services
$8 to $14/night for RVs
according to your needs
closed to early April
ℜ
Km 1282 Alaska Hwy.
14km from Teslin
☎390-2310
The Dawson Peaks Resort is set in a beautiful environment near Teslin Lake and Morlay Bay. You can stay for the day or the week and benefit from amenities ideally suited to a stay in the North. If you want to stay here in a tent or RV, call for information about rates and services. The restaurant (see below) serves good food. Dozens of excursions, lasting anywhere from 2hrs to seven days, are organized: reserve in advance. The establishment will send brochures uPon request.

Westmark Inn Dawson
$99 to $169
tv, ℜ, P
P.O. Box 420
☎993-5542
☎800-544-0970
≈993-5623
Located in the heart of Dawson, the Westmark Inn Dawson has been completely renovated. The 131 rooms are very comfortable and well equipped. You can have something to eat and drink in the Keno Lounge, or savour the best steaks in town at the Klondike Barbecue (terrace in summer).

Watson Lake

Cedar Lodge Motel
$70
K, tv, P
Mile 633 Alaska Hwy.
P.O. Box 243
☎*536-7406*
The Cedar Lodge Motel is
the only cedar-built hotel
in Watson Lake. The establishment was recently
renovated and expanded.
The rooms are very pleas-
ant, and some are
equipped with a kitchen-
ette. A shuttle service
between the airport or
seaplane base and the
motel is also available.

Big Horn Hotel
$87 according to the size
of the room and
the season
tv, P
downtown
☎*536-2020*
The Big Horn Hotel is a
family-style hotel with
lovely, well-decorated
rooms. The owners do
their utmost to offer guests
the best Possible stay at
very reasonable prices.
Complimentary coffee.

Restaurants

Whitehorse

High Country Inn
$-$$
4051 Fourth Ave.
☎*667-4471*
The restaurant at the High
Country Inn makes the
best pancakes in the
North.

Angelo's Restaurant
$$
202 Strickland St.
☎*668-6266*
Angelo's Restaurant serves
high-quality Greek and
Italian cuisine. Very
friendly staff and interest-
ing selection of dishes.

Airport Chalet
$$
Mile 916 Alaska Hwy.
right across from the airport
☎*668-2166*
The restaurant at the
Airport Chalet serves fresh
and varied cuisine in a
family atmosphere.

Dawson

Dawson Peaks Resort
$-$$
Km 1282 Alaska Hwy.
14km from Teslin
☎*390-2310*
The restaurant at the
Dawson Peaks Resort
serves good food.

Haines Junction

The Raven
$$
Oct to Apr
The Raven Haines Junction Hotel
☎*634-2804 or 634-2500*
The Raven offers choice
dishes to gourmands. The
restaurant was awarded
Where to Eat in Canada's
"Silver Star."

Entertainment

Whitehorse

Big events mark the pass-
ing months in Whitehorse.
In mid-February, the town
is set astir by the **Yukon
Sourdough Rendez-vous**, a
winter festival featuring
myriad competitions and
activities. At this same time
of year, you can also at-
tend a music festival, an
air-balloon festival and the
start of a dogsledding race,
the **Annual Yukon Quest**
*(mid-Feb; Yukon Quest Inter-
national Association,*
☎*668-4711)*, in which the
best teams journey to Fair-
banks, Alaska, and vie for
approximately $140,000.
Another music festival as
well as a folk festival are
held in April. In May, the
town plays host to a major
meeting for quadrille en-
thusiasts. A storytellers'
festival takes place in June,
as does a special evening
celebrating the longest day
of the year. In addition to
the activities surrounding
Canada Day, a trip down
the Yukon River, a period-
costume day, golf tourna-
ments, a horse show and
an authentic rodeo are
held in July. Every August,
Discovery Days is com-
memorated all across the
territory, notably with a
boat race between White-
horse and Dawson. With a
multitude of sporting and
cultural events, the
Laberge Lake Aboriginal
festivities are also a must.
In October, francophones
take over with the
week-long Franco-fête.
Finally, if you still have
energy to spare, you can
enjoy musical revues such
as **The Canteen Show** *(103
Main St.,* ☎*667-4682)* at the
Capitol Hotel, and the
Westmark Whitehorse Ho-
tel's **Frantic Follies Vaudeville
Revue** *(at Second Ave. and
Wood St.,* ☎*668-2042)* in the
evening, featuring dinner,
music, magic and French
cancan dancers.

Dawson

Dawson also hosts a num-
ber of celebrations. In
1998, the **Annual Dawson City
Music Festival** *(*☎*993-5584)*
celebrates its 20th anniver-

sary under the midnight sun. The festival features Canadian and American performers who organize workshops and concerts as well as dances, meals and other fun activities. Gold was discovered in the region on August 16, 1896. Every year, the town commemorates this unique event with the **Discovery Days** celebration. The entire Population takes part in the parade, dances, tournaments and other festivities.

At night, visitors can choose between the **Palace Grand Revue – Gaslight Follies** and an evening at **Diamond Tooth Gertie's Gambling Casino** *(every night starting at 7pm).*

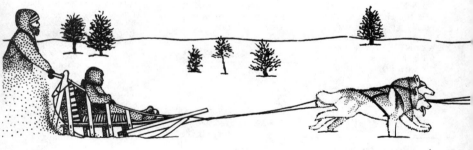

The Northwest Territories

All sorts of images come to mind when one thinks of the Canadian North.

O nce the domain of a few Aboriginal communities (mainly Dene and Inuit) surviving in extremely difficult living conditions, the Northwest Territories (N.W.T.) have attracted many adventurers and missionaries over the years, followed by an entire non-Aboriginal population from southern Canada, lured here by government jobs and the rich gold mines near Great Slave Lake.

T his enormous territory, over half the size of the United States, is still very sparsely populated, with only 41,000 inhabitants, 18,000 of whom live in Yellowknife, the capital.

O ver the past 40 years, living conditions have changed a lot for the Aboriginal peoples, who make up about 50% of the population. Even the region's most isolated communities have joined the modern world, relegating tipis, igloos and dogsleds to folklore. Despite this, Aboriginal people are still strongly attached to their traditions and culture, as evidenced by their festivities, crafts and even their style of government.

H owever, the N.W.T. is also a land of adventure, extremes and challenges. This region has a wealth of attractions to offer anyone who loves outdoor activities and is fascinated by unspoiled wilderness and the ancestral traditions of those who make their home there. The N.W.T. boasts two of the 10 biggest lakes in the world (Great Bear Lake and Great Slave Lake), whose icy surfaces are traversed by wide roads in winter; the majestic Virginia Falls, which are twice as high as Niagara Falls; and the impressive 1,800km-long Mackenzie River, which flows into the Beaufort Sea a few kilometres north of Inuvik.

F inally, the N.W.T. is also *the* place for wildlife preservation. There are four national parks here: Aulavik National Park, in the northwest; Nahanni National Park in the southwest; Tuktut Nogait National Park in the northeast; and lastly, on the Alberta border, Wood Buffalo National Park, home to the world's largest free-roaming herd of bison.

The many rich and varied attractions of this enormous region and the graciousness of its inhabitants make a visit to the N.W.T. a truly unforgettable experience.

Geography

Occupying the northernmost part of the North American continent, between the 60th and the 80th parallels, the N.W.T. encompasses 1,299,000km² . The N.W.T. is bounded by the Arctic Ocean to the north; the newly created Nunavut territory to the east; the provinces of Saskatchewan, Alberta and British Columbia to the south and the Yukon to the west. The region is made up of a huge continental shelf.

In the eastern region, two thirds of the Canadian Shield is characterized by a hilly, rocky terrain strewn with lakes. The western edge of the region, along the Yukon, consists of a jagged mountain range with summits about 2,000m high. The highest peak, as yet unnamed, rises 2,773m into the sky. The effects of successive periods of glaciation are particularly apparent in the soil, which is usually bare or extremely poor due to permafrost. As far as agriculture is concerned, only the land in the southernmost areas has any potential.

The glacial lakes in the N.W.T. are too numerous to list. To the west lie two of the 10 largest lakes in the world; Great Bear Lake and Great Slave Lake. The latter was actually named after an Aboriginal people, the Slaveys, who lived on its shores. The name Great Slave Lake is a corruption of Great Slavey Lake and has nothing to do with slavery, though the people are now known as Slaves. The waters of the two lakes, like those of most other lakes in the west, empty into the great Mackenzie River, which stretches 1,800km and spills into the Beaufort Sea, a part of the Arctic Ocean. In the centre of the region, two major waterways, the Coppermine and Back Rivers, also flow into the Arctic Ocean. To the east, the Thelon River runs into Hudson Bay.

Flora and Fauna

The tree line stretches diagonally from the mouth of the Mackenzie River northwest to Hudson Bay, on the Manitoba border. Even south of this limit, the vegetation is still fairly sparse, due to the rocky soil and the massif in the western part of the N.W.T. In fact, only a small proportion of this land is wooded.

The vegetation consists chiefly of firs, birches and larches. North of the tree line, in the Arctic tundra, nothing grows but small stunted shrubs, lichen and moss.

In the wooded areas, you might very well cross paths with some animals commonly found in the Canadian North – caribou, moose, black bears, the occasional grizzly, wolves, lynxes, beavers, martens, muskrats and wolverines. Wood Buffalo National Park, on the Alberta border, is home to the largest free-roaming bison herd on earth. It is also the last nesting place for whooping cranes. Other bird species found here include rock ptarmigans, Arctic terns, gyrfalcons and ravens.

The Arctic tundra is home to huge herds of caribou, as well as muskoxen, polar bears and arctic foxes. If you take a cruise on the Arctic Ocean, with a little luck you'll get to see some whales, arguably the most impressive of the sea mammals. You might also spot seals, walruses, and perhaps the odd narwhal. In the past, large numbers of whales, mostly belugas (small white whales), used to come here to breed in the cold, plankton-rich waters of the Arctic, but due to over-hunting there are a great deal fewer now.

Black Bear

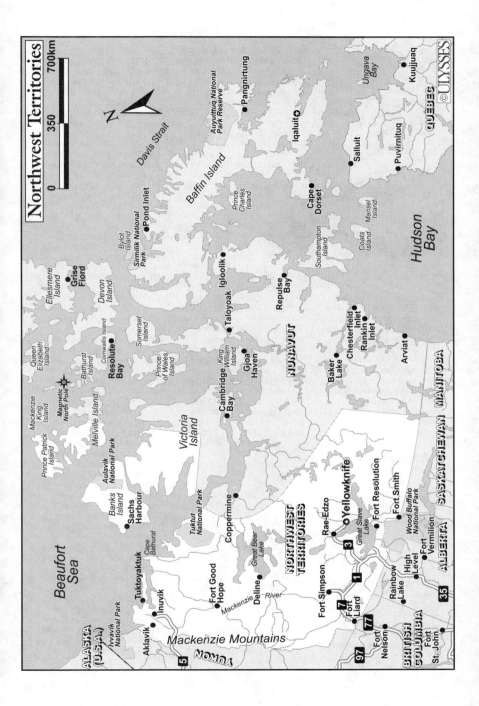

Walrus

Fishing is a very popular activity in the N.W.T. The lakes are teeming with trout, whitefish (fish with non-oily, white flesh), pike, Arctic char and grayling. Whether you eat them Aboriginal-style – dried or fried in fat – or prepared according to western recipes, you're sure to appreciate the delicate flavour of these delicious fish.

A Brief History

The Arctic was the last large region in the world to be inhabited by human beings. About 12,000 years ago, toward the end of the last ice age, tribes from northeastern Siberia crossed the Bering Strait to present-day Alaska. They probably did this during winter, when the ice forms a dangerous and unstable bridge between Asia and America. Within several generations, these tribes of Siberian descent had settled all over the North American Arctic, from Greenland to the north, to Labrador to the south. They developed a unique way of life that enabled them to survive the intense cold. The Inuit didn't arrive for another 3,000 years and they now live mainly in Nunavut (see "Nunavut").

It appears highly probable that between the start of the last millennium and the 1350s, European navigators sailed to the Canadian Arctic from Greenland and Iceland. Sir Henry Sinclair, a Scottish explorer, apparently came to Baffin Island in 1398. Officially, however, Sir Martin Frobisher, an English navigator, is recognized as the first European to explore the region. He landed on Baffin Island, now part of Nunavut, in 1577 and claimed it for the Crown of England. Explorers Henry Hudson, John Davis and William Baffin, to name a few, crisscrossed the Arctic Ocean and Hudson Bay in search of the Northwest Passage, a navigable route between Europe and the Orient. Two French explorers, Médard Chouard, known as Des Groseillers, and his brother-in-law, Pierre-Esprit Radisson, who had explored the Lake Superior and James Bay regions, realized that the best furs were found north of Lake Superior. Aware that the fur trade was expanding northwest on land, the two men tried to set up a commercial base on Hudson Bay, the inland sea discovered by Henry Hudson (whose life came to a tragic end when he was cast adrift on those same waters by his mutinous crew). This base would make it possible to sail into the heart of the northern regions where top-quality furs were more abundant. Unable to obtain backing from the French, Radisson and Des Groseillers went to England, where they found a sympathetic ear at King Charles II's court. The Hudson's Bay Company charter was drawn up in the spring of 1670 and signed by the king on May 2 of the same year. The two Frenchmen gained a trade monopoly and permission to colonize all land that drained into Hudson Bay. This huge territory, named Rupert's Land, encompassed northern Québec and Ontario, Manitoba, a part of Saskatchewan and Alberta, as well as part of the N.W.T. The Hudson's Bay Company was one of England's most successful colonial enterprises in Canada, playing a major role in commerce. For Europeans, the challenge presented by North America was clear: to scout out the unknown, exploit its resources, develop trade and settle the untamed wilderness. Tradesmen and explorers took up this challenge with zeal, increasing geographical knowledge of this immense territory at lightning speed. In the early 18th century, Canadian explorer Henry Kelsey, an employee of the Hudson's Bay Company, was the first European to enter the N.W.T. overland from Hudson Bay. The rival North West Company was also involved in the initial exploration of the N.W.T. In fact, an American explorer by the name of Peter Pond, who worked for that company, made the first map of the Great Slave Lake region. In 1789, Alexander Mackenzie, also employed by the North West Company, sailed down the huge river that now bears his name, to the Arctic Ocean. A few years before, in 1770, Samuel Hearne had left the post at Hudson Bay to sail through the land of the Chipewyans on the Coppermine River and had reached Great Slave Lake.

The search for a northern shipping route linking the east to the west continued into the 19th century. Many explorers searched in vain, but their efforts gave much insight into the Arctic Archipelago.

At the instigation of Prime Minister John Alexander Macdonald, the N.W.T. was purchased by the Canadian government and joined Confederation on July 15, 1870. The region's borders as they stood until 1999, when Nunavut was created, were not drawn until 1912. It took six months of negotiations between the Canadian government and the Hudson's Bay Company to reach a buy-back agreement. The Hudson's Bay Company was hoping to get a substantial sum for Rupert's Land, since the United States had paid Russia $7.2 million for Alaska in 1867 without any knowledge of the area's possible resources. Nevertheless, the agreement turned out to be advantageous for the Canadian government, which only had to pay $1.5 million for this vast region and gave a twentieth of the arable land back to the company. The newly acquired Rupert's Land was divided up into the province of Manitoba, the district of Keewatin in 1867, the districts of Franklin and Mackenzie in 1895 and the Yukon Territory in 1898. Part of the remaining land was added to the provinces of Alberta and Saskatchewan.

Aboriginal Peoples

There are eight official languages in the N.W.T.: English and French, the two official languages of Canada, and six aboriginal languages: Chipewyan, Cree, Dogrib, Gwich'in, Inuktitut and Slave.

Eight Aboriginal communities share the vast expanse of the N.W.T. The Inuvialuit, who number about 1,600, speak an Inuktitut dialect known as Inuvialuktun. In the same region, around Aklavik, there are 1,150 Gwich'in, who speak Dene. Five thousand Metis live in the western part of the N.W.T. Of Cree (or Dene) and French Canadian ancestry, these Aboriginal peoples played an important role in the fur trade, as they were bilingual. Today, they are represented politically by the Metis Nation of the N.W.T. The Dene who live northeast and south of Great Slave Lake, only 2,150 in all, speak Chipewyan. The Deh Cho Dene make their home in the southwestern part of the N.W.T., in the Fort Simpson area. Their population numbers about 2,000 and they speak Southern Slave. There are 1,025 Sahtu Dene, a Slave-speaking people who live west of Great Bear Lake, in Fort Good Hope, Norman Wells and Fort Norman. The Rae-Edzo and Rae Lakes area, north of Great Bear Lake, is home to 3,000 Dogrib. Finally, the Inuit, who number about 4,000, occupy the eastern part of the N.W.T. They speak Inuktitut and Inuvialuktun.

Politics

The N.W.T. does not have provincial status in Canadian confederation. The region is one of the three territories that make up the Canadian North, the others being the Yukon and Nunavut. Though the N.W.T. has its own parliament, the federal government still exercises a great deal of influence here. The head of the N.W.T. government presides over a seven-member executive cabinet and a Legislative Assembly. The interests of the federal government are represented by a commissioner who carries out the instructions of the Minister of the Department of Indian and Northern Affairs or the Governor General of Canada. The Legislative Assembly comprises 14 members elected to four-year terms. The political system is not based on negotiation between political parties but rather on decisions made by consensus. The N.W.T. is represented at the national parliament in Ottawa by a senator designated by the Governor General of Canada, and at the House of Commons by two members elected for five-year terms.

Economics

The economy of the N.W.T., once based exclusively on trapping and the fur trade, got its second wind when a large oil field was discovered in Norman Wells in 1920. During the Second World War, the U.S. helped fund the development of this oil field and the transportation of the precious liquid to refineries. In 1930, pitchblende and silver mines were discovered on the

Northwest Territories

eastern shore of Great Slave Lake, making Canada one of the world's leading producers of radium and uranium, the main constituents of pitchblende. A few years later, more immense riches hidden away in the N.W.T.'s subsoil were revealed when extensive gold deposits were found on the northern and southern shores of Great Slave Lake, in the Yellowknife area. Zinc was also found. The 1970s brought the discovery of major oil and natural gas deposits near Tuktoyaktuk, at the mouth of the Mackenzie River. Finally, the recent discovery of what might be one of the world's largest diamond mines created a sensation and rekindled prospectors' enthusiasm. The subsoil of the N.W.T. might well hold even more surprises. Apart from mining resources, the region's economy is based on forestry, tourism and local crafts.

Finding Your Way Around

The N.W.T. is on Mountain time (GMT -7).

The Territory is divided into five tourists regions:

• **DehCho** (Fort Simson, Nahanni National Park)

• **Inuvik** (in the northwest)

• **North Slave** (Yellowknife)

• **South Slave** (Hay River)

• **Sahtu** (Norman Wells and the Middle West)

By Plane

There is no international airport in the N.W.T., so you will probably have to fly through Edmonton, Alberta, to get to the capital, Yellowknife.

Air Canada, through connector airline NWT Air, and Canadian Regional Airlines, both offer regular flights to Yellowknife and Iqaluit. As far as smaller destinations are concerned, every community in the North is accessible by air thanks to companies like First Air, Air Inuit and Skyward Aviation. On the down side, the fares can be extremely high. Those wishing to visit several isolated northern communities are therefore advised to discuss their plans with the airlines, which offer more economical ticket options covering a limited number of stops in certain communities. These tickets are still fairly expensive, however. There is no regular air service to some parts of the N.W.T., including the Nahanni River region. The only way to get there is by air-taxi. You'll find a number of small air-taxi companies in the major towns of the N.W.T. All you have to do is look in the Yellow Pages and shop around for the best fare.

Adlair Aviation
Box 2946
Yellowknife, NT
X1A 2R3
☎*(867) 873-5161*
⇌*(867) 873-8475*

Aero Arctic Helicopters
Box 1496
Yellowknife, NT, X1A 2P1
☎*(867) 873-5230*
⇌*(867) 920-4488*

Air Tindi
Box 1693
☎*(867) 920-4177*
⇌*(867) 920-2836*

Buffalo Airways
Box 1479
Hay River, NT, X0E 0R0
☎*(867) 874-3333*
⇌*(867) 874-3572*

Keewatin Air
Box 38, Rankin Inlet
☎*(819) 645-2992*
⇌*(819) 645-2330*

First Air
Box 100
Yellowknife, NT, X1A 2N1
☎*(867) 873-4461*
☎*(800) 661-0808*
⇌*(867) 873-5209*

Skyward Aviation
Box 562
Rankin Inlet
NT, X0C 0G0
☎*(819) 645-3200*
⇌*(819) 645-3208*

By Car

Generally speaking, only small sections of the major roads in the N.W.T., near the larger towns, are paved. The remaining parts are dirt and gravel but still in good condition. In the south, the Mackenzie Highway (Hwy. 1) leads into the N.W.T. from the province of Alberta. The Liard Highway (Hwy. 7) links British Columbia to the N.W.T. and then connects with the Mackenzie Highway. The latter also intersects with Highway 3, which leads to Yellowknife; Highway 2, which leads to Hay River; Highway 6, which leads to Fort Resolution; and Highway 5, which leads to Fort Smith. In the north, the Dempster Highway (Hwy. 8) connects the town of Dawson (Yukon) to Inuvik, located at the mouth of the Mackenzie River. Two other highways, Canol Road (Hwy. 9) and Nahanni Range Road (Hwy. 10), lead from the Yukon to the N.W.T., but both end at the border between the two territories in the Mackenzie Mountains.

Highways 1, 3 and 8 all cross large rivers. During summer, a free ferry service is available to motorists, while in winter the ice on the rivers is so thick that it provides a perfectly safe natural bridge over which to travel. However, during the freezing and thawing periods, there are neither ferries nor ice bridges to get from one shore to the other. These periods generally last about four weeks, so if you're planning to go to the N.W.T. at the beginning or end of winter, make sure to call the following numbers to see if river crossings are possible:

For roads in the south: ☎*800-661-0750*
For ferry service in the south: ☎*800-661-1751*
For road and ferry service in the north: ☎*800-661-0752*

A Few Words of Advice about Driving in the North

Though the roads are kept in fairly good condition, it is wise to take a few precautions when embarking on a long car trip.

As the distances between communities can be huge, it is imperative to check how much gas you have before setting out, since you won't find a gas station along the way. Dust clouds, pebbles hitting the car, mud, and rocks obstructing the road are some of the difficulties motorists might encounter

on the highways of the north. To minimize the risk of accident, it is important to:

- Make sure that your vehicle is in good condition.

- Bring along a spare tire or two (flats are common), an emergency kit, a snow shovel in winter, a towline, an axe and matches.

- Always drive with your headlights on.

- Put protectors on your lights to prevent them from being damaged by small rocks thrown up by the wheels of other cars.

- Slow down when you pass another car to prepare for the dust cloud and flying rocks that this will occasion.

- Drive with your windows and air vents closed to limit the amount of dust inside the car.

- Bring along food and water in case you have to wait for help.

- Bring along some mosquito repellent in the summer and a warm change of clothing, a sleeping bag for each passenger and candles in the winter. A lit candle can make the interior of the car several degrees warmer without wasting gas.

By Bus

Greyhound
☎*(867) 256-9111*
The Greyhound bus company offers service between Edmonton, Alberta, and Yellowknife, with a connection to Enterprise. Though it's a long trip, this is an affordable option for travellers on a tight budget.

Practical Information

The area code for the **N.W.T.** is *867*.

For information on the various national parks, contact the **Canadian Parks Service** *(Box 1166, Yellowknife, NT, X1A 2N8)* or the **Ministry of Economic Development and Tourism** *(Yellowknife, NT, X1A 2L9; ☎867-873-7200 or 800-661-0788, ⇥867-873-4059).*

Tourist Information

N.W.T Arctic Tourism, in partnership with the N.W.T's Department of Resources, Wildlife and Economic Development, provides tourist information on the N.W.T. It produces an annual Explorer's Guide.

P.O. Box 610
Yellowknife, NT
X1A 2N5
☎*873-5007*
☎*800-661-0788*
⇥*873-4059*
www.nwttravel.nt.ca
nwtat@nwttravel.nt.ca

Liquor Laws

The minimum drinking age in the territories is 19. In bars, you may be requested to show identification proving that you are of legal age. It should be noted that some communities have decided by public consensus to curb the alcohol problem by banning all sales and consumption of alcohol within their jurisdiction. In these "dry" communities, it is absolutely forbidden to be in possession of wine, beer or spirits. To find out more about your rights, contact the local branch of the Royal Canadian Mounted Police.

Exploring

★ ★ ★

From Great Slave Lake to Nahanni National Park

★
Yellowknife

The capital of the N.W.T. since 1967, Yellowknife lies in the administrative region of Fort Smith. Located on the shores of Yellowknife Bay, at the mouth of the Yellowknife River, this town of 18,000 was founded on the north shore of Great Slave Lake.

Originally, Yellowknife was simply a small trading post established in 1789 by explorer Samuel Hearne, an employee of the Hudson's Bay Company. Hearne did not call the town Yellowknife because

of the gold mines, which weren't discovered until much later, but because an Aboriginal peoples that lived on the shores of the lake made knives with copper blades. The tribe was wiped out by a string of epidemics that broke out when Europeans arrived here, and by a fratricidal war with the Dogrib, who were trying to drive them off their land.

In 1896, miners heading for the Klondike in the Yukon discovered gold in the region. The gold proved very difficult to extract, however, and these veins were never mined. The N.W.T. didn't attract prospectors again until 1930, when a large deposit of pitchblende was discovered in the Great Bear Lake region. Thanks to the rapid development of aviation, scores of gold miners were able to scour the Yellowknife area, and numerous concessions were granted between 1934 and 1936. Here on the shores of the bay, Yellowknife rose from its ashes, becoming the little town known now as the old town. Few prospectors struck it rich, however, and the veins were almost exhausted when another, bigger lode was discovered at the end of World War II. Though extracting the gold proved very expensive, this mine is still in operation today. Hopes were so high that a new wave of miners arrived in Yellowknife. Very soon, the small town on the shores of Yellowknife Bay had to expand, and a new, modern town was built on the other side of the hill, a little farther inland. Designated the territorial capital in 1967, the town attracted a large number of bureaucrats from the south. To this day, the territorial government is the region's

primary employer, along with the gold mines. In the early 1990s, the miners, hoping to obtain better and safer working conditions, launched a major strike. The management, unwilling to give in to pressure from the workers, resorted to using scabs. Things heated up between striking and non-striking employees, and management was forced to post security guards at the mine entrances to protect the workers and the facilities. Nevertheless, frequent altercations broke out, both in the workplace and in local bars. This violent situation reached its climax on the morning of September 18, 1992, when a bomb exploded in one of the mine galleries, killing nine miners. After a long investigation conducted in a climate of anger and suspicion, the bomber was finally arrested and tried. The conflict was not resolved until 18 months later.

At first glance, Yellowknife is a small town made up of a few skyscrapers and some little wooden houses against a vast backdrop of rocks, lakes and twisted trees. The best place to start off a tour of Yellowknife and the surrounding area is the **tourist office** *(Northern Frontier Visitors Centre, near Frame Lake, 4807 49th St., ☎873-4262, www.northernfrontier.com)*, where you'll find all the maps and information you need.

The **old town**, located on a peninsula in Yellowknife Bay, looks out on Latham Island. Access is gained by Franklin Avenue (50th Ave.), the main street, which runs all the way through town. The old town marks the site originally chosen by the first gold prospectors to

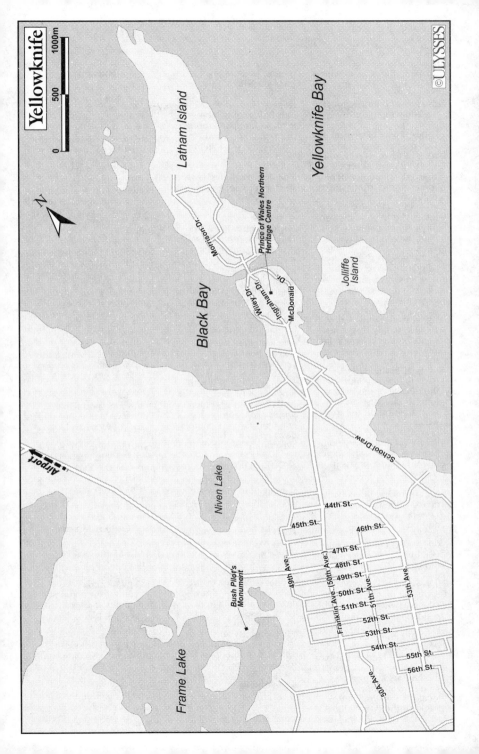

arrive in the region, who built small houses on piles because of the shifting of the ground during freezing and thawing periods.

A **Bush Pilot's Monument ★** was erected on the highest rock in town to pay homage to the pilots who opened up the northern route. At the top of the rock, you can take in a view of the entire old town, the Nerco-Con gold mine (the white tower with the red roof) and the skyscrapers. You'll notice that outcrops of the block of granite on which the new town are erected are visible all over, lending the town a very distinctive, desert-like atmosphere. To the northwest lies little Jolliffe Island, now a residential area accessible by car during winter, when the bay ices over, but only by boat in the summer. Near the island, right in the middle of the bay, a few houseboats can be seen floating on the calm waters. Although these homes are fairly rustic, they were once very common because of the exorbitant housing prices in Yellowknife. With no running water and a generator for electricity, houseboats enabled their owners to save on the price of land and on local taxes.

McDonald Drive will take you all the way around the old town. To the northeast, Latham Island is now accessible by a small bridge at the end of McDonald Drive. It, too, is residential. From the island, you can watch the constant comings and goings of the little seaplanes that land in the bay and conjure up images of the famous bush pilots who flew in supplies for local prospecting camps. Back on the peninsula, near the Bush Pilot's Mon-

ument, you can stop at the pleasant **Wildcat Café** (see p 676), set up inside a log house. This modest restaurant has become somewhat of an institution over the years, and local residents often get together here during summer.

The **Prince of Wales Northern Heritage Centre ★★** *(donation suggested; Jun to Aug, every day 10:30am to 5:30pm; Sep to May, Tue to Fri 10:30am to 5pm; on Frame Lake; take 50th St., near the Ingraham Trail, ☎873-7551)* is a major ethnological research centre in this region. A well-detailed exhibition traces the colonization of the N.W.T. and explains the Dene and Inuit way of life. Beautiful sculptures and other Aboriginal crafts are displayed here as well. You can also ask to consult the archives, which contain pictures of the first settlers who came to the area, as well as books and manuscripts dating from that era. One room is entirely devoted to the history of aviation in the North.

Dettah

This small town on the other side of Yellowknife Bay is accessible during summer by the Ingraham Trail. Its site was originally occupied by a seasonal Dene fishing camp. Today, it is the year-round home of about 100 Aboriginal people, who live in small wooden houses. They have the advantage of living close to Yellowknife and all its services, while continuing to support themselves by hunting and fishing, just like their ancestors. During winter, you get here by taking the road across the ice.

Rae-Edzo

These two little villages, located on either side of Marian Lake, the extension of the North Arm of Great Slave Lake, make up the largest Dene community in the N.W.T. Rae-Edzo is accessible by Highway 3 and lies about 100km northwest of Yellowknife. The two villages are linked by a small road about 10km long, which skirts round Marian Lake.

In 1852, explorer John Rae set up a trading post called Fort Rae for the Hudson's Bay Company. In 1904, the post was moved a few kilometres to the site of present-day Rae. Over the years, the local Dene left their isolated camps to settle in Rae-Edzo and send their children to the local school. To this day, the Dene embrace the traditional way of life of their ancestors, surviving on hunting and fishing. The women still embroider pieces of cloth and hide. These local crafts can be found in the handful of stores in Rae-Edzo. The parvis of the Rae church will catch your eye, since it is made up of poles reminiscent of tepee frames.

Lac La Martre

Lac La Martre is a Dogrib community located about 250km northwest of Yellowknife, on the shores of the lake of the same name. In summer, it is only accessible by plane, but in winter you can take the ice road that heads up to Rae Lakes. The site was chosen for a trading post in 1793 by the North West Company, a rival of the Hudson's Bay Company. Today, it is home to a picturesque cluster of wooden houses. Like the majority of Aboriginal people in small communities in the N.W.T., the local residents live on trapping, hunting and fishing. For a few years now, however, more and more tourists have been coming here to admire the landscape and the waterfalls and to fish in the well-stocked waters of Lac La Martre.

Rae Lakes

Rae Lakes is the northernmost community in this region. Very isolated, this Dogrib village has managed to preserve its old way of life. A single small motel, which also serves as a store and a restaurant, makes it possible for visitors to stay here long enough for an excursion in the area or a weekend of fishing. Rae Lakes is only accessible by plane during summer, though Aboriginal residents of Rae-Edzo sometimes come here by canoe. During winter, the ice road that serves as a continuation of Highway 3 stops at the edge of the little village.

Fort Smith

Nicknamed the "Garden City of the North," Fort Smith is located on the 60th parallel, on the Alberta border, 269km southeast of Hay River by Highway 5. The capital of the N.W.T. until 1967, this town of over 2,500 inhabitants is still an important administrative centre for the region. It is also home to Arctic College, which welcomes students from all over the N.W.T.

The Slave River was originally an important canoe route for the explorers and trappers of the North. However, its extremely dangerous rapids, impassable by canoe, forced

paddlers to stop and portage about 25km before they could take the river back down to Great Slave Lake. Because of this unavoidable stop, the Hudson's Bay Company set up a trading post called Fort Fitzgerald upstream from the rapids in 1872. Two years later, another fort, Fort Smith, was built downstream. Today, the rapids are a nesting place for white pelicans.

Though most tourists come to Fort Smith to visit **Wood Buffalo National Park ★** (see p 672), home of the largest free-roaming herd of bison in the world and the last remaining nesting place of the endangered whooping crane, the town has other attractions as well. Start off your tour of Fort Smith at the **Tourism Information Bureau** *(Jun to Sep, every day 10am to 10pm; Portage Rd.)*, which distributes maps of Wood Buffalo National Park and provides information on the excursions and wildlife interpretation programs organized in the park in July and August.

The **Northern Life Museum and National Exhibition Centre** *(free; Jun to Sep, Mon to Fri 9am to 5pm, Sat and Sun 1pm to 5pm, reduced hours in winter; 110 King St.; ☎872-2859)* houses a collection of objects made during the fur-trading era and gathered together by missionaries. The museum also explains the history and lifestyle of the local Aboriginal peoples, displays Inuit sculptures, dog sleds and harnesses, and presents an exhibition on bison.

If you walk downriver on Marine Drive, you'll find a lookout where you can observe through a telescope white pelicans frol-

icking in the choppy waters of the Slave River.

The **Monument to the Slave River Rapids** was erected in memory of the daring 19th-century explorers who travelled down the Slave River to open up the route to the Arctic.

Fort Fitzgerald, the first trading post established by the Hudson's Bay Company upriver from the rapids, lies 25km from Fort Smith. The old fort, once bustling with activity, is now abandoned, and all that remains are the vestiges of a former mission and a few houses.

Lutselk'e (Snowdrift)

In 1925, the Hudson's Bay Company set up a fur trading post on the west arm of Great Slave Lake. The Chipewyan in the area soon settled around the trading post, forming a small village which is only accessible by plane during summer. In Athabascan, Chipewyan means "pointed skin," a reference to their habit of leaving the tails on the pelts they used for their clothing. The area is popular with fishermen, since this part of Great Slave Lake, known as Christie Bay, is teeming with fish. In fact, it is one of the best places in the North for trout fishing. The steep cliffs that plunge into the deep, clear waters of the bay make for a wild and striking landscape.

Fort Resolution

Fort Resolution is a small Chipewyan village about 155km east of Hay River, on Highway 6. Located on the south shore of Great Slave Lake, near the mouth of the Slave River, it is one of the oldest communities in the N.W.T. The trading post was originally set up at the mouth of the river by the Hudson's Bay Company in 1786, then was moved to the present site of Fort Resolution in 1821. Its Chipewyan and Metis inhabitants live the same way their ancestors did, hunting and trapping animals in the Slave River delta.

Pine Point

In 1951, the Pine Point Mines company began extracting lead and zinc ore from an open-pit mine here. A small town was built to house the 2,000 people involved in the project. In 1965, a railway line reached Pine Point, and the mining company was able to increase its operations, attracting more miners and their families. The little town grew and built a hospital and a school. Unfortunately, a drop in world zinc and lead prices forced Pine Point Mines to shut down the mine. However, one of the clauses of the mining concession that had been granted to the company required the management of the mine to leave the area in its original state once all mining activities had been terminated. As a result, the town, devoted entirely to mining, was abandoned, and its buildings were taken down and reconstructed in other communities in the N.W.T. Today, all that remains of Pine Point are heaps of refuse from the mine and a few traces of the ghost town.

Hay River

Hay River is the largest town in the Big River administrative region. Located on the south shore

of Great Slave Lake, it is accessible by Highway 2 and by airplane. There are regular flights from Yellowknife and Edmonton.

Recent archaeological excavations have turned up ancient vestiges indicating that thousands of years ago, the site of the Hay River was occupied by the Slavey, a nomadic people belonging to the Dene family. Though the community began to appear on maps officially in 1854, it wasn't until 1868 that the Hudson's Bay Company established a trading post on the east bank of the mouth of the Hay River. A few years later, a small mission was set up here to convert the local Aboriginal peoples to Christianity. The community gradually expanded, and a school and a small port were constructed. Starting in 1939, the northern route leading through Hay River supplanted the one that ran along the Slave River and passed through Fort Smith, therefore increasing Hay River's commercial activities. The opening of the Pine Point mine and the construction of a railway line accelerated the town's development. Today, Hay River has a population of about 3,200 and is a hub for river transportation. Barges carrying supplies for other communities in the N.W.T. set out regularly from its port. The town has a modern appearance now, complete with several skyscrapers. The **Tourist Information Centre** (*Jul and Aug 9am to 9pm; Capital Cresc., near the post office, by the river,* ☎874-3180) has maps and books on the region.

West Channel Village was built on the west shore of **Vale Island**, at the mouth of the Hay River. The little

community was founded when commercial fishing began on Great Slave Lake. Before long, fisheries became the town's main employer. Today, West Channel Village is the commercial fishing headquarters on Great Slave Lake, supplying North America with whitefish, known for its white, nonoily flesh. At the end of West Channel Road, there is a beach that is very popular with local residents on weekends.

From atop the **Mackenzie Place Apartment Building**, a 17-storey tower in the middle of the downtown area, you can take in a great view of West Channel Village, the surrounding boreal forest and Great Slave Lake.

The **Hay River Native Reserve** is located on the opposite shore. The Aboriginal community settled on the town's former site in the 1800s. Here, you can see the old buildings of the Hudson's Bay Company's trading post and the first church built in the days of the missionaries.

Enterprise

This tiny town, located about 30km south of Hay River, is important only because it lies at the junction of Highways 1 and 2. There is an Esso station here, and you should fill up your tank and get something to eat before continuing northward. The gas station also has a small tourist information centre.

Fort Providence

This small Slave community lies on the road to Yellowknife, just past the ferry that shuttles across the Mackenzie River in summer. To get to Fort

Providence from Enterprise, take the Mackenzie Highway (1) for 85km, then turn right onto Highway 3. After 24km, you'll come to the ferry (which does not operate when the ice is forming or breaking up). Call the company (see p 665) to see if the ferry is running.

The **Mackenzie Bison Sanctuary ★**, near Fort Providence, is worth a visit (see p 672).

Fort Simpson

Located on the Mackenzie Highway, at the confluence of the Mackenzie and Liard Rivers, this little town of 1,000, originally named Fort of the Forks, was built in 1804. It was renamed in 1821 after George Simpson, the first governor of the North West and Hudson's Bay Companies, and soon became a large fur trading post. Also, its strategic location on two of the major waterways of the western N.W.T. made it a hub for the transportation of pelts and supplies. In the 1960s, Fort Simpson became a base camp for oil prospectors working in the Mackenzie River valley. Today, these commercial activities have ceased altogether, and the town is the perfect place from which to explore the surrounding area, and one of the main gateways to Nahanni National Park.

The Western Arctic

One of the most scenic highways in the Canadian North runs through this part of the N.W.T. Driving up the Dempster Highway, which starts in the Yukon and leads to the Mackenzie River delta, is a true feast for the eyes. Winding through mountains and then through the desert-like tundra, this road will take you across the Arctic Circle to Inuvik, the main town in the Western Arctic region.

Fort McPherson

The first town you'll reach, about 75km from the Yukon border, is Fort McPherson, perched on the banks of the Peel River between the mountains and the coastal plain that stretches out into the Arctic Ocean. The Gwich'in lived here for many years, trading with the nations living on the coast of British Columbia and the Inuit of the Arctic Ocean. When Alexander Mackenzie met them in 1789, this Gwich'in community already had iron spears and harpoon heads, as well as goods from Alaska. In the 1900s, Fort McPherson became an important base for the Royal Canadian Mounted Police. Standing by the Peel River is a monument to four Mounties who went to Dawson in 1910 and died on their way back.

Each summer, the community hosts a small music festival that attracts a sizable crowd.

The simple tourist information stand can provide you with information on boat rides on the Mackenzie River, as well as fishing trips.

Inuvik

Two hundred kilometres north of the Arctic Circle, at the end of the Dempster Highway, lies an amazing little town with a population of about 3,000. This modern community was designed in 1954 to replace the small town of Aklavik on the western arm of the Mackenzie River delta, which was believed to be sinking into the water. Inuvik thus became the first community north of the Arctic Circle to be equipped with all the sanitation facilities of a modern town. This was no easy task due to the permafrost. Visitors will find houses built on piles and amazing overhead metal conduits, used to carry drinking water and liquid waste, linking homes, businesses and public buildings. During the 1970s, the town enjoyed an economic boom, thanks to the prospectors looking for oil and natural gas in the Mackenzie delta. Though oil fever has subsided somewhat and local residents now lead a quiet existence, Inuvik is still the hub of the Arctic region.

Inuvik isn't a big place, so it won't take you long to see the town. You can start your tour at the **tourist information office** *(every day during summer 9am to 8pm, Mackenzie Rd., opposite the Mackenzie Hotel, ☎979-2678).*

The best-known building in Inuvik is definitely the igloo-shaped **Church of Our Lady of Victory** *(Mackenzie Rd., near the tourist information office).* Inquire at the presbytery if you'd like to see the interior, adorned with remarkable religious scenes painted by Mona Trasher, an Inuit artist renowned in the N.W.T.

The **Inuvik Research Centre** *(Mon to Fri 9am to 5pm, Mackenzie Rd.),* located in front of the tourist information office, can provide you with information on all scientific research being carried out in the Arctic region.

For a lovely view of the Mackenzie delta, go to the top of the **Chuck Park observation tower** *(Mackenzie Rd.)*, south of town, toward the airport. In the same direction, you'll also find **Lunar Links**, an amazing 18-hole golf course – of course at this latitude, there is no green! Maps of the course are available at the tourist information office.

Tuktoyaktuk

Home of the Karngmalit Inuit, Tuktoyaktuk (often shortened to "Tuk") is located in a sandpit on the shores of the Beaufort Sea. Inuvialuit traditions are still very much alive here. Some of the most distinctive features of the Tuk peninsula are its small hills of ice, up to 45km high, known locally as *pingos*. These cone-shaped promontories, which can grow 1.5m in a year, generally develop in places where the permafrost is several hundred metres thick. There are no fewer than 1,400 *pingos* on the peninsula, the highest of which, **Ibyuk**, is visible from Tuktoyaktuk. Nearby, you can visit a house made of earth and grass, the Inuvialuit version of the igloo. However, the region's major tourist attractions are the low altitude flight over the peninsula, which offers a chance to take in some gorgeous views of the Mackenzie delta, and cruises that take passengers out to see the belugas and other whales swimming peacefully offshore. For fare information, contact the **Western Arctic Tourism Association** *(Dept. EG, Box 2600, Inuvik, NT, XOE OTO, ☎979-4321, or ☎800-661-0788; ≈979-2434)*.

Sachs Harbour

The northernmost community on this tour, the town of Sachs Harbour, is located on Banks Island. This region remained uninhabited for a very long time. It was the quest for the Northwest Passage that eventually brought an expedition here in 1918. Today, Sachs Harbour is the gateway to **Aulavik National Park ★**.

Parks

The N.W.T. is a veritable paradise for anyone who loves nature, fresh air and vast stretches of pristine land. Numerous wilderness parks have been established here to protect various plant and animal species. Those who appreciate a landscape shaped by the extreme conditions of a harsh climate will find extraordinary adventure here.

Topping the list of spectacular spots are four national parks, whose beauty could astonish even the most blasé globetrotter: Nahanni National Park, on the Yukon border; Wood Buffalo National Park, which straddles the Northwest Territories and Alberta; Aulavik National Park on Banks Island, and Tuktut Noggit National Park on the Northeastern tip of the mainland. In addition to these three major national parks, the N.W.T. boasts many wildlife reserves that are home to numerous protected species.

★
From Great Slave Lake to Nahanni National Park

Highway 3, which leads to Yellowknife, runs for about 50km alongside the **Mackenzie Bison Sanctuary ★**, located on the west shore of Great Slave Lake. Originally, Wood Buffalo National Park was to be the home of the last herd of northern Canadian wood buffalo, but a number of plains buffalo were also brought here, and the two species interbred. As a result, the "purebred" wood buffalo was on its way to extinction. In an effort to preserve the species, 18 wood buffalo were sent in 1963 to this 10,000km² sanctuary on the shores of Great Slave Lake. Since then, the little herd has grown considerably, numbering over 2,000 today.

Wood Buffalo National Park ★★ is accessible from the communities of Fort Chipewyan, Alberta, and Fort Smith, N.W.T. Fort Chipewyan can be reached by plane from Fort McMurray twice a day, Sunday through Friday. In summer, motorboats travel the Athabasca and Embarras Rivers. There is a winter road open from December to March between Fort McMurray and Fort Chipewyan, but this route is not recommended. Finally, for the really adventurous, it is possible to enter the park by canoe via the Peace and Athabasca Rivers.

The park is home to the largest free-roaming, self-regulating herd of bison in the world. It is also the only remaining nesting ground of the whooping crane. Wood Buffalo was designated a UNESCO World Heritage Site as a result of these two facts. The park was initially established to protect the last remaining herd of wood bison in northern Canada. But when plains bison were shipped to the park between 1925 and 1928 (because plains in Buffalo National Park in Wainwright, Alberta, were overgrazed), the plains bison interbred with the wood bison, causing the extinction of "pure" wood bison. Or so they thought. A herd was discovered in Elk Island National Park (see p 549), and part of it was brought to Mackenzie Bison Sanctuary in the N.W.T. As a result, there are actually no pure wood buffalo in Wood Buffalo National Park.

Those who make the effort will enjoy hiking (most trails are in the vicinity of Fort Smith), canoeing, camping and the chance to experience Canada's northern wilderness in the country's largest national park. Careful advance planning is essential to a successful trip to this huge wilderness area and a Park Use Permit is required for all overnight stays in the park. Also remember to bring lots of insect repellent. For more information contact the park *(Box 750, Fort Smith, NWT, X0E 0P0, ☎872-7900, or Fort Chipewyan 697-3662, ⇒697-3560).*

Nahanni National Park ★★★ *(Nahanni Ram Tourism Association, Dept. EG, Box 177, Fort Simpson, NT, X0E 0N0, ☎695-3182 or 800-661-0788)* is probably the most beautiful park in the N.W.T. However, because there are no roads leading there, few people visit it. If you want

to be among them, you'll have to take a boat or go to the little town of Fort Simpson and rent an air-taxi, which will drop you off in the heart of the park. Designated a World Heritage Site by UNESCO, Nahanni National Park offers outdoor enthusiasts and adventurers some awe-inspiring landscapes. Experienced canoeists can paddle down the spectacular southern section of the Nahanni, the most beautiful undammed river in Canada. Others can go hiking along deep valleys, try whitewater rafting or admire the **Virginia Falls ★★**, twice as high as Niagara Falls, as well as some magnificent placid lakes. Nahanni National Park used to be called "Rivers of Myth and Mountains of Mystery." It is true that little was known about this region for a long time. The hostile wilderness, combined with the accounts of the missionaries and trappers who first scouted out the region, gave rise to numerous legends. This is indicated by the uninviting names of some of the valleys – Deadmen Valley, Hell's Gate, Devil's Kitchen and Death Canyon. If you aren't an adventurous soul but would still like to admire this unspoiled natural setting, you can enjoy a bird's-eye view of it aboard an air-taxi.

The 40km **Ingraham Trail** winds along the shores of several lakes (Prosperous, Madeline, Pontoon, Prelude, Hidden and Reid) east of Yellowknife. The most well laid out spot is the Prelude Lake park, which has a number of poorly marked trails and a hastily cleared picnic and camping area. Detailed maps of the Ingraham Trail are available at the tourist information office in Yellowknife. The wildlife is abundant, and it is common to see bald eagles, ospreys, grey jays, loons, bears and, in winter, caribou.

The Western Arctic

Aulavik National Park ★ (on Banks Island) is one of the best places in this part of the Territories for wildlife observation. It offers visitors the unique prospect of exploring an arctic region untouched by humans. Canoeists can paddle on the peaceful waters of the Thomson River, the northernmost river in Canada suitable for canoeing. The abundance of arctic foxes, polar bears, wolves and musk oxen made Banks Island a favourite of the Thule, who hunted here for centuries. However, it wasn't until the late 1920s that a few families settled in Sachs Harbour. The island is still considered one of the best places for trapping in the Arctic and is popular with photographers. In the spring, Inuvialuit guides organize dogsledding excur-sions for hunting and photographing polar bears and musk oxen. During summer, visitors can observe the migratory birds that stay in the park. For more information, contact the **Western Arctic Tourism Association** *(Dept. EG, Box 2600. Inuvik, NT, X0E 0T0,* ☎*979-4321 or 800-661-0788,* ⇄*979-2434).*

Outdoor Activities

Hiking

Hiking is obviously one of the best activities to enjoy in the parks of the N.W.T. One of the most magnificent settings is Nahanni, but the 40km Ingraham Trail, near Yellowknife, can be a wonderful option as well.

Whale-watching

The abundant plankton in the arctic waters makes this one of the best places in the world to observe certain species of whales, notably the beluga, and the narwhal near Pangnirtung. A number of naturalist guides offer sea excursions. One good outfit to try is:

Arctic Tour Company
Box 2021 E7
Inuvik, NT, X0E 0T0
⇄*979-2259*

Canoeing and Rafting

There is no shortage of lakes and rivers in this part of Canada, but the Nahanni is without question one of the most spectacular rivers. A number of organizations specializing in outdoor adventures offer excursions on the Nahanni. The prices depend on the itinerary and the length of the trip. It's a good idea to shop around.

Adventure Canada
14 Front Street South
Misissauga, ON, L5H 2C4
☎*(905) 271-4000*
☎*800-363-7566*
⇄*(905) 271-5595*
www.adventurecanada.com

Nahanni River Adventures
Box 4869 EX
Whitehorse, YT, Y1A 4N6
☎*668-3180*
☎*800-287-6927*
⇄*668-3056*

Fishing

The lakes and rivers of the N.W.T. are teeming with all sorts of fish like the famous Arctic char, and fishing enthusiasts can try their luck. Before setting out, make sure to inquire about the necessary fishing permits.

Arctic Safaris
Box 1294-X
Yellowknife, NT, X1A 2N9
☎*873-3212*
⇄*873-9008*

Blachford Lake Lodge
Box 1568
Yellowknife, NT, X1A 2P2
☎*873-3303*
⇄*920-4013*

Enodah Wilderness Travel
Box 2382
Yellowknife, NT, X1A 2P8
☎/⇄*873-4334*

Snowmobiling and Dogsledding

Ever dreamed of travelling across a snow-covered land with a team of dogs at your command? The Inuit still do sometimes, though most prefer the speedier snowmobile. Nowadays, visitors can enjoy both types of excursion all over the N.W.T.

Anderson River Nature's Best
Box 240
Tuktoyaktuk, NT, X0E 1C0
☎/⇄*977-2415*

Great Slave Sledging Company
Moraine Point Lodge
Box 2882, Yellowknife
NT, X1A 2R2
☎*873-6070*
☎*873-8249*
⇄*873-4790*

Beluga

Accommodations

From Great Slave Lake to Nahanni National Park

Yellowknife

Blue Raven Bed and Breakfast
$60 single
$75 double
Latham Island
37B Otto Drive, X1A 2T9
☎*873-6328*
The Blue Raven Bed and Breakfast, run by Tessa Macintosh, is a big blue and white house located in the old town, atop a hill overlooking Great Slave Lake. It has three spacious rooms, each with a lovely view of the water. Guests also enjoy a large terrace looking out over the lake and a pleasant common room with a fireplace. Non-smoking environment.

Igloo Inn
$99
tv, ℜ
Franklin Ave.
toward Latham Island
Box 596 X1A 2N4
☎*873-8511*
⇌*873-5547*
It would be hard to find a more dreary decor than that of the rooms at the Igloo Inn. This motel can be noisy at times, but the rooms are clean.

Discovery Inn
$120
tv, ℜ
on Franklin Ave.
near the Arctic Art Gallery
Box 784, X1A 2N6
☎*873-4151*
⇌*920-7948*
The Discovery Inn is as modest as the Igloo Inn but has the advantage of

being located closer to downtown. Some rooms have a kitchenette.

Explorer Hotel
$142
tv, ℜ, bar, ≡
near the tourist information office
48th St., toward the airport
Postal Service 7000
X1A 2R3
☎*873-3531*
☎*800-661-0892*
⇌*873-2789*
The Explorer Hotel is definitely the most attractive hotel in Yellowknife. Its rooms are bright and spacious, with fully equipped bathrooms, as well as fax and modem jacks for business travellers. The hotel also boasts one of the finest restaurants in town and offers a complimentary shuttle service to and from the airport. Finally, there is a small souvenir shop on the ground floor.

Yellowknife Inn
$150
tv, ℜ, bar
5010 49th St., Box 490
at the corner of Franklin Ave.
X1A 2N4
☎*873-2601*
☎*800-661-0580*
⇌*873-2602*
The Yellowknife Inn is the biggest hotel in town. Its pleasant little restaurant, the Lounge Café, makes it very popular with local civil servants, who come here for lunch. In addition to free access to a fitness centre, the hotel offers a complimentary shuttle service to the airport.

Rae Lakes

Gameti Motel
$175
tv
General Delivery
NT, X0E 1R0
☎*997-3031*
⇌*997-3099*
The Gameti Motel, located in town on the northeast shore of the lake, offers

modest rooms. The staff can also arrange a fishing trip for you.

Fort Smith

Pinecrest Hotel
$75
tv
163 McDougal Rd.
Box 127, NT, X0E 0P0
☎*872-2320*
The only thing going for the Pinecrest Hotel is that it offers the cheapest accommodations in Fort Smith.

Pelican Rapids Inn
$110
tv, ℜ
downtown
152 McDougal Rd.
Box 52, NT, X0E 0P0
☎*872-2789*
⇌*872-4727*
If you're looking for more comfortable lodgings, head to the Pelican Rapids Inn. Reservations recommended.

Snowdrift (Lutselk'e)

Snowdrift Co-op Hotel
$125
K, tv, sb
General Delivery
☎*370-3511*
⇌*370-3000*
The Snowdrift Co-op Hotel is the only hotel in this tiny community.

Hay River

Migrator Hotel
$80
tv, K
912 Mackenzie Hwy.
NT, X0E 0R8
☎*874-6792*
⇌*874-6704*
The Migrator Hotel has motel-style rooms, each with a kitchenette.

Caribou Motor Inn
$85
tv, K, ℜ, ◌
912 Mackenzie Hwy.
NT, X0E 0R8
☎*874-6706*
≈*874-6704*
Right next door, the Caribou Motor Inn, is similar to the Migrator.

Ptarmigan Inn Hotel
$113
tv, pb, ℜ
10 Gagnier St.
NT, X0E 1G1
☎*874-6591*
≈*874-3392*
For better accommodations, head to the Ptarmigan Inn Hotel, next to the tourist information office. A small souvenir shop, a hairdresser and a bank are all located near by.

Fort Providence

Snowshoe Inn
$80
tv, K, café
on the waterfront
Box 1000, NT, X0E 0L0
☎*699-4300*
The Snowshoe Inn has impersonal motel-style rooms.

Fort Simpson

The range of accommodations in Fort Simpson is hardly extensive. The local establishments offer basic rooms in the purest motel style. It doesn't make much difference whether you opt for the **Maroda Motel** *($120; 15 rooms; tv, K; Box 67, NT, X0E 0N0,* ☎*867-695-2602,* ≈*867-695-2273)* or the **Nahanni Inn** *($130; 35 rooms; tv, K, microwave, ℜ; Box 248, NT, X0E 0N0,* ☎*867-695-2201,* ≈*867-695-3000).*

The Western Arctic

Inuvik

Eskimo Inn
$115
tv, ℜ, café
133 Mackenzie Rd.
Box 1740, NT, X0E 0T0
☎*777-2801*
Though its rooms are impersonal, the Eskimo Inn is advantageously located in town.

Tuktoyaktuk

Pingo Park Lodge Ltd.
$125 to $175
tv
95-TDC, Box 290, NT, X0E 1C0
☎*977-2155*
≈*977-2416*
The Pingo Park Lodge Ltd. only has motel-style rooms. You'll also find a car-rental counter here.

Restaurants

From Great Slave Lake to Nahanni National Park

Yellowknife

Wildcat Café
$
summer only
in the old town
on Latham Island
3904 Wiley Rd.
The least expensive and most inviting place for a simple, frugal meal is definitely the Wildcat Café. This little café, set up inside a small log house, is a favourite with local residents. It only has a few tables and guests sit on wooden benches. Reservations are not accepted, so you have to get there early

or wait outside. In the latter case, you can take the opportunity to climb up to the Bush Pilot's Monument and admire the view of the town, the lake and the little seaplanes that land nearby.

Sam's Monkey Tree
$
483 Range Lake Rd.
☎*920-4914*
If you're looking for a family-style restaurant, try Sam's Monkey Tree. The decor is a little surreal for the area, but the food is simple and perfectly acceptable.

Our Place
$$
on the ground floor
of the Franklin Avenue
shopping centre
☎*920-2265*
Our Place is a good restaurant with a surprisingly varied menu that includes both French and Chinese dishes. The pink decor is unattractive, but the service is excellent and the food is tasty.

Explorer Hotel
$$$
47th St.
☎*873-3531*
On Sunday, local residents like to get together at the Explorer Hotel, which serves a terrific brunch. The dining room, graced with picture windows, is very pleasant and the food is some of the best in town. Arctic char is one of the specialties of the house. Courteous, attentive service.

Fort Smith

Pinerest
$
in the Pinecrest Hotel
☎*872-3161*
The Pinerest is the restaurant most often recommended by local residents. You'll find delicious cakes

at the **J-Bell Bakery** *(at the corner of McDougal Road and Portage Avenue).*

The Western Arctic

Inuvik

Green Briar Dining Room
$
in the Mackenzie Hotel
185 Mackenzie Rd.
☎777-2414
The Green Briar Dining Room serves dishes typical of the Canadian north. Here, too, caribou gets top billing.

Shopping

In every community in the Canadian north, residents will try to sell you all sorts of figurines carved out of caribou antlers, whale bones, stone or crafts made of hide or birch bark. Most of the time, you'll find items like these on sale at the local tourist information office.

In the larger communities, however, the art galleries that purchase these objects from the most renowned artists, many of whom live in remote communities, sell beautiful pieces. Like everything else in the Canadian north, they are often very expensive – but still reasonable in comparison to similar pieces sold in specialized galleries in Montréal, Toronto and Vancouver. If you are enchanted by these splendid Inuit sculptures, don't hesitate to buy one, as it will be a good investment. Aside from sculptures, you'll find leather gloves, mocassins and *mukluks* (boots), elegantly adorned with beads. Other commonly found Aboriginal crafts include birch bark boxes decorated with porcupine quills.

From Great Slave Lake to Nahanni National Park

Yellowknife

The **Arctic Art Gallery** *(Franklin Ave., at 48th Street)* is the largest art gallery in Yellowknife. All the biggest artists in the N.W.T. exhibit their work here. You'll find beautiful sculptures in all different price ranges, as well as engravings and paintings, including some by Mona Trasher, the Inuit artist who painted the interior of Inuvik's igloo-like church. A smaller art gallery is located nearby, to the east on 48th Street. It, too, has some magnificent sculptures. At the **tourist information office**, you can purchase leather goods or one of those famous birch bark boxes.

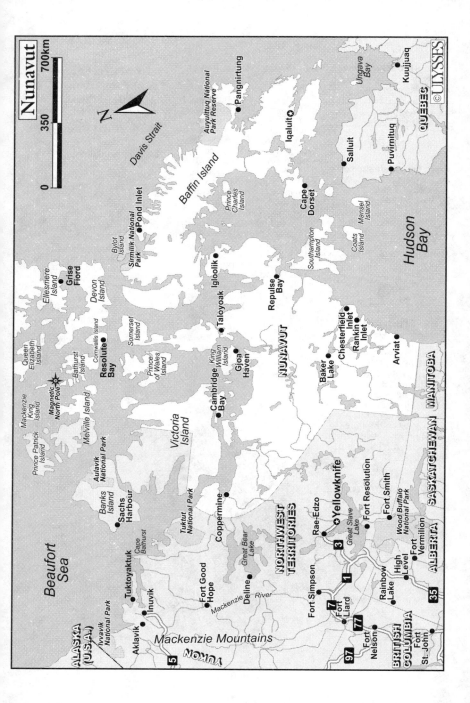

Nunavut

A s soon as visitors
step off the plane in this remote, alternatively spectacular and desolate territory, they are reminded that they are outsiders.

The excited cries of children shouting "qallunaat!" (KA-bloo-na – non-Inuit people) follow you everywhere. At once you realize that not only are you in a foreign and 'exotic' land, but that you too are considered strange and 'exotic.'

Home of the Inuit ("the people"), their ancestors and predecessors for 5,000 years, Nunavut's landscape ranges from rugged mountains and glaciers in the northeast, some of which reach heights of over 2,000m, to low, sandy marsh, muskeg, and long tidal flats in the southwest. But everywhere, the landscape is striking; so too is the thunderous silence, so unlike any sound heard elsewhere.

The Inuit share this land with wildlife such as caribou, polar bears, muskoxen, seals, walruses, and several species of whales, all of which they depend on, as they have for thousands of years, for food and clothing. But in addition to the 'traditional' way of life, there are signs

everywhere that the Inuit are as much a part of the 21st century as are southern Canadians. Snowmobiles and satellite dishes exist in Nunavut alongside dog teams and *komatiks* (wooden sleds).

And yet, there is so much more to this fascinating place than meets the eye. While its remoteness and limited degree of development may make it appear a pristine land, Nunavut suffers from some serious environmental threats produced great distances away. For example, it is predicted that greenhouse-

gas induced global warming will hit northern latitudes particularly hard, thinning the polar ice cap and threatening arctic animals like the polar bear. Similarly, persistent organic pollutants (POPs), like dioxins and PCBs, bioaccumulate in whales and polar bears in Canada's Far North, and are then passed on to the Inuit as they consume them.

Politics

On April 1, 1999, 60% of the Northwest Territories's eastern corner officially became the territory of Nunavut, "our land" in

Inuktitut. The territory, most of which consists of hundreds of islands, comprises nearly 2 million km², one-fifth the area of Canada; 150,000km² of its surface area are covered by ice caps and glaciers. Its population of some 25,000 people (1996), 85% of whom are Inuit, is scattered among 28 communities, from Arviat in the south to Grise Fiord in the north.

While Nunavut has the status of a territory (see "Northwest Territories") like the Yukon and Northwest Territories, its new political organization ensures Inuit self-government by virtue of their majority in the population. By contrast, within the new boundaries of the Northwest Territories, Inuit make up just 10% of the population. Nunavut's capital, Iqaluit, on Baffin Island, as well as Nunavut's decentralized administrative structure, are seen as better able to reflect the particular reality of the central and eastern Arctic. Yellowknife, the capital of the Northwest Territories, was a distant entity for the people of Nunavut.

In addition, the Inuit obtained a land-claim settlement that gives them ownership of 350,000km², 10% of which they have subsurface rights to, $1.1 billion in compensation from the federal government to be paid over 14 years, a share of resource royalties on Crown lands, and a greater involvement in managing the land and its resources.

Society and Economy

Government (municipal, territorial and federal) is the largest employer in Nunavut. Yet traditional activities like hunting, fishing and trapping remain vital to the economic, social and cultural well-being of Inuit. Until the 1950s and 1960s, when the Canadian government encouraged them to settle in communities, Inuit lived nomadically in camps, hunting for survival. Today, hunting demands snowmobiles, gasoline, and rifles, all of which are particularly expensive in the North.

During the 1960s and 1970s, the Inuit in the region derived most of their income through the sale of sealskins, by-products of the subsistence hunt. The 1983 ban on the importation of seal skins imposed by the European Community, combined with intense lobbying by environmental organizations, destroyed the market for sealskins and caused extreme economic hardship in many Nunavut communities.

The desolation of this area, the harshness of its climate, and the cost of transportation have been major obstacles to the development of its economy. As a result, resource exploitation (oil, gas and minerals) has played a major role in the territory's economy.

Today, tourism – ecotourism in particular – is seen as an environmentally and culturally sustainable source of income for Nunavut's communities. Guiding and arts and crafts production are the most

luctrative areas of this industry. Some residents even feel that tourists' interest in Inuit culture has the added benefit of stimulating, reviving and instilling pride amongst local people in their traditional way of life.

While the creation of Nunavut represents a great victory for the Inuit, they still face many challenges, such as an unemployment rate of nearly 30%, a very high cost of living, isolation, a low level of education and training, and a suicide rate nearly six times the national average. Furthermore, its population is the youngest in Canada. 56% of its population is under 25 years of age, a fact that lends urgency to the search for solutions. The territory's new premier Paul Okalik and his government, have recently announced plans to devote significant resources to suicide prevention; communities such as Igloolik have recently adopted programs that aim to increase self-esteem among local youth by teaching them about Inuit culture and helping them find jobs.

Finding Your Way Around

Virtually the only way to get to Nunavut from southern Canada is by plane. **First Air** (☎613-739-0200, ☎800-267-1247, ⇒613-688-2637) flies to Iqaluit from Montréal three times a week and from Ottawa every day; reserve seven days in advance to get the best rate. **Canadian Airlines International**

(☎800-665-1177 *in Canada,*
800-426-7000 from the U.S.)
also flies to Iqaluit from
Ottawa. From Iqaluit, both
airlines offer connecting
flights to the smaller communities in the region.
Calm Air, a Canadian Airlines partner, flies from
Winnipeg to western
Nunavut.

Practical Information

The area code for **Nunavut**
is *867*.

Time Zones

Nunavut currently operates
on three different time
zones: Eastern (GMT -5),
Central (GMT -6) and
Mountain (GMT-7).

Climate

The vastness of this territory encompasses many
regional climactic varia-
tions. For example, in
Rankin Inlet in western
Nunavut, summer temper-
atures range from 10° to
15°; in Cape Dorset, sum-
mer temperatures attain an
average high of 7.2° C,
dropping to a few degrees
below zero at night. Nev-
ertheless, it is not too
unusual for summer days
to warm up enough to
pack local watering holes
with delighted local youth.
Grise Fiord's July mean is
3.9° C, but many summer
days approach 10° C.
Winter temperatures in
Cape Dorset and Rankin
Inlet drop to between -25°
C and -35° C, and even
colder, while winter tem-
peratures in Grise Fiord
often plunge as low as
-40°C.

Be aware that many activities in this archipelago
depend on ice-freeze up
and break-up. Call the
community ahead of time
to be sure that ice conditions permit the particular
activity you intend to pur-
sue.

Midnight Sun

One of the attractions of
Nunavut is the opportunity
to see the 'midnight sun,'
the period of 24hr-a-day
light referred to locally as
'light season.' At extreme
latitudes, such as at Grise
Fiord, the summer sun
circles the sky, instead of
setting. Visitors are surprised to see people tending their boats and chil-
dren playing until late at
night, dependant on fa-
tigue, rather than a clock,
to signal bedtime. Of
course, the alternative is
also true: during 'dark
season – 'from the end of
October until mid-Febru-
ary – the sun disappears
entirely from the sky.
Locals continue to hunt
during this time, guided by
the light of the moon.
Farther south, such as in
Iqaluit or Cape Dorset,
there is a maximum of
20hrs of daylight in June
and July. Between October
and February, hours of
daylight decrease, with a
maximum of 5hrs of light
on the shortest days in
December.

Tourist Information

Nunavut Tourism
P. O. Box 1450
Iqaluit NT X0A 0H0
☎*800-491-7910*
(Canada and the U.S.)
☎*979-6551*
⇒*800-307-8223*
⇒*979-1261*
www.nunatour.net.ca
Nunavut Tourism provides
travel advice and produces

the 70-page *Arctic Traveller*
guide.

Nunavut.com
(*www.nunavut.com*) also
provides a wealth of information on the new terri-
tory.

Money and Banking

Iqaluit has a Royal Bank of
Canada. The Northern
Store (see p 686) and co-
operatives in smaller communities usually accept
traveller's cheques in
Canadian funds. It is a
good idea to carry some
cash because many busi-
nesses do not accept credit
cards.

Liquor Laws

Most of Nunavut's commu-
nities, excluding Iqaluit,
are "dry," that is, no alcohol is sold. Visitors are
discouraged from bringing
alcohol with them – if you
must, be discreet. For
more information, contact
the local detachment of
the Royal Canadian
Mounted Police.

Exploring

Just under half of the land
area of Nunavut lies on the
mainland. The remainder
is distributed throughout
an archipelago of hun-
dreds of islands like Baffin,
Ellesmere and Devon.
With an area of
507,500km^2, Baffin Island
accounts for more than a
quarter of Nunavut's territory. It is the sixth largest
island in the world after
Australia, Greenland, New
Guinea, Borneo and Mada-
gascar. Located on the
Arctic Circle, it is a land of

tundra, jagged mountains (it is sometimes referred to as "little Switzerland"), glaciers and ice caps. There are many reasons to visit Baffin and Ellesmere Islands. Few places in the world offer equal opportunities to gaze upon magnificent, completely untouched landscapes and embark on unforgettable adventures like those awaiting visitors to the northernmost part of Canada.

Iqaluit

The capital of Nunavut, Iqaluit, is the main population centre on Baffin Island and the administrative hub for the Arctic regions. Formerly known as Frobisher Bay after Sir Martin Frobisher, a sailor who came to this region in 1576 while looking for the Northwest Passage, it was renamed Iqaluit in 1987. During the 18th and 19th centuries, the town served as a base camp for whalers, but it wasn't until the second half of the 20th century that it became the administrative centre of the eastern Arctic. Now home to about 4,220 people, mostly Inuit, Iqaluit is facing the challenges presented by its new role as the capital of Nunavut. It is also the gateway to the Arctic for anyone wishing to explore the little communities on Baffin Island.

Iqaluit is not a very big place. You can start off your tour with a stop at the **Unikkaarik tourist information office** *(Mon to Fri 10am to noon and 1pm to 7pm, Sat and Sun noon to 7pm, in the southeast part of town, on the bay;* ☎*819-979-4636)*, where you'll find maps of the area and a list of outfitters

that offer fishing expeditions in Frobisher Bay, whose waters are teeming with fish. You can also see an audiovisual presentation on local attractions and the way of life in the 14 communities on Baffin Island.

Set up inside a restored house built by Hudson's Bay Company, the **Nunatta Sunagutangit Museum** *(closed Mon; right next to the tourist information office;* ☎*979-5537)* displays a collection of artifacts from the oldest settlements in the region. On the other side of town, near the airport, you'll find warehouses containing Inuit sculptures from various parts of the Arctic. Unless you are lucky enough to meet one of these artists in person in the course of your travels, this is one of the best places to find magnificent serpentine and soapstone sculptures at lower prices than in southern Canada. Many of these sculptures come from Cape Dorset, the cradle of new Inuit art in the 1950s.

Twelve kilometres west of Iqaluit there is a little island accessible only by boat. This island that was inhabited by the Thule, ancestors of contemporary Inuit, for 1,000 years. This island is now home to the **Quammaarviit Historic Park**. Archaeological excavations have uncovered many tools and bones dating back 2,600 years. As these digs have been completed, visitors can now stroll along little trails between sod houses (the Thule equivalent of the igloo) hearths that were in the middle of the tents that once stood here, and tombs.

Pangnirtung

A small community of about 1,000 Inuit, Pangnirtung is primarily of interest because of its location, at the entrance of **Auyuittuq National Park ★★★** (see p 683). Perched on the shore of a spectacular fiord, this small village is built around the landing strip used by airplanes to bring in supplies and by the few hikers who come to the park. Originally, the camp was established as a base for the whalers who crisscrossed the Arctic waters of this region. When whaling began to slow down, the Hudson's Bay Company decided to set up a furtrading post here. You'll find maps of the area and information on excursions from Pangnirtung at the Angmarlik Interpretive Centre *(every day during summer 9am to 9pm,* ☎*473-8737)*. For a **magnificent view** stretching all the way to the entrance of Auyuittuq National Park, take the 7km hiking trail from the Pisuktinu Tungavit campground, east of the village, to the top of **Mount Duval** (670 m). You'll have to exert yourself, but the panorama is ample compensation.

Cape Dorset ★★ is truly the artist colony of the North. Since the 1950s, the **West Baffin Eskimo Co-operative** *(*☎*897-8944,* ≈*897-8049; Mon to Fri 9:30am to 11:30am and 1:30pm to 4:30pm)* has made the community internationally famous for its print-making and carving. Group tours of the print shop can be arranged by calling in advance. Perhaps because of its role in the international arts scene, Cape

Dorset's residents seem more open to outsiders than more remote communities. Several worthwhile walks are accessible from town.

Pond Inlet

Wonderfully situated on the shores of Eclipse Sound, on northern Baffin Island, Pond Inlet faces the glaciers and rugged mountains of Bylot Island. The nomadic Thule and Inuit lived on north Baffin Island and its surrounding islands least 1,000 years ago. The area attracted Scottish whalers during the latter half of the 19thcentury, yet it was not until the 1920s, when the Hudson's Bay Company (1921), the RCMP (1923) and the Roman Catholic and Anglican missions (1929) appeared, that Inuit congregated in the area. Located within Sirmilik, the region's newest national park, it is, along with Arctic Bay to the west, the departure point for excursions on the surrounding land. The **Nattinak Centre** *(P.O. Box 281, Pond Inlet NT X0A 0S0, ☎899-8226, ⇋899-8246)* provides visitor information services, as well as cultural performances and walking tours of the community.

Resolute Bay

Tiny Resolute's sole claim to fame, so to speak, is that it is the starting point for all expeditions to the North Pole, so your visit here is likely to be a quick one.

Grise Fiord

At 76°24' N, Grise Fiord is Canada's most northerly community. Situated on the southern coast of Ellesmere Island, overlooking Jones Sound, the community rests at the foot of 600m-high mountains, 1,544km from the North Pole. The community was created in 1953 when the Canadian government relocated three families from Port Harrison (now Inukjuak), Québec, accompanied by a family from Pond Inlet. The government claimed that this resettlement was intended to improve the lives of these people, who suffered from bad hunting conditions at home. Critics charge that the intention had more to do with a need to populate the High Arctic in order to assert Canadian sovereignty over it. While the original inhabitants may not have selected Grise Fiord, the 170 people who live here today enjoy the peace and quiet it affords and the opportunity it provides to live close to the land.

Parks

To explore **Auyuittuq National Park**, on Baffin Island, or **Quttinirpaqq** (Ellesmere) National Park is to encounter nature in its most elementary state. These sorts of expeditions require lots of planning, however, and visitors who venture into the harsh, virgin territory of the Arctic parks will have no one to count on but themselves. You will need to carry on

your back everything necessary to cope with the sometimes abrupt changes in climate. Those who prepare carefully and stay in top physical shape will take home some indelible memories.

Auyuittuq National Park ★ ★ ★ *(Auyuittuq National Park, Pangnirtung, NT, X0A 0R0, ☎819-473-8828)*, on Baffin Island's Cumberland Peninsula, protects the northern Davis region. The amazing arctic landscape features the Pangnirtung Pass; the Penny Icecap, which covers a large part of the park; hanging valleys, glaciers and moraines. It was the Penny Icecap that inspired the name "Auyuittuq," which means "the land of eternal ice." Visitors should bear in mind that exploring the park is no easy task. Occasionally, you'll have to cross icy torrents, since only a few primitive cables or log bridges span the most dangerous streams. Getting around this harshly beautiful, untouched land, is not within everyone's reach, though its jagged peaks, like Mounts Thor, Asgard and Overlord, delight seasoned mountain climbers in search of extreme conditions. Visitors must take careful precautions, as the risk of hypothermia is great and no help is on hand. No infrastructure has been set up in the park, aside from a few shacks, built in case of emergency and located a good day's walk apart. There is a single radio station, which unfortunately does not always come in. Visitors have to carry all the equipment and supplies they will need for their expedition on their backs.

Nunavut

Anyone planning on coming to the park is required to register at the **Parks Canada** office in **Pangnirtung** (☎819-473-8828) or **Broughton Island** (☎819-927-8834) beforehand. Upon registration, you'll have to provide your itinerary and the amount of days you plan to spend in the park. You are also required to check in at the end of your expedition. Maps of the park may be purchased at these offices for $10. The Overlord guard post marks the entrance to the park. Despite its name, you won't find anyone there. It is located at the far end of the Pangnirtung fiord. Most people are brought there by boat or by snowmobile, depending on the season. You will find a list of experienced people who can take you at the park offices. The boat ride only takes about 1.5hr but costs a fortune – usually at least $300. You can always try to bargain, but make sure you're dealing with one of the guides on the list, since you'll have to make arrangements for him to pick you up on the appointed day.If the boat ride doesn't appeal to you, you can walk to the park entrance, located 32km from the village of Pangnirtung; unfortunately, this will cut your stay in the park short a few days.

Little has been done to make Auyuittuq Park more accessible to visitors. The Inukshuk have marked a trail to Pangnirtung Pass. This trail leads to some of the best stream crossings, steers clear of quicksand and helps prevent hikers from damaging the tundra. Though the land looks bare and desert-like due to the unforgiving arctic climate, during the brief summer season small clusters of pastel-coloured flowers grow amidst the rocks, somehow managing to withstand the wind, cold temperatures and lack of precipitation. These flowers lend the moraines a fragile beauty, and make the land seem both formidable and delicate.

Kekertin Historic Park is accessible by boat or by snowmobile from Pangnirtung. Inquire at the Angmarlik tourist information centre. Located on a small island south of Pangnirtung, this park was a whaling camp for nearly a century. Partially restored, it now has an interpretive site that examines the whalers' lifestyle and working conditions.

Covering an area of 37,775km², **Quttinirpaqq (Ellesmere)National Park** ★★ *(P.O. Box 353, Pangnirtung, NT, X0A 0R0, ☎819-473-8828)* is, as its Inuktitut name indicates, literally located on "top of the world," at the northern tip of Ellesmere Island. The advice we gave about preparing for an expedition in Auyuittuq National Park applies here as well. This magical place boasts spectacular glaciers and magnificent mountains, which plunge straight into the Arctic Ocean. Among them is one of the highest summits in Canada, **Mount Barbeau** (2,639m).

Most people begin their expedition at **Lake Hazen**, located right in the middle of the park. This area attracts many species of migratory birds during the brief arctic summer. Other animals commonly found here include foxes, white-furred arctic hare, musk oxen and wolves. With less than 10cm of precipitation per year, this desert-like region is one of the driest on earth. The park's main entrance is at the end of the Greely Fiord, at **Tanquary Fiord**. To get there, you have to take a small plane from Resolute. Unfortunately, the exorbitant fare (over $2,000) is likely to discourage many people. For further information on the park, write to **Parks Canada.**

Sirmilik National Park
★★*(interim mailing address: Sirmilik National Park, P.O. Box 353 Pangnirtung, Nunavut, XOA ORO, ☎473-8828, ≠473-8612 , Nunavut_Info@pch.gc.ca)* officially opened in 1999 but has no facilities or equipment as of yet. There are no official campsites either, but that shouldn't stop adventurous types from pitching their tents by any stream or river and enjoying the breath-taking landscapes and extreme isolation of this beautiful place. Extending over an area of 22,000km² along the northeastern corner of Baffin Island, its boundaries encompass the communities of Pond Inlet and Arctic Bay, as well as Bylot Island, a migratory bird sanctuary studded with rugged, snow-capped mountains and glaciers.

"Sirmilik," or "glacier" in Inuktitut, is indeed appropriately named. Bylot Island is home to thick-billed murres and black-legged kittiwakes and the coasts and waters around it are frequented by polar bears, seals, walruses and whales, including the narwhal – the unicorn of the sea. Access is provided by local outfitters in Pond Inlet or Arctic Bay. Count on paying about $400 per person from Pond Inlet to Bylot Island. Before you travel, make sure to call ahead to find out about the ice conditions on Eclipse Sound (ice break-up in July and freeze-up in October and November prevent both snowmobiles and boats from making the trip). Keep in mind that the Inuit have retained their right to hunt, fish and trap wildlife in the park, as well as to quarry carving stone.

Outdoor Activities

Nunavut is a paradise for outdoor enthusiasts. **Hikers** have it made: from mountains, glaciers and ice caps in the north, to vast plains in the west, the opportunities are endless and begin just about everywhere you turn. **Kaya-king** is popular, but those interested will have to come fully equipped: although the Inuit gave the world the kayak, it is a tradition that has been all but lost. However, some communities, such as Pelly Bay (Aqvilikjuaq) are experiencing a kayaking revival, spurred in part by tourism. Nunavut is a particularly good place for **whale-watching**, as belugas and narwhals, as well as some bowheads, can be seen.

Snowmobiling and **Dogsledding** trips are thrilling ways to discover this land and the traditions of the Inuit. **Bird-watchers** will be delighted by the territory's 10 bird sanctuaries and the opportunity to catch sight of thick-billed murres, snow geese, northern fulmars and black-legged kittiwakes, among others. For those who crave a taste of arctic char, there are many **fishing** camps in the region.

For most of these activities, you will need to make arrangements **in advance** with local outfitters. Contact Nunavut Tourism (see p 681) for a list of licensed outfitters.

Accommodations

Iqaluit

Bayshore Inn
$100
Box 1240
NT, X0A 0H0
☎*979-6733*
✻*979-4210*
The Bayshore Inn is the least expensive hotel in town, but the rates are nonetheless exorbitant for what you get.

Frobisher Inn
$150
tv, ℜ, café
Box 610, NT, X0A 0H0
☎*979-2222*
✻*979-0427*
The Frobisher Inn, a bit more expensive, offers a shuttle to the airport and has a fairly good restaurant. Guests can use the fax at the front desk.

Discovery Lodge Hotel
$160
tvc, radio, laundry facilities, ℜ
Box 387, NT, X0A 0H0
☎*979-4433*
✻*979-6591*
The Discovery Lodge Hotel also provides shuttle service to the airport.

Pangnirtung

Auyuittuq Lodge
$135
ℜ
NT, X0A 0R0
☎*473-8955*
✻*473-8611*
Aside from the free campground at the edge of town, toward Auyuittuq National Park, the Auyuittuq Lodge is the only place to stay in Pangnirtung. The rooms are very rustic, and you'll have to go down to the common room if you want to watch television. Still, after a long hike in the park, this place seems very inviting, if only because it offers the prospect of a shower and a hot meal (albeit a mediocre one). Reservations recommended during summer.

Resolute Bay

The **International Explorers' Home** *($120 fb; P.O. Box 200, NT, X0A 0V0,* ☎*819-252-3875)* and **Narwhal Arctic Services** *($195; tv, airport shuttle; NT, X0A 0V0,* ☎*819-252-3968,* ✻*819-252-3960)* are the only two places to stay in town.

Restaurants

While Iqaluit offers a selection of restaurants, keep in mind that in smaller communities choice is limited and prices are high. Many communities will only have one restaurant, which is usually situated in the hotel. Hours may also be limited. "Country food" (fish or meat caught by local fishers and hunters) is sometimes available, so ask the staff. Depending on the season and the community, treats may include smoked or fresh Arctic char, turbot, or caribou sausages, or muskox steaks (Ellesmere Island). Should you decide to cook for yourself, you may be able to purchase country food from the local Hunters and Trappers Association (HTA), some of which have modern packaging and smoking equipment.

Iqaluit

Every hotel in town has a restaurant. The one in the **Navigator Inn** *($$; opposite the Discovery Lodge,* ☎*979-8833)* serves pizza on certain evenings. Arctic char and caribou appear on all the menus. The **Kamotiq Inn** *($$;* ☎*979-5937)* is the only place in town that serves Mexican food. It also has a buffet.

Pangnirtung

Auyuittuq Lodge
$$$
☎*819-473-8955*
The only place to eat in this small village, aside from the little snack bar near the airport, is the Auyuittuq Lodge, which has a frugal set-price menu. After days of eating camping food, a meal in a warm place can be very enjoyable.

Shopping

Northern Stores, formerly the Hudson's Bay Company, are located in virtually every community in Nunavut. Locals shop here for everything from groceries to woollen socks, to ammunition. Visitors will also find arts and crafts, postcards and other souvenirs, the selection varying from community to community.

Iqaluit

Right next to the airport, you'll see a few warehouses full of carvings. There are also several galleries in town. The most beautiful pieces come from Cape Dorset and Pangnirtung. It is worth taking the time to browse through these places, as there are some wonderful finds to be made.

Caribou-antler jewellery, wall-hangings, as well as silver jewellery and prints depicting traditional or contemporary themes, are also available in Iqaluit, where Arctic College offers art courses to Inuit youth.

Cape Dorset (Kingait)

Most of the prints and carvings produced by the **West Baffin Eskimo Co-operative** (see "Exploring") are shipped south to galleries. Nevertheless, it retains some pieces for sale in its shop. There are several other spots in the community to find carvings. In fact, carvings have a way of "finding you." Carvers, finished product in hand, may approach you as you tour the community, or you may see them at work outside their homes.

Index

Index

Index

Index

Index

Index

Index

Travel Notes

Travel Notes

Order Form

Ulysses Travel Guides

☐ Atlantic Canada	$24.95 CAN $17.95 US	☐ Louisiana	$29.95 CAN $21.95 US
☐ Bahamas	$24.95 CAN $17.95 US	☐ Martinique	$24.95 CAN $17.95 US
☐ Beaches of Maine	$12.95 CAN $9.95 US	☐ Montréal	$19.95 CAN $14.95 US
☐ Bed & Breakfasts in Québec	$14.95 CAN $10.95 US	☐ New Orleans	$17.95 CAN $12.95 US
☐ Belize	$16.95 CAN $12.95 US	☐ New York City	$19.95 CAN $14.95 US
☐ Calgary	$17.95 CAN $12.95 US	☐ Nicaragua	$24.95 CAN $16.95 US
☐ Canada	$29.95 CAN $21.95 US	☐ Ontario	$27.95 CAN $19.95US
☐ Chicago	$19.95 CAN $14.95 US	☐ Ottawa	$17.95 CAN $12.95 US
☐ Chile	$27.95 CAN $17.95 US	☐ Panamá	$24.95 CAN $17.95 US
☐ Colombia	$29.95 CAN $21.95 US	☐ Peru	$27.95 CAN $19.95 US
☐ Costa Rica	$27.95 CAN $19.95 US	☐ Portugal	$24.95 CAN $16.95 US
☐ Cuba	$24.95 CAN $17.95 US	☐ Provence - Côte d'Azur	$29.95 CAN $21.95US
☐ Dominican Republic	$24.95 CAN $17.95 US	☐ Puerto Rico	$24.95 CAN $17.95 US
☐ Ecuador and Galapagos Islands	$24.95 CAN $17.95 US	☐ Québec	$29.95 CAN $21.95 US
☐ El Salvador	$22.95 CAN $14.95 US	☐ Québec and Ontario with Via	$9.95 CAN $7.95 US
☐ Guadeloupe	$24.95 CAN $17.95 US	☐ Seattle	$17.95 CAN $12.95 US
☐ Guatemala	$24.95 CAN $17.95 US	☐ Toronto	$18.95 CAN $13.95 US
☐ Honduras	$24.95 CAN $17.95 US	☐ Vancouver	$17.95 CAN $12.95 US
☐ Las Vegas	$17.95 $12.95	☐ Washington D.C.	$18.95 CAN $13.95 US
☐ Lisbon	$18.95 CAN $13.95 US	☐ Western Canada	$29.95 CAN $21.95 US

Ulysses Due South

☐ Acapulco	$14.95 CAN $9.95 US	☐ Los Cabos and La Paz	$14.95 CAN $7.99 US
☐ Belize	$16.95 CAN $12.95 US	☐ Puerto Plata - Sosua	$14.95 CAN $9.95 US
☐ Cartagena (Colombia)	$12.95 CAN $9.95 US	☐ Puerto Vallarta	$14.95 CAN $9.95 US
☐ Cancun Cozumel	$17.95 CAN $12.95 US	☐ St. Martin and St. Barts	$16.95 CAN $12.95 US
☐ Huatulco - Oaxaca Puerto Escondido	$17.95 CAN $12.95 US		

Ulysses Travel Journals

☐ Ulysses Travel Journal . $9.95 CAN
(Blue, Red, Green, Yellow, Sextant)
$7.95 US

☐ Ulysses Travel Journal . $14.95 CAN
(80 Days)
$9.95 US

Ulysses Green Escapes

☐ Cycling in France .... $22.95 CAN
$16.95 US
☐ Cycling in Ontario ...... $22.95 CAN
$16.95 US

☐ Hiking in the .... $19.95 CAN
Northeastern U.S.
$13.95 US
☐ Hiking in Québec .... $19.95 CAN
$13.95 US

Ulysses Conversation Guides

☐ French for Better Travel $9.95 CAN
$6.50 US

☐ Spanish for Better Travel $9.95 CAN
in Latin America
$6.50 US

Title	Qty	Price	Total

Name:

Address:

			Subtotal	
			Shipping	$4 CAN
			Subtotal	
			GST in Canada 7%	
			Total	

Tel: Fax:

E-mail:

Payment: ☐ Cheque ☐ Visa ☐ MasterCard

Card number_____ Expiry date_____

Signature_____

ULYSSES TRAVEL GUIDES

4176 St-Denis,
Montréal, Québec, H2W 2M5
(514) 843-9447 fax (514) 843-9448
Toll free: 1-877-542-7247
www.ulyssesguides.com
info@ulysses.ca